2 0 2 0
SECURITIES
REGULATION

SELECTED STATUTES, RULES, AND FORMS

2 0 2 0
SECURITIES
REGULATION

SELECTED STATUTES, RULES, AND FORMS

James D. Cox
Brainerd Currie Professor of Law
Duke University

Robert W. Hillman
Fair Business Practices Professor of Law
University of California, Davis

Donald C. Langevoort
Thomas Aquinas Reynolds Professor of Law
Georgetown University

Ann M. Lipton
Michael M. Fleishman Associate Professor in Business Law & Entrepreneurship
Tulane University

William Sjostrom
Professor of Law
University of Arizona

Published by Wolters Kluwer in New York.

Wolters Kluwer Legal & Regulatory U.S. serves customers worldwide with
CCH, Aspen Publishers, and Kluwer Law International products. (www.
WKLegaledu.com)

To contact Customer Service, e-mail customer.service@wolterskluwer.
com, call 1-800-234-1660, fax 1-800-901-9075, or mail correspondence to:

Wolters Kluwer
Attn: Order Department
PO Box 990
Frederick, MD 21705

Printed in the United States of America.

1 2 3 4 5 6 7 8 9 0

ISBN 978-1-5438-2033-1

About Wolters Kluwer Legal & Regulatory U.S.

Wolters Kluwer Legal & Regulatory U.S. delivers expert content and solutions in the areas of law, corporate compliance, health compliance, reimbursement, and legal education. Its practical solutions help customers successfully navigate the demands of a changing environment to drive their daily activities, enhance decision quality and inspire confident outcomes.

Serving customers worldwide, its legal and regulatory portfolio includes products under the Aspen Publishers, CCH Incorporated, Kluwer Law International, ftwilliam.com and MediRegs names. They are regarded as exceptional and trusted resources for general legal and practice-specific knowledge, compliance and risk management, dynamic workflow solutions, and expert commentary.

Summary of Contents

2 0 2 0
SECURITIES
REGULATION
SELECTED STATUTES, RULES, AND FORMS

SECURITIES ACT OF 1933

15 U.S.C. §§ 77a et seq.

Sec.1. SHORT TITLE

This title may be cited as the "Securities Act of 1933."

Sec.2. DEFINITIONS

(a) When used in this title, unless the context otherwise requires—

(1) [Security]

The term "security" means any note, stock, treasury stock, security future, security-based swap, bond, debenture, evidence of indebtedness, certificate of interest or participation in any profit-sharing agreement, collateral-trust certificate, preorganization certificate or subscription, transferable share, investment contract, voting-trust certificate, certificate of deposit for a security, fractional undivided interest in oil, gas, or other mineral rights, any put, call, straddle, option, or privilege on any security, certificate of deposit, or group or index of securities (including any interest therein or based on the value thereof), or any put, call, straddle, option, or privilege entered into on a national securities exchange relating to foreign currency, or, in general, any interest or instrument commonly known as a "security," or any certificate of interest or participation in, temporary or interim certificate for, receipt for, guarantee of, or warrant or right to subscribe to or purchase, any of the foregoing.

(2) [Person]

The term "person" means an individual, a corporation, a partnership, an association, a joint-stock company, a trust, any unincorporated organization, or a government or political subdivision thereof. As used in this paragraph the term "trust" shall include only a trust where the interest or interests of the beneficiary or beneficiaries are evidenced by a security.

(3) [Sale, Sell, Offer to Sell, Offer for Sale]

The term "sale" or "sell" shall include every contract of sale or disposition of a security or interest in a security, for value. The term "offer to sell", "offer for sale", or "offer" shall include every attempt or offer to dispose of, or solicitation of an offer to buy, a security or interest in a security, for value. The terms defined in this paragraph and the term "offer to buy" as used in subsection (c) of section 5 shall not include preliminary negotiations or agreements between an issuer (or any person directly or indirectly controlling or controlled by an issuer, or under direct or indirect common control with an issuer) and any underwriter or among underwriters who are or are to be in privity of contract with an issuer (or any person directly or indirectly controlling or controlled by an issuer, or under direct or indirect common control with an issuer). Any security given or delivered with, or as a bonus on account of, any purchase of securities or any other thing, shall be conclusively presumed to constitute a part of the subject of such purchase and to have been offered and sold for value. The issue or transfer of a right or privilege, when originally issued or transferred with a security, giving the holder of such security the right to convert such security into another security of the same issuer or of another person, or giving a right to subscribe to another security of the same issuer or of another person, which right cannot be exercised until some future date, shall not be deemed to be an offer or sale of such other security; but the issue or transfer of such other security upon the exercise of such right of conversion or subscription shall be deemed a sale of such other security. Any offer or sale of a security futures product by or on behalf of the issuer of the securities underlying the security futures product, an affiliate of the issuer, or an underwriter, shall constitute a contract for sale of, sale of, offer for sale, or offer to sell the underlying securities. Any offer or sale of a security-based swap by or on behalf of the issuer of the securities upon which such security-based swap is based or is referenced, an affiliate of the issuer, or an underwriter, shall constitute a contract for sale of, sale of, offer for sale,or offer to sell such securities. The publication or distribution by a broker or dealer of a research report about an emerging growth company that is the subject of a proposed public offering of the common equity securities of such emerging growth company pursuant to a registration statement that the issuer proposes to file, or has filed, or that is effective shall be deemed for purposes of paragraph (10) of this subsection and Section 5(c) not to constitute an offer for sale or offer to sell a security, even if the broker or dealer is participating or will participate in the registered offering of the securities of the issuer. As used in this paragraph, the term "research report" means a written, electronic, or oral communication that includes information, opinions, or recommendations with respect to securities of an issuer or an analysis of a security or an issuer, whether or not it provides information reasonably sufficient upon which to base an investment decision.

(4) [Issuer]

The term "issuer" means every person who issues or proposes to issue any security; except that with respect to certificates of deposit, voting-trust certificates, or collateral-trust certificates, or with respect to certificates of interest or shares in an unincorported investment trust not having a board of directors (or persons performing similar functions) or of the fixed, restricted management, or unit type, the term "issuer" means the person or persons performing the acts and assuming the duties of depositor or manager pursuant to the provision of the trust or other agreement or instrument under which such securities are issued; except that in the case of an unincorporated association which provides by its articles for limited liability of any or all of its members, or in the case of a trust, committee, or other legal entity, the trustees or members thereof shall not be individually liable as issuers of any security issued by the association, trust, committee, or other legal entity; except that with respect to equipment-trust certificates or like securities, the term "issuer" means the person by whom the equipment or property is or is to be used; and except that with respect to fractional undivided interest in oil, gas, or other mineral rights, the term "issuer" means the owner of any such right or of any interest in such right (whether whole or fractional) who creates fractional interests therein for the purpose of public offering.

(5) [Commission]

The term "Commission" means the Securities and Exchange Commission.

(6) [Territory]

The term "Territory" means Puerto Rico, the Virgin Islands, and the insular possessions of the United States.

(7) [Interstate Commerce]

The term "interstate commerce" means trade or commerce in securities or any transportation or communication relating thereto among the several States or between the District of Columbia or any Territory of the United States and any State or other Territory, or between any foreign country and any State, Territory, or the District of Columbia, or within the District of Columbia.

(8) [Registration Statement]

The term "registration statement" means the statement provided for in section 6, and includes any amendment thereto and any report, document, or memorandum filed as part of such statement or incorporated therein by reference.

(9) [Write, Written]

The term "write" or "written" shall include printed, lithographed, or any means of graphic communication.

(10) [Prospectus]

The term "prospectus" means any prospectus, notice, circular, advertisement, letter, or communication, written or by radio or television, which offers any security for sale or confirms the sale of any security; except that (a) a communication sent or given after the effective date of the registration statement (other than a prospectus permitted under subsection (b) of section 10) shall not be deemed a prospectus if it is proved that prior to or at the same time with such communication a written prospectus meeting the requirements of subsection (a) of section 10 at the time of such communication was sent or given to the person to whom the communication was made, and (b) a notice, circular, advertisement, letter, or communication in respect of a security shall not be deemed to be a prospectus if it states from whom a written prospectus meeting the requirements of section 10 may be obtained and, in addition, does no more than identify the security, state the price thereof, state by whom orders will be executed, and contain such other information as the Commission, by rules or regulations deemed necesssary or appropriate in the public interest and for the protection of investors, and subject to such terms and conditions as may be prescribed therein, may permit.

(11) [Underwriter]

The term "underwriter" means any person who has purchased from an issuer with a view to, or offers or sells for an issuer in connection with, the distribution of any security, or participates or has a direct or indirect participation in any such undertaking, or participates or has a participation in the direct or indirect underwriting of any such undertaking; but such term shall not include a person whose interest is limited to a commission from an underwriter or dealer not in excess of the usual and customary distributors' or sellers' commission. As used in this paragraph the term "issuer" shall include, in addition to an issuer, any person directly or indirectly controlling or controlled by the issuer, or any person under direct or indirect common control with the issuer.

(12) [Dealer]

The term "dealer" means any person who engages either for all or part of his time, directly or indirectly, as agent, broker, or principal, in the business of offering, buying, selling, or otherwise dealing or trading in securities issued by another person.

(13) [Insurance Company]

The term "insurance company" means a company which is organized as an insurance company whose primary and predominant business activity is the writing of insurance or the reinsuring of risks underwritten by insurance companies, and which is subject to supervision by the insurance commissioner, or a similar official or agency, of a State or territory or the District of Columbia; or any receiver or similar official or any liquidating agent for such company, in his capacity as such.

(14) [Separate Account]

The term "separate account" means an account established and maintained by an insurance company pursuant to the laws of any State or territory of the United States, the District of Columbia, or of Canada or any province thereof, under which income, gains and losses, whether or not realized, from assets allocated to such account are, in accordance with the applicable contract, credited to or charged against such account without regard to other income, gains, or losses of the insurance company.

(15) [Accredited Investor]

The term "accredited investor" shall mean—

(i) a bank as defined in section 3(a)(2) whether acting in its individual or fiduciary capacity; and insurance company as defined in paragraph (13) of this subsection; an investment company registered under the Investment Company Act of 1940 or a business development company as defined in section 2(a)(48) of that Act; a Small Business Investment Company licensed by the Small Business Administration; or an employee benefit plan, including an individual retirement account, which is subject to the provisions of the Employee Retirement Income Security Act of 1974, if the investment decision is made by a plan fiduciary, as defined in section 3(21) of such Act, which is either a bank, insurance company, or registered investment adviser; or

(ii) any person who, on the basis of such factors as financial sophistication, net worth, knowledge, and experience in financial matters, or amount of assets under management qualifies as an accredited investor under rules and regulations which the Commission shall prescribe.

(16) [Security Future; Narrow-Based Security Index; Security Futures Product]

The terms "security future," "narrowbased security index," and "security futures product" have the same meanings as provided in section 3(a)(55) of the Securities Exchange Act of 1934.

(17) [swap, security-based swap]

The terms "swap" and "security-based swap" have the same meanings as in section 1a of the Commodity Exchange Act (7 U.S.C. 1a).

(18) [purchase, sale]

The terms "purchase" or "sale" of a security-based swap shall be deemed to mean the execution, termination (prior to its scheduled maturity date), assignment, exchange, or similar transfer or conveyance of, or extinguishing of rights or obligations under, a security-based swap, as the context may require.

(19) [emerging growth company]

The term "emerging growth company" means an issuer that had total annual gross revenues of less than $1,000,000,000 (as such amount is indexed for inflation every 5 years by the Commission to reflect the change in the Consumer Price Index for All Urban Consumers published by the Bureau of Labor Statistics, setting the threshold to the nearest 1,000,000) during its most recently completed fiscal year. An issuer that is an emerging growth company as of the first day of that fiscal year shall continue to be deemed an emerging growth company until the earliest of—

(A) The last day of the fiscal year of the issuer during which it had total annual gross revenues of $1,000,000,000 (as such amount is indexed for inflation every 5 years by the Commission to reflect the change in the Consumer Price Index for All Urban Consumers published by the Bureau of Labor Statistics, setting the threshold to the nearest 1,000,000) or more;

(B) The last day of the fiscal year of the issuer following the fifth anniversary of the date of the first sale of common equity securities of the issuer pursuant to an effective registration statement under this title;

(C) The date on which such issuer has, during the previous 3-year period, issued more than $1,000,000,000 in non-convertible debt; or

(D) The date on which such issuer is deemed to be a "large accelerated filer," as defined in Section 240.12b-2 of Title 17, Code of Federal Regulations, or any successor thereto.

(b) [Efficiency, Competition and Capital Formation]

CONSIDERATION OF PROMOTION OF EFFICIENCY, COMPETITION, AND CAPITAL FORMATION. Whenever pursuant to this title the Commission is engaged in rulemaking and is required to consider or determine whether an action is necessary or appropriate in the public interest, the Commission shall also consider, in addition to the protection of investors, whether the action will promote efficiency, competition, and capital formation.

Sec. 2A. SWAP AGREEMENTS

(a) [*Reserved.*]

(b) SECURITY-BASED SWAP AGREEMENTS.—

(1) The definition of "security" in section 2(a)(1) of this title does not include any security-based swap agreement (as defined in section 3(a)(78) of the Securities Exchange Act of 1934).

(2) The Commission is prohibited from registering, or requiring, recommending, or suggesting, the registration under this title of any security-based swap agreement (as defined in section 3(a)(78) of the Securities Exchange Act of 1934). If the Commission becomes aware that a registrant has filed a registration statement with respect to such a swap

agreement, the Commission shall promptly so notify the registrant. Any such registration statement with respect to such a swap agreement shall be void and of no force or effect.

(3) The Commission is prohibited from—

(A) promulgating, interpreting, or enforcing rules; or

(B) issuing orders of general applicability;

under this title in a manner that imposes or specifies reporting or recordkeeping requirements, procedures, or standards as prophylactic measures against fraud, manipulation, or insider trading with respect to any security-based swap agreement (as defined in section 3(a)(78) of the Securities Exchange Act of 1934).

(4) References in this title to the "purchase" or "sale" of a security-based swap agreement shall be deemed to mean the execution, termination (prior to its scheduled maturity date), assignment, exchange, or similar transfer or conveyance of, or extinguishing of rights or obligations under, a security-based swap agreement (as defined in section 3(a)(78) of the Securities Exchange Act of 1934), as the context may require.

Sec.3. EXEMPTED SECURITIES

(a) Except as hereinafter expressly provided the provisions of this title shall not apply to any of the following classes of securities:

(1) [Reserved.]

(2) Any security issued or guaranteed by the United States or any territory thereof, or by the District of Columbia, or by any State of the United States, or by any political subdivision of a State or Territory, or by any public instrumentality of one or more States or Territories, or by any person controlled or supervised by and acting as an instrumentality of the Government of the United States pursuant to authority granted by the Congress of the United States; or any certificate of deposit for any of the foregoing; or any security issued or guaranteed by any bank; or any security issued by or representing an interest in or a direct obligation of a Federal Reserve bank; or any interest or participation in any common trust fund or similar fund that is excluded from the definition of the term "investment company" under section 3(c)(3) of the Investment Company Act of 1940; or any security which is an industrial development bond (as defined in section 103(c)(2) of the Internal Revenue Code of 1954) the interest on which is excludable from gross income under section 103(a)(1) of such Code if, by reason of the application of paragraph (4) or (6) of section 103(c) of such Code (determined as if paragraphs (4)(A), (5), and (7) were not included in such section 103(c)), paragraph (1) of such section 103(c) does not apply to such security; or any interest or participation in a single trust fund, or in a collective trust fund maintained by a bank, or any security arising out of a contract issued by an insurance company, which interest, participation, or security is issued in connection with (A) a stock bonus, pension, or profit-sharing plan which meets the requirements for qualification under section 401 of the Internal Revenue Code of 1954, (B) an annuity plan which meets the requirements for the deduction of the employer's contributions under section 404(a)(2) of such Code, or (C) a governmental plan as defined in section 414(d) of such Code which has been e stablished by an employer for the exclusive benefit of its employees or their beneficiaries for the purpose of distributing to such employees or their beneficiaries the corpus and income of the funds accumulated under such plan, if under such plan it is impossible, prior to the satisfaction of all liabilities with respect to such employees and their beneficiaries, for any part of the corpus or income to be used for, or diverted to, purposes other than the exclusive benefit of such employees or their beneficiaries, other than any plan described in clause (A), (B), or (C) of this paragraph (i) the contributions under which are held in a single trust fund or in a separate account maintained by an insurance company for a single employer and under which an amount in excess of the employer's contribution is allocated to the purchase of securities (other than interests or participations in the trust or separate account itself) issued by the employer or any company directly or indirectly controlling, controlled by, or under common control with the employer, (ii) which covers employ-

ees some or all of whom are employees within the meaning of section 401(c)(1) of such Code, (other than a person participating in a church plan who is described in section 414(e)(3)(B) of the Internal Revenue Code of 1986), or (iii) which is a plan funded by an annuity contract described in section 403(b) of such Code (other than a retirement income account described in section 403(b)(9) of the Internal Revenue Code of 1986, to the extent that the interest or participation in such single trust fund or collective trust fund is issued to a church, a convention or association of churches, or an organization described in section 414(e)(3)(A) of such Code establishing or maintaining the retirement income account or to a trust established by any such entity in connection with the retirement income account). The Commission, by rules and regulations or order, shall exempt from the provisions of section 5 of this title any interest or participation issued in connection with a stock bonus, pension, profit-sharing, or annuity plan which covers employees some or all of whom are employees within the meaning of section 401(c)(1) of the Internal Revenue Code of 1954, if and to the extent that the Commission determines this to be necessary or appropriate in the public interest and consistent with the protection of investors and the purposes fairly intended by the policy and provisions of this title. For the purposes of this paragraph, a security issued or guaranteed by a bank shall not include any interest or participation in any collective trust fund maintained by a bank; and the term "bank" means any national bank, or any banking institution organized under the laws of any State, Territory, or the District of Columbia, the business of which is substantially confined to banking and is supervised by the State or territorial banking commission or similar official; except that in the case of a common trust fund or similar fund, or a collective trust fund, the term "bank" has the same meaning as in the Investment Company Act of 1940;

(3) Any note, draft, bill of exchange, or banker's acceptance which arises out of a current transaction or the proceeds of which have been or are to be used for current transactions, and which has a maturity at the time of issuance of not exceeding nine months, exclusive of days of grace, or any renewal thereof the maturity of which is likewise limited;

(4) Any security issued by a person organized and operated exclusively for religious, educational, benevolent, fraternal, charitable, or reformatory purposes and not for pecuniary profit, and no part of the net earnings of which inures to the benefit of any person, private stockholder, or individual, or any security of a fund that is excluded from the definition of an investment company under section 3(c)(10)(B) of the Investment Company Act of 1940;

(5) Any security issued (A) by a savings and loan association, building and loan association, cooperative bank, homestead association, or similar institution, which is supervised and examined by State or Federal authority having supervision over any such institution; or (B) by (i) a farmer's cooperative organization exempt from tax under section 521 of the Internal Revenue Code of 1954, (ii) a corporation described in section 501(c)(16) of such Code and exempt from tax under section 501(a) of such Code, or (iii) a corporation described in section 501(c)(2) of such Code which is exempt from tax under section 501(a) of such Code and is organized for the exclusive purpose of holding title to property, collecting income therefrom, and turning over the entire amount thereof, less expenses, to an organization or corporation described in clause (i) or (ii);

(6) Any interest in a railroad equipment trust. For purposes of this paragraph "interest in a railroad equipment trust" means any interest in an equipment trust, lease, conditional sales contract or other similar arrangement entered into, issued, assumed, guaranteed by, or for the benefit of a common carrier to finance the acquisition of rolling stock including motive power;

(7) Certificates issued by a receiver or by a trustee or debtor in possession in a case under title 11 of the United States Code, with the approval of the court;

(8) Any insurance or endowment policy or annuity contract or optional annuity contract, issued by a corporation subject to the supervision of the insurance commissioner, bank commissioner, or any agency or officer performing like functions, of any State or Territory of the United States or the District of Columbia;

(9) Except with respect to a security exchanged in a case under title 11 of the United States Code, any security exchanged by the issuer with its existing security holders exlu-

sively where no commission or other remuneration is paid or given directly or indirectly for soliciting such exchange;

(10) Except with respect to a security exchanged in a case under title 11 of the United States Code, any security which is issued in exchange for one or more bona fide outstanding securities, claims or property interests, or partly in such exchange and partly for cash, where the terms and conditions of such issuance and exchange are approved, after a hearing upon the fairness of such terms and conditions at which all persons to whom it is proposed to issue securities in such exchange shall have the right to appear, by any court, or by any official or agency of the United States, or by any State or Territorial banking or insurance commission or other governmental authority expressly authorized by law to grant such approval;

(11) Any security which is a part of an issue offered and sold only to persons resident within a single State or Territory, where the issuer of such security is a person resident and doing business within, or, if a corporation, incorporated by and doing business within, such State or Territory.

(12) Any equity security issued in connection with the acquisition by a holding company of a bank under section 3(a) of the Bank Holding Company Act of 1956 or a savings association under section 10(e) of the Home Owners' Loan Act, if—

(A) the acquisition occurs solely as part of a reorganization in which security holders exchange their shares of a bank or savings association for shares of a newly formed holding company with no significant assets other than securities of the bank or savings association and the existing subsidiaries of the bank or savings association;

(B) the security holders receive, after that reorganization, substantially the same proportional share interests in the holding company as they held in the bank or savings association, except for nominal changes in shareholders' interests resulting from lawful elimination of fractional interests and the exercise of dissenting shareholders' rights under State or Federal law;

(C) the rights and interests of security holders in the holding company are substantially the same as those in the bank or savings association prior to the transaction, other than as may be required by law; and

(D) the holding company has substantially the same assets and liabilities, on a consolidated basis, as the bank or savings association had prior to the transaction.

For purposes of this paragraph, the term "savings association" means a savings association (as defined in section 3(b) of the Federal Deposit Insurance Act) the deposits of which are insured by the Federal Deposit Insurance Corporation.

(13) Any security issued by or any interest or participation in any church plan, company or account that is excluded from the definition of an investment company under section 3(c)(14) of the Investment Company Act of 1940.

(14) Any security futures product that is—

(A) cleared by a clearing agency registered under section 17A of the Securities Exchange Act of 1934 or exempt from registration under subsection (b)(7) of such section 17A; and

(B) traded on a national securities exchange or a national securities association registered pursuant to section 15A(a) of the Securities Exchange Act of 1934.

(b) Additional Exemptions.

(1) Small Issues Exemptive Authority. The Commission may from time to time by its rules and regulations and subject to such terms and conditions as may be prescribed there in, add any class of securities to the securities exempted as provided in this section, if it finds that the enforcement of this title with respect to such securities is not necessary in the public interest and for the protection of investors by reason of the small amount involved or the limited character of the public offering; but no issue of securities shall be exempted under this subsection where the aggregate amount at which such issue is offered to the public exceeds $5,000,000.

(2) Additional Issues. The Commission shall by rule or regulation add a class of securities to the securities exempted pursuant to this section in accordance with the following terms and conditions:

(A) The aggregate offering amount of all securities offered and sold within the prior 12-month period in reliance on the exemption added in accordance with this paragraph shall not exceed $50,000,000.

(B) The securities may be offered and sold publicly.

(C) The securities shall not be restricted securities within the meaning of the Federal securities laws and the regulations promulgated there under.

(D) The civil liability provision in Section 12(a)(2) shall apply to any person offering or selling such securities.

(E) The issuer may solicit interest in the offering prior to filing any offering statement, on such terms and conditions as the Commission may prescribe in the public interest or for the protection of investors.

(F) The Commission shall require the issuer to file audited financial statements with the Commission annually.

(G) Such other terms, conditions, or requirements as the Commission may determine necessary in the public interest and for the protection of investors, which may include—

(i) A requirement that the issuer prepare and electronically file with the Commission and distribute to prospective investors an offering statement, and any related documents, in such form and with such content as prescribed by the Commission, including audited financial statements, a description of the issuer's business operations, its financial condition, its corporate governance principles, its use of investor funds, and other appropriate matters; and

(ii) Disqualification provisions under which the exemption shall not be available to the issuer or its predecessors, affiliates, officers, directors, underwriters, or other related persons, which shall be substantially similar to the disqualification provisions contained in the regulations adopted in accordance with Section 926 of the Dodd-Frank Wall Street Reform and Consumer Protection Act (15 U.S.C. 77d note).

(3) Limitation. Only the following types of securities may be exempted under a rule or regulation adopted pursuant to paragraph (2): equity securities, debt securities, and debt securities convertible or exchangeable to equity interests, including any guarantees of such securities.

(4) Periodic Disclosures. Upon such terms and conditions as the Commission determines necessary in the public interest and for the protection of investors, the Commission by rule or regulation may require an issuer of a class of securities exempted under paragraph (2) to make available to investors and file with the Commission periodic disclosures regarding the issuer, its business operations, its financial condition, its corporate governance principles, its use of investor funds, and other appropriate matters, and also may provide for the suspension and termination of such a requirement with respect to that issuer.

(5) Adjustment. Not later than 2 years after the date of enactment of the Small Company Capital Formation Act of 2011 and every 2 years thereafter, the Commission shall review the offering amount limitation described in paragraph (2)(A) and shall increase such amount as the Commission determines appropriate. If the Commission determines not to increase such amount, it shall report to the Committee on Financial Services of the House of Representatives and the Committee on Banking, Housing, and Urban Affairs of the Senate on its reasons for not increasing the amount.

(c) The Commission may from time to time by its rules and regulations and subject to such terms and conditions as may be prescribed therein, add to the securities exempted as provided in this section any class of securities issued by a small business investment company under the Small Business Investment Act of 1958 if it finds, having regard to the purposes of that Act, that the enforcement of this Act with respect to such securities is not necessary in the public interest and for the protection of investors.

Sec.4. EXEMPTED TRANSACTIONS

(a) The provisions of section 5 shall not apply to—

(1) transactions by any person other than an issuer, underwriter, or dealer.

(2) transactions by an issuer not involving any public offering.

(3) transactions by a dealer (including an underwriter no longer acting as an underwriter in respect of the security involved in such transaction), except—

(A) transactions taking place prior to the expiration of forty days after the first date upon which the security was bona fide offered to the public by the issuer or by or through an underwriter,

(B) transactions in a security as to which a registration statement has been filed taking place prior to the expiration of forty days after the effective date of such registration statement or prior to the expiration of forty days after the first date upon which the security was bona fide offered to the public by the issuer or by or through an underwriter after such effective date, whichever is later (excluding in the computation of such forty days any time during which a stop order issued under section 8 is in effect as to the security), or such shorter period as the Commission may specify by rules and regulations or order, and

(C) transactions as to securities constituting the whole or a part of an unsold allotment to or subscription by such dealer as a participant in the distribution of such securities by the issuer or by or through an underwriter.

With respect to transactions referred to in clause (B), if securities of the issuer have not previously been sold pursuant to an earlier effective registration statement the applicable period, instead of forty days, shall be ninety days, or such shorter period as the Commission may specify by rules and regulations or order.

(4) brokers' transactions, executed upon customers' orders on any exchange or in the over-the-counter market but not the solicitation of such orders.

(5) transactions involving offers or sales by an issuer solely to one or more accredited investors, if the aggregate offering price of an issue of securities offered in reliance on this paragraph does not exceed the amount allowed under section 3(b)(1) of this title, if there is no advertising or public solicitation in connection with the transaction by the issuer or anyone acting on the issuer's behalf, and if the issuer files such notice with the Commission as the Commission shall prescribe.

(6) Transactions involving the offer or sale of securities by an issuer (including all entities controlled by or under common control with the issuer), provided that—

(A) The aggregate amount sold to all investors by the issuer, including any amount sold in reliance on the exemption provided under this paragraph during the 12-month period preceding the date of such transaction, is not more than $1,000,000;

(B) The aggregate amount sold to any investor by an issuer, including any amount sold in reliance on the exemption provided under this paragraph during the 12-month period preceding the date of such transaction, does not exceed—

(i) The greater of $2,000 or 5 percent of the annual income or net worth of such investor, as applicable, if either the annual income or the net worth of the investor is less than $100,000; and

(ii) 10 percent of the annual income or net worth of such investor, as applicable, not to exceed a maximum aggregate amount sold of $100,000, if either the annual income or net worth of the investor is equal to or more than $100,000;

(C) The transaction is conducted through a broker or funding portal that complies with the requirements of Section 4A(a); and

(D) The issuer complies with the requirements of Section 4A(b).

(7) Transactions meeting the requirements of subsection (d).

(b) Offers and sales exempt under Section 230.506 of Title 17, Code of Federal Regulations (as revised pursuant to Section 201 of the Jumpstart Our Business Startups Act) shall not be deemed public offerings under the Federal securities laws as a result of general advertising or general solicitation.

(c) (1) With respect to securities offered and sold in compliance with Rule 506 of Regulation D under this Act, no person who meets the conditions set forth in paragraph (2) shall be subject to registration as a broker or dealer pursuant to Section 15(a)(1) of this title, solely because—

(A) That person maintains a platform or mechanism that permits the offer, sale, purchase, or negotiation of or with respect to securities, or permits general solicitations, general advertisements, or similar or related activities by issuers of such securities, whether online, in person, or through any other means;

(B) That person or any person associated with that person co-invests in such securities; or

(C) That person or any person associated with that person provides ancillary services with respect to such securities.

(2) The exemption provided in paragraph (1) shall apply to any person described in such paragraph if—

(A) Such person and each person associated with that person receives no compensation in connection with the purchase or sale of such security;

(B) Such person and each person associated with that person does not have possession of customer funds or securities in connection with the purchase or sale of such security; and

(C) Such person is not subject to a statutory disqualification as defined in Section 3(a)(39) of this title and does not have any person associated with that person subject to such a statutory disqualification.

(3) For the purposes of this subsection, the term "ancillary services" means—

(A) The provision of due diligence services, in connection with the offer, sale, purchase, or negotiation of such security, so long as such services do not include, for separate compensation, investment advice or recommendations to issuers or investors; and

(B) The provision of standardized documents to the issuers and investors, so long as such person or entity does not negotiate the terms of the issuance for and on behalf of third parties and issuers are not required to use the standardized documents as a condition of using the service.

(d) Certain Accredited Investor Transactions.—The transactions referred to in subsection (a)(7) are transactions meeting the following requirements:

(1) Accredited Investor Requirement.—Each purchaser is an accredited investor, as that term is defined in section 230.501(a) of title 17, Code of Federal Regulations (or any successor regulation).

(2) Prohibition on General Solicitation or Advertising.—Neither the seller, nor any person acting on the seller's behalf, offers or sells securities by any form of general solicitation or general advertising.

(3) Information Requirement.—In the case of a transaction involving the securities of an issuer that is neither subject to section 13 or 15(d) of the Securities Exchange Act of 1934 (15 U.S.C. 78m; 78o(d)), nor exempt from reporting pursuant to section 240.12g3-2(b) of title 17, Code of Federal Regulations, nor a foreign government (as defined in section 230.405 of title 17, Code of Federal Regulations) eligible to register securities under Schedule B, the seller and a prospective purchaser designated by the seller obtain from the issuer, upon request of the seller, and the seller in all cases makes available to a prospective purchaser,

the following information (which shall be reasonably current in relation to the date of resale under this section):

(A) The exact name of the issuer and the issuer's predecessor (if any).

(B) The address of the issuer's principal executive offices.

(C) The exact title and class of the security.

(D) The par or stated value of the security.

(E) The number of shares or total amount of the securities outstanding as of the end of the issuer's most recent fiscal year.

(F) The name and address of the transfer agent, corporate secretary, or other person responsible for transferring shares and stock certificates.

(G) A statement of the nature of the business of the issuer and the products and services it offers, which shall be presumed reasonably current if the statement is as of 12 months before the transaction date.

(H) The names of the officers and directors of the issuer.

(I) The names of any persons registered as a broker, dealer, or agent that shall be paid or given, directly or indirectly, any commission or remuneration for such person's participation in the offer or sale of the securities.

(J) The issuer's most recent balance sheet and profit and loss statement and similar financial statements, which shall—

(i) Be for such part of the 2 preceding fiscal years as the issuer has been in operation;

(ii) Be prepared in accordance with generally accepted accounting principles or, in the case of a foreign private issuer, be prepared in accordance with generally accepted accounting principles or the International Financial Reporting Standards issued by the International Accounting Standards Board;

(iii) Be presumed reasonably current if—

(I) With respect to the balance sheet, the balance sheet is as of a date less than 16 months before the transaction date; and

(II) With respect to the profit and loss statement, such statement is for the 12 months preceding the date of the issuer's balance sheet; and

(iv) If the balance sheet is not as of a date less than 6 months before the transaction date, be accompanied by additional statements of profit and loss for the period from the date of such balance sheet to a date less than 6 months before the transaction date.

(K) To the extent that the seller is a control person with respect to the issuer, a brief statement regarding the nature of the affiliation, and a statement certified by such seller that they have no reasonable grounds to believe that the issuer is in violation of the securities laws or regulations.

(4) Issuers Disqualified.—The transaction is not for the sale of a security where the seller is an issuer or a subsidiary, either directly or indirectly, of the issuer.

(5) Bad Actor Prohibition.—Neither the seller, nor any person that has been or will be paid (directly or indirectly) remuneration or a commission for their participation in the offer or sale of the securities, including solicitation of purchasers for the seller is subject to an event that would disqualify an issuer or other covered person under Rule 506(d)(1) of Regulation D (17 CFR 230.506(d)(1)) or is subject to a statutory disqualification described under section 3(a)(39) of the Securities Exchange Act of 1934.

(6) Business Requirement.—The issuer is engaged in business, is not in the organizational stage or in bankruptcy or receivership, and is not a blank check, blind pool, or shell company that has no specific business plan or purpose or has indicated that the issuer's

primary business plan is to engage in a merger or combination of the business with, or an acquisition of, an unidentified person.

(7) Underwriter Prohibition.—The transaction is not with respect to a security that constitutes the whole or part of an unsold allotment to, or a subscription or participation by, a broker or dealer as an underwriter of the security or a redistribution.

(8) Outstanding Class Requirement.—The transaction is with respect to a security of a class that has been authorized and outstanding for at least 90 days prior to the date of the transaction.

(e) Additional Requirements.—

(1) In General.—With respect to an exempted transaction described under subsection (a)(7):

(A) Securities acquired in such transaction shall be deemed to have been acquired in a transaction not involving any public offering.

(B) Such transaction shall be deemed not to be a distribution for purposes of section 2(a)(11).

(C) Securities involved in such transaction shall be deemed to be restricted securities within the meaning of Rule 144 (17 CFR 230.144).

(2) Rule of Construction.—The exemption provided by subsection (a)(7) shall not be the exclusive means for establishing an exemption from the registration requirements of section 5.

SEC. 4A. REQUIREMENTS WITH RESPECT TO CERTAIN SMALL TRANSACTIONS

(a) Requirements on Intermediaries. A person acting as an intermediary in a transaction involving the offer or sale of securities for the account of others pursuant to Section 4(6) shall—

(1) Register with the Commission as—

(A) A broker; or

(B) A funding portal (as defined in Section 3(a)(80) of the Securities Exchange Act of 1934);

(2) Register with any applicable self-regulatory organization (as defined in Section 3(a)(26) of the Securities Exchange Act of 1934);

(3) Provide such disclosures, including disclosures related to risks and other investor education materials, as the Commission shall, by rule, determine appropriate;

(4) Ensure that each investor—

(A) Reviews investor-education information, in accordance with standards established by the Commission, by rule;

(B) Positively affirms that the investor understands that the investor is risking the loss of the entire investment, and that the investor could bear such a loss; and

(C) Answers questions demonstrating—

(i) An understanding of the level of risk generally applicable to investments in startups, emerging businesses, and small issuers;

(ii) An understanding of the risk of illiquidity; and

(iii) An understanding of such other matters as the Commission determines appropriate, by rule;

(5) Take such measures to reduce the risk of fraud with respect to such transactions, as established by the Commission, by rule, including obtaining a background and securities enforcement regulatory history check on each officer, director, and person holding more than 20 percent of the outstanding equity of every issuer whose securities are offered by such person;

(6) Not later than 21 days prior to the first day on which securities are sold to any investor (or such other period as the Commission may establish), make available to the

Commission and to potential investors any information provided by the issuer pursuant to subsection (b);

(7) Ensure that all offering proceeds are only provided to the issuer when the aggregate capital raised from all investors is equal to or greater than a target offering amount, and allow all investors to cancel their commitments to invest, as the Commission shall, by rule, determine appropriate;

(8) Make such efforts as the Commission determines appropriate, by rule, to ensure that no investor in a 12-month period has purchased securities offered pursuant to Section 4(6) that, in the aggregate, from all issuers, exceed the investment limits set forth in Section 4(6)(B);

(9) Take such steps to protect the privacy of information collected from investors as the Commission shall, by rule, determine appropriate;

(10) Not compensate promoters, finders, or lead generators for providing the broker or funding portal with the personal identifying information of any potential investor;

(11) Prohibit its directors, officers, or partners (or any person occupying a similar status or performing a similar function) from having any financial interest in an issuer using its services; and

(12) Meet such other requirements as the Commission may, by rule, prescribe, for the protection of investors and in the public interest.

(b) Requirements For Issuers. For purposes of Section 4(6), an issuer who offers or sells securities shall—

(1) File with the Commission and provide to investors and the relevant broker or funding portal, and make available to potential investors—

(A) The name, legal status, physical address, and website address of the issuer;

(B) The names of the directors and officers (and any persons occupying a similar status or performing a similar function), and each person holding more than 20 percent of the shares of the issuer;

(C) A description of the business of the issuer and the anticipated business plan of the issuer;

(D) A description of the financial condition of the issuer, including, for offerings that, together with all other offerings of the issuer under Section 4(6) within the preceding 12-month period, have, in the aggregate, target offering amounts of—

(i) $100,000 or less—

(I) The income tax returns filed by the issuer for the most recently completed year (if any); and

(II) Financial statements of the issuer, which shall be certified by the principal executive officer of the issuer to be true and complete in all material respects;

(ii) More than $100,000, but not more than $500,000, financial statements reviewed by a public accountant who is independent of the issuer, using professional standards and procedures for such review or standards and procedures established by the Commission, by rule, for such purpose; and

(iii) More than $500,000 (or such other amount as the Commission may establish, by rule), audited financial statements;

(E) A description of the stated purpose and intended use of the proceeds of the offering sought by the issuer with respect to the target offering amount;

(F) The target offering amount, the deadline to reach the target offering amount, and regular updates regarding the progress of the issuer in meeting the target offering amount;

(G) The price to the public of the securities or the method for determining the price, provided that, prior to sale, each investor shall be provided in writing the final price and all required disclosures, with a reasonable opportunity to rescind the commitment to purchase the securities;

(H) A description of the ownership and capital structure of the issuer, including—

(i) Terms of the securities of the issuer being offered and each other class of security of the issuer, including how such terms may be modified, and a summary of the differences between such securities, including how the rights of the securities being offered may be materially limited, diluted, or qualified by the rights of any other class of security of the issuer;

(ii) A description of how the exercise of the rights held by the principal shareholders of the issuer could negatively impact the purchasers of the securities being offered;

(iii) The name and ownership level of each existing shareholder who owns more than 20 percent of any class of the securities of the issuer;

(iv) How the securities being offered are being valued, and examples of methods for how such securities may be valued by the issuer in the future, including during subsequent corporate actions; and

(v) The risks to purchasers of the securities relating to minority ownership in the issuer, the risks associated with corporate actions, including additional issuances of shares, a sale of the issuer or of assets of the issuer, or transactions with related parties; and

(I) Such other information as the Commission may, by rule, prescribe, for the protection of investors and in the public interest;

(2) Not advertise the terms of the offering, except for notices which direct investors to the funding portal or broker;

(3) Not compensate or commit to compensate, directly or indirectly, any person to promote its offerings through communication channels provided by a broker or funding portal, without taking such steps as the Commission shall, by rule, require to ensure that such person clearly discloses the receipt, past or prospective, of such compensation, upon each instance of such promotional communication;

(4) Not less than annually, file with the Commission and provide to investors reports of the results of operations and financial statements of the issuer, as the Commission shall, by rule, determine appropriate, subject to such exceptions and termination dates as the Commission may establish, by rule; and

(5) Comply with such other requirements as the Commission may, by rule, prescribe, for the protection of investors and in the public interest.

(c) Liability For Material Misstatements and Omissions.

(1) Actions Authorized.

(A) In General. Subject to paragraph (2), a person who purchases a security in a transaction exempted by the provisions of Section 4(6) may bring an action against an issuer described in paragraph (2), either at law or in equity in any court of competent jurisdiction, to recover the consideration paid for such security with interest thereon, less the amount of any income received thereon, upon the tender of such security, or for damages if such person no longer owns the security.

(B) Liability. An action brought under this paragraph shall be subject to the provisions of Section 12(b) and Section 13, as if the liability were created under Section 12(a)(2).

(2) Applicability. An issuer shall be liable in an action under paragraph (1), if the issuer—

(A) By the use of any means or instruments of transportation or communication in interstate commerce or of the mails, by any means of any written or oral communication, in the offering or sale of a security in a transaction exempted by the provisions of Section 4(6), makes an untrue statement of a material fact or omits to state a material fact required to be stated or necessary in order to make the statements, in the light of the circumstances under which they were made, not misleading, provided that the purchaser did not know of such untruth or omission; and

(B) Does not sustain the burden of proof that such issuer did not know, and in the exercise of reasonable care could not have known, of such untruth or omission.

(3) Definition. As used in this subsection, the term "issuer" includes any person who is a director or partner of the issuer, and the principal executive officer or officers, principal financial officer, and controller or principal accounting officer of the issuer (and any person occupying a similar status or performing a similar function) that offers or sells a security in a transaction exempted by the provisions of Section 4(6), and any person who offers or sells the security in such offering.

(d) Information Available to States. The Commission shall make, or shall cause to be made by the relevant broker or funding portal, the information described in subsection (b) and such other information as the Commission, by rule, determines appropriate, available to the securities commission (or any agency or office performing like functions) of each State and territory of the United States and the District of Columbia.

(e) Restrictions On Sales. Securities issued pursuant to a transaction described in Section 4(6)—

(1) May not be transferred by the purchaser of such securities during the 1-yearperiod beginning on the date of purchase, unless such securities are transferred—

(A) To the issuer of the securities;

(B) To an accredited investor;

(C) As part of an offering registered with the Commission; or

(D) To a member of the family of the purchaser or the equivalent, or in connection with the death or divorce of the purchaser or other similar circumstance, in the discretion of the Commission; and

(2) Shall be subject to such other limitations as the Commission shall, by rule, establish.

(f) Applicability. Section 4(6) shall not apply to transactions involving the offer or sale of securities by any issuer that—

(1) Is not organized under and subject to the laws of a State or territory of the United States or the District of Columbia;

(2) Is subject to the requirement to file reports pursuant to Section 13 or Section15(d) of the Securities Exchange Act of 1934;

(3) Is an investment company, as defined in Section 3 of the Investment Company Act of 1940, or is excluded from the definition of investment company by Section 3(b) or Section 3(c) of that Act; or

(4) The Commission, by rule or regulation, determines appropriate.

(g) Rule of Construction. Nothing in this section or Section 4(6) shall be construed as preventing an issuer from raising capital through methods not described under Section 4(6).

(h) Certain Calculations.

(1) Dollar Amounts. Dollar amounts in Section 4(6) and subsection (b) of this section shall be adjusted by the Commission not less frequently than once every 5years, by notice published in the Federal Register to reflect any change in the Consumer Price Index for All Urban Consumers published by the Bureau of Labor Statistics.

(2) Income and Net Worth. The income and net worth of a natural person under Section 4(6)(B) shall be calculated in accordance with any rules of the Commission under this title regarding the calculation of the income and net worth, respectively, of an accredited investor.

Sec.5. PROHIBITIONS RELATING TO INTERSTATE COMMERCE AND THE MAILS

(a) Unless a registration statement is in effect as to a security, it shall be unlawful for any person, directly or indirectly—

(1) to make use of any means or instruments of transportation or communication in interstate commerce or of the mails to sell such security through the use or medium of any prospectus or otherwise; or

(2) to carry or cause to be carried through the mails or in interstate commerce, by any means or instruments of transportation, any such security for the purpose of sale or for delivery after sale.

(b) It shall be unlawful for any person, directly or indirectly—

(1) to make use of any means or instruments of transportation or communication in interstate commerce or of the mails to carry or transmit any prospectus relating to any security with respect to which a registration statement has been filed under this title, unless such prospectus meets the requirements of section 10, or

(2) to carry or to cause to be carried through the mails or in interstate commerce any such security for the purpose of sale or for delivery after sale, unless accompanied or preceded by a prospectus that meets the requirements of subsection (a) of section 10.

(c) It shall be unlawful for any person, directly or indirectly, to make use of any means or instruments of transportation or communication in interstate commerce or of the mails to offer to sell or offer to buy through the use or medium of any prospectus or otherwise any security, unless a registration statement has been filed as to such security, or while the registration statement is the subject of a refusal order or stop order or (prior to the effective date of the registration statement) any public proceeding of examination under section 8.

(d) Limitation. Notwithstanding any other provision of this section, an emerging growth company or any person authorized to act on behalf of an emerging growth company may engage in oral or written communications with potential investors that are qualified institutional buyers or institutions that are accredited investors, as such terms are respectively defined in Section 230.144A and Section 230.501(a) of Title 17, Code of Federal Regulations, or any successor thereto, to determine whether such investors might have an interest in a contemplated securities offering, either prior to or following the date of filing of a registration statement with respect to such securities with the Commission, subject to the requirement of subsection (b)(2).

(e) Notwithstanding the provisions of section 3 or 4, unless a registration statement meeting the requirements of section 10(a) is in effect as to a security-based swap, it shall be unlawful for any person, directly or indirectly, to make use of any means or instruments of transportation or communication in interstate commerce or of the mails to offer to sell, offer to buy or purchase or sell a security-based swap to any person who is not an eligible contract participant as defined in section 1a(18) of the Commodity Exchange Act (7 U.S.C. 1a(18)).

Sec.6. REGISTRATION OF SECURITIES AND SIGNING OF REGISTRATION STATEMENT

(a) Any security may be registered with the Commission under the terms and conditions hereinafter provided, by filing a registration statement in triplicate, at least one of which shall be signed by each issuer, its principal executive officer or officers, its principal financial officer, its comptroller or principal accounting officer, and the majority of its board of directors or persons performing similar functions (or, if there is no board of directors or persons performing similar functions, by the majority of the persons or board having the power of management of the issuer), and in case the issuer is a foreign or Territorial person by its duly authorized representative in the United States; except that when such registration statement relates to a security issued by a foreign government, or political subdivision thereof, it need be signed only by the underwriter of such security. Signatures of all such persons when written on the said registration statements shall be presumed to have been so written by authority of the person whose signature is so affixed and the burden of proof, in the event such authority shall be denied, shall be upon the party denying the same. The affixing of any signature without the authority of the purported signer shall constitute a violation of this title. A registration statement shall be deemed effective only as to the securities specified therein as proposed to be offered.

(b) Registration Fee.—

(1) Fee Payment Required.—At the time of filing a registration statement, the applicant shall pay to the Commission a fee at a rate that shall be equal to $92 per $1,000,000 of the

maximum aggregate price at which such securities are proposed to be offered, except that during fiscal year 2003 and any succeeding fiscal year such fee shall be adjusted pursuant to paragraph (2).

(2) Annual Adjustment.—For each fiscal year, the Commission shall by order adjust the rate required by paragraph (1) for such fiscal year to a rate that, when applied to the baseline estimate of the aggregate maximum offering prices for such fiscal year, is reasonably likely to produce aggregate fee collections under this subsection that are equal to the target fee collection amount for such fiscal year.

(3) Pro Rata Application.—The rates per $1,000,000 required by this subsection shall be applied pro rata to amounts and balances of less than $1,000,000.

(4) Review and Effective Date.—In exercising its authority under this subsection, the Commission shall not be required to comply with the provisions of section 553 of title 5, United States Code. An adjusted rate prescribed under paragraph (2) and published under paragraph (5) shall not be subject to judicial review. An adjusted rate prescribed under paragraph (2) shall take effect on the first day of the fiscal year to which such rate applies.

(5) Publication.—The Commission shall publish in the Federal Register notices of the rate applicable under this subsection and under Sections 13(e) and 14(g) for each fiscal year not later than August 31 of the fiscal year preceding the fiscal year to which such rate applies, together with any estimates or projections on which such rate is based.

(6) Definitions.—For purposes of this subsection:

(A) Target Fee Collection Amount. The target fee collection amount for each fiscal year is determined according to the following table:

Fiscal year:	Target fee collection amount	Fiscal year:	Target fee collection amount
2002	$ 377,000,000	2015	$ 515,000,000
2003	$ 435,000,000	2016	$ 550,000,000
2004	$ 467,000,000	2017	$ 585,000,000
2005	$ 570,000,000	2018	$ 620,000,000
2006	$ 689,000,000	2019	$ 660,000,000
2007	$ 214,000,000	2020	$ 705,000,000
2008	$ 234,000,000	2021 and each fiscal year thereafter	An amount that is equal to the target fee collection amount for the prior fiscal year, adjusted by the rate of inflation.
2009	$ 284,000,000		
2010	$ 334,000,000		
2011	$ 394,000,000		
2012	$ 425,000,000		
2013	$ 455,000,000		
2014	$ 485,000,000		

(B) Baseline Estimate of the Aggregate Maximum Offering Prices.— The baseline estimate of the aggregate maximum offering prices for any fiscal year is the baseline estimate of the aggregate maximum offering price at which securities are proposed to be offered pursuant to registration statements filed with the Commission during such fiscal year as determined by the Commission, after consultation with the Congressional Budget Office and the Office of anagement and Budget, using the methodology required for projections pursuant to Section 257 of the Balanced Budget and Emergency Deficit Control Act of 1985.

(c) The filing with the Commission of a registration statement, or of an amendment to a registration statement, shall be deemed to have taken place upon the receipt thereof, but the filing of a registration statement shall not be deemed to have taken place unless it is accompanied by a United States postal money order or a certified bank check or cash for the amount of the fee required under subsection (b).

(d) The information contained in or filed with any registration statement shall be made available to the public under such regulations as the Commission may prescribe, and copies thereof, photostatic or otherwise, shall be furnished to every applicant at such reasonable charge as the Commission may prescribe.

(e) Emerging Growth Companies.

(1) In General. Any emerging growth company, prior to its initial public offering date, may confidentially submit to the Commission a draft registration statement, for confidential nonpublic review by the staff of the Commission prior to public filing, provided that the initial confidential submission and all amendments thereto shall be publicly filed with the Commission not later than 15 days before the date on which the issuer conducts a road show, as such term is defined in Section 230.433(h)(4) of Title 17, Code of Federal Regulations, or any successor thereto. An issuer that was an emerging growth company at the time it submitted a confidential registration statement or, in lieu thereof, a publicly filed registration statement for review under this subsection but ceases to be an emerging growth company thereafter shall continue to be treated as an emerging market growth company for the purposes of this subsection through the earlier of the date on which the issuer consummates its initial public offering pursuant to such registrations statement or the end of the 1-year period beginning on the date the company ceases to be an emerging growth company.

(2) Confidentiality. Notwithstanding any other provision of this title, the Commission shall not be compelled to disclose any information provided to or obtained by the Commission pursuant to this subsection. For purposes of Section 552 of Title 5, United States Code, this subsection shall be considered a statute described in subsection (b)(3)(B) of such Section 552. Information described in or obtained pursuant to this subsection shall be deemed to constitute confidential information for purposes of Section 24(b)(2) of the Securities Exchange Act of 1934.

Sec.7. INFORMATION REQUIRED IN REGISTRATION STATEMENT

(a) *Information Required in Registration Statement.*

(1) *In General.* The registration statement, when relating to a security other than a security issued by a foreign government, or political subdivision therof, shall contain the information, and be accompanied by the documents, specified in Schedule A, and when relating to a security issued by a foreign government, or political subdivision thereof, shall contain the information, and be accompanied by the documents, specified in Schedule B; except that the Commission may by rules or regulations provide that any such information or document need not be included in respect of any class of issuers or securities if it finds that the requirement of such information or document is inapplicable to such class and that disclosure fully adequate for the protection of investors is otherwise required to be included within the registration statement. If any accountant, engineer, or appraiser, or any person whose profession gives authority to a statement made by him, is named as having prepared or certified any part of the registration statement, or is named as having prepared or certified a report or valuation for use in connection with the registration statement, the written consent of such person shall be filed with the registration statement. If any such person is named as having prepared or certified a report or valuation (other than a public official document or statement) which is used in connection with the registration statement, but is not named as having prepared or certified such report or valuation for use in connection with the registration statement, the written consent of such person shall be filed with the registration statement unless the Commission dispenses with such filing as impracticable or as involving undue hardship on the person filing the registration statement. Any such registration statement shall contain such other information, and be accompanied by such other documents, as the Commission may by rules or regulations require as being necessary or appropriate in t he public interest or for the protection of investors.

(2) Treatment of Emerging Growth Companies. An emerging growth company—

(A) Need not present more than 2 years of audited financial statements in order for the registration statement of such emerging growth company with respect to an initial public offering of its common equity securities to be effective, and in any other registration statement to be filed with the Commission, an emerging growth company need not present selected financial data in accordance with Section 229.301 of Title 17, Code of Federal Regulations, for any period prior to the earliest audited period presented in connection with its initial public offering; and

(B) May not be required to comply with any new or revised financial accounting standard until such date that a company that is not an issuer (as defined under Section 2(a) of the Sarbanes-Oxley Act of 2002 (15 U.S.C. 7201(a))) is required to comply with such new or revised accounting standard, if such standard applies to companies that are not issuers.

(b)(1) The Commission shall prescribe special rules with respect to registration statements filed by any issuer that is a blank check company. Such rules may, as the Commission determines necessary or appropriate in the public interest or for the protection of investors—

(A) require such issuers to provide timely disclosure, prior to or after such statement becomes effective under section 8, of (i) information regarding the company to be acquired and the specific application of the proceeds of the offering, or (ii) additional information necessary to prevent such statement from being misleading;

(B) place limitations on the use of such proceeds and the distribution of securities by such issuer until the disclosures required under subparagraph (A) have been made; and

(C) provide a right of rescission to shareholders of such securities.

(2) The Commission may, as it determines consistent with the public interest and the protection of investors, by rule or order exempt any issuer or class of issuers from the rules prescribed under paragraph (1).

(3) For purposes of paragraph (1) of this subsection, the term "blank check company" means any development stage company that is issuing a penny stock (within the meaning of section 3(a)(51) of the Securities Exchange Act of 1934) and that—

(A) has no specific business plan or purpose; or

(B) has indicated that its business plan is to merge with an unidentified company or companies.

(c) *Disclosure Requirements.*

(1) *In General.* The Commission shall adopt regulations under this subsection requiring each issuer of an asset-backed security to disclose, for each tranche or class of security, information regarding the assets backing that security.

(2) *Content of Regulations.* In adopting regulations under this subsection, the Commission shall—

(A) Set standards for the format of the data provided by issuers of an asset-backed security, which shall, to the extent feasible, facilitate comparison of such data across securities in similar types of asset classes; and

(B) Require issuers of asset-backed securities, at a minimum, to disclose asset-level or loan-level data, if such data are necessary for investors to independently perform due diligence, including—

(i) Data having unique identifiers relating to loan brokers or originators;

(ii) The nature and extent of the compensation of the broker or originator of the assets backing the security; and

(iii) The amount of risk retention by the originator and the securitizer of such assets.

(d) *Registration Statement For Asset-Backed Securities.* Not later than 180 days after the date of enactment of this subsection, the Commission shall issue rules relating to the registration statement required to be filed by any issuer of an asset-backed security (as that term is defined in section 3(a)(77) of the Securities Exchange Act of 1934) that require any issuer of an asset-backed security—

(1) To perform a review of the assets underlying the asset-backed security; and

(2) To disclose the nature of the review under paragraph (1).

Sec.8. TAKING EFFECT OF REGISTRATION STATEMENTS AND AMENDMENTS THERETO

(a) Except as hereinafter provided, the effective date of a registration statement shall be the twentieth day after the filing thereof or such earlier date as the Commission may determine, having due regard to the adequacy of the information respecting the issuer theretofore available to the public, to the facility with which the nature of the securities to be registered, their relationship to the capital structure of the issuer and the rights of holders thereof can be understood, and to the public interest and the protection of investors. If any amendment to any such statement is filed prior to the effective date of such statement, the registration statement shall be deemed to have been filed when such amendment was filed; except that an amendment filed with the consent of the Commission, prior to the effective date of the registration statement, or filed pursuant to an order of the Commission, shall be treated as a part of the registration statement.

(b) If it appears to the Commission that a registration statement is on its face incomplete or inaccurate in any material respect, the Commission may, after notice by personal service or the sending of confirmed telegraphic notice not later than ten days after the filing of the registration statement, and opportunity for hearing (at a time fixed by the Commission) within ten days after such notice by personal service or the sending of such telegraphic notice, issue an order prior to the effective date of registration refusing to permit such statement to become effective until it has been amended in accordance with such order. When such statement has been amended in accordance with such order the Commission shall so declare and the registration shall become effective at the time provided in subsection (a) or upon the date of such declaration, whichever date is the later.

(c) An amendment filed after the effective date of the registration statement, if such amendment, upon its face, appears to the Commission not to be incomplete or inaccurate in any material respect, shall become effective on such date as the Commission may determine, having due regard to the public interest and the protection of investors.

(d) If it appears to the Commission at any time that the registration statement includes any untrue statement of a material fact or omits to state any material fact required to be stated therein or necessary to make the statements therein not misleading, the Commission may, after notice by personal service or the sending of confirmed telegraphic notice, and after opportunity for hearing (at a time fixed by the Commission) within fifteen days after such notice by personal service or the sending of such telegraphic notice, issue a stop order suspending the effectiveness of the registration statement. When such statement has been amended in accordance with such stop order the Commission shall so declare and thereupon the stop order shall cease to be effective.

(e) The Commission is hereby empowered to make an examination in any case in order to determine whether a stop order should issue under subsection (d). In making such examination the Commission or any officer or officers designated by it shall have access to and may demand the production of any books and papers of, and may administer oaths and affirmations to and examine, the issuer, underwriter, or any other person, in respect of any matter relevant to the examination, and may, in its discretion, require the production of a balance sheet exhibiting the assets and liabilities of the issuer, or its income statement, or both, to be certified to by a public or certified accountant approved by the Commission. If the issuer or underwriter shall fail to cooperate, or shall obstruct or refuse to permit the making of an examination, such conduct shall be proper ground for the issuance of a stop order.

(f) Any notice required under this section shall be sent to or served on the issuer, or, in case of a foreign government political subdivision thereof, to or on the underwriter, or, in the case of a foreign or Territorial person, to or on its duly authorized representative in the United

States named in the registration statement, properly directed in each case of telegraphic notice to the address given in such statement.

Sec.8A. CEASE-AND-DESIST PROCEEDINGS

(a) AUTHORITY OF THE COMMISSION.—If the Commission finds, after notice and opportunity for hearing, that any person is violating, has violated, or is about to violate any provision of this title, or any rule or regulation thereunder, the Commission may publish its findings and enter an order requiring such person, and any other person that is, was, or would be a cause of the violation, due to an act or omission the person knew or should have known would contribute to such violation, to cease and desist from committing or causing such violation and any future violation of the same provision, rule or regulation. Such order may, in addition to requiring a person to cease and desist from committing or causing a violation, require such person to comply, or to take steps to effect compliance, with such provision, rule, or regulation, upon such terms and conditions and within such time as the Commission may specify in such order. Any such order may, as the Commission deems appropriate, require future compliance or steps to effect future compliance, either permanently or for such period of time as the Commission may specify, with such provision, rule, or regulation with respect to any security, any issuer, or any other person.

(b) HEARING.—The notice instituting proceedings pursuant to subsection (a) shall fix a hearing date not earlier than 30 days nor later than 60 days after service of the notice unless an earlier or a later date is set by the Commission with the consent of any respondent so served.

(c) TEMPORARY ORDER.—

(1) IN GENERAL.—Whenever the Commission determines that the alleged violation or threatened violation specified in the notice instituting proceedings pursuant to subsection (a), or the continuation thereof, is likely to result in significant dissipation or conversion of assets, significant harm to investors, or substantial harm to the public interest, including, but not limited to, losses to the Securities Investor Protection Corporation, prior to the completion of the proceedings, the Commission may enter a temporary order requiring the respondent to cease and desist from the violation or threatened violation and to take such action to prevent the violation or threatened violation and to prevent dissipation or conversion of assets, significant harm to investors, or substantial harm to the public interest as the Commission deems appropriate pending completion of such proceeding. Such an order shall be entered only after notice and opportunity for a hearing, unless the Commission determines that notice and hearing prior to entry would be impracticable or contrary to the public interest. A temporary order shall become effective upon service upon the respondent and, unless set aside, limited, or suspended by the Commission or a court of competent jurisdiction, shall remain effective and enforceable pending the completion of the proceedings.

(2) APPLICABILITY.—This subsection shall apply only to a respondent that acts, or, at the time of the alleged misconduct acted, as a broker, dealer, investment adviser, investment company, municipal securities dealer, government securities broker, government securities dealer, or transfer agent, or is, or was at the time of the alleged misconduct, an associated person of, or a person seeking to become associated with, any of the foregoing.

(d) REVIEW OF TEMPORARY ORDERS.—

(1) COMMISSION REVIEW.—At any time after the respondent has been served with a temporary cease-and-desist order pursuant to subsection (c), the respondent may apply to the Commission to have the order set aside, limited, or suspended. If the respondent has been served with a temporary cease-and-desist order entered without a prior Commission hearing, the respondent may, within 10 days after the date on which the order was served, request a hearing on such application and the Commission shall hold a hearing and render a decision on such application at the earliest possible time.

(2) JUDICIAL REVIEW.—Within—

(A) 10 days after the date the respondent was served with a temporary cease-and-desist order entered with a prior Commission hearing, or

(B) 10 days after the Commission renders a decision on an application and hearing under paragraph (1), with respect to any temporary cease-and-desist order entered without a prior Commission hearing,

the respondent may apply to the United States district court for the district in which the respondent resides or has its principal place of business, or for the District of Columbia, for an order setting aside, limiting, or suspending the effectiveness or enforcement of the order, and the court shall have jurisdiction to enter such an order. A respondent served with a temporary cease-and-desist order entered without a prior Commission hearing may not apply to the court except after hearing and decision by the Commission on the respondent's application under paragraph (1) of this subsection.

(3) No AUTOMATIC STAY OF TEMPORARY ORDER.—The commencement of proceedings under paragraph (2) of this subsection shall not, unless specifically ordered by the court, operate as a stay of the Commission's order.

(4) EXCLUSIVE REVIEW.—Section 9(a) of this title shall not apply to a temporary order entered pursuant to this section.

(e) AUTHORITY TO ENTER AN ORDER REQUIRING AN ACCOUNTING and DISGORGEMENT.—In any cease-and-desist proceeding under subsection (a), the Commission may enter an order requiring accounting and disgorgement, including reasonable interest. The Commission is authorized to adopt rules, regulations, and orders concerning payments to investors, rates of interest, periods of accrual, and such other matters as it deems appropriate to implement this subsection.

(f) AUTHORITY OF THE COMMISSION TO PROHIBIT PERSONS FROM SERVING AS OFFICERS OR DIRECTORS.—In any cease-and-desist proceeding under subsection (a), the Commission may issue an order to prohibit, conditionally or unconditionally, and permanently or for such period of time as it shall determine, any person who has violated section 17(a)(1) or the rules or regulations thereunder, from acting as an officer or director of any issuer that has a class of securities registered pursuant to section 12 of the Securities Exchange Act of 1934, or that is required to file reports pursuant to section 15(d) of that Act, if the conduct of that person demonstrates unfitness to serve as an officer or director of any such issuer.

(g) AUTHORITY TO IMPOSE MONEY PENALTIES.—

(1) GROUNDS.— In any cease-and-desist proceeding under subsection (a), the Commission may impose a civil penalty on a person if the Commission finds, on the record, after notice and opportunity for hearing, that—

(A) Such person—

(i) Is violating or has violated any provision of this title, or any rule or regulation issued under this title; or

(ii) Is or was a cause of the violation of any provision of this title, or any rule or regulation thereunder; and

(B) Such penalty is in the public interest.

(2) MAXIMUM AMOUNT OF PENALTY.—

(A) FIRST TIER. The maximum amount of a penalty for each act or omission described in paragraph (1) shall be $7,500 for a natural person or $75,000 for any other person.

(B) SECOND TIER.— Notwithstanding subparagraph (A), the maximum amount of penalty for each such act or omission shall be $75,000 for a natural person or $375,000 for any other person, if the act or omission described in paragraph (1) involved fraud, deceit, manipulation, or deliberate or reckless disregard of a regulatory requirement.

(C) THIRD TIER.— Notwithstanding subparagraphs (A) and (B), the maximum amount of penalty for each such act or omission shall be $150,000 for a natural person or $725,000 for any other person, if—

(i) The act or omission described in paragraph (1) involved fraud, deceit, manipulation, or deliberate or reckless disregard of a regulatory requirement; and

(ii) Such act or omission directly or indirectly resulted in—

(I) Substantial losses or created a significant risk of substantial losses to other persons; or

(II) Substantial pecuniary gain to the person who committed the act or omission.

(3) EVIDENCE CONCERNING ABILITY TO PAY.— In any proceeding in which the Commission may impose a penalty under this section, a respondent may present evidence of the ability of the respondent to pay such penalty. The Commission may, in its discretion, consider such evidence in determining whether such penalty is in the public interest. Such evidence may relate to the extent of the ability of the respondent to continue in business and the collectability of a penalty, taking into account any other claims of the United States or third parties upon the assets of the respondent and the amount of the assets of the respondent.

Sec.9. COURT REVIEW OF ORDERS

(a) Any person aggrieved by an order to the Commission may obtain a review of such order in the court of appeals of the United States, within any circuit wherein such person resides or has his principal place of business, or in the United States Court of Appeals for the District of Columbia, by filing in such Court, within sixty days after the entry of such order, a written petition praying that the order of the Commission be modified or be set aside in whole or in part. A copy of such petition shall be forthwith transmitted by the clerk of the court to the Commission, and thereupon the Commission shall file in the court the record upon which the order complained of was entered, as provided in section 2112 of title 28, United States Code. No objection to the order of the Commission shall be considered by the courts unless such objection shall have been urged before the Commission. The finding of the Commission as to the facts, if supported by evidence, shall be conclusive. If either party shall apply to the court for leave to adduce additional evidence, and shall show to the satisfaction of the court that such additional evidence is material and that there were reasonable grounds for failure to adduce such evidence in the hearing before the Commission, the court may order such additional evidence to be taken before the Commission and to be adduced upon the hearing in such manner and upon such terms and conditions as to the court may seem proper. The Commission may modify its findings as to the facts, by reason of the additional evidence so taken, and it shall file such modified or new findings, which, if supported by evidence, shall be conclusive, and its recommendation, if any, for the modification or setting aside of the original order. The jurisdiction of the court shall be exclusive and its judgement and decree, affirming, modifying, or setting aside, in whole or in part, any order of the Commission, shall be final, subject to review by the Supreme Court of the United States upon certiorari or certification as provided in section 1254 of Title 28, United States Code.

(b) The commencement of proceedings under subsection (a) shall not, unless specifically ordered by the court, operate as a stay of the Commission's order.

Sec.10. INFORMATION REQUIRED IN PROSPECTUS

(a) Except to the extent otherwise permitted or required pursuant to this subsection or subsections (c), (d), or (e)—

(1) a prospectus relating to a security other than a security issued by a foreign government or political subdivision thereof, shall contain the information contained in the registration statement, but it need not include the documents referred to in paragraphs (28) to (32), inclusive, of Schedule A;

(2) a prospectus relating to a security issued by a foreign government or political subdivision thereof shall contain the information contained in the registration statement, but it need not include the documents referred to in paragraphs (13) and (14) of Schedule B;

(3) notwithstanding the provisions of paragraphs (1) and (2) of this subsection (a) when a prospectus is used more than nine months after the effective date of the registration

statement, the information contained therein shall be as of a date not more than sixteen months prior to such use so far as such information is known to the user of such prospectus or can be furnished by such user without unreasonable effort or expense;

(4) there may be omitted from any prospectus any of the statements required under such subsection (a) which the Commission may by rules or regulations designate as not being necessary or appropriate in the public interest or for the protection of investors.

(b) In addition to the prospectus permitted or required in subsection (a), the Commission shall by rules or regulations deemed necessary or appropriate in the public interest or for the protection of investors permit the use of a prospectus for the purposes of subsection (b)(1) of section 5 which omits in part or summarizes information in the prospectus specified in subsection (a). A prospectus permitted under this subsection shall, except to the extent the Commission by rules or regulations deemed necessary or appropriate in the public interest or for the protection of investors otherwise provides, be filed as part of the registration statement but shall not be deemed a part of such registration statement for the purposes of section 11. The Commission may at any time issue an order preventing or suspending the use of a prospectus permitted under this subsection (b), if it has reason to believe that such prospectus has not been filed (if required to be filed as part of the registration statement) or includes any untrue statement of a material fact or omits to state any material fact required to be stated therein or necessary to make the statements therein, in the light of the circumstances under which such prospectus is or is to be used, not misleading. Upon issuance of an order under this subsection, the Commission shall give notice of the issuance of such order and opportunity for hearing by personal service or the sending of confirmed telegraphic notice. The Commission shall vacate or modify the order at any time for good cause or if such prospectus has been filed or amended in accordance with such order.

(c) Any prospectus shall contain such other information as the Commission may by rules or regulations require as being necessary or appropriate in the public interest or for the protection of investors.

(d) In the exercise of its powers under subsections (a), (b), or (c), the Commission shall have authority to classify prospectuses according to the nature and circumstances of their use or the nature of the security, issue, issuer, or otherwise, and, by rules and regulations and subject to such terms and conditions as it shall specify therein, to prescribe as to each class the form and contents which it may find appropriate and consistent with the public interest and the protection of investors.

(e) The statements or information required to be included in a prospectus by or under authority of subsections (a), (b), (c), or (d), when written, shall be placed in a conspicuous part of the prospectus and, except as otherwise permitted by rules or regulations, in type as large as that used generally in the body of the prospectus.

(f) In any case where a prospectus consists of a radio or television broadcast, copies thereof shall be filed with the Commission under such rules and regulations as it shall prescribe. The Commission may by rules and regulations require the filing with it of forms of prospectuses used in connection with the sale of securities registered under this title.

Sec. 11. CIVIL LIABILITIES ON ACCOUNT OF FALSE REGISTRATION STATEMENT

(a) In case any part of the registration statement, when such part became effective, contained an untrue statement of a material fact or omitted to state a material fact required to be stated therein or necessary to make the statements therein not misleading, any person acquiring such security (unless it is proved that at the time of such acquisition he knew of such untruth or omission) may, either at law or in equity, in any court of competent jurisdiction, sue—

(1) every person who signed the registration statement;

(2) every person who was a director of (or person performing similar functions), or partner in, the issuer at the time of the filing of the part of the registration statement with respect to which his liability is asserted;

(3) every person who, with his consent, is named in the registration statement as being or about to become a director, person performing similar functions, or partner;

(4) every accountant engineer, or appraiser, or any person whose profession gives authority to a statement made by him, who has with his consent been named as having prepared or certified any part of the registration statement, or as having prepared or certified any report or valuation which is used in connection with the registration statement, with respect to the statement in such registration statement, report, or valuation, which purports to have been prepared or certified by him;

(5) every underwriter with respect to such security.

If such person acquired the security after the issuer has made generally available to its security holders an earning statement covering a period of at least twelve months beginning after the effective date of the registration statement, then the right of recovery under this subsection shall be conditioned on proof that such person acquired the securities relying on such untrue statement in the registration statement or relying upon the registration statement and not knowing of such omission, but such reliance may be established without proof of the reading of the registration statement by such person.

(b) Notwithstanding the provisions of subsection (a) no person, other than the issuer, shall be liable as provided therein who shall sustain the burden of proof—

(1) that before the effective date of the part of the registration statement with respect to which his liability is asserted (A) he had resigned from or had taken such steps as are permitted by law to resign from, or ceased or refused to act in, every office, capacity, or relationship in which he was described in the registration statement as acting or agreeing to act, and (B) he had advised the Commission and the issuer in writing, that he had taken such action and that he would not be responsible for such part of the registration statement; or

(2) that if such part of the registration statement became effective without his knowledge, upon becoming aware of such fact he forthwith acted and advised the Commission, in accordance with paragraph (1), and, in addition, gave reasonable public notice that such part of the registration statement had become effective without his knowledge; or

(3) that (A) as regards any part of the registration statement not purporting to be made on the authority of an expert, and not purporting to be a copy of or extract from a report or valuation of an expert and not purporting to be made on the authority of a public official document or statement, he had, after reasonable investigation, reasonable ground to believe and did believe, at the time such part of the registration statement became effective, that the statements therein were true and that there was no omission to state a material fact required to be stated therein or necessary to make the statements therein not misleading; and

(B) as regards any part of the registration statement purporting to be made upon his authority as an expert or purporting to be a copy of or extract from a report or valuation of himself as an expert, (i) he had, after reasonable investigation, reasonable ground to believe and did believe, at the time such part of the registration statement became effective, that the statements therein were true and that there was no omission to state a material fact required to be stated therein or necessary to make the statements therein not misleading, or (ii) such part of the registration statement did not fairly represent his statement as an expert or was not a fair copy of or extract from his report or valuation as an expert; and

(C) as regards any part of the registration statement purporting to be made on the authority of an expert (other than himself) or purporting to be a copy of or extract from a report or valuation of an expert (other than himself), he had no reasonable ground to believe and did not believe, at the time such part of the registration statement became effective, that the statements therein were untrue or that there was an omission to state a material fact required to be stated therein or necessary to make the statements therein not misleading, or that such part of the registration statement did not fairly represent the statement of the expert or was not a fair copy of or extract from the report or valuation of the expert; and

(D) as regards any part of the registration statement purporting to be a statement made by an official person or purporting to be a copy of or extract from a public official document, he had no reasonable ground to believe and did not believe, at the time such part of the registration statement became effective, that the statements therein were untrue, or that there was an omission to state a material fact required to be stated therein or necessary to make the statements therein not misleading, or that such part of the registration statement did not fairly represent the statement made by the official person or was not a fair copy of or extract from the public official document.

(c) In determining, for the purpose of paragraph (3) of subsection (b) of this section, what constitutes reasonable investigation and reasonable ground for belief, the standard of reasonableness shall be that required of a prudent man in the management of his own property.

(d) If any person becomes an underwriter with respect to the security after the part of the registration statement with respect to which his liability is asserted has become effective, then for the purposes of paragraph (3) of subsection (b) of this section such part of the registration statement shall be considered as having become effective with respect to such person as of the time when he became an underwriter.

(e) The suit authorized under subsection (a) may be to recover such damages as shall represent the difference between the amount paid for the security (not exceeding the price at which the security was offered to the public) and (1) the value thereof as of the time such suit was brought, or (2) the price at which such security shall have been disposed of in the market before suit, or (3) the price at which such security shall have been disposed of after suit but before judgment if such damages shall be less than the damages representing the difference between the amount paid for the security (not exceeding the price at which the security was offered to the public) and the value thereof as of the time such suit was brought: Provided, That if the defendant proves that any portion or all of such damages represents other than the depreciation in value of such security resulting from such part of the registration statement, with respect to which his liability is asserted, not being true or omitting to state a material fact required to be stated therein or necessary to make the statements therein not misleading, such portion of or all such damages shall not be recoverable. In no event shall any underwriter (unless such underwriter shall have knowingly received from the issuer for acting as an underwriter some benefit, directly or indirectly in which all other underwriters similarly situated did not share in proportion to their respective interests in the underwriting) be liable in any suit or as a consequence of suits authorized under subsection (a) for damages in excess of the total price at which the securities underwritten by him and distributed to the public were offered to the public. In any suit under this or any other section of this title the court may, in its discretion, require an undertaking for the payment of the costs of such suit, including reasonable attorney's fees, and if judgment shall be rendered against a party litigant, upon the motion of the other party litigant, such costs may be assessed in favor of such party litigant (whether or not such undertaking has been required) if the court believes the suit or the defense to have been without merit, in an amount sufficient to reimburse him for the reasonable expenses incurred by him, in connection with such suit, such costs to be taxed in the manner usually provided for taxing of costs in the court in which the suit was heard.

(f)(1) Except as provided in paragraph (2), all or any one or more of the persons specified in subsection (a) shall be jointly and severally liable, and every person who becomes liable to make any payment under this section may recover contribution as in cases of contract from any person who, if sued separately, would have been liable to make the same payment, unless the person who has become liable was, and the other was not, guilty of fraudulent misrepresentation.

(2)(A) The liability of an outside director under subsection (e) shall be determined in accordance with section 21D(f) of the Securities Exchange Act of 1934.

(B) For purposes of this paragraph, the term "outside director" shall have the meaning given such term by rule or regulation of the Commission.

(g) In no case shall the amount recoverable under this section exceed the price at which the security was offered to the public.

Sec. 12. CIVIL LIABILITIES ARISING IN CONNECTION WITH PROSPECTUSES AND COMMUNICATIONS

(a) IN GENERAL.—Any person who—

(1) offers or sells a security in violation of section 5, or

(2) offers or sells a security (whether or not exempted by the provisions of section 3, other than paragraphs (2) and (14) of subsection (a) thereof), by the use of any means or instruments of transportation or communication in interstate commerce or of the mails, by means of a prospectus or oral communication, which includes an untrue statement of a material fact or omits to state a material fact necessary in order to make the statements, in the light of the circumstances under which they were made, not misleading (the purchaser not knowing of such untruth or omission), and who shall not sustain the burden of proof that he did not know, and in the exercise of reasonable care could not have known, of such untruth or omission,

shall be liable, subject to subsection (b), to the person purchasing such security from him, who may sue either at law or in equity in any court of competent jurisdiction, to recover the consideration paid for such security with interest thereon, less the amount of any income received thereon, upon the tender of such security, or for damages if he no longer owns the security.

(b) LOSS CAUSATION.—In an action described in subsection (a)(2), if the person who offered or sold such security proves that any portion or all of the amount recoverable under subsection (a)(2) represents other than the depreciation in value of the subject security resulting from such part of the prospectus or oral communication, with respect to which the liability of that person is asserted, not being true or omitting to state a material fact required to be stated therein or necessary to make the statement not misleading, then such portion or amount, as the case may be, shall not be recoverable.

Sec. 13. LIMITATION OF ACTIONS

No action shall be maintained to enforce any liability created under section 11 or section 12(a)(2) unless brought within one year after the discovery of the untrue statement or the omission, or after such discovery should have been made by the exercise of reasonable diligence, or, if the action is to enforce a liability created under section 12(a)(1), unless brought within one year after the violation upon which it is based. In no event shall any such action be brought to enforce a liability created under section 11 or section 12(a)(1) more than three years after the security was bona fide offered to the public, or under section 12(a)(2) more than three years after the sale.

Sec. 14. CONTRARY STIPULATIONS VOID

Any condition, stipulation, or provision binding any person acquiring any security to waive compliance with any provision of this title or of the rules and regulations of the Commission shall be void.

Sec. 15. LIABILITY OF CONTROLLING PERSONS

(a) Controlling Person.—Every person who, by or through stock ownership, agency, or otherwise, or who, pursuant to or in connection with an agreement or understanding with one or more other persons by or through stock ownership, agency, or otherwise, controls any person liable under section 11, or 12, shall also be liable jointly and severally with and to the same extent as such controlled person to any person to whom such controlled person is liable, unless the controlling person had no knowledge of or reasonable ground to believe in the existence of the facts by reason of which the liability of the controlled person is alleged to exist.

(b) Prosecution of Persons Who Aid and Abet Violations.—For purposes of any action brought by the Commission under subparagraph (b) or (d) of section 20, any person that knowingly or recklessly provides substantial assistance to another person in violation of a provision of this Act, or of any rule or regulation issued under this Act, shall be deemed to be in violation of such provision to the same extent as the person to whom such assistance is provided.

Sec. 16. ADDITIONAL REMEDIES; LIMITATIONS ON REMEDIES

(a) Remedies Additional.—Except as provided in subsection (b), the rights and remedies provided by this title shall be in addition to any and all other rights and remedies that may exist at law or in equity.

(b) Class Action Limitations.—No covered class action based upon the statutory or common law of any State or subdivision thereof may be maintained in any State or Federal court by any private party alleging—

(1) an untrue statement or omission of a material fact in connection with the purchase or sale of a covered security; or

(2) that the defendant used or employed any manipulative or deceptive device or contrivance in connection with the purchase or sale of a covered security.

(c) Removal of Covered Class Actions.—Any covered class action brought in any State court involving a covered security, as set forth in subsection (b), shall be removable to the Federal district court for the district in which the action is pending, and shall be subject to subsection (b).

(d) Preservation of Certain Actions.—

(1) Actions under state law of state of incorporation.—

(A) Actions preserved.—Notwithstanding subsection (b) or (c), a covered class action described in subparagraph (B) of this paragraph that is based upon the statutory or common law of the State in which the issuer is incorporated (in the case of a corporation) or organized (in the case of any other entity) may be maintained in a State or Federal court by a private party.

(B) Permissible actions.—A covered class action is described in this subparagraph if it involves—

(i) the purchase or sale of securities by the issuer or an affiliate of the issuer exclusively from or to holders of equity securities of the issuer; or

(ii) any recommendation, position, or other communication with respect to the sale of securities of the issuer that—

(I) is made by or on behalf of the issuer or an affiliate of the issuer to holders of equity securities of the issuer; and

(II) concerns decisions of those equity holders with respect to voting their securities, acting in response to a tender or exchange offer, or exercising dissenters' or appraisal rights.

(2) State actions.—

(A) In general.—Notwithstanding any other provision of this section, nothing in this section may be construed to preclude a State or political subdivision thereof or a State pension plan from bringing an action involving a covered security on its own behalf, or as a member of a class comprised solely of other States, political subdivisions, or State pension plans that are named plaintiffs, and that have authorized participation, in such action.

(B) State pension plan defined.—For purposes of this paragraph, the term "State pension plan" means a pension plan established and maintained for its employees by the government of the State or political subdivision thereof, or by any agency or instrumentality thereof.

(3) Actions under contractual agreements between issuers and indenture trustees.—Notwithstanding subsection (b) or (c), a covered class action that seeks to enforce a contractual agreement between an issuer and an indenture trustee may be maintained in a State or Federal court by a party to the agreement or a successor to such party.

(4) Remand of removed actions.—In an action that has been removed from a State court pursuant to subsection (c), if the Federal court determines that the action may be maintained in State court pursuant to this subsection, the Federal court shall remand such action to such State court.

(e) Preservation of State Jurisdiction.—The securities commission (or any agency or office performing like functions) of any State shall retain jurisdiction under the laws of such State to investigate and bring enforcement actions.

(f) Definitions.—For purposes of this section, the following definitions shall apply:

(1) Affiliate of the issuer.—The term "affiliate of the issuer" means a person that directly or indirectly, through one or more intermediaries, controls or is controlled by or is under common control with, the issuer.

(2) Covered class action.—

(A) In general.—The term "covered class action" means—

(i) any single lawsuit in which—

(I) damages are sought on behalf of more than 50 persons or prospective class members, and questions of law or fact common to those persons or members of the prospective class, without reference to issues of individualized reliance on an alleged misstatement or omission, predominate over any questions affecting only individual persons or members; or

(II) one or more named parties seek to recover damages on a representative basis on behalf of themselves and other unnamed parties similarly situated, and questions of law or fact common to those persons or members of the prospective class predominate over any questions affecting only individual persons or members; or

(ii) any group of lawsuits filed in or pending in the same court and involving common questions of law or fact, in which—

(I) damages are sought on behalf of more than 50 persons; and

(II) the lawsuits are joined, consolidated, or otherwise proceed as a single action for any purpose.

(B) Exception for derivative actions.—Notwithstanding subparagraph (A), the term "covered class action" does not include an exclusively derivative action brought by one or more shareholders on behalf of a corporation.

(C) Counting of certain class members.—For purposes of this paragraph, a corporation, investment company, pension plan, partnership, or other entity, shall be treated as one person or prospective class member, but only if the entity is not established for the purpose of participating in the action.

(D) Rule of construction.—Nothing in this paragraph shall be construed to affect the discretion of a State court in determining whether actions filed in such court should be joined, consolidated, or otherwise allowed to proceed as a single action.

(3) Covered security.—The term "covered security" means a security that satisfies the standards for a covered security specified in paragraph (1) or (2) of section 18(b) at the time during which it is alleged that the misrepresentation, omission, or manipulative or deceptive conduct occurred, except that such term shall not include any debt security that is exempt from registration under this title pursuant to rules issued by the Commission under section 4(2).

Sec.17. FRAUDULENT INTERSTATE TRANSACTIONS

(a) It shall be unlawful for any person in the offer or sale of any securities (including security-based swaps) or any security-based swap agreement (as defined in section 3(a)(78) of the Securities Exchange Act) by the use of any means or instruments of transportation or communication in interstate commerce or by use of the mails, directly or indirectly—

(1) to employ any device, scheme, or artifice to defraud, or

(2) to obtain money or property by means of any untrue statement of a material fact or any omission to state a material fact necessary in order to make the statements made, in light of the circumstances under which they were made, not misleading; or

(3) to engage in any transaction, practice, or course of business which operates or would operate as a fraud or deceit upon the purchaser.

(b) It shall be unlawful for any person, by the use of any means or instruments of transportation or communication in interstate commerce or by the use of the mails, to publish, give publicity to, or circulate any notice, circular, advertisement, newspaper, article, letter, investment service, or communication which, though not purporting to offer a security for sale, describes such security for a consideration received or to be received, directly or indirectly, from an issuer, underwriter, or dealer, without fully disclosing the receipt, whether past or prospective, of such consideration and the amount thereof.

(c) The exemptions provided in section 3 shall not apply to the provisions of this section.

(d) The authority of the Commission under this section with respect to security-based swap agreements (as defined in section 3(a)(78) of the Securities Exchange Act of 1934) shall be subject to the restrictions and limitations of section 2A(b) of this title.

Sec. 18. EXEMPTION FROM STATE REGULATION OF SECURITIES OFFERINGS

(a) SCOPE OF EXEMPTION.—Except as otherwise provided in this section, no law, rule, regulation, or order, or other administrative action of any State or any political subdivision thereof—

(1) requiring, or with respect to, registration or qualification of securities, or registration or qualification of securities transactions, shall directly or indirectly apply to a security that—

(A) is a covered security; or

(B) will be a covered security upon completion of the transaction;

(2) shall directly or indirectly prohibit, limit, or impose any conditions upon the use of—

(A) with respect to a covered security described in subsection (b), any offering document that is prepared by or on behalf of the issuer; or

(B) any proxy statement, report to shareholders, or other disclosure document relating to a covered security or the issuer thereof that is required to be and is filed with the Commission or any national securities organization registered under section 15A of the Securities Exchange Act of 1934, except that this subparagraph does not apply to the laws, rules, regulations, or orders, or other administrative actions of the State of incorporation of the issuer; or

(3) shall directly or indirectly prohibit, limit, or impose conditions, based on the merits of such offering or issuer, upon the offer or sale of any security described in paragraph (1).

(b) COVERED SECURITIES—For purposes of this section, the following are covered securities:

(1) Exclusive federal registration of nationally traded securities.—A security is a covered security if such security is—

(A) listed, or authorized for listing, on the New York Stock Exchange or the American Stock Exchange, or listed, or authorized for listing, on the National Market System of the Nasdaq Stock Market (or any successor to such entities);

(B) listed, or authorized for listing, on a national securities exchange (or tier or segment thereof) that has listing standards that the Commission determines by rule (on its own initiative or on the basis of a petition) are substantially similar to the listing standards applicable to securities described in subparagraph (A); or

(C) a security of the same issuer that is equal in seniority or that is a senior security to a security described in subparagraph (A) or (B).

(2) Exclusive federal registration of investment companies.—A security is a covered security if such security is a security issued by an investment company that is registered, or that has filed a registration statement, under the Investment Company Act of 1940.

(3) Sales to qualified purchasers.—A security is a covered security with respect to the offer or sale of the security to qualified purchasers, as defined by the Commission by rule. In prescribing such rule, the Commission may define the term "qualified purchaser" differently with respect to different categories of securities, consistent with the public interest and the protection of investors.

(4) Exemption in connection with certain exempt offerings.—A security is a covered security with respect to a transaction that is exempt from registration under this title pursuant to—

(A) paragraph (1) or (3) of section 4, and the issuer of such security files reports with the Commission pursuant to section 13 or 15(d) of the Securities Exchange Act of 1934;

(B) section 4(4);

(C) Section 4(6);

(D) A rule or regulation adopted pursuant to Section 3(b)(2) and such security is—

(i) Offered or sold on a national securities exchange; or

(ii) Offered or sold to a qualified purchaser, as defined by the Commission pursuant to paragraph (3) with respect to that purchase or sale;

(E) section 3(a), other than the offer or sale of a security that is exempt from such registration pursuant to paragraph (4), (10), or (11) of such section, except that a municipal security that is exempt from such registration pursuant to paragraph (2) of such section is not a covered security with respect to the offer or sale of such security in the State in which the issuer of such security is located;

(F) Commission rules or regulations issued under section 4(2), except that this subparagraph does not prohibit a State from imposing notice filing requirements that are substantially similar to those required by rule or regulation under section 4(2) that are in effect on September 1, 1996; or

(G) Section 4(a)(7).

(c) PRESERVATION OF AUTHORITY.—

(1) Fraud authority.—Consistent with this section, the securities commission (or any agency or office performing like functions) of any State shall retain jurisdiction under the laws of such State to investigate and bring enforcement actions in connection with securities or securities transactions.

(A) With respect to—

(i) Fraud or deceit; or

(ii) Unlawful conduct by a broker or dealer, or funding portal; and

(B) In connection to a transaction described under Section 4(6), with respect to—

(i) Fraud or deceit; or

(ii) Unlawful conduct by a broker, dealer, funding portal, or issuer.

(2) Preservation of filing requirements.—

(A) Notice filings permitted.—Nothing in this section prohibits the securities commission (or any agency or office performing like functions) of any State from requiring the filing of any document filed with the Commission pursuant to this title, together with annual or periodic reports of the value of securities sold or offered to be sold to persons located in the State (if such sales data is not included in documents filed with the Commission), solely for notice purposes and the assessment of any fee, together with a consent to service of process and any required fee.

(B) Preservation of fees.—

(i) In general.—Until otherwise provided by law, rule, regulation, or order, or other administrative action of any State or any political subdivision thereof, adopted after the date of enactment of the National Securities Markets Improvement Act of 1996, filing or registration fees with respect to securities or securities transactions shall continue to be collected in amounts determined pursuant to State law as in effect on the day before such date.

---

*As so numbered by Section 401(b) of the JOBS Act; this duplicates the redesignation as given by Section 305(a)(1) of the Act.—EDS.

(ii) Schedule.—The fees required by this subparagraph shall be paid, and all necessary supporting data on sales or offers for sales required under subparagraph (A), shall be reported on the same schedule as would have been applicable had the issuer not relied on the exemption provided in subsection (a).

(C) Availability of preemption contingent on payment of fees.—

(i) In general.—During the period beginning on the date of enactment of the National Securities Markets Improvement Act of 1996 and ending 3 years after that date of enactment, the securities commission (or any agency or office performing like functions) of any State may require the registration of securities issued by any issuer who refuses to pay the fees required by subparagraph (B).

(ii) Delays.—For purposes of this subparagraph, delays in payment of fees or underpayments of fees that are promptly remedied shall not constitute a refusal to pay fees.

(D) Fees not permitted on listed securities.—Notwithstanding subparagraphs (A), (B), and (C), no filing or fee may be required with respect to any security that is a covered security pursuant to subsection (b)(1), or will be such a covered security upon completion of the transaction, or is a security of the same issuer that is equal in seniority or that is a senior security to a security that is a covered security pursuant to subsection (b)(1).

*(F) Fees Not Permitted on Crowd funded Securities. Notwithstanding subparagraphs (A), (B), and (C), no filing or fee may be required with respect to any security that is a covered security pursuant to subsection (b)(4)(B), or will be such a covered security upon completion of the transaction, except for the securities commission (or any agency or office performing like functions) of the State of the principal place of business of the issuer, or any State in which purchasers of 50 percent or greater of the aggregate amount of the issue are residents, provided that for purposes of this subparagraph, the term "State" includes the District of Columbia and the territories of the United States.

(3) Enforcement of requirements.—Nothing in this section shall prohibit the securities commission (or any agency or office performing like functions) of any State from suspending the offer or sale of securities within such State as a result of the failure to submit any filing or fee required under law and permitted under this section.

(d) DEFINITIONS.—For purposes of this section, the following definitions shall apply:

(1) Offering document.—The term "offering document"—

(A) has the meaning given the term "prospectus" in section 2(a)(10), but without regard to the provisions of subparagraphs (a) and (b) of that section; and

(B) includes a communication that is not deemed to offer a security pursuant to a rule of the Commission.

(2) Prepared by or on behalf of the issuer.—Not later than 6 months after the date of enactment of the National Securities Markets Improvement Act of 1996, the Commission shall, by rule, define the term "prepared by or on behalf of the issuer" for purposes of this section.

(3) State.—The term "State" has the same meaning as in section 3 of the Securities Exchange Act of 1934.

(4) Senior security.—The term "senior security" means any bond, debenture, note, or similar obligation or instrument constituting a security and evidencing indebtedness, and any stock of a class having priority over any other class as to distribution of assets or payment of dividends.

Sec.19. SPECIAL POWERS OF COMMISSION

(a) The Commission shall have authority from time to time to make, amend, and rescind such rules and regulations as may be necessary to carry out the provisions of this title, includ-

---

* As so designated by Section 305(c) of the Act; there is no subparagraph (E).—EDS.

ing rules and regulations governing registration statements and prospectuses for various classes of securities and issuers, and defining accounting, technical and trade terms used in this title. Among other things, the Commission shall have authority, for the purposes of this title, to prescribe the form or forms in which required information shall be set forth, the items or details to be shown in the balance sheet and earning statement, and the methods to be followed in the preparation of accounts, in the appraisal or valuation of assets and liabilities, in the determination of depreciation and depletion, in the differentiation of recurring and non-recurring income, in the differentiation of investment and operating income, and in the preparation, where the Commission deems it necessary or desirable, of consolidated balance sheets or income accounts of any person directly or indirectly controlling or controlled by the issuer, or any person under direct or indirect common control with the issuer. The rules and regulations of the Commission shall be effective upon publication in the manner which the Commission shall prescribe. No provision of this title imposing any liability shall apply to any act done or omitted in good faith in conformity with any rule or regulation of the Commission, notwithstanding that such rule or regulation may, after such act or omission be amended or rescinded or be determined by judicial or other authority to be invalid for any reason.

(b) RECOGNITION OF ACCOUNTING STANDARDS.—

(1) IN GENERAL.—In carrying out its authority under subsection (a) and under section 13(b) of the Securities Exchange Act of 1934, the Commission may recognize, as "generally accepted" for purposes of the securities laws, any accounting principles established by a standard setting body—

(A) that—

(i) is organized as a private entity;

(ii) has, for administrative and operational purposes, a board of trustees (or equivalent body) serving in the public interest, the majority of whom are not, concurrent with their service on such board, and have not been during the 2-year period preceding such service, associated persons of any registered public accounting firm;

(iii) is funded as provided in section 109 of the Sarbanes-Oxley Act of 2002;

(iv) has adopted procedures to ensure prompt consideration, by majority vote of its members, of changes to accounting principles necessary to reflect emerging accounting issues and changing business practices; and

(v) considers, in adopting accounting principles, the need to keep standards current in order to reflect changes in the business environment, the extent to which international convergence on high quality accounting standards is necessary or appropriate in the public interest and for the protection of investors; and

(B) that the Commission determines has the capacity to assist the Commission in fulfilling the requirements of subsection (a) and section 13(b) of the Securities Exchange Act of 1934, because, at a minimum, the standard setting body is capable of improving the accuracy and effectiveness of financial reporting and the protection of investors under the securities laws.

(2) ANNUAL REPORT.—A standard setting body described in paragraph (1) shall submit an annual report to the Commission and the public, containing audited financial statements of that standard setting body.

(c) For the purpose of all investigations which, in the opinion of the Commission, are necessary and proper for the enforcement of this title, any member of the Commission or any officer or officers designated by it are empowered to administer oaths and affirmations, subpena witnesses, take evidence, and require the production of any books, papers, or other documents which the Commission deems relevant or material to the inquiry. Such attendance of witnesses and the production of such documentary evidence may be required from any place in the United States or any Territory at any designated place of hearing.

(d) (1) The Commission is authorized to cooperate with any association composed of duly constituted representatives of State governments whose primary assignment is the regulation of the securities business within those States, and which, in the judgment of the Commission, could assist in effectuating greater uniformity in Federal-State securities matters. The Commission shall, at its discretion, cooperate, coordinate, and share information with such an association for the purposes of carrying out the policies and projects set forth in paragraphs (2) and (3).

(2) It is the declared policy of this subsection that there should be greater Federal and State cooperation in securities matters, including—

(A) maximum effectiveness of regulation,

(B) maximum uniformity in Federal and State regulatory standards,

(C) minimum interference with the business of capital formation, and

(D) a substantial reduction in costs and paperwork to diminish the burdens of raising investment capital (particularly by small business) and to diminish the costs of the administration of the Government programs involved.

(3) The purpose of this subsection is to engender cooperation between the Commission, any such association of State securities officials, and other duly constituted securities associations in the following areas:

(A) the sharing of information regarding the registration or exemption of securities issues applied for in the various States;

(B) the development and maintenance of uniform securities forms and procedures; and

(C) the development of a uniform exemption from registration for small issuers which can be agreed upon among several States or between the States and the Federal Government. The Commission shall have the authority to adopt such an exemption as agreed upon for Federal purposes. Nothing in this Act shall be construed as authorizing preemption of State law.

(4) In order to carry out these policies and purposes, the Commission shall conduct an annual conference as well as such other meetings as are deemed necessary, to which representatives from such securities associations, securities self-regulatory organizations, agencies, and private organizations involved in capital formation shall be invited to participate.

(5) For fiscal year 1982, and for each of the three succeeding fiscal years, there are authorized to be appropriated such amounts as may be necessary and appropriate to carry out the policies, provisions, and purposes of this subsection. Any sums so appropriated shall remain available until expended.

(6) Notwithstanding any other provision of law, neither the Commission nor any other person shall be required to establish any procedures not specifically required by the securities laws, as that term is defined in section 3(a)(47) of the Securities Exchange Act of 1934, or by chapter 5 of title 5, United States Code, in connection with cooperation, coordination, or consultation with—

(A) any association referred to in paragraph (1) or (3) or any conference or meeting referred to in paragraph (4), while such association, conference, or meeting is carrying out activities in furtherance of the provisions of this subsection; or

(B) any forum, agency, or organization, or group referred to in section 503 of the Small Business Investment Incentive Act of 1980, while such forum, agency, organization, or group is carrying out activities in furtherance of the provisions of such section 503.

As used in this paragraph, the terms "association", "conference", "meeting", "forum", "agency", "organization", and "group" include any committee, subgroup, or representative of such entities.

(e) EVALUATION OF RULES OR PROGRAMS.— For the purpose of evaluating any rule or program of the Commission issued or carried out under any provision of the securities laws, as defined in section 3 of the Securities Exchange Act of 1934 (15 U.S.C. 78c), and the purposes of considering, proposing, adopting, or engaging in any such rule or program or developing new rules or programs, the Commission may—

(1) Gather information from and communicate with investors or other members of the public;

(2) Engage in such temporary investor testing programs as the Commission determines are in the public interest or would protect investors; and

(3) Consult with academics and consultants, as necessary to carry out this subsection.

(f) RULE OF CONSTRUCTION.— For purposes of the Paperwork Reduction Act (44 U.S.C. 3501 et seq.), any action taken under subsection (e) shall not be construed to be a collection of information.

(g) FUNDING FOR THE GASB.—

(1) IN GENERAL.— The Commission may, subject to the limitations imposed by section 15B of the Securities Exchange Act of 1934 (15 U.S.C. 78o-4), require a national securities association registered under the Securities Exchange Act of 1934 to establish—

(A) A reasonable annual accounting support fee to adequately fund the annual budget of the Governmental Accounting Standards Board (referred to in this subsection as the "GASB"); and

(B) Rules and procedures, in consultation with the principal organizations representing State governors, legislators, local elected officials, and State and local finance officers, to provide for the equitable allocation, assessment, and collection of the accounting support fee established under subparagraph (A) from the members of the association, and the remittance of all such accounting support fees to the Financial Accounting Foundation.

(2) ANNUAL BUDGET.— For purposes of this subsection, the annual budget of the GASB is the annual budget reviewed and approved according to the internal procedures of the Financial Accounting Foundation.

(3) USE OF FUNDS.— Any fees or funds collected under this subsection shall be used to support the efforts of the GASB to establish standards of financial accounting and reporting recognized as generally accepted accounting principles applicable to State and local governments of the United States.

(4) LIMITATION ON FEE.— The annual accounting support fees collected under this subsection for a fiscal year shall not exceed the recoverable annual budgeted expenses of the GASB (which may include operating expenses, capital, and accrued items).

(5) RULES OF CONSTRUCTION.—

(A) FEES NOT PUBLIC MONIES.— Accounting support fees collected under this subsection and other receipts of the GASB shall not be considered public monies of the United States.

(B) LIMITATION ON AUTHORITY OF THE COMMISSION.— Nothing in this subsection shall be construed to—

(i) Provide the Commission or any national securities association direct or indirect oversight of the budget or technical agenda of the GASB; or

(ii) Affect the setting of generally accepted accounting principles by the GASB.

(C) NONINTERFERENCE WITH STATES.— Nothing in this subsection shall be construed to impair or limit the authority of a State or local government to establish accounting and financial reporting standards.

Sec. 20. INJUNCTIONS AND PROSECUTION OF OFFENSES

(a) Whenever it shall appear to the Commission, either upon complaint or otherwise, that the provisions of this title, or of any rule or regulation prescribed under authority thereof, have been or are about to be violated, it may, in its discretion, either require or permit such person to file with it a statement in writing, under oath, or otherwise, as to all the facts and circumstances concerning the subject matter which it believes to be in the public interest to investigate, and may investigate such facts.

(b) Whenever it shall appear to the Commission that any person is engaged or about to engage in any acts or practices which constitute or will constitute a violation of the provisions of this title, or of any rule or regulation prescribed under authority thereof, the Commission may, in its discretion, bring an action in any district court of the United States, or United States court of any Territory, to enjoin such acts or practices, and upon a proper showing, a permanent or temporary injunction or restraining order shall be granted without bond. The Commission may transmit such evidence as may be available concerning such acts or practices to the Attorney General who may, in his discretion, institute the necessary criminal proceedings under this title. Any such criminal proceeding may be brought either in the district wherein the transmittal of the prospectus or security complained of begins, or in the district wherein such prospectus or security is received.

(c) Upon application of the Commission, the district courts of the United States and the United States courts of any Territory shall have jurisdiction to issue writs of mandamus commanding any person to comply with the provisions of this title or any order of the Commission made in pursuance thereof.

(d) MONEY PENALTIES IN CIVIL ACTIONS.—

(1) AUTHORITY OF COMMISSION.—Whenever it shall appear to the Commission that any person has violated any provision of this title, the rules or regulations thereunder, or a cease-and-desist order entered by the Commission pursuant to section 8A of this title, other than by committing a violation subject to a penalty pursuant to section 21A of the Securities Exchange Act of 1934, the Commission may bring an action in a United States district court to seek, and the court shall have jurisdiction to impose, upon a proper showing, a civil penalty to be paid by the person who committed such violation.

(2) AMOUNT OF PENALTY.—

(A) FIRST TIER.—The amount of the penalty shall be determined by the court in light of the facts and circumstances. For each violation, the amount of the penalty shall not exceed the greater of (i) $5,000 for a natural person or $50,000 for any other person, or (ii) the gross amount of pecuniary gain to such defendant as a result of the violation.

(B) SECOND TIER.—Notwithstanding subparagraph (A), the amount of penalty for each such violation shall not exceed the greater of (i) $50,000 for a natural person or $250,000 for any other person, or (ii) the gross amount of pecuniary gain to such defendant as a result of the violation, if the violation described in paragraph (1) involved fraud, deceit, manipulation, or deliberate or reckless disregard of a regulatory requirement.

(C) THIRD TIER.—Notwithstanding subparagraphs (A) and (B), the amount of penalty for each such violation shall not exceed the greater of (i) $100,000 for a natural person or $500,000 for any other person, or (ii) the gross amount of pecuniary gain to such defendant as a result of the violation, if—

(I) the violation described in paragraph (1) involved fraud, deceit, manipulation, or deliberate or reckless disregard of a regulatory requirement; and

(II) such violation directly or indirectly resulted in substantial losses or created a significant risk of substantial losses to other persons.

(3) PROCEDURES FOR COLLECTION.—

(A) PAYMENT OF PENALTY TO TREASURY.—A penalty imposed under this section shall be payable into the Treasury of the United States, except as otherwise provided in section 308 of the Sarbanes-Oxley Act of 2002 and Section 21F of the Securities Exchange Act of 1934.

(B) COLLECTION OF PENALTIES.—If a person upon whom such a penalty is imposed shall fail to pay such penalty within the time prescribed in the court's order, the Commission may refer the matter to the Attorney General who shall recover such penalty by action in the appropriate United States district court.

(C) REMEDY NOT EXCLUSIVE.—The actions authorized by this subsection may be brought in addition to any other action that the Commission or the Attorney General is entitled to bring.

(D) JURISDICTION AND VENUE.—For purposes of section 22 of this title, actions under this section shall be actions to enforce a liability or a duty created by this title.

(4) SPECIAL PROVISIONS RELATING TO A VIOLATION OF A CEASE-AND-DESIST ORDER.—In an action to enforce a cease-and-desist order entered by the Commission pursuant to section

8A, each separate violation of such order shall be a separate offense, except that in the case of a violation through a continuing failure to comply with such an order, each day of the failure to comply with the order shall be deemed a separate offense.

(e) AUTHORITY OF A COURT TO PROHIBIT PERSONS FROM SERVING AS OFFICERS AND DIRECTORS.—In any proceeding under subsection (b), the court may prohibit, conditionally or unconditionally, and permanently or for such period of time as it shall determine, any person who violated section 17(a)(1) of this title from acting as an officer or director of any issuer that has a class of securities registered pursuant to section 12 of the Securities Exchange Act of 1934 or that is required to file reports pursuant to section 15(d) of such Act if the person's conduct demonstrates unfitness to serve as an officer or director of any such issuer.

(f) PROHIBITION OF ATTORNEYS' FEES PAID FROM COMMISSION DISGORGEMENT FUNDS.— Except as otherwise ordered by the court upon motion by the Commission, or, in the case of an administrative action, as otherwise ordered by the Commission, funds disgorged as the result of an action brought by the Commission in Federal court, or as a result of any Commission administrative action, shall not be distributed as payment for attorneys' fees or expenses incurred by private parties seeking distribution of the disgorged funds.

(g) AUTHORITY OF A COURT TO PROHIBIT PERSONS FROM PARTICIPATING IN AN OFFERING OF PENNY STOCK.—

(1) IN GENERAL.—In any proceeding under subsection (a) against any person participating in, or, at the time of the alleged misconduct, who was participating in, an offering of penny stock, the court may prohibit that person from participating in an offering of penny stock, conditionally or unconditionally, and permanently or for such period of time as the court shall determine.

(2) DEFINITION.—For purposes of this subsection, the term "person participating in an offering of penny stock" includes any person engaging in activities with a broker, dealer, or issuer for purposes of issuing, trading, or inducing or attempting to induce the purchase or sale of, any penny stock. The Commission may, by rule or regulation, define such term to include other activities, and may, by rule, regulation, or order, exempt any person or class of persons, in whole or in part, conditionally or unconditionally, from inclusion in such term.

Sec. 21. HEARINGS BY COMMISSION

All hearings shall be public and may be held before the Commission or an officer or officers of the Commission designated by it, and appropriate records thereof shall be kept.

Sec. 22. JURISDICTION OF OFFENSES AND SUITS

(a) The district courts of the United States and United States courts of any Territory shall have jurisdiction of offenses and violations under this title and under the rules and regulations promulgated by the Commission in respect thereto, and, concurrent with State and Territorial courts, except as provided in section 16 with respect to covered class actions, of all suits in equity and actions at law brought to enforce any liability or duty created by this title. Any such suit or action may be brought in the district wherein the defendant is found or is an inhabitant or transacts business, or in the district where the offer or sale took place, if the defendant participated therein, and process in such cases may be served in any other district of which the defendant is an inhabitant or wherever the defendant may be found. In any action or proceeding instituted by the Commission under this title in a United States district court for any judicial district, a subpoena issued to compel the attendance of a witness or the production of documents or tangible things (or both) at a hearing or trial may be served at any place within the United States. Rule 45(c)(3)(A)(ii) of the Federal Rules of Civil Procedure shall not apply to a subpoena issued under the preceding sentence. Judgments and decrees so rendered shall be subject to review as provided in sections 1254, 1291, 1292, and 1294 of title 28, United States Code. Except as provided in section 16(c), no case arising under this title and brought in any State court of competent jurisdiction shall be removed to any court of the United States. No costs shall be assessed for or against the Commission in any proceeding under this title brought by or against it in the Supreme Court or such other courts.

(b) In case of contumacy or refusal to obey a subpena issued to any person, any of the said United States courts within the jurisdiction of which said person guilty of contumacy or refusal to obey is found or resides, upon application by the Commission may issue to such person an order requiring such person to appear before the Commission, or one of its examiners designated by it, there to produce documentary evidence if so ordered, or there to give evidence touching the matter in question; and any failure to obey such order of the court may be punished by said court as a contempt thereof.

(c) Extraterritorial Jurisdiction.— The district courts of the United States and the United tates courts of any Territory shall have jurisdiction of an action or proceeding brought or instituted by the Commission or the United States alleging a violation of section 17(a) involving—

(1) Conduct within the United States that constitutes significant steps in furtherance of the violation, even if the securities transaction occurs outside the United States and involves only foreign investors; or

(2) Conduct occurring outside the United States that has a foreseeable substantial effect within the United States.

Sec.23. UNLAWFUL REPRESENTATIONS

Neither the fact that the registration statement for a security has been filed or is in effect nor the fact that a stop order is not in effect with respect thereto shall be deemed a finding by the Commission that the registration statement is true and accurate on its face or that it does not contain an untrue statement of fact or omit to state a material fact, or be held to mean that the Commission has in any way passed upon the merits of, or given approval to, such security. It shall be unlawful to make, or cause to be made, to any prospective purchaser any representation contrary to the foregoing provisions of this section.

Sec.24. PENALTIES

Any person who willfully violates any of the provisions of this title, or the rules and regulations promulgated by the Commission under authority thereof, or any person who willfully, in a registration statement filed under this title, makes any untrue statement of a material fact or omits to state any material fact required to be stated therein or necessary to make the statements therein not misleading, shall upon conviction be fined not more than $10,000 or imprisoned not more than five years, or both.

Sec.25. JURISDICTION OF OTHER GOVERNMENT AGENCIES OVER SECURITIES

Nothing in this title shall relieve any person from submitting to the respective supervisory units of the Government of the United States information, reports, or other documents that are now or may hereafter be required by any provision of law.

Sec.26. SEPARABILITY OF PROVISIONS

If any provision of this Act, or the application of such provision to any person or circumstance, shall be held invalid, the remainder of this Act, or the application of such provision to persons or circumstances other than those as to which it is held invalid, shall not be affected thereby.

Sec.27. PRIVATE SECURITIES LITIGATION

(a) PRIVATE CLASS ACTIONS.—

(1) IN GENERAL.—The provisions of this subsection shall apply to each private action arising under this title that is brought as a plaintiff class action pursuant to the Federal Rules of Civil Procedure.

(2) CERTIFICATION FILED WITH COMPLAINT.—

(A) IN GENERAL.—Each plaintiff seeking to serve as a representative party on behalf of a class shall provide a sworn certification, which shall be personally signed by such plaintiff and filed with the complaint, that—

(i) states that the plaintiff has reviewed the complaint and authorized its filing;

(ii) states that the plaintiff did not purchase the security that is the subject of the complaint at the direction of plaintiff's counsel or in order to participate in any private action arising under this title;

(iii) states that the plaintiff is willing to serve as a representative party on behalf of a class, including providing testimony at deposition and trial, if necessary;

(iv) sets forth all of the transactions of the plaintiff in the security that is the subject of the complaint during the class period specified in the complaint;

(v) identifies any other action under this title, filed during the 3-year period preceding the date on which the certification is signed by the plaintiff, in which the plaintiff has sought to serve, or served, as a representative party on behalf of a class; and

(vi) states that the plaintiff will not accept any payment for serving as a representative party on behalf of a class beyond the plaintiff's pro rata share of any recovery, except as ordered or approved by the court in accordance with paragraph (4).

(B) NONWAIVER OF ATTORNEY-CLIENT PRIVILEGE.—The certification filed pursuant to subparagraph (A) shall not be construed to be a waiver of the attorney-client privilege.

(3) APPOINTMENT OF LEAD PLAINTIFF.—

(A) EARLY NOTICE TO CLASS MEMBERS.—

(i) IN GENERAL.—Not later than 20 days after the date on which the complaint is filed, the plaintiff or plaintiffs shall cause to be published, in a widely circulated national business-oriented publication or wire service, a notice advising members of the purported plaintiff class—

(I) of the pendency of the action, the claims asserted therein, and the purported class period; and

(II) that, not later than 60 days after the date on which the notice is published, any member of the purported class may move the court to serve as lead plaintiff of the purported class.

(ii) MULTIPLE ACTIONS.—If more than one action on behalf of a class asserting substantially the same claim or claims arising under this title is filed, only the plaintiff or plaintiffs in the first filed action shall be required to cause notice to be published in accordance with clause (i).

(iii) ADDITIONAL NOTICES MAY BE REQUIRED UNDER FEDERAL RULES.—Notice required under clause (i) shall be in addition to any notice required pursuant to the Federal Rules of Civil Procedure.

(B) APPOINTMENT OF LEAD PLAINTIFF.—

(i) IN GENERAL.—Not later than 90 days after the date on which a notice is published under subparagraph (A)(i), the court shall consider any motion made by a purported class member in response to the notice, including any motion by a class member who is not individually named as a plaintiff in the complaint or complaints, and shall appoint as lead plaintiff the member or members of the purported plaintiff class that the court determines to be most capable of adequately representing the interests of class members (hereafter in this paragraph referred to as the "most adequate plaintiff") in accordance with this subparagraph.

(ii) CONSOLIDATED ACTIONS.—If more than one action on behalf of a class asserting substantially the same claim or claims arising under this title has been filed, and any party has sought to consolidate those actions for pretrial purposes or for trial, the court shall not make the determination required by clause (i) until after the decision on the motion to consolidate is rendered. As soon as practicable after such decision is rendered, the court shall appoint the most adequate plaintiff as lead plaintiff for the consolidated actions in accordance with this subparagraph.

(iii) REBUTTABLE PRESUMPTION.—

(I) IN GENERAL.—Subject to subclause (II), for purposes of clause (i), the court shall adopt a presumption that the most adequate plaintiff in any private action arising under this title is the person or group of persons that—

(aa) has either filed the complaint or made a motion in response to a notice under subparagraph (A)(i);

(bb) in the determination of the court, has the largest financial interest in the relief sought by the class; and

(cc) otherwise satisfies the requirements of Rule 23 of the Federal Rules of Civil Procedure.

(II) REBUTTAL EVIDENCE.—The presumption described in subclause (I) may be rebutted only upon proof by a member of the purported plaintiff class that the presumptively most adequate plaintiff—

(aa) will not fairly and adequately protect the interests of the class; or

(bb) is subject to unique defenses that render such plaintiff incapable of adequately representing the class.

(iv) DISCOVERY.—For purposes of this subparagraph, discovery relating to whether a member or members of the purported plaintiff class is the most adequate plaintiff may be conducted by a plaintiff only if the plaintiff first demonstrates a reasonable basis for a finding that the presumptively most adequate plaintiff is incapable of adequately representing the class.

(v) SELECTION OF LEAD COUNSEL.—The most adequate plaintiff shall, subject to the approval of the court, select and retain counsel to represent the class.

(vi) RESTRICTIONS ON PROFESSIONAL PLAINTIFFS.—Except as the court may otherwise permit, consistent with the purposes of this section, a person may be a lead plaintiff, or an officer, director, or fiduciary of a lead plaintiff, in no more than 5 securities class actions brought as plaintiff class actions pursuant to the Federal Rules of Civil Procedure during any 3-year period.

(4) RECOVERY BY PLAINTIFFS.—The share of any final judgment or of any settlement that is awarded to a representative party serving on behalf of a class shall be equal, on a per share basis, to the portion of the final judgment or settlement awarded to all other members of the class. Nothing in this paragraph shall be construed to limit the award of reasonable costs and expenses (including lost wages) directly relating to the representation of the class to any representative party serving on behalf of the class.

(5) RESTRICTIONS ON SETTLEMENTS UNDER SEAL.—The terms and provisions of any settlement agreement of a class action shall not be filed under seal, except that on motion of any party to the settlement, the court may order filing under seal for those portions of a settlement agreement as to which good cause is shown for such filing under seal. For purposes of this paragraph, good cause shall exist only if publication of a term or provision of a settlement agreement would cause direct and substantial harm to any party.

(6) RESTRICTIONS ON PAYMENT OF ATTORNEYS' FEES AND EXPENSES.—Total attorneys' fees and expenses awarded by the court to counsel for the plaintiff class shall not exceed a reasonable percentage of the amount of any damages and prejudgment interest actually paid to the class.

(7) DISCLOSURE OF SETTLEMENT TERMS TO CLASS MEMBERS.—Any proposed or final settlement agreement that is published or otherwise disseminated to the class shall include each of the following statements, along with a cover page summarizing the information contained in such statements:

(A) STATEMENT OF PLAINTIFF RECOVERY.—The amount of the settlement proposed to be distributed to the parties to the action, determined in the aggregate and on an average per share basis.

(B) STATEMENT OF POTENTIAL OUTCOME OF CASE.—

(i) AGREEMENT ON AMOUNT OF DAMAGES.—If the settling parties agree on the average amount of damages per share that would be recoverable if the plaintiff prevailed on each claim alleged under this title, a statement concerning the average amount of such potential damages per share.

(ii) DISAGREEMENT ON AMOUNT OF DAMAGES.—If the parties do not agree on the average amount of damages per share that would be recoverable if the plaintiff prevailed on each claim alleged under this title, a statement from each settling party concerning the issue or issues on which the parties disagree.

(iii) INADMISSIBILITY FOR CERTAIN PURPOSES.—A statement made in accordance with clause (i) or (ii) concerning the amount of damages shall not be admissible in any Federal or State judicial action or administrative proceeding, other than an action or proceeding arising out of such statement.

(C) STATEMENT OF ATTORNEYS' FEES OR COSTS SOUGHT.—If any of the settling parties or their counsel intend to apply to the court for an award of attorneys' fees or costs from any fund established as part of the settlement, a statement indicating which parties or counsel intend to make such an application, the amount of fees and costs that will be sought (including the amount of such fees and costs determined on an average per share basis), and a brief explanation supporting the fees and costs sought.

(D) IDENTIFICATION OF LAWYERS' REPRESENTATIVES.—The name, telephone number, and address of one or more representatives of counsel for the plaintiff class who will be reasonably available to answer questions from class members concerning any matter contained in any notice of settlement published or otherwise disseminated to the class.

(E) REASONS FOR SETTLEMENT.—A brief statement explaining the reasons why the parties are proposing the settlement.

(F) OTHER INFORMATION.—Such other information as may be required by the court.

(8) ATTORNEY CONFLICT OF INTEREST.—If a plaintiff class is represented by an attorney who directly owns or otherwise has a beneficial interest in the securities that are the subject of the litigation, the court shall make a determination of whether such ownership or other interest constitutes a conflict of interest sufficient to disqualify the attorney from representing the plaintiff class.

(b) STAY OF DISCOVERY; PRESERVATION OF EVIDENCE.—

(1) IN GENERAL.—In any private action arising under this title, all discovery and other proceedings shall be stayed during the pendency of any motion to dismiss, unless the court finds, upon the motion of any party, that particularized discovery is necessary to preserve evidence or to prevent undue prejudice to that party.

(2) PRESERVATION OF EVIDENCE.—During the pendency of any stay of discovery pursuant to this subsection, unless otherwise ordered by the court, any party to the action with actual notice of the allegations contained in the complaint shall treat all documents, data compilations (including electronically recorded or stored data), and tangible objects that are in the custody or control of such person and that are relevant to the allegations, as if they were the subject of a continuing request for production of documents from an opposing party under the Federal Rules of Civil Procedure.

(3) SANCTION FOR WILLFUL VIOLATION.—A party aggrieved by the willful failure of an opposing party to comply with paragraph (2) may apply to the court for an order awarding appropriate sanctions.

(4) CIRCUMVENTION OF STAY OF DISCOVERY.—Upon a proper showing, a court may stay discovery proceedings in any private action in a State court as necessary in aid of its jurisdiction, or to protect or effectuate its judgments, in an action subject to a stay of discovery pursuant to this subsection.

(c) SANCTIONS FOR ABUSIVE LITIGATION.—

(1) MANDATORY REVIEW BY COURT.—In any private action arising under this title, upon final adjudication of the action, the court shall include in the record specific findings regarding compliance by each party and each attorney representing any party with each requirement of Rule 11(b) of the Federal Rules of Civil Procedure as to any complaint, responsive pleading, or dispositive motion.

(2) MANDATORY SANCTIONS.—If the court makes a finding under paragraph (1) that a party or attorney violated any requirement of Rule 11(b) of the Federal Rules of Civil Procedure as to any complaint, responsive pleading, or dispositive motion, the court shall impose sanctions on such party or attorney in accordance with Rule 11 of the Federal Rules of Civil Procedure. Prior to making a finding that any party or attorney has violated Rule 11 of the Federal Rules of Civil Procedure, the court shall give such party or attorney notice and an opportunity to respond.

(3) PRESUMPTION IN FAVOR OF ATTORNEYS' FEES AND COSTS.—

(A) IN GENERAL.—Subject to subparagraphs (B) and (C), for purposes of paragraph (2), the court shall adopt a presumption that the appropriate sanction—

(i) for failure of any responsive pleading or dispositive motion to comply with any requirement of Rule 11(b) of the Federal Rules of Civil Procedure is an award to the opposing party of the reasonable attorneys' fees and other expenses incurred as a direct result of the violation; and

(ii) for substantial failure of any complaint to comply with any requirement of Rule 11(b) of the Federal Rules of Civil Procedure is an award to the opposing party of the reasonable attorneys' fees and other expenses incurred in the action.

(B) REBUTTAL EVIDENCE.—The presumption described in subparagraph (A) may be rebutted only upon proof by the party or attorney against whom sanctions are to be imposed that—

(i) the award of attorneys' fees and other expenses will impose an unreasonable burden on that party or attorney and would be unjust, and the failure to make such an award would not impose a greater burden on the party in whose favor sanctions are to be imposed; or

(ii) the violation of Rule 11(b) of the Federal Rules of Civil Procedure was de minimis.

(C) SANCTIONS.—If the party or attorney against whom sanctions are to be imposed meets its burden under subparagraph (B), the court shall award the sanctions that the court deems appropriate pursuant to Rule 11 of the Federal Rules of Civil Procedure.

(d) DEFENDANT'S RIGHT TO WRITTEN INTERROGATORIES.—In any private action arising under this title in which the plaintiff may recover money damages only on proof that a defendant acted with a particular state of mind, the court shall, when requested by a defendant, submit to the jury a written interrogatory on the issue of each such defendant's state of mind at the time the alleged violation occurred.

Sec.27A. APPLICATION OF SAFE HARBOR FOR FORWARD-LOOKING STATEMENTS

(a) APPLICABILITY.—This section shall apply only to a forward-looking statement made by—

(1) an issuer that, at the time that the statement is made, is subject to the reporting requirements of section 13(a) or section 15(d) of the Securities Exchange Act of 1934;

(2) a person acting on behalf of such issuer;

(3) an outside reviewer retained by such issuer making a statement on behalf of such issuer; or

(4) an underwriter, with respect to information provided by such issuer or information derived from information provided by the issuer.

(b) EXCLUSIONS.—Except to the extent otherwise specifically provided by rule, regulation, or order of the Commission, this section shall not apply to a forward-looking statement—

(1) that is made with respect to the business or operations of the issuer, if the issuer—

(A) during the 3-year period preceding the date on which the statement was first made—

(i) was convicted of any felony or misdemeanor described in clauses (i) through (iv) of section 15(b)(4)(B) of the Securities Exchange Act of 1934; or

(ii) has been made the subject of a judicial or administrative decree or order arising out of a governmental action that—

(I) prohibits future violations of the antifraud provisions of the securities laws;

(II) requires that the issuer cease and desist from violating the antifraud provisions of the securities laws; or

(III) determines that the issuer violated the antifraud provisions of the securities laws;

(B) makes the forward-looking statement in connection with an offering of securities by a blank check company;

(C) issues penny stock;

(D) makes the forward-looking statement in connection with a rollup transaction; or

(E) makes the forward-looking statement in connection with a going private transaction; or

(2) that is—

(A) included in a financial statement prepared in accordance with generally accepted accounting principles;

(B) contained in a registration statement of, or otherwise issued by, an investment company;

(C) made in connection with a tender offer;

(D) made in connection with an initial public offering;

(E) made in connection with an offering by, or relating to the operations of, a partnership, limited liability company, or a direct participation investment program; or

(F) made in a disclosure of beneficial ownership in a report required to be filed with the Commission pursuant to section 13(d) of the Securities Exchange Act of 1934.

(c) SAFE HARBOR.—

(1) IN GENERAL.—Except as provided in subsection (b), in any private action arising under this title that is based on an untrue statement of a material fact or omission of a material fact necessary to make the statement not misleading, a person referred to in subsection (a) shall not be liable with respect to any forward-looking statement, whether written or oral, if and to the extent that—

(A) the forward-looking statement is—

(i) identified as a forward-looking statement, and is accompanied by meaningful cautionary statements identifying important factors that could cause actual results to differ materially from those in the forward-looking statement; or

(ii) immaterial; or

(B) the plaintiff fails to prove that the forward-looking statement—

(i) if made by a natural person, was made with actual knowledge by that person that the statement was false or misleading; or

(ii) if made by a business entity was—

(I) made by or with the approval of an executive officer of that entity, and

(II) made or approved by such officer with actual knowledge by that officer that the statement was false or misleading.

(2) ORAL FORWARD-LOOKING STATEMENTS.—In the case of an oral forward-looking statement made by an issuer that is subject to the reporting requirements of section 13(a) or section 15(d) of the Securities Exchange Act of 1934, or by a person acting on behalf of such issuer, the requirement set forth in paragraph (1)(A) shall be deemed to be satisfied—

(A) if the oral forward-looking statement is accompanied by a cautionary statement—

(i) that the particular oral statement is a forward-looking statement; and

(ii) that the actual results could differ materially from those projected in the forward-looking statement; and

(B) if—

(i) the oral forward-looking statement is accompanied by an oral statement that additional information concerning factors that could cause actual results to differ materially from those in the forward-looking statement is contained in a readily available written document, or portion thereof;

(ii) the accompanying oral statement referred to in clause (i) identifies the document, or portion thereof, that contains the additional information about those factors relating to the forward-looking statement; and

(iii) the information contained in that written document is a cautionary statement that satisfies the standard established in paragraph (1)(A).

(3) AVAILABILITY.—Any document filed with the Commission or generally disseminated shall be deemed to be readily available for purposes of paragraph (2).

(4) EFFECT ON OTHER SAFE HARBORS.—The exemption provided for in paragraph (1) shall be in addition to any exemption that the Commission may establish by rule or regulation under subsection (g).

(d) DUTY TO UPDATE.—Nothing in this section shall impose upon any person a duty to update a forward-looking statement.

(e) DISPOSITIVE MOTION.—On any motion to dismiss based upon subsection (c)(1), the court shall consider any statement cited in the complaint and cautionary statement accompanying the forward-looking statement, which are not subject to material dispute, cited by the defendant.

(f) STAY PENDING DECISION ON MOTION.—In any private action arising under this title, the court shall stay discovery (other than discovery that is specifically directed to the applicability of the exemption provided for in this section) during the pendency of any motion by a defendant for summary judgment that is based on the grounds that—

(1) the statement or omission upon which the complaint is based is a forward-looking statement within the meaning of this section; and

(2) the exemption provided for in this section precludes a claim for relief.

(g) EXEMPTION AUTHORITY.—In addition to the exemptions provided for in this section, the Commission may, by rule or regulation, provide exemptions from or under any provision of this title, including with respect to liability that is based on a statement or that is based on projections or other forward-looking information, if and to the extent that any such exemption is consistent with the public interest and the protection of investors, as determined by the Commission.

(h) EFFECT ON OTHER AUTHORITY OF COMMISSION.—Nothing in this section limits, either expressly or by implication, the authority of the Commission to exercise similar authority or to adopt similar rules and regulations with respect to forward-looking statements under any other statute under which the Commission exercises rulemaking authority.

(i) DEFINITIONS.—For purposes of this section, the following definitions shall apply:

(1) FORWARD-LOOKING STATEMENT.—The term "forward-looking statement" means—

(A) a statement containing a projection of revenues, income (including income loss), earnings (including earnings loss) per share, capital expenditures, dividends, capital structure, or other financial items;

(B) a statement of the plans and objectives of management for future operations, including plans or objectives relating to the products or services of the issuer;

(C) a statement of future economic performance, including any such statement contained in a discussion and analysis of financial condition by the management or in the results of operations included pursuant to the rules and regulations of the Commission;

(D) any statement of the assumptions underlying or relating to any statement described in subparagraph (A), (B), or (C);

(E) any report issued by an outside reviewer retained by an issuer, to the extent that the report assesses a forward-looking statement made by the issuer; or

(F) a statement containing a projection or estimate of such other items as may be specified by rule or regulation of the Commission.

(2) INVESTMENT COMPANY.—The term "investment company" has the same meaning as in section 3(a) of the Investment Company Act of 1940.

(3) PENNY STOCK.—The term "penny stock" has the same meaning as in section 3(a)(51) of the Securities Exchange Act of 1934, and the rules and regulations, or orders issued pursuant to that section.

(4) GOING PRIVATE TRANSACTION.—The term "going private transaction" has the meaning given that term under the rules or regulations of the Commission issued pursuant to section 13(e) of the Securities Exchange Act of 1934.

(5) SECURITIES LAWS.—The term "securities laws" has the same meaning as in section 3 of the Securities Exchange Act of 1934.

(6) PERSON ACTING ON BEHALF OF AN ISSUER.—The term "person acting on behalf of an issuer" means an officer, director, or employee of the issuer.

(7) OTHER TERMS.—The terms "blank check company", "rollup transaction", "partnership", "limited liability company", "executive officer of an entity" and "direct participation investment program", have the meanings given those terms by rule or regulation of the Commission.

Sec. 27B. CONFLICTS OF INTEREST RELATING TO CERTAIN SECURITIZATIONS

(a) IN GENERAL.— An underwriter, placement agent, initial purchaser, or sponsor, or any affiliate or subsidiary of any such entity, of an asset-backed security (as such term is defined in section 3 of the Securities and Exchange Act of 1934 (15 U.S.C. 78c), which for the purposes of this section shall include a synthetic asset-backed security), shall not, at any time for a period ending on the date that is one year after the date of the first closing of the sale of the asset-backed security, engage in any transaction that would involve or result in any material conflict of interest with respect to any investor in a transaction arising out of such activity.

(b) RULEMAKING.— Not later than 270 days after the date of enactment of this section, the Commission shall issue rules for the purpose of implementing subsection (a).

(c) EXCEPTION.— The prohibitions of subsection (a) shall not apply to—

(1) Risk-mitigating hedging activities in connection with positions or holdings arising out of the underwriting, placement, initial purchase, or sponsorship of an asset-backed security, provided that such activities are designed to reduce the specific risks to the underwriter, placement agent, initial purchaser, or sponsor associated with positions or holdings arising out of such underwriting, placement, initial purchase, or sponsorship; or

(2) Purchases or sales of asset-backed securities made pursuant to and consistent with—

(A) Commitments of the underwriter, placement agent, initial purchaser, or sponsor, or any affiliate or subsidiary of any such entity, to provide liquidity for the asset-backed security, or

(B) Bona fide market-making in the asset backed security.

(d) RULE OF CONSTRUCTION.—This subsection shall not otherwise limit the application of section 15G of the Securities Exchange Act of 1934.

Sec.28. GENERAL EXEMPTIVE AUTHORITY

GENERAL EXEMPTIVE AUTHORITY

The Commission, by rule or regulation, may conditionally or unconditionally exempt any person, security, or transaction, or any class or classes of persons, securities, or transactions, from any provision or provisions of this title or of any rule or regulation issued under this title, to the extent that such exemption is necessary or appropriate in the public interest, and is consistent with the protection of investors.

SCHEDULE A

(1) The name under which the issuer is doing or intends to do business;

(2) the name of the State or other sovereign power under which the issuer is organized;

(3) the location of the issuer's principal business office, and if the issuer is a foreign or territorial person, the name and address of its agent in the United States authorized to receive notice;

(4) the names and addresses of the directors or persons performing similar functions, and the chief executive, financial and accounting officers, chosen or to be chosen if the issuer be a corporation, association, trust or other entity; of all partners, if the issuer be a partnership; and of the issuer, if the issuer be an individual; and of the promoters in the case of a business to be formed, or formed within two years prior to the filing of the registration statement;

(5) the names and addresses of the underwriters;

(6) the names and addresses of all persons, if any, owning of record or beneficially, if known, more than 10 per centum of any class of stock of the issuer, or more than 10 per centum in the aggregate of the outstanding stock of the issuer as of a date within 20 days prior to the filing of the registration statement;

(7) the amount of securities of the issuer held by any person specified in paragraphs (4), (5), and (6) of this schedule, as of a date within 20 days prior to the filing of the registration statement, and, if possible, as of one year prior thereto, and the amount of the securities, for which the registration statement is filed, to which such persons have indicated their intention to subscribe;

(8) the general character of the business actually transacted or to be transacted by the issuer;

(9) a statement of the capitalization of the issuer, including the authorized and outstanding amounts of its capital stock and the proportion thereof paid up, the number and classes of shares in which such capital stock is divided, par value thereof, or if it has no par value, the stated or assigned value thereof, a description of the respective voting rights, preferences, conversion and exchange rights, rights to dividends, profits, or capital of each class, with respect to each other class, including the retirement and liquidation rights or values thereof;

(10) a statement of the securities, if any, covered by options outstanding or to be created in connection with the security to be offered, together with the names and addresses of all persons, if any, to be allotted more than 10 per centum in the aggregate of such options;

(11) the amount of capital stock of each class issued or included in the shares of stock to be offered;

(12) the amount of the funded debt outstanding and to be created by the security to be offered, with a brief description of the date, maturity, and character of such debt, rate of interest, character of amortization provisions, and the security, if any, therefor. If substitution of any security is permissible, a summarized statement of the conditions under which such substitution is permitted. If substitution is permissible without notice, a specific statement to that effect;

(13) the specific purposes in detail and the approximate amounts to be devoted to such purposes, so far as determinable, for which the security to be offered is to supply funds, and if the funds are to be raised in part from other sources, the amounts thereof and the sources thereof, shall be stated;

(14) the remuneration, paid or estimated to be paid, by the issuer or its predecessor, directly or indirectly, during the past year and ensuing year to (a) the directors or persons performing similar functions, and (b) its officers and other persons, naming them wherever such remuneration exceeded $25,000 during any such year;

(15) the estimated net proceeds to be derived from the security to be offered;

(16) the price at which it is proposed that the security shall be offered to the public or the method by which such price is computed and any variation therefrom at which any portion of such security is proposed to be offered to any persons or classes of persons, other than the underwriters, naming them or specifying the class. A variation in price may be proposed prior to the date of the public offering of the security, but the Commission shall immediately be notified of such variation;

(17) all commissions or discounts paid or to be paid, directly or indirectly, by the issuer to the underwriters in respect of the sale of the security to be offered. Commissions shall include all cash, securities, contracts, or anything else of value, paid, to be set aside, disposed of, or understandings with or for the benefit of any other persons in which any underwriter is interested, made, in connection with the sale of such security. A commission paid or to be paid in connection with the sale of such security by a person in which the issuer has an interest or which is controlled or directed by, or under common control with, the issuer shall be deemed to have been paid by the issuer. Where any such commission is paid, the amount of such commission paid to each underwriter shall be stated;

(18) the amount or estimated amounts, itemized in reasonable detail, of expenses, other than commissions specified in paragraph (17) of this schedule, incurred or borne by or for the account of the issuer in connection with the sale or the security to be offered or properly chargeable thereto, including legal, engineering, certification, authentication, and other charges;

(19) the net proceeds derived from any security sold by the issuer during the two years preceding the filing of the registration statement, the price at which such security was offered to the public, and the names of the principal underwriters of such security;

(20) any amount paid within two years preceding the filing of the registration statement or intended to be paid to any promoter and the consideration for any such payment;

(21) the names and addresses of the vendors and the purchase price of any property, or good will, acquired or to be acquired, not in the ordinary course of business, which is to be defrayed in whole or in part from the proceeds of the security to be offered, the amount of any commission payable to any person in connection with such acquisition, and the name or names of such person or persons, together with any expense incurred or to be incurred in connection with such acquisition, including the cost of borrowing money to finance such acquisition;

(22) full particulars of the nature and extent of the interest, if any, of every director, principal executive officer, and of every stockholder holding more than 10 per centum of any class of stock or more than 10 per centum in the aggregate of the stock of the issuer, in any property acquired, not in the ordinary course of business of the issuer, within two years preceding the filing of the registration statement or proposed to be acquired at such date;

(23) the names and addresses of counsel who have passed on the legality of the issue;

(24) dates of and parties to, and the general effect concisely stated of every material contract made, not in the ordinary course of business, which contract is to be executed in whole or in part at or after the filing of the registration statement or which contract has been made not more than two years before such filing. Any management contract or contract providing for special bonuses or profit-sharing arrangements, and every material patent or contract for a material patent right, and every contract by or with a public utility company or an affiliate thereof, providing for the giving or receiving of technical of financial advice or service (if such contract may involve a charge to any party thereto at a rate in excess of $2,500 per year in cash or securities or anything else of value), shall be deemed a material contract;

(25) a balance sheet as of a date not more than ninety days prior to the date of the filing of the registration statement showing all of the assets of the issuer, the nature and cost thereof, whenever determinable, in such detail and in such form as the Commission shall prescribe (with intangible items segregated), including any loan in excess of $20,000 to any officer, director, stockholder or person directly or indirectly controlling or controlled by the issuer, or person under direct or indirect common control with the issuer. All the liabilities of the issuer in such detail and such form as the Commission shall prescribe, including surplus of the issuer showing how and from what sources such surplus was created, all as of a date not more than ninety days prior to the filing of the registration statement. If such statement be not certified by an independent public or certified accountant, in addition to the balance sheet required to be submitted under this schedule, a similar detailed balance sheet of the assets and liabilities of the issuer, certified by an independent public or certified accountant, of a date not more than one year prior to the filing of the registration statement, shall be submitted;

(26) a profit and loss statement of the issuer showing earnings and income, the nature and source thereof, and the expenses and fixed charges in such detail and such form as the Commission shall prescribe for the latest fiscal year for which such statement is available and for the two preceding fiscal years, year by year, or, if such issuer has been in actual business for less than three years, then for such time as the issuer has been in actual business, year by year. If the date of the filing of the registration statement is more than six months after the close of the last fiscal year, a statement from such closing date to the latest practicable date. Such statement shall show what the practice of the issuer has been during the three years or lesser period as to the character of the charges, dividends or other distributions made against its various surplus accounts, and as to depreciation, depletion, and maintenance charges, in such detail and form as the Commission shall prescribe, and if stock dividends or avails from the sale of rights have been credited to income, they shall be shown separately with a statement of the basis upon which the credit is computed. Such statement shall also differentiate between any recurring and non-recurring income and between any investment and operating income. Such statement shall be certified by an independent public or certified accountant;

(27) if the proceeds, or any part of the proceeds, of the security to be issued is to be applied directly or indirectly to the purchase of any business, a profit and loss statement of such business certified by an independent public or certified accountant, meeting the requirements of paragraph (26) of this schedule, for the three preceding fiscal years, together with a balance sheet, similarly certified, of such business, meeting the requirements of paragraph (25) of this schedule of a date not more than ninety days prior to the filing of the registration statement or at the date such business was acquired by the issuer if the business was acquired by the issuer more than ninety days prior to the filing of the registration statement;

(28) a copy of any agreement or agreements (or, if identical agreements are used, the forms thereof) made with any underwriter, including all contracts and agreements referred to in paragraph (17) of this schedule;

(29) a copy of the opinion or opinions of counsel in respect to the legality of the issue, with a translation of such opinion, when necessary, into the English language;

(30) a copy of all material contracts referred to in paragraph (24) of this schedule, but no disclosure shall be required of any portion of any such contract if the Commission determines that disclosure of such portion would impair the value of the contract and would not be necessary for the protection of investors;

(31) unless previously filed and registered under the provisions of this title, and brought up to date, (a) a copy of its articles of incorporation, with all amendments thereof and of its existing by-laws or instruments corresponding thereto, whatever the name, if the issuer be a corporation; (b) copy of all instruments by which the trust is created or declared, if the issuer is a trust; (c) a copy of its articles of partnership or association and all other papers pertaining to its organization, if the issuer is a partnership, unincorporated association, joint-stock company, or any other form of organization; and

(32) a copy of the underlying agreements or indentures affecting any stock, bonds, or debentures offered or to be offered.

In case of certificates of deposit, voting trust certificates, collateral trust certificates, certificates of interest or shares in unincorporated investment trusts, equipment trust certificates, interim or other receipts for certificates, and like securities, the Commission shall establish rules and regulations requiring the submission of information of a like character applicable to such cases, together with such other information as it may deem appropriate and necessary regarding the character, financial or otherwise, of the actual issuer of the securities and/or the person performing the acts and assuming the duties of depositor or manager.

SCHEDULE B

(1) Name of borrowing government or subdivision thereof;

(2) specific purposes in detail and the approximate amounts to be devoted to such purposes, so far as determinable, for which the security to be offered is to supply funds, and if the funds are to be raised in part from other sources, the amounts thereof and the sources thereof, shall be stated;

(3) the amount of the funded debt and the estimated amount of the floating debt outstanding and to be created by the security to be offered, excluding intergovernmental debt, and a brief description of the date, maturity, character of such debt, rate of interest, character of amortization provisions, and the security, if any, therefor. If substitution or any security is permissible, a statement of the conditions under which such substitution is permitted. If substitution is permissible without notice, a specific statement to that effect;

(4) whether or not the issuer or its predecessor has, within a period of twenty years prior to the filing of the registration statement, defaulted on the principal or interest of any external security, excluding intergovernmental debt, and, if so, the date, amount, and circumstances of such default, and the terms of the succeeding arrangement, if any;

(5) the receipts, classified by source, and the expenditures, classified by purpose, in such detail and form as the Commission shall prescribe for the latest fiscal year for which such information is available and the two preceding fiscal years, year by year;

(6) the names and addresses of the underwriters;

(7) the names and address of its authorized agent, if any, in the United States;

(8) the estimated net proceeds to be derived from the sale in the United States of the security to be offered;

(9) the price at which it is proposed that the security shall be offered in the United States to the public or the method by which such price is computed. A variation in price may be proposed prior to the date of the public offering of the security, but the Commission shall immediately be notified of such variation;

(10) all commissions paid or to be paid, directly or indirectly, by the issuer to the underwriters in respect of the sale of the security to be offered. Commissions shall include all cash, securities, contracts, or anything else of value, paid, to be set aside, disposed of, or understandings with or for the benefit of any other persons in which the underwriter is

interested, made, in connection with the sale of such security. Where any such commission is paid, the amount of such commission paid to each underwriter shall be stated;

(11) the amount of estimated amounts, itemized in reasonable detail, of expenses, other than the commissions specified in paragraph (10) of this schedule, incurred or borne by or for the account of the issuer in connection with the sale of the security to be offered or properly chargeable thereto, including legal, engineering, certification, and other charges;

(12) the names and addresses of counsel who have passed upon the legality of the issue;

(13) a copy of any agreement or agreements made with any underwriter governing the sale of the security within the United States; and

(14) an agreement of the issuer to furnish a copy of the opinion or opinions of counsel in respect to the legality of the issue, with a translation, where necessary, into the English language. Such opinion shall set out in full all laws, decrees, ordinances, or other acts of Government under which the issue of such security has been authorized.

SECURITIES ACT RULES

17 C.F.R. §§ 230.100-230.905

Regulation D—Rules Governing the Limited Offer and Sale of Securities Without Registration Under the Securities Act of 1933

Regulation E—Exemption for Securities of Small Business Investment Companies

Regulation S—Rules Governing Offers and Sales Made Outside the United States Without Registration Under the Securities Act of 1933

**Regulation CE—Coordinated Exemptions for Certain Issues of Securities
Exempt Under State Law**

1001					Exemption for transactions exempt from qualification under Sec. 25102(n) of the California Corporations Code

NASAA Uniform Limited Offering Exemption

GENERAL

Rule 100. Definitions of Terms Used in the Rules and Regulations

(a) As used in the rules and regulations prescribed by the Securities and Exchange Commission pursuant to the Securities Act of 1933, unless the context otherwise requires:

(1) The term "Commission" means the Securities and Exchange Commission.

(2) The term "Act" means the Securities Act of 1933.

(3) The term "rules and regulations" refers to all rules and regulations adopted by the Commission pursuant to the Act, including the forms for registration and accompanying instructions thereto.

(4) The term "registrant" means the issuer of securities for which a registration statement is filed.

(5) The term "agent for service" means the person authorized in the registration statement to receive notices and communications from the Commission.

(6) The term "electronic filer" means a person or an entity that submits filings electronically pursuant to Rules 101, 901, 902 or 903 of Regulation S-T (§§ 232.101, 232.901, 232.902 or 232.903 of this chapter, respectively).

(7) The term "electronic filing" means a document under the federal securities laws that is transmitted or delivered to the Commission in electronic format.

(b) Unless otherwise specifically provided, the terms used in the rules and regulations shall have the meanings defined in the Act.

(c) A rule in the General Rules and Regulations which defines a term without express reference to the Act or to the rules and regulations or to a portion thereof defines such term for all purposes as used both in the Act and in the rules and regulations, unless the context otherwise requires.

Rule 110. Business Hours of the Commission

(a) *General.* The principal office of the Commission, at 100 F Street, NE, Washington, DC 20549, is open each day, except Saturdays, Sundays, and Federal holidays, from 9 a.m. to 5:30 p.m., Eastern Standard Time or Eastern Daylight Saving Time, whichever is currently in effect, *provided that* hours for the filing of documents pursuant to the Act or the rules and regulations thereunder are as set forth in paragraphs (b), (c) and (d) of this section.

(b) *Submissions made in paper.* Paper documents filed with or otherwise furnished to the Commission may be submitted each day, except Saturdays, Sundays and federal holidays, from 8 a.m. to 5:30 p.m., Eastern Standard Time or Eastern Daylight Saving Time, whichever is currently in effect.

(c) *Filings by direct transmission.* Filings made by direct transmission may be submitted to the Commission each day, except Saturdays, Sundays and federal holidays, from 8:00 a.m. to 10:00 p.m., Eastern Standard Time or Eastern Daylight Saving Time, whichever is currently in effect.

(d) *Filings by facsimile*. Registration statements and post-effective amendments thereto filed by facsimile transmission pursuant to Rule 462(b) (§ 230.462(b)) and Rule 455 (§ 230.455) may be filed with the Commission each day, except Saturdays, Sundays and federal holidays, from 5:30 p.m. to 10:00 p.m., Eastern Standard Time or Eastern Daylight Savings Time, whichever is currently in effect.

Rule 111. Payment of Fees

All payments of fees for registration statements under the Act shall be made by wire transfer, or by certified check, bank cashier's check, United States postal money order, or bank money order payable to the Securities and Exchange Commission, omitting the name or title of any official of the Commission. There will be no refunds. Payment of fees required by this section shall be made in accordance with the directions set forth in § 202.3a of this chapter.

Rule 120. Inspection of Registration Statements

Except for material contracts or portions thereof accorded confidential treatment pursuant to § 230.406, all registration statements are available for public inspection, during business hours, at the principal office of the Commission in Washington, D.C. Electronic registration statements made through the Electronic Data Gathering, Analysis, and Retrieval system are publicly available through the Commission's Web site (http://www.sec.gov).

Rule 122. Non-disclosure of Information Obtained in the Course of Examinations and Investigations

Information or documents obtained by officers or employees of the Commission in the course of any examination or investigation pursuant to Section 8(e) or 20(a) shall, unless made a matter of public record, be deemed confidential. Except as provided by 17 CFR 203.2, officers and employees are hereby prohibited from making such confidential information or documents or any other non-public records of the Commission available to anyone other than a member, officer or employee of the Commission, unless the Commission or the General Counsel, pursuant to delegated authority, authorizes the disclosure of such information or the production of such documents as not being contrary to the public interest. Any officer or employee who is served with a subpoena requiring the disclosure of such information or the production of such documents shall appear in court and, unless the authorization described in the preceding sentence shall have been given, shall respectfully decline to disclose the information or produce the documents called for, basing his refusal upon this rule. Any officer or employee who is served with such a subpoena shall promptly advise the General Counsel of the service of such subpoena, the nature of the information or documents sought, and any circumstances which may bear on the desirability of making available such information or documents.

Rule 130. Definition of "Rules and Regulations" as Used in Certain Sections of the Act

The term "rules and regulations" as used in Sections 7, 10(a), (c) and (d) and 19(a) of the Act, shall include the forms for registration of securities under the Act and the related instructions thereto.

Rule 131. Definition of Security Issued Under Governmental Obligations

(a) Any part of an obligation evidenced by any bond, note, debenture, or other evidence of indebtedness issued by any governmental unit specified in Section 3(a)(2) of the Act which is payable from payments to be made in respect of property or money which is or will be used, under a lease, sale, or loan arrangement, by or for industrial or commercial enterprise, shall be deemed to be a separate "security" within the meaning of Section 2(1) of the Act, issued by the lessee or obligor under the lease, sale or loan arrangement.

(b) An obligation shall not be deemed a separate "security" as defined in paragraph (a) hereof if, (1) the obligation is payable from the general revenues of a governmental unit, specified in Section 3(a)(2) of the Act, having other resources which may be used for payment of the obligation, or (2) the obligation relates to a public project or facility owned and operated by or on behalf of and under the control of a governmental unit specified in such section, or (3) the obligation relates to a facility which is leased to and under the control of an industrial or commercial enterprise but is a part of a public project which, as a whole, is owned by and under the general control of a governmental unit specified in such section, or an instrumentality thereof.

(c) This rule shall apply to transactions of the character described in paragraph (a) only with respect to bonds, notes, debentures or other evidences of indebtedness sold after December 31, 1968.

Rule 132. Definition of "Common Trust Fund" as Used in Section 3(a)(2) of the Act

The term "common trust fund" as used in section 3(a)(2) of the Act [15 U.S.C. 77c(a)(2)] shall include a common trust fund which is maintained by a bank which is a member of an affiliated group, as defined in section 1504(a) of the Internal Revenue Code of 1954 [26 U.S.C. 1504(a)], and which is maintained exclusively for the collective investment and reinvestment of monies contributed thereto by one or more bank members of such affiliated group in the capacity of trustee, executor, administrator, or guardian, provided that:

(a) the common trust fund is operated in compliance with the same state and federal regulatory requirements as would apply if the bank maintaining such fund and any other contributing banks were the same entity; and

(b) the rights of persons for whose benefit a contributing bank acts as trustee, executor, administrator, or guardian would not be diminished by reason of the maintenance of such common trust fund by another bank member of the affiliated group. (15 U.S.C. 77s(a)).

Rule 134. Communications Not Deemed a Prospectus

Except as provided in paragraphs (e) and (g) of this section, the terms "prospectus" as defined in section 2(a)(10) of the Act or "free writing prospectus" as defined in Rule 405 (§ 230.405) shall not include a communication limited to the statements required or permitted by this section, provided that the communication is published or transmitted to any person only after a registration statement relating to the offering that includes a prospectus satisfying the requirements of section 10 of the Act (except as otherwise permitted in paragraph (a) of this section) has been filed.

(a) Such communication may include any one or more of the following items of information, which need not follow the numerical sequence of this paragraph, provided that, except as to paragraphs (a)(4) through (6) of this section, the prospectus included in the filed registration statement does not have to include a price range otherwise required by rule:

(1) Factual information about the legal identity and business location of the issuer limited to the following: the name of the issuer of the security, the address, phone number, and e-mail address of the issuer's principal offices and contact for investors, the issuer's country of organization, and the geographic areas in which it conducts business;

(2) The title of the security or securities and the amount or amounts being offered, which title may include a designation as to whether the securities are convertible, exercisable, or exchangeable, and as to the ranking of the securities;

(3) A brief indication of the general type of business of the issuer, limited to the following:

(i) In the case of a manufacturing company, the general type of manufacturing, the principal products or classes of products manufactured, and the segments in which the company conducts business;

(ii) In the case of a public utility company, the general type of services rendered, a brief indication of the area served, and the segments in which the company conducts business;

(iii) In the case of an asset-backed issuer, the identity of key parties, such as sponsor, depositor, issuing entity, servicer or servicers, and trustee, the asset class of the transaction, and the identity of any credit enhancement or other support; and

(iv) In the case of any other type of company, a corresponding statement;

(4) The price of the security, or if the price is not known, the method of its determination or the bona fide estimate of the price range as specified by the issuer or the managing underwriter or underwriters;

(5) In the case of a fixed income security, the final maturity and interest rate provisions or, if the final maturity or interest rate provisions are not known, the probable final maturity or interest rate provisions, as specified by the issuer or the managing underwriter or underwriters;

(6) In the case of a fixed income security with a fixed (non-contingent) interest rate provision, the yield or, if the yield is not known, the probable yield range, as specified by the issuer or the managing underwriter or underwriters and the yield of fixed income securities with comparable maturity and security rating;

(7) A brief description of the intended use of proceeds of the offering, if then disclosed in the prospectus that is part of the filed registration statement;

(8) The name, address, phone number, and e-mail address of the sender of the communication and the fact that it is participating, or expects to participate, in the distribution of the security;

(9) The type of underwriting, if then included in the disclosure in the prospectus that is part of the filed registration statement;

(10) The names of underwriters participating in the offering of the securities, and their additional roles, if any, within the underwriting syndicate;

(11) The anticipated schedule for the offering (including the approximate date upon which the proposed sale to the public will begin) and a description of marketing events (including the dates, times, locations, and procedures for attending or otherwise accessing them);

(12) A description of the procedures by which the underwriters will conduct the offering and the procedures for transactions in connection with the offering with the issuer or an underwriter or participating dealer (including procedures regarding account-opening and submitting indications of interest and conditional offers to buy), and procedures regarding directed share plans and other participation in offerings by officers, directors, and employees of the issuer;

(13) Whether, in the opinion of counsel, the security is a legal investment for savings banks, fiduciaries, insurance companies, or similar investors under the laws of any State or Territory or the District of Columbia, and the permissibility or status of the investment under the Employee Retirement Income Security Act of 1974 [29 U.S.C. 1001 et seq.];

(14) Whether, in the opinion of counsel, the security is exempt from specified taxes, or the extent to which the issuer has agreed to pay any tax with respect to the security or measured by the income therefrom;

(15) Whether the security is being offered through rights issued to security holders, and, if so, the class of securities the holders of which will be entitled to subscribe, the subscription ratio, the actual or proposed record date, the date upon which the rights were issued or are expected to be issued, the actual or anticipated date upon which they will expire, and the approximate subscription price, or any of the foregoing;

(16) Any statement or legend required by any state law or administrative authority;

(17) [Reserved.]

(18) The names of selling security holders, if then disclosed in the prospectus that is part of the filed registration statement;

(19) The names of securities exchanges or other securities markets where any class of the issuer's securities are, or will be, listed;

(20) The ticker symbols, or proposed ticker symbols, of the issuer's securities;

(21) The CUSIP number as defined in Rule 17Ad-19(a)(5) of the Securities Exchange Act of 1934 (§ 240.17Ad-19(a)(5) of this chapter) assigned to the securities being offered; and

(22) Information disclosed in order to correct inaccuracies previously contained in a communication permissibly made pursuant to this section.

(b) Except as provided in paragraph (c) of this section, every communication used pursuant to this section shall contain the following:

(1) If the registration statement has not yet become effective, the following statement:

A registration statement relating to these securities has been filed with the Securities and Exchange Commission but has not yet become effective. These securities may not be sold nor may offers to buy be accepted prior to the time the registration statement becomes effective; and

(2) The name and address of a person or persons from whom a written prospectus for the offering meeting the requirements of section 10 of the Act (other than a free writing prospectus as defined in Rule 405) including as to the identified paragraphs above a price range where required by rule, may be obtained.

(c) Any of the statements or information specified in paragraph (b) of this section may, but need not, be contained in a communication which:

(1) Does no more than state from whom and include the uniform resource locator (URL) where a written prospectus meeting the requirements of section 10 of the Act (other than a free writing prospectus as defined in Rule 405) may be obtained, identify the security, state the price thereof and state by whom orders will be executed; or

(2) Is accompanied or preceded by a prospectus or a summary prospectus, other than a free writing prospectus as defined in Rule 405, which meets the requirements of section 10 of the Act, including a price range where required by rule, at the date of such preliminary communication.

(d) A communication sent or delivered to any person pursuant to this section which is accompanied or preceded by a prospectus which meets the requirements of section 10 of the Act (other than a free writing prospectus as defined in Rule 405), including a price range where required by rule, at the date of such communication, may solicit from the recipient of the communication an offer to buy the security or request the recipient to indicate whether he or she might be interested in the security, if the communication contains substantially the following statement:

No offer to buy the securities can be accepted and no part of the purchase price can be received until the registration statement has become effective, and any such offer may be withdrawn or revoked, without obligation or commitment of any kind, at any time prior to notice of its acceptance given after the effective date.

Provided, that such statement need not be included in such a communication to a dealer.

(e) A section 10 prospectus included in any communication pursuant to this section shall remain a prospectus for all purposes under the Act.

(f) The provision in paragraphs (c)(2) and (d) of this section that a prospectus that meets the requirements of section 10 of the Act precede or accompany a communication will be satisfied if such communication is an electronic communication containing an active hyperlink to such prospectus.

(g) This section does not apply to a communication relating to an investment company registered under the Investment Company Act of 1940 (15 U.S.C. 80a-1 et seq.) or a business development company as defined in section 2(a)(48) of the Investment Company Act of 1940 (15 U.S.C. 80a-2(a)(48)).

Rule 134a. Options Material Not Deemed a Prospectus

Written materials, including advertisements, relating to standardized options, as that term is defined in Rule 9b-1 under the Securities Exchange Act of 1934, shall not be deemed to be a prospectus for the purposes of Section 2(10) of the Securities Act of 1933: *Provided,* That such materials are limited to explanatory information describing the general nature of the standardized options markets or one or more strategies: *And, Provided Further,* That:

(a) The potential risks related to options trading generally and to each strategy addressed are explained;

(b) No past or projected performance figures, including annualized rates of return are used;

(c) No recommendation to purchase or sell any option contract is made;

(d) No specific security is identified, other than

(i) An option or other security exempt from registration under the Act, or

(ii) An index option, including the component securities of the index; and

(e) If there is a definitive options disclosure document, as defined in Rule 9b-1 under the Securities Exchange Act of 1934, the materials shall contain the name and address of a person or persons from whom a copy of such document may be obtained.

Rule 134b. Statement of Additional Information

For the purpose only of Section 5(b) of the Act (15 U.S.C. 77e(b)), the term "prospectus" as defined in Section 2(a)(10) of the Act (15 U.S.C. 77b(a)(10)) does not include a Statement of Additional Information filed as part of a registration statement on Form N-1A (§239.15A and §274.11A of this chapter), Form N-2 (§239.14 and §274.11a-1 of this chapter), Form N-3 (§239.17a and §274.11b of this chapter), Form N-4 (§239.17b and §274.11c of this chapter), or Form N-6 (§239.17c and §274.11d of this chapter) transmitted prior to the effective date of the registration statement if it is accompanied or preceded by a preliminary prospectus meeting the requirements of §230.430.

Rule 135. Notice of Proposed Registered Offerings

(a) For purposes of Section 5 of the Act (15 U.S.C. 77e) only, an issuer or a selling security holder (and any person acting on behalf of either of them) that publishes through any medium a notice of a proposed offering to be registered under the Act will not be deemed to offer its securities for sale through that notice if:

(1) *Legend.* The notice includes a statement to the effect that it does not constitute an offer of any securities for sale; and

(2) *Limited notice content.* The notice otherwise includes no more than the following information:

(i) The name of the issuer;

(ii) The title, amount and basic terms of the securities offered;

(iii) The amount of the offering, if any, to be made by selling security holders;

(iv) The anticipated timing of the offering;

(v) A brief statement of the manner and the purpose of the offering, without naming the underwriters;

(vi) Whether the issuer is directing its offering to only a particular class of purchasers;

(vii) Any statements or legends required by the laws of any state or foreign country or administrative authority; and

(viii) In the following offerings, the notice may contain additional information, as follows:

(A) *Rights offering.* In a rights offering to existing security holders:

(*1*) The class of security holders eligible to subscribe;

(*2*) The subscription ratio and expected subscription price;

(*3*) The proposed record date;

(*4*) The anticipated issuance date of the rights; and

(*5*) The subscription period or expiration date of the rights offering.

(B) *Offering to employees.* In an offering to employees of the issuer or an affiliated company:

(*1*) The name of the employer;

(*2*) The class of employees being offered the securities;

(*3*) The offering price; and

(*4*) The duration of the offering period.

(*C*) *Exchange offer.* In an exchange offer:

(*1*) The basic terms of the exchange offer;

(*2*) The name of the subject company;

(*3*) The subject class of securities sought in the exchange offer.

(D) *Rule 145(a) offering.* In a § 230.145(a) offering:

(*1*) The name of the person whose assets are to be sold in exchange for the securities to be offered;

(*2*) The names of any other parties to the transaction;

(*3*) A brief description of the business of the parties to the transaction;

(*4*) The date, time and place of the meeting of security holders to vote on or consent to the transaction; and

(*5*) A brief description of the transaction and the basic terms of the transaction.

(b) *Corrections of misstatements about the offering.* A person that publishes a notice in reliance on this section may issue a notice that contains no more information than is necessary to correct inaccuracies published about the proposed offering.

Note to § 230.135: Communications under this section relating to business combination transactions must be filed as required by § 230.425(b).

Rule 135a. Generic Advertising

For the purposes only of Section 5 of the Act, a notice, circular, advertisement, letter, sign or other communication, published or transmitted to any person which does not specifically refer by name to the securities of a particular investment company, to the investment company itself, or to any other securities not exempt under Section 3(a) of the Act, will not be deemed to offer any security for sale, provided:

(a) such communication is limited to any one or more of the following:

1. Explanatory information relating to securities of investment companies generally or to the nature of investment companies, or to services offered in connection with the ownership of such securities.

2. The mention or explanation of investment companies of different generic types or having various investment objectives, such as "balanced funds", "growth funds", "income funds", "leveraged funds", "specialty funds", "variable annuities", "bond funds", and "no-load funds",

3. Offers, descriptions and explanation of various products and services not constituting a security subject to registration under the Act, provided that such offers, descriptions and explanations do not relate directly to the desirability of owning or purchasing a security issued by a registered investment company,

4. Invitation to inquire for further information and

(b) such communication contains the name and address of a registered broker or dealer or other person sponsoring the communication.

If such communication contains a solicitation of inquiries and prospectuses for investment company securities are to be sent or delivered in response to such inquiries, the number of such investment companies and, if applicable, the fact that the sponsor of the communication is the principal underwriter or investment adviser in respect to such investment companies shall be stated.

(c) With respect to any communication describing any type of security, service or product, the broker, dealer or other person sponsoring such communication must offer for sale a security, service or product of the type described in such communication.

Rule 135b. Materials Not Deemed an Offer to Sell or Offer to Buy Nor a Prospectus

Materials meeting the requirements of § 240.9b-1 of this chapter shall not be deemed an offer to sell or offer to buy a security for purposes solely of Section 5 (15 U.S.C. 77e) of the Act, nor shall such materials be deemed a prospectus for purposes of Sections 2(a)(10) and 12(a)(2) (15 U.S.C. 77b(a)(10) and 77l(a)(2)) of the Act, even if such materials are referred to in, deemed to be incorporated by reference into, or otherwise in any manner deemed to be a part of a Form S-20 prospectus.

Rule 135c. Notice of Certain Proposed Unregistered Offerings

(a) For the purposes only of Section 5 of the Act, a notice given by an issuer required to file reports pursuant to Section 13 or 15(d) of the Securities Exchange Act of 1934 or a foreign issuer that is exempt from registration under the Securities Exchange Act of 1934 pursuant to § 240.12g3-2(b) of this chapter that it proposes to make, is making or has made an offering of securities not registered or required to be registered under the Act shall not be deemed to offer any securities for sale if:

(1) Such notice is not used for the purpose of conditioning the market in the United States for any of the securities offered;

(2) Such notice states that the securities offered will not be or have not been registered under the Act and may not be offered or sold in the United States absent registration or an applicable exemption from registration requirements; and

(3) Such notice contains no more than the following additional information:

(i) The name of the issuer;

(ii) The title, amount and basic terms of the securities offered, the amount of the offering, if any, made by selling security holders, the time of the offering and a brief statement of the manner and purpose of the offering without naming the underwriters;

(iii) In the case of a rights offering to security holders of the issuer, the class of securities the holder of which will be or were entitled to subscribe to the securities offered, the subscription ratio, the record date, the date upon which the rights are proposed to be or were issued, the term or expiration date of the rights and the subscription price, or any of the foregoing;

(iv) In the case of an offering of securities in exchange for other securities of the issuer or of another issuer, the name of the issuer and the title of the securities to be surrendered in exchange for the securities offered, the basis upon which the exchange may be made, or any of the foregoing;

(v) In the case of an offering to employees of the issuer or to employees of any affiliate of the issuer, the name of the employer and class or classes of employees to whom the securities are offered, the offering price or basis of the offering and the period during which the offering is to be or was made or any of the foregoing; and

(vi) Any statement or legend required by State or foreign law or administrative authority.

(b) Any notice contemplated by this section may take the form of a news release or a written communication directed to security holders or employees, as the case may be, or other published statements.

(c) Notwithstanding the provisions of paragraphs (a) and (b) of this section, in the case of a rights offering of a security listed or subject to unlisted trading privileges on a national securities exchange or quoted on the NASDAQ inter-dealer quotation system information with respect to the interest rate, conversion ratio and subscription price may be disseminated through the facilities of the exchange, the consolidated transaction reporting system, the NASDAQ system or the Dow Jones broad tape, provided such information is already disclosed in a Form 8-K (§ 249.308 of this chapter) on file with the Commission, in a Form 6-K (§ 249.306 of this chapter) furnished to the Commission or, in the case of an issuer relying on § 240.12g3-2(b) of this chapter, in a submission made pursuant to that Section to the Commission.

(d) The issuer shall file any notice contemplated by this section with the Commission under cover of Form 8-K (§ 249.308 of this chapter) or furnish such notice under Form 6-K (§ 249.306 of this chapter), as applicable, and, if relying on § 240.12g3-2(b) of this chapter, shall furnish such notice to the Commission in accordance with the provisions of that exemptive Section.

Rule 135e. Offshore Press Conferences, Meetings with Issuer Representatives Conducted Offshore, and Press-Related Materials Released Offshore

(a) For the purposes only of Section 5 of the Act [15 U.S.C. 77e], an issuer that is a foreign private issuer (as defined in § 230.405) or a foreign government issuer, a selling security holder of the securities of such issuers, or their representatives will not be deemed to offer any security for sale by virtue of providing any journalist with access to its press conferences held outside of the United States, to meetings with issuer or selling security holder representatives conducted outside of the United States, or to written press-related materials released outside the United States, at or in which a present or proposed offering of securities is discussed, if:

(1) The present or proposed offering is not being, or to be, conducted solely in the United States;

Note to Paragraph (a)(1): An offering will be considered not to be made solely in the United States under this paragraph (a)(1) only if there is an intent to make a bona fide offering offshore.

(2) Access is provided to both U.S. and foreign journalists; and

(3) Any written press-related materials pertaining to transactions in which any of the securities will be or are being offered in the United States satisfy the requirements of paragraph (b) of this section.

(b) Any written press-related materials specified in paragraph (a)(3) of this section must:

(1) State that the written press-related materials are not an offer of securities for sale in the United States, that securities may not be offered or sold in the United States absent registration or an exemption from registration, that any public offering of securities to be made in the United States will be made by means of a prospectus that may be obtained from the issuer or the selling security holder and that will contain detailed information about the company and management, as well as financial statements;

(2) If the issuer or selling security holder intends to register any part of the present or proposed offering in the United States, include a statement regarding this intention; and

(3) Not include any purchase order, or coupon that could be returned indicating interest in the offering, as part of, or attached to, the written press-related materials.

(c) For the purposes of this section, "United States" means the United States of America, its territories and possessions, any State of the United States, and the District of Columbia.

Rule 136. Definition of Certain Terms in Relation to Assessable Stock

(a) An "offer," "offer to sell" or "offer for sale" of securities shall be deemed to be made to the holders of assessable stock of a corporation when such corporation shall give notice of an assessment to the holders of such assessable stock. A "sale" shall be deemed to occur when a stockholder shall pay or agree to pay all or any part of such an assessment.

(b) The term "transactions by any person other than an issuer, underwriter or dealer" in section 4(1) of the Act shall not be deemed to include the offering or sale of assessable stock, at public auction or otherwise, upon the failure of the holder of such stock to pay an assessment levied thereon by the issuer, where the offer or sale is made for the purpose of realizing the amount of the assessment and any of the proceeds of such sale are to be received by the issuer. However, any person whose functions are limited to acting as auctioneer at such an auction sale shall not be deemed to be an underwriter of the securities offered or sold at the auction sale. Any person who acquires assessable stock at any such public auction or other sale with a view to the distribution thereof shall be deemed to be an underwriter of such assessable stock.

(c) The term "assessable stock" means stock which is subject to resale by the issuer pursuant to statute or otherwise in the event of a failure of the holder of such stock to pay any assessment levied thereon.

Rule 137. Publications or Distributions of Research Reports by Brokers or Dealers That Are Not Participating in an Issuer's Registered Distribution of Securities

Under the following conditions, the terms "offers," "participates," or "participation" in section 2(a)(11) of the Act shall not be deemed to apply to the publication or distribution of research reports with respect to the securities of an issuer which is the subject of an offering pursuant to a registration statement that the issuer proposes to file, or has filed, or that is effective:

(a) The broker or dealer (and any affiliate) that has distributed the report and, if different, the person (and any affiliate) that has published the report have not participated, are not participating, and do not propose to participate in the distribution of the securities that are or will be the subject of the registered offering.

(b) In connection with the publication or distribution of the research report, the broker or dealer (and any affiliate) that has distributed the report and, if different, the person (and any affiliate) that has published the report are not receiving and have not received consideration directly or indirectly from, and are not acting under any direct or indirect arrangement or understanding with:

(1) The issuer of the securities;

(2) A selling security holder;

(3) Any participant in the distribution of the securities that are or will be the subject of the registration statement; or

(4) Any other person interested in the securities that are or will be the subject of the registration statement.

Instruction to § 230.137(b). This paragraph (b) does not preclude payment of:

1. The regular price being paid by the broker or dealer for independent research, so long as the conditions of this paragraph (b) are satisfied; or

2. The regular subscription or purchase price for the research report.

(c) The broker or dealer publishes or distributes the research report in the regular course of its business.

(d) The issuer is not and during the past three years neither the issuer nor any of its predecessors was:

(1) A blank check company as defined in Rule 419(a)(2) (§ 230.419(a)(2));

(2) A shell company, other than a business combination related shell company, each as defined in Rule 405 (§ 230.405); or

(3) An issuer for an offering of penny stock as defined in Rule 3a51-1 of the Securities Exchange Act of 1934 (§ 240.3a51-1 of this chapter).

(e) Definition of research report. For purposes of this section, research report means a written communication, as defined in Rule 405, that includes information, opinions, or recommendations with respect to securities of an issuer or an analysis of a security or an issuer, whether or not it provides information reasonably sufficient upon which to base an investment decision.

Rule 138. Publications or Distributions of Research Reports by Brokers or Dealers About Securities Other Than Those They Are Distributing

(a) Registered offerings. Under the following conditions, a broker's or dealer's publication or distribution of research reports about securities of an issuer shall be deemed for purposes of sections 2(a)(10) and 5(c) of the Act not to constitute an offer for sale or offer to sell a security which is the subject of an offering pursuant to a registration statement that the issuer proposes to file, or has filed, or that is effective, even if the broker or dealer is participating or will participate in the registered offering of the issuer's securities:

(1)(i) The research report relates solely to the issuer's common stock, or debt securities, or preferred stock convertible into its common stock, and the offering involves solely the issuer's non-convertible debt securities or non-convertible, non-participating preferred stock; or

(ii) The research report relates solely to the issuer's non-convertible debt securities or non-convertible, non-participating preferred stock, and the offering involves solely the issuer's common stock, or debt securities, or preferred stock convertible into its common stock.

Instruction to paragraph (a)(1): If the issuer has filed a shelf registration statement under Rule 415(a)(1)(x) (§ 230.415(a)(1)(x)) or pursuant to General Instruction I.D. of Form S-3, General Instruction I.C. of Form F-3 (§ 239.13 or § 239.33 of this chapter), or pursuant to General Instructions A.2 and B of Form N-2 (§ 239.14 and § 274.11a-1 of this chapter) with respect to multiple classes of securities, the conditions of paragraph (a)(1) of this section must be satisfied for the offering in which the broker or dealer is participating or will participate.

(2) The issuer as of the date of reliance on this section:

(i) (A) Is required to file reports, and has filed all periodic reports required during the preceding 12 months (or such shorter time that the issuer was required to file such reports) on Forms 10-K (§ 249.310 of this chapter), 10-Q (§ 249.308a of this chapter), and 20-F (§ 249.220f of this chapter) pursuant to Section 13 or Section 15(d) of the Securities Exchange Act of 1934 (15 U.S.C. 78m or 78*o*(d)); or

(B) (*1*) Is a registered closed-end investment company; and

(*2*) Is required to file reports, and has filed all periodic reports required during the preceding 12 months (or such shorter time that the issuer was required to file such reports) on Forms N-CSR (§§ 249.331 and 274.128 of this chapter), N-PORT (§ 274.150 of this chapter), and N-CEN (§§ 249.330 and 274.101 of this chapter) pursuant to Section 30 of the Investment Company Act; or

(ii) Is a foreign private issuer that:

(A) Meets all of the registrant requirements of Form F-3 other than the reporting history provisions of General Instructions I.A.1. and I.A.2(a) of Form F-3;

(B) Either:

(1) Satisfies the public float threshold in General Instruction I.B.1. of Form F-3; or

(2) Is issuing non-convertible securities, other than common equity, and the issuer meets the provisions of General Instruction I.B.2.of Form F-3 (referenced in 17 CFR239.33 of this chapter); and

(C) Either:

(1) Has its equity securities trading on a designated offshore securities market as defined in Rule 902(b) (§ 230.902(b)) and has had them so traded for at least 12 months; or

(2) Has a worldwide market value of its outstanding common equity held by non-affiliates of $700 million or more.

(3) The broker or dealer publishes or distributes research reports on the types of securities in question in the regular course of its business; and

(4) The issuer is not, and during the past three years neither the issuer nor any of its predecessors was:

(i) A blank check company as defined in Rule 419(a)(2) (§ 230.419(a)(2));

(ii) A shell company, other than a business combination related shell company, each as defined in Rule 405 (§ 230.405); or

(iii) An issuer for an offering of penny stock as defined in Rule 3a51-1 of the Securities Exchange Act of 1934 (§ 240.3a51-1 of this chapter).

(b) Rule 144A offerings. If the conditions in paragraph (a) of this section are satisfied, a broker's or dealer's publication or distribution of a research report shall not be considered an offer for sale or an offer to sell a security or general solicitation or general advertising, in connection with an offering relying on Rule 144A (§ 230.144A).

(c) Regulation S offerings. If the conditions in paragraph (a) of this section are satisfied, a broker's or dealer's publication or distribution of a research report shall not:

(1) Constitute directed selling efforts as defined in Rule 902(c) (§ 230.902(c)) for offerings under Regulation S (§ 230.901 through § 230.905); or

(2) Be inconsistent with the offshore transaction requirement in Rule 902(h) (§ 230.902(h)) for offerings under Regulation S.

(d) Definition of research report. For purposes of this section, research report means a written communication, as defined in Rule 405, that includes information, opinions, or recommendations with respect to securities of an issuer or an analysis of a security or an issuer, whether or not it provides information reasonably sufficient upon which to base an investment decision.

Rule 139. Publications or Distributions of Research Reports by Brokers or Dealers Distributing Securities.

(a) *Registered Offerings.* Under the conditions of paragraph (a)(1) or (2) of this section, a broker's or dealer's publication or distribution of a research report about an issuer or any of its securities shall be deemed for purposes of sections 2(a)(10) and 5(c) of the Act not to constitute an offer for sale or offer to sell a security that is the subject of an offering pursuant to a registration statement that the issuer proposes to file, or has filed, or that is effective, even if the broker or dealer is participating or will participate in the registered offering of the issuer's securities. For purposes of the Fair Access to Investment Research Act of 2017 [Pub. L. 115-66, 146 131 Stat. 1196 (2017)], a safe harbor has been established for covered investment fund research reports, and the specific terms of that safe harbor are set forth in § 230.139b.

(1) Issuer-specific research reports.

(i) The issuer either:

(A)(1) At the later of the time of filing its most recent Form S-3 (§ 239.13 of this chapter) or Form F-3 (§ 239.33 of this chapter) or the time of its most recent amendment to such registration statement for purposes of complying with section 10(a)(3) of the Act or, if no Form S-3 or Form F-3 has been filed, at the date of reliance on this section, meets the registrant requirements of such Form S-3 or Form F-3 and:

(*i*) At such date, meets the minimum float provisions of General Instruction I.B.1 of such Forms; or (*ii*) At the date of reliance on this section, is, or if a registration statement has not been filed, will be, offering non-convertible securities, other than common equity, and meets the requirements for the General Instruction I.B.2. of Form S-3 or Form F-3 (referenced in 17 CFR 239.13 and 17 CFR 239.33 of this chapter); or

(*iii*) At the date of reliance on this section is a well-known seasoned issuer as defined in Rule 405 (§ 230.405), other than a majority-owned subsidiary that is a well known seasoned issuer by virtue of paragraph (1)(ii) of the definition of well-known seasoned issuer in Rule 405; and

(2) As of the date of reliance on this section, has filed all periodic reports required during the preceding 12 months on Forms 10-K (§ 249.310 of this chapter), 10-Q (§ 249.308a of this chapter), and 20-F (§ 249.220f of this chapter) pursuant to section 13 or section 15(d) of the Securities Exchange Act of 1934 (15 U.S.C. 78m or 78o(d)); or

(B) Is a foreign private issuer that as of the date of reliance on this section:

(1) Meets all of the registrant requirements of Form F-3 other than the reporting history provisions of General Instructions I.A.1. and I.A.2(a) of Form F-3;

(2) Either:

(*i*) Satisfies the public float threshold in General Instruction I.B.1. of Form F-3; or

(*ii*) Is issuing non-convertible securities, other than common equity, and meets the provisions of General Instruction I.B.2. of Form F-3 (referenced in 17 CFR 239.33 of this chapter); and

(3) Either:

(*i*) Has its equity securities trading on a designated offshore securities market as defined in Rule 902(b) (§ 230.902(b)) and has had them so traded for at least 12 months; or

(*ii*) Has a worldwide market value of its outstanding common equity held by non-affiliates of $700 million or more;

(ii) The issuer is not and during the past three years neither the issuer nor any of its predecessors was:

(A) A blank check company as defined in Rule 419(a)(2) (§ 230.419(a)(2));

(B) A shell company, other than a business combination related shell company, each as defined in Rule 405 (§ 230.405); or

(C) An issuer for an offering of penny stock as defined in Rule 3a51-1 of the Securities Exchange Act of 1934 (§ 240.3a51-1 of this chapter); and

(iii) The broker or dealer publishes or distributes research reports in the regular course of its business and such publication or distribution does not represent the initiation of publication of research reports about such issuer or its securities or reinitiation of such publication following discontinuation of publication of such research reports.

(2) Industry reports.

(i) The issuer is required to file reports pursuant to section 13 or section 15(d) of the Securities Exchange Act of 1934 or satisfies the conditions in paragraph (a)(1)(i)(B) of this section;

(ii) The condition in paragraph (a)(1)(ii) of this section is satisfied;

(iii) The research report includes similar information with respect to a substantial number of issuers in the issuer's industry or sub-industry, or contains a comprehensive list of securities currently recommended by the broker or dealer;

(iv) The analysis regarding the issuer or its securities is given no materially greater space or prominence in the publication than that given to other securities or issuers; and

(v) The broker or dealer publishes or distributes research reports in the regular course of its business and, at the time of the publication or distribution of the research report, is including similar information about the issuer or its securities in similar reports.

(b) *Rule 144A offerings.* If the conditions in paragraph (a)(1) or (a)(2) of this section are satisfied, a broker's or dealer's publication or distribution of a research report shall not be considered an offer for sale or an offer to sell a security or general solicitation or general advertising, in connection with an offering relying on Rule 144A (§ 230.144A).

(c) *Regulation S offerings.* If the conditions in paragraph (a)(1) or (a)(2) of this section are satisfied, a broker's or dealer's publication or distribution of a research report shall not:

(1) Constitute directed selling efforts as defined in Rule 902(c) (§ 230.902(c)) for offerings under Regulation S (§§ 230.901 through 230.905); or

(2) Be inconsistent with the offshore transaction requirement in Rule 902(h) (§ 230.902(h)) for offerings under Regulation S.

(d) *Definition of research report.* For purposes of this section, research report means a written communication, as defined in Rule 405, that includes information, opinions, or recommendations with respect to securities of an issuer or an analysis of a security or an issuer, whether or not it provides information reasonably sufficient upon which to base an investment decision.

Instruction to § 230.139. Projections. A projection constitutes an analysis or information falling within the definition of research report. When a broker or dealer publishes or distributes projections of an issuer's sales or earnings in reliance on paragraph (a)(2) of this section, it must:

1. Have previously published or distributed projections on a regular basis in order to satisfy the "regular course of its business" condition;

2. At the time of publishing or disseminating a research report, be publishing or distributing projections with respect to that issuer; and

3. For purposes of paragraph (a)(2)(iii) of this section, include projections covering the same or similar periods with respect to either a substantial number of issuers in the issuer's industry or sub-industry or substantially all issuers represented in the comprehensive list of securities contained in the research report.

Rule 139b. Publications or Distributions of Covered Investment Fund Research Reports By Brokers or Dealers Distributing Securities

(a) *Registered Offerings.* Under the conditions of paragraph (a)(1) or (2) of this section, the publication or distribution of a covered investment fund research report by a broker or dealer that is not an investment adviser to the covered investment fund and is not an affiliated person of the investment adviser to the covered investment fund shall be deemed for purposes of sections 2(a)(10) and 5(c) of the Act not to constitute an offer for sale or offer to sell a security that is the subject of an offering pursuant to a registration statement of the covered investment fund that is effective, even if the broker or dealer is participating or may participate in the registered offering of the covered investment fund's securities. This section does not affect the availability of any other exemption or exclusion from sections 2(a)(10) or 5(c) of the Act available to the broker or dealer.

(1) *Issuer-Specific Research Reports.*

(i) At the date of reliance on this section:

(A) The covered investment fund:

(*1*) Has been subject to the reporting requirements of section 30 of the Investment Company Act of 1940 (the "Investment Company Act") (15 U.S.C. 80a-29) for a period of at least 12 calendar months and has filed in a timely manner all of the reports required, as applicable, to be filed for the immediately preceding 12 calendar months on Forms N-CSR (§§ 249.331 and 274.128 of this chapter), [N-Q (§§ 249.332 and 274.130 of this chapter),] N-PORT (§ 274.150 of this chapter), N-MFP (§ 274.201 of this chapter), and N-CEN (§§ 249.330 and 274.101 of this chapter) pursuant to section 30 of the Investment Company Act; or

(*2*) If the covered investment fund is not a registered investment company under the Investment Company Act, has been subject to the reporting requirements of section 13 or section 15(d) of the Securities Exchange Act of 1934 (the "Exchange Act") (15 U.S.C. 78m or 78o(d)) for a period of at least 12 calendar months and has filed in a timely manner all of the reports required to be filed for the immediately preceding 12 calendar months on Forms 10-K (§ 249.310 of this chapter) and 10-Q (§ 249.308a of this chapter), or 20-F (§ 249.220f of this chapter) pursuant to section 13 or section 15(d) of the Exchange Act; and

(B) At the time of the broker's or dealer's initial publication or distribution of a research report on the covered investment fund (or reinitation [*sic*] thereof), and at least quarterly thereafter;

(*1*) If the covered investment fund is of the type defined in paragraph (c)(2)(i) of this section, the aggregate market value of voting and non-voting common equity held by affiliates and non-affiliates equals or exceeds the aggregate market value specified in General Instruction I.B.1 of Form S-3 (§ 239.13 of this chapter);

(*2*) If the covered investment fund is of the type defined in paragraph (c)(2)(ii) of this section, the aggregate market value of voting and non-voting common equity held by non-affiliates equals or exceeds the aggregate market value specified in General Instruction I.B.1 of Form S-3 (§ 239.13 of this chapter); or

(*3*) If the covered investment fund is a registered open-end investment company (other than an exchange-traded fund) its net asset value (inclusive of shares held by affiliates and non-affiliates) equals or exceeds the aggregate market value specified in General Instruction I.B.1 of Form S-3 (§ 239.13 of this chapter); and

(ii) The broker or dealer publishes or distributes research reports in the regular course of its business and, in the case of a research report regarding a covered investment fund that does not have a class of securities in substantially continuous distribution, such publication or distribution does not represent the initiation of publication of research reports about such covered investment fund or its securities or reinitiation of such publication following discontinuation of publication of such research reports.

(2) *Industry Reports*.

(i) The covered investment fund is subject to the reporting requirements of section 30 of the Investment Company Act or, if the covered investment fund is not a registered investment company under the Investment Company Act, is subject to the reporting requirements of section 13 or section 15(d) of the Exchange Act;

(ii) The covered investment fund research report:

(A) Includes similar information with respect to a substantial number of covered investment fund issuers of the issuer's type (*e.g.*, money market fund, bond fund, balanced fund, etc.), or investment focus (*e.g.*, primarily invested in the same industry or sub-industry, or the same country or geographic region); or

(B) Contains a comprehensive list of covered investment fund securities currently recommended by the broker or dealer (other than securities of a covered investment fund that is an affiliate of the broker or dealer, or for which the broker or dealer serves as investment adviser (or for which the broker or dealer is an affiliated person of the investment adviser));

(iii) The analysis regarding the covered investment fund issuer or its securities is given no materially greater space or prominence in the publication than that given to other covered investment fund issuers or securities; and

(iv) The broker or dealer publishes or distributes research reports in the regular course of its business and, at the time of the publication or distribution of the research report (in the case of a research report regarding a covered investment fund that does not have a class of securities in substantially continuous distribution), is including similar information about the issuer or its securities in similar reports.

(3) *Disclosure of Standardized Performance*. In the case of a research report about a covered investment fund that is a registered open-end management investment company or a trust account (or series or class thereof), any quotation of the issuer's performance must be presented in accordance with the conditions of paragraphs (d), (e), and (g) of § 230.482. In the case of a research report about a covered investment fund that is a registered closed-end investment company, any quotation of the issuer's performance must be presented in a manner that is in accordance with instructions to item 4.1(g) of Form N-2 (§§ 239.14 and

274.11a-1 of this chapter), provided, however, that other historical measures of performance may also be included if any other measurement is set out with no greater prominence than the measurement that is in accordance with the instructions to item 4.1(g) of Form N-2.

(b) *Self-Regulatory Organization Rules.* A self-regulatory organization shall not maintain or enforce any rule that would prohibit the ability of a member to publish or distribute a covered investment fund research report solely because the member is also participating in a registered offering or other distribution of any securities of such covered investment fund; or to participate in a registered offering or other distribution of securities of a covered investment fund solely because the member has published or distributed a covered investment fund research report about such covered investment fund or its securities. For purposes of section 19(b) of the Exchange Act (15 U.S.C. 78s(b)), this paragraph (b) shall be deemed a rule under that Act.

(c) *Definitions.* For purposes of this section:

(1) *Affiliated person* has the meaning given the term in section 2(a) of the Investment Company Act.

(2) *Covered investment fund* means:

(i) An investment company (or a series or class thereof) registered under, or that has filed an election to be treated as a business development company under, the Investment Company Act and that has filed a registration statement under the Act for the public offering of a class of its securities, which registration statement has been declared effective by the Commission; or

(ii) A trust or other person:

(A) Issuing securities in an offering registered under the Act and which class of securities is listed for trading on a national securities exchange;

(B) The assets of which consist primarily of commodities, currencies, or derivative instruments that reference commodities or currencies, or interests in the foregoing; and

(C) That provides in its registration statement under the Act that a class of its securities are purchased or redeemed, subject to conditions or limitations, for a ratable share of its assets.

(3) *Covered investment fund research report* means a research report published or distributed by a broker or dealer about a covered investment fund or any securities issued by the covered investment fund, but does not include a research report to the extent that the research report is published or distributed by the covered investment fund or any affiliate of the covered investment fund, or any research report published or distributed by any broker or dealer that is an investment adviser (or any affiliated person of an investment adviser) for the covered investment fund.

(4) *Exchange-traded fund* has the meaning given the term in General Instruction A to Form N-1A (§§ 239.15A and 274.11A of this chapter).

(5) *Investment adviser* has the meaning given the term in section 2(a) of the Investment Company Act.

(6) *Research report* means a written communication, as defined in § 230.405 that includes information, opinions, or recommendations with respect to securities of an issuer or an analysis of a security or an issuer, whether or not it provides information reasonably sufficient upon which to base an investment decision.

Rule 140. Definition of "Distribution" in Section 2(11) for Certain Transactions

A person, the chief part of whose business consists of the purchase of the securities of one issuer, or of two or more affiliated issuers, and the sale of its own securities, including the levying of assessments on its assessable stock and the resale of such stock upon the failure of the holder thereof to pay any assessment levied thereon, to furnish the proceeds with which to acquire the securities of such issuer or affiliated issuers, is to be regarded as engaged in the distribution of the securities of such issuer or affiliated issuers within the meaning of Section 2(11) of the Act.

Rule 141. Definition of "Commission from an Underwriter or Dealer Not in Excess of the Usual and Customary Distributors' or Sellers' Commissions" in Section 2(11), for Certain Transactions

(a) The term "commission" in Section 2(11) shall include such remuneration, commonly known as a spread, as may be received by a distributor or dealer as a consequence of reselling securities bought from an underwriter or dealer at a price below the offering price of such securities, where such resales afford the distributor or dealer a margin of profit not in excess of what is usual and customary in such transactions.

(b) The term "commission from an underwriter or dealer" in Section 2(11) shall include commissions paid by an underwriter or dealer directly or indirectly controlling or controlled by, or under direct or indirect common control with the issuer.

(c) The term "usual and customary distributors' or sellers' commission" in Section 2(11) shall mean a commission or remuneration, commonly known as a spread, paid to or received by any person selling securities either for his own account or for the account of others, which is not in excess of the amount usual and customary in the distribution and sale of issues of similar type and size, and not in excess of the amount allowed to other persons, if any, for comparable service in the distribution of the particular issue; but such term shall not include amounts paid to any person whose function is the management of the distribution of all or a substantial part of the particular issue, or who performs the functions normally performed by an underwriter or underwriting syndicate.

Rule 142. Definition of "Participates" and "Participation", as Used in Section 2(11), in Relation to Certain Transactions

(a) The terms "participates" and "participations" in section 2(11) shall not include the interest of a person (1) who is not in privity of contract with the issuer nor directly or indirectly controlling, controlled by, or under common control with, the issuer, and (2) who has no association with any principal underwriter of the securities being distributed, and (3) whose function in the distribution is confined to an undertaking to purchase all or some specified proportion of the securities remaining unsold after the lapse of some specified period of time, and (4) who purchase such securities for investment and not with a view to distribution.

(b) As used in this rule—

(1) The term "issuer" shall have the meaning defined in section 2(4) and in the last sentence of section 2(11).

(2) The term "association" shall include a relationship between two persons under which one—

(i) Is directly or indirectly controlling, controlled by, or under common control with, the other, or

(ii) Has, in common with the other, one or more partners, officers, directors, trustees, branch managers, or other persons occupying a similar status or performing similar functions, or

(iii) Has a participation, direct or indirect, in the profits of the other, or has a financial stake, by debtor-creditor relationship, stock ownership, contract or otherwise, in the income or business of the other.

(3) The term "principal underwriter" shall have the meaning defined in Reg. § 230.405.

Rule 143. Definition of "Has Purchased", "Sells For", "Participates", and "Participation", as Used in Section 2(11), in Relation to Certain Transactions of Foreign Governments for War Purposes

The terms "has purchased", "sells for", "participates", and "participation", in section 2(11), shall not be deemed to apply to any action of a foreign government in acquiring, for war purposes and by or in anticipation of the exercise of war powers, from any person subject to its jurisdiction securities of a person organized under the laws of the United States or any State or Territory, or in disposing of such securities with a view to their distribution by under-writers in the United States, notwithstanding the fact that the price to be paid to such foreign government upon the disposition of such securities by it may be measured by or may be in direct or indirect relation to such price as may be realized by the underwriters.

Rule 144. Persons Deemed Not to Be Engaged in a Distribution and Therefore Not Underwriters

Preliminary Note to Rule 144

Certain basic principles are essential to an understanding of the registration requirements in the Securities Act of 1933 (the Act or the Securities Act) and the purposes underlying Rule 144:

1. If any person sells a non-exempt security to any other person, the sale must be registered unless an exemption can be found for the transaction.

2. Section 4(1) of the Securities Act provides one such exemption for a transaction "by a person other than an issuer, underwriter, or dealer." Therefore, an understanding of the term "underwriter" is important in determining whether or not the Section 4(1) exemption from registration is available for the sale of the securities. The term "underwriter" is broadly defined in Section 2(a)(11) of the Securities Act to mean any person who has purchased from an issuer with a view to, or offers or sells for an issuer in connection with, the distribution of any security, or participates, or has a direct or indirect participation in any such undertaking, or participates or has a participation in the direct or indirect underwriting of any such undertaking. The interpretation of this definition traditionally has focused on the words "with a view to" in the phrase "purchased from an issuer with a view to . . . distribution." An investment banking firm which arranges with an issuer for the public sale of its securities is clearly an "underwriter" under that section. However, individual investors who are not professionals in the securities business also may be "underwriters" if they act as links in a chain of transactions through which securities move from an issuer to the public.

Since it is difficult to ascertain the mental state of the purchaser at the time of an acquisition of securities, prior to and since the adoption of Rule 144, subsequent acts and circumstances have been considered to determine whether the purchaser took the securities "with a view to distribution" at the time of the acquisition. Emphasis has been placed on factors such as the length of time the person held the securities and whether there has been an unforeseeable change in circumstances of the holder. Experience has shown, however, that reliance upon such factors alone has led to uncertainty in the application of the registration provisions of the Act.

The Commission adopted Rule 144 to establish specific criteria for determining whether a person is not engaged in a distribution. Rule 144 creates a safe harbor from the Section 2(a)(11) definition of "underwriter." A person satisfying the applicable conditions of the Rule 144 safe harbor is deemed not to be engaged in a distribution of the securities and therefore not an underwriter of the securities for purposes of Section 2(a)(11). Therefore, such a person is deemed not to be an underwriter when determining whether a sale is eligible for the Section 4(1) exemption for "transactions by any person other than an issuer, underwriter, or dealer." If a sale of securities complies with all of the applicable conditions of Rule 144:

1. Any affiliate or other person who sells restricted securities will be deemed not to be engaged in a distribution and therefore not an underwriter for that transaction;

2. Any person who sells restricted or other securities on behalf of an affiliate of the issuer will be deemed not to be engaged in a distribution and therefore not an underwriter for that transaction; and

3. The purchaser in such transaction will receive securities that are not restricted securities.

Rule 144 is not an exclusive safe harbor. A person who does not meet all of the applicable conditions of Rule 144 still may claim any other available exemption under the Act for the sale of the securities. The Rule 144 safe harbor is not available to any person with respect to any transaction or series of transactions that, although in technical compliance with Rule 144, is part of a plan or scheme to evade the registration requirements of the Act.

Rule 144

(a) *Definitions.* The following definitions shall apply for the purposes of this rule.

(1) An "affiliate" of an issuer is a person that directly, or indirectly through one or more intermediaries, controls, or is controlled by, or is under common control with, such issuer.

(2) The term "person" when used with reference to a person for whose account securities are to be sold in reliance upon this rule includes, in addition to such person, all of the following persons:

(i) Any relative or spouse of such person, or any relative of such spouse, any one of whom has the same home as such person;

(ii) Any trust or estate in which such person or any of the persons specified in paragraph (a)(2)(i) of this section collectively own ten percent or more of the total beneficial interest or of which any of such persons serve as trustee, executor or in any similar capacity; and

(iii) Any corporation or other organization (other than the issuer) in which such person or any of the persons specified in paragraph (a)(2)(i) of this section are the beneficial owners collectively of ten percent or more of any class of equity securities or ten percent or more of the equity interest.

(3) The term *restricted securities* means:

(i) Securities acquired directly or indirectly from the issuer, or from an affiliate of the issuer, in a transaction or chain of transactions not involving any public offering;

(ii) Securities acquired from the issuer that are subject to the resale limitations of § 230.502(d) under Regulation D or § 230.701(c);

(iii) Securities acquired in a transaction or chain of transactions meeting the requirements of § 230.144A;

(iv) Securities acquired from the issuer in a transaction subject to the conditions of Regulation CE (§ 230.1001);

(v) Equity securities of domestic issuers acquired in a transaction or chain of transactions subject to the conditions of § 230.901 or § 230.903 under Regulation S (§ 230.901 through § 230.905, and Preliminary Notes);

(vi) Securities acquired in a transaction made under § 230.801 to the same extent and proportion that the securities held by the security holder of the class with respect to which the rights offering was made were, as of the record date for the rights offering, "restricted securities" within the meaning of this paragraph (a)(3);

(vii) Securities acquired in a transaction made under § 230.802 to the same extent and proportion that the securities that were tendered or exchanged in the exchange offer or business combination were "restricted securities" within the meaning of this paragraph (a)(3); and

(viii) Securities acquired from the issuer in a transaction subject to an exemption under section 4(5) (15 U.S.C. 77d(5)) of the Act.

(4) The term *debt securities* means:

(i) Any security other than an equity security as defined in § 230.405;

(ii) Non-participatory preferred stock, which is defined as non-convertible capital stock, the holders of which are entitled to a preference in payment of dividends and in distribution of assets on liquidation, dissolution, or winding up of the issuer, but are not entitled to participate in residual earnings or assets of the issuer; and

(iii) Asset-backed securities, as defined in § 229.1101 of this chapter.

(b) *Conditions To Be Met.* Subject to paragraph (i) of this section, the following conditions must be met:

(1) *Non-Affiliates.*

(i) If the issuer of the securities is, and has been for a period of at least 90 days immediately before the sale, subject to the reporting requirements of section 13 or 15(d) of the Securities Exchange Act of 1934 (the Exchange Act), any person who is not an affiliate of the issuer at the time of the sale, and has not been an affiliate during the preceding three months, who sells restricted securities of the issuer for his or her own account shall be deemed not to be an underwriter of those securities within the meaning of section 2(a)(11) of the Act if all of the conditions of paragraphs (c)(1) and (d) of this section are met. The requirements of paragraph (c)(1) of this section shall not apply to restricted securities sold for the account of a person who is not an affiliate of the issuer at the time of the sale and has not been an affiliate during the preceding three months, provided a period of one year has elapsed since the later of the date the securities were acquired from the issuer or from an affiliate of the issuer.

(ii) If the issuer of the securities is not, or has not been for a period of at least 90 days immediately before the sale, subject to the reporting requirements of section 13 or 15(d) of the Exchange Act, any person who is not an affiliate of the issuer at the time of the sale, and has not been an affiliate during the preceding three months, who sells restricted securities of the issuer for his or her own account shall be deemed not to be an underwriter of those securities within the meaning of section 2(a)(11) of the Act if the condition of paragraph (d) of this section is met.

(2) *Affiliates or Persons Selling on Behalf of Affiliates.* Any affiliate of the issuer, or any person who was an affiliate at any time during the 90 days immediately before the sale, who sells restricted securities, or any person who sells restricted or any other securities for the account of an affiliate of the issuer of such securities, or any person who sells restricted or any other securities for the account of a person who was an affiliate at any time during the 90 days immediately before the sale, shall be deemed not to be an underwriter of those securities within the meaning of section 2(a)(11) of the Act if all of the conditions of this section are met.

(c) *Current Public Information.* Adequate current public information with respect to the issuer of the securities must be available. Such information will be deemed to be available only if the applicable condition set forth in this paragraph is met:

(1) Reporting Issuers. The issuer is, and has been for a period of at least 90 days immediately before the sale, subject to the reporting requirements of section 13 or 15(d) of the Exchange Act and has:

(i) Filed all required reports under section 13 or 15(d) of the Exchange Act, as applicable, during the 12 months preceding such sale (or for such shorter period that the issuer was required to file such reports), other than Form 8-K reports (§ 249.308 of this chapter); and

(ii) Submitted electronically every Interactive Data File (§ 232.11 of this chapter) required to be submitted pursuant to § 232.405 of this chapter, during the 12 months preceding such sale (or for such shorter period that the issuer was required to submit such files); or

(2) *Non-Reporting Issuers.* If the issuer is not subject to the reporting requirements of section 13 or 15(d) of the Exchange Act, there is publicly available the information concerning the issuer specified in paragraphs (a)(5)(i) to (xiv), inclusive, and paragraph (a)(5)(xvi) of § 240.15c2-11 of this chapter, or, if the issuer is an insurance company, the information specified in section 12(g)(2)(G)(i) of the Exchange Act (15 U.S.C. 78*l*(g)(2)(G)(i)).

Note to Paragraph (c). With respect to paragraph (c)(1), the person can rely upon:

1. A statement in whichever is the most recent report, quarterly or annual, required to be filed and filed by the issuer that such issuer has:

a. Filed all reports required under section 13 or 15(d) of the Exchange Act, as applicable, during the preceding 12 months (or for such shorter period that the issuer was required to file such reports), other than Form 8-K reports (§ 249.308 of this chapter), and has been subject to such filing requirements for the past 90 days; and

b. Submitted electronically every Interactive Data File (§ 232.11 of this chapter) required to be submitted pursuant to § 232.405 of this chapter, during the 12 months preceding such sale (or for such shorter period that the issuer was required to submit such files); or

2. A written statement from the issuer that it has complied with such reporting or submission requirements.

3. Neither type of statement may be relied upon, however, if the person knows or has reason to believe that the issuer has not complied with such requirements.

(d) *Holding Period For Restricted Securities.* If the securities sold are restricted securities, the following provisions apply:

(1) *General Rule.*

(i) If the issuer of the securities is, and has been for a period of at least 90 days immediately before the sale, subject to the reporting requirements of section 13 or 15(d) of the Exchange Act, a minimum of six months must elapse between the later of the date of the acquisition of the securities from the issuer, or from an affiliate of the issuer, and any resale of such securities in reliance on this section for the account of either the acquiror or any subsequent holder of those securities.

(ii) If the issuer of the securities is not, or has not been for a period of at least 90 days immediately before the sale, subject to the reporting requirements of section 13 or 15(d) of the Exchange Act, a minimum of one year must elapse between the later of the date of the acquisition of the securities from the issuer, or from an affiliate of the issuer, and any resale of such securities in reliance on this section for the account of either the acquiror or any subsequent holder of those securities.

(iii) If the acquiror takes the securities by purchase, the holding period shall not begin until the full purchase price or other consideration is paid or given by the person acquiring the securities from the issuer or from an affiliate of the issuer.

(2) *Promissory Notes, Other Obligations or Installment Contracts.* Giving the issuer or affiliate of the issuer from whom the securities were purchased a promissory note or other obligation to pay the purchase price, or entering into an installment purchase contract with such seller, shall not be deemed full payment of the purchase price unless the promissory note, obligation or contract:

(i) Provides for full recourse against the purchaser of the securities;

(ii) Is secured by collateral, other than the securities purchased, having a fair market value at least equal to the purchase price of the securities purchased; and

(iii) Shall have been discharged by payment in full prior to the sale of the securities.

(3) *Determination of Holding Period.* The following provisions shall apply for the purpose of determining the period securities have been held:

(i) *Stock Dividends, Splits and Recapitalizations.* Securities acquired from the issuer as a dividend or pursuant to a stock split, reverse split or recapitalization shall be deemed to have been acquired at the same time as the securities on which the dividend or, if more than one, the initial dividend was paid, the securities involved in the split or reverse split, or the securities surrendered in connection with the recapitalization.

(ii) *Conversions and Exchanges.* If the securities sold were acquired from the issuer solely in exchange for other securities of the same issuer, the newly acquired securities shall be deemed to have been acquired at the same time as the securities surrendered for conversion or exchange, even if the securities surrendered were not convertible or exchangeable by their terms.

Note to § 230.144(d)(3)(ii). If the surrendered securities originally did not provide for cashless conversion or exchange by their terms and the holder provided consideration, other than solely securities of the same issuer, in connection with the amendment of the surrendered securities to permit cashless conversion or exchange, then the newly acquired securities shall be deemed to have been acquired at the same time as such amendment to the surrendered securities, so long as, in the conversion or exchange, the securities sold were acquired from the issuer solely in exchange for other securities of the same issuer.

(iii) *Contingent Issuance of Securities.* Securities acquired as a contingent payment of the purchase price of an equity interest in a business, or the assets of a business, sold to the issuer or an affiliate of the issuer shall be deemed to have been acquired at the time of such sale if the issuer or affiliate was then committed to issue the securities subject only to conditions other than the payment of further consideration for such securities. An agreement entered into in connection with any such purchase to remain in the employment of, or not to compete with, the issuer or affiliate or the rendering of services pursuant to such agreement shall not be deemed to be the payment of further consideration for such securities;

(iv) *Pledged Securities.* Securities which are *bona fide* pledged by an affiliate of the issuer when sold by the pledgee, or by a purchaser, after a default in the obligation secured by the pledge, shall be deemed to have been acquired when they were acquired by the pledgor, except that if the securities were pledged without recourse they shall be deemed to have been acquired by the pledgee at the time of the pledge or by the purchaser at the time of purchase;

(v) *Gifts of Securities.* Securities acquired from an affiliate of the issuer by gift shall be deemed to have been acquired by the donee when they were acquired by the donor;

(vi) *Trusts.* Where a trust settlor is an affiliate of the issuer, securities acquired from the settlor by the trust, or acquired from the trust by the beneficiaries thereof, shall be deemed to have been acquired when such securities were acquired by the settlor;

(vii) *Estates.* Where a deceased person was an affiliate of the issuer, securities held by the estate of such person or acquired from such estate by the estate beneficiaries shall be deemed to have been acquired when they were acquired by the deceased person, except that no holding period is required if the estate is not an affiliate of the issuer or if the securities are sold by a beneficiary of the estate who is not such an affiliate.

Note to § 230.144(d)(3)(vii). While there is no holding period or amount limitation for estates and estate beneficiaries which are not affiliates of the issuer, paragraphs (c) and (h) of this section apply to securities sold by such persons in reliance upon this section.

(viii) *Rule 145(a) Transactions.* The holding period for securities acquired in a transaction specified in § 230.145(a) shall be deemed to commence on the date the securities were acquired by the purchaser in such transaction, except as otherwise provided in paragraphs (d)(3)(ii) and (ix) of this section.

(ix) *Holding Company Formations.* Securities acquired from the issuer in a transaction effected solely for the purpose of forming a holding company shall be deemed to have been acquired at the same time as the securities of the predecessor issuer exchanged in the holding company formation where:

(A) The newly formed holding company's securities were issued solely in exchange for the securities of the predecessor company as part of a reorganization of the predecessor company into a holding company structure;

(B) Holders received securities of the same class evidencing the same proportional interest in the holding company as they held in the predecessor, and the rights and interests of the holders of such securities are substantially the same as those they possessed as holders of the predecessor company's securities; and

(C) Immediately following the transaction, the holding company has no significant assets other than securities of the predecessor company and its existing subsidiaries and has substantially the same assets and liabilities on a consolidated basis as the predecessor company had before the transaction.

(x) *Cashless Exercise of Options and Warrants.* If the securities sold were acquired from the issuer solely upon cashless exercise of options or warrants issued by the issuer, the newly acquired securities shall be deemed to have been acquired at the same time as the exercised options or warrants, even if the options or warrants exercised originally did not provide for cashless exercise by their terms.

Note 1 to § 230.144(d)(3)(x). If the options or warrants originally did not provide for cashless exercise by their terms and the holder provided consideration, other than solely securities of the same issuer, in connection with the amendment of the options or warrants to permit cashless exercise, then the newly acquired securities shall be deemed to have been acquired at the same time as such amendment to the options or warrants so long as the exercise itself was cashless.

Note 2 to § 230.144(d)(3)(x). If the options or warrants are not purchased for cash or property and do not create any investment risk to the holder, as in the case of employee stock options, the newly acquired securities shall be deemed to have been acquired at the time the options or warrants are exercised, so long as the full purchase price or other consideration for the newly acquired securities has been paid or given by the person acquiring the securities from the issuer or from an affiliate of the issuer at the time of exercise.

(e) *Limitation on Amount of Securities Sold.* Except as hereinafter provided, the amount of securities sold for the account of an affiliate of the issuer in reliance upon this section shall be determined as follows:

(1) If any securities are sold for the account of an affiliate of the issuer, regardless of whether those securities are restricted, the amount of securities sold, together with all sales of securities of the same class sold for the account of such person within the preceding three months, shall not exceed the greatest of:

(i) one percent of the shares or other units of the class outstanding as shown by the most recent report or statement published by the issuer; or

(ii) the average weekly reported volume of trading in such securities on all national securities exchanges and/or reported through the automated quotation system of a registered securities association during the four calendar weeks preceding the filing of notice required by paragraph (h), or if no such notice is required the date of receipt of the order to execute the transaction by the broker or the date of execution of the transaction directly with a market maker; or

(iii) The average weekly volume of trading in such securities reported pursuant to an *effective transaction reporting plan* or an *effective national market system plan* as those terms are defined in § 242.600 of this chapter during the four-week period specified in paragraph (e)(1)(ii) of this section.

(2) If the securities sold are debt securities, then the amount of debt securities sold for the account of an affiliate of the issuer, regardless of whether those securities are restricted, shall not exceed either the limitation set forth in paragraph (e)(1) of this section or, together with all sales of securities of the same tranche (or class when the securities are non-participatory preferred stock) sold for the account of such person within the preceding three months, ten percent of the principal amount of the tranche (or class when the securities are non-participatory preferred stock) attributable to the securities sold.

(3) *Determination of Amount.* For the purpose of determining the amount of securities specified in paragraph (e)(1) of this section and, as applicable, paragraph (e)(2) of this section, the following provisions shall apply:

(i) Where both convertible securities and securities of the class into which they are convertible are sold, the amount of convertible securities sold shall be deemed to be the amount of securities of the class into which they are convertible for the purpose of determining the aggregate amount of securities of both classes sold;

(ii) The amount of securities sold for the account of a pledgee of those securities, or for the account of a purchaser of the pledged securities, during any period of three months within six months (or within one year if the issuer of the securities is not, or has not been for a period of at least 90 days immediately before the sale, subject to the reporting requirements of section 13 or 15(d) of the Exchange Act) after a default in the obligation secured by the pledge, and the amount of securities sold during the same three-month period for the account of the pledgor shall not exceed, in the aggregate, the amount specified in paragraph (e)(1) or (2) of this section, whichever is applicable;

Note to § 230.144(e)(3)(ii). Sales by a pledgee of securities pledged by a borrower will not be aggregated under paragraph (e)(3)(ii) with sales of the securities of the same issuer by other pledgees of such borrower in the absence of concerted action by such pledgees.

(iii) The amount of securities sold for the account of a donee of those securities during any three-month period within six months (or within one year if the issuer of the securities is not, or has not been for a period of at least 90 days immediately before the sale, subject to the reporting requirements of section 13 or 15(d) of the Exchange Act) after the donation, and the amount of securities sold during the same three-month period for the account of the donor, shall not exceed, in the aggregate, the amount specified in paragraph (e)(1) or (2) of this section, whichever is applicable;

(iv) Where securities were acquired by a trust from the settlor of the trust, the amount of such securities sold for the account of the trust during any three-month period within six months (or within one year if the issuer of the securities is not, or has not been for a period of at least 90 days immediately before the sale, subject to the reporting requirements of section 13 or 15(d) of the Exchange Act) after the acquisition of the securities by the trust, and the amount of securities sold during the same three-month period for the account of the settlor, shall not exceed, in the aggregate, the amount specified in paragraph (e)(1) or (2) of this section, whichever is applicable;

(v) The amount of securities sold for the account of the estate of a deceased person, or for the account of a beneficiary of such estate, during any three-month period and the amount of securities sold during the same three-month period for the account of the deceased person prior to his death shall not exceed, in the aggregate, the amount specified in paragraph (e)(1) or (2) of this section, whichever is applicable; *provided*, that no limitation on amount shall apply if the estate or beneficiary of the estate is not an affiliate of the issuer;

(vi) When two or more affiliates or other persons agree to act in concert for the purpose of selling securities of an issuer, all securities of the same class sold for the account of all such persons during any three-month period shall be aggregated for the purpose of determining the limitation on the amount of securities sold;

(vii) The following sales of securities need not be included in determining the amount of securities to be sold in reliance upon this section:

(A) Securities sold pursuant to an effective registration statement under the Act;

(B) Securities sold pursuant to an exemption provided by Regulation A (§ 230.251 through § 230.263) under the Act;

(C) Securities sold in a transaction exempt pursuant to section 4 of the Act (15 U.S.C. 77d) and not involving any public offering; and

(D) Securities sold offshore pursuant to Regulation S (§ 230.901 through § 230.905, and Preliminary Notes) under the Act.

(f) *Manner of Sale.*

(1) The securities shall be sold in one of the following manners:

(i) *brokers' transactions* within the meaning of section 4(4) of the Act;

(ii) transactions directly with a *market maker*, as that term is defined in section 3(a)(38) of the Exchange Act; or

(iii) *riskless principal transactions* where:

(A) the offsetting trades must be executed at the same price (exclusive of an explicitly disclosed markup or markdown, commission equivalent, or other fee);

(B) the transaction is permitted to be reported as riskless under the rules of a self regulatory organization; and

(C) the requirements of paragraphs (g)(2) (applicable to any markup or markdown, commission equivalent, or other fee), (g)(3), and (g)(4) of this section are met.

Note to § 230.144(f)(1).

For purposes of this section, a *riskless principal transaction* means a principal transaction where, after having received from a customer an order to buy, a broker or dealer purchases the security as principal in the market to satisfy the order to buy or, after having received from a customer an order to sell, sells the security as principal to the market to satisfy the order to sell.

(2) The person selling the securities shall not:

(i) Solicit or arrange for the solicitation of orders to buy the securities in anticipation of or in connection with such transaction, or

(ii) Make any payment in connection with the offer or sale of the securities to any person other than the broker or dealer who executes the order to sell the securities.

(3) Paragraph (f) of this section shall not apply to:

(i) Securities sold for the account of the estate of a deceased person or for the account of a beneficiary of such estate provided the estate or estate beneficiary is not an affiliate of the issuer; or

(ii) Debt securities.

(g) *Brokers' Transactions.* The term "brokers' transactions" in Section 4(4) of the Act shall for the purposes of this rule be deemed to include transactions by a broker in which such broker:

(1) Does no more than execute the order or orders to sell the securities as agent for the person for whose account the securities are sold;

(2) Receives no more than the usual and customary broker's commission;

(3) Neither solicits nor arranges for the solicitation of customers' orders to buy the securities in anticipation of or in connection with the transaction; *provided,* that the foregoing shall not preclude:

(i) inquiries by the broker of other brokers or dealers who have indicated an interest in the securities within the preceding 60 days;

(ii) inquiries by the broker of his customers who have indicated an unsolicited bona fide interest in the securities within the preceding 10 business days;

(iii) the publication by the broker of bid and ask quotations for the security in an interdealer quotation system provided that such quotations are incident to the maintenance of a bona fide inter-dealer market for the security for the broker's own account and that the broker has published bona fide bid and ask quotations for the security in an interdealer quotation system on each of at least twelve days within the preceding thirty calendar days with no more than four business days in succession without such two way quotations; or

(iv) the publication by the broker of bid and ask quotations for the security in an alternative trading system, as defined in § 242.300 of this chapter, provided that the broker has published bona fide bid and ask quotations for the security in the alternative trading system on each of the last twelve business days; and

Note to § 230.144(g)(3)(ii). The broker should obtain and retain in his files written evidence of indications of bona fide unsolicited interest by his customers in the securities at the time such indications are received.

(4) After reasonable inquiry is not aware of circumstances indicating that the person for whose account the securities are sold is an underwriter with respect to the securities or that the transaction is a part of a distribution of securities of the issuer. Without limiting the foregoing, the broker shall be deemed to be aware of any facts or statements contained in the notice required by paragraph (h) below.

Notes. (i) The broker, for his own protection, should obtain and retain in his files a copy of the notice required by paragraph (h).

(ii) The reasonable inquiry required by paragraph (g)(3) of this section should include, but not necessarily be limited to, inquiry as to the following matters:

(*a*) The length of time the securities have been held by the person for whose account they are to be sold. If practicable, the inquiry should include physical inspection of the securities;

(*b*) The nature of the transaction in which the securities were acquired by such person;

(*c*) The amount of securities of the same class sold during the past three months by all persons whose sales are required to be taken into consideration pursuant to paragraph (e) of this section;

(*d*) Whether such person intends to sell additional securities of the same class through any other means;

(*e*) Whether such person has solicited or made any arrangement for the solicitation of buy orders in connection with the proposed sale of securities;

(*f*)Whether such person has made any payment to any other person in connection with the proposed sale of the securities; and

(*g*) The number of shares or other units of the class outstanding, or the relevant trading volume.

(h) *Notice of Proposed Sale.*

(1) If the amount of securities to be sold in reliance upon this rule during any period of three months exceeds 5,000 shares or other units or has an aggregate sale price in excess of $50,000, three copies of a notice on Form 144 (§ 239.144 of this chapter) shall be filed with the Commission. If such securities are admitted to trading on any national securities exchange, one copy of such notice also shall be transmitted to the principal exchange on which such securities are admitted.

(2) The Form 144 shall be signed by the person for whose account the securities are to be sold and shall be transmitted for filing concurrently with either the placing with a broker of an order to execute a sale of securities in reliance upon this rule or the execution directly with a market maker of such a sale. Neither the filing of such notice nor the failure of the Commission to comment on such notice shall be deemed to preclude the Commission from taking any action that it deems necessary or appropriate with respect to the sale of the securities referred to in such notice. The person filing the notice required by this paragraph shall have a bona fide intention to sell the securities referred to in the notice within a reasonable time after the filing of such notice.

(i) *Unavailability to Securities of Issuers With No or Nominal Operations and No or Nominal Non-Cash Assets.*

(1) This section is not available for the resale of securities initially issued by an issuer defined below:

(i) An issuer, other than a business combination related shell company, as defined in § 230.405, or an asset-backed issuer, as defined in Item 1101(b) of Regulation AB (§ 229.1101(b) of this chapter), that has:

(A) No or nominal operations; and

(B) Either:

(*1*) No or nominal assets;

(*2*) Assets consisting solely of cash and cash equivalents; or

(*3*) Assets consisting of any amount of cash and cash equivalents and nominal other assets; or

(ii) An issuer that has been at any time previously an issuer described in paragraph (i)(1)(i).

(2) Notwithstanding paragraph (i)(1), if the issuer of the securities previously had been an issuer described in paragraph (i)(1)(i) but has ceased to be an issuer described in paragraph (i)(1)(i); is subject to the reporting requirements of section 13 or 15(d) of the Exchange Act; has filed all reports and other materials required to be filed by section 13 or 15(d) of the Exchange Act, as applicable, during the preceding 12 months (or for such

shorter period that the issuer was required to file such reports and materials), other than Form 8-K reports (§ 249.308 of this chapter); and has filed current "Form 10 information" with the Commission reflecting its status as an entity that is no longer an issuer described in paragraph (i)(1)(i), then those securities may be sold subject to the requirements of this section after one year has elapsed from the date that the issuer filed "Form 10 information" with the Commission.

(3) The term "Form 10 information" means the information that is required by Form 10 or Form 20-F (§ 249.210 or § 249.220f of this chapter), as applicable to the issuer of the securities, to register under the Exchange Act each class of securities being sold under this rule. The issuer may provide the Form 10 information in any filing of the issuer with the Commission. The Form 10 information is deemed filed when the initial filing is made with the Commission.

Rule 144A. Private Resales of Securities to Institutions

Preliminary Notes to Rule 144A

1. This section relates solely to the application of Section 5 of the Act and not to antifraud or other provisions of the federal securities laws.

2. Attempted compliance with this section does not act as an exclusive election; any seller hereunder may also claim the availability of any other applicable exemption from the registration requirements of the Act.

3. In view of the objective of this section and the policies underlying the Act, this section is not available with respect to any transaction or series of transactions that, although in technical compliance with this section, is part of a plan or scheme to evade the registration provisions of the Act. In such cases, registration under the Act is required.

4. Nothing in this section obviates the need for any issuer or any other person to comply with the securities registration or broker-dealer registration requirements of the Securities Exchange Act of 1934 (the "Exchange Act"), whenever such requirements are applicable.

5. Nothing in this section obviates the need for any person to comply with any applicable state law relating to the offer or sale of securities.

6. Securities acquired in a transaction made pursuant to the provisions of this section are deemed to be "restricted securities" within the meaning of § 230.144(a)(3) of this chapter.

7. The fact that purchasers of securities from the issuer thereof may purchase such securities with a view to reselling such securities pursuant to this section will not affect the availability to such issuer of an exemption under Section 4(a)(2) of the Act, or Regulation D under the Act, from the registration requirements of the Act.

Rule 144A.

(a) *Definitions*

(1) For purposes of this section, "qualified institutional buyer" shall mean:

(i) Any of the following entities, acting for its own account or the accounts of other qualified institutional buyers, that in the aggregate owns and invests on a discretionary basis at least $100 million in securities of issuers that are not affiliated with the entity:

(A) Any *insurance company* as defined in section 2(a)(13) of the Act;

NOTE: A purchase by an insurance company for one or more of its separate accounts, as defined by section 2(a)(37) of the Investment Company Act of 1940 (the "Investment Company Act"), which are neither registered under section 8 of the Investment Company Act nor required to be so registered, shall be deemed to be a purchase for the account of such insurance company.

(B) Any *investment company* registered under the Investment Company Act or any *business development company* as defined in Section 2(a)(48) of that Act;

(C) Any *Small Business Investment Company* licensed by the U.S. Small Business Administration under Section 301(c) or (d) of the Small Business Investment Act of 1958;

(D) Any *Plan* established and maintained by a state, its political subdivisions, or any agency or instrumentality of state or its political subdivisions, for the benefit of its employees;

(E) Any *employee benefit plan* within the meaning of Title I of the Employee Retirement Income Security Act of 1974;

(F) Any *trust fund* whose trustee is a bank or trust company and whose participants are exclusively plans of the types identified in paragraph (a)(1)(i)(D) or (E) of this section, except trust funds that include as participants individual retirement accounts or H.R. 10 plans.

(G) Any *business development company* as defined in Section 202(a)(22) of the Investment Advisers Act of 1940;

(H) Any *organization described in Section 501(c)(3)* of the Internal Revenue Code, *corporation (other than a bank as defined in Section 3(a)(2) of the Act or a savings and loan association or other institution referenced in Section 3(a)(5)(A) of the Act or a foreign bank or savings and loan association or equivalent institution), partnership, or Massachusetts or similar business trust;* and

(I) Any *investment adviser* registered under the Investment Advisers Act.

(ii) Any *dealer* registered pursuant to Section 15 of the Exchange Act, acting for its own account or the accounts of other qualified institutional buyers, that in the aggregate owns and invests on a discretionary basis at least $10 million of securities of issuers that are not affiliated with the dealer, *provided that* securities constituting the whole or a part of an unsold allotment to or subscription by a dealer as a participant in a public offering shall not be deemed to be owned by such dealer;

(iii) Any *dealer* registered pursuant to Section 15 of the Exchange Act acting in a riskless principal transaction on behalf of a qualified institutional buyer;

NOTE: A registered dealer may act as agent, on a non-discretionary basis, in a transaction with a qualified institutional buyer without itself having to be a qualified institutional buyer.

(iv) Any investment company registered under the Investment Company Act, acting for its own account or for the accounts of other qualified institutional buyers, that is part of a *family of investment companies* which own in the aggregate at least $100 million in securities of issuers other than issuers that are affiliated with the investment company or are part of such family of investment companies. "Family of investment companies" means any two or more investment companies registered under the Investment Company Act, except for a unit investment trust whose assets consist solely of shares of one or more registered investment companies, that have the same investment adviser (or, in the case of unit investment trusts, the same depositor), *provided that,* for purposes of this section:

(A) each series of a series company (as defined in Rule 18f-2 under the Investment Company Act [17 CFR 270.18f-2]) shall be deemed to be a separate investment company; and

(B) investment companies shall be deemed to have the same adviser (or depositor) if their advisers (or depositors) are majority-owned subsidiaries of the same parent, or if one investment company's adviser (or depositor) is a majority-owned subsidiary of the other investment company's adviser (or depositor);

(v) Any entity, all of the equity owners of which are qualified institutional buyers, acting for its own account or the accounts of other qualified institutional buyers; and

(vi) Any *bank* as defined in Section 3(a)(2) of the Act, any *savings and loan association* or other institution as referenced in Section 3(a)(5)(A) of the Act, *or any foreign bank or savings and loan association or equivalent institution,* acting for its own account or the accounts of other qualified institutional buyers, that in the aggregate owns and invests on a discretionary basis at least $100 million in securities of issuers that are not affiliated with it and that has an audited net worth of at least $25 million as demonstrated in its latest annual financial statements, as of a date not more than 16 months preceding the date of sale under the Rule in the case of a U.S. bank or savings and loan association, and not more than 18 months preceding such date of sale for a foreign bank or savings and loan association or equivalent institution.

(2) In determining the aggregate amount of securities owned and invested on a discretionary basis by an entity, the following instruments and interests shall be excluded: bank deposit notes and certificates of deposit; loan participations; repurchase agreements; securities owned but subject to a repurchase agreement; and currency, interest rate and commodity swaps.

(3) The aggregate value of securities owned and invested on a discretionary basis by an entity shall be the cost of such securities, except where the entity reports its securities holdings in its financial statements on the basis of their market value, and no current information with respect to the cost of those securities has been published. In the latter event, the securities may be valued at market for purposes of this section.

(4) In determining the aggregate amount of securities owned by an entity and invested on a discretionary basis, securities owned by subsidiaries of the entity that are consolidated with the entity in its financial statements prepared in accordance with generally accepted accounting principles may be included if the investments of such subsidiaries are managed under the direction of the entity, except that, unless the entity is a reporting company under Section 13 or 15(d) of the Exchange Act, securities owned by such subsidiaries may not be included if the entity itself is a majority-owned subsidiary that would be included in the consolidated financial statements of another enterprise.

(5) For purposes of this section, "riskless principal transaction" means a transaction in which a dealer buys a security from any person and makes a simultaneous offsetting sale of such security to a qualified institutional buyer, including another dealer acting as riskless principal for a qualified institutional buyer.

(6) For purposes of this section, "effective conversion premium" means the amount, expressed as a percentage of the security's conversion value, by which the price at issuance of a convertible security exceeds its conversion value.

(7) For purposes of this section, "effective exercise premium" means the amount, expressed as a percentage of the warrant's exercise value, by which the sum of the price at issuance and the exercise price of a warrant exceeds its exercise value.

(b) *Sales by Persons other than Issuers or Dealers.* Any person, other than the issuer or a dealer, who offers or sells securities in compliance with the conditions set forth in paragraph (d) of this section shall be deemed not to be engaged in a distribution of such securities and therefore not to be an underwriter of such securities within the meaning of sections 2(a)(11) and 4(a)(1) of the Act.

(c) *Sales by Dealers.* Any dealer who offers or sells securities in compliance with the conditions set forth in paragraph (d) of this section shall be deemed not to be a participant in a distribution of such securities within the meaning of Section 4(a)(3)(C) of the Act and not to be an underwriter of such securities within the meaning of Section 2(a)(11) of the Act, and such securities shall be deemed not to have been offered to the public within the meaning of section 4(a)(3)(A) of the Act.

(d) *Conditions to be Met.* To qualify for exemption under this section, an offer or sale must meet the following conditions:

(1) The securities are sold only to a qualified institutional buyer or to a purchaser that the seller and any person acting on behalf of the seller reasonably believe is a qualified institutional buyer. In determining whether a prospective purchaser is a qualified institutional buyer, the seller and any person acting on its behalf shall be entitled to rely upon the following non-exclusive methods of establishing the prospective purchaser's ownership and discretionary investments of securities:

(i) The prospective purchaser's most recent publicly available financial statements, *provided that* such statements present the information as of a date within 16 months preceding the date of sale of securities under this section in the case of a U.S. purchaser and within 18 months preceding such date of sale for a foreign purchaser;

(ii) The most recent publicly available information appearing in documents filed by the prospective purchaser with the Commission or another United States federal, state, or local governmental agency or self-regulatory organization, or with a foreign governmental agency or self-regulatory organization, *provided that* any such information is as of a date within 16 months preceding the date of sale of securities under this section in the case of a U.S. purchaser and within 18 months preceding such date of sale for a foreign purchaser;

(iii) The most recent publicly available information appearing in a recognized securities manual, *provided that* such information is as of a date within 16 months preceding the date of sale of securities under this section in the case of a U.S. purchaser and within 18 months preceding such date of sale for a foreign purchaser; or

(iv) A certification by the chief financial officer, a person fulfilling an equivalent function, or other executive officer of the purchaser, specifying the amount of securities owned and invested on a discretionary basis by the purchaser as of a specific date on or since the close of the purchaser's most recent fiscal year, or, in the case of a purchaser that is a member of a family of investment companies, a certification by an executive officer of the investment adviser specifying the amount of securities owned by the family of investment companies as of a specific date on or since the close of the purchaser's most recent fiscal year;

(2) The seller and any person acting on its behalf takes reasonable steps to ensure that the purchaser is aware that the seller may rely on the exemption from the provisions of Section 5 of the Act provided by this section;

(3) The securities offered or sold:

(i) Were not, when issued, of the same class as securities listed on a national securities exchange registered under Section 6 of the Exchange Act or quoted in a U.S. automated inter-dealer quotation system; *Provided,* that securities that are convertible or exchangeable into securities so listed or quoted at the time of issuance and that had an effective conversion premium of less than 10 percent, shall be treated as securities of the class into which they are convertible or exchangeable; and that warrants that may be exercised for securities so listed or quoted at the time of issuance, for a period of less than 3 years from the date of issuance, or that had an effective exercise premium of less than 10 percent, shall be treated as securities of the class to be issued upon exercise; and *provided further* that the Commission may from time to time, taking into account then-existing market practices, designate additional securities and classes of securities that will not be deemed of the same class as securities listed on a national securities exchange or quoted in a U.S. automated inter-dealer quotation system; and

(ii) Are not securities of an open-end investment company, unit investment trust or face-amount certificate company that is or is required to be registered under Section 8 of the Investment Company Act; and

(4) (i) In the case of securities of an issuer that is neither subject to Section 13 or 15(d) of the Exchange Act, nor exempt from reporting pursuant to Rule 12g3-2(b) (§ 240.12g3-2(b) of this chapter) under the Exchange Act, nor a foreign government as defined in Rule 405 (§ 230.405 of this chapter) eligible to register securities under Schedule B of the Act, the holder and a prospective purchaser designated by the holder have the right to obtain from the issuer, upon request of the holder, and the prospective purchaser has received from the issuer, the seller, or a person acting on either of their behalf, at or prior to the time of sale, upon such prospective purchaser's request to the holder or the issuer, the following information (which shall be reasonably current in relation to the date of resale under this section): a very brief statement of the nature of the business of the issuer and the products and services it offers; and the issuer's most recent balance sheet and profit and loss and retained earnings statements, and similar financial statements for such part of the two preceding fiscal years as the issuer has been in operation (the financial statements should be audited to the extent reasonably available).

(ii) The requirement that the information be "reasonably current" will be presumed to be satisfied if:

(A) the balance sheet is as of a date less than 16 months before the date of resale, the statements of profit and loss and retained earnings are for the 12 months preceding the date of such balance sheet, and if such balance sheet is not as of a date less than 6 months before the date of resale, it shall be accompanied by additional statements of profit and loss and retained earnings for the period from the date of such balance sheet to a date less than 6 months before the date of resale; and

(B) the statement of the nature of the issuer's business and its products and services offered is as of a date within 12 months prior to the date of resale; or

(C) with regard to foreign private issuers, the required information meets the timing requirements of the issuer's home country or principal trading markets.

(e) Offers and sales of securities pursuant to this section shall be deemed not to affect the availability of any exemption or safe harbor relating to any previous or subsequent offer or sale of such securities by the issuer or any prior or subsequent holder thereof.

Rule 145. Reclassifications of Securities, Mergers, Consolidations and Acquisitions of Assets

Preliminary Note

Rule 145 (§ 230.145 of this chapter) is designed to make available the protection provided by registration under the Securities Act of 1933, as amended (Act), to persons who are offered securities in a business combination of the type described in paragraphs (a)(1), (2) and (3) of the rule. The thrust of the rule is that an *offer, offer to sell, offer for sale*, or *sale* occurs when there is submitted to security holders a plan or agreement pursuant to which such holders are required to elect, on the basis of what is in substance a new investment decision, whether to accept a new or different security in exchange for their existing security. Rule 145 embodies the Commission's determination that such transactions are subject to the registration requirements of the Act, and that the previously existing *no-sale* theory of Rule 133 is no longer consistent with the statutory purposes of the Act. *See* Release No. 33-5316 (October 6, 1972) [37 FR 23631]. Securities issued in transactions described in paragraph (a) of Rule 145 may be registered on Form S-4 or F-4 (§ 239.25 or § 239.34 of this chapter) or Form N-14 (§ 239.23 of this chapter) under the Act.

Transactions for which statutory exemptions under the Act, including those contained in sections 3(a)(9), (10), (11) and 4(a)(2), are otherwise available are not affected by Rule 145. Reference is made to Rule 153a (§ 230.153a of this chapter) describing the prospectus delivery required in a transaction of the type referred to in Rule 145. A reclassification of securities covered by Rule 145 would be exempt from registration pursuant to section 3(a)(9) or (11) of the Act if the conditions of either of these sections are satisfied.

(a) *Transactions within this section.* An *offer, offer to sell, offer for sale* or *sale* shall be deemed to be involved, within the meaning of section 2(3) of the Act, so far as the security holders of a corporation or other person are concerned where, pursuant to statutory provisions of the jurisdiction under which such corporation or other person is organized, or pursuant to provisions contained in its certificate of incorporation or similar controlling instruments, or otherwise, there is submitted for the vote or consent of such security holders a plan or agreement for:

(1) *Reclassifications.* A reclassification of securities of such corporation or other person, other than a stock split, reverse stock split, or change in par value, which involves the substitution of a security for another security;

(2) *Mergers or Consolidations.* A statutory merger or consolidation or similar plan or acquisition in which securities of such corporation or other person held by such security holders will become or be exchanged for securities of any person, unless the sole purpose of the transaction is to change an issuer's domicile solely within the United States; or

(3) *Transfers of assets.* A transfer of assets of such corporation or other person, to another person in consideration of the issuance of securities of such other person or any of its affiliates, if:

(i) Such plan or agreement provides for dissolution of the corporation or other person whose security holders are voting or consenting; or

(ii) Such plan or agreement provides for a pro rata or similar distribution of such securities to the security holders voting or consenting; or

(iii) The board of directors or similar representatives of such corporation or other person, adopts resolutions relative to paragraph (a)(3)(i) or (ii) of this section within 1 year after the taking of such vote or consent; or

(iv) The transfer of assets is a part of a pre-existing plan for distribution of such securities, notwithstanding paragraph (a)(3)(i), (ii), or (iii) of this section.

(b) *Communications before a Registration Statement is filed.* Communications made in connection with or relating to a transaction described in paragraph (a) of this section that will be registered under the Act may be made under § 230.135, § 230.165 or § 230.166.

(c) *Persons and Parties Deemed To Be Underwriters.* For purposes of this section, if any party to a transaction specified in paragraph (a) of this section is a shell company, other than a business combination related shell company, as those terms are defined in § 230.405, any party to that transaction, other than the issuer, or any person who is an affiliate of such party at the time such transaction is submitted for vote or consent, who publicly offers or sells securities of the issuer acquired in connection with any such transaction, shall be deemed to be engaged in a distribution and therefore to be an underwriter thereof within the meaning of Section 2(a)(11) of the Act.

(d) *Resale Provisions for Persons and Parties Deemed Underwriters.* Notwithstanding the provisions of paragraph (c), a person or party specified in that paragraph shall not be deemed to be engaged in a distribution and therefore not to be an underwriter of securities acquired in a transaction specified in paragraph (a) that was registered under the Act if:

(1) The issuer has met the requirements applicable to an issuer of securities in paragraph (i)(2) of § 230.144; and

(2) One of the following three conditions is met:

(i) Such securities are sold by such person or party in accordance with the provisions of paragraphs (c), (e), (f), and (g) of § 230.144 and at least 90 days have elapsed since the date the securities were acquired from the issuer in such transaction; or

(ii) Such person or party is not, and has not been for at least three months, an affiliate of the issuer, and at least six months, as determined in accordance with paragraph (d) of § 230.144, have elapsed since the date the securities were acquired from the issuer in such transaction, and the issuer meets the requirements of paragraph (c) of § 230.144; or

(iii) Such person or party is not, and has not been for at least three months, an affiliate of the issuer, and at least one year, as determined in accordance with paragraph (d) of § 230.144, has elapsed since the date the securities were acquired from the issuer in such transaction.

Note to § 230.145(c) and (d). Paragraph (d) is not available with respect to any transaction or series of transactions that, although in technical compliance with the rule, is part of a plan or scheme to evade the registration requirements of the Act.

(e) *Definitions.*

(1) The term *affiliate* as used in paragraphs (c) and (d) of this section shall have the same meaning as the definition of that term in § 230.144.

(2) The term *party* as used in paragraphs (c) and (d) of this section shall mean the corporations, business entities, or other persons, other than the issuer, whose assets or capital structure are affected by the transactions specified in paragraph (a) of this section.

(3) The term *person* as used in paragraphs (c) and (d) of this section, when used in reference to a person for whose account securities are to be sold, shall have the same meaning as the definition of that term in paragraph (a)(2) of § 230.144.

Rule 146. Rules Under Section 18 of the Act

(a) *Prepared by or on behalf of the issuer.* An offering document (as defined in Section 18(d)(1) of the Act [15 U.S.C. 77r(d)(1)]) is "prepared by or on behalf of the issuer" for purposes of Section 18 of the Act, if the issuer or an agent or representative:

(1) Authorizes the document's production, and

(2) Approves the document before its use.

(b) *Covered Securities for Purposes of Section 18.*

(1) For purposes of Section 18(b) of the Act (15 U.S.C. 77r), the Commission finds that the following national securities exchanges, or segments or tiers thereof, have listing standards that are substantially similar to those of the New York Stock Exchange ("NYSE"), the NYSE American LLC ("NYSE American"), or the National Market System of the Nasdaq Stock Market ("Nasdaq/NGM"), and that securities listed, or authorized for listing, on such exchanges shall be deemed covered securities:

    (i)   Tier I of the NYSE Arca, Inc.;

    (ii) Tier I of the NASDAQ PHLX LLC;

    (iii) The Chicago Board Options Exchange, Incorporated;

    (iv) Options listed on Nasdaq ISE, LLC;

    (v)   The Nasdaq Capital Market;

    (vi) Tier I and Tier II of Bats BZX Exchange, Inc.; and

    (vii) Investors Exchange LLC.

(2) The designation of securities in paragraphs (b)(1)(i) through (vii) of this section as covered securities is conditioned on such exchanges' listing standards (or segments or tiers thereof) continuing to be substantially similar to those of the NYSE, NYSE American, or Nasdaq/NGM.

Rule 147. Intrastate Offers and Sales

(a) This section shall not raise any presumption that the exemption provided by section 3(a)(11) of the Act (15 U.S.C. 77c(a)(11)) is not available for transactions by an issuer which do not satisfy all of the provisions of this section.

(b) *Manner of Offers and Sales.* An issuer, or any person acting on behalf of the issuer, shall be deemed to conduct an offering in compliance with section 3(a)(11) of the Act (15 U.S.C. 77c(a)(11)), where offers and sales are made only to persons resident within the same state or territory in which the issuer is resident and doing business, within the meaning of section 3(a)(11) of the Act, so long as the issuer complies with the provisions of paragraphs (c), (d), and (f) through (h) of this section.

(c) *Nature of the Issuer.* The issuer of the securities shall at the time of any offers and sales be a person resident and doing business within the state or territory in which all of the offers and sales are made.

(1) The issuer shall be deemed to be a resident of the state or territory in which:

    (i) It is incorporated or organized, and it has its principal place of business, if a corporation, limited partnership, trust or other form of business organization that is organized under state or territorial law. The issuer shall be deemed to have its principal place of business in a state or territory in which the officers, partners or managers of the issuer primarily direct, control and coordinate the activities of the issuer;

    (ii) It has its principal place of business, as defined in paragraph (c)(1)(i) of this section, if a general partnership or other form of business organization that is not organized under any state or territorial law;

    (iii) Such person's principal residence is located, if an individual.

Instruction to Paragraph (c)(1): An issuer that has previously conducted an intrastate offering pursuant to this section (§ 230.147) or Rule 147A (§ 230.147A) may not conduct another intrastate offering pursuant to this section (§ 230.147) in a different state or territory, until the expiration of the time period specified in paragraph (e) of this section (§ 230.147(e)) or paragraph (e) of Rule 147A (§ 230.147A(e)), calculated on the basis of the date of the last sale in such offering.

(2) The issuer shall be deemed to be doing business within a state or territory if the issuer satisfies at least one of the following requirements:

(i) The issuer derived at least 80% of its consolidated gross revenues from the operation of a business or of real property located in or from the rendering of services within such state or territory;

Instruction to Paragraph (c)(2)(i): Revenues must be calculated based on the issuer's most recent fiscal year, if the first offer of securities pursuant to this section is made during the first six months of the issuer's current fiscal year, and based on the first six months of the issuer's current fiscal year or during the twelve-month fiscal period ending with such six-month period, if the first offer of securities pursuant to this section is made during the last six months of the issuer's current fiscal year.

(ii) The issuer had at the end of its most recent semi-annual fiscal period prior to an initial offer of securities in any offering or subsequent offering pursuant to this section, at least 80% of its assets and those of its subsidiaries on a consolidated basis located within such state or territory;

(iii) The issuer intends to use and uses at least 80% of the net proceeds to the issuer from sales made pursuant to this section (§ 230.147) in connection with the operation of a business or of real property, the purchase of real property located in, or the rendering of services within such state or territory; or

(iv) A majority of the issuer's employees are based in such state or territory.

(d) *Residence of Offerees and Purchasers.* Offers and sales of securities pursuant to this section (§ 230.147) shall be made only to residents of the state or territory in which the issuer is resident, as determined pursuant to paragraph (c) of this section, or who the issuer reasonably believes, at the time of the offer and sale, are residents of the state or territory in which the issuer is resident. For purposes of determining the residence of offerees and purchasers:

(1) A corporation, partnership, limited liability company, trust or other form of business organization shall be deemed to be a resident of a state or territory if, at the time of the offer and sale to it, it has its principal place of business, as defined in paragraph (c)(1)(i) of this section, within such state or territory.

Instruction to Paragraph (d)(1): A trust that is not deemed by the law of the state or territory of its creation to be a separate legal entity is deemed to be a resident of each state or territory in which its trustee is, or trustees are, resident.

(2) Individuals shall be deemed to be residents of a state or territory if such individuals have, at the time of the offer and sale to them, their principal residence in the state or territory.

(3) A corporation, partnership, trust or other form of business organization, which is organized for the specific purpose of acquiring securities offered pursuant to this section (§ 230.147), shall not be a resident of a state or territory unless all of the beneficial owners of such organization are residents of such state or territory.

Instruction to Paragraph (d): Obtaining a written representation from purchasers of in-state residency status will not, without more, be sufficient to establish a reasonable belief that such purchasers are in-state residents.

(e) *Limitation on Resales*. For a period of six months from the date of the sale by the issuer of a security pursuant to this section (§ 230.147), any resale of such security shall be made only to persons resident within the state or territory in which the issuer was resident, as determined pursuant to paragraph (c) of this section, at the time of the sale of the security by the issuer.

Instruction to Paragraph (e): In the case of convertible securities, resales of either the convertible security, or if it is converted, the underlying security, could be made during the period described in paragraph (e) only to persons resident within such state or territory. For purposes of this paragraph (e), a conversion in reliance on section 3(a)(9) of the Act (15 U.S.C. 77c(a)(9)) does not begin a new period.

(f) *Precautions Against Interstate Sales.*

(1) The issuer shall, in connection with any securities sold by it pursuant to this section:

(i) Place a prominent legend on the certificate or other document evidencing the security stating that: "Offers and sales of these securities were made under an exemption from registration and have not been registered under the Securities Act of 1933. For a period of six months from the date of the sale by the issuer of these securities, any resale of these securities (or the underlying securities in the case of convertible securities) shall be made only to persons resident within the state or territory of [identify the name of the state or territory in which the issuer was resident at the time of the sale of the securities by the issuer].";

(ii) Issue stop transfer instructions to the issuer's transfer agent, if any, with respect to the securities, or, if the issuer transfers its own securities, make a notation in the appropriate records of the issuer; and

(iii) Obtain a written representation from each purchaser as to his or her residence.

(2) The issuer shall, in connection with the issuance of new certificates for any of the securities that are sold pursuant to this section (§ 230.147) that are presented for transfer during the time period specified in paragraph (e), take the steps required by paragraphs (f)(1)(i) and (ii) of this section.

(3) The issuer shall, at the time of any offer or sale by it of a security pursuant to this section (§ 230.147), prominently disclose to each offeree in the manner in which any such offer is communicated and to each purchaser of such security in writing a reasonable period of time before the date of sale, the following: "Sales will be made only to residents of [identify the name of the state or territory in which the issuer was resident at the time of the sale of the securities by the issuer]. Offers and sales of these securities are made under an exemption from registration and have not been registered under the Securities Act of 1933. For a period of six months from the date of the sale by the issuer of the securities, any resale of the securities (or the underlying securities in the case of convertible securities) shall be made only to persons resident within the state or territory of [identify the name of the state or territory in which the issuer was resident at the time of the sale of the securities by the issuer]."

(g) *Integration With Other Offerings*. Offers or sales made in reliance on this section will not be integrated with:

(1) Offers or sales of securities made prior to the commencement of offers and sales of securities pursuant to this section (§ 230.147); or

(2) Offers or sales made after completion of offers and sales of securities pursuant to this section (§ 230.147) that are:

(i) Registered under the Act, except as provided in paragraph (h) of this section (§ 230.147);

(ii) Exempt from registration under Regulation A (§§ 230.251 through 230.263);

(iii) Exempt from registration under Rule 701 (§ 230.701);

(iv) Made pursuant to an employee benefit plan;

(v) Exempt from registration under Regulation S (§§ 230.901 through 230.905);

(vi) Exempt from registration under section 4(a)(6) of the Act (15 U.S.C. 77d(a)(6)); or

(vii) Made more than six months after the completion of an offering conducted pursuant to this section (§ 230.147).

Instruction to Paragraph (g): If none of the safe harbors applies, whether subsequent offers and sales of securities will be integrated with any securities offered or sold pursuant to this section (§ 230.147) will depend on the particular facts and circumstances.

(h) *Offerings Limited to Qualified Institutional Buyers and Institutional Accredited Investors*. Where an issuer decides to register an offering under the Act after making offers in reliance on this section (§ 230.147) limited only to qualified institutional buyers and institutional accredited investors referenced in section 5(d) of the Act, such offers will not be subject to integration with any subsequent registered offering. If the issuer makes offers in reliance on this section (§ 230.147) to persons other than qualified institutional buyers and institutional accredited investors referenced in section 5(d) of the Act, such offers will not be subject to integration if the issuer (and any underwriter, broker, dealer, or agent used by the issuer in connection with the proposed offering) waits at least 30 calendar days between the last such offer made in reliance on this section (§ 230.147) and the filing of the registration statement with the Commission.

Rule 147A. Intrastate Sales Exemption

(a) *Scope of the Exemption.* Offers and sales by or on behalf of an issuer of its securities made in accordance with this section (§ 230.147A) are exempt from section 5 of the Act (15 U.S.C. 77e). This exemption is not available to an issuer that is an investment company registered or required to be registered under the Investment Company Act of 1940 (15 U.S.C. 80a-1 *et seq.*).

(b) *Manner of Offers and Sales.* An issuer, or any person acting on behalf of the issuer, may rely on this exemption to make offers and sales using any form of general solicitation and general advertising, so long as the issuer complies with the provisions of paragraphs (c), (d), and (f) through (h) of this section.

(c) *Nature of the Issuer.* The issuer of the securities shall at the time of any offers and sales be a person resident and doing business within the state or territory in which all of the sales are made.

(1) The issuer shall be deemed to be a resident of the state or territory in which it has its principal place of business. The issuer shall be deemed to have its principal place of business in a state or territory in which the officers, partners or managers of the issuer primarily direct, control and coordinate the activities of the issuer.

(2) The issuer shall be deemed to be doing business within a state or territory if the issuer satisfies at least one of the following requirements:

(i) The issuer derived at least 80% of its consolidated gross revenues from the operation of a business or of real property located in or from the rendering of services within such state or territory;

Instruction to Paragraph (c)(2)(i): Revenues must be calculated based on the issuer's most recent fiscal year, if the first offer of securities pursuant to this section is made during the first six months of the issuer's current fiscal year, and based on the first six months of the issuer's current fiscal year or during the twelve-month fiscal period ending with such six-month period, if the first offer of securities pursuant to this section is made during the last six months of the issuer's current fiscal year.

(ii) The issuer had at the end of its most recent semi-annual fiscal period prior to an initial offer of securities in any offering or subsequent offering pursuant to this section, at least 80% of its assets and those of its subsidiaries on a consolidated basis located within such state or territory;

(iii) The issuer intends to use and uses at least 80% of the net proceeds to the issuer from sales made pursuant to this section (§ 230.147A) in connection with the operation of a business or of real property, the purchase of real property located in, or the rendering of services within such state or territory; or

(iv) A majority of the issuer's employees are based in such state or territory.

Instruction to Paragraph (c): An issuer that has previously conducted an intrastate offering pursuant to this section (§ 230.147A) or Rule 147 (§ 230.147) may not conduct another intrastate offering pursuant to this section (§ 230.147A) in a different state or territory, until the expiration of the time period specified in paragraph (e) of this section (§ 230.147A(e)) or paragraph (e) of Rule 147 (§ 230.147(e)), calculated on the basis of the date of the last sale in such offering.

(d) *Residence of Purchasers.* Sales of securities pursuant to this section (§ 230.147A) shall be made only to residents of the state or territory in which the issuer is resident, as determined pursuant to paragraph (c) of this section, or who the issuer reasonably believes, at the time of sale, are residents of the state or territory in which the issuer is resident. For purposes of determining the residence of purchasers:

(1) A corporation, partnership, limited liability company, trust or other form of business organization shall be deemed to be a resident of a state or territory if, at the time of sale to it, it has its principal place of business, as defined in paragraph (c)(1) of this section, within such state or territory.

Instruction to Paragraph (d)(1): A trust that is not deemed by the law of the state or territory of its creation to be a separate legal entity is deemed to be a resident of each state or territory in which its trustee is, or trustees are, resident.

(2) Individuals shall be deemed to be residents of a state or territory if such individuals have, at the time of sale to them, their principal residence in the state or territory.

(3) A corporation, partnership, trust or other form of business organization, which is organized for the specific purpose of acquiring securities offered pursuant to this section (§ 230.147A), shall not be a resident of a state or territory unless all of the beneficial owners of such organization are residents of such state or territory.

Instruction to Paragraph (d): Obtaining a written representation from purchasers of in-state residency status will not, without more, be sufficient to establish a reasonable belief that such purchasers are in-state residents.

(e) *Limitation on Resales.* For a period of six months from the date of the sale by the issuer of a security pursuant to this section (§ 230.147A), any resale of such security shall be made only to persons resident within the state or territory in which the issuer was resident, as determined pursuant to paragraph (c) of this section, at the time of the sale of the security by the issuer.

Instruction to Paragraph (e): In the case of convertible securities, resales of either the convertible security, or if it is converted, the underlying security, could be made during the period described in paragraph (e) only to persons resident within such state or territory. For purposes of this paragraph (e), a conversion in reliance on section 3(a)(9) of the Act (15 U.S.C. 77c(a)(9)) does not begin a new period.

(f) *Precautions Against Interstate Sales.*

(1) The issuer shall, in connection with any securities sold by it pursuant to this section:

(i) Place a prominent legend on the certificate or other document evidencing the security stating that: "Offers and sales of these securities were made under an exemption from registration and have not been registered under the Securities Act of 1933. For a period of six months from the date of the sale by the issuer of these securities, any resale of these securities (or the underlying securities in the case of convertible securities) shall be made only to persons resident within the state or territory of [identify the name of the state or territory in which the issuer was resident at the time of the sale of the securities by the issuer].";

(ii) Issue stop transfer instructions to the issuer's transfer agent, if any, with respect to the securities, or, if the issuer transfers its own securities, make a notation in the appropriate records of the issuer; and

(iii) Obtain a written representation from each purchaser as to his or her residence.

(2) The issuer shall, in connection with the issuance of new certificates for any of the securities that are sold pursuant to this section (§ 230.147A) that are presented for transfer during the time period specified in paragraph (e), take the steps required by paragraphs (f)(1)(i) and (ii) of this section.

(3) The issuer shall, at the time of any offer or sale by it of a security pursuant to this section (§ 230.147A), prominently disclose to each offeree in the manner in which any such offer is communicated and to each purchaser of such security in writing a reasonable period of time before the date of sale, the following: "Sales will be made only to residents of the state or territory of [identify the name of the state or territory in which the issuer was resident at the time of the sale of the securities by the issuer]. Offers and sales of these securities are made under an exemption from registration and have not been registered under the Securities Act of 1933. For a period of six months from the date of the sale by the issuer of the securities, any resale of the securities (or the underlying securities in the case of convertible securities) shall be made only to persons resident within the state or territory of [identify the name of the state or territory in which the issuer was resident at the time of the sale of the securities by the issuer]."

(g) *Integration With Other Offerings.* Offers or sales made in reliance on this section will not be integrated with:

(1) Offers or sales of securities made prior to the commencement of offers and sales of securities pursuant to this section (§ 230.147A); or

(2) Offers or sales of securities made after completion of offers and sales of securities pursuant to this section (§ 230.147A) that are:

(i) Registered under the Act, except as provided in paragraph (h) of this section (§ 230.147A);

(ii) Exempt from registration under Regulation A (§§ 230.251 through 230.263);

(iii) Exempt from registration under Rule 701 (§ 230.701);

(iv) Made pursuant to an employee benefit plan;

(v) Exempt from registration under Regulation S (§§ 230.901 through 230.905);

(vi) Exempt from registration under section 4(a)(6) of the Act (15 U.S.C. 77d(a)(6)); or

(vii) Made more than six months after the completion of an offering conducted pursuant to this section (§ 230.147A).

Instruction to Paragraph (g): If none of the safe harbors applies, whether subsequent offers and sales of securities will be integrated with any securities offered or sold pursuant to this section (§ 230.147A) will depend on the particular facts and circumstances.

(h) *Offerings Limited to Qualified Institutional Buyers and Institutional Accredited Investors.* Where an issuer decides to register an offering under the Act after making offers in reliance on this section (§ 230.147A) limited only to qualified institutional buyers and institutional accredited investors referenced in section 5(d) of the Act, such offers will not be subject to integration with any subsequent registered offering. If the issuer makes offers in reliance on this section (§ 230.147A) to persons other than qualified institutional buyers and institutional accredited investors referenced in section 5(d) of the Act, such offers will not be subject to integration if the issuer (and any underwriter, broker, dealer, or agent used by the issuer in connection with the proposed offering) waits at least 30 calendar days between the last such offer made in reliance on this section (§ 230.147A) and the filing of the registration statement with the Commission.

Rule 148. Persons Not Deemed to be Underwriters of Securities Issued or Sold in Connection with Bankruptcy Proceedings

[Removed and reserved in Release No. 33-7300, May 31, 1996, effective July 15, 1996, 61 F.R. 30397.]

Rule 149. Definition of "Exchanged" in Section 3(a)(9), for Certain Transactions

The term "exchanged" in section 3(a)(9) shall be deemed to include the issuance of a security in consideration of the surrender by the existing security holders of the issuer, of outstanding securities of the issuer, notwithstanding the fact that the surrender of the outstanding securities may be required by the terms of the plan of exchange to be accompanied by such payment in cash by the security holder as may be necessary to effect an equitable adjustment, in respect of dividends or interest paid or payable on the securities involved in the exchange, as between such security holder and other security holders of the same class accepting the offer of exchange.

Rule 150. Definition of "Commission or Other Remuneration" in Section 3(a)(9), for Certain Transactions

The term "commission or other remuneration" in Section 3(a)(9) shall not include payments made by the issuer, directly or indirectly, to its security holders in connection with an exchange of securities for outstanding securities, when such payments are part of the terms of the offer of exchange.

Rule 151. Safe Harbor Definition of Certain "Annuity Contracts or Optional Annuity Contracts" Within the Meaning of Section 3(a)(8)

(a) Any annuity contract or optional annuity contract (a *contract*) shall be deemed to be within the provisions of section 3(a)(8) of the Securities Act of 1933 (15 U.S.C. 77c(a)(8)), *Provided,* That

(1) The annuity or optional annuity contract is issued by a corporation (the *insurer*) subject to the supervision of the insurance commissioner, bank commissioner, or any agency or officer performing like functions, of any State or Territory of the United States or the District of Columbia;

(2) The insurer assumes the investment risk under the contract as prescribed in paragraph (b) of this section; and

(3) The contract is not marketed primarily as an investment.

(b) The insurer shall be deemed to assume the investment risk under the contract if:

(1) The value of the contract does not vary according to the investment experience of a separate account;

(2) The insurer for the life of the contract

(i) Guarantees the principal amount of purchase payments and interest credited thereto, less any deduction (without regard to its timing) for sales, administrative or other expenses or charges; and

(ii) Credits a specified rate of interest (as defined in paragraph (c) of this section to net purchase payments and interest credited thereto; and

(3) The insurer guarantees that the rate of any interest to be credited in excess of that described in paragraph (b)(2)(ii) of this section will not be modified more frequently than once per year.

(c) The term *specified rate of interest,* as used in paragraph (b)(2)(ii) of this section, means a rate of interest under the contract that is at least equal to the minimum rate required to be credited by the relevant nonforfeiture law in the jurisdiction in which the contract is issued. If that jurisdiction does not have any applicable nonforfeiture law at the time the contract is issued (or if the minimum rate applicable to an existing contract is no longer mandated in that jurisdiction), the specified rate under the contract must at least be equal to the minimum rate then required for individual annuity contracts by the NAIC Standard Nonforfeiture Law.

Rule 151A. Certain Contracts Not "Annuity Contracts" or "Optional Annuity Contracts" Under Section 3(a)(8) (Postponed)

[Withdrawn as of October 20, 2010. SEC Release No. 33-9152; October 14, 2010.]

Rule 152. Definition of "Transactions by an Issuer Not Involving Any Public Offering" in Section 4(2), for Certain Transactions

The phrase "transactions by an issuer not involving any public offering" in Section 4(a)(2) shall be deemed to apply to transactions not involving any public offering at the time of said transactions although subsequently thereto the issuer decides to make a public offering and/or files a registration statement.

Rule 152a. Offer or Sale of Certain Fractional Interests

Any offer or sale of a security, evidenced by a scrip certificate, order form or similar document which represents a fractional interest in a share of stock or similar security shall be deemed a transaction by a person other than an issuer, underwriter or dealer, within the meaning of Section 4(1) of the Act, if the fractional interest (a) resulted from a stock dividend, stock split, reverse stock split, conversion, merger or similar transaction, and (b) is offered or sold pursuant to arrangements for the purchase and sale of fractional interests among the persons entitled to such fractional interests for the purpose of combining such interests into whole shares, and for the sale of such number of whole shares as may be necessary to compensate security holders for any remaining fractional interests not so combined, notwithstanding that the issuer or an affiliate of the issuer may act on behalf of or as agent for the security holders in effecting such transactions.

Rule 153. Definition of "Preceded by a Prospectus" as Used in Section 5(b)(2) of the Act, in Relation to Certain Transactions

(a) Definition of preceded by a prospectus. The term preceded by a prospectus as used in section 5(b)(2) of the Act, regarding any requirement of a broker or dealer to deliver a prospectus to a broker or dealer as a result of a transaction effected between such parties on or through a national securities exchange or facility thereof, trading facility of a national securities association, or an alternative trading system, shall mean the satisfaction of the conditions in paragraph (b) of this section.

(b) Conditions. Any requirement of a broker or dealer to deliver a prospectus for transactions covered by paragraph (a) of this section will be satisfied if:

(1) Securities of the same class as the securities that are the subject of the transaction are trading on that national securities exchange or facility thereof, trading facility of a national securities association, or alternative trading system;

(2) The registration statement relating to the offering is effective and is not the subject of any pending proceeding or examination under Section 8(d) or 8(e) of the Act;

(3) Neither the issuer, nor any underwriter or participating dealer is the subject of a pending proceeding under Section 8A of the Act in connection with the offering; and

(4) The issuer has filed or will file with the Commission a prospectus that satisfies the requirements of section 10(a) of the Act.

(c) Definitions.

(1) The term national securities exchange, as used in this section, shall mean a securities exchange registered as a national securities exchange under Section 6 of the Securities Exchange Act of 1934 (15 U.S.C. 78f).

(2) The term trading facility, as used in this section, shall mean a trading facility sponsored and governed by the rules of a registered securities association or a national securities exchange.

(3) The term alternative trading system, as used in this section, shall mean an alternative trading system as defined in Rule 300(a) of Regulation ATS under the Securities Exchange Act of 1934 (§ 242.300(a) of this chapter) registered with the Commission pursuant to Rule 301 of Regulation ATS under the Securities Exchange Act of 1934 (§ 242.301(a) of this chapter).

Rule 153a. Definition of "Preceded by a Prospectus" as Used in Section 5(b) in Relation to Certain Transactions Requiring Approval of Security Holders

The term "preceded by a prospectus", as used in Section 5(b)(2) of the Act with respect to any requirement for the delivery of a prospectus to security holders of a corporation or other person, in connection with transactions of the character specified in paragraph (a) of Rule 145 under the Act, shall mean the delivery of a prospectus:

(i) prior to the vote of security holders on such transaction; or,

(ii) with respect to actions taken by consent, prior to the earliest date on which the corporate action may be taken;

to all security holders of record of such corporation or other person, entitled to vote on or consent to the proposed transaction, at their address of record on the transfer records of the corporation or other person:

Rule 153b. Definition of "Preceded by a Prospectus," as Used in Section 5(b)(2), in Connection with Certain Transactions in Standardized Options

The term "preceded by a prospectus", as used in Section 5(b)(2) of the Act with respect to any requirement for the delivery of a prospectus relating to standardized options registered on Form S-20, shall mean the delivery, prior to any transactions, of copies of such prospectus to each options market upon which the options are traded, for the purpose of redelivery to options customers upon their request, *Provided* That:

(a) Such options market shall thereto have requested of the issuer, from time to time, such number of copies of such prospectus as may have appeared reasonably necessary to comply with the requests of options customers, and shall have delivered promptly from its supply on hand a copy to any options customer making a request thereof; and

(b) The issuer shall have furnished such options market with such reasonable number of copies of such prospectus as may have been requested by the options market for the purpose stated above.

Rule 154. Delivery of Prospectuses to Investors at the Same Address

(a) *Delivery of a single prospectus.* If you must deliver a prospectus under the federal securities laws, for purposes of sections 5(b) and 2(a)(10) of the Act (15 U.S.C. 77e(b) and 77b(a)(10)) or §240.15c2-8(b) of this chapter, you will be considered to have delivered a prospectus to investors who share an address if:

(1) You deliver a prospectus to the shared address;

(2) You address the prospectus to the investors as a group (for example, "ABC Fund [or Corporation] Shareholders," "Jane Doe and Household," "The Smith Family") or to each of the investors individually (for example, "John Doe and Richard Jones"); and

(3) The investors consent in writing to delivery of one prospectus.

(b) *Implied consent.* You do not need to obtain written consent from an investor under paragraph (a)(3) of this section if all of the following conditions are met:

(1) The investor has the same last name as the other investors, or you reasonably believe that the investors are members of the same family;

(2) You have sent the investor a notice at least 60 days before you begin to rely on this section concerning delivery of prospectuses to that investor. The notice must be a separate written statement and:

(i) State that only one prospectus will be delivered to the shared address unless you receive contrary instructions;

(ii) Include a toll-free telephone number or be accompanied by a reply form that is pre-addressed with postage provided, that the investor can use to notify you that he or she wishes to receive a separate prospectus;

(iii) State the duration of the consent;

(iv) Explain how an investor can revoke consent;

(v) State that you will begin sending individual copies to an investor within 30 days after you receive revocation of the investor's consent; and

(vi) Contain the following prominent statement, or similar clear and understandable statement, in bold-face type: "Important Notice Regarding Delivery of Shareholder Documents." This statement also must appear on the envelope in which the notice is delivered. Alternatively, if the notice is delivered separately from other communications to investors, this statement may appear either on the notice or on the envelope in which the notice is delivered;

NOTE to Sec. 230.154(b)(2): The notice should be written in plain English. See §230.421(d)(2) of this chapter for a discussion of plain English principles.

(3) You have not received the reply form or other notification indicating that the investor wishes to continue to receive an individual copy of the prospectus, within 60 days after you sent the notice; and

(4) You deliver the prospectus to a post office box or to a residential street address. You can assume a street address is a residence unless you have information that indicates it is a business.

(c) *Revocation of consent.* If an investor, orally or in writing, revokes consent to delivery of one prospectus to a shared address (provided under paragraphs (a)(3) or (b) of this section), you must begin sending individual copies to that investor within 30 days after you receive the revocation. If the individual's consent concerns delivery of the prospectus of a registered open-end management investment company, at least once a year you must explain to investors who have consented how they can revoke their consent. The explanation must be reasonably designed to reach these investors.

(d) *Definition of address.* For purposes of this section, *address* means a street address, a post office box number, an electronic mail address, a facsimile telephone number, or other similar destination to which paper or electronic documents are delivered, unless otherwise provided in this section. If you have reason to believe that an address is the street address of a multi-unit building, the address must include the unit number.

Rule 155. Integration of Abandoned Offerings

Compliance with paragraph (b) or (c) of this Rule 155 provides a non-exclusive safe harbor from integration of private and registered offerings. Because of the objectives of Rule 155 and the policies underlying the Act, Rule 155 is not available to any issuer for any transaction or series of transactions that, although in technical compliance with the rule, is part of a plan or scheme to evade the registration requirements of the Act.

(a) *Definition of terms.* For the purposes of this section only, a *private offering* means an unregistered offering of securities that is exempt from registration under Section 4(a)(2) or 4(5) of the Act (15 U.S.C. §§ 77d(2) and 77d(5)) or § 230.506 of Regulation D.

(b) *Abandoned private offering followed by a registered offering.* A private offering of securities will not be considered part of an offering for which the issuer later files a registration statement if:

(1) No securities were sold in the private offering;

(2) The issuer and any person(s) acting on its behalf terminate all offering activity in the private offering before the issuer files the registration statement;

(3) The Section 10(a) final prospectus and any Section 10 preliminary prospectus used in the registered offering disclose information about the abandoned private offering, including:

(i) The size and nature of the private offering;

(ii) The date on which the issuer abandoned the private offering;

(iii) That any offers to buy or indications of interest given in the private offering were rejected or otherwise not accepted; and

(iv) That the prospectus delivered in the registered offering supersedes any offering materials used in the private offering; and

(4) The issuer does not file the registration statement until at least 30 calendar days after termination of all offering activity in the private offering, unless the issuer and any person acting on its behalf offered securities in the private offering only to persons who were (or who the issuer reasonably believes were):

(i) Accredited investors (as that term is defined in § 230.501(a)); or

(ii) Persons who satisfy the knowledge and experience standard of § 230.506(b)(2)(ii).

(c) *Abandoned registered offering followed by a private offering.* An offering for which the issuer filed a registration statement will not be considered part of a later commenced private offering if:

(1) No securities were sold in the registered offering;

(2) The issuer withdraws the registration statement under § 230.477;

(3) Neither the issuer nor any person acting on the issuer's behalf commences the private offering earlier than 30 calendar days after the effective date of withdrawal of the registration statement under § 230.477;

(4) The issuer notifies each offeree in the private offering that:

(i) The offering is not registered under the Act;

(ii) The securities will be "restricted securities" (as that term is defined in § 230.144(a)(3)) and may not be resold unless they are registered under the Act or an exemption from registration is available;

(iii) Purchasers in the private offering do not have the protection of Section 11 of the Act (15 U.S.C. 77k); and

(iv) A registration statement for the abandoned offering was filed and withdrawn, specifying the effective date of the withdrawal; and

(5) Any disclosure document used in the private offering discloses any changes in the issuer's business or financial condition that occurred after the issuer filed the registration statement that are material to the investment decision in the private offering.

Rule 156. Investment Company Sales Literature

(a) Under the federal securities laws, including section 17(a) of the Securities Act of 1933 [15 U.S.C. 77q(a)] and section 10(b) of the Securities Exchange Act of 1934 [15 U.S.C. 78j(b)] and Rule 10b-5 thereunder [17 CFR Part 240], it is unlawful for any person, directly or indirectly, by the use of any means or instrumentality of interstate commerce or of the mails, to use sales literature which is materially misleading in connection with the offer or sale of securities issued by an investment company. Under these provisions, sales literature is materially misleading if it: (1) contains an untrue statement of a material fact or (2) omits to state a material fact necessary in order to make a statement made, in the light of the circumstances of its use, not misleading.

(b) Whether or not a particular description, representation, illustration, or other statement involving a material fact is misleading depends on evaluation of the context in which it is made. In considering whether a particular statement involving a material fact is or might be misleading, weight should be given to all pertinent factors, including, but not limited to, those listed below:

(1) A statement could be misleading because of:

(i) Other statements being made in connection with the offer of sale or sale of the securities in question;

(ii) The absence of explanations, qualifications, limitations or other statements necessary or appropriate to make such statement not misleading; or

(iii) General economic or financial conditions or circumstances.

(2) Representations about past or future investment performance could be misleading because of statements or omissions made involving a material fact, including situations where:

(i) Portrayals of past income, gain, or growth of assets convey an impression of the net investment results achieved by an actual or hypothetical investment which would not be justified under the circumstances, including portrayals that omit explanations, qualifications, limitations, or other statements necessary or appropriate to make the portrayals not misleading; and

(ii) Representations, whether express or implied, about future investment performance, including: (A) Representations, as to security of capital, possible future gains or income, or expenses associated with an investment; (B) Representations implying that future gain or income may be inferred from or predicted based on past investment performance; or (C) Portrayals of past performance, made in a manner which would imply that gains or income realized in the past would be repeated in the future.

(3) A statement involving a material fact about the characteristics or attributes of an investment company could be misleading because of:

(i) Statements about possible benefits connected with or resulting from services to be provided or methods of operation which do not give equal prominence to discussion of any risks or limitations associated therewith;

(ii) Exaggerated or unsubstantiated claims about management skill or techniques, characteristics of the investment company or an investment in securities issued by such company, services, security of investment or funds, effects of government supervision, or other attributes; and

(iii) Unwarranted or incompletely explained comparisons to other investment vehicles or to indexes.

(c) For purposes of this section, the term *sales literature* shall be deemed to include any communication (whether in writing, by radio, or by television) used by any person to offer to sell or induce the sale of securities of any investment company. Communications between issuers, underwriters and dealers are included in this definition of sales literature if such communications, or the information contained therein, can be reasonably expected to be communicated to prospective investors in the offer or sale of securities or are designed to be employed in either written or oral form in the sale of securities.

(d) Nothing in this section may be construed to prevent a business development company or a registered closed-end investment company, from qualifying for an exemption under § 230.168 of this chapter or § 230.169 of this chapter.

Rule 157. Small Entities Under the Securities Act for Purposes of the Regulatory Flexibility Act

For purposes of Commission rulemaking in accordance with the provisions of Chapter Six of the Administrative Procedure Act [5 U.S.C. § 601 *et seq.*], and unless otherwise defined for purposes of a particular rulemaking proceeding, the term "small business" or "small organization" shall—

(a) When used with reference to an issuer, other than an investment company, for purposes of the Securities Act of 1933, mean an issuer whose total assets on the last day of its most recent fiscal year were $5,000,000 or less and that is engaged or proposing to engage in small business financing. An issuer is considered to be engaged or proposing to engage in small business financing under this section if it is conducting or proposes to conduct an offering of securities which does not exceed the dollar limitation prescribed by section 3(b) of the Securities Act.

(b) When used with reference to an investment company that is an issuer for purposes of the Act, have the meaning ascribed to those terms by § 270.0-10 of this chapter.

Rule 158. Definitions of Certain Terms in the Last Paragraph of Section 11(a)

(a) An "earning statement" made generally available to security holders of the registrant pursuant to the last paragraph of Section 11(a) of the Act shall be sufficient for the purposes of such paragraph if:

(1) There is included the information required for statements of comprehensive income (as defined in § 210.1-02 of Regulation S-X of this chapter) contained either:

(i) In Item 8 of Form 10-K (§ 239.310 of this chapter), part I, Item 1 of Form 10-Q (§ 240.308a of this chapter), or Rule 14a-3(b) (§ 240.14a-3(b) of this chapter) under the Securities Exchange Act of 1934;

(ii) in Item 17 of Form 20-F, if appropriate; or

(iii) in Form 40-F; and

(2) The information specified in the last paragraph of Section 11(a) is contained in one report or any combination of reports either:

(i) On Form 10-K, Form 10-Q, Form 8-K (§ 249.308 of this chapter), or in the annual report to security holders pursuant to Rule 14a-3 under the Securities Exchange Act of 1934 (§ 240.14a-3 of this chapter); or

(ii) on Form 20-F, Form 40-F or Form 6-K.

Note 1 to Paragraph (a). A subsidiary issuing debt securities guaranteed by its parent will be deemed to have met the requirements of this paragraph if the parent's income statements satisfy the criteria of this paragraph and information respecting the subsidiary is included to the same extent as was presented in the registration statement. An "earning statement" not meeting the requirements of this paragraph may otherwise be sufficient for purposes of the last paragraph of Section 11(a).

(b) For purposes of the last paragraph of section 11(a) only, the "earning statement" contemplated by paragraph (a) of this section shall be deemed to be "made generally available to its security holders" if the registrant:

(1) Is required to file reports pursuant to section 13 or 15(d) of the Securities Exchange Act of 1934 and

(2) Has filed its report or reports on Form 10-K and Form 10-KSB, Form 10-Q and Form 10-QSB, Form 8-K, Form 20-F, Form 40-F, or Form 6-K, or has supplied to the Commission copies of the annual report sent to security holders pursuant to Rule 14a-3(c), (§ 240.14a-3(c) of this chapter) containing such information. A registrant may use other methods to make an earning statement "generally available to its security holders" for purposes of the last paragraph of section 11(a).

A registrant may use other methods to make an earning statement "generally available to its securityholders" for purposes of the last paragraph of section 11(a).

(c) For purposes of the last paragraph of section 11(a) of the Act only, the effective date of the registration statement is deemed to be the date of the latest to occur of:

(1) The effective date of the registration statement;

(2) The effective date of the last post-effective amendment to the registration statement next preceding a particular sale of the issuer's registered securities to the public filed for the purposes of:

(i) Including any prospectus required by section 10(a)(3) of the Act; or

(ii) Reflecting in the prospectus any facts or events arising after the effective date of the registration statement (or the most recent post-effective amendment thereof) which, individually or in the aggregate, represent a fundamental change in the information set forth in the registration statement;

(3) The date of filing of the last report of the issuer incorporated by reference into the prospectus that is part of the registration statement or the date that a form of prospectus filed pursuant to Rule 424(b) or Rule 497(b), (c), (d), or (e) (§ 230.424(b) or § 230.497(b), (c), (d), or (e)) is deemed part of and included in the registration statement, and relied upon in either case in lieu of filing a post-effective amendment for purposes of paragraphs (c)(2)(i) and (ii) of this section next preceding a particular sale of the issuer's registered securities to the public; or

(4) As to the issuer and any underwriter at that time only, the most recent effective date of the registration statement for purposes of liability under section 11 of the Act of the issuer and any such underwriter only at the time of or next preceding a particular sale of the issuer's registered securities to the public determined pursuant to Rule 430B (§ 230.430B).

(d) If an earnings statement was made available by "other methods" than those specified in paragraphs (a) and (b) of this section, the earnings statement must be filed as exhibit 99 to the next periodic report required by section 13 or 15(d) of the Exchange Act covering the period in which the earnings statement was released.

Rule 159. Information Available to Purchaser at Time of Contract of Sale

(a) For purposes of section 12(a)(2) of the Act only, and without affecting any other rights a purchaser may have, for purposes of determining whether a prospectus or oral statement included an untrue statement of a material fact or omitted to state a material fact necessary in order to make the statements, in the light of the circumstances under which they were made, not misleading at the time of sale (including, without limitation, a contract of sale), any information conveyed to the purchaser only after such time of sale (including such contract of sale) will not be taken into account.

(b) For purposes of section 17(a)(2) of the Act only, and without affecting any other rights the Commission may have to enforce that section, for purposes of determining whether a statement includes or represents any untrue statement of a material fact or any omission to state a material fact necessary in order to make the statements made, in light of the circumstances under which they were made, not misleading at the time of sale (including, without limitation, a contract of sale), any information conveyed to the purchaser only after such time of sale (including such contract of sale) will not be taken into account.

(c) For purposes of section 12(a)(2) of the Act only, knowing of such untruth or omission in respect of a sale (including, without limitation, a contract of sale), means knowing at the time of such sale (including such contract of sale).

Rule 159A. Certain Definitions for Purposes of Section 12(a)(2) of the Act

(a) *Definition of seller for purposes of section 12(a)(2) of the Act.* For purposes of Section 12(a)(2) of the Act only, in a primary offering of securities of the issuer, regardless of the underwriting method used to sell the issuer's securities, seller shall include the issuer of the securities sold to a person as part of the initial distribution of such securities, and the issuer shall be considered to offer or sell the securities to such person, if the securities are offered or sold to such person by means of any of the following communications:

(1) Any preliminary prospectus or prospectus of the issuer relating to the offering required to be filed pursuant to Rule 424 (§ 230.424) or Rule 497 (§ 230.497);

(2) Any free writing prospectus as defined in Rule 405 (§ 230.405) relating to the offering prepared by or on behalf of the issuer or used or referred to by the issuer and, in the case of an issuer that is an open-end management company registered under the Investment Company Act of 1940 (15 U.S.C. 80a-1 et seq.), any summary prospectus, relating to the offering provided pursuant to Rule 498 (§ 230.498);

(3) The portion of any other free writing prospectus (or, in the case of an issuer that is an investment company registered under the Investment Company Act of 1940 or a business development company as defined in section 2(a)(48) of the Investment Company Act of 1940 (15 U.S.C. 80a-2(a)(48)), any advertisement pursuant to Rule 482 (§ 230.482)) relating to the offering containing material information about the issuer or its securities provided by or on behalf of the issuer; and

(4) Any other communication that is an offer in the offering made by the issuer to such person.

Notes to paragraph (a) of Rule 159A: 1. For purposes of paragraph (a) of this section, information is provided or a communication is made by or on behalf of an issuer if an issuer or an agent or representative of the issuer authorizes or approves the information or communication before its provision or use. An offering participant other than the issuer shall not be an agent or representative of the issuer solely by virtue of its acting as an offering participant.

2. Paragraph (a) of this section shall not affect in any respect the determination of whether any person other than an issuer is a "seller" for purposes of section 12(a)(2) of the Act.

(b) *Definition of by means of for purposes of section 12(a)(2) of the Act.*

(1) For purposes of section 12(a)(2) of the Act only, an offering participant other than the issuer shall not be considered to offer or sell securities that are the subject of a registration statement by means of a free writing prospectus as to a purchaser unless one or more of the following circumstances shall exist:

(i) The offering participant used or referred to the free writing prospectus in offering or selling the securities to the purchaser;

(ii) The offering participant offered or sold securities to the purchaser and participated in planning for the use of the free writing prospectus by one or more other offering participants and such free writing prospectus was used or referred to in offering or selling securities to the purchaser by one or more of such other offering participants; or

(iii) The offering participant was required to file the free writing prospectus pursuant to the conditions to use in Rule 433 (§ 230.433).

(2) For purposes of section 12(a)(2) of the Act only, a person will not be considered to offer or sell securities by means of a free writing prospectus solely because another person has used or referred to the free writing prospectus or filed the free writing prospectus with the Commission pursuant to Rule 433.

Rule 161. Amendments to Rules and Regulations Governing Exemptions

The rules and regulations governing the exemption of securities under Section 3(b) of the Act, as in effect at the time the securities are first bona fide offered to the public in conformity therewith, shall continue to govern the exemption of such securities notwithstanding the subsequent amendment of such rules and regulations. This rule shall not apply, however, to any new offering of such securities by an issuer or underwriter after the effective date of any such amendment, nor shall it apply to any offering after January 1, 1959, of securities by an issuer or underwriter pursuant to Regulation D or pursuant to Regulation A as in effect at any time prior to July 23, 1956.

Rule 162. Submission of Tenders in Registered Exchange Offers

(a) Notwithstanding section 5(a) of the Act (15 U.S.C. 77e(a)), an offeror may solicit tenders of securities in an exchange offer before a registration statement is effective as to the security offered, so long as no securities are purchased until the registration statement is effective and the tender offer has expired in accordance with the tender offer rules, and either:

(1) The exchange offer is subject to § 240.13e-4 or §§ 240.14d-1 through 14d-11 of this chapter; or

(2) The offeror provides withdrawal rights to the same extent as would be required if the exchange offer were subject to the requirements of § 240.13e-4 or §§ 240.14d-1 through 14d-11 of this chapter; and if a material change occurs in the information published, sent or given to security holders, the offeror complies with the provisions of § 240.13e-4(e)(3) or § 240.14d-4(b) and (d) of this chapter in disseminating information about the material change to security holders, and including the minimum periods during which the offer must remain open (with withdrawal rights) after notice of the change is provided to security holders.

(b) Notwithstanding Section 5(b)(2) of the Act (15 U.S.C. 77e(b)(2)), a prospectus that meets the requirements of Section 10(a) of the Act (15 U.S.C. 77j(a)) need not be delivered to security holders in an exchange offer that commences before the effectiveness of a registration statement in accordance with the provisions of § 230.162(a) of this section, so long as a preliminary prospectus, prospectus supplements and revised prospectuses are delivered to security holders in accordance with § 240.13e4(e)(2) or § 240.14d-4(b) of this chapter. This applies not only to exchange offers subject to those provisions, but also to exchange offers not subject to those provisions that meet the conditions in § 230.162(a)(2) of this section.

Instruction to § 230.162 of this section: Notwithstanding the provisions of § 230.162 of this section above, for going private transactions (as defined by § 240.13e-3) and roll-up transactions (as described by Item 901 of Regulation S-K (§ 229.901 of this chapter)), a registration statement registering the securities to be offered must have become effective and only a prospectus that meets the requirements of Section 10(a) of the Securities Act may be delivered to security holders on the date of commencement.

Rule 163. Exemption from Section 5(c) of the Act for Certain Communications by or on Behalf of Well-Known Seasoned Issuers

Preliminary Note to Rule 163

Attempted compliance with this section does not act as an exclusive election and the issuer also may claim the availability of any other applicable exemption or exclusion. Reliance on this section does not affect the availability of any other exemption or exclusion from the requirements of section 5 of the Act.

(a) In an offering by or on behalf of a well-known seasoned issuer, as defined in Rule 405 (§ 230.405), that will be or is at the time intended to be registered under the Act, an offer by or on behalf of such issuer is exempt from the prohibitions in section 5(c) of the Act on offers to sell, offers for sale, or offers to buy its securities before a registration statement has been filed, provided that:

(1) Any written communication that is an offer made in reliance on this exemption will be a free writing prospectus as defined in Rule 405 and a prospectus under section 2(a)(10) of the Act relating to a public offering of securities to be covered by the registration statement to be filed; and

(2) The exemption from Section 5(c) of the Act provided in this section for such written communication that is an offer shall be conditioned on satisfying the conditions in paragraph (b) of this section.

(b) Conditions.

(1) Legend.

(i) Every written communication that is an offer made in reliance on this exemption shall contain substantially the following legend:

The issuer may file a registration statement (including a prospectus) with the SEC for the offering to which this communication relates. Before you invest, you should read the prospectus in that registration statement and other documents the issuer has filed with the SEC for more complete information about the issuer and this offering. You may get these documents for free by visiting EDGAR on the SEC Web site at www.sec.gov. Alternatively, the company will arrange to send you the prospectus after filing if you request it by calling toll-free 1-8[xx-xxx-xxxx].

(ii) The legend also may provide an e-mail address at which the documents can be requested and may indicate that the documents also are available by accessing the issuer's Web site, and provide the Internet address and the particular location of the documents on the Web site.

(iii) An immaterial or unintentional failure to include the specified legend in a free writing prospectus required by this section will not result in a violation of section 5(c) of the Act or the loss of the ability to rely on this section so long as:

(A) A good faith and reasonable effort was made to comply with the specified legend condition;

(B) The free writing prospectus is amended to include the specified legend as soon as practicable after discovery of the omitted or incorrect legend; and

(C) If the free writing prospectus has been transmitted without the specified legend, the free writing prospectus is retransmitted with the legend by substantially the same means as, and directed to substantially the same prospective purchasers to whom, the free writing prospectus was originally transmitted.

(2) Filing condition.

(i) Subject to paragraph (b)(2)(ii) of this section, every written communication that is an offer made in reliance on this exemption shall be filed by the issuer with the Commission promptly upon the filing of the registration statement, if one is filed, or an amendment, if one is filed, covering the securities that have been offered in reliance on this exemption.

(ii) The condition that an issuer shall file a free writing prospectus with the Commission under this section shall not apply in respect of any communication that has previously been filed with, or furnished to, the Commission or that the issuer would not be required to file with the Commission pursuant to the conditions of Rule 433 (§ 230.433) if the communication was a free writing prospectus used after the filing of the registration statement. The condition that the issuer shall file a free writing prospectus with the Commission under this section shall be satisfied if the issuer satisfies the filing conditions (other than timing of filing which is provided in this section) that would apply under Rule 433 if the communication was a free writing prospectus used after the filing of the registration statement.

(iii) An immaterial or unintentional failure to file or delay in filing a free writing prospectus to the extent provided in this section will not result in a violation of section 5(c) of the Act or the loss of the ability to rely on this section so long as:

(A) A good faith and reasonable effort was made to comply with the filing condition; and

(B) The free writing prospectus is filed as soon as practicable after discovery of the failure to file.

(3) Ineligible offerings. The exemption in paragraph (a) of this section shall not be available to:

(i) Communications relating to business combination transactions that are subject to Rule 165 (§ 230.165) or Rule 166 (§ 230.166); or

(ii) Communications by an issuer that is an investment company registered under the Investment Company Act of 1940 (15 U.S.C. 80a-1 et seq.).

(c) For purposes of this section, a communication is made by or on behalf of an issuer if the issuer or an agent or representative of the issuer, other than an offering participant who is an underwriter or dealer, authorizes or approves the communication before it is made.

(d) For purposes of this section, a communication for which disclosure would be required under section 17(b) of the Act as a result of consideration given or to be given, directly or indirectly, by or on behalf of an issuer is deemed to be an offer by the issuer and, if a written communication, is deemed to be a free writing prospectus of the issuer.

(e) A communication exempt from section 5(c) of the Act pursuant to this section will not be considered to be in connection with a securities offering registered under the Securities Act for purposes of Rule 100(b)(2)(iv) of Regulation FD under the Securities Exchange Act of 1934 (§ 243.100(b)(2)(iv) of this chapter).

Rule 163A. Exemption from Section 5(c) of the Act for Certain Communications Made by or on Behalf of Issuers More Than 30 Days Before a Registration Statement Is Filed

Preliminary Note to Rule 163A

Attempted compliance with this section does not act as an exclusive election and the issuer also may claim the availability of any other applicable exemption or exclusion. Reliance on this section does not affect the availability of any other exemption or exclusion from the requirements of Section 5 of the Act.

(a) Except as excluded pursuant to paragraph (b) of this section, in all registered offerings by issuers, any communication made by or on behalf of an issuer more than 30 days before the date of the filing of the registration statement that does not reference a securities offering that is or will be the subject of a registration statement shall not constitute an offer to sell, offer for sale, or offer to buy the securities being offered under the registration statement for purposes of section 5(c) of the Act, provided that the issuer takes reasonable steps within its control to prevent further distribution or publication of such communication during the 30 days immediately preceding the date of filing the registration statement.

(b) The exemption in paragraph (a) of this section shall not be available with respect to the following communications:

(1) Communications relating to business combination transactions that are subject to Rule 165 (§ 230.165) or Rule 166 (§ 230.166);

(2) Communications made in connection with offerings registered on Form S-8 (§ 239.16b of this chapter), other than by well-known seasoned issuers;

(3) Communications in offerings of securities of an issuer that is, or during the past three years was (or any of whose predecessors during the last three years was):

(i) A blank check company as defined in Rule 419(a)(2) (§ 230.419(a)(2));

(ii) A shell company, other than a business combination related shell company, each as defined in Rule 405 (§ 230.405); or

(iii) An issuer for an offering of penny stock as defined in Rule 3a51-1 of the Securities Exchange Act of 1934 (§ 240.3a51-1 of this chapter); or

(4) Communications made by an issuer that is an investment company registered under the Investment Company Act of 1940 (15 U.S.C. 80a-1 et seq.), other than a registered closed-end investment company.

(c) For purposes of this section, a communication is made by or on behalf of an issuer if the issuer or an agent or representative of the issuer, other than an offering participant who is an underwriter or dealer, authorizes or approves the communication before it is made.

(d) A communication exempt from section 5(c) of the Act pursuant to this section will not be considered to be in connection with a securities offering registered under the Securities Act for purposes of Rule 100(b)(2)(iv) of Regulation FD under the Securities Exchange Act of 1934 (§ 243.100(b)(2)(iv) of this chapter).

Rule 163B. Exemption From Section 5(b)(1) and Section 5(c) of the Act For Certain Communications to Qualified Institutional Buyers or Institutional Accredited Investors

(a) Attempted compliance with this rule does not act as an exclusive election, and the issuer also may claim the availability of any other applicable exemption or exclusion. Reliance on this rule does not affect the availability of any other exemption or exclusion from the requirements of section 5 of the Act (15 U.S.C. 77e).

(b)(1) An issuer, or any person authorized to act on behalf of an issuer, may engage in oral or written communications with potential investors described in paragraph (c) of this section to determine whether such investors might have an interest in a contemplated registered securities offering, either prior to or following the date of filing of a registration statement with respect to such securities with the Commission. Communications under this rule will be exempt from section 5(b)(1) (15 U.S.C. 77e(b)(1)) and section 5(c) of the Act (15 U.S.C. 77e(c)).

(2) Any oral or written communication by an issuer, or any person authorized to act on behalf of an issuer, made in reliance on this rule will be deemed an "offer" as defined in section 2(a)(3) of the Act (15 U.S.C.77b(a)(3)).

(3) Any oral or written communication by an issuer, or any person authorized to act on behalf of an issuer, made in reliance on this rule is not required to be filed with the Commission, including pursuant to § 230.424(a) or § 230.497(a) of Regulation C under the Act or section 24(b) of the Investment Company Act of 1940 (15 U.S.C. 80a-24(b)) and the rules and regulations thereunder.

(c) Communications under this rule may be made with potential investors that are, or that an issuer or person authorized to act on its behalf reasonably believes are:

(1) Qualified institutional buyers, as defined in § 230.144A; or

(2) Institutions that are accredited investors, as defined in §§ 230.501(a)(1), (a)(2), (a)(3), (a)(7), or (a)(8).

Rule 164. Post-Filing Free Writing Prospectuses in Connection with Certain Registered Offerings

Preliminary Notes to Rule 164

1. This section is not available for any communication that, although in technical compliance with this section, is part of a plan or scheme to evade the requirements of Section 5 of the Act.

2. Attempted compliance with this section does not act as an exclusive election and the person relying on this section also may claim the availability of any other applicable exemption or exclusion. Reliance on this section does not affect the availability of any other exemption or exclusion from the requirements of section 5 of the Act.

(a) In connection with a registered offering of an issuer meeting the requirements of this section, a free writing prospectus, as defined in Rule 405 (§ 230.405), of the issuer or any other offering participant, including any underwriter or dealer, after the filing of the registration statement will be a section 10(b) prospectus for purposes of section 5(b)(1) of the Act provided that the conditions set forth in Rule 433 (§ 230.433) are satisfied.

(b) An immaterial or unintentional failure to file or delay in filing a free writing prospectus as necessary to satisfy the filing conditions contained in Rule 433 will not result in a violation of ection 5(b)(1) of the Act or the loss of the ability to rely on this section so long as:

(1) A good faith and reasonable effort was made to comply with the filing condition; and

(2) The free writing prospectus is filed as soon as practicable after discovery of the failure to file.

(c) An immaterial or unintentional failure to include the specified legend in a free writing prospectus as necessary to satisfy the legend condition contained in Rule 433 will not result in a violation of section 5(b)(1) of the Act or the loss of the ability to rely on this section so long as:

(1) A good faith and reasonable effort was made to comply with the legend condition;

(2) The free writing prospectus is amended to include the specified legend as soon as practicable after discovery of the omitted or incorrect legend; and

(3) If the free writing prospectus has been transmitted without the specified legend, the free writing prospectus must be retransmitted with the legend by substantially the same means as, and directed to substantially the same prospective purchasers to whom, the free writing prospectus was originally transmitted.

(d) Solely for purposes of this section, an immaterial or unintentional failure to retain a free writing prospectus as necessary to satisfy the record retention condition contained in Rule 433 will not result in a violation of section 5(b)(1) of the Act or the loss of the ability to rely on this section so long as a good faith and reasonable effort was made to comply with the record retention condition. Nothing in this paragraph will affect, however, any other record retention provisions applicable to the issuer or any offering participant.

(e) Ineligible issuers

(1) This section and Rule 433 are available only if at the eligibility determination date for the offering in question, determined pursuant to paragraph (h) of this section, the issuer is not an ineligible issuer as defined in Rule 405 (or in the case of any offering participant, other than the issuer, the participant has a reasonable belief that the issuer is not an ineligible issuer);

(2) Notwithstanding paragraph (e)(1) of this section, this section and Rule 433 are available to an ineligible issuer with respect to a free writing prospectus that contains only descriptions of the terms of the securities in the offering or the offering (or in the case of an offering of asset-backed securities, contains only information specified in paragraphs (a)(1), (2), (3), (4), (6), (7), and (8) of the definition of ABS informational and computational materials in Item 1101 of Regulation AB (§ 229.1101 of this chapter), unless the issuer is or during the last three years the issuer or any of its predecessors was:

(i) A blank check company as defined in Rule 419(a)(2) (§ 230.419(a)(2));

(ii) A shell company, other than a business combination related shell company, as defined in Rule 405; or

(iii) An issuer for an offering of penny stock as defined in Rule 3a51-1 of the Securities Exchange Act of 1934 (§ 240.3a51-1 of this chapter).

(f) *Excluded issuers.* This section and Rule 433 are not available if the issuer is an investment company registered under the Investment Company Act of 1940 (15 U.S.C. 80a-1 et seq.) other than a registered closed-end investment company.

(g) *Excluded offerings.* This section and Rule 433 are not available if the issuer is registering a business combination transaction as defined in Rule 165(f)(1) (§ 230.165(f)(1)) or the issuer, other than a well-known seasoned issuer, is registering an offering on Form S-8 (§ 239.16b of this chapter).

(h) For purposes of this section and Rule 433, the determination date as to whether an issuer is an ineligible issuer in respect of an offering shall be:

(1) Except as provided in paragraph (h)(2) of this section, the time of filing of the registration statement covering the offering; or

(2) If the offering is being registered pursuant to Rule 415 (§ 230.415), the earliest time after the filing of the registration statement covering the offering at which the issuer, or in the case of an underwritten offering the issuer or another offering participant, makes a bona fide offer, including without limitation through the use of a free writing prospectus, in the offering.

Rule 165. Offers Made in Connection with a Business Combination Transaction

Preliminary Note

This section is available only to communications relating to business combinations. The exemption does not apply to communications that may be in technical compliance with this section, but have the primary purpose or effect of conditioning the market for another transaction, such as a capital-raising or resale transaction.

(a) *Communications before a registration statement is filed.* Notwithstanding Section 5(c) of the Act (15 U.S.C. 77e(c)), the offeror of securities in a business combination transaction to be registered under the Act may make an offer to sell or solicit an offer to buy those securities from and including the first public announcement until the filing of a registration statement related to the transaction, so long as any written communication (other than non-public communications among participants) made in connection with or relating to the transaction (*i.e.*, prospectus) is filed in accordance with § 230.425 and the conditions in paragraph (c) of this section are satisfied.

(b) *Communications after a registration statement is filed.* Notwithstanding Section 5(b)(1) of the Act (15 U.S.C. 77e(b)(1)), any written communication (other than non-public communications among participants) made in connection with or relating to a business combination transaction (*i.e.*, prospectus) after the filing of a registration statement related to the transaction need not satisfy the requirements of Section 10 (15 U.S.C. 77j) of the Act, so long as the prospectus is filed in accordance with § 230.424 or § 230.425 and the conditions in paragraph (c) of this section are satisfied.

(c) *Conditions.* To rely on paragraphs (a) and (b) of this section:

(1) Each prospectus must contain a prominent legend that urges investors to read the relevant documents filed or to be filed with the Commission because they contain important information. The legend also must explain to investors that they can get the documents for free at the Commission's web site and describe which documents are available free from the offeror; and

(2) In an exchange offer, the offer must be made in accordance with the applicable tender offer rules (§§ 240.14d-1 through 240.14e-8 of this chapter); and, in a transaction involving the vote of security holders, the offer must be made in accordance with the applicable proxy or information statement rules (§§ 240.14a-1 through 240.14a-101 and §§ 240.14c-1 through 240.14c-101 of this chapter).

(d) This section is applicable not only to the offeror of securities in a business combination transaction, but also to any other participant that may need to rely on and complies with this section in communicating about the transaction.

(e) An immaterial or unintentional failure to file or delay in filing a prospectus described in this section will not result in a violation of Section 5(b)(1) or (c) of the Act (15 U.S.C. 77e(b)(1) and (c)), so long as:

(1) A good faith and reasonable effort was made to comply with the filing requirement; and

(2) The prospectus is filed as soon as practicable after discovery of the failure to file.

(f) *Definitions*.

(1) A *business combination transaction* means any transaction specified in § 230.145(a) or exchange offer;

(2) A *participant* is any person or entity that is a party to the business combination transaction and any persons authorized to act on their behalf; and

(3) *Public announcement* is any oral or written communication by a participant that is reasonably designed to, or has the effect of, informing the public or security holders in general about the business combination transaction.

Rule 166. Exemption from Section 5(c) for Certain Communications in Connection with Business Combination Transactions

Preliminary Note

This section is available only to communications relating to business combinations. The exemption does not apply to communications that may be in technical compliance with this section, but have the primary purpose or effect of conditioning the market for another transaction, such as a capital-raising or resale transaction.

(a) *Communications*. In a registered offering involving a business combination transaction, any communication made in connection with or relating to the transaction before the first public announcement of the offering will not constitute an offer to sell or a solicitation of an offer to buy the securities offered for purposes of Section 5(c) of the Act (15 U.S.C. 77e(c)), so long as the participants take all reasonable steps within their control to prevent further distribution or publication of the communication until either the first public announcement is made or the registration statement related to the transaction is filed.

(b) *Definitions*. The terms business combination transaction, participant and public announcement have the same meaning as set forth in § 230.165(f) of this chapter.

Rule 168. Exemption from Sections 2(a)(10) and 5(c) of the Act for Certain Communications of Regularly Released Factual Business Information and Forward-Looking Information

Preliminary Notes to Rule 168

1. This section is not available for any communication that, although in technical compliance with this section, is part of a plan or scheme to evade the requirements of section 5 of the Act.

2. This section provides a non-exclusive safe harbor for factual business information and forward-looking information released or disseminated as provided in this section. Attempted compliance with this section does not act as an exclusive election and the issuer also may claim the availability of any other applicable exemption or exclusion. Reliance on this section does not affect the availability of any other exemption or exclusion from the definition of prospectus in section 2(a)(10) or the requirements of section 5 of the Act.

3. The availability of this section for a release or dissemination of a communication that contains or incorporates factual business information or forward-looking information will not be affected by another release or dissemination of a communication that contains all or a portion of the same factual business information or forward-looking information that does not satisfy the conditions of this section.

(a) For purposes of sections 2(a)(10) and 5(c) of the Act, the regular release or dissemination by or on behalf of an issuer (and, in the case of an asset-backed issuer, the other persons specified in paragraph (a)(3) of this section) of communications containing factual business information or forward-looking information shall be deemed not to constitute an offer to sell or offer for sale of a security which is the subject of an offering pursuant to a registration statement that the issuer proposes to file, or has filed, or that is effective, if the conditions of this section are satisfied by any of the following:

(1) An issuer that is required to file reports pursuant to section 13 or section 15(d) of the Securities Exchange Act of 1934 (15 U.S.C. 78m or 78o(d));

(2) A foreign private issuer that:

(i) Meets all of the registrant requirements of Form F-3 (§ 239.33 of this chapter) other than the reporting history provisions of General Instructions I.A.1. and I.A.2.(a) of Form F-3;

(ii) Either:

(A) Satisfies the public float threshold in General Instruction I.B.1. of Form F-3; or

(B) Is issuing non-convertible securities, other than common equity, and meets the provisions of General Instruction I.B.2. of Form F-3 (referenced in 17 CFR 239.33 of this chapter); and

(iii) Either:

(A) Has its equity securities trading on a designated offshore securities market as defined in Rule 902(b) (§ 230.902(b)) and has had them so traded for at least 12 months; or

(B) Has a worldwide market value of its outstanding common equity held by non-affiliates of $700 million or more; or

(3) An asset-backed issuer or a depositor, sponsor, or servicer (as such terms are defined in Item 1101 of Regulation AB (§ 229.1101 of this chapter)) or an affiliated depositor, whether or not such other person is the issuer.

(b) Definitions.

(1) Factual business information means some or all of the following information that is released or disseminated under the conditions in paragraph (d) of this section, including, without limitation, such factual business information contained in reports or other materials filed with, furnished to, or submitted to the Commission pursuant to the Securities Exchange Act of 1934 (15 U.S.C. 78a et. seq.) or the Investment Company Act of 1940 (15 U.S.C. 80a-1 et seq.):

(i) Factual information about the issuer, its business or financial developments, or other aspects of its business;

(ii) Advertisements of, or other information about, the issuer's products or services; and

(iii) Dividend notices.

(2) Forward-looking information means some or all of the following information that is released or disseminated under the conditions in paragraph (d) of this section, including, without limitation, such forward-looking information contained in reports or other materials filed with, furnished to, or submitted to the Commission pursuant to the Securities Exchange Act of 1934 or the Investment Company Act of 1940:

(i) Projections of the issuer's revenues, income (loss), earnings (loss) per share, capital expenditures, dividends, capital structure, or other financial items;

(ii) Statements about the issuer management's plans and objectives for future operations, including plans or objectives relating to the products or services of the issuer;

(iii) Statements about the issuer's future economic performance, including statements of the type contemplated by the management's discussion and analysis of financial condition and results of operation described in Item 303 of Regulations S-B and S-K (§ 228.303 and § 229.303 of this chapter) or the operating and financial review and prospects described in Item 5 of Form 20-F (§ 249.220f of this chapter); and

(iv) Assumptions underlying or relating to any of the information described in paragraphs (b)(2)(i), (b)(2)(ii) and (b)(2)(iii) of this section.

(3) For purposes of this section, the release or dissemination of a communication is by or on behalf of the issuer if the issuer or an agent or representative of the issuer, other than an offering participant who is an underwriter or dealer, authorizes or approves such release or dissemination before it is made.

(4) For purposes of this section, in the case of communications of a person specified in paragraph (a)(3) of this section other than the asset-backed issuer, the release or dissemination of a communication is by or on behalf of such other person if such other person or its agent or representative, other than an underwriter or dealer, authorizes or approves such release or dissemination before it is made.

(c) Exclusion. A communication containing information about the registered offering or released or disseminated as part of the offering activities in the registered offering is excluded from the exemption of this section.

(d) Conditions to exemption. The following conditions must be satisfied:

(1) The issuer (or in the case of an asset-backed issuer, the issuer and the other persons specified in paragraph (a)(3) of this section, taken together) has previously released or disseminated information of the type described in this section in the ordinary course of its business;

(2) The timing, manner, and form in which the information is released or disseminated is consistent in material respects with similar past releases or disseminations; and

(3) The issuer is not an investment company registered under the Investment Company Act of 1940 (15 U.S.C. 80a-1 et seq.) or a business development company as defined in section 2(a)(48) of the Investment Company Act of 1940 (15 U.S.C. 80a-2(a)(48)), other than a registered closed-end investment company.

Rule 169. Exemption from Sections 2(a)(10) and 5(c) of the Act for Certain Communications of Regularly Released Factual Business Information

Preliminary Notes to Rule 169

1. This section is not available for any communication that, although in technical compliance with this section, is part of a plan or scheme to evade the requirements of section 5 of the Act.

2. This section provides a non-exclusive safe harbor for factual business information released or disseminated as provided in this section. Attempted compliance with this section does not act as an exclusive election and the issuer also may claim the availability of any other applicable exemption or exclusion. Reliance on this section does not affect the availability of any other exemption or exclusion from the definition of prospectus in section 2(a)(10) or the requirements of section 5 of the Act.

3. The availability of this section for a release or dissemination of a communication that contains or incorporates factual business information will not be affected by another release or dissemination of a communication that contains all or a portion of the same factual business information that does not satisfy the conditions of this section.

(a) For purposes of sections 2(a)(10) and 5(c) of the Act, the regular release or dissemination by or on behalf of an issuer of communications containing factual business information shall be deemed not to constitute an offer to sell or offer for sale of a security by an issuer which is the subject of an offering pursuant to a registration statement that the issuer proposes to file, or has filed, or that is effective, if the conditions of this section are satisfied.

(b) Definitions.

(1) Factual business information means some or all of the following information that is released or disseminated under the conditions in paragraph (d) of this section:

(i) Factual information about the issuer, its business or financial developments, or other aspects of its business; and

(ii) Advertisements of, or other information about, the issuer's products or services.

(2) For purposes of this section, the release or dissemination of a communication is by or on behalf of the issuer if the issuer or an agent or representative of the issuer, other than an offering participant who is an underwriter or dealer, authorizes or approves such release or dissemination before it is made.

(c) Exclusions. A communication containing information about the registered offering or released or disseminated as part of the offering activities in the registered offering is excluded from the exemption of this section.

(d) Conditions to exemption. The following conditions must be satisfied:

(1) The issuer has previously released or disseminated information of the type described in this section in the ordinary course of its business;

(2) The timing, manner, and form in which the information is released or disseminated is consistent in material respects with similar past releases or disseminations;

(3) The information is released or disseminated for intended use by persons, such as customers and suppliers, other than in their capacities as investors or potential investors in the issuer's securities, by the issuer's employees or agents who historically have provided such information; and

(4) The issuer is not an investment company registered under the Investment Company Act of 1940 (15 U.S.C. 80a-1 et seq.), other than a registered closed-end investment company.

Rule 170. Prohibition of Use of Certain Financial Statements

Financial statements which purport to give effect to the receipt and application of any part of the proceeds from the sale of securities for cash shall not be used unless such securities are to be offered through underwriters and the underwriting arrangements are such that the underwriters are or will be committed to take and pay for all of the securities, if any are taken, prior to or within a reasonable time after the commencement of the public offering, or if the securities are not so taken to refund to all subscribers the full amount of all subscription payments made for the securities. The caption of any such financial statement shall clearly set forth the assumptions upon which such statement is based. The caption shall be in type at least as large as that used generally in the body of the statement.

Rule 171. Disclosure Detrimental to the National Security

(a) Any requirement to the contrary notwithstanding, no registration statement, prospectus, or other document filed with the Commission or used in connection with the offering or sale of any securities shall contain any document or information which, pursuant to Executive order, has been classified by an appropriate department or agency of the United States for protection in the interest of national defense or foreign policy.

(b) Where a document or information is omitted pursuant to paragraph (a) of this section, there shall be filed, in lieu of such document or information, a statement from an appropriate department or agency of the United States to the effect that such document or information has been classified or that the status thereof is awaiting determination. Where a document is omitted pursuant to paragraph (a) of this section, but information relating to the subject-matter of such document is nevertheless included in material filed with the Commission pursuant to a determination of an appropriate department or agency of the United States that disclosure of such information would not be contrary to the interests of national defense or foreign policy, a statement from such department or agency to that effect shall be submitted for the information of the Commission. A registrant may rely upon any such statement in filing or omitting any document or information to which the statement relates.

(c) The Commission may protect any information in its possession which may require classification in the interests of national defense or foreign policy pending determination by an appropriate department or agency as to whether such information should be classified.

(d) It shall be the duty of the registrant to submit the documents or information referred to in paragraph (a) of this section to the appropriate department or agency of the United States prior to filing them with the Commission and to obtain and submit to the Commission, at the time of filing such documents or information, or in lieu thereof, as the case may be, the statements from such department or agency required by paragraph (b) of this section. All such statements shall be in writing.

Rule 172. Delivery of Prospectuses

(a) Sending confirmations and notices of allocations. After the effective date of a registration statement, the following are exempt from the provisions of section 5(b)(1) of the Act if the conditions set forth in paragraph (c) of this section are satisfied:

(1) Written confirmations of sales of securities in an offering pursuant to a registration statement that contain information limited to that called for in Rule 10b-10 under the Securities Exchange Act of 1934 (§ 240.10b-10 of this chapter) and other information customarily included in written confirmations of sales of securities, which may include notices provided pursuant to Rule 173 (§ 230.173); and

(2) Notices of allocation of securities sold or to be sold in an offering pursuant to the registration statement that may include information identifying the securities (including the CUSIP number) and otherwise may include only information regarding pricing, allocation and settlement, and information incidental thereto.

(b) Transfer of the security. Any obligation under section 5(b)(2) of the Act to have a prospectus that satisfies the requirements of section 10(a) of the Act precede or accompany the carrying or delivery of a security in a registered offering is satisfied if the conditions in paragraph (c) of this section are met.

(c) Conditions.

(1) The registration statement relating to the offering is effective and is not the subject of any pending proceeding or examination under section 8(d) or 8(e) of the Act;

(2) Neither the issuer, nor an underwriter or participating dealer is the subject of a pending proceeding under section 8A of the Act in connection with the offering; and

(3) The issuer has filed with the Commission a prospectus with respect to the offering that satisfies the requirements of section 10(a) of the Act or the issuer will make a good faith and reasonable effort to file such a prospectus within the time required under Rule 424 (§ 230.424) and, in the event that the issuer fails to file timely such a prospectus, the issuer files the prospectus as soon as practicable thereafter.

(4) The condition in paragraph (c)(3) of this section shall not apply to transactions by dealers requiring delivery of a final prospectus pursuant to section 4(3) of the Act.

(d) Exclusions. This section shall not apply to any:

(1) Offering of any investment company registered under the Investment Company Act of 1940 (15 U.S.C. 80a-1 et seq.), other than a registered closed-end investment company;

(2) A business combination transaction as defined in Rule 165(f)(1) (§ 230.165(f)(1); or

(3) Offering registered on Form S-8 (§ 239.16b of this chapter).

Rule 173. Notice of Registration

(a) In a transaction that represents a sale by the issuer or an underwriter, or a sale where there is not an exclusion or exemption from the requirement to deliver a final prospectus meeting the requirements of section 10(a) of the Act pursuant to section 4(3) of the Act or Rule 174 (§ 230.174), each underwriter or dealer selling in such transaction shall provide to each purchaser from it, not later than two business days following the completion of such sale, a copy of the final prospectus or, in lieu of such prospectus, a notice to the effect that the sale was made pursuant to a registration statement or in a transaction in which a final prospectus would have been required to have been delivered in the absence of Rule 172 (§ 230.172).

(b) If the sale was by the issuer and was not effected by or through an underwriter or dealer, the responsibility to send a prospectus, or in lieu of such prospectus, such notice as set forth in paragraph (a) of this section, shall be the issuer's.

(c) Compliance with the requirements of this section is not a condition to reliance on Rule 172.

(d) A purchaser may request from the person responsible for sending a notice a copy of the final prospectus if one has not been sent.

(e) After the effective date of the registration statement with respect to an offering, notices as set forth in paragraph (a) of this section, are exempt from the provisions of section 5(b)(1) of the Act.

(f) Exclusions. This section shall not apply to any:

(1) Transaction solely between brokers or dealers in reliance on Rule 153 (§ 230.153);

(2) Offering of any investment company registered under the Investment Company Act of 1940 (15 U.S.C. 80a-1 et seq.), other than a registered closed-end investment company;

(3) Offering of any business development company as defined in section 2(a)(48) of the Investment Company Act of 1940 (15 U.S.C. 80a-2(a)(48));

(4) A business combination transaction as defined in Rule 165(f)(1) (§ 230.165(f)(1)); or

(5) Offering registered on Form S-8 (§ 239.16b of this chapter).

Rule 174. Delivery of Prospectus by Dealers; Exemptions under Section 4(3) of the Act

The obligations of a dealer (including an underwriter no longer acting as an underwriter in respect of the security involved in such transactions) to deliver a prospectus in transactions in a security as to which a registration statement has been filed taking place prior to the expiration of the 40 or 90 day period specified in Section 4(3) of the Act after the effective date of such registration statement or prior to the expiration of such period after the first date upon which the security was bona fide offered to the public by the issuer or by or through an underwriter after such effective date, whichever is later, shall be subject to the following provisions:

(a) No prospectus need be delivered if the registration statement is on Form F-6 (§ 239.36 of this chapter).

(b) No prospectus need be delivered if the issuer is subject, immediately prior to the time of filing the registration statement, to the reporting requirements of Section 13 or 15(d) of the Securities Exchange Act of 1934.

(c) Where a registration statement relates to offerings to be made from time to time no prospectus need be delivered after the expiration of the initial prospectus delivery period specified in Section 4(3) of the Act following the first bona fide offering of securities under such registration statement.

(d) If (1) the registration statement relates to the security of an issuer that is not subject, immediately prior to the time of filing the registration statement, to the reporting requirements of Section 13 or 15(d) of the Securities Exchange Act of 1934, and (2) as of the offering date, the security is listed on a registered national securities exchange or authorized for inclusion in an electronic inter-dealer quotation system sponsored and governed by the rules of a registered securities association, no prospectus need be delivered after the expiration of twenty-five calendar days after the offering date. For purposes of this provision, the term "offering date" refers to the later of the effective date of the registration statement or the first date on which the security was bona fide offered to the public.

(e) Notwithstanding the foregoing, the period during which a prospectus must be delivered by a dealer shall be:

(1) As specified in Section 4(3) of the Act if the registration statement was the subject of a stop order issued under Section 8 of the Act; or

(2) As the Commission may provide upon application or on its own motion in a particular case.

(f) Nothing in this section shall affect the obligation to deliver a prospectus pursuant to the provisions of Section 5 of the Act by a dealer who is acting as an underwriter with respect to the securities involved or who is engaged in a transaction as to securities constituting the whole or a part of an unsold allotment to or subscription by such dealer as a participant in the distribution of such securities by the issuer or by or through an underwriter.

(g) If the registration statement relates to an offering of securities of a "blank check company," as defined in Rule 419 under the Act [17 CFR 230.419], the statutory period for prospectus delivery specified in Section 4(3) of the Act shall not terminate until 90 days after the date funds and securities are released from the escrow or trust account pursuant to Rule 419 under the Act.

(h) Any obligation pursuant to Section 4(3) of the Act and this section to deliver a prospectus, other than pursuant to paragraph (g) of this section, may be satisfied by compliance with the provisions of Rule 172 (§ 230.172).

Rule 175. Liability for Certain Statements by Issuers

(a) A statement within the coverage of paragraph (b) of this section which is made by or on behalf of an issuer or by an outside reviewer retained by the issuer shall be deemed not to be a fraudulent statement (as defined in paragraph (d) of this section), unless it is shown that such statement was made or reaffirmed without a reasonable basis or was disclosed other than in good faith.

(b) This rule applies to the following statements:

(1) A forward-looking statement (as defined in paragraph (c) of this section) made in a document filed with the Commission, in Part I of a quarterly report on Form 10-Q, (§ 249.308a of this chapter), or in an annual report to security holders meeting the requirements of Rule 14a-3(b) and (c) or 14c-3(a) and (b) under the Securities Exchange Act of 1934 (§§ 240.14a-3(b) and (c) or 240.14c-3(a) and (b) of this chapter), a statement reaffirming such forward-looking statement after the date the document was filed or the annual report was made publicly available, or a forward looking statement made before the date the document was filed or the date the annual report was publicly available if such statement is reaffirmed in a filed document, in Part I of a quarterly report on Form 10-Q, or in an annual report made publicly available within a reasonable time after the making of such forward-looking statement;

Provided, that

(i) At the time such statements are made or reaffirmed, either the issuer is subject to the reporting requirements of section 13(a) or 15(d) of the Securities Exchange Act of 1934 and has complied with the requirements of Rule 13a-1 or 15d-1 (§§ 239.13a- 1 or 239.15d-1 of this chapter) thereunder, if applicable, to file its most recent annual report on Form 10-K, Form 20-F, or Form 40-F; or if the issuer is not subject to the reporting requirements of Section 13(a) or 15(d) of the Securities Exchange Act of 1934, the statements are made in a registration statement filed under the Act, offering statement or solicitation of interest, written document or broadcast script under Regulation A or pursuant to sections 12(b) or (g) of the Securities Exchange Act of 1934; and

(ii) The statements are not made by or on behalf of an issuer that is an investment company registered under the Investment Company Act of 1940; and

(2) Information that is disclosed in a document filed with the Commission, in Part I of a quarterly report on Form 10-Q (§ 249.308a of this chapter) or in an annual report to shareholders meeting the requirements of Rules 14a-3 (b) and (c) or 14c-3 (a) and (b) under the Securities Exchange Act of 1934 (§§ 240.14a-3(b) and (c) or 240.14c-3(a) and (b) of this chapter) and that relates to:

(i) The effects of changing prices on the business enterprise, presented voluntarily or pursuant to Item 303 of Regulation S-K (§ 229.303 of this chapter), "Management's Discussion and Analysis of Financial Condition and Results of Operations," Item 5 of Form 20-F (§ 249.220(f) of this chapter), "Operating and Financial Review and Prospects," Item 302 of Regulation S-K (§ 229.302 of this chapter), "Supplementary Financial Information," or Rule 3-20(c) of Regulation S-X (§ 210.3-20(c) of this chapter); or

(ii) The value of proved oil and gas reserves (such as a standardized measure of discounted future net cash flows relating to proved oil and gas reserves as set forth in FASB ASC paragraphs 932-235-50-29 through 932-235-50-36 (Extractive Activities—Oil and Gas Topic)) presented voluntarily or pursuant to Item 302 of Regulation S-K (§ 229.302 of this chapter).

(c) For the purpose of this rule the term "forward-looking statement" shall mean and shall be limited to:

(1) A statement containing a projection of revenues, income (loss), earnings (loss) per share, capital expenditures, dividends, capital structure or other financial items;

(2) A statement of management's plans and objectives for future operations;

(3) A statement of future economic performance contained in management's discussion and analysis of financial condition and results of operations included pursuant to Item 303 of Regulation S-K or Item 5 of Form 20-F; or

(4) Disclosed statements of the assumptions underlying or relating to any of the statements described in paragraph (c)(1), (2), or (3) above.

(d) For the purpose of this rule the term "fraudulent statement" shall mean a statement which is an untrue statement of a material fact, a statement false or misleading with respect to any material fact, an omission to state a material fact necessary to make a statement not misleading, or which constitutes the employment of a manipulative, deceptive, or fraudulent device, contrivance, scheme, transaction, act, practice, course of business, or an artifice to defraud, as those terms are used in the Securities Act of 1933 or the rules or regulations promulgated thereunder.

Rule 176. Circumstances Affecting the Determination of What Constitutes Reasonable Investigation and Reasonable Grounds for Belief Under Section 11 of the Securities Act

In determining whether or not the conduct of a person constitutes a reasonable investigation or a reasonable ground for belief meeting the standard set forth in section 11(c), relevant circumstances include, with respect to a person other than the issuer.

(a) The type of issuer;

(b) The type of security;

(c) The type of person;

(d) The office held when the person is an officer;

(e) The presence or absence of another relationship to the issuer when the person is a director or proposed director;

(f) Reasonable reliance on officers, employees, and others whose duties should have given them knowledge of the particular facts (in the light of the functions and responsibilities of the particular person with respect to the issuer and the filing);

(g) When the person is an underwriter, the type of underwriting arrangement, the role of the particular person as an underwriter and the availability of information with respect to the registration; and

(h) Whether, with respect to a fact or document incorporated by reference, the particular person had any responsibility for the fact or document at the time of the filing from which it was incorporated.

Rule 215. Accredited Investor

The term "accredited investor" as used in section 2(15)(ii) of the Securities Act of 1933 [15 U.S.C. 77b(15)(ii)] shall include the following persons:

(a) Any savings and loan association or other institution specified in section 3(a)(5)(A) of the Act whether acting in its individual or fiduciary capacity; any broker or dealer registered pursuant to section 15 of the Securities Exchange Act of 1934; any plan established and maintained by a state, its political subdivisions, or any agency or instrumentality of a state or its political subdivisions, for the benefit of its employees, if such plan has total assets in excess of $5,000,000; any employee benefit plan within the meaning of Title I of the Employee Retirement Income Security Act of 1974, if the investment decision is made by a plan fiduciary, as defined in section 3(21) of such Act, which is a savings and loan association, or if the employee benefit plan has total assets in excess of $5,000,000 or, if a self-directed plan, with investment decisions made solely by persons that are accredited investors;

(b) Any private business development company as defined in section 202(a)(22) of the Investment Advisers Act of 1940;

(c) Any organization described in section 501(c)(3) of the Internal Revenue Code, corporation, Massachusetts or similar business trust, or partnership, not formed for the specific purpose of acquiring the securities offered, with total assets in excess of $5,000,000;

(d) Any director, executive officer, or general partner of the issuer of the securities being offered or sold, or any director, executive officer, or general partner of a general partner of that issuer;

(e) Any natural person whose individual net worth, or joint net worth with that person's spouse, exceeds $ 1,000,000.

(1) Except as provided in paragraph (e)(2) of this section, for purposes of calculating net worth under this paragraph (e):

(i) The person's primary residence shall not be included as an asset;

(ii) Indebtedness that is secured by the person's primary residence, up to the estimated fair market value of the primary residence at the time of the sale of securities, shall not be included as a liability (except that if the amount of such indebtedness outstanding at the time of the sale of securities exceeds the amount outstanding 60 days before such time, other than as a result of the acquisition of the primary residence, the amount of such excess shall be included as a liability); and

(iii) Indebtedness that is secured by the person's primary residence in excess of the estimated fair market value of the primary residence shall be included as a liability.

(2) Paragraph (e)(1) of this section will not apply to any calculation of a person's net worth made in connection with a purchase of securities in accordance with a right to purchase such securities, provided that:

(i) Such right was held by the person on July 20, 2010;

(ii) The person qualified as an accredited investor on the basis of net worth at the time the person acquired such right; and

(iii) The person held securities of the same issuer, other than such right, on July 20, 2010

(f) Any natural person who had an individual income in excess of $200,000 in each of the two most recent years or joint income with that person's spouse in excess of $300,000 in each of those years and has a reasonable expectation of reaching the same income level in the current year;

(g) Any trust, with total assets in excess of $5,000,000, not formed for the specific purpose of acquiring the securities offered, whose purchase is directed by a sophisticated person as described in § 230.506(b)(2)(ii); and

(h) Any entity in which all of the equity owners are accredited investors.

SPECIAL EXEMPTIONS

Rule 236. Exemption of Shares Offered in Connection with Certain Transactions

Shares of stock or similar security offered to provide funds to be distributed to shareholders of the issuer of such securities in lieu of issuing fractional shares, scrip certificates or order forms, in connection with a stock dividend, stock split, reverse stock split, conversion, merger or similar transaction, shall be exempt from registration under the Act if the following conditions are met:

(a) The issuer of such shares is required to file and has filed reports with the Commission pursuant to Section 13 or 15(d) of the Securities Exchange Act of 1934.

(b) The aggregate gross proceeds from the sale of all shares offered in connection with the transaction for the purpose of providing such funds does not exceed $300,000.

(c) At least ten days prior to the offering of the shares, the issuer shall furnish to the Commission in writing the following information: (1) that it proposes to offer shares in reliance upon the exemption provided by this rule; (2) the estimated number of shares to be so offered; (3) the aggregate market value of such shares as of the latest practicable date; and (4) a brief description of the transaction in connection with which the shares are to be offered.

Rule 238. Exemption for Standarized Options

(a) *Exemption*. Except as expressly provided in paragraphs (b) and (c) of this section, the Act does not apply to any standardized option, as that term is defined by section 240.9b-1(a)(4) of this chapter, that is:

(1) Issued by a clearing agency registered under section 17A of the Securities Exchange Act of 1934 (15 U.S.C. 78q-1); and

(2) Traded on a national securities exchange registered pursuant to section 6(a) of the Securities Exchange Act of 1934 (15 U.S.C. 78f(a)) or on a national securities association registered pursuant to section 15A(a) of the Securities Exchange Act of 1934 (15 U.S.C. 78o-3(a)).

(b) *Limitation*. The exemption provided in paragraph (a) of this section does not apply to the provisions of section 17 of the Act (15 U.S.C. 77q).

(c) *Offers and sales*. Any offer or sale of a standardized option by or on behalf of the issuer of the securities underlying the standardized option, an affiliate of the issuer, or an underwriter, will constitute a contract for sale of, sale of, offer for sale, or offer to sell the underlying securities as defined in section 2(a)(3) of the Act (15 U.S.C. 77b(a)(3)).

Rule 239. Exemption for Offers and Sales of Certain Security-Based Swaps

(a) Provided that the conditions of paragraph (b) of this section are satisfied and except as expressly provided in paragraph (c) of this section, the Act does not apply to any offer or sale of a security-based swap that:

(1) Is issued or will be issued by a clearing agency that is either registered as a clearing agency under Section 17A of the Securities Exchange Act of 1934 (15 U.S.C.78q-1) or exempt from registration under Section 17A of the Securities Exchange Act of 1934 pursuant to a rule, regulation, or order of the Commission ("eligible clearing agency"), and

(2) The Commission has determined is required to be cleared or that is permitted to be cleared pursuant to the eligible clearing agency's rules.

(b) The exemption provided in paragraph (a) of this section applies only to an offer or sale of a security-based swap described in paragraph (a) of this section if the following conditions are satisfied:

(1) The security-based swap is offered or sold in a transaction involving the eligible clearing agency in its function as a central counterparty with respect to such security-based swap;

(2) The security-based swap is sold only to an eligible contract participant (as defined in Section 1a(18) of the Commodity Exchange Act (7 U.S.C. 1a(18))); and

(3) The eligible clearing agency posts on its publicly available Web site at a specified Internet address or includes in its agreement covering the security-based swap that the eligible clearing agency provides or makes available to its counterparty the following:

(i) A statement identifying any security, issuer, loan, or narrow-based security index underlying the security-based swap;

(ii) A statement indicating the security or loan to be delivered (or class of securities or loans), or if cash settled, the security, loan, or narrow-based security index (or class of securities or loans) whose value is to be used to determine the amount of the settlement obligation under the security-based swap; and

(iii) A statement of whether the issuer of any security or loan, each issuer of a security in a narrow-based security index, or each referenced issuer underlying the security-based swap is subject to the reporting requirements of Sections 13 or 15(d) of the Securities Exchange Act of 1934 (15 U.S.C. 78m and 78o) and, if not subject to such reporting requirements, whether public information, including financial information, about any such issuer is available and where the information is available.

(c) The exemption provided in paragraph (a) of this section does not apply to the provisions of Section 17(a) of the Act (15 U.S.C. 77q(a)).

REGULATION A—GENERAL EXEMPTIONS
REGULATION A—CONDITIONAL SMALL ISSUES EXEMPTION

Mini-registration

Rule 251. Scope of Exemption

(a) *Tier 1 and Tier 2.* A public offer or sale of eligible securities, as defined in Rule 261 (§ 230.261), pursuant to Regulation A shall be exempt under section 3(b) from the registration requirements of the Securities Act of 1933 (the "Securities Act") (15 U.S.C. 77a *et seq.*).

(1) *Tier 1.* Offerings pursuant to Regulation A in which the sum of all cash and other consideration to be received for the securities being offered ("aggregate offering price") plus the gross proceeds for all securities sold pursuant to other offering statements within the 12 months before the start of and during the current offering of securities ("aggregate sales") does not exceed $20,000,000, including not more than $6,000,000 offered by all selling security-holders that are affiliates of the issuer ("Tier 1 offerings").

(2) *Tier 2.* Offerings pursuant to Regulation A in which the sum of the aggregate offering price and aggregate sales does not exceed $50,000,000, including not more than $15,000,000 offered by all selling security-holders that are affiliates of the issuer ("Tier 2 offerings").

(3) *Additional limitation on secondary sales in first year.* The portion of the aggregate offering price attributable to the securities of selling security-holders shall not exceed 30% of the aggregate offering price of a particular offering in:

(i) The issuer's first offering pursuant to Regulation A; or

(ii) Any subsequent Regulation A offering that is qualified within one year of the qualification date of the issuer's first offering.

Note to Paragraph (a): Where a mixture of cash and non-cash consideration is to be received, the aggregate offering price must be based on the price at which the securities are offered for cash. Any portion of the aggregate offering price or aggregate sales attributable to cash received in a foreign currency must be translated into United States currency at a currency exchange rate in effect on, or at a reasonable time before, the date of the sale of the securities. If securities are not offered for cash, the aggregate offering price or aggregate sales must be based on the value of the consideration as established by bona fide sales of that consideration made within a reasonable time, or, in the absence of sales, on the fair value as determined by an accepted standard. Valuations of non-cash consideration must be reasonable at the time made. If convertible securities or warrants are being offered and such securities are convertible, exercisable, or exchangeable within one year of the offering statement's qualification or at the discretion of the issuer, the underlying securities must also be qualified and the aggregate offering price must include the actual or maximum estimated conversion, exercise, or exchange price of such securities.

(b) *Issuer.* The issuer of the securities:

(1) Is an entity organized under the laws of the United States or Canada, or any State, Province, Territory or possession thereof, or the District of Columbia, with its principal place of business in the United States or Canada;

(2) [Reserved];

(3) Is not a development stage company that either has no specific business plan or purpose, or has indicated that its business plan is to merge with or acquire an unidentified company or companies;

(4) Is not an investment company registered or required to be registered under the Investment Company Act of 1940 (15 U.S.C. 80a-1 *et seq.*) or a business development company as defined in section 2(a)(48) of the Investment Company Act of 1940 (15 U.S.C. 80a-2(a)(48));

(5) Is not issuing fractional undivided interests in oil or gas rights, or a similar interest in other mineral rights;

(6) Is not, and has not been, subject to any order of the Commission entered pursuant to Section 12(j) (15 U.S.C. 78l(j)) of the Securities Exchange Act of 1934 (the "Exchange Act") (15 U.S.C. 78a et seq.) within five years before the filing of the offering statement;

(7) Has filed with the Commission all reports required to be filed, if any, pursuant to Rule 257 (§ 230.257) during the two years before the filing of the offering statement (or for such shorter period that the issuer was required to file such reports); and

(8) Is not disqualified under Rule 262 (§ 230.262).

(c) *Integration with other offerings.* Offers or sales made in reliance on this Regulation A will not be integrated with:

(1) Prior offers or sales of securities; or

(2) Subsequent offers or sales of securities that are:

(i) Registered under the Securities Act, except as provided in Rule 255(e) (§ 230.255(e));

(ii) Exempt from registration under Rule 701 (§ 230.701);

(iii) Made pursuant to an employee benefit plan;

(iv) Exempt from registration under Regulation S (§ 230.901-905);

(v) Made more than six months after the completion of the Regulation A offering; or

(vi) Exempt from registration under Section 4(a)(6) of the Securities Act (15 U.S.C. 77d(a)(6)).

Note to Paragraph (c): If these safe harbors do not apply, whether subsequent offers and sales of securities will be integrated with the Regulation A offering will depend on the particular facts and circumstances.

(d) *Offering conditions*—(1) *Offers.*

(i) Except as allowed by Rule 255 (§ 230.255), no offer of securities may be made unless an offering statement has been filed with the Commission.

(ii) After the offering statement has been filed, but before it is qualified:

(A) Oral offers may be made;

(B) Written offers pursuant to Rule 254 (§ 230.254) may be made; and

(C) Solicitations of interest and other communications pursuant to Rule 255 (§ 230.255) may be made.

(iii) Offers may be made after the offering statement has been qualified, but any written offers must be accompanied with or preceded by the most recent offering circular filed with the Commission for such offering.

(2) *Sales.*

(i) No sale of securities may be made:

(A) Until the offering statement has been qualified;

(B) By issuers that are not currently required to file reports pursuant to Rule 257(b) (§ 230.257(b)), until a Preliminary Offering Circular is delivered at least 48 hours before the sale to any person that before qualification of the offering statement had indicated an interest in purchasing securities in the offering, including those persons that responded to an issuer's solicitation of interest materials; and

(C) In a Tier 2 offering of securities that are not listed on a registered national securities exchange upon qualification, unless the purchaser is either an accredited investor (as defined in Rule 501 (§ 230.501)) or the aggregate purchase price to be paid by the purchaser for the securities (including the actual or maximum estimated conversion, exercise, or exchange price for any underlying securities that have been qualified) is no more than ten percent (10%) of the greater of such purchaser's:

(1) Annual income or net worth if a natural person (with annual income and net worth for such natural person purchasers determined as provided in Rule 501 (§ 230.501)); or

(2) Revenue or net assets for such purchaser's most recently completed fiscal year end if a non-natural person.

Note to Paragraph (d)(2)(i)(C): When securities underlying warrants or convertible securities are being qualified pursuant to Tier 2 of Regulation A one year or more after the qualification of an offering for which investment limitations previously applied, purchasers of the underlying securities for which investment limitations would apply at that later date may determine compliance with the ten percent (10%) investment limitation using the conversion, exercise, or exchange price to acquire the underlying securities at that later time without aggregating such price with the price of the overlying warrants or convertible securities.

(D) The issuer may rely on a representation of the purchaser when determining compliance with the ten percent (10%) investment limitation in this paragraph (d)(2)(i)(C), provided that the issuer does not know at the time of sale that any such representation is untrue.

(ii) In a transaction that represents a sale by the issuer or an underwriter, or a sale by a dealer within 90 calendar days after qualification of the offering statement, each underwriter or dealer selling in such transaction must deliver to each purchaser from it, not later than two business days following the completion of such sale, a copy of the Final Offering Circular, subject to the following provisions:

(A) If the sale was by the issuer and was not effected by or through an underwriter or dealer, the issuer is responsible for delivering the Final Offering Circular as if the issuer were an underwriter;

(B) For continuous or delayed offerings pursuant to paragraph (d)(3) of this rule, the 90 calendar day period for dealers shall commence on the day of the first bona fide offering of securities under such offering statement;

(C) If the security is listed on a registered national securities exchange, no offering circular need be delivered by a dealer more than 25 calendar days after the later of the qualification date of the offering statement or the first date on which the security was bona fide offered to the public;

(D) No offering circular need be delivered by a dealer if the issuer is subject, immediately prior to the time of the filing of the offering statement, to the reporting requirements of Rule 257(b) (§ 230.257(b)); and

(E) The Final Offering Circular delivery requirements set forth in this paragraph may be satisfied by delivering a notice to the effect that the sale was made pursuant to a qualified offering statement that includes the uniform resource locator ("URL"), which, in the case of an electronic-only offering, must be an active hyperlink, where the Final Offering Circular, or the offering statement of which such Final Offering Circular is part, may be obtained on the Commission's Electronic Data Gathering, Analysis and Retrieval System ("EDGAR") and contact information sufficient to notify a purchaser where a request for a Final Offering Circular can be sent and received in response.

(3) *Continuous or delayed offerings.*

(i) Continuous or delayed offerings may be made under this Regulation A, so long as the offering statement pertains only to:

(A) Securities that are to be offered or sold solely by or on behalf of a person or persons other than the issuer, a subsidiary of the issuer, or a person of which the issuer is a subsidiary;

(B) Securities that are to be offered and sold pursuant to a dividend or interest reinvestment plan or an employee benefit plan of the issuer;

(C) Securities that are to be issued upon the exercise of outstanding options, warrants, or rights;

(D) Securities that are to be issued upon conversion of other outstanding securities;

(E) Securities that are pledged as collateral; or

(F) Securities the offering of which will be commenced within two calendar days after the qualification date, will be made on a continuous basis, may continue for a period in excess of 30 calendar days from the date of initial qualification, and will be offered in an amount that, at the time the offering statement is qualified, is reasonably expected to be offered and sold within two years from the initial qualification date. These securities may be offered and sold only if not more than three years have elapsed since the initial qualification date of the offering statement under which they are being offered and sold; provided, however, that if a new offering statement has been filed pursuant to this paragraph (d)(3)(i)(F), securities covered by the prior offering statement may continue to be offered and sold until the earlier of the qualification date of the new offering statement or 180 calendar days after the third anniversary of the initial qualification date of the prior offering statement. Before the end of such three-year period, an issuer may file a new offering statement covering the securities. The new offering statement must include all the information that would be required at that time in an offering statement relating to all offerings that it covers. Before the qualification date of the new offering statement, the issuer may include as part of such new offering statement any unsold securities covered by the earlier offering statement by identifying on the cover page of the new offering circular, or the latest amendment, the amount of such unsold securities being included. The offering of securities on the earlier offering statement will be deemed terminated as of the date of qualification of the new offering statement. Securities may be sold pursuant to this paragraph (d)(3)(i)(F) only if the issuer is current in its annual and semiannual filings pursuant to Rule 257(b) (§ 230.257(b)), at the time of such sale.

(ii) At the market offerings, by or on behalf of the issuer or otherwise, are not permitted under this Regulation A. As used in this paragraph (d)(3)(ii), the term *at the market offering* means an offering of equity securities into an existing trading market for outstanding shares of the same class at other than a fixed price.

(e) *Confidential treatment.* A request for confidential treatment may be made under Rule 406 (§ 230.406) for information required to be filed, and Rule 83 (§ 200.83) for information not required to be filed.

(f) *Electronic filing.* Documents filed or otherwise provided to the Commission pursuant to this Regulation A must be submitted in electronic format by means of EDGAR in accordance with the EDGAR rules set forth in Regulation S-T (17 CFR Part 232).

Rule 252. Offering Statement

(a) *Documents to be included.* The offering statement consists of the contents required by Form 1-A (§ 239.90 of this chapter) and any other material information necessary to make the required statements, in light of the circumstances under which they are made, not misleading.

(b) *Paper, printing, language and pagination.* Except as otherwise specified in this rule, the requirements for offering statements are the same as those specified in Rule 403 (§ 230.403) for registration statements under the Act. No fee is payable to the Commission upon either the submission or filing of an offering statement on Form 1-A, or any amendment to an offering statement.

(c) *Signatures.* The issuer, its principal executive officer, principal financial officer, principal accounting officer, and a majority of the members of its board of directors or other governing body, must sign the offering statement in the manner prescribed by Form 1-A. If a signature is by a person on behalf of any other person, evidence of authority to sign must be filed, except where an executive officer signs for the issuer.

(d) *Non-public submission.* An issuer whose securities have not been previously sold pursuant to a qualified offering statement under this Regulation A or an effective registration statement under the Securities Act may submit a draft offering statement to the Commission for non-public review by the staff of the Commission before public filing, provided that the offering statement shall not be qualified less than 21 calendar days after the public filing with the Commission of:

(1) the initial non-public submission;

(2) all non-public amendments; and

(3) all non-public correspondence submitted by or on behalf of the issuer to the Commission staff regarding such submissions (subject to any separately approved confidential treatment request under Rule 251(e) (§ 230.251(e)).

(e) *Qualification.* An offering statement and any amendment thereto can be qualified only at such date and time as the Commission may determine.

(f) *Amendments.* (1) (i) Amendments to an offering statement must be signed and filed with the Commission in the same manner as the initial filing. Amendments to an offering statement must be filed under cover of Form 1-A and must be numbered consecutively in the order in which filed.

(ii) Every amendment that includes amended audited financial statements must include the consent of the certifying accountant to the use of such accountant's certification in connection with the amended financial statements in the offering statement or offering circular and to being named as having audited such financial statements.

(iii) Amendments solely relating to Part III of Form 1-A must comply with the requirements of paragraph (f)(1)(i) of this rule, except that such amendments may be limited to Part I of Form 1-A, an explanatory note, and all of the information required by Part III of Form 1-A.

(2) Post-qualification amendments must be filed in the following circumstances for ongoing offerings:

(i) At least every 12 months after the qualification date to include the financial statements that would be required by Form 1-A as of such date; or

(ii) To reflect any facts or events arising after the qualification date of the offering statement (or the most recent post-qualification amendment thereof) which, individually or in the aggregate, represent a fundamental change in the information set forth in the offering statement.

Rule 253. Offering Circular

(a) *Contents.* An offering circular must include the information required by Form 1-A for offering circulars.

(b) *Information that may be omitted.* Notwithstanding paragraph (a) of this rule, a qualified offering circular may omit information with respect to the public offering price, underwriting syndicate (including any material relationships between the issuer or selling security-holders and the unnamed underwriters, brokers or dealers), underwriting discounts or commissions, discounts or commissions to dealers, amount of proceeds, conversion rates, call prices and other items dependent upon the offering price, delivery dates, and terms of the securities dependent upon the offering date; provided, that the following conditions are met:

(1) The securities to be qualified are offered for cash.

(2) The outside front cover page of the offering circular includes a bona fide estimate of the range of the maximum offering price and the maximum number of shares or other units of securities to be offered or a bona fide estimate of the principal amount of debt securities offered, subject to the following conditions:

(i) The range must not exceed $2 for offerings where the upper end of the range is $10 or less or 20% if the upper end of the price range is over $10; and

(ii) The upper end of the range must be used in determining the aggregate offering price under Rule 251(a) (§ 230.251(a)).

(3) The offering statement does not relate to securities to be offered by competitive bidding.

(4) The volume of securities (the number of equity securities or aggregate principal amount of debt securities) to be offered may not be omitted in reliance on this paragraph (b).

Note to paragraph (b): A decrease in the volume of securities offered or a change in the bona fide estimate of the offering price range from that indicated in the offering circular filed as part of a qualified offering statement may be disclosed in the offering circular filed with the Commission pursuant to Rule 253(g) (§ 230.253(g)), so long as the decrease in the volume of securities offered or change in the price range would not materially change the disclosure contained in the offering statement at qualification. Notwithstanding the foregoing, any decrease in the volume of securities offered and any deviation from the low or high end of the price range may be reflected in the offering circular supplement filed with the Commission pursuant to Rule 253(g)(1) or (3) (§ 230.253(g)(1) or (3)) if, in the aggregate, the decrease in volume and/or change in price represent no more than a 20% change from the maximum aggregate offering price calculable using the information in the qualified offering statement. In no circumstances may this paragraph be used to offer securities where the maximum aggregate offering price would result in the offering exceeding the limit set forth in Rule 251(a) (§ 230.251(a)) or if the change would result in a Tier 1 offering becoming a Tier 2 offering. An offering circular supplement may not be used to increase the volume of securities being offered. Additional securities may only be offered pursuant to a new offering statement or post-qualification amendment qualified by the Commission.

(c) *Filing of omitted information.* The information omitted from the offering circular in reliance upon paragraph (b) of this rule must be contained in an offering circular filed with the Commission pursuant to paragraph (g) of this rule; except that if such offering circular is not so filed by the later of 15 business days after the qualification date of the offering statement or 15 business days after the qualification of a post-qualification amendment thereto that contains an offering circular, the information omitted in reliance upon paragraph (b) of this rule must be contained in a qualified post-qualification amendment to the offering statement.

(d) *Presentation of information.*

(1) Information in the offering circular must be presented in a clear, concise and understandable manner and in a type size that is easily readable. Repetition of information should be avoided; cross-referencing of information within the document is permitted.

(2) Where an offering circular is distributed through an electronic medium, issuers may satisfy legibility requirements applicable to printed documents by presenting all required information in a format readily communicated to investors.

(e) *Date.* An offering circular must be dated approximately as of the date it was filed with the Commission.

(f) *Cover page legend.* The cover page of every offering circular must display the following statement highlighted by prominent type or in another manner:

The United States Securities and Exchange Commission does not pass upon the merits of or give its approval to any securities offered or the terms of the offering, nor does it pass upon the accuracy or completeness of any offering circular or other solicitation materials. These securities are offered pursuant to an exemption from registration with the Commission; however, the Commission has not made an independent determination that the securities offered are exempt from registration.

(g) *Offering circular supplements.*

(1) An offering circular that discloses information previously omitted from the offering circular in reliance upon Rule 253(b) (§ 230.253(b)) must be filed with the Commission no later than two business days following the earlier of the date of determination of the offering price or the date such offering circular is first used after qualification in connection with a public offering or sale.

(2) An offering circular that reflects information other than that covered in paragraph (g)(1) of this rule that constitutes a substantive change from or addition to the information set forth in the last offering circular filed with the Commission must be filed with the Commission no later than five business days after the date it is first used after qualification in connection with a public offering or sale. If an offering circular filed pursuant to this paragraph (g)(2) consists of an offering circular supplement attached to an offering circular that previously had been filed or was not required to be filed pursuant to paragraph (g) of this rule because it did not contain substantive changes from an offering circular that previously was filed, only the offering circular supplement need be filed under paragraph (g) of this rule, provided that the cover page of the offering circular supplement identifies the date(s) of the related offering circular and any offering circular supplements thereto that together constitute the offering circular with respect to the securities currently being offered or sold.

(3) An offering circular that discloses information, facts or events covered in both paragraphs (g)(1) and (2) must be filed with the Commission no later than two business days following the earlier of the date of the determination of the offering price or the date it is first used after qualification in connection with a public offering or sale.

(4) An offering circular required to be filed pursuant to paragraph (g) of this rule that is not filed within the time frames specified in paragraphs (g)(1)-(3), as applicable, must be filed pursuant to this paragraph (g)(4) as soon as practicable after the discovery of such failure to file.

(5) Each offering circular filed under this rule must contain in the upper right corner of the cover page the paragraph and subparagraph of this rule under which the filing is made, and the file number of the offering statement to which the offering circular relates.

Rule 254. Preliminary Offering Circular

After the filing of an offering statement, but before its qualification, written offers of securities may be made if they meet the following requirements:

(a) *Outside front cover page.* The outside front cover page of the material bears the caption *Preliminary Offering Circular*, the date of issuance, and the following legend, which must be highlighted by prominent type or in another manner:

An offering statement pursuant to Regulation A relating to these securities has been filed with the Securities and Exchange Commission. Information contained in this Preliminary Offering Circular is subject to completion or amendment. These securities may not be sold nor may offers to buy be accepted before the offering statement filed with the Commission is qualified. This Preliminary Offering Circular shall not constitute an offer to sell or the solicitation of an offer to buy nor may there be any sales of these securities in any state in which such offer, solicitation or sale would be unlawful before registration or qualification under the laws of any such state. We may elect to satisfy our obligation to deliver a Final Offering Circular by sending you a notice within two business days after the completion of our sale to you that contains the URL where the Final Offering Circular or the offering statement in which such Final Offering Circular was filed may be obtained.

(b) *Other contents*. The Preliminary Offering Circular contains substantially the information required to be in an offering circular by Form 1-A (§ 239.90 of this chapter), except that certain information may be omitted under Rule 253(b) (§ 230.253(b)) subject to the conditions set forth in such rule.

(c) *Filing*. The Preliminary Offering Circular is filed as a part of the offering statement.

Rule 255. Solicitations of Interest and Other Communications

(a) *Solicitation of interest*. At any time before the qualification of an offering statement, including before the non-public submission or public filing of such offering statement, an issuer or any person authorized to act on behalf of an issuer may communicate orally or in writing to determine whether there is any interest in a contemplated securities offering. Such communications are deemed to be an offer of a security for sale for purposes of the antifraud provisions of the federal securities laws. No solicitation or acceptance of money or other consideration, nor of any commitment, binding or otherwise, from any person is permitted until qualification of the offering statement.

(b) *Conditions*. The communications must:

(1) State that no money or other consideration is being solicited, and if sent in response, will not be accepted;

(2) State that no offer to buy the securities can be accepted and no part of the purchase price can be received until the offering statement is qualified, and any such offer may be withdrawn or revoked, without obligation or commitment of any kind, at any time before notice of its acceptance given after the qualification date;

(3) State that a person's indication of interest involves no obligation or commitment of any kind; and

(4) After the public filing of the offering statement:

(i) State from whom a copy of the most recent version of the Preliminary Offering Circular may be obtained, including a phone number and address of such person;

(ii) Provide the URL where such Preliminary Offering Circular, or the offering statement in which such Preliminary Offering Circular was filed, may be obtained; or

(iii) Include a complete copy of the Preliminary Offering Circular.

(c) *Indications of interest*. Any written communication under this rule may include a means by which a person may indicate to the issuer that such person is interested in a potential offering. This issuer may require the name, address, telephone number, and/or e-mail address in any response form included pursuant to this paragraph (c).

(d) *Revised solicitations of interest*. If solicitation of interest materials are used after the public filing of the offering statement and such solicitation of interest materials contain information that is inaccurate or inadequate in any material respect, revised solicitation of interest materials must be redistributed in a substantially similar manner as such materials were originally distributed. Notwithstanding the foregoing in this paragraph (d), if the only information that is inaccurate or inadequate is contained in a Preliminary Offering Circular provided with the solicitation of interest materials pursuant to paragraphs (b)(4)(i) or (b)(4)(ii) of this rule, no such redistribution is required in the following circumstances:

(1) in the case of paragraph (b)(4)(i) of this rule, the revised Preliminary Offering Circular will be provided to any persons making new inquiries and will be recirculated to any persons making any previous inquiries; or

(2) in the case of paragraph (b)(4)(ii) of this rule, the URL continues to link directly to the most recent Preliminary Offering Circular or to the offering statement in which such revised Preliminary Offering Circular was filed.

(e) *Abandoned offerings*. Where an issuer decides to register an offering under the Securities Act after soliciting interest in a contemplated, but subsequently abandoned, Regulation A offering, the abandoned Regulation A offering would not be subject to integration with the registered offering if the issuer engaged in solicitations of interest pursuant to this rule only to qualified institutional buyers and institutional accredited investors permitted by Section 5(d) of the Securities Act. If the issuer engaged in solicitations of interest to persons other than qualified institutional buyers and institutional accredited investors, an abandoned Regulation A offering would not be subject to integration if the issuer (and any underwriter, broker, dealer, or agent used by the issuer in connection with the proposed offering) waits at least 30 calendar days between the last such solicitation of interest in the Regulation A offering and the filing of the registration statement with the Commission.

Rule 256. Definition of "qualified purchaser"

For purposes of Section 18(b)(3) of the Securities Act [15 USC 77r(b)(3)], a "qualified purchaser" means any person to whom securities are offered or sold pursuant to a Tier 2 offering of this Regulation A.

Rule 257. Periodic and Current Reporting; Exit Report

(a) *Tier 1: Exit report.* Each issuer that has filed an offering statement for a Tier 1 offering that has been qualified pursuant to this Regulation A must file an exit report on Form 1-Z (§ 239.94) not later than 30 calendar days after the termination or completion of the offering.

(b) *Tier 2: Periodic and current reporting.* Each issuer that has filed an offering statement for a Tier 2 offering that has been qualified pursuant to this Regulation A must file with the Commission the following periodic and current reports:

(1) *Annual reports.* An annual report on Form 1-K (§ 239.91) for the fiscal year in which the offering statement became qualified and for any fiscal year thereafter, unless the issuer's obligation to file such annual report is suspended under paragraph (d) of this rule. Annual reports must be filed within the period specified in Form 1-K.

(2) *Special financial report.* (i) A special financial report on Form 1-K or Form 1-SA if the offering statement did not contain the following:

(A) audited financial statements for the issuer's most recent fiscal year (or for the life of the issuer if less than a full fiscal year) preceding the fiscal year in which the issuer's offering statement became qualified; or

(B) unaudited financial statements covering the first six months of the issuer's current fiscal year if the offering statement was qualified during the last six months of that fiscal year.

(ii) The special financial report described in paragraph (b)(2)(i)(A) of this rule must be filed under cover of Form 1-K within 120 calendar days after the qualification date of the offering statement and must include audited financial statements for such fiscal year or other period specified in that paragraph, as the case may be. The special financial report described in paragraph (b)(2)(i)(B) of this rule must be filed under cover of Form 1-SA within 90 calendar days after the qualification date of the offering statement and must include the semiannual financial statements for the first six months of the issuer's fiscal year, which may be unaudited.

(iii) A special financial report must be signed in accordance with the requirements of the form on which it is filed.

(3) *Semiannual report.* A semiannual report on Form 1-SA (§ 239.92) within the period specified in Form 1-SA. Semiannual reports must cover the first six months of each fiscal year of the issuer, commencing with the first six months of the fiscal year immediately following the most recent fiscal year for which full financial statements were included in the offering statement, or, if the offering statement included financial statements for the first six months of the fiscal year following the most recent full fiscal year, for the first six months of the following fiscal year.

(4) *Current reports.* Current reports on Form 1-U (§ 239.93) with respect to the matters and within the period specified in that form, unless substantially the same information has

been previously reported to the Commission by the issuer under cover of Form 1-K or Form 1-SA.

(5) *Reporting by successor issuers.* Where in connection with a succession by merger, consolidation, exchange of securities, acquisition of assets or otherwise, securities of any issuer that is not required to file reports pursuant to paragraph (b) of this rule are issued to the holders of any class of securities of another issuer that is required to file such reports, the duty to file reports pursuant to paragraph (b) of this rule shall be deemed to have been assumed by the issuer of the class of securities so issued. The successor issuer must, after the consummation of the succession, file reports in accordance with paragraph (b) of this rule, unless that issuer is exempt from filing such reports or the duty to file such reports is terminated or suspended under paragraph (d).

(6) *Exchange Act Reporting Requirements.* The duty to file reports under this rule shall be deemed to have been met if the issuer is subject to the reporting requirements of Section 13 or 15(d) of the Exchange Act (15 U.S.C. 78m or 15 U.S.C. 78o) and, as of each Form 1-K and Form 1-SA due date, has filed all reports required to be filed by Section 13 or 15(d) of the Exchange Act (15 U.S.C. 78m or 15 U.S.C. 78o) during the 12 months (or such shorter period that the registrant was required to file such reports) preceding such due date.

(7) *Exemption For Subsidiary Issuers of Guaranteed Securities and Subsidiary Guarantors.* Any issuer of a guaranteed security, or guarantor of a security, that is permitted to omit financial statements by Item (b)(7)(i) of Part F/S of Form 1-A (referenced in § 239.90), Item 7(g)(1) of Part II of Form 1-K (referenced in § 239.91), and Item 3(e) of Form 1-SA (referenced in § 239.92), is exempt from the requirements of Rule 257(b).

(c) *Amendments.* All amendments to the reports described in paragraphs (a) and (b) of this rule must be filed under cover of the form amended, marked with the letter *A* to designate the document as an amendment, *e.g.*, "1-K/A," and in compliance with pertinent requirements applicable to such reports. Amendments filed pursuant to this paragraph (c) must set forth the complete text of each item as amended, but need not include any items that were not amended. Amendments must be numbered sequentially and be filed separately for each report amended. Amendments must be signed on behalf of the issuer by a duly authorized representative of the issuer. An amendment to any report required to include certifications as specified in the applicable form must include new certifications by the appropriate persons.

(d) *Suspension of duty to file reports.*

(1) [Reserved.]

(2) The duty to file reports under paragraph (b) of this rule with respect to a class of securities held of record (as defined in Rule 12g5-1 (§ 240.12g5-1)) by less than 300 persons, or less than 1,200 persons for a bank (as defined in Section 3(a)(6) of the Exchange Act (15 U.S.C. 78c(a)(6)), or a bank holding company (as defined in section 2 of the Bank Holding Company Act of 1956 (12 U.S.C. 1841)), shall be suspended for such class of securities immediately upon filing with the Commission an exit report on Form 1-Z (§ 239.94) if the issuer of such class has filed all reports due pursuant to this rule before the date of such Form 1-Z filing for the shorter of:

(i) The period since the issuer became subject to such reporting obligation; or

(ii) Its most recent three fiscal years and the portion of the current year preceding the date of filing Form 1-Z.

(3) For the purposes of paragraph (d)(2), the term *class* shall be construed to include all securities of an issuer that are of substantially similar character and the holders of which enjoy substantially similar rights and privileges. If the Form 1-Z is subsequently withdrawn or if it is denied because the issuer was ineligible to use the form, the issuer must, within 60 calendar days, file with the Commission all reports which would have been required if such exit report had not been filed. If the suspension resulted from the issuer's merger into, or consolidation with, another issuer or issuers, the notice must be filed by the successor issuer.

(4) The ability to suspend reporting, as described in paragraph (d)(2) of this rule, is not available for any class of securities if:

(i) During that fiscal year a Tier 2 offering statement was qualified;

(ii) The issuer has not filed an annual report under this rule or the Exchange Act for the fiscal year in which a Tier 2 offering statement was qualified; or

(iii) Offers or sales of securities of that class are being made pursuant to a Tier 2 Regulation A offering.

(e) *Termination of Duty to File Reports.* If the duty to file reports is deemed to have been met pursuant to paragraph (b)(6) of this section and such status ends because the issuer terminates or suspends its duty to file reports under the Exchange Act, the issuer's obligation to file reports under paragraph (b) of this section shall:

(1) Automatically terminate if the issuer is eligible to suspend its duty to file reports under paragraphs (d)(2) and (3) of this section; or

(2) Recommence with the report covering the most recent financial period after that included in any effective registration statement or filed Exchange Act report.

(f) *Temporary Relief From Ongoing Reporting Requirements.*

(1) An issuer that is not able to meet a filing deadline for any report or form required to be filed by § 230.252(f)(2)(i) or paragraphs (a) through (c) of this section during the period from and including March 26, 2020, to May 31, 2020, due to circumstances relating to coronavirus disease 2019 (COVID-19) shall be deemed to have satisfied the filing deadline for such report or form if:

(i) The issuer promptly discloses on its public website or provides direct notification to its investors that it is relying on this paragraph (f); and

(ii) The issuer files such report or form with the Commission no later than 45 days after the original filing deadline of the report or form.

(2) In any report or form filed pursuant to paragraph (f)(1)(ii) of this section, the issuer must disclose that it is relying on this paragraph (f) and state the reasons why, in good faith, it could not file such report or form on a timely basis.

Rule 258. Suspension of the Exemption

(a) *Suspension.* The Commission may at any time enter an order temporarily suspending a Regulation A exemption if it has reason to believe that:

(1) No exemption is available or any of the terms, conditions or requirements of Regulation A have not been complied with;

(2) The offering statement, any sales or solicitation of interest material, or any report filed pursuant to Rule 257 (§ 230.257) contains any untrue statement of a material fact or omits to state a material fact necessary in order to make the statements made, in light of the circumstances under which they are made, not misleading;

(3) The offering is being made or would be made in violation of section 17 of the Securities Act;

(4) An event has occurred after the filing of the offering statement that would have rendered the exemption hereunder unavailable if it had occurred before such filing;

(5) Any person specified in Rule 262(a) (§ 230.262(a)) has been indicted for any crime or offense of the character specified in Rule 262(a)(1) (§ 230.262(a)(1)), or any proceeding has been initiated for the purpose of enjoining any such person from engaging in or continuing any conduct or practice of the character specified in Rule 262(a)(2) (§ 230.262(a)(2)), or any proceeding has been initiated for the purposes of Rule 262(a)(3)-(8) (§ 230.262(a)(3)-(8)); or

(6) The issuer or any promoter, officer, director, or underwriter has failed to cooperate, or has obstructed or refused to permit the making of an investigation by the Commission in connection with any offering made or proposed to be made in reliance on Regulation A.

(b) *Notice and hearing.* Upon the entry of an order under paragraph (a) of this rule, the Commission will promptly give notice to the issuer, any underwriter, and any selling security-holder:

(1) That such order has been entered, together with a brief statement of the reasons for the entry of the order; and

(2) That the Commission, upon receipt of a written request within 30 calendar days after the entry of the order, will, within 20 calendar days after receiving the request, order a hearing at a place to be designated by the Commission.

(c) *Suspension order.* If no hearing is requested and none is ordered by the Commission, an order entered under paragraph (a) of this rule shall become permanent on the 30th calendar day after its entry and shall remain in effect unless or until it is modified or vacated by the Commission. Where a hearing is requested or is ordered by the Commission, the Commission will, after notice of and opportunity for such hearing, either vacate the order or enter an order permanently suspending the exemption.

(d) *Permanent suspension.* The Commission may, at any time after notice of and opportunity for hearing, enter an order permanently suspending the exemption for any reason upon which it could have entered a temporary suspension order under paragraph (a) of this rule. Any such order shall remain in effect until vacated by the Commission.

(e) *Notice procedures.* All notices required by this rule must be given by personal service, registered or certified mail to the addresses given by the issuer, any underwriter and any selling security-holder in the offering statement.

Rule 259. Withdrawal or Abandonment of Offering Statements

(a) *Withdrawal.* If none of the securities that are the subject of an offering statement has been sold and such offering statement is not the subject of a proceeding under Rule 258 (§ 230.258), the offering statement may be withdrawn with the Commission's consent. The application for withdrawal must state the reason the offering statement is to be withdrawn and must be signed by an authorized representative of the issuer. Any withdrawn document will remain in the Commission's files, as well as the related request for withdrawal.

(b) *Abandonment.* When an offering statement has been on file with the Commission for nine months without amendment and has not become qualified, the Commission may, in its discretion, declare the offering statement abandoned. If the offering statement has been amended, the nine-month period shall be computed from the date of the latest amendment.

Rule 260. Insignificant Deviations from a Term, Condition or Requirement of Regulation A

(a) *Failure to comply.* A failure to comply with a term, condition or requirement of Regulation A will not result in the loss of the exemption from the requirements of section 5 of the Securities Act for any offer or sale to a particular individual or entity, if the person relying on the exemption establishes that:

(1) The failure to comply did not pertain to a term, condition or requirement directly intended to protect that particular individual or entity;

(2) The failure to comply was insignificant with respect to the offering as a whole, provided that any failure to comply with paragraphs (a), (b), (d)(1) and (3) of Rule 251 (§ 230.251) shall be deemed to be significant to the offering as a whole; and

(3) A good faith and reasonable attempt was made to comply with all applicable terms, conditions and requirements of Regulation A.

(b) *Action by Commission.* A transaction made in reliance upon Regulation A must comply with all applicable terms, conditions and requirements of the regulation. Where an exemption is established only through reliance upon paragraph (a) of this rule, the failure to comply shall nonetheless be actionable by the Commission under section 20 of the Securities Act.

(c) *Suspension.* This provision provides no relief or protection from a proceeding under Rule 258 (§ 230.258).

Rule 261. Definitions

As used in this Regulation A, all terms have the same meanings as in Rule 405 (§ 230.405), except that all references to *registrant* in those definitions shall refer to the issuer of the securities to be offered and sold under Regulation A. In addition, these terms have the following meanings:

(a) *Affiliated issuer.* An affiliate (as defined in Rule 501 (§ 230.501)) of the issuer that is issuing securities in the same offering.

(b) *Business day.* Any day except Saturdays, Sundays or United States federal holidays.

(c) *Eligible securities.* Equity securities, debt securities, and securities convertible or exchangeable to equity interests, including any guarantees of such securities, but not including asset-backed securities as such term is defined in Item 1101(c) of Regulation AB.

(d) *Final order.* A written directive or declaratory statement issued by a federal or state agency described in Rule 262(a)(3) (§ 230.262(a)(3)) under applicable statutory authority that provides for notice and an opportunity for hearing, which constitutes a final disposition or action by that federal or state agency.

(e) *Final offering circular.* The more recent of: the current offering circular contained in a qualified offering statement; and any offering circular filed pursuant to Rule 253(g) (§ 230.253(g)). If, however, the issuer is relying on Rule 253(b) ((§ 230.253(b)), the Final Offering Circular is the most recent of the offering circular filed pursuant to Rule 253(g)(1) or (3) (§ 230.253(g)(1) or (3)) and any subsequent offering circular filed pursuant to Rule 253(g) (§ 230.253(g)).

(f) *Offering statement.* An offering statement prepared pursuant to Regulation A.

(g) *Preliminary offering circular.* The offering circular described in Rule 254 (§ 230.254).

Rule 262. Disqualification Provisions

(a) *Disqualification events.* No exemption under this Regulation A shall be available for a sale of securities if the issuer; any predecessor of the issuer; any affiliated issuer; any director, executive officer, other officer participating in the offering, general partner or managing member of the issuer; any beneficial owner of 20% or more of the issuer's outstanding voting equity securities, calculated on the basis of voting power; any promoter connected with the issuer in any capacity at the time of filing, any offer after qualification, or such sale; any person that has been or will be paid (directly or indirectly) remuneration for solicitation of purchasers in connection with such sale of securities; any general partner or managing member of any such solicitor; or any director, executive officer or other officer participating in the offering of any such solicitor or general partner or managing member of such solicitor:

(1) Has been convicted, within ten years before the filing of the offering statement (or five years, in the case of issuers, their predecessors and affiliated issuers), of any felony or misdemeanor:

(i) In connection with the purchase or sale of any security;

(ii) Involving the making of any false filing with the Commission; or

(iii) Arising out of the conduct of the business of an underwriter, broker, dealer, municipal securities dealer, investment adviser or paid solicitor of purchasers of securities;

(2) Is subject to any order, judgment or decree of any court of competent jurisdiction, entered within five years before the filing of the offering statement, that, at the time of such filing, restrains or enjoins such person from engaging or continuing to engage in any conduct or practice:

(i) In connection with the purchase or sale of any security;

(ii) Involving the making of any false filing with the Commission; or

(iii) Arising out of the conduct of the business of an underwriter, broker, dealer, municipal securities dealer, investment adviser or paid solicitor of purchasers of securities;

(3) Is subject to a final order (as defined in Rule 261 (§ 230.261)) of a state securities commission (or an agency or officer of a state performing like functions); a state authority that supervises or examines banks, savings associations, or credit unions; a state insurance commission (or an agency or officer of a state performing like functions); an appropriate federal banking agency; the U.S. Commodity Futures Trading Commission; or the National Credit Union Administration that:

(i) At the time of the filing of the offering statement, bars the person from:

(A) Association with an entity regulated by such commission, authority, agency, or officer;

(B) Engaging in the business of securities, insurance or banking; or

(C) Engaging in savings association or credit union activities; or

(ii) Constitutes a final order based on a violation of any law or regulation that prohibits fraudulent, manipulative, or deceptive conduct entered within ten years before such filing of the offering statement;

(4) Is subject to an order of the Commission entered pursuant to section 15(b) or 15B(c) of the Securities Exchange Act of 1934 (15 U.S.C. 78o(b) or 78o-4(c)) or section 203(e) or (f) of the Investment Advisers Act of 1940 (15 U.S.C. 80b-3(e) or (f)) that, at the time of the filing of the offering statement:

(i) Suspends or revokes such person's registration as a broker, dealer, municipal securities dealer or investment adviser;

(ii) Places limitations on the activities, functions or operations of such person; or

(iii) Bars such person from being associated with any entity or from participating in the offering of any penny stock;

(5) Is subject to any order of the Commission entered within five years before the filing of the offering statement that, at the time of such filing, orders the person to cease and desist from committing or causing a violation or future violation of:

(i) Any scienter-based anti-fraud provision of the federal securities laws, including without limitation section 17(a)(1) of the Securities Act of 1933 (15 U.S.C. 77q(a)(1)), section 10(b) of the Securities Exchange Act of 1934 (15 U.S.C. 78j(b)) and 17 CFR 240.10b-5, section 15(c)(1) of the Securities Exchange Act of 1934 (15 U.S.C. 78o(c)(1)) and section 206(1) of the Investment Advisers Act of 1940 (15 U.S.C. 80b-6(1)), or any other rule or regulation thereunder; or

(ii) Section 5 of the Securities Act of 1933 (15 U.S.C. 77e).

(6) Is suspended or expelled from membership in, or suspended or barred from association with a member of, a registered national securities exchange or a registered national or affiliated securities association for any act or omission to act constituting conduct inconsistent with just and equitable principles of trade;

(7) Has filed (as a registrant or issuer), or was or was named as an underwriter in, any registration statement or offering statement filed with the Commission that, within five years before the filing of the offering statement, was the subject of a refusal order, stop order, or order suspending the Regulation A exemption, or is, at the time of such filing, the subject of an investigation or proceeding to determine whether a stop order or suspension order should be issued; or

(8) Is subject to a United States Postal Service false representation order entered within five years before the filing of the offering statement, or is, at the time of such filing, subject to a temporary restraining order or preliminary injunction with respect to conduct alleged by the United States Postal Service to constitute a scheme or device for obtaining money or property through the mail by means of false representations.

(b) *Transition, waivers, reasonable care exception.* Paragraph (a) of this rule shall not apply:

(1) With respect to any order under § 230.262(a)(3) or (a)(5) that occurred or was issued before June 19, 2015;

(2) Upon a showing of good cause and without prejudice to any other action by the Commission, if the Commission determines that it is not necessary under the circumstances that an exemption be denied;

(3) If, before the filing of the offering statement, the court or regulatory authority that entered the relevant order, judgment or decree advises in writing (whether contained in the relevant judgment, order or decree or separately to the Commission or its staff) that disqualification under paragraph (a) of this rule should not arise as a consequence of such order, judgment or decree; or

(4) If the issuer establishes that it did not know and, in the exercise of reasonable care, could not have known that a disqualification existed under paragraph (a) of this rule.

Instruction to paragraph (b)(4). An issuer will not be able to establish that it has exercised reasonable care unless it has made, in light of the circumstances, factual inquiry into whether any disqualifications exist. The nature and scope of the factual inquiry will vary based on the facts and circumstances concerning, among other things, the issuer and the other offering participants.

(c) *Affiliated issuers.* For purposes of paragraph (a) of this rule, events relating to any affiliated issuer that occurred before the affiliation arose will be not considered disqualifying if the affiliated entity is not:

(1) In control of the issuer; or

(2) Under common control with the issuer by a third party that was in control of the affiliated entity at the time of such events.

(d) *Disclosure of prior "bad actor" events.* The issuer must include in the offering circular a description of any matters that would have triggered disqualification under paragraphs (a)(3) and (a)(5) of this rule but occurred before June 19, 2015. The failure to provide such information shall not prevent an issuer from relying on Regulation A if the issuer establishes that it did not know and, in the exercise of reasonable care, could not have known of the existence of the undisclosed matter or matters.

NOTE: An issuer will not be able to establish that it has exercised reasonable care unless it has made, in light of the circumstances, factual inquiry into whether any disqualifications exist. The nature and scope of the factual inquiry will vary based on the facts and circumstances concerning, among other things, the issuer and the other offering participants.

Rule 263. Consent to Service of Process

(a) If the issuer is not organized under the laws of any of the states or territories of the United States of America, it shall furnish to the Commission a written irrevocable consent and power of attorney on Form F-X (§ 239.42 of this chapter) at the time of filing the offering statement required by Rule 252 (§ 230.252).

(b) Any change to the name or address of the agent for service of the issuer shall be communicated promptly to the Commission through amendment of the requisite form and referencing the file number of the relevant offering statement.

REGULATION C—REGISTRATION

Rule 400. Application of § 230.400 to § 230.494, Inclusive

Sections 230.400 to 230.494 shall govern every registration of securities under the Act, except that any provision in a form, or an item of Regulation S-K (17 CFR 229.001 *et seq.*) referred to in such form, covering the same subject matter as any such rule shall be controlling unless otherwise specifically provided in §§ 230.400 to 230.494.

Rule 402. Number of Copies—Binding—Signatures

(a) Three copies of the complete registration statement, including exhibits and all other papers and documents filed as a part of the statement, shall be filed with the Commission. Each copy shall be bound, in one or more parts, without stiff covers. The binding shall be made on the side or stitching margin in such manner as to leave the reading matter legible. At least one such copy of every registration shall be signed by the persons specified in section 6(a) of the Act. Unsigned copies shall be conformed.

(b) Ten additional copies of the registration statement, similarly bound, shall be furnished for use in the examination of the registration statement, public inspection, copying and other purposes. Where a registration statement incorporates into the prospectus documents which are required to be delivered with the prospectus in lieu of prospectus presentation, the ten additional copies of the registration statement shall be accompanied by ten copies of such documents. No other exhibits are required to accompany such additional copies.

(c) Notwithstanding any other provision of this section, if a registration statement is filed on Form S-8 (§ 239.16b of this chapter), three copies of the complete registration statement, including exhibits and all other papers and documents filed as a part of the statement, shall be filed with the Commission. Each copy shall be bound, in one or more parts, without stiff covers. The binding shall be made on the side or stitching margin in such manner as to leave the reading matter legible. At least one such copy shall be signed by the persons specified in Section 6(a) of the Act. Unsigned copies shall be conformed. Three additional copies of the registration statement, similarly bound, also shall be furnished to the Commission for use in the examination of the registration statement, public inspection, copying and other purposes. No exhibits are required to accompany the additional copies of registration statements filed on Form S-8.

(d) Notwithstanding any other provision of this section, if a registration statement is filed pursuant to Rule 462(b) (§ 230.462(b)) and Rule 110(d) (§ 230.110(d)), one copy of the complete registration statement, including exhibits and all other papers and documents filed as a part thereof shall be filed with the Commission. Such copy should not be bound and may contain facsimile versions of manual signatures in accordance with paragraph (e) of this section.

(e) *Signatures.* Where the Act or the rules thereunder, including paragraphs (a) and (c) of this section, require a document filed with or furnished to the Commission to be signed, such document shall be manually signed, or signed using either typed signatures or duplicated or facsimile versions of manual signatures. Where typed, duplicated or facsimile signatures are used, each signatory to the filing shall manually sign a signature page or other document authenticating, acknowledging or otherwise adopting his or her signature that appears in the filing. Such document shall be executed before or at the time the filing is made and shall be retained by the registrant for a period of five years. Upon request, the registrant shall furnish to the Commission or its staff a copy of any or all documents retained pursuant to this section.

Rule 404. Preparation of Registration Statement

(a) A registration statement shall consist of the facing sheet of the applicable form a prospectus containing the information called for by Part 1 of such form; the information, list of exhibits, undertakings and signatures required to be set forth in Part II of such form; financial statements and schedules; exhibits; any other information or documents filed as part of the registration statement; and all documents or information incorporated by reference in the foregoing (whether or not required to be filed).

(b) All general instructions, instructions to items of the form, and instructions as to financial statements, exhibits, or prospectuses are to be omitted from the registration statement in all cases.

(c) The prospectus shall contain the information called for by all of the items of Part I of the applicable form, except that unless otherwise specified, no reference need be made to inapplicable items, and negative answers to any item in Part I may be omitted. A copy of the prospectus may be filed as a part of the registration statement in lieu of furnishing the information in item-and-answer form. Wherever a copy of the prospectus is filed in lieu of information in item-and-answer form, the text of the items of the form is to be omitted from the registration statement, as well as from the prospectus, except to the extent provided in paragraph (d) of this rule.

security, limited partnership interest, interest in a joint venture, or certificate of interest in a business trust; any security future on any such security; or any security convertible, with or without consideration into such a security, or carrying any warrant or right to subscribe to or purchase such a security; or any such warrant or right; or any put, call, straddle, or other option or privilege of buying such a security from or selling such a security to another without being bound to do so.

Exchange-Traded Vehicle Security. The term "exchange-traded vehicle security" means a security (A) of an issuer (i) that is not a registered investment company under the Investment Company Act of 1940 and (ii) the assets of which consist primarily of commodities, currencies, or derivative instruments that reference commodities or currencies, or interests in the foregoing, (B) offered or sold in a registered offering on a continuous basis pursuant to Rule 415 by or on behalf of the issuer, (C) of a class of securities that is listed for trading on a national securities exchange at or immediately after the time of effectiveness of the registration statement, and (D) which is able to be purchased or redeemed, subject to conditions or limitations as described in the registration statement for the offering of such security, by the issuer for a ratable share of the issuer's assets (or the cash equivalent thereof) at their net asset value each business day.

Executive officer. The term "executive officer," when used with reference to a registrant, means its president, any vice president of the registrant in charge of a principal business unit, division or function (such as sales, administration or finance), any other officer who performs a policy making function or any other person who performs similar policy making functions for the registrant. Executive officers of subsidiaries may be deemed executive officers of the registrant if they perform such policy making functions for the registrant.

Fiscal year. The term "fiscal year" means the annual accounting period or, if no closing date has been adopted, the calendar year ending on December 31.

Foreign government. The term "foreign government" means the government of any foreign country or of any political subdivision of a foreign country.

Foreign issuer. The term "foreign issuer" means any issuer which is a foreign government, a national of any foreign country or a corporation or other organization incorporated or organized under the laws of any foreign country.

Foreign Private Issuer. (1) The term foreign private issuer means any foreign issuer other than a foreign government except an issuer meeting the following conditions as of the last business day of its most recently completed second fiscal quarter:

    (i) More than 50 percent of the outstanding voting securities of such issuer are directly or indirectly owned of record by residents of the United States; and

    (ii) Any of the following:

        (A) The majority of the executive officers or directors are United States citizens or residents;

        (B) More than 50 percent of the assets of the issuer are located in the United States; or

        (C) The business of the issuer is administered principally in the United States.

Note to Paragraph (1) of the Definition of Foreign Private Issuer: To determine the percentage of outstanding voting securities held by U.S. residents:

    A. Use the method of calculating record ownership in § 240.12g3-2(a) of this chapter, except that:

        (1) The inquiry as to the amount of shares represented by accounts of customers resident in the United States may be limited to brokers, dealers, banks and other nominees located in:

            (i) The United States,

            (ii) The issuer's jurisdiction of incorporation, and

            (iii) The jurisdiction that is the primary trading market for the issuer's voting securities, if different than the issuer's jurisdiction of incorporation; and

(2) Notwithstanding § 240.12g5-1(a)(8) of this chapter, the issuer shall not exclude securities held by persons who received the securities pursuant to an employee compensation plan.

B. If, after reasonable inquiry, the issuer is unable to obtain information about the amount of shares represented by accounts of customers resident in the United States, the issuer may assume, for purposes of this definition, that the customers are residents of the jurisdiction in which the nominee has its principal place of business.

C. Count shares of voting securities beneficially owned by residents of the United States as reported on reports of beneficial ownership provided to the issuer or filed publicly and based on information otherwise provided to the issuer.

(2) In the case of a new registrant with the Commission, the determination of whether an issuer is a foreign private issuer shall be made as of a date within 30 days prior to the issuer's filing of an initial registration statement under either the Act or the Securities Exchange Act of 1934.

(3) Once an issuer qualifies as a foreign private issuer, it will immediately be able to use the forms and rules designated for foreign private issuers until it fails to qualify for this status at the end of its most recently completed second fiscal quarter. An issuer's determination that it fails to qualify as a foreign private issuer governs its eligibility to use the forms and rules designated for foreign private issuers beginning on the first day of the fiscal year following the determination date. Once an issuer fails to qualify for foreign private issuer status, it will remain unqualified unless it meets the requirements for foreign private issuer status as of the last business day of its second fiscal quarter.

Free writing prospectus. Except as otherwise specifically provided or the context otherwise requires, a free writing prospectus is any written communication as defined in this section that constitutes an offer to sell or a solicitation of an offer to buy the securities relating to a registered offering that is used after the registration statement in respect of the offering is filed (or, in the case of a well-known seasoned issuer, whether or not such registration statement is filed) and is made by means other than:

(1) A prospectus satisfying the requirements of section 10(a) of the Act, Rule 430 (§ 230.430), Rule 430A (§ 230.430A), Rule 430B (§ 230.430B), Rule 430C (§ 230.430C), Rule 430D (§ 230.430D), or Rule 431 (§ 230.431);

(2) A written communication used in reliance on Rule 167 and Rule 426 (§ 230.167 and § 230.426);

(3) A written communication that constitutes an offer to sell or solicitation of an offer to buy such securities that falls within the exception from the definition of prospectus in clause (a) of section 2(a)(10) of the Act; or

(4) A written communication used in reliance on Rule 163B (§ 230.163B) or on section 5(d) of the Act.

Graphic communication. The term graphic communication, which appears in the definition of "write, written" in section 2(a)(9) of the Act and in the definition of written communication in this section, shall include all forms of electronic media, including, but not limited to, audiotapes, videotapes, facsimiles, CD-ROM, electronic mail, Internet Web sites, substantially similar messages widely distributed (rather than individually distributed) on telephone answering or voice mail systems, computers, computer networks and other forms of computer data compilation. Graphic communication shall not include a communication that, at the time of the communication, originates live, in real-time to a live audience and does not originate in recorded form or otherwise as a graphic communication, although it is transmitted through graphic means.

Ineligible issuer. (1) An ineligible issuer is an issuer with respect to which any of the following is true as of the relevant date of determination:

(i) Any issuer that is required to file reports pursuant to section 13 or 15(d) of the Securities Exchange Act of 1934 (15 U.S.C. 78m or 78*o*(d)) or section 30 of the Investment Company Act of 1940 (15 U.S.C. 80a-29) that has not filed all reports and other materials required to be filed during the preceding 12 months (or for such shorter period that the issuer was required to file such reports pursuant to sections 13 or 15(d) of the Securities Exchange Act of 1934 or section 30 of the Investment Company Act of 1940), other than reports on Form 8-K (§ 249.308 of this chapter) required solely pursuant to an item specified in General Instruction I.A.3(b) of Form S-3 (§ 239.13 of this chapter) or General Instruction A.2.a of Form N-2 (§ 239.14 and § 274.11a-1 of this chapter) (or in the case of an asset-backed issuer, to the extent the depositor or any issuing entity previously established, directly or indirectly, by the depositor (as such terms are defined in Item 1101 of Regulation AB (§ 229.1101 of this chapter) are or were at any time during the preceding 12 calendar months required to file reports pursuant to section 13 or 15(d) of the Securities Exchange Act of 1934 with respect to a class of asset-backed securities involving the same asset class, such depositor and each such issuing entity must have filed all reports and other material required to be filed for such period (or such shorter period that each such entity was required to file such reports), other than reports on Form 8-K required solely pursuant to an item specified in General Instruction I.A.2 of Form SF-3);

(ii) The issuer is, or during the past three years the issuer or any of its predecessors was:

(A) A blank check company as defined in Rule 419(a)(2) (§ 230.419(a)(2));

(B) A shell company, other than a business combination related shell company, each as defined in this section;

(C) An issuer in an offering of penny stock as defined in Rule 3a51-1 of the Securities Exchange Act of 1934 (§ 240.3a51-1 of this chapter);

(iii) The issuer is a limited partnership that is offering and selling its securities other than through a firm commitment underwriting;

(iv) Within the past three years, a petition under the federal bankruptcy laws or any state insolvency law was filed by or against the issuer, or a court appointed a receiver, fiscal agent or similar officer with respect to the business or property of the issuer subject to the following:

(A) In the case of an involuntary bankruptcy in which a petition was filed against the issuer, ineligibility will occur upon the earlier to occur of:

(1) 90 days following the date of the filing of the involuntary petition (if the case has not been earlier dismissed); or

(2) The conversion of the case to a voluntary proceeding under federal bankruptcy or state insolvency laws; and

(B) Ineligibility will terminate under this paragraph (1)(iv) if an issuer has filed an annual report with audited financial statements subsequent to its emergence from that bankruptcy, insolvency, or receivership process;

(v) Within the past three years, the issuer or any entity that at the time was a subsidiary of the issuer was convicted of any felony or misdemeanor described in paragraphs (i) through (iv) of section 15(b)(4)(B) of the Securities Exchange Act of 1934 (15 U.S.C. 78o(b)(4)(B)(i) through (iv));

(vi) Within the past three years (but in the case of a decree or order agreed to in a settlement, not before [insert date 120 days after publication in the Federal Register]), the issuer or any entity that at the time was a subsidiary of the issuer was made the subject of any judicial or administrative decree or order arising out of a governmental action that:

(A) Prohibits certain conduct or activities regarding, including future violations of, the anti-fraud provisions of the federal securities laws;

(B) Requires that the person cease and desist from violating the anti-fraud provisions of the federal securities laws; or

(C) Determines that the person violated the anti-fraud provisions of the federal securities laws;

(vii) The issuer has filed a registration statement that is the subject of any pending proceeding or examination under section 8 of the Act or has been the subject of any refusal order or stop order under section 8 of the Act within the past three years;

(viii) The issuer is the subject of any pending proceeding under section 8A of the Act in connection with an offering; or

(ix) In the case of an issuer that is a registered closed-end investment company or a business development company, within the past three years any person or entity that at the time was an investment adviser to the issuer, including any sub-adviser, was made the subject of any judicial or administrative decree or order arising out of a governmental action that determines that the investment adviser aided, abetted or caused the issuer to have violated the anti-fraud provisions of the federal securities laws.

(2) An issuer shall not be an ineligible issuer if the Commission determines, upon a showing of good cause, that it is not necessary under the circumstances that the issuer be considered an ineligible issuer. Any such determination shall be without prejudice to any other action by the Commission in any other proceeding or matter with respect to the issuer or any other person.

(3) The date of determination of whether an issuer is an ineligible issuer is as follows:

(i) For purposes of determining whether an issuer is a well-known seasoned issuer, at the date specified for purposes of such determination in paragraph (2) of the definition of well-known seasoned issuer in this section; and

(ii) For purposes of determining whether an issuer or offering participant may use free writing prospectuses in respect of an offering in accordance with the provisions of Rules 164 and 433 (§ 230.164 and § 230.433), at the date in respect of the offering specified in paragraph (h) of Rule 164.

Majority-owned subsidiary. The term "majority-owned subsidiary" means a subsidiary more than 50 percent of whose outstanding securities representing the right, other than as affected by events of default, to vote for the election of directors, is owned by the subsidiary's parent and/or one or more of the parent's other majority-owned subsidiaries.

Material. The term "material," when used to qualify a requirement for the furnishing of information as to any subject, limits the information required to those matters to which there is a substantial likelihood that a reasonable investor would attach importance in determining whether to purchase the security registered.

Officer. The term "officer" means a president, vice president, secretary, treasurer or principal financial officer, comptroller or principal accounting officer, and any person routinely performing corresponding functions with respect to any organization whether incorporated or unincorporated.

Parent. A "parent" of a specified person is an affiliate controlling such person directly, or indirectly through one or more intermediaries.

Predecessor. The term "predecessor" means a person the major portion of the business and assets of which another person acquired in a single succession, or in a series of related successions in each of which the acquiring person acquired the major portion of the business and assets of the acquired person.

Principal underwriter. The term "principal underwriter" means an underwriter in privity of contract with the issuer of the securities as to which he is underwriter, the term "issuer" having the meaning given in sections 2(4) and 2(11) of the Act.

Promoter. (1) The term "promoter" includes—

(i) Any person who, acting alone or in conjunction with one or more other persons, directly or indirectly takes initiative in founding and organizing the business or enterprise of an issuer; or

(ii) Any person who, in connection with the founding and organizing of the business or enterprise of an issuer, directly or indirectly receives in consideration of services or property, or both services and property, 10 percent or more of any class of securities of the issuer or 10 percent or more of the proceeds from the sale of any class of such securities. However, a person who receives such securities or proceeds either solely as underwriting commissions or solely in consideration of property shall not be deemed a promoter within the meaning of this paragraph if such person does not otherwise take part in founding and organizing the enterprise.

(2) All persons coming within the definition of "promoter" in paragraph (1) of this section may be referred to as "founders" or "organizers" or by another term provided that such term is reasonably descriptive of those persons' activities with respect to the issuer.

Prospectus. Unless otherwise specified or the context otherwise requires, the term "prospectus" means a prospectus meeting the requirements of section 10(a) of the Act.

Registered Closed-End Investment Company. The term registered closed-end investment company means a closed-end company, as defined in section 5(a)(2) of the Investment Company Act of 1940 (15 U.S.C. 80a-5(a)(2)), that is registered under the Investment Company Act.

Registrant. The term "registrant" means the issuer of the securities for which the registration statement is filed.

Share. The term "share" means a share of stock in a corporation or unit of interest in an unincorporated person.

Shell company. The term *shell company* means a registrant, other than an asset-backed issuer as defined in Item 1101(b) of Regulation AB, that has:

(1) No or nominal operations; and

(2) Either:

(i) No or nominal assets;

(ii) Assets consisting solely of cash and cash equivalents; or

(iii) Assets consisting of any amount of cash and cash equivalents and nominal other assets.

Significant Subsidiary. The term "significant subsidiary" means a subsidiary, including its subsidiaries, which meets any of the following conditions:

(1) The registrant's and its other subsidiaries' investments in and advances to the subsidiary exceed 10 percent of the total assets of the registrant and its subsidiaries consolidated as of the end of the most recently completed fiscal year (for a proposed combination between entities under common control, this condition is also met when the number of common shares exchanged or to be exchanged by the registrant exceeds 10 percent of its total common shares outstanding at the date the combination is initiated); or

(2) The registrant's and its other subsidiaries' proportionate share of the total assets (after intercompany eliminations) of the subsidiary exceeds 10 percent of the total assets of the registrant and its subsidiaries consolidated as of the end of the most recently completed fiscal year; or

(3) The registrant's and its other subsidiaries' equity in the income from continuing operations before income taxes of the subsidiary exclusive of amounts attributable to any noncontrolling interests exceeds 10 percent of such income of the registrant and its subsidiaries consolidated for the most recently completed fiscal year.

Note 1: A registrant that files its financial statements in accordance with or provides a reconciliation to U.S. Generally Accepted Accounting Principles shall make the prescribed tests using amounts determined under U.S. Generally Accepted Accounting Principles. A foreign private issuer that files its financial statements in accordance with IFRS as issued by the IASB shall make the prescribed tests using amounts determined under IFRS as issued by the IASB.

Computational Note 1 to Paragraph (3): For purposes of making the prescribed income test the following guidance should be applied:

1. When a loss exclusive of amounts attributable to any noncontrolling interests has been incurred by either the parent and its subsidiaries consolidated or the tested subsidiary, but not both, the equity in the income or loss of the tested subsidiary exclusive of amounts

attributable to any noncontrolling interests should be excluded from such income of the registrant and its subsidiaries consolidated for purposes of the computation.

2. If income of the registrant and its subsidiaries consolidated exclusive of amounts attributable to any noncontrolling interests for the most recent fiscal year is at least 10 percent lower than the average of the income for the last five fiscal years, such average income should be substituted for purposes of the computation. Any loss years should be omitted for purposes of computing average income.

Smaller Reporting Company. As used in this part, the term *smaller reporting company* means an issuer that is not an investment company, an asset-backed issuer (as defined in § 229.1101 of this chapter), or a majority-owned subsidiary of a parent that is not a smaller reporting company and that:

(1) Had a public float of less than $250 million; or

(2) Had annual revenues of less than $100 million and either:

(i) No public float; or

(ii) A public float of less than $700 million.

(3) Whether an issuer is a smaller reporting company is determined on an annual basis.

(i) For issuers that are required to file reports under section 13(a) or 15(d) of the Exchange Act:

(A) Public float is measured as of the last business day of the issuer's most recently completed second fiscal quarter and computed by multiplying the aggregate worldwide number of shares of its voting and non-voting common equity held by non-affiliates by the price at which the common equity was last sold, or the average of the bid and asked prices of common equity, in the principal market for the common equity;

(B) Annual revenues are as of the most recently completed fiscal year for which audited financial statements are available; and

(C) An issuer must reflect the determination of whether it came within the definition of smaller reporting company in its quarterly report on Form 10-Q for the first fiscal quarter of the next year, indicating on the cover page of that filing, and in subsequent filings for that fiscal year, whether it is a smaller reporting company, except that, if a determination based on public float indicates that the issuer is newly eligible to be a smaller reporting company, the issuer may choose to reflect this determination beginning with its first quarterly report on Form 10-Q following the determination, rather than waiting until the first fiscal quarter of the next year.

(ii) For determinations based on an initial registration statement under the Securities Act or Exchange Act for shares of its common equity:

(A) Public float is measured as of a date within 30 days of the date of the filing of the registration statement and computed by multiplying the aggregate worldwide number of shares of its voting and non-voting common equity held by non-affiliates before the registration plus, in the case of a Securities Act registration statement, the number of shares of its voting and non-voting common equity included in the registration statement by the estimated public offering price of the shares;

(B) Annual revenues are as of the most recently completed fiscal year for which audited financial statements are available; and

(C) The issuer must reflect the determination of whether it came within the definition of smaller reporting company in the registration statement and must appropriately indicate on the cover page of the filing, and subsequent filings for the fiscal year in which the filing is made, whether it is a smaller reporting company. The issuer must re-determine its status at the end of its second fiscal quarter and then reflect any change in status as provided in paragraph (3)(i)(C) of this definition. In the case of a determination based on an initial Securities Act registration statement, an issuer that was not determined to be a smaller reporting company has the option to re-determine its status at the conclusion of the offering covered by the registration statement based on the actual offering price and number of shares sold.

(iii) Once an issuer determines that it does not qualify for smaller reporting company status because it exceeded one or more of the current thresholds, it will remain unqualified unless when making its annual determination either:

(A) It determines that it's public float was less than $200 million; or

(B) It determines that its public float and its annual revenues meet the requirements for subsequent qualification included in the following chart:

Prior Annual Revenues	Prior Public Float	
	None or less than $700 million	$700 million or more
Less than $100 million	Neither threshold exceeded.	Public float—Less than $560 million; and Revenues—Less than $100 million.
$100 million or more	Public float—None or less than $700 million; and Revenues—Less than $80 million.	Public float—Less than $560 million; and Revenues—Less than $80 million.

Instruction 1 to Definition of "Smaller Reporting Company": A registrant that qualifies as a smaller reporting company under the public float thresholds identified in paragraphs (1) and (3)(iii)(A) of this definition will qualify as a smaller reporting company regardless of its revenues.

Instruction 2 to Definition of "Smaller Reporting Company": A foreign private issuer is not eligible to use the requirements for smaller reporting companies unless it uses the forms and rules designated for domestic issuers and provides financial statements prepared in accordance with U.S. Generally Accepted Accounting Principles.

Subsidiary. A "subsidiary" of a specified person is an affiliate controlled by such person directly, or indirectly through one or more intermediaries. (See also "majority owned subsidiary," "significant subsidiary," "totally held subsidiary" and "wholly owned subsidiary.")

Sub-underwriter. The term *sub-underwriter* means a dealer that is participating as an underwriter in an offering by committing to purchase securities from a principal underwriter for the securities but is not itself in privity of contract with the issuer of the securities.

Succession. The term "succession" means the direct acquisition of the assets comprising a going business, whether by merger, consolidation, purchase, or other direct transfer. The term does not include the acquisition of control of a business unless followed by the direct acquisition of its assets. The terms "succeed" and "successor" have meanings correlative to the foregoing.

Totally held subsidiary. The term "totally held subsidiary" means a subsidiary (1) substantially all of whose outstanding securities are owned by its parent and/or the parent's other totally held subsidiaries, and (2) which is not indebted to any person other than its parent and/or the parent's other totally held subsidiaries in an amount which is material in relation to the particular subsidiary, excepting indebtedness incurred in the ordinary course of business which is not overdue and which matures within one year from the date of its creation, whether evidenced by securities or not.

Voting securities. The term "voting securities" means securities the holders of which are presently entitled to vote for the election of directors.

Well-known seasoned issuer. A well-known seasoned issuer is an issuer that, as of the most recent determination date determined pursuant to paragraph (2) of this definition:

(1)(i) Meets all the registrant requirements of General Instruction I.A. of Form S-3 or Form F-3 (§239.13 or §239.33 of this chapter), or General Instructions A.2.a and A.2.b of Form N-2 (§239.14 and §274.11a-1 of this chapter) and either;

(A) As of a date within 60 days of the determination date, has a worldwide market value of its outstanding voting and non-voting common equity held by non-affiliates of $700 million or more; or

(B) (1) As of a date within 60 days of the determination date, has issued in the last three years at least $1 billion aggregate principal amount of non-convertible securities, other than common equity, in primary offerings for cash, not exchange, registered under the Act; and

(2) Will register only non-convertible securities, other than common equity, and full and unconditional guarantees permitted pursuant to paragraph (1)(ii) of this definition unless, at the determination date, the issuer also is eligible to register a primary offering of its securities relying on General Instruction I.B.1. of Form S-3 or Form F-3 or is eligible to register a primary offering described in General Instruction I.B.1. of Form S-3 relying on General Instruction A.2 of Form N-2.

(3) Provided that as to a parent issuer only, for purposes of calculating the aggregate principal amount of outstanding non-convertible securities under paragraph (1)(i)(B)(1) of this definition, the parent issuer may include the aggregate principal amount of non-convertible securities, other than common equity, of its majority-owned subsidiaries issued in registered primary offerings for cash, not exchange, that it has fully and unconditionally guaranteed, within the meaning of Rule 3-10 of Regulation S-X (§ 210.3-10 of this chapter) in the last three years; or

(ii) Is a majority-owned subsidiary of a parent that is a well-known seasoned issuer pursuant to paragraph (1)(i) of this definition and, as to the subsidiaries' securities that are being or may be offered on that parent's registration statement:

(A) The parent has provided a full and unconditional guarantee, as defined in Rule 3-10 of Regulation S-X, of the payment obligations on the subsidiary's securities and the securities are non-convertible securities, other than common equity;

(B) The securities are guarantees of:

(1) Non-convertible securities, other than common equity, of its parent being registered; or

(2) Non-convertible securities, other than common equity, of another majority-owned subsidiary being registered where there is a full and unconditional guarantee, as defined in Rule 3-10 of Regulation S-X, of such non-convertible securities by the parent; or

(C) The securities of the majority-owned subsidiary meet the conditions of General Instruction I.B.2 of Form S-3 or Form F-3.

(iii) Is not an ineligible issuer as defined in this section.

(iv) Is not an asset-backed issuer as defined in Item 1101 of Regulation AB (§ 229.1101(b) of this chapter).

(v) Is not an investment company registered under the Investment Company Act of 1940 (15 U.S.C. 80a-1 et seq.) other than a registered closed-end investment company.

(2) For purposes of this definition, the determination date as to whether an issuer is a well-known seasoned issuer shall be the latest of:

(i) The time of filing of its most recent shelf registration statement; or

(ii) The time of its most recent amendment (by post-effective amendment, incorporated report filed pursuant to section 13 or 15(d) of the Securities Exchange Act of 1934 (15 U.S.C. 78m or 78o(d) of this chapter), or form of prospectus) to a shelf registration statement for purposes of complying with section 10(a)(3) of the Act (or if such amendment has not been made within the time period required by section 10(a)(3) of the Act, the date on which such amendment is required); or

(iii) In the event that the issuer has not filed a shelf registration statement or amended a shelf registration statement for purposes of complying with section 10(a)(3) of the Act for sixteen months, the time of filing of the issuer's most recent annual report on Form 10-K (§ 249.310 of this chapter), Form 20-F (§ 249.220f of this chapter), or Form N-CSR (§ 249.331 and § 274.128 of this chapter) (or if such report has not been filed by its due date, such due date.

Wholly owned subsidiary. The term "wholly owned subsidiary" means a subsidiary substantially all of whose outstanding voting securities are owned by its parent and/or the parent's other wholly owned subsidiaries.

Written communication. Except as otherwise specifically provided or the context otherwise requires, a written communication is any communication that is written, printed, a radio or television broadcast, or a graphic communication as defined in this section.

Note to definition of "written communication."

A communication that is a radio or television broadcast is a written communication regardless of the means of transmission of the broadcast.

Rule 406. Confidential Treatment of Information Filed with the Commission

Preliminary Notes:

(1) Confidential treatment of supplemental information or other information not required to be filed under the Act should be requested under 17 CFR § 200.83 and not under this rule.

(2) All confidential treatment requests shall be submitted in paper format only, whether or not the filer is an electronic filer. *See* Rule 101(c)(1)(i) of Regulation S-T (§ 232.101(c)(1)(i) of this chapter.

(a) Any person submitting any information in a document required to be filed under the Act may make written objection to its public disclosure by following the procedure in paragraph (b) of this section, which shall be the exclusive means of requesting confidential treatment of information included in any document (hereinafter referred to as the "material filed") required to be filed under the Act, *except* that if the material filed is a registration statement on Form S-8 (§ 239.16b of this chapter) or on Form S-3, F-2, F-3 (§ 239.13, 32 or 33 of this chapter) relating to a dividend or interest reinvestment plan, or on Form S-4 (§ 239.25 of this chapter) complying with General Instruction G of that Form, or if the material filed is a registration statement that does not contain a delaying amendment pursuant to Rule 473 (§ 230.473 of this chapter), the person shall comply with the procedure in paragraph (b) *prior* to the filing of a registration statement.

(b) The person shall omit from the material filed the portion thereof which it desires to keep undisclosed (hereinafter called the "confidential portion"). In lieu thereof, the person shall indicate at the appropriate place in the material filed that the confidential portion has been so omitted and filed separately with the Commission. The person shall file with the material filed:

(1) One copy of the confidential portion, marked "Confidential Treatment", of the material filed with the Commission. The copy shall contain an appropriate identification of the item or other requirement involved and, notwithstanding that the confidential portion does not constitute the whole of the answer or required disclosure, the entire answer or required disclosure, except that in the case where the confidential portion is part of a financial statement or schedule, only the particular financial statement or schedule need be included. The copy of the confidential portion shall be in the same form as the remainder of the material filed;

(2) An application making objection to the disclosure of the confidential portion. Such application shall be on a sheet or sheets separate from the confidential portion, and shall contain (i) an identification of the portion; (ii) a statement of the grounds of the objection referring to and analyzing the applicable exemption(s) from disclosure under § 200.80 of this chapter, the Commission's rule adopted under the Freedom of Information Act (5 U.S.C. 552), and a justification of the period of time for which confidential treatment is sought; (iii) a detailed explanation of why, based on the facts and circumstances of the particular case, disclosure of the information is unnecessary for the protection of investors; (iv) a written consent to the furnishing of the confidential portion to

other government agencies, offices or bodies and to the Congress; and (v) the name, address and telephone number of the person to whom all notices and orders issued under this rule at any time should be directed.

(3) The copy of the confidential portion and the application filed in accordance with this paragraph (b) shall be enclosed in a separate envelope marked "Confidential Treatment" and addressed to the Secretary, Securities and Exchange Commission, Washington, D.C. 20549.

(c) Pending a determination as to the objection, the material for which confidential treatment has been applied will not be made available to the public.

(d) If it is determined by the Division, acting pursuant to delegated authority, that the application should be granted, an order to that effect will be entered, and a notation to that effect will be made at the appropriate place in the material filed. Such a determination will not preclude reconsideration whenever appropriate, such as upon receipt of any subsequent request under the Freedom of Information Act and, if appropriate, revocation of the confidential status of all or a portion of the information in question.

(e) If the Commission denies the application, or the Division, acting pursuant to delegated authority, denies the application and Commission review is not sought pursuant to § 201.431 of this chapter, confirmed telegraphic notice of the order of denial will be sent to the person named in the application pursuant to paragraph (b)(2)(v) of this section. In such case, if the material filed may be withdrawn pursuant to an applicable statute, rule, or regulation, the registrant shall have the right to withdraw the material filed in accordance with the terms of the applicable statute, rule, or regulation, but without the necessity of stating any grounds for the withdrawal or of obtaining the further assent of the Commission. In the event of such withdrawal, the confidential portion will be returned to the registrant. If the material filed may not be so withdrawn, the confidential portion will be made available for public inspection in the same manner as if confidential treatment had been revoked under paragraph (h) of this section.

(f) If a right of withdrawal pursuant to paragraph (e) of this section is not exercised, the confidential portion will be made available for public inspection as part of the material filed, and the registrant shall amend the material filed to include all information required to be set forth in regard to such confidential portion.

(g) In any case where a prior grant of confidential treatment has been revoked, the person named in the application pursuant to paragraph (b)(2)(v) of this section will be so informed by registered or certified mail. Pursuant to § 201.26 of this chapter, persons making objections to disclosure may petition the Commission for review of a determination by the Division revoking confidential treatment.

(h) Upon revocation of confidential treatment, the confidential portion shall be made available to the public at the time and according to the conditions specified in paragraphs (h)(1)—(2):

(1) Upon the lapse of five days after the dispatch of notice by registered or certified mail of a determination disallowing an objection, if prior to the lapse of such five days the person shall not have communicated to the Secretary of the Commission his intention to seek review by the Commission under § 201.431 of this chapter of the determination made by the Division; or

(2) If such a petition for review shall have been filed under § 201.431 of this chapter, upon final disposition adverse to the petitioner.

(i) If the confidential portion is made available to the public, one copy thereof shall be attached to each copy of the material filed with the Commission.

Rule 408. Additional Information

(a) In addition to the information expressly required to be included in a registration statement, there shall be added such further material information, if any, as may be necessary to make the required statements, in the light of the circumstances under which they are made, not misleading.

(b) Notwithstanding paragraph (a) of this section, unless otherwise required to be included in the registration statement, the failure to include in a registration statement information included in a free writing prospectus will not, solely by virtue of inclusion of the information in a free writing prospectus (as defined in Rule 405 (§ 230.405)), be considered an omission of material information required to be included in the registration statement.

Rule 409. Information Unknown or Not Reasonably Available

Information required need be given only insofar as it is known or reasonably available to the registrant. If any required information is unknown and not reasonably available to the registrant, either because the obtaining thereof would involve unreasonable effort or expense, or because it rests peculiarly within the knowledge of another person not affiliated with the registrant, the information may be omitted, subject to the following conditions:

(a) The registrant shall give such information on the subject as it possesses or can acquire without unreasonable effort or expense, together with the sources thereof.

(b) The registrant shall include a statement either showing that unreasonable effort or expense would be involved or indicating the absence of any affiliation with the person within whose knowledge the information rests and stating the result of a request made to such person for the information.

Rule 410. Disclaimer of Control

If the existence of control is open to reasonable doubt in any instance, the registrant may disclaim the existence of control and any admission thereof; in such case, however, the registrant shall state the material facts pertinent to the possible existence of control.

Rule 411. Incorporation By Reference

(a) *Prospectus.* Except as provided by this section, Item 1100(c) of Regulation AB (§ 229.1100(c) of this chapter) for registered offerings of asset-backed securities, or unless otherwise provided in the appropriate form, information must not be incorporated by reference into the prospectus. Where a summary or outline of the provisions of any document is required in the prospectus, the summary or outline may incorporate by reference particular items, sections or paragraphs of any exhibit and may be qualified in its entirety by such reference. In any financial statements, incorporating by reference, or cross-referencing to, information outside of the financial statements is not permitted unless otherwise specifically permitted or required by the Commission's rules or by U.S. Generally Accepted Accounting Principles or International Financial Reporting Standards as issued by the International Accounting Standards Board, whichever is applicable.

(b) *Information Not Required in a Prospectus.* Information may be incorporated by reference in answer, or partial answer, to any item of a registration statement that calls for information not required to be included in a prospectus. Except as provided in the Commission's rules or by U.S. Generally Accepted Accounting Principles or International Financial Reporting Standards as issued by the International Accounting Standards Board, whichever is applicable, financial information required to be given in comparative form for two or more fiscal years or periods must not be incorporated by reference unless the information incorporated by reference includes the entire period for which the comparative data is given. In any financial statements, incorporating by reference, or cross-referencing to, information outside of the financial statements is not permitted unless otherwise specifically permitted or required by the Commission's rules or by U.S. Generally Accepted Accounting Principles or International Financial Reporting Standards as issued by the International Accounting Standards Board, whichever is applicable.

(c) *Exhibits.* Any document or part thereof filed with the Commission pursuant to any Act administered by the Commission may be incorporated by reference as an exhibit to any registration statement filed with the Commission by the same or any other person. If any modification has occurred in the text of any document incorporated by reference since the filing thereof, the registrant must file with the reference a statement containing the text of such modification and the date thereof.

(d) *Hyperlinks.* Include an active hyperlink to information incorporated into a registration statement or prospectus by reference if such information is publicly available on the Commission's Electronic Data Gathering, Analysis and Retrieval System ("EDGAR") at the time the registration statement or prospectus is filed. For hyperlinking to exhibits, please refer to Item 601 of Regulation S-K (§ 229.601 of this chapter) or the appropriate form.

(e) *General.* Include an express statement clearly describing the specific location of the information you are incorporating by reference. The statement must identify the document where the information was originally filed or submitted and the location of the information within that document. The statement must be made at the particular place where the information is required, if applicable. Information must not be incorporated by reference in any case where such incorporation would render the disclosure incomplete, unclear, or confusing. For example, unless expressly permitted or required, disclosure must not be incorporated by reference from a second document if that second document incorporates information pertinent to such disclosure by reference to a third document.

Rule 412. Modified or Superseded Documents

(a) Any statement contained in a document incorporated or deemed to be incorporated by reference or deemed to be part of a registration statement or the prospectus that is part of the registration statement shall be deemed to be modified or superseded for purposes of the registration statement or the prospectus that is part of the registration statement to the extent that a statement contained in the prospectus that is part of the registration statement or in any other subsequently filed document which also is or is deemed to be incorporated by reference or deemed to be part of the registration statement or prospectus that is part of the registration statement modifies or replaces such statement. Any statement contained in a document that is deemed to be incorporated by reference or deemed to be part of a registration statement or the prospectus that is part of the registration statement after the most recent effective date or after the date of the most recent prospectus that is part of the registration statement may modify or replace existing statements contained in the registration statement or the prospectus that is part of the registration statement.

(b) The modifying or superseding statement may, but need not, state that it has modified or superseded a prior statement or include any other information set forth in the document which is not so modified or superseded. The making of a modifying or superseding statement shall not be deemed an admission that the modified or superseded statement, when made, constituted an untrue statement of a material fact, an omission to state a material fact necessary to make a statement not misleading, or the employment of a manipulative, deceptive, or fraudulent device, contrivance, scheme, transaction, act, practice, course of business or artifice to defraud, as those terms are used in the Act, the Securities Exchange Act of 1934, the Investment Company Act of 1940, or the rules and regulations thereunder.

(c) Any statement so modified shall not be deemed in its unmodified form to constitute part of the registration statement or prospectus for purpose of the Act. Any statement so superseded shall not be deemed to constitute a part of the registration statement or the prospectus for purpose of the Act.

Rule 413. Registration of Additional Securities and Additional Classes of Securities

(a) Except as provided in section 24(f) of the Investment Company Act of 1940 (15 U.S.C. 80a-24(f)) and in paragraph (b) of this section, where a registration statement is already in effect, the registration of additional securities shall only be effected through a separate registration statement relating to the additional securities.

(b) Notwithstanding paragraph (a) of this section, the following additional securities or additional classes of securities may be added to an automatic shelf registration statement already in effect by filing a post-effective amendment to that automatic shelf registration statement:

(1) Securities of a class different than those registered on the effective automatic shelf registration statement identified as provided in Rule 430B(a) (§ 230.430B(a)); or

(2) Securities of a majority-owned subsidiary that are permitted to be included in an automatic shelf registration statement, provided that the subsidiary and the securities are identified as provided in Rule 430B and the subsidiary satisfies the signature requirements of an issuer in the post-effective amendment.

Rule 415. Delayed or Continuous Offering and Sale of Securities

(a) Securities may be registered for an offering to be made on a continuous or delayed basis in the future. *Provided,* That—

(1) The registration statement pertains only to:

(i) Securities which are to be offered or sold solely by or on behalf of a person or persons other than the registrant, a subsidiary of the registrant or a person of which the registrant is a subsidiary;

(ii) Securities which are to be offered and sold pursuant to a dividend or interest reinvestment plan or an employee benefit plan of the registrant;

(iii) Securities which are to be issued upon the exercise of outstanding options, warrants or rights;

(iv) Securities which are to be issued upon conversion of other outstanding securities;

(v) Securities which are pledged as collateral;

(vi) Securities which are registered on Form F-6 (§ 239.36 of this chapter);

(vii) Asset-backed securities (as defined in 17 CFR 229.1101(c)) registered (or qualified to be registered) on Form SF-3 (§ 239.45 of this chapter) which are to be offered and sold on an immediate or delayed basis by or on behalf of the registrant;

Instruction to Paragraph (a)(1)(vii): The requirements of General Instruction I.B.1 of Form SF-3 (§ 239.45 of this chapter) must be met for any offerings of an asset-backed security (as defined in 17 CFR 229.1101(c)) registered in reliance on this paragraph (a)(1)(vii).

(viii) Securities which are to be issued in connection with business combination transactions;

(ix) Securities, other than asset-backed securities (as defined in 17 CFR 229.1101(c)), the offering of which will be commenced promptly, will be made on a continuous basis and may continue for a period in excess of 30 days from the date of initial effectiveness;

(x) Securities registered (or qualified to be registered) on Form S-3 or Form F-3 (§ 239.13 or § 239.33 of this chapter), or on Form N-2 (§ 239.14 and § 274.11a-1 of this chapter) pursuant to General Instruction A.2 of that form, which are to be offered and sold on an immediate, continuous or delayed basis by or on behalf of the registrant, a majority-owned subsidiary of the registrant or a person of which the registrant is a majority-owned subsidiary; or

(xi) Shares of common stock which are to be offered and sold on a delayed or continuous basis by or on behalf of a registered closed-end investment company or business development company that makes periodic repurchase offers pursuant to § 270.23c-3 of this chapter.

(xii) Asset-backed securities (as defined in 17 CFR 229.1101(c)) that are to be offered and sold on a continuous basis if the offering is commenced promptly and being conducted on the condition that the consideration paid for such securities will be promptly refunded to the purchaser unless:

(A) All of the securities being offered are sold at a specified price within a specified time; and

(B) The total amount due to the seller is received by him by a specified date.

(2) Securities in paragraph (a)(1)(viii) of this section and securities in paragraph (a)(1)(ix) of this section that are not registered on Form S-3 or Form F-3 (§ 239.13 or § 239.33 of this chapter), or on Form N-2 (§ 239.14 and § 274.11a-1 of this chapter) pursuant to General Instruction A.2 of that form, may only be registered in an amount which, at the time the registration statement becomes effective, is reasonably expected to be offered and sold within two years from the initial effective date of the registration.

(3) The registrant furnishes the undertakings required by Item 512(a) of Regulation S-K (§ 229.512(a) of this chapter) except that a registrant that is an investment company filing on Form N-2 must furnish the undertakings required by Item 34.4 of Form N-2 (§§ 239.14 and 274.11a-1 of this chapter).

(4) In the case of a registration statement pertaining to an at the market offering of equity securities by or on behalf of the registrant, the offering must come within paragraph (a)(1)(x) of this section. As used in this paragraph, the term "at the market offering" means an offering of equity securities into an existing trading market for outstanding shares of the same class at other than a fixed price.

(5) Securities registered on an automatic shelf registration statement and securities described in paragraphs (a)(1)(vii), (ix), and (x) of this section may be offered and sold only if not more than three years have elapsed since the initial effective date of the registration statement under which they are being offered and sold, provided, however, that if a new registration statement has been filed pursuant to paragraph (a)(6) of this section:

(i) If the new registration statement is an automatic shelf registration statement, it shall be immediately effective pursuant to Rule 462(e) (§ 230.462(e)); or

(ii) If the new registration statement is not an automatic shelf registration statement:

(A) Securities covered by the prior registration statement may continue to be offered and sold until the earlier of the effective date of the new registration statement or 180 days after the third anniversary of the initial effective date of the prior registration statement; and

(B) A continuous offering of securities covered by the prior registration statement that commenced within three years of the initial effective date may continue until the effective date of the new registration statement if such offering is permitted under the new registration statement.

(6) Prior to the end of the three-year period described in paragraph (a)(5) of this section, an issuer may file a new registration statement covering securities described in such paragraph (a)(5) of this section, which may, if permitted, be an automatic shelf registration statement. The new registration statement and prospectus included therein must include all the information that would be required at that time in a prospectus relating to all offering(s) that it covers. Prior to the effective date of the new registration statement (including at the time of filing in the case of an automatic shelf registration statement), the issuer may include on such new registration statement any unsold securities covered by the earlier registration statement by identifying on the bottom of the facing page of the new registration statement or latest amendment thereto the amount of such unsold securities being included and any filing fee paid in connection with such unsold securities, which will continue to be applied to such unsold securities. The offering of securities on the earlier registration statement will be deemed terminated as of the date of effectiveness of the new registration statement.

(b) This section shall not apply to any registration statement pertaining to securities issued by a face-amount certificate company or redeemable securities issued by an open-end management company or unit investment trust under the Investment Company Act of 1940 or any registration statement filed by any foreign government or political subdivision thereof.

Rule 418. Supplemental Information

(a) The Commission or its staff may, where it is deemed appropriate, request supplemental information concerning the registrant, the registration statement, the distribution of the securities, market activities and underwriters' activities. Such information includes, but is not limited to, the following items which the registrant should be prepared to furnish promptly upon request:

(1) (i) Any reports or memoranda which have been prepared for external use by the registrant or a principal underwriter, as defined in Rule 405 (§ 230.405), in connection with the proposed offering;

(ii) A statement as to the actual or proposed use and distribution of the reports or memoranda specified in paragraph (a) (1) (i) of this section, identifying each class of persons who have received or will receive such reports or memoranda and the number of copies distributed to each such class;

(2) In the case of a registration statement relating to a business combination as defined in Rule 145(a) (17 CFR 230.145(a)), exchange offer, tender offer or similar transaction, any feasibility studies, management analyses, fairness opinions or similar reports prepared by or for any of the parties to the subject transaction in connection with such transaction;

(3) Except in the case of a registrant eligible to use Form S-3 (§ 239.13 of this chapter) or Form N-2 (§ 239.14 and § 274.11a-1 of this chapter) under General Instruction A.2 of that form, any engineering, management or similar reports or memoranda relating to broad aspects of the business, operations or products of the registrant, which have been prepared within the past twelve months for or by the registrant and any affiliate of the registrant or any principal underwriter, as defined in Rule 405 (§ 230.405), of the securities being registered except for:

(i) Reports solely comprised of recommendations to buy, sell or hold the securities of the registrant, unless such recommendations have changed within the past six months; and

(ii) Any information contained in documents already filed with the Commission.

(4) Where there is a registration of an at-the-market offering, as defined in § 242.100 of this chapter, of more than 10 percent of the securities outstanding, where the offering includes securities owned by officers, directors or affiliates of the registrant and where there is no underwriting agreement, information (i) concerning contractual arrangements between selling security holders of a limited group or of several groups of related share-holders to comply with the anti-manipulation rules until the offering by all members of the group is completed and to inform the exchange, brokers and selling security holders when the distribution by the members of the group is over, or (ii) concerning the registrant's efforts to notify members of a large group of unrelated sellers of the applicable Commission rules and regulations;

(5) Where the registrant recently has introduced a new product or has begun to do business in a new industry segment or has made public its intentions to introduce a new product or to do business in a new industry segment, and this action requires the investment of a material amount of the assets of the registrant or otherwise is material, copies of any studies prepared for the registrant by outside persons or any internal studies, documents, reports or memoranda the contents of which were material to the decision to develop the product or to do business in the new segment including, but not limited to, documents relating to financial requirements and engineering, competitive, environmental and other considerations, but excluding technical documents;

(6) Where reserve estimates are referred to in a document, a copy of the full report of the engineer or other expert who estimated the reserves;

(7) With respect to the extent of the distribution of a preliminary prospectus, information concerning:

(i) The date of the preliminary prospectus distributed;

(ii) The dates of approximate dates of distribution;

(iii) The number of prospective underwriters and dealers to whom the preliminary prospectus was furnished;

(iv) The number of prospectuses so distributed;

(v) The number of prospectuses distributed to others, identifying them in general terms; and

(vi) The steps taken by such underwriters and dealers to comply with the provisions of Rule 15c2-8 under the Securities Exchange Act of 1934 (§ 240.15c2-8 of this chapter).

(8) Any free writing prospectuses used in connection with the offering.

(b) Supplemental information described in paragraph (a) of this section shall not be required to be filed with or deemed part of and included in the registration statement, unless otherwise required. The information shall be returned to the registrant upon request, provided that:

(1) Such request is made at the time such information is furnished to the staff;

(2) The return of such information is consistent with the protection of investors;

(3) The return of such information is consistent with the provisions of the Freedom of Information Act [5 U.S.C. 552];

(4) The information was not filed in electronic format.

Rule 419. Offerings by Blank Check Companies

(a) *Scope of the Rule and Definitions.*

(1) The provisions of this section shall apply to every registration statement filed under the Act relating to an offering by a blank check company.

(2) For purposes of this Section, the term "blank check company" shall mean a company that:

(i) is a development stage company that has no specific business plan or purpose or has indicated that its business plan is to engage in a merger or acquisition with an unidentified company or companies, or other entity or person; and

(ii) is issuing "penny stock," as defined in Rule 3a51-1 [17 CFR 240.3a51-1] under the Securities Exchange Act of 1934 ("Exchange Act").

(3) For purposes of this section, the term "purchaser" shall mean any person acquiring securities directly or indirectly in the offering, for cash or otherwise, including promoters or others receiving securities as compensation in connection with the offering.

(b) *Deposit of Securities and Proceeds in Escrow or Trust Account.*

(1) *General.*

(i) Except as otherwise provided in this section or prohibited by other applicable law, all securities issued in connection with an offering by a blank check company and the gross proceeds from the offering shall be deposited promptly into:

(A) an escrow account maintained by an "insured depository institution," as that term is defined in Section 3(c)(2) of the Federal Deposit Insurance Act [12 U.S.C. 1813(c)(2) (1991)]; or

(B) a separate bank account established by a broker or dealer registered under the Exchange Act maintaining net capital equal to or exceeding $25,000 (as calculated pursuant to Exchange Act Rule 15c3-1 [17 CFR 240.15c3-1]), in which the broker or dealer acts as trustee for persons having the beneficial interests in the account.

(ii) If funds and securities are deposited into an escrow account maintained by an insured depository institution, the deposit account records of the insured depository institution must provide that funds in the escrow account are held for the benefit of the purchasers named and identified in accordance with section 330.1 of the regulations of the Federal Deposit Insurance Corporation [12 CFR 330.1], and the records of the escrow agent, maintained in good faith and in the regular course of business, must show the name and interest of each party to the account. If funds and securities are deposited in a separate bank account established by a broker or dealer acting as a trustee, the books and records of the broker-dealer must indicate the name, address, and interest of each person for whom the account is held.

(2) *Deposit and Investment of Proceeds.*

(i) All offering proceeds, after deduction of cash paid for underwriting commissions, underwriting expenses and dealer allowances, and amounts permitted to be released to the registrant pursuant to (b)(2)(vi) of this section, shall be deposited promptly into the escrow or trust account; *provided, however,* that no deduction may be made for underwriting commissions, underwriting expenses or dealer allowances payable to an affiliate of the registrant.

(ii) Deposited proceeds shall be in the form of checks, drafts, or money orders payable to the order of the escrow agent or trustee.

(iii) Deposited proceeds and interest or dividends thereon, if any, shall be held for the sole benefit of the purchasers of the securities.

(iv) Deposited proceeds shall be invested in one of the following:

(A) an obligation that constitutes a "deposit," as that term is defined in section 3(*l*) of the Federal Deposit Insurance Act [12 U.S.C. 1813(*l*) (1991)];

(B) securities of any open-end investment company registered under the Investment Company Act of 1940 [15 U.S.C. 80a-1 *et. seq.*] that holds itself out as a money market fund meeting the conditions of paragraph (d) of Rule 2a-7 [17 CFR 270.2a-7] under the Investment Company Act; or

(C) securities that are direct obligations of, or obligations guaranteed as to principal or interest by, the United States.

Note to Rule 419(b)(2)(iv): Issuers are cautioned that investments in government securities are inappropriate unless such securities can be readily sold or otherwise disposed of for cash at the time required without any dissipation of offering proceeds invested.

(v) Interest or dividends earned on the funds, if any, shall be held in the escrow or trust account until the funds are released in accordance with the provisions of this section. If funds held in the escrow or trust account are released to a purchaser of the securities, the purchasers shall receive interest or dividends earned, if any, on such funds up to the date of release. If funds held in the escrow or trust account are released to the registrant, interest or dividends earned on such funds up to the date of release may be released to the registrant.

(vi) The registrant may receive up to 10 percent of the proceeds remaining after payment of underwriting commissions, underwriting expenses and dealer allowances permitted by paragraph (b)(2)(i) of this section, exclusive of interest or dividends, as those proceeds are deposited into the escrow or trust account.

(3) *Deposit of Securities.*

(i) All securities issued in connection with the offering, whether or not for cash consideration, and any other securities issued with respect to such securities, including securities issued with respect to stock splits, stock dividends, or similar rights, shall be deposited directly into the escrow or trust account promptly upon issuance. The identity of the purchaser of the securities shall be included on the stock certificates or other documents evidencing such securities. *See also* 17 CFR 240.15g-8 regarding restrictions on sales of, or offers to sell, securities deposited in the escrow or trust account.

(ii) Securities held in the escrow or trust account are to remain as issued and deposited and shall be held for the sole benefit of the purchasers, who shall have voting rights, if any, with respect to securities held in their names, as provided by applicable state law. No transfer or other disposition of securities held in the escrow or trust account or any interest related to such securities shall be permitted other than by will or the laws of descent and distribution, or pursuant to a qualified domestic relations order as defined by the Internal Revenue Code of 1986 as amended [26 U.S.C. 1 *et seq.*], or Title 1 of the Employee Retirement Income Security Act [29 U.S.C. 1001 *et seq.*], or the rules thereunder.

(iii) Warrants, convertible securities or other derivative securities relating to securities held in the escrow or trust account may be exercised or converted in accordance with their terms; *provided, however,* that securities received upon exercise or conversion, together with any cash or other consideration paid in connection with the exercise or conversion, are promptly deposited into the escrow or trust account.

(4) *Escrow or Trust Agreement.* A copy of the executed escrow or trust agreement shall be filed as an exhibit to the registration statement and shall contain the provisions of paragraphs (b)(2), and (e)(3) of this section.

(5) *Request for Supplemental Information.* Upon request by the Commission or the staff, the registrant shall furnish as supplemental information the names and addresses of persons for whom securities are held in the escrow or trust account.

Note to Rule 419(b): With respect to a blank check offering subject to both Rule 419 and Exchange Act Rule 15c2-4 17 CFR 240.15c2-4], the requirements of Rule 15c2-4 are applicable only until the conditions of the offering governed by tha Rule are met (*e.g.,* reaching the minimum in a "part-or-none" offering). When those conditions are satisfied, Rule 419 continues to govern the use of offering proceeds.

(c) *Disclosure of Offering Terms.*

The initial registration statement shall disclose the specific terms of the offering, including, but not limited to:

(1) the terms and provisions of the escrow or trust agreement and the effect thereof upon the registrant's right to receive funds and the effect of the escrow or trust agreement upon the purchaser's funds and securities required to be deposited into the escrow or trust account, including, if applicable, any material risk of non-insurance of purchasers' funds resulting from deposits in excess of the insured amounts; and

(2) the obligation of the registrant to provide, and the right of the purchaser to receive, information regarding an acquisition, including the requirement that pursuant to this section, purchasers confirm in writing their investment in the registrant's securities as specified in paragraph (e) of this section.

(d) *Probable Acquisition Post-Effective Amendment Requirement.*

If, during any period in which offers or sales are being made, a significant acquisition becomes probable, the registrant shall file promptly a post-effective amendment disclosing the information specified by the applicable registration statement form and Industry Guides, including financial statements of the registrant and the company to be acquired a well as pro forma financial information required by the form and applicable rules and regulations. Where warrants, rights or other derivative securities issued in the initial offering are exercisable, there is a continuous offering of the underlying security.

(e) *Release of Deposited and Funds Securities.*

(1) *Post-Effective Amendment for Acquisition Agreement.* Upon execution of an agrement(s) for the acquisition(s) of a business(es) or assets that will constitute the business (or a line of business) of the registrant and for which the fair value of the business(es) or net assets to be acquired represents at least 80 percent of the maximum offering proceeds, including proceeds received or to be received upon the exercise or conversion of any securities offered, but excluding amounts payable to non-affiliates for underwriting commissions, underwriting expenses, and dealer allowances, the registrant shall file a post-effective amendment that:

(i) discloses the information specified by the applicable registration statement form and Industry Guides, including financial statements of the registrant and the company acquired or to be acquired and pro forma financial information required by the form and applicable rules and regulations;

(ii) discloses the results of the initial offering, including but not limited to:

(A) the gross offering proceeds received to date, specifying the amounts paid for underwriter commissions, underwriting expenses and dealer allowances, amounts disbursed to the registrant, and amounts remaining in the escrow or trust account; and

(B) the specific amount, use and application of funds disbursed to the registrant to date, including, but not limited to, the amounts paid to officers, directors, promoters, controlling shareholders or affiliates, either directly or indirectly, specifying the amounts and purposes of such payments; and

(iii) discloses the terms of the offering as described pursuant to paragraph (e)(2) of this section.

(2) *Terms of the Offering.* The terms of the offering must provide, and the registrant must satisfy, the following conditions:

(i) within five business days after the effective date of the post-effective amendment(s), the registrant shall send by first class mail or other equally prompt means, to each purchaser of securities held in escrow or trust, a copy of the prospectus contained in the post-effective amendment and any amendment or supplement thereto;

(ii) each purchaser shall have no fewer than 20 business days and no more than 45 business days from the effective date of the post-effective amendment to notify the registrant in writing that the purchaser elects to remain an investor. If the registrant has not received such written notification by the 45th business day following the effective date of the post-effective amendment, funds and interest or dividends, if any, held in the escrow or trust account shall be sent by first class mail or other equally prompt means to the purchaser within five business days;

(iii) the acquisition(s) meeting the criteria set forth in paragraph (e)(1) of this section will be consummated if a sufficient number of purchasers confirm their investments; and

(iv) if a consummated acquisition(s) meeting the requirements of this section has not occurred by a date 18 months after the effective date of the initial registration statement, funds held in the escrow or trust account shall be returned by first class mail or equally prompt means to the purchaser within five business days following that date.

(3) *Conditions for Release of Deposited Securities and Funds.* Funds held in the escrow or trust account may be released to the registrant and securities may be delivered to the purchaser or other registered holder identified on the deposited securities only at the same time as or after:

(i) the escrow agent or trustee has received a signed representation from the registrant, together with other evidence acceptable to the escrow agent or trustee, that the requirements of paragraphs (e)(1) and (e)(2) of this section have been met; and

(ii) consummation of an acquisition(s) meeting the requirements of paragraph (e)(2)(iii) of this section.

(4) *Prospectus Supplement.* If funds and securities are released from the escrow or trust account to the registrant pursuant to this paragraph, the prospectus shall be supplemented to indicate the amount of funds and securities released and the date of release.

Notes to Rule 419(e)

Note 1. With respect to a blank check offering subject to both Rule 419 and Exchange Act Rule 10b-9 [17 CFR 240.10b-9], the requirements of Rule 10b-9 are applicable only until the conditions of the offering governed by that Rule are met (*e.g.,* reaching the minimum in a "part-or-none" offering). When those conditions are satisfied, Rule 419 continues to govern the use of offering proceeds.

Note 2. If the business(es) or assets are acquired for cash, the fair value shall be presumed to be equal to the cash paid. If all or part of the consideration paid consists of securities or other non-cash consideration, the fair value shall be determined by an accepted standard, such as bona fide sales of the assets or similar assets made within a reasonable time, forecasts of expected cash flows, independent appraisals, etc. Such valuation must be reasonable at the time made.

(f) *Financial Statements.*

The registrant shall:

(1) Furnish to security holders audited financial statements for the first full fiscal year of operations following consummation of an acquisition pursuant to paragraph (e) of this section, together with the information required by Item 303(a) of Regulation S-K [17 CFR 229.303(a)], no later than 90 days after the end of such fiscal year; and

(2) File the financial statements and additional information with the Commission under cover of Form 8-K [17 CFR 249.308]; *provided, however,* that such financial statements and related information need not be filed separately if the registrant is filing reports pursuant to Section 13(a) or 15(d) of the Exchange Act.

Rule 420. Legibility of Prospectus

(a) The body of all printed prospectuses and all notes to financial statements and other tabular data included therein shall be in roman type at least as large and as legible as 10-point modern type. However, (1) to the extent necessary for convenient presentation, financial statements and other tabular data, including tabular data in notes, and (2) prospectuses deemed to be omitting prospectuses under rule 482 [17 CFR 230.482] may be in roman type at least and as legible as 8-point modern type. All such type shall be leaded at least 2-points.

(b) Where a prospectus is distributed through an electronic medium, issuers may satisfy legibility requirements applicable to printed documents, such as paper size, type size and font, bold-face type, italics and red ink, by presenting all required information in a format readily communicated to investors, and where indicated, in a manner reasonably calculated to draw investor attention to specific information.

Rule 421. Presentation of Information in Prospectuses

(a) The information required in a prospectus need not follow the order of the items or other requirements in the form. Such information shall not, however, be set forth in such fashion as to obscure any of the required information or any information necessary to keep the required information from being incomplete or misleading. Where an item requires information to be given in a prospectus in tabular form it shall be given in substantially the tabular form specified in the item.

(b) You must present the information in a prospectus in a clear, concise and understandable manner. You must prepare the prospectus using the following standards:

(1) Present information in clear, concise sections, paragraphs, and sentences. Whenever possible, use short, explanatory sentences and bullet lists;

(2) Use descriptive headings and subheadings;

(3) Avoid frequent reliance on glossaries or defined terms as the primary means of explaining information in the prospectus. Define terms in a glossary or other section of the document only if the meaning is unclear from the context. Use a glossary only if it facilitates understanding of the disclosure; and

(4) Avoid legal and highly technical business terminology.

Note to § 230.421(b): In drafting the disclosure to comply with this section, you should avoid the following:

1. Legalistic or overly complex presentations that make the substance of the disclosure difficult to understand;

2. Vague "boilerplate" explanations that are imprecise and readily subject to different interpretations;

3. Complex information copied directly from legal documents without any clear and concise explanation of the provision(s); and

4. Disclosure repeated in different sections of the document that increases the size of the document but does not enhance the quality of the information.

(c) All information required to be included in a prospectus shall be clearly understandable without the necessity of referring to the particular form or to the general rules and regulations. Except as to financial statements and information required in a tabular form, the information set forth in a prospectus may be expressed in condensed or summarized form. In lieu of repeating information in the form of notes to financial statements, references may be made to other parts of the prospectus where such information is set forth.

(d) (1) To enhance the readability of the prospectus, you must use plain English principles in the organization, language, and design of the front and back cover pages, the summary, and the risk factors section.

(2) You must draft the language in these sections so that at a minimum it substantially complies with each of the following plain English writing principles:

(i) Short sentences;

(ii) Definite, concrete, everyday words;

(iii) Active voice;

(iv) Tabular presentation or bullet lists for complex material, whenever possible;

(v) No legal jargon or highly technical business terms; and

(vi) No multiple negatives.

(3) In designing these sections or other sections of the prospectus, you may include pictures, logos, charts, graphs, or other design elements so long as the design is not misleading and the required information is clear. You are encouraged to use tables, schedules, charts and graphic illustrations of the results of operations, balance sheet, or other financial data that present the data in an understandable manner. Any presentation must be consistent with the financial statements and non-financial information in the prospectus. You must draw the graphs and charts to scale. Any information you provide must not be misleading.

(e) A summary prospectus prepared and filed (except a summary prospectus filed by an open-end management investment company registered under the Investment Company Act of 1940 (15 U.S.C. 80a-1 *et seq.*) or a separate account (as defined in section 2(a) (14) of the Securities Act (15 U.S.C. 77b(a) (14)) registered under the Investment Company Act of 1940 on §§ 239.17a and 274.11b of this chapter (Form N-3), §§ 239.17b and 274.11c of this chapter (Form N-4), or §§ 239.17c and 274.11d of this chapter (Form N-6)) as part of a registration statement in accordance with this rule shall be deemed to be a prospectus permitted under section 10(b) of the Act (15 U.S.C. 77j(b)) for the purposes of section 5(b)(1) of the Act (15 U.S.C. 77e(b) (1)) if the form used for registration of the securities to be offered provides for the use of a summary prospectus and the following conditions are met: [*sic*]

Instruction to § 230.421: You should read Securities Act Release No. 33-7497 (January 28, 1998) for information on plain English principles.

Rule 423.　Date of Prospectuses

Except for a form of prospectus used after the effective date of the registration statement and before the determination of the offering price as permitted by Rule 430A(c) under the Securities Act (§ 230.430A(c) of this chapter) or before the opening of bids as permitted by Rule 445(c) under the Securities Act (§ 230.445(c) of this chapter), each prospectus used after the effective date of the registration statement shall be dated approximately as of such effective date; provided, however, that a revised or amended prospectus used thereafter need only bear the approximate date of its issuance. Each supplement to a prospectus shall be dated separately the approximate date of its issuance.

Rule 424.　Filing of Prospectuses, Number of Copies

(a) Except as provided in paragraph (f) of this section, five copies of every form of prospectus sent or given to any person prior to the effective date of the registration statement which varies from the form or forms of prospectus included in the registrant statement as filed pursuant to § 230.402(a) of this chapter shall be filed as a part of the registration statement not later than the date such form of prospectus is first sent or given to any person: *Provided, however,* That only a form of prospectus that contains substantive changes from or additions to a prospectus previously filed with the Commission as part of a registration statement need be filed pursuant to this paragraph (a).

(b) Ten copies of each form of prospectus purporting to comply with section 10 of the Act, except for documents constituting a prospectus pursuant to Rule 428(a) (§ 230.428(a)) or free writing prospectuses pursuant to Rule 164 and Rule 433 (§ 230.164 and § 230.433), shall be filed with the Commission in the form in which it is used after the effectiveness of the registration statement and identified as required by paragraph (e) of this section; provided, however, that only a form of prospectus that contains substantive changes from or additions to a previously filed prospectus is required to be filed; Provided, further, that this paragraph (b) shall not apply in respect of a form of prospectus contained in a registration statement and relating solely to securities offered at competitive bidding, which prospectus is intended for use prior to the opening of bids. Ten copies of the form of prospectus shall be filed or transmitted for filing as follows:

(1) A form of prospectus that discloses information previously omitted from the prospectus filed as part of an effective registration statement in reliance upon Rule 430A under the Securities Act [§ 230.430A of this chapter] shall be filed with the Commission no later than the second business day following the earlier of the date of determination of the offering price or the date it is first used after effectiveness in connection with a public offering or sales, or transmitted by a means reasonably calculated to result in filing with the Commission by that date.

(2) A form of prospectus that is used in connection with a primary offering of securities pursuant to Rule 415(a)(1)(x) (§ 230.415(a)(1)(x)) or a primary offering of securities registered for issuance on a delayed basis pursuant to Rule 415(a)(1)(vii) or (viii) (§ 230.415(a)(1)(vii) or (viii)) and that, in the case of Rule 415(a)(1)(viii) discloses the public offering price, description of securities or similar matters, and in the case of Rule 415(a)(1)(vii) and (x) discloses information previously omitted from the prospectus filed as part of an effective registration statement in reliance on Rule 430B (§ 230.430B), or, in the case of asset-backed securities, Rule 430D (§ 230.430D), shall be filed with the Commission no later than the second business day following the earlier of the date of the determination of the offering price or the date it is first used after effectiveness in connection with a public offering or sales, or transmitted by a means reasonably calculated to result in filing with the Commission by that date.

(3) A form of prospectus that reflects facts or events other than those covered in paragraphs (b)(1), (2) and (6) of this section that constitute a substantive change from or addition to the information set forth in the last form of prospectus filed with the Commission under this section or as part of a registration statement under the Securities Act shall be filed with the Commission no later than the fifth business day after the date it is first used after effectiveness in connection with a public offering or sales, or transmitted by a means reasonably calculated to result in filing with the Commission by that date.

(4) A form of prospectus that discloses information, facts or events covered in both paragraphs (b)(1) and (3) shall be filed with the Commission no later than the second business day following the earlier of the date of the determination of the offering price or the date it is first used after effectiveness in connection with a public offering or sales, or transmitted by a means reasonably calculated to result in filing with the Commission by that date.

(5) A form of prospectus that discloses information, facts or events covered in both paragraphs (b)(2) and (3) shall be filed with the Commission no later than the second business day following the earlier of the date of the determination of the offering price or the date it is first used after effectiveness in connection with a public offering or sales, or transmitted by a means reasonably calculated to result in filing with the Commission by that date.

(6) A form of prospectus used in connection with an offering of securities under Canada's National Policy Statement No. 45 pursuant to Rule 415 under the Securities Act (§ 230.415 of this chapter) that is not made in the United States shall be filed with the Commission no later than the date it is first used in Canada, or transmitted by a means reasonably calculated to result in filing with the Commission by that date.

(7) A form of prospectus that identifies selling security holders and the amounts to be sold by them that was previously omitted from the registration statement and the prospectus in reliance upon Rule 430B (§ 230.430B) shall be filed with the Commission no later than the second business day following the earlier of the date of sale or the date of first use or transmitted by a means reasonably calculated to result in filing with the Commission by that date.

(8) A form of prospectus otherwise required to be filed pursuant to paragraph (b) of this section that is not filed within the time frames specified in paragraph (b) of this section must be filed pursuant to this paragraph as soon as practicable after the discovery of such failure to file.

Instruction to Paragraph (b): Notwithstanding § 230.424(b)(2) and (b)(5) above, a form of prospectus or prospectus supplement relating to an offering of asset-backed securities under § 230.415(a)(1)(vii) or 230.415(a)(1)(xii) that is required to be filed pursuant to paragraph (b) of this section shall be filed with the Commission no later than the second business day following the date it is first used after effectiveness in connection with a public offering or sales, or transmitted by a means reasonably calculated to result in filing with the Commission by that date.

(c) If a form of prospectus, other than one filed pursuant to paragraph (b)(1) or (b)(4) of this Rule, consists of a prospectus supplement attached to a form of prospectus that (1) previously has been filed or (2) was not required to be filed pursuant to paragraph (b) because it did not contain substantive changes from a prospectus that previously was filed, only the prospectus supplement need be filed under paragraph (b) of this rule, provided that the first page of each prospectus supplement includes a cross reference to the date(s) of the related prospectus and any prospectus supplements thereto that together constitute the prospectus required to be delivered by Section 5(b) of the Securities Act [15 U.S.C. 77e(b)] with respect to the securities currently being offered or sold. The cross reference may be set forth in longhand, provided it is legible.

NOTE: Any prospectus supplement being filed separately that is smaller than a prospectus page should be attached to an 8″ × 11″ sheet of paper.

(d) Every prospectus consisting of a radio or television broadcast shall be reduced to writing. Five copies of every such prospectus shall be filed with the Commission in accordance with the requirements of this section.

(e) Each copy of a form of prospectus filed under this rule shall contain in the upper right corner of the cover page the paragraph of this rule, including the subparagraph if applicable, under which the filing is made, and the file number of the registration statement to which the prospectus relates. The information required by this paragraph may be set forth in longhand, provided it is legible.

(f) This rule shall not apply with respect to prospectuses of an investment company registered under the Investment Company Act of 1940, other than a registered closed-end investment company. References to "form of prospectus" in paragraphs (a), (b), and (c) of this section shall be deemed also to refer to the form of Statement of Additional Information.

(g) A form of prospectus filed pursuant to this section that operates to reflect the payment of filing fees for an offering or offerings pursuant to Rule 456(b) (§ 230.456(b)) must include on its cover page the calculation of registration fee table reflecting the payment of such filing fees for the securities that are the subject of the payment.

(h)(1) Three copies of a form of prospectus relating to an offering of asset-backed securities pursuant to § 230.415(a)(1)(vii) or § 230.415(a)(1)(xii) disclosing information previously omitted from the prospectus filed as part of an effective registration statement in reliance on § 230.430D shall be filed with the Commission at least three business days before the date of the first sale in the offering, or if used earlier, the earlier of:

(i) The applicable number of business days before the date of the first sale; or

(ii) The second business day after first use.

(2) Three copies of a prospectus supplement relating to an offering of asset-backed securities pursuant to § 230.415(a)(1)(vii) or § 230.415(a)(1)(xii) that reflects any material

change from the information contained in a prospectus filed in accordance with § 230.424(h)(1) shall be filed with the Commission at least forty-eight hours before the date and time of the first sale in the offering. The prospectus supplement must clearly delineate what material information has changed and how the information has changed from the prospectus filed in accordance with paragraph (h)(1) of this section.

Instruction to Paragraph (h): The filing requirements of this paragraph (h) do not apply if a filing is made solely to add fees pursuant to § 230.457 and for no other purpose.

(i)(1) A form of prospectus filed pursuant to this section that operates to reflect the payment of filing fees for an offering of an indeterminate amount of exchange-traded vehicle securities pursuant to Rule 456(d) and Rule 457(u) (§ 230.456(d) and § 230.457(u)) shall be filed with the Commission within the time period set forth in Rule 456(d). The form of prospectus must be accompanied by the appropriate registration fee.

(2) The form of prospectus must include the following information:

(i) The name and address of issuer;

(ii) The name of the securities for which the prospectus is filed;

(iii) The Securities Act file number(s) of the registration statement(s) associated with the offering;

(iv) The last day of the fiscal year for the issuer for which the prospectus is filed;

(v) The calculation of registration fee information calculated pursuant to Rule 457(u); and

(vi) The total interest due pursuant to Rule 456(d)(5) and the total amount of registration fee due including any such interest, if the prospectus is being filed more than 90 days after the end of the issuer's fiscal year.

Rule 425. Filing of Certain Prospectuses and Communications under § 230.135 in Connection with Business Combination Transactions

(a) All written communications made in reliance on § 230.165 are prospectuses that must be filed with the Commission under this section on the date of first use.

(b) All written communications that contain no more information than that specified in § 230.135 must be filed with the Commission on or before the date of first use except as provided in paragraph (d)(1) of this section. A communication limited to the information specified in § 230.135 will not be deemed an offer in accordance with § 230.135 even though it is filed under this section.

(c) Each prospectus or § 230.135 communication filed under this section must identify the filer, the company that is the subject of the offering and the Commission file number for the related registration statement or, if that file number is unknown, the subject company's Exchange Act or Investment Company Act file number, in the upper right corner of the cover page.

(d) Notwithstanding paragraph (a), the following need not be filed under this section:

(1) Any written communication that is limited to the information specified in § 230.135 and does not contain new or different information from that which was previously publicly disclosed and filed under this section.

(2) Any research report used in reliance on § 230.137, § 230.138 and § 230.139;

(3) Any confirmation described in § 240.10b-10 of this chapter; and

(4) Any prospectus filed under § 230.424.

Notes to § 230.425: 1. File five copies of the prospectus or § 230.135 communication if paper filing is permitted.

2. No filing is required under § 240.13e-4(c), § 240.14a-12(b), § 240.14d-2(b), or § 240.14d-9(a), if the communication is filed under this section. Communications filed under this section also are deemed filed under the other applicable sections.

Rule 427. Contents of Prospectus Used After Nine Months

There may be omitted from any prospectus used more than 9 months after the effective date of the registration statement any information previously required to be contained in the prospectus insofar as later information covering the same subjects, including the latest available certified financial statement, as of a date not more than 16 months prior to the use of the prospectus is contained therein.

Rule 428. Documents Constituting a Section 10(a) prospectus for Form S-8 Registration Statement; Requirements Relating to Offerings of Securities Registered on Form S-8.

(a) (1) Where securities are to be offered pursuant to a registration statement on Form S-8 (§ 239.16b of this chapter), the following, taken together, shall constitute a prospectus that meets the requirements of Section 10(a) of the Act: (i) the document(s), or portions thereof as permitted by paragraph (b)(1)(ii) of this section, containing the employee benefit plan information required by Item 1 of the Form; (ii) the statement of availability of registrant information, employee benefit plan annual reports and other information required by Item 2; and (iii) the documents containing registrant information and employee benefit plan annual reports that are incorporated by reference in the registration statement pursuant to Item 3.

(2) The registrant shall maintain a file of the documents that, pursuant to paragraph (a) of this section, at any time are part of the Section 10(a) prospectus, except for documents required to be incorporated by reference in the registration statement pursuant to Item 3 of Form S-8. Each such document shall be included in the file until five years after it is last used as part of the Section 10(a) prospectus to offer or sell securities pursuant to the plan. With respect to documents containing specifically designated portions that constitute part of the Section 10(a) prospectus pursuant to paragraph (b)(1)(ii) of this section, the entire document shall be maintained in the file. Upon request, the registrant shall furnish to the Commission or its staff a copy of any or all of the documents included in the file.

(b) Where securities are offered pursuant to a registration statement on Form S-8:

(1)(i) The registrant shall deliver or cause to be delivered, to each employee who is eligible to participate (or selected by the registrant to participate, in the case of a stock option or other plan with selective participation) in an employee benefit plan to which the registration statement relates, the information required by Part I of Form S-8. The information shall be in written form and shall be updated in writing in a timely manner to reflect any material changes during any period in which offers or sales are being made. When updating information is furnished, documents previously furnished need not be re-delivered, but the registrant shall furnish promptly without charge to each employee, upon written or oral request, a copy of all documents containing the plan information required by Part I that then constitute part of the Section 10(a) prospectus.

(ii) The registrant may designate an entire document or only portions of a document as constituting part of the Section 10(a) prospectus. If the registrant designates only portions of a document as constituting part of the prospectus, rather than the entire document, a statement clearly identifying such portions, for example, by reference to section headings, section numbers, paragraphs or page numbers within the document must be included in a conspicuous place in the forepart of the document, or such portions must be specifically designated throughout the text of the document. Registrants shall not designate only words or sentences within a paragraph as part of a prospectus. Unless the portions of a document constituting part of the Section 10(a) prospectus are clearly identified, the entire document shall constitute part of the prospectus.

(iii) The registrant shall date any document constituting part of the Section 10(a) prospectus or containing portions constituting part of the prospectus and shall include the following printed, stamped or typed legend in a conspicuous place in the forepart of the document, substituting the bracketed language as appropriate: "This document [Specifically designated portions of this document] constitutes [constitute] part of a prospectus covering securities that have been registered under the Securities Act of 1933."

(iv) The registrant shall revise the document(s) containing the plan information sent or given to newly eligible participants pursuant to paragraph (b)(1)(i) of this section, if documents containing updating information would obscure the readability of the plan information.

(2) The registrant shall deliver or cause to be delivered with the document(s) containing the information required by Part I of Form S-8, to each employee to whom such information is sent or given, a copy of any one of the following:

(i) the registrant's annual report to security holders containing the information required by Rule 14a-3(b) (§ 240.14a-3(b) of this chapter) under the Securities Exchange Act of 1934 (*Exchange Act*) for its latest fiscal year;

(ii) The registrant's annual report on Form 10-K (§ 249.310 of this chapter), 20-F (§ 249.220f of this chapter) or, in the case of registrants described in General Instruction A.(2) of Form 40-F (§ 249.240f of this chapter), for its latest fiscal year;

(iii) The latest prospectus filed pursuant to Rule 424(b) (§ 230.424(b)) under the Act that contains audited financial statements for the registrant's latest fiscal year, *Provided* that the financial statements are not incorporated by reference from another filing, and *Provided* further that such prospectus contains substantially the information required by Rule 14a-3(b) (§ 240.14a-3(b) of this chapter) or the registration statement was on Form S-1 (§ 239.11 of this chapter) or F-1 (§ 239.31 of this chapter); or

(iv) The registrant's effective Exchange Act registration statement on Form 10 (§ 249.210 of this chapter), 20-F or, in the case of registrants described in General Instruction A.(2) of Form 40-F, containing audited financial statements for the registrant's latest fiscal year.

Instructions.

1. If a registrant has previously sent or given an employee a copy of any document specified in clauses (i)-(iv) of paragraph (b)(2) for the latest fiscal year, it need not be re-delivered, but the registrant shall furnish promptly, without charge, a copy of such document upon written or oral request of the employee.

2. If the latest fiscal year of the registrant has ended within 120 days (or 190 days with respect to foreign private issuers) prior to the delivery of the documents containing the information specified by Part I of Form S-8, the registrant may deliver a document containing financial statements for the fiscal year preceding the latest fiscal year, *provided that* within the 120 or 190 day period a document containing financial statements for the latest fiscal year is furnished to each employee.

(3) The registrant shall deliver or cause to be delivered promptly, without charge, to each employee to whom information is required to be delivered, upon written or oral request, a copy of the information that has been incorporated by reference pursuant to Item 3 of Form S-8 (not including exhibits to the information that is incorporated by reference unless such exhibits are specifically incorporated by reference into the information that the registration statement incorporates).

(4) Where interests in a plan are registered, the registrant shall deliver or cause to be delivered promptly, without charge, to each employee to whom information is required to be delivered, upon written or oral request, a copy of the then latest annual report of the plan filed pursuant to section 15(d) of the Exchange Act, whether on Form 11-K (§ 249.311 of this chapter) or included as part of the registrant's annual report on Form 10-K.

(5) The registrant shall deliver or cause to be delivered to all employees participating in a stock option plan or plan fund that invests in registrant securities (and other plan participants who request such information orally or in writing) who do not otherwise receive such material, copies of all reports, proxy statements and other communications distributed to its security holders generally, provided that such material is sent or delivered no later than the time it is sent to security holders.

(c) As used in this Rule, the term "employee benefit plan" is defined in Rule 405 of Regulation C (§ 230.405 of this chapter) and the term "employee" is defined in General Instruc-tion A.1 of Form S-8.

Rule 430. Prospectus For Use Prior to Effective Date

(a) A form of prospectus filed as a part of the registration statement shall be deemed to meet the requirements of section 10 of the Act for the purpose of section 5(b)(1) thereof prior to the effective date of the registration statement, provided such form of prospectus contains substantially the information required by the Act and the rules and regulations thereunder to be included in a prospectus meeting the requirements of section 10(a) of the Act for the securities being registered, or contains substantially that information except for the omission of information with respect to the offering price, underwriting discounts or commissions, discounts or commissions to dealers, amount of proceeds, conversion rates, call prices, or other matters dependent upon the offering price. Every such form of prospectus shall be deemed to have been filed as a part of the registration statement for the purpose of section 7 of the Act.

(b) A form of prospectus filed as part of a registration statement on Form N-1A (§ 239.15A and § 274.11A of this chapter), Form N-2 (§ 239.14 and § 274.11a-1 of this chapter), Form N-3 (§ 239.17a and § 274.11b of this chapter), Form N-4 (§ 239.17b and § 274.11c of this chapter), or Form N-6 (§ 239.17c and § 274.11d of this chapter) shall be deemed to meet the requirements of Section 10 of the Act (15 U.S.C. 77j) for the purpose of Section 5(b)(1) thereof (15 U.S.C. 77e(b)(1)) prior to the effective date of the registration statement, provided that:

(1) Such form of prospectus meets the requirements of paragraph (a) of this section; and

(2) Such registration statement contains a form of Statement of Additional Information that is made available to persons receiving such prospectus upon written or oral request, and without charge, unless the form of prospectus contains the information otherwise required to be disclosed in the form of Statement of Additional Information. Every such form of prospectus shall be deemed to have been filed as part of the registration statement for the purpose of section 7 of the Act.

Rule 430A. Prospectus in a Registration Statement at the Time of Effectiveness

(a) The form of prospectus filed as part of a registration statement that is declared effective may omit information with respect to the public offering price, underwriting syndicate (including any material relationships between the registrant and underwriters not named therein), underwriting discounts or commissions, discounts or commissions to dealers, amount of proceeds, conversion rates, call prices and other items dependent upon the offering price, delivery dates, and terms of the securities dependent upon the offering date; and such form of prospectus need not contain such information in order for the registration statement to meet the requirements of Section 7 of the Securities Act [15 U.S.C. 77g] for the purposes of Section 5 thereof [15 U.S.C. 77e], *Provided that:*

(1) the securities to be registered are offered for cash;

(2) the registrant furnishes the undertakings required by Item 512(i) of Regulation S-K (§ 229.512(i) of this chapter), or the undertakings required by Item 34.4 of Form N-2 (§ 239.14 and § 274.11a-1 of this chapter); and

(3) the information omitted in reliance upon paragraph (a) from the form of prospectus filed as part of a registration statement that is declared effective is contained in a form of prospectus filed with the Commission pursuant to Rule 424(b) or Rule 497(h) under the Securities Act [§§ 230.424(b) or 230.497(h) of this chapter]; except that if such form of prospectus is not so filed by the later of fifteen business days after the effective date of the registration statement or fifteen business days after the effectiveness of a post-effective amendment thereto that contains a form of prospectus, or transmitted by a means reasonably calculated to result in filing with the Commission by that date, the information omitted in reliance upon paragraph (a) must be contained in an effective post-effective amendment to the registration statement.

Instruction to paragraph (a): A decrease in the volume of securities offered or changed in the bona fide estimate of the maximum offering price range from that indicated in the form of prospectus filed as part of a registration statement that is declared effective may be disclosed in the form of prospectus filed with the Commission pursuant to § 230.424(b) or § 230.497(h) under the Securities Act so long as the decrease in the volume or change in the price range would not materially change the disclosure contained in the registration statement at effectiveness. Notwithstanding the foregoing, any increase or decrease in volume (if the total dollar value of securities offered would not exceed that which was registered) and any deviation from the low or high end of the range may be reflected in the form of prospectus filed with the Commission pursuant to Rule 424(b)(1) (§ 230.424(b)(1)) or Rule 497(h) (§ 230.497(h)) if, in the aggregate, the changes in volume and price represent no more than a 20% change in the maximum aggregate offering price set forth in the "Calculation of Registration Fee" table in the effective registration statement.

(b) The information omitted in reliance upon paragraph (a) from the form of prospectus filed as part of an effective registration statement, and contained in the form of prospectus filed with the Commission pursuant to Rule 424(b) or Rule 497(h) under the Securities Act [§§ 230.424(b) or 230.497(h) of this chapter], shall be deemed to be a part of the registration statement as of the time it was declared effective.

(c) When used prior to determination of the offering price of the securities, a form of prospectus relating to the securities offered pursuant to a registration statement that is declared effective with information omitted from the form of prospectus filed as part of such effective registration statement in reliance upon this Rule 430A need not contain information omitted pursuant to paragraph (a), in order to meet the requirements of Section 10 of the Securities Act [15 U.S.C. 77j] for the purpose of Section 5(b)(1) [15 U.S.C. 77e(b)(1)] thereof. This provision shall not limit the information required to be contained in a form of prospectus meeting the requirements of Section 10(a) of the Act for the purposes of Section 5(b)(2) thereof or exception (a) of Section 2(10) [15 U.S.C. 77b(10)] thereof.

(d) This rule shall not apply to registration statements for securities to be offered by competitive bidding.

(e) In the case of a registration statement filed on Form N-1A (§ 239.15A and § 274.11A of this chapter), Form N-2 (§ 239.14 and § 274.11a-1 of this chapter), Form N-3 (§ 239.17a and § 274.11b of this chapter), Form N-4 (§ 239.17b and § 274.11c of this chapter), or Form N-6 (§ 239.17c and § 274.11d of this chapter), the references to "form of prospectus" in paragraphs (a) and (b) of this section and the accompanying Note shall be deemed also to refer to the form of Statement of Additional Information filed as part of such a registration statement.

(f) This section may apply to registration statements that are immediately effective pursuant to Rule 462(e) and (f) (§ 230.462(e) and (f)).

NOTE: If information is omitted in reliance upon paragraph (a) from the form of prospectus filed as part of an effective registration statement, or effective post-effective amendment thereto, the registrant must ascertain promptly whether a form of prospectus transmitted for filing under Rule 424(b) or Rule 497(h) under the Securities Act actually was received for filing by the Commission and, in the event that it was not, promptly file such prospectus.

Rule 430B. Prospectus in a Registration Statement After Effective Date

(a) A form of prospectus filed as part of a registration statement for offerings pursuant to Rule 415(a)(1)(x) (§ 230.415(a)(1)(x)) may omit from the information required by the form to be in the prospectus information that is unknown or not reasonably available to the issuer pursuant to Rule 409 (§ 230.409). In addition, a form of prospectus filed as part of an automatic shelf registration statement for offerings pursuant to Rule 415(a) (§ 230.415(a)), other than Rule 415(a)(1)(viii), also may omit information as to whether the offering is a primary offering or an offering on behalf of persons other than the issuer, or a combination thereof, the plan of distribution for the securities, a description of the securities registered other than an identification of the name or class of such securities, and the identification of other issuers. Each such form of prospectus shall be deemed to have been filed as part of the registration statement for the purpose of section 7 of the Act.

(b) A form of prospectus filed as part of a registration statement for offerings pursuant to Rule 415(a)(1)(i) by an issuer eligible to use Form S-3 or Form F-3 (§ 239.13 or § 239.33 of this chapter) for primary offerings pursuant to General Instruction I.B.1 of such forms or an issuer eligible to register such a primary offering under General Instruction A.2 of Form N-2 (§ 239.14 and § 274.11a-1 of this chapter), may omit the information specified in paragraph (a) of this section, and may also omit the identities of selling security holders and amounts of securities to be registered on their behalf if:

(1) The registration statement is an automatic shelf registration statement as defined in Rule 405 (§ 230.405); or

(2) All of the following conditions are satisfied:

(i) The initial offering transaction of the securities (or securities convertible into such securities) the resale of which are being registered on behalf of each of the selling security holders, was completed;

(ii) The securities (or securities convertible into such securities) were issued and outstanding prior to the original date of filing the registration statement covering the resale of the securities;

(iii) The registration statement refers to any unnamed selling security holders in a generic manner by identifying the initial offering transaction in which the securities were sold; and

(iv) The issuer is not and during the past three years neither the issuer nor any of its predecessors was:

(A) A blank check company as defined in Rule 419(a)(2) (§ 230.419(a)(2));

(B) A shell company, other than a business combination related shell company, each as defined in Rule 405; or

(C) An issuer in an offering of penny stock as defined in Rule 3a51-1 of the Securities Exchange Act of 1934 (§ 240.3a51-1 of this chapter).

(c) A form of prospectus that is part of a registration statement that omits information in reliance upon paragraph (a) or (b) of this section meets the requirements of section 10 of the Act for the purpose of section 5(b)(1) thereof. This provision shall not limit the information required to be contained in a form of prospectus in order to meet the requirements of section 10(a) of the Act for the purposes of section 5(b)(2) thereof or exception (a) of section 2(a)(10) thereof.

(d) Information omitted from a form of prospectus that is part of an effective registration statement in reliance on paragraph (a) or (b) of this section may be included subsequently in the prospectus that is part of a registration statement by:

(1) A post-effective amendment to the registration statement;

(2) A prospectus filed pursuant to Rule 424(b) (§ 230.424(b)); or

(3) If the applicable form permits, including the information in the issuer's periodic or current reports filed pursuant to section 13 or 15(d) of the Securities Exchange Act of 1934 (15 U.S.C. 78m or 78o(d)) that are incorporated or deemed incorporated by reference into the prospectus that is part of the registration statement in accordance with applicable requirements, subject to the provisions of paragraph (h) of this section.

(e) Information omitted from a form of prospectus that is part of an effective registration statement in reliance on paragraph (a) or (b) of this section and contained in a form of prospectus required to be filed with the Commission pursuant to Rule 424(b), other than as provided in paragraph (f) of this section, shall be deemed part of and included in the registration statement as of the date such form of filed prospectus is first used after effectiveness.

(f)(1) Information omitted from a form of prospectus that is part of an effective registration statement in reliance on paragraph (a) or (b) of this section and is contained in a form of prospectus required to be filed with the Commission pursuant to Rule 424(b)(2), (b)(5), or (b)(7), shall be deemed to be part of and included in the registration statement on the earlier of the date such subsequent form of prospectus is first used or the date and time of the first contract of sale of securities in the offering to which such subsequent form of prospectus relates.

(2) The date on which a form of prospectus is deemed to be part of and included in the registration statement pursuant to paragraph (f)(1) of this section shall be deemed, for purposes of liability under section 11 of the Act of the issuer and any underwriter at the time only, to be a new effective date of the part of such registration statement relating to the securities to which such form of prospectus relates, such part of the registration statement consisting of all information included in the registration statement and any prospectus relating to the offering of such securities (including information relating to the offering in a prospectus already included in the registration statement) as of such date and all information relating to the offering included in reports and materials incorporated by reference into such registration statement and prospectus as of such date, and in each case not modified or superseded pursuant to Rule 412 (§ 230.412). The offering of such securities at that time shall be deemed to be the initial bona fide offering thereof.

(3) If a registration statement is amended to include or is deemed to include, through incorporation by reference or otherwise, except as otherwise provided in Rule 436 (§ 230.436), a report or opinion of any person made on such person's authority as an expert whose consent would be required under section 7 of the Act because of being named as having prepared or certified part of the registration statement, then for purposes of this section and for liability purposes under section 11 of the Act, the part of the registration statement for which liability against such person is asserted shall be considered as having become effective with respect to such person as of the time the report or opinion is deemed to be part of the registration statement and a consent required pursuant to section 7 of the Act has been provided as contemplated by section 11 of the Act.

(4) Except for an effective date resulting from the filing of a form of prospectus filed for purposes of including information required by section 10(a)(3) of the Act or pursuant to Item 512(a)(1)(ii) of Regulation S-K (§ 229.512(a)(1)(ii) of this chapter) or Item 34.3.a(2) of Form N-2 (§ 239.14 and § 274.11a-1 of this chapter), the date a form of prospectus is deemed part of and included in the registration statement pursuant to this paragraph shall not be an effective date established pursuant to paragraph (f)(2) of this section as to:

(i) Any director (or person acting in such capacity) of the issuer;

(ii) Any person signing any report or document incorporated by reference into the registration statement, except for such a report or document incorporated by reference for purposes of including information required by section 10(a)(3) of the Act or pursuant to Item 512(a)(1)(ii) of Regulation S-K or Item 34.3.a(2) of Form N-2 (§ 239.14 and § 274.11a-1 of this chapter) (such person except for such reports being deemed not to be a person who signed the registration statement within the meaning of section 11(a) of the Act).

(5) The date a form of prospectus is deemed part of and included in the registration statement pursuant to paragraph (f)(2) of this section shall not be an effective date established pursuant to paragraph (f)(2) of this section as to:

(i) Any accountant with respect to financial statements or other financial information contained in the registration statement as of a prior effective date and for which the accountant previously provided a consent to be named as required by section 7 of the Act, unless the form of prospectus contains new audited financial statements or other financial information as to which the accountant is an expert and for which a new consent is required pursuant to section 7 of the Act or Rule 436; and

(ii) Any other person whose report or opinion as an expert or counsel has, with their consent, previously been included in the registration statement as of a prior effective date, unless the form of prospectus contains a new report or opinion for which a new consent is required pursuant to section 7 of the Act or Rule 436.

(g) Notwithstanding paragraph (e) or (f) of this section or paragraph (a) of Rule 412, no statement made in a registration statement or prospectus that is part of the registration statement or made in a document incorporated or deemed incorporated by reference into the registration statement or prospectus that is part of the registration statement after the effective date of such registration statement or portion thereof in respect of an offering determined pursuant to this section will, as to a purchaser with a time of contract of sale prior to such effective date, supersede or modify any statement that was made in the registration statement or prospectus that was part of the registration statement or made in any such document immediately prior to such effective date.

(h) Where a form of prospectus filed pursuant to Rule 424(b) relating to an offering does not include disclosure of omitted information regarding the terms of the offering, the securities, or the plan of distribution, or selling security holders for the securities that are the subject of the form of prospectus, because such omitted information has been included in periodic or current reports filed pursuant to section 13 or 15(d) of the Securities Exchange Act of 1934 incorporated or deemed incorporated by reference into the prospectus, the issuer shall file a form of prospectus identifying the periodic or current reports that are incorporated or deemed incorporated by reference into the prospectus that is part of the registration statement that contain such omitted information. Such form of prospectus shall be required to be filed, depending on the nature of the incorporated information, pursuant to Rule 424(b)(2), (b)(5), or (b)(7).

(i) Issuers relying on this section shall furnish the undertakings required by Item 512(a) of Regulation S-K or Item 34.3 of Form N-2 (§ 239.14 and § 274.11a-1 of this chapter) as applicable.

Note to Rule 430B: The provisions of paragraph (b) of Rule 401 (§ 230.401(b)) shall apply to any prospectus filed for purposes of including information required by section 10(a)(3) of the Act.

Rule 430C. Prospectus in a Registration Statement Pertaining to an Offering Other Than Pursuant to Rule 430A or Rule 430B After the Effective Date

(a) In offerings made other than in reliance on Rule 430B (§ 230.430B) or Rule 430D (§ 230.430D) and other than for prospectuses filed in reliance on Rule 430A (§ 230.430A), information contained in a form of prospectus required to be filed with the Commission pursuant to Rule 424(b) (§ 230.424(b)) or Rule 497(b), (c), (d), or (e) (§ 230.497(b), (c), (d) or (e)), shall be deemed to be part of and included in the registration statement on the date it is first used after effectiveness.

(b) Notwithstanding paragraph (a) of this section or paragraph (a) of Rule 412 (§ 230.412), no statement made in a registration statement or prospectus that is part of the registration statement or made in a document incorporated or deemed incorporated by reference into the registration statement or prospectus that is part of the registration statement will, as to a purchaser with a time of contract of sale prior to such first use, supersede or modify any statement that was made in the registration statement or prospectus that was part of the registration statement or made in any such document immediately prior to such date of first use.

(c) Nothing in this section shall affect the information required to be included in an issuer's registration statement and prospectus.

(d) Issuers subject to paragraph (a) of this section shall furnish the undertakings required by Item 512(a) of Regulation S-K (§ 229.512(a) of this chapter) or Item 34.4 of Form N-2 (§§ 239.14 and 274.11a-1 of this chapter), as applicable.

Rule 430D. Prospectus in a Registration Statement After Effective Date For Asset-Backed Securities Offerings

(a) A form of prospectus filed as part of a registration statement for primary offerings of asset-backed securities pursuant to § 230.415(a)(1)(vii) or § 230.415(a)(1)(xii) may omit from the information required by the form to be in the prospectus information that is unknown or not reasonably available to the issuer pursuant to § 230.409.

(b) Information omitted from a form of prospectus that is part of an effective registration statement in reliance on paragraph (a) of this section (other than information with respect to offering price, underwriting syndicate (including any material relationships between the registrant and underwriters not named therein), underwriting discounts or commissions, discounts or commissions to dealers, amount of proceeds or other matters dependent upon the offering price to the extent such information is unknown or not reasonably available to the issuer pursuant to § 230.409) shall be disclosed in a form of prospectus required to be filed with the Commission pursuant to § 230.424(h). Each such form of prospectus shall be deemed to have been filed as part of the registration statement for the purpose of section 7 of the Act (15 U.S.C. 77g).

(c) A form of prospectus filed as part of a registration statement that omits information in reliance upon paragraph (a) of this section meets the requirements of section 10 of the Act (15 U.S.C. 77j) for the purpose of section 5(b)(1) of the Act (15 U.S.C. 77e(b)(1)). This provision shall not limit the information required to be contained in a form of prospectus in order to meet the requirements of section 10(a) of the Act for the purposes of section 5(b)(2) (15 U.S.C. 77e(b)(2)) or exception (a) of section 2(a)(10) of the Act (15 U.S.C. 77b(a)(10)(a)).

(d)(1) Except as provided in paragraph (b) or (d)(2) of this section, information omitted from a form of prospectus that is part of an effective registration statement in reliance on paragraph (a) of this section may be included subsequently in the prospectus that is part of a registration statement by:

(i) A post-effective amendment to the registration statement;

(ii) A prospectus filed pursuant to § 230.424(b); or

(iii) If the applicable form permits, including the information in the issuer's periodic or current reports filed pursuant to section 13 or 15(d) of the Securities Exchange Act of 1934 (15 U.S.C. 78m or 78o(d)) that are incorporated or deemed incorporated by reference into the prospectus that is part of the registration statement in accordance with the applicable requirements, subject to the provisions of paragraph (h) of this section.

(2) Information omitted from a form of prospectus that is part of an effective registration statement in reliance on paragraph (a) of this section that adds a new structural feature or credit enhancement must be included subsequently in the prospectus that is part of a registration statement by a post-effective amendment to the registration statement.

(e)(1) Information omitted from a form of prospectus that is part of an effective registration statement in reliance on paragraph (a) of this section and contained in a form of prospectus required to be filed with the Commission pursuant to § 230.424(b), other than as provided in paragraph (f) of this section, shall be deemed part of and included in the registration statement as of the date such form of filed prospectus is first used after effectiveness.

(2) Information omitted from a form of prospectus that is part of an effective registration statement in reliance on paragraph (a) of this section and contained in a form of prospectus required to be filed with the Commission pursuant to § 230.424(h) shall be deemed part of and included in the registration statement the earlier of the date such form of filed prospectus is filed with the Commission pursuant to § 230.424(h) or, if used earlier than the date of filing, the date it is first used after effectiveness.

(f)(1) Information omitted from a form of prospectus that is part of an effective registration statement in reliance on paragraph (a) of this section, and is contained in a form of prospectus required to be filed with the Commission pursuant to § 230.424(b)(2) or (b)(5), shall be deemed to be part of and included in the registration statement on the earlier of the date such subsequent form of prospectus is first used or the date and time of the first contract of sale of securities in the offering to which such subsequent form of prospectus relates.

(2) The date on which a form of prospectus is deemed to be part of and included in the registration statement pursuant to paragraph (f)(1) of this section shall be deemed, for purposes of liability under section 11 of the Act (15 U.S.C. 77k) of the issuer and any underwriter at the time only, to be a new effective date of the part of such registration statement relating to the securities to which such form of prospectus relates, such part of the registration statement consisting of all information included in the registration statement and any prospectus relating to the offering of such securities (including information relating to the offering in a prospectus already included in the registration statement) as of such date and all information relating to the offering included in reports and materials

incorporated by reference into such registration statement and prospectus as of such date, and in each case not modified or superseded pursuant to § 230.412. The offering of such securities at that time shall be deemed to be the initial bona fide offering thereof.

(3) If a registration statement is amended to include or is deemed to include, through incorporation by reference or otherwise, except as otherwise provided in § 230.436, a report or opinion of any person made on such person's authority as an expert whose consent would be required under section 7 of the Act (15 U.S.C. 77g) because of being named as having prepared or certified part of the registration statement, then for purposes of this section and for liability purposes under section 11 of the Act (15 U.S.C. 77k), the part of the registration statement for which liability against such person is asserted shall be considered as having become effective with respect to such person as of the time the report or opinion is deemed to be part of the registration statement and a consent required pursuant to section 7 of the Act has been provided as contemplated by section 11 of the Act.

(4) Except for an effective date resulting from the filing of a form of prospectus filed for purposes of including information required by section 10(a)(3) of the Act (15 U.S.C. 77j(a)(3)) or pursuant to Item 512(a)(1)(ii) of Regulation S-K (§ 229.512(a)(1)(ii) of this chapter), the date a form of prospectus is deemed part of and included in the registration statement pursuant to this paragraph shall not be an effective date established pursuant to paragraph (f)(2) of this section as to:

(i) Any director (or person acting in such capacity) of the issuer;

(ii) Any person signing any report or document incorporated by reference into the registration statement, except for such a report or document incorporated by reference for purposes of including information required by section 10(a)(3) of the Act (15 U.S.C. 77j(a)(3)) or pursuant to Item 512(a)(1)(ii) of Regulation S-K (§ 229.512(a)(1)(ii) of this chapter) (such person except for such reports being deemed not to be a person who signed the registration statement within the meaning of section 11(a) of the Act (15 U.S.C. 77k(a)).

(5) The date a form of prospectus is deemed part of and included in the registration statement pursuant to paragraph (f)(2) of this section shall not be an effective date established pursuant to paragraph (f)(2) of this section as to:

(i) Any accountant with respect to financial statements or other financial information contained in the registration statement as of a prior effective date and for which the accountant previously provided a consent to be named as required by section 7 of the Act (15 U.S.C. 77g), unless the form of prospectus contains new audited financial statements or other financial information as to which the accountant is an expert and for which a new consent is required pursuant to section 7 of the Act or § 230.436; and

(ii) Any other person whose report or opinion as an expert or counsel has, with their consent, previously been included in the registration statement as of a prior effective date, unless the form of prospectus contains a new report or opinion for which a new consent is required pursuant to section 7 of the Act (15 U.S.C. 77g) or § 230.436.

(g) Notwithstanding paragraph (e) or (f) of this section or § 230.412(a), no statement made in a registration statement or prospectus that is part of the registration statement or made in a document incorporated or deemed incorporated by reference into the registration statement or prospectus that is part of the registration statement after the effective date of such registration statement or portion thereof in respect of an offering determined pursuant to this section will, as to a purchaser with a time of contract of sale prior to such effective date, supersede or modify any statement that was made in the registration statement or prospectus that was part of the registration statement or made in any such document immediately prior to such effective date.

(h) Where a form of prospectus filed pursuant to § 230.424(b) relating to an offering does not include disclosure of omitted information regarding the terms of the offering, the securities or the plan of distribution for the securities that are the subject of the form of prospectus, because such omitted information has been included in periodic or current reports filed pursuant to section 13 or 15(d) of the Securities Exchange Act of 1934 (15 U.S.C. 78m or 78o(d)) incorporated or deemed incorporated by reference into the prospectus, the issuer shall file a form of prospectus identifying the periodic or current reports that are incorporated or deemed incorporated by reference into the prospectus that is part of the registration statement that contain such omitted information. Such form of prospectus shall be required to be filed, depending on the nature of the incorporated information, pursuant to § 230.424(b)(2) or (b)(5).

(i) Issuers relying on this section shall furnish the undertakings required by Item 512(a) of Regulation S-K (§ 229.512(a) of this chapter).

Rule 431. Summary Prospectuses

(a) A summary prospectus prepared and filed (except a summary prospectus filed by an open-end management investment company registered under the Investment Company Act of 1940 (15 U.S.C. 80a-1 *et seq.*) or a separate account (as defined in section 2(a)(14) of the Securities Act (15 U.S.C. 77b(a)(14)) registered under the Investment Company Act of 1940 on §§ 239.17a and 274.11b of this chapter (Form N-3), §§ 239.17b and 274.11c of this chapter (Form N-4), or §§ 239.17c and 274.11d of this chapter (Form N-6) as part of a registration statement in accordance with this section shall be deemed to be a prospectus permitted under section 10(b) of the Act (15 U.S.C. 77j(b)) for the purposes of section 5(b)(1) of the Act (15 U.S.C. 77e(b)(1)) if the form used for registration of the securities to be offered provides for the use of a summary prospectus and the following conditions are met:

(1)(i) The registrant is organized under the laws of the United States or any State or Territory or the District of Columbia and has its principal business operations in the United States or its territories; or

(ii) The registrant is a foreign private issuer eligible to use Form F-2 (§ 239.32 of this chapter);

(2) The registrant has a class of securities registered pursuant to section 12(b) of the Securities Exchange Act of 1934 or has a class of equity securities registered pursuant to section 12(g) of that Act or is required to file reports pursuant to section 15(d) of that Act;

(3) The registrant: (i) has been subject to the requirements of section 12 or 15(d) of the Securities Exchange Act of 1934 and has filed all the material required to be filed pursuant to sections 13, 14 or 15(d) of that Act for a period of at least thirty-six calendar months immediately preceding the filing of the registration statement; and (ii) has filed in a timely manner all reports required to be filed during the twelve calendar months and any portion of a month immediately preceding the filing of the registration statement and, if the registrant has used (during the twelve calendar months and any portion of a month immediately preceding the filing of the registration statement) Rule 12b-25(b) under the Securities Exchange Act of 1934 (§ 240.12b-25 of this chapter) with respect to a report or portion of a report, that report or portion thereof has actually been filed within the time period prescribed by that Rule; and

(4) Neither the registrant nor any of its consolidated or unconsolidated subsidiaries has, since the end of its last fiscal year for which certified financial statements of the registrant and its consolidated subsidiaries were included in a report filed pursuant to section 13(a) or 15(d) of the Securities Exchange Act of 1934; (i) failed to pay any dividend or sinking fund installment on preferred stock; or (ii) defaulted on any installment or installments on indebtedness for borrowed money, or on any rental on one or more long term leases, which defaults in the aggregate are material to the financial position of the registrant and its consolidated and unconsolidated subsidiaries, taken as a whole.

(b) A summary prospectus shall contain the information specified in the instructions as to summary prospectuses in the form used for registration of the securities to be offered. Such prospectus may include any other information the substance of which is contained in the registration statement except as otherwise specifically provided in the instructions as to summary prospectuses in the form used for registration. It shall not include any information the substance of which is not contained in the registration statement except that a summary prospectus may contain any information specified in Rule 134(a) (§ 230.134(a)). No reference need be made to inapplicable terms and negative answers to any item of the form may be omitted.

(c) All information included in a summary prospectus, other than the statement required by paragraph (e) of this section, may be expressed in such condensed or summarized form as may be appropriate in the light of the circumstances under which the prospectus is to be used. The information need not follow the numerical sequence of the items of the form used for registration. Every summary prospectus shall be dated approximately as of the date of its first use.

(d) When used prior to the effective date of the registration statement, a summary prospectus shall be captioned a "Preliminary Summary Prospectus" and shall comply with the applicable requirements relating to a preliminary prospectus.

(e) A statement to the following effect shall be prominently set forth in conspicuous print at the beginning or at the end of every summary prospectus:

"Copies of a more complete prospectus may be obtained from" (insert name(s), address(es) and telephone number(s)). Copies of a summary prospectus filed with the Commission pursuant to paragraph (g) of this section may omit the names of persons from whom the complete prospectus may be obtained.

(f) Any summary prospectus published in a newspaper, magazine or other periodical need only be set in type at least as large as 7 point modern type. Nothing in this rule shall prevent the use of reprints of a summary prospectus published in a newspaper, magazine, or other periodical, if such reprints are clearly legible.

(g) Eight copies of every proposed summary prospectus shall be filed as a part of the registration statement, or as an amendment thereto, at least 5 days (exclusive of Saturdays, Sundays and holidays) prior to the use thereof, or prior to the release for publication by any newspaper, magazine or other person, whichever is earlier. The Commission may, however, in its discretion, authorize such use or publication prior to the expiration of the 5-day period upon a written request for such authorization. Within 7 days after the first use or publication thereof, 5 additional copies shall be filed in the exact form in which it was used or published.

Rule 432. Additional Information Required to be Included in Prospectuses Relating to Tender Offers

Notwithstanding the provisions of any form for the registration of securities under the Act, any prospectus relating to securities to be offered in connection with a tender offer for, or a request or invitation for tenders of, securities subject to either § 240.13e-4 or section 14(d) of the Securities Exchange Act of 1934 (15 U.S.C. 78n(d)) must include the information required by § 240.13e-4(d) (1) or § 240.14d-6(d)(1) of this chapter, as applicable, in all tender offers, requests or invitations that are published, sent or given to security holders.

Rule 433. Conditions to Permissible Post-Filing Free Writing Prospectuses

(a) Scope of section. This section applies to any free writing prospectus with respect to securities of any issuer (except as set forth in Rule 164 (§ 230.164)) that are the subject of a registration statement that has been filed under the Act. Such a free writing prospectus that satisfies the conditions of this section may include information the substance of which is not included in the registration statement. Such a free writing prospectus that satisfies the conditions of this section will be a prospectus permitted under section 10(b) of the Act for purposes of sections 2(a)(10), 5(b)(1), and 5(b)(2) of the Act and will, for purposes of considering it a prospectus, be deemed to be public, without regard to its method of use or distribution, because it is related to the public offering of securities that are the subject of a filed registration statement.

(b) Permitted use of free writing prospectus. Subject to the conditions of this paragraph (b) and satisfaction of the conditions set forth in paragraphs (c) through (g) of this section, a free writing prospectus may be used under this section and Rule 164 in connection with a registered offering of securities:

(1) Eligibility and prospectus conditions for seasoned issuers and well-known seasoned issuers. Subject to the provisions of Rule 164(e), (f), and (g), the issuer or any other offering participant may use a free writing prospectus in the following offerings after a registration statement relating to the offering has been filed that includes a prospectus that, other than by reason of this section or Rule 431, satisfies the requirements of section 10 of the Act:

(i) Offerings of securities registered on Form S-3 (§ 239.33 of this chapter) pursuant to General Instruction I.C., or I.D. thereof or on Form SF-3 (§ 239.45 of this chapter) or on Form N-2 (§ 239.14 and § 274.11a-1 of this chapter) pursuant to General Instruction A.2 with respect to the same transactions;

(ii) Offerings of securities registered on Form F-3 (§ 239.13 of this chapter) pursuant to General Instruction I.A.5, I.B.1, I.B.2, or I.C. thereof;

(iii) Any other offering not excluded from reliance on this section and Rule 164 of securities of a well-known seasoned issuer; and

(iv) Any other offering not excluded from reliance on this section and Rule 164 of securities of an issuer eligible to use Form S-3 or Form F-3 for primary offerings pursuant to General Instruction I.B.1 of such Forms or an issuer eligible to use General Instruction A.2 of Form N-2 to register a primary offering described in General Instruction I.B.1 of Form S-3.

(2) Eligibility and prospectus conditions for non-reporting and unseasoned issuers. If the issuer does not fall within the provisions of paragraph (b)(1) of this section, then, subject to the provisions of Rule 164(e), (f), and (g), any person participating in the offer or sale of the securities may use a free writing prospectus as follows:

(i) If the free writing prospectus is or was prepared by or on behalf of or used or referred to by an issuer or any other offering participant, if consideration has been or will be given by the issuer or other offering participant for the dissemination (in any format) of any free writing prospectus (including any published article, publication, or advertisement), or if section 17(b) of the Act requires disclosure that consideration has been or will be given by the issuer or other offering participant for any activity described therein in connection with the free writing prospectus, then a registration statement relating to the offering must have been filed that includes a prospectus that, other than by reason of this section or Rule 431, satisfies the requirements of section 10 of the Act, including a price range where required by rule, and the free writing prospectus shall be accompanied or preceded by the most recent such prospectus; provided, however, that use of the free writing prospectus is not conditioned on providing the most recent such prospectus if a prior such prospectus has been provided and there is no material change from the prior prospectus reflected in the most recent prospectus; provided, further that after effectiveness and availability of a final prospectus meeting the requirements of section 10(a) of the Act, no such earlier prospectus may be provided in satisfaction of this condition, and such final prospectus must precede or accompany any free writing prospectus provided after such availability, whether or not an earlier prospectus had been previously provided.

Notes to paragraph (b)(2)(i) of Rule 433. 1. The condition that a free writing prospectus shall be accompanied or preceded by the most recent prospectus satisfying the requirements of section 10 of the Act would be satisfied if a free writing prospectus that is an electronic communication contained an active hyperlink to such most recent prospectus; and

2. A communication for which disclosure would be required under section 17(b) of the Act as a result of consideration given or to be given, directly or indirectly, by or on behalf of an issuer or other offering participant is an offer by the issuer or such other offering participant as the case may be and is, if written, a free writing prospectus of the issuer or other offering participant.

(ii) Where paragraph (b)(2)(i) of this section does not apply, a registration statement relating to the offering has been filed that includes a prospectus that, other than by reason of this section or Rule 431 satisfies the requirements of section 10 of the Act, including a price range where required by rule. For purposes of paragraph (f) of this section, the prospectus included in the registration statement relating to the offering that has been filed does not have to include a price range otherwise required by rule.

(3) *Successors.* A successor issuer will be considered to satisfy the applicable provisions of this paragraph (b) if:

(i) Its predecessor and it, taken together, satisfy the conditions, provided that the succession was primarily for the purpose of changing the state or other jurisdiction of incorporation of the predecessor or forming a holding company and the assets and liabilities of the successor at the time of succession were substantially the same as those of the predecessor; or

(ii) All predecessors met the conditions at the time of succession and the issuer has continued to do so since the succession.

(c) *Information in a free writing prospectus.*

(1) A free writing prospectus used in reliance on this section may include information the substance of which is not included in the registration statement but such information shall not conflict with:

(i) Information contained in the filed registration statement, including any prospectus or prospectus supplement that is part of the registration statement (including pursuant to Rule 430B (§ 230.430B), Rule 430C (§ 230.430C) or Rule 430D (§ 230.430D) and not superseded or modified; or

(ii) Information contained in the issuer's periodic and current reports filed or furnished to the Commission pursuant to section 13 or 15(d) of the Securities Exchange Act of 1934 (15 U.S.C. 78m or 78o(d)) that are incorporated by reference into the registration statement and not superseded or modified, or pursuant to section 30 of the Investment Company Act of 1940 (15 U.S.C. 80a-29).

(2) (i) A free writing prospectus used in reliance on this section shall contain substantially the following legend:

The issuer has filed a registration statement (including a prospectus) with the SEC for the offering to which this communication relates. Before you invest, you should read the prospectus in that registration statement and other documents the issuer has filed with the SEC for more complete information about the issuer and this offering. You may get these documents for free by visiting EDGAR on the SEC Web site at www.sec.gov. Alternatively, the issuer, any underwriter or any dealer participating in the offering will arrange to send you the prospectus if you request it by calling toll-free 1-8[xx-xxx-xxxx].

(ii) The legend also may provide an e-mail address at which the documents can be requested and may indicate that the documents also are available by accessing the issuer's Web site and provide the Internet address and the particular location of the documents on the Web site.

(d) *Filing conditions.*

(1) Except as provided in paragraphs (d)(3), (d)(4), (d)(5), (d)(6), (d)(7), (d)(8), and (f) of this section, the following shall be filed with the Commission under this section by a means reasonably calculated to result in filing no later than the date of first use. The free writing prospectus filed for purposes of this section will not be filed as part of the registration statement:

(i) The issuer shall file:

(A) Any issuer free writing prospectus, as defined in paragraph (h) of this section;

(B) Any issuer information that is contained in a free writing prospectus prepared by or on behalf of or used by any other offering participant (but not information prepared by or on behalf of a person other than the issuer on the basis of or derived from that issuer information); and

(C) A description of the final terms of the issuer's securities in the offering or of the offering contained in a free writing prospectus or portion thereof prepared by or on behalf of the issuer or any offering participant, after such terms have been established for all classes in the offering; and

(ii) Any offering participant, other than the issuer, shall file any free writing prospectus that is used or referred to by such offering participant and distributed by or on behalf of such person in a manner reasonably designed to lead to its broad unrestricted dissemination.

(2) Each free writing prospectus or issuer information contained in a free writing prospectus filed under this section shall identify in the filing the Commission file number for the related registration statement or, if that file number is unknown, a description sufficient to identify the related registration statement.

(3) The condition to file a free writing prospectus under paragraph (d)(1) of this section shall not apply if the free writing prospectus does not contain substantive changes from or additions to a free writing prospectus previously filed with the Commission.

(4) The condition to file issuer information contained in a free writing prospectus of an offering participant other than the issuer shall not apply if such information is included (including through incorporation by reference) in a prospectus or free writing prospectus previously filed that relates to the offering.

(5) Notwithstanding the provisions of paragraph (d)(1) of this section:

(i) To the extent a free writing prospectus or portion thereof otherwise required to be filed contains a description of terms of the issuer's securities in the offering or of the offering that does not reflect the final terms, such free writing prospectus or portion thereof is not required to be filed; and

(ii) A free writing prospectus or portion thereof that contains only a description of the final terms of the issuer's securities in the offering or of the offerings shall be filed by the issuer within two days of the later of the date such final terms have been established for all classes of the offering and the date of first use.

(6)(i) Notwithstanding the provisions of paragraph (d) of this section, in an offering of asset-backed securities, a free writing prospectus or portion thereof required to be filed that contains only ABS informational and computational materials as defined in Item 1101(a) of Regulation AB (§ 229.1101 of this chapter), may be filed under this section within the time-frame permitted by Rule 426(b) (§ 230.426(b)) and such filing will satisfy the filing conditions under this section.

(ii) In the event that a free writing prospectus is used in reliance on this section and Rule 164 and the conditions of this section and Rule 164 (which may include the conditions of paragraph (d)(6)(i) of this section) are satisfied with respect thereto, then the use of that free writing prospectus shall not be conditioned on satisfaction of the provisions, including without limitation the filing conditions, of Rule 167 and Rule 426 (§ 230.167 and § 230.426). In the event that ABS informational and computational materials are used in reliance on Rule 167 and Rule 426 and the conditions of those rules are satisfied with respect thereto, then the use of those materials shall not be conditioned on the satisfaction of the conditions of Rule 164 and this section.

(7) The condition to file a free writing prospectus or issuer information pursuant to this paragraph (d) for a free writing prospectus used at the same time as a communication in a business combination transaction subject to Rule 425 (§ 230.425) shall be satisfied if:

(i) The free writing prospectus or issuer information is filed in accordance with the provisions of Rule 425, including the filing timeframe of Rule 425;

(ii) The filed material pursuant to Rule 425 indicates on the cover page that it also is being filed pursuant to Rule 433; and

(iii) The filed material pursuant to Rule 425 contains the information specified in paragraph (c)(2) of this section.

(8) Notwithstanding any other provision of this paragraph (d):

(i) A road show for an offering that is a written communication is a free writing prospectus, provided that, except as provided in paragraph (d)(8)(ii) of this section, a written communication that is a road show shall not be required to be filed; and

(ii) In the case of a road show that is a written communication for an offering of common equity or convertible equity securities by an issuer that is, at the time of the filing of the registration statement for the offering, not required to file reports with the Commission pursuant to section 13 or section 15(d) of the Securities Exchange Act of 1934, such a road show is required to be filed pursuant to this section unless the issuer of the securities makes at least one version of a bona fide electronic road show available without restriction by means of graphic communication to any person, including any potential investor in the securities (and if there is more than one version of a road show for the offering that is a written communication, the version available without restriction is made available no later than the other versions).

Note to paragraph (d)(8): A communication that is provided or transmitted simultaneously with a road show and is provided or transmitted in a manner designed to make the communication available only as part of the road show and not separately is deemed to be part of the road show. Therefore, if the road show is not a written communication, such a simultaneous communication (even if it would otherwise be a graphic communication or other written communication) is also deemed not to be written. If the road show is written and not required to be filed, such a simultaneous communication is also not required to be filed. Otherwise, a written communication that is an offer contained in a separate file from a road show, whether or not the road show is a written communication, or otherwise transmitted separately from a road show, will be a free writing prospectus subject to any applicable filing conditions of paragraph (d) of this section.

(e) Treatment of information on, or hyperlinked from, an issuer's Web site.

(1) An offer of an issuer's securities that is contained on an issuer's Web site or hyperlinked by the issuer from the issuer's Web site to a third party's Web site is a written offer of such securities by the issuer and, unless otherwise exempt or excluded from the requirements of section 5(b)(1) of the Act, the filing conditions of paragraph (d) of this section apply to such offer.

(2) Notwithstanding paragraph (e)(1) of this section, historical issuer information that is identified as such and located in a separate section of the issuer's Web site containing historical issuer information, that has not been incorporated by reference into or otherwise included in a prospectus of the issuer for the offering and that has not otherwise been used or referred to in connection with the offering, will not be considered a current offer of the issuer's securities and therefore will not be a free writing prospectus.

(f) Free writing prospectuses published or distributed by media. Any written offer for which an issuer or any other offering participant or any person acting on its behalf provided, authorized, or approved information that is prepared and published or disseminated by a person unaffiliated with the issuer or any other offering participant that is in the business of publishing, radio or television broadcasting or otherwise disseminating written communications would be considered at the time of publication or dissemination to be a free writing prospectus prepared by or on behalf of the issuer or such other offering participant for purposes of this section subject to the following:

(1) The conditions of paragraph (b)(2)(i) of this section will not apply and the conditions of paragraphs (c)(2) and (d) of this section will be deemed to be satisfied if:

(i) No payment is made or consideration given by or on behalf of the issuer or other offering participant for the written communication or its dissemination; and

(ii) The issuer or other offering participant in question files the written communication with the Commission, and includes in the filing the legend required by paragraph (c)(2) of this section, within four business days after the issuer or other offering participant becomes aware of the publication, radio or television broadcast, or other dissemination of the written communication.

(2) The filing obligation under paragraph (f)(1)(ii) of this section shall be subject to the following:

(i) The issuer or other offering participant shall not be required to file a free writing prospectus if the substance of that free writing prospectus has previously been filed with the Commission;

(ii) Any filing made pursuant to paragraph (f)(1)(ii) of this section may include information that the issuer or offering participant in question reasonably believes is necessary or appropriate to correct information included in the communication; and

(iii) In lieu of filing the actual written communication as published or disseminated as required by paragraph (f)(1)(ii) of this section, the issuer or offering participant in question may file a copy of the materials provided to the media, including transcripts of interviews or similar materials, provided the copy or transcripts contain all the information provided to the media.

(3) For purposes of this paragraph (f) of this section, an issuer that is in the business of publishing or radio or television broadcasting may rely on this paragraph (f) as to any publication or radio or television broadcast that is a free writing prospectus in respect of an offering of securities of the issuer if the issuer or an affiliate:

(i) Is the publisher of a bona fide newspaper, magazine, or business or financial publication of general and regular circulation or bona fide broadcaster of news including business and financial news;

(ii) Has established policies and procedures for the independence of the content of the publications or broadcasts from the offering activities of the issuer; and

(iii) Publishes or broadcasts the communication in the ordinary course.

(g) Record retention. Issuers and offering participants shall retain all free writing prospectuses they have used, and that have not been filed pursuant to paragraph (d) or (f) of this section, for three years following the initial bona fide offering of the securities in question.

Note to paragraph (g) of § 230.433. To the extent that the record retention requirements of Rule 17a-4 of the Securities Exchange Act of 1934 (§ 240.17a-4 of this chapter) apply to free writing prospectuses required to be retained by a broker-dealer under this section, such free writing prospectuses are required to be retained in accordance with such requirements.

(h) Definitions. For purposes of this section:

(1) An issuer free writing prospectus means a free writing prospectus prepared by or on behalf of the issuer or used or referred to by the issuer and, in the case of an asset-backed issuer, prepared by or on behalf of a depositor, sponsor, or servicer (as defined in Item 1101 of Regulation AB) or affiliated depositor or used or referred to by any such person.

(2) Issuer information means material information about the issuer or its securities that has been provided by or on behalf of the issuer.

(3) A written communication or information is prepared or provided by or on behalf of a person if the person or an agent or representative of the person authorizes the communication or information or approves the communication or information before it is used. An offering participant other than the issuer shall not be an agent or representative of the issuer solely by virtue of its acting as an offering participant.

(4) A road show means an offer (other than a statutory prospectus or a portion of a statutory prospectus filed as part of a registration statement) that contains a presentation regarding an offering by one or more members of the issuer's management (and in the case of an offering of asset-backed securities, management involved in the securitization or servicing function of one or more of the depositors, sponsors, or servicers (as such terms are defined in Item 1101 of Regulation AB) or an affiliated depositor) and includes discussion of one or more of the issuer, such management, and the securities being offered; and

(5) A bona fide electronic road show means a road show that is a written communication transmitted by graphic means that contains a presentation by one or more officers of an issuer or other persons in an issuer's management (and in the case of an offering of asset-backed securities, management involved in the securitization or servicing function of one or more of the depositors, sponsors, or servicers (as such terms are defined in Item 1101 of

Regulation AB) or an affiliated depositor) and, if more than one road show that is a written communication is being used, includes discussion of the same general areas of information regarding the issuer, such management, and the securities being offered as such other issuer road show or shows for the same offering that are written communications.

Note to § 230.433. This section does not affect the operation of the provisions of clause (a) of section 2(a)(10) of the Act providing an exception from the definition of "prospectus."

Rule 436. Consents Required in Special Cases

(a) If any portion of the report or opinion of an expert or counsel is quoted or summarized as such in the registration statement or in a prospectus, the written consent of the expert or counsel shall be filed as an exhibit to the registration statement and shall expressly state that the expert or counsel consents to such quotation or summarization.

(b) If it is stated that any information contained in the registration statement has been reviewed or passed upon by any persons and that such information is set forth in the registration statement upon the authority of or in reliance upon such persons as experts, the written consents of such persons shall be filed as exhibits to the registration statement.

(c) Notwithstanding the provisions of paragraph (b) of this section, a report on unaudited interim financial information (as defined in paragraph (d) of this section) by an independent accountant who has conducted a review of such interim financial information shall not be considered a part of a registration statement prepared or certified by an accountant or a report prepared or certified by an accountant within the meaning of sections 7 and 11 of the Act.

(d) The term "report on unaudited interim financial information" shall mean a report which consists of the following: (1) a statement that the review of interim financial information was made in accordance with established professional standards for such reviews; (2) an identification of the interim financial information reviewed; (3) a description of the procedures for a review of interim financial information; (4) a statement that a review of interim financial information is substantially less in scope than an audit conducted in accordance with the standards of the Public Company Accounting Oversight Board (United States) ("PCAOB"), the objective of which is an expression of opinion regarding the financial statements taken as a whole, and, accordingly, no such opinion is expressed; and (5) a statement about whether the accountant is aware of any material modifications that should be made to the accompanying financial information so that it conforms with generally accepted accounting principles.

(e) Where a counsel is named as having acted for the underwriters or selling security holders, no consent will be required by reason of his being named as having act in such capacity.

(f) Where the opinion of one counsel relies upon the opinion of another counsel, the consent of the counsel whose prepared opinion is relied upon need not be furnished.

*(g)(1) Notwithstanding the provisions of paragraphs (a) and (b) of this section, the security rating assigned to a class of debt securities, a class of convertible debt securities, or a class of preferred stock by a nationally recognized statistical rating organization, or with respect to registration statements on Form F-9 (§ 239.39 of this chapter) by any other rating organization specified in the Instruction to paragraph (a)(2) of General Instruction I of Form F-9, shall not be considered a part of the registration statement prepared or certified by a person within the meaning of sections 7 and 11 of the Act.

(2) For the purpose of paragraph (g)(1) of this section, the term "nationally recognized statistical rating organization" shall have the same meaning as used in Rule 15c3-1(c)(2)(vi)(F) [17 CFR 240.15c3-1(c)(2)(vi)(F)].

---

* Pursuant to Section 939G of the Dodd-Frank Wall Street Reform and Consumer Protection Act Rule 436(g) shall have no force or effect.

(h) Notwithstanding the provisions of paragraphs (a) and (b) of this section, any description about matters identified by a qualified person pursuant to § 229.1302(f) of this chapter shall not be considered a part of the registration statement prepared or certified by the qualified person within the meaning of Sections 7 and 11 of the Securities Act.

Rule 455. Place of Filing

All registration statements and other papers filed with the Commission shall be filed at its principal office. Such material may be filed by delivery to the Commission; provided, however, that only registration statements and post-effective amendments thereto filed pursuant to Rule 462(b) (§ 230.462(b)) and Rule 110(d) (§ 230.110(d)) may be filed by means of facsimile transmission.

Rule 456. Date of Filing; Timing of Fee Payment

(a) The date on which any papers are actually received by the Commission shall be the date of filing thereof, if all requirements of the Act and the rules with respect to such filing have been complied with and the required fee paid. The failure to pay an insignificant amount of the required fee at the time of filing, as the result of a bona fide error, shall not be deemed to affect the date of filing.

(b)(1) Notwithstanding paragraph (a) of this section, a well-known seasoned issuer that registers securities offerings on an automatic shelf registration statement, or registers additional securities or classes of securities thereon pursuant to Rule 413(b) (§ 230.413(b)), may, but is not required to, defer payment of all or any part of the registration fee to the Commission required by section 6(b)(2) of the Act on the following conditions:

(i) If the issuer elects to defer payment of the registration fee, it shall pay the registration fees (pay-as-you-go registration fees) calculated in accordance with Rule 457(r) (§ 230.457(r)) in advance of or in connection with an offering of securities from the registration statement within the time required to file the prospectus supplement pursuant to Rule 424(b) (§ 230.424(b)) for the offering, provided, however, that if the issuer fails, after a good faith effort to pay the filing fee within the time required by this section, the issuer may still be considered to have paid the fee in a timely manner if it is paid within four business days of its original due date; and

(ii) The issuer reflects the amount of the pay-as-you-go registration fee paid or to be paid in accordance with paragraph (b)(1)(i) of this section by updating the "Calculation of Registration Fee" table to indicate the class and aggregate offering price of securities offered and the amount of registration fee paid or to be paid in connection with the offering or offerings either in a post-effective amendment filed at the time of the fee payment or on the cover page of a prospectus filed pursuant to Rule 424(b) (§ 230.424(b)).

(2) A registration statement filed relying on the pay-as-you-go registration fee payment provisions of paragraph (b)(1) of this section will be considered filed as to the securities or classes of securities identified in the registration statement for purposes of this section and section 5 of the Act when it is received by the Commission, if it complies with all other requirements of the Act and the rules with respect to it.

(3) The securities sold pursuant to a registration statement will be considered registered, for purposes of section 6(a) of the Act, if the pay-as-you-go registration fee has been paid and the post-effective amendment or prospectus including the amended "Calculation of Registration Fee" table is filed pursuant to paragraph (b)(1) of this section.

(c)(1) Notwithstanding paragraph (a) of this section, an asset-backed issuer that registers asset-backed securities offerings on Form SF-3 (§ 239.45 of this chapter), may, but is not required to, defer payment of all or any part of the registration fee to the Commission required by section 6(b)(1) of the Act (15 U.S.C. 77f(b)(1)) on the following conditions:

(i) If the issuer elects to defer payment of the registration fee, it shall pay the registration fees (pay-as-you-go registration fees) calculated in accordance with § 230.457(s) in advance of or in connection with an offering of securities from the registration statement at the time of filing the prospectus pursuant to § 230.424(h) for the offering; and

(ii) The issuer reflects the amount of the pay-as-you-go registration fee paid or to be paid in accordance with paragraph (c)(1)(i) of this section by updating the "Calculation of Registration Fee" table to indicate the class and aggregate offering price of securities offered and the amount of registration fee paid or to be paid in connection with the offering or offerings on the cover page of a prospectus filed pursuant to § 230.424(h).

(2) A registration statement filed relying on the pay-as-you-go registration fee payment provisions of paragraph (c)(1) of this section will be considered filed as to the securities or classes of securities identified in the registration statement for purposes of this section and section 5 of the Act (15 U.S.C. 77e) when it is received by the Commission, if it complies with all other requirements of the Act and the rules with respect to it.

(3) The securities sold pursuant to a registration statement will be considered registered, for purpose of section 6(a) of the Act (15 U.S.C. 77f(a)), if the pay-as-you-go registration fee has been paid and the prospectus including the amended "Calculation of Registration Fee" table is filed pursuant to paragraph (c)(1) of this section.

(d)(1) Notwithstanding paragraph (a) of this section, where a registration statement relates to an offering of exchange-traded vehicle securities, an issuer may elect to register an offering of an indeterminate amount of such securities if it meets the following conditions:

(i) The issuer must state in the "Calculation of Registration Fee" table that it is offering an indeterminate amount of such securities; and

(ii) The issuer must, not later than 90 days after the end of any fiscal year during which it has publicly offered such securities, pay a registration fee to the Commission calculated in accordance with Rule 457(u) (§ 230.457(u)) and file a prospectus in accordance with Rule 424(i) (§ 230.424(i)).

Instruction to Paragraph (d)(1)(ii): To determine the date on which the registration fee must be paid, the first day of the 90-day period is the first calendar day of the fiscal year following the fiscal year for which the registration fee is to be paid. If the last day of the 90-day period falls on a Saturday, Sunday, or federal holiday, the registration fee is due on the first business day thereafter.

(2) If a registrant elects to register an offering of an indeterminate amount of exchange-traded vehicle securities pursuant to paragraph (d)(1), the securities sold will be considered registered, for purposes of section 6(a) of the Act, if the registration fee has been paid and a prospectus is filed pursuant to paragraph (d)(1) of this section not later than the end of the 90-day period.

(3) A registration statement filed relying on the registration fee payment provisions of paragraph (d)(1) of this section will be considered filed as to the securities identified in the registration statement for purposes of this section and section 5 of the Act when it is received by the Commission, if it complies with all other requirements of the Act and the rules with respect to it.

(4) *Issuer Ceasing Operations; Mergers and Other Transactions.* For purposes of this section, if an issuer ceases operations, the date the issuer ceases operations will be deemed to be the end of its fiscal year. In the case of a liquidation, merger, or sale of all or substantially all of the assets ("merger") of the issuer, the issuer will be deemed to have ceased operations for the purposes of this section on the date the merger is consummated; provided, however, that in the case of a merger of an issuer or a series of an issuer ("Predecessor Issuer") with another issuer or a series of an issuer ("Successor Issuer"), the Predecessor Issuer will not be deemed to have ceased operations and the Successor Issuer will assume the obligations, fees, and redemption credits of the Predecessor Issuer incurred pursuant to this section if the Successor Issuer:

(i) Had no assets or liabilities, other than nominal assets or liabilities, and no operating history immediately prior to the merger;

(ii) Acquired substantially all of the assets and assumed substantially all of the liabilities and obligations of the Predecessor Issuer; and

(iii) The merger is not designed to result in the Predecessor Issuer merging with, or substantially all of its assets being acquired by, an issuer (or a series of an issuer) that would not meet the conditions of paragraph (d)(4)(i) of this section.

(5) An issuer paying the fee required by paragraph (d)(1) or any portion thereof more than 90 days after the end of the fiscal year of the issuer shall pay to the Commission interest on unpaid amounts, calculated based on the interest rate in effect at the time of the interest payment by reference to the "current value of funds rate" on the Treasury Department's Financial Management Service Internet site at *http://www.fms.treas.gov*, or by calling (202) 874-6995, and using the following formula: $I = (X)\ (Y)\ (Z/365)$, where: I = Amount of interest due; X = Amount of registration fee due; Y = Applicable interest rate, expressed as a fraction; Z = Number of days by which the registration fee payment is late. The payment of interest pursuant to this paragraph shall not preclude the Commission from bringing an action to enforce the requirements of this paragraph (d).

(6) *Failure to Comply.* An immaterial or unintentional failure to comply with a requirement of Rule 456(d) will not result in a violation of section 6(a) of the Act (15 U.S.C. 77f(a)), so long as:

(i) A good faith and reasonable effort was made to comply with the requirement; and

(ii) In the case of a late payment of a registration fee, the issuer pays the registration fee and any interest due thereon as soon as practicable after discovery of the failure to pay the registration fee.

Rule 460. Distribution of Preliminary Prospectus

(a) Pursuant to the statutory requirement that the Commission in ruling upon requests for acceleration of the effective date of a registration statement shall have due regard to the adequacy of the information respecting the issuer theretofore available to the public, the Commission may consider whether the persons making the offering have taken reasonable steps to make the information contained in the registration statement conveniently available to underwriters and dealers who it is reasonably anticipated will be invited to participate in the distribution of the security to be offered or sold.

(b)(1) As a minimum, reasonable steps to make the information conveniently available would involve the distribution, to each underwriter and dealer who it is reasonably anticipated will be invited to participate in the distribution of the security, a reasonable time in advance of the anticipated effective date of the registration statement, of as many copies of the proposed form of preliminary prospectus permitted by Rule 430 (§230.430) as appears to be reasonable to secure adequate distribution of the preliminary prospectus.

(2) In the case of a registration statement filed by a closed-end investment company on Form N-2 (§239.14 and §274.11a-1 of this chapter), reasonable steps to make information conveniently available would involve distribution of a sufficient number of copies of the Statement of Additional Information required by §230.430(b) as it appears to be reasonable to secure their adequate distribution either to each underwriter or dealer who it is reasonably anticipated will be invited to participate in the distribution of the security, or to the underwriter, dealer or other source named on the cover page of the preliminary prospectus as being the person investors should contract in order to obtain in the Statement of Additional Information.

(c) The granting of acceleration will not be conditioned upon

(1) The distribution of a preliminary prospectus in any state where such distribution would be illegal; or

(2) The distribution of a preliminary prospectus (i) in the case of a registration statement relating solely to securities to be offered at competitive bidding, provided the undertaking in Item 512(d)(1) of Regulation S-K (§229.512(d)(2) of this chapter) is included in the registration statement and distribution of prospectuses pursuant to such undertaking is

made prior to the publication or distribution of the invitation for bids, or (ii) in the case of a registration statement relating to a security issued by a face-amount certificate company or a redeemable security issued by an open-end management company or unit investment trust if any other security of the same class is currently being offered or sold, pursuant to an effective registration statement by the issuer or by or through an underwriter, or (iii) in the case of an offering of subscription rights unless it is contemplated that the distribution will be made through dealers and the underwriters intend to make the offering during the stockholders' subscription period, in which case copies of the preliminary prospectus must be distributed to dealers prior to the effective date of the registration statement in the same fashion as is required in the case of other offerings through underwriters, or (iv) in the case of a registration statement pertaining to a security to be offered pursuant to an exchange offer or transaction described in Rule 145 (§ 230.145).

Rule 461. Acceleration of Effective Date

(a) Requests for acceleration of the effective date of a registration statement shall be made by the registrant and the managing underwriters of the proposed issue, or, if there are no managing underwriters, by the principal underwriters of the proposed issue, and shall state the date upon which it is desired that the registration statement shall become effective. Such requests may be made in writing or orally, provided that, if an oral request is to be made, a letter indicating that fact and stating that the registrant and the managing or principal underwriters are aware of their obligations under the Act must accompany the registration statement (or a pre-effective amendment thereto) at the time of filing with the Commission. Written requests may be sent to the Commission by facsimile transmission. If by reason of the expected arrangement in connection with the offering, it is to be requested that the registration statement shall become effective at a particular hour of the day, the Commission must be advised to that effect not later than the second business day before the day which it is desired that the registration statement shall become effective. A person's request for acceleration will be considered confirmation of such person's awareness of the person's obligations under the Act. Not later than the time of filing the last amendment prior to the effective date of the registration statement, the registrant shall inform the Commission as to whether or not the amount of compensation to be allowed or paid to the underwriters and any other arrangements among the registrant, the underwriters and other broker dealers participating in the distribution, as described in the registration statement, have been reviewed to the extent required by the National Association of Securities Dealers, Inc. and such Association has issued a statement expressing no objections to the compensation and other arrangements.

(b) Having due regard to the adequacy of information respecting the registrant theretofore available to the public, to the facility with which the nature of the securities to be registered, their relationship to the capital structure of the registrant issuer and the rights of holders thereof can be understood, and to the public interest and the protection of investors, as provided in section 8(a) of the Act, it is the general policy of the Commission, upon request, as provided in paragraph (a) of this section, to permit acceleration of the effective date of the registration statement as soon as possible after the filing of appropriate amendments, if any. In determining the date on which a registration statement shall become effective, the following are included in the situations in which the Commission considers that the statutory standards of section 8(a) may not be met and may refuse to accelerate the effective date:

(1) Where there has not been a bona fide effort to make the prospectus reasonably concise, readable, and in compliance with the plain English requirements of Rule 421(d) of Regulation C (17 CFR 230.421(d)) in order to facilitate an understanding of the information in the prospectus.

(2) Where the form of preliminary prospectus, which has been distributed by the issuer or underwriter, is found to be inaccurate or inadequate in any material respect, until the Commission has received satisfactory assurance that appropriate correcting material has been sent to all underwriters and dealers who received such preliminary prospectus or

prospectuses in quantity sufficient for their information and the information of others to whom the inaccurate or inadequate material was sent.

(3) Where the Commission is currently making an investigation of the issuer, a person controlling the issuer, or one of the underwriters, if any, of the securities to be offered, pursuant to any of the Acts administered by the Commission.

(4) Where one or more of the underwriters, although firmly committed to purchase securities covered by the registration statement, is subject to and does not meet the financial responsibility requirements of Rule 15c3-1 under the Securities Exchange Act of 1934 (§ 240.15c3-1 of this chapter). For the purposes of this paragraph underwriters will be deemed to be firmly committed even though the obligation to purchase is subject to the usual conditions as to receipt of opinions of counsel, accountants, etc., the accuracy of warranties or representations, the happening of calamities or the occurrence of other events the determination of which is not expressed to be in the sole or absolute discretion of the underwriters.

(5) Where there have been transactions in securities of the registrant by persons connected with or proposed to be connected with the offering which may have artificially affected or may artificially affect the market price of the security being offered.

(6) Where the amount of compensation to be allowed or paid to the underwriters and any other arrangements among the registrant, the underwriters and other broker dealers participating in the distribution, as described in the registration statement, if required to be reviewed by the National Association of Securities Dealers, Inc. (NASD), have been reviewed by the NASD and the NASD has not issued a statement expressing no objections to the compensation and other arrangements.

(7) Where, in the case of a significant secondary offering at the market, the registrant, selling security holders and underwriters have not taken sufficient measures to insure compliance with Regulation M (§§ 242.100 through 242.105 of this chapter).

(c) Insurance against liabilities arising under the Act, whether the cost of insurance is borne by the registrant, the insured or some other person, will not be considered a bar to acceleration, unless the registrant is a registered investment company or a business development company and the cost of such insurance is borne by other than an insured officer or director of the registrant. In the case of such a registrant, the Commission may refuse to accelerate the effective date of the registration statement when the registrant is organized or administered pursuant to any instrument (including a contract for insurance against liabilities arising under the Act) that protects or purports to protect any director or officer of the company against any liability to the company or its security holders to which he or she would otherwise be subject by reason of willful misfeasance, bad faith, gross negligence or reckless disregard of the duties involved in the conduct of his or her office.

Rule 462. Immediate Effectiveness of Certain Registration Statements and Post-Effective Amendments

(a) A registration statement on Form S-8 (§ 239.16b of this chapter) and a registration statement on Form S-3 (§ 239.13 of this chapter) or on Form F-3 (§ 239.33 of this chapter) for a dividend or interest reinvestment plan shall become effective upon filing with the Commission.

(b) A registration statement and any post-effective amendment thereto shall become effective upon filing with the Commission if:

(1) The registration statement is for registering additional securities of the same class(es) as were included in an earlier registration statement for the same offering and declared effective by the Commission;

(2) The new registration statement is filed prior to the time confirmations are sent or given; and

(3) The new registration statement registers additional securities in an amount and at a price that together represent no more than 20% of the maximum aggregate offering price set

forth for each class of securities in the "Calculation of Registration Fee" table contained in such earlier registration statement.

(c) If the prospectus contained in a post-effective amendment filed prior to the time confirmations are sent or given contains no substantive changes from or additions to the prospectus previously filed as part of the effective registration statement, other than price-related information omitted from the registration statement in reliance on Rule 430A of the Act (§ 230.430A), such post-effective amendment shall become effective upon filing with the Commission.

(d) A post-effective amendment filed solely to add exhibits to a registration statement shall become effective upon filing with the Commission.

(e) An automatic shelf registration statement, including an automatic shelf registration statement filed in accordance with Rule 415(a)(6) (§ 230.415(a)(6)), and any post-effective amendment thereto, including a post-effective amendment filed to register additional classes of securities pursuant to Rule 413(b) (§ 230.413(b)), shall become effective upon filing with the Commission.

(f) A post-effective amendment filed pursuant to paragraph (e) of this section for purposes of adding a new issuer and its securities as permitted by Rule 413(b) (§ 230.413(b)) that satisfies the requirements of Form S-3 or Form F-3 or General Instruction A.2 of Form N-2 (§ 239.13, § 239.33, or § 239.14 and § 274.11a-1 of this chapter), as applicable, including the signatures required by Rule 402(e) (§ 230.402(e)), and contains a prospectus satisfying the requirements of Rule 430B (§ 230.430B), shall become effective upon filing with the Commission.

Rule 463. Report of Offering of Securities and Use of Proceeds Therefrom

(a) Except as provided in this section, following the effective date of the first registration statement filed under the Act by an issuer, the issuer or successor issuer shall report the use of proceeds pursuant to Item 701 of Regulation S-B or S-K or Item 14(e) of Form 20-F, as applicable, on its first periodic report filed pursuant to Sections 13(a) and 15(d) (15 U.S.C. 78m(a) and 78o(d)) of the Securities Exchange Act of 1934 after effectiveness, and thereafter on each of its subsequent periodic reports filed pursuant to Sections 13(a) and 15(d) of the Securities Exchange Act of 1934 through the later of disclosure of the application of all the offering proceeds or disclosure of the termination of the offering.

(b) A successor issuer shall comply with paragraph (a) of this section only if a report of the use of proceeds is required with respect to the first effective registration statement of the predecessor issuer.

(c) For purposes of this section:

(1) The term "offering proceeds" shall not include any amount(s) received for the account(s) of any selling security holder(s).

(2) The term "application" shall not include the temporary investment of proceeds by the issuer pending final application.

(d) This section shall not apply to any effective registration statement for securities to be issued:

(1) In a business combination described in Rule 145(a) (§ 230.145(a));

(2) By an issuer which pursuant to a business combination described in Rule 145(a) has succeeded to another issuer that prior to such business combination had a registration statement become effective under the Act and on the date such business combination was not subject to paragraph (a) of this section;

(3) Pursuant to an employee benefit plan;

(4) Pursuant to a dividend or interest reinvestment plan;

(5) As American depository receipts for foreign securities;

(6) By any investment company registered under the Investment Company Act of 1940 and any issuer that has elected to be regulated as a business development company

under sections 54 through 65 of the Investment Company Act of 1940 (15 U.S.C. 80a-53 through 80a-64);

(7) By any public utility company or public utility holding company required to file reports with any State or Federal authority;

(8) In a merger in which a vote or consent of the security holders of the company being acquired is not required pursuant to applicable state law; or

(9) In an exchange offer for the securities of the issuer or another entity.

Rule 464. Effective Date of Post-Effective Amendments to Registration Statements Filed on Form S-8 and on Certain Forms S-3, S-4, F-2 and F-3

Provided. That, at the time of filing of each post-effective amendment with the Commission, the issuer continues to meet the requirements of filing on Form S-8 (§ 239.16b of this chapter); or on Form S-3, F-2 or F-3 (§ 239.13, 32 or 33 of this chapter) for a registration statement relating to a dividend or interest reinvestment plan; or in the case of a registration statement on Form S-4 (§ 239.25 of this chapter) that there is continued compliance with General Instruction G of that Form:

(a) The post-effective amendment shall become effective upon filing with the Commission; and

(b) With respect to securities sold on or after the filing date pursuant to a prospectus which forms a part of a Form S-8 registration statement; or a Form S-3, F-2, or F-3 registration statement relating to a dividend or interest reinvestment plan; or a Form S-4 registration statement complying with General Instruction G of that Form and which has been amended to include or incorporate new full year financial statements or to comply with the provisions of section 10(a)(3) of the Act, the effective date of the registration statement shall be deemed to be the filing date of the post-effective amendment.

Rule 473. Delaying Amendments

(a) An amendment in the following form filed with a registration statement, or as an amendment to a registration statement which has not become effective, shall be deemed, for the purpose of section 8(a) of the Act, to be filed on such date or dates as may be necessary to delay the effective date of such registration statement (1) until the registrant shall file a further amendment which specifically states as provided in paragraph (b) of this section that such registration statement shall thereafter become effective in accordance with section 8(a) of the Act, or (2) until the registration statement shall become effective on such date as the Commission, acting pursuant to section 8(a), may determine:

The registrant hereby amends this registration statement on such date or dates as may be necessary to delay its effective date until the registrant shall file a further amendment which specifically states that this registration statement shall thereafter become effective in accordance with section 8(a) of the Securities Act of 1933 or until the registration statement shall become effective on such date as the Commission acting pursuant to said section 8(a), may determine.

(b) An amendment which for the purpose of paragraph (a)(1) of this section specifically states that a registration statement shall thereafter become effective in accordance with section 8(a) of the Act, shall be in the following form:

This registration statement shall hereafter become effective in accordance with the provisions of section 8(a) of the Securities Act of 1933.

(c) An amendment pursuant to paragraph (a) of this section which is filed with a registration statement shall be set forth on the facing page thereof following the calculation of the registration fee. Any such amendment filed after the filing of the registration statement, any amendment altering the proposed date of public sale of the securities being registered, or any amendment filed pursuant to paragraph (b) of this section may be made by telegram, letter or facsimile transmission. Each such telegraphic amendment shall be confirmed in writing within a reasonable time by the filing of a signed copy of the amendment. Such confirmation shall not be deemed an amendment.

(d) No amendments pursuant to paragraph (a) of this section may be filed with a registration statement on Form F-7, F-8 or F-80 (§ 239.37, § 239.38 or § 239.41 of this chapter); on Form F-10 (§ 239.40 of this chapter) relating to an offering being made contemporaneously in the United States and the issuer's home jurisdiction; on Form S-8 (§ 239.16b of this chapter); on Form S-3 or F-3 (§ 239.13 or § 239.33 of this chapter) relating to a dividend or interest reinvestment plan; on Form S-3 or Form F-3 relating to an automatic shelf registration statement; or on Form S-4 (§ 239.25 of this chapter) complying with General Instruction G of that Form.

Rule 474. Date of Filing of Amendments

The date on which amendments are actually received by the Commission shall be the date of filing thereof, if all of the requirements of the Act and the rules with respect to such filing have been complied with.

Rule 477. Withdrawal of Registration Statement or Amendment

(a) Except as provided in paragraph (b) of this section, any registration statement or any amendment or exhibit thereto may be withdrawn upon application if the Commission, finding such withdrawal consistent with the public interest and the protection of investors, consents thereto.

(b) Any application for withdrawal of a registration statement filed on Form F-2 (§ 239.32 of this chapter) relating to a dividend or interest reinvestment plan, or on Form S-4 (§ 239.25 of this chapter) complying with General Instruction G of that Form, and/or any pre-effective amendment thereto, will be deemed granted upon filing if such filing is made prior to the effective date. Any other application for withdrawal of an entire registration statement made before the effective date of the registration statement will be deemed granted at the time the application is filed with the Commission unless, within 15 calendar days after the registrant files the application, the Commission notifies the registrant that the application for withdrawal will not be granted.

(c) The registrant must sign any application for withdrawal and must state fully in it the grounds on which the registrant makes the application. The fee paid upon the filing of the registration statement will not be refunded to the registrant. The registrant must state in the application that no securities were sold in connection with the offering. If the registrant applies for withdrawal in anticipation of reliance on § 230.155(c), the registrant must, without discussing any terms of the private offering, state in the application that the registrant may undertake a subsequent private offering in reliance on § 230.155(c).

(d) Any withdrawn document will remain in the Commission's public files, as well as the related request for withdrawal.

Rule 478. Powers to Amend or Withdraw Registration Statement

All persons signing a registration statement shall be deemed, in the absence of a statement to the contrary, to confer upon the registrant, and upon the agent for service named in the registration statement, the following powers:

(a) A power to amend the registration statement (1) by filing an amendment as provided in § 230.473; (2) by filing any written consent; (3) by correcting typographical errors; (4) by reducing the amount of securities registered, pursuant to an undertaking contained in the registration statement.

(b) A power to make application pursuant to § 230.475 for the Commission's consent to the filing of an amendment.

(c) A power to withdraw the registration statement or any amendment or exhibit thereto.

(d) A power to consent to the entry of an order under Section 8(b) of the Act, waiving notice and hearing, such order being entered without prejudice to the right of the registrant thereafter to have the order vacated upon a showing to the Commission that the registration statement as amended is no longer incomplete or inaccurate on its face in any material respect.

Investment Companies; Business Development Companies

Note: The rules in this section of Regulation C (§§ 230.480 to 230.488 and §§ 230.495 to 230.498) apply only to investment companies and business development companies. Section 230.489 applies to certain entities excepted from the definition of investment company by rules under the Investment Company Act of 1940. The rules in the rest of Regulation C (§§ 230.400 to 230.479 and §§ 230.490 to 230.494), unless the context specifically indicates otherwise, also apply to investment companies and business development companies. See § 230.400.

Rule 482. Advertising by an Investment Company as Satisfying Requirements of Section 10

(a) *Scope of Rule*. This section applies to an advertisement or other sales material (*advertisement*) with respect to securities of an investment company registered under the Investment Company Act of 1940 (15 U.S.C. 80a-1 *et seq*.) (*1940 Act*), or a business development company, that is selling or proposing to sell its securities pursuant to a registration statement that has been filed under the Act. This section does not apply to an advertisement that is excepted from the definition of prospectus by section 2(a)(10) of the Act (15 U.S.C. 77b(a)(10)), § 230.498(d), § 230.498A(g) or (j)(2), or to a summary prospectus under § 230.498 or § 230.498A. An advertisement that complies with this section, which may include information the substance of which is not included in the prospectus specified in section 10(a) of the Act (15 U.S.C 77j(a)), will be deemed to be a prospectus under section 10(b) of the Act (15 U.S.C. 77j(b)) for the purposes of section 5(b)(1) of the Act (15 U.S.C. 77e(b)(1)).

Note 1 to Paragraph (a): The fact that an advertisement complies with this section does not relieve the investment company, underwriter, or dealer of any obligations with respect to the advertisement under the antifraud provisions of the Federal securities laws. For guidance about factors to be weighed in determining whether statements, representations, illustrations, and descriptions contained in investment company advertisements are misleading, see § 230.156. In addition, an advertisement that complies with this section is subject to the legibility requirements of § 230.420.

(b) *Required disclosure*. This paragraph describes information that is required to be included in an advertisement in order to comply with this section.

(1) *Availability of Additional Information*. An advertisement must include a statement that advises an investor to consider the investment objectives, risks, and charges and expenses of the investment company carefully before investing; explains that the prospectus and, if available, the summary prospectus contain this and other information about the investment company; identifies a source from which an investor may obtain a prospectus and, if available, a summary prospectus; and states that the prospectus and, if available, the summary prospectus should be read carefully before investing.

(2) *Advertisements used prior to effectiveness of registration statement*. An advertisement that is used prior to effectiveness of the investment company's registration statement or the determination of the public offering price (in the case of a registration statement that becomes effective omitting information from the prospectus contained in the registration statement in reliance upon § 230.430A) must include the "Subject to Completion" legend required by § 230.481(b)(2).

(3) *Advertisements including performance data*. An advertisement that includes performance data of an open-end management investment company or a separate account registered under the 1940 Act as a unit investment trust offering variable annuity contracts (*trust account*) must include the following:

(i) A legend disclosing that the performance data quoted represents past performance; that past performance does not guarantee future results; that the investment return and principal value of an investment will fluctuate so that an investor's shares, when redeemed, may be worth more or less than their original cost; and that current performance may be lower or higher than the performance data quoted. The legend should also identify either a toll-free (or collect) telephone number or a website where an investor may obtain performance data current to the most recent month-end unless the advertisement includes total return quotations current to the most recent month ended seven business days prior to the date of use. An advertisement for a money market fund that is a government money market fund, as defined in § 270.2a-7(a)(16) of this chapter, or a retail money market fund, as defined in § 270.2a-7(a)(25) of this chapter may omit the disclosure about principal value fluctuation; and

Note to paragraph (b)(3)(i): The date of use refers to the date or dates when an advertisement is used by investors, not the date on which an advertisement is published or submitted for publication. The date of use refers to the entire period of use by investors and not simply the first date on which an advertisement is used.

(ii) If a sales load or any other nonrecurring fee is charged, the maximum amount of the load or fee, and if the sales load or fee is not reflected, a statement that the performance data does not reflect the deduction of the sales load or fee, and that, if reflected, the load or fee would reduce the performance quoted.

(4) *Money market funds.* (i) An advertisement for an investment company that holds itself out to be a money market fund, that is not a government money market fund, as defined in § 270.2a-7(a)(16) of this chapter, or a retail money market fund, as defined in § 270.2a-7(a)(25) of this chapter, must include the following statement:

You could lose money by investing in the Fund. Because the share price of the Fund will fluctuate, when you sell your shares they may be worth more or less than what you originally paid for them. The Fund may impose a fee upon sale of your shares or may temporarily suspend your ability to sell shares if the Fund's liquidity falls below required minimums because of market conditions or other factors. An investment in the Fund is not insured or guaranteed by the Federal Deposit Insurance Corporation or any other government agency. The Fund's sponsor has no legal obligation to provide financial support to the Fund, and you should not expect that the sponsor will provide financial support to the Fund at any time.

(ii) An advertisement for an investment company that holds itself out to be a money market fund, that is a government money market fund, as defined in § 270.2a-7(a)(16) of this chapter or a retail money market fund, as defined in § 270.2a-7(a)(25) of this chapter, and that is subject to the requirements of § 270.2a-7(c)(2)(i) and/or (ii) of this chapter (or is not subject to the requirements of § 270.2a-7(c)(2)(i) and/or (ii) of this chapter pursuant to § 270.2a-7(c)(2)(iii) of this chapter, but has chosen to rely on the ability to impose liquidity fees and suspend redemptions consistent with the requirements of § 270.2a-7(c)(2)(i) and/or (ii)), must include the following statement:

You could lose money by investing in the Fund. Although the Fund seeks to preserve the value of your investment at $1.00 per share, it cannot guarantee it will do so. The Fund may impose a fee upon sale of your shares or may temporarily suspend your ability to sell shares if the Fund's liquidity falls below required minimums because of market conditions or other factors. An investment in the Fund is not insured or guaranteed by the Federal Deposit Insurance Corporation or any other government agency. The Fund's sponsor has no legal obligation to provide financial support to the Fund, and you should not expect that the sponsor will provide financial support to the Fund at any time.

(iii) An advertisement for an investment company that holds itself out to be a money market fund, that is a government money market fund, as defined in § 270.2a-7(a)(16) of this chapter, that is not subject to the requirements of § 270.2a-7(c)(2)(i) and/or (ii) of this chapter pursuant to § 270.2a-7(c)(2)(iii) of this chapter, and that has not chosen to rely on the ability to impose liquidity fees and suspend redemptions consistent with the requirements of § 270.2a-7(c)(2)(i) and/or (ii), must include the following statement:

> You could lose money by investing in the Fund. Although the Fund seeks to preserve the value of your investment at $1.00 per share, it cannot guarantee it will do so. An investment in the Fund is not insured or guaranteed by the Federal Deposit Insurance Corporation or any other government agency. The Fund's sponsor has no legal obligation to provide financial support to the Fund, and you should not expect that the sponsor will provide financial support to the Fund at any time.

Note to Paragraph (b)(4). If an affiliated person, promoter, or principal underwriter of the Fund, or an affiliated person of such a person, has contractually committed to provide financial support to the Fund, the statement may omit the last sentence ("The Fund's sponsor has no legal obligation to provide financial support to the Fund, and you should not expect that the sponsor will provide financial support to the Fund at any time.") for the term of the agreement. For purposes of this Note, the term "financial support" includes any capital contribution, purchase of a security from the Fund in reliance on § 270.17a-9 of this chapter, purchase of any defaulted or devalued security at par, execution of letter of credit or letter of indemnity, capital support agreement (whether or not the Fund ultimately received support), performance guarantee, or any other similar action reasonably intended to increase or stabilize the value or liquidity of the fund's portfolio; however, the term "financial support" excludes any routine waiver of fees or reimbursement of fund expenses, routine inter-fund lending, routine inter-fund purchases of fund shares, or any action that would qualify as financial support as defined above, that the board of directors has otherwise determined not to be reasonably intended to increase or stabilize the value or liquidity of the fund's portfolio.

(5) *Presentation.* In a print advertisement, the statements required by paragraphs (b)(1) through (b)(4) of this section must be presented in a type size at least as large as and of a style different from, but at least as prominent as, that used in the major portion of the advertisement, provided that when performance data is presented in a type size smaller than that of the major portion of the advertisement, the statements required by paragraph (b)(3) of this section may appear in a type size no smaller than that of the performance data. If an advertisement is delivered through an electronic medium, the legibility requirements for the statements required by paragraphs (b)(1) through (b)(4) of this section relating to type size and style may be satisfied by presenting the statements in any manner reasonably calculated to draw investor attention to them. In a radio or television advertisement, the statements required by paragraphs (b)(1) through (b)(4) of this section must be given emphasis equal to that used in the major portion of the advertisement. The statements required by paragraph (b)(3) of this section must be presented in close proximity to the performance data, and, in a print advertisement, must be presented in the body of the advertisement and not in a footnote.

(6) *Commission legend.* An advertisement that complies with this section need not contain the Commission legend required by § 230.481(b)(1).

(c) *Use of Applications.* An advertisement that complies with this section may not contain or be accompanied by any application by which a prospective investor may invest in the investment company, except that a prospectus meeting the requirements of section 10(a) of the Act (15 U.S.C. 77j(a)) by which a unit investment trust offers variable annuity or variable life insurance contracts may contain a contract application although the prospectus includes, or is accompanied by, information about an investment company in which the unit investment trust invests that, pursuant to this section, is deemed a prospectus under section 10(b) of the Act (15 U.S.C. 77j(b)).

(2) *Profile.* An advertisement that complies with this section may be used with a Profile that includes, or is accompanied by, an application to purchase shares of the investment company as permitted under § 230.498.

(d) *Performance data for non-money market funds.* In the case of an open-end management investment company or a trust account (other than a money market fund referred to in paragraph (e) of this section), any quotation of the company's performance contained in an advertisement shall be limited to quotations of:

(1) *Current yield.* A current yield that:

(i) Is based on the methods of computation prescribed in Form N-1A (§§ 239.15A and 274.11A of this chapter), N-3 (§§ 239.17a and 274.11b of this chapter), or N-4 (§§ 239.17b and 274.11c of this chapter);

(ii) Is accompanied by quotations of total return as provided for in paragraph (d)(3) of this section;

(iii) Is set out in no greater prominence than the required quotations of total return; and

(iv) Adjacent to the quotation and with no less prominence than the quotation, identifies the length of and the date of the last day in the base period used in computing the quotation.

(2) *Tax-equivalent yield.* A tax-equivalent yield that:

(i) Is based on the methods of computation prescribed in Form N-1A (§§ 239.15A and 274.11A of this chapter), N-3 (§§ 239.17a and 274.11b of this chapter), or N-4 (§§ 239.17b and 274.11c of this chapter);

(ii) Is accompanied by quotations of yield as provided for in paragraph (d)(1) of this section and total return as provided for in paragraph (d)(3) of this section;

(iii) Is set out in no greater prominence than the required quotations of yield and total return;

(iv) Relates to the same base period as the required quotation of yield; and

(v) Adjacent to the quotation and with no less prominence than the quotation, identifies the length of and the date of the last day in the base period used in computing the quotation.

(3) *Average annual total return.* Average annual total return for one, five, and ten year periods, except that if the company's registration statement under the Act (15 U.S.C. 77a *et seq.*) has been in effect for less than one, five, or ten years, the time period during which the registration statement was in effect is substituted for the period(s) otherwise prescribed. The quotations must:

(i) Be based on the methods of computation prescribed in Form N-1A (§§ 239.15A and 274.11A of this chapter), N-3 (§§ 239.17a and 274.11b of this chapter), or N-4 (§§ 239.17b and 274.11c of this chapter);

(ii) Be current to the most recent calendar quarter ended prior to the submission of the advertisement for publication;

(iii) Be set out with equal prominence; and

(iv) Adjacent to the quotation and with no less prominence than the quotation, identify the length of and the last day of the one, five, and ten year periods.

(4) *After-tax return.* For an open-end management investment company, average annual total return (after taxes on distributions) and average annual total return (after taxes on distributions and redemption) for one, five, and ten year periods, except that if the company's registration statement under the Act (15 U.S.C. 77a *et seq.*) has been in effect for less than one, five, or ten years, the time period during which the registration statement was in effect is substituted for the period(s) otherwise prescribed. The quotations must:

(i) Be based on the methods of computation prescribed in Form N-1A (§§ 239.15A and 274.11A of this chapter);

(ii) Be current to the most recent calendar quarter ended prior to the submission of the advertisement for publication;

(iii) Be accompanied by quotations of total return as provided for in paragraph (d)(3) of this section;

(iv) Include both average annual total return (after taxes on distributions) and average annual total return (after taxes on distributions and redemption);

(v) Be set out with equal prominence and be set out in no greater prominence than the required quotations of total return; and

(vi) Adjacent to the quotations and with no less prominence than the quotations, identify the length of and the last day of the one, five, and ten year periods.

(5) *Other performance measures.* Any other historical measure of company performance (not subject to any prescribed method of computation) if such measurement:

(i) Reflects all elements of return;

(ii) Is accompanied by quotations of total return as provided for in paragraph (d)(3) of this section;

(iii) In the case of any measure of performance adjusted to reflect the effect of taxes, is accompanied by quotations of total return as provided for in paragraph (d)(4) of this section;

(iv) Is set out in no greater prominence than the required quotations of total return; and

(v) Adjacent to the measurement and with no less prominence than the measurement, identifies the length of and the last day of the period for which performance is measured.

(e) *Performance data for money market funds.* In the case of a money market fund:

(1) *Yield.* Any quotation of the money market fund's yield in an advertisement shall be based on the methods of computation prescribed in Form N-1A (§§ 239.15A and 274.11A of this chapter), N-3 (§§ 239.17a and 274.11b of this chapter), or N-4 (§§ 239.17b and 274.11c of this chapter) and may include:

(i) A quotation of current yield that, adjacent to the quotation and with no less prominence than the quotation, identifies the length of and the date of the last day in the base period used in computing that quotation;

(ii) A quotation of effective yield if it appears in the same advertisement as a quotation of current yield and each quotation relates to an identical base period and is presented with equal prominence; or

(iii) A quotation or quotations of tax-equivalent yield or tax-equivalent effective yield if it appears in the same advertisement as a quotation of current yield and each quotation relates to the same base period as the quotation of current yield, is presented with equal prominence, and states the income tax rate used in the calculation.

(2) *Total return.* Accompany any quotation of the money market fund's total return in an advertisement with a quotation of the money market fund's current yield under paragraph (e)(1)(i) of this section. Place the quotations of total return and current yield next to each other, in the same size print, and if there is a material difference between the quoted total return and the quoted current yield, include a statement that the yield quotation more closely reflects the current earnings of the money market fund than the total return quotation.

(f) *Advertisements that make tax representations.* An advertisement for an open-end management investment company (other than a company that is permitted under § 270.35d-1(a)(4) of this chapter to use a name suggesting that the company's distributions are exempt from federal income tax or from both federal and state income tax) that represents or implies that the company is managed to limit or control the effect of taxes on company performance must accompany any quotation of the company's performance permitted by paragraph (d) of this section with quotations of total return as provided for in paragraph (d)(4) of this section.

(g) *Timeliness of performance data.* All performance data contained in any advertisement must be as of the most recent practicable date considering the type of investment company and the media through which the data will be conveyed, except that any advertisement containing total return quotations will be considered to have complied with this paragraph provided that:

(1) (i) The total return quotations are current to the most recent calendar quarter ended prior to the submission of the advertisement for publication; and

(ii) Total return quotations current to the most recent month ended seven business days prior to the date of use are provided at the toll-free (or collect) telephone number or website identified pursuant to paragraph (b)(3)(i) of this section; or

(2) The total return quotations are current to the most recent month ended seven business days prior to the date of use of the advertisement.

Note to paragraph (g): The date of use refers to the date or dates when an advertisement is used by investors, not the date on which an advertisement is published or submitted for publication. The date of use refers to the entire period of use by investors and not simply the first date on which an advertisement is used.

(h) *Filing.* An advertisement that complies with this section need not be filed as part of the registration statement filed under the Act.

Note to paragraph (h): These advertisements, unless filed with NASD Regulation, Inc., are required to be filed in accordance with the requirements of § 230.497.

REGULATION D—RULES GOVERNING THE LIMITED OFFER AND SALE OF SECURITIES WITHOUT REGISTRATION UNDER THE SECURITIES ACT OF 1933

Rule 500. Use of Regulation D

Users of Regulation D (§§ 230.500 et seq.) should note the following:

(a) Regulation D relates to transactions exempted from the registration requirements of Section 5 of the Securities Act of 1933 (the "Act") (15 U.S.C. 77a et seq., as amended). Such transactions are not exempt from the antifraud, civil liability, or other provisions of the federal securities laws. Issuers are reminded of their obligation to provide such further material information, if any, as may be necessary to make the information required under Regulation D, in light of the circumstances under which it is furnished, not misleading.

(b) Nothing in Regulation D obviates the need to comply with any applicable state law relating to the offer and sale of securities. Regulation D is intended to be a basic element in a uniform system of federal-state limited offering exemptions consistent with the provisions of Sections 18 and 19(c) of the Act (15 U.S.C. 77r and 77(s)(c)). In those states that have adopted Regulation D, or any version of Regulation D, special attention should be directed to the applicable state laws and regulations, including those relating to registration of persons who receive remuneration in connection with the offer and sale of securities, to disqualification of issuers and other persons associated with offerings based on state administrative orders or judgments, and to requirements for filings of notices of sales.

(c) Attempted compliance with any rule in Regulation D does not act as an exclusive election; the issuer can also claim the availability of any other applicable exemption. For instance, an issuer's failure to satisfy all the terms and conditions of Rule 506(b) (§ 230.506(b)) shall not raise any presumption that the exemption provided by Section 4(a)(2) of the Act (15 U.S.C. 77d(2)) is not available.

(d) Regulation D is available only to the issuer of the securities and not to any affiliate of that issuer or to any other person for resales of the issuer's securities. Regulation D provides an exemption only for the transactions in which the securities are offered or sold by the issuer, not for the securities themselves.

(e) Regulation D may be used for business combinations that involve sales by virtue of Rule 145(a) (§ 230.145(a)) or otherwise.

(f) In view of the objectives of Regulation D and the policies underlying the Act, Regulation D is not available to any issuer for any transaction or chain of transactions that, although in technical compliance with Regulation D, is part of a plan or scheme to evade the registration provisions of the Act. In such cases, registration under the Act is required.

(g) Securities offered and sold outside the United States in accordance with Regulation S (§ 230.901 through 905) need not be registered under the Act. See Release No. 33-6863. Regulation S may be relied upon for such offers and sales even if coincident offers and sales are made in accordance with Regulation D inside the United States. Thus, for example, persons who are offered and sold securities in accordance with Regulation S would not be counted in the calculation of the number of purchasers under Regulation D. Similarly, proceeds from such sales would not be included in the aggregate offering price. The provisions of this paragraph (g), however, do not apply if the issuer elects to rely solely on Regulation D for offers or sales to persons made outside the United States.

Rule 501. Definitions and Terms Used in Regulation D

As used in Regulation D [§ 230.500 *et seq.* of this chapter], the following terms shall have the meaning indicated:

(a) *Accredited investor.* "Accredited investor" shall mean any person who comes within any of the following categories, or who the issuer reasonably believes comes within any of the following categories, at the time of the sale of the securities to that person:

(1) Any bank as defined in section 3(a)(2) of the Act, or any savings and loan association or other institution as defined in section 3(a)(5)(A) of the Act whether acting in its individual or fiduciary capacity; any broker or dealer registered pursuant to section 15 of the Securities Exchange Act of 1934; any insurance company as defined in section 2(a)(13) of the Act; any investment company registered under the Investment Company Act of 1940 or a business development company as defined in section 2(a)(48) of that Act; any Small Business Investment Company licensed by the U.S. Small Business Administration under section 301(c) or (d) of the Small Business Investment Act of 1958; any plan established and maintained by a state, its political subdivisions, or any agency or instrumentality of a state or its political subdivisions, for the benefit of its employees, if such plan has total assets in excess of $5,000,000; any employee benefit plan within the meaning of the Employee Retirement Income Security Act of 1974 if the investment decision is made by a plan fiduciary, as defined in section 3(21) of such Act, which is either a bank, savings and loan association, insurance company, or registered investment adviser, or if the employee benefit plan has total assets in excess of $5,000,000 or, if a self-directed plan, with investment decisions made solely by persons that are accredited investors;

(2) Any private business development company as defined in section 202(a)(22) of the Investment Advisers Act of 1940;

(3) Any organization described in section 501(c)(3) of the Internal Revenue Code, corporation, Massachusetts or similar business trust, or partnership, not formed for the specific purpose of acquiring the securities offered, with total assets in excess of $5,000,000;

(4) Any director, executive officer, or general partner of the issuer of the securities being offered or sold, or any director, executive officer, or general partner of a general partner of that issuer;

(5) Any natural person whose individual net worth, or joint net worth with that person's spouse, exceeds $1,000,000.

(i) Except as provided in paragraph (a)(5)(ii) of this section, for purposes of calculating net worth under this paragraph (a)(5):

(A) The person's primary residence shall not be included as an asset;

(B) Indebtedness that is secured by the person's primary residence, up to the estimated fair market value of the primary residence at the time of the sale of securities, shall not be included as a liability (except that if the amount of such indebtedness outstanding at the time of sale of securities exceeds the amount outstanding 60 days before such time, other than as a result of the acquisition of the primary residence, the amount of such excess shall be included as a liability); and

(C) Indebtedness that is secured by the person's primary residence in excess of the estimated fair market value of the primary residence at the time of the sale of securities shall be included as a liability;

(ii) Paragraph (a)(5)(i) of this section will not apply to any calculation of a person's net worth made in connection with a purchase of securities in accordance with a right to purchase such securities, provided that:

(A) Such right was held by the person on July 20, 2010;

(B) The person qualified as an accredited investor on the basis of net worth at the time the person acquired such right; and

(C) The person held securities of the same issuer, other than such right, on July 20, 2010.

(6) Any natural person who had an individual income in excess of $200,000 in each of the two most recent years or joint income with that person's spouse in excess of $300,000 in each of those years and has a reasonable expectation of reaching the same income level in the current year;

(7) Any trust, with total assets in excess of $5,000,000, not formed for the specific purpose of acquiring the securities offered, whose purchase is directed by a sophisticated person as described in § 230.506(b)(2)(ii); and

(8) Any entity in which all of the equity owners are accredited investors.

(b) *Affiliate.* An "affiliate" of, or person "affiliated" with, a specified person shall mean a person that directly, or indirectly through one or more intermediaries, controls or is controlled by, or is under common control with, the person specified.

(c) *Aggregate offering price.* "Aggregate offering price" shall mean the sum of all cash, services, property, notes, cancellation of debt, or other consideration to be received by an issuer for issuance of its securities. Where securities are being offered for both cash and non-cash consideration, the aggregate offering price shall be based on the price at which the securities are offered for cash. Any portion of the aggregate offering price attributable to cash received in a foreign currency shall be translated into United States currency at the currency exchange rate in effect at a reasonable time prior to or on the date of the sale of the securities. If securities are not offered for cash, the aggregate offering price shall be based on the value of the consideration as established by bona fide sales of that consideration made within a reasonable time, or, in the absence of sales, on the fair value as determined by an accepted standard. Such valuations of non-cash consideration must be reasonable at the time made.

(d) *Business combination.* "Business combination" shall mean any transaction of the type specified in paragraph (a) of Rule 145 under the Act (17 CFR 230.145) and any transaction involving the acquisition by one issuer, in exchange for all or a part of its own or its parent's stock, of stock of another issuer if, immediately after the acquisition, the acquiring issuer has control of the other issuer (whether or not it had control before the acquisition).

(e) *Calculation of number of purchasers.* For purposes of calculating the number of purchasers under § 230.506(b) only, the following shall apply:

(1) The following purchasers shall be excluded:

(i) Any relative, spouse or relative of the spouse of a purchaser who has the same primary residence as the purchaser;

(ii) Any trust or estate in which a purchaser and any of the persons related to him as specified in paragraph (e)(1)(i) or (e)(1)(iii) of this § 230.501 collectively have more than 50 percent of the beneficial interest (excluding contingent interests);

(iii) Any corporation or other organization of which a purchaser and any of the persons related to him as specified in paragraph (e)(1)(i) or (e)(1)(ii) of this § 230.501 collectively are beneficial owners of more than 50 percent of the equity securities (excluding directors' qualifying shares) or equity interests; and

(iv) Any accredited investor.

(2) A corporation, partnership or other entity shall be counted as one purchaser. If, however, that entity is organized for the specific purpose of acquiring the securities offered and is not an accredited investor under paragraph (a)(8) of this section, then each beneficial owner of equity securities or equity interests in the entity shall count as a separate purchaser for all provisions of Regulation D (§§ 230.501-230.508), except to the extent provided in paragraph (e)(1) of this section.

(3) A non-contributory employee benefit plan within the meaning of Title I of the Employee Retirement Income Security Act of 1974 shall be counted as one purchaser where the trustee makes all investment decisions for the plan.

Note: The issuer must satisfy all the other provisions of Regulation D for all purchasers whether or not they are included in calculating the number of purchasers. Clients of an investment adviser or customers of a broker or dealer shall be considered the "purchasers" under Regulation D regardless of the amount of discretion given to the investment adviser or broker or dealer to act on behalf of the client or customer.

(f) *Executive officer.* "Executive officer" shall mean the president, any vice president in charge of a principal business unit, division or function (such as sales, administration or finance), any other officer who performs a policy making function, or any other person who performs similar policy making functions for the issuer. Executive officers of subsidiaries may be deemed executive officers of the issuer if they perform such policy making functions for the issuer.

(g) *Final Order.* Final order shall mean a written directive or declaratory statement issued by a federal or state agency described in § 230.506(d)(1)(iii) under applicable statutory authority that provides for notice and an opportunity for hearing, which constitutes a final disposition or action by that federal or state agency.

(h) *Issuer.* The definition of the term "issuer" in section 2(a)(4) of the Act shall apply, except that in the case of a proceeding under the Federal Bankruptcy Code [11 U.S.C. 101 et seq.], the trustee or debtor in possession shall be considered the issuer in an offering under a plan or reorganization, if the securities are to be issued under the plan.

(i) *Purchaser representative.* "Purchaser representative" shall mean any person who satisfies all of the following conditions or who the issuer reasonably believes satisfies all of the following conditions:

(1) Is not an affiliate, director, officer or other employee of the issuer, or beneficial owner of 10 percent or more of any class of the equity securities or 10 percent or more of the equity interest in the issuer, except where the purchaser is:

(i) A relative of the purchaser representative by blood, marriage or adoption and not more remote than a first cousin;

*(ii) A trust or estate in which the purchaser representative and any persons related to him as specified in paragraph (h)(1)(i) or (h)(1)(iii) of this § 230.501 collectively have more than 50 percent of the beneficial interest (excluding contingent interest) or of which the purchaser representative serves as trustee, executor, or in any similar capacity; or

**(iii) A corporation or other organization of which the purchaser representative and any persons related to him as specified in paragraph (h)(1)(i) or (h)(1)(ii) of this § 230.501 collectively are the beneficial owners of more than 50 percent of the equity securities (excluding directors' qualifying shares) or equity interests;

(2) Has such knowledge and experience in financial and business matters that he is capable of evaluating, alone, or together with other purchaser representatives of the purchaser, or together with the purchaser, the merits and risks of the prospective investment;

(3) Is acknowledged by the purchaser in writing, during the course of the transaction, to be his purchaser representative in connection with evaluating the merits and risks of the prospective investment; and

---

* Cross-references in paragraph (i)(1)(ii) to (h)(1)(i) and (h)(1)(iii) should probably read (i)(1)(i) and (i)(1)(iii) but the SEC did not update these cross-references when it added a new paragraph (g) and redesignated paragraph (h) as paragraph (i).–EDS.

** Cross-references in paragraph (i)(1)(iii) to (h)(1)(i) and (h)(1)(iii) should probably read (i)(1)(i) and (i)(1)(iii) but the SEC did not update these cross-references when it added a new paragraph (g) and redesignated paragraph (h) as paragraph (i).–Eds.

(4) Discloses to the purchaser in writing a reasonable time prior to the sale of securities to that purchaser any material relationship between himself or his affiliates and the issuer or its affiliates that then exists, that is mutually understood to be contemplated, or that has existed at any time during the previous two years, and any compensation received or to be received as a result of such relationship.

Note 1 to § 230.501. A person acting as a purchaser representative should consider the applicability of the registration and antifraud provisions relating to brokers and dealers under the Securities Exchange Act of 1934 ("Exchange Act") [15 U.S.C. 78a et seq., as amended] and relating to investment advisers under the Investment Advisers Act of 1940.

Note 2 to § 230.501. The acknowledgement required by paragraph (h)(3) and the disclosure required by paragraph (h)(4) of this § 230.501 must be made with specific reference to each prospective investment. Advance blanket acknowledgment, such as for "all securities transactions" or "all private placements," is not sufficient.

Note 3 to § 230.501. Disclosure of any material relationships between the purchaser representative or his affiliates and the issuer or its affiliates does not relieve the purchaser representative of his obligation to act in the interest of the purchaser.

Rule 502. General Conditions to be Met

The following conditions shall be applicable to offers and sales made under Regulation D (§§ 230.500 *et seq.* of this chapter):

(a) *Integration.* All sales that are part of the same Regulation D offering must meet all of the terms and conditions of Regulation D. Offers and sales that are made more than six months before the start of a Regulation D offering or are made more than six months after completion of a Regulation D offering will not be considered part of that Regulation D offering, so long as during those six month periods there are no offers or sales of securities by or for the issuer that are of the same or a similar class as those offered or sold under Regulation D, other than those offers or sales of securities under an employee benefit plan as defined in Rule 405 under the Act [17 CFR 230.405].

Note: The term "offering" is not defined in the Act or in Regulation D. If the issuer offers or sells securities for which the safe harbor rule in paragraph (a) of this § 230.502 is unavailable, the determination as to whether separate sales of securities are part of the same offering (i.e. are considered "integrated") depends on the particular facts and circumstances. Generally, transactions otherwise meeting the requirements of an exemption will not be integrated with simultaneous offerings being made outside the United States in compliance with Regulation S. See Release No. 33-6863.

The following factors should be considered in determining whether offers and sales should be integrated for purposes of the exemptions under Regulation D:

(a) whether the sales are part of a single plan of financing;

(b) whether the sales involve issuance of the same class of securities;

(c) whether the sales have been made at or about the same time;

(d) whether the same type of consideration is being received; and

(e) whether the sales are made for the same general purpose.

See Release No. 33-4552 (November 6, 1962) [27 FR 11316].

(b) *Information requirements.*

(1) *When information must be furnished.*

If the issuer sells securities under § 230.506(b) to any purchaser that is not an accredited investor, the issuer shall furnish the information specified in paragraph (b)(2) of this section to such purchaser a reasonable time prior to sale. The issuer is not required to furnish the specified information to purchasers when it sells securities under § 230.504, or to any accredited investor.

Note: When an issuer provides information to investors pursuant to paragraph (b)(1), it should consider providing such information to accredited investors as well, in view of the anti-fraud provisions of the federal securities laws.

(2) *Type of information to be furnished.*

(i) If the issuer is not subject to the reporting requirements of section 13 or 15(d) of the Exchange Act, at a reasonable time prior to the sale of securities the issuer shall furnish to the purchaser, to the extent material to an understanding of the issuer, its business and the securities being offered:

(A) *Non-financial statement information.* If the issuer is eligible to use Regulation A (§ 230.251-263), the same kind of information as would be required in Part II of Form 1-A (§ 239.90 of this chapter). If the issuer is not eligible to use Regulation A, the same kind of information as required in Part I of a registration statement filed under the Securities Act on the form that the issuer would be entitled to use.

(B) *Financial Statement Information.*

(*1*) *Offerings up to $2,000,000.* The information required in Article 8 of Regulation S-X (§ 210.8 of this chapter), except that only the issuer's balance sheet, which shall be dated within 120 days of the start of the offering, must be audited.

(*2*) *Offerings up to $7,500,000.* The financial statement information required in Form S-1 (§ 239.10 of this chapter) for smaller reporting companies. If an issuer, other than a limited partnership, cannot obtain audited financial statements without unreasonable effort or expense, then only the issuer's balance sheet, which shall be dated within 120 days of the start of the offering, must be audited. If the issuer is a limited partnership and cannot obtain the required financial statements without unreasonable effort or expense, it may furnish financial statements that have been prepared on the basis of Federal income tax requirements and examined and reported on in accordance with generally accepted auditing standards by an independent public or certified accountant.

(*3*) *Offerings over $7,500,000.* The financial statement as would be required in a registration statement filed under the Act on the form that the issuer would be entitled to use. If an issuer, other than a limited partnership, cannot obtain audited financial statements without unreasonable effort or expense, then only the issuer's balance sheet, which shall be dated within 120 days of the start of the offering, must be audited. If the issuer is a limited partnership and cannot obtain the required financial statements without unreasonable effort or expense, it may furnish financial statements that have been prepared on the basis of Federal income tax requirements and examined and reported on in accordance with generally accepted auditing standards by an independent public or certified accountant.

(C) If the issuer is a foreign private issuer eligible to use Form 20-F (§ 249.220f of this chapter), the issuer shall disclose the same kind of information required to be included in a registrtion statement filed under the Act on the form that the issuer would be entitled to use. The financial statements need be certified only to the extent required by paragraph (b)(2)(i)(B)(*1*), (*2*) or (*3*) of this section, as appropriate.

(ii) If the issuer is subject to the reporting requirements of section 13 or 15(d) of the Exchange Act, at a reasonable time prior to the sale of securities, the issuer shall furnish to the purchaser the information specified in paragraph (b)(2)(ii)(A) or (B) of this section, and in either event the information specified in paragraph (b)(2)(ii)(C) of this section:

(A) The issuer's annual report to shareholders for the most recent fiscal year, if such annual report meets the requirements of Rules 14a-3 or 14c-3 under the Exchange Act (§ 240.14a-3 or § 240.14c-3 of this chapter), the definitive proxy statement filed in connection with that annual report, and if requested by the purchaser in writing, a copy of the issuer's most recent Form 10-K (§ 249.310 of this chapter) under the Exchange Act.

(B) The information contained in an annual report on Form 10-K (§ 249.310 of this chapter) under the Exchange Act or in a registration statement on Form S-1 (§ 239.11 of this chapter) or S-11 (§ 239.18 of this chapter) under the Act or on Form 10 (§ 249.210 of this chapter) under the Exchange Act, whichever filing is the most recent required to be filed.

(C) The information contained in any reports or documents required to be filed by the issuer under sections 13(a), 14(a), 14(c), and 15(d) of the Exchange Act since the distribution or filing of the report or registration statement specified in paragraph (A) or (B), and a brief description of the securities being offered, the use of the proceeds from the offering, and any material changes in the issuer's affairs that are not disclosed in the documents furnished.

(D) If the issuer is a foreign private issuer, the issuer may provide in lieu of the information specified in paragraph (b)(2)(ii)(A) or (B) of this section, the information contained in its most recent filing on Form 20-F or Form F-1 (§ 239.31 of the chapter).

(iii) Exhibits required to be filed with the Commission as part of a registration statement or report, other than an annual report to shareholders or parts of that report incorporated by reference in a Form 10-K report, need not be furnished to each purchaser that is not an accredited investor if the contents of material exhibits are identified and such exhibits are made available to a purchaser, upon his or her written request, a reasonable time before his or her purchase.

(iv) At a reasonable time prior to the sale of securities to any purchaser that is not an accredited investor in a transaction under § 230.506(b), the issuer shall furnish to the purchaser a brief description in writing of any material written information concerning the offering that has been provided by the issuer to any accredited investor but not previously delivered to such unaccredited purchaser. The issuer shall furnish any portion or all of this information to the purchaser, upon his written request a reasonable time prior to his purchase.

(v) The issuer shall also make available to each purchaser at a reasonable time prior to his purchase of securities in a transaction under § 230.506 the opportunity to ask questions and receive answers concerning the terms and conditions of the offering and to obtain any additional information which the issuer possesses or can acquire without unreasonable effort or expense that is necessary to verify the accuracy of information furnished under paragraph (b)(2)(i) or (ii) of this § 230.502.

(vi) For business combinations or exchange offers, in addition to information required by Form S-4 [17 CFR 239.25], the issuer shall provide to each purchaser at the time the plan is submitted to security holders, or, with an exchange, during the course of the transaction and prior to sale, written information about any terms or arrangements of the proposed transactions that are materially different from those for all other security holders. For purposes of this subsection, an issuer which is not subject to the reporting requirements of section 13 or 15(d) of the Exchange Act may satisfy the requirements of Part I.B. or C. of Form S-4 by compliance with paragraph (b)(2)(i) of this § 230.502.

(vii) At a reasonable time prior to the sale of securities to any purchaser that is not an accredited investor in a transaction under § 230.506(b), the issuer shall advise the purchaser of the limitations on resale in the manner contained in paragraph (d)(2) of this section. Such disclosure may be contained in other materials required to be provided by this paragraph.

(c) *Limitation on Manner of Offering.* Except as provided in § 230.504(b)(1) or § 230.506(c), neither the issuer nor any person acting on its behalf shall offer or sell the securities by any form of general solicitation or general advertising, including, but not limited to, the following:

(1) Any advertisement, article, notice or other communication published in any newspaper, magazine, or similar media or broadcast over television or radio; and

(2) Any seminar or meeting whose attendees have been invited by any general solicitation or general advertising;

Provided, however, that publication by an issuer of a notice in accordance with § 230.135c or filing with the Commission by an issuer of a notice of sales on Form D (17 CFR 239.500) in which the issuer has made a good faith and reasonable attempt to comply with the requirements of such form, shall not be deemed to constitute general solicitation or general advertising for purposes of this section;

Provided further, that, if the requirements of § 230.135e are satisfied, providing any journalist with access to press conferences held outside of the United States, to meetings with issuer or selling security holder representatives conducted outside of the United States, or to written press-related materials released outside the United States, at or in which a present or proposed offering of securities is discussed, will not be deemed to constitute general solicitation or general advertising for purposes of this section.

(d) *Limitations on resale.* Except as provided in § 230.504(b)(1), securities acquired in a transaction under Regulation D shall have the status of securities acquired in a transaction under section 4(a)(2) of the Act and cannot be resold without registration under the Act or an exemption therefrom. The issuer shall exercise reasonable care to assure that the purchasers of the securities are not underwriters within the meaning of section 2(11) of the Act, which reasonable care may be demonstrated by the following;

Provided, however, that publication by an issuer of a notice in accordance with § 230.135c shall not be deemed to constitute general solicitation or general advertising for purposes of this section.

(1) Reasonable inquiry to determine if the purchaser is acquiring the securities for himself or for other persons;

(2) Written disclosure to each purchaser prior to sale that the securities have not been registered under the Act and, therefore, cannot be resold unless they are registered under the Act or unless an exemption from registration is available; and

(3) Placement of a legend on the certificate or other document that evidences the securities stating that the securities have not been registered under the Act and setting forth or referring to the restrictions on transferability and sale of the securities.

While taking these actions will establish the requisite reasonable care, it is not the exclusive method to demonstrate such care. Other actions by the issuer may satisfy this provision. In addition, § 230.502(b)(2)(vii) requires the delivery of written disclosure of the limitations on resale to investors in certain instances.

Rule 503. Filing of Notice of Sales

(a) *When Notice of Sales on Form D is Required and Permitted to be Filed.*

(1) An issuer offering or selling securities in reliance on § 230.504 or § 230.506 must file with the Commission a notice of sales containing the information required by Form D (17 CFR 239.500) for each new offering of securities no later than 15 calendar days after the first sale of securities in the offering, unless the end of that period falls on a Saturday, Sunday or holiday, in which case the due date would be the first business day following.

(2) An issuer may file an amendment to a previously filed notice of sales on Form D at any time.

(3) An issuer must file an amendment to a previously filed notice of sales on Form D for an offering:

(i) To correct a material mistake of fact or error in the previously filed notice of sales on Form D, as soon as practicable after discovery of the mistake or error;

(ii) To reflect a change in the information provided in the previously filed notice of sales on Form D, as soon as practicable after the change, except that no amendment is required to reflect a change that occurs after the offering terminates or a change that occurs solely in the following information:

(A) The address or relationship to the issuer of a related person identified in response to Item 3 of the notice of sales on Form D;

(B) An issuer's revenues or aggregate net asset value;

(C) The minimum investment amount, if the change is an increase, or if the change, together with all other changes in that amount since the previously filed notice of sales on Form D, does not result in a decrease of more than 10%;

(D) Any address or state(s) of solicitation shown in response to Item 12 of the notice of sales on Form D;

(E) The total offering amount, if the change is a decrease, or if the change, together with all other changes in that amount since the previously filed notice of sales on Form D, does not result in an increase of more than 10%;

(F) The amount of securities sold in the offering or the amount remaining to be sold;

(G) The number of non-accredited investors who have invested in the offering, as long as the change does not increase the number to more than 35;

(H) The total number of investors who have invested in the offering; or

(I) The amount of sales commissions, finders' fees or use of proceeds for payments to executive officers, directors or promoters, if the change is a decrease, or if the change, together with all other changes in that amount since the previously filed notice of sales on Form D, does not result in an increase of more than 10%; and

(iii) Annually, on or before the first anniversary of the filing of the notice of sales on Form D or the filing of the most recent amendment to the notice of sales on Form D, if the offering is continuing at that time.

(4) An issuer that files an amendment to a previously filed notice of sales on Form D must provide current information in response to all requirements of the notice of sales on Form D regardless of why the amendment is filed.

(b) *How Notice of Sales on Form D Must Be Filed and Signed.*

(1) A notice of sales on Form D must be filed with the Commission in electronic format by means of the Commission's Electronic Data Gathering, Analysis, and Retrieval System (EDGAR) in accordance with EDGAR rules set forth in Regulation S-T (17 CFR Part 232).

(2) Every notice of sales on Form D must be signed by a person duly authorized by the issuer.

Rule 504. Exemption for Limited Offerings and Sales of Securities Not Exceeding $5,000,000

(a) *Exemption.* Offers and sales of securities that satisfy the conditions in paragraph (b) of this § 230.504 by an issuer that is not:

(1) subject to the reporting requirements of section 13 or 15(d) of the Exchange Act;

(2) an investment company; or

(3) a development stage company that either has no specific business plan or purpose or has indicated that its business plan is to engage in a merger or acquisition with an unidentified company or companies, or other entity or person, shall be exempt from the provision of section 5 of the Act under section 3(b) of the Act.

(b) *Conditions to be met.*

(1) *General conditions.* To qualify for exemption under this 230.504, offers and sales must satisfy the terms and conditions of 230.501 and 230.502(a), (c) and (d), except that the provisions of 230.502(c) and (d) will not apply to offers and sales of securities under this 230.504 that are made:

(i) Exclusively in one or more states that provide for the registration of the securities, and require the public filing and delivery to investors of a substantive disclosure document before sale, and are made in accordance with those state provisions;

(ii) In one or more states that have no provision for the registration of the securities or the public filing or delivery of a disclosure document before sale, if the securities have been registered in at least one state that provides for such registration, public filing and delivery before sale, offers and sales are made in that state in accordance with such provisions, and the disclosure document is delivered before sale to all purchasers (including those in the states that have no such procedure); or

(iii) Exclusively according to state law exemptions from registration that permit general solicitation and general advertising so long as sales are made only to "accredited investors" as defined in 230.501(a).

(2) The aggregate offering price for an offering of securities under this § 230.504, as defined in § 230.501(c), shall not exceed $5,000,000, less the aggregate offering price for all securities sold within the twelve months before the start of and during the offering of securities under this § 230.504 or in violation of section 5(a) of the Securities Act.

Instruction to Paragraph (b)(2): If a transaction under § 230.504 fails to meet the limitation on the aggregate offering price, it does not affect the availability of this § 230.504 for the other transactions considered in applying such limitation. For example, if an issuer sold $5,000,000 of its securities on January 1, 2014 under this § 230.504 and an additional $500,000 of its securities on July 1, 2014, this § 230.504 would not be available for the later sale, but would still be applicable to the January 1, 2014 sale.

(3) Disqualifications. No exemption under this section shall be available for the securities of any issuer if such issuer would be subject to disqualification under § 230.506(d) on or after January 20, 2017; provided that disclosure of prior "bad actor" events shall be required in accordance with § 230.506(e).

Instruction to Paragraph (b)(3): For purposes of disclosure of prior "bad actor" events pursuant to § 230.506(e), an issuer shall furnish to each purchaser, a reasonable time prior to sale, a description in writing of any matters that would have triggered disqualification under this paragraph (b)(3) but occurred before January 20, 2017.

Rule 505. Exemption for Limited Offers and Sales of Securities Not Exceeding $5,000,000

[*Removed and Reserved.* Release Nos. 33-10238; 34-79161; October 26, 2016.]

Rule 506. Exemption for Limited Offers and Sales Without Regard to Dollar Amount of Offering

(a) *Exemption.* Offers and sales of securities by an issuer that satisfy the conditions in paragraph (b) or (c) of this § 230.506 shall be deemed to be transactions not involving any public offering within the meaning of section 4(a)(2) of the Act.

(b) *Conditions to be met in offerings subject to limitation on manner of offering.*

(1) *General conditions.* To qualify for exemption under this section, offers and sales must satisfy all the terms and conditions of §§ 230.501 and 230.502.

(2) *Specific conditions.*

(i) *Limitation on number of purchasers.* There are no more than or the issuer reasonably believes that there are no more than 35 purchasers of securities from the issuer in any offering under this § 230.506.

Note to Paragraph (b)(2)(i). See § 230.501(e) for the calculation of the number of purchasers and § 230.502(a) for what may or may not constitute an offering under Paragraph b of this section.

    (ii) *Nature of purchasers.* Each purchaser who is not an accredited investor either alone or with his purchaser representative(s) has such knowledge and experience in financial and business matters that he is capable of evaluating the merits and risks of the prospective investment, or the issuer reasonably believes immediately prior to making any sale that such purchaser comes within this description.

  (c) *Conditions to be met in offerings not subject to limitation on manner of offering.*

    (1) *General conditions.* To qualify for exemption under this section, sales must satisfy all the terms and conditions of § § 230.501 and 230.502(a) and (d).

    (2) *Specific conditions.*

    (i) *Nature of purchasers.* All purchasers of securities sold in any offering under paragraph (c) of this section are accredited investors.

    (ii) *Verification of accredited investor status.* The issuer shall take reasonable steps to verify that purchasers of securities sold in any offering under paragraph (c) of this section are accredited investors. The issuer shall be deemed to take reasonable steps to verify if the issuer uses, at its option, one of the following non-exclusive and non-mandatory methods of verifying that a natural person who purchases securities in such offering is an accredited investor; provided, however, that the issuer does not have knowledge that such person is not an accredited investor:

    (A) In regard to whether the purchaser is an accredited investor on the basis of income, reviewing any Internal Revenue Service form that reports the purchaser's income for the two most recent years (including, but not limited to, Form W-2, Form 1099, Schedule K-1 to Form 1065, and Form 1040) and obtaining a written representation from the purchaser that he or she has a reasonable expectation of reaching the income level necessary to qualify as an accredited investor during the current year;

    (B) In regard to whether the purchaser is an accredited investor on the basis of net worth, reviewing one or more of the following types of documentation dated within the prior three months and obtaining a written representation from the purchaser that all liabilities necessary to make a determination of net worth have been disclosed:

    (1) With respect to assets: Bank statements, brokerage statements and other statements of securities holdings, certificates of deposit, tax assessments, and appraisal reports issued by independent third parties; and

    (2) With respect to liabilities: A consumer report from at least one of the nationwide consumer reporting agencies; or

    (C) Obtaining a written confirmation from one of the following persons or entities that such person or entity has taken reasonable steps to verify that the purchaser is an accredited investor within the prior three months and has determined that such purchaser is an accredited investor:

    (1) A registered broker-dealer;

    (2) An investment adviser registered with the Securities and Exchange Commission;

    (3) A licensed attorney who is in good standing under the laws of the jurisdictions in which he or she is admitted to practice law; or

    (4) A certified public accountant who is duly registered and in good standing under the laws of the place of his or her residence or principal office.

    (D) In regard to any person who purchased securities in an issuer's Rule 506(b) offering as an accredited investor prior to September 23, 2013 and continues to hold such securities, for the same issuer's Rule 506(c) offering, obtaining a certification by such person at the time of sale that he or she qualifies as an accredited investor.

Instructions to paragraph (c)(2)(ii)(A) through (D) of this section:

1. The issuer is not required to use any of these methods in verifying the accredited investor status of natural persons who are purchasers. These methods are examples of the types of non-exclusive and non-mandatory methods that satisfy the verification requirement in § 230.506(c)(2)(ii).

2. In the case of a person who qualifies as an accredited investor based on joint income with that person's spouse, the issuer would be deemed to satisfy the verification requirement in § 230.506(c)(2)(ii)(A) by reviewing copies of Internal Revenue Service forms that report income for the two most recent years in regard to, and obtaining written representations from, both the person and the spouse.

3. In the case of a person who qualifies as an accredited investor based on joint net worth with that person's spouse, the issuer would be deemed to satisfy the verification requirement in § 230.506(c)(2)(ii)(B) by reviewing such documentation in regard to, and obtaining written representations from, both the person and the spouse.

(d) *"Bad Actor" disqualification.*

(1) No exemption under this section shall be available for a sale of securities if the issuer; any predecessor of the issuer; any affiliated issuer; any director, executive officer, other officer participating in the offering, general partner or managing member of the issuer; any beneficial owner of 20% or more of the issuer's outstanding voting equity securities, calculated on the basis of voting power; any promoter connected with the issuer in any capacity at the time of such sale; any investment manager of an issuer that is a pooled investment fund; any person that has been or will be paid (directly or indirectly) remuneration for solicitation of purchasers in connection with such sale of securities; any general partner or managing member of any such investment manager or solicitor; or any director, executive officer or other officer participating in the offering of any such investment manager or solicitor or general partner or managing member of such investment manager or solicitor:

(i) Has been convicted, within ten years before such sale (or five years, in the case of issuers, their predecessors and affiliated issuers), of any felony or misdemeanor:

(A) In connection with the purchase or sale of any security;

(B) Involving the making of any false filing with the Commission; or (C) Arising out of the conduct of the business of an underwriter, broker, dealer, municipal securities dealer, investment adviser or paid solicitor of purchasers of securities;

(ii) Is subject to any order, judgment or decree of any court of competent jurisdiction, entered within five years before such sale, that, at the time of such sale, restrains or enjoins such person from engaging or continuing to engage in any conduct or practice:

(A) In connection with the purchase or sale of any security;

(B) Involving the making of any false filing with the Commission; or

(C) Arising out of the conduct of the business of an underwriter, broker, dealer, municipal securities dealer, investment adviser or paid solicitor of purchasers of securities;

(iii) Is subject to a final order of a state securities commission (or an agency or officer of a state performing like functions); a state authority that supervises or examines banks, savings associations, or credit unions; a state insurance commission (or an agency or officer of a state performing like functions); an appropriate federal banking agency; the U.S. Commodity Futures Trading Commission; or the National Credit Union Administration that:

(A) At the time of such sale, bars the person from:

(1) Association with an entity regulated by such commission, authority, agency, or officer;

(2) Engaging in the business of securities, insurance or banking; or

(3) Engaging in savings association or credit union activities; or

(B) Constitutes a final order based on a violation of any law or regulation that prohibits fraudulent, manipulative, or deceptive conduct entered within ten years before such sale;

(iv) Is subject to an order of the Commission entered pursuant to section 15(b) or 15B(c) of the Securities Exchange Act of 1934 (15 U.S.C. 78o(b) or 78o-4(c)) or section 203(e) or (f) of the Investment Advisers Act of 1940 (15 U.S.C. 80b-3(e) or (f)) that, at the time of such sale:

(A) Suspends or revokes such person's registration as a broker, dealer, municipal securities dealer or investment adviser;

(B) Places limitations on the activities, functions or operations of such person; or

(C) Bars such person from being associated with any entity or from participating in the offering of any penny stock;

(v) Is subject to any order of the Commission entered within five years before such sale that, at the time of such sale, orders the person to cease and desist from committing or causing a violation or future violation of:

(A) Any scienter-based anti-fraud provision of the federal securities laws, including without limitation section 17(a)(1) of the Securities Act of 1933 (15 U.S.C. 77q(a)(1)), section 10(b) of the Securities Exchange Act of 1934 (15 U.S.C. 78j(b)) and 17 CFR 240.10b-5, section 15(c)(1) of the Securities Exchange Act of 1934 (15 U.S.C. 78o(c)(1)) and section 206(1) of the Investment Advisers Act of 1940 (15 U.S.C. 80b-6(1)), or any other rule or regulation thereunder; or

(B) Section 5 of the Securities Act of 1933 (15 U.S.C. 77e).

(vi) Is suspended or expelled from membership in, or suspended or barred from association with a member of, a registered national securities exchange or a registered Rule 506 17 national or affiliated securities association for any act or omission to act constituting conduct inconsistent with just and equitable principles of trade;

(vii) Has filed (as a registrant or issuer), or was or was named as an underwriter in, any registration statement or Regulation A offering statement filed with the Commission that, within five years before such sale, was the subject of a refusal order, stop order, or order suspending the Regulation A exemption, or is, at the time of such sale, the subject of an investigation or proceeding to determine whether a stop order or suspension order should be issued; or

(viii) Is subject to a United States Postal Service false representation order entered within five years before such sale, or is, at the time of such sale, subject to a temporary restraining order or preliminary injunction with respect to conduct alleged by the United States Postal Service to constitute a scheme or device for obtaining money or property through the mail by means of false representations.

(2) Paragraph (d)(1) of this section shall not apply:

(i) With respect to any conviction, order, judgment, decree, suspension, expulsion or bar that occurred or was issued before September 23, 2013;

(ii) Upon a showing of good cause and without prejudice to any other action by the Commission, if the Commission determines that it is not necessary under the circumstances that an exemption be denied;

(iii) If, before the relevant sale, the court or regulatory authority that entered the relevant order, judgment or decree advises in writing (whether contained in the relevant judgment, order or decree or separately to the Commission or its staff) that disqualification under paragraph (d)(1) of this section should not arise as a consequence of such order, judgment or decree; or

(iv) If the issuer establishes that it did not know and, in the exercise of reasonable care, could not have known that a disqualification existed under paragraph (d)(1) of this section.

Instruction to paragraph (d)(2)(iv). An issuer will not be able to establish that it has exercised reasonable care unless it has made, in light of the circumstances, factual inquiry into whether any disqualifications exist. The nature and scope of the factual inquiry will vary based on the facts and circumstances concerning, among other things, the issuer and the other offering participants.

(3) For purposes of paragraph (d)(1) of this section, events relating to any affiliated issuer that occurred before the affiliation arose will be not considered disqualifying if the affiliated entity is not:

(i) In control of the issuer; or

(ii) Under common control with the issuer by a third party that was in control of the affiliated entity at the time of such events.

(e) *Disclosure of prior "Bad Actor" events.* The issuer shall furnish to each purchaser, a reasonable time prior to sale, a description in writing of any matters that would have triggered disqualification under paragraph (d)(1) of this section but occurred before September 23, 2013. The failure to furnish such information timely shall not prevent an issuer from relying on this section if the issuer establishes that it did not know and, in the exercise of reasonable care, could not have known of the existence of the undisclosed matter or matters.

Instruction to paragraph (e). An issuer will not be able to establish that it has exercised reasonable care unless it has made, in light of the circumstances, factual inquiry into whether any disqualifications exist. The nature and scope of the factual inquiry will vary based on the facts and circumstances concerning, among other things, the issuer and the other offering participants.

Rule 507. Disqualifying Provision Relating to Exemptions Under §§ 230.504 and 230.506

(a) No exemption under § 230.504 or § 230.506 shall be available for an issuer if such issuer, any of its predecessors or affiliates have been subject to any order, judgment, or decree of any court of competent jurisdiction temporarily, preliminarily or permanently enjoining such person for failure to comply with § 230.503.

(b) Paragraph (a) of this section shall not apply if the Commission determines, upon a showing of good cause, that it is not necessary under the circumstances that exemption be denied.

Rule 508. Insignificant Deviations From a Term, Condition or Requirement of Regulation D

(a) A failure to comply with a term, condition or requirement of § 230.504 or § 230.506 will not result in the loss of the exemption from the requirements of section 5 of the Act for any offer or sale to a particular individual or entity, if the person relying on the exemption shows:

(1) the failure to comply did not pertain to a term, condition or requirement directly intended to protect that particular individual or entity; and

(2) the failure to comply was insignificant with respect to the offering as a whole, provided that any failure to comply with paragraph (c) of § 230.502, paragraph (b)(2) of § 230.504 and paragraph (b)(2)(i) of § 230.506 shall be deemed to be significant to the offering as a whole; and

(3) a good faith and reasonable attempt was made to comply with all applicable terms, conditions and requirements of § 230.504 or § 230.506.

(b) A transaction made in reliance on § 230.504 or § 230.506 shall comply with all applicable terms, conditions and requirements of Regulation D. Where an exemption is established only through reliance upon paragraph (a) of this section, the failure to comply shall nonetheless be actionable by the Commission under section 20 of the Act.

REGULATION E—EXEMPTION FOR SECURITIES OF BUSINESS INVESTMENT COMPANIES

Rule 701. Exemption For Offers and Sales of Securities Pursuant to Certain Compensatory Benefit Plans and Contracts Relating to Compensation

Preliminary Notes

1. This section relates to transactions exempted from the registration requirements of section 5 of the Act (15 U.S.C. 77e). These transactions are not exempt from the antifraud, civil liability, or other provisions of the federal securities laws. Issuers and persons acting on their behalf have an obligation to provide investors with disclosure adequate to satisfy the antifraud provisions of the federal securities laws.

2. In addition to complying with this section, the issuer also must comply with any applicable state law relating to the offer and sale of securities.

3. An issuer that attempts to comply with this section, but fails to do so, may claim any other exemption that is available.

4. This section is available only to the issuer of the securities. Affiliates of the issuer may not use this section to offer or sell securities. This section also does not cover resales of securities by any person. This section provides an exemption only for the transactions in which the securities are offered or sold by the issuer, not for the securities themselves.

5. The purpose of this section is to provide an exemption from the registration requirements of the Act for securities issued in compensatory circumstances. This section is not available for plans or schemes to circumvent this purpose, such as to raise capital. This section also is not available to exempt any transaction that is in technical compliance with this section but is part of a plan or scheme to evade the registration provisions of the Act. In any of these cases, registration under the Act is required unless another exemption is available.

Rule 701. (a) *Exemption.* Offers and sales made in compliance with all of the conditions of this section are exempt from section 5 of the Act (15 U.S.C. 77e).

(b) *Issuers eligible to use this section.*

(1) *General.* This section is available to any issuer that is not subject to the reporting requirements of section 13 or 15(d) of the Securities Exchange Act of 1934 (the "Exchange Act") (15 U.S.C. 78m or 78o(d)) and is not an investment company registered or required to be registered under the Investment Company Act of 1940 (15 U.S.C. 80a-1 *et seq.*).

(2) *Issuers that become subject to reporting.* If an issuer becomes subject to the reporting requirements of section 13 or 15(d) of the Exchange Act (15 U.S.C. 78m or 78o(d)) after it has made offers complying with this section, the issuer may nevertheless rely on this section to sell the securities previously offered to the persons to whom those offers were made.

(3) *Guarantees by reporting companies.* An issuer subject to the reporting requirements of section 13 or 15(d) of the Exchange Act (15 U.S.C. 78m, 78o(d)) may rely on this section if it is merely guaranteeing the payment of a subsidiary's securities that are sold under this section.

(c) *Transactions exempted by this section.* This section exempts offers and sales of securities (including plan interests and guarantees pursuant to paragraph (d)(2)(ii) of this section) under a written compensatory benefit plan (or written compensation contract) established by the issuer, its parents, its majority-owned subsidiaries or majority-owned subsidiaries of the issuer's parent, for the participation of their employees, directors, general partners, trustees (where the issuer is a business trust), officers, or consultants and advisors, and their family members who acquire such securities from such persons through gifts or domestic relations orders. This section exempts offers and sales to former employees, directors, general partners, trustees, officers, consultants and advisors only if such persons were employed by or providing services to the issuer at the time the securities were offered. In addition, the term "employee" includes insurance agents who are exclusive agents of the issuer, its subsidiaries or parents, or derive more than 50% of their annual income from those entities.

(1) *Special requirements for consultants and advisors.* This section is available to consultants and advisors only if:

(i) They are natural persons;

(ii) They provide *bona fide* services to the issuer, its parents, its majority-owned subsidiaries or majority-owned subsidiaries of the issuer's parent; and

(iii) The services are not in connection with the offer or sale of securities in a capital-raising transaction, and do not directly or indirectly promote or maintain a market for the issuer's securities.

(2) *Definition of "Compensatory Benefit Plan."* For purposes of this section, a *compensatory benefit plan* is any purchase, savings, option, bonus, stock appreciation, profit sharing, thrift, incentive, deferred compensation, pension or similar plan.

(3) *Definition of "Family Member."* For purposes of this section, *family member* includes any child, stepchild, grandchild, parent, stepparent, grandparent, spouse, former spouse, sibling, niece, nephew, mother-in-law, father-in-law, son-in-law, daughter-in-law, brother-in-law, or sister-in-law, including adoptive relationships, any person sharing the employee's household (other than a tenant or employee), a trust in which these persons have more than fifty percent of the beneficial interest, a foundation in which these persons (or the employee) control the management of assets, and any other entity in which these persons (or the employee) own more than fifty percent of the voting interests.

(d) *Amounts that may be sold.*

(1) *Offers.* Any amount of securities may be offered in reliance on this section. However, for purposes of this section, sales of securities underlying options must be counted as sales on the date of the option grant.

(2) *Sales.* The aggregate sales price or amount of securities sold in reliance on this section during any consecutive 12-month period must not exceed the greatest of the following:

(i) $1,000,000;

(ii) 15% of the total assets of the issuer (or of the issuer's parent if the issuer is a wholly-owned subsidiary and the securities represent obligations that the parent fully and unconditionally guarantees), measured at the issuer's most recent balance sheet date (if no older than its last fiscal year end); or

(iii) 15% of the outstanding amount of the class of securities being offered and sold in reliance on this section, measured at the issuer's most recent balance sheet date (if no older than its last fiscal year end).

(3) *Rules for calculating prices and amounts.*

(i) *Aggregate sales price.* The term *aggregate sales price* means the sum of all cash, property, notes, cancellation of debt or other consideration received or to be received by the issuer for the sale of the securities. Non-cash consideration must be valued by reference to *bona fide* sales of that consideration made within a reasonable time or, in the absence of such sales, on the fair value as determined by an accepted standard. The value of services exchanged for securities issued must be measured by reference to the value of the securities issued. Options must be valued based on the exercise price of the option.

(ii) *Time of the calculation.* With respect to options to purchase securities, the aggregate sales price is determined when an option grant is made (without regard to when the option becomes exercisable). With respect to other securities, the calculation is made on the date of sale. With respect to deferred compensation or similar plans, the calculation is made when the irrevocable election to defer is made.

(iii) *Derivative securities.* In calculating outstanding securities for purposes of paragraph (d)(2)(iii) of this section, treat the securities underlying all currently exercisable or convertible options, warrants, rights or other securities, other than those issued under this exemption, as outstanding. In calculating the amount of securities sold for other purposes of paragraph (d)(2) of this section, count the amount of securities that would be acquired upon exercise or conversion in connection with sales of options, warrants, rights or other exercisable or convertible securities, including those to be issued under this exemption.

(iv) *Other exemptions.* Amounts of securities sold in reliance on this section do not affect "aggregate offering prices" in other exemptions, and amounts of securities sold in reliance on other exemptions do not affect the amount that may be sold in reliance on this section.

(e) *Disclosure that must be provided.* The issuer must deliver to investors a copy of the compensatory benefit plan or the contract, as applicable. In addition, if the aggregate sales price or amount of securities sold during any consecutive 12-month period exceeds $10 million, the issuer must deliver the following disclosure to investors a reasonable period of time before the date of sale:

(1) If the plan is subject to the Employee Retirement Income Security Act of 1974 ("ERISA") (29 U.S.C. 1104 – 1107), a copy of the summary plan description required by ERISA;

(2) If the plan is not subject to ERISA, a summary of the material terms of the plan;

(3) Information about the risks associated with investment in the securities sold pursuant to the compensatory benefit plan or compensation contract; and

(4) Financial statements required to be furnished by Part F/S of Form 1-A (Regulation A Offering Statement) (§ 239.90 of this chapter) under Regulation A (§§ 230.251 through 230.263). Foreign private issuers as defined in Rule 405 must provide a reconciliation to generally accepted accounting principles in the United States (U.S. GAAP) if their financial statements are not prepared in accordance with U.S. GAAP or International Financial Reporting Standards as issued by the International Accounting Standards Board (Item 17 of Form 20-F (§ 249.220f of this chapter)). The financial statements required by this section must be as of a date no more than 180 days before the sale of securities in reliance on this exemption.

(5) If the issuer is relying on paragraph (d)(2)(ii) of this section to use its parent's total assets to determine the amount of securities that may be sold, the parent's financial statements must be delivered. If the parent is subject to the reporting requirements of section 13 or 15(d) of the Exchange Act (15 U.S.C. 78m or 78o(d)), the financial statements of the parent required by Rule 10-01 of Regulation S-X (§ 210.10-01 of this chapter) and Item 310 of Regulation S-B (§ 228.310 of this chapter), as applicable, must be delivered.

(6) If the sale involves a stock option or other derivative security, the issuer must deliver disclosure a reasonable period of time before the date of exercise or conversion. For deferred compensation or similar plans, the issuer must deliver disclosure to investors a reasonable period of time before the date the irrevocable election to defer is made.

(f) *No integration with other offerings.* Offers and sales exempt under this section are deemed to be a part of a single, discrete offering and are not subject to integration with any other offers or sales, whether registered under the Act or otherwise exempt from the registration requirements of the Act.

(g) *Resale limitations.*

(1) Securities issued under this section are deemed to be "restricted securities" as defined in § 230.144.

(2) Resales of securities issued pursuant to this section must be in compliance with the registration requirements of the Act or an exemption from those requirements.

(3) Ninety days after the issuer becomes subject to the reporting requirements of section 13 or 15(d) of the Exchange Act (15 U.S.C. 78m or 78o(d)), securities issued under this section may be resold by persons who are not affiliates (as defined in

§ 230.144) in reliance on § 230.144 without compliance with paragraphs (c) and (d) of § 230.144, and by affiliates without compliance with paragraph (d) of § 230.144.

REGULATION S—RULES GOVERNING OFFERS AND SALES MADE OUTSIDE THE UNITED STATES WITHOUT REGISTRATION UNDER THE SECURITIES ACT OF 1933

Preliminary Notes

1. The following rules relate solely to the application of Section 5 of the Securities Act of 1933 (the "Act") [15 U.S.C. § 77e] and not to antifraud or other provisions of the federal securities laws.

2. In view of the objective of these rules and the policies underlying the Act, Regulation S is not available with respect to any transaction or series of transactions that, although in technical compliance with these rules, is part of a plan or scheme to evade the registration provisions of the Act. In such cases, registration under the Act is required.

3. Nothing in these rules obviates the need for any issuer or any other person to comply with the securities registration or broker-dealer registration requirements of the Securities Exchange Act (the "Exchange Act"), whenever such requirements are applicable.

4. Nothing in these rules obviates the need to comply with any applicable state law relating to the offer and sale of securities.

5. Attempted compliance with any rule in Regulation S does not act as an exclusive election; a person making an offer or sale of securities may also claim the availability of any other applicable exemption from the registration requirements of the Act. The availability of the Regulation S safe harbor to offers and sales that occur outside of the United States will not be affected by the subsequent offer and sale of these securities into the United States or to U.S. persons during the distribution compliance period, as long as the subsequent offer and sale are made pursuant to registration or an exemption therefrom under the Act.

6. Regulation S is available only for offers and sales of securities outside the United States. Securities acquired overseas, whether or not pursuant to Regulation S, may be resold in the United States only if they are registered under the Act or an exemption from registration is available.

7. Nothing in these rules precludes access by journalists for publications with a general circulation in the United States to offshore press conferences, press releases and meetings with company press spokespersons in which an offshore offering or tender offer is discussed, provided that the information is made available to the foreign and United States press generally and is not intended to induce purchases of securities by persons in the United States or tenders of securities by United States holders in the case of exchange offers. Where applicable, issuers and bidders may also look to § 230.135e and § 240.14d-1(c) of this chapter.

8. The provisions of this Regulation S shall not apply to offers and sales of securities issued by open-end investment companies or unit investment trusts registered or required to be registered or closed-end investment companies required to be registered, but not registered, under the Investment Company Act of 1940 [15 U.S.C. § 80a-1 *et seq.*] (the "1940 Act").

Rule 901. General Statement

For the purposes only of section 5 of the Act (15 U.S.C. § 77e), the terms "offer," "offer to sell," "offer for sell," "sell," "sale," and "offer to buy" shall be deemed to include offers and sales that occur within the United States and shall be deemed not to include offers and sales that occur outside the United States.

Rule 902. Definitions

As used in Regulation S, the following terms shall have the meanings indicated.

(a) *Debt securities.* "Debt securities" of an issuer is defined to mean any security other than an equity security as defined in § 230.405, as well as the following:

(1) Non-participatory preferred stock, which is defined as non-convertible capital stock, the holders of which are entitled to a preference in payment of dividends and in distribution of assets on liquidation, dissolution, or winding up of the issuer, but are not entitled to participate in residual earnings or assets of the issuer; and

(2) Asset-backed securities, which are securities of a type that either:

(i) Represent an ownership interest in a pool of discrete assets, or certificates of interest or participation in such assets (including any rights designed to assure servicing, or the receipt or timeliness of receipt by holders of such assets, or certificates of interest or participation in such assets, of amounts payable thereunder), provided that the assets are not generated or originated between the issuer of the security and its affiliates; or

(ii) Are secured by one or more assets or certificates of interest or participation in such assets, and the securities, by their terms, provide for payments of principal and interest (if any) in relation to payments or reasonable projections of payments on assets meeting the requirements of paragraph (a)(2)(i) of this section, or certificates of interest or participations in assets meeting such requirements.

(iii) For purposes of paragraph (a)(2) of this section, the term "assets" means securities, installment sales, accounts receivable, notes, leases or other contracts, or other assets that by their terms convert into cash over a finite period of time.

(b) *Designated offshore securities market.* "Designated offshore securities market" means:

(1) The Eurobond market, as regulated by the International Securities Market Association; the Alberta Stock Exchange; the Amsterdam Stock Exchange; the Australian Stock Exchange Limited; the Bermuda Stock Exchange; the Bourse de Bruxelles; the Copenhagen Stock Exchange; the European Association of Securities Dealers Automated Quotation; the Frankfurt Stock Exchange; the Helsinki Stock Exchange; The Stock Exchange of Hong Kong Limited; the Irish Stock Exchange; the Istanbul Stock Exchange; the Johannesburg Stock Exchange; the London Stock Exchange; the Bourse de Luxembourg; the Mexico Stock Exchange; the Borsa Valori di Milan; the Montreal Stock Exchange; the Oslo Stock Exchange; the Bourse de Paris; the Stock Exchange of Singapore Ltd.; the Stockholm Stock Exchange; the Tokyo Stock Exchange; the Toronto Stock Exchange; the Vancouver Stock Exchange; the Warsaw Stock Exchange and the Zurich Stock Exchange; and

(2) Any foreign securities exchange or non-exchange market designated by the Commission. Attributes to be considered in determining whether to designate an offshore securities market, among others, include:

(i) Organization under foreign law;

(ii) Association with a generally recognized community of brokers, dealers, banks, or other professional intermediaries with an established operating history;

(iii) Oversight by a governmental or self-regulatory body;

(iv) Oversight standards set by an existing body of law;

(v) Reporting of securities transactions on a regular basis to a governmental or self-regulatory body;

(vi) A system for exchange of price quotations through common communications media; and

(vii) An organized clearance and settlement system.

(c) *Directed selling efforts.*

(1) "Directed selling efforts" means any activity undertaken for the purpose of, or that could reasonably be expected to have the effect of, conditioning the market in the United States for any of the securities being offered in reliance on this Regulation S (§ 230.901 through § 230.905, and Preliminary Notes). Such activity

includes placing an advertisement in a publication "with a general circulation in the United States" that refers to the offering of securities being made in reliance upon this Regulation S.

(2) Publication "with a general circulation in the United States":

(i) Is defined as any publication that is printed primarily for distribution in the United States, or has had, during the preceding twelve months, an average circulation in the United States of 15,000 or more copies per issue; and

(ii) Will encompass only the U.S. edition of any publication printing a separate U.S. edition if the publication, without considering its U.S. edition, would not constitute a publication with a general circulation in the United States.

(3) The following are not "directed selling efforts":

(i) Placing an advertisement required to be published under U.S. or foreign law, or under rules or regulations of a U.S. or foreign regulatory or self-regulatory authority, provided the advertisement contains no more information than legally required and includes a statement to the effect that the securities have not been registered under the Act and may not be offered or sold in the United States (or to a U.S. person, if the advertisement relates to an offering under Category 2 or 3 (paragraph (b)(2) or (b)(3)) in §230.903) absent registration or an applicable exemption from the registration requirements;

(ii) Contact with persons excluded from the definition of "U.S. person" pursuant to paragraph (k)(2)(vi) of this section or persons holding accounts excluded from the definition of "U.S. person" pursuant to paragraph (k)(2)(i) of this section, solely in their capacities as holders of such accounts;

(iii) A tombstone advertisement in any publication with a general circulation in the United States, provided:

(A) The publication has less than 20% of its circulation, calculated by aggregating the circulation of its U.S. and comparable non-U.S. editions, in the United States;

(B) Such advertisement contains a legend to the effect that the securities have not been registered under the Act and may not be offered or sold in the United States (or to a U.S. person, if the advertisement relates to an offering under Category 2 or 3 (paragraph (b)(2) or (b)(3)) in §230.903) absent registration or an applicable exemption from the registration requirements; and

(C) Such advertisement contains no more information than:

(*1*) The issuer's name;

(*2*) The amount and title of the securities being sold;

(*3*) A brief indication of the issuer's general type of business;

(*4*) The price of the securities;

(*5*) The yield of the securities, if debt securities with a fixed (non-contingent) interest provision;

(*6*) The name and address of the person placing the advertisement, and whether such person is participating in the distribution;

(*7*) The names of the managing underwriters;

(*8*) The dates, if any, upon which the sales commenced and concluded;

(*9*) Whether the securities are offered or were offered by rights issued to security holders and, if so, the class of securities that are entitled or were entitled to subscribe, the subscription ratio, the record date, the dates (if any) upon which the rights were issued and expired, and the subscription price; and

(*10*) Any legend required by law or any foreign or U.S. regulatory or self-regulatory authority;

(iv) Bona fide visits to real estate, plants or other facilities located in the United States and tours thereof conducted for a prospective investor by an issuer, a distributor, any of their respective affiliates or a person acting on behalf of any of the foregoing;

(v) Distribution in the United States of a foreign broker-dealer's quotations by a third-party system that distributes such quotations primarily in foreign countries if:

(A) Securities transactions cannot be executed between foreign broker-dealers and persons in the United States through the system; and

(B) The issuer, distributors, their respective affiliates, persons acting on behalf of any of the foregoing, foreign broker-dealers and other participants in the system do not initiate contacts with U.S. persons or persons within the United States, beyond those contacts exempted under § 240.15a-6 of this chapter.

(vi) Publication by an issuer of a notice in accordance with § 230.135 or § 230.135c.

(vii) Providing any journalist with access to press conferences held outside of the United States, to meetings with the issuer or selling security holder representatives conducted outside the United States, or to written press-related materials released outside the United States, at or in which a present or proposed offering of securities is discussed, if the requirements of § 230.135e are satisfied; and

(viii) Publication or distribution of a research report by a broker or dealer in accordance with Rule 138(c) (§ 230.138(c)) or Rule 139(b) (§ 230.139(b)).

(d) *Distributor.* "Distributor" means any underwriter, dealer, or other person who participates, pursuant to a contractual arrangement, in the distribution of the securities offered or sold in reliance on this Regulation S (§ 230.901 through § 230.905, and Preliminary Notes).

(e) *Domestic issuer/Foreign issuer.* "Domestic issuer" means any issuer other than a "foreign government" or "foreign private issuer" (both as defined in § 230.405). "Foreign issuer" means any issuer other than a "domestic issuer."

(f) *Distribution compliance period.* "Distribution compliance period" means a period that begins when the securities were first offered to persons other than distributors in reliance upon this Regulation S (§ 230.901 through § 230.905, and Preliminary Notes) or the date of closing of the offering, whichever is later, and continues until the end of the period of time specified in the relevant provision of § 230.903, except that:

(1) All offers and sales by a distributor of an unsold allotment or subscription shall be deemed to be made during the distribution compliance period;

(2) In a continuous offering, the distribution compliance period shall commence upon completion of the distribution, as determined and certified by the managing underwriter or person performing similar functions;

(3) In a continuous offering of non-convertible debt securities offered and sold in identifiable tranches, the distribution compliance period for securities in a tranche shall commence upon completion of the distribution of such tranche, as determined and certified by the managing underwriter or person performing similar functions; and

(4) That in a continuous offering of securities to be acquired upon the exercise of warrants, the distribution compliance period shall commence upon completion of the distribution of the warrants, as determined and certified by the managing underwriter or person performing similar functions, if requirements of § 230.903(b)(5) are satisfied.

(g) *Offering restrictions.* "Offering restrictions" means:

(1) Each distributor agrees in writing:

(i) That all offers and sales of the securities prior to the expiration of the distribution compliance period specified in Category 2 or 3 (paragraph (b)(2) or (b)(3)) in § 230.903, as applicable, shall be made only in accordance with the provisions of § 230.903 or § 230.904; pursuant to registration of the securities under the Act; or pursuant to an available exemption from the registration requirements of the Act; and

(ii) For offers and sales of equity securities of domestic issuers, not to engage in hedging transactions with regard to such securities prior to the expiration of the distribution compliance period specified in Category 2 or 3 (paragraph (b)(2) or (b)(3)) in § 230.903, as applicable, unless in compliance with the Act; and

(2) All offering materials and documents (other than press releases) used in connection with offers and sales of the securities prior to the expiration of the distribution compliance period specified in Category 2 or 3 (paragraph (b)(2) or (b)(3)) in § 230.903, as applicable, shall include statements to the effect that the securities have not been registered under the Act and may not be offered or sold in the United States or to U.S. persons (other than distributors) unless the securities are registered under the Act, or an exemption from the registration requirements of the Act is available. For offers and sales of equity securities of domestic issuers, such offering materials and documents also must state that hedging transactions involving those securities may not be conducted unless in compliance with the Act. Such statements shall appear:

(i) On the cover or inside cover page of any prospectus or offering circular used in connection with the offer or sale of the securities;

(ii) In the underwriting section of any prospectus or offering circular used in connection with the offer or sale of the securities; and

(iii) In any advertisement made or issued by the issuer, any distributor, any of their respective affiliates, or any person acting on behalf of any of the foregoing. Such statements may appear in summary form on prospectus cover pages and in advertisements.

(h) *Offshore transaction.*

(1) An offer or sale of securities is made in an "offshore transaction" if:

(i) The offer is not made to a person in the United States; and

(ii) Either:

(A) At the time the buy order is originated, the buyer is outside the United States, or the seller and any person acting on its behalf reasonably believe that the buyer is outside the United States; or

(B) For purposes of:

(*1*) § 230.903, the transaction is executed in, on or through a physical trading floor of an established foreign securities exchange that is located outside the United States; or

(*2*) § 230.904, the transaction is executed in, on or through the facilities of a designated offshore securities market described in paragraph (b) of this section, and neither the seller nor any person acting on its behalf knows that the transaction has been pre-arranged with a buyer in the United States.

(2) Notwithstanding paragraph (h)(1) of this section, offers and sales of securities specifically targeted at identifiable groups of U.S. citizens abroad, such as members of the U.S. armed forces serving overseas, shall not be deemed to be made in "offshore transactions."

(3) Notwithstanding paragraph (h)(1) of this section, offers and sales of securities to persons excluded from the definition of "U.S. person" pursuant to paragraph (k)(2)(vi) of this section or persons holding accounts excluded from the definition of "U.S. person" pursuant to paragraph (k)(2)(i) of this section, solely in their capacities as holders of such accounts, shall be deemed to be made in "offshore transactions."

(4) Notwithstanding paragraph (h)(1) of this section, publication or distribution of a research report in accordance with Rule 138(c) (§ 230.138(c)) or Rule 139(b) (§ 230.139(b)) by a broker or dealer at or around the time of an offering in reliance on Regulation S (§§ 230.901 through 230.905) will not cause the transaction to fail to be an offshore transaction as defined in this section.

(i) *Reporting issuer.* "Reporting issuer" means an issuer other than an investment company registered or required to register under the 1940 Act that:

(1) Has a class of securities registered pursuant to Section 12(b) or 12(g) of the Exchange Act (15 U.S.C. §§ 78*l*(b) or 78*l*(g)) or is required to file reports pursuant to Section 15(d) of the Exchange Act (15 U.S.C. § 78*o*(d)); and

(2) Has filed all the material required to be filed pursuant to Section 13(a) or 15(d) of the Exchange Act (15 U.S.C. §§ 78m(a) or 78*o*(d)) for a period of at least twelve months immediately preceding the offer or sale of securities made in reliance upon this Regulation S (§ 230.901 through § 230.905, and Preliminary Notes) (or for such shorter period that the issuer was required to file such material).

(j) *Substantial U.S. market interest.*

(1) "Substantial U.S. market interest" with respect to a class of an issuer's equity securities means:

(i) The securities exchanges and inter-dealer quotation systems in the United States in the aggregate constituted the single largest market for such class of securities in the shorter of the issuer's prior fiscal year or the period since the issuer's incorporation; or

(ii) 20 percent or more of all trading in such class of securities took place in, on or through the facilities of securities exchanges and inter-dealer quotation systems in the United States and less than 55 percent of such trading took place in, on or through the facilities of securities markets of a single foreign country in the shorter of the issuer's prior fiscal year or the period since the issuer's incorporation.

(2) "Substantial U.S. market interest" with respect to an issuer's debt securities means:

(i) Its debt securities, in the aggregate, are held of record (as that term is defined in § 240.12g5-1 of this chapter and used for purposes of paragraph (j)(2) of this section) by 300 or more U.S. persons;

(ii) $1 billion or more of: the principal amount outstanding of its debt securities, the greater of liquidation preference or par value of its securities described in § 230.902(a)(1), and the principal amount or principal balance of its securities described in § 230.902(a)(2), in the aggregate, is held of record by U.S. persons; and

(iii) 20 percent or more of: the principal amount outstanding of its debt securities, the greater of liquidation preference or par value of its securities described in § 230.902(a)(1), and the principal amount or principal balance of its securities described in § 230.902(a)(2), in the aggregate, is held of record by U.S. persons.

(3) Notwithstanding paragraph (j)(2) of this section, substantial U.S. market interest with respect to an issuer's debt securities is calculated without reference to securities that qualify for the exemption provided by Section 3(a)(3) of the Act (15 U.S.C. § 77c(a)(3)).

(k) *U.S. person.*

(1) "U.S. person" means:

(i) Any natural person resident in the United States;

(ii) Any partnership or corporation organized or incorporated under the laws of the United States;

(iii) Any estate of which any executor or administrator is a U.S. person;

(iv) Any trust of which any trustee is a U.S. person;

(v) Any agency or branch of a foreign entity located in the United States;

(vi) Any non-discretionary account or similar account (other than an estate or trust) held by a dealer or other fiduciary for the benefit or account of a U.S. person;

(vii) Any discretionary account or similar account (other than an estate or trust) held by a dealer or other fiduciary organized, incorporated, or (if an individual) resident in the United States; and

(viii) Any partnership or corporation if:

(A) Organized or incorporated under the laws of any foreign jurisdiction; and

(B) Formed by a U.S. person principally for the purpose of investing in securities not registered under the Act, unless it is organized or incorporated, and owned, by accredited investors (as defined in § 230.501(a)) who are not natural persons, estates or trusts.

(2) The following are not "U.S. persons":

(i) Any discretionary account or similar account (other than an estate or trust) held for the benefit or account of a non-U.S. person by a dealer or other professional fiduciary organized, incorporated, or (if an individual) resident in the United States;

(ii) Any estate of which any professional fiduciary acting as executor or administrator is a U.S. person if:

(A) An executor or administrator of the estate who is not a U.S. person has sole or shared investment discretion with respect to the assets of the estate; and

(B) The estate is governed by foreign law;

(iii) Any trust of which any professional fiduciary acting as trustee is a U.S. person, if a trustee who is not a U.S. person has sole or shared investment discretion with respect to the trust assets, and no beneficiary of the trust (and no settlor if the trust is revocable) is a U.S. person;

(iv) An employee benefit plan established and administered in accordance with the law of a country other than the United States and customary practices and documentation of such country;

(v) Any agency or branch of a U.S. person located outside the United States if:

(A) The agency or branch operates for valid business reasons; and

(B) The agency or branch is engaged in the business of insurance or banking and is subject to substantive insurance or banking regulation, respectively, in the jurisdiction where located; and

(vi) The International Monetary Fund, the International Bank for Reconstruction and Development, the Inter-American Development Bank, the Asian Development Bank, the African Development Bank, the United Nations, and their agencies, affiliates and pension plans, and any other similar international organizations, their agencies, affiliates and pension plans.

(l) *United States.* "United States" means the United States of America, its territories and possessions, any State of the United States, and the District of Columbia.

Rule 903. Offers or Sales of Securities by the Issuer, a Distributor, Any of Their Respective Affiliates, or Any Person Acting on Behalf of Any of the Foregoing; Conditions Relating to Specific Securities

An offer or sale of securities by the issuer, a distributor, any of their respective affiliates, or any person acting on behalf of any of the foregoing, shall be deemed to occur outside the United States within the meaning of § 230.901 if:

(1) The offer or sale is made in an offshore transaction;

(2) No directed selling efforts are made in the United States by the issuer, a distributor, any of their respective affiliates, or any person acting on behalf of any of the foregoing; and

(3) The conditions of paragraph (b) of this section, as applicable, are satisfied.

(b) *Additional Conditions.*

(1) *Category 1.* No conditions other than those set forth in § 230.903(a) apply to securities in this category. Securities are eligible for this category if:

(i) The securities are issued by a foreign issuer that reasonably believes at the commencement of the offering that:

(A) There is no substantial U.S. market interest in the class of securities to be offered or sold (if equity securities are offered or sold);

(B) There is no substantial U.S. market interest in its debt securities (if debt securities are offered or sold);

(C) There is no substantial U.S. market interest in the securities to be purchased upon exercise (if warrants are offered or sold); and

(D) There is no substantial U.S. market interest in either the convertible securities or the underlying securities (if convertible securities are offered or sold);

(ii) The securities are offered and sold in an overseas directed offering, which means:

(A) An offering of securities of a foreign issuer that is directed into a single country other than the United States to the residents thereof and that is made in accordance with the local laws and customary practices and documentation of such country; or

(B) An offering of non-convertible debt securities of a domestic issuer that is directed into a single country other than the United States to the residents thereof and that is made in accordance with the local laws and customary practices and documentation of such country, provided that the principal and interest of the securities (or par value, as applicable) are denominated in a currency other than U.S. dollars and such securities are neither convertible into U.S. dollar-denominated securities nor linked to U.S. dollars (other than through related currency or interest rate swap transactions that are commercial in nature) in a manner that in effect converts the securities to U.S. dollar-denominated securities.

(iii) The securities are backed by the full faith and credit of a foreign government; or

(iv) The securities are offered and sold to employees of the issuer or its affiliates pursuant to an employee benefit plan established and administered in accordance with the law of a country other than the United States, and customary practices and documentation of such country, provided that:

(A) The securities are issued in compensatory circumstances for bona fide services rendered to the issuer or its affiliates in connection with their businesses and such services are not rendered in connection with the offer or sale of securities in a capital-raising transaction;

(B) Any interests in the plan are not transferable other than by will or the laws of descent or distribution;

(C) The issuer takes reasonable steps to preclude the offer and sale of interests in the plan or securities under the plan to U.S. residents other than employees on temporary assignment in the United States; and

(D) Documentation used in connection with any offer pursuant to the plan contains a statement that the securities have not been registered under the Act and may not be offered or sold in the United States unless registered or an exemption from registration is available.

(2) *Category 2.* The following conditions apply to securities that are not eligible for Category 1 (paragraph (b)(1)) of this section and that are equity securities of a reporting foreign issuer, or debt securities of a reporting issuer or of a non-reporting foreign issuer.

(i) Offering restrictions are implemented;

(ii) The offer or sale, if made prior to the expiration of a 40-day distribution compliance period, is not made to a U.S. person or for the account or benefit of a U.S. person (other than a distributor); and

(iii) Each distributor selling securities to a distributor, a dealer, as defined in section 2(a)(12) of the Act (15 U.S.C. § 77b(a)(12)), or a person receiving a selling concession, fee or other remuneration in respect of the securities sold, prior to the expiration of a 40-day distribution compliance period, sends a confirmation or other notice to the purchaser stating that the purchaser is subject to the same restrictions on offers and sales that apply to a distributor.

(3) *Category 3.* The following conditions apply to securities that are not eligible for Category 1 or 2 (paragraph (b)(1) or (b)(2)) of this section:

(i) Offering restrictions are implemented;

(ii) In the case of debt securities:

(A) The offer or sale, if made prior to the expiration of a 40-day distribution compliance period, is not made to a U.S. person or for the account or benefit of a U.S. person (other than a distributor); and

(B) The securities are represented upon issuance by a temporary global security which is not exchangeable for definitive securities until the expiration of the 40-day distribution compliance period and, for persons other than distributors, until certification of beneficial ownership of the securities by a non-U.S. person or a U.S. person who purchased securities in a transaction that did not require registration under the Act;

(iii) In the case of equity securities:

(A) The offer or sale, if made prior to the expiration of a one-year distribution compliance period (or six-month distribution compliance period if the issuer is a reporting issuer), is not made to a U.S. person or for the account or benefit of a U.S. person (other than a distributor); and

(B) The offer or sale, if made prior to the expiration of a one-year distribution compliance period (or six-month distribution compliance period if the issuer is a reporting issuer), is made pursuant to the following conditions:

(*1*) The purchaser of the securities (other than a distributor) certifies that it is not a U.S. person and is not acquiring the securities for the account or benefit of any U.S. person or is a U.S. person who purchased securities in a transaction that did not require registration under the Act;

(*2*) The purchaser of the securities agrees to resell such securities only in accordance with the provisions of this Regulation S (§ 230.901 through § 230.905, and Preliminary Notes), pursuant to registration under the Act, or pursuant to an available exemption from registration; and agrees not to engage in hedging transactions with regard to such securities unless in compliance with the Act;

(*3*) The securities of a domestic issuer contain a legend to the effect that transfer is prohibited except in accordance with the provisions of this Regulation S (§ 230.901 through § 230.905, and Preliminary Notes), pursuant to registration under the Act, or pursuant to an available exemption from registration; and that hedging transactions involving those securities may not be conducted unless in compliance with the Act;

(*4*) The issuer is required, either by contract or a provision in its bylaws, articles, charter or comparable document, to refuse to register any transfer of the securities not made in accordance with the provisions of this Regulation S (§ 230.901 through § 230.905, and Preliminary Notes), pursuant to registration under the Act, or pursuant to an available exemption from registration; *provided, however,* that if the securities are in bearer form or foreign law prevents the issuer of the securities from refusing to register securities transfers, other reasonable procedures (such as a legend described in paragraph (b)(3)(iii)(B)(*3*) of this section) are implemented to prevent any transfer of the securities not made in accordance with the provisions of this Regulation S; and

(iv) Each distributor selling securities to a distributor, a dealer (as defined in section 2(a)(12) of the Act (15 U.S.C. 77b(a)(12)), or a person receiving a selling concession, fee or other remuneration, prior to the expiration of a 40-day distribution compliance period in the case of debt securities, or a one-year distribution compliance period (or six-month distribution compliance period if the issuer is a reporting issuer) in the case of equity securities, sends a confirmation or other notice to the purchaser stating that the purchaser is subject to the same restrictions on offers and sales that apply to a distributor.

(4) *Guaranteed securities.* Notwithstanding paragraphs (b)(1) through (b)(3) of this section, in offerings of debt securities fully and unconditionally guaranteed as to principal and interest by the parent of the issuer of the debt securities, only the requirements of paragraph (b) of this section that are applicable to the offer and sale of the guarantee must be satisfied with respect to the offer and sale of the guaranteed debt securities.

(5) *Warrants.* An offer or sale of warrants under Category 2 or 3 (paragraph (b)(2) or (b)(3)) of this section also must comply with the following requirements:

(i) Each warrant must bear a legend stating that the warrant and the securities to be issued upon its exercise have not been registered under the Act and that the warrant may not be exercised by or on behalf of any U.S. person unless registered under the Act or an exemption from such registration is available;

(ii) Each person exercising a warrant is required to give:

(A) Written certification that it is not a U.S. person and the warrant is not being exercised on behalf of a U.S. person; or

(B) A written opinion of counsel to the effect that the warrant and the securities delivered upon exercise thereof have been registered under the Act or are exempt from registration thereunder; and

(iii) Procedures are implemented to ensure that the warrant may not be exercised within the United States, and that the securities may not be delivered within the United States upon exercise, other than in offerings deemed to meet the definition of "offshore transaction" pursuant to § 230.902(h), unless registered under the Act or an exemption from such registration is available.

Rule 904. Offshore Resales

(a) An offer or sale of securities by any person other than the issuer, a distributor, any of their respective affiliates (except any officer or director who is an affiliate solely by virtue of holding such position), or any person acting on behalf of any of the foregoing, shall be deemed to occur outside the United States within the meaning of § 230.901 if:

(1) The offer or sale are made in an offshore transaction;

(2) No directed selling efforts are made in the United States by the seller, an affiliate, or any person acting on their behalf; and

(3) The conditions of paragraph (b) of this section, if applicable, are satisfied.

(b) *Additional conditions.*

(1) *Resales by dealers and persons receiving selling concessions.* In the case of an offer or sale of securities prior to the expiration of the distribution compliance period specified in Category 2 or 3 (paragraph (b)(2) or (b)(3)) of § 230.903, as applicable, by a dealer, as defined in Section 2(a)(12) of the Act (15 U.S.C. § 77b(a)(12)), or a person receiving a selling concession, fee or other remuneration in respect of the securities offered or sold:

(i) Neither the seller nor any person acting on its behalf knows that the offeree or buyer of the securities is a U.S. person; and

(ii) If the seller or any person acting on the seller's behalf knows that the purchaser is a dealer, as defined in Section 2(a)(12) of the Act (15 U.S.C. § 77b(a)(12)), or is a person receiving a selling concession, fee or other remuneration in respect of the securities sold, the seller or a person acting on the seller's behalf sends to the purchaser a confirmation or other notice stating that the securities may be offered and sold during the distribution compliance period only in accordance with the provisions of this Regulation S (§ 230.901 through § 230.905, and Preliminary Notes); pursuant to registration of the securities under the Act; or pursuant to an available exemption from the registration requirements of the Act.

(2) *Resales by certain affiliates.* In the case of an offer or sale of securities by an officer or director of the issuer or a distributor, who is an affiliate of the issuer or distributor solely by virtue of holding such position, no selling concession, fee or other remuneration is paid in connection with such offer or sale other than the usual and customary broker's commission that would be received by a person executing such transaction as agent.

Rule 905. Resale Limitations

Equity securities of domestic issuers acquired from the issuer, a distributor, or any of their respective affiliates in a transaction subject to the conditions of § 230.901 or § 230.903 are deemed to be "restricted securities" as defined in § 230.144. Resales of any of such restricted securities by the offshore purchaser must be made in accordance with this Regulation S (§ 230.901 through § 230.905, and Preliminary Notes), the registration requirements of the Act or an exemption therefrom. Any "restricted securities," as defined in § 230.144, that are equity securities of a domestic issuer will continue to be deemed to be restricted securities, notwithstanding that they were acquired in a resale transaction made pursuant to § 230.901 or § 230.904.

REGULATION CE—COORDINATED EXEMPTIONS FOR CERTAIN ISSUES OF SECURITIES EXEMPT UNDER STATE LAW

Preliminary Notes

(1) Nothing in this section is intended to be or should be construed as in any way relieving issuers or persons acting on behalf of issuers from providing disclosure to prospective investors necessary to satisfy the antifraud provisions of the federal securities laws. This section only provides an exemption from the registration requirements of the Securities Act of 1933 ("the Act") [15 U.S.C. 77a et seq.].

(2) Nothing in this section obviates the need to comply with any applicable state law relating to the offer and sales of securities.

(3) Attempted compliance with this section does not act as an exclusive election; the issuer also can claim the availability of any other applicable exemption.

(4) This exemption is not available to any issuer for any transaction which, while in technical compliance with the provision of this section, is part of a plan or scheme to evade the registration provisions of the Act. In such cases, registration under the Act is required.

Rule 1001. Exemption for Transactions Exempt From Qualification Under Sec. 25102(n) of the California Corporations Code

(a) Exemption. Offers and sales of securities that satisfy the conditions of paragraph (n) of Sec. 25102 of the California Corporations Code, and paragraph (b) of this section, shall be exempt from the provisions of Section 5 of the Securities Act of 1933 by virtue of Section 3(b) of that Act.

(b) Limitation on and computation of offering price. The sum of all cash and other consideration to be received for the securities shall not exceed $5,000,000, less the aggregate offering price for all other securities sold in the same offering of securities, whether pursuant to this or another exemption.

(c) Resale limitations. Securities issued pursuant to this Sec. 230.1001 are deemed to be "restricted securities" as defined in Securities Act Rule 144 [Sec. 230.144]. Resales of such securities must be made in compliance with the registration requirements of the Act or an exemption therefrom.

NASAA UNIFORM LIMITED OFFERING EXEMPTION (ULOE)
Adopted September 21, 1983
North American Securities Administrators Association, Inc.
Preliminary Notes

1. Nothing in this exemption is intended to or should be construed as in any way relieving issuers or persons acting on behalf of issuers from providing disclosure to prospective investors adequate to satisfy the anti-fraud provisions of this state's securities law.

2. In view of the objective of this rule and the purposes and policies underlying this act, the exemption is not available to any issuer with respect to any transaction which, although in technical compliance with this rule, is part of a plan or scheme to evade registration or the conditions or limitations explicitly stated in this rule.

3. Nothing in this rule is intended to relieve registered broker/dealers or agents from the due diligence, suitability, or know your customer standards or any other requirements of law otherwise applicable to such registered persons.

RULE

By authority delegated the administrator in Section—of this act to promulgate rules, the following transaction is determined to be exempt from the registration provisions of this act:

1. Any offer or sale of securities offered or sold in compliance with Securities Act of 1933, Regulation D, Rules 230.505 and/or 230.506[1], including any offer or sale made exempt by application of Rule 508(a), as made effective in Release No. 33-6389 and as amended in Release Nos. 33-6437, 33-6663, 33-6758, and 33-6825, and which satisfies the following further conditions and limitations:

---

[1] In those states where facts and circumstances permit, it would not be inconsistent with the regulatory objectives of this exemption for a state to elect to accept Rule 506 offerings within the ambit of this exemption. In doing so, however, the state disqualification provisions of this rule and the federal disqualification provisions of Rule 505 should be made applicable.

With inclusion of Rule 506, the major objective of the exemption is not limited to facilitating the capital-raising ability of small business. The removal of the dollar limit makes the exemption available to private placements of all sizes. In large private offerings, the problems associated with determining that all the investors are experienced enough to fully understand the risks of the offering and controlling the manner and scope of the offering so that it does not become a public offering are magnified. Also, and largely because of the removal of the dollar limit, the exemption becomes more attractive to tax shelter investments.

Tax shelter offerings that would be permitted by Rule 506, particularly those with abusively high write-off ratios, involve special facts and circumstances, and enforcement experience shows that they have a greater potential for regulatory concerns and many lack economic substance and fail to contribute to job creation. In recognition of these concerns, Rule 506 is not adopted as part of the basic ULOE.

In those states where facts and circumstances permit, it would not be inconsistent with the regulatory objectives of this exemption to further condition the exemption with the following provision:

"In the case of offerings of direct participation programs as defined in Section 34 or Article III of the National Association of Securities Dealers, Inc., Rules of Fair Practice, delivery of a disclosure document containing the information required by Rule 502(b) of Regulation D to individuals covered by subsections (5) and (6) of Rule 501(a) of Regulation D is required."

A. No commission, fee or other remuneration shall be paid or given, directly or indirectly, to any person for soliciting any prospective purchaser in this state unless such person is appropriately registered in this state.[2&3]

It is a defense to a violation of this subsection if the issuer sustains the burden of proof to establish that he or she did not know and in the exercise of reasonable care could not have known that the person who received a commission, fee or other remuneration was not appropriately registered in this state.

B. No exemption under this rule shall be available for the securities of any issuer if any of the parties described in Securities Act of 1933, Regulation A, Rule 230.252 sections (c), (d), (e) or (f):

1. Has filed a registration statement which is subject of a currently effective registration stop order entered pursuant to any state's securities law within five years prior to the filing of the notice required under this exemption.

2. Has been convicted within five years prior to the filing of the notice required under this exemption of any felony or misdemeanor in connection with the offer, purchase or sale of any security or any felony involving fraud or deceit, including but not limited to forgery, embezzlement, obtaining money under false pretenses, larceny or conspiracy to defraud.

3. Is currently subject to any state administrative enforcement order or judgment entered by that state's securities administrator within five years prior to the filing of the notice required under this exemption or is subject to any state's administrative enforcement order or judgment in which fraud or deceit, including but not limited to making untrue statements of material facts and omitting to state material facts, was found and the order or judgment was entered within five years prior to the filing of the notice required under this exemption.

4. Is subject to any state's administrative enforcement order or judgment which prohibits, denies or revokes the use of any exemption from registration in connection with the offer, purchase or sale of securities.

5. Is currently subject to any order, judgment, or decree of any court of competent jurisdiction temporarily or preliminarily restraining or enjoining, or is subject to any order, judgment or decree of any court of competent jurisdiction, permanently restraining or enjoining, such party from engaging in or continuing any conduct or practice in connection with the purchase or sale of any security or involving the making of any false filing with the state entered within five years prior to the filing of the notice required under this exemption.

6. The prohibitions of paragraphs 1-3 and 5 above shall not apply if the person subject to the disqualification is duly licensed or registered to conduct securities related business in the state in which the administrative order or judgment was entered against such

---

[2] In those states where facts and circumstances permit, it would not be inconsistent with the regulatory objectives of this exemption for a state to substitute the following for section 1.A.

a. All persons who offer or sell securities in this state to nonaccredited and/or accredited investors as defined in Securities Act of 1933, Regulation D, Rule 230.501(a)(5)—(6) shall be appropriately registered in accordance with this state's securities law.

It is a defense to a violation of this subsection if the issuer sustains the burden of proof to establish that he or she did not know and in the exercise of reasonable care could not have known that the person who received a commission fee or other remuneration was not appropriately registered in this state.

[3] In those states where facts and circumstances permit, it would not be inconsistent with the regulatory objectives of this exemption for a state to provide for a system or process to simplify and facilitate the registration of broker/dealers and agents which would not otherwise be required to be registered except for this exemption. Such a system or process should as a minimum, grant jurisdiction as well as the ability to effectively limit and control persons offering and selling securities within the state.

person or if the broker/dealer employing such party is licensed or registered in this state and the Form B-D filed with this state discloses the order, conviction, judgment or decree relating to such person. No person disqualified under this subsection may act in a capacity other than that for which the person is licensed or registered.

7. Any disqualification caused by this section is automatically waived if the state securities administrator or agency of the state which created the basis for disqualification determines upon a showing of good cause that it is not necessary under the circumstances that the exemption be denied.

It is a defense to a violation of this subsection if issuer sustains the burden of proof to establish that he or she did not know and in the exercise of reasonable care could not have known that a disqualification under this subsection existed.

C. The issuer shall file with the state administrator a notice on Form D (17CFR239.500):

1. No later than (10 days prior)[4] to the receipt of consideration or the delivery of a subscription agreement by an investor in this state which results from an offer being made in reliance upon this exemption and at such other times and in the form required under Regulation D, Rule 230.503 to be filed with the Securities and Exchange Commission.

2. The notice shall contain an undertaking by the issuer to furnish to the state securities administrator, upon written request, the information furnished by the issuer to offerees, except where the state administrator pursuant to regulation requires that the information be filed at the same time with the filing of the notice.[5]

3. Unless otherwise available, included with or in the initial notice shall be a consent to service of process.

4. Every person filing the initial notice provided for in 1 above shall pay a filing fee of. . . .

D. In all sales to nonaccredited investors in this state one of the following conditions must be satisfied or the issuer and any person acting on its behalf shall have reasonable grounds to believe and after making reasonable inquiry shall believe that one of the following conditions is satisfied:

1. The investment is suitable for the purchaser upon the basis of the facts, if any, disclosed by the purchaser as to the purchaser's other security holdings, financial situation and needs. For the purpose of this condition only, it may be presumed that if the investment does not exceed 10% of the investor's net worth, it is suitable.

2. The purchaser either alone or with his/her purchaser representative(s) has such knowledge and experience in financial and business matters that he/she is or they are capable of evaluating the merits and risks of the prospective investment.

2. A failure to comply with a term, condition or requirement of Sections 1.A, [C[6]], and D of this rule will not result in loss of the exemption from the requirements of section [301] of this act for any offer or sale to a particular individual or entity if the person relying on the exemption shows:

A. the failure to comply did not pertain to a term, condition or requirement directly intended to protect that particular individual or entity; and

---

[4] In those states where facts and circumstances permit, it would not be inconsistent with the Regulatory objectives of this exemption for a state to consider a post-sale notice patterned after the notice provisions of Regulation D (Rule 230.503).

[5] This latter filing requirement is not intended to provide the basis for a fairness type of review of the offering.

[6] In those states which have adopted a post-sale notice patterned after the notice provisions of Regulation D (Rule 230.503) it would not be inconsistent with the regulatory objectives of this exemption to include the notice filing requirements of section 1.C within the substantial compliance provisions of section 2 or to eliminate the filing as a condition and adopt a rule similar to Rule 230.507.

B. the failure to comply was insignificant with respect to the offering as a whole; and

C. a good faith and reasonable attempt was made to comply with all applicable terms, conditions and requirements of Sections 1.A [C[6]], and D.

3. Where an exemption is established only through reliance upon section 2 of this rule, the failure to comply shall nonetheless be actionable by the [administrator] under section [408] of the Act.[7]

4. Transactions which are exempt under this rule may not be combined with offers and sales exempt under any other rule or section of this act; however, nothing in this limitation shall act as an election. Should for any reason the offer and sale fail to comply with all of the conditions for this exemption, the issuer may claim the availability of any other applicable exemption.

5. The administrator may, by rule or order, increase the number of purchasers or waive any other conditions of this exemption.

6. The exemption authorized by this rule shall be known and may be cited as the "Uniform Limited Offering Exemption."

---

[7] The cited reference is to the section of the Uniform Securities Act which authorizes the state administrator to bring a civil action to enjoin rule violations. Those states which have authority to bring an administrative enforcement action for rule violations may wish to include a reference to that statutory authority. If the administrator lacks authority to bring enforcement actions based solely on rule violations, he/she may wish to consider a statutory amendment.

SECURITIES ACT—SELECTED FORMS

Selected Forms Under the Securities Act of 1933

Form	Subject
	Registration Statements
S-1	General form of registration statement
S-3	For registration under the Securities Act of 1933 of securities of certain issuers offered pursuant to certain types of transactions
S-8	For securities to be offered to employees pursuant to certain plans
F-6	For registration under the Securities Act of 1933 of depositary shares represented by American depositary receipts
	Regulation A Notification and Consents
1-A	Offering statement under Regulation A
	Regulation D or Section 4(6) Notification
D	Notice of sales of securities pursuant to Regulation D or Section 4(6)
	Rule 144 Notification
144	Notice of proposed sale of securities pursuant to Rule 144

FORM S-1

UNITED STATES SECURITIES AND EXCHANGE COMMISSION
WASHINGTON, D.C. 20549

FORM S-1

REGISTRATION STATEMENT UNDER THE SECURITIES ACT OF 1933

....
(Exact name of registrant as specified in its charter)

....
(State or other jurisdiction of incorporation or organization)

....
(Primary Standard Industrial Classification Code Number)

....
(I.R.S. Employer Identification Number)

....
(Address, including zip code, and telephone number, including area code, of
registrant's principal executive offices)

....
(Name, address, including zip code, and telephone number, including area code,
of agent for service)

....
Approximate date of commencement of proposed sale to the public ....

If any of the securities being registered on this Form are to be offered on a delayed or continuous basis pursuant to Rule 415 under the Securities Act, check the following box: ☐

If this Form is filed to register additional securities for an offering pursuant to Rule 462(b) under the Securities Act, please check the following box and list the Securities Act registration statement number of the earlier effective registration statement for the same offering. ☐

If this Form is a post-effective amendment filed pursuant to Rule 462(c) under the Securities Act, check the following box and list the Securities Act registration statement number of the earlier effective registration statement for the same offering. ☐

If this Form is a post-effective amendment filed pursuant to Rule 462(d) under the Securities Act, check the following box and list the Securities Act registration statement number of the earlier effective registration statement for the same offering. ☐

Indicate by check mark whether the registrant is a large accelerated filer, an accelerated filer, a non-accelerated filer, smaller reporting company, or an emerging growth company. See the definitions of "large accelerated filer," "accelerated filer," "smaller reporting company," and "emerging growth company" in Rule 12b-2 of the Exchange Act.

Large accelerated filer ☐   Accelerated filer   ☐
Non-accelerated filer ☐   Smaller reporting company ☐
                                     Emerging growth company ☐

If an emerging growth company, indicate by check mark if the registrant has elected not to use extended transition period for complying with any new or revised financial accounting standards provided pursuant to Section 7(a)(2)(B) of the Securities Act. ☐

Calculation of Registration Fee

Title of each class of securities to be registered	Amount to be registered	Proposed maximum offering price per unit	Proposed maximum aggregate offering price	Amount of registration fee

Note: Specific details relating to the fee calculation shall be furnished in notes to the table, including references to provisions of Rule 457 (§ 230.457 of this chapter) relied upon, if the basis of the calculation is not otherwise evident from the information presented in the table. If the filing fee is calculated pursuant to Rule 457(*o*) under the Securities Act, only the title of the class of securities to be registered, the proposed maximum aggregate offering price for that class of securities and the amount of registration fee need to appear in the Calculation of Registration Fee table. If an offering of an indeterminate amount of exchange-traded vehicle securities is being registered, state that the registration statement covers an indeterminate amount of securities to be offered or sold and that the filing fee will be calculated and paid in accordance with Rule 456(d) and Rule 457(u) (§ 230.456(d) and § 230.457(u) of this chapter), respectively. Any difference between the dollar amount of securities registered for such offerings and the dollar amount of securities sold may be carried forward on a future registration statement pursuant to Rule 429 under the Securities Act.

GENERAL INSTRUCTIONS

I. Eligibility Requirements for Use of Form S-1

This Form shall be used for the registration under the Securities Act of 1933 ("Securities Act") of securities of all registrants for which no other form is authorized or prescribed, except that this Form shall not be used for securities of foreign governments or political subdivisions thereof or asset-backed securities, as defined in 17 CFR 229.1101(c).

II. Application of General Rules and Regulations

A. Attention is directed to the General Rules and Regulations under the Securities Act, particularly those comprising *Regulation C* (17 CFR 230.400 to 230.494) thereunder. That Regulation contains general requirements regarding the preparation and filing of the registration statement.

B. Attention is directed to *Regulation S-K* (17 CFR Part 229) for the requirements applicable to the content of the non-financial statement portions of registration statements under the Securities Act. Where this Form directs the registrant to furnish information required by Regulation S-K and the item of Regulation S-K so provides, information need only be furnished to the extent appropriate.

C. A registration statement filed (or submitted for confidential review) under Section 6 of the Securities Act (15 U.S.C. 77f) by an emerging growth company, defined in Section 2(a)(19) of the Securities Act (15 U.S.C. 77b(a)(19)), prior to an initial public offering may omit financial information for historical periods otherwise required by Regulation S-X (17 CFR Part 210) as of the time of filing (or confidential submission) of the registration statement, provided that:

1. The omitted financial information relates to a historical period that the registrant reasonably believes will not be required to be included in this Form at the time of the contemplated offering; and

2. Prior to the registrant distributing a preliminary prospectus to investors, the registration statement is amended to include all financial information required by Regulation S-X at the date of the amendment.

III. Exchange Offers

If any of the securities being registered are to be offered in exchange for securities of any other issuer, the prospectus shall also include the information which would be required by item 11 if the securities of such other issuer were registered on this Form. There shall also be included the information concerning such securities of such other issuer which would be called for by Item 9 if such securities were being registered. In connection with this instruction, reference is made to *Rule 409*.

IV. Roll-up Transactions

If the securities to be registered on this Form will be is[s]ued in a roll-up trans[a]ction as defined in *Item 901(c)* of Regulation S-K (17 CFR 229.901(c)), attention is directed to the requirements of Form S-4 applicable to roll-up transactions, including, but not limited to, General Instruction I.

V. Registration of Additional Securities

With respect to the registration of additional securities for an offering pursuant to *Rule 462(b)* under the Securities Act, the registrant may file a registration statement consisting only of the following: the facing page; a statement that the contents of the earlier registration statement, identified by file number, are incorporated by reference; required opinions and consents; the signature page; and any price-related information omitted from the earlier registration statement in reliance on *Rule 430A* that the registrant chooses to include in the new registration statement. The information contained in such a Rule 462(b) registration statement shall be deemed to be a part of the earlier registration statement as of the date of effectiveness of the Rule 462(b) registration statement. Any opinion or consent required in the Rule 462(b) registration statement may be incorporated by reference from the earlier registration statement with respect to the offering, if: (i) such opinion or consent expressly provides for such incorporation; and (ii) such opinion relates to the securities registered pursuant to Rule 462(b). *See Rule 439(b)* under the Securities Act.

. . .

VI. Offerings of Asset-Backed Securities

The following applies if a registration statement on this Form S-1 is being used to register an offering of asset-backed securities. Terms used in this General Instruction VI. have the same meaning as in Item 1101 of Regulation AB (17 CFR 229.1101).

A. Items that May Be Omitted. Such registrants may omit the information called for by Item 11, Information with Respect to the Registrant.

B. Substitute Information to Be Included. In addition to the Items that are otherwise required by this Form, the registrant must furnish in the prospectus the information required by Items 1102 through 1120 of Regulation AB (17 CFR 229.1102 through 229.1120).

C. Signatures. The registration statement must be signed by the depositor, the depositor's principal executive officer or officers, principal financial officer and controller or principal accounting officer, and by at least a majority of the depositor's board of directors or persons performing similar functions.

VII. Eligibility to Use Incorporation by Reference

If a registrant meets the following requirements in paragraphs A?F immediately prior to the time of filing a registration statement on this Form, it may elect to provide information required by Items 3 through 11 of this Form in accordance with Item 11A and Item 12 of this Form. Notwithstanding the foregoing, in the financial statements, incorporating by reference or cross-referencing to information outside of the financial statements is not permitted unless otherwise specifically permitted or required by the Commission's rules or by U.S. Generally Accepted Accounting Principles or International Financial Reporting Standards as issued by the International Accounting Standards Board, whichever is applicable.

A. The registrant is subject to the requirement to file reports pursuant to Section 13 or Section 15(d) of the Securities Exchange Act of 1934 ("Exchange Act").

B. The registrant has filed all reports and other materials required to be filed by Sections 13(a), 14, or 15(d) of the Exchange Act during the preceding 12 months (or for such shorter period that the registrant was required to file such reports and materials).

C. The registrant has filed an annual report required under Section 13(a) or Section 15(d) of the Exchange Act for its most recently completed fiscal year.

D. The registrant is not:

1. And during the past three years neither the registrant nor any of its predecessors was:

(a) A blank check company as defined in Rule 419(a)(2) (§ 230.419(a)(2));

(b) A shell company, other than a business combination related shell company, each as defined in Rule 405 (§ 230.405); or

(c) A registrant for an offering of penny stock as defined in Rule 3a51-1 of the Exchange Act (§ 240.3a51-1 of this chapter).

2. Registering an offering that effectuates a business combination transaction as defined in Rule 165(f)(1) (§ 230.165(f)(1) of this chapter).

E. If a registrant is a successor registrant it shall be deemed to have satisfied conditions A., B., C., and D.2 above if:

1. Its predecessor and it, taken together, do so, provided that the succession was primarily for the purpose of changing the state of incorporation of the predecessor or forming a holding company and that the assets and liabilities of the successor at the time of succession were substantially the same as those of the predecessor; or

2. All predecessors met the conditions at the time of succession and the registrant has continued to do so since the succession.

F. The registrant makes its periodic and current reports filed pursuant to Section 13 or Section 15(d) of the Exchange Act that are incorporated by reference pursuant to Item 11A or Item 12 of this Form readily available and accessible on a Web site maintained by or for the registrant and containing information about the registrant.

PART I—INFORMATION REQUIRED IN PROSPECTUS

Item 1. Forepart of the Registration Statement and Outside Front Cover Page of Prospectus

Set forth in the forepart of the registration statement and on the outside front cover page of the prospectus the information required by *Item 501* of Regulation S-K (§ 229.501 of this chapter).

Item 2. Inside Front and Outside Back Cover Pages of Prospectus

Set forth on the inside front cover page of the prospectus or, where permitted, on the outside back cover page, the information required by *Item 502* of Regulation S-K (§ 229.502 of this chapter).

Item 3. Summary Information and Risk Factors

Furnish the information required by *Items 105 and 503* of Regulation S-K (§ 229.105 and § 229.503 of this chapter).

Item 4. Use of Proceeds

Furnish the information required by *Item 504* of Regulation S-K (§ 229.504 of this chapter).

Item 5. Determination of Offering Price

Furnish the information required by *Item 505* of Regulation S-K (§ 229.505 of this chapter).

Item 6. Dilution

Furnish the information required by *Item 506* of Regulation S-K (§ 229.506 of this chapter).

Item 7. Selling Security Holders

Furnish the information required by *Item 507* of Regulation S-K (§ 229.507 of this chapter).

Item 8. Plan of Distribution

Furnish the information required by *Item 508* of Regulation S-K (§ 229.508 of this chapter).

Item 9. Description of Securities to be Registered

Furnish the information required by *Item 202* of Regulation S-K (§ 229.202 of this chapter).

Item 10. Interests of Named Experts and Counsel

Furnish the information required by *Item 509* of Regulation S-K (§ 229.509 of this chapter).

Item 11. Information with Respect to the Registrant

Furnish the following information with respect to the registrant:

(a) Information required by *Item 101* of Regulation S-K (§ 229.101 of this chapter), description of business;

(b) Information required by *Item 102* of Regulation S-K (§ 229.102 of this chapter), description of property;

(c) Information required by *Item 103* of Regulation S-K (§ 229.103 of this chapter), legal proceedings;

(d) Where common equity securities are being offered, information required by *Item 201* of Regulation S-K (§ 229.201 of this chapter), market price of and dividends on the registrant's common equity and related stockholder matters;

(e) Financial statements meeting the requirements of Regulation S-X (17 CFR Part 210) (Schedules required under Regulation S-X shall be filed as "Financial Statements Schedules" pursuant to Item 15, Exhibits and Financial Statement Schedules, of this form), as well as any financial information required by Rule 3-05 and Article 11 of Regulation S-X. A smaller reporting company may provide the information in Rule 8-04 and 8-05 of Regulation S-X in lieu of the financial information required by Rule 3-05 and Article 11 of Regulation S-X;

(f) Information required by *Item 301* of Regulation S-K (§ 229.301 of this chapter), selected financial data;

(g) Information required by *Item 302* of Regulation S-K (§ 229.302 of this chapter), supplementary financial in formation;

(h) Information required by *Item 303* of Regulation S-K (§ 229.303 of this chapter), management's discussion and analysis of financial condition and results of operations;

(i) Information required by *Item 304* of Regulation S-K (§ 229.304 of this chapter), changes in and disagreements with accountants on accounting and financial disclosure;

(j) Information required by *Item 305* of Regulation S-K (§ 229.305 of this chapter), quantitative and qualitative disclosures about market risk.

(k) Information required by *Item 401* of Regulation S-K (§ 229.401 of this chapter), directors and executive officers;

(l) Information required by Item 402 of Regulation S-K (§ 229.402 of this chapter), executive compensation, and information required by paragraph (e)(4) of Item 407 of Regulation S-K (§ 229.407 of this chapter), corporate governance;

(m) Information required by *Item 403* of Regulation S-K (§ 229.403 of this chapter), security ownership of certain beneficial owners and management; and

(n) Information required by Item 404 of Regulation S-K (§ 229.404 of this chapter), transactions with related persons, promoters and certain control persons, and Item 407(a) of Regulation S-K (§ 229.407(a) of this chapter), corporate governance.

Item 11A. Material Changes.

If the registrant elects to incorporate information by reference pursuant to General Instruction VII, describe any and all material changes in the registrant's affairs that have occurred since the end of the latest fiscal year for which audited financial statements were included in the latest Form 10-K and that have not been described in a Form 10-Q or Form 8-K filed under the Exchange Act.

Item 12. Incorporation of Certain Information by Reference.

If the registrant elects to incorporate information by reference pursuant to General Instruction VII.:

(a) It must specifically incorporate by reference into the prospectus contained in the registration statement the following documents by means of a statement to that effect in the prospectus listing all such documents:

(1) The registrant's latest annual report on Form 10-K filed pursuant to Section 13(a) or Section 15(d) of the Exchange Act that contains financial statements for the registrant's latest fiscal year for which a Form 10-K was required to have been filed; and

(2) All other reports filed pursuant to Section 13(a) or 15(d) of the Exchange Act or proxy or information statements filed pursuant to Section 14 of the Exchange Act since the end of the fiscal year covered by the annual report referred to in paragraph (a)(1) above.

Note to Item 12(a). Attention is directed to Rule 439 (Í230.439) regarding consent to use of material incorporated by reference.

(b) In addition to the incorporation by reference permitted pursuant to paragraph (a) of this Item, a smaller reporting company, as defined in Rule 405 (17 CFR 230.405), may elect to incorporate by reference information filed after the effective date of the registration statement. A smaller reporting company making this election must state in the prospectus contained in the registration statement that all documents subsequently filed by the registrant pursuant to Sections 13(a), 13(c), 14 or 15(d) of the Exchange Act, prior to the termination of the offering shall be deemed to be incorporated by reference into the prospectus.

(c)(1) The registrant must state:

(i) That it will provide to each person, including any beneficial owner, to whom a prospectus is delivered, a copy of any or all of the reports or documents that have been incorporated by reference in the prospectus contained in the registration statement but not delivered with the prospectus;

(ii) That it will provide these reports or documents upon written or oral request;

(iii) That it will provide these reports or documents at no cost to the requester;

(iv) The name, address, telephone number, and e-mail address, if any, to which the request for these reports or documents must be made; and

(v) The registrant's Web site address, including the uniform resource locator (URL) where the incorporated reports and other documents may be accessed.

Note to Item 12(c)(1). If the registrant sends any of the information that is incorporated by reference in the prospectus contained in the registration statement to security holders, it also must send any exhibits that are specifically incorporated by reference in that information.

(2) The registrant must:

(i) Identify the reports and other information that it files with the SEC; and

(ii) State that the SEC maintains an internet site that contains reports, proxy and information statements, and other information regarding issuers that file electronically with the SEC and state the address of that site (http://www.sec.gov).

Item 12A. Disclosure of Commission Position on Indemnification for Securities Act Liabilities

Furnish the information required by *Item 510* of Regulation S-K (§ 229.510 of this chapter).

PART II—INFORMATION NOT REQUIRED IN PROSPECTUS

Item 13. Other Expenses of Issuance and Distribution

Furnish the information required by *Item 511* of Regulation S-K (§ 229.511 of this chapter).

Item 14. Indemnification of Directors and Officers

Furnish the information required by *Item 702* of Regulation S-K (§ 229.702 of this chapter).

Item 15. Recent Sales of Unregistered Securities

Furnish the information required by *Item 701* of Regulation S-K (§ 229.701 of this chapter).

Item 16. Exhibits and Financial Statement Schedules

(a) Subject to the rules regarding incorporation by reference, furnish the exhibits as required by *Item 601* of Regulation S-K (§ 229.601 of this chapter).

(b) Furnish the financial statement schedules required by *Regulation S-X* (17 CFR Part 210) and Item 11(e) of this Form. These schedules shall be lettered or numbered in the manner described for exhibits in paragraph (a).

Item 17. Undertakings

Furnish the undertakings required by *Item 512* of Regulation S-K (§ 229.512 of this chapter).

SIGNATURES

Pursuant to the requirements of the Securities Act of 1933, the registrant has duly caused this registration statement to be signed on its behalf by the undersigned, thereunto duly authorized in the City of .... , State of .... , on .... , 19 ....

(Registrant)

By (Signature and Title)

Pursuant to the requirements of the Securities Act of 1933, this registration statement has been signed by the following persons in the capacities and on the dates indicated.

(Signature)

(Title)

(Date)

Instructions.

1. The registration statement shall be signed by the registrant, its principal executive officer or officers, its principal financial officer, its controller or principal accounting officer and by at least a majority of the board of directors or persons performing similar functions. If the registrant is a foreign person, the registration statement shall also be signed by its authorized representative in the United States. Where the registrant is a limited partnership, the registration statement shall be signed by a majority of the board of directors of any corporate general partner signing the registration statement.

2. The name of each person who signs the registration statement shall be typed or printed beneath his signature. Any person who occupies more than one of the specified positions shall indicate each capacity in which he signs the registration statement. Attention is directed to *Rule 402* concerning manual signatures and to *Item 601* of Regulation S-K concerning signatures pursuant to powers of attorney.

INSTRUCTIONS AS TO SUMMARY PROSPECTUSES

1. A summary prospectus used pursuant to *Rule 431* (§ 230.431 of this chapter), shall at the time of its use contain much of the information specified below as is then included in the registration statement. All other information and documents contained in the registration statement may be omitted.

(a) As to Item 1, the aggregate offering price to the public, the aggregate underwriting discounts and commissions and the offering price per unit to the public;

(b) As to Item 4, a brief statement of the principal purposes for which the proceeds are to be used;

(c) As to Item 7, a statement as to the amount of the offering, if any, to be made for the account of security holders;

(d) As to Item 8, the name of the managing underwriter or underwriters and a brief statement as to the nature of the underwriter's obligation to take the securities; if any securities to be registered are to be offered otherwise than through underwriters, a brief statement as to the manner of distribution; and, if securities are to be offered otherwise than for cash. a brief statement as to the general purposes of the distribution, the basis upon which the securities are to be offered, the amount of compensation and other expenses of distribution, and by whom they are to be borne;

(e) As to Item 9, a brief statement as to dividend rights, voting rights, conversion rights, interest, maturity;

(f) As to Item 11, a brief statement of the general character of the business done and intended to be done, the selected financial data (*Item 301* of Regulation S-K (§ 229.301 of this chapter)) and a brief statement of the nature and present status of any material pending legal proceedings; and

(g) A tabular presentation of notes payable, long term debt, deferred credits, minority interests, if material, and the equity section of the latest balance sheet filed, as may be appropriate.

2. The summary prospectus shall not contain a summary or condensation of any other required financial information except as provided above.

3. Where securities being registered are to be offered in exchange for securities of any other issuer, the summary prospectus also shall contain that information as to Items 9 and 11 specified in paragraphs (e) and (f) above which would be required if the securities of such other issuer were registered on this Form.

4. The Commission may, upon the request of the registrant, and where consistent with the protection of investors, permit the omission of any of the information herein required or the furnishing in substitution therefor of appropriate information of comparable character. The Commission may also require the inclusion of other information in addition to, or in substitution for, the information herein required in any case where such information is necessary or appropriate for the protection of investors.

FORM S-3

UNITED STATES SECURITIES AND EXCHANGE COMMISSION
WASHINGTON, D.C. 20549

FORM S-3

REGISTRATION STATEMENT UNDER THE SECURITIES ACT OF 1933

....
(Exact name of registrant as specified in its charter)

....
(State or other jurisdiction of incorporation or organization)

....
(I.R.S. Employer Identification No.)

....
(Address, including zip code, and telephone number, including area code, of registrant's
principal executive offices)

....
(Name, address, including zip code, and telephone number, including area code, of
agent for service)

Approximate date of commencement of proposed sale to the public..........................

If the only securities being registered on this Form are being offered pursuant to dividend or interest reinvestment plans, please check the following box. ☐

If any of the securities being registered on this Form are to be offered on a delayed or continuous basis pursuant to Rule 415 under the Securities Act of 1933, other than securities offered only in connection with dividend or interest reinvestment plans, check the following box. ☐

If this Form is filed to register additional securities for an offering pursuant to Rule 462(b) under the Securities Act, please check the following box and list the Securities Act registration statement number of the earlier effective registration statement for the same offering. ☐

If this Form is a post-effective amendment filed pursuant to Rule 462(c) under the Securities Act, check the following box and list the Securities Act registration statement number of the earlier effective registration statement for the same offering. ☐

If this Form is a registration statement pursuant to General Instruction I.D. or a post-effective amendment thereto that shall become effective upon filing with the Commission pursuant to Rule 462(e) under the Securities Act, check the following box. ☐

If this Form is a post-effective amendment to a registration statement filed pursuant to General Instruction I.D. filed to register additional securities or additional classes of securities pursuant to Rule 413(b) under the Securities Act, check the following box. ☐

Indicate by check mark whether the registrant is a large accelerated filer, an accelerated filer, a non-accelerated filer, smaller reporting company, or an emerging growth company. See the definitions of "large accelerated filer," "accelerated filer," "smaller reporting company," and "emerging growth company" in Rule 12b-2 of the Exchange Act.

Large accelerated filer ☐   Accelerated filer   ☐
Non-accelerated filer   ☐   Smaller reporting company ☐
                                                Emerging growth company ☐

If an emerging growth company, indicate by check mark if the registrant has elected not to use extended transition period for complying with any new or revised financial accounting standards provided pursuant to Section 7(a)(2)(B) of the Securities Act. ☐

Calculation of Registration Fee

Title of securities to be registered	Amount to be registered	Proposed maximum offering price per share	Proposed maximum aggregate offering price	Amount of registration fee

Notes to the "Calculation of Registration Fee" Table ("Fee Table"):

1. Specific details relating to the fee calculation shall be furnished in notes to the Fee Table, including references to provisions of Rule 457 (§ 230.457 of this chapter) relied upon, if the basis of the calculation is not otherwise evident from the information presented in the Fee Table.

2. If the filing fee is calculated pursuant to Rule 457(o) under the Securities Act, only the title of the class of securities to be registered, the proposed maximum aggregate offering price for that class of securities, and the amount of registration fee need to appear in the Fee Table. Where two or more classes of securities are being registered pursuant to General Instruction II.D., however, the Fee Table need only specify the maximum aggregate offering price for all classes; the Fee Table need not specify by each class the proposed maximum aggregate offering price (see General Instruction II.D.).

3. If the filing fee is calculated pursuant to Rule 457(r) under the Securities Act, the Fee Table must state that it registers an unspecified amount of securities of each identified class of securities and must provide that the issuer is relying on Rule 456(b) and Rule 457(r). If the Fee Table is amended in a post-effective amendment to the registration statement or in a prospectus filed in accordance with Rule 456(b)(1)(ii) (§ 230.456(b)(1)(ii) of this chapter), the Fee Table must specify the aggregate offering price for all classes of securities in the referenced offering or offerings and the applicable registration fee.

4. Any difference between the dollar amount of securities registered for such offerings and the dollar amount of securities sold may be carried forward on a future registration statement pursuant to Rule 457 under the Securities Act.

5. If an offering of an indeterminate amount of exchange-traded vehicle securities is being registered, the Fee Table must state that the registration statement covers an indeterminate amount of securities to be offered or sold and the filing fee will be calculated and paid in accordance with Rule 456(d) and Rule 457(u) (§ 230.456(d) and § 230.457(u) of this chapter), respectively.

GENERAL INSTRUCTIONS

I. Eligibility Requirements for Use of Form S-3

This instruction sets forth registrant requirements and transaction requirements for the use of Form S-3. Any registrant which meets the requirements of I.A. below ("Registrant Requirements") may use this Form for the registration of securities under the Securities Act of 1933 ("Securities Act") which are offered in any transaction specified in I.B. below ("Transaction Requirement") provided that the requirement applicable to the specified transaction are met. With respect to majority-owned subsidiaries, see Instruction I.C. below. With respect to well-known seasoned issuers and majority-owned subsidiaries of well-known seasoned issuers, see Instruction I.D. below.

A. *Registrant Requirements*. Registrants must meet the following conditions in order to use this form for registration under the Securities Act of securities offered in the transactions specified in I.B. below:

1. The registrant is organized under the laws of the United States, or any state or territory or the District of Columbia, and has its principal business operations in the United states or its territories.

2. The registrant has a class of securities registered pursuant to Section 12(b) of the Securities Exchange Act of 1934 ("Exchange Act") or a class of equity securities registered pursuant to Section 12(g) of the Exchange Act, or is required to file reports pursuant to Section 15(d) of the Exchange Act.

3. The registrant:

(a) has been subject to the requirements of Section 12 or 15(d) of the Exchange Act and has filed all the material required to be filed pursuant to Section 13, 14 or 15(d) for a period of at least twelve calendar months immediately preceding the filing of the registration statement on this Form; and

(b) has filed in a timely manner all reports required to be filed during the twelve calendar months and any portion of a month immediately preceding the filing of the registration statement, other than a report that is required solely pursuant to Item 1.01, 1.02, 2.03, 2.04, 2.05, 2.06, 4.02(a) or 5.02(e) of Form 8-K (§ 249.308 of this chapter). If the registrant has used (during the twelve calendar months and any portion of a month immediately preceding the filing of the registration statement) Rule 12b-25(b) (§ 240.12b-25(b) of this chapter) under the Exchange Act with respect to a report or a portion of a report, that report or portion thereof has actually been filed within the time period prescribed by that rule.

4. Neither the registrant nor any of its consolidated or unconsolidated subsidiaries have, since the end of the last fiscal year for which certified financial statements of the registrant and its consolidated subsidiaries were included in a report filed pursuant to Section 13(a) or 15(d) of the Exchange Act: (a) failed to pay any dividend or sinking fund installment on preferred stock; or (b) defaulted: (i) on any installment or installments on indebtedness for borrowed money, or (ii) on any rental on one or more long-term leases, which defaults in the aggregate are material to the financial position of the registrant and its consolidated and unconsolidated subsidiaries, taken as a whole.

5. A foreign issuer, other than a foreign government, which satisfies all of the above provisions of these registrant eligibility requirements except the provisions in I.A.1. relating to organization and principal business shall be deemed to have met these registrant eligibility requirements provided that such foreign issuer files the same reports with the Commission under Section 13(a) or 15(d) of the Exchange Act as a domestic registrant pursuant to I.A.3. above.

6. If the registrant is a successor registrant, it shall be deemed to have met conditions 1, 2, 3 and 5 above if: (a) its predecessor and it, taken together, do so, provided that the succession was primarily for the purpose of changing the state of incorporation of the predecessor or forming a holding company, and that the assets and liabilities of the successor at the time of succession were substantially the same as those of the predecessor, or (b) if all predecessors met the conditions at the time of succession and the registrant has continued to do so since the succession.

7. *Electronic Filings.* In addition to satisfying the foregoing conditions, a registrant subject to the electronic filing requirements of Rule 101 of Regulation S-T (§ 232.101 of this chapter) shall have:

(a) Filed with the Commission all required electronic filings, including electronic copies of documents submitted in paper pursuant to a hardship exemption as provided by Rule 201 or Rule 202(d) of Regulation S-T (§ 232.201 or § 232.202(d) of this chapter); and

(b) Submitted electronically to the Commission all Interactive Data Files required to be submitted pursuant to Rule 405 of Regulation S-T (§ 232.405 of this chapter) during the twelve calendar months and any portion of a month immediately preceding the filing of the registration statement on this Form (or for such shorter period of time that the registrant was required to submit and post such files).

B. *Transaction Requirements.* Security offerings meeting any of the following conditions and made by a registrant meeting the Registrant Requirements specified in I.A. above may be registered on this form:

1. *Primary Offerings by Certain Registrants.* Securities to be offered for cash by or on behalf of a registrant, or outstanding securities to be offered for cash for the account of any person other than the registrant, including securities acquired by standby underwriters in connection with the call or redemption by the registrant of warrants or a class of convertible securities; provided that the aggregate market value of the voting and nonvoting common equity held by non-affiliates of the registrant is $75 million or more.

Instruction. For the purposes of this form, "common equity" is as defined in Securities Act Rule 405. The aggregate market value of the registrant's outstanding voting and non-voting common equity shall be computed by use of the price at which the common equity was last sold, or the average of the bid and asked prices of such common equity, in the principal market for such common equity as of a date within 60 days prior to the date of filing. See the definition of "affiliate" in Securities Act Rule 405.

    2. Primary Offerings of Non-Convertible Securities Other than Common Equity. Non-convertible securities, other than common equity, to be offered for cash by or on behalf of a registrant, provided the registrant (i) has issued (as of a date within 60 days prior to the filing of the registration statement) at least $1 billion in non-convertible securities, other than common equity, in primary offerings for cash, not exchange, registered under the Securities Act, over the prior three years; or (ii) has outstanding (as of a date within 60 days prior to the filing of the registration statement) at least $750 million of non-convertible securities, other than common equity, issued in primary offerings for cash, not exchange, registered under the Securities Act; or (iii) is a wholly-owned subsidiary of a well-known seasoned issuer (as defined in 17 CFR 230.405); or (iv) is a majority-owned operating partnership of a real estate investment trust that qualifies as a well-known seasoned issuer (as defined in 17 CFR 230.405).

Instruction. For purposes of Instruction I.B.2(i) above, an insurance company, as defined in Section 2(a)(13) of the Securities Act, when using this Form to register offerings of securities subject to regulation under the insurance laws of any State or Territory of the United States or the District of Columbia ("insurance contracts"), may include purchase payments or premium payments for insurance contracts, including purchase payments or premium payments for variable insurance contracts (not including purchase payments or premium payments initially allocated to investment options that are not registered under the Securities Act), issued in offerings registered under the Securities Act over the prior three years. For purposes of Instruction I.B.2(ii) above, an insurance company, as defined in Section 2(a)(13) of the Securities Act, when using this Form to register offerings of insurance contracts, may include the contract value, as of the measurement date, of any outstanding insurance contracts, including variable insurance contracts (not including the value allocated as of the measurement date to investment options that are not registered under the Securities Act), issued in offerings registered under the Securities Act.

    3. Transactions Involving Secondary Offerings. Outstanding securities to be offered for the account of any person other than the issuer, including securities acquired by standby underwriters in connection with the call or redemption by the issuer of warrants or a class of convertible securities, if securities of the same class are listed and registered on a national securities exchange or are quoted on the automated quotation system of a national securities association. (In addition, attention is directed to General Instruction C to Form S-8 for the registration of employee benefit plan securities for resale.)

    4. Rights Offerings, Dividend or Interest Reinvestment Plans, and Conversions, Warrants and Options.

    (a) Securities to be offered

        (1) Upon the exercise of outstanding rights granted by the issuer of the securities to be offered, if such rights are granted on a *pro rata* basis to all existing security holders of the class of securities to which the rights attach,

        (2) Under a dividend or interest reinvestment plan, or

        (3) Upon the conversion of outstanding convertible securities or the exercise of outstanding warrants or options issued by the issuer of the securities to be offered, or an affiliate of that issuer.

    (b) However, Form S-3 is available for registering these securities only if the issuer has sent, within the twelve calendar months immediately before the registration statement is filed, material containing the information required by Rule 14a-3(b) under the Exchange Act to:

        (1) All record holders of the rights,

(2) All participants in the plans, or

(3) All record holders of the convertible securities, warrants or options, respectively.

(c) The issuer also must have provided, within the twelve calendar months immediately before the Form S-3 registration statement is filed, the information required by Items 401, 402, 403 and 407(c)(3), (d)(4), (d)(5) and (e)(4) of Regulation S-K (§ 229.401–§ 229.403 and § 229.407(c)(3), (d)(4), (d)(5) and (e)(4) of this chapter) to:

(1) Holders of rights exercisable for common stock,

(2) Holders of securities convertible into common stock, and

(3) Participants in plans that may invest in common stock, securities convertible into common stock, or warrants or options exercisable for common stock, respectively.

5. This Form shall not be used to register offerings of asset-backed securities, as defined in 17 CFR 229.1101(c).

6. Limited Primary Offerings by Certain Other Registrants. Securities to be offered for cash by or on behalf of a registrant; *provided that*:

(a) the aggregate market value of securities sold by or on behalf of the registrant pursuant to this Instruction I.B.6. during the period of 12 calendar months immediately prior to, and including, the sale is no more than one-third of the aggregate market value of the voting and non-voting common equity held by non-affiliates of the registrant;

(b) the registrant is not a shell company (as defined in § 230.405 of this chapter) and has not been a shell company for at least 12 calendar months previously and if it has been a shell company at any time previously, has filed current Form 10 information with the Commission at least 12 calendar months previously reflecting its status as an entity that is not a shell company; and

(c) the registrant has at least one class of common equity securities listed and registered on a national securities exchange.

Instructions.

1. "Common equity" is as defined in Securities Act Rule 405 (§ 230.405 of this chapter). For purposes of computing the aggregate market value of the registrant's outstanding voting and non-voting common equity pursuant to General Instruction I.B.6., registrants shall use the price at which the common equity was last sold, or the average of the bid and asked prices of such common equity, in the principal market for such common equity as of a date within 60 days prior to the date of sale. See the definition of "affiliate" in Securities Act Rule 405 (§ 230.405 of this chapter).

2. For purposes of computing the aggregate market value of all securities sold by or on behalf of the registrant in offerings pursuant to General Instruction I.B.6. during any period of 12 calendar months, registrants shall aggregate the gross proceeds of such sales; *provided*, that, in the case of derivative securities convertible into or exercisable for shares of the registrant's common equity, registrants shall calculate the aggregate market value of any underlying equity shares in lieu of the market value of the derivative securities. The aggregate market value of the underlying equity shall be calculated by multiplying the maximum number of common equity shares into which the derivative securities are convertible or for which they are exercisable as of a date within 60 days prior to the date of sale, by the same per share market price of the registrant's equity used for purposes of calculating the aggregate market value of the registrant's outstanding voting and non-voting common equity pursuant to Instruction 1 to General Instruction I.B.6. If the derivative securities have been converted or exercised, the aggregate market value of the underlying equity shall be calculated by multiplying the actual number of shares into which the securities were converted or received upon exercise, by the market price of such shares on the date of conversion or exercise.

3. If the aggregate market value of the registrant's outstanding voting and nonvoting common equity computed pursuant to General Instruction I.B.6. equals or exceeds $75 million subsequent to the effective date of this registration statement, then the one-third

limitation on sales specified in General Instruction I.B.6(a) shall not apply to additional sales made pursuant to this registration statement on or subsequent to such date and instead the registration statement shall be considered filed pursuant to General Instruction I.B.1.

4. The term "Form 10 information" means the information that is required by Form 10 or Form 20-F (§ 249.210 or § 249.220f of this chapter), as applicable to the registrant, to register under the Securities Exchange Act of 1934 each class of securities being registered using this form. A registrant may provide the Form 10 information in another Commission filing with respect to the registrant.

5. The date used in Instruction 2 to General Instruction I.B.6. shall be the same date used in Instruction 1 to General Instruction I.B.6.

6. A registrant's eligibility to register a primary offering on Form S-3 pursuant to General Instruction I.B.6. does not mean that the registrant meets the requirements of Form S-3 for purposes of any other rule or regulation of the Commission apart from Rule 415(a)(1)(x) (§ 230.415(a)(1)(x) of this chapter).

7. Registrants must set forth on the outside front cover of the prospectus the calculation of the aggregate market value of the registrant's outstanding voting and nonvoting common equity pursuant to General Instruction I.B.6. and the amount of all securities offered pursuant to General Instruction I.B.6. during the prior 12 calendar month period that ends on, and includes, the date of the prospectus.

8. For purposes of General Instruction I.B.6(c), a "national securities exchange" shall mean an exchange registered as such under Section 6(a) of the Securities Exchange Act of 1934.

C. *Majority-Owned Subsidiaries.* If a registrant is a majority-owned subsidiary, security offerings may be registered on this form if:

1. The registrant-subsidiary itself meets the Registrant Requirements and the applicable Transaction Requirement;

2. The parent of the registrant-subsidiary meets the Registrant Requirements and the conditions of Transaction Requirement B.2. (Primary Offerings of Non-Convertible Securities Other than Common Equity) are met;

3. The parent of the registrant-subsidiary meets the Registrant Requirements and the applicable Transaction Requirement, and provides a full and unconditional guarantee, as defined in Rule 3-10 of Regulation S-X (§ 210.3-10 of this chapter), of the payment obligations on the securities being registered, and the securities being registered are non-convertible securities, other than common equity;

4. The parent of the registrant-subsidiary meets the Registrant Requirements and the applicable Transaction Requirement, and the securities of the registrant-subsidiary being registered are full and unconditional guarantees, as defined in Rule 3-10 of Regulation S-X, of the payment obligations on the parent's non-convertible securities, other than common equity, being registered; or

5. The parent of the registrant-subsidiary meets the Registrant Requirements and the applicable Transaction Requirement, and the securities of the registrant-subsidiary being registered are guarantees of the payment obligations on the non-convertible securities, other than common equity, being registered by another majority-owned subsidiary of the parent where the parent provides a full and unconditional guarantee, as defined in Rule 3-10 of Regulation S-X, of such non-convertible securities.

Note to General Instruction I.C.: With regard to paragraphs I.C.3, I.C.4, and I.C.5 above, the guarantor is the issuer of a separate security consisting of the guarantee, which must be concurrently registered, but may be registered on the same registration statement as are the non-convertible guaranteed securities.

D. *Automatic Shelf Offerings by Well-Known Seasoned Issuers.* Any registrant that is a well-known seasoned issuer, as defined in Rule 405, at the most recent eligibility determination date specified in paragraph (2) of that definition may use this Form for registration under the Securities Act of securities offerings, other than pursuant to Rule 415(a)(1)(vii) or (viii) (§ 230.415(a)(1)(vii) or (viii) of this chapter), as follows:

1. The securities to be offered are:

(a) Any securities to be offered pursuant to Rule 415, Rule 430A, or Rule 430B (§ 230.415, § 230.430A, or § 230.430B of this chapter) by:

(i) A registrant that is a well-known seasoned issuer by reason of paragraph (1)(i)(A) of the definition in Rule 405; or

(ii) A registrant that is a well-known seasoned issuer only by reason of paragraph (1)(i)(B) of the definition in Rule 405 if the registrant also is eligible to register a primary offering of its securities pursuant to Transaction Requirement I.B.1 of this Form;

(b) Non-convertible securities, other than common equity, to be offered pursuant to Rule 415, Rule 430A, or Rule 430B by a registrant that is a well-known seasoned issuer only by reason of paragraph (1)(i)(B) of the definition in Rule 405 and does not fall within Transaction Requirement I.B.1 of this Form;

(c) Securities of majority-owned subsidiaries of the parent registrant to be offered pursuant to Rule 415, Rule 430A, or Rule 430B if the parent registrant is a well known seasoned issuer and the securities of the majority-owned subsidiary being registered meet the following requirements:

(i) Securities of a majority-owned subsidiary that is a well-known seasoned issuer at the time it becomes a registrant, other than by virtue of paragraph (1)(ii) of the definition of well-known seasoned issuer in Rule 405;

(ii) Securities of a majority-owned subsidiary that are non-convertible securities, other than common equity, and the parent registrant provides a full and unconditional guarantee, as defined in Rule 3-10 of Regulation S-X, of the payment obligations on the non-convertible securities;

(iii) Securities of a majority-owned subsidiary that are a guarantee of:

(A) Non-convertible securities, other than common equity, of the parent registrant being registered;

(B) Non-convertible securities, other than common equity, of another majority owned subsidiary being registered and the parent registrant has provided a full and unconditional guarantee, as defined in Rule 3-10 of Regulation S-X, of the payment obligations on such non-convertible securities; or

(iv) Securities of a majority-owned subsidiary that meet the conditions of Transaction Requirement I.B.2. of this Form (Primary Offerings of Non-Convertible Securities Other than Common Equity).

(d) Securities to be offered for the account of any person other than the issuer ("selling security holders"), provided that the registration statement and the prospectus are not required to separately identify the selling security holders or the securities to be sold by such persons until the filing of a prospectus, prospectus supplement, posteffective amendment to the registration statement, or periodic or current report under the Exchange Act that is incorporated by reference into the registration statement and prospectus, identifying the selling security holders and the amount of securities to be sold by each of them and, if included in a periodic or current report, a prospectus or prospectus supplement is filed, as required by Rule 430B, pursuant to Rule 424(b)(7) (§ 230.424(b)(7) of this chapter).

2. The registrant pays the registration fee pursuant to Rules 456(b) and 457(r) or in accordance with Rule 456(a).

3. If the registrant is a majority-owned subsidiary, it is required to file and has filed reports pursuant to Section 13 or Section 15(d) of the Exchange Act and satisfies the requirements of the Form with regard to incorporation by reference or information about the majority-owned subsidiary is included in the registration statement (or a post-effective amendment to the registration statement).

4. The registrant may register additional securities or classes of its or its majority owned subsidiaries' securities on a post-effective amendment pursuant to Rule 413(b) (§ 203.413(b) of this chapter).

5. An automatic shelf registration statement and post-effective amendment will become effective immediately pursuant to Rule 462(e) and (f) (§ 230.462(e) and (f) of this chapter) upon filing. All filings made on or in connection with automatic shelf registration statements on this Form become public upon filing with the Commission.

II. Application of General Rules and Regulations

A. Attention is directed to the General Rules and Regulations under the Securities Act, particularly Regulation C thereunder. That regulation contains general requirements regarding the preparation and filing of registration statements.

B. Attention is directed to Regulation S-K for the requirements applicable to the content of the non-financial statement portions of registration statements under the Securities Act. Where this form directs the registrant to furnish information required by Regulation S-K and the item of Regulation S-K so provides, information need only be furnished to the extent appropriate. Notwithstanding Items 501 and 502 of Regulation S-K, no table of contents is required to be included in the prospectus or registration statement prepared on this form. In addition to the information expressly required to be included in a registration statement on this Form S-3, registrants also may provide such other information as they deem appropriate.

C. A smaller reporting company, defined in Rule 405 (17 CFR 230.405), that is eligible to use Form S-3 shall use the disclosure items in Regulation S-K (17 CFR 229.10 *et seq.*) with specific attention to the scaled disclosure provided for smaller reporting companies, if any. Smaller reporting companies may provide the financial information called for by Article 8 of Regulation S-X in lieu of the financial information called for by Item 11 in this form.

D. *Non-Automatic Shelf Registration Statements.* Where two or more classes of securities being registered on this Form pursuant to General Instruction I.B.1. or I.B.2. are to be offered pursuant to Rule 415(a)(1)(x) (§ 230.415(a)(1)(x) of this chapter), and where this Form is not an automatic shelf registration statement, Rule 457(o) permits the registration fee to be calculated on the basis of the maximum offering price of all the securities listed in the Fee Table. In this event, while the Fee Table would list each of the classes of securities being registered and the aggregate proceeds to be raised, the Fee Table need not specify by each class information as to the amount to be registered, proposed maximum offering price per unit, and proposed maximum aggregate offering price.

E. *Automatic Shelf Registration Statements.* Where securities are being registered on this Form pursuant to General Instruction I.D., Rule 456(b) permits, but does not require, the registrant to pay the registration fee on a pay-as-you-go basis and Rule 457(r) permits, but does not require, the registration fee to be calculated on the basis of the aggregate offering price of the securities to be offered in an offering or offerings off the registration statement. If a registrant elects to pay all or a portion of the registration fee on a deferred basis, the Fee Table in the initial filing must identify the classes of securities being registered and provide that the registrant elects to rely on Rule 456(b) and Rule 457(r), but the Fee Table does not need to specify any other information. When the registrant amends the Fee Table in accordance with Rule 456(b)(1)(ii), the amended Fee Table must include either the dollar amount of securities being registered if paid in advance of or in connection with an offering or offerings or the aggregate offering price for all classes of securities referenced in the offerings and the applicable registration fee.

F. *Information in Automatic and Non-Automatic Shelf Registration Statements.* Where securities are being registered on this Form pursuant to General Instruction I.B.1, I.B.2, I.C., or I.D., information is only required to be furnished as of the date of initial effectiveness of the registration statement to the extent required by Rule 430A or Rule 430B. Required information about a specific transaction must be included in the prospectus in the registration statement by means of a prospectus that is deemed to be part of and included in the registration statement pursuant to Rule 430A or Rule 430B, a post-effective amendment to the registration statement, or a periodic or current report under the Exchange Act incorporated by reference into the registration statement and the prospectus and identified in a prospectus filed, as required by Rule 430B, pursuant to Rule 424(b) (§ 230.424(b) of this chapter).

G. *Selling Security Holder Offerings*. Where a registrant eligible to register primary offerings on this Form pursuant to General Instruction I.B.1 registers securities offerings on this Form pursuant to General Instruction I.B.1 or I.B.3 for the account of persons other than the registrant, if the offering of the securities, or securities convertible into such securities, that are being registered on behalf of the selling security holders was completed and the securities, or securities convertible into such securities, were issued and outstanding prior to the original date of filing the registration statement covering the resale of the securities, the registrant may, as permitted by Rule 430B(b), in lieu of identifying selling security holders prior to effectiveness of the resale registration statement, refer to unnamed selling security holders in a generic manner by identifying the initial transaction in which the securities were sold. Following effectiveness, the registrant must include in a prospectus filed pursuant to Rule 424(b)(7), a post-effective amendment to the registration statement, or an Exchange Act report incorporated by reference into the prospectus that is part of the registration statement (which Exchange Act report is identified in a prospectus filed, as required by Rule 430B, pursuant to Rule 424(b)(7)) the names of previously unidentified selling security holders and amounts of securities that they intend to sell. If this Form is being filed pursuant to General Instruction I.D. by a well-known seasoned issuer to register securities being offered for the account of persons other than the issuer, the registration statement and the prospectus included in the registration statement do not need to designate the securities that will be offered for the account of such persons, identify them, or identify the initial transaction in which the securities, or securities convertible into such securities, were sold until the registrant files a post-effective amendment to the registration statement, a prospectus pursuant to Rule 424(b), or an Exchange Act report (and prospectus filed, as required by Rule 430B, pursuant to Rule 424(b)(7)) containing information for the offering on behalf of such persons.

III. Dividend or Interest Reinvestment Plans; Filing and Effectiveness of Registration Statement; Requests For Confidential Treatment

A registration statement on this Form S-3 relating solely to securities offered pursuant to a dividend or interest reinvestment plan will become effective automatically (Rule 462 of this chapter) upon filing (Rule 456 of this chapter). Post-effective amendments to such a registration statement on this form shall become effective upon filing (Rule 464 of this chapter). All filings made on or in connection with this form become public upon filing with the Commission. As a result, requests for confidential treatment made under Rule 406 must be processed with the Commission staff prior to the filing of such a registration statement. The number of copies of the registration statement and of each amendment required by Rules 402 and 472 shall be filed with the Commission; *provided, however*, that the number of additional copies referred to in Rule 402(b) may be reduced from 10 to three and the number of additional copies referred to in Rule 472(a) may be reduced from eight to three, one of which shall be marked clearly and precisely to indicate changes.

IV. Registration of Additional Securities and Additional Classes of Securities.

A. *Registration of Additional Securities Pursuant to Rule 462(b)*.With respect to the registration of additional securities for an offering pursuant to Rule 462(b) under the Securities Act, the registrant may file a registration statement consisting only of the following: the facing page; a statement that the contents of the earlier registration statement, identified by file number, are incorporated by reference; required opinions and consents; the signature page; and any price-related information omitted from the earlier registration statement in reliance on Rule 430A that the registrant chooses to include in the new registration statement. The information contained in such a Rule 462(b) registration statement shall be deemed to be a part of the earlier registration statement as of the date of effectiveness of the Rule 462(b) registration statement. Any opinion or consent required in the Rule 462(b) registration statement may be incorporated by reference from the earlier registration statement with respect to the offering, if: (i) such opinion or consent expressly provides for such incorporation; and (ii) such opinion relates to the securities registered pursuant to Rule 462(b).

B. *Registration of Additional Securities or Classes of Securities or Additional Registrants After Effectiveness.* A well-known seasoned issuer relying on General Instruction I.D. of this Form may register additional securities or classes of securities, pursuant to Rule 413(b) by filing a post-effective amendment to the effective registration statement. The well-known seasoned issuer may add majority-owned subsidiaries as additional registrants whose securities are eligible to be sold as part of the automatic shelf registration statement by filing a post-effective amendment identifying the additional registrants, and the registrant and the additional registrants and other persons required to sign the registration statement must sign the post-effective amendment. The post-effective amendment must consist of the facing page; any disclosure required by this Form that is necessary to update the registration statement to reflect the additional securities, additional classes of securities, or additional registrants; any required opinions and consents; and the signature page. Required information, consents, or opinions may be included in the prospectus and the registration statement through a post-effective amendment or may be provided through a document incorporated or deemed incorporated by reference into the registration statement and the prospectus that is part of the registration statement, or, as to the required information only, contained in a prospectus filed pursuant to Rule 424(b) that is deemed part of and included in the registration statement and prospectus that is part of the registration statement.

PART I
INFORMATION REQUIRED IN PROSPECTUS

Item 1. Forepart of the Registration Statement and Outside Front Cover Page of Prospectus.

Set forth in the forepart of the registration statement and on the outside front cover page of the prospectus the information required by Item 501 of Regulation S-K.

Item 2. Inside Front and Outside Back Cover Pages of Prospectus

Set forth on the inside front cover page of the prospectus or, where permitted, on the outside back cover page, the information required by Item 502 of Regulation S-K.

Item 3. Summary Information, Risk Factors and Ratio of Earnings to Fixed Charges

Furnish the information required by Items 105 and 503 of Regulation S-K (§ 229.105 and § 229.503 of this chapter).

Item 4. Use of Proceeds

Furnish the information required by Item 504 of Regulation S-K.

Item 5. Determination of Offering Price

Furnish the information required by Item 505 of Regulation S-K.

Item 6. Dilution

Furnish the information required by Item 506 of Regulation S-K.

Item 7. Selling Security Holders

Furnish the information required by Item 507 of Regulation S-K.

Item 8. Plan of Distribution

Furnish the information required by Item 508 of Regulation S-K.

Item 9. Description of Securities to be Registered

Furnish the information required by Item 202 of Regulation S-K, unless capital stock is to be registered and securities of the same class are registered pursuant to Section 12 of the Exchange Act.

Item 10. Interests of Named Experts and Counsel

Furnish the information required by Item 509 of Regulation S-K.

Item 11. Material Changes

(a) Describe any and all material changes in the registrant's affairs that have occurred since the end of the latest fiscal year for which certified financial statements were included in the latest annual report to security holders and that have not been described in a report on Form 10-Q (§ 249.308a of this chapter) or Form 8-K (§ 249.308 of this chapter) filed under the Exchange Act.

(b) Include in the prospectus, if not incorporated by reference therein from the reports filed under the Exchange Act specified in Item 12(a), a proxy or information statement filed pursuant to Section 14 of the Exchange Act, a prospectus previously filed pursuant to Rule 424(b) or (c) under the Securities Act or, where no prospectus was required to be filed pursuant to Rule 424(b), the prospectus included in the registration statement at effectiveness, or a Form 8-K filed during either of the two preceding fiscal years: (i) information required by Rule 3-05 and Article 11 of Regulation S-X; (ii) restated financial statements prepared in accordance with Regulation S-X if there has been a change in accounting principles or a correction in an error where such change or correction requires a material retroactive restatement of financial statements; (iii) restated financial statements prepared in accordance with Regulation S-X where one or more business combinations accounted for by the pooling of interest method of accounting have been consummated subsequent to the most recent fiscal year and the acquired businesses, considered in the aggregate, are significant pursuant to Rule 11-01(b); or (iv) any financial information required because of a material disposition of assets outside the normal course of business.

Item 12. Incorporation of Certain Information by Reference

(a) The documents listed in (1) and (2) below shall be specifically incorporated by reference into the prospectus, by means of a statement to that effect in the prospectus listing all such documents:

(1) The registrant's latest annual report on Form 10-K (17 CFR 249.310) filed pursuant to Section 13(a) or 15(d) of the Exchange Act that contains financial statements for the registrant's latest fiscal year for which a Form 10-K was required to be filed; and

(2) All other reports filed pursuant to Section 13(a) or 15(d) of the Exchange Act since the end of the fiscal year covered by the annual report referred to in (1) above; and

(3) If capital stock is to be registered and securities of the same class are registered under Section 12 of the Exchange Act, the description of such class of securities which is contained in a registration statement filed under the Exchange Act, including any amendment or reports filed for the purpose of updating such description.

(b) The prospectus shall also state that all documents subsequently filed by the registrant pursuant to Section 13(a), 13(c), 14 or 15(d) of the Exchange Act, prior to the termination of the offering, shall be deemed to be incorporated by reference into the prospectus.

(c)(1) You must state

(i) that you will provide to each person, including any beneficial owner, to whom a prospectus is delivered, a copy of any or all of the information that has been incorporated by reference in the prospectus but not delivered with the prospectus:

(ii) that you will provide this information upon written or oral request;

(iii) that you will provide this information at no cost to the requester; and

(iv) the name, address, and telephone number to which the request for this information must be made.

Note to Item 12(c)(1): If you send any of the information that is incorporated by reference in the prospectus to security holders, you also must send any exhibits that are specifically incorporated by reference in that information.

(2) You must

(i) identify the reports and other information that you file with the SEC; and

(ii) state that the SEC maintains an internet site that contains reports, proxy and information statements, and other information regarding issuers that file electronically with the SEC and state the address of that site (http://www.sec.gov). Disclose your internet address, if available.

(d) Any information required in the prospectus in response to Item 3 through Item 11 of this Form may be included in the prospectus through documents filed pursuant to Section 13(a), 14, or 15(d) of the Exchange Act that are incorporated or deemed incorporated by reference into the prospectus that is part of the registration statement. Notwithstanding the foregoing, in the financial statements, incorporating by reference or cross-referencing to information outside of the financial statements is not permitted unless otherwise specifically permitted or required by the Commission's rules or by U.S. Generally Accepted Accounting Principles or International Financial Reporting Standards as issued by the International Accounting Standards Board, whichever is applicable.

Instruction. Attention is directed to Rule 439 regarding consent to use of material incorporated by reference.

Item 13. Disclosure of Commission Position on Indemnification For Securities Act Liabilities

Furnish the information required by Item 510 of Regulation S-K.

PART II
INFORMATION NOT REQUIRED IN PROSPECTUS

Item 14. Other Expenses of Issuance and Distribution.

Furnish the information required by Item 511 of Regulation S-K.

Item 15. Indemnification of Directors and Officers.

Furnish the information required by Item 702 of Regulation S-K.

Item 16. Exhibits.

Subject to the rules regarding incorporation by reference, furnish the exhibits required by Item 601 of Regulation S-K.

Item 17. Undertakings.

Furnish the undertakings required by Item 512 of Regulation S-K.

SIGNATURES

Pursuant to the requirements of the Securities Act of 1933, the registrant certifies that it has reasonable grounds to believe that it meets all of the requirements for filing on Form S-3 and has duly caused this registration statement to be signed on its behalf by the undersigned, thereunto duly authorized in the City of ...., State of .... , on .... , 19........................ (Registrant) ....
By (Signature and Title) ....

Pursuant to the requirements of the Securities Act of 1933, this registration statement has been signed by the following persons in the capacities and on the dates indicated.
(Signature) ....
(Title) ....
(Date) ....

Instructions. 1. The registration statement shall be signed by the registrant, its principal executive officer or officers, its principal financial officer, its controller or principal accounting officer, and by at least a majority of the board of directors or persons performing similar functions. If the registrant is a foreign person, the registration statement shall also be signed by its authorized representative in the United States. Where the registrant is a limited partnership, the registration statement shall be signed by a majority of the board of directors of any corporate general partner signing the registration statement.

2. The name of each person who signs the registration statement shall be typed or printed beneath his signature. Any person who occupies more than one of the specified positions shall indicate each capacity in which he signs the registration statement. Attention is directed to Rule 402 concerning manual signatures and Item 601 of Regulation S-K concerning signatures pursuant to powers of attorney.

FORM S-8

UNITED STATES SECURITIES AND EXCHANGE COMMISSION
Washington, D.C. 20549

FORM S-8

REGISTRATION STATEMENT UNDER THE SECURITIES ACT OF 1933

(Exact name of registrant as specified in its charter)

| (State or other jurisdiction of incorporation or organization) | (I.R.S. Employer Identification No.) |

(Address of Principal Executive Offices)   (Zip Code)

(Full title of the plan)

(Name and address of agent for service)

(Telephone number, including area code, of agent for service)

Indicate by check mark whether the registrant is a large accelerated filer, an accelerated filer, a non-accelerated filer, smaller reporting company, or an emerging growth company. See the definitions of "large accelerated filer," "accelerated filer," "smaller reporting company," and "emerging growth company" in Rule 12b-2 of the Exchange Act.

Large accelerated filer ☐   Accelerated filer ☐
Non-accelerated filer ☐   Smaller reporting company ☐
Non-accelerated filer ☐   Emerging growth company ☐

If an emerging growth company, indicate by check mark if the registrant has elected not to use extended transition period for complying with any new or revised financial accounting standards provided pursuant to Section 7(a)(2)(B) of the Securities Act.

CALCULATION OF REGISTRATION FEE

Title of securities to be registered	Amount to be registered	Proposed maximum offering price per share	Proposed maximum aggregate offering price	Amount of registration fee

Notes:

1. If plan interests are being registered, include the following: In addition, pursuant to Rule 416(c) under the Securities Act of 1933, this registration statement also covers an indeterminate amount of interests to be offered or sold pursuant to the employee benefit plan(s) described herein.

2. Specific details relating to the fee calculation shall be furnished in notes to the table, including references to provisions of Rule 457 (§ 230,457 of this chapter) relied upon, if the basis of the calculation is not otherwise evident from the information presented in the table.

GENERAL INSTRUCTIONS

A. Rule as to Use of Form S-8

1. Any registrant that, immediately prior to the time of filing a registration statement on this Form, is subject to the requirement to file reports pursuant to Section 13 (15 U.S.C. 78m) or 15(d) (15 U.S.C. 78o(d)) of the Securities Exchange Act of 1934 ("Exchange Act"); has filed all

reports and other materials required to be filed by such requirements during the preceding 12 months (or for such shorter period that the registrant was required to file such reports and materials); is not a shell company (as defined in § 230.405 of this chapter) and has not been a shell company for at least 60 calendar days previously (subject to the exception in paragraph (a)(7) of this Instruction A.1.); and if it has been a shell company at any time previously, has filed current Form 10 information with the Commission at least 60 calendar days previously reflecting its status as an entity that is not a shell company (subject to the exception in paragraph (a)(7) of this Instruction A.1.), may use this Form for registration under the Securities Act of 1933 ("Act") (15 U.S.C. 77a *et seq.*) of the following securities:

(a) Securities of the registrant to be offered under any employee benefit plan to its employees or employees of its subsidiaries or parents. For purposes of this form, the term "employee benefit plan" is defined in Rule 405 of Regulation C (230.405).

(1) For purposes of this form, the term "employee" is defined as any employee, director, general partner, trustee (where the registrant is a business trust), officer, or consultant or advisor. Form S-8 is available for the issuance of securities to consultants or advisors only if:

(i) they are natural persons;

(ii) They provide bona fide services to the registrant; and

(iii) the services are not in connection with the offeror sale of securities in a capital-raising transaction, and do not directly or indirectly promote or maintain a market for the registrant's securities.

(2) In addition, the term "employee" includes insurance agents who are exclusive agents of the registrant, its subsidiaries or parents, or derive more than 50% of their annual income from those entities.

(3) The term "employee" also includes former employees as well as executors, administrators or beneficiaries of the estates of deceased employees, guardians or members of a committee for incompetent former employees, or similar persons duly authorized by law to administer the estate or assets of former employees. The inclusion of all individuals described in the preceding sentence in the term "employee" is only to permit registration on Form S-8 of:

(i) the exercise of employee benefit plan stock options and the subsequent sale of the securities, if these exercises and sales are permitted under the terms of the plan; and

(ii) the acquisition of registrant securities pursuant to intra-plan transfers among plan funds, if these transfers are permitted under the terms of the plan.

(4) The term "registrant" as used in this Form means the company whose securities are to be offered pursuant to the plan, and also may mean the plan itself.

(5) The form also is available for the exercise of employee benefit plan options and the subsequent resale of the underlying securities by an employee's family member who has acquired the options from the employee through a gift or a domestic relations order. For purposes of this form, "family member" includes any child, stepchild, grandchild, parent, stepparent, grandparent, spouse, former spouse, sibling, niece, nephew, mother-in-law, father-in-law, son-in-law, daughter-in-law, brother-in-law, or sister-in-law, including adoptive relationships, any person sharing the employees household (other than a tenant or employee), a trust in which these persons have more than fifty percent of the beneficial interest, a foundation in which these persons (or the employee) control the management of assets, and any other entity in which these persons (or the employee) own more than fifty percent of the voting interests. Form S-8 is not available for the exercise of options transferred for value. The following transactions are not prohibited transfers for value:

(i) a transfer under a domestic relations order in settlement of marital property rights; and

(ii) a transfer to an entity in which more than fifty percent of the voting interests are owned by family members (or the employee) in exchange for an interest in that entity.

(6) The term "Form 10 information" means the information that is required by Form 10 or Form 20-F (§ 249.210, § 249.210b, or § 249.220f of this chapter), as applicable to the registrant, to register under the Securities Exchange Act of 1934 each class of securities being registered using this form. A registrant may provide the Form 10 information in another Commission filing with respect to the registrant.

(7) Notwithstanding the last two clauses of the first paragraph of this Instruction A.1., a business combination related shell company may use this form immediately after it:

(i) Ceases to be a shell company; and

(ii) Files current Form 10 information with the Commission reflecting its status as an entity that is not a shell company.

(b) Interests in the above plans, if such interests constitute securities and are required to be registered under the Act. (*See* Release No. 33-6188 (February 1, 1980) and Section 3(a)(2) of the Act.)

2. Where interests in a plan are being registered and the plan's latest annual report filed pursuant to Section 15(d) of the Exchange Act is to be incorporated by reference pursuant to the requirements of Form S-8, the plan shall either: (i) have been subject to the requirement to file reports pursuant to Section 15(d) and shall have filed all reports required to be filed by such requirements during the preceding 12 months (or for such shorter period that the plan was required to file such reports); or (ii) if the plan has not previously been subject to the reporting requirements of Section 15(d), concurrently with the filing of the registration statement on Form S-8, the plan shall file an annual report for its latest fiscal year (or if the plan has not yet completed its first fiscal year, then for a period ending not more than 90 days prior to the filing of this registration statement), *provided that* if the plan has not been in existence for at least 90 days prior to the filing date, the requirement to file an employee plan annual report concurrently with the Form S-8 registration statement shall not apply.

3. *Electronic Filings.* In addition to satisfying the foregoing conditions, a registrant subject to the electronic filing requirements of Rule 101 of Regulation S-T (§ 232.101 of this chapter) shall have:

(a) Filed with the Commission all required electronic filings, including electronic copies of documents submitted in paper pursuant to a hardship exemption as provided by Rule 201 or Rule 202(d) of Regulation S-T (§ 232.201 or § 232.202(d) of this chapter); and

(b) Submitted electronically to the Commission all Interactive Data Files required to be submitted pursuant to Rule 405 of Regulation S-T (§ 232.405 of this chapter) during the twelve calendar months and any portion of a month immediately preceding the filing of the registration statement on this Form (or for such shorter period of time that the registrant was required to submit and post such files).

B. Application of General Rules and Regulations

1. Attention is directed to the General Rules and Regulations under the Act, particularly those comprising Regulation C thereunder (17 CFR §§ 230.400 to 230.499). That Regulation contains general requirements regarding the preparation and filing of registration statements. However, any provision in this Form covering the same subject matter as any such requirement shall be controlling unless otherwise specifically provided in Regulation C (*see* § 230.400).

2. Attention is directed to Regulation S-K (17 CFR Part 229) for the requirements applicable to the content of the non-financial portions of registration statements under the Act. Where this Form directs the registrant to furnish information required by any item of Regulation S-K, information need only be furnished to the extent appropriate.

3. A "smaller reporting company," defined in § 230.405, shall use the disclosure items in Regulation S-K (17 CFR 229.10 *et seq.*) with specific attention to the scaled disclosure provided for smaller reporting companies, if any.

C. Reoffers and Resales

1. *Securities.* Reoffers and resales of the following securities may be made on a continuous or delayed basis in the future, as provided by Rule 415 (§ 230.415), pursuant to a registration statement on this Form by means of a separate prospectus ("reoffer prospectus"), which is prepared in accordance with the requirements of Part I of Form S-3 (or, if the registrant is a foreign private issuer, in accordance with Part I of Form F-3), and filed with the registration statement on Form S-8 or, in the case of control securities, a post-effective amendment thereto:

(a) *Control securities*, which are defined for purposes of this General Instruction C as securities acquired under a Securities Act registration statement held by affiliates of the registrant as defined in Rule 405 (§ 230.405). Control securities may be included in a reoffer prospectus only if they have been or will be acquired by the selling security holder pursuant to an employee benefit plan; or

(b) *Restricted securities*, which are defined for purposes of this General Instruction C as securities issued under any employee benefit plan of the registrant meeting the definition of, "restricted securities" in Rule 144(a)(3) (§ 230.144(a)(3)), whether or not held by affiliates of the registrant. Restricted securities may be included in a reoffer prospectus only if they have been acquired by the selling security holder prior to the filing of the registration statement.

2. *Limitations.* The reoffer prospectus may be used as follows:

(a) If the registrant, at the time of filing such prospectus, satisfies the registrant requirements for use of Form S-3 (or if the registrant is a foreign private issuer, the registrant requirements for use of Form F-3), then control and restricted securities may be registered for reoffer and resale without any limitations.

(b) If the registrant, at the time of filing such prospectus, does not satisfy the registrant requirements for use of Form S-3 or F-3, as appropriate, then the following limitation shall apply with respect to both control securities and restricted securities: the amount of securities to be offered or resold by means of the reoffer prospectus, by each person, and any other person with whom he or she is acting in concert for the purpose of selling securities of the registrant, may not exceed, during any three month period, the amount specified in Rule 144(e) (§ 230. 144(e)).

3. *Selling Security Holders.*

(a) *Control Securities.* If the names of the security holders who intend to resell are not known by the registrant at the time of filing the Form S-8 registration statement, the registrant may either: (1) refer to the selling security holders in a generic manner in the reoffer prospectus; later, as their names and the amounts of securities to be reoffered become known, the registrant must supplement the reoffer prospectus with that information; or (2) name in the reoffer prospectus all persons eligible to resell and the amounts of securities available to be resold, whether or not they have a present intent to do so; any additional persons must be added by prospectus supplement. Prospectus supplements must be filed with the Commission as required by Rule 424(b) (§ 230.424(b)). The registrant may file a reoffer prospectus covering control securities as part of the initial registration statement or by means of a post-effective amendment to the Form S-8 registration statement.

(b) *Restricted Securities.* All persons (including non-affiliates) holding restricted securities registered for reoffer or resale pursuant to a reoffer prospectus are to be named as selling shareholders in the reoffer prospectus; *provided, however*, that any non-affiliate who holds less than the lesser of 1000 shares or 1% of the shares issuable under the plan to which the Form S-8 registration statement relates need not be named if the reoffer prospectus indicates that certain unnamed non-affiliates, each of whom may sell up to that amount, may use the reoffer prospectus for reoffers and resales. The reoffer prospectus covering restricted securities must be filed with the initial registration statement, not a post-effective amendment thereto.

Notes to General Instruction C

1. The term "person" as used in this General Instruction C shall be the same as set forth in Rule 144(a)(2) (§ 230.144(a)(2)).

2. If the conditions of this General Instruction C are not satisfied, registration of reoffers or resales must be made by means of a separate registration statement using whichever form is applicable.

D. Filing and Effectiveness of Registration Statement; Requests for Confidential Treatment; Number of Copies

A registration statement on this Form S-8 will become effective automatically (Rule 462, §230.462) upon filing (Rule 456. §230.456). In addition, post-effective amendments on this Form shall become effective upon filing (Rules 464, §230.464 and 456). Delaying amendments are not permitted in connection with any registration statement on this Form (Rule 473(d), §230.473(d)), and any attempt to interpose a delaying amendment of any kind will be ineffective. All filings made on or in connection with this Form become public upon filing with the Commission. As a result, requests for confidential treatment made under either Rule 406 (§230.406), or Exchange Act Rule 24b-2 (§240.24b-2) in connection with documents incorporated by reference, must be acted upon, *i.e.*, granted or denied, by the Commission staff prior to the filing of the registration statement. The number of copies of the filing required by Rules 402(c) and 472(d) (§230.402(c), §230.472(d)) shall be filed with the Commission.

E. Registration of Additional Securities

With respect to the registration of additional securities of the same class as other securities for which a registration statement filed on this Form relating to an employee benefit plan is effective, the registrant may file a registration statement consisting only of the following: the facing page; a statement that the contents of the earlier registration statement, identified by file number, are incorporated by reference, required opinions and consents; the signature page; and any information required in the new registration statement that is not in the earlier registration statement. If the new registration statement covers restricted securities being offered for resale, it shall include the required reoffer prospectus. If the earlier registration statement included a reoffer prospectus, the new registration statement shall be deemed to include that reoffer prospectus, *provided, however*, that a revised reoffer prospectus shall be filed. if the reoffer prospectus is substantively different from that filed in the earlier registration statement. The filing fee required by the Act and Rule 457 (§230.457) shall be paid with respect to the additional securities only.

F. Registration of Plan Interests

Where a registration statement on this Form relates to securities to be offered pursuant to an employee stock purchase, savings, or similar plan, the registration statement shall be deemed to register an indeterminate amount of interests in such plan that are separate securities and required to be registered under the Securities Act. *See* Rule 416(c) (§230.416(c)).

G. Updating

Updating of information constituting the Section 10(a) prospectus pursuant to Rule 428(a) (§230.428(a)) during the offering of the securities shall be accomplished as follows:

1. Plan information specified by Item 1 of Form S-8 required to be sent or given to employees shall be updated as specified in Rule 428(b)(1) (§230.428(b)(1)). Such information need not be filed with the Commission.

2. Registrant information shall be updated by the filing of Exchange Act reports, which are incorporated by reference in the registration statement and the Section 10(a) prospectus. Any material changes in the registrant's affairs required to be disclosed in the registration statement but not required to be included in a specific Exchange Act report shall be reported on Form 8-K (§249.308) pursuant to Item 5 thereof (or, if the registrant is a foreign private issuer, on Form 6-K (§249.306)).

3. An employee plan annual report incorporated by reference in the registration statement from Form 11-K (or Form 10-K, as permitted by Rule 15d-21 (§ 240.15d-21)) shall be updated by the filing of a subsequent plan annual report on Form 11-K or 10-K.

Part I
INFORMATION REQUIRED IN THE SECTION 10(a) PROSPECTUS

Note:

The document(s) containing the information specified in this Part I will be sent or given to employees as specified by Rule 428(b)(1) (§ 230.428(b)(1)). Such documents need not be filed with the Commission either as part of this registration statement or us prospectuses or prospectus supplements pursuant to Rule 424 (§ 230.424). These documents and the documents incorporated by reference in the registration statement pursuant to Item 3 of Part II of this Form, taken together, constitute a prospectus that meets the requirements of Section 10(a) of the Securities Act. See Rule 428 (§ 230.428(a)(1)).

Item 1. Plan Information

The registrant shall deliver or cause to be delivered to each participant material information regarding the plan and its operations that will enable participants to make an informed decision regarding investment in the plan. This information shall include, to the extent material to the particular plan being described, but not be limited to, the disclosure specified in (a) through (j) below. Any unusual risks associated with participation in the plan not described pursuant to a specified item shall be prominently disclosed, as, for example, when the plan imposes a substantial restriction on the ability of a participant to withdraw contributions, or when plan participation may obligate the participant's general credit in connection with purchases on a margin basis. The information may be in one or several documents, provided that it is presented in a clear, concise and understandable manner. *See* Rule 421 (§ 230.421)

(a) General Plan Information

(1) Give the title of the plan and the name of the registrant whose securities are to be offered pursuant to the plan.

(2) Briefly state the general nature and purpose of the plan, its duration, and any provisions for its modification, earlier termination or extension to the extent that they affect the participants.

(3) Indicate whether the plan is subject to any provisions of the Employee Retirement Income Security Act of 1974 ("ERISA"), and if so, the general nature of those provisions to which it is subject.

(4) Give an address and a telephone number, including area code, which participants may use to obtain additional information about the plan and its administrators. State the capacity in which the plan administrators act (*e.g.*, trustees or managers) and the functions that they perform. If any person other than a participating employee has discretion with respect to the investment of all or any part of the assets of the plan in one or more investment media, name such person and describe the policies followed and to be followed with respect to the type and proportion of securities or other property in which funds of the plan may be invested. If the plan is not subject to ERISA: (i) state the nature of any material relationship between the administrators and the employees, the registrant or its affiliates; and (ii) describe the manner in which the plan administrators are selected, their term of office, and the manner in which they may be removed from office.

(b) Securities to be Offered

(1) State the title and total amount of securities to be offered pursuant to the plan.

(2) Furnish the information required by Item 202 of Regulation S-K (§ 229.202), except that if common stock registered under Section 12 of the Exchange Act is offered, such information is unnecessary. If plan interests are being registered, they need not be described pursuant to this item.

(c) Employees Who May Participate In the Plan

Indicate each class or group of employees that may participate in the plan and the basis upon which the eligibility of employees to participate therein is to be determined.

(d) Purchase of Securities Pursuant to the Plan and Payment for Securities Offered

(1) State the period of time within which employees may elect to participate in the plan, the price at which the securities may be purchased or the basis upon which such price is to be determined, and any terms regarding the amount of securities that an eligible employee can purchase.

(2) State when and the manner in which employees are to pay for the securities purchased pursuant to the plan, if payment is to be made by payroll deductions or other installment payments, state the percentage of wages or salaries or other basis for computing such payments, and the time and manner in which an employee may alter the amount of such deduction or payment.

(3) State the amount each employee is required or permitted to contribute or, if not a fixed amount, the percentage of wages or salaries or other basis of computing contributions.

(4) If contributions are to be made under the plan by the registrant or any employer, state who is to make such contributions, when they are to be made and the nature and amount of each contribution: If such contributions are not a fixed amount, state the basis for computing contributions.

(5) State the nature and frequency of any reports to be made to participating employees as to the amount and status of their accounts.

(6) If the plan is not subject to ERISA, state whether securities are to be purchased in the open market or otherwise. If they are not to be purchased in the open market, then state from whom they are to be purchased and describe the fees, commissions or other charges paid. If the employer or any of its affiliates, or any person having a material relationship with the employer or any of its affiliates, directly or indirectly, receives any part of the aggregate purchase price (including fees, commissions or other charges), explain the basis for compensation.

Note:

If the plan is one under which credit is extended to finance the acquisition of securities, consideration should be given to the applicability of Regulation G (12 CFR Part 207) or T (12 CFR Part 220).

(e) Resale Restrictions

Describe briefly any restriction on resale of the securities purchased under the plan which may be imposed upon the employee purchaser.

(f) Tax Effects of Plan Participation

Describe briefly the tax effect that may accrue to employees as a result of plan participation as well as the tax effects, if any, upon the registrant and whether or not the plan is qualified under Section 401(a) of the Internal Revenue Code.

Note:

If the plan is not qualified under Section 401 of the Internal Revenue Code of 1986, as amended, consideration should be given to the applicability of the Investment Company Act of 1940. *See* Securities Act Release No. 4790 (July 13, 1965).

(g) Investment of Funds

If participating employees may direct all or any part of the assets under the plan to two or more investment media, furnish a brief description of the provisions of the plan with respect to the alternative investment media; and provide a tabular or other meaningful presentation of financial data for each of the past three fiscal years (or such lesser period for which the data with respect to each investment medium is available) that, in the opinion of the registrant, will apprise employees

251

of material trends and significant changes in the performance of alternative investment media and enable them to make informed investment decisions. Financial data shall be presented for any additional fiscal years necessary to keep the information from being misleading or that the registrant deems appropriate, but the total period presented need not exceed five years.

(h) Withdrawal from the Plan; Assignment of Interest

(1) Describe the terms and conditions under which a participating employee may (i) withdraw from the plan and terminate his or her interest therein; or (ii) withdraw funds or investments held for the employee's account without terminating his or her interest in the plan.

(2) State whether, and the terms and conditions upon which, the plan permits an employee to assign or hypothecate his or her interest in the plan.

(3) No information need be provided as to the effect of a qualified domestic relations order as defined in ERISA Section 206(d) (29 U.S.C. 1056(d)).

(i) Forfeitures and Penalties

Describe briefly every event which could, under the plan, result in a forfeiture by, or a penalty to, a participant, and the consequences thereof.

(j) Charges and Deductions and Liens Therefor

(1) Describe all charges and deductions (other than deductions described in paragraph (d) and taxes) that may be made against employees participating in the plan or against funds. securities or other property held under the plan and indicate who will receive, directly or indirectly, any part thereof. Such description should include charges and deductions that may be made upon the termination of an employee's interest in the plan, or upon partial withdrawals from the employee's account thereunder.

(2) State whether or not under the plan, or pursuant to any contract in connection therewith, any person has or may create a lien on any funds, securities, or other property held under the plan. If so, describe fully the circumstances under which the lien was or may be created.

(3) No information need be provided as to the effect of a qualified domestic relations order as defined in ERISA Section 206(d) (29 U.S.C. 1056(d)).

Item 2. Registrant Information and Employee Plan Annual Information

The registrant shall provide a written statement to participants advising them of the availability without charge, upon written or oral request, of the documents incorporated by reference in Item 3 of Part II of the registration statement, and stating that these documents are incorporated by reference in the Section 10(a) prospectus. The statement also shall indicate the availability without charge, upon written or oral request, of other documents required to be delivered to employees pursuant to Rule 428(b) (§ 230.428(b)). The statement shall include the address (giving title or department) and telephone number to which the request is to be directed.

Part II
INFORMATION REQUIRED IN THE REGISTRATION STATEMENT

Item 3. Incorporation of Documents by Reference

The registrant, and where interests in the plan are being registered, the plan, shall state that the documents listed in (a) through (c) below are incorporated by reference in the registration statement; and shall state that all documents subsequently filed by it pursuant to Sections 13(a), 13(c), 14 and 15(d) of the Securities Exchange Act of 1934, prior to the filing of a post-effective amendment which indicates that all securities offered have been sold or which deregisters all securities then remaining unsold, shall be deemed to be incorporated by reference in the registration statement and to be part thereof from the date of filing of such documents. Copies of these documents are not required to be filed with the registration statement.

(a) The registrant's latest annual report. and where interests in the plan are being registered, the plan's latest annual report, filed pursuant to Section 13(a) or 15(d) of the Exchange Act, or in the case of the registrant either (1) the latest prospectus filed pursuant to Rule 424(b) under the Act that contains audited financial statements for the registrant's latest fiscal year for which such statements have been filed, or (2) the registrant's effective registration statement on Form 10, Form 20-F or, in the case of registrants described in General Instruction A.(2) of Form 40-F, on Form 40-F filed under the Exchange Act containing audited financial statements for the registrant's latest fiscal year.

(b) All other reports filed pursuant to Section 13(a) or 15(d) of the Exchange Act since the end of the fiscal year covered by the registrant document referred to in (a) above.

(c) If the class of securities to be offered is registered under Section 12 of the Exchange Act, the description of such class of securities contained in a registration statement filed under such Act, including any amendment or report filed for the purpose of updating such description.

Item 4. Description of Securities

If the class of securities to be offered is not registered under Section 12 of the Exchange Act, set forth the information required by Item 202 of Regulation S-K (§ 229.202 of this chapter). If plan interests are being registered, they need not be described pursuant to this item.

Item 5. Interests of Named Experts and Counsel

Furnish the information required by Item 509 of Regulation S-K (§ 229.509 of this chapter).

Item 6. Indemnification of Directors and Officers

Furnish the information required by Item 702 of Regulation S-K (§ 229.702 of this chapter).

Item 7. Exemption from Registration Claimed

With respect to restricted securities to be reoffered or resold pursuant to this registration statement, the registrant shall indicate the section of the Act or Rule of the Commission under which exemption from registration was claimed and set forth briefly the facts relied upon to make the exemption available.

Item 8. Exhibits

Furnish the exhibits required by Item 601 Regulation S-K (§ 229.601 of this chapter), except that with respect to Item 601(b)(5):

(a) An opinion of counsel as to the legality of the securities being registered is required only with respect to original issuance securities.

(b) Neither an opinion of counsel concerning compliance with the requirements of ERISA nor an Internal Revenue Service determination letter that the plan is qualified under Section 401 of the Internal Revenue Code shall be required if, in lieu thereof, the response to this Item 8 includes an undertaking that the registrant will submit or has submitted the plan and any amendment thereto to the Internal Revenue Service ("IRS") in a timely manner and has made or will make all changes required by the IRS in order to qualify the plan.

Item 9. Undertakings

Furnish the undertakings required by Item 512(a), (b) and (h) of Regulation S-K (§ 229.512(a), (b) and (h) of this chapter), as well as any other applicable undertakings in Item 512.

Notes to Item 9:

(1) The Regulation S-K Item 512(a) undertakings are usually required pursuant to this item since most registration statements on Form S-8 involve the continuous offering and sale of securities under Rule 415 (§ 230.415 of this chapter).

(2) With respect to registration statements filed on this Form, foreign private issuers are not required to furnish the Item 512(a)(4) undertaking.

SIGNATURES

The Registrant. Pursuant to the requirements of the Securities Act of 1933, the registrant certifies that it has reasonable grounds to believe that it meets all of the requirements for filing on Form S-8 and has duly caused this registration statement to be signed on its behalf by the undersigned, thereunto duly authorized, in the City of_____

State of _____,

on _____, 19 _____.

(Registrant)_____

By (Signature and Title)_____

Pursuant to the requirements of the Securities Act of 1933, this registration statement has been signed by the following persons in the capacities and on the date indicated.

(Signature)_____

(Title)_____

(Date)_____

The Plan. Pursuant to the requirements of the Securities Act of 1933, the trustees (or other persons who administer the employee benefit plan) have duly caused this registration statement to be signed on its behalf by the undersigned, thereunto duly authorized, in the City of_____

State of _____

on _____ 19 _____

(Plan)_____

By (Signature and Title) _____

Instructions.

1. The registration statement shall be signed by the registrant, its principal executive officer or officers, its principal financial officer, its controller or principal accounting officer, and at least a majority of the board of directors or persons performing similar functions. Where interests in the plan are being registered, the registration statement shall be signed by the plan. If the signing person is a foreign person, the registration statement shall also be signed by its authorized representative in the United States. Where the signing person is a limited partnership, the registration statement shall be signed by a majority of the board of directors of any corporate general partner signing the registration statement.

2. The name of each person who signs the registration statement shall be typed or printed beneath the signature. Any person who occupies more than one of the specified positions shall indicate each capacity in which he or she signs the registration statement. Attention is directed to Rule 402 (§ 230.402) concerning manual signatures and Item 601 (§ 229.601) of Regulation S-K concerning signatures pursuant to powers of attorney.

FORM F-6

REGISTRATION STATEMENT UNDER THE SECURITIES ACT OF 1933 FOR DEPOSITARY SHARES EVIDENCED BY AMERICAN DEPOSITARY RECEIPTS

....
(Exact name of issuer of deposited securities as specified in its charter)

....
(Translation of issuer's name into English)

....
(Jurisdiction of incorporation or organization of issuer)

....
(Exact name of depositary as specified in its charter)

....
(Address, including zip code, and telephone number, including area code, of
depositary's principal executive offices)

....
(Address, including zip code, and telephone number, including area code, of
agent for service)

It is proposed that this filing become effective under Rule 466
(check appropriate box)
[ ] immediately upon filing
[ ] on (Date) at (Time).

If a separate registration statement has been filed to register the
deposited shares, check the following box. [ ]

Calculation of Registration Fee

Title of each class of securities to be registered	Amount to be registered	Proposed maximum aggregate price per unit	Proposed maximum aggregate offering price	Amount of registration fee

GENERAL INSTRUCTIONS

I. Eligibility Requirements for Use of Form F-6

A. General. Form F-6 may be used for the registration under the Securities Act of 1933 (the "Securities Act") of Depositary Shares evidenced by American Depositary Receipts ("ADRs") issued by a depositary against the deposit of the securities of a foreign issuer (regardless of the physical location of the certificates) if the following conditions are met:

(1) The holder of the ADRs is entitled to withdraw the deposited securities at any time subject only to (i) temporary delays caused by closing transfer books of the depositary or the issuer of the deposited securities or the deposit of shares in connection with voting at a shareholders' meeting, or the payment of dividends, (ii) the payment of fees, taxes, and similar charges, and (iii) compliance with any laws or governmental regulations relating to ADRs or to the withdrawal of deposited securities;

(2) The deposited securities are offered or sold in transactions registered under the Securities Act or in transactions that would be exempt therefrom if made in the United States; and

(3) As of the filing date of this registration statement, the issuer of the deposited securities is reporting pursuant to the periodic reporting requirements of section 13(a) or 15(d) of the Securities Exchange Act of 1934 or the deposited securities are exempt therefrom by Rule 12g3-2(b) (§ 240.12g3-2(b) of this chapter) unless the issuer of the deposited securities concurrently files a registration statement on another form for the deposited securities.

B. Registration of Deposited Securities. Form F-6 is available for registration of the Depositary Shares only. The registration of the deposited securities, if necessary, shall be on any other form the registrant is eligible to use. Alternatively, Depositary Shares may also be registered on any form used to register the deposited securities if such registration statement also conforms to the requirements of Parts I and II of Form F-6 and either the depositary or the legal entity created by the agreement for the issuance of ADRs signs the registration statement with respect to the disclosure and undertakings made in response to such requirements. The amount of fees charged need not be disclosed in the prospectus if the depositary makes and follows the undertakings in Item 4(c) and if the prospectus lists the various services for which fees may be charged, states that such fees may differ from those other depositaries charge, states that the fee schedule is available without charge from the depositary, and states that each registered holder of an ADR will receive thirty days notice of a change in the fee schedule.

II. Amount of Securities; Filing Fee

An ADR evidences one or more Depositary Shares, as defined in Rule 405 (§ 230.405 of this chapter). The registration statement relates to Depositary Shares, not the number of physical certificates issued. For example, if an ADR is issued against a Depositary Share, which equals two common shares in a foreign issuer, the registration of 100,000 Depositary Shares represents 200,000 common shares. If the depositary issues a certificate for 10,000 Depositary Shares and another for 15,000 Depositary Shares, then 75,000 (100,000 minus 25,000) Depositary Shares (not 99,998) remain available for distribution under the registration statement.

Rule 457(k) (§ 230.457(k) of this chapter) describes the method of computing the filing fee.

III. Application of General Rules and Regulations

A. Attention is directed to the General Rules and Regulations under the Securities Act, particularly Regulation C (§ 230.400 et seq. of this chapter). That Regulation contains general requirements regarding the preparation and filing of registration statements.

B. The prospectus may consist of the ADR certificate if it includes the information required in Part I of this Form. Such prospectus need not conform to the requirements of Rule 420 (§ 240.420 of this chapter) except that the type shall be roman type at least as large as 5½-point modern type.

C. You must file the Form F-6 registration statement in electronic format via the Commission's Electronic Data Gathering, Analysis, and Retrieval (EDGAR) system in accordance with the EDGAR rules set forth in Regulation S-T (17 CFR Part 232). For assistance with technical questions about EDGAR or to request an access code, call the EDGAR Filer Support Office at (202) 551-8900.

If filing the registration statement in paper under a hardship exemption in Rule 201 or 202 of Regulation S-T (17 CFR 232.201 or 232.202), or as otherwise permitted, you must file the number of copies of the registration statement and of each amendment required by Securities Act Rules 402 and 472 (17 CFR 230.402 and 230.472), except that you need only file three additional copies instead of the ten referred to in Rule 402(b) (17 CFR 230.402(b)). You may also file only three additional copies instead of the eight referred to in Securities Act Rule 472(a) (17 CFR 230.472(a)).

PART I—INFORMATION REQUIRED IN PROSPECTUS

Item 1. Description of Securities to be Registered

Furnish the information required by Item 12.E. of Form 20-F (§ 249.220f of this chapter).

Item 2. Available Information

Provide the information in either (a) or (b) below, whichever is applicable.

(a) State that the foreign issuer publishes information in English required to maintain the exemption from registration under Rule 12g3-2(b) under the Securities Exchange [sic] of 1934 on its Internet Web site or through an electronic information delivery system generally available to the public in its primary trading market. Then disclose the address of the foreign issuer's Internet Web site or the electronic information delivery system in its primary trading market.

(b) State that the foreign issuer is subject to the periodic reporting requirements of the Securities Exchange Act of 1934 and accordingly files reports with the Commission. Then disclose that these reports are available for inspection and copying through the Commission's EDGAR system or at public reference facilities maintained by the Commission in Washington, D.C.

Note to Item 2: In the case of an unsponsored ADR facility, you may base your representation that the issuer publishes information in English required to maintain the exemption from registration under Exchange Act Rule 12g3-2(b) upon your reasonable, good faith belief after exercising reasonable diligence.

PART II—INFORMATION NOT REQUIRED IN PROSPECTUS

Item 3. Exhibits

Subject to the rules as to incorporation by reference, the exhibits specified below shall be filed as a part of the registration statement. Exhibits shall be appropriately lettered or numbered for convenient reference. Exhibits incorporated by reference may bear the designation given in the previous filing. Instruction 1 to Item 601 of Regulation S-K applies to this paragraph.

(a) A copy of the Deposit Agreement or Deposit Agreements under which the securities registered hereunder are issued. If the Deposit Agreement is amended during the offering of the Depositary Shares, such amendments shall be filed as amendments to the registration statement.

(b) Any other agreement, to which the depositary is a party relating to the issuance of the Depositary Shares registered hereby or the custody of the deposited securities represented thereby.

(c) Every material contract relating to the deposited securities between the depositary and the issuer of the deposited securities in effect at any time within the last three years.

(d) An opinion of counsel as to the legality of the securities being registered, indicating whether they will when sold be legally issued, and entitle the holders thereof to the rights specified therein.

(e) If the procedure in Rule 466 is being used, a certification in the following form:

Certification under Rule 466

The depositary, ... , represents and certifies the following:

(1) That it previously had filed a registration statement on Form F-6 (Name and File No.), which the Commission declared effective, with terms of deposit identical to the terms of deposit of this registration statement except for the number of foreign securities a Depositary Share represents.

(2) That is ability to designate the date and time of effectiveness under Rule 466 has not been suspended.

[Depositary] ....:.

By [Signature and Title] ....

Item 4. Undertakings

Notwithstanding the provisions of Rule 415(a)(2) (§230.415(a)(2) of this chapter), the undertakings in Item 512(a) of Regulation S-K are not required. Furnish the following undertakings:

(a) The depositary hereby undertakes to make available at the principal office of the depositary in the United States, for inspection by holders of the ADRs, any reports and communications received from the issuer of the deposited securities which are both (1) received by the depositary as the holder of the deposited securities; and (2) made generally available to the holders of the underlying securities by the issuer.

(b) If the amounts of fees charged are not disclosed in the prospectus, the depositary undertakes to prepare a separate document stating the amount of any fee charged and describing the service for which it is charged and to deliver promptly a copy of such fee schedule without charge to anyone upon request. The depositary undertakes to notify each registered holder of an ADR thirty days before any change in the fee schedule.

SIGNATURES

Pursuant to the requirements of the Securities Act of 1933, the registrant certifies that it has reasonable grounds to believe that all the requirements for filing on Form F-6 are met and has duly caused this registration statement to be signed on its behalf by the undersigned, thereunto duly authorized, in the City of .... , State of .... , on .... , 19........

[Legal entity created by the agreement

for the issuance of American Depositary

Receipts for shares of ....] ....

By [Signature and Title] ....

[Registrant] ....

By [Signature and Title] ....

Pursuant to the requirements of the Securities Act of 1933, this registration statement has been signed by the following persons in the capacities and on the dates indicated.

[Signature] ....

[Title] ....

[Date] ....

Instructions 1. The legal entity created by the agreement for the issuance of ADRs shall sign the registration statement as registrant. The depositary may sign on behalf of such entity, but the depositary for the issuance of ADRs itself shall not be deemed to be an issuer, a person signing the registration statement, or a person controlling such issuer. If the issuer of the deposited securities sponsors the ADR arrangement, the registration statement shall also be signed by the issuer and its principal executive officer or officers, its principal financial officer, its controller or principal accounting officer, at least a majority of the board of directors or persons performing similar functions, and its authorized representative in the United States.

2. The name of each person who signs the registration statement shall be typed or printed beneath his signature. Any person who occupies more than one of the specified positions shall indicate each capacity in which he signs the registration statement. Attention is directed to Rule 402 concerning manual signatures and Item 601 of Regulation S-K concerning signatures pursuant to powers of attorney.

UNITED STATES SECURITIES AND EXCHANGE COMMISSION
WASHINGTON, D.C. 20549

FORM 1-A

REGULATION A OFFERING STATEMENT UNDER THE SECURITIES ACT OF 1933

GENERAL INSTRUCTIONS

I. Eligibility Requirements For Use of Form 1-A.

This Form is to be used for securities offerings made pursuant to Regulation A (17 CFR 230.251 *et seq.*). Careful attention should be directed to the terms, conditions and requirements of Regulation A, especially Rule 251, because the exemption is not available to all issuers or for every type of securities transaction. Further, the aggregate offering price and aggregate sales of securities in any 12-month period is strictly limited to $20 million for Tier 1 offerings and $50 million for Tier 2 offerings, including no more than $6 million offered by all selling security-holders that are affiliates of the issuer for Tier 1 offerings and $15 million by all selling securityholders that are affiliates of the issuer for Tier 2 offerings. Please refer to Rule 251 of Regulation A for more details.

II. Preparation, Submission and Filing of the Offering Statement.

An offering statement must be prepared by all persons seeking exemption under the provisions of Regulation A. Parts I, II and III must be addressed by all issuers. Part II, which relates to the content of the required offering circular, provides alternative formats, of which the issuer must choose one. General information regarding the preparation, format, content, and submission or filing of the offering statement is contained in Rule 252. Information regarding non-public submission of the offering statement is contained in Rule 252(d). Requirements relating to the offering circular are contained in Rules 253 and 254. The offering statement must be submitted or filed with the Securities and Exchange Commission in electronic format by means of the Commission's Electronic Data Gathering, Analysis and Retrieval System (EDGAR) in accordance with the EDGAR rules set forth in Regulation S-T (17 CFR Part 232) for such submission or filing.

III. Incorporation By Reference and Cross-Referencing.

An issuer may incorporate by reference to other documents previously submitted or filed on EDGAR. Cross-referencing within the offering statement is also encouraged to avoid repetition of information. For example, you may respond to an item of this Form by providing a cross-reference to the location of the information in the financial statements, instead of repeating such information. Incorporation by reference and cross-referencing are subject to the following additional conditions:

(a) The use of incorporation by reference and cross-referencing in Part II of this Form is limited to the following items:

(1) Items 2-14 of Part II if following the Offering Circular format;

(2) Items 3-11 (other than Item 11(e)) of Form S-1 if following the Part I of Form S-1 format; or

(3) Items 3-26, 28, and 30 of Form S-11 if following the Part I of Form S-11 format.

(b) Descriptions of where the information incorporated by reference or cross-referenced can be found must be specific and must clearly identify the relevant document and portion thereof where such information can be found. For exhibits incorporated by reference, this description must be noted in the exhibits index for each relevant exhibit. All descriptions of where information incorporated by reference can be found must be accompanied by a hyperlink to the incorporated document on EDGAR, which hyperlink need not remain active after the filing of the offering statement. Inactive hyperlinks must be updated in any amendment to the offering statement otherwise required.

(c) Reference may not be made to any document if the portion of such document containing the pertinent information includes an incorporation by reference to another document. Incorporation by reference to documents not available on EDGAR is not permitted. Incorporating information into the financial statements from elsewhere is not permitted. Information shall not be incorporated by reference or cross-referenced in any case where such incorporation would render the statement or report incomplete, unclear, or confusing.

(d) If any substantive modification has occurred in the text of any document incorporated by reference since such document was filed, the issuer must file with the reference a statement containing the text and date of such modification.

IV. Supplemental Information.

The information specified below must be furnished to the Commission as supplemental information, if applicable. Supplemental information shall not be required to be filed with or deemed part of the offering statement, unless otherwise required. The information shall be returned to the issuer upon request made in writing at the time of submission, provided that the return of such information is consistent with the protection of investors and the provisions of the Freedom of Information Act [5 U.S.C. 552] and the information was not filed in electronic format.

(a) A statement as to whether or not the amount of compensation to be allowed or paid to the underwriter has been cleared with the Financial Industry Regulatory Authority (FINRA).

(b) Any engineering, management, market, or similar report referenced in the offering circular or provided for external use by the issuer or by a principal underwriter in connection with the proposed offering. There must also be furnished at the same time a statement as to the actual or proposed use and distribution of such report or memorandum. Such statement must identify each class of persons who have received or will receive the report or memorandum, and state the number of copies distributed to each such class along with a statement as to the actual or proposed use and distribution of such report or memorandum.

(c) Such other information as requested by the staff in support of statements, representations and other assertions contained in the offering statement or any correspondence to the staff.

Correspondence appropriately responding to any staff comments made on the offering statement must also be furnished electronically. When applicable, such correspondence must clearly indicate where changes responsive to the staff's comments may be found in the offering statement.

PART I—NOTIFICATION

The following information must be provided in the XML-based portion of Form 1-A available through the EDGAR portal and must be completed or updated before uploading each offering statement or amendment thereto. The format of Part I shown below may differ from the electronic version available on EDGAR. The electronic version of Part I will allow issuers to attach Part II and Part III for filing by means of EDGAR. All items must be addressed, unless otherwise indicated.

* * * * * *

☐ No changes to the information required by Part I have occurred since the last filing of this offering statement.

ITEM 1. Issuer Information.

Exact name of issuer as specified in the issuer's charter: _____

Jurisdiction of incorporation/organization: _____

Year of incorporation: _____

CIK: _____

Primary Standard Industrial Classification Code: _____

I.R.S. Employer Identification Number: _____

Total number of full-time employees: _____

Total number of part-time employees: _____

Contact Information

Address of Principal Executive Offices: _____

_____

Telephone: (_____)_____

Provide the following information for the person the Securities and Exchange Commission's staff should call in connection with any pre-qualification review of the offering statement:

Name: _____

Address: _____

Telephone: (_____)_____

Provide up to two e-mail addresses to which the Securities and Exchange Commission's staff may send any comment letters relating to the offering statement. After qualification of the offering statement, such e-mail addresses are not required to remain active:

Financial Statements

Industry Group (select one): ☐ Banking	☐ Insurance	☐ Other

Use the financial statements for the most recent fiscal period contained in this offering statement to provide the following information about the issuer. The following table does not include all of the line items from the financial statements. Long Term Debt would include notes payable, bonds, mortgages, and similar obligations. To determine "Total Revenues" for all companies selecting "Other" for their industry group, refer to Article 5-03(b)(1) of Regulation S-X. For companies selecting "Insurance," refer to Article 7-04 of Regulation S-X for calculation of "Total Revenues" and paragraphs 5 and 7(a) for "Costs and Expenses Applicable to Revenues".

[If "Other" is selected, display the following options in the Financial Statements table:]

Balance Sheet Information
Cash and Cash Equivalents: _____
Investment Securities: _____
Accounts and Notes Receivable: _____

Property, Plant and Equipment (PP&E): _____
Total Assets: _____
Accounts Payable and Accrued Liabilities: _____
Long Term Debt: _____
Total Liabilities: _____
Total Stockholders' Equity: _____
Total Liabilities and Equity: _____

Statement of Comprehensive Income Information
Total Revenues: _____
Costs and Expenses Applicable to Revenues: _____
Depreciation and Amortization: _____
Net Income: _____
Earnings Per Share – Basic: _____
Earnings Per Share – Diluted: _____

[If "Banking" is selected, display the following options in the Financial Statements table:]

Balance Sheet Information
Cash and Cash Equivalents: _____
Investment Securities: _____
Loans: _____
Property and Equipment: _____
Total Assets: _____
Accounts Payable and Accrued Liabilities: _____
Deposits: _____
Long Term Debt: _____
Total Liabilities: _____
Total Stockholders' Equity: _____
Total Liabilities and Equity: _____

Statement of Comprehensive Income Information
Total Interest Income: _____
Total Interest Expense: _____
Depreciation and Amortization: _____
Net Income: _____
Earnings Per Share – Basic: _____
Earnings Per Share – Diluted: _____

[If "Insurance" is selected, display the following options in the Financial Statements table:]

Balance Sheet Information
Cash and Cash Equivalents: _____
Total Investments: _____
Accounts and Notes Receivable: _____
Property and Equipment: _____
Total Assets: _____
Accounts Payable and Accrued Liabilities: _____
Policy Liabilities and Accruals: _____
Long Term Debt: _____
Total Liabilities: _____
Total Stockholders' Equity: _____
Total Liabilities and Equity: _____

Statement of Comprehensive Income Information
Total Revenues: _____
Costs and Expenses Applicable to Revenues: _____
Depreciation and Amortization: _____
Net Income: _____
Earnings Per Share – Basic: _____
Earnings Per Share – Diluted: _____

[End of section that varies based on the selection of Industry Group]

Name of Auditor (if any):_____

Outstanding Securities

	Name of Class (if any)	Units Outstanding	CUSIP (if any)	Name of Trading Center or Quotation Medium (if any)
Common Equity				
Preferred Equity				
Debt Securities				

ITEM 2. Issuer Eligibility.

☐ Check this box to certify that all of the following statements are true for the issuer(s):

• Organized under the laws of the United States or Canada, or any State, Province, Territory or possession thereof, or the District of Columbia.

• Principal place of business is in the United States or Canada.

• Not a development stage company that either (a) has no specific business plan or purpose, or (b) has indicated that its business plan is to merge with an unidentified company or companies.

• Not an investment company registered or required to be registered under the Investment Company Act of 1940.

• Not issuing fractional undivided interests in oil or gas rights, or a similar interest in other mineral rights.

• Not issuing asset-backed securities as defined in Item 1101(c) of Regulation AB.

• Not, and has not been, subject to any order of the Commission entered pursuant to Section 12(j) of the Exchange Act (15 U.S.C. 78*l*(j)) within five years before the filing of this offering statement.

• Has filed with the Commission all the reports it was required to file, if any, pursuant to Rule 257 during the two years immediately before the filing of the offering statement (or for such shorter period that the issuer was required to file such reports).

ITEM 3. Application of Rule 262.

☐ Check this box to certify that, as of the time of this filing, each person described in Rule 262 of Regulation A is either not disqualified under that rule or is disqualified but has received a waiver of such disqualification.

☐ Check this box if "bad actor" disclosure under Rule 262(d) is provided in Part II of the offering statement.

ITEM 4. Summary Information Regarding the Offering and Other Current or Proposed Offerings.

Check the appropriate box to indicate whether you are conducting a Tier 1 or Tier 2 offering:

☐ Tier 1	☐ Tier 2

Check the appropriate box to indicate whether the annual financial statements have been audited:

☐ Unaudited	☐ Audited

Types of Securities Offered in this Offering Statement (select all that apply):

☐ Equity (common or preferred stock)
☐ Debt
☐ Option, warrant or other right to acquire another security
☐ Security to be acquired upon exercise of option, warrant or other right to acquire security
☐ Tenant-in-common securities
☐ Other (describe)

Does the issuer intend to offer the securities on a delayed or continuous basis pursuant to Rule 251(d)(3)?

Yes ☐ No ☐

Does the issuer intend this offering to last more than one year?

Yes ☐ No ☐

Does the issuer intend to price this offering after qualification pursuant to Rule 253(b)?

Yes ☐ No ☐

Will the issuer be conducting a best efforts offering?

Yes ☐ No ☐

Has the issuer used solicitation of interest communications in connection with the proposed offering?

Yes ☐ No ☐

Does the proposed offering involve the resale of securities by affiliates of the issuer?

Yes ☐ No ☐

Number of securities offered: _____

Number of securities of that class already outstanding: _____

The information called for by this item below may be omitted if undetermined at the time of filing or submission, except that if a price range has been included in the offering statement, the midpoint of that range must be used to respond. Please refer to Rule 251(a) for the definition of "aggregate offering price" or "aggregate sales" as used in this item. Please leave the field blank if undetermined at this time and include a zero if a particular item is not applicable to the offering.

Price per security: $ _____

The portion of the aggregate offering price attributable to securities being offered on behalf of the issuer:

$ _____

The portion of the aggregate offering price attributable to securities being offered on behalf of selling securityholders:

$ _____

The portion of aggregate offering attributable to all the securities of the issuer sold pursuant to a qualified offering statement within the 12 months before the qualification of this offering statement:

$ _____

The estimated portion of aggregate sales attributable to securities that may be sold pursuant to any other qualified offering statement concurrently with securities being sold under this offering statement:

$ _____

Total: $ _____ (the sum of the aggregate offering price and aggregate sales in the four preceding paragraphs).

Anticipated fees in connection with this offering and names of service providers:

	Name of Service Provider	Fees
Underwriters:	_____	$_____
Sales Commissions:	_____	$_____
Finders' Fees:	_____	$_____
Audit:	_____	$_____
Legal:	_____	$_____
Promoters:	_____	$_____
Blue Sky Compliance:	_____	$_____

CRD Number of any broker or dealer listed: _____

Estimated net proceeds to the issuer: $ _____

Clarification of responses (if necessary): _____

ITEM 5. Jurisdictions in Which Securities Are to Be Offered.

Using the list below, select the jurisdictions in which the issuer intends to offer the securities:

[List will include all U.S. and Canadian jurisdictions, with an option to add and remove them individually, add all and remove all.]

Using the list below, select the jurisdictions in which the securities are to be offered by underwriters, dealers or sales persons or check the appropriate box:

☐ None

☐ Same as the jurisdictions in which the issuer intends to offer the securities.

[List will include all U.S. and Canadian jurisdictions, with an option to add and remove them individually, add all and remove all.]

ITEM 6. Unregistered Securities Issued or Sold Within One Year.

☐ None

As to any unregistered securities issued by the issuer or any of its predecessors or affiliated issuers within one year before the filing of this Form 1-A, state:

(a) Name of such issuer.

(b) (1) Title of securities issued

(2) Total amount of such securities issued

(3) Amount of such securities sold by or for the account of any person who at the time was a director, officer, promoter or principal securityholder of the issuer of such securities, or was an underwriter of any securities of such issuer

(c) (1) Aggregate consideration for which the securities were issued and basis for computing the amount thereof.

_____

_____

_____

(2) Aggregate consideration for which the securities listed in (b)(3) of this item (if any) were issued and the basis for computing the amount thereof (if different from the basis described in (c)(1)).

(d) Indicate the section of the Securities Act or Commission rule or regulation relied upon for exemption from the registration requirements of such Act and state briefly the facts relied upon for such exemption: _____

PART II—INFORMATION REQUIRED IN OFFERING CIRCULAR

(a) Financial statement requirements regardless of the applicable disclosure format are specified in Part F/S of this Form 1-A. The narrative disclosure contents of offering circulars are specified as follows:

(1) The information required by:

(i) The Offering Circular format described below; or

(ii) The information required by Part I of Form S-1 (17 CFR 239.11) or Part I of Form S-11 (17 CFR 239.18), except for the financial statements, selected financial data, and supplementary financial information called for by those forms. An issuer choosing to follow the Form S-1 or Form S-11 format may follow the requirements for smaller reporting companies if it meets the definition of that term in Rule 405 (17 CFR 230.405). An issuer may only use the Form S-11 format if the offering is eligible to be registered on that form;

The cover page of the offering circular must identify which disclosure format is being followed.

(2) The offering circular must describe any matters that would have triggered disqualification under Rule 262(a)(3) or (a)(5) but for the provisions set forth in Rule 262(b)(1);

(3) The legend required by Rule 253(f) of Regulation A must be included on the offering circular cover page (for issuers following the S-1 or S-11 disclosure models this legend must be included instead of the legend required by Item 501(b)(7) of Regulation S-K);

(4) For preliminary offering circulars, the legend required by Rule 254(a) must be included on the offering circular cover page (for issuers following the S-1 or S-11 disclosure models, this legend must be included instead of the legend required by Item 501(b)(10) of Regulation S-K); and

(5) For Tier 2 offerings where the securities will not be listed on a registered national securities exchange upon qualification, the offering circular cover page must include the following legend highlighted by prominent type or in another manner:

Generally, no sale may be made to you in this offering if the aggregate purchase price you pay is more than 10% of the greater of your annual income or net worth. Different rules apply to accredited investors and non-natural persons. Before making any representation that your investment does not exceed applicable thresholds, we encourage you to review Rule 251(d)(2)(i)(C) of Regulation A. For general information on investing, we encourage you to refer to www.investor.gov.

(b) The Commission encourages the use of management's projections of future economic performance that have a reasonable basis and are presented in an appropriate format. See Rule 175, 17 CFR 230.175.

(c) Offering circulars need not follow the order of the items or the order of other requirements of the disclosure form except to the extent otherwise specifically provided. Such information may not, however, be set forth in such a fashion as to obscure any of the required information or any information necessary to keep the required information from being incomplete or misleading. Information requested to be presented in a specified tabular format must be given in substantially the tabular format specified. For incorporation by reference, please refer to General Instruction III of this Form.

OFFERING CIRCULAR

Item 1. Cover Page of Offering Circular.

The cover page of the offering circular must be limited to one page and must include the information specified in this item.

(a) Name of the issuer.

Instruction to Item 1(a):

If your name is the same as, or confusingly similar to, that of a company that is well known, include information to eliminate any possible confusion with the other company. If your name indicates a line of business in which you are not engaged or you are engaged only to a limited extent, include information to eliminate any misleading inference as to your business. In some circumstances, disclosure may not be sufficient and you may be required to change your name. You will not be required to change your name if you are an established company, the character of your business has changed, and the investing public is generally aware of the change and the character of your current business.

(b) Full mailing address of the issuer's principal executive offices and the issuer's telephone number (including the area code) and, if applicable, website address.

(c) Date of the offering circular.

(d) Title and amount of securities offered. Separately state the amount of securities offered by selling securityholders, if any. Include a cross-reference to the section where the disclosure required by Item 14 of Part II of this Form 1-A has been provided;

(e) The information called for by the applicable table below as to all the securities being offered, in substantially the tabular format indicated. If necessary, you may estimate any underwriting discounts and commissions and the proceeds to the issuer or other persons.

	Price to public	Underwriting discount and commissions	Proceeds to issuer	Proceeds to other persons
Per share/unit:	_____	_____	_____	_____
Total:	_____	_____	_____	_____

If the securities are to be offered on a best efforts basis, the cover page must set forth the termination date, if any, of the offering, any minimum required sale and any arrangements to place the funds received in an escrow, trust, or similar arrangement. The following table must be used instead of the preceding table.

	Price to public	Underwriting discount and commissions	Proceeds to issuer	Proceeds to other persons
Per share/ unit:				
Total Minimum:				
Total Maximum:				

Instructions to Item 1(e):

1. The term "commissions" includes all cash, securities, contracts, or anything else of value, paid, to be set aside, disposed of, or understandings with or for the benefit of any other persons in which any underwriter is interested, made in connection with the sale of such security.

2. Only commissions paid by the issuer in cash are to be indicated in the table. Commissions paid by other persons or any form of non-cash compensation must be briefly identified in a footnote to the table with a cross-reference to a more complete description elsewhere in the offering circular.

3. Before the commencement of sales pursuant to Regulation A, the issuer must inform the Commission whether or not the amount of compensation to be allowed or paid to the underwriters, as described in the offering statement, has been cleared with FINRA.

4. If the securities are not to be offered for cash, state the basis upon which the offering is to be made.

5. Any finder's fees or similar payments must be disclosed on the cover page with a reference to a more complete discussion in the offering circular. Such disclosure must identify the finder, the nature of the services rendered and the nature of any relationship between the finder and the issuer, its officers, directors, promoters, principal stockholders and underwriters (including any affiliates of such persons).

6. The amount of the expenses of the offering borne by the issuer, including underwriting expenses to be borne by the issuer, must be disclosed in a footnote to the table.

(f) The name of the underwriter or underwriters.

(g) Any legend or information required by the law of any state in which the securities are to be offered.

(h) A cross-reference to the risk factors section, including the page number where it appears in the offering circular. Highlight this cross-reference by prominent type or in another manner.

(i) Approximate date of commencement of proposed sale to the public.

(j) If the issuer intends to rely on Rule 253(b) and a preliminary offering circular is circulated, provide (1) a bona fide estimate of the range of the maximum offering price and the maximum number of securities offered or (2) a bona fide estimate of the principal amount of the debt securities offered. The range must not exceed $2 for offerings where the upper end of the range is $10 or less and 20% if the upper end of the price range is over $10.

Instruction to Item 1(j):

The upper limit of the price range must be used in determining the aggregate offering price for purposes of Rule 251(a).

Item 2. Table of Contents.

On the page immediately following the cover page of the offering circular, provide a reasonably detailed table of contents. It must show the page numbers of the various sections or subdivisions of the offering circular. Include a specific listing of the risk factors section required by Item 3 of Part II of this Form 1-A.

Item 3. Summary and Risk Factors.

(a) An issuer may provide a summary of the information in the offering circular where the length or complexity of the offering circular makes a summary useful. The summary should be brief and must not contain all of the detailed information in the offering circular.

(b) Immediately following the Table of Contents required by Item 2 or the Summary, there must be set forth under an appropriate caption, a carefully organized series of short, concise paragraphs, summarizing the most significant factors that make the offering speculative or substantially risky. Issuers should avoid generalized statements and include only factors that are specific to the issuer.

Item 4. Dilution.

Where there is a material disparity between the public offering price and the effective cash cost to officers, directors, promoters and affiliated persons for shares acquired by them in a transaction during the past year, or that they have a right to acquire, there must be included a comparison of the public contribution under the proposed public offering and the average effective cash contribution of such persons.

Item 5. Plan of Distribution and Selling Securityholders.

(a) If the securities are to be offered through underwriters, give the names of the principal underwriters, and state the respective amounts underwritten. Identify each such underwriter having a material relationship to the issuer and state the nature of the relationship. State briefly the nature of the underwriters' obligation to take the securities.

Instructions to Item 5(a):

1. All that is required as to the nature of the underwriters' obligation is whether the underwriters are or will be committed to take and to pay for all of the securities if any are taken, or whether it is merely an agency or the type of best efforts arrangement under which the underwriters are required to take and to pay for only such securities as they may sell to the public. Conditions precedent to the underwriters' taking the securities, including market outs, need not be described except in the case of an agency or best efforts arrangement.

2. It is not necessary to disclose each member of a selling group. Disclosure may be limited to those underwriters who are in privity of contract with the issuer with respect to the offering.

(b) State briefly the discounts and commissions to be allowed or paid to dealers, including all cash, securities, contracts or other consideration to be received by any dealer in connection with the sale of the securities.

(c) Outline briefly the plan of distribution of any securities being issued that are to be offered through the selling efforts of brokers or dealers or otherwise than through underwriters.

(d) If any of the securities are to be offered for the account of securityholders, identify each selling securityholder, state the amount owned by the securityholder prior to the offering, the amount offered for his or her account and the amount to be owned after the offering. Provide such disclosure in a tabular format. At the bottom of the table, provide the total number of securities being offered for the account of all securityholders and describe what percent of the pre-offering outstanding securities of such class the offering represents.

Instruction to Item 5(d):

The term "securityholder" in this paragraph refers to beneficial holders, not nominee holders or other such holders of record. If the selling securityholder is an entity, disclosure of the persons who have sole or shared voting or investment power must be included.

(e) Describe any arrangements for the return of funds to subscribers if all of the securities to be offered are not sold. If there are no such arrangements, so state.

(f) If there will be a material delay in the payment of the proceeds of the offering by the underwriter to the issuer, the salient provisions in this regard and the effects on the issuer must be stated.

(g) Describe any arrangement to (1) limit or restrict the sale of other securities of the same class as those to be offered for the period of distribution, (2) stabilize the market for any of the securities to be offered, or (3) withhold commissions, or otherwise to hold each underwriter or dealer responsible for the distribution of its participation.

(h) Identify any underwriter that intends to confirm sales to any accounts over which it exercises discretionary authority and include an estimate of the amount of securities so intended to be confirmed.

Instruction to Item 5:

Attention is directed to the provisions of Rules 10b-9 [17 CFR 240.10b-9] and 15c2-4 [17 CFR 240.15c2-4] under the Securities Exchange Act of 1934. These rules outline, among other things, antifraud provisions concerning the return of funds to subscribers and the transmission of proceeds of an offering to a seller.

Item 6. Use of Proceeds to Issuer.

State the principal purposes for which the net proceeds to the issuer from the securities to be offered are intended to be used and the approximate amount intended to be used for each such purpose. If the issuer will not receive any of proceeds from the offering, so state.

Instructions to Item 6:

1. If any substantial portion of the proceeds has not been allocated for particular purposes, a statement to that effect must be made together with a statement of the amount of proceeds not so allocated.

2. State whether or not the proceeds will be used to compensate or otherwise make payments to officers or directors of the issuer or any of its subsidiaries.

3. For best efforts offerings, describe any anticipated material changes in the use of proceeds if all of the securities being qualified on the offering statement are not sold.

4. If an issuer must provide the disclosure described in Item 9(c) the use of proceeds and plan of operations should be consistent.

5. If any material amounts of other funds are to be used in conjunction with the proceeds, state the amounts and sources of such other funds and whether such funds are firm or contingent.

6. If any material part of the proceeds is to be used to discharge indebtedness, describe the material terms of such indebtedness. If the indebtedness to be discharged was incurred within one year, describe the use of the proceeds arising from such indebtedness.

7. If any material amount of the proceeds is to be used to acquire assets, otherwise than in the ordinary course of business, briefly describe and state the cost of the assets. If the assets are to be acquired from affiliates of the issuer or their associates, give the names of the persons from whom they are to be acquired and set forth the basis used in determining the purchase price to the issuer.

8. The issuer may reserve the right to change the use of proceeds, so long as the reservation is prominently disclosed in the section where the use of proceeds is discussed. It is not necessary to describe the possible alternative uses of proceeds unless the issuer believes that a change in circumstances leading to an alternative use of proceeds is likely to occur.

Item 7. Description of Business.

(a) *Narrative Description of Business.*

(1) Describe the business done and intended to be done by the issuer and its subsidiaries and the general development of the business during the past three years or such shorter period as the issuer may have been in business. Such description must include, but not be limited to, a discussion of the following factors if such factors are material to an understanding of the issuer's business:

(i) The principal products and services of the issuer and the principal market for and method of distribution of such products and services.

(ii) The status of a product or service if the issuer has made public information about a new product or service that would require the investment of a material amount of the assets of the issuer or is otherwise material.

(iii) [Reserved.]

(iv) The total number of persons employed by the issuer, indicating the number employed full time.

(v) Any bankruptcy, receivership or similar proceeding.

(vi) Any legal proceedings material to the business or financial condition of the issuer.

(vii) Any material reclassification, merger, consolidation, or purchase or sale of a significant amount of assets not in the ordinary course of business.

(2) The issuer must also describe those distinctive or special characteristics of the issuer's operation or industry that are reasonably likely to have a material impact upon the issuer's future financial performance. Examples of factors that might be discussed include dependence on one or a few major customers or suppliers (including suppliers of raw materials or financing), effect of existing or probable governmental regulation (including environmental regulation), material terms of and/or expiration of material labor contracts or patents, trademarks, licenses, franchises, concessions or royalty agreements, unusual competitive conditions in the industry, cyclicality of the industry and anticipated raw material or energy shortages to the extent management may not be able to secure a continuing source of supply.

(b) [Reserved.]

(c) *Industry Guides*. The disclosure guidelines in all Securities Act Industry Guides must be followed. To the extent that the industry guides are codified into Regulation S-K, the Regulation S-K industry disclosure items must be followed.

(d) For offerings of limited partnership or limited liability company interests, an issuer must comply with the Commission's interpretive views on substantive disclosure requirements set forth in Securities Act Release No. 6900 (June 17, 1991).

Item 8. Description of Property.

(a) State briefly the location and general character of any principal plants or other material physical properties of the issuer and its subsidiaries. If any such property is not held in fee or is held subject to any major encumbrance, so state and briefly describe how held. Include information regarding the suitability, adequacy, productive capacity and extent of utilization of the properties and facilities used in the issuer's business.

(b) Issuers engaged in mining operations must refer to and, if required, provide the disclosure under subpart 1300 of Regulation S-K (§ § 229.1300 through 1305), in addition to any disclosure required by this Item.

Instruction to Item 8:

Except as required by paragraph (b) of this Item, detailed descriptions of the physical characteristics of individual properties or legal descriptions by metes and bounds are not required and should not be given.

Item 9. Management's Discussion and Analysis of Financial Condition and Results of Operations.

Discuss the issuer's financial condition, changes in financial condition and results of operations for each year and interim period for which financial statements are required, including the causes of material changes from year to year or period to period in financial statement line items, to the extent necessary for an understanding of the issuer's business as a whole. Information provided also must relate to the segment information of the issuer. Provide the information specified below as well as such other information that is necessary for an investor's understanding of the issuer's financial condition, changes in financial condition and results of operations.

(a) *Operating Results.* Provide information regarding significant factors, including unusual or infrequent events or transactions or new developments, materially affecting the issuer's income from operations, and, in each case, indicating the extent to which income was so affected. Describe any other significant component of revenue or expenses necessary to understand the issuer's results of operations. To the extent that the financial statements disclose material changes in net sales or revenues, provide a narrative discussion of the extent to which such changes are attributable to changes in prices or to changes in the volume or amount of products or services being sold or to the introduction of new products or services.

Instruction to Item 9(a):

1. The discussion and analysis shall focus specifically on material events and uncertainties known to management that would cause reported financial information not to be necessarily indicative of future operating results or of future financial condition. This would include descriptions and amounts of (A) matters that would have an impact on future operations that have not had an impact in the past, and (B) matters that have had an impact on reported operations that are not expected to have an impact upon future operations.

2. Where the consolidated financial statements reveal material changes from year to year in one or more line items, the causes for the changes shall be described to the extent necessary to an understanding of the issuer's businesses as a whole. If the causes for a change in one line item also relate to other line items, no repetition is required and a line-by-line analysis of the financial statements as a whole is not required or generally appropriate. Issuers need not recite the amounts of changes from year to year which are readily computable from the financial statements. The discussion must not merely repeat numerical data contained in the consolidated financial statements.

3. When interim period financial statements are included, discuss any material changes in financial condition from the end of the preceding fiscal year to the date of the most recent interim balance sheet provided. Discuss any material changes in the issuer's results of operations with respect to the most recent fiscal year-to-date period for which a statement of comprehensive income (or statement of net income if comprehensive income is presented in two separate but consecutive financial statements or if no other comprehensive income) is provided and the corresponding year-to-date period of the preceding fiscal year.

(b) *Liquidity and Capital Resources.* Provide information regarding the following:

(1) The issuer's liquidity (both short and long term), including a description and evaluation of the internal and external sources of liquidity and a brief discussion of any material unused sources of liquidity. If a material deficiency in liquidity is identified, indicate the course of action that the issuer has taken or proposes to take to remedy the deficiency.

(2) The issuer's material commitments for capital expenditures as of the end of the latest fiscal year and any subsequent interim period and an indication of the general purpose of such commitments and the anticipated sources of funds needed to fulfill such commitments.

(c) *Plan of Operations.* Issuers (including predecessors) that have not received revenue from operations during each of the three fiscal years immediately before the filing of the offering statement (or since inception, whichever is shorter) must describe, if formulated, their plan of operation for the 12 months following the commencement of the proposed offering. If such information is not available, the reasons for its unavailability must be stated. Disclosure relating to any plan must include, among other things, a statement indicating whether, in the issuer's opinion, the proceeds from the offering will satisfy its cash requirements or whether it anticipates it will be necessary to raise additional funds in the next six months to implement the plan of operations.

(d) *Trend Information.* The issuer must identify the most significant recent trends in production, sales and inventory, the state of the order book and costs and selling prices since the latest financial year. The issuer also must discuss, for at least the current financial year, any known trends, uncertainties, demands, commitments or events that are reason-ably likely to have a material effect on the issuer's net sales or revenues, income from continuing operations, profitability, liquidity or capital resources, or that would cause reported financial information not necessarily to be indicative of future operating results or financial condition.

Item 10. Directors, Executive Officers and Significant Employees.

(a) For each of the directors, persons nominated or chosen to become directors, executive officers, persons chosen to become executive officers, and significant employees, provide the information specified below in substantially the following tabular format:

Name	Position	Age	Term of Office[1]	Approximate hours per week for part-time employees[2]
Executive Officers:				
Directors:				
Significant Employees:				

[1] Provide the month and year of the start date and, if applicable, the end date. To the extent you are unable to provide specific dates, provide such other description in the table or in an appropriate footnote clarifying the term of office. If the person is a nominee or chosen to become a director or executive officer, it must be indicated in this column or by footnote.

[2] For executive officers and significant employees that are working part-time, indicate approximately the average number of hours per week or month such person works or is anticipated to work. This column may be left blank for directors. The entire column may be omitted if all those listed in the table work full time for the issuer.

In a footnote to the table, briefly describe any arrangement or understanding between the persons described above and any other persons (naming such persons) pursuant to which the person was or is to be selected to his or her office or position.

Instructions to Item 10(a):

1. No nominee or person chosen to become a director or person chosen to be an executive officer who has not consented to act as such may be named in response to this item.

2. The term "executive officer" means the president, secretary, treasurer, any vice president in charge of a principal business function (such as sales, administration, or finance) and any other person who performs similar policy making functions for the issuer.

3. The term "significant employee" means persons such as production managers, sales managers, or research scientists, who are not executive officers, but who make or are expected to make significant contributions to the business of the issuer.

(b) *Family Relationships.* State the nature of any family relationship between any director, executive officer, person nominated or chosen by the issuer to become a director or executive officer or any significant employee.

Instruction to Item 10(b):

The term *"family relationship"* means any relationship by blood, marriage, or adoption, not more remote than *first cousin.*

(c) *Business Experience.* Give a brief account of the business experience during the past five years of each director, executive officer, person nominated or chosen to become a director or executive officer, and each significant employee, including his or her principal occupations and employment during that period and the name and principal business of any corporation or other organization in which such occupations and employment were carried on. When an executive officer or significant employee has been employed by the issuer for less than five years, a brief explanation must be included as to the nature of the responsibilities undertaken by the individual in prior positions to provide adequate disclosure of this prior business experience. What is required is information relating to the level of the employee's professional competence, which may include, depending upon the circumstances, such specific information as the size of the operation supervised.

(d) *Involvement in Certain Legal Proceedings.* Describe any of the following events which occurred during the past five years and which are material to an evaluation of the ability or integrity of any director, person nominated to become a director or executive officer of the issuer:

(1) A petition under the federal bankruptcy laws or any state insolvency law was filed by or against, or a receiver, fiscal agent or similar officer was appointed by a court for the business or property of such person, or any partnership in which he was general partner at or within two years before the time of such filing, or any corporation or business association of which he was an executive officer at or within two years before the time of such filing; or

(2) Such person was convicted in a criminal proceeding (excluding traffic violations and other minor offenses).

Item 11. Compensation of Directors and Executive Officers.

(a) Provide, in substantially the tabular format indicated, the annual compensation of each of the three highest paid persons who were executive officers or directors during the issuer's last completed fiscal year.

Name	Capacities in which compensation was received (*e.g.,* Chief Executive Officer, director, etc.)	Cash compensation ($)	Other compensation ($)	Total compensation ($)

(b) Provide the aggregate annual compensation of the issuer's directors as a group for the issuer's last completed fiscal year. Specify the total number of directors in the group.

(c) For Tier 1 offerings, the annual compensation of the three highest paid persons who were executive officers or directors and the aggregate annual compensation of the issuer's directors may be provided as a group, rather than as specified in paragraphs (a) and (b) of this item. In such case, issuers must specify the total number of persons in the group.

(d) Briefly describe all proposed compensation to be made in the future pursuant to any ongoing plan or arrangement to the individuals specified in paragraphs (a) and (b) of this item. The description must include a summary of how each plan operates, any performance formula or measure in effect (or the criteria used to determine payment amounts), the time periods over which the measurements of benefits will be determined, payment schedules, and any recent material amendments to the plan. Information need not be included with respect to any group life, health, hospitalization, or medical reimbursement plans that do not discriminate in scope, terms or operation in favor of executive officers or directors of the issuer and that are available generally to all salaried employees.

Instructions to Item 11:

1. In case of compensation paid or to be paid otherwise than in cash, if it is impracticable to determine the cash value thereof, state in a note to the table the nature and amount thereof.

2. This item is to be answered on an accrual basis if practicable; if not so answered, state the basis used.

Item 12. Security Ownership of Management and Certain Securityholders.

(a) Include the information specified in paragraph (b) of this item as of the most recent practicable date (stating the date used), in substantially the tabular format indicated, with respect to voting securities beneficially owned by:

(1) All executive officers and directors as a group, individually naming each director or executive officer who beneficially owns more than 10% of any class of the issuer's voting securities;

(2) Any other securityholder who beneficially owns more than 10% of any class of the issuer's voting securities as such beneficial ownership would be calculated if the issuer were subject to Rule 13d-3(d)(1) of the Securities Exchange Act of 1934.

(b) Beneficial Ownership Table:

Title of class	Name and address of beneficial owner[1]	Amount and nature of beneficial ownership	Amount and nature of beneficial ownership acquirable[2]	Percent of class[3]

[1] The address given in this column may be a business, mailing, or residential address. The address may be included in an appropriate footnote to the table rather than in this column.

[2] This column must include the amount of equity securities each beneficial owner has the right to acquire using the manner specified in Rule 13d-3(d)(1) of the Securities Exchange Act of 1934. An appropriate footnote must be included if the column heading does not sufficiently describe the circumstances upon which such securities could be acquired.

[3] This column must use the amounts contained in the two preceding columns to calculate the percent of class owned by such beneficial owner.

Item 13. Interest of Management and Others in Certain Transactions.

(a) Describe briefly any transactions or any currently proposed transactions during the issuer's last two completed fiscal years and the current fiscal year, to which the issuer or any of its subsidiaries was or is to be a participant and the amount involved exceeds $50,000 for Tier 1 or the lesser of $120,000 and one percent of the average of the issuer's total assets at year end for the last two completed fiscal years for Tier 2, and in which any of the following persons had or is to have a direct or indirect material interest, naming the person and stating his or her relationship to the issuer, the nature of the person's interest in the transaction and, where practicable, the amount of such interest:

(1) Any director or executive officer of the issuer;

(2) Any nominee for election as a director;

(3) Any securityholder named in answer to Item 12(a)(2);

(4) If the issuer was incorporated or organized within the past three years, any promoter of the issuer; or

(5) Any immediate family member of the above persons. An "immediate family member" of a person means such person's child, stepchild, parent, stepparent, spouse, sibling, mother-in-law, father-in-law, son-in-law, daughter-in-law, brother-in-law, sister-in-law, or any person (other than a tenant or employee) sharing such person's household.

Instructions to Item 13(a):

1. For purposes of calculating the amount of the transaction described above, all periodic installments in the case of any lease or other agreement providing for periodic payments must be aggregated to the extent they occurred within the time period described in this item.

2. No information need be given in answer to this item as to any transaction where:

(a) The rates of charges involved in the transaction are determined by competitive bids, or the transaction involves the rendering of services as a common or contract carrier at rates or charges fixed in conformity with law or governmental authority;

(b) The transaction involves services as a bank depositary of funds, transfer agent, registrar, trustee under a trust indenture, or similar services;

(c) The interest of the specified person arises solely from the ownership of securities of the issuer and the specified person receives no extra or special benefit not shared on a pro-rata basis by all of the holders of securities of the class.

3. This item calls for disclosure of indirect as well as direct material interests in transactions. A person who has a position or relationship with a firm, corporation, or other entity which engages in a transaction with the issuer or its subsidiaries may have an indirect interest in such transaction by reason of the position or relationship. However, a person is deemed not to have a material indirect interest in a transaction within the meaning of this item where:

(a) The interest arises only (i) from the person's position as a director of another corporation or organization (other than a partnership) that is a party to the transaction, or (ii) from the direct or indirect ownership by the person and all other persons specified in paragraphs (1) through (5) of this item, in the aggregate, of less than a 10 percent equity interest in another person (other than a partnership) that is a party to the transaction, or (iii) from both such position and ownership;

(b) The interest arises only from the person's position as a limited partner in a partnership in which the person and all other persons specified in paragraphs (1) through (5) of this item had an interest of less than 10 percent; or

(c) The interest of the person arises solely from the holding of an equity interest (unless the equity interest confers management rights similar to a general partner interest) or a creditor interest in another person that is a party to the transaction with the issuer or any of its subsidiaries and the transaction is not material to the other person.

4. Include the name of each person whose interest in any transaction is described and the nature of the relationships by reason of which such interest is required to be described. The amount of the interest of any specified person must be computed without regard to the amount of the profit or loss involved in the transaction. Where it is not practicable to state the approximate amount of the interest, the approximate amount involved in the transaction must be disclosed.

5. Information must be included as to any material underwriting discounts and commissions upon the sale of securities by the issuer where any of the specified persons was or is to be a principal underwriter or is a controlling person, or member, of a firm which was or is to be a principal underwriter. Information need not be given concerning ordinary management fees paid by underwriters to a managing underwriter pursuant to an agreement among underwriters, the parties to which do not include the issuer or its subsidiaries.

6. As to any transaction involving the purchase or sale of assets by or to any issuer or any subsidiary, otherwise than in the ordinary course of business, state the cost of the assets to the purchaser and, if acquired by the seller within two years before the transaction, the cost to the seller.

7. Information must be included in answer to this item with respect to transactions not excluded above which involve compensation from the issuer or its subsidiaries, directly or indir-

ectly, to any of the specified persons for services in any capacity unless the interest of such persons arises solely from the ownership individually and in the aggregate of less than 10 percent of any class of equity securities of another corporation furnishing the services to the issuer or its subsidiaries.

(b) If any expert named in the offering statement as having prepared or certified any part of the offering statement was employed for such purpose on a contingent basis or, at the time of such preparation or certification or at any time thereafter, had a material interest in the issuer or any of its parents or subsidiaries or was connected with the issuer or any of its subsidiaries as a promoter, underwriter, voting trustee, director, officer or employee, describe the nature of such contingent basis, interest or connection.

Item 14. Securities Being Offered.

(a) If capital stock is being offered, state the title of the class and furnish the following information regarding all classes of capital stock outstanding:

(1) Outline briefly: (i) dividend rights; (ii) voting rights; (iii) liquidation rights; (iv) preemptive rights; (v) conversion rights; (vi) redemption provisions; (vii) sinking fund provisions; (viii) liability to further calls or to assessment by the issuer; (ix) any classification of the Board of Directors, and the impact of classification where cumulative voting is permitted or required; (x) restrictions on alienability of the securities being offered; (xi) any provision discriminating against any existing or prospective holder of such securities as a result of such securityholder owning a substantial amount of securities; and (xii) any rights of holders that may be modified otherwise than by a vote of a majority or more of the shares outstanding, voting as a class.

(2) Briefly describe potential liabilities imposed on securityholders under state statutes or foreign law, for example, to employees of the issuer, unless such disclosure would be immaterial because the financial resources of the issuer or other factors are such as to make it unlikely that the liability will ever be imposed.

(3) If preferred stock is to be offered or is outstanding, describe briefly any restriction on the repurchase or redemption of shares by the issuer while there is any arrearage in the payment of dividends or sinking fund installments. If there is no such restriction, so state.

(b) If debt securities are being offered, outline briefly the following:

(1) Provisions with respect to interest, conversion, maturity, redemption, amortization, sinking fund or retirement.

(2) Provisions with respect to the kind and priority of any lien securing the issue, together with a brief identification of the principal properties subject to such lien.

(3) Material affirmative and negative covenants.

Instruction to Item 14(b):

In the case of secured debt there must be stated: (i) the approximate amount of unbonded property available for use against the issuance of bonds, as of the most recent practicable date, and (ii) whether the securities being issued are to be issued against such property, against the deposit of cash, or otherwise.

(c) If securities described are to be offered pursuant to warrants, rights, or convertible securities, state briefly:

(1) The amount of securities issuable upon the exercise or conversion of such warrants, convertible securities or rights;

(2) The period during which and the price at which the warrants, convertible securities or rights are exercisable;

(3) The amounts of warrants, convertible securities or rights outstanding; and

(4) Any other material terms of such securities.

(d) In the case of any other kind of securities, include a brief description with comparable information to that required in (a), (b) and (c) of Item 14.

PART F/S

(a) General Rules.

(1) The appropriate financial statements set forth below of the issuer, or the issuer and its predecessors or any businesses to which the issuer is a successor must be filed as part of the offering statement and included in the offering circular that is distributed to investors.

(2) Unless the issuer is a Canadian company, financial statements must be prepared in accordance with generally accepted accounting principles in the United States (US GAAP). If the issuer is a Canadian company, such financial statements must be prepared in accordance with either US GAAP or International Financial Reporting Standards (IFRS) as issued by the International Accounting Standards Board (IASB). If the financial statements comply with IFRS, such compliance must be explicitly and unreservedly stated in the notes to the financial statements and if the financial statements are audited, the auditor's report must include an opinion on whether the financial statements comply with IFRS as issued by the IASB.

(3) The issuer may elect to delay complying with any new or revised financial accounting standard until the date that a company that is not an issuer (as defined under section 2(a) of the Sarbanes-Oxley Act of 2002 (15 U.S.C. 7201(a)) is required to comply with such new or revised accounting standard, if such standard also applies to companies that are not issuers. Issuers electing such extension of time accommodation must disclose it at the time the issuer files its offering statement and apply the election to all standards. Issuers electing not to use this accommodation must forgo this accommodation for all financial accounting standards and may not elect to rely on this accommodation in any future filings.

(b) Financial Statements for Tier 1 Offerings.

(1) The financial statements prepared pursuant to this paragraph (b), including (b)(7), need not be prepared in accordance with Regulation S-X.

(2) The financial statements prepared pursuant to paragraph (b), including (b)(7), need not be audited. If the financial statements are not audited, they shall be labeled as "unaudited". However, if an audit of these financial statements is obtained for other purposes and that audit was performed in accordance with either U.S. generally accepted auditing standards or the Standards of the Public Company Accounting Oversight Board by an auditor that is independent pursuant to either the independence standards of the American Institute of Certified Public Accountants (AICPA) or Rule 2-01 of Regulation S-X, those audited financial statements must be filed, and an audit opinion complying with Rule 2-02 of Regulation S-X must be filed along with such financial statements. The auditor may, but need not, be registered with the Public Company Accounting Oversight Board.

(3) *Consolidated Balance Sheets.* Age of balance sheets at filing and at qualification:

(A) If the filing is made, or the offering statement is qualified, more than three months but no more than nine months after the most recently completed fiscal year end, include a balance sheet as of the two most recently completed fiscal year ends.

(B) If the filing is made, or the offering statement is qualified, more than nine months after the most recently completed fiscal year end, include a balance sheet as of the two most recently completed fiscal year ends and an interim balance sheet as of a date no earlier than six months after the most recently completed fiscal year end.

(C) If the filing is made, or the offering statement is qualified, within three months after the most recently completed fiscal year end, include a balance sheet as of the two fiscal year ends preceding the most recently completed fiscal year end and an interim balance sheet as of a date no earlier than six months after the date of the most recent fiscal year end balance sheet that is required.

(D) If the filing is made, or the offering statement is qualified, during the period from inception until three months after reaching the annual balance sheet date for the first time, include a balance sheet as of a date within nine months of filing or qualification.

(4) *Statements of Comprehensive Income, Cash Flows, and Changes in Stockholders' Equity.* File consolidated statements of comprehensive income (either in a single continuous finan-

cial statement or in two separate but consecutive financial statements; or a statement of net income if there was no other comprehensive income), cash flows, and changes in stockholders' equity for each of the two fiscal years preceding the date of the most recent balance sheet being filed or such shorter period as the issuer has been in existence.

(5) *Interim Financial Statements.*

(i) If a consolidated interim balance sheet is required by (b)(3) of Part F/S, consolidated interim statements of comprehensive income (either in a single continuous financial statement or in two separate but consecutive financial statements; or a statement of net income if there was no other comprehensive income) and cash flows shall be provided and must cover at least the first six months of the issuer's fiscal year and the corresponding period of the preceding fiscal year. An analysis of the changes in each caption of stockholders' equity presented in the balance sheets must be provided in a note or separate statement. This analysis shall be presented in the form of a reconciliation of the beginning balance to the ending balance for each period for which a statement of comprehensive income is required to be filed with all significant reconciling items described by appropriate captions with contributions from and distributions to owners shown separately. Dividends per share for each class of shares shall also be provided.

(ii) Interim financial statements of issuers that report under U.S. GAAP may be condensed as described in Rule 8-03(a) of Regulation S-X.

(iii) The interim statements of comprehensive income for all issuers must be accompanied by a statement that in the opinion of management all adjustments necessary in order to make the interim financial statements not misleading have been included.

(6) *Oil and Gas Producing Activities.* Issuers engaged in oil and gas producing activities must follow the financial accounting and reporting standards specified in Rule 4-10 of Regulation S-X.

(7) *Financial Statements of and Disclosures About Other Entities.* The circumstances described below may require you to file financial statements of, or provide disclosures about, other entities in the offering statement. The financial statements of other entities must be presented for the same periods as if the other entity was the issuer as described above in paragraphs (b)(3) and (b)(4) unless a shorter period is specified by the rules below. The financial statements of other entities shall follow the same audit requirement as paragraph (b)(2) of this Part F/S:

(i) *Financial Statements of and Disclosures About Guarantors and Issuers of Guaranteed Securities.* The requirements of Rule 3-10 of Regulation S-X are applicable to financial statements of a subsidiary that issues securities guaranteed by the parent company or guarantees securities issued by the parent company. However, the reference in Rule 3-10(a) of Regulation S-X to "an issuer or guarantor of a guaranteed security that is registered or being registered is required to file financial statements required by Regulation S-X with respect to the guarantee or guaranteed security" instead refers to "an issuer or guarantor of a guaranteed security that is qualified or being qualified pursuant to Regulation A is required to file financial statements required by Part F/S of Form 1-A with respect to the guarantee or guaranteed security." The definition of "parent company" is the same as in Rule 3-10(b)(1) of Regulation S-X, except that Rule 3-10(b)(1)(ii) instead reads as follows: "Is, or as a result of the subject offering statement will be, required to file reports with the Commission pursuant to Rule 257(b) of Regulation A (§§ 230.251-230.263), or is an Exchange Act reporting company." The parent company must also provide the disclosures required by Rule 13-01 of Regulation S-X. The parent company may elect to provide these disclosures in a footnote to its consolidated financial statements or alternatively, in management's discussion and analysis of financial condition and results of operations described in Item 9 of Form 1-A in its offering statement on Form 1-A filed in connection with the offer and sale of the subject securities.

(ii) *Financial Statements of and Disclosures About Affiliates Whose Securities Collateralize an Issuance.* The requirements of Rules 3-16 or 13-02 of Regulation S-X are applicable if an issuer's securities that are qualified or being qualified pursuant to Regulation A are collateralized by the securities of the issuer's affiliates. Rule 13-02 of Regulation S-X must be followed unless Rule 3-16 of Regulation S-X applies. The issuer may elect to provide the disclosures specified in Rule 13-02 of Regulation S-X in a footnote to its consolidated financial statements or alternatively, in management's discussion and analysis of financial condition and results of operations described in Item 9 of Form 1-A in its offering statement on Form 1-A filed in connection with the offer and sale of the subject securities.

Instructions to Paragraph (b) in Part F/S:

1. Issuers should refer to Rule 257(b)(2) to determine whether a special financial report will be required after qualification of the offering statement.

2. If the last day that the financial statements included in the offering statement can be accepted, according to the age requirements of this item falls on a Saturday, Sunday, or holiday, such offering statement may be filed on the first business day following the last day of the specified period.

3. As an alternative, an issuer may—but need not—elect to comply with the provisions of paragraph (c).

(c) Financial Statement Requirements For Tier 2 Offerings.

(1) In addition to the general rules in paragraph (a), provide the financial statements required by paragraph (b) of this Part F/S, except the following rules should be followed in the preparation of the financial statements:

(i) Issuers that report under U.S. GAAP and, when applicable, other entities for which financial statements are required, must comply with Article 8 of Regulation S-X, as if they were conducting a registered offering on Form S-1, except the age of financial statements may follow paragraphs (b)(3)–(4) of this Part F/S.

(ii) Audited financial statements are required for Tier 2 offerings for the issuer and, when applicable, for financial statements of other entities. However, interim financial statements may be unaudited.

(iii) The audit must be conducted in accordance with either U.S. Generally Accepted Auditing Standards or the standards of the Public Company Accounting Oversight Board (United States) and the report and qualifications of the independent accountant shall comply with the requirements of Article 2 of Regulation S-X. Accounting firms conducting audits for the financial statements included in the offering circular may, but need not, be registered with the Public Company Accounting Oversight Board.

PART III—EXHIBITS

Item 16. Index to Exhibits.

(a) An exhibits index must be presented at the beginning of Part III.

(b) Each exhibit must be listed in the exhibit index according to the number assigned to it under Item 17 below.

(c) For incorporation by reference, please refer to General Instruction III of this Form.

Item 17. Description of Exhibits.

As appropriate, the following documents must be filed as exhibits to the offering statement.

1. *Underwriting Agreement*—Each underwriting contract or agreement with a principal underwriter or letter pursuant to which the securities are to be distributed; where the terms have yet to be finalized, proposed formats may be provided.

2. *Charter and Bylaws*—The charter and bylaws of the issuer or instruments corresponding thereto as currently in effect and any amendments thereto.

3. *Instruments Defining the Rights of Securityholders*—

(a) All instruments defining the rights of any holder of the issuer's securities, including but not limited to (i) holders of equity or debt securities being issued; (ii) holders of long-term debt of the issuer, and of all subsidiaries for which consolidated or unconsolidated financial statements are required to be filed.

(b) The following instruments need not be filed if the issuer agrees to file them with the Commission upon request: (i) instruments defining the rights of holders of long-term debt of the issuer and all of its subsidiaries for which consolidated financial statements are required to be filed if such debt is not being issued pursuant to this Regulation A offering and the total amount of such authorized issuance does not exceed 5% of the total assets of the issuer and its subsidiaries on a consolidated basis; (ii) any instrument with respect to a class of securities that is to be retired or redeemed before the issuance or upon delivery of the securities being issued pursuant to this Regulation A offering and appropriate steps have been taken to assure such retirement or redemption; and (iii) copies of instruments evidencing scrip certificates or fractions of shares.

4. *Subscription Agreement*—The form of any subscription agreement to be used in connection with the purchase of securities in this offering.

5. *Voting Trust Agreement*—Any voting trust agreements and amendments.

6. *Material Contracts*—

(a) Every contract not made in the ordinary course of business that is material to the issuer and is to be performed in whole or in part at or after the filing of the offering statement or was entered into not more than two years before such filing. Only contracts need be filed as to which the issuer or subsidiary of the issuer is a party or has succeeded to a party by assumption or assignment or in which the issuer or such subsidiary has a beneficial interest. Schedules (or similar attachments) to material contracts may be excluded if not material to an investment decision or if the material information contained in such schedules is otherwise disclosed in the agreement or the offering statement. The material contract filed must contain a list briefly identifying the contents of all omitted schedules, together with an agreement to furnish supplementally a copy of any omitted schedule to the Commission upon request.

(b) If the contract is such as ordinarily accompanies the kind of business conducted by the issuer and its subsidiaries, it is made in the ordinary course of business and need not be filed unless it falls within one or more of the following categories, in which case it must be filed except where immaterial in amount or significance: (i) any contract to which directors, officers, promoters, voting trustees, securityholders named in the offering statement, or underwriters are parties, except where the contract merely involves the purchase or sale of current assets having a determinable market price, at such market price; (ii) any contract upon which the issuer's business is substantially dependent, as in the case of continuing contracts to sell the major part of the issuer's products or services or to purchase the major part of the issuer's requirements of goods, services or raw materials or any franchise or license or other agreement to use a patent, formula, trade secret, process or trade name upon which the issuer's business depends to a material extent; (iii) any contract calling for the acquisition or sale of any property, plant or equipment for a consideration exceeding 15% of such fixed assets of the issuer on a consolidated basis; or (iv) any material lease under which a part of the property described in the offering statement is held by the issuer.

(c) Any management contract or any compensatory plan, contract or arrangement including, but not limited to, plans relating to options, warrants or rights, pension, retirement or deferred compensation or bonus, incentive or profit sharing (or if not set forth in any formal document, a written description) is deemed material and must be filed except for the following: (i) ordinary purchase and sales agency agreements; (ii) agreements with managers of stores in a chain organization or similar organization; (iii) contracts providing for labor or salesperson's bonuses or payments to a class of securityholders, as such; (iv) any compensatory plan, contract or arrangement that pursuant to its terms is available to employees generally and that in operation provides for the same method of allocation of benefits between management and non-management participants.

7. *Plan of Acquisition, Reorganization, Arrangement, Liquidation, or Succession*—Any material plan of acquisition, disposition, reorganization, readjustment, succession, liquidation or arrangement and any amendments thereto described in the offering statement. Schedules

(or similar attachments) to these exhibits must not be filed unless such schedules contain information that is material to an investment decision and that is not otherwise disclosed in the agreement or the offering statement. The plan filed must contain a list briefly identifying the contents of all omitted schedules, together with an agreement to furnish supplementally a copy of any omitted schedule to the Commission upon request.

8. *Escrow Agreements*—Any escrow agreement or similar arrangement which has been executed in connection with the Regulation A offering.

9. *Letter Re Change in Certifying Accountant*—A letter from the issuer's former independent accountant regarding its concurrence or disagreement with the statements made by the issuer in the current report concerning the resignation or dismissal as the issuer's principal accountant.

10. *Power of Attorney*—If any name is signed to the offering statement pursuant to a power of attorney, signed copies of the power of attorney must be filed. Where the power of attorney is contained elsewhere in the offering statement or documents filed therewith, a reference must be made in the index to the part of the offering statement or document containing such power of attorney. In addition, if the name of any officer signing on behalf of the issuer is signed pursuant to a power of attorney, certified copies of a resolution of the issuer's board of directors authorizing such signature must also be filed. A power of attorney that is filed with the Commission must relate to a specific filing or an amendment thereto. A power of attorney that confers general authority may not be filed with the Commission.

11. *Consents*—

(a) Experts: The written consent of (i) any accountant, counsel, engineer, geologist, appraiser or any persons whose profession gives authority to a statement made by them and who is named in the offering statement as having prepared or certified any part of the document or is named as having prepared or certified a report or evaluation whether or not for use in connection with the offering statement; (ii) the expert that authored any portion of a report quoted or summarized as such in the offering statement, expressly stating their consent to the use of such quotation or summary; (iii) any persons who are referenced as having reviewed or passed upon any information in the offering statement, and that such information is being included on the basis of their authority or in reliance upon their status as experts.

(b) All written consents must be dated and signed.

12. *Opinion Re Legality*—An opinion of counsel as to the legality of the securities covered by the Offering Statement, indicating whether they will when sold, be legally issued, fully paid and non-assessable, and if debt securities, whether they will be binding obligations of the issuer.

13. *"Testing the Waters" Materials*—Any written communication or broadcast script used under the authorization of Rule 255. Such materials need not be filed if they are substantively the same as materials previously filed with the offering statement.

14. *Appointment of Agent For Service of Process*—A Canadian issuer must file Form F-X.

15. *The Technical Report Summary Under Item 601(b)(96) of Regulation S-K*—An issuer that is required to file a technical report summary pursuant to Item 1302(b)(2) of Regulation S-K must provide the information specified in Item 601(b)(96) of Regulation S-K as an exhibit to Form 1-A.

16. *Additional Exhibits*—

(a) Any non-public, draft offering statement previously submitted pursuant to Rule 252(d) and any related, non-public correspondence submitted by or on behalf of the issuer.

(b) Any additional exhibits which the issuer may wish to file, which must be so marked as to indicate clearly the subject matters to which they refer.

17. *Subsidiary Guarantors and Issuers of Guaranteed Securities and Affiliates Whose Securities Collateralize Securities of the Issuer.* List each of the entities in paragraphs (a) and (b) below under an appropriately captioned heading that identifies the associated securities. An entity need not be listed more than once so long as its role as issuer, co-issuer, or guarantor of a guaranteed

security and/or as affiliate whose security is pledged as collateral for an issuer's security is clearly indicated with respect to each applicable security:

(a) For an issuer that is the parent company (as that term is defined in paragraph (b)(7)(i) of Part F/S) and subject to § 210.13-01 as described in paragraph (b)(7)(i) of Part F/S, each of the issuer's subsidiaries that is a guarantor, issuer, or co-issuer of the guaranteed security for which the issuer is required to file reports with the Commission pursuant to Rule 257(b) of Regulation A, or is an Exchange Act reporting company subject to Section 13(a) or Section 15(d) of the Securities Exchange Act of 1934, or the offer and sale of which is qualified or being qualified pursuant to Regulation A; and

(b) For an issuer that is subject to § 210.13-02 as described in paragraph (b)(7)(i) of Part F/S, each of the issuer's affiliates whose security is pledged as collateral for the issuer's security for which the issuer is required to file reports with the Commission pursuant to Rule 257(b) of Regulation A, or is an Exchange Act reporting company subject to Section 13(a) or Section 15(d) of the Securities Exchange Act of 1934, or the offer and sale of which is qualified or being qualified pursuant to Regulation A. For each affiliate, also identify the security or securities pledged as collateral.

SIGNATURES

Pursuant to the requirements of Regulation A, the issuer certifies that it has reasonable grounds to believe that it meets all of the requirements for filing on Form 1-A and has duly caused this offering statement to be signed on its behalf by the undersigned, thereunto duly authorized, in the City of ,State of ,on *(date)*.

(Exact name of issuer as specified in its charter) _____

By (Signature and Title) _____

This offering statement has been signed by the following persons in the capacities and on the dates indicated.

(Signature) _____

(Title) _____

(Date) _____

Instructions to Signatures:

1. The offering statement must be signed by the issuer, its principal executive officer, principal financial officer, principal accounting officer, and a majority of the members of its board of directors or other governing body. If a signature is by a person on behalf of any other person, evidence of authority to sign must be filed with the offering statement, except where an executive officer signs on behalf of the issuer.

2. The offering statement must be signed using a typed signature. Each signatory to the filing must also manually sign a signature page or other document authenticating, acknowledging or otherwise adopting his or her signature that appears in the filing. Such document must be executed before or at the time the filing is made and must be retained by the issuer for a period of five years. Upon request, the issuer must furnish to the Commission or its staff a copy of any or all documents retained pursuant to this section.

3. The name and title of each person signing the offering statement must be typed or printed beneath the signature.

FORM D

Form D

http://www.rbsourcefilings.com/document/read/R24-IDANDNQ-R24-IDAWXYZ

United States
Securities and Exchange Commission
Washington, DC 20549
FORM D
NOTICE OF EXEMPT OFFERING OF SECURITIES

Intentional misstatements or omissions of fact constitute federal criminal violations. See 18 U.S.C. 1001.

You must follow the accompanying <u>instructions</u> in submitting this notice.

Item 1. <u>Issuer's Identity</u>

<u>Name of Issuer</u> _____

<u>Previous Name(s)</u> _____ □ None

<u>Jurisdiction of Incorporation/Organization</u> (dropdown or other list selection feature)

<u>Entity Type</u> (dropdown or other list selection feature)

<u>Year of Incorporation/Organization</u> (dropdown or other list selection feature to select year or "Yet to Be Formed")

_____
Add Issuer

Item 2. <u>Principal Place of Business and Contact Information</u>

<u>Street Address</u> _____

City _____ State/Province _____ (<u>dropdown</u> or other list selection feature)

Zip/Postal Code _____

Country

-
  - U.S.
  - Canada
  - Other (<u>dropdown</u> or other list selection feature for countries if answer is "Other" than U.S. or Canada)

<u>Telephone Number</u> _____

_____
Add Information for Additional Issuer(s)

Item 3. <u>Related Persons</u>

<u>Full Name</u>	<u>Relationship</u>	<u>Address</u>

	[ ] Executive Director	_____
_____	[ ] Director	_____
	[ ] Promoter	_____

Clarification of Response (if Necessary): _____

Add Related Person

Item 4. <u>Industry Group (dropdown or other list selection feature)</u>

Item 5. <u>Issuer Size</u>

Revenue Range (for issuers that do not specify "Hedge Fund" or "Other Investment Fund" in response to <u>Item 4</u>**)**

- o No Revenues
- o $1 – $1,000,000
- o $1,000,001 – $5,000,000
- o $5,000,001 – $25,000,000
- o $25,000,001 – $100,000,000
- o Over $100,000,000
- o Decline to Disclose
- o Not Applicable

OR

Aggregate Net Asset Value Range (for issuers that specify "Hedge Fund" or "Other Investment Fund" in response to <u>Item 4</u>**)**

- o No Aggregate Net Asset Value
- o $1 – $5,000,000
- o $5,000,001 – $25,000,000
- o $25,000,001 – $50,000,000
- o $50,000,001 – $100,000,000
- o Over $100,000,000
- o Decline to Disclose
- o Not Applicable

Item 6. <u>Federal Exemption(s) and Exclusion(s) Claimed</u> (select all that apply)

[ ] <u>Rule 504(b)(1)</u> (not <u>(i)</u>, <u>(ii)</u> or <u>(iii)</u>)	[ ] <u>Rule 506(b)</u>
[ ] <u>Rule 504(b)(1)(i)</u>	[ ] <u>Rule 506(c)</u>
[ ] <u>Rule 504(b)(1)(ii)</u>	[ ] <u>Section 4(a)(5)</u>
[ ] <u>Rule 504(b)(1)(iii)</u>	[ ] <u>Investment Company Act Section 3(c)</u>[1]

[1] If the filer selects the <u>Investment Company Act Section 3(c)</u> checkbox, a pop-up or other feature will require the filer to select all claimed exclusions from the definition of "investment company" from among <u>Sections 3(c)(1)</u> through <u>Section 3(c)(14)</u> (except for <u>Section 3(c)(8)</u>).

Item 7. <u>Type of Filing</u>

- [ ] New Notice (dropdown or other feature to select "Date of First Sale" or "First Sale Yet to Occur")
- [ ] Amendment

Item 8. <u>Duration of Offering</u>

Does the issuer intend this offering to last more than one year?

- o [ ] Yes
- o [ ] No

Item 9. <u>Type(s) of Securities Offered</u> (select all that apply)

- [ ] Equity
- [ ] Debt
- [ ] Option, Warrant or Other Right to Acquire Another Security
- [ ] Security to be Acquired Upon Exercise of Option, Warrant or Other Right to Acquire Security
- [ ] Pooled Investment Fund Interests
- [ ] Tenant-in-Common Securities
- [ ] Mineral Property Securities
- [ ] Other (Describe: _____)

Item 10. <u>Business Combination Transaction</u>

Is this offering being made in connection with a business combination transaction, such as a merger, acquisition or exchange offer?

- o [ ] Yes
- o [ ] No

Clarification of Response (if Necessary): _____

Item 11. <u>Minimum Investment</u>

Minimum investment accepted from any outside investor $ _____

Item 12. <u>Sales Compensation</u>

Recipient	Recipient CRD Number	Associated Broker or Dealer	Broker or Dealer CRD Number	Street Address	State(s) of Solicitation (dropdown or other list selection feature)

Add Recipient

Item 13. <u>Offering and Sales Amounts</u>

Total Offering Amount $ _____   or [ ] Indefinite

Total Amount Sold $ _____

Total Remaining to be Sold $[auto subtract] _____   or [ ] Indefinite

Clarification of Response (if Necessary): _____

Item 14. <u>Investors</u>

- [ ] Select if securities in the offering have been or may be sold to persons who do not qualify as *accredited investors,* and enter the number of such non-accredited investors who already have invested in the offering: _____
- Regardless whether securities in the offering have been or may be sold to persons who do not qualify as accredited investors, enter the total number of investors who already have invested in the offering: _____

Item 15. <u>Sales Commissions and Finders' Fees Expenses</u>

Provide separately the amounts of sales commissions and finders' fees expenses, if any. If the amount of an expenditure is not known, provide an estimate and check the box next to the amount(s).

Sales Commissions $_____   [ ] Estimate
Finders' Fees $_____   [ ] Estimate

Clarification of Response (if Necessary): _____

Item 16. <u>Use of Proceeds</u>

Provide the amount of the gross proceeds of the offering that has been or is proposed to be used for payments to any of the persons required to be named as executive officers, directors or promoters in response to <u>Item 3</u> above. If the amount is unknown, provide an estimate and check the box next to the amount.

$ _____   [ ] Estimate
Clarification of Response (if Necessary): _____

Signature and Submission

Terms of   Please verify the information you have entered and review the Terms of
Submission: Submission below before signing and clicking SUBMIT below to file
                    this notice.

<u>Printable Version</u>

In submitting this notice, each issuer named above is:

- Notifying the SEC and/or each State in which this notice is filed of the offering of securities described and undertaking to furnish them, upon written request in accordance with applicable law, the information furnished to offerees.*
- Irrevocably appointing each of the Secretary of the SEC and the Securities Administrator or other legally designated officer of the State in which the issuer maintains its principal place of business and any State in which this notice is filed, as its agents for service of process, and agreeing that these persons may accept service on its behalf, of any notice, process or pleading, and further agreeing that such service may be made by registered or certified mail, in any Federal or state action, administrative proceeding, or arbitration brought against the issuer in any place subject to the jurisdiction of the United States, if the action, proceeding or arbitration (a) arises out of any activity in connection with the offering of securities that is the subject of this notice, and (b) is founded, directly or indirectly, upon the provisions of: (i) the Securities

Act of 1933, the Securities Exchange Act of 1934, the Trust Indenture Act of 1939, the Investment Company Act of 1940, or the Investment Advisers Act of 1940, or any rule or regulation under any of these statutes; or (ii) the laws of the State in which the issuer maintains its principal place of business or any State in which this notice is filed.

- Certifying that, if the issuer is claiming a Regulation D exemption for the offering, the issuer is not disqualified from relying on Rule 504 or Rule 506 for one of the reasons stated in Rule 504(b)(3) or Rule 506(d).

* This undertaking does not affect any limits Section 102(a) of the National Securities Markets Improvement Act of 1996 ("NSMIA") [Pub. L. No. 104-290, 110 Stat. 3416 (Oct. 11, 1996)] imposes on the ability of States to require information. As a result, if the securities that are the subject of this Form D are "covered securities" for purposes of NSMIA, whether in all instances or due to the nature of the offering that is the subject of this Form D, States cannot routinely require offering materials under this undertaking or otherwise and can require offering materials only to the extent NSMIA permits them to do so under NSMIA's preservation of their anti-fraud authority.

Each issuer identified above has read this notice, knows the contents to be true, and has duly caused this notice to be signed on its behalf by the undersigned duly authorized person.

Signature

Signature:_____ Title:_____ Date:_____

By clicking on SUBMIT below, you are agreeing to the Terms of Submission above.

| SUBMIT |

Persons who respond to the collection of information contained in this form are not required to respond unless the form displays a currently valid OMB control number.

Instructions for Submitting Notice

General Instructions

- **Who must file:**
  - Each issuer of securities that sells its securities in reliance on an exemption provided in Regulation D or Section 4(a)(5) of the Securities Act of 1933 must file this notice containing the information requested with the U.S. Securities and Exchange Commission (SEC) and with the state(s) requiring it. If more than one issuer has sold its securities in the same transaction, all issuers should be identified in one filing with the SEC, but some states may require a separate filing for each issuer or security sold.
- **When to file:**
  - An issuer must file a new notice with the SEC for each new offering of securities no later than 15 calendar days after the "date of first sale" of securities in the offering as explained in Instruction 7. For this purpose, the date of first sale is the date on which the first investor is irrevocably contractually committed to invest, which, depending on the terms and conditions of the contract, could be the date on which the issuer receives the investor's subscription agreement or check. An issuer may file the notice at any time before that if it has determined to make the offering. An issuer must file a new notice with each state that requires it at the time set by the state. For state filing information, go to www.NASAA.org. A mandatory capital commitment call does not constitute a new offering, but is made under the original offering, so no new Form D filing is required.
  - An issuer may file an amendment to a previously filed notice at any time.
  - An issuer must file an amendment to a previously filed notice for an offering:
    - to correct a material mistake of fact or error in the previously filed notice, as soon as practicable after discovery of the mistake or error;
    - to reflect a change in the information provided in the previously filed notice, except as provided below, as soon as practicable after the change; and

- annually, on or before the first anniversary of the most recent previously filed notice, if the offering is continuing at that time.

- **When amendment is not required:** An issuer is not required to file an amendment to a previously filed notice to reflect a change that occurs after the offering terminates or a change that occurs solely in the following information:
  - the address or relationship to the issuer of a related person identified in response to Item 3;
  - an issuer's revenues or aggregate net asset value;
  - the minimum investment amount, if the change is an increase, or if the change, together with all other changes in that amount since the previously filed notice, does not result in a decrease of more than 10%;
  - any address or state(s) of solicitation shown in response to Item 12;
  - the total offering amount, if the change is a decrease, or if the change, together with all other changes in that amount since the previously filed notice, does not result in an increase of more than 10%;
  - the amount of securities sold in the offering or the amount remaining to be sold;
  - the number of non-accredited investors who have invested in the offering, as long as the change does not increase the number to more than 35;
  - the total number of investors who have invested in the offering;
  - the amount of sales commissions, finders' fees or use of proceeds for payments to executive officers, directors or promoters, if the change is a decrease, or if the change, together with all other changes in that amount since the previously filed notice, does not result in an increase of more than 10%.
- **Saturdays, Sundays and Holidays:** If the date on which a notice or an amendment to a previously filed notice is required to be filed falls on a Saturday, Sunday or holiday, the due date is the first business day following.
- **Amendment content:** An issuer that files an amendment to a previously filed notice must provide current information in response to all items of this Form D, regardless of why the amendment is filed.
- **How to File:** Issuers must file this notice with the SEC in electronic format. For state filing information, go to www.NASAA.org.
- **Filing Fee:** There is no federal filing fee. For information on state filing fees, go to www.NASAA.org.
- **Definitions of Terms:** Terms used but not defined in this form that are defined in Rule 405 and Rule 501 under the Securities Act of 1933, 17 CFR 230.405 and 230.501, have the meanings given to them in those rules.

Item-by-Item Instructions

Item 1. Issuer's Identity.

Identify each legal entity issuing any securities being reported as being offered by entering its full name; any previous name used within the past five years; and its jurisdiction of incorporation or organization, type of legal entity, and year of incorporation or organization within the past five years or status as formed over five years ago or not yet formed. If more than one entity is issuing the securities, identify a primary issuer in the first fields shown and identify additional issuers in the fields that appear.

Item 2. Principal Place of Business and Contact Information.

Enter a full street address of the issuer's principal place of business. Post office box numbers and "In care of" addresses are not acceptable. Enter a contact telephone number for the issuer. If you identified more than one issuer in response to Item 1, enter the requested information for the primary issuer you identified in response to that item and, at your option, for any or all of the other issuers you identified in the fields that appear.

Item 3. Related Persons.

Enter the full name and address of each person having the specified relationships with any issuer and identify each relationship:

- Each *executive officer* and *director* of the issuer and person performing similar functions (title alone is not determinative) for the issuer, such as the general and managing partners of partnerships and managing members of limited liability companies; and
- Each person who has functioned directly or indirectly as a *promoter* of the issuer within the past five years of the later of the first sale of securities or the date upon which the Form D

filing was required to be made.

If necessary to prevent the information supplied from being misleading, also provide a clarification in the space provided.

Item 4. Industry Group.

Select the issuer's industry group. If the issuer or issuers can be categorized in more than one industry group, select the industry group that most accurately reflects the use of the bulk of the proceeds of the offering. For purposes of this filing, use the ordinary dictionary and commonly understood meanings of the terms identifying the industry group.

Item 5. Issuer Size.

- *Revenue Range* (for issuers that do not specify "Hedge Fund" or "Other Investment Fund" in response to Item 4): Enter the revenue range of the issuer or of all the issuers together for the most recently completed fiscal year available, or, if not in existence for a fiscal year, revenue range to date. Domestic SEC reporting companies should state revenues in accordance with Regulation S-X under the Securities Exchange Act of 1934. Domestic non-reporting companies should state revenues in accordance with U.S. Generally Accepted Accounting Principles (GAAP). Foreign issuers should calculate revenues in U.S. dollars and state them in accordance with U.S. GAAP, home country GAAP or International Financial Reporting Standards. If the issuer(s) declines to disclose its revenue range, enter "Decline to Disclose." If the issuer's(s') business is intended to produce revenue but did not, enter "No Revenues." If the business is not intended to produce revenue (for example, the business seeks asset appreciation only), enter "Not Applicable."
- *Aggregate Net Asset Value* (for issuers that specify "Hedge Fund" or "Other Investment Fund" in response to Item 4): Enter the aggregate net asset value range of the issuer or of all the issuers together as of the most recent practicable date. If the issuer(s) declines to disclose its aggregate net asset value range, enter "Decline to Disclose."

Item 6. Federal Exemption(s) and Exclusion(s) Claimed.

Select the provision(s) being claimed to exempt the offering and resulting sales from the federal registration requirements under the Securities Act of 1933 and, if applicable, to exclude the issuer from the definition of "investment company" under the Investment Company Act of 1940. Select "Rule 504(b)(1) (not (i), (ii) or (iii))" only if the issuer is relying on the exemption in the introductory sentence of Rule 504 for offers and sales that satisfy all the terms and conditions of Rules 501 and 502(a), (c) and (d).

Item 7. Type of Filing.

Indicate whether the issuer is filing a new notice or an amendment to a notice that was filed previously. If this is a new notice, enter the date of the first sale of securities in the offering or indicate that the first sale has "Yet to Occur." For this purpose, the date of first sale is the date on which the first investor is irrevocably contractually committed to invest, which, depending on the terms and conditions of the contract, could be the date on which the issuer receives the investor's subscription agreement or check.

Item 8. Duration of Offering.

Indicate whether the issuer intends the offering to last for more than one year.

Item 9. Type(s) of Securities Offered.

Select the appropriate type or types of securities offered as to which this notice is filed. If the securities are debt convertible into other securities, however, select "Debt" and any other appropriate types of securities except for "Equity." For purposes of this filing, use the ordinary dictionary and commonly understood meanings of these categories. For instance, equity securities would be securities that represent proportional ownership in an issuer, such as ordinary common and preferred stock of corporations and partnership and limited liability company interests; debt securities would be securities representing money loaned to an issuer that must be repaid to the investor at a later date; pooled investment fund interests would be securities that represent ownership interests in a pooled or collective investment vehicle; tenant-in-common securities would be securities that include an undivided fractional interest in real property other than a mineral property; and mineral property securities would be securities that include an undivided interest in an oil, gas or other mineral property.

Item 10. Business Combination Transaction.

Indicate whether or not the offering is being made in connection with a business combination, such as an exchange (tender) offer or a merger, acquisition, or other transaction of the type described in paragraph (a)(1), (2) or (3) of Rule 145 under the Securities Act of 1933. Do not include an exchange (tender) offer for a class of the issuer's own securities. If necessary to prevent the information supplied from being misleading, also provide a clarification in the space provided.

Item 11. Minimum Investment.

Enter the minimum dollar amount of investment that will be accepted from any outside investor. If the offering provides a minimum investment amount for outside investors that can be waived, provide the lowest amount below which a waiver will not be granted. If there is no minimum investment amount, enter "0." Investors will be considered outside investors if they are not employees, officers, directors, general partners, trustees (where the issuer is a business trust), consultants, advisors or vendors of the issuer, its parents, its majority owned subsidiaries, or majority owned subsidiaries of the issuer's parent.

Item 12. Sales Compensation.

Enter the requested information for each person that has been or will be paid directly or indirectly any commission or other similar compensation in cash or other consideration in connection with sales of securities in the offering, including finders. Enter the CRD number for every person identified and any broker and dealer listed that has a CRD number. CRD numbers can be found at *http://brokercheck.finra.org*. A person that does not have a CRD number need not obtain one in order to be listed, and must be listed when required regardless of whether the person has a CRD number. In addition, enter the State(s) in which the named person has solicited or intends to solicit investors. If more than five persons to be listed are associated persons of the same broker or dealer, enter only the name of the broker or dealer, its CRD number and street address, and the State(s) in which the named person has solicited or intends to solicit investors.

Item 13. Offering and Sales Amounts.

Enter the dollar amount of securities being offered under a claim of federal exemption identified in Item 6 above. Also enter the dollar amount of securities sold in the offering as of the filing date. Select the "Indefinite" box if the amount being offered is undetermined or cannot be calculated at the present time, such as if the offering includes securities to be acquired upon the exercise or exchange of other securities or property and the exercise price or exchange value is not currently known or knowable. If an amount is definite but difficult to calculate without unreasonable effort or expense, provide a good faith estimate. The total offering and sold amounts should include all cash and other consideration to be received for the securities, including cash to be paid in the future under mandatory capital commitments. In offerings for consideration other than cash, the amounts entered should be based on the issuer's good faith valuation of the consideration. If necessary to prevent the information supplied from being misleading, also provide a clarification in the space provided.

Item 14. Investors.

Indicate whether securities in the offering have been or may be sold to persons who do not qualify as accredited investors as defined in Rule 501(a) and provide the number of such investors who already have already invested in the offering. In addition, regardless whether securities in the offering have been or may be sold to persons who do not qualify as accredited investors, specify the total number of investors who already have invested.

Item 15. Sales Commission and Finders' Fees Expenses.

The information on sales commissions and finders' fees expenses may be given as subject to future contingencies.

Item 16. Use of Proceeds.

No additional instructions.

Signature and Submission. An individual who is a duly authorized representative of each issuer identified must sign, date and submit this notice for the issuer. The capacity in which the individual signed should be set forth in the "Title" space. Each individual must:

- sign with a typed signature; and
- manually sign a signature page or other document authenticating, acknowledging or otherwise adopting the signature that appears in typed form in the Form D filing on or before the time of filing the Form D.

Each issuer must:

- retain the manually signed document signed on its behalf for five years; and
- provide a copy of the manually signed document to the SEC or its staff upon request.

Entity Type (for Item 1)

- [ ] Corporation
- [ ] Limited Partnership
- [ ] Limited Liability Company
- [ ] General Partnership
- [ ] Business Trust
- [ ] Other (Specify)

Year of Incorporation/Organization (for Item 1)

- [ ] Yet to Be Formed
- [ ] Within Last Five Years (Specify Year)
- [ ] Over Five Years Ago

Industry Groups (for Item 4)

- [ ] Agriculture
- Banking & Financial Services
  - ○ [ ] Commercial Banking
  - ○ [ ] Insurance
  - ○ [ ] Investing
  - ○ [ ] Investment Banking
  - ○ [ ] Pooled Investment Fund[*]
    - ▪ [ ] Hedge Fund
    - ▪ [ ] Private Equity Fund
    - ▪ [ ] Venture Capital Fund
    - ▪ [ ] Other Investment Fund
  - ○ [ ] Other Banking & Financial Services
- [ ] Business Services Energy
  - ○ [ ] Coal Mining
  - ○ [ ] Electric Utilities
  - ○ [ ] Energy Conservation
  - ○ [ ] Environmental Services
  - ○ [ ] Oil & Gas
  - ○ [ ] Other Energy
- Health Care
  - ○ [ ] Biotechnology
  - ○ [ ] Health Insurance
  - ○ [ ] Hospitals & Physicians
  - ○ [ ] Pharmaceuticals
  - ○ [ ] Other Health Care

- [ ] Manufacturing
- Real Estate
  - o [ ] Commercial
  - o [ ] Construction
  - o [ ] REITS & Finance
  - o [ ] Residential
  - o [ ] Other Real Estate
- [ ] Retailing
- [ ] Restaurants
- Technology
  - o [ ] Computers
  - o [ ] Telecommunications
  - o [ ] Other Technology
- Travel
  - o [ ] Airlines & Airports
  - o [ ] Lodging & Conventions
  - o [ ] Tourism & Travel Services
  - o [ ] Other Travel
- [ ] Other

Footnotes

* If the Pooled Investment Fund checkbox is selected, pop-ups or other features also will require the filer to select one of the lower level checkboxes designating a specific type of investment fund and select a "yes" or "no" checkbox as to whether the filer is registered as an investment company under the Investment Company Act of 1940. If the "Hedge Fund" or "Other Investment Fund" option is selected, the filer will be asked to specify its aggregate net asset value range or to "Decline to Disclose" that value or specify that the information request is "Not Applicable."

**UNITED STATES
SECURITIES AND EXCHANGE COMMISSION**
Washington, D.C. 20549

FORM 144

**NOTICE OF PROPOSED SALE OF SECURITIES
PURSUANT TO RULE 144 UNDER THE SECURITIES ACT OF 1933**

ATTENTION: *Transmit for filing 3 copies of this form concurrently with either placing an order with a broker to execute sale or executing a sale directly with a market maker.*

SEC USE ONLY
DOCUMENT SEQUENCE NO.
CUSIP NUMBER
WORK LOCATION

1(a) NAME OF ISSUER *(Please type or print)*		(b) IRS IDENT. NO.	(c) S.E.C. FILE NO.

1(d) ADDRESS OF ISSUER	STREET	CITY	STATE	ZIP CODE

	(e) TELEPHONE NO.	
	AREA CODE	NUMBER

2(a) NAME OF PERSON FOR WHOSE ACCOUNT THE SECURITIES ARE TO BE SOLD	(b) RELATIONSHIP TO ISSUER

(c) ADDRESS STREET	CITY	STATE	ZIP CODE

INSTRUCTION: The person filing this notice should contact the issuer to obtain the I.R.S. Identification Number and the S.E.C. File Number.

3(a) Title of the Class of Securities To Be Sold	(b) Name and Address of Each Broker Through Whom the Securities are to be Offered or Each Market Maker who is Acquiring the Securities	(c) SEC USE ONLY Broker-Dealer File Number	(c) Number of Shares or Other Units To Be Sold *(See instr. 3(c))*	(d) Aggregate Market Value *(See instr. 3(d))*	(e) Number of Shares or Other Units Outstanding *(See instr. 3(e))*	(f) Approximate Date of Sale *(See instr. 3(f))* (MO. DAY YR.)	(g) Name of Each Securities Exchange *(See instr. 3(g))*

INSTRUCTIONS:

1. (a) Name of issuer
   (b) Issuer's I.R.S. Identification Number
   (c) Issuer's S.E.C. file number, if any
   (d) Issuer's address, including zip code
   (e) Issuer's telephone number, including area code

2. (a) Name of person for whose account the securities are to be sold
   (b) Such person's relationship to the issuer, (e.g., officer, director, 10% stockholder, or member of immediate family of any of the foregoing)
   (c) Such person's address, including zip code

3. (a) Title of the class of securities to be sold
   (b) Name and address of each broker through whom the securities are intended to be sold
   (c) Number of shares or other units to be sold (if debt securities, give the aggregate face amount)
   (d) Aggregate market value of the securities to be sold as of a specified date within 10 days prior to filing of this notice
   (e) Number of shares or other units of the class outstanding, or if debt securities the face amount thereof outstanding, as shown by the most recent report or statement published by the issuer
   (f) Approximate date on which the securities are to be sold
   (g) Name of each securities exchange, if any, on which the securities are intended to be sold

Potential persons who are to respond to the collection of information contained in this form are not required to respond unless the form displays a currently valid OMB control number.

TABLE I—SECURITIES TO BE SOLD

Furnish the following information with respect to the acquisition of the securities to be sold and with respect to the payment of all or any part of the purchase price or other consideration therefor:

Title of the Class	Date you Acquired	Name of Acquisition Transaction	Name of Person from Whom Acquired (If gift, also give date donor acquired)	Amount of Securities Acquired	Date of Payment	Nature of Payment

INSTRUCTIONS: If the securities were purchased and full payment therefor was not made in cash at the time of purchase, explain in the table or in a note thereto the nature of the consideration given. If the consideration consisted of any note or other obligation, or if payment was made in installments describe the arrangement and state when the note or other obligation was discharged in full or the last installment paid.

TABLE II—SECURITIES SOLD DURING THE PAST 3 MONTHS

Furnish the following information as to all securities of the issuer sold during the past 3 months by the person for whose account the securities are so be sold.

Name and Address of Seller	Title of Securities Sold	Date of Sale	Amount of Securities Sold	Gross Proceeds

REMARKS:

INSTRUCTIONS:
See the definition of "person" in paragraph (a) of Rule 144. Information is to be given not only as to the person for whose account the securities are to be sold but also as to all other persons included in that definition. In addition, information shall be given as to sales by all persons whose sales are required by paragraph (e) of Rule 144 to be aggregated with sales for the account of the person filing this notice.

ATTENTION:
The person for whose account the securities to which this notice relates are to be sold hereby represents by signing this notice that he does not know any material adverse information in regard to the current and prospective operations of the Issuer of the securities to be sold which has not been publicly disclosed. If such person has adopted a written trading plan or given trading instructions to satisfy Rule 10b5-1 under the Exchange Act, by signing the form and indicating the date that the plan was adopted or the instruction given, that person makes such representation as of the plan adoption or instruction date.

The notice shall be signed by the person for whose account the securities are to be sold. At least one copy of the notice shall be manually signed. Any copies not manually signed shall bear typed or printed signatures.

_____
(SIGNATURE)

_____
DATE OF NOTICE

_____
DATE OF PLAN ADOPTION OR GIVING OF INSTRUCTION, IF RELYING ON RULE 10B5-1

ATTENTION: Intentional misstatements or omission of facts constitute Federal Criminal Violations (See 18 U.S.C. 1001)

SEC 1147 (04-07)

REGULATION CROWDFUNDING, GENERAL RULES AND REGULATIONS—SELECTED PROVISIONS

17 C.F.R. §§ 227.100 et. seq.

Rule 100. Crowdfunding exemption and requirements

(a) *Exemption.* An issuer may offer or sell securities in reliance on section 4(a)(6) of the Securities Act of 1933 (the "Securities Act") (15 U.S.C. 77d(a)(6)), provided that:

(1) The aggregate amount of securities sold to all investors by the issuer in reliance on section 4(a)(6) of the Securities Act (15 U.S.C. 77d(a)(6)) during the 12-month period preceding the date of such offer or sale, including the securities offered in such transaction, shall not exceed $1,070,000;

(2) The aggregate amount of securities sold to any investor across all issuers in reliance on section 4(a)(6) of the Securities Act (15 U.S.C. 77d(a)(6)) during the 12-month period preceding the date of such transaction, including the securities sold to such investor in such transaction, shall not exceed:

(i) The greater of $2,200 or 5 percent of the lesser of the investor's annual income or net worth if either the investor's annual income or net worth is less than $107,000; or

(ii) 10 percent of the lesser of the investor's annual income or net worth, not to exceed an amount sold of $107,000, if both the investor's annual income and net worth are equal to or more than $107,000;

Instruction 1 to paragraph (a)(2). To determine the investment limit for a natural person, the person's annual income and net worth shall be calculated as those values are calculated for purposes of determining accredited investor status in accordance with § 230.501 of this chapter.

Instruction 2 to paragraph (a)(2). A person's annual income and net worth may be calculated jointly with that person's spouse; however, when such a joint calculation is used, the aggregate investment of the investor spouses may not exceed the limit that would apply to an individual investor at that income or net worth level.

Instruction 3 to paragraph (a)(2). An issuer offering and selling securities in reliance on section 4(a)(6) of the Securities Act (15 U.S.C. 77d(a)(6)) may rely on the efforts of an intermediary required by § 227.303(b) to ensure that the aggregate amount of securities purchased by an investor in offerings pursuant to section 4(a)(6) of the Securities Act will not cause the investor to exceed the limit set forth in section 4(a)(6) of the Securities Act and § 227.100(a)(2), *provided that* the issuer does not know that the investor has exceeded the investor limits or would exceed the investor limits as a result of purchasing securities in the issuer's offering.

(3) The transaction is conducted through an intermediary that complies with the requirements in section 4A(a) of the Securities Act (15 U.S.C. 77d-1(a)) and the related requirements in this part, and the transaction is conducted exclusively through the intermediary's platform; and

Instruction to paragraph (a)(3). An issuer shall not conduct an offering or concurrent offerings in reliance on section 4(a)(6) of the Securities Act of 1933 (15 U.S.C. 77d(a)(6)) using more than one intermediary.

(4) The issuer complies with the requirements in section 4A(b) of the Securities Act (15 U.S.C. 77d-1(b)) and the related requirements in this part; *provided, however,* that the failure to comply with §§ 227.202, 227.203(a)(3) and 227.203(b) shall not prevent an issuer from relying on the exemption provided by section 4(a)(6) of the Securities Act (15 U.S.C. 77d(a)(6)).

(b) *Applicability.* The crowdfunding exemption shall not apply to transactions involving the offer or sale of securities by any issuer that:

(1) Is not organized under, and subject to, the laws of a State or territory of the United States or the District of Columbia;

(2) Is subject to the requirement to file reports pursuant to section 13 or section 15(d) of the Securities Exchange Act of 1934 (the "Exchange Act") (15 U.S.C. 78m or 78o(d));

(3) Is an investment company, as defined in section 3 of the Investment Company Act of 1940 (15 U.S.C. 80a-3), or is excluded from the definition of investment company by section 3(b) or section 3(c) of that Act (15 U.S.C. 80a-3(b) or 80a-3(c));

(4) Is not eligible to offer or sell securities in reliance on section 4(a)(6) of the Securities Act (15 U.S.C. 77d(a)(6)) as a result of a disqualification as specified in § 227.503(a);

(5) Has sold securities in reliance on section 4(a)(6) of the Securities Act (15 U.S.C. 77d(a)(6)) and has not filed with the Commission and provided to investors, to the extent required, the ongoing annual reports required by this part during the two years immediately preceding the filing of the required offering statement; or

Instruction to paragraph (b)(5). An issuer delinquent in its ongoing reports can again rely on section 4(a)(6) of the Securities Act (15 U.S.C. 77d(a)(6)) once it has filed with the Commission and provided to investors both of the annual reports required during the two yearsimmediately preceding the filing of the required offering statement.

(6) Has no specific business plan or has indicated that its business plan is to engage in a merger or acquisition with an unidentified company or companies.

(c) *Issuer.* For purposes of § 227.201(r), calculating aggregate amounts offered and sold in § 227.100(a) and § 227.201(t), and determining whether an issuer has previously sold securities in § 227.201(t)(3), *issuer* includes all entities controlled by or under common control with the issuer and any predecessors of the issuer.

Instruction to paragraph (c). The term *control* means the possession, direct or indirect, of the power to direct or cause the direction of the management and policies of the entity, whether through the ownership of voting securities, by contract or otherwise.

(d) *Investor.* For purposes of this part, *investor* means any investor or any potential investor, as the context requires.

Rule 201. Disclosure requirements

An issuer offering or selling securities in reliance on section 4(a)(6) of the Securities Act (15 U.S.C. 77d(a)(6)) and in accordance with section 4A of the Securities Act (15 U.S.C. 77d-1) and this part must file with the Commission and provide to investors and the relevant intermediary the following information:

(a) The name, legal status (including its form of organization, jurisdiction in which it is organized and date of organization), physical address and Web site of the issuer;

(b) The names of the directors and officers (and any persons occupying a similar status or performing a similar function) of the issuer, all positions and offices with the issuer held by such persons, the period of time in which such persons served in the position or office and their business experience during the past three years, including:

(1) Each person's principal occupation and employment, including whether any officer is employed by another employer; and

(2) The name and principal business of any corporation or other organization in which such occupation and employment took place.

Instruction to paragraph (b). For purposes of this paragraph (b), the term *officer* means a president, vice president, secretary, treasurer or principal financial officer, comptroller or principal accounting officer, and any person routinely performing similar functions.

(c) The name of each person, as of the most recent practicable date but no earlier than 120 days prior to the date the offering statement or report is filed, who is a beneficial owner of 20 percent or more of the issuer's outstanding voting equity securities, calculated on the basis of voting power;

(d) A description of the business of the issuer and the anticipated business plan of the issuer;

(e) The current number of employees of the issuer;

(f) A discussion of the material factors that make an investment in the issuer speculative or risky;

(g) The target offering amount and the deadline to reach the target offering amount, including a statement that if the sum of the investment commitments does not equal or exceed the target offering amount at the offering deadline, no securities will be sold in the offering, investment commitments will be cancelled and committed funds will be returned;

(h) Whether the issuer will accept investments in excess of the target offering amount and, if so, the maximum amount that the issuer will accept and how oversubscriptions will be allocated, such as on a pro-rata, first come-first served, or other basis;

(i) A description of the purpose and intended use of the offering proceeds;

Instruction to paragraph (i). An issuer must provide a reasonably detailed description of any intended use of proceeds, such that investors are provided with enough information to understand how the offering proceeds will be used. If an issuer has identified a range of possible uses, the issuer should identify and describe each probable use and the factors the issuer may consider in allocating proceeds among the potential uses. If the issuer will accept proceeds in excess of the target offering amount, the issuer must describe the purpose, method for allocating oversubscriptions, and intended use of the excess proceeds with similar specificity.

Rule 202. Ongoing reporting requirements

(a) An issuer that has offered and sold securities in reliance on section 4(a)(6) of the Securities Act (15 U.S.C. 77d(a)(6)) and in accordance with section 4A of the Securities Act (15 U.S.C. 77d-1) and this part must file with the Commission and post on the issuer's Web site an annual report along with the financial statements of the issuer certified by the principal executive officer of the issuer to be true and complete in all material respects and a description of the financial condition of the issuer as described in § 227.201(s). If, however, an issuer has available financial statements that have either been reviewed or audited by a public accountant that is independent of the issuer, those financial statements must be provided and the certification by the principal executive officer will not be required. The annual report also must include the disclosure required by paragraphs (a), (b), (c), (d), (e), (f), (m), (p), (q), (r), and (x) of § 227.201. The report must be filed in accordance with the requirements of § 227.203 and Form C (§ 239.900 of this chapter) and no later than 120 days after the end of the fiscal year covered by the report.

Instruction 1 to paragraph (a). Instructions (3), (8), (9), (10), and (11) to paragraph (t) of § 227.201 shall apply for purposes of this section.

Instruction 2 to paragraph (a). An issuer providing financial statements that are not audited or reviewed must have its principal executive officer provide the following certification:

I, [identify the certifying individual], certify that the financial statements of [identify the issuer] included in this Form are true and complete in all material respects.

[Signature and title].

(b) An issuer must continue to comply with the ongoing reporting requirements until one of the following occurs:

(1) The issuer is required to file reports under section 13(a) or section 15(d) of the Exchange Act (15 U.S.C. 78m(a) or 78o(d));

(2) The issuer has filed, since its most recent sale of securities pursuant to this part, at least one annual report pursuant to this section and has fewer than 300 holders of record;

(3) The issuer has filed, since its most recent sale of securities pursuant to this part, the annual reports required pursuant to this section for at least the three most recent years and has total assets that do not exceed $10,000,000;

(4) The issuer or another party repurchases all of the securities issued in reliance on section 4(a)(6) of the Securities Act (15 U.S.C. 77d(a)(6)), including any payment in full of debt securities or any complete redemption of redeemable securities; or

(5) The issuer liquidates or dissolves its business in accordance with state law.

(c) [Expired October 29, 2018. See SEC Release No. 33-10556; September 19, 2018.]

Rule 203. Filing requirements and form

(a) *Form C—Offering statement and amendments* (§ 239.900 of this chapter).

(1) *Offering statement.* An issuer offering or selling securities in reliance on section 4(a)(6) of the Securities Act (15 U.S.C. 77d(a)(6)) and in accordance with section 4A of

the Securities Act (15 U.S.C. 77d-1) and this part must file with the Commission and provide to investors and the relevant intermediary a Form C: Offering Statement (Form C) (§ 239.900 of this chapter) prior to the commencement of the offering of securities. The Form C must include the information required by § 227.201.

(2) *Amendments to offering statement.* An issuer must file with the Commission and provide to investors and the relevant intermediary an amendment to the offering statement filed on Form C (§ 239.900 of this chapter) to disclose any material changes, additions or updates to information that it provides to investors through the intermediary's platform, for any offering that has not yet been completed or terminated. The amendment must be filed on Form C: Amendment (Form C/A) (§ 239.900 of this chapter), and if the amendment reflects material changes, additions or updates, the issuer shall check the box indicating that investors must reconfirm an investment commitment within five business days or the investor's commitment will be considered cancelled.

(3) *Progress updates.*

(i) An issuer must file with the Commission and provide to investors and the relevant intermediary a Form C: Progress Update (Form C-U) (§ 239.900 of this chapter) to disclose its progress in meeting the target offering amount no later than five business days after each of the dates when the issuer reaches 50 percent and 100 percent of the target offering amount.

(ii) If the issuer will accept proceeds in excess of the target offering amount, the issuer must file with the Commission and provide to investors and the relevant intermediary, no later than five business days after the offering deadline, a final Form C-U (§ 239.900 of this chapter) to disclose the total amount of securities sold in the offering.

(iii) The requirements of paragraphs (a)(3)(i) and (ii) of this section shall not apply to an issuer if the relevant intermediary makes publicly available on the intermediary's platform frequent updates regarding the progress of the issuer in meeting the target offering amount; however, the issuer must still file a Form C-U (§ 239.900 of this chapter) to disclose the total amount of securities sold in the offering no later than five business days after the offering deadline.

Instruction to paragraph (a)(3). If multiple Forms C-U (§ 239.900 of this chapter) are triggered within the same five business day period, the issuer may consolidate such progress updates into one Form C-U, so long as the Form C-U discloses the most recent threshold that was met and the Form C-U is filed with the Commission and provided to investors and the relevant intermediary by the day on which the first progress update is due.

Instruction 1 to paragraph (a). An issuer would satisfy the requirement to provide to the relevant intermediary the information required by this paragraph (a) if it provides to the relevant intermediary a copy of the disclosures filed with the Commission.

Instruction 2 to paragraph (a). An issuer would satisfy the requirement to provide to investors the information required by this paragraph (a) if the issuer refers investors to the information on the intermediary's platform by means of a posting on the issuer's Web site or by email.

(b) *Form C: Annual report and termination of reporting* (§ 239.900 of this chapter). (1) *Annual reports.* An issuer that has sold securities in reliance on section 4(a)(6) of the Securities Act (15 U.S.C. 77d(a)(6)) and in accordance with section 4A of the Securities Act (15 U.S.C. 77d-1) and this part must file an annual report on Form C: Annual Report (Form C-AR) (§ 239.900 of this chapter) with the Commission no later than 120 days after the end of the fiscal year covered by the report. The annual report shall include the information required by § 227.202(a).

(1) Annual Reports. An issuer that has sold securities in reliance on section 4(a)(6) of the Securities Act (15 U.S.C. 77d(a)(6)) and in accordance with section 4A of the Securities Act (15 U.S.C. 77d-1) and this part must file an annual report on Form C: Annual Report (Form C-AR) (§ 239.900 of this chapter) with the Commission no later than 120 days after the end of the fiscal year covered by the report. The annual report shall include the information required by § 227.202(a).

(2) *Amendments to annual report.* An issuer must file with the Commission an amendment to the annual report filed on Form C: Annual Report (Form C-AR) (§ 239.900 of this chapter) to make a material change to the previously filed annual report as soon as practicable after discovery of the need for the material change. The amendment must be filed on Form C: Amendment to Annual Report (Form C-AR/A) (§ 239.900 of this chapter).

(3) *Termination of reporting.* An issuer eligible to terminate its obligation to file annual reports with the Commission pursuant to § 227.202(b) must file with the Commission, within five business days from the date on which the issuer becomes eligible to terminate its reporting obligation, Form C: Termination of Reporting (Form C-TR) (§ 239.900 of this chapter) to advise investors that the issuer will cease reporting pursuant to this part.

Rule 204. Advertising

(a) An issuer may not, directly or indirectly, advertise the terms of an offering made in reliance on section 4(a)(6) of the Securities Act (15 U.S.C. 77d(a)(6)), except for notices that meet the requirements of paragraph (b) of this section.

Instruction to paragraph (a). For purposes of this paragraph (a), *issuer* includes persons acting on behalf of the issuer.

(b) A notice may advertise any of the terms of an issuer's offering made in reliance on section 4(a)(6) of the Securities Act (15 U.S.C. 77d(a)(6)) if it directs investors to the intermediary's platform and includes no more than the following information:

(1) A statement that the issuer is conducting an offering pursuant to section 4(a)(6) of the Securities Act (15 U.S.C. 77d(a)(6)), the name of the intermediary through which the offering is being conducted and a link directing the potential investor to the intermediary's platform;

(2) The terms of the offering; and

(3) Factual information about the legal identity and business location of the issuer, limited to the name of the issuer of the security, the address, phone number and Web site of the issuer, the email address of a representative of the issuer and a brief description of the business of the issuer.

(c) Notwithstanding the prohibition on advertising any of the terms of the offering, an issuer, and persons acting on behalf of the issuer, may communicate with investors and potential investors about the terms of the offering through communication channels provided by the intermediary on the intermediary's platform, provided that an issuer identifies itself as the issuer in all communications. Persons acting on behalf of the issuer must identify their affiliation with the issuer in all communications on the intermediary's platform.

Instruction to § 227.204. For purposes of this section, *terms of the offering* means the amount of securities offered, the nature of the securities, the price of the securities and the closing date of the offering period.

Rule 205. Promoter compensation

(a) An issuer, or person acting on behalf of the issuer, shall be permitted to compensate or commit to compensate, directly or indirectly, any person to promote the issuer's offerings made in reliance on section 4(a)(6) of the Securities Act (15 U.S.C. 77d(a)(6)) through communication channels provided by an intermediary on the intermediary's platform, but only if the issuer or person acting on behalf of the issuer, takes reasonable steps to ensure that the person promoting the offering clearly discloses the receipt, past or prospective, of such compensation with any such communication.

Instruction to paragraph (a). The disclosure required by this paragraph is required, with each communication, for persons engaging in promotional activities on behalf of the issuer through the communication channels provided by the intermediary, regardless of whether or not the compensation they receive is specifically for the promotional activities. This includes persons hired specifically to promote the offering as well as to persons who are otherwise employed by the issuer or who undertake promotional activities on behalf of the issuer.

(b) Other than as set forth in paragraph (a) of this section, an issuer or person acting on behalf of the issuer shall not compensate or commit to compensate, directly or indirectly, any person to promote the issuer's offerings made in reliance on section 4(a)(6) of the Securities Act (15 U.S.C. 77d(a)(6)), unless such promotion is limited to notices permitted by, and in compliance with, § 227.204.

Rule 300. Intermediaries

(a) *Requirements.* A person acting as an intermediary in a transaction involving the offer or sale of securities in reliance on section 4(a)(6) of the Securities Act (15 U.S.C. 77d(a)(6)) must:

(1) Be registered with the Commission as a broker under section 15(b) of the Exchange Act (15 U.S.C. 78 *o* (b)) or as a funding portal in accordance with the requirements of § 227.400; and

(2) Be a member a national securities association registered under section 15A of the Exchange Act (15 U.S.C. 78 *o*-3).

(b) *Financial interests.* Any director, officer or partner of an intermediary, or any person occupying a similar status or performing a similar function, may not have a financial interest in an issuer that is offering or selling securities in reliance on section 4(a)(6) of the Securities Act (15 U.S.C. 77d(a)(6)) through the intermediary's platform, or receive a financial interest in an issuer as compensation for the services provided to or for the benefit of the issuer in connection with the offer or sale of such securities. An intermediary may not have a financial interest in an issuer that is offering or selling securities in reliance on section 4(a)(6) of the Securities Act (15 U.S.C. 77d(a)(6)) through the intermediary's platform unless:

(1) The intermediary receives the financial interest from the issuer as compensation for the services provided to, or for the benefit of, the issuer in connection with the offer or sale of the securities being offered or sold in reliance on section 4(a)(6) of the Securities Act (15 U.S.C. 77d(a)(6)) through the intermediary's platform; and

(2) the financial interest consists of securities of the same class and having the same terms, conditions and rights as the securities being offered or sold in reliance on section 4(a)(6) of the Securities Act (15 U.S.C. 77d(a)(6)) through the intermediary's platform. For purposes of this paragraph, a *financial interest in an issuer* means a direct or indirect ownership of, or economic interest in, any class of the issuer's securities.

(c) *Definitions.* For purposes of this part:

(1) *Associated person of a funding portal* or *person associated with a funding portal* means any partner, officer, director or manager of a funding portal (or any person occupying a similar status or performing similar functions), any person directly orindirectly controlling or controlled by such funding portal, or any employee of a funding portal, except that any person associated with a funding portal whose functions are solely clerical or ministerial shall not be included in the meaning of such term for purposes of section 15(b) of the Exchange Act (15 U.S.C. 78 *o* (b)) (other than paragraphs (4) and (6) of section 15(b) of the Exchange Act).

(2) *Funding portal* means a broker acting as an intermediary in a transaction involving the offer or sale of securities in reliance on section 4(a)(6) of the Securities Act (15 U.S.C. 77d(a)(6)), that does not:

(i) Offer investment advice or recommendations;

(ii) Solicit purchases, sales or offers to buy the securities displayed on its platform;

(iii) Compensate employees, agents, or other persons for such solicitation or based on the sale of securities displayed or referenced on its platform; or

(iv) Hold, manage, possess, or otherwise handle investor funds or securities.

(3) *Intermediary* means a broker registered under section 15(b) of the Exchange Act (15 U.S.C. 78 *o* (b)) or a funding portal registered under § 227.400 and includes, where relevant, an associated person of the registered broker or registered funding portal.

(4) *Platform* means a program or application accessible via the Internet or other similar electronic communication medium through which a registered broker or a registered funding portal acts as an intermediary in a transaction involving the offer or sale of securities in reliance on section 4(a)(6) of the Securities Act (15 U.S.C. 77d(a)(6)).

Instruction to paragraph (c)(4). An intermediary through which a crowdfunding transaction is conducted may engage in back office or other administrative functions other than on the intermediary's platform.

Rule 301. Measures to reduce risk of fraud

An intermediary in a transaction involving the offer or sale of securities in reliance on section 4(a)(6) of the Securities Act (15 U.S.C. 77d(a)(6)) must:

(a) Have a reasonable basis for believing that an issuer seeking to offer and sell securities in reliance on section 4(a)(6) of the Securities Act (15 U.S.C. 77d(a)(6)) through the intermediary's platform complies with the requirements in section 4A(b) of the Act (15 U.S.C. 77d-1(b)) and the related requirements in this part. In satisfying this requirement, an intermediary may rely on the representations of the issuer concerning compliance with these requirements unless the intermediary has reason to question the reliability of those representations;

(b) Have a reasonable basis for believing that the issuer has established means to keep accurate records of the holders of the securities it would offer and sell through the intermediary's platform, provided that an intermediary may rely on the representations of the issuer concerning its means of recordkeeping unless the intermediary has reason to question the reliability of those representations. An intermediary will be deemed to have satisfied this requirement if the issuer has engaged the services of a transfer agent that is registered under Section 17A of the Exchange Act (15 U.S.C. 78q-1(c)).

(c) Deny access to its platform to an issuer if the intermediary:

(1) Has a reasonable basis for believing that the issuer or any of its officers, directors (or any person occupying a similar status or performing a similar function) or beneficial owners of 20 percent or more of the issuer's outstanding voting equity securities, calculated on the basis of voting power, is subject to a disqualification under § 227.503. In satisfying this requirement, an intermediary must, at a minimum, conduct a background and securities enforcement regulatory history check on each issuer whose securities are to be offered by the intermediary and on each officer, director or beneficial owner of 20 percent or more of the issuer's outstanding voting equity securities, calculated on the basis of voting power.

(2) Has a reasonable basis for believing that the issuer or the offering presents the potential for fraud or otherwise raises concerns about investor protection. In satisfying this requirement, an intermediary must deny access if it reasonably believes that it is unable to adequately or effectively assess the risk of fraud of the issuer or its potential offering. In addition, if an intermediary becomes aware of information after it has granted access that causes it to reasonably believe that the issuer or the offering presents the potential for fraud or otherwise raises concerns about investor protection, the intermediary must promptly remove the offering from its platform, cancel the offering, and return (or, for funding portals, direct the return of) any funds that have been committed by investors in the offering.

Rule 302. Account opening

(a) *Accounts and Electronic Delivery.*

(1) No intermediary or associated person of an intermediary may accept an investment commitment in a transaction involving the offer or sale of securities in reliance on section 4(a)(6) of the Securities Act (15 U.S.C. 77d(a)(6)) until the investor has opened an account with the intermediary and the intermediary has obtained from the investor consent to electronic delivery of materials.

(2) An intermediary must provide all information that is required to be provided by the intermediary under subpart C (§ § 227.300 through 227.305), including, but not limited to, educational materials, notices and confirmations, through electronic means. Unless otherwise indicated in the relevant rule of subpart C, in satisfying this requirement, an intermediary must provide the information through an electronic message that contains the information, through an electronic message that includes a specific link to the information as posted on intermediary's platform, or through an electronic message that provides notice of what the information is and that it is located on the intermediary's platform or on the issuer's Web site. Electronic messages include, but are not limited to, email, social media messages, instant messages or other electronic media messages.

(b) *Educational Materials.*

(1) In connection with establishing an account for an investor, an intermediary must deliver educational materials to such investor that explain in plain language and are otherwise designed to communicate effectively and accurately:

(i) The process for the offer, purchase and issuance of securities through the intermediary and the risks associated with purchasing securities offered and sold in reliance on section 4(a)(6) of the Securities Act (15 U.S.C. 77d(a)(6));

(ii) The types of securities offered and sold in reliance on section 4(a)(6) of the Securities Act (15 U.S.C. 77d(a)(6)) available for purchase on the intermediary's platform and the risks associated with each type of security, including the risk of having limited voting power as a result of dilution;

(iii) The restrictions on the resale of a security offered and sold in reliance on section 4(a)(6) of the Securities Act (15 U.S.C. 77d(a)(6));

(iv) The types of information that an issuer is required to provide under § 227.202, the frequency of the delivery of that information and the possibility that those obligations may terminate in the future;

(v) The limitations on the amounts an investor may invest pursuant to § 227.100(a)(2);

(vi) The limitations on an investor's right to cancel an investment commitment and the circumstances in which an investment commitment may be cancelled by the issuer;

(vii) The need for the investor to consider whether investing in a security offered and sold in reliance on Section 4(a)(6) of the Securities Act (15 U.S.C. 77d(a)(6)) is appropriate for that investor;

(viii) That following completion of an offering conducted through the intermediary, there may or may not be any ongoing relationship between the issuer and intermediary; and

(ix) That under certain circumstances an issuer may cease to publish annual reports and, therefore, an investor may not continually have current financial information about the issuer.

(2) An intermediary must make the most current version of its educational material available on its platform at all times and, if at any time, the intermediary makes a material revision to its educational materials, it must make the revised educational materials available to all investors before accepting any additional investment commitments or effecting any further transactions in securities offered and sold in reliance on section 4(a)(6) of the Securities Act (15 U.S.C. 77d(a)(6)).

(c) *Promoters.* In connection with establishing an account for an investor, an intermediary must inform the investor that any person who promotes an issuer's offering for compensation, whether past or prospective, or who is a founder or an employee of an issuer that engages in promotional activities on behalf of the issuer on the intermediary's platform, must clearly disclose in all communications on the intermediary's platform, respectively, the receipt of the compensation and that he or she is engaging in promotional activities on behalf of the issuer.

(d) *Compensation Disclosure.* When establishing an account for an investor, an intermediary must clearly disclose the manner in which the intermediary is compensated in connection with offerings and sales of securities in reliance on section 4(a)(6) of the Securities Act (15 U.S.C. 77d(a)(6)).

Rule 303. Requirements with respect to transactions

(a) *Issuer information.* An intermediary in a transaction involving the offer or sale of securities in reliance on section 4(a)(6) of the Securities Act (15 U.S.C. 77d(a)(6)) must make available to the Commission and to investors any information required to be provided by the issuer of the securities under §§ 227.201 and 227.203(a).

(1) This information must be made publicly available on the intermediary's platform, in a manner that reasonably permits a person accessing the platform to save, download, or otherwise store the information;

(2) This information must be made publicly available on the intermediary's platform for a minimum of 21 days before any securities are sold in the offering, during which time the intermediary may accept investment commitments;

(3) This information, including any additional information provided by the issuer, must remain publicly available on the intermediary's platform until the offer and sale of securities in reliance on section 4(a)(6) of the Securities Act (15 U.S.C. 77d(a)(6)) is completed or cancelled; and

(4) An intermediary may not require any person to establish an account with the intermediary to access this information.

(b) *Investor qualification.* Each time before accepting any investment commitment (including any additional investment commitment from the same person), an intermediary must:

(1) Have a reasonable basis for believing that the investor satisfies the investment limitations established by section 4(a)(6)(B) of the Act (15 U.S.C. 77d(a)(6)(B)) and this part. An intermediary may rely on an investor's representations concerning compliance with the investment limitation requirements concerning the investor's annual income, net worth, and the amount of the investor's other investments made pursuant to section 4(a)(6) of the Securities Act (15 U.S.C. 77d(a)(6)) unless the intermediary has reason to question the reliability of the representation.

(2) Obtain from the investor:

(i) A representation that the investor has reviewed the intermediary's educational materials delivered pursuant to § 227.302(b), understands that the entire amount of his or her investment may be lost, and is in a financial condition to bear the loss of the investment; and

(ii) A questionnaire completed by the investor demonstrating the investor's understanding that:

(A) There are restrictions on the investor's ability to cancel an investment commitment and obtain a return of his or her investment;

(B) It may be difficult for the investor to resell securities acquired in reliance on section 4(a)(6) of the Securities Act (15 U.S.C. 77d(a)(6)); and

(C) Investing in securities offered and sold in reliance on section 4(a)(6) of the Securities Act (15 U.S.C. 77d(a)(6)) involves risk, and the investor should not invest any funds in an offering made in reliance on section 4(a)(6) of the Securities Act unless he or she can afford to lose the entire amount of his or her investment.

(c) *Communication channels.* An intermediary must provide on its platform communication channels by which persons can communicate with one another and with representatives of the issuer about offerings made available on the intermediary's platform, provided:

(1) If the intermediary is a funding portal, it does not participate in these communications other than to establish guidelines for communication and remove abusive or potentially fraudulent communications;

(2) The intermediary permits public access to view the discussions made in the communication channels;

(3) The intermediary restricts posting of comments in the communication channels to those persons who have opened an account with the intermediary on its platform; and

(4) The intermediary requires that any person posting a comment in the communication channels clearly and prominently disclose with each posting whether he or she is a founder or an employee of an issuer engaging in promotional activities on behalf of the issuer, or is otherwise compensated, whether in the past or prospectively, to promote the issuer's offering.

Rule 304. Completion of offerings, cancellations and reconfirmations

(a) *Generally.* An investor may cancel an investment commitment for any reason until 48 hours prior to the deadline identified in the issuer's offering materials. During the 48 hours prior to such deadline, an investment commitment may not be cancelled except as provided in paragraph (c) of this section.

(b) *Early completion of offering.* If an issuer reaches the target offering amount prior to the deadline identified in its offering materials pursuant to § 227.201(g), the issuer may close the offering on a date earlier than the deadline identified in its offering materials pursuant to § 227.201(g), *provided that:*

(1) The offering remains open for a minimum of 21 days pursuant to § 227.303(a);

(2) The intermediary provides notice to any potential investors, and gives or sends notice to investors that have made investment commitments in the offering, of:

(i) The new, anticipated deadline of the offering;

(ii) The right of investors to cancel investment commitments for any reason until 48 hours prior to the new offering deadline; and

(iii) Whether the issuer will continue to accept investment commitments during the 48-hour period prior to the new offering deadline.

(3) The new offering deadline is scheduled for and occurs at least five business days after the notice required in paragraph (b)(2) of this section is provided; and

(4) At the time of the new offering deadline, the issuer continues to meet or exceed the target offering amount.

(c) *Cancellations and reconfirmations based on material changes.*

(1) If there is a material change to the terms of an offering or to the information provided by the issuer, the intermediary must give or send to any investor who has made an investment commitment notice of the material change and that the investor's investment commitment will be cancelled unless the investor reconfirms his or her investment commitment within five business days of receipt of the notice. If the investor fails to reconfirm his or her investment within those five business days, the intermediary within five business days thereafter must:

(i) Give or send the investor a notification disclosing that the commitment was cancelled, the reason for the cancellation and the refund amount that the investor is expected to receive; and

(ii) Direct the refund of investor funds.

(2) If material changes to the offering or to the information provided by the issuer regarding the offering occur within five business days of the maximum number of days that an offering is to remain open, the offering must be extended to allow for a period of five business days for the investor to reconfirm his or her investment.

(d) *Return of funds if offering is not completed.* If an issuer does not complete an offering, an intermediary must within five business days:

(1) Give or send each investor a notification of the cancellation, disclosing the reason for the cancellation, and the refund amount that the investor is expected to receive;

(2) Direct the refund of investor funds; and

(3) Prevent investors from making investment commitments with respect to that offering on its platform.

Rule 401. Exemption

A funding portal that is registered with the Commission pursuant to § 227.400 is exempt from the broker registration requirements of section 15(a)(1) of the Exchange Act (15 U.S.C. 78 *o* (a)(1)) in connection with its activities as a funding portal.

Rule 402. Conditional safe harbor

(a) *General.* Under section 3(a)(80) of the Exchange Act (15 U.S.C. 78c(a)(80)), a funding portal acting as an intermediary in a transaction involving the offer or sale of securities in reliance on section 4(a)(6) of the Securities Act (15 U.S.C. 77d(a)(6)) may not: offer investment advice or recommendations; solicit purchases, sales, or offers to buy the securities offered or displayed on its platform or portal; compensate employees, agents, or other persons for such solicitation or based on the sale of securities displayed or referenced on its platform or portal; hold, manage, possess, or otherwise handle investor funds or securities; or engage in such other activities as the Commission, by rule, determines appropriate. This section is intended to provide clarity with respect to the ability of a funding portal to engage in certain activities, consistent with the prohibitions under section 3(a)(80) of the Exchange Act. No presumption shall arise that a funding portal has violated the prohibitions under section 3(a)(80) of the Exchange Act or this part by reason of the funding portal or its associated persons engaging in activities in connection with the offer or sale of securities in reliance on section 4(a)(6) of the Securities Act that do not meet the conditions specified in paragraph (b) of this section. The antifraud provisions and all other applicable provisions of the federal securities laws continue to apply to the activities described in paragraph (b) of this section.

Rule 501. Restrictions on resales

(a) Securities issued in a transaction exempt from registration pursuant to section 4(a)(6) of the Securities Act (15 U.S.C. 77d(a)(6)) and in accordance with section 4A of the Securities Act (15 U.S.C. 77d-1) and this part may not be transferred by any purchaser of such securities during the one-year period beginning when the securities were issued in a transaction exempt from registration pursuant to section 4(a)(6) of the Securities Act (15 U.S.C. 77d(a)(6)), unless such securities are transferred:

(1) To the issuer of the securities;

(2) To an accredited investor;

(3) As part of an offering registered with the Commission; or

(4) To a member of the family of the purchaser or the equivalent, to a trust controlled by the purchaser, to a trust created for the benefit of a member of the family of the purchaser or the equivalent, or in connection with the death or divorce of the purchaser or other similar circumstance.

(b) For purposes of this § 227.501, the term *accredited investor* shall mean any person who comes within any of the categories set forth in § 230.501(a) of this chapter, or who the seller reasonably believes comes within any of such categories, at the time of the sale of the securities to that person.

(c) For purposes of this section, the term *member of the family of the purchaser or the equivalent* includes a child, stepchild, grandchild, parent, stepparent, grandparent, spouse or spousal equivalent, sibling, mother-in-law, father-in-law, son-in-law, daughter-in-law, brother-in-law, or sister-in-law of the purchaser, and shall include adoptive relationships. For purposes of this paragraph (c), the term *spousal equivalent* means a cohabitant occupying a relationship generally equivalent to that of a spouse.

Rule 502. Insignificant deviations from a term, condition or requirement of this part (Regulation Crowdfunding)

(a) A failure to comply with a term, condition, or requirement of this part will not result in the loss of the exemption from the requirements of Section 5 of the Securities Act (15 U.S.C. 77e) for any offer or sale to a particular individual or entity, if the issuer relying on the exemption shows:

(1) The failure to comply was insignificant with respect to the offering as a whole;

(2) The issuer made a good faith and reasonable attempt to comply with all applicable terms, conditions and requirements of this part; and

(3) The issuer did not know of such failure where the failure to comply with a term, condition or requirement of this part was the result of the failure of the intermediary to comply with the requirements of section 4A(a) of the Securities Act (15 U.S.C. 77d-1(a)) and the related rules, or such failure by the intermediary occurred solely in offerings other than the issuer's offering.

(b) Paragraph (a) of this section shall not preclude the Commission from bringing an enforcement action seeking any appropriate relief for an issuer's failure to comply with all applicable terms, conditions and requirements of this part.

SECURITIES EXCHANGE ACT OF 1934—SELECTED PROVISIONS

15 U.S.C. §§ 78a et seq.

N.B. The following is not a complete text of the Securities Exchange Act of 1934. It omits a number of statutory provisions entirely, and also omits certain subsections of provisions that are partially included.

Section	15 U.S.C. Section	Subject
1	78a	Short title
2	78b	Necessity for regulation as provided in this title
3(a)	78c	Definitions and application of title
(1)		Exchange
(4)		Broker
(5)		Dealer
(7)		Director
(8)		Issuer
(9)		Person
(10)		Security
(11)		Equity security
(12)		Exempted security or exempted securities
(13)		Buy, purchase
(14)		Sale, sell
(17)		Interstate commerce
(18)		Person associated with a broker or dealer
(26)		Self-regulatory organization
(29)		Municipal securities
(30)		Municipal securities dealer
(31)		Municipal securities broker
(37)		Records
(38)		Market maker
(39)		Statutory disqualification
(42)		Government securities
(51)		Penny stock
(58)		Audit committee
(65)		Eligible Contract Participant
(66)		Major Swap Participant
(67)		Major Security-Based Swap Participant
(68)		Security-Based Swap
(69)		Swap
(70)		Person Associated With a Security-Based Swap Dealer or Major Security-Based Swap Participant
(71)		Security-Based Swap Dealer
(72)		Appropriate Federal Banking Agency
(73)		Board
(74)		Prudential Regulator
(75)		Security-Based Swap Data Repository

TITLE I
Regulation of Securities Exchanges

Sec. 1. SHORT TITLE

This Act may be cited as the "Securities Exchange Act of 1934."

Sec. 2. NECESSITY FOR REGULATION AS PROVIDED IN THIS TITLE

For the reasons hereinafter enumerated, transactions in securities as commonly conducted upon securities exchanges and over-the-counter markets are effected with a national public interest which makes it necessary to provide for regulation and control of such transactions and of practices and matters related thereto, including transactions by officers, directors, and principal security holders, to require appropriate reports, to remove impediments to and perfect the mechanisms of a national market system for securities and a national system for the clearance and settlement of securities transactions and the safeguarding of securities and funds related thereto, and to impose requirements necessary to make such regulation and control reasonably complete and effective, in order to protect interstate commerce, the national credit, the Federal taxing power, to protect and make more effective the national banking system and Federal Reserve System, and to insure the maintenance of fair and honest markets in such transactions:

(1) Such transactions (a) are carried on in large volume by the public generally and in large part originate outside the States in which the exchanges and over-the-counter markets are located and/or are effected by means of the mails and instrumentalities of interstate commerce; (b) constitute an important part of the current of interstate commerce; (c) involve in large part the securities of issuers engaged in interstate commerce; (d) involve the use of credit, directly affect the financing of trade, industry, and transportation in interstate commerce, and directly affect and influence the volume of interstate commerce; and affect the national credit.

(2) The prices established and offered in such transactions are generally disseminated and quoted throughout the United States and foreign countries and constitute a basis for determining and establishing the prices at which securities are bought and sold, the amount of certain taxes owing to the United States and to the several States by owners, buyers, and sellers of securities, and the value of collateral for bank loans.

(3) Frequently the prices of securities on such exchanges and markets are susceptible to manipulation and control, and the dissemination of such prices gives rise to excessive speculation, resulting in sudden and unreasonanble fluctuations in the prices of securities which (a) cause alternately unreasonable expansion and unreasonable contraction of the volume of credit available for trade, transportation, and industry in interstate commerce, (b) hinder the proper appraisal of the value of securities and thus prevent a fair calculation of taxes owing to the United States and to the several States by owners, buyers, and sellers of securities, and (c) prevent the fair valuation of collateral for bank loans and/or obstruct the effective operation of the national banking system and Federal Reserve System.

(4) National emergencies, which produce widespread unemployment and the dislocation of trade, transportation, and industry, and which burden interstate commerce and adversely affect the general welfare, are precipitated, intensified, and prolonged by manipulation and sudden and unreasonable fluctuations of security prices and by excessive speculation on such exchanges and markets, and to meet such emergencies the Federal Government is put to such great expense as to burden the national credit.

Sec. 3. DEFINITIONS AND APPLICATION OF TITLE

(a) When used in this title, unless the context otherwise requires—

(1) [Exchange]

The term "exchange" means any organization, association, or group of persons, whether incorporated or unincorporated, which constitutes, maintains, or provides a market place or facilities for bringing together purchasers and sellers of securities or for otherwise performing with respect to securities the functions commonly performed by a stock exchange as that term is generally understood, and includes the market place and the market facilities maintained by such exchange.

(4) [Broker]

(A) IN GENERAL.—The term "broker" means any person engaged in the business of effecting transactions in securities for the account of others.

(5) [Dealer]

(A) IN GENERAL.—The term "dealer" means any person engaged in the business of buying and selling securities (not including security-based swaps, other than security-based swaps with or for persons that are not eligible contract participants) for such person's own account through a broker or otherwise.

(B) EXCEPTION FOR PERSON NOT ENGAGED IN THE BUSINESS OF DEAL-ING.—The term "dealer" does not include a person that buys or sells securities (not including security-based swaps, other than security-based swaps with or for persons that are not eligible contract participants) for such person's own account, either individually or in a fiduciary capacity, but not as a part of a regular business.

(7) [Director]

The term "director" means any director of a corporation or any person performing similar functions with respect to any organization, whether incorporated or unincorporated.

(8) [Issuer]

The term "issuer" means any person who issues or proposes to issue any security; except that with respect to certificates of deposit for securities, voting-trust certificates, or collateral-trust certificates, or with respect to certificates of interest or shares in an unincorporated investment trust not having a board of directors or of the fixed, restricted management, or unit type, the term "issuer" means the person or persons performing the acts and assuming the duties of depositor or manager pursuant to the provisions of the trust or other agreement or instrument under which such securities are issued; and except that with respect to equipment-trust certificates or like securities, the term "issuer" means the person by whom the equipment or property is, or is to be, used.

(9) [Person]

The term "person" means a natural person, company, government, or political subdivision, agency, or instrumentality of a government.

(10) [Security]

The term "security" means any note, stock, treasury stock, security future, security-based swap, bond, debenture, certificate of interest or participation in any profit-sharing agreement or in any oil, gas, or other mineral royalty or lease, any collateral-trust certificate, preorganization certificate or subscription, transferable share, investment contract, voting-trust certificate, certificate of deposit for a security, any put, call, straddle, option, or privilege on any security, certificate of deposit, or group or index of securities (including any interest therein or based on the value thereof), or any put, call, straddle, option, or privilege entered into on a national securities exchange relating to foreign currency, or in general, any instrument commonly known as a "security"; or any certificate of interest or participation in, temporary or interim certificate for, receipt for, or warrant or right to subscribe to or purchase, any of the foregoing; but shall not include currency or any note, draft, bill of exchange, or banker's acceptance which has a maturity at the time of issuance of not exceeding nine months, exclusive of days of grace, or any renewal thereof the maturity of which is likewise limited.

(11) [Equity Security]

The term "equity security" means any stock or similar security; or any security future on any such security; or any security convertible, with or without consideration, into such a security, or carrying any warrant or right to subscribe to or purchase such a security; or any such warrant or right; or any other security which the Commission shall deem to be of similar nature and consider necessary or appropriate, by such rules and regulations as it may prescribe in the public interest or for the protection of investors, to treat as an equity security.

(12) [Exempted Security or Exempted Securities]

(A) The term "exempted security" or "exempted securities" includes—

(i) government securities, as defined in paragraph (42) of this subsection;

(ii) municipal securities, as defined in paragraph (29) of this subsection;

(iii) any interest or participation in any common trust fund or similar fund that is excluded from the definition of the term 'investment company' under section 3(c)(3) of the Investment Company Act of 1940;

(iv) any interest or participation in a single trust fund, or a collective trust fund maintained by a bank, or any security arising out of a contract issued by an insurance company, which interest, participation, or security is issued in connection with a qualified plan as defined in subparagraph (C) of this paragraph;

(v) any security issued by or any interest or participation in any pooled income fund, collective trust fund, collective investment fund, or similar fund that is excluded from the definition of an investment company under section 3(c)(10)(B) of the Investment Company Act of 1940;

(vi) solely for purposes of sections 12, 13, 14, and 16 of this title, any security issued by or any interest or participation in any church plan, company, or account that is excluded from the definition of an investment company under section 3(c)(14) of the Investment Company Act of 1940; and

(vii) such other securities (which may include, among others, unregistered securities, the market in which is predominantly intrastate) as the Commission may, by such rules and regulations as it deems consistent with the public interest and the protection of investors, either unconditionally or upon specified terms and conditions or for stated periods, exempt from the operation of any one or more provisions of this title which by their terms do not apply to an "exempted security" or to "exempted securities."

(B)(i) Notwithstanding subparagraph (A)(i) of this paragraph, government securities shall not be deemed to be "exempted securities" for the purposes of section 17A of this title.

(ii) Notwithstanding subparagraph (A)(ii) of this paragraph, municipal securities shall not be deemed to be "exempted securities" for the purposes of sections 15 and 17A of this title.

(C) For purposes of subparagraph (A)(iv) of this paragraph, the term "qualified plan" means (i) a stock bonus, pension, or profit-sharing plan which meets the requirements for qualification under section 401 of the Internal Revenue Code of 1954, (ii) an annuity plan which meets the requirements for the deduction of the employer's contribution under section 404(a)(2) of such Code, or (iii) a governmental plan as defined in section 414(d) of such Code which has been established by an employer for the exclusive benefit of its employees or their beneficiaries for the purpose of distributing to such employees or their beneficiaries the corpus and income of the funds accumulated under such plan, if under such plan it is impossible, prior to the satisfaction of all liabilities with respect to such employees and their beneficiaries, for any part of the corpus or income to be used for, or diverted to, purposes other than the exclusive benefit of such employees or their beneficiaries, other than any plan described in clause (i), (ii), or (iii) of this subparagraph which (I) covers employees some or all of whom are employees within the meaning of section 401(c) of such Code, or (II) is a plan funded by an annuity contract described in section 403(b) of such Code.

(13) [Buy, Purchase]

The terms "buy" and "purchase" each include any contract to buy, purchase, or otherwise acquire. For security futures products, such term includes any contract, agreement, or transaction for future delivery. For security-based swaps, such terms include the execution, termination (prior to its scheduled maturity date), assignment, exchange, or similar transfer or conveyance of, or extinguishing of rights or obligations under, a security-based swap, as the context may require.

(14) [Sale, Sell]

The terms "sale" and "sell" each include any contract to sell or otherwise dispose of. For security futures products, such term includes any contract, agreement, or transaction for future delivery. For security-based swaps, such terms include the execution, termination (prior to its scheduled maturity date), assignment, exchange, or similar transfer or conveyance of, or extinguishing of rights or obligations under, a security-based swap, as the context may require.

(17) [Interstate Commerce]

The term "interstate commerce" means trade, commerce, transportation, or communication among the several States, or between any foreign country and any State, or between any State and any place or ship outside thereof. The term includes intrastate use of (A) any facility of a national securities exchange or of a telephone or other interstate means of communication, or (B) any other interstate instrumentality.

(18) [Person Associated with Broker]

The term "person associated with a broker or dealer" or "associated person of a broker or dealer" means any partner, officer, director, or branch manager of such broker or dealer (or any person occupying a similar status or performing similar functions), any person directly or indirectly controlling, controlled by, or under common control with such broker or dealer, or any employee of such broker or dealer, except that any person associated with a broker or dealer whose functions are solely clerical or ministerial shall not be inclued in the meaning of such term for purposes of section 15(b) of this title (other than paragraph (6) thereof).

(26) [Self-Regulatory Organization]

The term "self-regulatory organization" means any national securities exchange, registered securities association, or registered clearing agency, or (solely for purposes of sections 19(b), 19(c), and 23(b) of this title) the Municipal Securities Rulemaking Board established by section 15B of this title.

(29) [Municipal Securities]

The term "municipal securities" means securities which are direct obligations of, or obligations guaranteed as to principal or interest by, a State or any political subdivision thereof, or any agency or instrumentality of a State or any political subdivision thereof, or any municipal corporate instrumentality of one or more States, or any security which is an industrial development bond (as defined in section 103(c)(2) of the Internal Revenue Code of 1954) the interest on which is excludable from gross income under section 103(a)(1) of such Code if, by reason of the application of paragraph (4) or (6) of section 103(c) of such Code (determined as if paragraphs 4(A), (5), and (7) were not included in such section 103(c)), paragraph (1) of such section 103(c) does not apply to such security.

(30) [Municipal Securities Dealer]

The term "municipal securities dealer" means any person (including a separately identifiable department or division of a bank) engaged in the business of buying and selling municipal securities for his own account, through a broker or otherwise, but does not include—

(A) any person insofar as he buys or sells such securities for his own account, either individually or in some fiduciary capacity, but not as a part of a regular business; or

(B) a bank, unless the bank is engaged in the business of buying and selling municipal securities for its own account other than in a fiduciary capacity, through a broker or otherwise: *Provided, however,* That if the bank is engaged in such business through a separately identifiable department or division (as defined by the Municipal Securities Rulemaking Board in accordance with Section 15B(b)(2)(H) of this title), the department or division and not the bank itself shall be deemed to be the municipal securities dealer.

(31) [Municipal Securities Broker]

The term "municipal securities broker" means a broker engaged in the business of effecting transactions in municipal securities for the account of others.

(37) [Records]

The term "records" means accounts, correspondence, memorandums, tapes, discs, papers, books, and other documents or transcribed information of any type, whether expressed in ordinary or machine language.

(38) [Market Maker]

The term "market maker" means any specialist permitted to act as a dealer, any dealer acting in the capacity of block positioner, and any dealer who, with respect to a security, holds himself out (by entering quotations in an inter-dealer communications system or otherwise) as being willing to buy and sell such security for his own account on a regular or continuous basis.

(39) [Statutory Disqualification]

A person is subject to a "statutory disqualification" with respect to membership or participation in, or association with a member of, a self-regulatory organization, if such person—

(A) has been and is expelled or suspended from membership or participation in, or barred or suspended from being associated with a member of, any self-regulatory organization, foreign equivalent of a self-regulatory organization, foreign or international securities exchange, contract market designated pursuant to section 5 of the Commodity Exchange Act (7 U.S.C. 7), or any substantially equivalent foreign statute or regulation or futures associates registered under section 17 of such Act (7 U.S.C. 21), or any substantially foreign statute or regulation or has been and is denied trading privileges on any such contract market or foreign equivalent;

(B) is subject to—

(i) an order of the Commission, other appropriate regulatory agency, or foreign financial regulatory authority—

(I) denying, suspending for a period not exceeding 12 months, or revoking his registration as a broker, dealer, municipal securities dealer, government securities broker, government securities dealer, security-based swap dealer, or major security-based swap participant or limiting his activities as a foreign person performing a function substantially equivalent to any of the above; or

(II) barring or suspending for a period not exceeding 12 months his being associated with a broker, dealer, municipal securities dealer, government securities broker, government securities dealer, security-based swap dealer, major security-based swap participant, or foreign person performing a function substantially equivalent to any of the above;

(ii) an order of the Commodity Futures Trading Commission denying, suspending, or revoking his registration under the Commodity Exchange Act (7 U.S.C. 1 et seq.); or

(iii) an order by a foreign financial regulatory authority denying, suspending, or revoking the person's authority to engage in transactions in contracts of sale of a commodity for future delivery or other instruments traded on or subject to the rules of a contract market, board of trade, or foreign equivalent thereof,

(C) by his conduct while associated with a broker, dealer, municipal securities dealer, government securities broker, government securities dealer, security-based swap dealer, or major security-based swap participant, or while associated with an entity or person required to be registered under the Commodity Exchange Act, has been found to be a cause of any effective suspension, expulsion, or order of the character described in subparagraph (A) or (B) of this paragraph, and in entering such a suspension, expulsion, or order, the Commission, an appropriate regulatory agency, or any such self-regulatory organization shall have jurisdiction to find whether or not any person was a cause thereof;

(D) by his conduct while associated with any broker, dealer, municipal securities dealer, government securities broker, government securities dealer, security-based swap dealer, major security-based swap participant, or any other entity engaged in transactions in securities, or while associated with an entity engaged in transactions in contracts of sale of a commodity for future delivery or other instruments traded on or subject to the rules of a contract market, board of trade, or foreign equivalent thereof, has been found to be a cause of any effective suspension, expulsion, or order by a foreign or international securities exchange or foreign financial regulatory authority empowered by a foreign government to administer or enforce its laws relating to financial transactions as described in subparagraphs (A) or (B) of this paragraph,

(E) has associated with him any person who is known, or in the exercise of reasonable care should be known, to him to be a person described by subparagraph (A), (B), (C), or (D) of this paragraph; or

(F) has committed or omitted any act enumerated in subparagraph (D), (E), or (G) of paragraph (4) of section 15(b) of this title, has been convicted of any offense specified in subparagraph (B) of such paragraph (4) or any other felony within ten years of the date of the filing of an application for membership or participation in, or to become associated with a member of, such self-regulatory organization, is enjoined from any action, conduct, or practice specified in subparagraph (C) of such paragraph (4), has willfully made or caused to be made in any application for membership or participation in, or to become associated with a member of, a self-regulatory organization, report required to be filed with a self-regulatory organization, or proceeding before a self-regulatory organization, any statement which was at the time, and in the light of the circumstances under which it was made, false or misleading with respect to any material fact, or has omitted to state in any such application, report, or proceeding any material fact which is required to be stated therein.

(42) [Government Securities]

The term "government securities" means—

(A) securities which are direct obligations of, or obligations guaranteed as to principal or interest by, the United States;

(B) securities which are issued or guaranteed by corporations in which the United States has a direct or indirect interest and which are designated by the Secretary of the Treasury for exemption as necessary or appropriate in the public interest or for the protection of investors;

(C) securities issued or guaranteed as to principal or interest by any corporation the securities of which are designated, by statute specifically naming such corporation, to constitute exempt securities within the meaning of the laws administered by the Commission;

(D) for purposes of sections 15C and 17A, any put, call, straddle, option, or privilege on a security described in subparagraph (A), (B), or (C) other than a put, call, straddle, option, or privilege—

(i) that is traded on one or more national securities exchanges; or

(ii) for which quotations are disseminated through an automated quotation system operated by a registered securities association; or

(E) for purposes of sections 15, 15C, and 17A as applied to a bank, a qualified Canadian government obligation as defined in section 5136 of the Revised Statutes of the United States.

(51) [Penny Stock]

(A) The term "penny stock" means any equity security other than a security that is—

(i) registered or approved for registration and traded on a national securities exchange that meets such criteria as the Commission shall prescribe by rule or regulation for purposes of this paragraph;

(ii) authorized for quotation on an automated quotation system sponsored by a registered securities association, if such system (I) was established and in operation before January 1, 1990, and (II) meets such criteria as the Commission shall prescribe by rule or regulation for purposes of this paragraph;

(iii) issued by an investment company registered under the Investment Company Act of 1940;

(iv) excluded, on the basis of exceeding a minimum price, net tangible assets of the issuer, or other relevant criteria, from the definition of such term by rule or regulation which the Commission shall prescribe for purposes of this paragraph; or

(v) exempted, in whole or in part, conditionally or unconditionally, from the definition of such term by rule, regulation, or order prescribed by the Commission.

(B) The Commission may, by rule, regulation, or order, designate any equity security or class of equity securities described in clause (i) or (ii) of subparagraph (A) as within the meaning of the term "penny stock" if such security or class of securities is traded other than on a national securities exchange or through an automated quotation system described in clause (ii) of subparagraph (A).

(C) In exercising its authority under this paragraph to prescribe rules, regulations, and orders, the Commission shall determine that such rule, regulation, or order is consistent with the public interest and the protection of investors.

(58) [Audit Committee]

The term "audit committee" means—

(A) a committee (or equivalent body) established by and amongst the board of directors of an issuer for the purpose of overseeing the accounting and financial reporting processes of the issuer and audits of the financial statements of the issuer; and

(B) if no such committee exists with respect to an issuer, the entire board of directors of the issuer.

(65) [Eligible Contract Participant]

The term "eligible contract participant" has the same meaning as in section 1a of the Commodity Exchange Act (7 U.S.C. 1a).

(66) [Major Swap Participant]

The term "major swap participant" has the same meaning as in section 1a of the Commodity Exchange Act (7 U.S.C. 1a).

(67) [Major Security-Based Swap Participant]

(A) IN GENERAL. The term "major security-based swap participant" means any person—

(i) Who is not a security-based swap dealer; and

(ii) (I) Who maintains a substantial position in security-based swaps for any of the major security-based swap categories, as such categories are determined by the Commission, excluding positions held for hedging or mitigating commercial risk;

(II) Whose outstanding security-based swaps create substantial counterparty exposure that could have serious adverse effects on the financial stability of the United States banking system or financial markets; or

(III) That is a financial entity that—

(aa) Is highly leveraged relative to the amount of capital such entity holds and that is not subject to capital requirements established by an appropriate Federal banking regulator; and

(bb) Maintains a substantial position in outstanding security-based swaps in any major security-based swap category, as such categories are determined by the Commission.

(B) DEFINITION OF SUBSTANTIAL POSITION. For purposes of subparagraph (A), the Commission shall define, by rule or regulation, the term "substantial position" at the threshold that the Commission determines to be prudent for the effective monitoring, management, and oversight of entities that are systemically important or can significantly impact the financial system of the United States. In setting such definitions, the Commission shall consider the person's relative position in uncleared as opposed to cleared security-based swaps and may take into consideration the value and quality of collateral held against counterparty exposures.

(C) SCOPE OF DESIGNATION. For purposes of subparagraph (A), a person may be designated as a major security-based swap participant for 1 or more categories of security-based swaps without being classified as a major security-based swap participant for all classes of security-based swaps.

(68) [Security-Based Swap]

(A) IN GENERAL. Except as provided in subparagraph (B), the term "security-based swap" means any agreement, contract, or transaction that—

(i) Is a swap, as that term is defined under section 1a of the Commodity Exchange Act (without regard to paragraph (47)(B)(x) of such section); and

(ii) Is based on—

(I) An index that is a narrow-based security index, including any interest therein or on the value thereof;

(II) A single security or loan, including any interest therein or on the value thereof; or

(III) The occurrence, nonoccurrence, or extent of the occurrence of an event relating to a single issuer of a security or the issuers of securities in a narrow-based security index, provided that such event directly affects the financial statements, financial condition, or financial obligations of the issuer.

(B) RULE OF CONSTRUCTION REGARDING MASTER AGREEMENTS. The term "security-based swap" shall be construed to include a master agreement that provides for an agreement, contract, or transaction that is a security-based swap pursuant to subparagraph (A), together with all supplements to any such master agreement, without regard to whether the master agreement contains an agreement, contract, or transaction that is not a security-based swap pursuant to subparagraph (A), except that the master agreement shall be considered to be a security-based swap only with respect to each agreement, contract, or transaction under the master agreement that is a security-based swap pursuant to subparagraph (A).

(C) EXCLUSIONS. The term "security-based swap" does not include any agreement, contract, or transaction that meets the definition of a security-based swap only because such agreement, contract, or transaction references, is based upon, or settles through the transfer, delivery, or receipt of an exempted security under paragraph (12), as in effect on the date of enactment of the Futures Trading Act of 1982 (other than any municipal security as defined in paragraph (29) as in effect on the date of enactment of the Futures Trading Act of 1982), unless such agreement, contract, or transaction is of the character of, or is commonly known in the trade as, a put, call, or other option.

(D) MIXED SWAP. The term "security-based swap" includes any agreement, contract, or transaction that is as described in subparagraph (A) and also is based on the value of 1 or more interest or other rates, currencies, commodities, instruments of indebtedness, indices, quantitative measures, other financial or economic interest or property of any kind (other than a single security or a narrow-based security index), or the occurrence, non-occurrence, or the extent of the occurrence of an event or contingency associated with a potential financial, economic, or commercial consequence (other than an event described in subparagraph (A)(ii)(III)).

(E) RULE OF CONSTRUCTION REGARDING USE OF THE TERM INDEX. The term "index" means an index or group of securities, including any interest therein or based on the value thereof.

(69) [Swap]

The term "swap" has the same meaning as in section 1a of the Commodity Exchange Act (7 U.S.C. 1a).

(70) [Person Associated With a Security-Based Swap Dealer or Major Security-Based Swap Participant]

(A) IN GENERAL. The term "person associated with a security-based swap dealer or major security-based swap participant" or "associated person of a security-based swap dealer or major security-based swap participant" means—

(i) Any partner, officer, director, or branch manager of such security-based swap dealer or major security-based swap participant (or any person occupying a similar status or performing similar functions);

(ii) Any person directly or indirectly controlling, controlled by, or under common control with such security-based swap dealer or major security-based swap participant; or

(iii) Any employee of such security-based swap dealer or major security-based swap participant.

(B) EXCLUSION. Other than for purposes of section 15F(l)(2), the term "person associated with a security-based swap dealer or major security-based swap participant" or "associated person of a security-based swap dealer or major security-based swap participant" does not include any person associated with a security-based swap dealer or major security-based swap participant whose functions are solely clerical or ministerial.

(71) [Security-Based Swap Dealer]

(A) IN GENERAL. The term "security-based swap dealer" means any person who—

(i) Holds themself out as a dealer in security-based swaps;

(ii) Makes a market in security-based swaps;

(iii) Regularly enters into security-based swaps with counterparties as an ordinary course of business for its own account; or

(iv) Engages in any activity causing it to be commonly known in the trade as a dealer or market maker in security-based swaps.

(B) DESIGNATION BY TYPE OR CLASS. A person may be designated as a security-based swap dealer for a single type or single class or category of security-based swap or activities and considered not to be a security-based swap dealer for other types, classes, or categories of security-based swaps or activities.

(C) EXCEPTION. The term "security-based swap dealer" does not include a person that enters into security-based swaps for such person's own account, either individually or in a fiduciary capacity, but not as a part of regular business.

(D) DE MINIMIS EXCEPTION. The Commission shall exempt from designation as a security-based swap dealer an entity that engages in a de minimis quantity of security-based swap dealing in connection with transactions with or on behalf of its customers.

The Commission shall promulgate regulations to establish factors with respect to the making of any determination to exempt.

(72) [Appropriate Federal Banking Agency]

The term "appropriate Federal banking agency" has the same meaning as in section 3(q) of the Federal Deposit Insurance Act (12 U.S.C. 1813(q)).

(73) [Board]

The term "Board" means the Board of Governors of the Federal Reserve System.

(74) [Prudential Regulator]

The term "prudential regulator" has the same meaning as in section 1a of the Commodity Exchange Act (7 U.S.C. 1a).

(75) [Security-Based Swap Data Repository]

The term "security-based swap data repository" means any person that collects and maintains information or records with respect to transactions or positions in, or the terms and conditions of, security-based swaps entered into by third parties for the purpose of providing a centralized recordkeeping facility for security-based swaps.

(76) [Swap Dealer]

The term "swap dealer" has the same meaning as in section 1a of the Commodity Exchange Act (7 U.S.C. 1a).

(77) [Security-Based Swap Execution Facility]

The term "security-based swap execution facility" means a trading system or platform in which multiple participants have the ability to execute or trade security-based swaps by accepting bids and offers made by multiple participants in the facility or system, through any means of interstate commerce, including any trading facility, that—

(A) Facilitates the execution of security-based swaps between persons; and

(B) Is not a national securities exchange.

(78) [Security-Based Swap Agreement]

(A) IN GENERAL. For purposes of sections 9, 10, 16, 20, and 21A of this Act, and section 17 of the Securities Act of 1933 (15 U.S.C. 77q), the term "security-based swap agreement" means a swap agreement as defined in section 206A of the Gramm-Leach-Bliley Act (15 U.S.C. 78c note) of which a material term is based on the price, yield, value, or volatility of any security or any group or index of securities, or any interest therein.

(B) EXCLUSIONS. The term "security-based swap agreement" does not include any security-based swap.

(79) [Asset-Backed Security]

The term "asset-backed security"—

(A) Means a fixed-income or other security collateralized by any type of self-liquidating financial asset (including a loan, a lease, a mortgage, or a secured or unsecured receivable) that allows the holder of the security to receive payments that depend primarily on cash flow from the asset, including—

(i) A collateralized mortgage obligation;

(ii) A collateralized debt obligation;

(iii) A collateralized bond obligation;

(iv) A collateralized debt obligation of asset-backed securities;

(v) A collateralized debt obligation of collateralized debt obligations; and

(vi) A security that the Commission, by rule, determines to be an asset-backed security for purposes of this section; and

(B) Does not include a security issued by a finance subsidiary held by the parent company or a company controlled by the parent company, if none of the securities issued by the finance subsidiary are held by an entity that is not controlled by the parent company.

*(80) Emerging Growth Company.

The term "emerging growth company" means an issuer that had total annual gross revenues of less than $1,000,000,000 (as such amount is indexed for inflation every 5 years by the Commission to reflect the change in the Consumer Price Index for All Urban Consumers published by the Bureau of Labor Statistics, setting the threshold to the nearest 1,000,000) during its most recently completed fiscal year. An issuer that is an emerging growth company as of the first day of that fiscal year shall continue to be deemed an emerging growth company until the earliest of—

(A) The last day of the fiscal year of the issuer during which it had total annual gross revenues of $1,000,000,000 (as such amount is indexed for inflation every 5 years by the Commission to reflect the change in the Consumer Price Index for All Urban Consumers published by the Bureau of Labor Statistics, setting the threshold to the nearest 1,000,000) or more;

(B) The last day of the fiscal year of the issuer following the fifth anniversary of the date of the first sale of common equity securities of the issuer pursuant to an effective registration statement under the Securities Act of 1933;

(C) The date on which such issuer has, during the previous 3-year period, issued more than $1,000,000,000 in non-convertible debt; or

(D) The date on which such issuer is deemed to be a "large accelerated filer," as defined in section 240.12b-2 of title 17, Code of Federal Regulations, or any success or thereto.

*(80) Funding Portal.

The term "funding portal" means any person acting as an intermediary in a transaction involving the offer or sale of securities for the account of others, solely pursuant to section 4(6) of the Securities Act of 1933 (15 U.S.C. 77d(6)),that does not—

(A) Offer investment advice or recommendations;

(B) Solicit purchases, sales, or offers to buy the securities offered or displayed on its website or portal;

(C) Compensate employees, agents, or other persons for such solicitation or based on the sale of securities displayed or referenced on its website or portal;

(D) Hold, manage, possess, or otherwise handle investor funds or securities; or

(E) Engage in such other activities as the Commission, by rule, determines appropriate.

(b) [Power to Define Terms]

The Commission and the Board of Governors of the Federal Reserve System, as to matters within their respective jurisdictions, shall have power by rules and regulations to define technical, trade, accounting, and other terms used in this title, consistently with the provisions and purposes of this title.

---

*Two paragraphs 80 were enacted.—EDS.

(c) [Exemption of Governmental Departments and Agencies from Act]

No provision of this title shall apply to, or be deemed to include, any executive department or independent establishment of the United States, or any lending agency which is wholly owned, directly or indirectly, by the United States, or any officer, agent, or employee of any such department, establishment, or agency, acting in the course of his official duty as such, unless such provision makes specific reference to such department, establishment, or agency.

(f) [Consideration of Promotion of Efficiency, Competition, and Capital Formation]

CONSIDERATION OF PROMOTION OF EFFICIENCY, COMPETITION, AND CAPITAL FORMATION. Whenever pursuant to this title the Commission is engaged in rulemaking, or in the review of a rule of a self-regulatory organization, and is required to consider or determine whether an action is necessary or appropriate in the public interest, the Commission shall also consider, in addition to the protection of investors, whether the action will promote efficiency, competition, and capital formation.

(h) [Limited Exemption For Funding Portals]

(1) In General. The Commission shall, by rule, exempt, conditionally or unconditionally, a registered funding portal from the requirement to register as a broker or dealer under section 15(a)(1), provided that such funding portal—

(A) Remains subject to the examination, enforcement, and other rulemaking authority of the Commission;

(B) Is a member of a national securities association registered under section 15A; and

(C) Is subject to such other requirements under this title as the Commission determines appropriate under such rule.

(2) National Securities Association Membership. For purposes of sections 15(b)(8) and 15A, the term "broker or dealer" includes a funding portal and the term" registered broker or dealer" includes a registered funding portal, except to the extent that the Commission, by rule, determines otherwise, provided that a national securities association shall only examine for and enforce against a registered funding portal rules of such national securities association written specifically for registered funding portals.

Sec. 3A. SWAP AGREEMENTS

(a) [Reserved.]

(b) SECURITY-BASED SWAP AGREEMENTS.—

(1) The definition of "security" in section 3(a)(10) of this title does not include any security-based swap agreement.

(2) The Commission is prohibited from registering, or requiring, recommending, or suggesting, the registration under this title of any security-based swap agreement. If the Commission becomes aware that a registrant has filed a registration application with respect to such a swap agreement, the Commission shall promptly so notify the registrant. Any such registration with respect to such a swap agreement shall be void and of no force or effect.

(3) Except as provided in section 16(a) with respect to reporting requirements, the Commission is prohibited from—

(A) promulgating, interpreting, or enforcing rules; or

(B) issuing orders of general applicability; under this title in a manner that imposes or specifies reporting or recordkeeping requirements, procedures, or standards as prophylactic measures against fraud, manipulation, or insider trading with respect to any security-based swap agreement.

(4) References in this title to the "purchase" or "sale" of a security-based swap agreement shall be deemed to mean the execution, termination (prior to its scheduled maturity

date), assignment, exchange, or similar transfer or conveyance of, or extinguishing of rights or obligations under, a security-based swap agreement, as the context may require.

Sec. 3B. SECURITIES-RELATED DERIVATIVES

(a) Any agreement, contract, or transaction (or class thereof) that is exempted by the Commodity Futures Trading Commission pursuant to section 4(c)(1) of the Commodity Exchange Act (7 U.S.C. 6(c)(1)) with the condition that the Commission exercise concurrent jurisdiction over such agreement, contract, or transaction (or class thereof) shall be deemed a security for purposes of the securities laws.

(b) With respect to any agreement, contract, or transaction (or class thereof) that is exempted by the Commodity Futures Trading Commission pursuant to section 4(c)(1) of the Commodity Exchange Act (7 U.S.C. 6(c)(1)) with the condition that the Commission exercise concurrent jurisdiction over such agreement, contract, or transaction (or class thereof), references in the securities laws to the "purchase" or "sale" of a security shall be deemed to include the execution, termination (prior to its scheduled maturity date), assignment, exchange, or similar transfer or conveyance of, or extinguishing of rights or obligations under such agreement, contract, or transaction, as the context may require.

Sec. 3C. CLEARING FOR SECURITY-BASED SWAPS

(a) IN GENERAL.

(1) Standard For Clearing. It shall be unlawful for any person to engage in a security-based swap unless that person submits such security-based swap for clearing to a clearing agency that is registered under this Act or a clearing agency that is exempt from registration under this Act if the security-based swap is required to be cleared.

(2) Open Access. The rules of a clearing agency described in paragraph (1) shall—

(A) Prescribe that all security-based swaps submitted to the clearing agency with the same terms and conditions are economically equivalent within the clearing agency and may be offset with each other within the clearing agency; and

(B) Provide for non-discriminatory clearing of a security-based swap executed bilaterally or on or through the rules of an unaffiliated national securities exchange or security-based swap execution facility.

(b) COMMISSION REVIEW.

(1) Commission-Initiated Review.

(A) The Commission on an ongoing basis shall review each security-based swap, or any group, category, type, or class of security-based swaps to make a determination that such security-based swap, or group, category, type, or class of security-based swaps should be required to be cleared.

(B) The Commission shall provide at least a 30-day public comment period regarding any determination under subparagraph (A).

(2) Swap Submissions.

(A) A clearing agency shall submit to the Commission each security-based swap, or any group, category, type, or class of security-based swaps that it plans to accept for clearing and provide notice to its members (in a manner to be determined by the Commission) of such submission.

(B) Any security-based swap or group, category, type, or class of security-based swaps listed for clearing by a clearing agency as of the date of enactment of this subsection shall be considered submitted to the Commission.

(C) The Commission shall—

(i) Make available to the public any submission received under subparagraphs (A) and (B);

(ii) Review each submission made under subparagraphs (A) and (B), and determine whether the security-based swap, or group, category, type, or class of security-based swaps, described in the submission is required to be cleared; and (iii) Provide at least a 30-day public comment period regarding its determination whether the clearing requirement under subsection (a)(1) shall apply to the submission.

(3) Deadline. The Commission shall make its determination under paragraph (2)(C) not later than 90 days after receiving a submission made under paragraphs (2)(A) and (2)(B), unless the submitting clearing agency agrees to an extension for the time limitation established under this paragraph.

(4) Determination.

(A) In reviewing a submission made under paragraph (2), the Commission shall review whether the submission is consistent with section 17A.

(B) In reviewing a security-based swap, group of security-based swaps or class of security-based swaps pursuant to paragraph (1) or a submission made under paragraph (2), the Commission shall take into account the following factors:

(i) The existence of significant outstanding notional exposures, trading liquidity and adequate pricing data.

(ii) The availability of rule framework, capacity, operational expertise and resources, and credit support infrastructure to clear the contract on terms that are consistent with the material terms and trading conventions on which the contract is then traded.

(iii) The effect on the mitigation of systemic risk, taking into account the size of the market for such contract and the resources of the clearing agency available to clear the contract.

(iv) The effect on competition, including appropriate fees and charges applied to clearing.

(v) The existence of reasonable legal certainty in the event of the insolvency of the relevant clearing agency or 1 or more of its clearing members with regard to the treatment of customer and security-based swap counterparty positions, funds, and property.

(C) In making a determination under subsection (b)(1) or paragraph (2)(C) that the clearing requirement shall apply, the Commission may require such terms and conditions to the requirement as the Commission determines to be appropriate.

(5) Rules. Not later than 1 year after the date of the enactment of this section, the Commission shall adopt rules for a clearing agency's submission for review, pursuant to this subsection, of a security-based swap, or a group, category, type or class of security-based swaps, that it seeks to accept for clearing. Nothing in this paragraph limits the Commission from making a determination under paragraph (2)(C) for security-based swaps described in paragraph (2)(B).

(c) STAY OF CLEARING REQUIREMENT.

(1) In General. After making a determination pursuant to subsection (b)(2), the Commission, on application of a counterparty to a security-based swap or on its own initiative, may stay the clearing requirement of subsection (a)(1) until the Commission completes a review of the terms of the security-based swap (or the group, category, type, or class of security-based swaps) and the clearing arrangement.

(2) Deadline. The Commission shall complete a review undertaken pursuant to paragraph (1) not later than 90 days after issuance of the stay, unless the clearing agency that clears the security-based swap, or group, category, type, or class of security-based swaps, agrees to an extension of the time limitation established under this paragraph.

(3) Determination. Upon completion of the review undertaken pursuant to paragraph (1), the Commission may—

(A) Determine, unconditionally or subject to such terms and conditions as the Commission determines to be appropriate, that the security-based swap, or group, category, type, or class of security-based swaps, must be cleared pursuant to this subsection if it finds that such clearing is consistent with subsection (b)(4); or

(B) Determine that the clearing requirement of subsection (a)(1) shall not apply to the security-based swap, or group, category, type, or class of security-based swaps.

(4) Rules. Not later than 1 year after the date of the enactment of this section, the Commission shall adopt rules for reviewing, pursuant to this subsection, a clearing agency's clearing of a security-based swap, or a group, category, type or class of security-based swaps, that it has accepted for clearing.

(d) PREVENTION OF EVASION.

(1) In General. The Commission shall prescribe rules under this section (and issue interpretations of rules prescribed under this section), as determined by the Commission to be necessary to prevent evasions of the mandatory clearing requirements under this Act.

(2) Duty of Commission to Investigate and Take Certain Actions. To the extent the Commission finds that a particular security-based swap or any group, category, type, or class of security-based swaps that would otherwise be subject to mandatory clearing but no clearing agency has listed the security-based swap or the group, category, type, or class of security-based swaps for clearing, the Commission shall—

(A) Investigate the relevant facts and circumstances;

(B) Within 30 days issue a public report containing the results of the investigation; and

(C) Take such actions as the Commission determines to be necessary and in the public interest, which may include requiring the retaining of adequate margin or capital by parties to the security-based swap or the group, category, type, or class of security-based swaps.

(3) Effect on Authority. Nothing in this subsection—

(A) Authorize the Commission to adopt rules requiring a clearing agency to list for clearing a security-based swap or any group, category, type, or class of security-based swaps if the clearing of the security-based swap or the group, category, type, or class of security-based swaps would threaten the financial integrity of the clearing agency; and

(B) Affect the authority of the Commission to enforce the open access provisions of subsection (a)(2) with respect to a security-based swap or the group, category, type, or class of security-based swaps that is listed for clearing by a clearing agency.

(e) REPORTING TRANSITION RULES. Rules adopted by the Commission under this section shall provide for the reporting of data, as follows:

(1) Security-based swaps entered into before the date of the enactment of this section shall be reported to a registered security-based swap data repository or the Commission no later than 180 days after the effective date of this section.

(2) Security-based swaps entered into on or after such date of enactment shall be reported to a registered security-based swap data repository or the Commission no later than the later of—

(A) 90 days after such effective date; or

(B) Such other time after entering into the security-based swap as the Commission may prescribe by rule or regulation.

(f) CLEARING TRANSITION RULES.

(1) Security-based swaps entered into before the date of the enactment of this section are exempt from the clearing requirements of this subsection if reported pursuant to subsection (e)(1).

(2) Security-based swaps entered into before application of the clearing requirement pursuant to this section are exempt from the clearing requirements of this section if reported pursuant to subsection (e)(2).

(g) EXCEPTIONS.

(1) In General. The requirements of subsection (a)(1) shall not apply to a security-based swap if 1 of the counterparties to the security-based swap—

(A) Is not a financial entity;

(B) Is using security-based swaps to hedge or mitigate commercial risk; and

(C) Notifies the Commission, in a manner set forth by the Commission, how it generally meets its financial obligations associated with entering into non-cleared security-based swaps.

(2) Option to Clear. The application of the clearing exception in paragraph (1) is solely at the discretion the counterparty to the security-based swap that meets the conditions of subparagraphs (A) through (C) of paragraph (1).

(3) Financial Entity Definition.

(A) In General. For the purposes of this subsection, the term "financial entity" means—

(i) A swap dealer;

(ii) A security-based swap dealer;

(iii) A major swap participant;

(iv) A major security-based swap participant;

(v) A commodity pool as defined in section 1a(10) of the Commodity Exchange Act;

(vi) A private fund as defined in section 202(a) of the Investment Advisers Act of 1940 (15 U.S.C. 80-b-2(a));

(vii) An employee benefit plan as defined in paragraphs (3) and (32) of section 3 of the Employee Retirement Income Security Act of 1974 (29 U.S.C. 1002);

(viii) A person predominantly engaged in activities that are in the business of banking or financial in nature, as defined in section 4(k) of the Bank Holding Company Act of 1956.

(B) Exclusion. The Commission shall consider whether to exempt small banks, savings associations, farm credit system institutions, and credit unions, including—

(i) Depository institutions with total assets of $10,000,000,000 or less;

(ii) Farm credit system institutions with total assets of $10,000,000,000 or less; or

(iii) Credit unions with total assets of $10,000,000,000 or less.

(4) Treatment of Affiliates.

(A) In General. An affiliate of a person that qualifies for an exception under this subsection (including affiliate entities predominantly engaged in providing financing for the purchase of the merchandise or manufactured goods of the person) may qualify for the exception only if the affiliate—

(i) Enters into the security-based swap to hedge or mitigate the commercial risk of the person or other affiliate of the person that is not a financial entity, and the commercial risk that the affiliate is hedging or mitigating has been transferred to the affiliate;

(ii) Is directly and wholly-owned by another affiliate qualified for the exception under this paragraph or an entity that is not a financial entity;

(iii) Is not indirectly majority-owned by a financial entity;

(iv) Is not ultimately owned by a parent company that is a financial entity; and

(v) Does not provide any services, financial or otherwise, to any affiliate that is a nonbank financial company supervised by the Board of Governors (as defined under section 102 of the Financial Stability Act of 2010).

(B) Limitation on Qualifying Affiliates. The exception in subparagraph (A) shall not apply if the affiliate is—

(i) A swap dealer;

(ii) A security-based swap dealer;

(iii) A major swap participant;

(iv) A major security-based swap participant;

(v) A commodity pool;

(vi) A bank holding company;

(vii) A private fund, as defined in section 202(a) of the Investment Advisers Act of 1940 (15 U.S.C. 80-b-2(a) [sic]);

(viii) An employee benefit plan or government plan, as defined in paragraphs (3) and (32) of section 3 of the Employee Retirement Income Security Act of 1974 (29 U.S.C. 1002);

(ix) An insured depository institution;

(x) A farm credit system institution;

(xi) A credit union;

(xii) A nonbank financial company supervised by the Board of Governors (as defined under section 102 of the Financial Stability Act of 2010); or

(xiii) An entity engaged in the business of insurance and subject to capital requirements established by an insurance governmental authority of a State, a territory of the United States, the District of Columbia, a country other than the United States, or a political subdivision of a country other than the United States that is engaged in the supervision of insurance companies under insurance law.

(C) Limitation on Affiliates' Affiliates. Unless the Commission determines, by order, rule, or regulation, that it is in the public interest, the exception in subparagraph (A) shall not apply with respect to an affiliate if such affiliate is itself affiliated with—

(i) A major security-based swap participant;

(ii) A security-based swap dealer;

(iii) A major swap participant; or

(iv) A swap dealer.

(D) Conditions on Transactions. With respect to an affiliate that qualifies for the exception in subparagraph (A)—

(i) Such affiliate may not enter into any security-based swap other than for the purpose of hedging or mitigating commercial risk; and

(ii) Neither such affiliate nor any person affiliated with such affiliate that is not a financial entity may enter into a security-based swap with or on behalf of any affiliate that is a financial entity or otherwise assume, net, combine, or consolidate the risk of security-based swaps entered into by any such financial entity, except one that is an affiliate that qualifies for the exception under subparagraph (A).

(E) Transition Rule For Affiliates. An affiliate, subsidiary, or a wholly owned entity of a person that qualifies for an exception under subparagraph (A) and is predominantly engaged in providing financing for the purchase or lease of merchandise or manufactured goods of the person shall be exempt from the margin requirement described in section 15F(e) and the clearing requirement described in subsection (a) with regard to security-based swaps entered into to mitigate the risk of the financing activities for not less than a 2-year period beginning on the date of enactment of this clause.

(F) *Risk Management Program.* Any security-based swap entered into by an affiliate that qualifies for the exception in subparagraph (A) shall be subject to a centralized risk management program of the affiliate, which is reasonably designed both to monitor and manage the risks associated with the security-based swap and to identify each of the affiliates on whose behalf a security-based swap was entered into.

(5) Election of Counterparty.

(A) Security-Based Swaps Required to Be Cleared. With respect to any security-based swap that is subject to the mandatory clearing requirement under subsection (a) and entered into by a security-based swap dealer or a major security-based swap participant with a counterparty that is not a swap dealer, major swap participant security-based swap dealer, or major security-based swap participant, the counterparty shall have the sole right to select the clearing agency at which the security-based swap will be cleared.

(B) Security-Based Swaps Not Required to Be Cleared. With respect to any security-based swap that is not subject to the mandatory clearing requirement under subsection (a) and entered into by a security-based swap dealer or a major security-based swap participant with a counterparty that is not a swap dealer, major swap participant, security-based swap dealer, or major security-based swap participant, the counterparty—

(i) May elect to require clearing of the security-based swap; and

(ii) Shall have the sole right to select the clearing agency at which the security-based swap will be cleared.

(6) Abuse of Exception. The Commission may prescribe such rules or issue interpretations of the rules as the Commission determines to be necessary to prevent abuse of the exceptions described in this subsection. The Commission may also request information from those persons claiming the clearing exception as necessary to prevent abuse of the exceptions described in this subsection.

(h) TRADE EXECUTION.

(1) In General. With respect to transactions involving security-based swaps subject to the clearing requirement of subsection (a)(1), counter-parties shall—

(A) Execute the transaction on an exchange; or

(B) Execute the transaction on a security-based swap execution facility registered under section 3D or a security-based swap execution facility that is exempt from registration under section 3D(e) of this Act.

(2) Exception. The requirements of subparagraphs (A) and (B) of paragraph (1) shall not apply if no exchange or security-based swap execution facility makes the security-based swap available to trade or for security-based swap transactions subject to the clearing exception under subsection (g).

(i) BOARD APPROVAL.

Exemptions from the requirements of this section to clear a security-based swap or execute a security-based swap through a national securities exchange or security-based swap execution facility shall be available to a counterparty that is an issuer of securities that are registered under section 12 or that is required to file reports pursuant to section 15(d), only if an appropriate committee of the issuer's board or governing body has reviewed and approved the issuer's decision to enter into security-based swaps that are subject to such exemptions.

(j) DESIGNATION OF CHIEF COMPLIANCE OFFICER.

(1) In General. Each registered clearing agency shall designate an individual to serve as a chief compliance officer.

(2) Duties. The chief compliance officer shall—

(A) Report directly to the board or to the senior officer of the clearing agency;

(B) In consultation with its board, a body performing a function similar thereto, or the senior officer of the registered clearing agency, resolve any conflicts of interest that may arise;

(C) Be responsible for administering each policy and procedure that is required to be established pursuant to this section;

(D) Ensure compliance with this title (including regulations issued under this title) relating to agreements, contracts, or transactions, including each rule prescribed by the Commission under this section;

(E) Establish procedures for the remediation of noncompliance issues identified by the compliance officer through any—

(i) Compliance office review;

(ii) Look-back;

(iii) Internal or external audit finding;

(iv) Self-reported error; or

(v) Validated complaint; and

(F) Establish and follow appropriate procedures for the handling, management response, remediation, retesting, and closing of non-compliance issues.

(3) Annual Reports.

(A) In General. In accordance with rules prescribed by the Commission, the chief compliance officer shall annually prepare and sign a report that contains a description of—

(i) The compliance of the registered clearing agency or security-based swap execution facility of the compliance officer with respect to this title (including regulations under this title); and

(ii) Each policy and procedure of the registered clearing agency of the compliance officer (including the code of ethics and conflict of interest policies of the registered clearing agency).

(B) Requirements. A compliance report under subparagraph (A) shall—

(i) Accompany each appropriate financial report of the registered clearing agency that is required to be furnished to the Commission pursuant to this section; and

(ii) Include a certification that, under penalty of law, the compliance report is accurate and complete.

Sec. 3D. SECURITY-BASED SWAP EXECUTION FACILITIES

(a) REGISTRATION.

(1) In General. No person may operate a facility for the trading or processing of security-based swaps, unless the facility is registered as a security-based swap execution facility or as a national securities exchange under this section.

(2) Dual Registration. Any person that is registered as a security-based swap execution facility under this section shall register with the Commission regardless of whether the person also is registered with the Commodity Futures Trading Commission as a swap execution facility.

(b) TRADING AND TRADE PROCESSING. A security-based swap execution facility that is registered under subsection (a) may—

(1) Make available for trading any security-based swap; and

(2) Facilitate trade processing of any security-based swap.

(c) IDENTIFICATION OF FACILITY USED TO TRADE SECURITY-BASED SWAPS BY NATIONAL SECURITIES EXCHANGES. A national securities exchange shall, to the extent that the exchange also operates a security-based swap execution facility and uses the same electronic trade execution system for listing and executing trades of security-based swaps on or through the exchange and the facility, identify whether electronic trading of such security-based swaps is taking place on or through the national securities exchange or the security-based swap execution facility.

(d) CORE PRINCIPLES FOR SECURITY-BASED SWAP EXECUTION FACILITIES.

(1) Compliance With Core Principles.

(A) In General. To be registered, and maintain registration, as a security-based swap execution facility, the security-based swap execution facility shall comply with—

(i) The core principles described in this subsection; and

(ii) Any requirement that the Commission may impose by rule or regulation.

(B) Reasonable Discretion of Security-Based Swap Execution Facility. Unless otherwise determined by the Commission, by rule or regulation, a security-based swap execution facility described in subparagraph (A) shall have reasonable discretion in establishing the manner in which it complies with the core principles described in this subsection.

(2) Compliance with Rules. A security-based swap execution facility shall—

(A) Establish and enforce compliance with any rule established by such security-based swap execution facility, including—

(i) The terms and conditions of the security-based swaps traded or processed on or through the facility; and

(ii) Any limitation on access to the facility;

(B) Establish and enforce trading, trade processing, and participation rules that will deter abuses and have the capacity to detect, investigate, and enforce those rules, including means—

(i) To provide market participants with impartial access to the market; and

(ii) To capture information that may be used in establishing whether rule violations have occurred; and

(C) Establish rules governing the operation of the facility, including rules specifying trading procedures to be used in entering and executing orders traded or posted on the facility, including block trades.

(3) Security-Based Swaps Not Readily Susceptible to Manipulation. The security-based swap execution facility shall permit trading only in security-based swaps that are not readily susceptible to manipulation.

(4) Monitoring of Trading and Trade Processing. The security-based swap execution facility shall—

(A) Establish and enforce rules or terms and conditions defining, or specifications detailing—

(i) Trading procedures to be used in entering and executing orders traded on or through the facilities of the security-based swap execution facility; and

(ii) Procedures for trade processing of security-based swaps on or through the facilities of the security-based swap execution facility; and

(B) Monitor trading in security-based swaps to prevent manipulation, price distortion, and disruptions of the delivery or cash settlement process through surveillance, compliance, and disciplinary practices and procedures, including methods for conducting real-time monitoring of trading and comprehensive and accurate trade reconstructions.

(5) Ability to Obtain Information. The security-based swap execution facility shall—

(A) Establish and enforce rules that will allow the facility to obtain any necessary information to perform any of the functions described in this subsection;

(B) Provide the information to the Commission on request; and

(C) Have the capacity to carry out such international information-sharing agreements as the Commission may require.

(6) Financial Integrity of Transactions. The security-based swap execution facility shall establish and enforce rules and procedures for ensuring the financial integrity of security-based swaps entered on or through the facilities of the security-based swap execution facility, including the clearance and settlement of security-based swaps pursuant to section 3C(a)(1).

(7) Emergency Authority. The security-based swap execution facility shall adopt rules to provide for the exercise of emergency authority, in consultation or cooperation with the Commission, as is necessary and appropriate, including the authority to liquidate or transfer open positions in any security-based swap or to suspend or curtail trading in a security-based swap.

(8) Timely Publication of Trading Information.

(A) In General. The security-based swap execution facility shall make public timely information on price, trading volume, and other trading data on security-based swaps to the extent prescribed by the Commission.

(B) Capacity of Security-Based Swap Execution Facility. The security-based swap execution facility shall be required to have the capacity to electronically capture and transmit and disseminate trade information with respect to transactions executed on or through the facility.

(9) Recordkeeping and Reporting.

(A) In General. A security-based swap execution facility shall—

(i) Maintain records of all activities relating to the business of the facility, including a complete audit trail, in a form and manner acceptable to the Commission for a period of 5 years; and

(ii) Report to the Commission, in a form and manner acceptable to the Commission, such information as the Commission determines to be necessary or appropriate for the Commission to perform the duties of the Commission under this title.

(B) Requirements. The Commission shall adopt data collection and reporting requirements for security-based swap execution facilities that are comparable to corresponding requirements for clearing agencies and security-based swap data repositories.

(10) Antitrust Considerations. Unless necessary or appropriate to achieve the purposes of this title, the security-based swap execution facility shall not—

(A) Adopt any rules or taking any actions that result in any unreasonable restraint of trade; or

(B) Impose any material anticompetitive burden on trading or clearing.

(11) Conflicts of Interest. The security-based swap execution facility shall—

(A) Establish and enforce rules to minimize conflicts of interest in its decision-making process; and

(B) Establish a process for resolving the conflicts of interest.

(12) Financial Resources.

(A) In General. The security-based swap execution facility shall have adequate financial, operational, and managerial resources to discharge each responsibility of the security-based swap execution facility, as determined by the Commission.

(B) Determination of Resource Adequacy. The financial resources of a security-based swap execution facility shall be considered to be adequate if the value of the financial resources—

(i) Enables the organization to meet its financial obligations to its members and participants notwithstanding a default by the member or participant creating the largest financial exposure for that organization in extreme but plausible market conditions; and

(ii) Exceeds the total amount that would enable the security-based swap execution facility to cover the operating costs of the security-based swap execution facility for a 1-year period, as calculated on a rolling basis.

(13) System Safeguards. The security-based swap execution facility shall—

(A) Establish and maintain a program of risk analysis and oversight to identify and minimize sources of operational risk, through the development of appropriate controls and procedures, and automated systems, that—

(i) Are reliable and secure; and

(ii) Have adequate scalable capacity;

(B) Establish and maintain emergency procedures, backup facilities, and a plan for disaster recovery that allow for—

(i) The timely recovery and resumption of operations; and

(ii) The fulfillment of the responsibilities and obligations of the security-based swap execution facility; and

(C) Periodically conduct tests to verify that the backup resources of the security-based swap execution facility are sufficient to ensure continued—

(i) Order processing and trade matching;

(ii) Price reporting;

(iii) Market surveillance; and

(iv) Maintenance of a comprehensive and accurate audit trail.

(14) Designation of Chief Compliance Officer.

(A) In General. Each security-based swap execution facility shall designate an individual to serve as a chief compliance officer.

(B) Duties. The chief compliance officer shall—

(i) Report directly to the board or to the senior officer of the facility;

(ii) Review compliance with the core principles in this subsection;

(iii) In consultation with the board of the facility, a body performing a function similar to that of a board, or the senior officer of the facility, resolve any conflicts of interest that may arise;

(iv) Be responsible for establishing and administering the policies and procedures required to be established pursuant to this section;

(v) Ensure compliance with this title and the rules and regulations issued under this title, including rules prescribed by the Commission pursuant to this section;

(vi) Establish procedures for the remediation of noncompliance issues found during—

(I) Compliance office reviews;

(II) Look backs;

(III) Internal or external audit findings;

(IV) Self-reported errors; or

(V) Through validated complaints; and

(vii) Establish and follow appropriate procedures for the handling, management response, remediation, retesting, and closing of noncompliance issues.

(C) Annual Reports.

(i) In General. In accordance with rules prescribed by the Commission, the chief compliance officer shall annually prepare and sign a report that contains a description of—

(I) The compliance of the security-based swap execution facility with this title; and

(II) The policies and procedures, including the code of ethics and conflict of interest policies, of the security-based swap execution facility.

(ii) Requirements. The chief compliance officer shall—

(I) Submit each report described in clause (i) with the appropriate financial report of the security-based swap execution facility that is required to be submitted to the Commission pursuant to this section; and

(II) Include in the report a certification that, under penalty of law, the report is accurate and complete.

(e) EXEMPTIONS. The Commission may exempt, conditionally or unconditionally, a security-based swap execution facility from registration under this section if the Commission finds that the facility is subject to comparable, comprehensive supervision and regulation on a consolidated basis by the Commodity Futures Trading Commission.

(f) RULES. The Commission shall prescribe rules governing the regulation of security-based swap execution facilities under this section.

Sec. 3E. SEGREGATION OF ASSETS HELD AS COLLATERAL IN SECURITY-BASED SWAP TRANSACTIONS

(a) REGISTRATION REQUIREMENT. It shall be unlawful for any person to accept any money, securities, or property (or to extend any credit in lieu of money, securities, or property) from, for, or on behalf of a security-based swaps customer to margin, guarantee, or secure a security-based swap cleared by or through a clearing agency (including money, securities, or property accruing to the customer as the result of such a security-based swap), unless the person shall have registered under this title with the Commission as a broker, dealer, or security-based swap dealer, and the registration shall not have expired nor been suspended nor revoked.

(b) CLEARED SECURITY-BASED SWAPS.

(1) Segregation Required. A broker, dealer, or security-based swap dealer shall treat and deal with all money, securities, and property of any security-based swaps customer received to margin, guarantee, or secure a security-based swap cleared by or though a clearing agency (including money, securities, or property accruing to the security-based swaps customer as the result of such a security-based swap) as belonging to the security-based swaps customer.

(2) Commingling Prohibited. Money, securities, and property of a security-based swaps customer described in paragraph (1) shall be separately accounted for and shall not be commingled with the funds of the broker, dealer, or security-based swap dealer or be used to margin, secure, or guarantee any trades or contracts of any security-based swaps customer or person other than the person for whom the same are held.

(c) EXCEPTIONS.

(1) Use of Funds.

(A) In General. Notwithstanding subsection (b), money, securities, and property of a security-based swaps customer of a broker, dealer, or security-based swap dealer described in subsection (b) may, for convenience, be commingled and deposited in the same 1 or more accounts with any bank or trust company or with a clearing agency.

(B) Withdrawal. Notwithstanding subsection (b), such share of the money, securities, and property described in subparagraph (A) as in the normal course of business shall be necessary to margin, guarantee, secure, transfer, adjust, or settle a cleared security-based swap with a clearing agency, or with any member of the clearing agency, may be withdrawn and applied to such purposes, including the payment of commissions, brokerage, interest, taxes, storage, and other charges, lawfully accruing in connection with the cleared security-based swap.

(2) Commission Action. Notwithstanding subsection (b), in accordance with such terms and conditions as the Commission may prescribe by rule, regulation, or order, any money, securities, or property of the security-based swaps customer of a broker, dealer, or security-based swap dealer described in subsection (b) may be commingled and deposited as provided in this section with any other money, securities, or property received by the broker, dealer, or security-based swap dealer and required by the Commission to be separately accounted for and treated and dealt with as belonging to the security-based swaps customer of the broker, dealer, or security-based swap dealer.

(d) PERMITTED INVESTMENTS. Money described in subsection (b) may be invested in obligations of the United States, in general obligations of any State or of any political subdivision of a State, and in obligations fully guaranteed as to principal and interest by the United States, or in any other investment that the Commission may by rule or regulation prescribe, and such investments shall be made in accordance with such rules and regulations and subject to such conditions as the Commission may prescribe.

(e) PROHIBITION. It shall be unlawful for any person, including any clearing agency and any depository institution, that has received any money, securities, or property for deposit in a separate account or accounts as provided in subsection (b) to hold, dispose of, or use any such money, securities, or property as belonging to the depositing broker, dealer, or security-based swap dealer or any person other than the swaps customer of the broker, dealer, or security-based swap dealer.

(f) SEGREGATION REQUIREMENTS FOR UNCLEARED SECURITY-BASED SWAPS.

(1) Segregation of Assets Held as Collateral In Uncleared Security-Based Swap Transactions.

(A) Notification. A security-based swap dealer or major security-based swap participant shall be required to notify the counterparty of the security-based swap dealer or major security-based swap participant at the beginning of a security-based swap transaction that the counterparty has the right to require segregation of the funds of other property supplied to margin, guarantee, or secure the obligations of the counterparty.

(B) Segregation and Maintenance of Funds. At the request of a counterparty to a security-based swap that provides funds or other property to a security-based swap dealer or major security-based swap participant to margin, guarantee, or secure the obligations of the counterparty, the security-based swap dealer or major security-based swap participant shall—

(i) Segregate the funds or other property for the benefit of the counterparty; and

(ii) In accordance with such rules and regulations as the Commission may promulgate, maintain the funds or other property in a segregated account separate from the assets and other interests of the security-based swap dealer or major security-based swap participant.

(2) Applicability. The requirements described in paragraph (1) shall—

(A) Apply only to a security-based swap between a counterparty and a security-based swap dealer or major security-based swap participant that is not submitted for clearing to a clearing agency;

(B) (i) Not apply to variation margin payments; or

(ii) Not preclude any commercial arrangement regarding—

(I) The investment of segregated funds or other property that may only be invested in such investments as the Commission may permit by rule or regulation; and

(II) The related allocation of gains and losses resulting from any investment of the segregated funds or other property.

(3) Use of Independent Third-Party Custodians. The segregated account described in paragraph (1) shall be—

(A) Carried by an independent third-party custodian; and

(B) Designated as a segregated account for and on behalf of the counterparty.

(4) Reporting Requirement. If the counterparty does not choose to require segregation of the funds or other property supplied to margin, guarantee, or secure the obligations of the counterparty, the security-based swap dealer or major security-based swap participant shall report to the counterparty of the security-based swap dealer or major security-based swap participant on a quarterly basis that the back office procedures of the security-based swap dealer or major security-based swap participant relating to margin and collateral requirements are in compliance with the agreement of the counterparties.

(g) BANKRUPTCY. A security-based swap, as defined in section 3(a)(68) shall be considered to be a security as such term is used in section 101(53A)(B) and subchapter III of title 11, United States Code. An account that holds a security-based swap, other than a portfolio margining account referred to in section 15(c)(3)(C) shall be considered to be a securities account, as that term is defined in section 741 of title 11, United States Code. The definitions of the terms "purchase" and "sale" in section 3(a)(13) and (14) shall be applied to the terms "purchase" and "sale", as used in section 741 of title 11, United States Code. The term "customer", as defined in section 741 of title 11, United States Code, excludes any person, to the extent that such person has a claim based on any open repurchase agreement, open reverse repurchase agreement, stock borrowed agreement, non-cleared option, or non-cleared security-based swap except to the extent of any margin delivered to or by the customer with respect to which there is a customer protection requirement under section 15(c)(3) or a segregation requirement.

Sec. 4. SECURITIES AND EXCHANGE COMMISSION

(a) There is hereby established a Securities and Exchange Commission (hereinafter referred to as the "Commission") to be composed of five commissioners to be appointed by the President by and with the advice and consent of the Senate. Not more than three of such commissioners shall be members of the same political party, and in making appointments members of different political parties shall be appointed alternately as nearly as may be practicable. No commissioner shall engage in any other business, vocation, or employment than that of serving as commissioner, nor shall any commissioner participate, directly or indirectly, in any stock-market operations or transactions of a character subject to regulation by the Commission pursuant to this title. Each commissioner shall hold office for a term of five years and until his successor is appointed and has qualified, except that he shall not so continue to serve beyond the expiration of the next session of Congress subsequent to the expiration of said fixed term of office, and except (1) any Commissioner appointed to fill a vacancy occurring prior to the expiration of the term for which his predecessor was appointed shall be appointed for the remainder of such term, and (2) the terms of office of the Commissioners first taking office after the enactment of this title shall expire as designated by the President at the time of nomination, one at the end of one year, one at the end of two years, one at the end of three years, one at the end of four years, and one at the end of five years, after the date of the enactment of this title.

(b) APPOINTMENT AND COMPENSATION OF STAFF AND LEASING AUTHORITY.—

(1) APPOINTMENT AND COMPENSATION.—The Commission shall appoint and compensate officers, attorneys, economists, examiners, and other employees in accordance with section 4802 of title 5, United States Code.

(2) REPORTING OF INFORMATION.—In establishing and adjusting schedules of compensation and benefits for officers, attorneys, economists, examiners, and other employees of the Commission under applicable provisions of law, the Commission shall inform the heads of the agencies referred to under section 1206 of the Financial Institutions Reform, Recovery, and Enforcement Act of 1989 (12 U.S.C. 1833b) and Congress of such compensation and benefits and shall seek to maintain comparability with such agencies regarding compensation and benefits.

(3) LEASING AUTHORITY.—Notwithstanding any other provision of law, the Commission is authorized to enter directly into leases for real property for office, meeting, storage, and such other space as is necessary to carry out its functions, and shall be exempt from any General Services Administration space management regulations or directives.

(c) Notwithstanding any other provision of law, in accordance with regulations which the Commission shall prescribe to prevent conflicts of interest, the Commission may accept payment and reimbursement, in cash or in kind, from non-Federal agencies, organizations, and individuals for travel, subsistence, and other necessary expenses incurred by Commission members and employees in attending meetings and conferences concerning the functions or activities of the Commission. Any payment or reimbursement accepted shall be credited to the appropriated funds of the Commission. The amount of travel, subsistence, and other necessary expenses for members and employees paid or reimbursed under this subsection may exceed per diem amounts established in official travel regulations, but the Commission may include in its regulations under this subsection a limitation on such amounts.

(d) Notwithstanding any other provision of law, former employers of participants in the Commission's professional fellows programs may pay such participants their actual expenses for relocation to Washington, District of Columbia, to facilitate their participation in such programs, and program participants may accept such payments.

(e) Notwithstanding any other provision of law, whenever any fee is required to be paid to the Commission pursuant to any provision of the securities laws or any other law, the Commission may provide by rule that such fee shall be paid in a manner other than in cash and the

Commission may also specify the time that such fee shall be determined and paid relative to the filing of any statement or document with the Commission.

(f) REIMBURSEMENT OF EXPENSES FOR ASSISTING FOREIGN SECURITIES AUTHORITIES.—Notwithstanding any other provision of law, the Commission may accept payment and reimbursement, in cash or in kind, from a foreign securities authority, or made on behalf of such authority, for necessary expenses incurred by the Commission, its members, and employees in carrying out any investigation pursuant to section 21(a)(2) of this title or in providing any other assistance to a foreign securities authority. Any payment or reimbursement accepted shall be considered a reimbursement to the appropriated funds of the Commission.

(g) OFFICE OF THE INVESTOR ADVOCATE.

(1) Office Established. There is established within the Commission the Office of the Investor Advocate (in this subsection referred to as the "Office").

(2) Investor Advocate.

(A) In General. The head of the Office shall be the Investor Advocate, who shall—

(i) Report directly to the Chairman; and

(ii) Be appointed by the Chairman, in consultation with the Commission, from among individuals having experience in advocating for the interests of investors in securities and investor protection issues, from the perspective of investors.

(B) Compensation. The annual rate of pay for the Investor Advocate shall be equal to the highest rate of annual pay for other senior executives who report to the Chairman of the Commission.

(C) Limitation on Service. An individual who serves as the Investor Advocate may not be employed by the Commission—

(i) During the 2-year period ending on the date of appointment as Investor Advocate; or

(ii) During the 5-year period beginning on the date on which the person ceases to serve as the Investor Advocate.

(3) Staff of Office. The Investor Advocate, after consultation with the Chairman of the Commission, may retain or employ independent counsel, research staff, and service staff, as the Investor Advocate deems necessary to carry out the functions, powers, and duties of the Office.

(4) Functions of the Investor Advocate. The Investor Advocate shall—

(A) Assist retail investors in resolving significant problems such investors may have with the Commission or with self-regulatory organizations;

(B) Identify areas in which investors would benefit from changes in the regulations of the Commission or the rules of self-regulatory organizations;

(C) Identify problems that investors have with financial service providers and investment products;

(D) Analyze the potential impact on investors of—

(i) Proposed regulations of the Commission; and

(ii) Proposed rules of self-regulatory organizations registered under this title; and

(E) To the extent practicable, propose to the Commission changes in the regulations or orders of the Commission and to Congress any legislative, administrative, or personnel changes that may be appropriate to mitigate problems identified under this paragraph and to promote the interests of investors.

(5) Access to Documents. The Commission shall ensure that the Investor Advocate has full access to the documents of the Commission and any self-regulatory organization, as necessary to carry out the functions of the Office.

(6) Annual Reports.

(A) Report on Objectives.

(i) In General. Not later than June 30 of each year after 2010, the Investor Advocate shall submit to the Committee on Banking, Housing, and Urban Affairs of the Senate and the Committee on Financial Services of the House of Representatives a report on the objectives of the Investor Advocate for the following fiscal year.

(ii) Contents. Each report required under clause (i) shall contain full and substantive analysis and explanation.

(B) Report on Activities.

(i) In General. Not later than December 31 of each year after 2010, the Investor Advocate shall submit to the Committee on Banking, Housing, and Urban Affairs of the Senate and the Committee on Financial Services of the House of Representatives a report on the activities of the Investor Advocate during the immediately preceding fiscal year.

(ii) Contents. Each report required under clause (i) shall include—

(I) Appropriate statistical information and full and substantive analysis;

(II) Information on steps that the Investor Advocate has taken during the reporting period to improve investor services and the responsiveness of the Commission and self-regulatory organizations to investor concerns;

(III) A summary of the most serious problems encountered by investors during the reporting period;

(IV) An inventory of the items described in subclause (III) that includes—

(aa) Identification of any action taken by the Commission or the self-regulatory organization and the result of such action;

(bb) The length of time that each item has remained on such inventory; and

(cc) For items on which no action has been taken, the reasons for inaction, and an identification of any official who is responsible for such action;

(V) Recommendations for such administrative and legislative actions as may be appropriate to resolve problems encountered by investors; and

(VI) Any other information, as determined appropriate by the Investor Advocate.

(iii) Independence. Each report required under this paragraph shall be provided directly to the Committees listed in clause (i) without any prior review or comment from the Commission, any commissioner, any other officer or employee of the Commission, or the Office of Management and Budget.

(iv) Confidentiality. No report required under clause (i) may contain confidential information.

(7) Regulations. The Commission shall, by regulation, establish procedures requiring a formal response to all recommendations submitted to the Commission by the Investor Advocate, not later than 3 months after the date of such submission.

(8) Ombudsman.

(A) Appointment. Not later than 180 days after the date on which the first Investor Advocate is appointed under paragraph (2)(A)(i), the Investor Advocate shall appoint an Ombudsman, who shall report directly to the Investor Advocate.

(B) Duties. The Ombudsman appointed under subparagraph (A) shall—

(i) Act as a liaison between the Commission and any retail investor in resolving problems that retail investors may have with the Commission or with self-regulatory organizations;

(ii) Review and make recommendations regarding policies and procedures to encourage persons to present questions to the Investor Advocate regarding compliance with the securities laws; and

(iii) Establish safeguards to maintain the confidentiality of communications between the persons described in clause (ii) and the Ombudsman.

(C) Limitation. In carrying out the duties of the Ombudsman under subparagraph (B), the Ombudsman shall utilize personnel of the Commission to the extent practicable. Nothing in this paragraph shall be construed as replacing, altering, or diminishing the activities of any ombudsman or similar office of any other agency.

(D) Report. The Ombudsman shall submit a semiannual report to the Investor Advocate that describes the activities and evaluates the effectiveness of the Ombudsman during the preceding year. The Investor Advocate shall include the reports required under this section in the reports required to be submitted by the Inspector Advocate under paragraph (6).

(h) EXAMINERS.

(1) Division of Trading and Markets. The Division of Trading and Markets of the Commission, or any successor organizational unit, shall have a staff of examiners who shall—

(A) Perform compliance inspections and examinations of entities under the jurisdiction of that Division; and

(B) Report to the Director of that Division.

(2) Division of Investment Management. The Division of Investment Management of the Commission, or any successor organizational unit, shall have a staff of examiners who shall—

(A) Perform compliance inspections and examinations of entities under the jurisdiction of that Division; and

(B) Report to the Director of that Division.

(i) SECURITIES AND EXCHANGE COMMISSION RESERVE FUND.

(1) Reserve Fund Established. There is established in the Treasury of the United States a separate fund, to be known as the "Securities and Exchange Commission Reserve Fund" (referred to in this subsection as the "Reserve Fund").

(2) Reserve Fund Amounts.

(A) In General. Except as provided in subparagraph (B), any registration fees collected by the Commission under section 6(b) of the Securities Act of 1933 (15 U.S.C. 77f(b)) or section 24(f) of the Investment Company Act of 1940 (15 U.S.C. 80a-24(f)) shall be deposited into the Reserve Fund.

(B) Limitations. For any 1 fiscal year—

(i) The amount deposited in the Fund may not exceed $50,000,000; and

(ii) The balance in the Fund may not exceed $100,000,000.

(C) Excess Fees. Any amounts in excess of the limitations described in subparagraph (B) that the Commission collects from registration fees under section 6(b) of the Securities Act of 1933 (15 U.S.C. 77f(b)) or section 24(f) of the Investment Company Act of 1940 (15 U.S.C. 80a-24(f)) shall be deposited in the General Fund of the Treasury of the United States and shall not be available for obligation by the Commission.

(3) Use of Amounts in Reserve Fund. The Commission may obligate amounts in the Reserve Fund, not to exceed a total of $100,000,000 in any 1 fiscal year, as the Commission determines is necessary to carry out the functions of the Commission. Any amounts in the reserve fund shall remain available until expended. Not later than 10 days after the date on which the Commission obligates amounts under this paragraph, the Commission shall notify Congress of the date, amount, and purpose of the obligation.

(4) Rule of Construction. Amounts collected and deposited in the Reserve Fund shall not be construed to be Government funds or appropriated monies and shall not be subject to apportionment for the purpose of chapter 15 of title 31, United States Code, or under any other authority.

(j) OFFICE OF THE ADVOCATE FOR SMALL BUSINESS CAPITAL FORMATION.

(1) Office Established. There is established within the Commission the Office of the Advocate for Small Business Capital Formation (hereafter in this subsection referred to as the "Office").

(2) Advocate For Small Business Capital Formation.

(A) In General. The head of the Office shall be the Advocate for Small Business Capital Formation, who shall—

(i) Report directly to the Commission; and

(ii) Be appointed by the Commission, from among individuals having experience in advocating for the interests of small businesses and encouraging small business capital formation.

(B) Compensation. The annual rate of pay for the Advocate for Small Business Capital Formation shall be equal to the highest rate of annual pay for other senior executives who report directly to the Commission.

(C) No Current Employee of the Commission. An individual may not be appointed as the Advocate for Small Business Capital Formation if the individual is currently employed by the Commission.

(3) Staff of Office. The Advocate for Small Business Capital Formation, after consultation with the Commission, may retain or employ independent counsel, research staff, and service staff, as the Advocate for Small Business Capital Formation determines to be necessary to carry out the functions of the Office.

(4) Functions of the Advocate For Small Business Capital Formation. The Advocate for Small Business Capital Formation shall—

(A) Assist small businesses and small business investors in resolving significant problems such businesses and investors may have with the Commission or with self-regulatory organizations;

(B) Identify areas in which small businesses and small business investors would benefit from changes in the regulations of the Commission or the rules of self-regulatory organizations;

(C) Identify problems that small businesses have with securing access to capital, including any unique challenges to minority-owned small businesses, women-owned small businesses, and small businesses affected by hurricanes or other natural disasters.

(D) Analyze the potential impact on small businesses and small business investors of—

(i) Proposed regulations of the Commission that are likely to have a significant economic impact on small businesses and small business capital formation; and

(ii) Proposed rules that are likely to have a significant economic impact on small businesses and small business capital formation of self-regulatory organizations registered under this title;

(E) Conduct outreach to small businesses and small business investors, including through regional roundtables, in order to solicit views on relevant capital formation issues;

(F) To the extent practicable, propose to the Commission changes in the regulations or orders of the Commission and to Congress any legislative, administrative, or personnel changes that may be appropriate to mitigate problems identified under this paragraph and to promote the interests of small businesses and small business investors;

(G) Consult with the Investor Advocate on proposed recommendations made under subparagraph (F); and

(H) Advise the Investor Advocate on issues related to small businesses and small business investors.

(5) Access to Documents. The Commission shall ensure that the Advocate for Small Business Capital Formation has full access to the documents and information of the Commission and any self-regulatory organization, as necessary to carry out the functions of the Office.

(6) Annual Report on Activities.

(A) In General. Not later than December 31 of each year after 2015, the Advocate for Small Business Capital Formation shall submit to the Committee on Banking, Housing, and Urban Affairs of the Senate and the Committee on Financial Services of the House of Representatives a report on the activities of the Advocate for Small Business Capital Formation during the immediately preceding fiscal year.

(B) Contents. Each report required under subparagraph (A) shall include—

(i) Appropriate statistical information and full and substantive analysis;

(ii) Information on steps that the Advocate for Small Business Capital Formation has taken during the reporting period to improve small business services and the responsiveness of the Commission and self-regulatory organizations to small business and small business investor concerns;

(iii) A summary of the most serious issues encountered by small businesses and small business investors, including any unique issues encountered by minority-owned small businesses, women-owned small businesses, and small businesses affected by hurricanes or other natural disasters and their investors, during the reporting period;

(iv) An inventory of the items summarized under clause (iii) (including items summarized under such clause for any prior reporting period on which no action has been taken or that have not been resolved to the satisfaction of the Advocate for Small Business Capital Formation as of the beginning of the reporting period covered by the report) that includes—

(I) Identification of any action taken by the Commission or the self-regulatory organization and the result of such action;

(II) The length of time that each item has remained on such inventory; and

(III) For items on which no action has been taken, the reasons for inaction, and an identification of any official who is responsible for such action;

(v) Recommendations for such changes to the regulations, guidance and orders of the Commission and such legislative actions as may be appropriate to resolve problems with the Commission and self-regulatory organizations encountered by small businesses and small business investors and to encourage small business capital formation; and

(vi) Any other information, as determined appropriate by the Advocate for Small Business Capital Formation.

(C) Confidentiality. No report required by subparagraph (A) may contain confidential information.

(D) Independence. Each report required under subparagraph (A) shall be provided directly to the committees of Congress listed in such subparagraph without any prior review or comment from the Commission, any commissioner, any other officer or employee of the Commission, or the Office of Management and Budget.

(7) Regulations. The Commission shall establish procedures requiring a formal response to all recommendations submitted to the Commission by the Advocate for Small Business Capital Formation, not later than 3 months after the date of such submission.

(8) Government-Business Forum on Small Business Capital Formation. The Advocate for Small Business Capital Formation shall be responsible for planning, organizing, and executing the annual Government-Business Forum on Small Business Capital Formation described in section 503 of the Small Business Investment Incentive Act of 1980 (15 U.S.C. 80c-1).

(9) Rule of Construction. Nothing in this subsection may be construed as replacing or reducing the responsibilities of the Investor Advocate with respect to small business investors.

Sec. 4A. DELEGATION OF FUNCTIONS BY COMMISSION

(a) In addition to its existing authority, the Securities and Exchange Commission shall have the authority to delegate, by published order or rule, any of its functions to a division of the Commission, an individual Commissioner, an administrative law judge, or an employee or employee board, including functions with respect to hearing, determining, ordering, certifying, reporting, or otherwise acting as to any work, business, or matter. Nothing in this section shall be deemed to supersede the provisions of section 556(b) of title 5, or to authorize the delegation of the function of rule-making as defined in subchapter II of chapter 5 of title 5, United States Code, with reference to general rules as distinguished from rules of particular applicability, or of the making of any rule pursuant to section 19(c) of this title.

(b) With respect to the delegation of any of its functions, as provided in subsection (a) of this section, the Commission shall retain a discretionary right to review the action of any such division of the Commission, individual Commissioner, administrative law judge, employee, or employee board, upon its own initiative or upon petition of a party to or intervenor in such action, within such time and in such manner as the Commission by rule shall prescribe. The vote of one member of the Commission shall be sufficient to bring any such action before the Commission for review. A person or party shall be entitled to review by the Commission if he or it is adversely affected by action at a delegated level which (1) denies any request for action pursuant to section 8(a) or section 8(c) of the Securities Act of 1933 or the first sentence of section 12(d) of this title; (2) suspends trading in a security pursuant to section 12(k) of this title; or (3) is pursuant to any provision of this title in a case of adjudication, as defined in section 551 of title 5, United States Code, not required by this title to be determined on the record after notice and opportunity for hearing (except to the extent there is involved a matter described in section 554(a) (1) through (6) of such title 5).

(c) If the right to exercise such review is declined, or if no such review is sought within the time stated in the rules promulgated by the Commission, then the action of any such division of the Commission, individual Commissioner, administrative law judge, employee, or employee board, shall for all purposes, including appeal or review thereof, be deemed the action of the Commission.

Sec. 4C. APPEARANCE AND PRACTICE BEFORE THE COMMISSION

(a) AUTHORITY TO CENSURE.—The Commission may censure any person, or deny, temporarily or permanently, to any person the privilege of appearing or practicing before the Commission in any way, if that person is found by the Commission, after notice and opportunity for hearing in the matter—

(1) not to possess the requisite qualifications to represent others;

(2) to be lacking in character or integrity, or to have engaged in unethical or improper professional conduct; or

(3) to have willfully violated, or willfully aided and abetted the violation of, any provision of the securities laws or the rules and regulations issued thereunder.

(b) DEFINITION.—With respect to any registered public accounting firm or associated person, for purposes of this section, the term "improper professional conduct" means—

(1) intentional or knowing conduct, including reckless conduct, that results in a violation of applicable professional standards; and

(2) negligent conduct in the form of—

(A) a single instance of highly unreasonable conduct that results in a violation of applicable professional standards in circumstances in which the registered public accounting firm or associated person knows, or should know, that heightened scrutiny is warranted; or

(B) repeated instances of unreasonable conduct, each resulting in a violation of applicable professional standards, that indicate a lack of competence to practice before the Commission.

Sec. 4D. ADDITIONAL DUTIES OF INSPECTOR GENERAL

(a) SUGGESTION SUBMISSIONS BY COMMISSION EMPLOYEES.

(1) Hotline Established. The Inspector General of the Commission shall establish and maintain a telephone hotline or other electronic means for the receipt of—

(A) Suggestions by employees of the Commission for improvements in the work efficiency, effectiveness, and productivity, and the use of the resources, of the Commission; and

(B) Allegations by employees of the Commission of waste, abuse, misconduct, or mismanagement within the Commission.

(2) Confidentiality. The Inspector General shall maintain as confidential—

(A) The identity of any individual who provides information by the means established under paragraph (1), unless the individual requests otherwise, in writing; and

(B) At the request of any such individual, any specific information provided by the individual.

(b) CONSIDERATION OF REPORTS. The Inspector General shall consider any suggestions or allegations received by the means established under subsection (a)(1), and shall recommend appropriate action in relation to such suggestions or allegations.

(c) RECOGNITION. The Inspector General may recognize any employee who makes a suggestion under subsection (a)(1) (or by other means) that would or does—

(1) Increase the work efficiency, effectiveness, or productivity of the Commission; or

(2) Reduce waste, abuse, misconduct, or mismanagement within the Commission.

(d) REPORT. The Inspector General of the Commission shall submit to Congress an annual report containing a description of—

(1) The nature, number, and potential benefits of any suggestions received under subsection (a);

(2) The nature, number, and seriousness of any allegations received under subsection (a);

(3) Any recommendations made or actions taken by the Inspector General in response to substantiated allegations received under subsection (a); and

(4) Any action the Commission has taken in response to suggestions or allegations received under subsection (a).

(e) FUNDING. The activities of the Inspector General under this subsection shall be funded by the Securities and Exchange Commission Investor Protection Fund established under section 21F.

Sec. 4E. DEADLINE FOR COMPLETING ENFORCEMENT INVESTIGATIONS AND COMPLIANCE EXAMINATIONS AND INSPECTIONS

(a) ENFORCEMENT INVESTIGATIONS.

(1) In General. Not later than 180 days after the date on which Commission staff provide a written Wells notification to any person, the Commission staff shall either file an action against such person or provide notice to the Director of the Division of Enforcement of its intent to not file an action.

(2) Exceptions For Certain Complex Actions. Notwithstanding paragraph (1), if the Director of the Division of Enforcement of the Commission or the Director's designee determines that a particular enforcement investigation is sufficiently complex such that a determination regarding the filing of an action against a person cannot be completed within the deadline specified in paragraph (1), the Director of the Division of Enforcement of the Commission or the Director's designee may, after providing notice to the Chairman of the Commission, extend such deadline as needed for one additional 180-day period. If after the additional 180-day period the Director of the Division of Enforcement of the Commission or the Director's designee determines that a particular enforcement investigation is sufficiently complex such that a determination regarding the filing of an action against a person cannot be completed within the additional 180-day period, the Director of the Division of

Enforcement of the Commission or the Director's designee may, after providing notice to and receiving approval of the Commission, extend such deadline as needed for one or more additional successive 180-day periods.

(b) COMPLIANCE EXAMINATIONS AND INSPECTIONS.

(1) In General. Not later than 180 days after the date on which Commission staff completes the on-site portion of its compliance examination or inspection or receives all records requested from the entity being examined or inspected, whichever is later, Commission staff shall provide the entity being examined or inspected with written notification indicating either that the examination or inspection has concluded, has concluded without findings, or that the staff requests the entity undertake corrective action.

(2) Exception For Certain Complex Actions. Notwithstanding paragraph (1), if the head of any division or office within the Commission responsible for compliance examinations and inspections or his designee determines that a particular compliance examination or inspection is sufficiently complex such that a determination regarding concluding the examination or inspection, or regarding the staff requests the entity undertake corrective action, cannot be completed within the deadline specified in paragraph (1), the head of any division or office within the Commission responsible for compliance examinations and inspections or his designee may, after providing notice to the Chairman of the Commission, extend such deadline as needed for one additional 180-day period.

Sec. 5. TRANSACTIONS ON UNREGISTERED EXCHANGES

It shall be unlawful for any broker, dealer, or exchange, directly or indirectly, to make use of the mails or any means or instrumentality of interstate commerce for the purpose of using any facility of an exchange within or subject to the jurisdiction of the United States to effect any transaction in a security or to report any such transaction, unless such exchange (1) is registered as a national securities exchange under section 6 of this title, or (2) is exempted from such registration upon application by the exchange because, in the opinion of the Commission, by reason of the limited volume of transactions effected on such exchange, it is not practicable and not necessary or appropriate in the public interest or for the protection of investors to require such registration.

Sec. 6. NATIONAL SECURITIES EXCHANGES

(a) An exchange may be registered as a national securities exchange under the terms and conditions hereinafter provided in this section and in accordance with the provisions of section 19(a) of this title, by filing with the Commission an application for registration in such form as the Commission, by rule, may prescribe containing the rules of the exchange and such other information and documents as the Commission, by rule, may prescribe as necessary or appropriate in the public interest or for the protection of investors.

(b) An exchange shall not be registered as a national securities exchange unless the Commission determines that—

(1) Such exchange is so organized and has the capacity to be able to carry out the purposes of this title and to comply, and (subject to any rule or order of the Commission pursuant to section 17(d) or 19(g)(2) of this title) to enforce compliance by its members and peron pursuant to section 17(d) or 19(g)(2) of this title) to enforce compliance by its members and persons associated with its members, with the provisions of this title, the rules and regulations thereunder, and the rules of the exchange.

(2) Subject to the provisions of subsection (c) of this section, the rules of the exchange provide that any registered broker or dealer or natural person associated with a registered broker or dealer may become a member of such exchange and any person may become associated with a member thereof.

(3) The rules of the exchange assure a fair representation of its members in the selection of its directors and administration of its affairs and provide that one or more directors

shall be representative of issuers and investors and not be associated with a member of the exchange, broker, or dealer.

(4) The rules of the exchange provide for the equitable allocation of reasonable dues, fees, and other charges among its members and issuers and other persons using its facilities.

(5) The rules of the exchange are designed to prevent fraudulent and manipulative acts and practices, to promote just and equitable principles of trade, to foster cooperation and coordination with persons engaged in regulating, clearing, settling, processing information with respect to, and facilitating transactions in securities, to remove impediments to and perfect the mechanism of a free and open market and a national market system, and, in general, to protect investors and the public interest; and are not designed to permit unfair discrimination between customers, issuers, brokers, or dealers, or to regulate by virtue of any authority conferred by this title matters not related to the purposes of this title or the administration of the exchange.

(6) The rules of the exchange provide that (subject to any rule or order to the Commission pursuant to section 17(d) or 19(g)(2) of this title) its members and persons associated with its members shall be appropriately disciplined for violation of the provisions of this title, the rules or regulations thereunder, or the rules of the exchange, by expulsion, suspension, limitation of activities, functions, and operations, fine, censure, being suspended or barred from being associated with a member, or any other fitting sanction.

(7) The rules of the exchange are in accordance with the provisions of subsection (d) of this section, and, in general, provide a fair procedure for the disciplining of members and persons associated with members, the denial of membership to any person seeking membership therein, the barring of any person from becoming associated with a member thereof, and the prohibition or limitation by the exchange of any person with respect to access to services offered by the exchange or a member thereof.

(8) The rules of the exchange do not impose any burden on competition not necessary or appropriate in furtherance of the purposes of this title.

(9)(A) The rules of the exchange prohibit the listing of any security issued in a limited partnership rollup transaction (as such term is defined in paragraphs (4) and (5) of section 14(h)), unless such transaction was conducted in accordance with procedures designed to protect the rights of limited partners, including—

(i) the right of dissenting limited partners to one of the following:

(I) an appraisal and compensation:

(II) retention of a security under substantially the same terms and conditions as the original issue;

(III) approval of the limited partnership rollup transaction by not less than 75 percent of the outstanding securities of each of the participating limited partnerships;

(IV) the use of a committee of limited partners that is independent, as determined in accordance with rules prescribed by the exchange, of the general partner of sponsor, that has been approved by a majority of the outstanding units of each of the participating limited partnerships, and that has such authority as is necessary to protect, the interest of limited partners, including the authority to hire independent advisors, to negotiate with the general partner or sponsor on behalf of the limited partners, and to make a recommendation to the limited partners with respect to the proposed transaction; or

(V) other comparable rights that are prescribed by rule by the exchange and that are designed to protect dissenting limited partners;

(ii) the right not to have their voting power unfairly reduced or abridged;

(iii) the right not to bear an unfair protion of the costs of a proposed limited partnership rollup transaction that is rejected; and

(iv) restrictions on the conversion of contingent interests of fees into non-contingent interests or fees and restrictions on the receipt of a non-contingent equity interest in exchange for fees for services which have not yet been provided.

(B) As used in this paragraph, the term "dissenting limited partner" means a person who, on the date on which soliciting material is mailed to investors, is a holder of a beneficial interest in a limited partnership that is the subject of a limited partnership rollup transaction, and who casts a vote against the transaction and complies with procedures established by the exchange, except that for purposes of an exchange or tender offer, such person shall file an objection in writing under the rules of the exchange during the period during which the offer is outstanding.

(10) (A) The rules of the exchange prohibit any member that is not the beneficial owner of a security registered under section 12 from granting a proxy to vote the security in connection with a shareholder vote described in subparagraph (B), unless the beneficial owner of the security has instructed the member to vote the proxy in accordance with the voting instructions of the beneficial owner.

(B) A shareholder vote described in this subparagraph is a shareholder vote with respect to the election of a member of the board of directors of an issuer, executive compensation, or any other significant matter, as determined by the Commission, by rule, and does not include a vote with respect to the uncontested election of a member of the board of directors of any investment company registered under the Investment Company Act of 1940 (15 U.S.C. 80b-1 et seq.).

(C) Nothing in this paragraph shall be construed to prohibit a national securities exchange from prohibiting a member that is not the beneficial owner of a security registered under section 12 from granting a proxy to vote the security in connection with a shareholder vote not described in subparagraph (A).

(c) (1) A national securities exchange shall deny membership to (A) any person, other than a natural person, which is not a registered broker or dealer or (B) any natural person who is not, or is not associated with, a registered broker or dealer.

(2) A national securities exchange may, and in cases in which the Commission, by order, directs as necessary or appropriate in the public interest or for the protection of investors shall, deny membership to any registered broker or dealer or natural person associated with a registered broker or dealer, and bar from becoming associated with a member any person, who is subject to a statutory disqualification. A national securities exchange shall file notice with the Commission not less than thirty days prior to admitting any person to membership or permitting any person to become associated with a member, if the exchange knew, or in the exercise of reasonable care should have known, that such person was subject to a statutory disqualification. The notice shall be in such form and contain such information as the Commission, by rule, may prescribe as necessary or appropriate in the public interest or for the protection of investors.

(e) (1) On and after the date of enactment of the Securities Acts Amendments of 1975, no national securities exchange may impose any schedule or fix rates of commissions, allowances, discounts, or other fees to be charged by its members: Provided, however, That until May 1, 1976, the preceding provisions of this paragraph shall not prohibit any such exchange from imposing or fixing any schedule of commissions, allowances, discounts, or other fees to be charged by its members for acting as broker on the floor of the exchange or as odd-lot dealer: And provided further, That the Commission, in accordance with the provisions of section 19(b) of this title as modified by the provisions of paragraph (3) of this subsection, may—

(A) permit a national securities exchange, by rule, to impose a reasonable schedule or fix reasonable rates of commissions, allowances, discounts, or other fees to be charged by its members for effecting transactions on such exchange prior to November 1, 1976, if the Commission finds that such schedule or fixed rates of commissions, allowances, discounts, or other fees are in the public interest; and

(B) permit a national securities exchange, by rule, to impose a schedule or fix rates of commissions, allowances, discounts, or other fees to be charged by its members for effecting transactions on such exchange after November 1, 1976, if the Commission finds that such schedule or fixed rates of commissions, allowances, discounts, or other fees (i) are reasonable in relation to the costs of providing the service for which such fees are charged (and the Commission publishes the standards employed in adjudging reasonableness) and (ii) do not impose any burden on competition not necessary or appropriate in furtherance of the purposes of this title, taking into consideration the competitive effects of permitting such schedule or fixed rates weighed against the competitive effects of other lawful actions which the Commission is authorized to take under this title.

Sec. 7. MARGIN REQUIREMENTS

(a) For the purpose of preventing the excessive use of credit for the purchase or carrying of securities, the Board of Governors of the Federal Reserve System shall, prior to the effective date of this section and from time to time thereafter, prescribe rules and regulations with respect to the amount of credit that may be initially extended and subsequently maintained on any security (other than an exempted security or a security futures product). For the initial extension of credit, such rules and regulations shall be based upon the following standard: An amount not greater than whichever is the higher of—

(1) 55 per centum of the current market price of the security, or

(2) 100 per centum of the lowest market price of the security during the preceding thirty-six calendar months, but not more than 75 per centum of the current market price.

Such rules and regulations may make appropriate provision with respect to the carrying of undermargined accounts for limited periods and under specified conditions; the withdrawal of funds or securities; the substitution or additional purchases of securities; the transfer of accounts from one lender to another; special or different margin requirements for delayed deliveries, short sales, arbitrage transactions, and securities to which paragraph (2) of this subsection does not apply; the bases and the methods to be used in calculating loans, and margins and market prices; and similar administrative adjustments and details. For the purposes of paragraph (2) of this subsection, until July 1, 1936, the lowest price at which a security has sold on or after July 1, 1933, shall be considered as the lowest price at which such security has sold during the preceding thirty-six calendar months.

(b) Notwithstanding the provisions of subsection (a) of this section, the Board of Governors of the Federal Reserve System, may, from time to time, with respect to all or specified securities or transactions, or classes of securities, or classes of transactions, by such rules and regulations (1) prescribe such lower margin requirements for the initial extension or maintenance of credit as it deems necessary or appropriate for the accommodation of commerce and industry, having due regard to the general credit situation of the country, and (2) prescribe such higher margin requirements for the initial extension or maintenance of credit as it may deem necessary or appropriate to prevent the excessive use of credit to finance transactions in securities.

(c) UNLAWFUL CREDIT EXTENSION TO CUSTOMERS.—

(1) Prohibition.—It shall be unlawful for any member of a national securities exchange or any broker or dealer, directly or indirectly, to extend or maintain credit or arrange for the extension or maintenance of credit to or for any customer—

(A) on any security (other than an exempted security except as provided in paragraph (2)), in contravention of the rules and regulations which the Board of Governors of the Federal Reserve System (hereafter in this section referred to as the "Board") shall prescribe under subsections (a) and (b); or

(B) without collateral or on any collateral other than securities, except in accordance with such rules and regulations as the Board may prescribe—

(i) to permit under specified conditions and for a limited period any such member, broker, or dealer to maintain a credit initially extended in conformity with the rules and regulations of the Board; and

(ii) to permit the extension or maintenance of credit in cases where the extension or maintenance of credit is not for the purpose of purchasing or carrying securities or of evading or circumventing the provisions of subparagraph (A).

(d) Unlawful Credit Extension in Violation of Rules and Regulations; Exceptions to Application of Rules, Etc.—

(1) Prohibition.—It shall be unlawful for any person not subject to subsection (c) to extend or maintain credit or to arrange for the extension or maintenance of credit for the purpose of purchasing or carrying any security, in contravention of such rules and regulations as the Board shall prescribe to prevent the excessive use of credit for the purchasing or carrying of or trading in securities in circumvention of the other provisions of this section. Such rules and regulations may impose upon all loans made for the purpose of purchasing or carrying securities limitations similar to those imposed upon members, brokers, or dealers by subsection (c) and the rules and regulations thereunder.

(2) Exceptions.—This subsection and the rules and regulations issued under this subsection shall not apply to any credit extended, maintained, or arranged—

(A) by a person not in the ordinary course of business;

(B) on an exempted security;

(C) to or for a member of a national securities exchange or a registered broker or dealer—

(i) a substantial portion of whose business consists of transactions with persons other than brokers or dealers; or

(ii) to finance its activities as a market maker or an underwriter;

(D) by a bank on a security other than an equity security; or

(E) as the Board shall, by such rules, regulations, or orders as it may deem necessary or appropriate in the public interest or for the protection of investors, exempt, either unconditionally or upon specified terms and conditions or for stated periods, from the operation of this subsection and the rules and regulations thereunder.

(3) Board authority.—The Board may impose such rules and regulations, in whole or in part, on any credit otherwise exempted by subparagraph (C) if it determines that such action is necessary or appropriate in the public interest or for the protection of investors.

(f)(1) It is unlawful for any United States person, or any foreign person controlled by a United States person or acting on behalf of or in conjunction with such person, to obtain, receive, or enjoy the beneficial use of a loan or other extension or credit from any lender (without regard to whether the lender's office or place of business is in a State or the transaction occurred in whole or in part within a State) for the purpose of (A) purchasing or carrying United States securities, or (B) purchasing or carrying within the United States of any other securities, if, under this section or rules and regulations prescribed thereunder, the loan or other credit transaction is prohibited or would be prohibited if it had been made or the transaction had otherwise occurred in a lender's office or other place of business in a State.

(2) For the purposes of this subsection—

(A) The term "United States person" includes a person which is organized or exists under the laws of any State or, in the case of a natural person, a citizen or resident of the United States; a domestic estate; or a trust in which one or more of the foregoing persons has a cumulative direct or indirect beneficial interest in excess of 50 per centum of the value of the trust.

(B) The term "United States security" means a security (other than an exempted security) issued by a person incorporated under the laws of any State, or whose principal place of business is within a State.

(C) The term "foreign person controlled by a United States person" includes any noncorporate entity in which United States persons directly or indirectly have more than a 50 per centum beneficial interest, and any corporation in which one or more United States persons, directly or indirectly, own stock possessing more than 50 per centum of the total combined voting power of all classes of stock entitled to vote, or more than 50 per centum of the total value of shares of all classes of stock.

(3) The Board of Governors of the Federal Reserve System may, in its discretion and with due regard for the purposes of this section, by rule or regulation exempt any class of United States persons or foreign persons controlled by a United States person from the application of this subsection.

(g) Subject to such rules and regulations as the Board of Governors of the Federal Reserve System may adopt in the public interest and for the protection of investors, no member of a national securities exchange or broker or dealer shall be deemed to have extended or maintained credit or arranged for the extension or maintenance of credit for the purpose of purchasing a security, within the meaning of this section, by reason of a bona fide agreement for delayed delivery of a mortgage related security or a small business related security against full payment of the purchase price thereof upon such delivery within one hundred and eighty days after the purchase, or within such shorter period as the Board of Governors of the Federal Reserve System may prescribe by rule or regulation.

PROHIBITION AGAINST MANIPULATION OF SECURITY PRICES

Sec. 9.   (a) It shall be unlawful for any person, directly or indirectly, by the use of the mails or any means or instrumentality of interstate commerce, or of any facility of any national securities exchange, or for any member of a national securities exchange—

(1) For the purpose of creating a false or misleading appearance of active trading in any security other than a government security, or a false or misleading appearance with respect to the market for any such security, (A) to effect any transaction in such security which involves no change in the beneficial ownership thereof, or (B) to enter an order or orders for the purchase of such security with the knowledge that an order or orders of substantially the same size, at substantially the same time, and at substantially the same price, for the sale of any such security, has been or will be entered by or for the same or different parties, or (C) to enter any order or orders for the sale of any such security with the knowledge that an order or orders of substantially the same size, at substantially the same time, and at substantially the same price, for the purchase of such security, has been or will be entered by or for the same or different parties.

(2) To effect, alone or with 1 or more other persons, a series of transactions in any security registered on a national securities exchange, any security not so registered, or in connection with any security-based swap or security-based swap agreement with respect to such security creating actual or apparent active trading in such security, or raising or depressing the price of such security, for the purpose of inducing the purchase or sale of such security by others.

(3) If a dealer, broker, security-based swap dealer, major security-based swap participant, or other person selling or offering for sale or purchasing or offering to purchase the security, a security-based swap, or a security-based swap agreement with respect to such security, to induce the purchase or sale of any security registered on a national securities exchange, any security not so registered, any security-based swap, or any security-based swap agreement with respect to such security by the circulation or dissemination in the ordinary course of business of information to the effect that the price of any such security will or is likely to rise or fall because of market operations of any 1 or more persons conducted for the purpose of raising or depressing the price of such security.

(4) If a dealer, broker, security-based swap dealer, major security-based swap participant, or other person selling or offering for sale or purchasing or offering to purchase the security, a security-based swap, or security-based swap agreement with respect to such security, to make, regarding any security registered on a national securities exchange, any security not so registered, any security-based swap, or any security-based swap agreement with respect to such security, for the purpose of inducing the purchase or sale of such security, such security-based swap, or such the circumstances under which it was made, false or misleading with respect to any material fact, and which that person knew or had reasonable ground to believe was so false or misleading.

(5) For a consideration, received directly or indirectly from a broker, dealer, security-based swap dealer, major security-based swap participant, or other person selling or offering for sale or purchasing or offering to purchase the security, a security-based swap, or security-based swap agreement with respect to such security, to induce the purchase of any security registered on a national securities exchange, any security not so registered, any security-based swap, or any security-based swap agreement with respect to such security by the circulation or dissemination of information to the effect that the price of any such security will or is likely to rise or fall because of the market operations of any 1 or more persons conducted for the purpose of raising or depressing the price of such security.

(6) To effect either alone or with one or more other persons any series of transactions for the purchase and/or sale of any security other than a government security for the purpose of pegging, fixing, or stabilizing the price of such security in contravention of such rules and regulations as the Commission may prescribe as necessary or appropriate in the public interest or for the protection of investors.

(b) It shall be unlawful for any person to effect in contravention of such rules and regulations as the Commission may prescribe as necessary or appropriate in the public interest or for the protection of investors—

(1) Any transaction in connection with any security whereby any party to such transaction acquires—

(A) Any put, call, straddle, or other option or privilege of buying the security from or selling the security to another without being bound to do so;

(B) Any security futures product on the security; or

(C) Any security-based swap involving the security or the issuer of the security;

(2) Any transaction in connection with any security with relation to which such person has, directly or indirectly, any interest in any—

(A) Such put, call, straddle, option, or privilege;

(B) Such security futures product; or

(C) Such security-based swap; or

(3) Any transaction in any security for the account of any person who such person has reason to believe has, and who actually has, directly or indirectly, any interest in any—

(A) Such put, call, straddle, option, or privilege;

(B) Such security futures product with relation to such security; or

(C) Any security-based swap involving such security or the issuer of such security.

(c) It shall be unlawful for any broker, dealer, or member of a national securities exchange directly or indirectly to endorse or guarantee the performance of any put, call, straddle, option, or privilege in relation to any security other than a government security in contravention of such rules and regulations as the Commission may prescribe as necessary or appropriate in the public interest or for the protection of investors.

(d) Transactions Relating to Short Sales of Securities. It shall be unlawful for any person, directly or indirectly, by the use of the mails or any means or instrumentality of interstate commerce, or of any facility of any national securities exchange, or for any member of a national securities exchange to effect, alone or with one or more other persons, a manipulative short sale of any security. The Commission shall issue such other rules as are necessary or appropriate to ensure that the appropriate enforcement options and remedies are available for violations of this subsection in the public interest or for the protection of investors.

(e) The terms "put," "call," "straddle," "option," or "privilege" as used in this section shall not include any registered warrant, right, or convertible security.

(f) Any person who willfully participates in any act or transaction in violation of subsection (a), (b), or (c) of this section, shall be liable to any person who shall purchase or sell any security at a price which was affected by such act or transaction, and the person so injured may sue in law or in equity in any court of competent jurisdiction to recover the damages sustained as a result of any such act or transaction. In any such suit the court may, in its discretion, require an undertaking for the payment of the costs of such suit, and assess reasonable costs, including reasonable attorneys fees, against either party litigant. Every person who becomes liable to make any payment under this subsection may recover contribution as in cases of contract from any person who, if joined in the original suit, would have been liable to make the same payment. No action shall be maintained to enforce any liability created under this section, unless brought within one year after the discovery of the facts constituting the violation and within three years after such violation.

(g) The provisions of subsection (a) shall not apply to an exempted security.

(h)(1) Notwithstanding any other provision of law, the Commission shall have the authority to regulate the trading of any put, call, straddle, option, or privilege on any security, certificate of deposit, or group or index of securities (including any interest therein or based on the value thereof), or any put, call, straddle, option, or privilege entered into on a national securities exchange relating to foreign currency (but not, with respect to any of the foregoing, an option on a contract for future delivery other than a security futures product).

(2) Notwithstanding the Commodity Exchange Act, the Commission shall have the authority to regulate the trading of any security futures product to the extent provided in the securities laws.

(i) LIMITATIONS ON PRACTICES THAT AFFECT MARKET VOLATILITY.—It shall be unlawful for any person, by the use of the mails or any means or instrumentality of interstate commerce or of any facility of any national securities exchange, to use or employ any act or practice in connection with the purchase or sale of any equity security in contravention of such rules or regulations as the Commission may adopt, consistent with the public interest, the protection of investors, and the maintenance of fair and orderly markets—

(1) to prescribe means reasonably designed to prevent manipulation of price levels of the equity securities market or a substantial segment thereof; and

(2) to prohibit or constrain, during periods of extraordinary market volatility, any trading practice in connection with the purchase or sale of equity securities that the Commission determines (A) has previously contributed significantly to extraordinary levels of volatility that have threatened the maintenance of fair and orderly markets; and (B) is reasonably certain to engender such levels of volatility if not prohibited or constrained. In adopting rules under paragraph (2), the Commission shall, consistent with the purposes of this subsection, minimize the impact on the normal operations of the market and a natural person's freedom to buy or sell any equity security.

(j) The authority of the Commission under this section with respect to security-based swap agreements shall be subject to the restrictions and limitations of section 3A(b) of this title.

(j)* It shall be unlawful for any person, directly or indirectly, by the use of any means or instrumentality of interstate commerce or of the mails, or of any facility of any national securities exchange, to effect any transaction in, or to induce or attempt to induce the purchase or sale of, any security-based swap, in connection with which such person engages in any fraudulent, deceptive, or manipulative act or practice, makes any fictitious quotation, or engages in any transaction, practice, or course of business which operates as a fraud or deceit upon any person. The Commission shall, for the purposes of this subsection, by rules and regulations define, and prescribe means reasonably designed to prevent, such transactions, acts, practices, and courses of business as are fraudulent, deceptive, or manipulative, and such quotations as are fictitious.

REGULATION OF THE USE OF MANIPULATIVE AND DECEPTIVE DEVICES

Sec. 10. It shall be unlawful for any person, directly or indirectly, by the use of any means or instrumentality of interstate commerce or of the mails, or of any facility of any national securities exchange

---

*[This subsection was not redesignated as (k) when §929X of the Dodd-Frank Wall Street Reform and Consumer Protection Act redesignated the prior subsections. —EDS.]

(a) (1) To effect a short sale, or to use or employ any stop-loss order in connection with the purchase or sale, of any security other than a government security in contravention of such rules and regulations as the Commission may prescribe as necessary or appropriate in the public interest or for the protection of investors.

(2) Paragraph (1) of this subsection shall not apply to security futures products.

(b) To use or employ, in connection with the purchase or sale of any security registered on a national securities exchange or any security not so registered, or any securities-based swap agreement any manipulative or deceptive device or contrivance in contravention of such rules and regulations as the commission may prescribe as necessary or appropriate in the public interest or for the protection of investors.

Rules promulgated under subsection (b) that prohibit fraud, manipulation, or insider trading (but not rules imposing or specifying reporting or recordkeeping requirements, procedures, or standards as prophylactic measures against fraud, manipulation, or insider trading), and judicial precedents decided under subsection (b) and rules promulgated thereunder that prohibit fraud, manipulation, or insider trading, shall apply to security-based swap agreements to the same extent as they apply to securities. Judicial precedents decided under section 17(a) of the Securities Act of 1933 and sections 9, 15, 16, 20, and 21A of this title, and judicial precedents decided under applicable rules promulgated under such sections, shall apply to security-based swap agreements to the same extent as they apply to securities.

(c) (1) To effect, accept, or facilitate a transaction involving the loan or borrowing of securities in contravention of such rules and regulations as the Commission may prescribe as necessary or appropriate in the public interest or for the protection of investors.

(2) Nothing in paragraph (1) may be construed to limit the authority of the appropriate Federal banking agency (as defined in section 3(q) of the Federal Deposit Insurance Act (12 U.S.C. 1813(q))), the National Credit Union Administration, or any other Federal department or agency having a responsibility under Federal law to prescribe rules or regulations restricting transactions involving the loan or borrowing of securities in order to protect the safety and soundness of a financial institution or to protect the financial system from systemic risk.

AUDIT REQUIREMENTS

Sec. 10A (a) IN GENERAL.—Each audit required pursuant to this title of the financial statements of an issuer by a registered public accounting firm shall include, in accordance with generally accepted auditing standards, as may be modified or supplemented from time to time by the Commission—

(1) procedures designed to provide reasonable assurance of detecting illegal acts that would have a direct and material effect on the determination of financial statement amounts;

(2) procedures designed to identify related party transactions that are material to the financial statements or otherwise require disclosure therein; and

(3) an evaluation of whether there is substantial doubt about the ability of the issuer to continue as a going concern during the ensuing fiscal year.

(b) REQUIRED RESPONSE TO AUDIT DISCOVERIES.—

(1) INVESTIGATION AND REPORT TO MANAGEMENT.—If, in the course of conducting an audit pursuant to this title to which subsection (a) applies, the registered public accounting firm detects or otherwise becomes aware of information indicating that an illegal act (whether or not perceived to have a material effect on the financial statements of the issuer) has or may have occurred, the firm shall, in accordance with generally accepted auditing standards, as may be modified or supplemented from time to time by the Commission—

(A) (i) determine whether it is likely that an illegal act has occurred; and

(ii) if so, determine and consider the possible effect of the illegal act on the financial statements of the issuer, including any contingent monetary effects, such as fines, penalties, and damages; and

(B) as soon as practicable, inform the appropriate level of the management of the issuer and assure that the audit committee of the issuer, or the board of directors of the issuer in the absence of such a committee, is adequately informed with respect to illegal acts that have been detected or have otherwise come to the attention of such firm in the course of the audit, unless the illegal act is clearly inconsequential.

(2) Response to failure to take remedial action.—If, after determining that the audit committee of the board of directors of the issuer, or the board of directors of the issuer in the absence of an audit committee, is adequately informed with respect to illegal acts that have been detected or have otherwise come to the attention of the firm in the course of the audit of such firm, the registered public accounting firm concludes that—

(A) the illegal act has a material effect on the financial statements of the issuer;

(B) the senior management has not taken, and the board of directors has not caused senior management to take, timely and appropriate remedial actions with respect to the illegal act; and

(C) the failure to take remedial action is reasonably expected to warrant departure from a standard report of the auditor, when made, or warrant resignation from the audit engagement; the registered public accounting firm shall, as soon as practicable, directly report its conclusions to the board of directors.

(3) Notice to commission; response to failure to notify.—An issuer whose board of directors receives a report under paragraph (2) shall inform the Commission by notice not later than 1 business day after the receipt of such report and shall furnish the registered public accounting firm making such report with a copy of the notice furnished to the Commission. If the registered public accounting firm fails to receive a copy of the notice before the expiration of the required 1-business-day period, the registered public accounting firm shall—

(A) resign from the engagement; or

(B) furnish to the Commission a copy of its report (or the documentation of any oral report given) not later than 1 business day following such failure to receive notice.

(4) Report after resignation.—If a registered public accounting firm resigns from an engagement under paragraph (3)(A), the firm shall, not later than 1 business day following the failure by the issuer to notify the Commission under paragraph (3), furnish to the Commission a copy of the report of the firm (or the documentation of any oral report given).

(c) AUDITOR LIABILITY LIMITATION.—No registered public accounting firm shall be liable in a private action for any finding, conclusion, or statement expressed in a report made pursuant to paragraph (3) or (4) of subsection (b), including any rule promulgated pursuant thereto.

(d) CIVIL PENALTIES IN CEASE-AND-DESIST PROCEEDINGS.—If the Commission finds, after notice and opportunity for hearing in a proceeding instituted pursuant to section 21C, that a registered public accounting firm has willfully violated paragraph (3) or (4) of subsection (b), the Commission may, in addition to entering an order under section 21C, impose a civil penalty against the registered public accounting firm and any other person that the Commission finds was a cause of such violation. The determination to impose a civil penalty and the amount of the penalty shall be governed by the standards set forth in section 21B.

(e) PRESERVATION OF EXISTING AUTHORITY.—Except as provided in subsection (d), nothing in this section shall be held to limit or otherwise affect the authority of the Commission under this title.

(f) DEFINITIONS.—As used in this section, the term "illegal act" means an act or omission that violates any law, or any rule or regulation having the force of law. As used in this section, the term "issuer" means an issuer (as defined in section 3), the securities of which are registered under section 12, or that is required to file reports pursuant to section 15(d), or that files or has filed a registration statement that has not yet become effective under the Securities Act of 1933 (15 U.S.C. 77a et seq.), and that it has not withdrawn.

(g) PROHIBITED ACTIVITIES.—Except as provided in subsection (h), it shall be unlawful for a registered public accounting firm (and any associated person of that firm, to the extent determined appropriate by the Commission) that performs for any issuer any audit required by this title or the rules of the Commission under this title or, beginning 180 days after the date of commencement of the operations of the Public Company Accounting Oversight Board established under section 101 of the Sarbanes-Oxley Act of 2002 (in this section referred to as the "Board"), the rules of the Board, to provide to that issuer, contemporaneously with the audit, any non-audit service, including—

(1) bookkeeping or other services related to the accounting records or financial statements of the audit client;

(2) financial information systems design and implementation;

(3) appraisal or valuation services, fairness opinions, or contribution-in-kind reports;

(4) actuarial services;

(5) internal audit outsourcing services;

(6) management functions or human resources;

(7) broker or dealer, investment adviser, or investment banking services;

(8) legal services and expert services unrelated to the audit; and

(9) any other service that the Board determines, by regulation, is impermissible.

(h) PREAPPROVAL REQUIRED FOR NON-AUDIT SERVICES.—A registered public accounting firm may engage in any non-audit service, including tax services, that is not described in any of paragraphs (1) through (9) of subsection (g) for an audit client, only if the activity is approved in advance by the audit committee of the issuer, in accordance with subsection (i).

(i) PREAPPROVAL REQUIREMENTS.—

(1) IN GENERAL.—

(A) AUDIT COMMITTEE ACTION.—All auditing services (which may entail providing comfort letters in connection with securities underwritings or statutory audits required for insurance companies for purposes of State law) and non-audit services, other than as provided in subparagraph (B), provided to an issuer by the auditor of the issuer shall be preapproved by the audit committee of the issuer.

(B) DE MINIMIS EXCEPTION.—The preapproval requirement under subparagraph (A) is waived with respect to the provision of non-audit services for an issuer, if—

(i) the aggregate amount of all such non-audit services provided to the issuer constitutes not more than 5 percent of the total amount of revenues paid by the issuer to its auditor during the fiscal year in which the non-audit services are provided;

(ii) such services were not recognized by the issuer at the time of the engagement to be non-audit services; and

(iii) such services are promptly brought to the attention of the audit committee of the issuer and approved prior to the completion of the audit by the audit committee or by 1 or more members of the audit committee who are members of the board of directors to whom authority to grant such approvals has been delegated by the audit committee.

(2) DISCLOSURE TO INVESTORS.—Approval by an audit committee of an issuer under this subsection of a non-audit service to be performed by the auditor of the issuer shall be disclosed to investors in periodic reports required by section 13(a).

(3) DELEGATION OF AUTHORITY.—The audit committee of an issuer may delegate to 1 or more designated members of the audit committee who are independent directors of the board of directors, the authority to grant preapprovals required by this subsection. The decisions of any member to whom authority is delegated under this paragraph to preapprove an activity under this subsection shall be presented to the full audit committee at each of its scheduled meetings.

(4) APPROVAL OF AUDIT SERVICES FOR OTHER PURPOSES.—In carrying out its duties under subsection (m)(2), if the audit committee of an issuer approves an audit service within the scope of the engagement of the auditor, such audit service shall be deemed to have been preapproved for purposes of this subsection.

(j) AUDIT PARTNER ROTATION.—It shall be unlawful for a registered public accounting firm to provide audit services to an issuer if the lead (or coordinating) audit partner (having primary responsibility for the audit), or the audit partner responsible for reviewing the audit, has performed audit services for that issuer in each of the 5 previous fiscal years of that issuer.

(k) REPORTS TO AUDIT COMMITTEES.—Each registered public accounting firm that performs for any issuer any audit required by this title shall timely report to the audit committee of the issuer—

(1) all critical accounting policies and practices to be used;

(2) all alternative treatments of financial information within generally accepted accounting principles that have been discussed with management officials of the issuer, ramifications of the use of such alternative disclosures and treatments, and the treatment preferred by the registered public accounting firm; and

(3) other material written communications between the registered public accounting firm and the management of the issuer, such as any management letter or schedule of unadjusted differences.

(l) CONFLICTS OF INTEREST.—It shall be unlawful for a registered public accounting firm to perform for an issuer any audit service required by this title, if a chief executive officer, controller, chief financial officer, chief accounting officer, or any person serving in an equivalent position for the issuer, was employed by that registered independent public accounting firm and participated in any capacity in the audit of that issuer during the 1-year period preceding the date of the initiation of the audit.

(m) STANDARDS RELATING TO AUDIT COMMITTEES.—

(1) COMMISSION RULES.—

(A) IN GENERAL.—Effective not later than 270 days after the date of enactment of this subsection, the Commission shall, by rule, direct the national securities exchanges and national securities associations to prohibit the listing of any security of an issuer that is not in compliance with the requirements of any portion of paragraphs (2) through (6).

(B) OPPORTUNITY TO CURE DEFECTS.—The rules of the Commission under subparagraph (A) shall provide for appropriate procedures for an issuer to have an opportunity to cure any defects that would be the basis for a prohibition under subparagraph (A), before the imposition of such prohibition.

(2) RESPONSIBILITIES RELATING TO REGISTERED PUBLIC ACCOUNTING FIRMS.—The audit committee of each issuer, in its capacity as a committee of the board of directors, shall be directly responsible for the appointment, compensation, and oversight of the work of any registered public accounting firm employed by that issuer (including resolution of disagreements between management and the auditor regarding financial reporting) for the purpose of preparing or issuing an audit report or related work, and each such registered public accounting firm shall report directly to the audit committee.

(3) INDEPENDENCE.—

(A) IN GENERAL.—Each member of the audit committee of the issuer shall be a member of the board of directors of the issuer, and shall otherwise be independent.

(B) CRITERIA.—In order to be considered to be independent for purposes of this paragraph, a member of an audit committee of an issuer may not, other than in his or her capacity as a member of the audit committee, the board of directors, or any other board committee—

(i) accept any consulting, advisory, or other compensatory fee from the issuer; or

(ii) be an affiliated person of the issuer or any subsidiary thereof.

(C) EXEMPTION AUTHORITY.—The Commission may exempt from the requirements of subparagraph (B) a particular relationship with respect to audit committee members, as the Commission determines appropriate in light of the circumstances.

(4) COMPLAINTS.—Each audit committee shall establish procedures for—

(A) the receipt, retention, and treatment of complaints received by the issuer regarding accounting, internal accounting controls, or auditing matters; and

(B) the confidential, anonymous submission by employees of the issuer of concerns regarding questionable accounting or auditing matters.

(5) AUTHORITY TO ENGAGE ADVISERS.—Each audit committee shall have the authority to engage independent counsel and other advisers, as it determines necessary to carry out its duties.

(6) FUNDING.—Each issuer shall provide for appropriate funding, as determined by the audit committee, in its capacity as a committee of the board of directors, for payment of compensation—

(A) to the registered public accounting firm employed by the issuer for the purpose of rendering or issuing an audit report; and

(B) to any advisers employed by the audit committee under paragraph (5).

POSITION LIMITS AND POSITION ACCOUNTABILITY FOR SECURITY-BASED SWAPS AND LARGE TRADER REPORTING

Sec. 10B. (a) POSITION LIMITS. As a means reasonably designed to prevent fraud and manipulation, the Commission shall, by rule or regulation, as necessary or appropriate in the public interest or for the protection of investors, establish limits (including related hedge exemption provisions) on the size of positions in any security-based swap that may be held by any person. In establishing such limits, the Commission may require any person to aggregate positions in—

(1) Any security-based swap and any security or loan or group of securities or loans on which such security-based swap is based, which such security-based swap references, or to which such security-based swap is related as described in paragraph (68) of section 3(a), and any other instrument relating to such security or loan or group or index of securities or loans; or

(2) Any security-based swap and—

(A) Any security or group or index of securities, the price, yield, value, or volatility of which, or of which any interest therein, is the basis for a material term of such security-based swap as described in paragraph (68) of section 3(a); and

(B) Any other instrument relating to the same security or group or index of securities described under subparagraph (A).

(b) EXEMPTIONS. The Commission, by rule, regulation, or order, may conditionally or unconditionally exempt any person or class of persons, any security-based swap or class of security-based swaps, or any transaction or class of transactions from any requirement the Commission may establish under this section with respect to position limits.

(c) SRO RULES.

(1) IN GENERAL. As a means reasonably designed to prevent fraud or manipulation, the Commission, by rule, regulation, or order, as necessary or appropriate in the public interest, for the protection of investors, or otherwise in furtherance of the purposes of this title, may direct a self-regulatory organization—

(A) To adopt rules regarding the size of positions in any security-based swap that may be held by—

(i) Any member of such self-regulatory organization; or

(ii) Any person for whom a member of such self-regulatory organization effects transactions in such security-based swap; and

(B) To adopt rules reasonably designed to ensure compliance with requirements prescribed by the Commission under this subsection.

(2) REQUIREMENT TO AGGREGATE POSITIONS. In establishing the limits under paragraph (1), the self-regulatory organization may require such member or person to aggregate positions in—

(A) Any security-based swap and any security or loan or group or narrow-based security narrow-based security index of securities or loans on which such security-based swap is based, which such security-based swap references, or to which such security-based swap is related as described in section 3(a)(68), and any other instrument relating to such security or loan or group or narrow-based security index of securities or loans; or

(B)(i) Any security-based swap; and

(ii) Any security-based swap and any other instrument relating to the same security or group or narrow-based security index of securities.

(d) LARGE TRADER REPORTING. The Commission, by rule or regulation, may require any person that effects transactions for such person's own account or the account of others in any securities-based swap or uncleared security-based swap and any security or loan or group or narrow-based security index of securities or loans as set forth in paragraphs (1) and (2) of subsection (a) under this section to report such information as the Commission may prescribe regarding any position or positions in any security-based swap or uncleared security-based swap and any security or loan or group or narrow-based security index of securities or loans and any other instrument relating to such security or loan or group or narrow-based security index of securities or loans as set forth in paragraphs (1) and (2) of subsection (a) under this section.

COMPENSATION COMMITTEES

Sec. 10C. (a) INDEPENDENCE OF COMPENSATION COMMITTEES.

(1) LISTING STANDARDS. The Commission shall, by rule, direct the national securities exchanges and national securities associations to prohibit the listing of any equity security of an issuer, other than an issuer that is a controlled company, limited partnership, company in bankruptcy proceedings, open-ended management investment company that is registered under the Investment Company Act of 1940, or a foreign private issuer that provides annual disclosures to shareholders of the reasons that the foreign private issuer does not have an independent compensation committee, that does not comply with the requirements of this subsection.

(2) INDEPENDENCE OF COMPENSATION COMMITTEES. The rules of the Commission under paragraph (1) shall require that each member of the compensation committee of the board of directors of an issuer be—

(A) A member of the board of directors of the issuer; and

(B) Independent.

(3) INDEPENDENCE. The rules of the Commission under paragraph (1) shall require that, in determining the definition of the term "independence" for purposes of paragraph (2), the national securities exchanges and the national securities associations shall consider relevant factors, including—

(A) The source of compensation of a member of the board of directors of an issuer, including any consulting, advisory, or other compensatory fee paid by the issuer to such member of the board of directors; and

(B) Whether a member of the board of directors of an issuer is affiliated with the issuer, a subsidiary of the issuer, or an affiliate of a subsidiary of the issuer.

(4) EXEMPTION AUTHORITY. The rules of the Commission under paragraph (1) shall permit a national securities exchange or a national securities association to exempt a particular relationship from the requirements of paragraph (2), with respect to the members of a compensation committee, as the national securities exchange or national securities association determines is appropriate, taking into consideration the size of an issuer and any other relevant factors.

(b) INDEPENDENCE OF COMPENSATION CONSULTANTS AND OTHER COMPENSATION COMMITTEE ADVISERS.

(1) IN GENERAL. The compensation committee of an issuer may only select a compensation consultant, legal counsel, or other adviser to the compensation committee after taking into consideration the factors identified by the Commission under paragraph (2).

(2) RULES. The Commission shall identify factors that affect the independence of a compensation consultant, legal counsel, or other adviser to a compensation committee of an issuer. Such factors shall be competitively neutral among categories of consultants, legal counsel, or other advisers and preserve the ability of compensation committees to retain the services of members of any such category, and shall include—

(A) The provision of other services to the issuer by the person that employs the compensation consultant, legal counsel, or other adviser;

(B) The amount of fees received from the issuer by the person that employs the compensation consultant, legal counsel, or other adviser, as a percentage of the total revenue of the person that employs the compensation consultant, legal counsel, or other adviser;

(C) The policies and procedures of the person that employs the compensation consultant, legal counsel, or other adviser that are designed to prevent conflicts of interest;

(D) Any business or personal relationship of the compensation consultant, legal counsel, or other adviser with a member of the compensation committee; and

(E) Any stock of the issuer owned by the compensation consultant, legal counsel, or other adviser.

(c) COMPENSATION COMMITTEE AUTHORITY RELATING TO COMPENSATION CONSULTANTS.

(1) AUTHORITY TO RETAIN COMPENSATION CONSULTANT.

(A) IN GENERAL. The compensation committee of an issuer, in its capacity as a committee of the board of directors, may, in its sole discretion, retain or obtain the advice of a compensation consultant.

(B) DIRECT RESPONSIBILITY OF COMPENSATION COMMITTEE. The compensation committee of an issuer shall be directly responsible for the appointment, compensation, and oversight of the work of a compensation consultant.

(C) RULE OF CONSTRUCTION. This paragraph may not be construed—

(i) To require the compensation committee to implement or act consistently with the advice or recommendations of the compensation consultant; or

(ii) To affect the ability or obligation of a compensation committee to exercise its own judgment in fulfillment of the duties of the compensation committee.

(2) DISCLOSURE. In any proxy or consent solicitation material for an annual meeting of the shareholders (or a special meeting in lieu of the annual meeting) occurring on or after the date that is 1 year after the date of enactment of this section, each issuer shall disclose in the proxy or consent material, in accordance with regulations of the Commission, whether—

(A) The compensation committee of the issuer retained or obtained the advice of a compensation consultant; and

(B) The work of the compensation consultant has raised any conflict of interest and, if so, the nature of the conflict and how the conflict is being addressed.

(d) AUTHORITY TO ENGAGE INDEPENDENT LEGAL COUNSEL AND OTHER ADVISERS.

(1) IN GENERAL. The compensation committee of an issuer, in its capacity as a committee of the board of directors, may, in its sole discretion, retain and obtain the advice of independent legal counsel and other advisers.

(2) DIRECT RESPONSIBILITY OF COMPENSATION COMMITTEE. The compensation committee of an issuer shall be directly responsible for the appointment, compensation, and oversight of the work of independent legal counsel and other advisers.

(3) RULE OF CONSTRUCTION. This subsection may not be construed—

(A) To require a compensation committee to implement or act consistently with the advice or recommendations of independent legal counsel or other advisers under this subsection; or

(B) To affect the ability or obligation of a compensation committee to exercise its own judgment in fulfillment of the duties of the compensation committee.

(e) COMPENSATION OF COMPENSATION CONSULTANTS, INDEPENDENT LEGAL COUNSEL, AND OTHER ADVISERS. Each issuer shall provide for appropriate funding, as determined by the compensation committee in its capacity as a committee of the board of directors, for payment of reasonable compensation—

(1) To a compensation consultant; and

(2) To independent legal counsel or any other adviser to the compensation committee.

(f) COMMISSION RULES.

(1) IN GENERAL. Not later than 360 days after the date of enactment of this section, the Commission shall, by rule, direct the national securities exchanges and national securities associations to prohibit the listing of any security of an issuer that is not in compliance with the requirements of this section.

(2) OPPORTUNITY TO CURE DEFECTS. The rules of the Commission under paragraph (1) shall provide for appropriate procedures for an issuer to have a reasonable opportunity to cure any defects that would be the basis for the prohibition under paragraph (1), before the imposition of such prohibition.

(3) EXEMPTION AUTHORITY.

(A) IN GENERAL. The rules of the Commission under paragraph (1) shall permit a national securities exchange or a national securities association to exempt a category of issuers from the requirements under this section, as the national securities exchange or the national securities association determines is appropriate.

(B) CONSIDERATIONS. In determining appropriate exemptions under subparagraph (A), the national securities exchange or the national securities association shall take into account the potential impact of the requirements of this section on smaller reporting issuers.

(g) CONTROLLED COMPANY EXEMPTION.

(1) IN GENERAL. This section shall not apply to any controlled company.

(2) DEFINITION. For purposes of this section, the term "controlled company" means an issuer—

(A) That is listed on a national securities exchange or by a national securities association; and

(B) That holds an election for the board of directors of the issuer in which more than 50 percent of the voting power is held by an individual, a group, or another issuer.

RECOVERY OF ERRONEOUSLY AWARDED COMPENSATION POLICY

Sec. 10D. (a) LISTING STANDARDS. The Commission shall, by rule, direct the national securities exchanges and national securities associations to prohibit the listing of any security of an issuer that does not comply with the requirements of this section.

(b) RECOVERY OF FUNDS. The rules of the Commission under subsection (a) shall require each issuer to develop and implement a policy providing—

(1) For disclosure of the policy of the issuer on incentive-based compensation that is based on financial information required to be reported under the securities laws; and

(2) That, in the event that the issuer is required to prepare an accounting restatement due to the material noncompliance of the issuer with any financial reporting requirement under the securities laws, the issuer will recover from any current or former executive officer of the issuer who received incentive-based compensation (including stock options awarded as compensation) during the 3-year period preceding the date on which the issuer

is required to prepare an accounting restatement, based on the erroneous data, in excess of what would have been paid to the executive officer under the accounting restatement.

NATIONAL MARKET SYSTEM FOR SECURITIES; SECURITIES INFORMATION PROCESSORS

Sec. 11A. (a)(1) The Congress finds that—

(A) The securities markets are an important national asset which must be preserved and strengthened.

(B) New data processing and communications techniques create the opportunity for more efficient and effective market operations.

(C) It is in the public interest and appropriate for the protection of investors and the maintenance of fair and orderly markets to assure—

(i) economically efficient execution of securities transactions;

(ii) fair competition among brokers and dealers, among exchange markets, and between exchange markets and markets other than exchange markets;

(iii) the availability to brokers, dealers, and investors of information with respect to quotations for and transactions in securities;

(iv) the practicability of brokers executing investors' orders in the best market; and

(v) an opportunity, consistent with the provisions of clauses (i) and (iv) of this subparagraph, for investors' orders to be executed without the participation of a dealer.

(D) The linking of all markets for qualified securities through communication and data processing facilities will foster efficiency, enhance competition, increase the information available to brokers, dealers, and investors, facilitate the offsetting of investors' orders, and contribute to best execution of such orders.

(2) The Commission is directed, therefore, having due regard for the public interest, the protection of investors, and the maintenance of fair and orderly markets, to use its authority under this title to facilitate the establishment of a national market system for securities (which may include subsystems for particular types of securities with unique trading characteristics) in accordance with the findings and to carry out the objectives set forth in paragraph (1) of this subsection. The Commission, by rule, shall designate the securities or classes of securities qualified for trading in the national market system from among securities other than exempted securities. (Securities or classes of securities so designated hereinafter in this section referred to as "qualified securities".)

REGISTRATION REQUIREMENTS FOR SECURITIES

Sec. 12. (a) It shall be unlawful for any member, broker, or dealer to effect any transaction in any security (other than an exempted security) on a national securities exchange unless a registration is effective as to such security for such exchange in accordance with the provisions of this title, and the rules and regulations thereunder. The provisions of this subsection shall not apply in respect of a security futures product traded on a national securities exchange.

(b) A security may be registered on a national securities exchange by the issuer filing an application with the exchange (and filing with the Commission such duplicate originals thereof as the Commission may require), which application shall contain—

(1) Such information, in such detail, as to the issuer and any person directly or indirectly controlling or controlled by, or under direct or indirect common control with, the issuer, and any guarantor of the security as to principal or interest or both, as the Commission may by rules and regulations require, as necessary or appropriate in the public interest or for the protection of investors, in respect of the following:

(A) the organization, financial structure and nature of the business;

(B) the terms, position, rights, and privileges of the different classes of securities outstanding;

(C) the terms on which their securities are to be, and during the preceding three years have been, offered to the public or otherwise;

(D) the directors, officers, and underwriters, and each security holder of record holding more than 10 per centum of any class of any equity security of the issuer (other than an exempted security), their remuneration and their interests in the securities of, and their material contracts with, the issuer and any person directly or indirectly controlling or controlled by, or under direct or indirect common control with, the issuer;

(E) remuneration to others than directors and officers exceeding $20,000 per annum;

(F) bonus and profit-sharing arrangements;

(G) management and service contracts;

(H) options existing or to be created in respect of their securities;

(I) material contracts, not made in the ordinary course of business, which are to be executed in whole or in part at or after the filing of the application or which were made not more than two years before such filing, and every material patent or contract for a material patent right shall be deemed a material contract;

(J) balance sheets for not more than the three preceding fiscal years, certified if required by the rules and regulations of the Commission by a registered public accounting firm;

(K) profit and loss statements for not more than the three preceding fiscal years, certified if required by the rules and regulations of the Commission by a registered public accounting firm; and

(L) any further financial statements which the Commission may deem necessary or appropriate for the protection of investors.

(2) Such copies of articles of incorporation, bylaws, trust indentures, or corresponding documents by whatever name known, underwriting arrangements, and other similar documents of, and voting trust agreements with respect to, the issuer and any person directly or indirectly controlling or controlled by, or under direct or indirect common control with, the issuer as the Commission may require as necessary or appropriate for the proper protection of investors and to insure fair dealing in the security.

(3) Such copies of material contracts, referred to in paragraph (1) (I) above, as the Commission may require as necessary or appropriate for the proper protection of investors and to insure fair dealing in the security.

(c) If in the judgment of the Commission any information required under subsection (b) is inapplicable to any specified class or classes of issuers, the Commission shall require in lieu thereof the submission of such other information of comparable character as it may deem applicable to such class of issuers.

(d) If the exchange authorities certify to the Commission that the security has been approved by the exchange for listing and registration, the registration shall become effective thirty days after the receipt of such certification by the Commission or within such shorter period of time as the Commission may determine. A security registered with a national securities exchange may be withdrawn or stricken from listing and registration in accordance with the rules of the exchange and, upon such terms as the Commission may deem necessary to impose for the protection of investors, upon application by the issuer or the exchange to the Commission; whereupon the issuer shall be relieved from further compliance with the provisions of this section and section 13 of this title and any rules or regulations under such sections as to the securities so withdrawn or stricken.

An unissued security may be registered only in accordance with such rules and regulations as the Commission may prescribe as necessary or appropriate in the public interest or for the protection of investors.

(g) (1) Every issuer which is engaged in interstate commerce, or in a business affecting interstate commerce, or whose securities are traded by use of the mails or any means or instrumentality of interstate commerce shall—

(A) Within 120 days after the last day of its first fiscal year ended on which the issuer has total assets exceeding $10,000,000 and a class of equity security (other than an exempted security) held of record by either—

(i) 2,000 persons, or

(ii) 500 persons who are not accredited investors (as such term is defined by the Commission), and

(B) In the case of an issuer that is a bank, a savings and loan holding company (as defined in section 10 of the Home Owners' Loan Act), or a bank holding company, as such term is defined in section 2 of the Bank Holding Company Act of 1956 (12 U.S.C. 1841), not later than 120 days after the last day of its first fiscal year ended after the effective date of this subsection, on which the issuer has total assets exceeding $10,000,000 and a class of equity security (other than an exempted security) held of record by 2,000 or more persons,

register such security by filing with the Commission a registration statement (and such copies thereof as the Commission may require) with respect to such security containing such information and documents as the Commission may specify comparable to that which is required in an application to register a security pursuant to subsection (b) of this section. Each such registration statement shall become effective sixty days after filing with the Commission or within such shorter period as the Commission may direct. Until such registration statement becomes effective it shall not be deemed filed for the purposes of section 18 of this title. Any issuer may register any class of equity security not required to be registered by filing a registration statement pursuant to the provisions of this paragraph. The Commission is authorized to extend the date upon which any issuer or class of issuers is required to register a security pursuant to the provisions of this paragraph.

(2) The provisions of this subsection shall not apply in respect of—

(A) any security listed and registered on a national securities exchange.

(B) any security issued by an investment company registered pursuant to section 8 of the Investment Company Act of 1940.

(C) any security, other than permanent stock, guaranty stock, permanent reserve stock, or any similar certificate evidencing nonwithdrawable capital, issued by a savings and loan association, building and loan association, cooperative bank, homestead association, or similar institution, which is supervised and examined by State or Federal authority having supervision over any such institution.

(D) any security of an issuer organized and operated exclusively for religious, educational, benevolent, fraternal, charitable, or reformatory purposes and not for pecuniary profit, and no part of the net earnings of which inures to the benefit of any private shareholder or individual; or any security of a fund that is excluded from the definition of an investment company under section 3(c)(10)(B) of the Investment Company Act of 1940.

(E) any security of an issuer which is a "cooperative association" as defined in the Agricultural Marketing Act, approved June 15, 1929, as amended, or a federation of such cooperative associations, if such federation possesses no greater powers or purposes than cooperative associations so defined.

(F) any security issued by a mutual or cooperative organization which supplies a commodity or service primarily for the benefit of its members and operates not for pecuniary profit, but only if the security is part of a class issuable only to persons who purchase commodities or services from the issuer, the security is transferable only to a successor in interest or occupancy of premises serviced or to be served by the issuer, and no dividends are payable to the holder of the security.

(G) any security issued by an insurance company if all of the following conditions are met:

(i) Such insurance company is required to and does file an annual statement with the Commissioner of Insurance (or other officer or agency performing a similar function) of its domiciliary State, and such annual statement conforms to that prescribed by the National Association of Insurance Commissioners or in the determination of such State commissioner, officer or agency substantially conforms to that so prescribed.

(ii) Such insurance company is subject to regulation by its domiciliary State of proxies, consents, or authorizations in respect of securities issued by such company and such regulation conforms to that prescribed by the National Association of Insurance Commissioners.

(iii) After July 1, 1966, the purchase and sales of securities issued by such insurance company by beneficial owners, directors, or officers of such company are subject to regulation (including reporting) by its domiciliary State substantially in the manner provided in section 16 of this title.

(H) any interest or participation in any collective trust funds maintained by a bank or in a separate account maintained by an insurance company which interest or participation is issued in connection with (i) a stock-bonus, pension, or profit-sharing plan which meets the requirements for qualification under section 401 of the Internal Revenue Code of 1954, or (ii) an annuity plan which meets the requirements for deduction of the employer's contribution under section 404(a)(2) of such Code.

(3) The Commission may by rules or regulations or, on its own motion, after notice and opportunity for hearing, by order, exempt from this subsection any security of a foreign issuer, including any certificate of deposit for such a security, if the Commission finds that such exemption is in the public interest and is consistent with the protection of investors.

(4) Registration of any class of security pursuant to this subsection shall be terminated ninety days, or such shorter period as the Commission may determine, after the issuer files a certification with the Commission that the number of holders of record of such class of security is reduced to less than 300 persons, or, in the case of a bank, a savings and loan holding company (as defined in section 10 of the Home Owners' Loan Act), or a bank holding company, as such term is defined in section 2 of the Bank Holding Company Act of 1956 (12 U.S.C. 1841), 1,200 persons. The Commission shall after notice and opportunity for hearing deny termination of registration if it finds that the certification is untrue. Termination of registration shall be deferred pending final determination on the question of denial.

(5) For the purposes of this subsection the term "class" shall include all securities of an issuer which are of substantially similar character and the holders of which enjoy substantially similar rights and privileges. The Commission may for the purpose of this subsection define by rules and regulations the terms "total assets" and "held of record" as it deems necessary or appropriate in the public interest or for the protection of investors in order to prevent circumvention of the provisions of this subsection. For purposes of this subsection, a security futures product shall not be considered a class of equity security of the issuer of the securities underlying the security futures product. For purposes of determining whether an issuer is required to register a security with the Commission pursuant to paragraph (1), the definition of "held of record" shall not include securities held by persons who received the securities pursuant to an employee compensation plan in transactions exempted from the registration requirements of section 5 of the Securities Act of 1933.

(6) Exclusion For Persons Holding Certain Securities. The Commission shall, by rule, exempt, conditionally or unconditionally, securities acquired pursuant to an offering made under section 4(6) of the Securities Act of 1933 from the provisions of this subsection.

(h) The Commission may by rules and regulations, or upon application of an interested person, by order, after notice and opportunity for hearing, exempt in whole or in part any issuer or class of issuers from the provisions of subsection (g) of this section or from section 13, 14, or 15(d) or may exempt from section 16 any officer, director, or beneficial owner of securities of any issuer, any security of which is required to be registered pursuant to subsection (g) hereof, upon such terms and conditions and for such period as it deems necessary or appropriate, if the

Commission finds, by reason of the number of public investors, amount of trading interest in the securities, the nature and extent of the activities of the issuer, income or assets of the issuer, or otherwise, that such action is not inconsistent with the public interest or the protection of investors. The Commission may, for the purposes of any of the above-mentioned sections or subsections of this title, classify issuers and prescribe requirements appropriate for each such class.

(i) In respect of any securities issued by banks and savings associations, the deposits of which are insured in accordance with the Federal Deposit Insurance Act, the powers, functions, and duties vested in the Commission to administer and enforce sections 10A(m), 12, 13, 14(a), 14(c), 14(d), 14(f), and 16 of this Act, and sections 302, 303, 304, 306, 401(b), 404, 406, and 407 of the Sarbanes-Oxley Act of 2002 (1) with respect to national banks and Federal savings associations, the accounts of which are insured by the Federal Deposit Insurance Corporation are vested in the Comptroller of the Currency, (2) with respect to all other member banks of the Federal Reserve System, are vested in the Board of Governors of the Federal Reserve System, and (3) with respect to all other insured banks and State savings associations, the accounts of which are insured by the Federal Deposit Insurance Corporation, are vested in the Federal Deposit Insurance Corporation. The Comptroller of the Currency, the Board of Governors of the Federal Reserve System, and the Federal Deposit Insurance Corporation shall have the power to make such rules and regulations as may be necessary for the execution of the functions vested in them as provided in this subsection. In carrying out their responsibilities under this subsection, the agencies named in the first sentence of this subsection shall issue substantially similar regulations to regulations and rules issued by the Commission under sections 10A(m), 12, 13, 14(a), 14(c), 14(d), 14(f) and 16 of this Act, and sections 302, 303, 304, 306, 401(b), 404, 406, and 407 of the Sarbanes-Oxley Act of 2002, unless they find that implementation of substantially similar regulations with respect to insured banks and insured institutions are not necessary or appropriate in the public interest or for protection of investors, and publish such findings, and the detailed reasons therefor, in the Federal Register. Such regulations of the above-named agencies, or the reasons for failure to publish such substantially similar regulations to those of the Commission, shall be published in the Federal Register within 120 days of the date of enactment of this subsection, and, thereafter, within 60 days of any changes made by the Commission in its relevant regulations and rules.

(j) The Commission is authorized, by order, as it deems necessary or appropriate for the protection of investors to deny, to suspend the effective date of, to suspend for a period not exceeding twelve months, or to revoke the registration of a security, if the Commission finds, on the record after notice and opportunity for hearing, that the issuer of such security has failed to comply with any provision of this title or the rules and regulations thereunder. No member of a national securities exchange, broker, or dealer shall make use of the mails or any means or instrumentality of interstate commerce to effect any transaction in, or to induce the purchase or sale of, any security the registration of which has been and is suspended or revoked pursuant to the preceding sentence.

(k) TRADING SUSPENSIONS; EMERGENCY AUTHORITY.—

(1) TRADING SUSPENSIONS.—If in its opinion the public interest and the protection of investors so require, the Commission is authorized by order—

(A) summarily to suspend trading in any security (other than an exempted security) for a period not exceeding 10 business days, and

(B) summarily to suspend all trading on any national securities exchange or otherwise, in securities other than exempted securities, for a period not exceeding 90 calendar days.

The action described in subparagraph (B) shall not take effect unless the Commission notifies the President of its decision and the President notifies the Commission that the President does not disapprove of such decision.

If the actions described in subparagraph (A) or (B) involve a security futures product, the Commission shall consult with and consider the views of the Commodity Futures Trading Commission.

(2) EMERGENCY ORDERS.—(A) The Commission, in an emergency, may by order summarily take such action to alter, supplement, suspend, or impose requirements or restrictions with respect to any matter or action subject to regulation by the Commission or a self-regulatory organization under this title, as the Commission determines is necessary in the public interest and for the protection of investors—

 (i) to maintain or restore fair and orderly securities markets (other than markets in exempted securities); or

 (ii) to ensure prompt, accurate, and safe clearance and settlement of transactions in securities (other than exempted securities).

(B) An order of the Commission under this paragraph (2) shall continue in effect for the period specified by the Commission, and may be extended, except that in no event shall the Commission's action continue in effect for more than 10 business days, including extensions. If the actions described in subparagraph (A) involve a security futures product, the Commission shall consult with and consider the views of the Commodity Futures Trading Commission. In exercising its authority under this paragraph, the Commission shall not be required to comply with the provisions of section 553 of title 5, United States Code, or with the provisions of section 19(c) of this title.

(3) TERMINATION OF EMERGENCY ACTIONS BY PRESIDENT.—The President may direct that action taken by the Commission under paragraph (1)(B) or paragraph (2) of this subsection shall not continue in effect.

(4) COMPLIANCE WITH ORDERS.—No member of a national securities exchange, broker, or dealer shall make use of the mails or any means or instrumentality of interstate commerce to effect any transaction in, or to induce the purchase or sale of, any security in contravention of an order of the Commission under this subsection unless such order has been stayed, modified, or set aside as provided in paragraph (5) of this subsection or has ceased to be effective upon direction of the President as provided in paragraph (3).

(5) LIMITATIONS ON REVIEW OF ORDERS.—An order of the Commission pursuant to this subsection shall be subject to review only as provided in section 25(a) of this title. Review shall be based on an examination of all the information before the Commission at the time such order was issued. The reviewing court shall not enter a stay, writ of mandamus, or similar relief unless the court finds, after notice and hearing before a panel of the court, that the Commission's action is arbitrary, capricious, an abuse of discretion, or otherwise not in accordance with law.

(6) CONSULTATION.—Prior to taking any action described in paragraph (1)(B), the Commission shall consult with and consider the views of the Secretary of the Treasury, the Board of Governors of the Federal Reserve System, and the Commodity Futures Trading Commission, unless such consultation is impracticable in light of the emergency.

(7) DEFINITION. For purposes of this subsection, the term "emergency" means—

 (A) A major market disturbance characterized by or constituting—

  (i) Sudden and excessive fluctuations of securities prices generally, or a substantial threat thereof, that threaten fair and orderly markets; or

  (ii) A substantial disruption of the safe or efficient operation of the national system for clearance and settlement of transactions in securities, or a substantial threat thereof; or

 (B) A major disturbance that substantially disrupts, or threatens to substantially disrupt—

  (i) The functioning of securities markets, investment companies, or any other significant portion or segment of the securities markets; or

  (ii) The transmission or processing of securities transactions.

(l) It shall be unlawful for an issuer, any class of whose securities is registered pursuant to this section or would be required to be so registered except for the exemption from registration provided by subsection (g)(2)(B) or (g)(2)(G) of this section, by the use of any means or instrumentality of interstate commerce, or of the mails, to issue, either originally or upon transfer, any of such securities in a form or with a format which contravenes such rules and regulations as the Commission may prescribe as necessary or appropriate for the prompt and accurate clearance and settlement of transactions in securities. The provisions of this subsection shall not apply to variable annuity contracts or variable life policies issued by an insurance company or its separate accounts.

PERIODICAL AND OTHER REPORTS

Sec. 13. (a) Every issuer of a security registered pursuant to section 12 of this title shall file with the Commission, in accordance with such rules and regulations as the Commission may prescribe as necessary or appropriate for the proper protection of investors and to insure fair dealing in the security—

(1) such information and documents (and such copies thereof) as the Commission shall require to keep reasonably current the information and documents required to be included in or filed with an application or registration statement filed pursuant to section 12, except that the Commission may not require the filing of any material contract wholly executed before July 1, 1962.

(2) such annual reports (and such copies thereof), certified if required by the rules and regulations of the Commission by independent public accountants, and such quarterly reports (and such copies thereof), as the Commission may prescribe.

Every issuer of a security registered on a national securities exchange shall also file a duplicate original of such information, documents, and reports with the exchange.

In any registration statement, periodic report, or other reports to be filed with the Commission, an emerging growth company need not present selected financial data in accordance with section 229.301 of title 17, Code of Federal Regulations, for any period prior to the earliest audited period presented in connection with its first registration statement that became effective under this Act or the Securities Act of 1933 and, with respect to any such statement or reports, an emerging growth company may not be required to comply with any new or revised financial accounting standard until such date that a company that is not an issuer (as defined under section 2(a) of the Sarbanes-Oxley Act of 2002 (15 U.S.C. 7201(a))) is required to comply with such new or revised accounting standard, if such standard applies to companies that are not issuers.

(b) (1) The Commission may prescribe, in regard to reports made pursuant to this title, the form or forms in which the required information shall be set forth, the items or details to be shown in the balance sheet and the earnings statement, and the methods to be followed in the preparation of reports, in the appraisal or valuation of assets and liabilities, in the determination of depreciation and depletion, in the differentiation of recurring and nonrecurring income, in the differentiation of investment and operating income, and in the preparation, where the Commission deems it necessary or desirable, of separate and/or consolidated balance sheets or income accounts of any person directly or indirectly controlling or controlled by the issuer, or any person under direct or indirect common control with the issuer; but in the case of the reports of any person whose methods of accounting are prescribed under the provisions of any law of the United States, or any rule or regulation thereunder, the rules and regulations of the Commission with respect to reports shall not be inconsistent with the requirements imposed by such law or rule or regulation in respect of the same subject matter, (except that such rules and regulations of the Commission may be inconsistent with such requirements to the extent that the Commission determines that the public interest or the protection of investors so requires).

(2) Every issuer which has a class of securities registered pursuant to section 12 of this title and every issuer which is required to file reports pursuant to section 15(d) of this title shall—

(A) make and keep books, records, and accounts, which, in reasonable detail, accurately and fairly reflect the transactions and dispositions of the assets of the issuer;

(B) devise and maintain a system of internal accounting controls sufficient to provide reasonable assurances that—

(i) transactions are executed in accordance with management's general or specific authorization;

(ii) transactions are recorded as necessary (I) to permit preparation of financial statements in conformity with generally accepted accounting principles or any other criteria applicable to such statements, and (II) to maintain accountability for assets;

(iii) access to assets is permitted only in accordance with management's general or specific authorization; and

(iv) the recorded accountability for assets is compared with the existing assets at reasonable intervals and appropriate action is taken with respect to any differences; and

(C) notwithstanding any other provision of law, pay the allocable share of such issuer of a reasonable annual accounting support fee or fees, determined in accordance with section 109 of the Sarbanes-Oxley Act of 2002.

(3) (A) With respect to matters concerning the national security of the United States, no duty or liability under paragraph (2) of this subsection shall be imposed upon any person acting in cooperation with the head of any Federal department or agency responsible for such matters if such act in cooperation with such head of a department or agency was done upon the specific, written directive of the head of such department or agency pursuant to Presidential authority to issue such directives. Each directive issued under this paragraph shall set forth the specific facts and circumstances with respect to which the provisions of this paragraph are to be invoked. Each such directive shall, unless renewed in writing, expire one year after the date of issuance.

(B) Each head of a Federal department or agency of the United States who issues a directive pursuant to this paragraph shall maintain a complete file of all such directives and shall, on October 1 of each year, transmit a summary of matters covered by such directives in force at any time during the previous year to the Permanent Select Committee on Intelligence of the House of Representatives and the Select Committee on Intelligence of the Senate.

(4) No criminal liability shall be imposed for failing to comply with the requirements of paragraph (2) of this subsection except as provided in paragraph (5) of this subsection.

(5) No person shall knowingly circumvent or knowingly fail to implement a system of internal accounting controls or knowingly falsify any book, record, or account described in paragraph (2).

(6) Where an issuer which has a class of securities registered pursuant to section 12 of this title or an issuer which is required to file reports pursuant to section 15(d) of this title holds 50 per centum or less of the voting power with respect to a domestic or foreign firm, the provisions of paragraph (2) require only that the issuer proceed in good faith to use its influence, to the extent reasonable under the issuer's circumstances, to cause such domestic or foreign firm to devise and maintain a system of internal accounting controls consistent with paragraph (2). Such circumstances include the relative degree of the issuer's ownership of the domestic or foreign firm and the laws and practices governing the business operations of the country in which such firm is located. An issuer which demonstrates good faith efforts to use such influence shall be conclusively presumed to have complied with the requirements of paragraph (2).

(7) For the purpose of paragraph (2) of this subsection, the terms "reasonable assurances" and "reasonable detail" mean such level of detail and degree of assurance as would satisfy prudent officials in the conduct of their own affairs.

(c) If in the judgment of the Commission any report required under subsection (a) is inapplicable to any specified class or classes of issuers, the Commission shall require in lieu thereof the submission of such reports of comparable character as it may deem applicable to such class or classes of issuers.

(d) (1) Any person who, after acquiring directly or indirectly the beneficial ownership of any equity security of a class which is registered pursuant to section 12 of this title, or any equity security of an insurance company which would have been required to be so registered except for the exemption contained in section 12(g)(2)(G) of this title, or any equity security issued by a closed-end investment company registered under the Investment Company Act of 1940 or any equity security by a Native Corporation pursuant to section 37(d)(6) of the Alaska Native

Claims Settlement Act or otherwise becomes or is deemed to become a beneficial owner of any of the foregoing upon the purchase or sale of a security-based swap that the Commission may define by rule, and, is directly or indirectly the beneficial owner of more than 5 per centum of such class shall, within ten days after such acquisition or within such shorter time as the Commission may establish by rule, file with the Commission, a statement containing such of the following information, and such additional information, as the Commission may by rules and regulations prescribe as necessary or appropriate in the public interest or for the protection of investors—

(A) The background, and identity, residence, and citizenship of, and the nature of such beneficial ownership by, such person and all other persons by whom or on whose behalf the purchases have been or are to be effected;

(B) the source and amount of the funds or other consideration used or to be used in making the purchases, and if any part of the purchase price or proposed purchase price is represented or is to be represented by funds or other consideration borrowed or otherwise obtained for the purpose of acquiring, holding, or trading such security, a description of the transaction and the names of the parties thereto, except that where a source of funds is a loan made in the ordinary course of business by a bank, as defined in section 3(a)(6) of this title, if the person filing such statement so requests, the name of the bank shall not be made available to the public;

(C) if the purpose of the purchases or prospective purchases is to acquire control of the business of the issuer of the securities, any plans or proposals which such persons may have to liquidate such issuer, to sell its assets to or merge it with any other persons, or to make any other major change in its business or corporate structure;

(D) the number of shares of such security which are beneficially owned, and the number of shares concerning which there is a right to acquire, directly or indirectly, by (i) such person, and (ii) by each associate of such person, giving the background, identity, residence and citizenship of each such associate; and

(E) information as to any contracts, arrangements, or understandings with any person with respect to any securities of the issuer, including but not limited to transfer of any of the securities, joint ventures, loan or option arrangements, puts or calls, guaranties of loans, guaranties against loss or guaranties of profits, division of losses or profits, or the giving or withholding of proxies, naming the persons with whom such contracts, arrangements, or understandings have been entered into, and giving the details thereof.

(2) If any material change occurs in the facts set forth in the statement filed with the Commission, an amendment shall be filed with the Commission, in accordance with such rules and regulations as the Commission may prescribe as necessary or appropriate in the public interest or for the protection of investors.

(3) When two or more persons act as a partnership, limited partnership, syndicate, or other group for the purpose of acquiring, holding, or disposing of securities of an issuer, such syndicate or group shall be deemed a "person" for the purposes of this subsection.

(4) In determining, for purposes of this subsection, any percentage of a class of any security, such class shall be deemed to consist of the amount of the outstanding securities of such class, exclusive of any securities of such class held by or for the account of the issuer or a subsidiary of the issuer.

(5) The Commission, by rule or regulation or by order, may permit any person to file in lieu of the statement required by paragraph (1) of this subsection or the rules and regulations thereunder, a notice stating the name of such person, the number of shares of any equity securities subject to paragraph (1) which are owned by him, the date of their acquisition and such other information as the Commission may specify, if it appears to the Commission that such securities were acquired by such person in the ordinary course of his business and were not acquired for the purpose of and do not have the effect of changing or influencing the control of the issuer nor in connection with or as a participant in any transaction having such purpose or effect.

(6) The provisions of this subsection shall not apply to—

(A) any acquisition or offer to acquire securities made or proposed to be made by means of a registration statement under the Securities Act of 1933;

(B) any acquisition of the beneficial ownership of a security which, together with all other acquisitions by the same person of securities of the same class during the preceding twelve months, does not exceed 2 per centum of that class;

(C) any acquisition of an equity security by the issuer of such security;

(D) any acquisition or proposed acquisition of a security which the Commission, by rules or regulations or by order, shall exempt from the provisions of this subsection as not entered into for the purpose of, and not having the effect of, changing or influencing the control of the issuer or otherwise as not comprehended within the purposes of this subsection.

(e)(1) It shall be unlawful for an issuer which has a class of equity securities registered pursuant to section 12 of this title, or which is a closed-end investment company registered under the Investment Company Act of 1940, to purchase any equity security issued by it if such purchase is in contravention of such rules and regulations as the Commission, in the public interest or for the protection of investors, may adopt (A) to define acts and practices which are fraudulent, deceptive, or manipulative, and (B) to prescribe means reasonably designed to prevent such acts and practices. Such rules and regulations may require such issuer to provide holders of equity securities of such class with such information relating to the reasons for such purchase, the source of funds, the number of shares to be purchased, the price to be paid for such securities, the method of purchase, and such additional information, as the Commission deems necessary or appropriate in the public interest or for the protection of investors, or which the Commission deems to be material to a determination whether such security should be sold.

(2) For the purpose of this subsection, a purchase by or for the issuer, or any person controlling, controlled by, or under the common control with the issuer, or a purchase subject to control of the issuer or any such person, shall be deemed to be a purchase by the issuer. The Commission shall have power to make rules and regulations implementing this paragraph in the public interest and for the protection of investors, including exemptive rules and regulations covering situations in which the Commission deems it unnecessary or inappropriate that a purchase of the type described in this paragraph shall be deemed to be a purchase by the issuer for purposes of some or all of the provisions of paragraph (1) of this subsection.

(f)(1) Every institutional investment manager which uses the mails, or any means or instrumentality of interstate commerce in the course of its business as an institutional investment manager and which exercises investment discretion with respect to accounts holding equity securities of a class described in section 13(d)(1) or otherwise becomes or is deemed to become a beneficial owner of any security of a class described in subsection (d)(1) upon the purchase or sale of a security-based swap that the Commission may define by rule of this title having an aggregate fair market value on the last trading day in any of the preceding twelve months of at least $100,000,000 or such lesser amount (but in no case less than $10,000,000) as the Commission, by rule, may determine, shall file reports with the Commission in such form, for such periods, and at such times after the end of such periods as the Commission, by rule, may prescribe, but in no event shall such reports be filed for periods longer than one year or shorter than one quarter. Such reports shall include for each such equity security held on the last day of the reporting period by accounts (in aggregate or by type as the Commission, by rule, may prescribe) with respect to which the institutional investment manager exercises investment discretion (other than securities held in amounts which the Commission, by rule, determines to be insignificant for purposes of this subsection), the name of the issuer and the title, class, CUSIP number, number of shares or principal amount, and aggregate fair market value of each such security. Such reports may also include for accounts (in aggregate or by type) with respect to which the institutional investment manager exercises investment discretion such of the following information as the Commission, by rule, prescribes—

(A) the name of the issuer and the title, class, CUSIP number, number of shares or principal amount, and aggregate fair market value or cost or amortized cost of each other security (other than an exempted security) held on the last day of the reporting period by such accounts;

(B) the aggregate fair market value or cost or amortized cost of exempted securities (in aggregate or by class) held on the last day of the reporting period by such accounts;

(C) the number of shares of each equity security of a class described in section 13(d)(1) of this title held on the last day of the reporting period by such accounts with respect to which the institutional investment manager possesses sole or shared authority to exercise the voting rights evidenced by such securities;

(D) the aggregate purchases and aggregate sales during the reporting period of each security (other than an exempted security) effected by or for such accounts; and

(E) with respect to any transaction or series of transactions having a market value of at least $500,000 or such other amount as the Commission, by rule, may determine effected during the reporting period by or for such accounts in any equity security of a class described in section 13(d)(1) of this title—

(i) the name of the issuer and the title, class, and CUSIP number of the security;

(ii) the number of shares or principal amount of the security involved in the transaction;

(iii) whether the transaction was a purchase or sale;

(iv) the per share price or prices at which the transaction was effected;

(v) the date or dates of the transaction;

(vi) the date or dates of the settlement of the transaction;

(vii) the broker or dealer through whom the transaction was effected;

(viii) the market or markets in which the transaction was effected; and

(ix) such other related information as the Commission, by rule, may prescribe.

(2) The Commission shall prescribe rules providing for the public disclosure of the name of the issuer and the title, class, CUSIP number, aggregate amount of the number of short sales of each security, and any additional information determined by the Commission following the end of the reporting period. At a minimum, such public disclosure shall occur every month.

(3) The Commission, by rule or order, may exempt, conditionally or unconditionally, any institutional investment manager or security or any class of institutional investment managers or securities from any or all of the provisions of this subsection or the rules thereunder.

(4) The Commission shall make available to the public for a reasonable fee a list of all equity securities of a class described in section 13(d)(1) of this title, updated no less frequently than reports are required to be filed pursuant to paragraph (1) of this subsection. The Commission shall tabulate the information contained in any report filed pursuant to this subsection in a manner which will, in the view of the Commission, maximize the usefulness of the information to other Federal and State authorities and the public. Promptly after the filing of any such report, the Commission shall make the information contained therein conveniently available to the public for a reasonable fee in such form as the Commission, by rule, may prescribe, except that the Commission, as it determines to be necessary or appropriate in the public interest or for the protection of investors, may delay or prevent public disclosure of any such information in accordance with section 552 of title 5, United States Code. Notwithstanding the preceding sentence, any such information identifying the securities held by the account of a natural person or an estate or trust (other than a business trust or investment company) shall not be disclosed to the public.

(5) In exercising its authority under this subsection, the Commission shall determine (and so state) that its action is necessary or appropriate in the public interest and for the protection of investors or to maintain fair and orderly markets or, in granting an exemption, that its action is consistent with the protection of investors and the purposes of this subsection. In exercising such authority the Commission shall take such steps as are within its power, including consulting with the Comptroller General of the United States, the Director of the Office of Management and Budget, the appropriate regulatory agencies, Federal and State authorities which, directly or indirectly, require reports from institutional investment

managers of information substantially similar to that called for by this subsection, national securities exchanges, and registered securities associations, (A) to achieve uniform, centralized reporting of information concerning the securities holdings of and transactions by or for accounts with respect to which institutional investment managers exercise investment discretion, and (B) consistently with the objective set forth in the preceding subparagraph, to avoid unnecessarily duplicative reporting by, and minimize the compliance burden on, institutional investment managers. Federal authorities which, directly or indirectly, require reports from institutional investment managers of information substantially similar to that called for by this subsection shall cooperate with the Commission in the performance of its responsibilities under the preceding sentence. An institutional investment manager which is a bank, the deposits of which are insured in accordance with the Federal Deposit Insurance Act, shall file with the appropriate regulatory agency a copy of every report filed with the Commission pursuant to this subsection.

(6)(A) For purposes of this subsection the term "institutional investment manager" includes any person, other than a natural person, investing in or buying and selling securities for its own account, and any person exercising investment discretion with respect to the account of any other person.

(B) The Commission shall adopt such rules as it deems necessary or appropriate to prevent duplicative reporting pursuant to this subsection by two or more institutional investment managers exercising investment discretion with respect to the same amount.

(g)(1) Any person who is directly or indirectly the beneficial owner of more than 5 per centum of any security of a class described in subsection (d)(1) of this section or otherwise becomes or is deemed to become a beneficial owner of any security of a class described in subsection (d)(1) upon the purchase or sale of a security-based swap that the Commission may define by rule, shall file with the Commission a statement setting forth, in such form and at such time as the Commission may, by rule, prescribe—

(A) such person's identity, residence, and citizenship; and

(B) the number and description of the shares in which such person has an interest and the nature of such interest.

(2) If any material change occurs in the facts set forth in the statement filed with the Commission, an amendment shall be filed with the Commission, in accordance with such rules and regulations as the Commission may prescribe as necessary or appropriate in the public interest or for the protection of investors.

(3) When two or more persons act as a partnership, limited partnership, syndicate, or other group for the purpose of acquiring, holding, or disposing of securities of an issuer, such syndicate or group shall be deemed a "person" for the purposes of this subsection.

(4) In determining, for purposes of this subsection, any percentage of a class of any security, such class shall be deemed to consist of the amount of the outstanding securities of such class, exclusive of any securities of such class held by or for the account of the issuer or a subsidiary of the issuer.

(5) In exercising its authority under this subsection, the Commission shall take such steps as it deems necessary or appropriate in the public interest or for the protection of investors (A) to achieve centralized reporting of information regarding ownership, (B) to avoid unnecessarily duplicative reporting by and minimize the compliance burden on persons required to report, and (C) to tabulate and promptly make available the information contained in any report filed pursuant to this subsection in a manner which will, in the view of the Commission, maximize the usefulness of the information to other Federal and State agencies and the public.

(6) The Commission may, by rule or order, exempt, in whole or in part, any person or class of persons from any or all of the reporting requirements of this subsection as it deems necessary or appropriate in the public interest or for the protection of investors.

(i) ACCURACY OF FINANCIAL REPORTS.—Each financial report that contains financial statements, and that is required to be prepared in accordance with (or reconciled to) generally accepted accounting principles under this title and filed with the Commission shall reflect all material correcting adjustments that have been identified by a registered public accounting firm in accordance with generally accepted accounting principles and the rules andregulations of the Commission.

(j) OFF-BALANCE SHEET TRANSACTIONS.—Not later than 180 days after the date of enactment of the Sarbanes-Oxley Act of 2002, the Commission shall issue final rules providing that each annual and quarterly financial report required to be filed with the Commission shall disclose all material off-balance sheet transactions, arrangements, obligations (including contingent obligations), and other relationships of the issuer with unconsolidated entities or other persons, that may have a material current or future effect on financial condition, changes in financial condition, results of operations, liquidity, capital expenditures, capital resources, or significant components of revenues or expenses.

(k) PROHIBITION ON PERSONAL LOANS TO EXECUTIVES.—

(1) IN GENERAL.—It shall be unlawful for any issuer (as defined in section 2 of the Sarbanes-Oxley Act of 2002), directly or indirectly, including through any subsidiary, to extend or maintain credit, to arrange for the extension of credit, or to renew an extension of credit, in the form of a personal loan to or for any director or executive officer (or equivalent thereof) of that issuer. An extension of credit maintained by the issuer on the date of enactment of this subsection shall not be subject to the provisions of this subsection, provided that there is no material modification to any term of any such extension of credit or any renewal of any such extension of credit on or after that date of enactment.

(2) LIMITATION.—Paragraph (1) does not preclude any home improvement and manufactured home loans (as that term is defined in section 5 of the Home Owners' Loan Act (12 U.S.C. 1464)), consumer credit (as defined in section 103 of the Truth in Lending Act (15 U.S.C. 1602)), or any extension of credit under an open end credit plan (as defined in section 103 of the Truth in Lending Act (15 U.S.C. 1602)), or a charge card (as defined in section 127(c)(4)(e) of the Truth in Lending Act (15 U.S.C. 1637(c)(4)(e)), or any extension of credit by a broker or dealer registered under section 15 of this title to an employee of that broker or dealer to buy, trade, or carry securities, that is permitted under rules or regulations of the Board of Governors of the Federal Reserve System pursuant to section 7 of this title (other than an extension of credit that would be used to purchase the stock of that issuer), that is—

(A) made or provided in the ordinary course of the consumer credit business of such issuer;

(B) of a type that is generally made available by such issuer to the public; and

(C) made by such issuer on market terms, or terms that are no more favorable than those offered by the issuer to the general public for such extensions of credit.

(3) RULE OF CONSTRUCTION FOR CERTAIN LOANS.—Paragraph (1) does not apply to any loan made or maintained by an insured depository institution (as defined in section 3 of the Federal Deposit Insurance Act (12 U.S.C. 1813)), if the loan is subject to the insider lending restrictions of section 22(h) of the Federal Reserve Act (12 U.S.C. 375b).

(l) REAL TIME ISSUER DISCLOSURES.—Each issuer reporting under section 13(a) or 15(d) shall disclose to the public on a rapid and current basis such additional information concerning material changes in the financial condition or operations of the issuer, in plain English, which may include trend and qualitative information and graphic presentations, as the Commission determines, by rule, is necessary or useful for the protection of investors and in the public interest.

(m) PUBLIC AVAILABILITY OF SECURITY-BASED SWAP TRANSACTION DATA.

(1) IN GENERAL.

(A) DEFINITION OF REAL-TIME PUBLIC REPORTING. In this paragraph, the term "real-time public reporting" means to report data relating to a security-based swap transaction, including price and volume, as soon as technologically practicable after the time at which the security-based swap transaction has been executed.

(B) PURPOSE. The purpose of this section is to authorize the Commission to make security-based swap transaction and pricing data available to the public in such form and at such times as the Commission determines appropriate to enhance price discovery.

(C) GENERAL RULE. The Commission is authorized to provide by rule for the public availability of security-based swap transaction, volume, and pricing data as follows:

(i) With respect to those security-based swaps that are subject to the mandatory clearing requirement described in section 3C(a)(1) (including those security-based swaps that are excepted from the requirement pursuant to section 3C(g)), the Commission shall require real-time public reporting for such transactions.

(ii) With respect to those security-based swaps that are not subject to the mandatory clearing requirement described in section 3C(a)(1), but are cleared at a registered clearing agency, the Commission shall require real-time public reporting for such transactions.

(iii) With respect to security-based swaps that are not cleared at a registered clearing agency and which are reported to a security-based swap data repository or the Commission under section 3C(a)(6), the Commission shall require real-time public reporting for such transactions, in a manner that does not disclose the business transactions and market positions of any person.

(iv) With respect to security-based swaps that are determined to be required to be cleared under section 3C(b) but are not cleared, the Commission shall require real-time public reporting for such transactions.

(D) REGISTERED ENTITIES AND PUBLIC REPORTING. The Commission may require registered entities to publicly disseminate the security-based swap transaction and pricing data required to be reported under this paragraph.

(E) RULEMAKING REQUIRED. With respect to the rule providing for the public availability of transaction and pricing data for security-based swaps described in clauses (i) and (ii) of subparagraph (C), the rule promulgated by the Commission shall contain provisions—

(i) To ensure such information does not identify the participants;

(ii) To specify the criteria for determining what constitutes a large notional security-based swap transaction (block trade) for particular markets and contracts;

(iii) To specify the appropriate time delay for reporting large notional security-based swap transactions (block trades) to the public; and

(iv) That take into account whether the public disclosure will materially reduce market liquidity.

(F) TIMELINESS OF REPORTING. Parties to a security-based swap (including agents of the parties to a security-based swap) shall be responsible for reporting security-based swap transaction information to the appropriate registered entity in a timely manner as may be prescribed by the Commission.

(G) REPORTING OF SWAPS TO REGISTERED SECURITY-BASED SWAP DATA REPOSITORIES. Each security-based swap (whether cleared or uncleared) shall be reported to a registered security-based swap data repository.

(H) REGISTRATION OF CLEARING AGENCIES. A clearing agency may register as a security-based swap data repository.

(2) SEMIANNUAL AND ANNUAL PUBLIC REPORTING OF AGGREGATE SECURITY-BASED SWAP DATA.

(A) IN GENERAL. In accordance with subparagraph (B), the Commission shall issue a written report on a semiannual and annual basis to make available to the public information relating to—

(i) The trading and clearing in the major security-based swap categories; and

(ii) The market participants and developments in new products.

(B) USE; CONSULTATION. In preparing a report under subparagraph (A), the Commission shall—

(i) Use information from security-based swap data repositories and clearing agencies; and

(ii) Consult with the Office of the Comptroller of the Currency, the Bank for International Settlements, and such other regulatory bodies as may be necessary.

(C) AUTHORITY OF COMMISSION. The Commission may, by rule, regulation, or order, delegate the public reporting responsibilities of the Commission under this paragraph in accordance with such terms and conditions as the Commission determines to be appropriate and in the public interest.

(n) SECURITY-BASED SWAP DATA REPOSITORIES.

(1) REGISTRATION REQUIREMENT. It shall be unlawful for any person, unless registered with the Commission, directly or indirectly, to make use of the mails or any means or instrumentality of interstate commerce to perform the functions of a security-based swap data repository.

(2) INSPECTION AND EXAMINATION. Each registered security-based swap data repository shall be subject to inspection and examination by any representative of the Commission.

(3) COMPLIANCE WITH CORE PRINCIPLES.

(A) IN GENERAL. To be registered, and maintain registration, as a security-based swap data repository, the security-based swap data repository shall comply with—

(i) The requirements and core principles described in this subsection; and

(ii) Any requirement that the Commission may impose by rule or regulation.

(B) REASONABLE DISCRETION OF SECURITY-BASED SWAP DATA REPOSITORY. Unless otherwise determined by the Commission, by rule or regulation, a security-based swap data repository described in subparagraph (A) shall have reasonable discretion in establishing the manner in which the security-based swap data repository complies with the core principles described in this subsection.

(4) STANDARD SETTING.

(A) DATA IDENTIFICATION.

(i) In General. In accordance with clause (ii), the Commission shall prescribe standards that specify the data elements for each security-based swap that shall be collected and maintained by each registered security-based swap data repository.

(ii) Requirement. In carrying out clause (i), the Commission shall prescribe consistent data element standards applicable to registered entities and reporting counterparties.

(B) DATA COLLECTION AND MAINTENANCE. The Commission shall prescribe data collection and data maintenance standards for security-based swap data repositories.

(C) COMPARABILITY. The standards prescribed by the Commission under this subsection shall be comparable to the data standards imposed by the Commission on clearing agencies in connection with their clearing of security-based swaps.

(5) DUTIES. A security-based swap data repository shall—

(A) Accept data prescribed by the Commission for each security-based swap under subsection (b);

(B) Confirm with both counterparties to the security-based swap the accuracy of the data that was submitted;

(C) Maintain the data described in subparagraph (A) in such form, in such manner, and for such period as may be required by the Commission;

(D) (i) Provide direct electronic access to the Commission (or any designee of the Commission, including another registered entity); and

(ii) Provide the information described in subparagraph (A) in such form and at such frequency as the Commission may require to comply with the public reporting requirements set forth in subsection (m);

(E) At the direction of the Commission, establish automated systems for monitoring, screening, and analyzing security-based swap data;

(F) Maintain the privacy of any and all security-based swap transaction information that the security-based swap data repository receives from a security-based swap dealer, counterparty, or any other registered entity; and

(G) On a confidential basis pursuant to section 24, upon request, and after notifying the Commission of the request, make available security-based swap data obtained by the security-based swap data repository, including individual counterparty trade and position data, to—

(i) Each appropriate prudential regulator;

(ii) The Financial Stability Oversight Council;

(iii) The Commodity Futures Trading Commission;

(iv) The Department of Justice; and

(v) Any other person that the Commission determines to be appropriate, including—

(I) Foreign financial supervisors (including foreign futures authorities);

(II) Foreign central banks;

(III) Foreign ministries; and

(IV) Other foreign authorities.

(H) *Confidentiality Agreement.* Before the security-based swap data repository may share information with any entity described in subparagraph (G), the security-based swap data repository shall receive a written agreement from each entity stating that the entity shall abide by the confidentiality requirements described in section 24 relating to the information on security-based swap transactions that is provided.

(6) DESIGNATION OF CHIEF COMPLIANCE OFFICER.

(A) IN GENERAL. Each security-based swap data repository shall designate an individual to serve as a chief compliance officer.

(B) DUTIES. The chief compliance officer shall—

(i) Report directly to the board or to the senior officer of the security-based swap data repository;

(ii) Review the compliance of the security-based swap data repository with respect to the requirements and core principles described in this subsection;

(iii) In consultation with the board of the security-based swap data repository, a body performing a function similar to the board of the security-based swap data repository, or the senior officer of the security-based swap data repository, resolve any conflicts of interest that may arise;

(iv) Be responsible for administering each policy and procedure that is required to be established pursuant to this section;

(v) Ensure compliance with this title (including regulations) relating to agreements, contracts, or transactions, including each rule prescribed by the Commission under this section;

(vi) Establish procedures for the remediation of noncompliance issues identified by the chief compliance officer through any—

(I) Compliance office review;

(II) Look-back;

(III) Internal or external audit finding;

(IV) Self-reported error; or

(V) Validated complaint; and

(vii) Establish and follow appropriate procedures for the handling, management response, remediation, retesting, and closing of noncompliance issues.

(C) ANNUAL REPORTS.

(i) In General. In accordance with rules prescribed by the Commission, the chief compliance officer shall annually prepare and sign a report that contains a description of—

(I) The compliance of the security-based swap data repository of the chief compliance officer with respect to this title (including regulations); and

(II) Each policy and procedure of the security-based swap data repository of the chief compliance officer (including the code of ethics and conflict of interest policies of the security-based swap data repository).

(ii) Requirements. A compliance report under clause (i) shall—

(I) Accompany each appropriate financial report of the security-based swap data repository that is required to be furnished to the Commission pursuant to this section; and

(II) Include a certification that, under penalty of law, the compliance report is accurate and complete.

(7) CORE PRINCIPLES APPLICABLE TO SECURITY-BASED SWAP DATA REPOSITORIES.

(A) ANTITRUST CONSIDERATIONS. Unless necessary or appropriate to achieve the purposes of this title, the swap data repository shall not—

(i) Adopt any rule or take any action that results in any unreasonable restraint of trade; or

(ii) Impose any material anticompetitive burden on the trading, clearing, or reporting of transactions.

(B) GOVERNANCE ARRANGEMENTS. Each security-based swap data repository shall establish governance arrangements that are transparent—

(i) To fulfill public interest requirements; and

(ii) To support the objectives of the Federal Government, owners, and participants.

(C) Conflicts of Interest. Each security-based swap data repository shall—

(i) Establish and enforce rules to minimize conflicts of interest in the decision-making process of the security-based swap data repository; and

(ii) Establish a process for resolving any conflicts of interest described in clause (i).

(D) ADDITIONAL DUTIES DEVELOPED BY COMMISSION.

(i) In General. The Commission may develop 1 or more additional duties applicable to security-based swap data repositories.

(ii) Consideration of Evolving Standards. In developing additional duties under subparagraph (A), the Commission may take into consideration any evolving standard of the United States or the international community.

(iii) Additional Duties For Commission Designees. The Commission shall establish additional duties for any registrant described in section 13(m)(2)(C) in order to minimize conflicts of interest, protect data, ensure compliance, and guarantee the safety and security of the security-based swap data repository.

(8) REQUIRED REGISTRATION FOR SECURITY-BASED SWAP DATA REPOSITORIES. Any person that is required to be registered as a security-based swap data repository under this subsection shall register with the Commission, regardless of whether that person is also licensed under the Commodity Exchange Act as a swap data repository.

(9) RULES. The Commission shall adopt rules governing persons that are registered under this subsection.

(o) BENEFICIAL OWNERSHIP. For purposes of this section and section 16, a person shall be deemed to acquire beneficial ownership of an equity security based on the purchase or sale of a security-based swap, only to the extent that the Commission, by rule, determines after consultation with the prudential regulators and the Secretary of the Treasury, that the purchase or sale of the security-based swap, or class of security-based swap, provides incidents of ownership comparable to direct ownership of the equity security, and that it is necessary to achieve the purposes of this section that the purchase or sale of the security-based swaps, or class of security-based swap, be deemed the acquisition of beneficial ownership of the equity security.

(p) DISCLOSURES RELATING TO CONFLICT MINERALS ORIGINATING IN THE DEMOCRATIC REPUBLIC OF THE CONGO.

(1) REGULATIONS.

(A) IN GENERAL. Not later than 270 days after the date of the enactment of this subsection, the Commission shall promulgate regulations requiring any person described in paragraph (2) to disclose annually, beginning with the person's first full fiscal year that begins after the date of promulgation of such regulations, whether conflict minerals that are necessary as described in paragraph (2)(B), in the year for which such reporting is required, did originate in the Democratic Republic of the Congo or an adjoining country and, in cases in which such conflict minerals did originate in any such country, submit to the Commission a report that includes, with respect to the period covered by the report—

(i) A description of the measures taken by the person to exercise due diligence on the source and chain of custody of such minerals, which measures shall include an independent private sector audit of such report submitted through the Commission that is conducted in accordance with standards established by the Comptroller General of the United States, in accordance with rules promulgated by the Commission, in consultation with the Secretary of State; and

(ii) A description of the products manufactured or contracted to be manufactured that are not DRC conflict free ("DRC conflict free" is defined to mean the products that do not contain minerals that directly or indirectly finance or benefit armed groups in the Democratic Republic of the Congo or an adjoining country), the entity that conducted the independent private sector audit in accordance with clause (i), the facilities used to process the conflict minerals, the country of origin of the conflict minerals, and the efforts to determine the mine or location of origin with the greatest possible specificity.

(B) CERTIFICATION. The person submitting a report under subparagraph (A) shall certify the audit described in clause (i) of such subparagraph that is included in such report. Such a certified audit shall constitute a critical component of due diligence in establishing the source and chain of custody of such minerals.

(C) UNRELIABLE DETERMINATION. If a report required to be submitted by a person under subparagraph (A) relies on a determination of an independent private sector audit, as described under subparagraph (A)(i), or other due diligence processes previously determined by the Commission to be unreliable, the report shall not satisfy the requirements of the regulations promulgated under subparagraph (A)(i).

(D) DRC CONFLICT FREE. For purposes of this paragraph, a product may be labeled as "DRC conflict free" if the product does not contain conflict minerals that directly or indirectly finance or benefit armed groups in the Democratic Republic of the Congo or an adjoining country.

(E) INFORMATION AVAILABLE TO THE PUBLIC. Each person described under paragraph (2) shall make available to the public on the Internet website of such person the information disclosed by such person under subparagraph (A).

(2) PERSON DESCRIBED. A person is described in this paragraph if—

(A) The person is required to file reports with the Commission pursuant to paragraph (1)(A); and

(B) Conflict minerals are necessary to the functionality or production of a product manufactured by such person.

(3) REVISIONS AND WAIVERS. The Commission shall revise or temporarily waive the requirements described in paragraph (1) if the President transmits to the Commission a determination that—

(A) Such revision or waiver is in the national security interest of the United States and the President includes the reasons therefor; and

(B) Establishes a date, not later than 2 years after the initial publication of such exemption, on which such exemption shall expire.

(4) TERMINATION OF DISCLOSURE REQUIREMENTS. The requirements of paragraph (1) shall terminate on the date on which the President determines and certifies to the appropriate congressional committees, but in no case earlier than the date that is one day after the end of the 5-year period beginning on the date of the enactment of this subsection, that no armed groups continue to be directly involved and benefitting from commercial activity involving conflict minerals.

(5) DEFINITIONS. For purposes of this subsection, the terms "adjoining country", "appropriate congressional committees", "armed group", and "conflict mineral" have the meaning given those terms under section 1502 of the Dodd-Frank Wall Street Reform and Consumer Protection Act.

(q) DISCLOSURE OF PAYMENTS BY RESOURCE EXTRACTION ISSUERS.

(1) DEFINITIONS. In this subsection—

(A) The term "commercial development of oil, natural gas, or minerals" includes exploration, extraction, processing, export, and other significant actions relating to oil, natural gas, or minerals, or the acquisition of a license for any such activity, as determined by the Commission;

(B) The term "foreign government" means a foreign government, a department, agency, or instrumentality of a foreign government, or a company owned by a foreign government, as determined by the Commission;

(C) The term "payment"—

(i) Means a payment that is—

(I) Made to further the commercial development of oil, natural gas, or minerals; and

(II) Not de minimis; and

(ii) Includes taxes, royalties, fees (including license fees), production entitlements, bonuses, and other material benefits, that the Commission, consistent with the guidelines of the Extractive Industries Transparency Initiative (to the extent practicable), determines are part of the commonly recognized revenue stream for the commercial development of oil, natural gas, or minerals;

(D) The term "resource extraction issuer" means an issuer that—

(i) Is required to file an annual report with the Commission; and

(ii) Engages in the commercial development of oil, natural gas, or minerals;

(E) The term "interactive data format" means an electronic data format in which pieces of information are identified using an interactive data standard; and

(F) The term "interactive data standard" means standardized list of electronic tags that mark information included in the annual report of a resource extraction issuer.

(2) DISCLOSURE.

(A) INFORMATION REQUIRED. Not later than 270 days after the date of enactment of the Dodd-Frank Wall Street Reform and Consumer Protection Act, the Commission shall issue final rules that require each resource extraction issuer to include in an annual report of the resource extraction issuer information relating to any payment made by the resource extraction issuer, a subsidiary of the resource extraction issuer, or an entity under the control of the resource extraction issuer to a foreign government or the Federal Government for the purpose of the commercial development of oil, natural gas, or minerals, including—

(i) The type and total amount of such payments made for each project of the resource extraction issuer relating to the commercial development of oil, natural gas, or minerals; and

(ii) The type and total amount of such payments made to each government.

(B) CONSULTATION IN RULEMAKING. In issuing rules under subparagraph (A), the Commission may consult with any agency or entity that the Commission determines is relevant.

(C) INTERACTIVE DATA FORMAT. The rules issued under subparagraph (A) shall require that the information included in the annual report of a resource extraction issuer be submitted in an interactive data format.

(D) INTERACTIVE DATA STANDARD.

(i) In General. The rules issued under subparagraph (A) shall establish an interactive data standard for the information included in the annual report of a resource extraction issuer.

(ii) Electronic Tags. The interactive data standard shall include electronic tags that identify, for any payments made by a resource extraction issuer to a foreign government or the Federal Government—

(I) The total amounts of the payments, by category;

(II) The currency used to make the payments;

(III) The financial period in which the payments were made;

(IV) The business segment of the resource extraction issuer that made the payments;

(V) The government that received the payments, and the country in which the government is located;

(VI) The project of the resource extraction issuer to which the payments relate; and

(VII) Such other information as the Commission may determine is necessary or appropriate in the public interest or for the protection of investors.

(E) INTERNATIONAL TRANSPARENCY EFFORTS. To the extent practicable, the rules issued under subparagraph (A) shall support the commitment of the Federal Government to international transparency promotion efforts relating to the commercial development of oil, natural gas, or minerals.

(F) EFFECTIVE DATE. With respect to each resource extraction issuer, the final rules issued under subparagraph (A) shall take effect on the date on which the resource extraction issuer is required to submit an annual report relating to the fiscal year of the resource extraction issuer that ends not earlier than 1 year after the date on which the Commission issues final rules under subparagraph (A).

(3) PUBLIC AVAILABILITY OF INFORMATION.

(A) IN GENERAL. To the extent practicable, the Commission shall make available online, to the public, a compilation of the information required to be submitted under the rules issued under paragraph (2)(A).

(B) OTHER INFORMATION. Nothing in this paragraph shall require the Commission to make available online information other than the information required to be submitted under the rules issued under paragraph (2)(A).

(4) AUTHORIZATION OF APPROPRIATIONS. There are authorized to be appropriated to the Commission such sums as may be necessary to carry out this subsection.

(r) DISCLOSURE OF CERTAIN ACTIVITIES RELATING TO IRAN.

(1) IN GENERAL. Each issuer required to file an annual or quarterly report under subsection (a) shall disclose in that report the information required by paragraph (2) if, during the period covered by the report, the issuer or any affiliate of the issuer—

(A) Knowingly engaged in an activity described in subsection (a) or (b) of section 5 of the Iran Sanctions Act of 1996 (Public Law 104–172; 50 U.S.C. 1701 note);

(B) Knowingly engaged in an activity described in subsection (c)(2) of section 104 of the Comprehensive Iran Sanctions, Accountability, and Divestment Act of 2010 (22 U.S.C. 8513) or a transaction described in subsection (d)(1) of that section;

(C) Knowingly engaged in an activity described in section 105A(b)(2) of that Act; or

(D) Knowingly conducted any transaction or dealing with—

(i) Any person the property and interests in property of which are blocked pursuant to Executive Order No. 13224 (66 Fed. Reg. 49079; relating to blocking property and prohibiting transactions with persons who commit, threaten to commit, or support terrorism);

(ii) Any person the property and interests in property of which are blocked pursuant to Executive Order No. 13382 (70 Fed. Reg. 38567; relating to blocking of property of weapons of mass destruction proliferators and their supporters); or

(iii) Any person or entity identified under section 560.304 of title 31, Code of Federal Regulations (relating to the definition of the Government of Iran) without the specific authorization of a Federal department or agency.

(2) INFORMATION REQUIRED. If an issuer or an affiliate of the issuer has engaged in any activity described in paragraph (1), the issuer shall disclose a detailed description of each such activity, including—

(A) The nature and extent of the activity;

(B) The gross revenues and net profits, if any, attributable to the activity; and

(C) Whether the issuer or the affiliate of the issuer (as the case may be) intends to continue the activity.

(3) NOTICE OF DISCLOSURES. If an issuer reports under paragraph (1) that the issuer or an affiliate of the issuer has knowingly engaged in any activity described in that paragraph, the issuer shall separately file with the Commission, concurrently with the annual or quarterly report under subsection (a), a notice that the disclosure of that activity has been included in that annual or quarterly report that identifies the issuer and contains the information required by paragraph (2).

(4) PUBLIC DISCLOSURE OF INFORMATION. Upon receiving a notice under paragraph (3) that an annual or quarterly report includes a disclosure of an activity described in paragraph (1), the Commission shall promptly—

(A) Transmit the report to—

(i) The President;

(ii) The Committee on Foreign Affairs and the Committee on Financial Services of the House of Representatives; and

(iii) The Committee on Foreign Relations and the Committee on Banking, Housing, and Urban Affairs of the Senate; and

(B) Make the information provided in the disclosure and the notice available to the public by posting the information on the Internet website of the Commission.

(5) INVESTIGATIONS. Upon receiving a report under paragraph (4) that includes a disclosure of an activity described in paragraph (1) (other than an activity described in subparagraph (D)(iii) of that paragraph), the President shall—

(A) Initiate an investigation into the possible imposition of sanctions under the Iran Sanctions Act of 1996 (Public Law 104–172; 50 U.S.C. 1701 note), section 104 or 105A of the Comprehensive Iran Sanctions, Accountability, and Divestment Act of 2010, an Executive order specified in clause (i) or (ii) of paragraph (1)(D), or any other provision of law relating to the imposition of sanctions with respect to Iran, as applicable; and

(B) Not later than 180 days after initiating such an investigation, make a determination with respect to whether sanctions should be imposed with respect to the issuer or the affiliate of the issuer (as the case may be).

(6) SUNSET. The provisions of this subsection shall terminate on the date that is 30 days after the date on which the President makes the certification described in section 401(a) of the Comprehensive Iran Sanctions, Accountability, and Divestment Act of 2010 (22 U.S.C. 8551(a)).

REPORTING AND RECORDKEEPING FOR CERTAIN SECURITY-BASED SWAPS

Sec. 13A. (a) REQUIRED REPORTING OF SECURITY-BASED SWAPS NOT ACCEPTED BY ANY CLEARING AGENCY OR DERIVATIVES CLEARING ORGANIZATION.

(1) IN GENERAL. Each security-based swap that is not accepted for clearing by any clearing agency or derivatives clearing organization shall be reported to—

(A) A security-based swap data repository described in section 13(n); or

(B) In the case in which there is no security-based swap data repository that would accept the security-based swap, to the Commission pursuant to this section within such time period as the Commission may by rule or regulation prescribe.

(2) TRANSITION RULE FOR PREENACTMENT SECURITY-BASED SWAPS.

(A) Security-Based Swaps Entered Into Before the Date of Enactment of The Wall Street Transparency and Accountability Act of 2010. Each security-based swap entered into before the date of enactment of the Wall Street Transparency and Accountability Act of 2010, the terms of which have not expired as of the date of enactment of that Act, shall be reported to a registered security-based swap data repository or the Commission by a date that is not later than—

(i) 30 days after issuance of the interim final rule; or

(ii) Such other period as the Commission determines to be appropriate.

(B) COMMISSION RULEMAKING. The Commission shall promulgate an interim final rule within 90 days of the date of enactment of this section providing for the reporting of each security-based swap entered into before the date of enactment as referenced in subparagraph (A).

(C) EFFECTIVE DATE. The reporting provisions described in this section shall be effective upon the date of the enactment of this section.

(3) REPORTING OBLIGATIONS.

(A) SECURITY-BASED SWAPS IN WHICH ONLY 1 COUNTERPARTY IS A SECURITY-BASED SWAP DEALER OR MAJOR SECURITY-BASED SWAP PARTICIPANT. With respect to a security-based swap in which only 1 counterparty is a security-based swap dealer or major security-based swap participant, the security-based swap dealer or major security-based swap participant shall report the security-based swap as required under paragraphs (1) and (2).

(B) SECURITY-BASED SWAPS IN WHICH 1 COUNTERPARTY IS A SECURITY-BASED SWAP DEALER AND THE OTHER A MAJOR SECURITY-BASED SWAP PARTICIPANT. With respect to a security-based swap in which 1 counterparty is a security-based swap dealer and the other a major security-based swap participant, the security-based swap dealer shall report the security-based swap as required under paragraphs (1) and (2).

(C) OTHER SECURITY-BASED SWAPS. With respect to any other security-based swap not described in subparagraph (A) or (B), the counterparties to the security-based swap shall select a counterparty to report the security-based swap as required under paragraphs (1) and (2).

(b) DUTIES OF CERTAIN INDIVIDUALS. Any individual or entity that enters into a security-based swap shall meet each requirement described in subsection (c) if the individual or entity did not—

(1) Clear the security-based swap in accordance with section 3C(a)(1); or

(2) Have the data regarding the security-based swap accepted by a security-based swap data repository in accordance with rules (including timeframes) adopted by the Commission under this title.

(c) REQUIREMENTS. An individual or entity described in subsection (b) shall—

(1) Upon written request from the Commission, provide reports regarding the security-based swaps held by the individual or entity to the Commission in such form and in such manner as the Commission may request; and

(2) Maintain books and records pertaining to the security-based swaps held by the individual or entity in such form, in such manner, and for such period as the Commission may require, which shall be open to inspection by—

(A) Any representative of the Commission;

(B) An appropriate prudential regulator;

(C) The Commodity Futures Trading Commission;

(D) The Financial Stability Oversight Council; and

(E) The Department of Justice.

(d) IDENTICAL DATA. In prescribing rules under this section, the Commission shall require individuals and entities described in subsection (b) to submit to the Commission a report that contains data that is not less comprehensive than the data required to be collected by security-based swap data repositories under this title.

PROXIES

Sec. 14. (a) (1) It shall be unlawful for any person, by the use of the mails or by any means or instrumentality of interstate commerce or of any facility of a national securities exchange or otherwise, in contravention of such rules and regulations as the Commission may prescribe as necessary or appropriate in the public interest or for the protection of investors, to solicit or to permit the use of his name to solicit any proxy or consent or authorization in respect of any security (other than an exempted security) registered pursuant to section 12 of this title.

(2) The rules and regulations prescribed by the Commission under paragraph (1) may include—

(A) A requirement that a solicitation of proxy, consent, or authorization by (or on behalf of) an issuer include a nominee submitted by a shareholder to serve on the board of directors of the issuer; and

(B) A requirement that an issuer follow a certain procedure in relation to a solicitation described in subparagraph (A).

(b) (1) It shall be unlawful for any member of a national securities exchange, or any broker or dealer registered under this title, or any bank, association, or other entity that exercises fiduciary powers, in contravention of such rules and regulations as the Commission may prescribe as necessary or appropriate in the public interest or for the protection of investors, to give, or to refrain from giving a proxy, consent, authorization, or information statement in respect of any security registered pursuant to section 12 of this title, or any security issued by an investment company registered under the Investment Company Act of 1940, and carried for the account of a customer.

(2) With respect to banks, the rules and regulations prescribed by the Commission under paragraph (1) shall not require the disclosure of the names of beneficial owners of securities in an account held by the bank on the date of enactment of this paragraph unless the beneficial owner consents to the disclosure. The provisions of this paragraph shall not apply in the case of a bank which the Commission finds has not made a good faith effort to obtain such consent from such beneficial owners.

(c) Unless proxies, consents, or authorizations in respect of a security registered pursuant to section 12 of this title, or a security issued by an investment company registered under the Investment Company Act of 1940, are solicited by or on behalf of the management of the issuer from the holders of record of such security in accordance with the rules and regulations prescribed under subsection (a) of this section, prior to any annual or other meeting of the holders of such security, such issuer shall, in accordance with rules and regulations prescribed by the Commission, file with the Commission and transmit to all holders of record of such security information substantially equivalent to the information which would be required to be transmitted if a solicitation were made, but no information shall be required to be filed or transmitted pursuant to this subsection before July 1, 1964.

(d) (1) It shall be unlawful for any person, directly or indirectly, by use of the mails or by any means or instrumentality of interstate commerce or of any facility of a national securities exchange or otherwise, to make a tender offer for, or a request or invitation for tenders of, any class of any equity security which is registered pursuant to section 12 of this title, or any equity of an insurance company which would have been required to be so registered except for the exemption contained in section 12(g)(2)(G) of this title, or any equity security issued by a closed-end investment company registered under the Investment Company Act of 1940, if, after consummation thereof, such person would, directly or indirectly, be the beneficial owner of more than 5 per centum of such class, unless at the time copies of the offer or request or invitation are first published or sent or given to security holders such person has filed with the Commission a statement containing such of the information specified in section 13(d) of this title, and such additional information as the Commission may by rules and regulations prescribe as necessary or appropriate in the public interest or for the protection of investors. All requests or invitations for tenders or advertisements making a tender offer or requesting or inviting tenders of such a security shall be filed as a part of such statement and shall contain such of the information contained in such statement as the Commission may by rules and regulations prescribe. Copies of any additional material soliciting or requesting such tender offers subsequent to the initial solicitation or request shall contain such information as the Commission may by rules and regulations prescribe as necessary or appropriate in the public interest or for the protection of investors, and shall be filed with the Commission not later than the time copies of such material are first published or sent or given to security holders. Copies of all statements, in the form in which such material is furnished to security holders and the Commission, shall be sent to the issuer not later than the date such material is first published or sent or given to any security holders.

(2) When two or more persons act as a partnership, limited partnership, syndicate, or other group for the purpose of acquiring, holding, or disposing of securities of an issuer, such syndicate or group shall be deemed a "person" for purposes of this subsection.

(3) In determining, for purposes of this subsection, any percentage of a class of any security, such class shall be deemed to consist of the amount of the outstanding securities of such class, exclusive of any securities of such class held by or for the account of the issuer or a subsidiary of the issuer.

(4) Any solicitation or recommendation to the holders of such a security to accept or reject a tender offer or request or invitation for tenders shall be made in accordance with such rules and regulations as the Commission may prescribe as necessary or appropriate in the public interest or for the protection of investors.

(5) Securities deposited pursuant to a tender offer or request or invitation for tenders may be withdrawn by or on behalf of the depositor at any time until the expiration of seven days after the time definitive copies of the offer or request or invitation are first published or sent or given to security holders, and at any time after sixty days from the date of the original tender offer or request or invitation, except as the Commission may otherwise prescribe by rules, regulations, or order as necessary or appropriate in the public interest or for the protection of investors.

(6) Where any person makes a tender offer, or request or invitation for tenders, for less than all the outstanding equity securities of a class, and where a greater number of securities is deposited pursuant thereto within ten days after copies of the offer or request or invitation are first published or sent or given to security holders than such person is bound or willing to take up and pay for, the securities taken up shall be taken up as nearly as may be pro rata, disregarding fractions, according to the number of securities deposited by each depositor. The provisions of this subsection shall also apply to securities deposited within ten days after notice of an increase in the consideration offered to security holders, as described in paragraph (7), is first published or sent or given to security holders.

(7) Where any person varies the terms of a tender offer or request or invitation for tenders before the expiration thereof by increasing the consideration offered to holders of such securities, such person shall pay the increased consideration to each security holder whose securities are taken up and paid for pursuant to the tender offer or request or invitation for tenders whether or not such securities have been taken up by such person before the variation of the tender offer or request or invitation.

(8) The provisions of this subsection shall not apply to any offer for, or request or invitation for tenders of, any security—

    (A) if the acquisition of such security, together with all other acquisitions by the same person of securities of the same class during the preceding twelve months, would not exceed 2 per centum of that class;

    (B) by the issuer of such security; or

    (C) which the Commission, by rules or regulations or by order, shall exempt from the provisions of this subsection as not entered into for the purpose of, and not having the effect of, changing or influencing the control of the issuer or otherwise as not comprehended within the purposes of this subsection.

(e) It shall be unlawful for any person to make any untrue statement of a material fact or omit to state any material fact necessary in order to make the statements made, in the light of the circumstances under which they are made, not misleading, or to engage in any fraudulent, deceptive, or manipulative acts or practices, in connection with any tender offer or request or invitation for tenders, or any solicitation of security holders in opposition to or in favor of any such offer, request, or invitation. The Commission shall, for the purposes of this subsection, by rules and regulations define, and prescribe means reasonably designed to prevent, such acts and practices as are fraudulent, deceptive, or manipulative.

(f) If, pursuant to any arrangement or understanding with the person or persons acquiring securities in a transaction subject to subsection (d) of this section or subsection (d) of section 13 of this title, any persons are to be elected or designated as directors of the issuer, otherwise than at a meeting of security holders, and the persons so elected or designated will constitute a majority of the directors of the issuer, then, prior to the time any such person takes office as a director, and in accordance with rules and regulations prescribed by the Commission, the issuer shall file with the Commission, and transmit to all holders of record of securities of the issuer who would be entitled to vote at a meeting for election of directors, information substantially equivalent to the information which would be required by subsection (a) or (c) of this section to be transmitted if such person or persons were nominees for election as directors at a meeting of such security holders.

(h) Proxy Solicitations and Tender Offers in Connection With Limited Partnership Rollup Transactions.—

(1) Proxy rules to contain special provisions.—It shall be unlawful for any person to solicit any proxy, consent, or authorization concerning a limited partnership rollup transaction, or to make any tender offer in furtherance of a limited partnership rollup transaction, unless such transaction is conducted in accordance with rules prescribed by the Commission under subsections (a) and (d) as required by this subsection. Such rules shall—

    (A) permit any holder of a security that is the subject of the proposed limited partnership rollup transaction to engage in preliminary communications for the purpose of determining whether to solicit proxies, consents, or authorizations in opposition to the proposed limited partnership rollup transaction, without regard to whether any such communication would otherwise be considered a solicitation of proxies, and without being required to file soliciting material with the Commission prior to making that determination, except that—

        (i) nothing in this subparagraph shall be construed to limit the application of any provision of this title prohibiting, or reasonably designed to prevent, fraudulent, deceptive, or manipulative acts or practices under this title; and

        (ii) any holder of not less than 5 percent of the outstanding securities that are the subject of the proposed limited partnership rollup transaction who engages in the business of buying and selling limited partnership interests in the secondary market shall be required to disclose such ownership interests and any potential conflicts of interests in such preliminary communications;

    (B) require the issuer to provide to holders of the securities that are the subject of the limited partnership rollup transaction such list of the holders of the issuer's securities as the Commission may determine in such form and subject to such terms and conditions as the Commission may specify;

(C) prohibit compensating any person soliciting proxies, consents, or authorizations directly from security holders concerning such a limited partnership rollup transaction—

(i) on the basis of whether the solicited proxy, consent, or authorization either approves or disapproves the proposed limited partnership rollup transaction; or

(ii) contingent on the approval, disapproval, or completion of the limited partnership rollup transaction;

(D) set forth disclosure requirements for soliciting material distributed in connection with a limited partnership rollup transaction, including requirements for clear, concise, and comprehensible disclosure with respect to—

(i) any changes in the business plan, voting rights, form of ownership interest, or the compensation of the general partner in the proposed limited partnership rollup transaction from each of the original limited partnerships;

(ii) the conflicts of interest, if any, of the general partner;

(iii) whether it is expected that there will be a significant difference between the exchange values of the limited partnerships and the trading price of the securities to be issued in the limited partnership rollup transaction;

(iv) the valuation of the limited partnerships and the method used to determine the value of the interests of the limited partners to be exchanged for the securities in the limited partnership rollup transaction;

(v) the differing risks and effects of the limited partnership rollup transaction for investors in different limited partnership proposed to be included, and the risks and effects of completing the limited partnership rollup transaction with less than all limited partnerships;

(vi) the statement by the general partner required under subparagraph (E);

(vii) such other matters deemed necessary or appropriate by the Commission;

(E) require a statement by the general partner as to whether the proposed limited partnership rollup transaction is fair or unfair to investors in each limited partnership, a discussion of the basis for that conclusion, and an evaluation and a description by the general partner of alternatives to the limited partnership rollup transaction, such as liquidation;

(F) provide that, if the general partner or sponsor has obtained any opinion (other than an opinion of counsel), appraisal, or report that is prepared by an outside party and that is materially related to the limited partnership rollup transaction, such soliciting materials shall contain or be accompanied by clear, concise, and comprehensible disclosure with respect to—

(i) the analysis of the transaction, scope of review, preparation of the opinion, and basis for and methods of arriving at conclusions, and any representations and undertakings with respect thereto;

(ii) the identity and qualifications of the person who prepared the opinion, the method of selection of such person, and any material past, existing, or contemplated relationships between the person or any of its affiliates and the general partner, sponsor, successor, or any other affiliate;

(iii) any compensation of the preparer of such opinion, appraisal, or report that is contingent on the transaction's approval or completion; and

(iv) any limitations imposed by the issuer on the access afforded to such preparer to the issuer's personnel, premises, and relevant books and records;

(G) provide that, if the general partner or sponsor has obtained any opinion, appraisal, or report as described in subparagraph (F) from any person whose compensation is contingent on the transaction's approval or completion or who has not been given access by the issuer to its personnel and premises and relevant books and records, the general partner or sponsor shall state the reasons therefor;

(H) provide that, if the general partner or sponsor has not obtained any opinion on the fairness of the proposed limited partnership rollup transaction to investors in each of the affected partnerships, such soliciting materials shall contain or be accompanied by a statement of such partner's or sponsor's reasons for concluding that such an opinion is not necessary in order to permit the limited partners to make an informed decision on the proposed transaction;

(I) require that the soliciting material include a clear, concise, and comprehensible summary of the limited partnership rollup transaction (including a summary of the matters referred to in clauses (i) through (vii) of subparagraph (D) and a summary of the matter referred to in subparagraphs (F), (G), and (H)), with the risks of the limited partnership rollup transaction set forth prominently in the fore part thereof;

(J) provide that any solicitation or offering period with respect to any proxy solicitation, tender offer, or information statement in a limited partnership rollup transaction shall be for not less than the lesser of 60 calendar days or the maximum number of days permitted under applicable State law; and

(K) contain such other provisions as the Commission determines to be necessary or appropriate for the protection of investors in limited partnership rollup transactions.

(2) EXEMPTIONS.—The Commission may, consistent with the public interest, the protection of investors, and the purposes of this title, exempt by rule or order any security or class of securities, any transaction or class of transactions, or any person or class of persons, in whole or in part, conditionally or unconditionally, from the requirements imposed pursuant to paragraph (1) or from the definition contained in paragraph (4).

(3) EFFECT ON COMMISSION AUTHORITY.—Nothing in this subsection limits the authority of the Commission under subsection (a) or (d) or any other provision of this title or precludes the Commission from imposing, under subsection (a) or (d) or any other provision of this title, a remedy or procedure required to be imposed under this subsection.

(4) DEFINITION OF LIMITED PARTNERSHIP ROLLUP TRANSACTION.—Except as provided in paragraph (5), as used in this subsection, the term "limited partnership rollup transaction" means a transaction involving the combination or reorganization of one or more limited partnerships, directly or indirectly, in which—

(A) some or all of the investors in any of such limited partnerships will receive new securities, or securities in another entity, that will be reported under a transaction reporting plan declared effective before the date of enactment of this subsection by the Commission under section 11A;

(B) any of the investors' limited partnership securities are not, as of the date of filing, reported under a transaction reporting plan declared effective before the date of enactment of this subsection by the Commission under section 11A;

(C) investors in any of the limited partnerships involved in the transaction are subject to a significant adverse change with respect to voting rights, the term of existence of the entity, management compensation, or investment objectives; and

(D) any of such investors are not provided an option to receive or retain a security under substantially the same terms and conditions as the original issue.

(5) EXCLUSIONS FROM DEFINITION.—Notwithstanding paragraph (4), the term "limited partnership rollup transaction" does not include—

(A) a transaction that involves only a limited partnership or partnerships having an operating policy or practice of retaining cash available for distribution and reinvesting proceeds from the sale, financing, or refinancing of assets in accordance with such criteria as the Commission determines appropriate;

(B) a transaction involving only limited partnerships wherein the interests of the limited partners are repurchased, recalled, or exchanged in accordance with the terms of the preexisting limited partnership agreements for securities in an operating company specifically identified at the time of the formation of the original limited partnership;

(C) a transaction in which the securities to be issued or exchanged are not required to be and are not registered under the Securities Act of 1933;

(D) a transaction that involves only issuers that are not required to register or report under section 12, both before and after the transaction;

(E) a transaction, except as the Commission may otherwise provide by rule for the protection of investors, involving the combination or reorganization of one or more limited partnerships in which a non-affiliated party succeeds to the interests of a general partner or sponsor, if—

(i) such action is approved by not less than $66\frac{2}{3}$ percent of the outstanding units of each of the participating limited partnerships; and

(ii) as a result of the transaction, the existing general partners will receive only compensation to which they are entitled as expressly provided for in the preexisting limited partnership agreements; or

(F) a transaction, except as the Commission may otherwise provide by rule for the protection of investors, in which the securities offered to investors are securities of another entity that are reported under a transaction reporting plan declared effective before the date of enactment of this subsection by the Commission under section 11A, if—

(i) such other entity was formed, and such class of securities was reported and regularly traded, not less than 12 months before the date on which soliciting material is mailed to investors; and

(ii) the securities of that entity issued to investors in the transaction do not exceed 20 percent of the total outstanding securities of the entity, exclusive of any securities of such class held by or for the account of the entity or a subsidiary of the entity.

(i) DISCLOSURE OF PAY VERSUS PERFORMANCE.— The Commission shall, by rule, require each issuer to disclose in any proxy or consent solicitation material for an annual meeting of the shareholders of the issuer a clear description of any compensation required to be disclosed by the issuer under section 229.402 of title 17, Code of Federal Regulations (or any successor thereto), including, for any issuer other than an emerging growth company, that shows the relationship between executive compensation actually paid and the financial performance of the issuer, taking into account any change in the value of the shares of stock and dividends of the issuer and any distributions. The disclosure under this subsection may include a graphic representation of the information required to be disclosed.

(j) DISCLOSURE OF HEDGING BY EMPLOYEES AND DIRECTORS.— The Commission shall, by rule, require each issuer to disclose in any proxy or consent solicitation material for an annual meeting of the shareholders of the issuer whether any employee or member of the board of directors of the issuer, or any designee of such employee or member, is permitted to purchase financial instruments (including prepaid variable forward contracts, equity swaps, collars, and exchange funds) that are designed to hedge or offset any decrease in the market value of equity securities—

(1) Granted to the employee or member of the board of directors by the issuer as part of the compensation of the employee or member of the board of directors; or

(2) Held, directly or indirectly, by the employee or member of the board of directors

SHAREHOLDER APPROVAL OF EXECUTIVE COMPENSATION

Sec. 14A (a) SEPARATE RESOLUTION REQUIRED.

(1) IN GENERAL. Not less frequently than once every 3 years, a proxy or consent or authorization for an annual or other meeting of the shareholders for which the proxy solicitation rules of the Commission require compensation disclosure shall include a separate resolution subject to shareholder vote to approve the compensation of executives,

as disclosed pursuant to section 229.402 of title 17, Code of Federal Regulations, or any successor thereto.

(2) FREQUENCY OF VOTE. Not less frequently than once every 6 years, a proxy or consent or authorization for an annual or other meeting of the shareholders for which the proxy solicitation rules of the Commission require compensation disclosure shall include a separate resolution subject to shareholder vote to determine whether votes on the resolutions required under paragraph (1) will occur every 1, 2, or 3 years.

(3) EFFECTIVE DATE. The proxy or consent or authorization for the first annual or other meeting of the shareholders occurring after the end of the 6-month period beginning on the date of enactment of this section shall include—

(A) The resolution described in paragraph (1); and

(B) A separate resolution subject to shareholder vote to determine whether votes on the resolutions required under paragraph (1) will occur every 1, 2, or 3 years.

(b) SHAREHOLDER APPROVAL OF GOLDEN PARACHUTE COMPENSATION.

(1) DISCLOSURE. In any proxy or consent solicitation material (the solicitation of which is subject to the rules of the Commission pursuant to subsection (a)) for a meeting of the shareholders occurring after the end of the 6-month period beginning on the date of enactment of this section, at which shareholders are asked to approve an acquisition, merger, consolidation, or proposed sale or other disposition of all or substantially all the assets of an issuer, the person making such solicitation shall disclose in the proxy or consent solicitation material, in a clear and simple form in accordance with regulations to be promulgated by the Commission, any agreements or understandings that such person has with any named executive officers of such issuer (or of the acquiring issuer, if such issuer is not the acquiring issuer) concerning any type of compensation (whether present, deferred, or contingent) that is based on or otherwise relates to the acquisition, merger, consolidation, sale, or other disposition of all or substantially all of the assets of the issuer and the aggregate total of all such compensation that may (and the conditions upon which it may) be paid or become payable to or on behalf of such executive officer.

(2) SHAREHOLDER APPROVAL. Any proxy or consent or authorization relating to the proxy or consent solicitation material containing the disclosure required by paragraph (1) shall include a separate resolution subject to shareholder vote to approve such agreements or understandings and compensation as disclosed, unless such agreements or understandings have been subject to a shareholder vote under subsection (a).

(c) RULE OF CONSTRUCTION. The shareholder vote referred to in subsections (a) and (b) shall not be binding on the issuer or the board of directors of an issuer, and may not be construed—

(1) As overruling a decision by such issuer or board of directors;

(2) To create or imply any change to the fiduciary duties of such issuer or board of directors;

(3) To create or imply any additional fiduciary duties for such issuer or board of directors; or

(4) To restrict or limit the ability of shareholders to make proposals for inclusion in proxy materials related to executive compensation.

(d) DISCLOSURE OF VOTES. Every institutional investment manager subject to section 13(f) shall report at least annually how it voted on any shareholder vote pursuant to subsections (a) and (b), unless such vote is otherwise required to be reported publicly by rule or regulation of the Commission.

(e) EXEMPTION.

(1) IN GENERAL. The Commission may, by rule or order, exempt any other issuer or class of issuers from the requirement under subsection (a) or (b). In determining whether to make an exemption under this subsection, the Commission shall take into account, among other considerations, whether the requirements under subsections (a) and (b) disproportionately burdens small issuers.

(2) TREATMENT OF EMERGING GROWTH COMPANIES

(A) IN GENERAL. An emerging growth company shall be exempt from the requirements of subsections (a) and (b).

(B) COMPLIANCE AFTER TERMINATION OF EMERGING GROWTH COMPANY TREATMENT. An issuer that was an emerging growth company but is no longer an emerging growth company shall include the first separate resolution described under subsection (a)(1) not later than the end of—

(i) In the case of an issuer that was an emerging growth company for less than 2 years after the date of first sale of common equity securities of the issuer pursuant to an effective registration statement under the Securities Act of 1933, the 3-year period beginning on such date; and

(ii) In the case of any other issuer, the 1-year period beginning on the date the issuer is no longer an emerging growth company.

CORPORATE GOVERNANCE

Sec. 14B. Not later than 180 days after the date of enactment of this subsection, the Commission shall issue rules that require an issuer to disclose in the annual proxy sent to investors the reasons why the issuer has chosen—

(1) The same person to serve as chairman of the board of directors and chief executive officer (or in equivalent positions); or

(2) Different individuals to serve as chairman of the board of directors and chief executive officer (or in equivalent positions of the issuer).

REGISTRATION AND REGULATION OF BROKERS AND DEALERS

Sec. 15. (a)(1) It shall be unlawful for any broker or dealer which is either a person other than a natural person or a natural person not associated with a broker or dealer which is a person other than a natural person (other than such a broker or dealer whose business is exclusively intrastate and who does not make use of any facility of a national securities exchange) to make use of the mails or any means or instrumentality of interstate commerce to effect any transactions in, or to induce or attempt to induce the purchase or sale of, any security (other than an exempted security or commercial paper, bankers' acceptances, or commercial bills) unless such broker or dealer is registered in accordance with subsection (b) of this section.

(2) The Commission, by rule or order, as it deems consistent with the public interest and the protection of investors, may conditionally or unconditionally exempt from paragraph (1) of this subsection any broker or dealer or class of broker[s] or dealer[s] specified in such rule or order.

(b)(1) A broker or dealer may be registered by filing with the Commission an application for registration in such form and containing such information and documents concerning such broker or dealer and any persons associated with such broker or dealer as the Commission, by rule, may prescribe as necessary or appropriate in the public interest or for the protection of investors. Within forty-five days of the date of the filing of such application (or within such longer period as to which the applicant consents), the Commission shall—

(A) by order grant registration, or

(B) institute proceedings to determine whether registration should be denied. Such proceedings shall include notice of the grounds for denial under consideration and opportunity for hearing and shall be concluded within one hundred twenty days of the date of the filing of the application for registration. At the conclusion of such proceedings, the Commission, by order, shall grant or deny such registration. The Commission may extend the time for conclusion of such proceedings for up to ninety days if it finds good cause for such extension and publishes its reasons for so finding or for such longer period as to which the applicant consents.

The Commission shall grant such registration if the Commission finds that the requirements of this section are satisfied. The order granting registration shall not be effective until such broker or dealer has become a member of a registered securities association, or until such broker or dealer has become a member of a national securities exchange, if such broker or dealer effects transactions solely on that exchange, unless the Commission has exempted such broker or dealer, by rule or order, from such membership. The Commission shall deny such registration if it does not make such a finding or if it finds that if the applicant were so registered, its registration would be subject to suspension or revocation under paragraph (4) of this subsection.

(2) (A) An application for registration of a broker or dealer to be formed or organized may be made by a broker or dealer to which the broker or dealer to be formed or organized is to be the successor. Such application, in such form as the Commission, by rule, may prescribe, shall contain such information and documents concerning the applicant, the successor, and any persons associated with the applicant or the successor, as the Commission, by rule, may prescribe as necessary or appropriate in the public interest or for the protection of investors. The grant or denial of registration to such an applicant shall be in accordance with the procedures set forth in paragraph (1) of this subsection. If the Commission grants such registration, the registration shall terminate on the forty-fifth day after the effective date thereof, unless prior thereto the successor shall, in accordance with such rules and regulations as the Commission may prescribe, adopt the application for registration as its own.

(B) Any person who is a broker or dealer solely by reason of acting as a municipal securities dealer or municipal securities broker, who so acts through a separately identifiable department or division, and who so acted in such a manner on the date of enactment of the Securities Acts Amendments of 1975, may, in accordance with such terms and conditions as the Commission, by rule, prescribes as necessary and appropriate in the public interest and for the protection of investors, register such separately identifiable department or division in accordance with this subsection. If any such department or division is so registered, the department or division and not such person himself shall be the broker or dealer for purposes of this title.

(C) Within six months of the date of the granting of registration to a broker or dealer, the Commission, or upon the authorization and direction of the Commission, a registered securities association or national securities exchange of which such broker or dealer is a member, shall conduct an inspection of the broker or dealer to determine whether it is operating in conformity with the provisions of this title and the rules and regulations thereunder: Provided, however, That the Commission may delay such inspection of any class of brokers or dealers for a period not to exceed six months.

(3) Any provision of this title (other than section 5 and subsection (a) of this section) which prohibits any act, practice, or course of business if the mails or any means or instrumentality of interstate commerce is used in connection therewith shall also prohibit any such act, practice, or course of business by any registered broker or dealer or any person acting on behalf of such a broker or dealer, irrespective of any use of the mails or any means or instrumentality of interstate commerce in connection therewith.

(4) The Commission, by order, shall censure, place limitations on the activities, functions, or operations of, suspend for a period not exceeding twelve months, or revoke the registration of any broker or dealer if it finds, on the record after notice and opportunity for hearing, that such censure, placing of limitations, suspension, or revocation is in the public interest and that such broker or dealer, whether prior or subsequent to becoming such, or any person associated with such broker or dealer, whether prior or subsequent to becoming so associated—

(A) has willfully made or caused to be made in any application for registration or report required to be filed with the Commission or with any other appropriate regulatory agency under this title, or in any proceeding before the Commission with respect to registration, any statement which was at the time and in the light of the circumstances under which it was made false or misleading with respect to any material fact, or has omitted to state in any such application or report any material fact which is required to be stated therein.

(B) has been convicted within ten years preceding the filing of any application for registration or at any time thereafter of any felony or misdemeanor or of a substantially equivalent crime by a foreign court of competent jurisdiction which the Commission finds—

(i) involves the purchase or sale of any security, the taking of a false oath, the making of a false report, bribery, perjury, burglary, any substantially equivalent activity however denominated by the laws of the relevant foreign government or conspiracy to commit any such offense;

(ii) Arises out of the conduct of the business of a broker, dealer, municipal securities dealer, municipal advisor, government securities broker, government securities dealer, investment adviser, bank, insurance company, fiduciary, transfer agent, nationally recognized statistical rating organization, foreign person performing a function substantially equivalent to any of the above, or entity or person required to be registered under the Commodity Exchange Act, or any substantially equivalent foreign statute or regulation;

(iii) involves the larceny, theft, robbery, extortion, forgery, counterfeiting, fraudulent concealment, embezzlement, fraudulent conversion, or misappropriation of funds, or securities, or substantially equivalent activity however denominated by the laws of the relevant foreign government, or

(iv) involves the violation of section 152, 1341, 1342, or 1343 or chapter 25 or 47 of title 18, United States Code, or a violation of a substantially equivalent foreign statute.

(C) Is permanently or temporarily enjoined by order, judgment, or decree of any court of competent jurisdiction from acting as an investment adviser, underwriter, broker, dealer, municipal securities dealer, municipal advisor, government securities broker, government securities dealer, security-based swap dealer, major security-based swap participant, transfer agent, nationally recognized statistical rating organization, foreign person performing a function substantially equivalent to any of the above, or entity or person required to be registered under the Commodity Exchange Act or any substantially equivalent foreign statute or regulation, or as an affiliated person or employee of any investment company, bank, insurance company, foreign entity substantially equivalent to any of the above, or entity or person required to be registered under the Commodity Exchange Act or any substantially equivalent foreign statute or regulation, or from engaging in or continuing any conduct or practice in connection with any such activity, or in connection with the purchase or sale of any security.

(D) has willfully violated any provision of the Securities Act of 1933, the Investment Advisers Act of 1940, the Investment Company Act of 1940, the Commodity Exchange Act, this title, the rules or regulations under any of such statutes, or the rules of the Municipal Securities Rulemaking Board, or is unable to comply with any such provision.

(E) has willfully aided, abetted, counseled, commanded, induced, or procured the violation by any person of any provision of the Securities Act of 1933, the Investment Advisers Act of 1940, the Investment Company Act of 1940, the Commodity Exchange Act, this title, the rules or regulations under any of such statutes, or the rules of the Municipal Securities Rulemaking Board, or has failed reasonably to supervise, with a view to preventing violations of the provisions of such statutes, rules, and regulations, another person who commits such a violation, if such other person is subject to his supervision. For the purposes of this subparagraph (E) no person shall be deemed to have failed reasonably to supervise any other person, if—

(i) there have been established procedures, and a system for applying such procedures, which would reasonably be expected to prevent and detect, insofar as practicable, any such violation by such other person, and

(ii) such person has reasonably discharged the duties and obligations incumbent upon him by reason of such procedures and system without reasonable cause to believe that such procedures and system were not being complied with.

(F) is subject to any order of the Commission barring or suspending the right of the person to be associated with a broker, dealer, security-based swap dealer, major security-based swap participant, and

(G) has been found a foreign financial regulatory authority to have—

(i) made or caused to made in any application for registration or report required to be filed with a foreign financial regulatory authority, or in any proceeding before a foreign financial regulatory authority with respect to registration, any statement that was at the time and in the light of the circumstances under which it was made false or misleading with respect to any material fact, or has omitted to state in any application or report to the foreign financial regulatory authority any material fact that is required to be stated therein;

(ii) violated any foreign statute or regulation regarding transactions in securities, or contracts of sale of a commodity for future delivery, traded on or subject to the rules of a contract market or any board of trade;

(iii) aided, abetted, counseled, commanded, induced, or procured the violation by any person of any provision of any statutory provisions enacted by a foreign government, or rules or regulations thereunder, empowering a foreign financial regulatory authority regarding transactions in securities, or contracts of sale of a commodity for future delivery, traded on or subject to the rules of a contract market or any board of trade, or has been found, by a foreign financial regulatory authority, to have failed reasonably to supervise, with a view to preventing violations of such statutory provisions, rules, and regulations, another person who commits such a violation, if such other person is subject to his supervision; or

(H) is subject to any final order of a State securities commission (or any agency or officer performing like functions), State authority that supervises or examines banks, savings associations, or credit unions, State insurance commission (or any agency or office performing like functions), an appropriate Federal banking agency (as defined in section 3 of the Federal Deposit Insurance Act (12 U.S.C. 1813(q))), or the National Credit Union Administration, that—

(i) bars such person from association with an entity regulated by such commission, authority, agency, or officer, or from engaging in the business of securities, insurance, banking, savings association activities, or credit union activities; or

(ii) constitutes a final order based on violations of any laws or regulations that prohibit fraudulent, manipulative, or deceptive conduct.

(5) Pending final determination whether any registration under this subsection shall be revoked, the Commission, by order, may suspend such registration, if such suspension appears to the Commission, after notice and opportunity for hearing, to be necessary or appropriate in the public interest or for the protection of investors. Any registered broker or dealer may, upon such terms and conditions as the Commission deems necessary or appropriate in the public interest or for the protection of investors, withdraw from registration by filing a written notice of withdrawal with the Commission. If the Commission finds that any registered broker or dealer is no longer in existence or has ceased to do business as a broker or dealer, the Commission, by order, shall cancel the registration of such broker or dealer.

(6) (A) With respect to any person who is associated, who is seeking to become associated, or, at the time of the alleged misconduct, who was associated or was seeking to become associated with a broker or dealer, or any person participating, or, at the time of the alleged misconduct, who was participating, in an offering of any penny stock, the Commission, by order, shall censure, place limitations on the activities or functions of such person, or suspend for a period not exceeding 12 months, or bar such person from being associated with a broker, dealer, investment adviser, municipal securities dealer, municipal advisor, transfer agent, or nationally recognized statistical rating organization, or from participating in an offering of penny stock, if the Commission finds, on the record after notice and opportunity for a hearing, that such censure, placing of limitations, suspension, or bar is in the public interest and that such person—

(i) has committed or omitted any act, or is subject to an order or finding, enumerated in subparagraph (A), (D), (E), (H), or (G) of paragraph (4) of this subsection;

(ii) has been convicted of any offense specified in subparagraph (B) of such paragraph (4) within 10 years of the commencement of the proceedings under this paragraph; or

(iii) is enjoined from any action, conduct, or practice specified in subparagraph (C) of such paragraph (4).

(B) It shall be unlawful—

(i) for any person as to whom an order under subparagraph (A) is in effect, without the consent of the Commission, willfully to become, or to be, associated with a broker or dealer in contravention of such order, or to participate in an offering of penny stock in contravention of such order;

(ii) for any broker or dealer to permit such a person, without the consent of the Commission, to become or remain, a person associated with the broker or dealer in contravention of such order, if such broker or dealer knew, or in the exercise of reasonable care should have known, of such order; or

(iii) for any broker or dealer to permit such a person, without the consent of the Commission, to participate in an offering of penny stock in contravention of such order, if such broker or dealer knew, or in the exercise of reasonable care should have known, of such order and of such participation.

(C) For purposes of this paragraph, the term "person participating in an offering of penny stock" includes any person acting as any promoter, finder, consultant, agent, or other person who engages in activities with a broker, dealer, or issuer for purposes of the issuance or trading in any penny stock, or inducing or attempting to induce the purchase or sale of any penny stock. The Commission may, by rule or regulation, define such term to include other activities, and may, by rule, regulation, or order, exempt any person or class of persons, in whole or in part, conditionally or unconditionally, from such term.

(7) No registered broker or dealer or government securities broker or government securities dealer registered (or required to register) under section 15C(a)(1)(A) shall effect any transaction in, or induce the purchase or sale of, any security unless such broker or dealer meets such standards of operational capability and such broker or dealer and all natural persons associated with such broker or dealer meet such standards of training, experience, competence, and such other qualifications as the Commission finds necessary or appropriate in the public interest or for the protection of investors. The Commission shall establish such standards by rules and regulations, which may—

(A) specify that all or any portion of such standards shall be applicable to any class of brokers and dealers and persons associated with brokers and dealers;

(B) require persons in any such class to pass tests prescribed in accordance with such rules and regulations, which tests shall, with respect to any class of partners, officers, or supervisory employees (which latter term may be defined by the Commission's rules and regulations and as so defined shall include branch managers of brokers or dealers) engaged in the management of the broker or dealer, include questions relating to bookkeeping, accounting, internal control over cash and securities, supervision of employees, maintenance of records, and other appropriate matters; and

(C) provide that persons in any such class other than brokers and dealers and partners, officers, and supervisory employees of brokers or dealers, may be qualified solely on the basis of compliance with such standards of training and such other qualifications as the Commission finds appropriate.

The Commission, by rule, may prescribe reasonable fees and charges to defray its costs in carrying out this paragraph, including, but not limited to, fees for any test administered by it or under its direction. The Commission may cooperate with registered securities associations and national securities exchanges in devising and administering tests and may require registered brokers and dealers and persons associated with such brokers and dealers to pass tests administered by or on behalf of any such association or exchange and to pay such association or exchange reasonable fees or charges to defray the costs incurred by such association or exchange in administering such tests.

(8) It shall be unlawful for any registered broker or dealer to effect any transaction in, or induce or attempt to induce the purchase or sale of, any security (other than commercial paper, bankers' acceptances, or commercial bills), unless such broker or dealer is a member of a securities association registered pursuant to section 15A of this title or effects transactions in securities solely on a national securities exchange of which it is a member.

(9) The Commission by rule or order, as it deems consistent with the public interest and the protection of investors, may conditionally or unconditionally exempt from paragraph (8) of this subsection any broker or dealer or class of brokers or dealers specified in such rule or order.

(10) For purposes of determining whether a person is subject to a statutory disqualification under section 6(c)(2), 15A(g)(2), or 17A(b)(4)(A) of this title, the term "Commission" in paragraph (4)(B) of this subsection shall mean "exchange", "association", or "clearing agency", respectively. . . .

(c)(1)(A) No broker or dealer shall make use of the mails or any means or instrumentality of interstate commerce to effect any transaction in, or to induce or attempt to induce the purchase or sale of, any security (other than commercial paper, bankers' acceptances, or commercial bills) or any security-based swap agreement by means of any manipulative, deceptive, or other fraudulent device or contrivance.

(B) No broker, dealer, or municipal securities dealer shall make use of the mails or any means or instrumentality of interstate commerce to effect any transaction in, or to induce or attempt to induce the purchase or sale of, any municipal security or any security-based swap agreement involving a municipal security by means of any manipulative, deceptive, or other fraudulent device or contrivance.

(C) No government securities broker or government securities dealer shall make use of the mails or any means or instrumentality of interstate commerce to effect any transaction in, or to induce or to attempt to induce the purchase or sale of, any government security or any security-based swap agreement involving a government security by means of any manipulative, deceptive, or other fraudulent device or contrivance.

(2)(A) No broker or dealer shall make use of the mails or any means or instrumentality of interstate commerce to effect any transaction in, or to induce or attempt to induce the purchase or sale of, any security (other than an exempted security or commercial paper, bankers' acceptances, or commercial bills) otherwise than on a national securities exchange of which it is a member, in connection with which such broker or dealer engages in any fraudulent, deceptive, or manipulative act or practice, or makes any fictitious quotation.

(B) No broker, dealer, or municipal securities dealer shall make use of the mails or any means or instrumentality of interstate commerce to effect any transaction in, or to induce or attempt to induce the purchase or sale of, any municipal security in connection with which such municipal securities dealer engages in any fraudulent, deceptive, or manipulative act or practice, or makes any fictitious quotation.

(C) No government securities broker or government securities dealer shall make use of the mails or any means or instrumentality of interstate commerce to effect any transaction in, or induce or attempt to induce the purchase or sale of, any government security in connection with which such government securities broker or government securities dealer engages in any fraudulent, deceptive, or manipulative act or practice, or makes any fictitious quotation.

(D) The Commission shall, for the purposes of this paragraph, by rules and regulations define, and prescribe means reasonably designed to prevent, such acts and practices as are fraudulent, deceptive, or manipulative and such quotations as are fictitious.

(E) The Commission shall, prior to adopting any rule or regulation under subparagraph (C), consult with and consider the views of the Secretary of the Treasury and each appropriate regulatory agency. If the Secretary of the Treasury or any appropriate regulatory agency comments in writing on a proposed rule or regulation of the Commission under such subparagraph (C) that has been published for comment, the Commission shall respond in writing to such written comment before adopting the proposed rule. If the Secretary of the Treasury determines, and notifies the Commission, that such rule or regulation, if implemented, would, or as applied does (i) adversely affect the liquidity or efficiency of the market for government securities; or (ii) impose any burden on competition not necessary or appropriate in furtherance of the purposes of this section, the Commission shall, prior to adopting the proposed rule or regulation, find that such rule or regulation is necessary and appropriate in furtherance of the purposes of this section notwithstanding the Secretary's determination.

(4) If the Commission finds, after notice and opportunity for hearing, that any person subject to the provisions of Section 12, 13, 14 or subsection (d) of Section 15 of this title or any rule or regulation thereunder has failed to comply with any such provision, rule, or regulation in any material respect, the Commission may publish its findings and issue an order requiring such person, and any person who was a cause of the failure to comply due to an act or omission the person knew or should have known would contribute to the failure to comply, to comply, or to take steps to effect compliance, with such provision or such rule or regulation thereunder upon such terms and conditions and within such time as the Commission may specify in such order.

(d) Supplementary and Periodic Information.

(1) In General. Each issuer which has filed a registration statement containing an undertaking which is or becomes operative under this subsection as in effect prior to the date of enactment of the Securities Acts Amendments of 1964, and each issuer which shall after such date file a registration statement which has become effective pursuant to the Securities Act of 1933, as amended, shall file with the Commission, in accordance with such rules and regulations as the Commission may prescribe as necessary or appropriate in the public interest or for the protection of investors, such supplementary and periodic information, documents, and reports as may be required pursuant to section 13 of this title in respect of a security registered pursuant to section 12 of this title. The duty to file under this subsection shall be automatically suspended if and so long as any issue of securities of such issuer is registered pursuant to section 12 of this title. The duty to file under this subsection shall also be automatically suspended as to any fiscal year, other than the fiscal year within which such registration statement became effective, if, at the beginning of such fiscal year, the securities of each class to which the registration statement relates are held of record by less than 300 persons, or, in the case of a bank, a savings and loan holding company (as defined in section 10 of the Home Owners' Loan Act), or a bank holding company, as such term is defined in section 2 of the Bank Holding Company Act of 1956 (12 U.S.C. 1841), 1,200 persons. For the purposes of this subsection, the term "class" shall be construed to include all securities of an issuer which are of substantially similar character and the holders of which enjoy substantially similar rights and privileges. The Commission may, for the purpose of this subsection, define by rules and regulations the term "held of record" as it deems necessary or appropriate in the public interest or for the protection of investors in order to prevent circumvention of the provisions of this subsection. Nothing in this subsection shall apply to securities issued by a foreign government or political subdivision thereof.

(2) Asset-Backed Securities.

(A) Suspension of Duty to File. The Commission may, by rule or regulation, provide for the suspension or termination of the duty to file under this subsection for any class of asset-backed security, on such terms and conditions and for such period or periods as the Commission deems necessary or appropriate in the public interest or for the protection of investors.

(B) Classification of Issuers. The Commission may, for purposes of this subsection, classify issuers and prescribe requirements appropriate for each class of issuers of asset-backed securities.

(e) Notices to Customers Regarding Securities Lending. Every registered broker or dealer shall provide notice to its customers that they may elect not to allow their fully paid securities to be used in connection with short sales. If a broker or dealer uses a customer's securities in connection with short sales, the broker or dealer shall provide notice to its customer that the broker or dealer may receive compensation in connection with lending the customer's securities. The Commission, by rule, as it deems necessary or appropriate in the public interest and for the protection of investors, may prescribe the form, content, time, and manner of delivery of any notice required under this paragraph.

(f) The Commission, by rule, as it deems necessary or appropriate in the public interest and for the protection of investors or to assure equal regulation, may require any member of a national securities exchange not required to register under section 15 of this title and any person associated with any such member to comply with any provision of this title (other than section 15(a)) or the rules or regulations thereunder which by its terms regulates or prohibits any act, practice, or course of business by a "broker or dealer" or "registered broker or dealer" or a "person associated with a broker or dealer," respectively.

(g) Every registered broker or dealer shall establish, maintain, and enforce written policies and procedures reasonably designed, taking into consideration the nature of such broker's or dealer's business, to prevent the misuse in violation of this title, or the rule or regulations thereunder, of material, nonpublic information by such broker or dealer or any person associated with such broker or dealer. The Commission, as it deems necessary or appropriate in the public interest or for the protection of investors, shall adopt rules or regulations to require specific policies or procedures reasonably designed to prevent misuse in violation of this title (or the rules or regulations thereunder) of material, nonpublic information.

(h) REQUIREMENTS FOR TRANSACTIONS IN PENNY STOCKS.—

(1) IN GENERAL.—No broker or dealer shall make use of the mails or any means or instrumentality of interstate commerce to effect any transaction in, or to induce or attempt to induce the purchase or sale of, any penny stock by any customer except in accordance with the requirements of this subsection and the rules and regulations prescribed under this subsection.

(2) RISK DISCLOSURE WITH RESPECT TO PENNY STOCKS.—Prior to effecting any transaction in any penny stock, a broker or dealer shall give the customer a risk disclosure document that—

(A) contains a description of the nature and level of risk in the market for penny stocks in both public offerings and secondary trading;

(B) contains a description of the broker's or dealer's duties to the customer and of the rights and remedies available to the customer with respect to violations of such duties or other requirements of Federal securities laws;

(C) contains a brief, clear, narrative description of a dealer market, including "bid" and "ask" prices for penny stocks and the significance of the spread between the bid and ask prices;

(D) contains the toll free telephone number for inquiries on disciplinary actions established pursuant to section 15A(i) of this title;

(E) defines significant terms used in the disclosure document or in the conduct of trading in penny stocks; and

(F) contains such other information, and is in such form (including language, type size, and format), as the Commission shall require by rule or regulation.

(3) COMMISSION RULES RELATING TO DISCLOSURE.—The Commission shall adopt rules setting forth additional standards for the disclosure by brokers and dealers to customers of information concerning transactions in penny stocks. Such rules—

(A) shall require brokers and dealers to disclose to each customer, prior to effecting any transaction in, and at the time of confirming any transaction with respect to any penny stock, in accordance with such procedures and methods as the Commission may require consistent with the public interest and the protection of investors—

(i) the bid and ask prices for penny stock, or such other information as the Commission may, by rule, require to provide customers with more useful and reliable information relating to the price of such stock;

(ii) the number of shares to which such bid and ask prices apply, or other comparable information relating to the depth and liquidity of the market for such stock; and

(iii) the amount and a description of any compensation that the broker or dealer and the associated person thereof will receive or has received in connection with such transaction;

(B) shall require brokers and dealers to provide, to each customer whose account with the broker or dealer contains penny stocks, a monthly statement indicating the market value of the penny stocks in that account or indicating that the market value of such stock cannot be determined because of the unavailability of firm quotes; and

(C) may, as the Commission finds necessary or appropriate in the public interest or for the protection of investors, require brokers and dealers to disclose to customers additional information concerning transactions in penny stocks.

(4) EXEMPTIONS.—The Commission, as it determines consistent with the public interest and the protection of investors, may by rule, regulation, or order exempt in whole or in part, conditionally or unconditionally, any person or class of persons, or any transaction or class of transactions, from the requirements of this subsection. Such exemptions shall include an exemption for brokers and dealers based on the minimal percentage of the broker's or dealer's commissions, commission-equivalents, and markups received from transactions in penny stocks.

(5) REGULATIONS.—It shall be unlawful for any person to violate such rules and regulations as the Commission shall prescribe in the public interest or for the protection of investors or to maintain fair and orderly markets—

(A) as necessary or appropriate to carry out this subsection; or

(B) as reasonably designed to prevent fraudulent, deceptive, or manipulative acts and practices with respect to penny stocks.

(k)* REGISTRATION OR SUCCESSION TO A UNITED STATES BROKER OR DEALER. In determining whether to permit a foreign person or an affiliate of a foreign person to register as a United States broker or dealer, or succeed to the registration of a United States broker or dealer, the Commission may consider whether, for a foreign person, or an affiliate of a foreign person that presents a risk to the stability of the United States financial system, the home country of the foreign person has adopted, or made demonstrable progress toward adopting, an appropriate system of financial regulation to mitigate such risk.

(l)* TERMINATION OF A UNITED STATES BROKER OR DEALER. For a foreign person or an affiliate of a foreign person that presents such a risk to the stability of the United States financial system, the Commission may determine to terminate the registration of such foreign person or an affiliate of such foreign person as a broker or dealer in the United States, if the Commission determines that the home country of the foreign person has not adopted, or made demonstrable progress toward adopting, an appropriate system of financial regulation to mitigate such risk.

(k)* STANDARD OF CONDUCT.

(1) IN GENERAL. Notwithstanding any other provision of this Act or the Investment Advisers Act of 1940, the Commission may promulgate rules to provide that, with respect to a broker or dealer, when providing personalized investment advice about securities to a retail customer (and such other customers as the Commission may by rule provide), the standard of conduct for such broker or dealer with respect to such customer shall be the same as the standard of conduct applicable to an investment adviser under section 211 of the Investment Advisers Act of 1940. The receipt of compensation based on commission or other standard compensation for the sale of securities shall not, in and of itself, be considered a violation of such standard applied to a broker or dealer. Nothing in this section shall require a broker or dealer or registered representative to have a continuing duty of care or loyalty to the customer after providing personalized investment advice about securities.

---

*[So numbered in the original.——EDS.]

(2) DISCLOSURE OF RANGE OF PRODUCTS OFFERED. Where a broker or dealer sells only proprietary or other limited range of products, as determined by the Commission, the Commission may by rule require that such broker or dealer provide notice to each retail customer and obtain the consent or acknowledgment of the customer. The sale of only proprietary or other limited range of products by a broker or dealer shall not, in and of itself, be considered a violation of the standard set forth in paragraph (1).

(l)* OTHER MATTERS. The Commission shall—

(1) Facilitate the provision of simple and clear disclosures to investors regarding the terms of their relationships with brokers, dealers, and investment advisers, including any material conflicts of interest; and

(2) Examine and, where appropriate, promulgate rules prohibiting or restricting certain sales practices, conflicts of interest, and compensation schemes for brokers, dealers, and investment advisers that the Commission deems contrary to the public interest and the protection of investors.

(m) HARMONIZATION OF ENFORCEMENT. The enforcement authority of the Commission with respect to violations of the standard of conduct applicable to a broker or dealer providing personalized investment advice about securities to a retail customer shall include—

(1) The enforcement authority of the Commission with respect to such violations provided under this Act; and

(2) The enforcement authority of the Commission with respect to violations of the standard of conduct applicable to an investment adviser under the Investment Advisers Act of 1940, including the authority to impose sanctions for such violations, and the Commission shall seek to prosecute and sanction violators of the standard of conduct applicable to a broker or dealer providing personalized investment advice about securities to a retail customer under this Act to same extent as the Commission prosecutes and sanctions violators of the standard of conduct applicable to an investment advisor under the Investment Advisers Act of 1940.

(n) DISCLOSURES TO RETAIL INVESTORS.

(1) IN GENERAL. Notwithstanding any other provision of the securities laws, the Commission may issue rules designating documents or information that shall be provided by a broker or dealer to a retail investor before the purchase of an investment product or service by the retail investor.

(2) CONSIDERATIONS. In developing any rules under paragraph (1), the Commission shall consider whether the rules will promote investor protection, efficiency, competition, and capital formation.

(3) FORM AND CONTENTS OF DOCUMENTS AND INFORMATION. Any documents or information designated under a rule promulgated under paragraph (1) shall—

(A) Be in a summary format; and

(B) Contain clear and concise information about—

(i) Investment objectives, strategies, costs, and risks; and

(ii) Any compensation or other financial incentive received by a broker, dealer, or other intermediary in connection with the purchase of retail investment products.

(o) AUTHORITY TO RESTRICT MANDATORY PREDISPUTE ARBITRATION. The Commission, by rule, may prohibit, or impose conditions or limitations on the use of, agreements that require customers or clients of any broker, dealer, or municipal securities dealer to arbitrate any future dispute between them arising under the Federal securities laws, the rules and regulations thereunder, or the rules of a self-regulatory organization if it finds that such prohibition, imposition of conditions, or limitations are in the public interest and for the protection of investors.

---

*Two paragraphs 80 were enacted.—EDS.

REGISTERED SECURITIES ASSOCIATIONS

Sec. 15A. (a) An association of brokers and dealers may be registered as a national securities association pursuant to subsection (b), or as an affiliated securities association pursuant to subsection (d), under the terms and conditions hereinafter provided in this section and in accordance with the provisions of section 19(a) of this title, by filing with the Commission an application for registration in such form as the Commission, by rule, may prescribe containing the rules of the association and such other information and documents as the Commission, by rule, may prescribe as necessary or appropriate in the public interest or for the protection of investors.

(b) An association of brokers and dealers shall not be registered as a national securities association unless the Commission determines that—

(1) By reason of the number and geographical distribution of its members and the scope of their transactions, such association will be able to carry out the purposes of this section.

(2) Such association is so organized and has the capacity to be able to carry out the purposes of this title and to comply, and (subject to any rule or order of the Commission pursuant to section 17(d) or 19(g)(2) of this title) to enforce compliance by its members and persons associated with its members, with the provisions of this title, the rules and regulations thereunder, the rules of the Municipal Securities Rulemaking Board, and the rules of the association.

(3) Subject to the provisions of subsection (g) of this section, the rules of the association provide that any registered broker or dealer may become a member of such association and any person may become associated with a member thereof.

(4) The rules of the association assure a fair representation of its members in the selection of its directors and administration of its affairs and provide that one or more directors shall be representative of issuers and investors and not be associated with a member of the association, broker, or dealer.

(5) The rules of the association provide for the equitable allocation of reasonable dues, fees, and other charges among members and issuers and other persons using any facility or system which the association operates or controls.

(6) The rules of the association are designed to prevent fraudulent and manipulative acts and practices, to promote just and equitable principles of trade, to foster cooperation and coordination with persons engaged in regulating, clearing, settling, processing information with respect to, and facilitating transactions in securities, to remove impediments to and perfect the mechanism of a free and open market and a national market system, and, in general, to protect investors and the public interest; and are not designed to permit unfair discrimination between customers, issuers, brokers, or dealers, to fix minimum profits, to impose any schedule or fix rates of commissions, allowances, discounts, or other fees to be charged by its members, or to regulate by virtue of any authority conferred by this title matters not related to the purposes of this title or the administration of the association.

(7) The rules of the association provide that (subject to any rule or order of the Commission pursuant to section 17(d) or 19(g)(2) of this title) its members and persons associated with its members shall be appropriately disciplined for violation of any provision of this title, the rules or regulations thereunder, the rules of the Municipal Securities Rulemaking Board, or the rules of the association, by expulsion, suspension, limitation of activities, functions, and operations, fine, censure, being suspended or barred from being associated with a member, or any other fitting sanction.

(8) The rules of the association are in accordance with the provisions of subsection (h) of this section, and, in general, provide a fair procedure for the disciplining of members and persons associated with members, the denial of membership to any person seeking membership therein, the barring of any person from becoming associated with a member thereof, and the prohibition or limitation by the association of any person with respect to access to services offered by the association or a member thereof.

(9) The rules of the association do not impose any burden on competition not necessary or appropriate in furtherance of the purposes of this title.

(10) The requirements of subsection (c), insofar as these may be applicable, are satisfied.

(11) The rules of the association include provisions governing the form and content of quotations relating to securities sold otherwise than on a national securities exchange which may be distributed or published by any member or person associated with a member, and the persons to whom such quotations may be supplied. Such rules relating to quotations shall be designed to produce fair and informative quotations, to prevent fictitious or misleading quotations, and to promote orderly procedures for collecting, distributing, and publishing quotations.

(14) The rules of the association include provisions governing the sales, or offers of sales, of securities on the premises of any military installation to any member of the Armed Forces or a dependent thereof, which rules require

(A) The broker or dealer performing brokerage services to clearly and conspicuously disclose to potential

(i) That the securities offered are not being offered or provided by the broker or dealer on behalf of the Federal Government, and that its offer is not sanctioned, recommended,or encouraged by the Federal Government; and

(ii) The identity of the registered broker-dealeroffering the securities;

(B) Such broker or dealer to perform an appropriate suitability determination, including consideration of costs and knowledge about securities, prior to making a recommendation of a security to a member of the Armed Forces or a dependent thereof; and

(C) That no person receive any referral fee or incentive compensation in connection with a sale or offer of sale of securities, unless such person is an associated person of a registered broker or dealer and is qualified pursuant to the rules of a selfregulatory organization.

(15) The rules of the association provide that the association shall—

(A) Request guidance from the Municipal Securities Rulemaking Board in interpretation of the rules of the Municipal Securities Rulemaking Board; and

(B) Provide information to the Municipal Securities Rulemaking Board about the enforcement actions and examinations of the association under section 15B(b)(2)(E), so that the Municipal Securities Rulemaking Board may—

(i) Assist in such enforcement actions and examinations; and

(ii) Evaluate the ongoing effectiveness of the rules of the Board.

(c) The Commission may permit or require the rules of an association applying for registration pursuant to subsection (b), to provide for the admission of an association registered as an affiliated securities association pursuant to subsection (d), to participation in said applicant association as an affiliate thereof, under terms permitting such powers and responsibilities to such affiliate, and under such other appropriate terms and conditions, as may be provided by the rules of said applicant association, if such rules appear to the Commission to be necessary or appropriate in the public interest or for the protection of investors and to carry out the purposes of this section. The duties and powers of the Commission with respect to any national securities association or any affiliated securities association shall in no way be limited by reason of any such affiliation.

(d) An applicant association shall not be registered as an affiliated securities association unless it appears to the Commission that:

(1) Such association, notwithstanding that it does not satisfy the requirements set forth in paragraph (1) of subsection (b), will, forthwith upon the registration thereof, be admitted to affiliation with an association registered as a national securities association pursuant to said subsection (b), in the manner and under the terms and conditions provided by the rules of said national securities association in accordance with subsection (c); and

(2) Such association and its rules satisfy the requirements set forth in paragraphs (2) to (10), inclusive and paragraph (12), of subsection (b); except that in the case of any such association any restrictions upon membership therein of the type authorized by paragraph (3) of subsection (b) shall not be less stringent than in the case of the national securities association with which such association is to be affiliated.

(e)(1) The rules of a registered securities association may provide that no member thereof shall deal with any nonmember professional (as defined in paragraph (2) of this subsection) except at the same prices, for the same commissions or fees, and on the same terms and conditions as are by such member accorded to the general public.

(2) For the purposes of this subsection, the term "nonmember professional" shall include: (A) with respect to transactions in securities other than municipal securities, any registered broker or dealer who is not a member of any registered securities association, except such a broker or dealer who deals exclusively in commercial paper, bankers' acceptances, and commercial bills, and (B) with respect to transactions in municipal securities, any municipal securities dealer (other than a bank or division or department of a bank) who is not a member of any registered securities association and any municipal securities broker who is not a member of any such association.

(3) Nothing in this subsection shall be so construed or applied as to prevent: (A) any member of a registered securities association from granting to any other member of any registered securities association any dealer's discount, allowance, commission, or special terms, in connection with the purchase or sale of securities, or (B) any member of a registered securities association or any municipal securities dealer which is a bank or a division or department of a bank from granting to any member of any registered securities association or any such municipal securities dealer any dealer's discount, allowance, commission, or special terms in connection with the purchase or sale of municipal securities: provided, however, that the granting of any such discount, allowance, commission, or special terms in connection with the purchase or sale of municipal securities shall be subject to rules of the Municipal Securities Rulemaking Board adopted pursuant to Section 15B(b)(2)(K) of this title.

(f) Nothing in subsection (b)(6) or (b)(11) of this section shall be construed to permit a registered securities association to make rules concerning any transaction by a registered broker or dealer in a municipal security.

(g)(1) A registered securities association shall deny membership to any person who is not a registered broker or dealer.

(2) A registered securities association may, and in cases in which the Commission, by order, directs as necessary or appropriate in the public interest or for the protection of investors shall, deny membership to any registered broker or dealer, and bar from becoming associated with a member any person, who is subject to a statutory disqualification. A registered securities association shall file notice with the Commission not less than 30 days prior to admitting any registered broker or dealer to membership or permitting any person to become associated with a member, if the association knew, or in the exercise of reasonable care should have known, that such broker or dealer or person was subject to a statutory disqualification. The notice shall be in such form and contain such information as the Commission, by rule, may prescribe as necessary or appropriate in the public interest or for the protection of investors.

(3)(A) A registered securities association may deny membership to, or condition the membership of, a registered broker or dealer if: (i) such broker or dealer does not meet such standards of financial responsibility or operational capability or such broker or dealer or any natural person associated with such broker or dealer does not meet such standards of training, experience and competence as are prescribed by the rules of the association, or (ii) such broker or dealer or person associated with such broker or dealer has engaged and there is a reasonable likelihood he will again engage in acts or practices inconsistent with just and equitable principles of trade. A registered securities association may examine and verify the qualifications of an applicant to become a member and the natural persons associated with such an applicant in accordance with procedures established by the rules of the association.

(B) A registered securities association may bar a natural person from becoming associated with a member or condition the association of a natural person with a member if such natural person: (i) does not meet such standards of training, experience, and competence as are prescribed by the rules of the association, or (ii) has engaged and there is a reasonable likelihood he will again engage in acts or practices inconsistent with just and equitable principles of trade. A registered securities association may examine and verify the qualifications of an applicant to become a person associated with a member in accordance with procedures established by the rules of the association and require a natural person associated with a member, or any class of such natural persons, to be registered with the association in accordance with procedures so established.

(C) A registered securities association may bar any person from becoming associated with a member if such person does not agree: (i) to supply the association with such information with respect to its relationship and dealings with the member as may and records to verify the accuracy of any information so supplied.

(D) Nothing in subparagraph (A), (B), or (C) of this paragraph shall be construed to permit a registered securities association to deny membership to or condition the membership of, or bar any person from becoming associated with or condition the association of any person with, a broker or dealer that engages exclusively in transactions in municipal securities.

(4) A registered securities association may deny membership to a registered broker or dealer not engaged in a type of business in which the rules of the association require members to be engaged: provided, however, that no registered securities association may deny membership to a registered broker or dealer by reason of the amount of such type of business done by such broker or dealer or the other types of business in which he is engaged.

(h)(1) In any proceeding by a registered securities association to determine whether a member or person associated with a member should be disciplined (other than a summary proceeding pursuant to paragraph (3) of this subsection) the association shall bring specific charges, notify such member or person of, and give him an opportunity to defend against, such charges, and keep a record. A determination by the association to impose a disciplinary sanction shall be supported by a statement setting forth:

(A) Any act or practice in which such member or person associated with a member has been found to have engaged, or which such member or person has been found to have omitted;

(B) The specific provision of this title, the rules or regulations thereunder, the rules of the Municipal Securities Rulemaking Board, or the rules of the association which any such act or practice, or omission to act, is deemed to violate; and

(C) The sanction imposed and the reason therefor.

(2) In any proceeding by a registered securities association to determine whether a person shall be denied membership, barred from becoming associated with a member, or prohibited or limited with respect to access to services offered by the association or member thereof (other than a summary proceeding pursuant to paragraph (3) of this subsection), the association shall notify such person of, and give him an opportunity to be heard upon, the specific grounds for denial, bar, or prohibition or limitation under consideration and keep a record. A determination by the association to deny membership, bar a person from becoming associated with a member, or prohibit or limit a person with respect to access to services offered by the association or a member thereof shall be supported by a statement setting forth the specific grounds on which the denial, bar, or prohibition or limitation is based.

(3) A registered securities association may summarily: (A) suspend a member or person associated with a member who has been and is expelled or suspended from any self-regulatory organization or barred or suspended from being associated with a member of

any self-regulatory organization, (B) suspend a member who is in such financial or operating difficulty that the association determines and so notifies the Commission that the member cannot be permitted to continue to do business as a member with safety to investors, creditors, other members, or the association, or (C) limit or prohibit any person with respect to access to services offered by the association if subparagraph (A) or (B) of this paragraph is applicable to such person or, in the case of a person who is not a member, if the association determines that such person does not meet the qualification requirements or other prerequisites for such access and such person cannot be permitted to continue to have such access with safety to investors, creditors, members, or the association. Any person aggrieved by any such summary action shall be promptly afforded an opportunity for a hearing by the association in accordance with the provisions of paragraph (1) or (2) of this subsection. The Commission, by order, may stay any such summary action on its own motion or upon application by any person aggrieved thereby, if the Commission determines summarily or after notice and opportunity for hearing (which hearing may consist solely of the submission of affidavits or presentation of oral arguments) that such stay is consistent with the public interest and the protection of investors.

(i) OBLIGATION TO MAINTAIN REGISTRATION, DISCIPLINARY, AND OTHER DATA.—

(1) MAINTENANCE OF SYSTEM TO RESPOND TO INQUIRIES.—A registered securities association shall—

(A) Establish and maintain a system for collecting and retaining registration information;

(B) Establish and maintain a toll-free telephone listing, and a readily accessible electronic or other process, to receive and promptly respond to inquiries regarding—

(i) Registration information on its members and their associated persons; and

(ii) Registration information on the members and their associated persons of any registered national securities exchange that uses the system described in subparagraph (A) for the registration of its members and their associated persons; and (C) Adopt rules governing the process for making inquiries and the type, scope, and presentation of information to be provided in response to such inquiries in consultation with any registered national securities exchange providing information pursuant to subparagraph (B)(ii).

(2) RECOVERY OF COSTS.—A registered securities association may charge persons making inquiries described in paragraph (1)(B), other than individual investors, reasonable fees for responses to such inquiries.

(3) PROCESS FOR DISPUTED INFORMATION.—Each registered securities association shall adopt rules establishing an administrative process for disputing the accuracy of information provided in response to inquiries under this subsection in consultation with any registered national securities exchange providing information pursuant to paragraph (1)(B)(ii).

(4) LIMITATION ON LIABILITY.—A registered securities association, or an exchange reporting information to such an association, shall not have any liability to any person for any actions taken or omitted in good faith under this subsection.

(5) DEFINITION.—For purposes of this subsection, the term "registration information" means the information reported in connection with the registration or licensing of brokers and dealers and their associated persons, including disciplinary actions, regulatory, judicial, and arbitration proceedings, and other information required by law, or exchange or association rule, and the source and status of such information.

(j) REGISTRATION FOR SALES OF PRIVATE SECURITIES OFFERINGS. A registered securities association shall create a limited qualification category for any associated person of a member who effects sales as part of a primary offering of securities not involving a public offering, pursuant to Section 3(b), 4(2), or 4(6) of the Securities Act of 1933 and the rules and regulations thereunder, and shall deem qualified in such limited qualification category, without testing, any bank employee who, in the six month period preceding the date of the enactment of the Gramm-Leach-Bliley Act, engaged in effecting such sales.

(k) LIMITED PURPOSE NATIONAL SECURITIES ASSOCIATION.

(1) REGULATION OF MEMBERS WITH RESPECT TO SECURITY FUTURES PRODUCTS. A futures association registered under Section 17 of the Commodity Exchange Act shall be a registered national securities association for the limited purpose of regulating the activities of members who are registered as brokers or dealers in security futures products pursuant to Section 15(b)(11).

(2) REQUIREMENTS FOR REGISTRATION. Such a securities association shall—

(A) Be so organized and have the capacity to carry out the purposes of the securities laws applicable to security futures products and to comply, and (subject to any rule or order of the Commission pursuant to Section 19(g)(2)) to enforce compliance by its members and persons associated with its members, with the provisions of the securities laws applicable to security futures products, the rules and regulations thereunder, and its rules;

(B) Have rules that—

(i) Are designed to prevent fraudulent and manipulative acts and practices, to promote just and equitable principles of trade, and, in general, to protect investors and the public interest, including rules governing sales practices and the advertising of security futures products reasonably comparable to those of other national securities associations registered pursuant to subsection (a) that are applicable to security futures products; and

(ii) Are not designed to regulate by virtue of any authority conferred by this title matters not related to the purposes of this title or the administration of the association;

(C) Have rules that provide that (subject to any rule or order of the Commission pursuant to Section 19(g)(2)) its members and persons associated with its members shall be appropriately disciplined for violation of any provision of the securities laws applicable to security futures products, the rules or regulations thereunder, or the rules of the association, by expulsion, suspension, limitation of activities, functions, and operations, fine, censure, being suspended or barred from being associated with a member, or any other fitting sanction; and

(D) Have rules that ensure that members and natural persons associated with members meet such standards of training, experience, and competence necessary to effect transactions in security futures products and are tested for their knowledge of securities and security futures products.

(3) EXEMPTION FROM RULE CHANGE SUBMISSION. Such a securities association shall be exempt from submitting proposed rule changes pursuant to Section 19(b) of this title, except that—

(A) The association shall file proposed rule changes related to higher margin levels, fraud or manipulation, recordkeeping, reporting, listing standards, or decimal pricing for security futures products, sales practices for, advertising of, or standards of training, experience, competence, or other qualifications for security futures products for persons who effect transactions in security futures products, or rules effectuating the association's obligation to enforce the securities laws pursuant to Section 19(b)(7);

(B) The association shall file pursuant to Sections 19(b)(1) and 19(b)(2) proposed rule changes related to margin, except for changes resulting in higher margin levels; and

(C) The association shall file pursuant to Section 19(b)(1) proposed rule changes that have been abrogated by the Commission pursuant to Section 19(b)(7)(C).

(4) OTHER EXEMPTIONS. Such a securities association shall be exempt from and shall not be required to enforce compliance by its members, and its members shall not, solely with respect to their transactions effected in security futures products, be required to comply, with the following provisions of this title and the rules thereunder:

(A) Section 8.

(B) Subsections (b)(1), (b)(3), (b)(4), (b)(5), (b)(8), (b)(10), (b)(11), (b)(12), (b)(13), (c), (d), (e), (f), (g), (h), and (i) of this section.

(C) Subsections (d), (f), and (k) of Section 17.

(D) Subsections (a), (f), and (h) of Section 19.

(*l*) Consistent with this title, each national securities association registered pursuant to subsection (a) of this section shall issue such rules as are necessary to avoid duplicative or conflicting rules applicable to any broker or dealer registered with the Commission pursuant to Section 15(b) (except paragraph (11) thereof), that is also registered with the Commodity Futures Trading Commission pursuant to Section 4f(a) of the Commodity Exchange Act (except paragraph (2) thereof), with respect to the application of—

(1) Rules of such national securities association of the type specified in Section 15(c)(3)(B) involving security futures products; and

(2) Similar rules of national securities associations registered pursuant to subsection (k) of this section and national securities exchanges registered pursuant to Section 6(g) involving security futures products.

(m) PROCEDURES AND RULES FOR SECURITY FUTURE PRODUCTS. A national securities association registered pursuant to subsection (a) shall, not later than 8 months after the date of the enactment of the Commodity Futures Modernization Act of 2000, implement the procedures specified in Section 6(h)(5)(A) of this title and adopt the rules specified in subparagraphs (B) and (C) of Section 6(h)(5) of this title.

MUNICIPAL SECURITIES

Sec. 15B. (a)(1)(A) it shall be unlawful for any municipal securities dealer (other than one registered as a broker or dealer under section 15 of this title) to make use of the mails or any means or instrumentality of interstate commerce to effect any transaction in, or to induce or attempt to induce the purchase or sale of, any municipal security unless such municipal securities dealer is registered in accordance with this subsection.

(B) It shall be unlawful for a municipal advisor to provide advice to or on behalf of a municipal entity or obligated person with respect to municipal financial products or the issuance of municipal securities, or to undertake a solicitation of a municipal entity or obligated person, unless the municipal advisor is registered in accordance with this subsection.

(2) A municipal securities dealer or municipal advisor may be registered by filing with the Commission an application for registration in such form and containing such information and documents concerning such municipal securities dealer or municipal advisor and any persons associated with such municipal securities dealer or municipal advisor as the Commission, by rule, may prescribe as necessary or appropriate in the public interest or for the protection of investors. Within forty-five days of the date of the filing of such application (or within such longer period as to which the applicant consents), the Commission shall—

(A) by order grant registration, or

(B) institute proceedings to determine whether registration should be denied. Such proceedings shall include notice of the grounds for denial under consideration and opportunity for hearing and shall be concluded within one hundred twenty days of the date of the filing of the application for registration. At the conclusion of such proceedings the Commission, by order, shall grant or deny such registration. The Commission may extend the time for the conclusion of such proceedings for up to ninety days if it finds good cause for such extension and publishes its reasons for so finding or for such longer period as to which the applicant consents.

The Commission shall grant the registration of a municipal securities dealer if the Commission finds that the requirements of this section are satisfied. The Commission shall deny such registration if it does not make such a finding or if it finds that if the applicant were so registered, its registration would be subject to suspension or revocation under subsection (c) of this section.

(3) Any provision of this title (other than section 5 or paragraph (1) of this subsection) which prohibits any act, practice, or course of business if the mails or any means or

instrumentality of interstate commerce is used in connection therewith shall also prohibit any such act, practice, or course of business by any registered municipal securities dealer or municipal advisor or any person acting on behalf of such municipal securities dealer or municipal advisor, irrespective of any use of the mails or any means or instrumentality of interstate commerce in connection therewith.

(4) The Commission, by rule or order, upon its own motion or upon application, may conditionally or unconditionally exempt any broker, dealer, municipal securities dealer, or municipal advisor or class of brokers, dealers, municipal securities dealers, or municipal advisor from any provision of this section or the rules or regulations thereunder, if the Commission finds that such exemption is consistent with the public interest, the protection of investors, and the purposes of this section.

(5) No municipal advisor shall make use of the mails or any means or instrumentality of interstate commerce to provide advice to or on behalf of a municipal entity or obligated person with respect to municipal financial products, the issuance of municipal securities, or to undertake a solicitation of a municipal entity or obligated person, in connection with which such municipal advisor engages in any fraudulent, deceptive, or manipulative act or practice.

(b)(1) The Municipal Securities Rulemaking Board shall be composed of 15 members, or such other number of members as specified by rules of the Board pursuant to paragraph (2)(B), which shall perform the duties set forth in this section. The members of the Board shall serve as members for a term of 3 years or for such other terms as specified by rules of the Board pursuant to paragraph (2)(B), and shall consist of (A) 8 individuals who are independent of any municipal securities broker, municipal securities dealer, or municipal advisor, at least 1 of whom shall be representative of institutional or retail investors in municipal securities, at least 1 of whom shall be representative of municipal entities, and at least 1 of whom shall be a member of the public with knowledge of or experience in the municipal industry (which members are hereinafter referred to as "public representatives"); and (B) 7 individuals who are associated with a broker, dealer, municipal securities dealer, or municipal advisor, including at least 1 individual who is associated with and representative of brokers, dealers, or municipal securities dealers that are not banks or subsidiaries or departments or divisions of banks (which members are hereinafter referred to as "broker-dealer representatives"), at least 1 individual who is associated with and representative of municipal securities dealers which are banks or subsidiaries or departments or divisions of banks (which members are hereinafter referred to as "bank representatives"), and at least 1 individual who is associated with a municipal advisor (which members are hereinafter referred to as "advisor representatives" and, together with the broker-dealer representatives and the bank representatives, are referred to as "regulated representatives"). Each member of the board shall be knowledgeable of matters related to the municipal securities markets. Prior to the expiration of the terms of office of the members of the Board, an election shall be held under rules adopted by the Board (pursuant to subsection (b)(2)(B) of this section) of the members to succeed such members.

(d)(1) Neither the Commission nor the Board is authorized under this title, by rule or regulation, to require any issuer of municipal securities, directly or indirectly through a purchaser or prospective purchaser of securities from the issuer, to file with the Commission or the Board prior to the sale of such securities by the issuer any application, report, or document in connection with the issuance, sale, or distribution of such securities.

(2) The Board is not authorized under this title to require any issuer of municipal securities, directly or indirectly through a municipal securities broker, municipal securities dealer, municipal advisor, or otherwise, to furnish to the Board or to a purchaser or prospective purchaser of such securities any application, report, document, or information with respect to such issuer: *Provided, however,* That the Board may require municipal securities brokers and municipal securities dealers or municipal advisors to furnish to the Board or purchaser or prospective purchasers of municipal securities applications, reports, documents, and information with respect to the issuer thereof which [are] generally available from a source other than such issuer. Nothing in this paragraph shall be construed to impair or limit the power of the Commission under any provision of this title.

GOVERNMENT SECURITIES BROKERS AND DEALERS

Sec. 15C. (a) (1) (A) It shall be unlawful for any government securities broker or government securities dealer (other than a registered broker or dealer or a financial institution) to make use of the mails or any means or instrumentality of interstate commerce to effect any transaction in, or to induce or attempt to induce the purchase or sale of, any government security unless such government securities broker or government securities dealer is registered in accordance with paragraph (2) of this subsection.

SECURITIES ANALYSTS AND RESEARCH REPORTS

Sec. 15D. (a) ANALYST PROTECTIONS.—The Commission, or upon the authorization and direction of the Commission, a registered securities association or national securities exchange, shall have adopted, not later than 1 year after the date of enactment of this section, rules reasonably designed to address conflicts of interest that can arise when securities analysts recommend equity securities in research reports and public appearances, in order to improve the objectivity of research and provide investors with more useful and reliable information, including rules designed—

(1) to foster greater public confidence in securities research, and to protect the objectivity and independence of securities analysts, by—

(A) restricting the prepublication clearance or approval of research reports by persons employed by the broker or dealer who are engaged in investment banking activities, or persons not directly responsible for investment research, other than legal or compliance staff;

(B) limiting the supervision and compensatory evaluation of securities analysts to officials employed by the broker or dealer who are not engaged in investment banking activities; and

(C) requiring that a broker or dealer and persons employed by a broker or dealer who are involved with investment banking activities may not, directly or indirectly, retaliate against or threaten to retaliate against any securities analyst employed by that broker or dealer or its affiliates as a result of an adverse, negative, or otherwise unfavorable research report that may adversely affect the present or prospective investment banking relationship of the broker or dealer with the issuer that is the subject of the research report, except that such rules may not limit the authority of a broker or dealer to discipline a securities analyst for causes other than such research report in accordance with the policies and procedures of the firm;

(2) to define periods during which brokers or dealers who have participated, or are to participate, in a public offering of securities as underwriters or dealers should not publish or otherwise distribute research reports relating to such securities or to the issuer of such securities;

(3) to establish structural and institutional safeguards within registered brokers or dealers to assure that securities analysts are separated by appropriate informational partitions within the firm from the review, pressure, or oversight of those whose involvement in investment banking activities might potentially bias their judgment or supervision; and

(4) to address such other issues as the Commission, or such association or exchange, determines appropriate.

(b) DISCLOSURE.—The Commission, or upon the authorization and direction of the Commission, a registered securities association or national securities exchange, shall have adopted, not later than 1 year after the date of enactment of this section, rules reasonably designed to require each securities analyst to disclose in public appearances, and each registered broker or dealer to disclose in each research report, as applicable, conflicts of interest that are known or should have been known by the securities analyst or the broker or dealer, to exist at the time of the appearance or the date of distribution of the report, including—

(1) the extent to which the securities analyst has debt or equity investments in the issuer that is the subject of the appearance or research report;

(2) whether any compensation has been received by the registered broker or dealer, or any affiliate thereof, including the securities analyst, from the issuer that is the subject of the appearance or research report, subject to such exemptions as the Commission may determine appropriate and necessary to prevent disclosure by virtue of this paragraph of material non-public information regarding specific potential future investment banking transactions of such issuer, as is appropriate in the public interest and consistent with the protection of investors;

(3) whether an issuer, the securities of which are recommended in the appearance or research report, currently is, or during the 1-year period preceding the date of the appearance or date of distribution of the report has been, a client of the registered broker or dealer, and if so, stating the types of services provided to the issuer;

(4) whether the securities analyst received compensation with respect to a research report, based upon (among any other factors) the investment banking revenues (either generally or specifically earned from the issuer being analyzed) of the registered broker or dealer; and

(5) such other disclosures of conflicts of interest that are material to investors, research analysts, or the broker or dealer as the Commission, or such association or exchange, determines appropriate.

(c) LIMITATION. Notwithstanding subsection (a) or any other provision of law, neither the Commission nor any national securities association registered under section 15A may adopt or maintain any rule or regulation in connection with an initial public offering of the common equity of an emerging growth company—

(1) Restricting, based on functional role, which associated persons of a broker, dealer, or member of a national securities association, may arrange for communications between a securities analyst and a potential investor; or

(2) Restricting a securities analyst from participating in any communications with the management of an emerging growth company that is also attended by any other associated person of a broker, dealer, or member of a national securities association whose functional role is other than as a securities analyst.

(d) DEFINITIONS.—In this section—

(1) the term "securities analyst" means any associated person of a registered broker or dealer that is principally responsible for, and any associated person who reports directly or indirectly to a securities analyst in connection with, the preparation of the substance of a research report, whether or not any such person has the job title of "securities analyst"; and

(2) the term "research report" means a written or electronic communication that includes an analysis of equity securities of individual companies or industries, and that provides information reasonably sufficient upon which to base an investment decision.

REGISTRATION OF NATIONALLY RECOGNIZED STATISTICAL RATING ORGANIZATIONS

Sec. 15E. (a) REGISTRATION PROCEDURES.—

(1) APPLICATION FOR REGISTRATION.—

(A) IN GENERAL.—A credit rating agency that elects to be treated as a nationally recognized statistical rating organization for purposes of this title (in this section referred to as the "applicant"), shall furnish to the Commission an application for registration, in such form as the Commission shall require, by rule or regulation issued in accordance with subsection (n), and containing the information described in subparagraph (B).

(B) REQUIRED INFORMATION.—An application for registration under this section shall contain information regarding—

(i) Credit ratings performance measurement statistics over short-term, mid-term, and long-term periods (as applicable) of the applicant;

(ii) The procedures and methodologies that the applicant uses in determining credit ratings;

(iii) Policies or procedures adopted and implemented by the applicant to prevent the misuse, in violation of this title (or the rules and regulations hereunder), of material, nonpublic information;

(iv) The organizational structure of the applicant;

(v) Whether or not the applicant has in effect a code of ethics, and if not, the reasons therefor;

(vi) Any conflict of interest relating to the issuance of credit ratings by the applicant;

(vii) The categories described in any of clauses (i) through (v) of section 3(a)(62)(B) with respect to which the applicant intends to apply for registration under this section;

(viii) On a confidential basis, a list of the 20 largest issuers and subscribers that use the credit rating services of the applicant, by amount of net revenues received therefrom in the fiscal year immediately preceding the date of submission of the application;

(ix) On a confidential basis, as to each applicable category of obligor described in any of clauses (i) through (v) of section 3(a)(62)(B), written certifications described in subparagraph (C), except as provided in subparagraph (D); and

(x) Any other information and documents concerning the applicant and any person associated with such applicant as the Commission, by rule, may prescribe as necessary or appropriate in the public interest or for the protection of investors.

(C) WRITTEN CERTIFICATIONS.—Written certifications required by subparagraph (B)(ix)—

(i) Shall be provided from not fewer than 10 qualified institutional buyers, none of which is affiliated with the applicant;

(ii) May address more than one category of obligors described in any of clauses (i) through (v) of section 3(a)(62)(B);

(iii) Shall include not fewer than 2 certifications for each such category of obligor; and

(iv) Shall state that the qualified institutional buyer—

(I) Meets the definition of a qualified institutional buyer under section 3(a)(64); and

(II) Has used the credit ratings of the applicant for at least the 3 years immediately preceding the date of the certification in the subject category or categories of obligors.

(D) EXEMPTION FROM CERTIFICATION REQUIREMENT.—A written certification under subparagraph (B)(ix) is not required with respect to any credit rating agency which has received, or been the subject of, a no-action letter from the staff of the Commission prior to August 2, 2006, stating that such staff would not recommend enforcement action against any broker or dealer that considers credit ratings issued by such credit rating agency to be ratings from a nationally recognized statistical rating organization.

(E) LIMITATION ON LIABILITY OF QUALIFIED INSTITUTIONAL BUYERS.—No qualified institutional buyer shall be liable in any private right of action for any opinion or statement expressed in a certification made pursuant to subparagraph (B)(ix).

(2) REVIEW OF APPLICATION.—

(A) INITIAL DETERMINATION.—Not later than 90 days after the date on which the application for registration is furnished to the Commission under paragraph (1) (or within such longer period as to which the applicant consents) the Commission shall—

(i) By order, grant such registration for ratings in the subject category or categories of obligors, as described in clauses (i) through (v) of section 3(a)(62)(B); or

(ii) Institute proceedings to determine whether registration should be denied.

(B) CONDUCT OF PROCEEDINGS.—

(i) CONTENT.—Proceedings referred to in subparagraph (A)(ii) shall—

(I) Include notice of the grounds for denial under consideration and an opportunity for hearing; and

(II) Be concluded not later than 120 days after the date on which the application for registration is furnished to the Commission under paragraph (1).

(ii) DETERMINATION.—At the conclusion of such proceedings, the Commission, by order, shall grant or deny such application for registration.

(iii) EXTENSION AUTHORIZED.—The Commission may extend the time for conclusion of such proceedings for not longer than 90 days, if it finds good cause for such extension and publishes its reasons for so finding, or for such longer period as to which the applicant consents.

(C) GROUNDS FOR DECISION.—The Commission shall grant registration under this subsection—

(i) If the Commission finds that the requirements of this section are satisfied; and

(ii) Unless the Commission finds (in which case the Commission shall deny such registration) that—

(I) The applicant does not have adequate financial and managerial resources to consistently produce credit ratings with integrity and to materially comply with the procedures and methodologies disclosed under paragraph (1)(B) and with subsections (g), (h), (i), and (j); or

(II) If the applicant were so registered, its registration would be subject to suspension or revocation under subsection (d).

(3) PUBLIC AVAILABILITY OF INFORMATION.—Subject to section 24, the Commission shall, by rule, require a nationally recognized statistical rating organization, upon the granting of registration under this section, to make the information and documents submitted to the Commission in its completed application for registration, or in any amendment submitted under paragraph (1) or (2) of subsection (b), publicly available on its website, or through another comparable, readily accessible means, except as provided in clauses (viii) and (ix) of paragraph (1)(B).

(b) UPDATE OF REGISTRATION.—

(1) UPDATE.—Each nationally recognized statistical rating organization shall promptly amend its application for registration under this section if any information or document provided therein becomes materially inaccurate, except that a nationally recognized statistical rating organization is not required to amend—

(A) The information required to be filed under subsection (a)(1)(B)(i) by filing information under this paragraph, but shall amend such information in the annual submission of the organization under paragraph (2) of this subsection; or

(B) The certifications required to be provided under subsection (a)(1)(B)(ix) by filing information under this paragraph.

(2) CERTIFICATION.—Not later than 90 days after the end of each calendar year, each nationally recognized statistical rating organization shall file with to the Commission an amendment to its registration, in such form as the Commission, by rule, may prescribe as necessary or appropriate in the public interest or for the protection of investors—

(A) Certifying that the information and documents in the application for registration of such nationally recognized statistical rating organization (other than the certifications required under subsection (a)(1)(B)(ix)) continue to be accurate; and

(B) Listing any material change that occurred to such information or documents during the previous calendar year.

(c) ACCOUNTABILITY FOR RATINGS PROCEDURES.—

(1) AUTHORITY.—The Commission shall have exclusive authority to enforce the provisions of this section in accordance with this title with respect to any nationally recognized statistical rating organization, if such nationally recognized statistical rating organization

issues credit ratings in material contravention of those procedures relating to such nationally recognized statistical rating organization, including procedures relating to the prevention of misuse of nonpublic information and conflicts of interest, that such nationally recognized statistical rating organization—

(A) Includes in its application for registration under subsection (a) (1) (B) (ii); or

(B) Makes and disseminates in reports pursuant to section 17(a) or the rules and regulations thereunder.

(2) LIMITATION.—The rules and regulations that the Commission may prescribe pursuant to this title, as they apply to nationally recognized statistical rating organizations, shall be narrowly tailored to meet the requirements of this title applicable to nationally recognized statistical rating organizations. Notwithstanding any other provision of this section, or any other provision of law, neither the Commission nor any State (or political subdivision thereof) may regulate the substance of credit ratings or the procedures and methodologies by which any nationally recognized statistical rating organization determines credit ratings.

(3) INTERNAL CONTROLS OVER PROCESSES FOR DETERMINING CREDIT RATINGS.

(A) IN GENERAL. Each nationally recognized statistical rating organization shall establish, maintain, enforce, and document an effective internal control structure governing the implementation of and adherence to policies, procedures, and methodologies for determining credit ratings, taking into consideration such factors as the Commission may prescribe, by rule.

(B) ATTESTATION REQUIREMENT. The Commission shall prescribe rules requiring each nationally recognized statistical rating organization to submit to the Commission an annual internal controls report, which shall contain—

(i) A description of the responsibility of the management of the nationally recognized statistical rating organization in establishing and maintaining an effective internal control structure under subparagraph (A);

(ii) An assessment of the effectiveness of the internal control structure of the nationally recognized statistical rating organization; and

(iii) The attestation of the chief executive officer, or equivalent individual, of the nationally recognized statistical rating organization.

(d) CENSURE, DENIAL, OR SUSPENSION OF REGISTRATION; NOTICE AND HEARING.—

(1) IN GENERAL. The Commission, by order, shall censure, place limitations on the activities, functions, or operations of, suspend for a period not exceeding 12 months, or revoke the registration of any nationally recognized statistical rating organization, or with respect to any person who is associated with, who is seeking to become associated with, or, at the time of the alleged misconduct, who was associated or was seeking to become associated with a nationally recognized statistical rating organization, the Commission, by order, shall censure, place limitations on the activities or functions of such person, suspend for a period not exceeding 1 year, or bar such person from being associated with a nationally recognized statistical rating organization, if the Commission finds, on the record after notice and opportunity for hearing, that such censure, placing of limitations, suspension, bar or revocation is necessary for the protection of investors and in the public interest and that such nationally recognized statistical rating organization, or any person associated with such an organization, whether prior to or subsequent to becoming so associated—

(A) Has committed or omitted any act, or is subject to an order or finding, enumerated in subparagraph (A), (D), (E), (H), or (G) of section 15(b) (4), has been convicted of any offense specified in section 15(b) (4) (B), or is enjoined from any action, conduct, or practice specified in subparagraph (C) of section 15(b) (4), during the 10-year period preceding the date of commencement of the proceedings under this subsection, or at any time thereafter;

(B) Has been convicted during the 10-year period preceding the date on which an application for registration is filed with the Commission under this section, or at any time thereafter, of—

(i) Any crime that is punishable by imprisonment for 1 or more years, and that is not described in section 15(b)(4)(B); or

(ii) A substantially equivalent crime by a foreign court of competent jurisdiction;

(C) Is subject to any order of the Commission barring or suspending the right of the person to be associated with a nationally recognized statistical rating organization;

(D) Fails to file the certifications required under subsection (b)(2);

(E) Fails to maintain adequate financial and managerial resources to consistently produce credit ratings with integrity;

(F) Has failed reasonably to supervise, with a view to preventing a violation of the securities laws, an individual who commits such a violation, if the individual is subject to the supervision of that person.

(e) TERMINATION OF REGISTRATION.—

(1) VOLUNTARY WITHDRAWAL.—A nationally recognized statistical rating organization may, upon such terms and conditions as the Commission may establish as necessary in the public interest or for the protection of investors, withdraw from registration by furnishing a written notice of withdrawal to the Commission.

(2) COMMISSION AUTHORITY.—In addition to any other authority of the Commission under this title, if the Commission finds that a nationally recognized statistical rating organization is no longer in existence or has ceased to do business as a credit rating agency, the Commission, by order, shall cancel the registration under this section of such nationally recognized statistical rating organization.

(f) REPRESENTATIONS.—

(1) BAN ON REPRESENTATIONS OF SPONSORSHIP BY UNITED STATES OR AGENCY THEREOF.—It shall be unlawful for any nationally recognized statistical rating organization to represent or imply in any manner whatsoever that such nationally recognized statistical rating organization has been designated, sponsored, recommended, or approved, or that the abilities or qualifications thereof have in any respect been passed upon, by the United States or any agency, officer, or employee thereof.

(2) BAN ON REPRESENTATION AS NRSRO OF UNREGISTERED CREDIT RATING AGENCIES.—It shall be unlawful for any credit rating agency that is not registered under this section as a nationally recognized statistical rating organization to state that such credit rating agency is a nationally recognized statistical rating organization registered under this title.

(3) STATEMENT OF REGISTRATION UNDER SECURITIES EXCHANGE ACT OF 1934 PROVISIONS.—No provision of paragraph (1) shall be construed to prohibit a statement that a nationally recognized statistical rating organization is a nationally recognized statistical rating organization under this title, if such statement is true in fact and if the effect of such registration is not misrepresented.

(g) PREVENTION OF MISUSE OF NONPUBLIC INFORMATION.—

(1) ORGANIZATION POLICIES AND PROCEDURES.—Each nationally recognized statistical rating organization shall establish, maintain, and enforce written policies and procedures reasonably designed, taking into consideration the nature of the business of such nationally recognized statistical rating organization, to prevent the misuse in violation of this title, or the rules or regulations hereunder, of material, nonpublic information by such nationally recognized statistical rating organization or any person associated with such nationally recognized statistical rating organization.

(2) COMMISSION AUTHORITY.—The Commission shall issue final rules in accordance with subsection (n) to require specific policies or procedures that are reasonably designed to prevent misuse in violation of this title (or the rules or regulations hereunder) of material, nonpublic information.

(h) MANAGEMENT OF CONFLICTS OF INTEREST.—

(1) ORGANIZATION POLICIES AND PROCEDURES.—Each nationally recognized statistical rating organization shall establish, maintain, and enforce written policies and procedures

reasonably designed, taking into consideration the nature of the business of such nationally recognized statistical rating organization and affiliated persons and affiliated companies thereof, to address and manage any conflicts of interest that can arise from such business.

(2) COMMISSION AUTHORITY.—The Commission shall issue final rules in accordance with subsection (n) to prohibit, or require the management and disclosure of, any conflicts of interest relating to the issuance of credit ratings by a nationally recognized statistical rating organization, including, without limitation, conflicts of interest relating to—

(A) The manner in which a nationally recognized statistical rating organization is compensated by the obligor, or any affiliate of the obligor, for issuing credit ratings or providing related services;

(B) The provision of consulting, advisory, or other services by a nationally recognized statistical rating organization, or any person associated with such nationally recognized statistical rating organization, to the obligor, or any affiliate of the obligor;

(C) Business relationships, ownership interests, or any other financial or personal interests between a nationally recognized statistical rating organization, or any person associated with such nationally recognized statistical rating organization, and the obligor, or any affiliate of the obligor;

(D) Any affiliation of a nationally recognized statistical rating organization, or any person associated with such nationally recognized statistical rating organization, with any person that underwrites the securities or money market instruments that are the subject of a credit rating; and

(E) Any other potential conflict of interest, as the Commission deems necessary or appropriate in the public interest or for the protection of investors.

(3) SEPARATION OF RATINGS FROM SALES AND MARKETING.

(A) RULES REQUIRED. The Commission shall issue rules to prevent the sales and marketing considerations of a nationally recognized statistical rating organization from influencing the production of ratings by the nationally recognized statistical rating organization.

(B) CONTENTS OF RULES. The rules issued under subparagraph (A) shall provide for—

(i) Exceptions for small nationally recognized statistical rating organizations with respect to which the Commission determines that the separation of the production of ratings and sales and marketing activities is not appropriate; and

(ii) Suspension or revocation of the registration of a nationally recognized statistical rating organization, if the Commission finds, on the record, after notice and opportunity for a hearing, that—

(I) The nationally recognized statistical rating organization has committed a violation of a rule issued under this subsection; and

(II) The violation of a rule issued under this subsection affected a rating.

(4) LOOK-BACK REQUIREMENT.

(A) REVIEW BY THE NATIONALLY RECOGNIZED STATISTICAL RATING ORGANIZATION. Each nationally recognized statistical rating organization shall establish, maintain, and enforce policies and procedures reasonably designed to ensure that, in any case in which an employee of a person subject to a credit rating of the nationally recognized statistical rating organization or the issuer, underwriter, or sponsor of a security or money market instrument subject to a credit rating of the nationally recognized statistical rating organization was employed by the nationally recognized statistical rating organization and participated in any capacity in determining credit ratings for the person or the securities or money market instruments during the 1-year period preceding the date an action was taken with respect to the credit rating, the nationally recognized statistical rating organization shall—

(i) Conduct a review to determine whether any conflicts of interest of the employee influenced the credit rating; and

(ii) Take action to revise the rating if appropriate, in accordance with such rules as the Commission shall prescribe.

(B) REVIEW BY COMMISSION.

(i) IN GENERAL. The Commission shall conduct periodic reviews of the policies described in subparagraph (A) and the implementation of the policies at each nationally recognized statistical rating organization to ensure they are reasonably designed and implemented to most effectively eliminate conflicts of interest.

(ii) TIMING OF REVIEWS. The Commission shall review the code of ethics and conflict of interest policy of each nationally recognized statistical rating organization—

(I) Not less frequently than annually; and

(II) Whenever such policies are materially modified or amended.

(5) REPORT TO COMMISSION ON CERTAIN EMPLOYMENT TRANSITIONS.

(A) REPORT REQUIRED. Each nationally recognized statistical rating organization shall report to the Commission any case such organization knows or can reasonably be expected to know where a person associated with such organization within the previous 5 years obtains employment with any obligor, issuer, underwriter, or sponsor of a security or money market instrument for which the organization issued a credit rating during the 12-month period prior to such employment, if such employee—

(i) Was a senior officer of such organization;

(ii) Participated in any capacity in determining credit ratings for such obligor, issuer, underwriter, or sponsor; or

(iii) Supervised an employee described in clause (ii).

(B) PUBLIC DISCLOSURE. Upon receiving such a report, the Commission shall make such information publicly available.

(i) PROHIBITED CONDUCT.—

(1) PROHIBITED ACTS AND PRACTICES.—The Commission shall issue final rules in accordance with subsection (n) to prohibit any act or practice relating to the issuance of credit ratings by a nationally recognized statistical rating organization that the Commission determines to be unfair, coercive, or abusive, including any act or practice relating to—

(A) Conditioning or threatening to condition the issuance of a credit rating on the purchase by the obligor or an affiliate thereof of other services or products, including pre-credit rating assessment products, of the nationally recognized statistical rating organization or any person associated with such nationally recognized statistical rating organization;

(B) Lowering or threatening to lower a credit rating on, or refusing to rate, securities or money market instruments issued by an asset pool or as part of any asset-backed or mortgage-backed securities transaction, unless a portion of the assets within such pool or part of such transaction, as applicable, also is rated by the nationally recognized statistical rating organization; or

(C) Modifying or threatening to modify a credit rating or otherwise departing from its adopted systematic procedures and methodologies in determining credit ratings, based on whether the obligor, or an affiliate of the obligor, purchases or will purchase the credit rating or any other service or product of the nationally recognized statistical rating organization or any person associated with such organization.

(2) RULE OF CONSTRUCTION.—Nothing in paragraph (1), or in any rules or regulations adopted thereunder, may be construed to modify, impair, or supersede the operation of any of the antitrust laws (as defined in the first section of the Clayton Act, except that such term includes section 5 of the Federal Trade Commission Act, to the extent that such section 5 applies to unfair methods of competition).

(j) DESIGNATION OF COMPLIANCE OFFICER.—

(1) IN GENERAL Each nationally recognized statistical rating organization shall designate an individual responsible for administering the policies and procedures that are required to be established pursuant to subsections (g) and (h), and for ensuring compliance

with the securities laws and the rules and regulations thereunder, including those promulgated by the Commission pursuant to this section.

(2) LIMITATIONS.

(A) IN GENERAL. Except as provided in subparagraph (B), an individual designated under paragraph (1) may not, while serving in the designated capacity—

(i) Perform credit ratings;

(ii) Participate in the development of ratings methodologies or models;

(iii) Perform marketing or sales functions; or

(iv) Participate in establishing compensation levels, other than for employees working for that individual.

(B) EXCEPTION. The Commission may exempt a small nationally recognized statistical rating organization from the limitations under this paragraph, if the Commission finds that compliance with such limitations would impose an unreasonable burden on the nationally recognized statistical rating organization.

(3) OTHER DUTIES. Each individual designated under paragraph (1) shall establish procedures for the receipt, retention, and treatment of—

(A) Complaints regarding credit ratings, models, methodologies, and compliance with the securities laws and the policies and procedures developed under this section; and

(B) Confidential, anonymous complaints by employees or users of credit ratings.

(4) COMPENSATION. The compensation of each compliance officer appointed under paragraph (1) shall not be linked to the financial performance of the nationally recognized statistical rating organization and shall be arranged so as to ensure the independence of the officer's judgment.

(5) ANNUAL REPORTS REQUIRED.

(A) Annual Reports Required. Each individual designated under paragraph (1) shall submit to the nationally recognized statistical rating organization an annual report on the compliance of the nationally recognized statistical rating organization with the securities laws and the policies and procedures of the nationally recognized statistical rating organization that includes—

(i) A description of any material changes to the code of ethics and conflict of interest policies of the nationally recognized statistical rating organization; and

(ii) A certification that the report is accurate and complete.

(B) Submission of Reports to the Commission. Each nationally recognized statistical rating organization shall file the reports required under subparagraph (A) together with the financial report that is required to be submitted to the Commission under this section.

(k) STATEMENTS OF FINANCIAL CONDITION.—Each nationally recognized statistical rating organization shall, on a confidential basis, file with the Commission, at intervals determined by the Commission, such financial statements, certified (if required by the rules or regulations of the Commission) by an independent public accountant, and information concerning its financial condition, as the Commission, by rule, may prescribe as necessary or appropriate in the public interest or for the protection of investors.

(l) SOLE METHOD OF REGISTRATION.—

(1) IN GENERAL.—On and after the effective date of this section, a credit rating agency may only be registered as a nationally recognized statistical rating organization for any purpose in accordance with this section.

(2) PROHIBITION ON RELIANCE ON NO-ACTION RELIEF.—On and after the effective date of this section—

(A) An entity that, before that date, received advice, approval, or a no-action letter from the Commission or staff thereof to be treated as a nationally recognized statistical rating organization pursuant to the Commission rule at section 240.15c3-1 of title 17,

Code of Federal Regulations, may represent itself or act as a nationally recognized statistical rating organization only—

(i) During Commission consideration of the application, if such entity has filed an application for registration under this section; and

(ii) On and after the date of approval of its application for registration under this section; and

(B) The advice, approval, or no-action letter described in subparagraph (A) shall be void.

(3) NOTICE TO OTHER AGENCIES.—Not later than 30 days after the date of enactment of this section, the Commission shall give notice of the actions undertaken pursuant to this section to each Federal agency which employs in its rules and regulations the term "nationally recognized statistical rating organization" (as that term is used under Commission rule 15c3-1 (17 C.F.R. 240.15c3-1), as in effect on the date of enactment of this section).

(m) ACCOUNTABILITY.

(1) IN GENERAL. The enforcement and penalty provisions of this title shall apply to statements made by a credit rating agency in the same manner and to the same extent as such provisions apply to statements made by a registered public accounting firm or a securities analyst under the securities laws, and such statements shall not be deemed forward-looking statements for the purposes of section 21E.

(2) RULEMAKING. The Commission shall issue such rules as may be necessary to carry out this subsection.

(n) REGULATIONS.—

(1) NEW PROVISIONS.—Such rules and regulations as are required by this section or are otherwise necessary to carry out this section, including the application form required under subsection (a)—

(A) Shall be issued by the Commission in final form, not later than 270 days after the date of enactment of this section; and

(B) Shall become effective not later than 270 days after the date of enactment of this section.

(2) REVIEW OF EXISTING REGULATIONS.—Not later than 270 days after the date of enactment of this section, the Commission shall—

(A) Review its existing rules and regulations which employ the term "nationally recognized statistical rating organization" or "NRSRO"; and

(B) Amend or revise such rules and regulations in accordance with the purposes of this section, as the Commission may prescribe as necessary or appropriate in the public interest or for the protection of investors.

(o) NRSROS SUBJECT TO COMMISSION AUTHORITY.—

(1) IN GENERAL.—No provision of the laws of any State or political subdivision thereof requiring the registration, licensing, or qualification as a credit rating agency or a nationally recognized statistical rating organization shall apply to any nationally recognized statistical rating organization or person employed by or working under the control of a nationally recognized statistical rating organization.

(2) LIMITATION.—Nothing in this subsection prohibits the securities commission (or any agency or office performing like functions) of any State from investigating and bringing an enforcement action with respect to fraud or deceit against any nationally recognized statistical rating organization or person associated with a nationally recognized statistical rating organization.

(p) REGULATION OF NATIONALLY RECOGNIZED STATISTICAL RATING ORGANIZATIONS.

(1) ESTABLISHMENT OF OFFICE OF CREDIT RATINGS.

(A) OFFICE ESTABLISHED. The Commission shall establish within the Commission an Office of Credit Ratings (referred to in this subsection as the "Office") to administer the rules of the Commission—

(i) With respect to the practices of nationally recognized statistical rating organizations in determining ratings, for the protection of users of credit ratings and in the public interest;

(ii) To promote accuracy in credit ratings issued by nationally recognized statistical rating organizations; and

(iii) To ensure that such ratings are not unduly influenced by conflicts of interest.

(B) DIRECTOR OF THE OFFICE. The head of the Office shall be the Director, who shall report to the Chairman.

(2) STAFFING. The Office established under this subsection shall be staffed sufficiently to carry out fully the requirements of this section. The staff shall include persons with knowledge of and expertise in corporate, municipal, and structured debt finance.

(3) COMMISSION EXAMINATIONS.

(A) ANNUAL EXAMINATIONS REQUIRED. The Office shall conduct an examination of each nationally recognized statistical rating organization at least annually.

(B) CONDUCT OF EXAMINATIONS. Each examination under subparagraph (A) shall include a review of—

(i) Whether the nationally recognized statistical rating organization conducts business in accordance with the policies, procedures, and rating methodologies of the nationally recognized statistical rating organization;

(ii) The management of conflicts of interest by the nationally recognized statistical rating organization;

(iii) Implementation of ethics policies by the nationally recognized statistical rating organization;

(iv) The internal supervisory controls of the nationally recognized statistical rating organization;

(v) The governance of the nationally recognized statistical rating organization;

(vi) The activities of the individual designated by the nationally recognized statistical rating organization under subsection (j)(1);

(vii) The processing of complaints by the nationally recognized statistical rating organization; and

(viii) The policies of the nationally recognized statistical rating organization governing the post-employment activities of former staff of the nationally recognized statistical rating organization.

(C) INSPECTION REPORTS. The Commission shall make available to the public, in an easily understandable format, an annual report summarizing—

(i) The essential findings of all examinations conducted under subparagraph (A), as deemed appropriate by the Commission;

(ii) The responses by the nationally recognized statistical rating organizations to any material regulatory deficiencies identified by the Commission under clause (i); and

(iii) Whether the nationally recognized statistical rating organizations have appropriately addressed the recommendations of the Commission contained in previous reports under this subparagraph.

(4) RULEMAKING AUTHORITY. THE COMMISSION SHALL—

(A) Establish, by rule, fines, and other penalties applicable to any nationally recognized statistical rating organization that violates the requirements of this section and the rules thereunder; and

(B) Issue such rules as may be necessary to carry out this section.

(q) TRANSPARENCY OF RATINGS PERFORMANCE.

(1) RULEMAKING REQUIRED. The Commission shall, by rule, require that each nationally recognized statistical rating organization publicly disclose information on the initial credit

ratings determined by the nationally recognized statistical rating organization for each type of obligor, security, and money market instrument, and any subsequent changes to such credit ratings, for the purpose of allowing users of credit ratings to evaluate the accuracy of ratings and compare the performance of ratings by different nationally recognized statistical rating organizations.

(2) CONTENT. The rules of the Commission under this subsection shall require, at a minimum, disclosures that—

(A) Are comparable among nationally recognized statistical rating organizations, to allow users of credit ratings to compare the performance of credit ratings across nationally recognized statistical rating organizations;

(B) Are clear and informative for investors having a wide range of sophistication who use or might use credit ratings;

(C) Include performance information over a range of years and for a variety of types of credit ratings, including for credit ratings withdrawn by the nationally recognized statistical rating organization;

(D) Are published and made freely available by the nationally recognized statistical rating organization, on an easily accessible portion of its website, and in writing, when requested;

(E) Are appropriate to the business model of a nationally recognized statistical rating organization; and

(F) Each nationally recognized statistical rating organization include an attestation with any credit rating it issues affirming that no part of the rating was influenced by any other business activities, that the rating was based solely on the merits of the instruments being rated, and that such rating was an independent evaluation of the risks and merits of the instrument.

(r) CREDIT RATINGS METHODOLOGIES. The Commission shall prescribe rules, for the protection of investors and in the public interest, with respect to the procedures and methodologies, including qualitative and quantitative data and models, used by nationally recognized statistical rating organizations that require each nationally recognized statistical rating organization—

(1) To ensure that credit ratings are determined using procedures and methodologies, including qualitative and quantitative data and models, that are—

(A) Approved by the board of the nationally recognized statistical rating organization, a body performing a function similar to that of a board; and

(B) In accordance with the policies and procedures of the nationally recognized statistical rating organization for the development and modification of credit rating procedures and methodologies;

(2) To ensure that when material changes to credit rating procedures and methodologies (including changes to qualitative and quantitative data and models) are made, that—

(A) The changes are applied consistently to all credit ratings to which the changed procedures and methodologies apply;

(B) To the extent that changes are made to credit rating surveillance procedures and methodologies, the changes are applied to then-current credit ratings by the nationally recognized statistical rating organization within a reasonable time period determined by the Commission, by rule; and

(C) The nationally recognized statistical rating organization publicly discloses the reason for the change; and

(3) To notify users of credit ratings—

(A) Of the version of a procedure or methodology, including the qualitative methodology or quantitative inputs, used with respect to a particular credit rating;

(B) When a material change is made to a procedure or methodology, including to a qualitative model or quantitative inputs;

(C) When a significant error is identified in a procedure or methodology, including a qualitative or quantitative model, that may result in credit rating actions; and

(D) Of the likelihood of a material change described in subparagraph (B) resulting in a change in current credit ratings.

(s) TRANSPARENCY OF CREDIT RATING METHODOLOGIES AND INFORMATION REVIEWED.

(1) FORM FOR DISCLOSURES. The Commission shall require, by rule, each nationally recognized statistical rating organization to prescribe a form to accompany the publication of each credit rating that discloses—

(A) Information relating to—

(i) The assumptions underlying the credit rating procedures and methodologies;

(ii) The data that was relied on to determine the credit rating; and

(iii) If applicable, how the nationally recognized statistical rating organization used servicer or remittance reports, and with what frequency, to conduct surveillance of the credit rating; and

(B) Information that can be used by investors and other users of credit ratings to better understand credit ratings in each class of credit rating issued by the nationally recognized statistical rating organization.

(2) FORMAT. The form developed under paragraph (1) shall—

(A) Be easy to use and helpful for users of credit ratings to understand the information contained in the report;

(B) Require the nationally recognized statistical rating organization to provide the content described in paragraph (3)(B) in a manner that is directly comparable across types of securities; and

(C) Be made readily available to users of credit ratings, in electronic or paper form, as the Commission may, by rule, determine.

(3) CONTENT OF FORM.

(A) Qualitative Content. Each nationally recognized statistical rating organization shall disclose on the form developed under paragraph (1)—

(i) The credit ratings produced by the nationally recognized statistical rating organization;

(ii) The main assumptions and principles used in constructing procedures and methodologies, including qualitative methodologies and quantitative inputs and assumptions about the correlation of defaults across underlying assets used in rating structured products;

(iii) The potential limitations of the credit ratings, and the types of risks excluded from the credit ratings that the nationally recognized statistical rating organization does not comment on, including liquidity, market, and other risks;

(iv) Information on the uncertainty of the credit rating, including—

(I) Information on the reliability, accuracy, and quality of the data relied on in determining the credit rating; and

(II) A statement relating to the extent to which data essential to the determination of the credit rating were reliable or limited, including—

(aa) Any limits on the scope of historical data; and

(bb) Any limits in accessibility to certain documents or other types of information that would have better informed the credit rating;

(v) Whether and to what extent third party due diligence services have been used by the nationally recognized statistical rating organization, a description of the information that such third party reviewed in conducting due diligence services, and a description of the findings or conclusions of such third party;

(vi) A description of the data about any obligor, issuer, security, or money market instrument that were relied upon for the purpose of determining the credit rating;

(vii) A statement containing an overall assessment of the quality of information available and considered in producing a rating for an obligor, security, or money market instrument, in relation to the quality of information available to the nationally recognized statistical rating organization in rating similar issuances;

(viii) Information relating to conflicts of interest of the nationally recognized statistical rating organization; and

(ix) Such additional information as the Commission may require.

(B) Quantitative Content. Each nationally recognized statistical rating organization shall disclose on the form developed under this subsection—

(i) An explanation or measure of the potential volatility of the credit rating, including—

(I) Any factors that might lead to a change in the credit ratings; and

(II) The magnitude of the change that a user can expect under different market conditions;

(ii) Information on the content of the rating, including—

(I) The historical performance of the rating; and

(II) The expected probability of default and the expected loss in the event of default;

(iii) Information on the sensitivity of the rating to assumptions made by the nationally recognized statistical rating organization, including—

(I) 5 assumptions made in the ratings process that, without accounting for any other factor, would have the greatest impact on a rating if the assumptions were proven false or inaccurate; and

(II) An analysis, using specific examples, of how each of the 5 assumptions identified under subclause (I) impacts a rating;

(iv) Such additional information as may be required by the Commission.

(4) Due Diligence Services For Asset-Backed Securities.

(A) Findings. The issuer or underwriter of any asset-backed security shall make publicly available the findings and conclusions of any third-party due diligence report obtained by the issuer or underwriter.

(B) Certification Required. In any case in which third-party due diligence services are employed by a nationally recognized statistical rating organization, an issuer, or an underwriter, the person providing the due diligence services shall provide to any nationally recognized statistical rating organization that produces a rating to which such services relate, written certification, as provided in subparagraph (C).

(C) Format and Content. The Commission shall establish the appropriate format and content for the written certifications required under subparagraph (B), to ensure that providers of due diligence services have conducted a thorough review of data, documentation, and other relevant information necessary for a nationally recognized statistical rating organization to provide an accurate rating.

(D) Disclosure of Certification. The Commission shall adopt rules requiring a nationally recognized statistical rating organization, at the time at which the nationally recognized statistical rating organization produces a rating, to disclose the certification described in subparagraph (B) to the public in a manner that allows the public to determine the adequacy and level of due diligence services provided by a third party.

(t) Corporate Governance, Organization, and Management of Conflicts of Interest.

(1) Board of Directors. Each nationally recognized statistical rating organization shall have a board of directors.

(2) Independent Directors.

(A) In General. At least 1/2 of the board of directors, but not fewer than 2 of the members thereof, shall be independent of the nationally recognized statistical rating agency. A portion of the independent directors shall include users of ratings from a nationally recognized statistical rating organization.

(B) INDEPENDENCE DETERMINATION. In order to be considered independent for purposes of this subsection, a member of the board of directors of a nationally recognized statistical rating organization—

(i) May not, other than in his or her capacity as a member of the board of directors or any committee thereof—

(I) Accept any consulting, advisory, or other compensatory fee from the nationally recognized statistical rating organization; or

(II) Be a person associated with the nationally recognized statistical rating organization or with any affiliated company thereof; and

(ii) Shall be disqualified from any deliberation involving a specific rating in which the independent board member has a financial interest in the outcome of the rating.

(C) COMPENSATION AND TERM. The compensation of the independent members of the board of directors of a nationally recognized statistical rating organization shall not be linked to the business performance of the nationally recognized statistical rating organization, and shall be arranged so as to ensure the independence of their judgment. The term of office of the independent directors shall be for a pre-agreed fixed period, not to exceed 5 years, and shall not be renewable.

(3) DUTIES OF BOARD OF DIRECTORS. In addition to the overall responsibilities of the board of directors, the board shall oversee—

(A) The establishment, maintenance, and enforcement of policies and procedures for determining credit ratings;

(B) The establishment, maintenance, and enforcement of policies and procedures to address, manage, and disclose any conflicts of interest;

(C) The effectiveness of the internal control system with respect to policies and procedures for determining credit ratings; and

(D) The compensation and promotion policies and practices of the nationally recognized statistical rating organization.

(4) TREATMENT OF NRSRO SUBSIDIARIES. If a nationally recognized statistical rating organization is a subsidiary of a parent entity, the board of the directors of the parent entity may satisfy the requirements of this subsection by assigning to a committee of such board of directors the duties under paragraph (3), if—

(A) At least 1/2 of the members of the committee (including the chairperson of the committee) are independent, as defined in this section; and

(B) At least 1 member of the committee is a user of ratings from a nationally recognized statistical rating organization.

(5) EXCEPTION AUTHORITY. If the Commission finds that compliance with the provisions of this subsection present an unreasonable burden on a small nationally recognized statistical rating organization, the Commission may permit the nationally recognized statistical rating organization to delegate such responsibilities to a committee that includes at least one individual who is a user of ratings of a nationally recognized statistical rating organization.

(u) DUTY TO REPORT TIPS ALLEGING MATERIAL VIOLATIONS OF LAW.

(1) DUTY TO REPORT. Each nationally recognized statistical rating organization shall refer to the appropriate law enforcement or regulatory authorities any information that the nationally recognized statistical rating organization receives from a third party and finds credible that alleges that an issuer of securities rated by the nationally recognized statistical rating organization has committed or is committing a material violation of law that has not been adjudicated by a Federal or State court.

(2) RULE OF CONSTRUCTION. Nothing in paragraph (1) may be construed to require a nationally recognized statistical rating organization to verify the accuracy of the information described in paragraph (1).

(v) INFORMATION FROM SOURCES OTHER THAN THE ISSUER. In producing a credit rating, a nationally recognized statistical rating organization shall consider information about an issuer that the nationally recognized statistical rating organization has, or receives from a source other than the issuer or underwriter, that the nationally recognized statistical rating organization finds credible and potentially significant to a rating decision.

REGISTRATION AND REGULATION OF SECURITY-BASED SWAP DEALERS AND MAJOR SECURITY-BASED SWAP PARTICIPANTS

Sec. 15F. (a) REGISTRATION.

(1) SECURITY-BASED SWAP DEALERS. It shall be unlawful for any person to act as a security-based swap dealer unless the person is registered as a security-based swap dealer with the Commission.

(2) MAJOR SECURITY-BASED SWAP PARTICIPANTS. It shall be unlawful for any person to act as a major security-based swap participant unless the person is registered as a major security-based swap participant with the Commission.

(b) REQUIREMENTS.

(1) IN GENERAL. A person shall register as a security-based swap dealer or major security-based swap participant by filing a registration application with the Commission.

(2) CONTENTS.

(A) IN GENERAL. The application shall be made in such form and manner as prescribed by the Commission, and shall contain such information, as the Commission considers necessary concerning the business in which the applicant is or will be engaged.

(B) CONTINUAL REPORTING. A person that is registered as a security-based swap dealer or major security-based swap participant shall continue to submit to the Commission reports that contain such information pertaining to the business of the person as the Commission may require.

(3) EXPIRATION. Each registration under this section shall expire at such time as the Commission may prescribe by rule or regulation.

(4) RULES. Except as provided in subsections (d) and (e), the Commission may prescribe rules applicable to security-based swap dealers and major security-based swap participants, including rules that limit the activities of non-bank security-based swap dealers and major security-based swap participants.

(5) TRANSITION. Not later than 1 year after the date of enactment of the Wall Street Transparency and Accountability Act of 2010, the Commission shall issue rules under this section to provide for the registration of security-based swap dealers and major security-based swap participants.

(6) STATUTORY DISQUALIFICATION. Except to the extent otherwise specifically provided by rule, regulation, or order of the Commission, it shall be unlawful for a security-based swap dealer or a major security-based swap participant to permit any person associated with a security-based swap dealer or a major security-based swap participant who is subject to a statutory disqualification to effect or be involved in effecting security-based swaps on behalf of the security-based swap dealer or major security-based swap participant, if the security-based swap dealer or major security-based swap participant knew, or in the exercise of reasonable care should have known, of the statutory disqualification.

(c) DUAL REGISTRATION.

(1) SECURITY-BASED SWAP DEALER. Any person that is required to be registered as a security-based swap dealer under this section shall register with the Commission, regardless of whether the person also is registered with the Commodity Futures Trading Commission as a swap dealer.

(2) MAJOR SECURITY-BASED SWAP PARTICIPANT. Any person that is required to be registered as a major security-based swap participant under this section shall register with the

Commission, regardless of whether the person also is registered with the Commodity Futures Trading Commission as a major swap participant.

(d) RULEMAKING.

(1) IN GENERAL. The Commission shall adopt rules for persons that are registered as security-based swap dealers or major security-based swap participants under this section.

(2) EXCEPTION FOR PRUDENTIAL REQUIREMENTS.

(A) IN GENERAL. The Commission may not prescribe rules imposing prudential requirements on security-based swap dealers or major security-based swap participants for which there is a prudential regulator.

(B) APPLICABILITY. Subparagraph (A) does not limit the authority of the Commission to prescribe rules as directed under this section.

(e) CAPITAL AND MARGIN REQUIREMENTS.

(1) IN GENERAL.

(A) SECURITY-BASED SWAP DEALERS AND MAJOR SECURITY-BASED SWAP PARTICIPANTS THAT ARE BANKS. Each registered security-based swap dealer and major security-based swap participant for which there is not a prudential regulator shall meet such minimum capital requirements and minimum initial and variation margin requirements as the prudential regulator shall by rule or regulation prescribe under paragraph (2)(A).

(B) SECURITY-BASED SWAP DEALERS AND MAJOR SECURITY-BASED SWAP PARTICIPANTS THAT ARE NOT BANKS. Each registered security-based swap dealer and major security-based swap participant for which there is not a prudential regulator shall meet such minimum capital requirements and minimum initial and variation margin requirements as the Commission shall by rule or regulation prescribe under paragraph (2)(B).

(2) RULES.

(A) SECURITY-BASED SWAP DEALERS AND MAJOR SECURITY-BASED SWAP PARTICIPANTS THAT ARE BANKS. The prudential regulators, in consultation with the Commission and the Commodity Futures Trading Commission, shall adopt rules for security-based swap dealers and major security-based swap participants, with respect to their activities as a swap dealer or major swap participant, for which there is a prudential regulator imposing—

(i) Capital requirements; and

(ii) Both initial and variation margin requirements on all security-based swaps that are not cleared by a registered clearing agency.

(B) SECURITY-BASED SWAP DEALERS AND MAJOR SECURITY-BASED SWAP PARTICIPANTS THAT ARE NOT BANKS. The Commission shall adopt rules for security-based swap dealers and major security-based swap participants, with respect to their activities as a swap dealer or major swap participant, for which there is not a prudential regulator imposing—

(i) Capital requirements; and

(ii) Both initial and variation margin requirements on all swaps that are not cleared by a registered clearing agency.

(3) STANDARDS FOR CAPITAL AND MARGIN.

(A) IN GENERAL. To offset the greater risk to the security-based swap dealer or major security-based swap participant and the financial system arising from the use of security-based swaps that are not cleared, the requirements imposed under paragraph (2) shall—

(i) Help ensure the safety and soundness of the security-based swap dealer or major security-based swap participant; and

(ii) Be appropriate for the risk associated with the non-cleared security-based swaps held as a security-based swap dealer or major security-based swap participant.

(B) RULE OF CONSTRUCTION.

(i) In General. Nothing in this section shall limit, or be construed to limit, the authority—

(I) Of the Commission to set financial responsibility rules for a broker or dealer registered pursuant to section 15(b) (except for section 15(b)(11) thereof) in accordance with section 15(c)(3); or

(II) Of the Commodity Futures Trading Commission to set financial responsibility rules for a futures commission merchant or introducing broker registered pursuant to section 4f(a) of the Commodity Exchange Act (except for section 4f(a)(3) thereof) in accordance with section 4f(b) of the Commodity Exchange Act.

(ii) Futures Commission Merchants and Other Dealers. A futures commission merchant, introducing broker, broker, or dealer shall maintain sufficient capital to comply with the stricter of any applicable capital requirements to which such futures commission merchant, introducing broker, broker, or dealer is subject to under this title or the Commodity Exchange Act.

(C) Margin Requirements. In prescribing margin requirements under this subsection, the prudential regulator with respect to security-based swap dealers and major security-based swap participants that are depository institutions, and the Commission with respect to security-based swap dealers and major security-based swap participants that are not depository institutions shall permit the use of noncash collateral, as the regulator or the Commission determines to be consistent with—

(i) Preserving the financial integrity of markets trading security-based swaps; and

(ii) Preserving the stability of the United States financial system.

(D) Comparability of Capital and Margin Requirements.

(i) In General. The prudential regulators, the Commission, and the Securities and Exchange Commission shall periodically (but not less frequently than annually) consult on minimum capital requirements and minimum initial and variation margin requirements.

(ii) Comparability. The entities described in clause (i) shall, to the maximum extent practicable, establish and maintain comparable minimum capital requirements and minimum initial and variation margin requirements, including the use of noncash collateral, for—

(I) Security-based swap dealers; and

(II) Major security-based swap participants.

(f) Reporting and Recordkeeping.

(1) In General. Each registered security-based swap dealer and major security-based swap participant—

(A) Shall make such reports as are required by the Commission, by rule or regulation, regarding the transactions and positions and financial condition of the registered security-based swap dealer or major security-based swap participant;

(B) (i) For which there is a prudential regulator, shall keep books and records of all activities related to the business as a security-based swap dealer or major security-based swap participant in such form and manner and for such period as may be prescribed by the Commission by rule or regulation; and

(ii) For which there is no prudential regulator, shall keep books and records in such form and manner and for such period as may be prescribed by the Commission by rule or regulation; and

(C) Shall keep books and records described in subparagraph (B) open to inspection and examination by any representative of the Commission.

(2) Rules. The Commission shall adopt rules governing reporting and recordkeeping for security-based swap dealers and major security-based swap participants

(g) Daily Trading Records.

(1) In General. Each registered security-based swap dealer and major security-based swap participant shall maintain daily trading records of the security-based swaps of the registered security-based swap dealer and major security-based swap participant and all

related records (including related cash or forward transactions) and recorded communications, including electronic mail, instant messages, and recordings of telephone calls, for such period as may be required by the Commission by rule or regulation.

(2) INFORMATION REQUIREMENTS. The daily trading records shall include such information as the Commission shall require by rule or regulation.

(3) COUNTERPARTY RECORDS. Each registered security-based swap dealer and major security-based swap participant shall maintain daily trading records for each counterparty in a manner and form that is identifiable with each security-based swap transaction.

(4) AUDIT TRAIL. Each registered security-based swap dealer and major security-based swap participant shall maintain a complete audit trail for conducting comprehensive and accurate trade reconstructions.

(5) RULES. The Commission shall adopt rules governing daily trading records for security-based swap dealers and major security-based swap participants.

(h) BUSINESS CONDUCT STANDARDS.

(1) IN GENERAL. Each registered security-based swap dealer and major security-based swap participant shall conform with such business conduct standards as prescribed in paragraph (3) and as may be prescribed by the Commission by rule or regulation that relate to—

(A) Fraud, manipulation, and other abusive practices involving security-based swaps (including security-based swaps that are offered but not entered into);

(B) Diligent supervision of the business of the registered security-based swap dealer and major security-based swap participant;

(C) Adherence to all applicable position limits; and

(D) Such other matters as the Commission determines to be appropriate.

(2) RESPONSIBILITIES WITH RESPECT TO SPECIAL ENTITIES.

(A) Advising Special Entities. A security-based swap dealer or major security-based swap participant that acts as an advisor to special entity regarding a security-based swap shall comply with the requirements of paragraph (4) with respect to such special entity.

(B) Entering of Swaps With Respect to Special Entities. A security-based swap dealer that enters into or offers to enter into security-based swap with a special entity shall comply with the requirements of paragraph (5) with respect to such special entity.

(C) Special Entity Defined. For purposes of this subsection, the term "special entity" means—

(i) A Federal agency;

(ii) A State, State agency, city, county, municipality, or other political subdivision of a State or;

(iii) Any employee benefit plan, as defined in section 3 of the Employee Retirement Income Security Act of 1974 (29 U.S.C. 1002);

(iv) Any governmental plan, as defined in section 3 of the Employee Retirement Income Security Act of 1974 (29 U.S.C. 1002); or

(v) Any endowment, including an endowment that is an organization described in section 501(c)(3) of the Internal Revenue Code of 1986.

(3) BUSINESS CONDUCT REQUIREMENTS. Business conduct requirements adopted by the Commission shall—

(A) Establish a duty for a security-based swap dealer or major security-based swap participant to verify that any counterparty meets the eligibility standards for an eligible contract participant;

(B) Require disclosure by the security-based swap dealer or major security-based swap participant to any counterparty to the transaction (other than a security-based swap dealer, major security-based swap participant, security-based swap dealer, or major security-based swap participant) of—

(i) Information about the material risks and characteristics of the security-based swap;

(ii) Any material incentives or conflicts of interest that the security-based swap dealer or major security-based swap participant may have in connection with the security-based swap; and

(iii) (I) For cleared security-based swaps, upon the request of the counterparty, receipt of the daily mark of the transaction from the appropriate derivatives clearing organization; and

(II) For uncleared security-based swaps, receipt of the daily mark of the transaction from the security-based swap dealer or the major security-based swap participant;

(C) Establish a duty for a security-based swap dealer or major security-based swap participant to communicate in a fair and balanced manner based on principles of fair dealing and good faith; and

(D) Establish such other standards and requirements as the Commission may determine are appropriate in the public interest, for the protection of investors, or otherwise in furtherance of the purposes of this Act.

(4) SPECIAL REQUIREMENTS FOR SECURITY-BASED SWAP DEALERS ACTING AS ADVISORS.

(A) In General. It shall be unlawful for a security-based swap dealer or major security-based swap participant—

(i) To employ any device, scheme, or artifice to defraud any special entity or prospective customer who is a special entity;

(ii) To engage in any transaction, practice, or course of business that operates as a fraud or deceit on any special entity or prospective customer who is a special entity; or

(iii) To engage in any act, practice, or course of business that is fraudulent, deceptive, or manipulative.

(B) Duty. Any security-based swap dealer that acts as an advisor to a special entity shall have a duty to act in the best interests of the special entity.

(C) Reasonable Efforts. Any security-based swap dealer that acts as an advisor to a special entity shall make reasonable efforts to obtain such information as is necessary to make a reasonable determination that any security-based swap recommended by the security-based swap dealer is in the best interests of the special entity, including information relating to—

(i) The financial status of the special entity;

(ii) The tax status of the special entity;

(iii) The investment or financing objectives of the special entity; and

(iv) Any other information that the Commission may prescribe by rule or regulation.

(5) SPECIAL REQUIREMENTS FOR SECURITY-BASED SWAP DEALERS AS COUNTERPARTIES TO SPECIAL ENTITIES.

(A) IN GENERAL. Any security-based swap dealer or major security-based swap participant that offers to or enters into a security-based swap with a special entity shall—

(i) Comply with any duty established by the Commission for a security-based swap dealer or major security-based swap participant, with respect to a counterparty that is an eligible contract participant within the meaning of subclause (I) or (II) of clause (vii) of section 1a(18) of the Commodity Exchange Act, that requires the security-based swap dealer or major security-based swap participant to have a reasonable basis to believe that the counterparty that is a special entity has an independent representative that—

(I) Has sufficient knowledge to evaluate the transaction and risks;

(II) Is not subject to a statutory disqualification;

(III) Is independent of the security-based swap dealer or major security-based swap participant;

(IV) Undertakes a duty to act in the best interests of the counterparty it represents;

(V) Makes appropriate disclosures;

(VI) Will provide written representations to the special entity regarding fair pricing and the appropriateness of the transaction; and

(VII) In the case of employee benefit plans subject to the Employee Retirement Income Security Act of 1974, is a fiduciary as defined in section 3 of that Act (29 U.S.C. 1002); and

(ii) Before the initiation of the transaction, disclose to the special entity in writing the capacity in which the security-based swap dealer is acting.

(B) COMMISSION AUTHORITY. The Commission may establish such other standards and requirements under this paragraph as the Commission may determine are appropriate in the public interest, for the protection of investors, or otherwise in furtherance of the purposes of this Act.

(6) RULES. The Commission shall prescribe rules under this subsection governing business conduct standards for security-based swap dealers and major security-based swap participants.

(7) APPLICABILITY. This subsection shall not apply with respect to a transaction that is—

(A) Initiated by a special entity on an exchange or security-based swaps execution facility; and

(B) The security-based swap dealer or major security-based swap participant does not know the identity of the counterparty to the transaction.

(i) DOCUMENTATION STANDARDS.

(1) IN GENERAL. Each registered security-based swap dealer and major security-based swap participant shall conform with such standards as may be prescribed by the Commission, by rule or regulation, that relate to timely and accurate confirmation, processing, netting, documentation, and valuation of all security-based swaps.

(2) RULES. The Commission shall adopt rules governing documentation standards for security-based swap dealers and major security-based swap participants.

(j) DUTIES. Each registered security-based swap dealer and major security-based swap participant shall, at all times, comply with the following requirements:

(1) MONITORING OF TRADING. The security-based swap dealer or major security-based swap participant shall monitor its trading in security-based swaps to prevent violations of applicable position limits.

(2) RISK MANAGEMENT PROCEDURES. The security-based swap dealer or major security-based swap participant shall establish robust and professional risk management systems adequate for managing the day-to-day business of the security-based swap dealer or major security-based swap participant.

(3) DISCLOSURE OF GENERAL INFORMATION. The security-based swap dealer or major security-based swap participant shall disclose to the Commission and to the prudential regulator for the security-based swap dealer or major security-based swap participant, as applicable, information concerning—

(A) Terms and conditions of its security-based swaps;

(B) Security-based swap trading operations, mechanisms, and practices;

(C) Financial integrity protections relating to security-based swaps; and

(D) Other information relevant to its trading in security-based swaps.

(4) ABILITY TO OBTAIN INFORMATION. The security-based swap dealer or major security-based swap participant shall—

(A) Establish and enforce internal systems and procedures to obtain any necessary information to perform any of the functions described in this section; and

(B) Provide the information to the Commission and to the prudential regulator for the security-based swap dealer or major security-based swap participant, as applicable, on request.

(5) CONFLICTS OF INTEREST. The security-based swap dealer and major security-based swap participant shall implement conflict-of-interest systems and procedures that—

(A) Establish structural and institutional safeguards to ensure that the activities of any person within the firm relating to research or analysis of the price or market for any security-based swap or acting in a role of providing clearing activities or making determinations as to accepting clearing customers are separated by appropriate informational partitions within the firm from the review, pressure, or oversight of persons whose involvement in pricing, trading, or clearing activities might potentially bias their judgment or supervision and contravene the core principles of open access and the business conduct standards described in this title; and

(B) Address such other issues as the Commission determines to be appropriate

(6) ANTITRUST CONSIDERATIONS. Unless necessary or appropriate to achieve the purposes of this title, the security-based swap dealer or major security-based swap participant shall not—

(A) Adopt any process or take any action that results in any unreasonable restraint of trade; or

(B) Impose any material anticompetitive burden on trading or clearing.

(7) RULES. The Commission shall prescribe rules under this subsection governing duties of security-based swap dealers and major security-based swap participants.

(k) DESIGNATION OF CHIEF COMPLIANCE OFFICER.

(1) IN GENERAL. Each security-based swap dealer and major security-based swap participant shall designate an individual to serve as a chief compliance officer.

(2) DUTIES. The chief compliance officer shall—

(A) Report directly to the board or to the senior officer of the security-based swap dealer or major security-based swap participant;

(B) Review the compliance of the security-based swap dealer or major security-based swap participant with respect to the security-based swap dealer and major security-based swap participant requirements described in this section;

(C) In consultation with the board of directors, a body performing a function similar to the board, or the senior officer of the organization, resolve any conflicts of interest that may arise;

(D) Be responsible for administering each policy and procedure that is required to be established pursuant to this section;

(E) Ensure compliance with this title (including regulations) relating to security-based swaps, including each rule prescribed by the Commission under this section;

(F) Establish procedures for the remediation of noncompliance issues identified by the chief compliance officer through any—

(i) Compliance office review;

(ii) Look-back;

(iii) Internal or external audit finding;

(iv) Self-reported error; or

(v) Validated complaint; and

(G) Establish and follow appropriate procedures for the handling, management response, remediation, retesting, and closing of noncompliance issues.

(3) ANNUAL REPORTS.

(A) In General. In accordance with rules prescribed by the Commission, the chief compliance officer shall annually prepare and sign a report that contains a description of—

(i) The compliance of the security-based swap dealer or major swap participant with respect to this title (including regulations); and swap participant of the chief compliance officer (including the code of ethics and conflict of interest policies).

(B) Requirements. A compliance report under subparagraph (A) shall—

(i) Accompany each appropriate financial report of the security-based swap dealer or major security-based swap participant that is required to be furnished to the Commission pursuant to this section; and

(ii) Include a certification that, under penalty of law, the compliance report is accurate and complete.

(*l*) ENFORCEMENT AND ADMINISTRATIVE PROCEEDING AUTHORITY.

(1) PRIMARY ENFORCEMENT AUTHORITY.

(A) Securities and Exchange Commission. Except as provided in subparagraph (B), the Commission shall have primary authority to enforce subtitle B, and the amendments made by subtitle B of the Wall Street Transparency and Accountability Act of 2010, with respect to any person.

(B) Prudential Regulators. The prudential regulators shall have exclusive authority to enforce the provisions of subsection (e) and other prudential requirements of this title (including risk management standards), with respect to security-based swap dealers or major security-based swap participants for which they are the prudential regulator.

(C) Referral.

(i) Violations of Nonprudential Requirements. If the appropriate Federal banking agency for security-based swap dealers or major security-based swap participants that are depository institutions has cause to believe that such security-based swap dealer or major security-based swap participant may have engaged in conduct that constitutes a violation of the nonprudential requirements of this section or rules adopted by the Commission thereunder, the agency may recommend in writing to the Commission that the Commission initiate an enforcement proceeding as authorized under this title. The recommendation shall be accompanied by a written explanation of the concerns giving rise to the recommendation.

(ii) Violations of Prudential Requirements. If the Commission has cause to believe that a securities-based swap dealer or major securities-based swap participant that has a prudential regulator may have engaged in conduct that constitute a violation of the prudential requirements of subsection (e) or rules adopted thereunder, the Commission may recommend in writing to the prudential regulator that the prudential regulator initiate an enforcement proceeding as authorized under this title. The recommendation shall be accompanied by a written explanation of the concerns giving rise to the recommendation.

(2) CENSURE, DENIAL, SUSPENSION; NOTICE AND HEARING. The Commission, by order, shall censure, place limitations on the activities, functions, or operations of, or revoke the registration of any security-based swap dealer or major security-based swap participant that has registered with the Commission pursuant to subsection (b) if the Commission finds, on the record after notice and opportunity for hearing, that such censure, placing of limitations, or revocation is in the public interest and that such security-based swap dealer or major security-based swap participant, or any person associated with such security-based swap dealer or major security-based swap participant effecting or involved in effecting transactions in security-based swaps on behalf of such security-based swap dealer or major security-based swap participant, whether prior or subsequent to becoming so associated—

(A) Has committed or omitted any act, or is subject to an order or finding, enumerated in subparagraph (A), (D), or (E) of paragraph (4) of section 15(b);

(B) Has been convicted of any offense specified in subparagraph (B) of such paragraph (4) within 10 years of the commencement of the proceedings under this subsection;

(C) Is enjoined from any action, conduct, or practice specified in subparagraph (C) of such paragraph (4);

(D) Is subject to an order or a final order specified in subparagraph (F) or (H), respectively, of such paragraph (4); or

(E) Has been found by a foreign financial regulatory authority to have committed or omitted any act, or violated any foreign statute or regulation, enumerated in subparagraph (G) of such paragraph (4).

(3) ASSOCIATED PERSONS. With respect to any person who is associated, who is seeking to become associated, or, at the time of the alleged misconduct, who was associated or was seeking to become associated with a security-based swap dealer or major security-based swap participant for the purpose of effecting or being involved in effecting security-based swaps on behalf of such security-based swap dealer or major security-based swap participant, the Commission, by order, shall censure, place limitations on the activities or functions of such person, or suspend for a period not exceeding 12 months, or bar such person from being associated with a security-based swap dealer or major security-based swap participant, if the Commission finds, on the record after notice and opportunity for a hearing, that such censure, placing of limitations, suspension, or bar is in the public interest and that such person—

(A) Has committed or omitted any act, or is subject to an order or finding, enumerated in subparagraph (A), (D), or (E) of paragraph (4) of section 15(b);

(B) Has been convicted of any offense specified in subparagraph (B) of such paragraph (4) within 10 years of the commencement of the proceedings under this subsection;

(C) Is enjoined from any action, conduct, or practice specified in subparagraph (C) of such paragraph (4);

(D) Is subject to an order or a final order specified in subparagraph (F) or (H), respectively, of such paragraph (4); or

(E) Has been found by a foreign financial regulatory authority to have committed or omitted any act, or violated any foreign statute or regulation, enumerated in subparagraph (G) of such paragraph (4).

(4) UNLAWFUL CONDUCT. It shall be unlawful—

(A) For any person as to whom an order under paragraph (3) is in effect, without the consent of the Commission, willfully to become, or to be, associated with a security-based swap dealer or major security-based swap participant in contravention of such order; or

(B) For any security-based swap dealer or major security-based swap participant to permit such a person, without the consent of the Commission, to become or remain a person associated with the security-based swap dealer or major security-based swap participant in contravention of such order, if such security-based swap dealer or major security-based swap participant knew, or in the exercise of reasonable care should have known, of such order.

CREDIT RISK RETENTION

Sec. 15G. (a) DEFINITIONS. In this section—

(1) The term "Federal banking agencies" means the Office of the Comptroller of the Currency, the Board of Governors of the Federal Reserve System, and the Federal Deposit Insurance Corporation;

(2) The term "insured depository institution" has the same meaning as in section 3(c) of the Federal Deposit Insurance Act (12 U.S.C. 1813(c));

(3) The term "securitizer" means—

(A) An issuer of an asset-backed security; or

(B) A person who organizes and initiates an asset-backed securities transaction by selling or transferring assets, either directly or indirectly, including through an affiliate, to the issuer; and

(4) The term "originator" means a person who—

(A) Through the extension of credit or otherwise, creates a financial asset that collateralizes an asset-backed security; and

(B) Sells an asset directly or indirectly to a securitizer.

(b) REGULATIONS REQUIRED.

(1) IN GENERAL. Not later than 270 days after the date of enactment of this section, the Federal banking agencies and the Commission shall jointly prescribe regulations to require any securitizer to retain an economic interest in a portion of the credit risk for any asset that the securitizer, through the issuance of an asset-backed security, transfers, sells, or conveys to a third party.

(2) RESIDENTIAL MORTGAGES. Not later than 270 days after the date of the enactment of this section, the Federal banking agencies, the Commission, the Secretary of Housing and Urban Development, and the Federal Housing Finance Agency, shall jointly prescribe regulations to require any securitizer to retain an economic interest in a portion of the credit risk for any residential mortgage asset that the securitizer, through the issuance of an asset-backed security, transfers, sells, or conveys to a third party.

(c) STANDARDS FOR REGULATIONS.

(1) STANDARDS. The regulations prescribed under subsection (b) shall—

(A) Prohibit a securitizer from directly or indirectly hedging or otherwise transferring the credit risk that the securitizer is required to retain with respect to an asset;

(B) Require a securitizer to retain—

(i) Not less than 5 percent of the credit risk for any asset—

(I) That is not a qualified residential mortgage that is transferred, sold, or conveyed through the issuance of an asset-backed security by the securitizer; or

(II) That is a qualified residential mortgage that is transferred, sold, or conveyed through the issuance of an asset-backed security by the securitizer, if 1 or more of the assets that collateralize the asset-backed security are not qualified residential mortgages; or

(ii) Less than 5 percent of the credit risk for an asset that is not a qualified residential mortgage that is transferred, sold, or conveyed through the issuance of an asset-backed security by the securitizer, if the originator of the asset meets the underwriting standards prescribed under paragraph (2)(B);

(C) Specify—

(i) The permissible forms of risk retention for purposes of this section;

(ii) The minimum duration of the risk retention required under this section; and

(iii) That a securitizer is not required to retain any part of the credit risk for an asset that is transferred, sold or conveyed through the issuance of an asset-backed security by the securitizer, if all of the assets that collateralize the asset-backed security are qualified residential mortgages;

(D) Apply, regardless of whether the securitizer is an insured depository institution;

(E) With respect to a commercial mortgage, specify the permissible types, forms, and amounts of risk retention that would meet the requirements of subparagraph (B), which in the determination of the Federal banking agencies and the Commission may include—

(i) Retention of a specified amount or percentage of the total credit risk of the asset;

(ii) Retention of the first-loss position by a third-party purchaser that specifically negotiates for the purchase of such first loss position, holds adequate financial resources to back losses, provides due diligence on all individual assets in the pool before the issuance of the asset-backed securities, and meets the same standards for risk retention as the Federal banking agencies and the Commission require of the securitizer;

(iii) A determination by the Federal banking agencies and the Commission that the underwriting standards and controls for the asset are adequate; and

(iv) Provision of adequate representations and warranties and related enforcement mechanisms; and

(F) Establish appropriate standards for retention of an economic interest with respect to collateralized debt obligations, securities collateralized by collateralized debt obligations, and similar instruments collateralized by other asset-backed securities; and

(G) Provide for—

(i) A total or partial exemption of any securitization, as may be appropriate in the public interest and for the protection of investors;

(ii) A total or partial exemption for the securitization of an asset issued or guaranteed by the United States, or an agency of the United States, as the Federal banking agencies and the Commission jointly determine appropriate in the public interest and for the protection of investors, except that, for purposes of this clause, the Federal National Mortgage Association and the Federal Home Loan Mortgage Corporation are not agencies of the United States;

(iii) A total or partial exemption for any asset-backed security that is a security issued or guaranteed by any State of the United States, or by any political subdivision of a State or territory, or by any public instrumentality of a State or territory that is exempt from the registration requirements of the Securities Act of 1933 by reason of section 3(a)(2) of that Act (15 U.S.C. 77c(a)(2)), or a security defined as a qualified scholarship funding bond in section 150(d)(2) of the Internal Revenue Code of 1986, as may be appropriate in the public interest and for the protection of investors; and

(iv) The allocation of risk retention obligations between a securitizer and an originator in the case of a securitizer that purchases assets from an originator, as the Federal banking agencies and the Commission jointly determine appropriate.

(2) ASSET CLASSES.

(A) Asset Classes. The regulations prescribed under subsection (b) shall establish asset classes with separate rules for securitizers of different classes of assets, including residential mortgages, commercial mortgages, commercial loans, auto loans, and any other class of assets that the Federal banking agencies and the Commission deem appropriate.

(B) Contents. For each asset class established under subparagraph (A), the regulations prescribed under subsection (b) shall include underwriting standards established by the Federal banking agencies that specify the terms, conditions, and characteristics of a loan within the asset class that indicate a low credit risk with respect to the loan.

(d) ORIGINATORS. In determining how to allocate risk retention obligations between a securitizer and an originator under subsection (c)(1)(E)(iv), the Federal banking agencies and the Commission shall—

(1) Reduce the percentage of risk retention obligations required of the securitizer by the percentage of risk retention obligations required of the originator; and

(2) Consider—

(A) Whether the assets sold to the securitizer have terms, conditions, and characteristics that reflect low credit risk;

(B) Whether the form or volume of transactions in securitization markets creates incentives for imprudent origination of the type of loan or asset to be sold to the securitizer; and

(C) The potential impact of the risk retention obligations on the access of consumers and businesses to credit on reasonable terms, which may not include the transfer of credit risk to a third party.

(e) EXEMPTIONS, EXCEPTIONS, AND ADJUSTMENTS.

(1) IN GENERAL. The Federal banking agencies and the Commission may jointly adopt or issue exemptions, exceptions, or adjustments to the rules issued under this section, including exemptions, exceptions, or adjustments for classes of institutions or assets relating to the risk retention requirement and the prohibition on hedging under subsection (c)(1).

(2) APPLICABLE STANDARDS. Any exemption, exception, or adjustment adopted or issued by the Federal banking agencies and the Commission under this paragraph shall—

(A) Help ensure high quality underwriting standards for the securitizers and originators of assets that are securitized or available for securitization; and

(B) Encourage appropriate risk management practices by the securitizers and originators of assets, improve the access of consumers and businesses to credit on reasonable terms, or otherwise be in the public interest and for the protection of investors.

(3) CERTAIN INSTITUTIONS AND PROGRAMS EXEMPT.

(A) Farm Credit System Institutions. Notwithstanding any other provision of this section, the requirements of this section shall not apply to any loan or other financial asset made, insured, guaranteed, or purchased by any institution that is subject to the supervision of the Farm Credit Administration, including the Federal Agricultural Mortgage Corporation.

(B) Other Federal Programs. This section shall not apply to any residential, multi-family, or health care facility mortgage loan asset, or securitization based directly or indirectly on such an asset, which is insured or guaranteed by the United States or an agency of the United States. For purposes of this subsection, the Federal National Mortgage Association, the Federal Home Loan Mortgage Corporation, and the Federal home loan banks shall not be considered an agency of the United States.

(4) EXEMPTION FOR QUALIFIED RESIDENTIAL MORTGAGES.

(A) In General. The Federal banking agencies, the Commission, the Secretary of Housing and Urban Development, and the Director of the Federal Housing Finance Agency shall jointly issue regulations to exempt qualified residential mortgages from the risk retention requirements of this subsection.

(B) Qualified Residential Mortgage. The Federal banking agencies, the Commission, the Secretary of Housing and Urban Development, and the Director of the Federal Housing Finance Agency shall jointly define the term "qualified residential mortgage" for purposes of this subsection, taking into consideration underwriting and product features that historical loan performance data indicate result in a lower risk of default, such as—

(i) Documentation and verification of the financial resources relied upon to qualify the mortgagor;

(ii) Standards with respect to—

(I) The residual income of the mortgagor after all monthly obligations;

(II) The ratio of the housing payments of the mortgagor to the monthly income of the mortgagor;

(III) The ratio of total monthly installment payments of the mortgagor to the income of the mortgagor;

(iii) Mitigating the potential for payment shock on adjustable rate mortgages through product features and underwriting standards;

(iv) Mortgage guarantee insurance or other types of insurance or credit enhancement obtained at the time of origination, to the extent such insurance or credit enhancement reduces the risk of default; and

(v) Prohibiting or restricting the use of balloon payments, negative amortization, prepayment penalties, interest-only payments, and other features that have been demonstrated to exhibit a higher risk of borrower default.

(C) LIMITATION ON DEFINITION. The Federal banking agencies, the Commission, the Secretary of Housing and Urban Development, and the Director of the Federal Housing

Finance Agency in defining the term "qualified residential mortgage", as required by subparagraph (B), shall define that term to be no broader than the definition "qualified mortgage" as the term is defined under section 129C (c) (2) of the Truth in Lending Act, as amended by the Consumer Financial Protection Act of 2010, and regulations adopted thereunder.

(5) CONDITION FOR QUALIFIED RESIDENTIAL MORTGAGE EXEMPTION. The regulations issued under paragraph (4) shall provide that an asset-backed security that is collateralized by tranches of other asset-backed securities shall not be exempt from the risk retention requirements of this subsection.

(6) CERTIFICATION. The Commission shall require an issuer to certify, for each issuance of an asset-backed security collateralized exclusively by qualified residential mortgages, that the issuer has evaluated the effectiveness of the internal supervisory controls of the issuer with respect to the process for ensuring that all assets that collateralize the asset-backed security are qualified residential mortgages.

(f) ENFORCEMENT. The regulations issued under this section shall be enforced by—

(1) The appropriate Federal banking agency, with respect to any securitizer that is an insured depository institution; and

(2) The Commission, with respect to any securitizer that is not an insured depository institution.

(g) AUTHORITY OF COMMISSION. The authority of the Commission under this section shall be in addition to the authority of the Commission to otherwise enforce the securities laws.

(h) AUTHORITY TO COORDINATE ON RULEMAKING. The Chairperson of the Financial Stability Oversight Council shall coordinate all joint rulemaking required under this section.

(i) EFFECTIVE DATE OF REGULATIONS. The regulations issued under this section shall become effective—

(1) With respect to securitizers and originators of asset-backed securities backed by residential mortgages, 1 year after the date on which final rules under this section are published in the Federal Register; and

(2) With respect to securitizers and originators of all other classes of asset-backed securities, 2 years after the date on which final rules under this section are published in the Federal Register.

[DIRECTORS, OFFICERS, AND PRINCIPAL STOCKHOLDERS]

Sec. 16. (a) DISCLOSURES REQUIRED.—

(1) DIRECTORS, OFFICERS, AND PRINCIPAL STOCKHOLDERS REQUIRED TO FILE.—Every person who is directly or indirectly the beneficial owner of more than 10 percent of any class of any equity security (other than an exempted security) which is registered pursuant to section 12, or who is a director or an officer of the issuer of such security, shall file the statements required by this subsection with the Commission.

(2) TIME OF FILING.—The statements required by this subsection shall be filed—

(A) at the time of the registration of such security on a national securities exchange or by the effective date of a registration statement filed pursuant to section 12(g);

(B) within 10 days after he or she becomes such beneficial owner, director, or officer;

(C) if there has been a change in such ownership, or if such person shall have purchased or sold a securitybased swap agreement involving such equity security, before the end of the second business day following the day on which the subject transaction has been executed, or at such other time as the Commission shall establish, by rule, in any case in which the Commission determines that such 2-day period is not feasible.

(3) CONTENTS OF STATEMENTS.—A statement filed—

(A) under subparagraph (A) or (B) of paragraph (2) shall contain a statement of the amount of all equity securities of such issuer of which the filing person is the beneficial owner; and

(B) under subparagraph (C) of such paragraph shall indicate ownership by the filing person at the date of filing, any such changes in such ownership, and such purchases and sales of the security-based swap agreements or security-based swaps as have occurred since the most recent such filing under such subparagraph.

(4) ELECTRONIC FILING AND AVAILABILITY.—Beginning not later than 1 year after the date of enactment of the Sarbanes-Oxley Act of 2002—

(A) a statement filed under subparagraph (C) of paragraph (2) shall be filed electronically;

(B) the Commission shall provide each such statement on a publicly accessible Internet site not later than the end of the business day following that filing; and

(C) the issuer (if the issuer maintains a corporate website) shall provide that statement on that corporate website, not later than the end of the business day following that filing.

(b) For the purpose of preventing the unfair use of information which may have been obtained by such beneficial owner, director, or officer by reason of his relationship to the issuer, any profit realized by him from any purchase and sale, or any sale and purchase, of any equity security of such issuer (other than an exempted security) or a security-based swap agreement involving any such equity security within any period of less than six months, unless such security or security-based swap agreement was acquired in good faith in connection with a debt previously contracted, shall inure to and be recoverable by the issuer, irrespective of any intention on the part of such beneficial owner, director, or officer in entering into such transaction of holding the security or security-based swap agreement purchased or of not repurchasing the security or security-based swap agreement sold for a period exceeding six months. Suit to recover such profit may be instituted at law or in equity in any court of competent jurisdiction by the issuer, or by the owner of any security of the issuer in the name and in behalf of the issuer if the issuer shall fail or refuse to bring such suit within sixty days after request or shall fail diligently to prosecute the same thereafter; but no such suit shall be brought more than two years after the date such profit was realized. This subsection shall not be construed to cover any transaction where such beneficial owner was not such both at the time of the purchase and sale, or the sale and purchase, of the security or security-based swap agreement involved or security-based swaps involved, or any transaction or transactions which the Commission by rules and regulations may exempt as not comprehended within the purpose of this subsection.

(c) It shall be unlawful for any such beneficial owner, director, or officer, directly or indirectly, to sell any equity security of such issuer (other than an exempted security), if the person selling the security or his principal (1) does not own the security sold, or (2) if owning the security, does not deliver it against such sale within twenty days thereafter, or does not within five days after such sale deposit it in the mails or other usual channels of transportation; but no person shall be deemed to have violated this subsection if he proves that notwithstanding the exercise of good faith he was unable to make such delivery or deposit within such time, or that to do so would cause undue inconvenience or expense.

(d) The provisions of subsection (b) of this section shall not apply to any purchase and sale, or sale and purchase, and the provisions of subsection (c) of this section shall not apply to any sale, of an equity security not then or theretofore held by him in an investment account, by a dealer in the ordinary course of his business and incident to the establishment or maintenance by him of a primary or secondary market (otherwise than on a national securities exchange or an exchange exempted from registration under section 5 of this title) for such security. The Commission may, by such rules and regulations as it deems necessary or appropriate in the public interest, define and prescribe terms and conditions with respect to securities held in an investment account and transactions made in the ordinary course of business and incident to the establishment or maintenance of a primary or secondary market.

(e) The provisions of this section shall not apply to foreign or domestic arbitrage transactions unless made in contravention of such rules and regulations as the Commission may adopt in order to carry out the purposes of this section.

(f) TREATMENT OF TRANSACTIONS IN SECURITY FUTURES PRODUCTS.—The provisions of this section shall apply to ownership of and transactions in security futures products.

(g) The authority of the Commission under this section with respect to security-based swap agreements shall be subject to the restrictions and limitations of section 3A(b) of this title.

ACCOUNTS AND RECORDS, REPORTS, EXAMINATIONS OF EXCHANGES, MEMBERS, AND OTHERS

Sec. 17. (a)(1) Every national securities exchange, member thereof, broker or dealer who transacts a business in securities through the medium of any such member, registered securities association, registered broker or dealer, registered municipal securities dealer, registered securities information processor, registered transfer agent, nationally recognized statistical rating organization and registered clearing agency and the Municipal Securities Rulemaking Board shall make and keep for prescribed periods such records, furnish such copies thereof, and make and disseminate such reports as the Commission, by rule, prescribes as necessary or appropriate in the public interest, for the protection of investors, or otherwise in furtherance of the purposes of this title. Any report that a nationally recognized statistical rating organization is required by Commission rules under this paragraph to make and disseminate to the Commission shall be deemed furnished to the Commission.

LIABILITY FOR MISLEADING STATEMENTS

Sec. 18. (a) Any person who shall make or cause to be made any statement in any application, report, or document filed pursuant to this title or any rule or regulation thereunder or any undertaking contained in a registration statement as provided in subsection (d) of section 15 of this title, which statement was at the time and in the light of the circumstances under which it was made false or misleading with respect to any material fact, shall be liable to any person (not knowing that such statement was false or misleading) who, in reliance upon such statement, shall have purchased or sold a security at a price which was affected by such statement, for damages caused by such reliance, unless the person sued shall prove that he acted in good faith and had no knowledge that such statement was false or misleading. A person seeking to enforce such liability may sue at law or in equity in any court of competent jurisdiction. In any such suit the court may, in its discretion, require an undertaking for the payment of the costs of such suit, and assess reasonable costs, including reasonable attorneys' fees, against either party litigant.

(b) Every person who becomes liable to make payment under this section may recover contribution as in cases of contract from any person who, if joined in the original suit, would have been liable to make the same payment.

(c) No action shall be maintained to enforce any liability created under this section unless brought within one year after the discovery of the facts constituting the cause of action and within three years after such cause of action accrued.

REGISTRATION, RESPONSIBILITIES, AND OVERSIGHT OF SELF-REGULATORY ORGANIZATIONS

Sec. 19. (a)(1) The Commission shall, upon the filing of an application for registration as a national securities exchange, registered securities association, or registered clearing agency, pursuant to section 6, 15A or 17A of this title, respectively, publish notice of the filing and afford interested persons an opportunity to submit written data, views, and arguments concerning such application. Within ninety days of the date of publication of such notice (or within such longer period as to which the applicant consents), the Commission shall—

(A) by order grant such registration, or

(B) institute proceedings to determine whether registration should be denied. Such proceedings shall include notice of the grounds for denial under consideration and opportunity for hearing and shall be concluded within one hundred eighty days of the date of publication of notice of the filing of the application for registration. At the conclusion of such proceedings the Commission, by order, shall grant or deny such registration. The Commission may extend the time for conclusion of such proceedings for up to ninety days if it finds good cause for such extension and publishes its reasons for so finding or for such longer period as to which the applicant consents.

The Commission shall grant such registration if it finds that the requirements of this title and the rules and regulations thereunder with respect to the applicant are satisfied. The Commission shall deny such registration if it does not make such finding.

(b)(1) Each self-regulatory organization shall file with the Commission, in accordance with such rules as the Commission may prescribe, copies of any proposed rule or any proposed change in, addition to, or deletion from the rules of such self-regulatory organization (hereinafter in this subsection collectively referred to as a "proposed rule change") accompanied by a concise general statement of the basis and purpose of such proposed rule change. The Commission shall, as soon as practicable after the date of the filing of any proposed rule change, publish notice thereof together with the terms of substance of the proposed rule change or a description of the subjects and issues involved. The Commission shall give interested persons an opportunity to submit written data, views, and arguments concerning such proposed rule change. No proposed rule change shall take effect unless approved by the Commission or otherwise permitted in accordance with the provisions of this subsection.

LIABILITY OF CONTROLLING PERSONS AND PERSONS WHO AID AND ABET VIOLATIONS

Sec. 20. (a) Every person who, directly or indirectly, controls any person liable under any provision of this title or of any rule or regulation thereunder shall also be liable jointly and severally with and to the same extent as such controlled person to any person to whom such controlled person is liable, (including to the Commission in any action brought under paragraph (1) or (3) of section 21(d)), unless the controlling person acted in good faith and did not directly or indirectly induce the act or acts constituting the violation or cause of action.

(b) It shall be unlawful for any person, directly or indirectly, to do any act or thing which it would be unlawful for such person to do under the provisions of this title or any rule or regulation thereunder through or by means of any other person.

(c) It shall be unlawful for any director or officer of, or any owner of any securities issued by, any issuer required to file any document, report, or information under this title or any rule or regulation thereunder without just cause to hinder, delay, or obstruct the making or filing of any such document, report, or information.

(d) Wherever communicating, or purchasing or selling a security while in possession of, material nonpublic information would violate, or result in liability to any purchaser or seller of the security under any provisions of this title, or any rule or regulation thereunder, such conduct in connection with a purchase or sale of a put, call, straddle, option, privilege or security-based swap agreement with respect to such security or with respect to a group or index of securities including such security, shall also violate and result in comparable liability to any purchaser or seller of that security under such provision, rule, or regulation.

(e) PROSECUTION OF PERSONS WHO AID AND ABET VIOLATIONS.—For purposes of any action brought by the Commission under paragraph (1) or (3) of section 21(d), any person that knowingly or recklessly provides substantial assistance to another person in violation of a provision of this title, or of any rule or regulation issued under this title, shall be deemed to be in violation of such provision to the same extent as the person to whom such assistance is provided.

(f) The authority of the Commission under this section with respect to security-based swap agreements shall be subject to the restrictions and limitations of section 3A(b) of this title.

LIABILITY TO CONTEMPORANEOUS TRADERS FOR INSIDER TRADING

Sec. 20A. (a) PRIVATE RIGHTS OF ACTION BASED ON CONTEMPORANEOUS TRADING.—Any person who violates any provision of this title or the rules or regulations thereunder by purchasing or selling a security while in possession of material, nonpublic information shall be liable in an action in any court of competent jurisdiction to any person who, contemporaneously with the purchase or sale of securities that is the subject of such violation, has purchased (where such violation is based on a sale of securities) or sold (where such violation is abased on a purchase of securities) securities of the same class.

(b) LIMITATIONS ON LIABILITY.—

(1) CONTEMPORANEOUS TRADING ACTIONS LIMITED TO PROFIT GAINED OR LOSS AVOIDED.— The total amount of damages imposed under subsection (a) shall not exceed the profit gained or loss avoided in the transaction or transactions that are the subject of the violation.

(2) OFFSETTING DISGORGEMENTS AGAINST LIABILITY.—The total amount of damages imposed against any person under subsection (a) shall be diminished by the amounts, if any, that such person may be required to disgorge, pursuant to a court order obtained at the instance of the Commission, in a proceeding brought under section 21(d) of this title relating to the same transaction or transactions.

(3) CONTROLLING PERSON LIABILITY.—No person shall be liable under this section solely by reason of employing another person who is liable under this section, but the liability of a controlling person under this section shall be subject to section 20(a) of this title.

(4) STATUTE OF LIMITATIONS.—No action may be brought under this section more than 5 years after the date of the last transaction that is the subject of the violation.

(c) JOINT AND SEVERAL LIABILITY FOR COMMUNICATING.—Any person who violates any provision of this title or the rules or regulations thereunder by communicating material, non-public information shall be jointly and severally liable under subsection (a) with, and to the same extent as, any person or persons liable under subsection (a) to whom the communication was directed.

(d) AUTHORITY NOT TO RESTRICT OTHER EXPRESS OR IMPLIED RIGHTS OF ACTION.—Nothing in this section shall be construed to limit or condition the right of any person to bring an action to enforce a requirement of this title or the availability of any cause of action implied from a provision of this title.

(e) PROVISIONS NOT TO AFFECT PUBLIC PROSECUTIONS.—This section shall not be construed to bar or limit in any manner any action by the Commission or the Attorney General under any other provision of this title, nor shall it bar or limit in any manner any action to recover penalties, or to seek any other order regarding penalties.

INVESTIGATIONS; INJUNCTIONS AND PROSECUTION OF OFFENSES

Sec. 21. (a)(1) The Commission may, in its discretion, make such investigations as it deems necessary to determine whether any person has violated, is violating, or is about to violate any provision of this title, the rules or regulations thereunder, the rules of a national securities exchange or registered securities association of which such person is a member or a person associated, or, as to any act or practice, or omission to act, while associated with a member, formerly associated with a member, the rules of a registered clearing agency in which such person is a participant, or, as to any act or practice, or omission to act, while a participant, was a participant the rules of the Public Company Accounting Oversight Board, of which such person is a registered public accounting firm , a person associated with such a firm, or, as to any act, practice, or omission to act, while associated with such firm, a person formerly associated with such a firm, or the rules of the Municipal Securities Rulemaking Board, and may require or permit any person to file with it a statement in writing, under oath or otherwise as the Commission shall determine, as to all the facts and circumstances concerning the matter to be investigated. The Commission is authorized, in its discretion, to publish information concerning any such violations, and to investigate any facts, conditions, practices, or matters which it may deem necessary or proper to aid in the enforcement of such provisions, in the prescribing of rules and regulations under this title, or in securing information to serve as a basis for recommending further legislation concerning the matters to which this title relates.

(2) On request from a foreign securities authority, the Commission may provide assistance in accordance with this paragraph if the requesting authority states that the requesting authority is conducting an investigation which it deems necessary to determine whether

any person has violated, is violating, or is about to violate any laws or rules relating to securities matters that the requesting authority administers or enforces. The Commission may, in its discretion, conduct such investigation as the Commission deems necessary to collect information and evidence pertinent to the request for assistance. Such assistance may be provided wihtout regard to whether the facts stated in the request would also constitute a violation of the laws of the United States. In deciding whether to provide such assistance, the Commission shall consider whether (A) the requesting authority has agreed to provide reciprocal assistance in securities matters to the Commission; and (B) compliance with the request would prejudice the public interest of the United States.

(b) For the purpose of any such investigation, or any other proceeding under this title, any member of the Commission or any officer designated by it is empowered to administer oaths and affirmations, subpena witnesses, compel their attendance, take evidence, and require the production of any books, papers, correspondence, memoranda, or other records which the Commission deems relevant or material to the inquiry. Such attendance of witnesses and the production of any such records may be required from any place in the United States or any State at any designated place of hearing.

(c) In case of contumacy by, or refusal to obey a subpena issued to, any person, the Commission may invoke the aid of any court of the United States within the jurisdiction of which such investigation or proceeding is carried on, or where such person resides or carries on business, in requiring the attendance and testimony of witnesses and the production of books, papers, correspondence, memoranda, and other records. And such court may issue an order requiring such person to appear before the Commission or member or officer designated by the Commission, there to produce records, if so ordered, or to give testimony touching the matter under investigation or in question; and any failure to obey such order of the court may be punished by such court as a contempt thereof. All process in any such case may be served in the judicial district whereof such person is an inhabitant or wherever he may be found. Any person who shall, without just cause, fail or refuse to attend and testify or to answer any lawful inquiry or to produce books, papers, correspondence, memoranda, and other records, if in his power so to do, in obedience to the subpena of the Commission, shall be guilty of a misdemeanor and, upon conviction, shall be subject to a fine of not more than $1,000 or to imprisonment for a term of not more than one year, or both.

(d) (1) Whenever it shall appear to the Commission that any person is engaged or is about to engage in any acts or practices constituting a violation of any provision of this title, the rules or regulations thereunder, the rules of a national securities exchange or registered securities association of which such person is a member or a person associated with a member, the rules of a registered clearing agency in which such person is a participant, the rules of the Public Company Accounting Oversight Board, of which such person is a registered public accounting firm or a person associated with such a firm, or the rules of the Municipal Securities Rulemaking Board, it may in its discretion bring an action in the proper district court of the United States, the United States District Court for the District of Columbia, or the United States courts of any territory or other place subject to the jurisdiction of the United States, to enjoin such acts or practices, and upon a proper showing a permanent or temporary injunction or restraining order shall be granted without bond. The Commission may transmit such evidence as may be available concerning such acts or practices as may constitute a violation of any provision of this title or the rules or regulations thereunder to the Attorney General, who may, in his discretion, institute the necessary criminal proceedings under this title.

(2) AUTHORITY OF A COURT TO PROHIBIT PERSONS FROM SERVING AS OFFICERS AND DIRECTORS.—In any proceeding under paragraph (1) of this subsection, the court may prohibit, conditionally or unconditionally, and permanently or for such period of time as it shall determine, any person who violated section 10(b) of this title or the rules or regulations thereunder from acting as an officer or director of any issuer that has a class of securities registered pursuant to section 12 of this title or that is required to file reports pursuant to section 15(d) of this title if the person's conduct demonstrates unfitness to serve as an officer or director of any such issuer.

(3) MONEY PENALTIES IN CIVIL ACTIONS.—

(A) AUTHORITY OF COMMISSION.—Whenever it shall appear to the Commission that any person has violated any provision of this title, the rules or regulations thereunder, or a cease-and-desist order entered by the Commission pursuant to section 21C of this title, other than by committing a violation subject to a penalty pursuant to section 21A, the Commission may bring an action in a United States district court to seek, and the court shall have jurisdiction to impose, upon a proper showing, a civil penalty to be paid by the person who committed such violation.

(B) AMOUNT OF PENALTY.—

(i) FIRST TIER.—The amount of the penalty shall be determined by the court in light of the facts and circumstances. For each violation, the amount of the penalty shall not exceed the greater of (I) $5,000 for a natural person or $50,000 for any other person, or (II) the gross amount of pecuniary gain to such defendant as a result of the violation.

(ii) SECOND TIER.—Notwithstanding clause (i), the amount of penalty for each such violation shall not exceed the greater of (I) $50,000 for a natural person or $250,000 for any other person, or (II) the gross amount of pecuniary gain to such defendant as a result of the violation, if the violation described in subparagraph (A) involved fraud, deceit, manipulation, or deliberate or reckless disregard of a regulatory requirement.

(iii) THIRD TIER.—Notwithstanding clauses (i) and (ii), the amount of penalty for each such violation shall not exceed the greater of (I) $100,000 for a natural person or $500,000 for any other person, or (II) the gross amount of pecuniary gain to such defendant as a result of the violation, if—

(aa) the violation described in subparagraph (A) involved fraud, deceit, manipulation, or deliberate or reckless disregard of a regulatory requirement; and

(bb) such violation directly or indirectly resulted in substantial losses or created a significant risk of substantial losses to other persons.

(C) PROCEDURES FOR COLLECTION.—

(i) PAYMENT OF PENALTY TO TREASURY.—A penalty imposed under this section shall be payable into the Treasury of the United States, except as otherwise provided in section 308 of the Sarbanes-Oxley Act of 2002 and Section 21F of this title.

(ii) COLLECTION OF PENALTIES.—If a person upon whom such a penalty is imposed shall fail to pay such penalty within the time prescribed in the court's order, the Commission may refer the matter to the Attorney General who shall recover such penalty by action in the appropriate United States district court.

(iii) REMEDY NOT EXCLUSIVE.—The actions authorized by this paragraph may be brought in addition to any other action that the Commission or the Attorney General is entitled to bring.

(iv) JURISDICTION AND VENUE.—For purposes of section 27 of this title, action under this paragraph shall be actions to enforce a liability or a duty created by this title.

(D) SPECIAL PROVISIONS RELATING TO A VIOLATION OF A CEASE-AND-DESIST ORDER.—In an action to enforce a cease-and-desist order entered by the Commission pursuant to section 21C, each separate violation of such order shall be a separate offense, except that in the case of a violation through a continuing failure to comply with the order, each day of the failure to comply shall be deemed a separate offense.

(4) PROHIBITION OF ATTORNEYS' FEES PAID FROM COMMISSION DISGORGEMENT FUNDS.—Except as otherwise ordered by the court upon motion by the Commission, or, in the case of an administrative action, as otherwise ordered by the Commission, funds disgorged as the result of an action brought by the Commission in Federal court, or as a result of any Commission administrative action, shall not be distributed as payment for attorneys' fees or expenses incurred by private parties seeking distribution of the disgorged funds.

(5) EQUITABLE RELIEF.—In any action or proceeding brought or instituted by the Commission under any provision of the securities laws, the Commission may seek, and any

Federal court may grant, any equitable relief that may be appropriate or necessary for the benefit of investors.

(6) AUTHORITY OF A COURT TO PROHIBIT PERSONS FROM PARTICIPATING IN AN OFFERING OF PENNY STOCK.—

(A) IN GENERAL.—In any proceeding under paragraph (1) against any person participating in, or, at the time of the alleged misconduct who was participating in, an offering of penny stock, the court may prohibit that person from participating in an offering of penny stock, conditionally or unconditionally, and permanently or for such period of time as the court shall determine.

(B) DEFINITION.—For purposes of this paragraph, the term "person participating in an offering of penny stock" includes any person engaging in activities with a broker, dealer, or issuer for purposes of issuing, trading, or inducing or attempting to induce the purchase or sale of, any penny stock. The Commission may, by rule or regulation, define such term to include other activities, and may, by rule, regulation, or order, exempt any person or class of persons, in whole or in part, conditionally or unconditionally, from inclusion in such term.

(e) Upon application of the Commission the district courts of the United States and the United States courts of any territory or other place subject to the jurisdiction of the United States shall also have jurisdiction to issue writs of mandamus, injunctions, and orders commanding (1) any person to comply with the provisions of this title, the rules, regulations, and orders thereunder, the rules of a national securities exchange or registered securities association of which such person is a member or person associated with a member, the rules of a registered clearing agency in which such person is a participant, the rules of the Public Company Accounting Oversight Board, of which such person is a registered public accounting firm or a person associated with such a firm, and the rules of the Municipal Securities Rulemaking Board, or any undertaking contained in a registration statement as provided in subsection (d) of section 15 of this title, (2) any national securities exchange or registered securities association to enforce compliance by its members and persons associated with its members with the provisions of this title, the rules, regulations, and orders thereunder, and the rules of such exchange or association, or (3) any registered clearing agency to enforce compliance by its participants with the provisions of the rules of such clearing agency.

(f) Notwithstanding any other provision of this title, the Commission shall not bring any action pursuant to subsection (d) or (e) of this section against any person for violation of, or to command compliance with, the rules of a self-regulatory organization or the Public Company Accounting Oversight Board unless it appears to the Commission that (1) such self-regulatory organization or the Public Company Accounting Oversight Board is unable or unwilling to take appropriate action against such person in the public interest and for the protection of investors, or (2) such action is otherwise necessary or appropriate in the public interest or for the protection of investors.

(g) Notwithstanding the provisions of section 1407(a) of title 28, United States Code, or any other provision of law, no action for equitable relief instituted by the Commission pursuant to the securities laws shall be consolidated or coordinated with other actions not brought by the Commission, even though such other actions may involve common questions of fact, unless such consolidation is consented to by the Commission.

(h)(1) The Right to Financial Privacy Act of 1978 shall apply with respect to the Commission, except as otherwise provided in this subsection.

(2) Notwithstanding section 1105 or 1107 of the Right to Financial Privacy Act of 1978, the Commission may have access to and obtain copies of, or the information contained in financial records of a customer from a financial institution without prior notice to the customer upon an ex parte showing to an appropriate United States district court that the Commission seeks such financial records pursuant to a subpoena issued in conformity with the requirements of section 19(b) of the Securities Act of 1933, section 21(b) of the Securities Exchange Act of 1934, section 42(b) of the Investment Company Act of 1940, or section 209(b) of the Investment Advisers Act of 1940, and that the Commission has reason to believe that—

(A) delay in obtaining access to such financial records, or the required notice, will result in—

(i) flight from prosecution;

(ii) destruction of or tampering with evidence;

(iii) transfer of assets or records outside the territorial limits of the United States;

(iv) improper conversion of investor assets; or

(v) impeding the ability of the Commission to identify or trace the source or disposition of funds involved in any securities transaction;

(B) such financial records are necessary to identify or trace the record or beneficial ownership interest in any security;

(C) the acts, practices or course of conduct under investigation involve—

(i) the dissemination of materially false or misleading informatioin concerning any security, issuer, or market, or the failure to make disclosures required under the securities law, which remain uncorrected; or

(ii) a financial loss to investors or other persons protected under the securities laws which remains substantially uncompensated; or

(D) the acts, practices or course of conduct under investigation—

(i) involve significant financial speculation in securities; or

(ii) endanger the stability of any financial or investment intermediary.

CIVIL PENALTIES FOR INSIDER TRADING

Sec. 21A. (a) AUTHORITY TO IMPOSE CIVIL PENALTIES.—

(1) JUDICIAL ACTIONS BY COMMISSION AUTHORIZED.—Whenever it shall appear to the Commission that any person has violated any provision of this title or the rules or regulations thereunder by purchasing or selling a security or security-based swap agreement while in possession of material, nonpublic information in, or has violated any such provision by communicating such information in connection with, a transaction on or through the facilities of a national securities exchange or from or through a broker or dealer, and which is not part of a public offering by an issuer of securities other than standardized options or security futures products, the Commission—

(A) may bring an action in a United States district court to seek, and the court shall have jurisdiction to impose, a civil penalty to be paid by the person who committed such violation; and

(B) may, subject to subsection (b)(1), bring an action in a United States district court to seek, and the court shall have jurisdiction to impose, a civil penalty to be paid by a person who, at the time of the violation, directly or indirectly controlled the person who committed such violation.

(2) AMOUNT OF PENALTY FOR PERSON WHO COMMITTED VIOLATION.—The amount of the penalty which may be imposed on the person who committed such violation shall be determined by the court in light of the facts and circumstances, but shall not exceed three times the profit gained or loss avoided as a result of such unlawful purchase, sale, or communication.

(3) AMOUNT OF PENALTY FOR CONTROLLING PERSON.—The amount of the penalty which may be imposed on any person who, at the time of the violation, directly or indirectly controlled the person who committed such violation, shall be determined by the court in light of the facts and circumstances, but shall not exceed the greater of $1,000,000, or three times the amount of the profit gained or loss avoided as a result of such controlled person's violation. If such controlled person's violation was a violation by communication, the profit gained or loss avoided as a result of the violation shall, for purposes of this paragraph only, be deemed to be limited to the profit gained or loss avoided by the person or persons to whom the controlled person directed such communication.

(b) LIMITATIONS ON LIABILITY.—

(1) LIABILITY OF CONTROLLING PERSONS.—No controlling person shall be subject to a penalty under subsection (a)(1)(B) unless the Commission establishes that—

(A) such controlling person knew or recklessly disregarded the fact that such controlled person was likely to engage in the act or acts constituting the violation and failed to take appropriate steps to prevent such act or acts before they occurred; or

(B) such controlling person knowingly or recklessly failed to establish, maintain, or enforce any policy or procedure required under section 15(f) of this title or section 204A of the Investment Advisers Act of 1940 and such failure substantially contributed to or permitted the occurrence of the act or acts constituting the violation.

(2) ADDITIONAL RESTRICTIONS ON LIABILITY.—No person shall be subject to a penalty under subsection (a) solely by reason of employing another person who is subject to a penalty under such subsection, unless such employing person is liable as a controlling person under paragraph (1) of this subsection. Section 20(a) of this title shall not apply to actions under subsection (a) of this section.

(c) AUTHORITY OF COMMISSION.—The Commissioner, by such rules, regulations, and orders as it considers necessary or appropriate in the public interest or for the protection of investors, may exempt, in whole or in part, either unconditionally or upon specific terms and conditions, any person or transaction or class of persons or transactions from this section.

(d) PROCEDURES FOR COLLECTION.—

(1) PAYMENT OF PENALTY TO TREASURY.—A penalty imposed under this section shall (subject to subsection (e)) be payable into the Treasury of the United States, except as otherwise provided in section 308 of the Sarbanes-Oxley Act of 2002 and Section 21F of this title.

(2) COLLECTION OF PENALTIES.—If a person upon whom such a penalty is imposed shall fail to pay such penalty within the time prescribed in the court's order, the Commission may refer the matter to the Attorney General who shall recover such penalty by action in the appropriate United States district court.

(3) REMEDY NOT EXCLUSIVE.—The actions authorized by this section may be brought in addition to any other actions that the Commission or the Attorney General are entitled to bring.

(4) JURISDICTION AND VENUE.—For purposes of section 27 of this title, actions under this section shall be actions to enforce a liability or a duty created by this title.

(5) STATUTE OF LIMITATIONS.—No action may be brought under this section more than 5 years after the date of the purchase or sale. This section shall not be construed to bar or limit in any manner any action by the Commission or the Attorney General under any other provision of this title, nor shall it bar or limit in any manner any action to recover penalties, or to seek any other order regarding penalties, imposed in an action commenced within 5 years of such transaction.

(e) DEFINITION.—For purposes of this section, "profit gained" or "loss avoided" is the difference between the purchase or sale price of the security and the value of that security as measured by the trading price of the security a reasonable period after public dissemination of the nonpublic information.

(f) The authority of the Commission under this section with respect to security-based swap agreements shall be subject to the restrictions and limitations of section 3A(b) of this title.

(g) DUTY OF MEMBERS AND EMPLOYEES OF CONGRESS.

(1) IN GENERAL. Subject to the rule of construction under Section 10 of the STOCK Act and solely for purposes of the insider trading prohibitions arising under this Act, including Section 10(b) and Rule 10b-5 there under, each Member of Congress or employee of Congress owes a duty arising from a relationship of trust and confidence to the Congress, the United States Government, and the citizens of the United States with respect to material, nonpublic information derived from such person's position as a Member of Congress or employee of Congress or gained from the performance of such person's official responsibilities.

(2) DEFINITIONS. In this subsection—

(A) The term "Member of Congress" means a member of the Senate or House of Representatives, a Delegate to the House of Representatives, and the Resident Commissioner from Puerto Rico; and

(B) The term "employee of Congress" means—

(i) Any individual (other than a Member of Congress), whose compensation is disbursed by the Secretary of the Senate or the Chief Administrative Officer of the House of Representatives; and

(ii) Any other officer or employee of the legislative branch (as defined in Section 109(11) of the Ethics in Government Act of 1978 (5 U.S.C. App. 109(11))).

(3) RULE OF CONSTRUCTION. Nothing in this subsection shall be construed to impair or limit the construction of the existing antifraud provisions of the securities laws or the authority of the Commission under those provisions.

(h) DUTY OF OTHER FEDERAL OFFICIALS.

(1) IN GENERAL. Subject to the rule of construction under section 10 of the STOCK Act and solely for purposes of the insider trading prohibitions arising under this Act, including section 10(b), and Rule 10b-5 there under, each executive branch employee, each judicial officer, and each judicial employee owes a duty arising from a relationship of trust and confidence to the United States Government and the citizens of the United States with respect to material, nonpublic information derived from such person's position as an executive branch employee, judicial officer, or judicial employee or gained from the performance of such person's official responsibilities.

(2) DEFINITIONS. In this subsection—

(A) The term "executive branch employee"—

(i) Has the meaning given the term "employee" under section 2105 of title 5, United States Code;

(ii) Includes—

(I) The President;

(II) The Vice President; and

(III) An employee of the United States Postal Service or the Postal Regulatory Commission;

(B) The term "judicial employee" has the meaning given that term in section 109(8) of the Ethics in Government Act of 1978 (5 U.S.C. App. 109(8)); and (C) The term" judicial officer" has the meaning given that term under section 109(10) of the Ethics in Government Act of 1978 (5 U.S.C. App. 109(10)).

(3) RULE OF CONSTRUCTION. Nothing in this subsection shall be construed to impair or limit the construction of the existing antifraud provisions of the securities laws or the authority of the Commission under those provisions.

(i) PARTICIPATION IN INITIAL PUBLIC OFFERINGS. An individual described in section 101(f) of the Ethics in Government Act of 1978 may not purchase securities that are the subject of an initial public offering (within the meaning given such term in section 12(f)(1)(G)(i)) in any manner other than is available to members of the public generally.

CIVIL REMEDIES IN ADMINISTRATIVE PROCEEDINGS

Sec. 21B. (a) COMMISSION AUTHORITY TO ASSESS MONEY PENALTIES.—

(1) IN GENERAL. In any proceeding instituted pursuant to sections 15(b)(4), 15(b)(6), 15D, 15B, 15C, 15E, or 17A of this title against any person, the Commission or the appropriate regulatory agency may impose a civil penalty if it finds, on the record after notice and opportunity for hearing, that such penalty is in the public interest and that such person:

(A) has willfully violated any provision of the Securities Act of 1933, the Investment Company Act of 1940, the Investment Advisers Act of 1940, or this title, or the rules or regulations thereunder, or the rules of the Municipal Securities Rulemaking Board;

(B) has willfully aided, abetted, counseled, commanded, induced, or procured such a violation by any other person;

(C) has willfully made or caused to be made in any application for registration or report required to be filed with the Commission or with any other appropriate regulatory agency under this title, or in any proceeding before the Commission with respect to registration, any statement which was, at the time and in the light of the circumstances under which it was made, false or misleading with respect to any material fact, or has omitted to state in any such application or report any material fact which is required to be stated therein; or

(D) has failed reasonably to supervise, within the meaning of section 15(b)(4)(E) of this title, with a view to preventing violations of the provisions of such statutes, rules and regulations, another person who commits such a violation, if such other person is subject to his supervision; and that such penalty is in the public interest.

(2) CEASE-AND-DESIST PROCEEDINGS. In any proceeding instituted under section 21C against any person, the Commission may impose a civil penalty, if the Commission finds, on the record after notice and opportunity for hearing, that such person—

(A) Is violating or has violated any provision of this title, or any rule or regulation issued under this title; or

(B) Is or was a cause of the violation of any provision of this title, or any rule or regulation issued under this title.

(b) MAXIMUM AMOUNT OF PENALTY.—

(1) FIRST TIER.—The maximum amount of penalty for each act or omission described in subsection (a) shall be $5,000 for a natural person or $50,000 for any other person.

(2) SECOND TIER.—Notwithstanding paragraph (1), the maximum amount of penalty for each such act or omission shall be $50,000 for a natural person or $250,000 for any other person if the act or omission described in subsection (a) involved fraud, deceit, manipulation, or deliberate or reckless disregard of a regulatory requirement.

(3) THIRD TIER.—Notwithstanding paragraphs (1) and (2), the maximum amount of penalty for each such act or omission shall be $100,000 for a natural person or $500,000 for any other person if—

(A) The act or omission described in subsection (a) involved fraud, deceit, manipulation, or deliberate or reckless disregard of a regulatory requirement; and

(B) such act or omission directly or indirectly resulted in substantial losses or created a significant risk of substantial losses to other persons or resulted in substantial pecuniary gain to the person who committed the act or omission.

(c) DETERMINATION OF PUBLIC INTEREST.—In considering under this section whether a penalty is in the public interest, the Commission or the appropriate regulatory agency may consider—

(1) whether the act or omission for which such penalty is assessed involved fraud, deceit, manipulation, or deliberate or reckless disregard of a regulatory requirement;

(2) the harm to other persons resulting either directly or indirectly from such act or omission;

(3) the extent to which any person was unjustly enriched, taking into account any restitution made to persons injured by such behavior;

(4) whether such person previously has been found by the Commission, another appropriate regulatory agency, or a self-regulatory organization to have violated the Federal securities laws, State securities laws, or the rules of a self-regulatory organization, has been enjoined by a court of competent jurisdiction from violations of such laws or rules, or has been convicted by a court of competent jurisdiction of violations of such laws or of any felony or misdemeanor described in section 15(b)(4)(B) of this title;

(5) the need to deter such person and other persons from committing such acts or omissions; and

(6) such other matters as justice may require.

(d) EVIDENCE CONCERNING ABILITY TO PAY.—In any proceeding in which the Commission or the appropriate regulatory agency may impose a penalty under this section, a respondent may present evidence of the respondent's ability to pay such penalty. The Commission or the appropriate regulatory agency may, in its discretion, consider such evidence in determining whether such penalty is in the public interest. Such evidence may relate to the extent of such person's ability to continue in business and the collectability of a penalty, taking into account any other claims of the United States or third parties upon such person's assets and the amount of such person's assets.

(e) AUTHORITY TO ENTER AN ORDER REQUIRING AN ACCOUNTING AND DISGORGEMENT.—In any proceeding in which the Commission or the appropriate regulatory agency may impose a penalty under this section, the Commission or the appropriate regulatory agency may enter an order requiring accounting and disgorgement, including reasonable interest. The Commission is authorized to adopt rules, regulations, and orders concerning payments to investors, rates of interest, periods of accrual, and such other matters as it deems appropriate to implement this subsection.

(f) SECURITY-BASED SWAPS.

(1) CLEARING AGENCY. Any clearing agency that knowingly or recklessly evades or participates in or facilitates an evasion of the requirements of section 3C shall be liable for a civil-money penalty in twice the amount otherwise available for a violation of section 3C.

(2) SECURITY-BASED SWAP DEALER OR MAJOR SECURITY-BASED SWAP PARTICIPANT. Any security-based swap dealer or major security-based swap participant that knowingly or recklessly evades or participates in or facilitates an evasion of the requirements of section 3C shall be liable for a civil money penalty in twice the amount otherwise available for a violation of section 3C.

CEASE-AND-DESIST PROCEEDINGS

Sec. 21C. (a) AUTHORITY OF THE COMMISSION.—If the Commission finds, after notice and opportunity for hearing, that any person is violating, has violated, or is about to violate any provision of this title, or any rule or regulation thereunder, the Commission may publish its findings and enter an order requiring such person, and any other person that is, was, or would be a cause of the violation, due to an act or omission the person knew or should have known would contribute to such violation, to cease and desist from committing or causing such violation and any future violation of the same provision, rule, or regulation. Such order may, in addition to requiring a person to cease and desist from committing or causing a violation, require such person to comply, or to take steps to effect compliance, with such provision, rule, or regulation, upon such terms and conditions and within such time as the Commission may specify in such order. Any such order may, as the Commission deems appropriate, require future compliance or steps to effect future compliance, either permanently or for such period of time as the Commission may specify, with such provision, rule, or regulation with respect to any security, any issuer, or any other person.

(b) HEARING.—The notice instituting proceedings pursuant to subsection (a) shall fix a hearing date not earlier than 30 days nor later than 60 days after service of the notice unless an earlier or a later date is set by the Commission with the consent of any respondent so served.

(c) TEMPORARY ORDER.—

(1) IN GENERAL.—Whenever the Commission determines that the alleged violation or threatened violation specified in the notice instituting proceedings pursuant to subsection (a), or the continuation thereof, is likely to result in significant dissipation or conversion of assets, significant harm to investors, or substantial harm to the public interest, including, but not limited to, losses to the Securities Investor Protection Corporation, prior to the

completion of the proceedings, the Commission may enter a temporary order requiring the respondent to cease and desist from the violation or threatened violation and to take such action to prevent the violation or threatened violation and to prevent dissipation or conversion of assets, significant harm to investors, or substantial harm to the public interest as the Commission deems appropriate pending completion of such proceedings. Such an order shall be entered only after notice and opportunity for a hearing, unless the Commission determines that notice and hearing prior to entry would be impracticable or contrary to the public interest. A temporary order shall become effective upon service upon the respondent and, unless set aside, limited, or suspended by the Commission or a court of competent jurisdiction, shall remain effective and enforceable pending the completion of the proceedings.

(2) APPLICABILITY.—Paragraph (1) shall apply only to a respondent that acts, or, at the time of the alleged misconduct acted, as a broker, dealer, investment adviser, investment company, municipal securities dealer, government securities broker, government securities dealer, registered public accounting firm (as defined in section 2 of the Sarbanes-Oxley Act of 2002), or transfer agent, or is, or was at the time of the alleged misconduct, an associated person of, or a person seeking to become associated with, any of the foregoing.

(3) TEMPORARY FREEZE.—

(A) IN GENERAL.—

(i) ISSUANCE OF TEMPORARY ORDER.—Whenever, during the course of a lawful investigation involving possible violations of the Federal securities laws by an issuer of publicly traded securities or any of its directors, officers, partners, controlling persons, agents, or employees, it shall appear to the Commission that it is likely that the issuer will make extraordinary payments (whether compensation or otherwise) to any of the foregoing persons, the Commission may petition a Federal district court for a temporary order requiring the issuer to escrow, subject to court supervision, those payments in an interest-bearing account for 45 days.

(ii) STANDARD.—A temporary order shall be entered under clause (i), only after notice and opportunity for a hearing, unless the court determines that notice and hearing prior to entry of the order would be impracticable or contrary to the public interest.

(iii) EFFECTIVE PERIOD.—A temporary order issued under clause (i) shall—

(I) become effective immediately;

(II) be served upon the parties subject to it; and

(III) unless set aside, limited or suspended by a court of competent jurisdiction, shall remain effective and enforceable for 45 days.

(iv) EXTENSIONS AUTHORIZED.—The effective period of an order under this subparagraph may be extended by the court upon good cause shown for not longer than 45 additional days, provided that the combined period of the order shall not exceed 90 days.

(B) PROCESS ON DETERMINATION OF VIOLATIONS.—

(i) VIOLATIONS CHARGED.—If the issuer or other person described in subparagraph (A) is charged with any violation of the Federal securities laws before the expiration of the effective period of a temporary order under subparagraph (A) (including any applicable extension period), the order shall remain in effect, subject to court approval, until the conclusion of any legal proceedings related thereto, and the affected issuer or other person, shall have the right to petition the court for review of the order.

(ii) VIOLATIONS NOT CHARGED.—If the issuer or other person described in subparagraph (A) is not charged with any violation of the Federal securities laws before the expiration of the effective period of a temporary order under subparagraph (A) (including any applicable extension period), the escrow shall terminate at the expiration of the 45-day effective period (or the expiration of any extension period, as applicable), and the disputed payments (with accrued interest) shall be returned to the issuer or other affected person.

(d) REVIEW OF TEMPORARY ORDERS.—

(1) COMMISSION REVIEW.—At any time after the respondent has been served with a temporary cease-and-desist order pursuant to subsection (c), the respondent may apply to the Commission to have the order set aside, limited, or suspended. If the respondent has been served with a temporary cease-and-desist order entered without a prior Commission hearing, the respondent may, within 10 days after the date on which the order was served, request a hearing on such application and the Commission shall hold a hearing and render a decision on such application at the earliest possible time.

(2) JUDICIAL REVIEW.—Within—

(A) 10 days ater the date the respondent was served with a temporary cease-and-desist order entered with a prior Commission hearing, or

(B) 10 days after the Commission renders a decision on an application and hearing under paragraph (1), with respect to any temporary cease-and-desist order entered without a prior Commission hearing, the respondent may apply to the United States district court for the district in which the respondent resides or has its principal place of business, or for the District of Columbia, for an order setting aside, limiting, or suspending the effectiveness or enforcement of the order, and the court shall have jurisdiction to enter such an order. A respondent served with a temporary cease-and-desist order entered without a prior Commission hearing may not apply to the court except after hearing and decision by the Commission on the respondent's application under paragraph (1) of this subsection.

(3) NO AUTOMATIC STAY OF TEMPORARY ORDER.—The commencement of proceedings under paragraph (2) of this subsection shall not, unless specifically ordered by the court, operate as a stay of the Commission's order.

(4) EXCLUSIVE REVIEW.—Section 25 of this title shall not apply to a temporary order entered pursuant to this section.

(e) AUTHORITY TO ENTER AN ORDER REQUIRING AN ACCOUNTING AND DISGORGEMENT.—In any cease-and-desist proceeding under subsection (a), the Commission may enter an order requiring accounting and disgorgement, including reasonable interest. The Commission is authorized to adopt rules, regulations, and orders concerning payments to investors, rates of interest, periods of accrual, and such other matters as it deems appropriate to implement this subsection.

(f) AUTHORITY OF THE COMMISSION TO PROHIBIT PERSONS FROM SERVING AS OFFICERS OR DIRECTORS.—In any cease-and-desist proceeding under subsection (a), the Commission may issue an order to prohibit, conditionally or unconditionally, and permanently or for such period of time as it shall determine, any person who has violated section 10(b) or the rules or regulations thereunder, from acting as an officer or director of any issuer that has a class of securities registered pursuant to section 12, or that is required to file reports pursuant to section 15(d), if the conduct of that person demonstrates unfitness to serve as an officer or director of any such issuer.

PRIVATE SECURITIES LITIGATION

Sec. 21D. (a) PRIVATE CLASS ACTIONS.—

(1) IN GENERAL.—The provisions of this subsection shall apply in each private action arising under this title that is brought as a plaintiff class action pursuant to the Federal Rules of Civil Procedure.

(2) CERTIFICATION FILED WITH COMPLAINT.—

(A) IN GENERAL.—Each plaintiff seeking to serve as a representative party on behalf of a class shall provide a sworn certification, which shall be personally signed by such plaintiff and filed with the complaint, that—

(i) states that the plaintiff has reviewed the complaint and authorized its filing;

(ii) states that the plaintiff did not purchase the security that is the subject of the complaint at the direction of plaintiff's counsel or in order to participate in any private action arising under this title;

(iii) states that the plaintiff is willing to serve as a representative party on behalf of a class, including providing testimony at deposition and trial, if necessary;

(iv) sets forth all of the transactions of the plaintiff in the security that is the subject of the complaint during the class period specified in the complaint;

(v) identifies any other action under this title, filed during the 3-year period preceding the date on which the certification is signed by the plaintiff, in which the plaintiff has sought to serve as a representative party on behalf of a class; and

(vi) states that the plaintiff will not accept any payment for serving as a representative party on behalf of a class beyond the plaintiff's pro rata share of any recovery, except as ordered or approved by the court in accordance with paragraph (4).

(B) NONWAIVER OF ATTORNEY-CLIENT PRIVILEGE.—The certification filed pursuant to subparagraph (A) shall not be construed to be a waiver of the attorney-client privilege.

(3) APPOINTMENT OF LEAD PLAINTIFF.—

(A) EARLY NOTICE TO CLASS MEMBERS.—

(i) IN GENERAL.—Not later than 20 days after the date on which the complaint is filed, the plaintiff or plaintiffs shall cause to be published, in a widely circulated national business-oriented publication or wire service, a notice advising members of the purported plaintiff class—

(I) of the pendency of the action, the claims asserted therein, and the purported class period; and

(II) that, not later than 60 days after the date on which the notice is published, any member of the purported class may move the court to serve as lead plaintiff of the purported class.

(ii) MULTIPLE ACTIONS.—If more than one action on behalf of a class asserting substantially the same claim or claims arising under this title is filed, only the plaintiff or plaintiffs in the first filed action shall be required to cause notice to be published in accordance with clause (i).

(iii) ADDITIONAL NOTICES MAY BE REQUIRED UNDER FEDERAL RULES.—Notice required under clause (i) shall be in addition to any notice required pursuant to the Federal Rules of Civil Procedure.

(B) APPOINTMENT OF LEAD PLAINTIFF.—

(i) IN GENERAL.—Not later than 90 days after the date on which a notice is published under subparagraph (A)(i), the court shall consider any motion made by a purported class member in response to the notice, including any motion by a class member who is not individually named as a plaintiff in the complaint or complaints, and shall appoint as lead plaintiff the member or members of the purported plaintiff class that the court determines to be most capable of adequately representing the interests of class members (hereafter in this paragraph referred to as the "most adequate plaintiff") in accordance with this subparagraph.

(ii) CONSOLIDATED ACTIONS.—If more than one action on behalf of a class asserting substantially the same claim or claims arising under this title has been filed, and any party has sought to consolidate those actions for pretrial purposes or for trial, the court shall not make the determination required by clause (i) until after the decision on the motion to consolidate is rendered. As soon as practicable after such decision is rendered, the court shall appoint the most adequate plaintiff as lead plaintiff for the consolidated actions in accordance with this paragraph.

(iii) REBUTTABLE PRESUMPTION.—

(I) IN GENERAL.—Subject to subclause (II), for purposes of clause (i), the court shall adopt a presumption that the most adequate plaintiff in any private action arising under this title is the person or group of persons that—

(aa) has either filed the complaint or made a motion in response to a notice under subparagraph (A)(i);

(bb) in the determination of the court, has the largest financial interest in the relief sought by the class; and

(cc) otherwise satisfies the requirements of Rule 23 of the Federal Rules of Civil Procedure.

(II) REBUTTAL EVIDENCE.—The presumption described in subclause (I) may be rebutted only upon proof by a member of the purported plaintiff class that the presumptively most adequate plaintiff—

(aa) will not fairly and adequately protect the interests of the class; or

(bb) is subject to unique defenses that render such plaintiff incapable of adequately representing the class.

(iv) DISCOVERY.—For purposes of this subparagraph, discovery relating to whether a member or members of the purported plaintiff class is the most adequate plaintiff may be conducted by a plaintiff only if the plaintiff first demonstrates a reasonable basis for a finding that the presumptively most adequate plaintiff is incapable of adequately representing the class.

(v) SELECTION OF LEAD COUNSEL.—The most adequate plaintiff shall, subject to the approval of the court, select and retain counsel to represent the class.

(vi) RESTRICTIONS ON PROFESSIONAL PLAINTIFFS.—Except as the court may otherwise permit, consistent with the purposes of this section, a person may be a lead plaintiff, or an officer, director, or fiduciary of a lead plaintiff, in no more than 5 securities class actions brought as plaintiff class actions pursuant to the Federal Rules of Civil Procedure during any 3-year period.

(4) RECOVERY BY PLAINTIFFS.—The share of any final judgment or of any settlement that is awarded to a representative party serving on behalf of a class shall be equal, on a per share basis, to the portion of the final judgment or settlement awarded to all other members of the class. Nothing in this paragraph shall be construed to limit the award of reasonable costs and expenses (including lost wages) directly relating to the representation of the class to any representative party serving on behalf of a class.

(5) RESTRICTIONS ON SETTLEMENTS UNDER SEAL.—The terms and provisions of any settlement agreement of a class action shall not be filed under seal, except that on motion of any party to the settlement, the court may order filing under seal for those portions of a settlement agreement as to which good cause is shown for such filing under seal. For purposes of this paragraph, good cause shall exist only if publication of a term or provision of a settlement agreement would cause direct and substantial harm to any party.

(6) RESTRICTIONS ON PAYMENT OF ATTORNEYS' FEES AND EXPENSES.—Total attorneys' fees and expenses awarded by the court to counsel for the plaintiff class shall not exceed a reasonable percentage of the amount of any damages and prejudgment interest actually paid to the class.

(7) DISCLOSURE OF SETTLEMENT TERMS TO CLASS MEMBERS.—Any proposed or final settlement agreement that is published or otherwise disseminated to the class shall include each of the following statements, along with a cover page summarizing the information contained in such statements:

(A) STATEMENT OF PLAINTIFF RECOVERY.—The amount of the settlement proposed to be distributed to the parties to the action, determined in the aggregate and on an average per share basis.

(B) STATEMENT OF POTENTIAL OUTCOME OF CASE.—

(i) AGREEMENT ON AMOUNT OF DAMAGES.—If the settling parties agree on the average amount of damages per share that would be recoverable if the plaintiff prevailed on each claim alleged under this title, a statement concerning the average amount of such potential damages per share.

(ii) DISAGREEMENT ON AMOUNT OF DAMAGES.—If the parties do not agree on the average amount of damages per share that would be recoverable if the plaintiff prevailed on each claim alleged under this title, a statement from each settling party concerning the issue or issues on which the parties disagree.

(iii) INADMISSIBILITY FOR CERTAIN PURPOSES.—A statement made in accordance with clause (i) or (ii) concerning the amount of damages shall not be admissible in any Federal or State judicial action or administrative proceeding, other than an action or proceeding arising out of such statement.

(C) STATEMENT OF ATTORNEYS' FEES OR COSTS SOUGHT.—If any of the settling parties or their counsel intend to apply to the court for an award of attorneys' fees or costs from any fund established as part of the settlement, a statement indicating which parties or counsel intend to make such an application, the amount of fees and costs that will be sought (including the amount of such fees and costs determined on an average per share basis), and a brief explanation supporting the fees and costs sought. Such information shall be clearly summarized on the cover page of any notice to a party of any proposed or final settlement agreement.

(D) IDENTIFICATION OF LAWYERS' REPRESENTATIVES.—The name, telephone number, and address of one or more representatives of counsel for the plaintiff class who will be reasonably available to answer questions from class members concerning any matter contained in any notice of settlement published or otherwise disseminated to the class.

(E) REASONS FOR SETTLEMENT.—A brief statement explaining the reasons why the parties are proposing the settlement.

(F) OTHER INFORMATION.—Such other information as may be required by the court.

(8) SECURITY FOR PAYMENT OF COSTS IN CLASS ACTIONS.—In any private action arising under this title that is certified as a class action pursuant to the Federal Rules of Civil Procedure, the court may require an undertaking from the attorneys for the plaintiff class, the plaintiff class, or both, or from the attorneys for the defendant, the defendant, or both, in such proportions and at such times as the court determines are just and equitable, for the payment of fees and expenses that may be awarded under this subsection.

(9) ATTORNEY CONFLICT OF INTEREST.—If a plaintiff class is represented by an attorney who directly owns or otherwise has a beneficial interest in the securities that are the subject of the litigation, the court shall make a determination of whether such ownership or other interest constitutes a conflict of interest sufficient to disqualify the attorney from representing the plaintiff class.

(b) REQUIREMENTS FOR SECURITIES FRAUD ACTIONS.—

(1) MISLEADING STATEMENTS AND OMISSIONS.—In any private action arising under this title in which the plaintiff alleges that the defendant—

(A) made an untrue statement of a material fact; or

(B) omitted to state a material fact necessary in order to make the statements made, in the light of the circumstances in which they were made, not misleading;

the complaint shall specify each statement alleged to have been misleading, the reason or reasons why the statement is misleading, and, if an allegation regarding the statement or omission is made on information and belief, the complaint shall state with particularity all facts on which that belief is formed.

(2) REQUIRED STATE OF MIND.—

IN GENERAL. Except as provided in subparagraph (B), in any private action arising under this title in which the plaintiff may recover money damages only on proof that the defendant acted with a particular state of mind, the complaint shall, with respect to each act or omission alleged to violate this title, state with particularity facts giving rise to a strong inference that the defendant acted with the required state of mind.

(B) EXCEPTION. In the case of an action for money damages brought against a credit rating agency or a controlling person under this title, it shall be sufficient, for purposes of pleading any required state of mind in relation to such action, that the complaint state with particularity facts giving rise to a strong inference that the credit rating agency knowingly or recklessly failed—

(i) To conduct a reasonable investigation of the rated security with respect to the factual elements relied upon by its own methodology for evaluating credit risk; or

(ii) To obtain reasonable verification of such factual elements (which verification may be based on a sampling technique that does not amount to an audit) from other sources that the credit rating agency considered to be competent and that were independent of the issuer and underwriter.

(3) MOTION TO DISMISS; STAY OF DISCOVERY.—

(A) DISMISSAL FOR FAILURE TO MEET PLEADING REQUIREMENTS.—In any private action arising under this title, the court shall, on the motion of any defendant, dismiss the complaint if the requirements of paragraphs (1) and (2) are not met.

(B) STAY OF DISCOVERY.—In any private action arising under this title, all discovery and other proceedings shall be stayed during the pendency of any motion to dismiss, unless the court finds upon the motion of any party that particularized discovery is necessary to preserve evidence or to prevent undue prejudice to that party.

(C) PRESERVATION OF EVIDENCE.—

(i) IN GENERAL.—During the pendency of any stay of discovery pursuant to this paragraph, unless otherwise ordered by the court, any party to the action with actual notice of the allegations contained in the complaint shall treat all documents, data compilations (including electronically recorded or stored data), and tangible objects that are in the custody or control of such person and that are relevant to the allegations, as if they were the subject of a continuing request for production of documents from an opposing party under the Federal Rules of Civil Procedure.

(ii) SANCTION FOR WILLFUL VIOLATION.—A party aggrieved by the willful failure of an opposing party to comply with clause (i) may apply to the court for an order awarding appropriate sanctions.

(D) CIRCUMVENTION OF STAY OF DISCOVERY.—Upon a proper showing, a court may stay discovery proceedings in any private action in a State court, as necessary in aid of its jurisdiction, or to protect or effectuate its judgments, in an action subject to a stay of discovery pursuant to this paragraph.

(4) LOSS CAUSATION.—In any private action arising under this title, the plaintiff shall have the burden of proving that the act or omission of the defendant alleged to violate this title caused the loss for which the plaintiff seeks to recover damages.

(c) SANCTIONS FOR ABUSIVE LITIGATION.—

(1) MANDATORY REVIEW BY COURT.—In any private action arising under this title, upon final adjudication of the action, the court shall include in the record specific findings regarding compliance by each party and each attorney representing any party with each requirement of Rule 11(b) of the Federal Rules of Civil Procedure as to any complaint, responsive pleading, or dispositive motion.

(2) MANDATORY SANCTIONS.—If the court makes a finding under paragraph (1) that a party or attorney violated any requirement of Rule 11(b) of the Federal Rules of Civil Procedure as to any complaint, responsive pleading, or dispositive motion, the court shall impose sanctions on such party or attorney in accordance with Rule 11 of the Federal Rules of Civil Procedure. Prior to making a finding that any party or attorney has violated Rule 11 of the Federal Rules of Civil Procedure, the court shall give such party or attorney notice and an opportunity to respond.

(3) PRESUMPTION IN FAVOR OF ATTORNEYS' FEES AND COSTS.—

(A) IN GENERAL.—Subject to subparagraphs (B) and (C), for purposes of paragraph (2), the court shall adopt a presumption that the appropriate sanction—

(i) for failure of any responsive pleading or dispositive motion to comply with any requirement of Rule 11(b) of the Federal Rules of Civil Procedure is an award to the opposing party of the reasonable attorneys' fees and other expenses incurred as a direct result of the violation; and

      (ii) for substantial failure of any complaint to comply with any requirement of Rule 11(b) of the Federal Rules of Civil Procedure is an award to the opposing party of the reasonable attorneys' fees and other expenses incurred in the action.

    (B) REBUTTAL EVIDENCE.—The presumption described in subparagraph (A) may be rebutted only upon proof by the party or attorney against whom sanctions are to be imposed that—

      (i) the award of attorneys' fees and other expenses will impose an unreasonable burden on that party or attorney and would be unjust, and the failure to make such an award would not impose a greater burden on the party in whose favor sanctions are to be imposed; or

      (ii) the violation of Rule 11(b) of the Federal Rules of Civil Procedure was de minimis.

    (C) SANCTIONS.—If the party or attorney against whom sanctions are to be imposed meets its burden under subparagraph (B), the court shall award the sanctions that the court deems appropriate pursuant to Rule 11 of the Federal Rules of Civil Procedure.

  (d) DEFENDANT'S RIGHT TO WRITTEN INTERROGATORIES.—In any private action arising under this title in which the plaintiff may recover money damages, the court shall, when requested by a defendant, submit to the jury a written interrogatory on the issue of each such defendant's state of mind at the time the alleged violation occurred.

  (e) LIMITATION ON DAMAGES.—

    (1) IN GENERAL.—Except as provided in paragraph (2), in any private action arising under this title in which the plaintiff seeks to establish damages by reference to the market price of a security, the award of damages to the plaintiff shall not exceed the difference between the purchase or sale price paid or received, as appropriate, by the plaintiff for the subject security and the mean trading price of that security during the 90-day period beginning on the date on which the information correcting the misstatement or omission that is the basis for the action is disseminated to the market.

    (2) EXCEPTION.—In any private action arising under this title in which the plaintiff seeks to establish damages by reference to the market price of a security, if the plaintiff sells or repurchases the subject security prior to the expiration of the 90-day period described in paragraph (1), the plaintiff's damages shall not exceed the difference between the purchase or sale price paid or received, as appropriate, by the plaintiff for the security and the mean trading price of the security during the period beginning immediately after dissemination of information correcting the misstatement or omission and ending on the date on which the plaintiff sells or repurchases the security.

    (3) DEFINITION.—For purposes of this subsection, the "mean trading price" of a security shall be an average of the daily trading price of that security, determined as of the close of the market each day during the 90-day period referred to in paragraph (1).

  (f) PROPORTIONATE LIABILITY.—

    (1) APPLICABILITY.—Nothing in this subsection shall be construed to create, affect, or in any manner modify, the standard for liability associated with any action arising under the securities laws.

    (2) LIABILITY FOR DAMAGES.—

      (A) JOINT AND SEVERAL LIABILITY.—Any covered person against whom a final judgment is entered in a private action shall be liable for damages jointly and severally only if the trier of fact specifically determines that such covered person knowingly committed a violation of the securities laws.

      (B) PROPORTIONATE LIABILITY.—

        (i) IN GENERAL.—Except as provided in subparagraph (A), a covered person against whom a final judgment is entered in a private action shall be liable solely for the portion of the judgment that corresponds to the percentage of responsibility of that covered person, as determined under paragraph (3).

(ii) RECOVERY BY AND COSTS OF COVERED PERSON.—In any case in which a contractual relationship permits, a covered person that prevails in any private action may recover the attorney's fees and costs of that covered person in connection with the action.

(3) DETERMINATION OF RESPONSIBILITY.—

(A) IN GENERAL.—In any private action, the court shall instruct the jury to answer special interrogatories, or if there is no jury, shall make findings, with respect to each covered person and each of the other persons claimed by any of the parties to have caused or contributed to the loss incurred by the plaintiff, including persons who have entered into settlements with the plaintiff or plaintiffs, concerning—

(i) whether such person violated the securities laws;

(ii) the percentage of responsibility of such person, measured as a percentage of the total fault of all persons who caused or contributed to the loss incurred by the plaintiff; and

(iii) whether such person knowingly committed a violation of the securities laws.

(B) CONTENTS OF SPECIAL INTERROGATORIES OR FINDINGS.—The responses to interrogatories, or findings, as appropriate, under subparagraph (A) shall specify the total amount of damages that the plaintiff is entitled to recover and the percentage of responsibility of each covered person found to have caused or contributed to the loss incurred by the plaintiff or plaintiffs.

(C) FACTORS FOR CONSIDERATION.—In determining the percentage of responsibility under this paragraph, the trier of fact shall consider—

(i) the nature of the conduct of each covered person found to have caused or contributed to the loss incurred by the plaintiff or plaintiffs; and

(ii) the nature and extent of the causal relationship between the conduct of each such person and the damages incurred by the plaintiff or plaintiffs.

(4) UNCOLLECTIBLE SHARE.—

(A) IN GENERAL.—Notwithstanding paragraph (2)(B), upon motion made not later than 6 months after a final judgment is entered in any private action, the court determines that all or part of the share of the judgment of the covered person is not collectible against that covered person, and is also not collectible against a covered person described in paragraph (2)(A), each covered person described in paragraph (2)(B) shall be liable for the uncollectible share as follows:

(i) PERCENTAGE OF NET WORTH.—Each covered person shall be jointly and severally liable for the uncollectible share if the plaintiff establishes that—

(I) the plaintiff is an individual whose recoverable damages under the final judgment are equal to more than 10 percent of the net worth of the plaintiff; and

(II) the net worth of the plaintiff is equal to less than $200,000.

(ii) OTHER PLAINTIFFS.—With respect to any plaintiff not described in subclauses (I) and (II) of clause (i), each covered person shall be liable for the uncollectible share in proportion to the percentage of responsibility of that covered person, except that the total liability of a covered person under this clause may not exceed 50 percent of the proportionate share of that covered person, as determined under paragraph (3)(B).

(iii) NET WORTH.—For purposes of this subparagraph, net worth shall be determined as of the date immediately preceding the date of the purchase or sale (as applicable) by the plaintiff of the security that is the subject of the action, and shall be equal to the fair market value of assets, minus liabilities, including the net value of the investments of the plaintiff in real and personal property (including personal residences).

(B) OVERALL LIMIT.—In no case shall the total payments required pursuant to subparagraph (A) exceed the amount of the uncollectible share.

(C) COVERED PERSONS SUBJECT TO CONTRIBUTION.—A covered person against whom judgment is not collectible shall be subject to contribution and to any continuing liability to the plaintiff on the judgment.

(5) RIGHT OF CONTRIBUTION.—To the extent that a covered person is required to make an additional payment pursuant to paragraph (4), that covered person may recover contribution—

(A) from the covered person originally liable to make the payment;

(B) from any covered person liable jointly and severally pursuant to paragraph (2) (A);

(C) from any covered person held proportionately liable pursuant to this paragraph who is liable to make the same payment and has paid less than his or her proportionate share of that payment; or

(D) from any other person responsible for the conduct giving rise to the payment that would have been liable to make the same payment.

(6) NONDISCLOSURE TO JURY.—The standard for allocation of damages under paragraphs (2) and (3) and the procedure for reallocation of uncollectible shares under paragraph (4) shall not be disclosed to members of the jury.

(7) SETTLEMENT DISCHARGE.—

(A) IN GENERAL.—A covered person who settles any private action at any time before final verdict or judgment shall be discharged from all claims for contribution brought by other persons. Upon entry of the settlement by the court, the court shall enter a bar order constituting the final discharge of all obligations to the plaintiff of the settling covered person arising out of the action. The order shall bar all future claims for contribution arising out of the action—

(i) by any person against the settling covered person; and

(ii) by the settling covered person against any person, other than a person whose liability has been extinguished by the settlement of the settling covered person.

(B) REDUCTION.—If a covered person enters into a settlement with the plaintiff prior to final verdict or judgment, the verdict or judgment shall be reduced by the greater of—

(i) an amount that corresponds to the percentage of responsibility of that covered person; or

(ii) the amount paid to the plaintiff by that covered person.

(8) CONTRIBUTION.—A covered person who becomes jointly and severally liable for damages in any private action may recover contribution from any other person who, if joined in the original action, would have been liable for the same damages. A claim for contribution shall be determined based on the percentage of responsibility of the claimant and of each person against whom a claim for contribution is made.

(9) STATUTE OF LIMITATIONS FOR CONTRIBUTION.—In any private action determining liability, an action for contribution shall be brought not later than 6 months after the entry of a final, nonappealable judgment in the action, except that an action for contribution brought by a covered person who was required to make an additional payment pursuant to paragraph (4) may be brought not later than 6 months after the date on which such payment was made.

(10) DEFINITIONS.—For purposes of this subsection—

(A) a covered person "knowingly commits a violation of the securities laws"—

(i) with respect to an action that is based on an untrue statement of material fact or omission of a material fact necessary to make the statement not misleading, if—

(I) that covered person makes an untrue statement of a material fact, with actual knowledge that the representation is false, or omits to state a fact necessary in order to make the statement made not misleading, with actual knowledge that, as a result of the omission, one of the material representations of the covered person is false; and

(II) persons are likely to reasonably rely on that misrepresentation or omission; and

(ii) with respect to an action that is based on any conduct that is not described in clause (i), if that covered person engages in that conduct with actual knowledge of the facts and circumstances that make the conduct of that covered person a violation of the securities laws;

(B) reckless conduct by a covered person shall not be construed to constitute a knowing commission of a violation of the securities laws by that covered person;

(C) the term "covered person" means—

(i) a defendant in any private action arising under this title; or

(ii) a defendant in any private action arising under section 11 of the Securities Act of 1933, who is an outside director of the issuer of the securities that are the subject of the action; and

(D) the term "outside director" shall have the meaning given such term by rule or regulation of the Commission.

APPLICATION OF SAFE HARBOR FOR FORWARD-LOOKING STATEMENTS

Sec. 21E. (a) APPLICABILITY.—This section shall apply only to a forward-looking statement made by—

(1) an issuer that, at the time that the statement is made, is subject to the reporting requirements of section 13(a) or section 15(d);

(2) a person acting on behalf of such issuer;

(3) an outside reviewer retained by such issuer making a statement on behalf of such issuer; or

(4) an underwriter, with respect to information provided by such issuer or information derived from information provided by such issuer.

(b) EXCLUSIONS.—Except to the extent otherwise specifically provided by rule, regulation, or order of the Commission, this section shall not apply to a forward-looking statement—

(1) that is made with respect to the business or operations of the issuer, if the issuer—

(A) during the 3-year period preceding the date on which the statement was first made—

(i) was convicted of any felony or misdemeanor described in clauses (i) through (iv) of section 15(b)(4)(B); or

(ii) has been made the subject of a judicial or administrative decree or order arising out of a governmental action that—

(I) prohibits future violations of the antifraud provisions of the securities laws;

(II) requires that the issuer cease and desist from violating the antifraud provisions of the securities laws; or

(III) determines that the issuer violated the antifraud provisions of the securities laws;

(B) makes the forward-looking statement in connection with an offering of securities by a blank check company;

(C) issues penny stock;

(D) makes the forward-looking statement in connection with a rollup transaction; or

(E) makes the forward-looking statement in connection with a going private transaction; or

(2) that is—

(A) included in a financial statement prepared in accordance with generally accepted accounting principles;

(B) contained in a registration statement of, or otherwise issued by, an investment company;

(C) made in connection with a tender offer;

(D) made in connection with an initial public offering;

(E) made in connection with an offering by, or relating to the operations of, a partnership, limited liability company, or a direct participation investment program; or

(F) made in a disclosure of beneficial ownership in a report required to be filed with the Commission pursuant to section 13(d).

(c) SAFE HARBOR.—

(1) IN GENERAL.—Except as provided in subsection (b), in any private action arising under this title that is based on an untrue statement of a material fact or omission of a material fact necessary to make the statement not misleading, a person referred to in subsection (a) shall not be liable with respect to any forward-looking statement, whether written or oral, if and to the extent that—

(A) the forward-looking statement is—

(i) identified as a forward-looking statement, and is accompanied by meaningful cautionary statements identifying important factors that could cause actual results to differ materially from those in the forward-looking statement; or

(ii) immaterial; or

(B) the plaintiff fails to prove that the forward-looking statement—

(i) if made by a natural person, was made with actual knowledge by that person that the statement was false or misleading; or

(ii) if made by a business entity; was—

(I) made by or with the approval of an executive officer of that entity; and

(II) made or approved by such officer with actual knowledge by that officer that the statement was false or misleading.

(2) ORAL FORWARD-LOOKING STATEMENTS.—In the case of an oral forward-looking statement made by an issuer that is subject to the reporting requirements of section 13(a) or section 15(d), or by a person acting on behalf of such issuer, the requirement set forth in paragraph (1)(A) shall be deemed to be satisfied—

(A) if the oral forward-looking statement is accompanied by a cautionary statement—

(i) that the particular oral statement is a forward-looking statement; and

(ii) that the actual results might differ materially from those projected in the forward-looking statement; and

(B) if—

(i) the oral forward-looking statement is accompanied by an oral statement that additional information concerning factors that could cause actual results to materially differ from those in the forward-looking statement is contained in a readily available written document, or portion thereof;

(ii) the accompanying oral statement referred to in clause (i) identifies the document, or portion thereof, that contains the additional information about those factors relating to the forward-looking statement; and

(iii) the information contained in that written document is a cautionary statement that satisfies the standard established in paragraph (1)(A).

(3) AVAILABILITY.—Any document filed with the Commission or generally disseminated shall be deemed to be readily available for purposes of paragraph (2).

(4) EFFECT ON OTHER SAFE HARBORS.—The exemption provided for in paragraph (1) shall be in addition to any exemption that the Commission may establish by rule or regulation under subsection (g).

(d) DUTY TO UPDATE.—Nothing in this section shall impose upon any person a duty to update a forward-looking statement.

(e) DISPOSITIVE MOTION.—On any motion to dismiss based upon subsection (c)(1), the court shall consider any statement cited in the complaint and any cautionary statement accompanying the forward-looking statement, which are not subject to material dispute, cited by the defendant.

(f) STAY PENDING DECISION ON MOTION.—In any private action arising under this title, the court shall stay discovery (other than discovery that is specifically directed to the applicability of the exemption provided for in this section) during the pendency of any motion by a defendant for summary judgment that is based on the grounds that—

(1) the statement or omission upon which the complaint is based is a forward-looking statement within the meaning of this section; and

(2) the exemption provided for in this section precludes a claim for relief.

(g) EXEMPTION AUTHORITY.—In addition to the exemptions provided for in this section, the Commission may, by rule or regulation, provide exemptions from or under any provision of this title, including with respect to liability that is based on a statement or that is based on projections or other forward-looking information, if and to the extent that any such exemption is consistent with the public interest and the protection of investors, as determined by the Commission.

(h) EFFECT ON OTHER AUTHORITY OF COMMISSION.—Nothing in this section limits, either expressly or by implication, the authority of the Commission to exercise similar authority or to adopt similar rules and regulations with respect to forward-looking statements under any other statute under which the Commission exercises rulemaking authority.

(i) DEFINITIONS.—For purposes of this section, the following definitions shall apply:

(1) FORWARD-LOOKING STATEMENT.—The term "forward-looking statement" means—

(A) a statement containing a projection of revenues, income (including income loss), earnings (including earnings loss) per share, capital expenditures, dividends, capital structure, or other financial items;

(B) a statement of the plans and objectives of management for future operations, including plans or objectives relating to the products or services of the issuer;

(C) a statement of future economic performance, including any such statement contained in a discussion and analysis of financial condition by the management or in the results of operations included pursuant to the rules and regulations of the Commission;

(D) any statement of the assumptions underlying or relating to any statement described in subparagraph (A), (B), or (C);

(E) any report issued by an outside reviewer retained by an issuer, to the extent that the report assesses a forward-looking statement made by the issuer; or

(F) a statement containing a projection or estimate of such other items as may be specified by rule or regulation of the Commission.

(2) INVESTMENT COMPANY.—The term "investment company" has the same meaning as in section 3(a) of the Investment Company Act of 1940.

(3) GOING PRIVATE TRANSACTION.—The term "going private transaction" has the meaning given that term under the rules or regulations of the Commission issued pursuant to section 13(e).

(4) PERSON ACTING ON BEHALF OF AN ISSUER.—The term "person acting on behalf of an issuer" means any officer, director, or employee of such issuer.

(5) OTHER TERMS.—The terms "blank check company", "rollup transaction", "partnership", "limited liability company", "executive officer of an entity" and "direct participation investment program", have the meanings given those terms by rule or regulation of the Commission.

SECURITIES WHISTLEBLOWER INCENTIVES AND PROTECTION

SEC. 21F. (a) DEFINITIONS. In this section the following definitions shall apply:

(1) COVERED JUDICIAL OR ADMINISTRATIVE ACTION. The term "covered judicial or administrative action" means any judicial or administrative action brought by the Commission under the securities laws that results in monetary sanctions exceeding $1,000,000.

(2) FUND. The term "Fund" means the Securities and Exchange Commission Investor Protection Fund.

(3) ORIGINAL INFORMATION. The term "original information" means information that—

(A) Is derived from the independent knowledge or analysis of a whistleblower;

(B) Is not known to the Commission from any other source, unless the whistleblower is the original source of the information; and

(C) Is not exclusively derived from an allegation made in a judicial or administrative hearing, in a governmental report, hearing, audit, or investigation, or from the news media, unless the whistleblower is a source of the information.

(4) MONETARY SANCTIONS. The term "monetary sanctions", when used with respect to any judicial or administrative action, means—

(A) Any monies, including penalties, disgorgement, and interest, ordered to be paid; and

(B) Any monies deposited into a disgorgement fund or other fund pursuant to section 308(b) of the Sarbanes-Oxley Act of 2002 (15 U.S.C. 7246(b)), as a result of such action or any settlement of such action.

(5) RELATED ACTION. The term "related action", when used with respect to any judicial or administrative action brought by the Commission under the securities laws, means any judicial or administrative action brought by an entity described in subclauses (I) through (IV) of subsection (h)(2)(D)(i) that is based upon the original information provided by a whistleblower pursuant to subsection (a) that led to the successful enforcement of the Commission action.

(6) WHISTLEBLOWER. The term "whistleblower" means any individual who provides, or 2 or more individuals acting jointly who provide, information relating to a violation of the securities laws to the Commission, in a manner established, by rule or regulation, by the Commission.

(b) AWARDS.

(1) IN GENERAL. In any covered judicial or administrative action, or related action, the Commission, under regulations prescribed by the Commission and subject to subsection (c), shall pay an award or awards to 1 or more whistleblowers who voluntarily provided original information to the Commission that led to the successful enforcement of the covered judicial or administrative action, or related action, in an aggregate amount equal to—

(A) Not less than 10 percent, in total, of what has been collected of the monetary sanctions imposed in the action or related actions; and

(B) Not more than 30 percent, in total, of what has been collected of the monetary sanctions imposed in the action or related actions.

(2) PAYMENT OF AWARDS. Any amount paid under paragraph (1) shall be paid from the Fund.

(c) DETERMINATION OF AMOUNT OF AWARD; DENIAL OF AWARD.

(1) DETERMINATION OF AMOUNT OF AWARD.

(A) Discretion. The determination of the amount of an award made under subsection (b) shall be in the discretion of the Commission.

(B) Criteria. In determining the amount of an award made under subsection (b), the Commission—

(i) Shall take into consideration—

(I) The significance of the information provided by the whistleblower to the success of the covered judicial or administrative action;

(II) The degree of assistance provided by the whistleblower and any legal representative of the whistleblower in a covered judicial or administrative action;

(III) The programmatic interest of the Commission in deterring violations of the securities laws by making awards to whistleblowers who provide information that lead to the successful enforcement of such laws; and

(IV) Such additional relevant factors as the Commission may establish by rule or regulation; and

(ii) Shall not take into consideration the balance of the Fund.

(2) DENIAL OF AWARD. No award under subsection (b) shall be made—

(A) To any whistleblower who is, or was at the time the whistleblower acquired the original information submitted to the Commission, a member, officer, or employee of—

(i) An appropriate regulatory agency;

(ii) The Department of Justice;

(iii) A self-regulatory organization;

(iv) The Public Company Accounting Oversight Board; or

(v) A law enforcement organization;

(B) To any whistleblower who is convicted of a criminal violation related to the judicial or administrative action for which the whistleblower otherwise could receive an award under this section;

(C) To any whistleblower who gains the information through the performance of an audit of financial statements required under the securities laws and for whom such submission would be contrary to the requirements of section 10A of the Securities Exchange Act of 1934 (15 U.S.C. 78j-1); or

(D) To any whistleblower who fails to submit information to the Commission in such form as the Commission may, by rule, require.

(d) REPRESENTATION.

(1) PERMITTED REPRESENTATION. Any whistleblower who makes a claim for an award under subsection (b) may be represented by counsel.

(2) REQUIRED REPRESENTATION.

(A) IN GENERAL. Any whistleblower who anonymously makes a claim for an award under subsection (b) shall be represented by counsel if the whistleblower anonymously submits the information upon which the claim is based.

(B) DISCLOSURE OF IDENTITY. Prior to the payment of an award, a whistleblower shall disclose the identity of the whistleblower and provide such other information as the Commission may require, directly or through counsel for the whistleblower.

(e) NO CONTRACT NECESSARY. No contract with the Commission is necessary for any whistleblower to receive an award under subsection (b), unless otherwise required by the Commission by rule or regulation.

(f) APPEALS. Any determination made under this section, including whether, to whom, or in what amount to make awards, shall be in the discretion of the Commission. Any such determination, except the determination of the amount of an award if the award was made in accordance with subsection (b), may be appealed to the appropriate court of appeals of the United States not more than 30 days after the determination is issued by the Commission. The court shall review the determination made by the Commission in accordance with section 706 of title 5, United States Code.

(g) INVESTOR PROTECTION FUND.

(1) FUND ESTABLISHED. There is established in the Treasury of the United States a fund to be known as the "Securities and Exchange Commission Investor Protection Fund".

(2) USE OF FUND. The Fund shall be available to the Commission, without further appropriation or fiscal year limitation, for—

(A) Paying awards to whistleblowers as provided in subsection (b); and

(B) Funding the activities of the Inspector General of the Commission under section 4(i).

(3) DEPOSITS AND CREDITS.

(A) IN GENERAL. There shall be deposited into or credited to the Fund an amount equal to—

(i) Any monetary sanction collected by the Commission in any judicial or administrative action brought by the Commission under the securities laws that is not added to a disgorgement fund or other fund under section 308 of the Sarbanes-Oxley Act of 2002 (15 U.S.C. 7246) or otherwise distributed to victims of a violation of the securities laws, or the rules and regulations thereunder, underlying such action, unless the balance of the Fund at the time the monetary sanction is collected exceeds $300,000,000;

(ii) Any monetary sanction added to a disgorgement fund or other fund under section 308 of the Sarbanes-Oxley Act of 2002 (15 U.S.C. 7246) that is not distributed to the victims for whom the Fund was established, unless the balance of the disgorgement fund at the time the determination is made not to distribute the monetary sanction to such victims exceeds $200,000,000; and

(iii) All income from investments made under paragraph (4).

(B) ADDITIONAL AMOUNTS. If the amounts deposited into or credited to the Fund under subparagraph (A) are not sufficient to satisfy an award made under subsection (b), there shall be deposited into or credited to the Fund an amount equal to the unsatisfied portion of the award from any monetary sanction collected by the Commission in the covered judicial or administrative action on which the award is based.

(4) INVESTMENTS.

(A) AMOUNTS IN FUND MAY BE INVESTED. The Commission may request the Secretary of the Treasury to invest the portion of the Fund that is not, in the discretion of the Commission, required to meet the current needs of the Fund.

(B) ELIGIBLE INVESTMENTS. Investments shall be made by the Secretary of the Treasury in obligations of the United States or obligations that are guaranteed as to principal and interest by the United States, with maturities suitable to the needs of the Fund as determined by the Commission on the record.

(C) INTEREST AND PROCEEDS CREDITED. The interest on, and the proceeds from the sale or redemption of, any obligations held in the Fund shall be credited to the Fund.

(5) REPORTS TO CONGRESS. Not later than October 30 of each fiscal year beginning after the date of enactment of this subsection, the Commission shall submit to the Committee on Banking, Housing, and Urban Affairs of the Senate, and the Committee on Financial Services of the House of Representatives a report on—

(A) The whistleblower award program, established under this section, including—

(i) A description of the number of awards granted; and

(ii) The types of cases in which awards were granted during the preceding fiscal year;

(B) The balance of the Fund at the beginning of the preceding fiscal year;

(C) The amounts deposited into or credited to the Fund during the preceding fiscal year;

(D) The amount of earnings on investments made under paragraph (4) during the preceding fiscal year;

(E) The amount paid from the Fund during the preceding fiscal year to whistleblowers pursuant to subsection (b);

(F) The balance of the Fund at the end of the preceding fiscal year; and

(G) A complete set of audited financial statements, including—

(i) A balance sheet;

(ii) Income statement; and

(iii) Cash flow analysis.

(h) PROTECTION OF WHISTLEBLOWERS.

(1) PROHIBITION AGAINST RETALIATION.

(A) IN GENERAL. No employer may discharge, demote, suspend, threaten, harass, directly or indirectly, or in any other manner discriminate against, a whistleblower in the terms and conditions of employment because of any lawful act done by the whistleblower—

(i) In providing information to the Commission in accordance with this section;

(ii) In initiating, testifying in, or assisting in any investigation or judicial or administrative action of the Commission based upon or related to such information; or

(iii) In making disclosures that are required or protected under the Sarbanes-Oxley Act of 2002 (15 U.S.C. 7201 et seq.), the Securities Exchange Act of 1934 (15 U.S.C. 78a et seq.), including section 10A(m) of such Act (15 U.S.C. 78f(m)), section 1513(e) of title 18, United States Code, and any other law, rule, or regulation subject to the jurisdiction of the Commission.

(B) Enforcement.

(i) Cause of Action. An individual who alleges discharge or other discrimination in violation of subparagraph (A) may bring an action under this subsection in the appropriate district court of the United States for the relief provided in subparagraph (C).

(ii) Subpoenas. A subpoena requiring the attendance of a witness at a trial or hearing conducted under this section may be served at any place in the United States.

(iii) Statute of Limitations.

(I) In General. An action under this subsection may not be brought—

(aa) More than 6 years after the date on which the violation of subparagraph (A) occurred; or

(bb) More than 3 years after the date when facts material to the right of action are known or reasonably should have been known by the employee alleging a violation of subparagraph (A).

(II) Required Action Within 10 Years. Notwithstanding subclause (I), an action under this subsection may not in any circumstance be brought more than 10 years after the date on which the violation occurs.

(C) RELIEF. Relief for an individual prevailing in an action brought under subparagraph (B) shall include—

(i) Reinstatement with the same seniority status that the individual would have had, but for the discrimination;

(ii) 2 times the amount of back pay otherwise owed to the individual, with interest; and

(iii) Compensation for litigation costs, expert witness fees, and reasonable attorneys' fees.

(2) CONFIDENTIALITY.

(A) IN GENERAL. Except as provided in subparagraphs (B) and (C), the Commission and any officer or employee of the Commission shall not disclose any information, including information provided by a whistleblower to the Commission, which could reasonably be expected to reveal the identity of a whistleblower, except in accordance with the provisions of section 552a of title 5, United States Code, unless and until required to be disclosed to a defendant or respondent in connection with a public proceeding instituted by the Commission or any entity described in subparagraph (C). For purposes of section 552 of title 5, United States Code, this paragraph shall be considered a statute described in subsection (b)(3)(B) of such section.

(B) EXEMPTED STATUTE. For purposes of section 552 of title 5, United States Code, this paragraph shall be considered a statute described in subsection (b)(3)(B) of such section 552.

(C) RULE OF CONSTRUCTION. Nothing in this section is intended to limit, or shall be construed to limit, the ability of the Attorney General to present such evidence to a grand jury or to share such evidence with potential witnesses or defendants in the course of an ongoing criminal investigation.

(D) AVAILABILITY TO GOVERNMENT AGENCIES.

(i) In General. Without the loss of its status as confidential in the hands of the Commission, all information referred to in subparagraph (A) may, in the discretion of the Commission, when determined by the Commission to be necessary to accomplish the purposes of this Act and to protect investors, be made available to—

(I) The Attorney General of the United States;

(II) An appropriate regulatory authority;

(III) A self-regulatory organization;

(IV) A State attorney general in connection with any criminal investigation;

(V) Any appropriate State regulatory authority;

(VI) The Public Company Accounting Oversight Board;

(VII) A foreign securities authority; and

(VIII) A foreign law enforcement authority.

(ii) Confidentiality.

(I) In General. Each of the entities described in subclauses (I) through (VI) of clause (i) shall maintain such information as confidential in accordance with the requirements established under subparagraph (A).

(II) Foreign Authorities. Each of the entities described in subclauses (VII) and (VIII) of clause (i) shall maintain such information in accordance with such assurances of confidentiality as the Commission determines appropriate.

(3) RIGHTS RETAINED. Nothing in this section shall be deemed to diminish the rights, privileges, or remedies of any whistleblower under any Federal or State law, or under any collective bargaining agreement.

(i) PROVISION OF FALSE INFORMATION. A whistleblower shall not be entitled to an award under this section if the whistleblower—

(1) Knowingly and willfully makes any false, fictitious, or fraudulent statement or representation; or

(2) Uses any false writing or document knowing the writing or document contains any false, fictitious, or fraudulent statement or entry.

(j) RULEMAKING AUTHORITY. The Commission shall have the authority to issue such rules and regulations as may be necessary or appropriate to implement the provisions of this section consistent with the purposes of this section.

HEARINGS BY COMMISSION

Sec. 22. Hearings may be public and may be held before the Commission, any member or members thereof, or any officer or officers of the Commission designated by it, and appropriate records thereof shall be kept.

RULES, REGULATIONS, AND ORDERS; ANNUAL REPORTS

Sec. 23. (a)(1) The Commission, the Board of Governors of the Federal Reserve System, and the other agencies enumerated in section 3(a)(34) of this title shall each have power to make such rules and regulations as may be necessary or appropriate to implement the provisions of this title for which they are responsible or for the execution of the functions vested in them by this title, and may for such purposes classify persons, securities, transactions, statements, applications, reports, and other matters within their respective jurisdictions, and prescribe greater, lesser, or different requirements for different classes thereof. No provision of this title imposing any liability shall apply to any act done or omitted in good faith in conformity with a rule, regulation, or order of the Commission, the Board of Governors of the Federal Reserve System, other agency enumerated in section 3(a)(34) of this title, or any self-regulatory organization, notwithstanding that such rule, regulation, or order may thereafter be amended or rescinded or determined by judicial or other authority to be invalid for any reason.

(2) The Commission and the Secretary of the Treasury, in making rules and regulations pursuant to any provisions of this title, shall consider among other matters the impact any such rule or regulation would have on competition. The Commission and the Secretary of the Treasury shall not adopt any such rule or regulation which would impose a burden on competition not necessary or appropriate in furtherance of the purposes of this title. The Commission and the Secretary of the Treasury shall include in the statement of basis and purpose incorporated in any rule or regulation adopted under this title, the reasons for the Commission's or the Secretary's determination that any burden on competition imposed by such rule or regulation is necessary or appropriate in furtherance of the purposes of this title.

(3) The Commission and the Secretary, in making rules and regulations pursuant to any provision of this title, considering any application for registration in accordance with section 19(a) of this title, or reviewing any proposed rule change of a self-regulatory organization in accordance with section 19(b) of this title, shall keep in a public file and make available for copying all written statements filed with the Commission and the Secretary and all written communications between the Commission or the Secretary and any person relating to the proposed rule, regulation, application, or proposed rule change; Provided, however, That the Commission and the Secretary shall not be required to keep in a public file or make available for copying any such statement or communication which it may withhold from the public in accordance with the provisions of section 552 of title 5, United States Code.

(c) The Commission, by rule, shall prescribe the procedure applicable to every case pursuant to this title of adjudication (as defined in section 551 of title 5, United States Code) not required to be determined on the record after notice and opportunity for hearing. Such rules shall, as a minimum, provide that prompt notice shall be given of any adverse action or final disposition and that such notice and the entry of any order shall be accompanied by a statement of written reasons.

(d) CEASE-AND-DESIST PROCEDURES.—Within 1 year after the date of enactment of this subsection, the Commission shall establish regulations providing for the expeditious conduct of hearings and rendering of decisions under section 21C of this title, section 8A of the Securities Act of 1933, section 9(f) of the Investment Company Act of 1940, and section 203(k) of the Investment Advisers Act of 1940.

PUBLIC AVAILABILITY OF INFORMATION

Sec. 24. (a) For purposes of section 552 of title 5, United States Code, the term "records" includes all applications, statements, reports, contracts, correspondence, notices, and other documents filed with or otherwise obtained by the Commission pursuant to this title or otherwise.

(b) It shall be unlawful for any member, officer, or employee of the Commission to disclose to any person other than a member, officer, or employee of the Commission, or to use for personal benefit, any information contained in any application, statement, report, contract, correspondence, notice, or other document filed with or otherwise obtained by the Commission (1) in contravention of the rules and regulations of the Commission under section 552 of title 5, United States Code, or (2) in circumstances where the Commission has determined pursuant to such rules to accord confidential treatment to such information.

(c) CONFIDENTIAL DISCLOSURES.—The Commission may, in its discretion and a showing that such information is needed, provide all "records" (as defined in subsection (a)) and other information in its possession to such persons, both domestic and foreign, as the Commission by rule deems appropriate if the person receiving such records or information provides such assurances of confidentiality as the Commission deems appropriate.

(d) RECORDS OBTAINED FROM FOREIGN SECURITIES AUTHORITIES.—Except as provided in subsection (g), the Commission shall not be compelled to disclose records obtained from a foreign securities authority if (1) the foreign securities authority has in good faith determined and represented to the Commission that public disclosure of such records would violate the laws applicable to that foreign securities authority, and (2) the Commission obtains such records pursuant to (A) such procedure as the Commission may authorize for use in connection with the administration or enforcement of the securities laws, or (B) a memorandum of understanding. For purposes of section 552 of title 5, United States Code, this subsection shall be considered a statute described in subsection (b)(3)(B) of such section 552.

(e) FREEDOM OF INFORMATION ACT. For purposes of section 552(b)(8) of title 5, United States Code, (commonly referred to as the Freedom of Information Act)—

(1) The Commission is an agency responsible for the regulation or supervision of financial institutions; and

(2) Any entity for which the Commission is responsible for regulating, supervising, or examining under this title is a financial institution.

(f) SHARING PRIVILEGED INFORMATION WITH OTHER AUTHORITIES.

(1) PRIVILEGED INFORMATION PROVIDED BY THE COMMISSION. The Commission shall not be deemed to have waived any privilege applicable to any information by transferring that information to or permitting that information to be used by—

(A) Any agency (as defined in section 6 of title 18, United States Code);

(B) The Public Company Accounting Oversight Board;

(C) Any self-regulatory organization;

(D) Any foreign securities authority;

(E) Any foreign law enforcement authority; or

(F) Any State securities or law enforcement authority.

(2) NONDISCLOSURE OF PRIVILEGED INFORMATION PROVIDED TO THE COMMISSION. The Commission shall not be compelled to disclose privileged information obtained from any foreign securities authority, or foreign law enforcement authority, if the authority has in good faith determined and represented to the Commission that the information is privileged.

(3) NONWAIVER OF PRIVILEGED INFORMATION PROVIDED TO THE COMMISSION.

(A) IN GENERAL. Federal agencies, State securities and law enforcement authorities, self-regulatory organizations, and the Public Company Accounting Oversight Board shall not be deemed to have waived any privilege applicable to any information by transferring that information to or permitting that information to be used by the Commission.

(B) EXCEPTION. The provisions of subparagraph (A) shall not apply to a self-regulatory organization or the Public Company Accounting Oversight Board with respect to information used by the Commission in an action against such organization.

(4) DEFINITIONS. For purposes of this subsection—

(A) The term "privilege" includes any work-product privilege, attorney-client privilege, governmental privilege, or other privilege recognized under Federal, State, or foreign law;

(B) The term "foreign law enforcement authority" means any foreign authority that is empowered under foreign law to detect, investigate or prosecute potential violations of law; and

(C) The term "State securities or law enforcement authority" means the authority of any State or territory that is empowered under State or territory law to detect, investigate, or prosecute potential violations of law.

(g) SAVINGS PROVISIONS.—Nothing in this section shall—

(1) alter the Commission's responsibilities under the Right to Financial Privacy Act (12 U.S.C. 3401 et seq.), as limited by section 21(h) of this Act, with respect to transfers of records covered by such statutes, or

(2) authorize the Commission to withhold information from the Congress or prevent the Commission from complying with an order of a court of the United States in an action commenced by the United States or the Commission.

COURT REVIEW OF ORDERS AND RULES

Sec. 25. (a)(1) A person aggrieved by a final order of the Commission entered pursuant to this title may obtain review of the order in the United States Court of Appeals for the circuit in which he resides or has his principal place of business, or for the District of Columbia Circuit, by filing in such court, within sixty days after the entry of the order, a written petition requesting that the order be modified or set aside in whole or in part.

(2) A copy of the petition shall be transmitted forthwith by the clerk of the court to a member of the Commission or an officer designated by the Commission for that purpose. Thereupon the Commission shall file in the court the record on which the order complained of is entered, as provided in section 2112 of title 28, United States Code, and the Federal Rules of Appellate Procedure.

(3) On the filing of the petition, the court has jurisdiction, which becomes exclusive on the filing of the record, to affirm or modify and enforce or to set aside the order in whole or in part.

(4) The findings of the Commission as to the facts, if supported by substantial evidence, are conclusive.

(5) If either party applies to the court for leave to adduce additional evidence and shows to the satisfaction of the court that the additional evidence is material and that there was reasonable ground for failure to adduce it before the Commission, the court may remand the case to the Commission for further proceedings, in whatever manner and on whatever conditions the court considers appropriate. If the case is remanded to the Commission, it shall file in the court a supplemental record containing any new evidence, any further or modified findings, and any new order.

(b)(1) A person adversely affected by a rule of the Commission promulgated pursuant to section 6, 9(h)(2), 11, 11A, 15(c)(5) or (6), 15A, 17, 17A, or 19 of this title may obtain review of this rule in the United States Court of Appeals for the circuit in which he resides or has his principal place of business or for the District of Columbia Circuit, by filing in such court, within sixty days after the promulgation of the rule, a written petition requesting that the rule be set aside.

(2) A copy of the petition shall be transmitted forthwith by the clerk of the court to a member of the Commission or an officer designated for that purpose. Thereupon, the Commission shall file in the court the rule under review and any documents referred to therein, the Commission's notice of proposed rulemaking and any documents referred to therein, all written submissions and the transcript of any oral presentations in the rulemaking, factual information not included in the foregoing that was considered by the Commission in the promulgation of the rule or proffered by the Commission as pertinent to the rule, the report of any advisory committee received or considered by the Commission in the rulemaking, and any other materials prescribed by the court.

(3) On the filing of the petition, the court has jurisdiction, which becomes exclusive on the filing of the materials set forth in paragraph (2) of this subsection, to affirm and enforce or to set aside the rule.

(4) The findings of the Commission as to the facts identified by the Commission as the basis, in whole or in part, of the rule, if supported by substantial evidence, are conclusive. The court shall affirm and enforce the rule unless the Commission's action in promulgating the rule is found to be arbitrary, capricious, an abuse of discretion, or otherwise not in accordance with law; contrary to constitutional right, power, privilege or immunity; in

excess of statutory jurisdiction, authority, or limitations, or short of statutory right; or without observance of procedure required by law.

(5) If proceedings have been instituted under this subsection in two or more courts of appeals with respect to the same rule, the Commission shall file the materials set forth in paragraph (2) of this subsection in that court in which a proceeding was first instituted. The other courts shall thereupon transfer all such proceedings to the court in which the materials have been filed. For the convenience of the parties in the interest of justice that court may thereafter transfer all the proceedings to any other court of appeals.

(c) (1) No objection to an order or rule of the Commission, for which review is sought under this section, may be considered by the court unless it was urged before the Commission or there was reasonable ground for failure to do so.

(2) The filing of a petition under this section does not operate as a stay of the Commission's order or rule. Until the court's jurisdiction becomes exclusive, the Commission may stay its order or rule pending judicial review if it finds that justice so requires. After the filing of a petition under this section, the court, on whatever conditions may be required and to the extent necessary to prevent irreparable injury, may issue all necessary and appropriate process to stay the order or rule or to preserve status or rights pending its review; but (notwithstanding section 705 of title 5, United States Code) no such process may be issued by the court before the filing of the record or the materials set forth in subsection (b) (2) of this section unless: (A) the Commission has denied a stay or failed to grant requested relief, (B) a reasonable period has expired since the filing of an application for a stay without a decision by the Commission, or (C) there was reasonable ground for failure to apply to the Commission.

(3) When the same order or rule is the subject of one or more petitions for review filed under this section and an action for enforcement filed in a district court of the United States under section 21 (d) or (e) of this title, that court in which the petition or the action is first filed has jurisdiction with respect to the order or rule to the exclusion of any other court, and thereupon all such proceedings shall be transferred to that court; but, for the convenience of the parties in the interest of justice, that court may thereafter transfer all the proceedings to any other court of appeals or district court of the United States, whether or not a petition for review or an action for enforcement was originally filed in the transferee court. The scope of review by a district court under section 21 (d) or (e) of this title is in all cases the same as by a court of appeals under this section.

(d) (1) For purposes of the preceding subsections of this section, the term "Commission" includes the agencies enumerated in section 3(a) (34) of this title insofar as such agencies are acting pursuant to this title and the Secretary of the Treasury insofar as he is acting pursuant to section 15C of this title.

(2) For purposes of subsection (a) (4) of this section and section 706 of title 5, United States Code, an order of the Commission pursuant to section 19(a) of this title denying registration to a clearing agency for which the Commission is not the appropriate regulatory agency or pursuant to section 19(b) of this title disapproving a proposed rule change by such a clearing agency shall be deemed to be an order of the appropriate regulatory agency for such clearing agency insofar as such order was entered by reason of a determination by such appropriate regulatory agency pursuant to section 19(a) (2) (C) or 19(b) (4) (C) of this title that such registration or proposed rule change would be inconsistent with the safeguarding of securities or funds.

UNLAWFUL REPRESENTATIONS

Sec. 26. No action or failure to act by the Commission or the Board of Governors of the Federal Reserve System, in the administration of this title shall be construed to mean that the particular authority has in any way passed upon the merits of, or given approval to, any security or any transaction or transactions therein, nor shall such action or failure to act with regard to any statement or report filed with or examined by such authority pursuant to this title or rules and regulations thereunder, be deemed a finding by such authority that such statement or report is true and accurate on its face or that it is not false or misleading. It shall be unlawful to make, or cause to be made, to any prospective purchaser or seller of a security any representation that any such action or failure to act by any such authority is to be so construed or has such effect.

JURISDICTION OF OFFENSES AND SUITS

Sec. 27. (a) IN GENERAL. The district courts of the United States and the United States courts of any Territory or other place subject to the jurisdiction of the United States shall have exclusive jurisdiction of violations of this title or the rules and regulations thereunder, and of all suits in equity and actions at law brought to enforce any liability or duty created by this title or the rules and regulations thereunder. Any criminal proceeding may be brought in the district wherein any act or transaction constituting the violation occurred. Any suit or action to enforce any liability or duty created by this title or rules and regulations thereunder, or to enjoin any violation of such title or rules and regulations, may be brought in any such district or in the district wherein the defendant is found or is an inhabitant or transacts business, and process in such cases may be served in any other district of which the defendant is an inhabitant or wherever the defendant may be found. In any action or proceeding instituted by the Commission under this title in a United States district court for any judicial district, a subpoena issued to compel the attendance of a witness or the production of documents or tangible things (or both) at a hearing or trial may be served at any place within the United States. Rule 45(c)(3)(A)(ii) of the Federal Rules of Civil Procedure shall not apply to a subpoena issued under the preceding sentence. Judgments and decrees so rendered shall be subject to review as provided in sections 1254, 1291, 1292, and 1294 of title 28, United States Code. No costs shall be assessed for or against the Commission in any proceeding under this title brought by or against it in the Supreme Court or such other courts.

(b) EXTRATERRITORIAL JURISDICTION. The district courts of the United States and the United States courts of any Territory shall have jurisdiction of an action or proceeding brought or instituted by the Commission or the United States alleging a violation of the antifraud provisions of this title involving—

(1) Conduct within the United States that constitutes significant steps in furtherance of the violation, even if the securities transaction occurs outside the United States and involves only foreign investors; or

(2) Conduct occurring outside the United States that has a foreseeable substantial effect within the United States.

SPECIAL PROVISION RELATING TO STATUTE OF LIMITATIONS ON PRIVATE CAUSES OF ACTION

Sec. 27A. (a) EFFECT ON PENDING CAUSES OF ACTION.—The limitation period for any private civil action implied under section 10(b) of this Act that was commenced on or before June 19, 1991, shall be the limitation period provided by the laws applicable in the jurisdiction, including principles of retroactivity, as such laws existed on June 19, 1991.

(b) EFFECT ON DISMISSED CAUSES OF ACTION.—Any private civil action implied under section 10(b) of this Act that was commenced on or before June 19, 1991—

(1) which was dismissed as time barred subsequent to June 19, 1991, and

(2) which would have been timely filed under the limitation period provided by the laws applicable in the jurisdiction, including principles of retroactivity, as such laws existed on June 19, 1991,

shall be reinstated on motion by the plaintiff not later than 60 days after the date of enactment of this section.

EFFECT ON EXISTING LAW

Sec. 28. (a) LIMITATION ON JUDGMENTS.

(1) IN GENERAL. No person permitted to maintain a suit for damages under the provisions of this title shall recover, through satisfaction of judgment in 1 or more actions, a total amount in excess of the actual damages to that person on account of the act complained of. Except as otherwise specifically provided in this title, nothing in this title shall affect the jurisdiction of the securities commission (or any agency or officer performing like functions) of any State over any security or any person insofar as it does not conflict with the provisions of this title or the rules and regulations under this title.

(2) RULE OF CONSTRUCTION. Except as provided in subsection (f), the rights and remedies provided by this title shall be in addition to any and all other rights and remedies that may exist at law or in equity.

(3) STATE BUCKET SHOP LAWS. No State law which prohibits or regulates the making or promoting of wagering or gaming contracts, or the operation of "bucket shops" or other similar or related activities, shall invalidate—

(A) Any put, call, straddle, option, privilege, or other security subject to this title (except any security that has a pari-mutuel payout or otherwise is determined by the Commission, acting by rule, regulation, or order, to be appropriately subject to such laws), or apply to any activity which is incidental or related to the offer, purchase, sale, exercise, settlement, or closeout of any such security;

(B) Any security-based swap between eligible contract participants; or

(C) Any security-based swap effected on a national securities exchange registered pursuant to section 6(b).

(4) OTHER STATE PROVISIONS. No provision of State law regarding the offer, sale, or distribution of securities shall apply to any transaction in a security-based swap or a security futures product, except that this paragraph may not be construed as limiting any State antifraud law of general applicability. A security-based swap may not be regulated as an insurance contract under any provision of State law.

(b) Nothing in this title shall be construed to modify existing law with regard to the binding effect (1) on any member of or participant in any self-regulatory organization of any action taken by the authorities of such organization to settle disputes between its members or participants, (2) on any municipal securities dealer or municipal securities broker of any action taken pursuant to a procedure established by the Municipal Securities Rulemaking Board to settle disputes between municipal securities dealers and municipal securities brokers, or (3) of any action described in paragraph (1) or (2) on any person who has agreed to be bound thereby.

(c) The stay, setting aside, or modification pursuant to section 19(e) of this title of any disciplinary sanction imposed by a self-regulatory organization on a member thereof, person associated with a member, or participant therein, shall not affect the validity or force of any action taken as a result of such sanction by the self-regulatory organization prior to such stay, setting aside, or modification: Provided, That such action is not inconsistent with the provisions of this title or the rules or regulations thereunder. The rights of any person acting in good faith which arise out of any such action shall not be affected in any way by such stay, setting aside, or modification.

(d) No State or political subdivision thereof shall impose any tax on any change in beneficial or record ownership of securities effected through the facilities of a registered clearing agency or registered transfer agent or any nominee thereof or custodian therefor or upon the delivery or transfer of securities to or through or receipt from such agency or agent or any nominee thereof or custodian therefor, unless such change in beneficial or record ownership or such transfer or delivery or receipt would otherwise be taxable by such State or political subdivision if the facilities of such registered clearing agency, registered transfer agent, or any nominee thereof or custodian therefor were not physically located in the taxing State or political subdivision. No State or political subdivision thereof shall impose any tax on securities which are deposited in or retained by a registered clearing agency, registered transfer agent, or any nominee thereof or custodian therefor, unless such securities would otherwise be taxable by such State or political subdivision if the facilities of such registered clearing agency, registered transfer agent, or any nominee thereof or custodian therefor were not physically located in the taxing State or political subdivision.

(e) (1) No person using the mails, or any means or instrumentality of interstate commerce, in the exercise of investment discretion with respect to an account shall be deemed to have acted unlawfully or to have breached a fiduciary duty under State or Federal law unless expressly provided to the contrary by a law enacted by the Congress or any State subsequent to the date of enactment of the Securities Acts Amendments of 1975 solely by reason of his having caused the account to pay a member of an exchange, broker, or dealer an amount of commission for effecting a securities transaction in excess of the amount of commission another member of an exchange, broker, or dealer would have charged for effecting that transaction, if such person determined in good faith that such amount of commission was reasonable in relation to the value of the brokerage and research services provided by such member, broker, or dealer, viewed in terms of either that particular transaction or his overall responsibilities with respect to the accounts as to which he exercises investment discretion. This subsection is exclusive and plenary insofar as conduct is covered by the foregoing, unless otherwise expressly provided by contract: Provided, however, That nothing in this subsection shall be construed to impair or limit the power of the Commission under any other provision of this title or otherwise.

(2) A person exercising investment discretion with respect to an account shall make such disclosure of his policies and practices with respect to commissions that will be paid for effecting securities transactions, at such times and in such manner, as the appropriate regulatory agency, by rule, may prescribe as necessary or appropriate in the public interest or for the protection of investors.

(3) For purposes of this subsection a person provides brokerage and research services insofar as he—

(A) furnishes advice, either directly or through publications or writings, as to the value of securities, the advisability of investing in, purchasing, or selling securities, and the availability of securities or purchasers or sellers of securities;

(B) furnishes analyses and reports concerning issuers, industries, securities, economic factors and trends, portfolio strategy, and the performance of accounts; or

(C) effects securities transactions and performs functions incidental thereto (such as clearance, settlement, and custody) or required in connection therewith by rules of the Commission or a self-regulatory organization of which such person is a member or person associated with a member or in which such person is a participant.

(4) The provisions of this subsection shall not apply with regard to securities that are security futures products.

(f) LIMITATIONS ON REMEDIES.—

(1) CLASS ACTION LIMITATIONS.—No covered class action based upon the statutory or common law of any State or subdivision thereof may be maintained in any State or Federal court by any private party alleging—

(A) a misrepresentation or omission of a material fact in connection with the purchase or sale of a covered security; or

(B) that the defendant used or employed any manipulative or deceptive device or contrivance in connection with the purchase or sale of a covered security.

(2) REMOVAL OF COVERED CLASS ACTIONS.—Any covered class action brought in any State court involving a covered security, as set forth in paragraph (1), shall be removable to the Federal district court for the district in which the action is pending, and shall be subject to paragraph (1).

(3) PRESERVATION OF CERTAIN ACTIONS.—

(A) Actions under state law of state of incorporation.—

(i) Actions preserved.—Notwithstanding paragraph (1) or (2), a covered class action described in clause (ii) of this subparagraph that is based upon the statutory or common law of the State in which the issuer is incorporated (in the case of a corporation) or organized (in the case of any other entity) may be maintained in a State or Federal court by a private party.

(ii) Permissible actions.—A covered class action is described in this clause if it involves—

(I) the purchase or sale of securities by the issuer or an affiliate of the issuer exclusively from or to holders of equity securities of the issuer; or

(II) any recommendation, position, or other communication with respect to the sale of securities of an issuer that—

(aa) is made by or on behalf of the issuer or an affiliate of the issuer to holders of equity securities of the issuer; and

(bb) concerns decisions of such equity holders with respect to voting their securities, acting in response to a tender or exchange offer, or exercising dissenters' or appraisal rights.

(B) State actions.—

(i) In general.—Notwithstanding any other provision of this subsection, nothing in this subsection may be construed to preclude a State or political subdivision thereof or a State pension plan from bringing an action involving a covered security on its own behalf, or as a member of a class comprised solely of other States, political subdivisions, or State pension plans that are named plaintiffs, and that have authorized participation, in such action.

(ii) State pension plan defined.—For purposes of this subparagraph, the term "State pension plan" means a pension plan established and maintained for its employees by the government of a State or political subdivision thereof, or by any agency or instrumentality thereof.

(C) Actions under contractual agreements between issuers and indenture trustees.—Notwithstanding paragraph (1) or (2), a covered class action that seeks to enforce a contractual agreement between an issuer and an indenture trustee may be maintained in a State or Federal court by a party to the agreement or a successor to such party.

(D) Remand of removed actions.—In an action that has been removed from a State court pursuant to paragraph (2), if the Federal court determines that the action may be maintained in State court pursuant to this subsection, the Federal court shall remand such action to such State court.

(4) PRESERVATION OF STATE JURISDICTION.—The securities commission (or any agency or office performing like functions) of any State shall retain jurisdiction under the laws of such State to investigate and bring enforcement actions.

(5) DEFINITIONS.—For purposes of this subsection, the following definitions shall apply:

(A) Affiliate of the issuer.—The term "affiliate of the issuer" means a person that directly or indirectly, through one or more intermediaries, controls or is controlled by or is under common control with, the issuer.

(B) Covered class action.—The term "covered class action" means—

(i) any single lawsuit in which—

(I) damages are sought on behalf of more than 50 persons or prospective class members, and questions of law or fact common to those persons or members of the prospective class, without reference to issues of individualized reliance on an alleged misstatement or omission, predominate over any questions affecting only individual persons or members; or

(II) one or more named parties seek to recover damages on a representative basis on behalf of themselves and other unnamed parties similarly situated, and questions of law or fact common to those persons or members of the prospective class predominate over any questions affecting only individual persons or members; or

(ii) any group of lawsuits filed in or pending in the same court and involving common questions of law or fact, in which—

(I) damages are sought on behalf of more than 50 persons; and

(II) the lawsuits are joined, consolidated, or otherwise proceed as a single action for any purpose.

(C) Exception for derivative actions.—Notwithstanding subparagraph (B), the term "covered class action" does not include an exclusively derivative action brought by one or more shareholders on behalf of a corporation.

(D) Counting of certain class members.—For purposes of this paragraph, a corporation, investment company, pension plan, partnership, or other entity, shall be treated as one person or prospective class member, but only if the entity is not established for the purpose of participating in the action.

(E) Covered security.—The term "covered security" means a security that satisfies the standards for a covered security specified in paragraph (1) or (2) of section 18(b) of the Securities Act of 1933, at the time during which it is alleged that the misrepresentation, omission, or manipulative or deceptive conduct occurred, except that such term shall not include any debt security that is exempt from registration under the Securities Act of 1933 pursuant to rules issued by the Commission under section 4(2) of that Act.

(F) Rule of construction.—Nothing in this paragraph shall be construed to affect the discretion of a State court in determining whether actions filed in such court should be joined, consolidated, or otherwise allowed to proceed as a single action.

VALIDITY OF CONTRACTS

Sec. 29. (a) Any condition, stipulation, or provision binding any person to waive compliance with any provision of this title or of any rule or regulation thereunder, or of any rule of a self-regulatory organization, shall be void.

(b) Every contract made in violation of any provision of this title or of any rule or regulation thereunder, and every contract (including any contract for listing a security on an exchange) heretofore or hereafter made the performance of which involves the violation of, or the continuance of any relationship or practice in violation of, any provision of this title or any rule or regulation thereunder, shall be void (1) as regards the rights of any person who, in violation of any such provision, rule, or regulation, shall have made or engaged in the performance of any such contract, and (2) as regards the rights of any person who, not being a party to such contract, shall have acquired any right thereunder with actual knowledge of the facts by reason of which the making or performance of such contract was in violation of any such provision, rule, or regulation: *Provided,* (A) That no contract shall be void by reason of this subsection because of any violation of any rule or regulation prescribed pursuant to paragraph (3) of subsection (c) of section 15 of this title, and (B) that no contract shall be deemed to be void by reason of this subsection in any action maintained in reliance upon this subsection, by any person to or for whom any broker or dealer sells, or from or for whom any broker or dealer purchases, a security in violation of any rule or regulation prescribed pursuant to paragraph (1) or (2) of subsection (c) of section 15 of this title, unless such action is brought within one year after the discovery that such sale or purchase involves such violation and within 3 years after such violation. The Commission may, in a rule or regulation prescribed pursuant to such paragraph (2), of such section 15(c), designate such rule or regulation, or portion thereof, as a rule or regulation, or portion thereof, a contract in violation of which shall not be void by reason of this subsection.

(c) Nothing in this title shall be construed (1) to affect the validity of any loan or extension of credit (or any extension or renewal thereof) made or of any lien created prior or subsequent to the enactment of this title, unless at the time of the making of such loan or extension of credit (or extension or renewal thereof) or the creating of such lien, the person making such loan or extension of credit (or extension or renewal thereof) or acquiring such lien shall have actual knowledge of facts by reason of which the making of such loan or extension of credit (or extension or renewal thereof) or the acquisition of such lien is a violation of the provisions of this title or any rule or regulation thereunder, or (2) to afford a defense to the collection of any debt or obligation or the enforcement of any lien by any person who shall have acquired such debt, obligation, or lien in good faith for value and without actual knowledge of the violation of any provision of this title or any rule or regulation thereunder affecting the legality of such debt, obligation, or lien.

FOREIGN SECURITIES EXCHANGES

Sec. 30. (a) It shall be unlawful for any broker or dealer, directly or indirectly, to make use of the mails or of any means or instrumentality of interstate commerce for the purpose of effecting on an exchange not within or subject to the jurisdiction of the United States, any transaction in any security the issuer of which is a resident of, or is organized under the laws of, or has its principal place of business in, a place within or subject to the jurisdiction of the United States, in contravention of such rules and regulations as the Commission may prescribe as necessary or appropriate in the public interest or for the protection of investors or to prevent the evasion of this chapter.

(b) The provisions of this chapter or of any rule or regulation thereunder shall not apply to any person insofar as he transacts a business in securities without the jurisdiction of the United States, unless he transacts such business in contravention of such rules and regulations as the Commission may prescribe as necessary or appropriate to prevent the evasion of this chapter.

(c) RULE OF CONSTRUCTION. No provision of this title that was added by the Wall Street Transparency and Accountability Act of 2010, or any rule or regulation thereunder, shall apply to any person insofar as such person transacts a business in security-based swaps without the jurisdiction of the United States, unless such person transacts such business in contravention of such rules and regulations as the Commission may prescribe as necessary or appropriate to prevent the evasion of any provision of this title that was added by the Wall Street Transparency and Accountability Act of 2010. This subsection shall not be construed to limit the jurisdiction of the Commission under any provision of this title, as in effect prior to the date of enactment of the Wall Street Transparency and Accountability Act of 2010.

PROHIBITED FOREIGN TRADE PRACTICES BY ISSUERS

Sec. 30A. (a) PROHIBITION.—It shall be unlawful for any issuer which has a class of securities registered pursuant to section 12 of this title or which is required to file reports under section 15(d) of this title, or for any officer, director, employee, or agent of such issuer or any stockholder thereof acting on behalf of such issuer, to make use of the mails or any means of instrumentality of interstate commerce corruptly in furtherance of an offer, payment, promise to pay, or authorization of the payment of any money, or offer, gift, promise to give, or authorization of the giving of anything of value to—

(1) any foreign official for purposes of—

(A)(i) influencing any act or decision of such foreign official in his official capacity, (ii) inducing such foreign official to do or omit to do any act in violation of the lawful duty of such official, or (iii) securing any improper advantage; or

(B) inducing such foreign official to use his influence with a foreign government or instrumentality thereof to affect or influence any act or decision of such government or instrumentality,

in order to assist such issuer in obtaining or retaining business for or with, or directing business to, any person;

(2) any foreign political party or official thereof or any candidate for foreign political office for purposes of—

(A)(i) influencing any act or decision of such party, official, or candidate in its or his official capacity, (ii) inducing such party, official, or candidate to do or omit to do an act in violation of the lawful duty of such party, official, or candidate, or (iii) securing any improper advantage; or

(B) inducing such party, official, or candidate to use its or his influence with a foreign government or instrumentality thereof to affect or influence any act or decision of such government or instrumentality,

in order to assist such issuer in obtaining or retaining business for or with, or directing business to, any person; or

(3) any person, while knowing that all or a portion of such money or thing of value will be offered, given, or promised, directly or indirectly, to any foreign official, to any foreign political party or official thereof, or to any candidate for foreign political office, for purposes of—

(A) (i) influencing any act or decision of such foreign official, political party, party official, or candidate in his or its official capacity, (ii) inducing such foreign official, political party, party official, or candidate to do or omit to do any act in violation of the lawful duty of such foreign official, political party, party official, or candidate, or (iii) securing any improper advantage;

(B) inducing such foreign official, political party, party official, or candidate to use his or its influence with a foreign government or instrumentality thereof to affect or influence any act or decision of such government or instrumentality,

in order to assist such issuer in obtaining or retaining business for or with, or directing business to, any person.

(b) Exception for Routine Governmental Action.—Subsections (a) and (g) shall not apply to any facilitating or expediting payment to a foreign official, political party, or party official the purpose of which is to expedite or to secure the performance of a routine governmental action by a foreign official, political party, or party official.

(c) Affirmative Defenses.—It shall be an affirmative defense to actions under subsection (a) or (g) that—

(1) the payment, gift, offer, or promise of anything of value that was made, was lawful under the written laws and regulations of the foreign official's, political party's, party official's, or candidate's country; or

(2) the payment, gift, offer, or promise of anything of value that was made, was a reasonable and bona fide expenditure, such as travel and lodging expenses, incurred by or on behalf of a foreign official, party, party official, or candidate and was directly related to—

(A) the promotion, demonstration, or explanation of products or services; or

(B) the execution or performance of a contract with a foreign government or agency thereof.

(d) Guidelines by the Attorney General.—Not later than one year after the date of the enactment of the Foreign Corrupt Practices Act Amendments of 1988, the Attorney General, after consultation with the Commission, the Secretary of Commerce, the United States Trade Representative, the Secretary of State, and the Secretary of the Treasury, and after obtaining the views of all interested persons through public notice and comment procedures, shall determine to what extent compliance with this section would be enhanced and the business community would be assisted by further clarification of the preceding provisions of this section and may, based on such determination and to the extent necessary and appropriate, issue—

(1) guidelines describing specific types of conduct, associated with common types of export sales arrangments and business contracts, which for purposes of the Department of Justice's present enforcement policy, the Attorney General determines would be in conformance with the preceding providisions of this section; and

(2) general precautionary procedures which issuers may use on a voluntary basis to conform their conduct to the Department of Justice's present enforcement policy regarding the preceding provisions of this section.

The Attorney General shall issue the guidelines and procedures referred to in the preceding sentence in accordance with the provisions of subchapter II of chapter 5 of title 5, United States Code, and those guidelines and procedures shall be subject to the provisions of chapter 7 of that title.

(e) OPINIONS OF THE ATTORNEY GENERAL.—(1) The Attorney General, after consultation with appropriate departments and agencies of the United States and after obtaining the views of all interested persons through public notice and comment procedures, shall establish a procedure to provide responses to specific inquiries by issuers concerning conformance of their conduct with the Department of Justice's present enforcement policy regarding the preceding provisions of this section. The Attorney General shall, within 30 days after receiving such a request, issue an opinion in response to that request. The opinion shall state whether or not certain specified prospective conduct would, for purposes of the Department of Justice's present enforcement policy, violate the preceding provisions of this section. Additional requests for opinions may be filed with the Attorney General regarding other specified prospective conduct that is beyond the scope of conduct specified in previous requests. In any action brought under the applicable provisions of this section, there shall be a rebuttable presumption that conduct, which is specified in a request by an issuer and for which the Attorney General has issued an opinion that such conduct is in conformity with the Department of Justice's present enforcement policy, is in compliance with the preceding provisions of this section. Such a presumption may be rebutted by a preponderance of the evidence. In considering the presumption for purposes of this paragraph, a court shall weigh all relevant factors, including but not limited to whether the information submitted to the Attorney General was accurate and complete and whether it was within the scope of the conduct specified in any request received by the Attorney General. The Attorney General shall establish the procedure required by this paragraph in accordance with the provisions of subchapter II of chapter 5 of title 5, United States Code, and that procedure shall be subject to the provis ions of chapter 7 of that title.

(2) Any document or other material which is provided to, received by, or prepared in the Department of Justice or any other department or agency of the United States in connection with a request by an issuer under the procedure established under paragraph (1), shall be exempt from disclosure under section 552 of title 5, United States Code, and shall not, except with the consent of the issuer, be made publicly available, regardless of whether the Attorney General responds to such a request or the issuer withdraws such request before receiving a response.

(3) Any issuer who has made a request to the Attorney General under paragraph (1) may withdraw such request prior to the time the Attorney General issues an opinion in response to such request. Any request so withdrawn shall have no force or effect.

(4) The Attorney General shall, to the maximum extent practicable, provide timely guidance concerning the Department of Justice's present enforcement policy with respect to the preceding provisions of this section to potential exporters and small businesses that are unable to obtain specialized counsel on issues pertaining to such provisions. Such guidance shall be limited to responses to requests under paragraph (1) concerning conformity of specified prospective conduct with the Department of Justice's present enforcement policy regarding the preceding provisions of this section and general explanations of compliance responsibilities and of potential liabilities under the preceding provisions of this section.

(f) DEFINITIONS.—For purposes of this section:

(1) The term "foreign official" means any officer or employee of a foreign government or any department, agency, or instrumentality thereof, or of a public international organization, or any person acting in an official capacity for or on behalf of any such government or department, agency, or instrumentality, or for or on behalf of any such public international organization.

(B) For purposes of subparagraph (A), the term "public international organization" means—

(i) an organization that is designated by Executive order pursuant to section 1 of the International Organizations Immunities Act (22 U.S.C. 288); or

(ii) any other international organization that is designated by the President by Executive order for the purposes of this section, effective as of the date of publication of such order in the Federal Register.

(2) (A) A person's state of mind is "knowing" with respect to conduct, a circumstance, or a result if—

(i) such person is aware that such person is engaging in such conduct, that such circumstance exists, or that such result is substantially certain to occur; or

(ii) such person has a firm belief that such circumstance exists or that such result is substantially certain to occur.

(B) When knowledge of the existence of a particular circumstance is required for an offense, such knowledge is established if a person is aware of a high probability of the existence of such circumstance, unless the person actually believes that such circumstance does not exist.

(3) (A) The term "routine governmental action" means only an action which is ordinarily and commonly performed by a foreign official in—

(i) obtaining permits, licenses, or other official documents to qualify a person to do business in a foreign country;

(ii) processing governmental papers, such as visas and work orders;

(iii) providing police protection, mail pick-up and delivery, or scheduling inspections associated with contract performance or inspections related to transit of goods across country;

(iv) providing phone service, power and water supply, loading and unloading cargo, or protecting perishable products or commodities from deterioration; or

(v) actions of a similar nature.

(B) The term "routine governmental action" does not include any decision by a foreign official whether, or on what terms, to award new business to or to continue business with a particular party, or any action taken by a foreign official involved in the decisionmaking process to encourage a decision to award new business to or continue business with a particular party.

(g) ALTERNATIVE JURISDICTION.—

(1) It shall also be unlawful for any issuer organized under the laws of the United States, or a State, territory, possession, or commonwealth of the United States or a political subdivision thereof and which has a class of securities registered pursuant to section 12 of this title or which is required to file reports under section 15(d) of this title, or for any United States person that is an officer, director, employee, or agent of such issuer or a stockholder thereof acting on behalf of such issuer, to corruptly do any act outside the United States in furtherance of an offer, payment, promise to pay, or authorization of the payment of any money, or offer, gift, promise to give, or authorization of the giving of anything of value to any of the persons or entities set forth in paragraphs (1), (2), and (3) of subsection (a) of this section for the purposes set forth therein, irrespective of whether such issuer or such officer, director, employee, agent, or stockholder makes use of the mails or any means or instrumentality of interstate commerce in furtherance of such offer, gift, payment, promise, or authorization.

(2) As used in this subsection, the term "United States person" means a national of the United States (as defined in section 101 of the Immigration and Nationality Act (8 U.S.C. 1101)) or any corporation, partnership, association, joint-stock company, business trust, unincorporated organization, or sole proprietorship organized under the laws of the United States or any State, territory, possession, or commonwealth of the United States, or any political subdivision thereof.

PENALTIES

Sec. 32. (a) Any person who willfully violates any provision of this title (other than section 30A), or any rule or regulation thereunder the violation of which is made unlawful or the observance of which is required under the terms of this title, or any person who willfully and knowingly makes, or causes to be made, any statement in any application, report, or document required to be filed under this title or any rule or regulation thereunder or any undertaking contained in a registration statement as provided in subsection (d) of section 15 of this title or by any self-regulatory organization in connection with an application for membership or participation therein or to become associated with a member thereof, which statement was false or misleading with respect to any material fact, shall upon conviction be fined not more than $5,000,000, or imprisoned not more than 20 years, or both, except that when such person is a person other than a natural person, a fine not exceeding $25,000,000 may be imposed; but no person shall be subject to imprisonment under this section for the violation of any rule or regulation if he proves that he had no knowledge of such rule or regulation.

(b) Any issuer which fails to file information, documents, or reports required to be filed under subsection (d) of section 15 of this title or any rule or regulation thereunder shall forfeit to the United States the sum of $100 for each and every day such failure to file shall continue. Such forfeiture, which shall be in lieu of any criminal penalty for such failure to file which might be deemed to arise under subsection (a) of this section, shall be payable into the Treasury of the United States and shall be recoverable in a civil suit in the name of the United States.

(c) (1) (A) Any issuer that violates subsection (a) or (g) of section 30A shall be fined not more than $2,000,000.

(B) Any issuer that violates subsection (a) or (g) of section 30A(a) shall be subject to a civil penalty of not more than $10,000 imposed in an action brought by the Commission.

(2) (A) Any officer, director, employee, or agent of an issuer, or stockholder acting on behalf of such issuer, who willfully violates subsection (a) or (g) of section 30A of this title shall be fined not more than $100,000, or imprisoned not more than 5 years, or both.

(B) Any officer, director, employee, or agent of an issuer, or stockholder acting on behalf of such issuer, who violates subsection (a) or (g) of section 30A of this title shall be subject to a civil penalty of not more than $10,000 imposed in an action brought by the Commission.

(3) Whenever a fine is imposed under paragraph (2) upon any officer, director, employee, agent, or stockholder of an issuer, such fine may not be paid, directly or indirectly, by such issuer.

SEPARABILITY OF PROVISIONS

Sec. 33. If any provision of this Act, or the application of such provision to any person or circumstances, shall be held invalid, the remainder of the Act, and the application of such provision to persons or circumstances other than those as to which it is held invalid, shall not be affected thereby.

REQUIREMENTS FOR THE EDGAR SYSTEM

Sec. 35A. The Commission, by rule or regulation—

(1) shall provide that any information in the EDGAR system that is required to be disseminated by the contractor—

(A) may be sold or disseminated by the contractor only pursuant to a uniform schedule of fees prescribed by the Commission;

(B) may be obtained by a purchaser by direct interconnection with the EDGAR system;

(C) shall be equally available on equal terms to all persons; and

(D) may be used, resold, or redisseminated by any person who has lawfully obtained such information without restriction and without payment of additional fees or royalties; and

(2) shall require that persons, or classes of persons, required to make filings with the Commission submit such filings in a form and manner suitable for entry into the EDGAR system and shall specify the date that such requirement is effective with respect to that person or class; except that the Commission may exempt persons or classes of persons, or filings or classes of filings, from such rules or regulations in order to prevent hardships or to avoid imposing unreasonable burdens or as otherwise may be necessary or appropriate.

GENERAL EXEMPTIVE AUTHORITY

Sec. 36. (a) AUTHORITY.—

(1) In general.—Except as provided in subsection (b), but notwithstanding any other provision of this title, the Commission, by rule, regulation, or order, may conditionally or unconditionally exempt any person, security, or transaction, or any class or classes of persons, securities, or transactions, from any provision or provisions of this title or of any rule or regulation thereunder, to the extent that such exemption is necessary or appropriate in the public interest, and is consistent with the protection of investors.

(2) Procedures.—The Commission shall, by rule or regulation, determine the procedures under which an exemptive order under this section shall be granted and may, in its sole discretion, decline to entertain any application for an order of exemption under this section.

(b) LIMITATION.—The Commission may not, under this section, exempt any person, security, or transaction, or any class or classes of persons, securities, or transactions from section 15C or the rules or regulations issued thereunder or (for purposes of section 15C and the rules and regulations issued thereunder) from any definition in paragraph (42), (43), (44), or (45) of section 3(a).

(c) DERIVATIVES.— Unless the Commission is expressly authorized by any provision described in this subsection to grant exemptions, the Commission shall not grant exemptions, with respect to amendments made by subtitle B of the Wall Street Transparency and Accountability Act of 2010, with respect to paragraphs (65), (66), (68), (69), (70), (71), (72), (73), (74), (75), (76), and (79) of section 3(a), and sections 10B(a), 10B(b), 10B(c), 13A, 15F, 17A(g), 17A(h), 17A(i), 17A(j), 17A(k), and 17A(l); provided that the Commission shall have exemptive authority under this title with respect to security-based swaps as to the same matters that the Commodity Futures Trading Commission has under the Wall Street Transparency and Accountability Act of 2010 with respect to swaps, including under section 4(c) of the Commodity Exchange Act.

INVESTOR ADVISORY COMMITTEE

Sec. 39. (a) ESTABLISHMENT AND PURPOSE.

(1) ESTABLISHMENT. There is established within the Commission the Investor Advisory Committee (referred to in this section as the "Committee").

(2) PURPOSE. The Committee shall—

(A) Advise and consult with the Commission on—

(i) Regulatory priorities of the Commission;

(ii) Issues relating to the regulation of securities products, trading strategies, and fee structures, and the effectiveness of disclosure;

(iii) Initiatives to protect investor interest; and

(iv) Initiatives to promote investor confidence and the integrity of the securities marketplace; and

(B) Submit to the Commission such findings and recommendations as the Committee determines are appropriate, including recommendations for proposed legislative changes.

(b) MEMBERSHIP.

(1) IN GENERAL. The members of the Committee shall be—

(A) The Investor Advocate;

(B) A representative of State securities commissions;

(C) A representative of the interests of senior citizens; and

(D) Not fewer than 10, and not more than 20, members appointed by the Commission, from among individuals who—

(i) Represent the interests of individual equity and debt investors, including investors in mutual funds;

(ii) Represent the interests of institutional investors, including the interests of pension funds and registered investment companies;

(iii) Are knowledgeable about investment issues and decisions; and

(iv) Have reputations of integrity.

(2) TERM. Each member of the Committee appointed under paragraph (1)(B) shall serve for a term of 4 years.

(3) MEMBERS NOT COMMISSION EMPLOYEES. Members appointed under paragraph (1)(B) shall not be deemed to be employees or agents of the Commission solely because of membership on the Committee.

(c) CHAIRMAN; VICE CHAIRMAN; SECRETARY; ASSISTANT SECRETARY.

(1) IN GENERAL. The members of the Committee shall elect, from among the members of the Committee—

(A) A chairman, who may not be employed by an issuer;

(B) A vice chairman, who may not be employed by an issuer;

(C) A secretary; and

(D) An assistant secretary.

(2) TERM. Each member elected under paragraph (1) shall serve for a term of 3 years in the capacity for which the member was elected under paragraph (1).

(d) MEETINGS.

(1) FREQUENCY OF MEETINGS. The Committee shall meet—

(A) Not less frequently than twice annually, at the call of the chairman of the Committee; and

(B) From time to time, at the call of the Commission.

(2) NOTICE. The chairman of the Committee shall give the members of the Committee written notice of each meeting, not later than 2 weeks before the date of the meeting.

(e) COMPENSATION AND TRAVEL EXPENSES. Each member of the Committee who is not a full-time employee of the United States shall—

(1) Be entitled to receive compensation at a rate not to exceed the daily equivalent of the annual rate of basic pay in effect for a position at level V of the Executive Schedule under section 5316 of title 5, United States Code, for each day during which the member is engaged in the actual performance of the duties of the Committee; and

(2) While away from the home or regular place of business of the member in the performance of services for the Committee, be allowed travel expenses, including per diem in lieu of subsistence, in the same manner as persons employed intermittently in the Government service are allowed expenses under section 5703(b) of title 5, United States Code.

(f) STAFF. The Commission shall make available to the Committee such staff as the chairman of the Committee determines are necessary to carry out this section.

(g) REVIEW BY COMMISSION. The Commission shall—

(1) Review the findings and recommendations of the Committee; and

(2) Each time the Committee submits a finding or recommendation to the Commission, promptly issue a public statement—

(A) Assessing the finding or recommendation of the Committee; and

(B) Disclosing the action, if any, the Commission intends to take with respect to the finding or recommendation.

(h) COMMITTEE FINDINGS. Nothing in this section shall require the Commission to agree to or act upon any finding or recommendation of the Committee.

(i) FEDERAL ADVISORY COMMITTEE ACT. The Federal Advisory Committee Act (5 U.S.C. App.) shall not apply with respect to the Committee and its activities.

(j) AUTHORIZATION OF APPROPRIATIONS. There is authorized to be appropriated to the Commission such sums as are necessary to carry out this section.

EXCHANGE ACT RULES—SELECTED PROVISIONS

17 C.F.R. §§ 240.10b to 240.19c4

Rule	Subject
14a-3	Information to be furnished security holders
14a-4	Requirements as to proxy
14a-5	Presentation of information in proxy statement
14a-6	Filing requirements
14a-7	Obligations of registrants to provide a list of, or mail soliciting material to, security holders
14a-8	Shareholder proposals
14a-9	False or misleading statements
14a-10	Prohibition of certain solicitations
14a-11	Shareholder nominations [Vacated.]
14a-12	Solicitation before furnishing a proxy statement
14a-13	Obligation of registrants in communicating with beneficial owners
14a-16	Internet availability of proxy materials
14a-17	Electronic shareholder forums
14a-21	Shareholder approval of executive compensation, frequency of votes for approval of executive compensation and shareholder approval of golden parachute compensation

Regulations 14D and 14E
Disclosure Requirements and Minimum Time for Tender Offers

Rule	Subject
14d-1	Scope of and definitions applicable to regulations 14D and 14E
14d-2	Commencement of a tender offer
14d-3	Filing and transmission of tender offer statement
14d-4	Dissemination of tender offers to security holders
14d-5	Dissemination of certain tender offers by the use of stockholder lists and security position listings
14d-6	Disclosure of tender offer information to security holders
14d-7	Additional withdrawal rights
14d-8	Exemption from statutory pro rata requirement
14d-9	Recommendation or solicitation by the subject company and others
14d-10	Equal treatment of security holders
14d-11	Subsequent offering period
14e-1	Unlawful tender offer practices
14e-2	Position of a subject company with respect to a tender offer
14e-3	Transactions in securities on the basis of material, nonpublic information in the context of tender offers
14e-4	Prohibited transactions in connection with partial tender offers
14e-5	Prohibiting purchases outside of a tender offer

Rules Relating to Over-the-Counter Markets

Rule	Subject
15c1-1	Definitions
15c1-2	Fraud and misrepresentation
15c1-6	Disclosure of interest in distribution
15c2-1	Hypothecation of customers' securities
15c2-8	Delivery of prospectus
15c2-11	Initiation or resumption of quotations without specified information
15c2-12	Municipal securities disclosure
15c3-5	Risk management controls for brokers or dealers with market access

Penny Stock Disclosures

Rule	Subject
15g-1	Exemptions for certain transactions

RULES OF GENERAL APPLICATION

Rule 0-4. Non-disclosure of Information Obtained in the Course of Examinations and Investigations

Information or documents obtained by officers or employees of the Commission in the course of any examination or investigation pursuant to Section 17(a) or 21(a) shall, unless made a matter of public record, be deemed confidential. Except as provided by 17 CFR 203.2, officers and employees are hereby prohibited from making such confidential information or documents or any other non-public records of the Commission available to anyone other than a member, officer or employee of the Commission, unless the Commission or the General Counsel, pursuant to delegated authority, authorizes the disclosure of such information or the production of such documents as not being contrary to the public interest. Any officer or employee who is served with a subpoena requiring the disclosure of such information or the production of such documents shall appear in court and, unless the authorization described in the preceding sentence shall have been given, shall respectfully decline to disclose the information or produce the documents called for, basing his refusal upon this rule. Any officer or employee who is served with such a subpoena shall promptly advise the General Counsel of the service of such subpoena, the nature of the information or documents sought, and any circumstances which may bear upon the desirability of making available such information or documents.

DEFINITION OF "EQUITY SECURITY" AS USED IN
SECTION 12(g) AND 16

Rule 3a11-1. Definition of the Term "Equity Security"

The term *equity security* is hereby defined to include any stock or similar security, certificate of interest or participation in any profit sharing agreement, preorganization certificate or subscription, transferable share, voting trust certificate or certificate of deposit for an equity security, limited partnership interest, interest in a joint venture, or certificate of interest in a business trust; any security future on any such security; or any security convertible, with or without consideration into such a security, or carrying any warrant or right to subscribe to or purchase such a security; or any such warrant or right; or any put, call, straddle, or other option or privilege of buying such a security from or selling such a security to another without being bound to do so.

MISCELLANEOUS EXEMPTIONS

Rule 3a12-3. Exemption from Sections 14(a), 14(b), 14(c), 14(f) and 16 for Securities of Certain Foreign Issuers

(a) Securities for which the filing of securities on Form 18 [17 CFR 249.218] are authorized shall be exempt from the operation of sections 14 and 16 of the Act.

(b) Securities registered by a foreign private issuer, as defined in Rule 3b-4 (§ 240.3b-4 of this chapter), shall be exempt from sections 14(a), 14(b), 14(c), 14(f) and 16 of the Act.

DEFINITIONS

Rule 3a51-1. Definition of "Penny Stock"

For purposes of section 3(a)(51) of the Act, the term "penny stock" shall mean any equity security other than a security:

(a) That is a reported security, as defined in § 242.600(b)(47), provided that:

(1) The security is registered, or approved for registration upon notice of issuance, on a national securities exchange that has been continuously registered as a national securities exchange since April 20, 1992 (the date of the adoption of Rule 3a51-1 (§ 240.3a51-1) by the Commission); and the national securities exchange has maintained quantitative listing standards that are substantially similar to or stricter than those listing standards that were in place on that exchange on January 8, 2004; or

(2) The security is registered, or approved for registration upon notice of issuance, on a national securities exchange, or is listed, or approved for listing upon notice of issuance on, an automated quotation system sponsored by a registered national securities association, that:

(i) Has established initial listing standards that meet or exceed the following criteria:

(A) The issuer shall have:

(1) Stockholders' equity of $5,000,000;

(2) Market value of listed securities of $50 million for 90 consecutive days prior to applying for the listing (market value means the closing bid price multiplied by the number of securities listed); or

(3) Net income of $750,000 (excluding extraordinary or non-recurring items) in the most recently completed fiscal year or in two of the last three most recently completed fiscal years;

(B) The issuer shall have an operating history of at least one year or a market value of listed securities of $50 million (market value means the closing bid price multiplied by the number of securities listed);

(C) The issuer's stock, common or preferred, shall have a minimum bid price of $4 per share;

(D) In the case of common stock, there shall be at least 300 round lot holders of the security (a round lot holder means a holder of a normal unit of trading);

(E) In the case of common stock, there shall be at least 1,000,000 publicly held shares and such shares shall have a market value of at least $5 million (market value means the closing bid price multiplied by number of publicly held shares, and shares held directly or indirectly by an officer or director of the issuer and by any person who is the beneficial owner of more than 10 percent of the total shares outstanding are not considered to be publicly held);

(F) In the case of a convertible debt security, there shall be a principal amount outstanding of at least $10 million;

(G) In the case of rights and warrants, there shall be at least 100,000 issued and the underlying security shall be registered on a national securities exchange or listed on an automated quotation system sponsored by a registered national securities association and shall satisfy the requirements of paragraph (a) or (e) of this section;

(H) In the case of put warrants (that is, instruments that grant the holder the right to sell to the issuing company a specified number of shares of the company's common stock, at a specified price until a specified period of time), there shall be at least 100,000 issued and the underlying security shall be registered on a national securities exchange or listed on an automated quotation system sponsored by a registered national securities association and shall satisfy the requirements of paragraph (a) or (e) of this section;

(I) In the case of units (that is, two or more securities traded together), all component parts shall be registered on a national securities exchange or listed on an automated quotation system sponsored by a registered national securities association and shall satisfy the requirements of paragraph (a) or (e) of this section; and

(J) In the case of equity securities (other than common and preferred stock, convertible debt securities, rights and warrants, put warrants, or units), including hybrid products and derivative securities products, the national securities exchange or registered national securities association shall establish quantitative listing standards that are substantially similar to those found in paragraphs (a)(2)(i)(A) through (a)(2)(i)(I) of this section; and

(ii) Has established quantitative continued listing standards that are reasonably related to the initial listing standards set forth in paragraph (a)(2)(i) of this section, and that are consistent with the maintenance of fair and orderly markets;

(b) that is issued by an investment company registered under the Investment Company Act of 1940;

(c) that is a put or call option issued by the Options Clearing Corporation;

(d) Except for purposes of Section 7(b) of the Securities Act and Rule 419 (17 CFR 230.419, that has a price of five dollars or more;

(1) For purposes of this paragraph (d) of this section:

(i) a security has a price of five dollars or more for a particular transaction if the security is purchased or sold in that transaction at a price of five dollars or more, excluding any broker or dealer commission, commission equivalent, mark-up, or mark-down; and

(ii) other than in connection with a particular transaction, a security has a price of five dollars or more at a given time if the inside bid quotation is five dollars or more; provided, however, that if there is no such inside bid quotation, a security has a price of five dollars or more at a given time if the average of three or more interdealer bid quotations at specified prices displayed at that time in an interdealer quotation system, as defined in 17 CFR 240.15c2-7, by three or more market makers in the security, is five dollars or more.

(iii) The term "inside bid quotation" shall mean the highest bid quotation for the security displayed by a market maker in the security on an automated interdealer quotation system that has the characteristics set forth in Section 17B(b)(2) of the Act, or such other automated interdealer quotation system designated by the Commission for purposes of this section, at any time in which at least two market makers are contemporaneously displaying on such system bid and offer quotations for the security at specified prices.

(2) If a security is a unit composed of one or more securities, the unit price divided by the number of shares of the unit that are not warrants, options, rights, or similar securities must be five dollars or more, as determined in accordance with paragraph (d)(1) of this section, and any share of the unit that is a warrant, option, right, or similar security, or a convertible security, must have an exercise price or conversion price of five dollars or more;

(e)(1) That is registered, or approved for registration upon notice of issuance, on a national securities exchange that makes transaction reports available pursuant to § 240.11Aa3-1, provided that:

(i) Price and volume information with respect to transactions in that security is required to be reported on a current and continuing basis and is made available to vendors of market information pursuant to the rules of the national securities exchange;

(ii) The security is purchased or sold in a transaction that is effected on or through the facilities of the national securities exchange, or that is part of the distribution of the security; and

(iii) The security satisfies the requirements of paragraph (a)(1) or (a)(2) of this section;

(2) A security that satisfies the requirements of this paragraph (e), but does not otherwise satisfy the requirements of paragraph (a), (b), (c), (d), (f), or (g) of this section, shall be a penny stock for purposes of section 15(b)(6) of the Act (15 U.S.C. 78o(b)(6));

(f) That is a security futures product listed on a national securities exchange or an automated quotation system sponsored by a registered national securities association; or

(g) whose issuer has:

(1) net tangible assets (*i.e.,* total assets less intangible assets and liabilities) in excess of $2,000,000, if the issuer has been in continuous operation for at least three years, or $5,000,000, if the issuer has been in continuous operation for less than three years; or

(2) average revenue of at least $6,000,000 for the last three years.

(3) For purposes of paragraph (g) of this section, net tangible assets or average revenues must be demonstrated by financial statements dated less than fifteen months prior to the date of the transaction that the broker or dealer has reviewed and has a reasonable basis for believing are accurate in relation to the date of the transaction, and:

(i) if the issuer is other than a foreign private issuer, are the most recent financial statements for the issuer that have been audited and reported on by an independent public accountant in accordance with the provisions of 17 CFR 210.2-02; or

(ii) if the issuer is a foreign private issuer, are the most recent financial statements for the issuer that have been filed with the Commission or furnished to the Commission pursuant to 17 CFR 240.12g3-2(b) of this chapter; provided, however, that if financial statements for the issuer dated less than fifteen months prior to the date of the transaction have not been filed with or furnished to the Commission, financial statements dated within fifteen months prior to the transaction shall be prepared in accordance with generally accepted accounting principles in the country of incorporation, audited in compliance with the requirements of that jurisdiction, and reported on by an accountant duly registered and in good standing in accordance with the regulations of that jurisdiction.

(4) The broker or dealer shall preserve, as part of its records, copies of the financial statements required by paragraph (g)(3) of this section for the period specified in 17 CFR 240.17a-4(b) of this chapter.

Rule 3b-2. Definition of "Officer"

The term "officer" means a president, vice president, secretary, treasurer or principal financial officer, comptroller or principal accounting officer, and any person routinely performing corresponding functions with respect to any organization whether incorporated or unincorporated.

Rule 3b-3. Definition of "Short Sale"

[*Removed and Reserved*. Release No. 34-50103; July 28, 2004.]

Rule 3b-4. Definition of "foreign government", "foreign issuer" and "foreign private issuer"

(a) The term "foreign government" means the government of any foreign country or of any political subdivision of a foreign country.

(b) The term "foreign issuer" means any issuer which is a foreign government, a national of any foreign country or a corporation or other organization incorporated or organized under the laws of any foreign country.

(c) The term foreign private issuer means any foreign issuer other than a foreign government except for an issuer meeting the following conditions as of the last business day of its most recently completed second fiscal quarter:

(1) More than 50 percent of the issuer's outstanding voting securities are directly or indirectly held of record by residents of the United States; and

(2) Any of the following:

(i) The majority of the executive officers or directors are United States citizens or residents;

(ii) More than 50 percent of the assets of the issuer are located in the United States; or

(iii) The business of the issuer is administered principally in the United States.

Note to paragraph (c)(1): To determine the percentage of outstanding voting securities held by U.S. residents:

A. Use the method of calculating record ownership in § 240.12g3-2(a), except that:

(1) Your inquiry as to the amount of shares represented by accounts of customers resident in the United States may be limited to brokers, dealers, banks and other nominees located in:

(i) The United States,

(ii) Your jurisdiction of incorporation, and

(iii) The jurisdiction that is the primary trading market for your voting securities, if different than your jurisdiction of incorporation; and

(2) Notwithstanding § 240.12g5-1(a)(8) of this chapter, you shall not exclude securities held by persons who received the securities pursuant to an employee compensation plan.

B. If, after reasonable inquiry, you are unable to obtain information about the amount of shares represented by accounts of customers resident in the United States, you may assume, for purposes of this definition, that the customers are residents of the jurisdiction in which the nominee has its principal place of business.

C. Count shares of voting securities beneficially owned by residents of the United States as reported on reports of beneficial ownership provided to you or filed publicly and based on information otherwise provided to you.

(d) Notwithstanding paragraph (c) of this section, in the case of a new registrant with the Commission, the determination of whether an issuer is a foreign private issuer will be made as of a date within 30 days prior to the issuer's filing of an initial registration statement under either the Act or the Securities Act of 1933.

(e) Once an issuer qualifies as a foreign private issuer, it will immediately be able to use the forms and rules designated for foreign private issuers until it fails to qualify for this status at the end of its most recently completed second fiscal quarter. An issuer's determination that it fails to qualify as a foreign private issuer governs its eligibility to use the forms and rules designated for foreign private issuers beginning on the first day of the fiscal year following the determination date. Once an issuer fails to qualify for foreign private issuer status, it will remain unqualified unless it meets the requirements for foreign private issuer status as of the last business day of its second fiscal quarter.

Rule 3b-6. Liability for Certain Statements by Issuers

(a) A statement within the coverage of paragraph (b) of this section which is made by or on behalf of an issuer or by an outside reviewer retained by the issuer shall be deemed not to be a fraudulent statement (as defined in paragraph (d) of this section), unless it is shown that such statement was made or reaffirmed without a reasonable basis or was disclosed other than in good faith.

(b) This rule applies to the following statements:

(1) A forward-looking statement (as defined in paragraph (c) of this section) made in a document filed with the Commission, in Part I of a quarterly report on Form 10-Q, § 249.308a of this chapter, or in an annual report to security holders meeting the requirements of Rules 14a-3(b) and (c) or 14c-3(a) and (b) (§§ 240.14a-3(b) and (c) or 240.14c-3(a) and (b)), a statement reaffirming such forward-looking statement after the date the document was filed

or the annual report was made publicly available, or a forward-looking statement made before the date the document was filed or the date the annual report was made publicly available if such statement is reaffirmed in a filed document, in Part I of a quarterly report on Form 10-Q, or in an annual report made publicly available within a reasonable time after the making of such forward-looking statement; *Provided,* that:

(i) At the time such statements are made or reaffirmed, either the issuer is subject to the reporting requirements of Section 13(a) or 15(d) of the Act and has complied with the requirements of Rule 13a-1 or 15d-1 thereunder, if applicable, to file its most recent annual report on Form 10-K, Form 20-F or Form 40-F; or if the issuer is not subject to the reporting requirements of Section 13(a) or 15(d) of the Act, the statements are made in a registration statement filed under the Securities Act of 1933 offering statement or solicitation of interest, written document or broadcast script under Regulation A or pursuant to Section 12(b) or (g) of the Securities Exchange Act of 1934; and

(2) Information that is disclosed in a document filed with the Commission in Part I of a quarterly report on Form 10-Q (§ 249.308a of this chapter) or in an annual report to security holders meeting the requirements of Rules 14a-3(b) and (c) or 14c-3(a) and (b) under the Act (§§ 240.14a-3(b) and (c) or 240.14c-3(a) and (b) of this chapter) and that relates to:

(i) The effects of changing prices on the business enterprise, presented voluntarily or pursuant to Item 303 of Regulation S-K (§ 229.303 of this chapter), "Management's Discussion and Analysis of Financial Condition and Results of Operations," Item 5 of Form 20-F (§ 240.220(f) of this chapter), "Operating and Financial Review and Prospects," Item 302 of Regulation S-K (§ 229.302 of this chapter) "Supplementary Financial Information," or Rule 3-20(c) of Regulation S-X (§ 210.3-20(c)) of this chapter); or

(ii) The value of proved oil and gas reserves (such as a standardized measure of discounted future net cash flows relating to proved oil and gas reserves as set forth in FASB ASC paragraphs 932-235-50-29 through 932-235-50-36 (Extractive Activities—Oil and Gas Topic)), presented voluntarily or pursuant to Item 302 of Regulation S-K (§ 229.302 of this chapter).

(c) For the purpose of this rule, the term *forward-looking statement* shall mean and shall be limited to:

(1) A statement containing a projection of revenues, income (loss), earnings (loss) per share, capital expenditures, dividends, capital structure or other financial items;

(2) A statement of management's plans and objectives for future operations;

(3) A statement of future economic performance contained in management's discussion and analysis of financial condition and results of operations included pursuant to Item 303 of Regulation S–K (§ 229.303 of this chapter) or Item 5 of Form 20–F or

(4) Disclosed statements of the assumptions underlying or relating to any of the statements described in paragraphs (c) (1), (2), or (3) of this section.

For the purpose of this rule the term *fraudulent statement* shall mean a statement which is an untrue statement of a material fact, a statement false or misleading with respect to any material fact, an omission to state a material fact necessary to make a statement not misleading, or which constitutes the employment of a manipulative, deceptive, or fraudulent device, contrivance, scheme, transaction, act, practice, course of business, or an artifice to defraud, as those terms are used in the Securities Exchange Act of 1934 or the rules or regulations promulgated thereunder.

Rule 3b-7. Definition of "Executive Officer"

The term "executive officer," when used with reference to a registrant, means its president, any vice president of the registrant in charge of a principal business unit, division or function (such as sales, administration, or finance), any other officer who performs a policy making function or any other person who performs similar policy making functions for the registrant. Executive officers of subsidiaries may be deemed executive officers of the registrant if they perform such policy making functions for the registrant.

MANIPULATIVE AND DECEPTIVE DEVICES AND CONTRIVANCES

Rule 10b-5. Employment of Manipulative and Deceptive Devices

It shall be unlawful for any person, directly or indirectly, by the use of any means or instrumentality of interstate commerce, or of the mails, or of any facility of any national securities exchange,

(a) to employ any device, scheme, or artifice to defraud,

(b) to make any untrue statement of a material fact or to omit to state a material fact necessary in order to make the statements made, in the light of the circumstances under which they were made, not misleading, or

(c) to engage in any act, practice, or course of business which operates or would operate as a fraud or deceit upon any person,

in connection with the purchase or sale of any security.

Rule 10b5-1. Trading "on the basis of" Material Nonpublic Information in Insider Trading Cases

Preliminary Note to § 240.10b5-1: This provision defines when a purchase or sale constitutes trading "on the basis of" material nonpublic information in insider trading cases brought under Section 10(b) of the Act and Rule 10b-5 thereunder. The law of insider trading is otherwise defined by judicial opinions construing Rule 10b-5, and Rule 10b5-1 does not modify the scope of insider trading law in any other respect.

(a) General. The "manipulative and deceptive devices" prohibited by Section 10(b) of the Act (15 U.S.C. 78j) and § 240.10b-5 thereunder include, among other things, the purchase or sale of a security of any issuer, on the basis of material nonpublic information about that security or issuer, in breach of a duty of trust or confidence that is owed directly, indirectly, or derivatively, to the issuer of that security or the shareholders of that issuer, or to any other person who is the source of the material nonpublic information.

(b) Definition of "on the basis of." Subject to the affirmative defenses in paragraph (c) of this section, a purchase or sale of a security of an issuer is "on the basis of" material nonpublic information about that security or issuer if the person making the purchase or sale was aware of the material nonpublic information when the person made the purchase or sale.

(c) Affirmative defenses. (1) (i) Subject to paragraph (c) (1) (ii) of this section, a person's purchase or sale is not "on the basis of" material nonpublic information if the person making the purchase or sale demonstrates that:

(A) Before becoming aware of the information, the person had:

(1) Entered into a binding contract to purchase or sell the security,

(2) Instructed another person to purchase or sell the security for the instructing person's account, or

(3) Adopted a written plan for trading securities;

(B) The contract, instruction, or plan described in paragraph (c) (1) (i) (A) of this Section:

(1) Specified the amount of securities to be purchased or sold and the price at which and the date on which the securities were to be purchased or sold;

(2) Included a written formula or algorithm, or computer program, for determining the amount of securities to be purchased or sold and the price at which and the date on which the securities were to be purchased or sold; or

(3) Did not permit the person to exercise any subsequent influence over how, when, or whether to effect purchases or sales; provided, in addition, that any other person who, pursuant to the contract, instruction, or plan, did exercise such influence must not have been aware of the material nonpublic information when doing so; and

(C) The purchase or sale that occurred was pursuant to the contract, instruction, or plan. A purchase or sale is not "pursuant to a contract, instruction, or plan" if, among other things, the person who entered into the contract, instruction, or plan altered or deviated from the contract, instruction, or plan to purchase or sell securities (whether by changing the amount, price, or timing of the purchase or sale), or entered into or altered a corresponding or hedging transaction or position with respect to those securities.

(ii) Paragraph (c)(1)(i) of this section is applicable only when the contract, instruction, or plan to purchase or sell securities was given or entered into in good faith and not as part of a plan or scheme to evade the prohibitions of this section.

(iii) This paragraph (c)(1)(iii) defines certain terms as used in paragraph (c) of this Section.

(A) Amount. "Amount" means either a specified number of shares or other securities or a specified dollar value of securities.

(B) Price. "Price" means the market price on a particular date or a limit price, or a particular dollar price.

(C) Date. "Date" means, in the case of a market order, the specific day of the year on which the order is to be executed (or as soon thereafter as is practicable under ordinary principles of best execution). "Date" means, in the case of a limit order, a day of the year on which the limit order is in force.

(2) A person other than a natural person also may demonstrate that a purchase or sale of securities is not "on the basis of" material nonpublic information if the person demonstrates that:

(i) The individual making the investment decision on behalf of the person to purchase or sell the securities was not aware of the information; and

(ii) The person had implemented reasonable policies and procedures, taking into consideration the nature of the person's business, to ensure that individuals making investment decisions would not violate the laws prohibiting trading on the basis of material nonpublic information. These policies and procedures may include those that restrict any purchase, sale, and causing any purchase or sale of any security as to which the person has material nonpublic information, or those that prevent such individuals from becoming aware of such information.

Rule 10b5-2. Duties of Trust or Confidence in Misappropriation Insider Trading Cases

Preliminary Note to § 240.10b5-2: This section provides a non-exclusive definition of circumstances in which a person has a duty of trust or confidence for purposes of the "misappropriation" theory of insider trading under Section 10(b) of the Act and Rule 10b-5. The law of insider trading is otherwise defined by judicial opinions construing Rule 10b-5, and Rule 10b5-2 does not modify the scope of insider trading law in any other respect.

(a) Scope of Rule. This section shall apply to any violation of Section 10(b) of the Act (15 U.S.C. 78j(b)) and § 240.10b-5 thereunder that is based on the purchase or sale of securities on the basis of, or the communication of, material nonpublic information misappropriated in breach of a duty of trust or confidence.

(b) Enumerated "duties of trust or confidence." For purposes of this section, a "duty of trust or confidence" exists in the following circumstances, among others:

(1) Whenever a person agrees to maintain information in confidence;

(2) Whenever the person communicating the material nonpublic information and the person to whom it is communicated have a history, pattern, or practice of sharing confidences, such that the recipient of the information knows or reasonably should know that the person communicating the material nonpublic information expects that the recipient will maintain its confidentiality; or

(3) Whenever a person receives or obtains material nonpublic information from his or her spouse, parent, child, or sibling; provided, however, that the person receiving or obtaining the information may demonstrate that no duty of trust or confidence existed with respect to the information, by establishing that he or she neither knew nor reasonably should have known that the person who was the source of the information expected that the person would keep the information confidential, because of the parties' history, pattern, or practice of sharing and maintaining confidences, and because there was no agreement or understanding to maintain the confidentiality of the information.

Rule 10b-10. Confirmation of Transactions

Preliminary Note. This section requires broker-dealers to disclose specified information in writing to customers at or before completion of a transaction. The requirements under this section that particular information be disclosed is not determinative of a broker-dealer's obligation under the general antifraud provisions of the federal securities laws to disclose additional information to a customer at the time of the customer's investment decision.

(a) *Disclosure Requirement*. It shall he unlawful for any broker or dealer to effect for or with an account of a customer any transaction in, or to induce the purchase or sale by such customer of, any security (other than U.S. Savings Bonds or municipal securities) unless such broker or dealer, at or before completion of such transaction, gives or sends to such customer written notification disclosing:

(1) The date and time of the transaction (or the fact that the time of the transaction will be furnished upon written request to such customer) and the identity, price, and number of shares or units (or principal amount) of such security purchased or sold by such customer; and

(2) Whether the broker or dealer is acting as agent for such customer, as agent for some other person, as agent for both such customer and some other person, or as principal for its own account; and if the broker or dealer is acting as principal, whether it is a market maker in the security (other than by reason of acting as a block positioner); and

(i) If the broker or dealer is acting as agent for such customer, for some other person, or for both such customer and some other person:

(A) The name of the person from whom the security was purchased, or to whom it was sold, for such customer or the fact that the information will be furnished upon written request of such customer; and

(B) The amount of any remuneration received or to be received by the broker from such customer in connection with the transaction unless remuneration paid by such customer is determined pursuant to written agreement with such customer, otherwise than on a transaction basis; and

(C) For a transaction in any NMS stock as defined in § 242.600 of this chapter or a security authorized for quotation on an automated interdealer quotation system that has the characteristics set forth in section 17B of the Act (15 U.S.C. 78q-2), a statement whether payment for order flow is received by the broker or dealer for transactions in such securities and the fact that the source and nature of the compensation received in connection with the particular transaction will be furnished upon written request of the customer; *provided, however,* that brokers or dealers that do not receive payment for order flow in connection with any transaction have no disclosure obligations under this paragraph; and

(D) The source and amount of any other remuneration received or to be received by the broker in connection with the transaction: *Provided, however,* that if, in the case of a purchase, the broker was not participating in a distribution, or in the case of a sale, was not participating in a tender offer, the written notification may state whether any other remuneration has been or will be received and the fact that the source and amount of such other remuneration will be furnished upon written request of such customer; or

(ii) If the broker or dealer is acting as principal for its own account:

(A) In the case where such broker or dealer is not a market maker in an equity security and, if, after having received an order to buy from a customer, the broker or dealer purchased the equity security from another person to offset a contemporaneous sale to such customer or, after having received an order to sell from a customer, the broker or dealer sold the security to another person to offset a contemporaneous purchase from such customer, the difference between the price to the customer and the dealer's contemporaneous purchase (for customer purchases) or sale price (for customer sales); or

(B) In the case of any other transaction in an NMS stock as defined by § 242.600 of this chapter, or an equity security that is traded on a national securities exchange and that is subject to last sale reporting, the reported trade price, the price to the customer in the transaction, and the difference, if any, between the reported trade price and the price to the customer.

(3) Whether any odd-lot differential or equivalent fee has been paid by such customer in connection with the execution of an order for an odd-lot number of shares or units (or principal amount) of a security and the fact that the amount of any such differential or fee will be furnished upon oral or written request: *Provided, however*, that such disclosure need not be made if the differential or fee is included in the remuneration disclosure, or exempted from disclosure, pursuant to paragraph (a)(2)(i)(B) of this section; and

(4) In the case of any transaction in a debt security subject to redemption before maturity, a statement to the effect that such debt security may be redeemed in whole or in part before maturity, that such a redemption could affect the yield represented and the fact that additional information is available upon request; and

(5) In the case of a transaction in a debt security effected exclusively on the basis of a dollar price:

(i) The dollar price at which the transaction was effected, and

(ii) The yield to maturity calculated from the dollar price: *Provided, however*, that this paragraph (a)(5)(ii) shall not apply to a transaction in a debt security that either:

(A) Has a maturity date that may be extended by the issuer thereof, with a variable interest payable thereon; or

(B) Is an asset-backed security, that represents an interest in or is secured by a pool of receivables or other financial assets that are subject continuously to prepayment; and

(6) In the case of a transaction in a debt security effected on the basis of yield:

(i) The yield at which the transaction was effected, including the percentage amount and its characterization (*e.g.*, current yield, yield to maturity, or yield to call) and if effected at yield to call, the type of call, the call date and call price; and

(ii) The dollar price calculated from the yield at which the transaction was effected; and

(iii) If effected on a basis other than yield to maturity and the yield to maturity is lower than the represented yield, the yield to maturity as well as the represented yield; *Provided, however*, that this paragraph (a)(6)(iii) shall not apply to a transaction in a debt security that either:

(A) Has a maturity date that may be extended by the issuer thereof, with a variable interest rate payable thereon; or

(B) Is an asset-backed security, that represents an interest in or is secured by a pool of receivables or other financial assets that are subject continuously to prepayment; and

(7) In the case of a transaction in a debt security that is an asset-backed security, which represents an interest in or is secured by a pool of receivables or other financial assets that are subject continuously to prepayment, a statement indicating that the actual yield of such asset-backed security may vary according to the rate at which the underlying receivables or other financial assets are prepaid and a statement of the fact that information concerning the factors that affect yield (including at a minimum estimated yield, weighted average life, and the prepayment assumptions underlying yield) will be furnished upon written request of such customer; and

(8) That the broker or dealer is not a member of the Securities Investor Protection Corporation (SIPC), or that the broker or dealer clearing or carrying the customer account is not a member of SIPC, if such is the case: *Provided, however*, that this paragraph (a)(9) shall not apply in the case of a transaction in shares of a registered open-end investment company or unit investment trust if:

(i) The customer sends funds or securities directly to, or received funds or securities directly from, the registered open-end investment company or unit investment trust, its transfer agent, its custodian, or other designated agent, and such person is not an associated person of the broker or dealer required by paragraph (a) of this section to send written notification to the customer; and

(ii) The written notification required by paragraph (a) of this section is sent on behalf of the broker or dealer to the customer by a person described in paragraph (a)(9)(i) of this section.

(b) *Alternative Periodic Reporting*. A broker or dealer may effect transactions for or with the account of a customer without giving or sending to such customer the written notification described in paragraph (a) of this section if:

(1) Such transactions are effected pursuant to a periodic plan or an investment company plan, or effected in shares of any open-end management investment company registered under the Investment Company Act of 1940 that holds itself out as a money market fund and attempts to maintain a stable net asset value per share: *Provided, however*, that no sales load is deducted upon the purchase or redemption of shares in the money market fund; and

(2) Such broker or dealer gives or sends to such customer within five business days after the end of each *quarterly* period, for transactions involving investment company and periodic plans, and after the end of each *monthly* period, for other transactions described in paragraph (b)(1) of this section, a written statement disclosing each purchase or redemption, effected for or with, and each dividend or distribution credited to or reinvested for, the account of such customer during the month; the date of such transaction; the identity, number, and price of any securities purchased or redeemed by such customer in each such transaction; the total number of shares of such securities in such customer's account; any remuneration received or to be received by the broker or dealer in connection therewith; and that any other information required by paragraph (a) of this section will be furnished upon written request: *Provided, however*, that the written statement may be delivered to some other person designated by the customer for distribution to the customer; and

(3) Such customer is provided with prior notification in writing disclosing the intention to send the written information referred to in paragraph (b)(1) of this section in lieu of an immediate confirmation.

(c) A broker or dealer shall give or send to a customer information requested pursuant to this rule within 5 business days of receipt of the request; *Provided, however,* That in the case of information pertaining to a transaction effected more than 30 days prior to receipt of the request, the information shall be given or sent to the customer within 15 business days.

(d) *Definitions.* For the purposes of this section:

(1) *Customer* shall not include a broker or dealer;

(2) *Completion of the transaction* shall have the meaning provided in Rule 15c1-1 under the Act;

(3) *Time of the transaction* means the time of execution, to the extent feasible, of the customer's order;

(4) *Debt security* as used in paragraphs (a)(3), (4), and (5) only, means any security, such as a bond, debenture, note, or any other similar instrument which evidences a liability of the issuer (including any such security that is convertible into stock or a similar security) and fractional or participation interests in one or more of any of the foregoing; *Provided, however,* that securities issued by an investment company registered under the Investment Company Act of 1940 shall not be included in this definition;

(5) *Periodic plan* means any written authorization for a broker acting as agent to purchase or sell for a customer a specific security or securities (other than securities issued by an open end investment company or unit investment trust registered under the Investment Company Act of 1940), in specific amounts (calculated in security units or dollars), at specific time intervals and setting forth the commissions or charges to be paid by the customer in connection therewith (or the manner of calculating them); and

(6) *Investment company plan* means any plan under which securities issued by an open-end investment company or unit investment trust registered under the Investment Company Act of 1940 are purchased by a customer (the payments being made directly to, or made payable to, the registered investment company, or the principal underwriter, custodian, trustee, or other designated agent of the registered investment company), or sold by a customer pursuant to:

(i) An individual retirement or individual pension plan qualified under the Internal Revenue Code;

(ii) A contractual or systematic agreement under which the customer purchases at the applicable public offering price, or redeems at the applicable redemption price, such securities in specified amounts (calculated in security units or dollars) at specified time intervals and setting forth the commissions or charges to be paid by such customer in connection therewith (or the manner of calculating them); or

(iii) Any other arrangement involving a group of two or more customers and contemplating periodic purchases of such securities by each customer through a person designated by the group; *Provided,* That such arrangement requires the registered investment company or its agent—

(A) To give or send to the designated person, at or before the completion of the transaction for the purchase of such securities, a written notification of the receipt of the total amount paid by the group;

(B) To send to anyone in the group who was a customer in the prior quarter and on whose behalf payment has not been received in the current quarter a quarterly written statement reflecting that a payment was not received on his behalf; and

(C) To advise each customer in the group if a payment is not received from the designated person on behalf of the group within 10 days of a date certain specified in the arrangement for delivery of that payment by the designated person and thereafter to send to each such customer the written notification described in paragraph (a) of this section for the next three succeeding payments.

(7) *NMS stock* shall have the meaning provided in § 242.600 of this chapter.

(8) *Effective transaction reporting plan* shall have the meaning provided in Rule 11Aa3-1 under the Act.

(9) *Payment for order flow* shall mean any monetary payment, service, property, or other benefit that results in remuneration, compensation, or consideration to a broker or dealer from any broker or dealer, national securities exchange, registered securities association, or exchange member in return for the routing of customer orders by such broker or dealer to any broker or dealer, national securities exchange, registered securities association, or exchange member for execution, including but not limited to: research, clearance, custody, products or services; reciprocal agreements for the provision of order flow; adjustment of a broker or dealer's unfavorable trading errors; offers to participate as underwriter in public offerings; stock loans or shared interest accrued thereon; discounts, rebates, or any other reductions of or credits against any fee to, or expense or other financial obligation of, the broker or dealer routing a customer order that exceeds that fee, expense or financial obligation.

(10) *Asset-backed security* means a security that is primarily serviced by the cashflows of a discrete pool of receivables or other financial assets, either fixed or revolving, that by their terms convert into cash within a finite time period plus any rights or other assets designed to assure the servicing or timely distribution of proceeds to the security holders.

(e) *Security futures products*. The provisions of paragraphs (a) and (b) of this section shall not apply to a broker or dealer registered pursuant to section 15(b)(11)(A) of the Act (15 U.S.C. 78o(b)(11)(A)) to the extent that it effects transactions for customers in security futures products in a futures account (as that term is defined in § 240.15c3-3(a)(15)) and a broker or dealer registered pursuant to section 15(b)(1) of the Act (15 U.S.C. 78o(b)(1)) that is also a futures commission merchant registered pursuant to section 4f(a)(1) of the Commodity Exchange Act (7 U.S.C. 6f(a)(1)), to the extent that it effects transactions for customers in security futures products in a futures account (as that term is defined in § 240.15c3-3(a)(15)), *Provided* that:

(1) The broker or dealer that effects any transaction for a customer in security futures products in a futures account gives or sends to the customer no later than the next business day after execution of any futures securities product transaction, written notification disclosing:

(i) The date the transaction was executed, the identity of the single security or narrow-based security index underlying the contract for the security futures product, the number of contracts of such security futures product purchased or sold, the price, and the delivery month;

(ii) The source and amount of any remuneration received or to be received by the broker or dealer in connection with the transaction, including, but not limited to, markups, commissions, costs, fees, and other charges incurred in connection with the transaction, provided, however, that if no remuneration is to be paid for an initiating transaction until the occurrence of the corresponding liquidating transaction, that the broker or dealer may disclose the amount of remuneration only on the confirmation for the liquidating transaction;

(iii) The fact that information about the time of the execution of the transaction, the identity of the other party to the contract, and whether the broker or dealer is acting as agent for such customer, as agent for some other person, as agent for both such customer and some other person, or as principal for its own account, and if the broker or dealer is acting as principal, whether it is engaging in a block transaction or an exchange of security futures products for physical securities, will be available upon written request of the customer; and

(iv) Whether payment for order flow is received by the broker or dealer for such transactions, the amount of this payment and the fact that the source and nature of the compensation received in connection with the particular transaction will be furnished upon written request of the customer; provided, however, that brokers or dealers that do not receive payment for order flow have no disclosure obligation under this paragraph.

(f) The Commission may exempt any broker or dealer from the requirements of paragraphs (a) and (b) of this section with regard to specific transactions or specific classes of transactions for which the broker or dealer will provide alternative procedures to effect the purposes of this section; any such exemption may be granted subject to compliance with such alternative procedures and upon such other stated terms and conditions as the Commission may impose.

Rule 10b-16. Disclosure of Credit Terms in Margin Transactions

(a) It shall be unlawful for any broker or dealer to extend credit, directly or indirectly, to any customer in connection with any securities transaction unless such broker or dealer has established procedures to assure that each customer

(1) is given or sent at the time of opening the account, a written statement or statements disclosing (i) the conditions under which an interest charge will be imposed; (ii) the annual rate or rates of interest that can be imposed; (iii) the method of computing interest; (iv) if rates of interest are subject to change without prior notice, the specific conditions under which they can be changed; (v) the method of determining the debit balance or balances on which interest is to be charged and whether credit is to be given for credit balances in cash accounts; (vi) what other charges resulting from the extension of credit, if any, will be made and under what conditions; and (vii) the nature of any interest or lien retained by the broker or dealer in the security or other property held as collateral and the conditions under which additional collateral can be required; *provided, however,* that the requirements of this Paragraph (a)(1) will be met in any case where the account is opened by telephone if the information required to be disclosed is orally communicated to the customer at that time and the required written statement or statements are sent to the customer immediately thereafter; and *provided, further,* that in the case of customers to whom credit is already being extended on the effective date of this Rule, the written statement or statements required hereunder must be given or sent to said customers within 90 days after the effective date of this Rule; and

(2) is given or sent a written statement or statements, at least quarterly, for each account in which credit was extended, disclosing (i) the balance at the beginning of the period; the date, amount and a brief description of each debit and credit entered during such period; the closing balance; and, if interest is charged for a period different from the period covered by the statement, the balance as of the last day of the interest period; (ii) the total interest charge for the period during which interest is charged (or, if interest is charged separately for separate accounts, the total interest charge for each such account), itemized to show the dates on which the interest period began and ended; the annual rate or rates of interest charged and the interest charge for each such different annual rate of interest; and either each different debit balance on which an interest calculation was based or the average debit balance for the interest period, except that if an average debit balance is used, a separate average debit balance must be disclosed for each interest rate applied; and (iii) all other charges resulting from the extension of credit in that account; *provided, however,* that if the interest charge disclosed on a statement is for a period different from the period covered by the statement, there must be printed on the statement appropriate language to the effect that it should be retained for use in conjunction with the next statement containing the remainder of the required information; and *provided further,* that in the case of "equity funding programs" registered under the Securities Act of 1933, the requirements of this Paragraph (a)(2) will be met if the broker or dealer furnishes to the customer, within one month after each extension of credit, a written statement or statements containing the information required to be disclosed under this Paragraph (a)(2).

(b) It shall be unlawful for any broker or dealer to make any changes in the terms and conditions under which credit charges will be made (as described in the initial statement made under Paragraph (a) of this Rule), unless the customer shall have been given not less than thirty (30) days written notice of such changes, except that no such prior notice shall be necessary where such changes are required by law; *provided, however,* that if any change for which prior notice would otherwise be required under this paragraph results in a lower interest charge to the customer than would have been imposed before the change, notice of such change may be given within a reasonable time after the effective date of the change.

Rule 10b-18. Purchases of Certain Equity Securities by the Issuer and Others

Preliminary Notes

1. Section 240.10b-18 provides an issuer (and its affiliated purchasers) with a "safe harbor" from liability for manipulation under sections 9(a)(2) of the Act and § 240.10b-5 under the Act *solely* by reason of the manner, timing, price, and volume of their repurchases when they repurchase the issuer's common stock in the market in accordance with the section's manner, timing, price, and volume conditions. As a safe harbor, compliance with § 240.10b-18 is voluntary. To come within the safe harbor, however, an issuer's repurchases must satisfy (on a daily basis) each of the section's four conditions. Failure to meet any one of the four conditions will remove all of the issuer's repurchases from the safe harbor for that day. The safe harbor, moreover, is not available for repurchases that, although made in technical compliance with the section, are part of a plan or scheme to evade the federal securities laws.

2. Regardless of whether the repurchases are effected in accordance with § 240.10b-18, reporting issuers must report their repurchasing activity as required by Item 703 of Regulations S-K and S-B (17 CFR 229.703 and 228.703) and Item 15(e) of Form 20-F (17 CFR 249.220f) (regarding foreign private issuers), and closed-end management investment companies that are registered under the Investment Company Act of 1940 must report their repurchasing activity as required by Item 8 of Form N-CSR (17 CFR 249.331; 17 CFR 274.128).

(a) *Definitions*. Unless otherwise provided, all terms used in this section shall have the same meaning as in the Act. In addition, the following definitions shall apply:

(1) *ADTV* means the average daily trading volume reported for the security during the four calendar weeks preceding the week in which the Rule 10b-18 purchase is to be effected.

(2) *Affiliate* means any person that directly or indirectly controls, is controlled by, or is under common control with, the issuer.

(3) *Affiliated purchaser* means:

(i) A person acting, directly or indirectly, in concert with the issuer for the purpose of acquiring the issuer's securities; or

(ii) An affiliate who, directly or indirectly, controls the issuer's purchases of such securities, whose purchases are controlled by the issuer, or whose purchases are under common control with those of the issuer; *Provided, however*, that "affiliated purchaser" shall not include a broker, dealer, or other person solely by reason of such broker, dealer, or other person effecting Rule 10b-18 purchases on behalf of the issuer or for its account, and shall not include an officer or director of the issuer solely by reason of that officer or director's participation in the decision to authorize Rule 10b-18 purchases by or on behalf of the issuer.

(4) *Agent independent of the issuer* has the meaning contained in § 242.100 of this chapter.

(5) *Block* means a quantity of stock that either:

(i) Has a purchase price of $200,000 or more; or

(ii) Is at least 5,000 shares and has a purchase price of at least $50,000; or

(iii) Is at least 20 round lots of the security and totals 150 percent or more of the trading volume for that security or, in the event that trading volume data are unavailable, is at least 20 round lots of the security and totals at least one-tenth of one percent (.001) of the outstanding shares of the security, exclusive of any shares owned by any affiliate;

Provided, however, That a block under paragraph (a)(5)(i), (ii), and (iii) shall not include any amount a broker or dealer, acting as principal, has accumulated for the purpose of sale or resale to the issuer or to any affiliated purchaser of the issuer if the issuer or such affiliated purchaser knows or has reason to know that such amount was accumulated for such purpose, nor shall it include any amount that a broker or dealer has sold short to the issuer or to any affiliated purchaser of the issuer if the issuer or such affiliated purchaser knows or has reason to know that the sale was a short sale.

(6) *Consolidated system* means a consolidated transaction or quotation reporting system that collects and publicly disseminates on a current and continuous basis transaction or quotation information in common equity securities pursuant to an effective transaction reporting plan or an effective national market system plan (as those terms are defined in § 242.600 of this chapter).

(7) *Market-wide trading suspension* means a market-wide trading halt of 30 minutes or more that is:

(i) Imposed pursuant to the rules of a national securities exchange or a national securities association in response to a market-wide decline during a single trading session; or

(ii) Declared by the Commission pursuant to its authority under section 12(k) of the Act (15 U.S.C. 78*l*(k)).

(8) *Plan* has the meaning contained in § 242.100 of this chapter.

(9) *Principal market* for a security means the single securities market with the largest reported trading volume for the security during the six full calendar months preceding the week in which the Rule 10b-18 purchase is to be effected.

(10) *Public float value* has the meaning contained in § 242.100 of this chapter.

(11) *Purchase price* means the price paid per share as reported, exclusive of any commission paid to a broker acting as agent, or commission equivalent, mark-up, or differential paid to a dealer.

(12) *Riskless principal transaction* means a transaction in which a broker or dealer after having received an order from an issuer to buy its security, buys the security as principal in the market at the same price to satisfy the issuer's buy order. The issuer's buy order must be effected at the same price per-share at which the broker or dealer bought the shares to satisfy the issuer's buy order, exclusive of any explicitly disclosed markup or markdown, commission equivalent, or other fee. In addition, only the first leg of the transaction, when the broker or dealer buys the security in the market as principal, is reported under the rules of a self-regulatory organization or under the Act. For purposes of this section, the broker or dealer must have written policies and procedures in place to assure that, at a minimum, the issuer's buy order was received prior to the offsetting transaction; the offsetting transaction is allocated to a riskless principal account or the issuer's account within 60 seconds of the execution; and the broker or dealer has supervisory systems in place to produce records that enable the broker or dealer to accurately and readily reconstruct, in a time-sequenced manner, all orders effected on a riskless principal basis.

(13) *Rule 10b-18 purchase* means a purchase (or any bid or limit order that would effect such purchase) of an issuer's common stock (or an equivalent interest, including a unit of beneficial interest in a trust or limited partnership or a depository share) by or for the issuer or any affiliated purchaser (including riskless principal transactions). However, it does *not* include any purchase of such security:

(i) Effected during the applicable restricted period of a distribution that is subject to § 242.102 of this chapter;

(ii) Effected by or for an issuer plan by an agent independent of the issuer;

(iii) Effected as a fractional share purchase (a fractional interest in a security) evidenced by a script certificate, order form, or similar document;

(iv) Effected during the period from the time of public announcement (as defined in § 230.165(f)) of a merger, acquisition, or similar transaction involving a recapitalization, until the earlier of the completion of such transaction or the completion of the vote by target shareholders.This exclusion does *not* apply to Rule 10b-18 purchases:

(A) Effected during such transaction in which the consideration is solely cash and there is no valuation period; or

(B) Where:

(*1*) The total volume of Rule 10b-18 purchases effected on any single day does not exceed the lesser of 25% of the security's four-week ADTV or the issuer's average daily Rule 10b-18 purchases during the three full calendar months preceding the date of the announcement of such transaction;

(2) The issuer's block purchases effected pursuant to paragraph (b)(4) of this section do not exceed the average size and frequency of the issuer's block purchases effected pursuant to paragraph (b)(4) of this section during the three full calendar months preceding the date of the announcement of such transaction; and

(3) Such purchases are not otherwise restricted or prohibited;

(v) Effected pursuant to § 240.13e-1;

(vi) Effected pursuant to a tender offer that is subject to § 240.13e-4 or specifically excepted from § 240.13e-4; or

(vii) Effected pursuant to a tender offer that is subject to section 14(d) of the Act (15 U.S.C. 78n(d)) and the rules and regulations thereunder.

(b) *Conditions to be met.* Rule 10b-18 purchases shall not be deemed to have violated the anti-manipulation provisions of sections 9(a)(2) or 10(b) of the Act (15 U.S.C. 78i(a)(2) or 78j(b)), or § 240.10b-5 under the Act, solely by reason of the time, price, or amount of the Rule 10b-18 purchases, or the number of brokers or dealers used in connection with such purchases, if the issuer or affiliated purchaser of the issuer effects the Rule 10b-18 purchases according to each of the following conditions:

(1) *One broker or dealer.* Rule 10b-18 purchases must be effected from or through only one broker or dealer on any single day; *Provided, however,* that:

(i) The "one broker or dealer"condition shall not apply to Rule 10b-18 purchases that are not solicited by or on behalf of the issuer or its affiliated purchaser(s);

(ii) Where Rule 10b-18 purchases are effected by or on behalf of more than one affiliated purchaser of the issuer (or the issuer and one or more of its affiliated purchasers) on a single day, the issuer and all affiliated purchasers must use the same broker or dealer; and

(iii) Where Rule 10b-18 purchases are effected on behalf of the issuer by a broker-dealer that is not an electronic communication network (ECN) or other alternative trading system (ATS), that broker-dealer can access ECN or other ATS liquidity in order to execute repurchases on behalf of the issuer (or any affiliated purchaser of the issuer) on that day.

(2) *Time of purchases.* Rule 10b-18 purchases must not be:

(i) The opening (regular way) purchase reported in the consolidated system;

(ii) Effected during the 10 minutes before the scheduled close of the primary trading session in the principal market for the security, and the 10 minutes before the scheduled close of the primary trading session in the market where the purchase is effected, for a security that has an ADTV value of $1 million or more and a public float value of $150 million or more; and

(iii) Effected during the 30 minutes before the scheduled close of the primary trading session in the principal market for the security, and the 30 minutes before the scheduled close of the primary trading session in the market where the purchase is effected, for all other securities;

(iv) However, for purposes of this section, Rule 10b-18 purchases may be effected following the close of the primary trading session until the termination of the period in which last sale prices are reported in the consolidated system so long as such purchases are effected at prices that do not exceed the lower of the closing price of the primary trading session in the principal market for the security and any lower bids or sale prices subsequently reported in the consolidated system, and all of this section's conditions are met. However, for purposes of this section, the issuer may use one broker or dealer to effect Rule 10b-18 purchases during this period that may be different from the broker or dealer that it used during the primary trading session. However, the issuer's Rule 10b-18 purchase may not be the opening transaction of the session following the close of the primary trading session.

(3) *Price of purchases.* Rule 10b-18 purchases must be effected at a purchase price that:

(i) Does not exceed the highest independent bid or the last independent transaction price, whichever is higher, quoted or reported in the consolidated system at the time the Rule 10b-18 purchase is effected;

(ii) For securities for which bids and transaction prices are not quoted or reported in the consolidated system, Rule 10b-18 purchases must be effected at a purchase price that does not exceed the highest independent bid or the last independent transaction price, whichever is higher, displayed and disseminated on any national securities exchange or on any inter-dealer quotation system (as defined in § 240.15c2-11) that displays at least two priced quotations for the security, at the time the Rule 10b-18 purchase is effected; and

(iii) For all other securities, Rule 10b-18 purchases must be effected at a price no higher than the highest independent bid obtained from three independent dealers.

(4) *Volume of purchases.* The total volume of Rule 10b-18 purchases effected by or for the issuer and any affiliated purchasers effected on any single day must not exceed 25 percent of the ADTV for that security; *However,* once each week, in lieu of purchasing under the 25 percent of ADTV limit for that day, the issuer or an affiliated purchaser of the issuer may effect one block purchase if:

(i) No other Rule 10b-18 purchases are effected that day, and

(ii) The block purchase is *not*included when calculating a security's four week ADTV under this section.

(c) *Alternative conditions.* The conditions of paragraph (b) of this section shall apply in connection with Rule 10b-18 purchases effected during a trading session following the imposition of a market-wide trading suspension, except:

(1) That the time of purchases condition in paragraph (b)(2) of this section shall not apply, either:

(i) From the reopening of trading until the scheduled close of trading on the day that the market-wide trading suspension is imposed; or

(ii) At the opening of trading on the next trading day until the scheduled close of trading that day, if a market-wide trading suspension was in effect at the close of trading on the preceding day; and

(2) The volume of purchases condition in paragraph (b)(4) of this section is modified so that the amount of Rule 10b-18 purchases must not exceed 100 percent of the ADTV for that security.

(d) *Other purchases.* No presumption shall arise that an issuer or an affiliated purchaser has violated the anti-manipulation provisions of sections 9(a)(2) or 10(b) of the Act (15 U.S.C. 78i(a)(2) or 78j(b)), or § 240.10b-5 under the Act, if the Rule 10b-18 purchases of such issuer or affiliated purchaser do not meet the conditions specified in paragraph (b) or (c) of this section.

Rule 10b-21. Deception in Connection with a Seller's Ability or Intent to Deliver Securities on the Date Delivery Is Due

PRELIMINARY NOTE to § 240.10b-21: This rule is not intended to limit, or restrict, the applicability of the general antifraud provisions of the federal securities laws, such as section 10(b) of the Act and rule 10b-5 thereunder.

(a) It shall also constitute a "manipulative or deceptive device or contrivance" as used in section 10(b) of this Act for any person to submit an order to sell an equity security if such person deceives a broker or dealer, a participant of a registered clearing agency, or a purchaser about its intention or ability to deliver the security on or before the settlement date, and such person fails to deliver the security on or before the settlement date.

(b) For purposes of this rule, the term settlement date shall mean the business day on which delivery of a security and payment of money is to be made through the facilities of a registered clearing agency in connection with the sale of a security.

NOTICE PURSUANT TO SECTION 10A OF THE ACT

Rule 10A-1. Notice to the Commission Pursuant to Section 10A of the Act

(a)(1) If any issuer with a reporting obligation under the Act receives a report requiring a notice to the Commission in accordance with section 10A(b)(3) of the Act, 15 U.S.C. 78j-1(b)(3), the issuer shall submit such notice to the Commission's Office of the Chief Accountant within the time period prescribed in that section. The notice may be provided by facsimile, telegraph, personal delivery, or any other means, provided it is received by the Office of the Chief Accountant within the required time period.

(2) The notice specified in paragraph (a)(1) of this section shall be in writing and:

(i) Shall identify the issuer (including the issuer's name, address, phone number, and file number assigned to the issuer's filings by the Commission) and the independent accountant (including the independent accountant's name and phone number, and the address of the independent accountant's principal office);

(ii) Shall state the date that the issuer received from the independent accountant the report specified in section 10A(b)(2) of the Act, 15 U.S.C. 78j-1(b)(2);

(iii) Shall provide, at the election of the issuer, either:

(A) A summary of the independent accountant's report, including a description of the act that the independent accountant has identified as a likely illegal act and the possible effect of that act on all affected financial statements of the issuer or those related to the most current three-year period, whichever is shorter; or

(B) A copy of the independent accountant's report; and

(iv) May provide additional information regarding the issuer's views of and response to the independent accountant's report.

(3) Reports of the independent accountant submitted by the issuer to the Commission's Office of the Chief Accountant in accordance with paragraph (a)(2)(iii)(B) of this section shall be deemed to have been made pursuant to section 10A(b)(3) or section 10A(b)(4) of the Act, 15 U.S.C. 78j-1(b)(3) or 78j-1(b)(4), for purposes of the safe harbor provided by section 10A(c) of the Act, 15 U.S.C. 78j-1(c).

(4) Submission of the notice in paragraphs (a)(1) and (a)(2) of this section shall not relieve the issuer from its obligations to comply fully with all other reporting requirements, including, without limitation:

(i) The filing requirements of Form 8-K, §249.308 of this chapter, and Form N-CSR, §274.128 of this chapter, regarding a change in the issuer's certifying accountant and

(ii) The disclosure requirements of item 304 of Regulation S-K, §229.304 of this chapter.

(b)(1) Any independent accountant furnishing to the Commission a copy of a report (or the documentation of any oral report) in accordance with section 10A(b)(3) or section 10A(b)(4) of the Act, 15 U.S.C. 78j-1(b)(3) or 78j-1(b)(4), shall submit that report (or documentation) to the Commission's Office of the Chief Accountant within the time period prescribed by the appropriate section of the Act. The report (or documentation) may be submitted to the Commission's Office of the Chief Accountant by facsimile, telegraph, personal delivery, or any other means, provided it is received by the Office of the Chief Accountant within the time period set forth in section 10A(b)(3) or 10A(b)(4) of the Act, 15 U.S.C. 78j-1(b)(3) or 78j-1(b)(4), whichever is applicable in the circumstances.

(2) If the report (or documentation) submitted to the Office of the Chief Accountant in accordance with paragraph (b)(1) of this section does not clearly identify both the issuer (including the issuer's name, address, phone number, and file number assigned to the issuer's filings with the Commission) and the independent accountant (including the independent accountant's name and phone number, and the address of the independent accountant's principal office), then the independent accountant shall place that information in a prominent attachment to the report (or documentation) and shall submit that attachment to the Office of the Chief Accountant at the same time and in the same manner as the report (or documentation) is submitted to that Office.

(3) Submission of the report (or documentation) by the independent accountant as described in paragraphs (b)(1) and (b)(2) of this section shall not replace, or otherwise satisfy the need for, the newly engaged and former accountants' letters under §§ 229.304(a)(2)(D) [sic] and 229.304(a)(3) of this chapter (Items 304(a)(2)(D) [sic] and 304(a)(3) of Regulation S-K, respectively) and shall not limit, reduce, or affect in any way the independent accountant's obligations to comply fully with all other legal and professional responsibilities, including, without limitation, those under the standards of the Public Company Accounting Oversight Board (United States) ("PCAOB") and the rules or interpretations of the Commission that modify or supplement those auditing standards.

(c) A notice or report submitted to the Office of the Chief Accountant in accordance with paragraphs (a) and (b) of this section shall be deemed to be an investigative record and shall be non-public and exempt from disclosure pursuant to the Freedom of Information Act to the same extent and for the same periods of time that the Commission's investigative records are non-public and exempt from disclosure under, among other applicable provisions, 5 U.S.C. 552(b)(7) and § 200.80(b)(7) of this chapter. Nothing in this paragraph, however, shall relieve, limit, delay, or affect in any way, the obligation of any issuer or any independent accountant to make all public disclosures required by law, by any Commission disclosure item, rule, report, or form, or by any applicable accounting, auditing, or professional standard.

Instruction to paragraph (c). Issuers and independent accountants may apply for additional bases for confidential treatment for a notice, report, or part thereof, in accordance with § 200.83 of this chapter. That section indicates, in part, that any person who, pursuant to any requirement of law, submits any information or causes or permits any information to be submitted to the Commission, may request that the Commission afford it confidential treatment by reason of personal privacy or business confidentiality, or for any other reason permitted by Federal law.

Rule 10A-2. Auditor Independence

It shall be unlawful for an auditor not to be independent under § 210.2-01(c)(2)(iii)(B), (c)(4), (c)(6), (c)(7), and § 210.2-07.

Rule 10A-3. Listing Standards Relating to Audit Committees

(a) Pursuant to section 10A(m) of the Act (15 U.S.C. 78j-1(m)) and section 3 of the Sarbanes-Oxley Act of 2002 (15 U.S.C. 7202):

(1) *National securities exchanges.* The rules of each national securities exchange registered pursuant to section 6 of the Act (15 U.S.C. 78f) must, in accordance with the provisions of this section, prohibit the initial or continued listing of any security of an issuer that is not in compliance with the requirements of any portion of paragraph (b) or (c) of this section.

(2) *National securities associations.* The rules of each national securities association registered pursuant to section 15A of the Act (15 U.S.C. 78o-3) must, in accordance with the provisions of this section, prohibit the initial or continued listing in an automated inter-dealer quotation system of any security of an issuer that is not in compliance with the requirements of any portion of paragraph (b) or (c) of this section.

(3) *Opportunity to cure defects.* The rules required by paragraphs (a)(1) and (a)(2) of this section must provide for appropriate procedures for a listed issuer to have an opportunity to cure any defects that would be the basis for a prohibition under paragraph (a) of this section, before the imposition of such prohibition. Such rules also may provide that if a member of an audit committee ceases to be independent in accordance with the requirements of this section for reasons outside the member's reasonable control, that person, with notice by the issuer to the applicable national securities exchange or national securities association, may remain an audit committee member of the listed issuer until the earlier of the next annual shareholders meeting of the listed issuer or one year from the occurrence of the event that caused the member to be no longer independent.

(4) *Notification of noncompliance.* The rules required by paragraphs (a)(1) and (a)(2) of this section must include a requirement that a listed issuer must notify the applicable national

securities exchange or national securities association promptly after an executive officer of the listed issuer becomes aware of any material noncompliance by the listed issuer with the requirements of this section.

(5) *Implementation*.

(i) The rules of each national securities exchange or national securities association meeting the requirements of this section must be operative, and listed issuers must be in compliance with those rules, by the following dates:

(A) July 31, 2005 for foreign private issuers and small reporting companies (as defined in § 240.12b-2); and

(B) For all other listed issuers, the earlier of the listed issuer's first annual shareholders meeting after January 15, 2004, or October 31, 2004.

(ii) Each national securities exchange and national securities association must provide to the Commission, no later than July 15, 2003, proposed rules or rule amendments that comply with this section.

(iii) Each national securities exchange and national securities association must have final rules or rule amendments that comply with this section approved by the Commission no later than December 1, 2003.

(b) *Required standards*.

(1) *Independence*.

(i) Each member of the audit committee must be a member of the board of directors of the listed issuer, and must otherwise be independent; provided that, where a listed issuer is one of two dual holding companies, those companies may designate one audit committee for both companies so long as each member of the audit committee is a member of the board of directors of at least one of such dual holding companies.

(ii) *Independence requirements for non-investment company issuers*. In order to be considered to be independent for purposes of this paragraph (b)(1), a member of an audit committee of a listed issuer that is not an investment company may not, other than in his or her capacity as a member of the audit committee, the board of directors, or any other board committee:

(A) Accept directly or indirectly any consulting, advisory, or other compensatory fee from the issuer or any subsidiary thereof, provided that, unless the rules of the national securities exchange or national securities association provide otherwise, compensatory fees do not include the receipt of fixed amounts of compensation under a retirement plan (including deferred compensation) for prior service with the listed issuer (provided that such compensation is not contingent in any way on continued service); or

(B) Be an affiliated person of the issuer or any subsidiary thereof.

(iii) *Independence requirements for investment company issuers*. In order to be considered to be independent for purposes of this paragraph (b)(1), a member of an audit committee of a listed issuer that is an investment company may not, other than in his or her capacity as a member of the audit committee, the board of directors, or any other board committee:

(A) Accept directly or indirectly any consulting, advisory, or other compensatory fee from the issuer or any subsidiary thereof, provided that, unless the rules of the national securities exchange or national securities association provide otherwise, compensatory fees do not include the receipt of fixed amounts of compensation under a retirement plan (including deferred compensation) for prior service with the listed issuer (provided that such compensation is not contingent in any way on continued service); or

(B) Be an "interested person" of the issuer as defined in section 2(a)(19) of the Investment Company Act of 1940 (15 U.S.C. 80a-2(a)(19)).

(iv) *Exemptions from the independence requirements*.

(A) For an issuer listing securities pursuant to a registration statement under section 12 of the Act (15 U.S.C. 78*l*), or for an issuer that has a registration statement under the Securities Act of 1933 (15 U.S.C.77a *et seq*.) covering an initial public offering of securities to be listed by the issuer, where in each case the listed issuer was not, immediately prior to the effective date of such registration statement, required to file reports with the Commission pursuant to section 13(a) or 15(d) of the Act (15 U.S.C. 78m(a) or 78o(d)):

(*1*) All but one of the members of the listed issuer's audit committee may be exempt from the independence requirements of paragraph (b)(1)(ii) of this section for 90 days from the date of effectiveness of such registration statement; and

(*2*) A minority of the members of the listed issuer's audit committee may be exempt from the independence requirements of paragraph (b)(1)(ii) of this section for one year from the date of effectiveness of such registration statement.

(B) An audit committee member that sits on the board of directors of a listed issuer and an affiliate of the listed issuer is exempt from the requirements of paragraph (b)(1)(ii)(B) of this section if the member, except for being a director on each such board of directors, otherwise meets the independence requirements of paragraph (b)(1)(ii) of this section for each such entity, including the receipt of only ordinary-course compensation for serving as a member of the board of directors, audit committee or any other board committee of each such entity.

(C) An employee of a foreign private issuer who is not an executive officer of the foreign private issuer is exempt from the requirements of paragraph (b)(1)(ii) of this section if the employee is elected or named to the board of directors or audit committee of the foreign private issuer pursuant to the issuer's governing law or documents, an employee collective bargaining or similar agreement or other home country legal or listing requirements.

(D) An audit committee member of a foreign private issuer may be exempt from the requirements of paragraph (b)(1)(ii)(B) of this section if that member meets the following requirements:

(*1*) The member is an affiliate of the foreign private issuer or a representative of such an affiliate;

(*2*) The member has only observer status on, and is not a voting member or the chair of, the audit committee; and

(*3*) Neither the member nor the affiliate is an executive officer of the foreign private issuer.

(E) An audit committee member of a foreign private issuer may be exempt from the requirements of paragraph (b)(1)(ii)(B) of this section if that member meets the following requirements:

(*1*) The member is a representative or designee of a foreign government or foreign governmental entity that is an affiliate of the foreign private issuer; and

(*2*) The member is not an executive officer of the foreign private issuer.

(F) In addition to paragraphs (b)(1)(iv)(A) through (E) of this section, the Commission may exempt from the requirements of paragraphs (b)(1)(ii) or (b)(1)(iii) of this section a particular relationship with respect to audit committee members, as the Commission determines appropriate in light of the circumstances.

(2) *Responsibilities relating to registered public accounting firms*. The audit committee of each listed issuer, in its capacity as a committee of the board of directors, must be directly responsible for the appointment, compensation, retention and oversight of the work of any registered public accounting firm engaged (including resolution of disagreements between management and the auditor regarding financial reporting) for the purpose of preparing or issuing an audit report or performing other audit, review or attest services for the listed issuer, and each such registered public accounting firm must report directly to the audit committee.

(3) *Complaints*. Each audit committee must establish procedures for:

(i) The receipt, retention, and treatment of complaints received by the listed issuer regarding accounting, internal accounting controls, or auditing matters; and

(ii) The confidential, anonymous submission by employees of the listed issuer of concerns regarding questionable accounting or auditing matters.

(4) *Authority to engage advisers*. Each audit committee must have the authority to engage independent counsel and other advisers, as it determines necessary to carry out its duties.

(5) *Funding*. Each listed issuer must provide for appropriate funding, as determined by the audit committee, in its capacity as a committee of the board of directors, for payment of:

(i) Compensation to any registered public accounting firm engaged for the purpose of preparing or issuing an audit report or performing other audit, review or attest services for the listed issuer;

(ii) Compensation to any advisers employed by the audit committee under paragraph (b)(4) of this section; and

(iii) Ordinary administrative expenses of the audit committee that are necessary or appropriate in carrying out its duties.

(c) *General exemptions*.

(1) At any time when an issuer has a class of securities that is listed on a national securities exchange or national securities association subject to the requirements of this section, the listing of other classes of securities of the listed issuer on a national securities exchange or national securities association is not subject to the requirements of this section.

(2) At any time when an issuer has a class of common equity securities (or similar securities) that is listed on a national securities exchange or national securities association subject to the requirements of this section, the listing of classes of securities of a direct or indirect consolidated subsidiary or an at least 50% beneficially owned subsidiary of the issuer (except classes of equity securities, other than non-convertible, non-participating preferred securities, of such subsidiary) is not subject to the requirements of this section.

(3) The listing of securities of a foreign private issuer is not subject to the requirements of paragraphs (b)(1) through (b)(5) of this section if the foreign private issuer meets the following requirements:

(i) The foreign private issuer has a board of auditors (or similar body), or has statutory auditors, established and selected pursuant to home country legal or listing provisions expressly requiring or permitting such a board or similar body;

(ii) The board or body, or statutory auditors is required under home country legal or listing requirements to be either:

(A) Separate from the board of directors; or

(B) Composed of one or more members of the board of directors and one or more members that are not also members of the board of directors;

(iii) The board or body, or statutory auditors, are not elected by management of such issuer and no executive officer of the foreign private issuer is a member of such board or body, or statutory auditors;

(iv) Home country legal or listing provisions set forth or provide for standards for the independence of such board or body, or statutory auditors, from the foreign private issuer or the management of such issuer;

(v) Such board or body, or statutory auditors, in accordance with any applicable home country legal or listing requirements or the issuer's governing documents, are responsible, to the extent permitted by law, for the appointment, retention and oversight of the work of any registered public accounting firm engaged (including, to the extent permitted by law, the resolution of disagreements between management and the auditor regarding financial reporting) for the purpose of preparing or issuing an audit report or performing other audit, review or attest services for the issuer; and

(vi) The audit committee requirements of paragraphs (b)(3), (b)(4) and (b)(5) of this section apply to such board or body, or statutory auditors, to the extent permitted by law.

(4) The listing of a security futures product cleared by a clearing agency that is registered pursuant to section 17A of the Act (15 U.S.C. 78q-1) or that is exempt from the registration requirements of section 17A pursuant to paragraph (b)(7)(A) of such section is not subject to the requirements of this section.

(5) The listing of a standardized option, as defined in §240.9b-1(a)(4), issued by a clearing agency that is registered pursuant to section 17A of the Act (15 U.S.C. 78q-1) is not subject to the requirements of this section.

(6) The listing of securities of the following listed issuers are not subject to the requirements of this section:

(i) Asset-Backed Issuers (as defined in §240.13a-14(g) and §240.15d-14(g));

(ii) Unit investment trusts (as defined in 15 U.S.C. 80a-4(2)); and

(iii) Foreign governments (as defined in §240.3b-4(a)).

(7) The listing of securities of a listed issuer is not subject to the requirements of this section if:

(i) The listed issuer, as reflected in the applicable listing application, is organized as a trust or other unincorporated association that does not have a board of directors or persons acting in a similar capacity; and

(ii) The activities of the listed issuer that is described in paragraph (c)(7)(i) of this section are limited to passively owning or holding (as well as administering and distributing amounts in respect of) securities, rights, collateral or other assets on behalf of or for the benefit of the holders of the listed securities.

(d) *Disclosure.* Any listed issuer availing itself of an exemption from the independence standards contained in paragraph (b)(1)(iv) of this section (except paragraph (b)(1)(iv)(B) of this section), the general exemption contained in paragraph (c)(3) of this section or the last sentence of paragraph (a)(3) of this section, must:

(1) Disclose its reliance on the exemption and its assessment of whether, and if so, how, such reliance would materially adversely affect the ability of the audit committee to act independently and to satisfy the other requirements of this section in any proxy or information statement for a meeting of shareholders at which directors are elected that is filed with the Commission pursuant to the requirements of section 14 of the Act (15 U.S.C. 78n); and

(2) Disclose the information specified in paragraph (d)(1) of this section in, or incorporate such information by reference from such proxy or information statement filed with the Commission into, its annual report filed with the Commission pursuant to the requirements of section 13(a) or 15(d) of the Act (15 U.S.C. 78m(a) or 78o(d)).

(e) *Definitions.* Unless the context otherwise requires, all terms used in this section have the same meaning as in the Act. In addition, unless the context otherwise requires, the following definitions apply for purposes of this section:

(1)(i) The term *affiliate* of, or a person *affiliated* with, a specified person, means a person that directly, or indirectly through one or more intermediaries, controls, or is controlled by, or is under common control with, the person specified.

(ii)(A) A person will be deemed not to be in control of a specified person for purposes of this section if the person:

(*1*) Is not the beneficial owner, directly or indirectly, of more than 10% of any class of voting equity securities of the specified person; and

(*2*) Is not an executive officer of the specified person.

(B) Paragraph (e)(1)(ii)(A) of this section only creates a safe harbor position that a person does not control a specified person. The existence of the safe harbor does not create a presumption in any way that a person exceeding the ownership requirement in paragraph (e)(1)(ii)(A)(*1*) of this section controls or is otherwise an affiliate of a specified person.

(iii) The following will be deemed to be affiliates:

(A) An executive officer of an affiliate;

(B) A director who also is an employee of an affiliate;

(C) A general partner of an affiliate; and

(D) A managing member of an affiliate.

(iv) For purposes of paragraph (e) (1) (i) of this section, dual holding companies will not be deemed to be affiliates of or persons affiliated with each other by virtue of their dual holding company arrangements with each other, including where directors of one dual holding company are also directors of the other dual holding company, or where directors of one or both dual holding companies are also directors of the businesses jointly controlled, directly or indirectly, by the dual holding companies (and, in each case, receive only ordinary-course compensation for serving as a member of the board of directors, audit committee or any other board committee of the dual holding companies or any entity that is jointly controlled, directly or indirectly, by the dual holding companies).

(2) In the case of foreign private issuers with a two-tier board system, the term *board of directors* means the supervisory or non-management board.

(3) In the case of a listed issuer that is a limited partnership or limited liability company where such entity does not have a board of directors or equivalent body, the term board of directors means the board of directors of the managing general partner, managing member or equivalent body.

(4) The term *control* (including the terms *controlling*, *controlled by* and under *common control with*) means the possession, direct or indirect, of the power to direct or cause the direction of the management and policies of a person, whether through the ownership of voting securities, by contract, or otherwise.

(5) The term *dual holding companies* means two foreign private issuers that:

(i) Are organized in different national jurisdictions;

(ii) Collectively own and supervise the management of one or more businesses which are conducted as a single economic enterprise; and

(iii) Do not conduct any business other than collectively owning and supervising such businesses and activities reasonably incidental thereto.

(6) The term *executive officer* has the meaning set forth in §240.3b-7.

(7) The term *foreign private issuer* has the meaning set forth in §240.3b-4(c).

(8) The term *indirect* acceptance by a member of an audit committee of any consulting, advisory or other compensatory fee includes acceptance of such a fee by a spouse, a minor child or stepchild or a child or stepchild sharing a home with the member or by an entity in which such member is a partner, member, an officer such as a managing director occupying a comparable position or executive officer, or occupies a similar position (except limited partners, non-managing members and those occupying similar positions who, in each case, have no active role in providing services to the entity) and which provides accounting, consulting, legal, investment banking or financial advisory services to the issuer or any subsidiary of the issuer.

(9) The terms *listed* and *listing* refer to securities listed on a national securities exchange or listed in an automated inter-dealer quotation system of a national securities association or to issuers of such securities.

Instructions to § 240.10A-3.

1. The requirements in paragraphs (b) (2) through (b) (5), (c) (3) (v) and (c) (3) (vi) of this section do not conflict with, and do not affect the application of, any requirement or ability under a listed issuer's governing law or documents or other home country legal or listing provisions that requires or permits shareholders to ultimately vote on, approve or ratify such requirements. The requirements instead relate to the assignment of responsibility as between the audit committee and management. In such an instance, however, if the listed issuer provides a recommendation or nomination regarding such responsibilities to shareholders, the audit committee of the listed issuer, or body performing similar functions, must be responsible for making the recommendation or nomination.

2. The requirements in paragraphs (b)(2) through (b)(5), (c)(3)(v), (c)(3)(vi) and Instruction 1 of this section do not conflict with any legal or listing requirement in a listed issuer's home jurisdiction that prohibits the full board of directors from delegating such responsibilities to the listed issuer's audit committee or limits the degree of such delegation. In that case, the audit committee, or body performing similar functions, must be granted such responsibilities, which can include advisory powers, with respect to such matters to the extent permitted by law, including submitting nominations or recommendations to the full board.

3. The requirements in paragraphs (b)(2) through (b)(5), (c)(3)(v) and (c)(3)(vi) of this section do not conflict with any legal or listing requirement in a listed issuer's home jurisdiction that vests such responsibilities with a government entity or tribunal. In that case, the audit committee, or body performing similar functions, must be granted such responsibilities, which can include advisory powers, with respect to such matters to the extent permitted by law.

4. For purposes of this section, the determination of a person's beneficial ownership must be made in accordance with § 240.13d-3.

REQUIREMENTS UNDER SECTION 10C

Rule 10C-1. Listing Standards Relating To Compensation Committees.

(a) Pursuant to section 10C(a) of the Act (15 U.S.C. 78j-3(a)) and section 952 of the Dodd-Frank Wall Street Reform and Consumer Protection Act of 2010 (Pub. L. 111-203, 124 Stat. 1900):

(1) *National Securities Exchanges.* The rules of each national securities exchange registered pursuant to section 6 of the Act (15 U.S.C. 78f), to the extent such national securities exchange lists equity securities, must, in accordance with the provisions of this section, prohibit the initial or continued listing of any equity security of an issuer that is not in compliance with the requirements of any portion of paragraph (b) or (c) of this section.

(2) *National Securities Associations.* The rules of each national securities association registered pursuant to section 15A of the Act (15 U.S.C. 78o-3), to the extent such national securities association lists equity securities in an automated inter-dealer quotation system, must, in accordance with the provisions of this section, prohibit the initial or continued listing in an automated inter-dealer quotation system of any equity security of an issuer that is not in compliance with the requirements of any portion of paragraph (b) or (c) of this section.

(3) *Opportunity To Cure Defects.* The rules required by paragraphs (a)(1) and (a)(2) of this section must provide for appropriate procedures for a listed issuer to have a reasonable opportunity to cure any defects that would be the basis for a prohibition under paragraph (a) of this section, before the imposition of such prohibition. Such rules may provide that if a member of a compensation committee ceases to be independent in accordance with the requirements of this section for reasons outside the member's reasonable control, that person, with notice by the issuer to the applicable national securities exchange or national securities association, may remain a compensation committee member of the listed issuer until the earlier of the next annual shareholders meeting of the listed issuer or one year from the occurrence of the event that caused the member to be no longer independent.

(4) *Implementation.*

(i) Each national securities exchange and national securities association that lists equity securities must provide to the Commission, no later than 90 days after publication of this section in the Federal Register, proposed rules or rule amendments that comply with this section. Each submission must include, in addition to any other information required under section 19(b) of the Act (15 U.S.C. 78s(b)) and the rules thereunder, a review of whether and how existing or proposed listing standards satisfy the requirements of this rule, a discussion of the consideration of factors relevant to compensation committee independence conducted by the national securities exchange or national securities association, and the definition of independence applicable to compensation committee members that the national securities exchange or national securities association proposes to adopt or retain in light of such review.

(ii) Each national securities exchange and national securities association that lists equity securities must have rules or rule amendments that comply with this section approved by the Commission no later than one year after publication of this section in the Federal Register.

(b) *Required Standards.* The requirements of this section apply to the compensation committees of listed issuers.

(1) *Independence.*

(i) Each member of the compensation committee must be a member of the board of directors of the listed issuer, and must otherwise be independent.

(ii) *Independence Requirements.* In determining independence requirements for members of compensation committees, the national securities exchanges and national securities associations shall consider relevant factors, including, but not limited to:

(A) The source of compensation of a member of the board of directors of an issuer, including any consulting, advisory or other compensatory fee paid by the issuer to such member of the board of directors; and

(B) Whether a member of the board of directors of an issuer is affiliated with the issuer, a subsidiary of the issuer or an affiliate of a subsidiary of the issuer.

(iii) *Exemptions From the Independence Requirements.*

(A) The listing of equity securities of the following categories of listed issuers is not subject to the requirements of paragraph (b)(1) of this section:

(1) Limited partnerships;

(2) Companies in bankruptcy proceedings;

(3) Open-end management investment companies registered under the Investment Company Act of 1940; and

(4) Any foreign private issuer that discloses in its annual report the reasons that the foreign private issuer does not have an independent compensation committee.

(B) In addition to the issuer exemptions set forth in paragraph (b)(1)(iii)(A) of this section, a national securities exchange or a national securities association, pursuant to section 19(b) of the Act (15 U.S.C. 78s(b)) and the rules thereunder, may exempt from the requirements of paragraph (b)(1) of this section a particular relationship with respect to members of the compensation committee, as each national securities exchange or national securities association determines is appropriate, taking into consideration the size of an issuer and any other relevant factors.

(2) *Authority To Retain Compensation Consultants, Independent Legal Counsel and Other Compensation Advisers.*

(i) The compensation committee of a listed issuer, in its capacity as a committee of the board of directors, may, in its sole discretion, retain or obtain the advice of a compensation consultant, independent legal counsel or other adviser.

(ii) The compensation committee shall be directly responsible for the appointment, compensation and oversight of the work of any compensation consultant, independent legal counsel and other adviser retained by the compensation committee.

(iii) Nothing in this paragraph (b)(2) shall be construed:

(A) To require the compensation committee to implement or act consistently with the advice or recommendations of the compensation consultant, independent legal counsel or other adviser to the compensation committee; or

(B) To affect the ability or obligation of a compensation committee to exercise its own judgment in fulfillment of the duties of the compensation committee.

(3) *Funding.* Each listed issuer must provide for appropriate funding, as determined by the compensation committee, in its capacity as a committee of the board of directors, for payment of reasonable compensation to a compensation consultant, independent legal counsel or any other adviser retained by the compensation committee.

(4) *Independence of Compensation Consultants and Other Advisers.* The compensation committee of a listed issuer may select a compensation consultant, legal counsel or other adviser to the compensation committee only after taking into consideration the following factors, as well as any other factors identified by the relevant national securities exchange or national securities association in its listing standards:

(i) The provision of other services to the issuer by the person that employs the compensation consultant, legal counsel or other adviser;

(ii) The amount of fees received from the issuer by the person that employs the compensation consultant, legal counsel or other adviser, as a percentage of the total revenue of the person that employs the compensation consultant, legal counsel or other adviser;

(iii) The policies and procedures of the person that employs the compensation consultant, legal counsel or other adviser that are designed to prevent conflicts of interest;

(iv) Any business or personal relationship of the compensation consultant, legal counsel or other adviser with a member of the compensation committee;

(v) Any stock of the issuer owned by the compensation consultant, legal counsel or other adviser; and

(vi) Any business or personal relationship of the compensation consultant, legal counsel, other adviser or the person employing the adviser with an executive officer of the issuer.

Instruction to Paragraph (b)(4) of This Section: A listed issuer's compensation committee is required to conduct the independence assessment outlined in paragraph (b)(4) of this section with respect to any compensation consultant, legal counsel or other adviser that provides advice to the compensation committee, other than in-house legal counsel.

(5) *General Exemptions.*

(i) The national securities exchanges and national securities associations, pursuant to section 19(b) of the Act (15 U.S.C. 78s(b)) and the rules thereunder, may exempt from the requirements of this section certain categories of issuers, as the national securities exchange or national securities association determines is appropriate, taking into consideration, among other relevant factors, the potential impact of such requirements on smaller reporting issuers.

(ii) The requirements of this section shall not apply to any controlled company or to any smaller reporting company.

(iii) The listing of a security futures product cleared by a clearing agency that is registered pursuant to section 17A of the Act (15 U.S.C. 78q-1) or that is exempt from the registration requirements of section 17A(b)(7)(A) (15 U.S.C. 78q-1(b)(7)(A)) is not subject to the requirements of this section.

(iv) The listing of a standardized option, as defined in § 240.9b-1(a)(4), issued by a clearing agency that is registered pursuant to section 17A of the Act (15 U.S.C. 78q-1) is not subject to the requirements of this section.

(c) *Definitions.* Unless the context otherwise requires, all terms used in this section have the same meaning as in the Act and the rules and regulations thereunder. In addition, unless the context otherwise requires, the following definitions apply for purposes of this section:

(1) In the case of foreign private issuers with a two-tier board system, the term board of directors means the supervisory or non-management board.

(2) The term *compensation committee* means:

(i) A committee of the board of directors that is designated as the compensation committee; or

(ii) In the absence of a committee of the board of directors that is designated as the compensation committee, a committee of the board of directors performing functions typically performed by a compensation committee, including oversight of executive compensation, even if it is not designated as the compensation committee or also performs other functions; or

(iii) For purposes of this section other than paragraphs (b)(2)(i) and (b)(3), in the absence of a committee as described in paragraphs (c)(2)(i) or (ii) of this section, the members of the board of directors who oversee executive compensation matters on behalf of the board of directors.

(3) The term *controlled company* means an issuer:

(i) That is listed on a national securities exchange or by a national securities association; and

(ii) Of which more than 50 percent of the voting power for the election of directors is held by an individual, a group or another company.

(4) The terms *listed and listing* refer to equity securities listed on a national securities exchange or listed in an automated inter-dealer quotation system of a national securities association or to issuers of such securities.

(5) The term *open-end management investment company* means an open-end company, as defined by Section 5(a)(1) of the Investment Company Act of 1940 (15 U.S.C. 80a-5(a)(1)), that is registered under that Act.

REGULATION 12B—REGISTRATION AND REPORTING
General Requirements as to Contents

Rule 12b-2. Definitions

Unless the context otherwise requires, the following terms, when used in the rules contained in this regulation or in Regulation 13A or 15D or in the forms for statements and reports filed pursuant to Section 12, 13 or 15(d) of the Act, shall have the respective meanings indicated in this rule:

Accelerated Filer and Large Accelerated Filer.

(1) *Accelerated Filer.* The term *accelerated filer* means an issuer after it first meets the following conditions as of the end of its fiscal year:

(i) The issuer had an aggregate worldwide market value of the voting and non-voting common equity held by its non-affiliates of $75 million or more, but less than $700 million, as of the last business day of the issuer's most recently completed second fiscal quarter;

(ii) The issuer has been subject to the requirements of section 13(a) or 15(d) of the Act (15 U.S.C. 78m or 78o(d)) for a period of at least twelve calendar months; and

(iii) The issuer has filed at least one annual report pursuant to section 13(a) or 15(d) of the Act; and

(iv) The issuer is not eligible to use the requirements for smaller reporting companies under the revenue test in paragraph (2) or (3)(iii)(B) of the "smaller reporting company" definition in this section, as applicable.

(2) *Large Accelerated Filer.* The term *large accelerated filer* means an issuer after it first meets the following conditions as of the end of its fiscal year:

(i) The issuer had an aggregate worldwide market value of the voting and non-voting common equity held by its non-affiliates of $700 million or more, as of the last business day of the issuer's most recently completed second fiscal quarter;

(ii) The issuer has been subject to the requirements of section 13(a) or 15(d) of the Act for a period of at least twelve calendar months; and

(iii) The issuer has filed at least one annual report pursuant to section 13(a) or 15(d) of the Act; and

(iv) The issuer is not eligible to use the requirements for smaller reporting companies under the revenue test in paragraph (2) or (3)(iii)(B) of the "smaller reporting company" definition in this section, as applicable.

(3) *Entering and Exiting Accelerated Filer and Large Accelerated Filer Status.*

(i) The determination at the end of the issuer's fiscal year for whether a non-accelerated filer becomes an accelerated filer, or whether a non-accelerated filer or accelerated filer becomes a large accelerated filer, governs the deadlines for the annual report to be filed for that fiscal year, the quarterly and annual reports to be filed for the subsequent fiscal year and all annual and quarterly reports to be filed thereafter while the issuer remains an accelerated filer or large accelerated filer.

(ii) Once an issuer becomes an accelerated filer, it will remain an accelerated filer unless: The issuer determines, at the end of a fiscal year, that the aggregate worldwide market value of the voting and non-voting common equity held by its non-affiliates was less than $60 million, as of the last business day of the issuer's most recently completed second fiscal quarter; or it determines that it is eligible to use the requirements for smaller reporting companies under the revenue test in paragraph (2) or (3)(iii)(B) of the "smaller reporting company" definition in this section, as applicable. An issuer that makes either of these determinations becomes a nonaccelerated filer. The issuer will not become an accelerated filer again unless it subsequently meets the conditions in paragraph (1) of this definition.

(iii) Once an issuer becomes a large accelerated filer, it will remain a large accelerated filer unless: It determines, at the end of a fiscal year, that the aggregate worldwide market value of the voting and non-voting common equity held by its non-affiliates ("aggregate worldwide market value") was less than $560 million, as of the last business day of the issuer's most recently completed second fiscal quarter or it determines that it is eligible to use the requirements for smaller reporting companies under the revenue test in paragraph (2) or (3)(iii)(B) of the "smaller reporting company" definition in this section, as applicable. If the issuer's aggregate worldwide market value was $60 million or more, but less than $560 million, as of the last business day of the issuer's most recently completed second fiscal quarter, and it is not eligible to use the requirements for smaller reporting companies under the revenue test in paragraph (2) or (3)(iii)(B) of the "smaller reporting company" definition in this section, as applicable, it becomes an accelerated filer. If the issuer's aggregate worldwide market value was less than $60 million, as of the last business day of the issuer's most recently completed second fiscal quarter, or it is eligible to use the requirements for smaller reporting companies under the revenue test in paragraph (2) or (3)(iii)(B) of the "smaller reporting company" definition in this section, it becomes a non-accelerated filer. An issuer will not become a large accelerated filer again unless it subsequently meets the conditions in paragraph (2) of this definition.

(iv) The determination at the end of the issuer's fiscal year for whether an accelerated filer becomes a non-accelerated filer, or a large accelerated filer becomes an accelerated filer or a non-accelerated filer, governs the deadlines for the annual report to be filed for that fiscal year, the quarterly and annual reports to be filed for the subsequent fiscal year and all annual and quarterly reports to be filed thereafter while the issuer remains an accelerated filer or non-accelerated filer.

(4) For purposes of paragraph (1), (2), and (3) of this definition only, a business development company is considered to be eligible to use the requirements for smaller reporting companies under the revenue test in paragraph (2) or (3)(iii)(B) of the "smaller reporting company" definition in this section, provided that the business development company meets the requirements of the test using annual investment income under Rule 6-07.1 of Regulation S-X (17 CFR 210.6-07.1) as the measure of its "annual revenues" for purposes of the test.

(ii) Once an issuer becomes an accelerated filer, it will remain an accelerated filer unless the issuer determines at the end of a fiscal year that the aggregate worldwide market value of the voting and non-voting common equity held by non-affiliates of the issuer was less than $50 million, as of the last business day of the issuer's most recently completed second fiscal quarter. An issuer making this determination becomes a nonaccelerated filer. The issuer will not become an accelerated filer again unless it subsequently meets the conditions in paragraph (1) of this definition.

(iii) Once an issuer becomes a large accelerated filer, it will remain a large accelerated filer unless the issuer determines at the end of a fiscal year that the aggregate worldwide market value of the voting and non-voting common equity held by non-affiliates of the issuer was less than $500 million, as of the last business day of the issuer's most recently completed second fiscal quarter. If the issuer's aggregate worldwide market value was $50 million or more, but less than $500 million, as of the last business day of the issuer's most recently completed second fiscal quarter, the issuer becomes an accelerated filer. If the issuer's aggregate worldwide market value was less than $50 million, as of the last business day of the issuer's most recently completed second fiscal quarter, the issuer becomes a non-accelerated filer. An issuer will not become a large accelerated filer again unless it subsequently meets the conditions in paragraph (2) of this definition.

(iv) The determination at the end of the issuer's fiscal year for whether an accelerated filer becomes a non-accelerated filer, or a large accelerated filer becomes an accelerated filer or a non-accelerated filer, governs the deadlines for the annual report to be filed for that fiscal year, the quarterly and annual reports to be filed for the subsequent fiscal year and all annual and quarterly reports to be filed thereafter while the issuer remains an accelerated filer or non-accelerated filer.

Note to Paragraphs (1), (2) and (3): The aggregate worldwide market value of the issuer's outstanding voting and non-voting common equity shall be computed by use of the price at which the common equity was last sold, or the average of the bid and asked prices of such common equity, in the principal market for such common equity.

Affiliate. An "affiliate" of, or a person "affiliated" with, a specified person, is a person that directly, or indirectly through one or more intermediaries, controls, or is controlled by, or is under common control with, the person specified.

Amount. The term "amount," when used in regard to securities, means the principal amount if relating to evidences of indebtedness, the number of shares if relating to shares, and the number of units if relating to any other kind of security.

Associate. The term "associate" used to indicate a relationship with any person, means: (1) any corporation or organization (other than the registrant or a majorityowned subsidiary of the registrant) of which such person is an officer or partner or is, directly or indirectly, the beneficial owner of 10 percent or more of any class of equity securities, (2) any trust or other estate in which such person has a substantial beneficial interest or as to which such person serves as trustee or in a similar fiduciary capacity, and (3) any relative or spouse of such person, or any relative of such spouse, who has the same home as such person or who is a director or officer of the registrant or any of its parents or subsidiaries.

Business Combination Related Shell Company. The term business combination related shell company means a shell company (as defined in § 240.12b-2) that is:

(1) Formed by an entity that is not a shell company solely for the purpose of changing the corporate domicile of that entity solely within the United States; or

(2) Formed by an entity that is not a shell company solely for the purpose of completing a business combination transaction (as defined in § 230.165(f) of this chapter) among one or more entities other than the shell company, none of which is a shell company.

Certified. The term "certified," when used in regard to financial statements, means examined and reported upon with an opinion expressed by an independent public or certified public accountant.

Charter. The term "charter" includes articles of incorporation, declarations of trust, articles of association or partnership, or any similar instrument, as amended, effecting (either with or without filing with any governmental agency) the organization or creation of an incorporated or unincorporated person.

Common Equity. The term "common equity" means any class of common stock or an equivalent interest, including but not limited to a unit of beneficial interest in a trust or a limited partnership interest.

Control. The term "control" (including the terms "controlling," "controlled by" and "under common control with") means the possession, direct or indirect, of the power to direct or cause the direction of the management and policies of a person, whether through the ownership of voting securities, by contract, or otherwise.

Depositary Share. The term "depositary share" means a security, evidenced by an American Depositary Receipt, that represents a foreign security or a multiple of or fraction thereof deposited with a depositary.

Emerging Growth Company. (1) The term emerging growth company means an issuer that had total annual gross revenues of less than $1,070,000,000 during its most recently completed fiscal year.

(2)   An issuer that is an emerging growth company as of the first day of that fiscal year shall continue to be deemed an emerging growth company until the earliest of:

(i)   The last day of the fiscal year of the issuer during which it had total annual gross revenues of $1,070,000,000 or more;

(ii) The last day of the fiscal year of the issuer following the fifth anniversary of the date of the first sale of common equity securities of the issuer pursuant to an effective registration statement under the Securities Act of 1933;

(iii) The date on which such issuer has, during the previous three year period, issued more than $1,000,000,000 in non-convertible debt; or

(iv) The date on which such issuer is deemed to be a large accelerated filer, as defined in Rule 12b-2 (§ 240.12b-2 of this chapter).

Employee. The term "employee" does not include a director, trustee, or officer.

Fiscal Year. The term "fiscal year" means the annual accounting period or, if no closing date has been adopted, the calendar year ending on December 31.

Majority-Owned Subsidiary. The term "majority-owned subsidiary" means a subsidiary more than 50 percent of whose outstanding securities representing the right, other than as affected by events of default, to vote for the election of directors, is owned by the subsidiary's parent and/or one or more of the parent's other majority-owned subsidiaries.

Managing Underwriter. The term "managing underwriter" includes an underwriter (or underwriters) who, by contract or otherwise, deals with the registrant; organizes the selling effort; receives some benefit directly or indirectly in which all other underwriters similarly situated do not share in proportion to their respective interests in the underwriting; or represents any other underwriters in such matters as maintaining the records of the distribution, arranging the allotments of securities offered or arranging for appropriate stabilization activities, if any.

Material. The term "material," when used to qualify a requirement for the furnishing of information as to any subject, limits the information required to those matters to which there is a substantial likelihood that a reasonable investor would attach importance in determining whether to buy or sell the securities registered.

Material Weakness. The term "material weakness" is a deficiency, or a combination of deficiencies, in internal control over financial reporting such that there is a reasonable possibility that a material misstatement of the registrant's annual or interim financial statements will not be prevented or detected on a timely basis.

Parent. A "parent" of a specified person is an affiliate controlling such person directly or indirectly through one or more intermediaries.

Predecessor. The term "predecessor" means a person the major portion of the business and assets of which another person acquired in a single succession or in a series of related successions, in each of which the acquiring person acquired the major portion of the business and assets of the acquired person.

Previously Filed or Reported. The terms "previously filed" and "previously reported" mean previously filed with, or reported in, a statement under Section 12, a report under Section 13 or 15(d), a definitive proxy statement or information statement under Section 14 of the Act, or a registration statement under the Securities Act of 1933: Provided, That information contained in any such document shall be deemed to have been previously filed with, or reported to, an exchange only if such document is filed with such exchange.

Principal Underwriter. The term "principal underwriter" means an underwriter in privity of contract with the issuer of the securities as to which he is underwriter.

Promoter.

(1) The term "promoter" includes:

(i) Any person who, acting alone or in conjunction with one or more other persons, directly or indirectly takes initiative in founding and organizing the business or enterprise of an issuer; or

(ii) Any person who, in connection with the founding and organizing of the business or enterprise of an issuer, directly or indirectly receives in consideration of services or property, or both services and property, 10 percent or more of any class of securities of the issuer or 10 percent or more of the proceeds from the sale of any class of such securities. However, a person who receives such securities or proceeds either solely as underwriting commissions or solely in consideration of property shall not be deemed a promoter within the meaning of this paragraph if such person does not otherwise take part in founding and organizing the enterprise.

(2) All persons coming within the definition of "promoter" in paragraph (1) of this definition may be referred to as "founders" or "organizers" or by another term provided that such term is reasonably descriptive of those persons' activities with respect to the issuer.

Prospectus. Unless otherwise specified or the context otherwise requires, the term "prospectus" means a prospectus meeting the requirements of Section 10(a) of the Securities Act of 1933 as amended.

Registrant. The term "registrant" means an issuer of securities with respect to which a registration statement or report is to be filed.

Registration Statement. The term "registration statement" or "statement," when used with reference to registration pursuant to Section 12 of the Act, includes both an application for registration of securities on a national securities exchange pursuant to Section 12(b) of the Act and a registration statement filed pursuant to Section 12(g) of the Act.

Share. The term "share" means a share of stock in a corporation or unit of interest in an unincorporated person.

Shell Company. The term shell company means a registrant, other than an assetbacked issuer as defined in Item 1101(b) of Regulation AB (§ 229.1101(b) of this chapter), that has:

(1) No or nominal operations; and

(2) Either:

(i) No or nominal assets;

(ii) Assets consisting solely of cash and cash equivalents; or

(iii) Assets consisting of any amount of cash and cash equivalents and nominal other assets.

Note: For purposes of this definition, the determination of a registrant's assets (including cash and cash equivalents) is based solely on the amount of assets that would be reflected on the registrant's balance sheet prepared in accordance with generally accepted accounting principles on the date of that determination.

Significant Deficiency. The term significant deficiency is a deficiency, or a combination of deficiencies, in internal control over financial reporting that is less severe than a material weakness, yet important enough to merit attention by those responsible for oversight of the registrant's financial reporting.

Significant Subsidiary. The term significant subsidiary means a subsidiary, including its subsidiaries, which meets any of the following conditions:

(1) The registrant's and its other subsidiaries' investments in and advances to the subsidiary exceed 10 percent of the total assets of the registrant and its subsidiaries consolidated as of the end of the most recently completed fiscal year (for a proposed combination between entities under common control, this condition is also met when the number of common shares exchanged or to be exchanged by the registrant exceeds 10 percent of its total common shares outstanding at the date the combination is initiated); or

(2) The registrant's and its other subsidiaries' proportionate share of the total assets (after intercompany eliminations) of the subsidiary exceeds 10 percent of the total assets of the registrant and its subsidiaries consolidated as of the end of the most recently completed fiscal year; or

(3) The registrant's and its other subsidiaries' equity in the income from continuing operations before income taxes of the subsidiary exclusive of amounts attributable to any noncontrolling interests exceeds 10 percent of such income of the registrant and its subsidiaries consolidated for the most recently completed fiscal year.

Note 1: A registrant that files its financial statements in accordance with or provides a reconciliation to U.S. Generally Accepted Accounting Principles shall make the prescribed tests using amounts determined under U.S. Generally Accepted Accounting Principles. A foreign private issuer that files its financial statements in accordance with IFRS as issued by the IASB shall make the prescribed tests using amounts determined under IFRS as issued by the IASB.

Computational Note 1 to Paragraph (3). For purposes of making the prescribed income test the following guidance should be applied:

1. When a loss exclusive of amounts attributable to any noncontrolling interests has been incurred by either the parent and its subsidiaries consolidated or the tested subsidiary, but not both, the equity in the income or loss of the tested subsidiary exclusive of amounts attributable to any noncontrolling interests should be excluded from such income of the registrant and its subsidiaries consolidated for purposes of the computation.

2. If income of the registrant and its subsidiaries consolidated exclusive of amounts attributable to any noncontrolling interests for the most recent fiscal year is at least 10 percent lower than the average of the income for the last five fiscal years, such average income should be substituted for purposes of the computation. Any loss years should be omitted for purposes of computing average income.

Smaller Reporting Company. As used in this part, the term *smaller reporting company* means an issuer that is not an investment company, an asset-backed issuer (as defined in § 229.1101 of this chapter), or a majority-owned subsidiary of a parent that is not a smaller reporting company and that:

(1) Had a public float of less than $250 million; or

(2) Had annual revenues of less than $100 million and either:

(i) No public float; or

(ii) A public float of less than $700 million.

(3) Whether an issuer is a smaller reporting company is determined on an annual basis.

(i) For issuers that are required to file reports under section 13(a) or 15(d) of the Exchange Act:

(A) Public float is measured as of the last business day of the issuer's most recently completed second fiscal quarter and computed by multiplying the aggregate worldwide number of shares of its voting and non-voting common equity held by non-affiliates by the price at which the common equity was last sold, or the average of the bid and asked prices of common equity, in the principal market for the common equity;

(B) Annual revenues are as of the most recently completed fiscal year for which audited financial statements are available; and

(C) An issuer must reflect the determination of whether it came within the definition of smaller reporting company in its quarterly report on Form 10-Q for the first fiscal quarter of the next year, indicating on the cover page of that filing, and in subsequent filings for that fiscal year, whether it is a smaller reporting company, except that, if a determination based on public float indicates that the issuer is newly eligible to be a smaller reporting company, the issuer may choose to reflect this determination beginning with its first quarterly report on Form 10-Q following the determination, rather than waiting until the first fiscal quarter of the next year.

(ii) For determinations based on an initial registration statement under the Securities Act or Exchange Act for shares of its common equity:

(A) Public float is measured as of a date within 30 days of the date of the filing of the registration statement and computed by multiplying the aggregate worldwide number of shares of its voting and non-voting common equity held by non-affiliates before the registration plus, in the case of a Securities Act registration statement, the number of shares of its voting and non-voting common equity included in the registration statement by the estimated public offering price of the shares;

(B) Annual revenues are as of the most recently completed fiscal year for which audited financial statements are available; and

(C) The issuer must reflect the determination of whether it came within the definition of smaller reporting company in the registration statement and must appropriately indicate on the cover page of the filing, and subsequent filings for the fiscal year in which the filing is made, whether it is a smaller reporting company. The issuer must re-determine its status at the end of its second fiscal quarter and then reflect any change in status as provided in paragraph (3)(i)(C) of this definition. In the case of a determination based on an initial Securities Act registration statement, an issuer that was not determined to be a smaller reporting company has the option to re-determine its status at the conclusion of the offering covered by the registration statement based on the actual offering price and number of shares sold.

(iii) Once an issuer determines that it does not qualify for smaller reporting company status because it exceeded one or more of the current thresholds, it will remain unqualified unless when making its annual determination either:

(A) It determines that its public float was less than $200 million; or

(B) It determines that its public float and its annual revenues meet the requirements for subsequent qualification included in the following chart:

Prior Annual Revenues	Prior Public Float	
	None or less than $700 million	$700 million or more
Less than $100 million	Neither threshold exceeded.	Public float—Less than $560 million; and Revenues—Less than $100 million.
$100 million or more	Public float—None or less than $700 million; and Revenues—Less than $80 million.	Public float—Less than $560 million; and Revenues—Less than $80 million.

Instruction 1 to Definition of "Smaller Reporting Company": A registrant that qualifies as a smaller reporting company under the public float thresholds identified in paragraphs (1) and

(3) (iii) (A) of this definition will qualify as a smaller reporting company regardless of its revenues.

Subsidiary. A "subsidiary" of a specified person is an affiliate controlled by such person directly, or indirectly through one or more intermediaries. (See also "majorityowned subsidiary," "significant subsidiary," and "totally-held subsidiary.")

Succession. The term succession means the direct acquisition of the assets comprising a going business, whether by merger, consolidation, purchase, or other direct transfer; or the acquisition of control of a shell company in a transaction required to be reported on Form 8-K (§ 249.308 of this chapter) in compliance with Item 5.01 of that Form or on Form 20-F (§ 249.220f of this chapter) in compliance with Rule 13a-19 (§ 240.13a-19) or Rule 15d-19 (§ 240.15d-19). Except for an acquisition of control of a shell company, the term does not include the acquisition of control of a business unless followed by the direct acquisition of its assets. The terms succeed and successor have meanings correlative to the foregoing.

Totally-Held Subsidiary. The term "totally-held subsidiary" means a subsidiary: (1) substantially all of whose outstanding securities are owned by its parent and/or the other parent's totally-held subsidiaries, and (2) which is not indebted to any person other than its parent and/ or the parent's other totally-held subsidiaries in an amount which is material in relation to the particular subsidiary, excepting indebtedness incurred in the ordinary course of business which is not overdue and which matures within one year from the date of its creation, whether evidenced by securities or not.

Voting Securities. The term "voting securities" means securities the holders of which are presently entitled to vote for the election of directors.

Wholly-Owned Subsidiary. The term "wholly-owned subsidiary" means a subsidiary substantially all of whose outstanding voting securities are owned by its parent and/or the parent's other wholly-owned subsidiaries.

Rule 12b-20. Additional Information

In addition to the information expressly required to be included in a statement or report, there shall be added such further material information, if any, as may be necessary to make the required statements, in the light of the circumstances under which they are made not misleading.

Rule 12b-21. Information Unknown or Not Available

Information required need be given only insofar as it is known or reasonably available to the registrant. If any required information is unknown and not reasonably available to the registrant, either because the obtaining thereof would involve unreasonable effort or expense, or because it rests peculiarly within the knowledge of another person not affiliated with the registrant, the information may be omitted, subject to the following conditions:

(a) The registrant shall give such information on the subject as it possesses or can acquire without unreasonable effort or expense, together with the sources thereof.

(b) The registrant shall include a statement either showing that unreasonable effort or expense would be involved or indicating the absence of any affiliation with the person within whose knowledge the information rests and stating the result of a request made to such person for the information.

Rule 12b-22. Disclaimer of Control

If the existence of control is open to reasonable doubt in any instance, the registrant may disclaim the existence of control and any admission thereof; in such case, however, the registrant shall state the material facts pertinent to the possible existence of control.

Rule 12b-25. Notification of Inability to Timely File All or Any Required Portion of a Form 10-K, 20-F, 11-K, N-CEN, N-CSR, 10-Q or 10-D

(a) If all or any required portion of an annual or transition report on Form 10-K, 20-F or 11-K (17 CFR 249.310, 249.220f or 249.311), a quarterly or transition report on Form 10-Q (17 CFR 249.308a), or a distribution report on Form 10-D (17 CFR 249.312) required to be filed pursuant to Section 13 or 15(d) of the Act (15 U.S.C. 78m or 78o(d)) and rules thereunder, or if all or any required portion of a semi-annual, annual or transition report on Form N-CSR (17 CFR 249.331; 17 CFR 274.128) or Form N-CEN (17 CFR 249.330; 17 CFR 274.101) required to be filed pursuant to Section 13 or 15(d) of the Act or section 30 of the Investment Company Act of 1940 (15 U.S.C. 80a-29) and the rules thereunder, is not filed within the time period prescribed for such report, the registrant, no later than one business day after the due date for such report, shall file a Form 12b-25 (17 CFR 249.322) with the Commission which shall contain disclosure of its inability to file the report timely and the reasons therefore in reasonable detail.

(b) With respect to any report or portion of any report described in paragraph (a) of this section which is not timely filed because the registrant is unable to do so without unreasonable effort or expense, such report shall be deemed to be filed on the prescribed due date for such report if:

(1) The registrant files the Form 12b-25 in compliance with paragraph (a) of this section and, when applicable, furnishes the exhibit required by paragraph (c) of this section;

(2) The registrant represents in the Form 12b-25 that:

(i) The reason(s) causing the inability to file timely could not be eliminated by the registrant without unreasonable effort or expense; and

(ii) The subject annual report, semi-annual report or transition report on Form 10-K, 20-F, 11-K, N-CEN, or N-CSR, or portion thereof, will be filed no later than the fifteenth calendar day following the prescribed due date; or the subject quarterly report or transition report on Form 10-Q or distribution report on Form 10-D, or portion thereof, will be filed no later than the fifth calendar day following the prescribed due date; and

(3) The report/portion thereof is actually filed within the period specified by paragraph (b)(2)(ii) of this section.

(c) If paragraph (b) of this section is applicable and the reason the subject report/portion thereof cannot be filed timely without unreasonable effort or expense relates to the inability of any person, other than the registrant, to furnish any required opinion, report or certification, the Form 12b-25 shall have attached as an exhibit a statement signed by such person stating the specific reasons why such person is unable to furnish the required opinion, report or certification on or before the date such report must be filed.

(d) Notwithstanding paragraph (b) of this section, a registrant will not be eligible to use any registration statement form under the Securities Act of 1933 the use of which is predicated on timely filed reports until the subject report is actually filed pursuant to paragraph (b)(3) of this section.

(e) If a Form 12b-25 filed pursuant to paragraph (a) of this section relates only to a portion of a subject report, the registrant shall:

(1) File the balance of such report and indicate on the cover page thereof which disclosure items are omitted; and

(2) Include, on the upper right corner of the amendment to the report which includes the previously omitted information, the following statement:

"The following items were the subject of a Form 12b-25 and are included herein: *(List Item Numbers)*."

(f) The provisions of this section shall not apply to financial statements to be filed by amendment to a form 10-K and 10-KSB as provided for by paragraph (a) of Rule 3-09 or schedules to be filed by amendment in accordance with General Instruction A to form 10-K and 10-KSB.

(g) *Electronic filings*. The provisions of this section shall not apply to reports required to be filed in electronic format if the sole reason the report is not filed within the time period prescribed is that the filer is unable to file the report in electronic format. Filers unable to submit a report in electronic format within the time period prescribed solely due to difficulties with electronic filing should comply with either Rule 201 or 202 of Regulation S-T (§ 232.201 and § 232.202 of this chapter), or apply for an adjustment of filing date pursuant to Rule 13(c) of Regulation S-T (232.13(c) of this chapter).

(h) *Interactive Data Submissions*. The provisions of this section shall not apply to the submission or posting of an Interactive Data File (§ 232.11 of this chapter). Filers unable to submit or post an Interactive Data File within the time period prescribed should comply with either Rule 201 or 202 of Regulation S-T (§ 232.201 and § 232.202 of this chapter).

EXTENSIONS AND TEMPORARY EXEMPTIONS—DEFINITIONS

Rule 12g-1. Registration of Securities; Exemption from Section 12(g)

An issuer is not required to register a class of equity securities pursuant to section 12(g)(1) of the Act (15 U.S.C. 78*l*(g)(1)) if on the last day of its most recent fiscal year:

(a) The issuer had total assets not exceeding $10 million; or

(b)(1) The class of equity securities was held of record by fewer than 2,000 persons and fewer than 500 persons were not accredited investors (as such term is defined in § 230.501(a) of this chapter, determined as of such day rather than at the time of the sale of the securities); or

(2) The class of equity securities was held of record by fewer than 2,000 persons in the case of a bank; a savings and loan holding company, as such term is defined in section 10 of the Home Owners' Loan Act (12 U.S.C. 1461); or a bank holding company, as such term is defined in section 2 of the Bank Holding Company Act of 1956 (12 U.S.C. 1841).

Rule 12g-2. Securities Deemed to Be Registered Pursuant to Section 12(g)(1) upon Termination of Exemption Pursuant to Section 12(g)(2)(A) or (B)

Any class of securities that would have been required to be registered pursuant to section 12(g)(1) of the Act (15 U.S.C. 78l(g)(1)) except for the fact that it was exempt from such registration by section 12(g)(2)(A) of the Act (15 U.S.C. 78l(g)(2)(A)) because it was listed and registered on a national securities exchange, or by section 12(g)(2)(B) of the Act (15 U.S.C. 78l(g)(2)(B)) because it was issued by an investment company registered pursuant to section 8 of the Investment Company Act of 1940 (15 U.S.C. 80a-8), shall upon the termination of the listing and registration of such class or the termination of the registration of such company and without the filing of an additional registration statement be deemed to be registered pursuant to section 12(g)(1) of the Act if at the time of such termination:

(a) The issuer of such class of securities has elected to be regulated as a business development company pursuant to sections 55 through 65 of the Investment Company Act of 1940 (15 U.S.C. 80a-54 through 64) and such election has not been withdrawn; or

(b) Securities of the class are not exempt from such registration pursuant to section 12 of the Act (15 U.S.C. 78l) or rules thereunder and all securities of such class are held of record by 300 or more persons, or 1,200 or more persons in the case of a bank; a savings and loan holding company, as such term is defined in section 10 of the Home Owners' Loan Act (12 U.S.C. 1461); or a bank holding company, as such term is defined in section 2 of the Bank Holding Company Act of 1956 (12 U.S.C. 1841).

Rule 12g-3. Registration of Securities of Successor Issuers Under Section 12(b) or 12(g)

(a) Where in connection with a succession by merger, consolidation, exchange of securities, acquisition of assets or otherwise, securities of an issuer that are not already registered pursuant to section 12 of the Act (15 U.S.C. 78l) are issued to the holders of any class of securities of another issuer that is registered pursuant to either section 12(b) or (g) of the Act (15 U.S.C. 78l(b) or (g)), the class of securities so issued shall be deemed to be registered under the same paragraph of section 12 of the Act unless upon consummation of the succession:

(1) Such class is exempt from such registration other than by § 240.12g3-2;

(2) All securities of such class are held of record by fewer than 300 persons, or 1,200 persons in the case of a bank; a savings and loan holding company, as such term is defined in section 10 of the Home Owners' Loan Act (12 U.S.C. 1461); or a bank holding company, as such term is defined in section 2 of the Bank Holding Company Act of 1956 (12 U.S.C. 1841); or

(3) The securities issued in connection with the succession were registered on Form F-8 or Form F-80 (§ 239.38 or § 239.41 of this chapter) and following succession the successor would not be required to register such class of securities under section 12 of the Act (15 U.S.C. 78l) but for this section.

(b) Where in connection with a succession by merger, consolidation, exchange of securities, acquisition of assets or otherwise, securities of an issuer that are not already registered pursuant to section 12 of the Act (15 U.S.C. 78l) are issued to the holders of any class of securities of another issuer that is required to file a registration statement pursuant to either section 12(b) or (g) of the Act (15 U.S.C. 78l(b) or (g)) but has not yet done so, the duty to file such statement shall be deemed to have been assumed by the issuer of the class of securities so issued. The successor issuer shall file a registration statement pursuant to the same paragraph of section 12 of the Act with respect to such class within the period of time the predecessor issuer would have been required to file such a statement unless upon consummation of the succession:

(1) Such class is exempt from such registration other than by § 240.12g3-2;

(2) All securities of such class are held of record by fewer than 300 persons, or 1,200 persons in the case of a bank; a savings and loan holding company, as such term is defined in section 10 of the Home Owners' Loan Act (12 U.S.C. 1461); or a bank holding company, as such term is defined in section 2 of the Bank Holding Company Act of 1956 (12 U.S.C. 1841); or

(3) The securities issued in connection with the succession were registered on Form F-8 or Form F-80 (§ 239.38 or § 239.41 of this chapter) and following the succession the successor would not be required to register such class of securities under section 12 of the Act (15 U.S.C. 78l) but for this section.

(c) Where in connection with a succession by merger, consolidation, exchange of securities, acquisition of assets or otherwise, securities of an issuer that are not already registered pursuant to section 12 of the Act (15 U.S.C. 78l) are issued to the holders of classes of securities of two or more other issuers that are each registered pursuant to section 12 of the Act, the class of securities so issued shall be deemed to be registered under section 12 of the Act unless upon consummation of the succession:

(1) Such class is exempt from such registration other than by § 240.12g3-2;

(2) All securities of such class are held of record by fewer than 300 persons, or 1,200 persons in the case of a bank; a savings and loan holding company, as such term is defined in section 10 of the Home Owners' Loan Act (12 U.S.C. 1461); or a bank holding company, as such term is defined in section 2 of the Bank Holding Company Act of 1956 (12 U.S.C. 1841); or

(3) The securities issued in connection with the succession were registered on Form F-8 or Form F-80 (§ 239.38 or § 239.41 of this chapter) and following succession the successor would not be required to register such class of securities under section 12 of the Act (15 U.S.C. 78l) but for this section.

(d) If the classes of securities issued by two or more predecessor issuers (as described in paragraph (c) of this section) are registered under the same paragraph of section 12 of the Act (15 U.S.C. 78l), the class of securities issued by the successor issuer shall be deemed registered under the same paragraph of section 12 of the Act. If the classes of securities issued by the predecessor issuers are not registered under the same paragraph of section 12 of the Act, the class of securities issued by the successor issuer shall be deemed registered under section 12(g) of the Act (15 U.S.C. 78l(g)).

(e) An issuer that is deemed to have a class of securities registered pursuant to section 12 of the Act (15 U.S.C. 78l) according to paragraph (a), (b), (c) or (d) of this section shall file reports on the same forms and such class of securities shall be subject to the provisions of sections 14 and 16 of the Act (15 U.S.C. 78n and 78p) to the same extent as the predecessor issuers, except as follows:

(1) An issuer that is not a foreign issuer shall not be eligible to file on Form 20-F (§ 249.220f of this chapter) or to use the exemption in § 240.3a12-3.

(2) A foreign private issuer shall be eligible to file on Form 20-F (§ 249.220f of this chapter) and to use the exemption in § 240.3a12-3.

(f) An issuer that is deemed to have a class of securities registered pursuant to section 12 of the Act (15 U.S.C. 78l) according to paragraphs (a), (b), (c) or (d) of this section shall indicate in the Form 8-K (§ 249.308 of this chapter) report filed with the Commission in connection with the succession, pursuant to the requirements of Form 8-K, the paragraph of section 12 of the Act under which the class of securities issued by the successor issuer is deemed registered by operation of paragraphs (a), (b), (c) or (d) of this section. If a successor issuer that is deemed registered under section 12(g) of the Act (15 U.S.C. 78l(g)) by paragraph (d) of this section intends to list a class of securities on a national securities exchange, it must file a registration statement pursuant to section 12(b) of the Act (15 U.S.C. 78l(b)) with respect to that class of securities.

(g) An issuer that is deemed to have a class of securities registered pursuant to section 12 of the Act (15 U.S.C. 78l) according to paragraph (a), (b), (c) or (d) of this section shall file an annual report for each fiscal year beginning on or after the date as of which the succession occurred. Annual reports shall be filed within the period specified in the appropriate form. Each such issuer shall file an annual report for each of its predecessors that had securities registered pursuant to section 12 of the Act (15 U.S.C. 78l) covering the last full fiscal year of the predecessor before the registrant's succession, unless such report has been filed by the predecessor. Such annual report shall contain information that would be required if filed by the predecessor.

Rule 12g3-2. Exemptions for American Depositary Receipts and Certain Foreign Securities

(a) Securities of any class issued by any foreign private issuer shall be exempt from section 12(g) (15 U.S.C. 78l(g)) of the Act if the class has fewer than 300 holders resident in the United States. This exemption shall continue until the next fiscal year end at which the issuer has a class of equity securities held by 300 or more persons resident in the United States. For the purpose of determining whether a security is exempt pursuant to this paragraph:

(1) Securities held of record by persons resident in the United States shall be determined as provided in § 240.12g5-1 except that securities held of record by a broker, dealer, bank or nominee for any of them for the accounts of customers resident in the United States shall be counted as held in the United States by the number of separate accounts for which the securities are held. The issuer may rely in good faith on information as to the number of such separate accounts supplied by all owners of the class of its securities which are brokers, dealers, or banks or a nominee for any of them.

(2) Persons in the United States who hold the security only through a Canadian Retirement Account (as that term is defined in rule 237(a)(2) under the Securities Act of 1933 (§ 230.237(a) (2) of this chapter)), shall not be counted as holders resident in the United States.

(b)(1) A foreign private issuer shall be exempt from the requirement to register a class of equity securities under section 12(g) of the Act (15 U.S.C. 78l(g)) if:

(i) The issuer is not required to file or furnish reports under section 13(a) of the Act (15 U.S.C. 78m(a)) or section 15(d) of the Act (15 U.S.C. 78o(d));

(ii) The issuer currently maintains a listing of the subject class of securities on one or more exchanges in a foreign jurisdiction that, either singly or together with the trading of the same class of the issuer's securities in another foreign jurisdiction, constitutes the primary trading market for those securities; and

(iii) The issuer has published in English, on its Internet Web site or through an electronic information delivery system generally available to the public in its primary trading market, information that, since the first day of its most recently completed fiscal year, it:

(A) Has made public or been required to make public pursuant to the laws of the country of its incorporation, organization or domicile;

(B) Has filed or been required to file with the principal stock exchange in its primary trading market on which its securities are traded and which has been made public by that exchange; and

(C) Has distributed or been required to distribute to its security holders.

Note 1 to Paragraph (b)(1): For the purpose of paragraph (b) of this section, primary trading market means that at least 55 percent of the trading in the subject class of securities on a worldwide basis took place in, on or through the facilities of a securities market or markets in a single foreign jurisdiction or in no more than two foreign jurisdictions during the issuer's most recently completed fiscal year. If a foreign private issuer aggregates the trading of its subject class of securities in two foreign jurisdictions for the purpose of this paragraph, the trading for the issuer's securities in at least one of the two foreign jurisdictions must be larger than the trading in the United States for the same class of the issuer's securities. When determining an issuer's primary trading market under this paragraph, calculate average daily trading volume in the United States and on a worldwide basis as under Rule 12h-6 under the Act (§ 240.12h-6).

Note 2 to Paragraph (b)(1): Paragraph (b)(1)(iii) of this section does not apply to an issuer when claiming the exemption under paragraph (b) upon the effectiveness of the termination of its registration of a class of securities under section 12(g) of the Act, or the termination of its obligation to file or furnish reports under section 15(d) of the Act.

Note 3 to Paragraph (b)(1): Compensatory stock options for which the underlying securities are in a class exempt under paragraph (b) of this section are also exempt under that paragraph.

(2)(i) In order to maintain the exemption under paragraph (b) of this section, a foreign private issuer shall publish, on an ongoing basis and for each subsequent fiscal year, in English, on its Internet Web site or through an electronic information delivery system generally available to the public in its primary trading market, the information specified in paragraph (b)(1)(iii) of this section.

(ii) An issuer must electronically publish the information required by paragraph (b)(2) of this section promptly after the information has been made public.

(3)(i) The information required to be published electronically under paragraph (b) of this section is information that is material to an investment decision regarding the subject securities, such as information concerning:

(A) Results of operations or financial condition;

(B) Changes in business;

(C) Acquisitions or dispositions of assets;

(D) The issuance, redemption or acquisition of securities;

(E) Changes in management or control;

(F) The granting of options or the payment of other remuneration to directors or officers; and

(G) Transactions with directors, officers or principal security holders.

(ii) At a minimum, a foreign private issuer shall electronically publish English translations of the following documents required to be published under paragraph (b) of this section if in a foreign language:

(A) Its annual report, including or accompanied by annual financial statements;

(B) Interim reports that include financial statements;

(C) Press releases; and

(D) All other communications and documents distributed directly to security holders of each class of securities to which the exemption relates.

(c) The exemption under paragraph (b) of this section shall remain in effect until:

(1) The issuer no longer satisfies the electronic publication condition of paragraph (b)(2) of this section;

(2) The issuer no longer maintains a listing of the subject class of securities on one or more exchanges in a primary trading market, as defined under paragraph (b)(1) of this section; or

(3) The issuer registers a class of securities under section 12 of the Act or incurs reporting obligations under section 15(d) of the Act.

(d) Depositary shares registered on Form F-6 (§ 239.36 of this chapter), but not the underlying deposited securities, are exempt from section 12(g) of the Act under this paragraph.

Rule 12g-4. Certifications of Termination of Registration under Section 12(g)

(a) Termination of registration of a class of securities under section 12(g) of the Act (15 U.S.C. 78l(g)) shall take effect 90 days, or such shorter period as the Commission may determine, after the issuer certifies to the Commission on Form 15 (§ 249.323 of this chapter) that the class of securities is held of record by:

(1) Fewer than 300 persons, or in the case of a bank; a savings and loan holding company, as such term is defined in section 10 of the Home Owners' Loan Act (12 U.S.C. 1461); or a bank holding company, as such term is defined in section 2 of the Bank Holding Company Act of 1956 (12 U.S.C. 1841), 1,200 persons; or

(2) Fewer than 500 persons, where the total assets of the issuer have not exceeded $10 million on the last day of each of the issuer's most recent three fiscal years.

(b) The issuer's duty to file any reports required under section 13(a) shall be suspended immediately upon filing a certification on Form 15. *Provided, however,* That if the certification on Form 15 is subsequently withdrawn or denied, the issuer shall, within 60 days after the date of such withdrawal or denial, file with the Commission all reports which would have been required had the certification on Form 15 not been filed. If the suspension resulted from the issuer's merger into, or consolidation with, another issuer or issuers, the certification shall be filed by the successor issuer.

Rule 12g5-1. Definition of Securities "Held of Record"

(a) For the purpose of determining whether an issuer is subject to the provisions of Sections 12(g) and 15(d) of the Act, securities shall be deemed to be "held of record" by each person who is identified as the owner of such securities on records of security holders maintained by or on behalf of the issue, subject to the following:

(1) In any case where the records of security holders have not been maintained in accordance with accepted practice, any additional person who would be identified as such an owner on such records if they had been maintained in accordance with accepted practice shall be included as a holder of record.

(2) Securities identified as held of record by a corporation, a partnership, a trust whether or not the trustees are named, or other organization shall be included as so held by one person.

(3) Securities identified as held of record by one or more persons as trustees, executors, guardians, custodians or in other fiduciary capacities with respect to a single trust, estate or account shall be included as held of record by one person.

(4) Securities held by two or more persons as co-owners shall be included as held by one person.

(5) Each outstanding unregistered or bearer certificate shall be included as held of record by a separate person, except to the extent that the issuer can establish that, if such securities were registered, they would be held of record, under the provisions of this rule, by a lesser number of persons.

(6) Securities registered in substantially similar names where the issuer has reason to believe because of the address or other indications that such names represent the same person, may be included as held of record by one person.

(7) Other than when determining compliance with Rule 257(d)(2) of Regulation A (§ 230.257(d)(2) of this chapter), the definition of "held of record" shall not include securities issued in a Tier 2 offering pursuant to Regulation A by an issuer that:

(i) Is required to file reports pursuant to Rule 257(b) of Regulation A (§ 230.257(b) of this chapter);

(ii) Is current in filing annual, semiannual and special financial reports pursuant to such rule as of its most recently completed fiscal year end;

(iii) Has engaged a transfer agent registered pursuant to Section 17A(c) of the Act to perform the function of a transfer agent with respect to such securities; and

(iv) Had a public float of less than $75 million as of the last business day of its most recently completed semiannual period, computed by multiplying the aggregate world-wide number of shares of its common equity securities held by non-affiliates by the price at which such securities were last sold (or the average bid and asked prices of such securities) in the principal market for such securities or, in the event the result of such public float calculation was zero, had annual revenues of less than $50 million as of its most recently completed fiscal year. An issuer that would be required to register a class of securities under Section 12(g) of the Act as a result of exceeding the applicable threshold in this paragraph (a)(7)(iv), may continue to exclude the relevant securities from the definition of "held of record" for a transition period ending on the penultimate day of the fiscal year two years after the date it became ineligible. The transition period terminates immediately upon the failure of an issuer to timely file any periodic report due pursuant to Rule 257 (§ 230.257 of this chapter) at which time the issuer must file a registration statement that registers that class of securities under the Act within 120 days.

(8)(i) For purposes of determining whether an issuer is required to register a class of equity securities with the Commission pursuant to section 12(g)(1) of the Act (15 U.S.C. 78*l*(g)(1)), an issuer may exclude securities:

(A) Held by persons who received the securities pursuant to an employee compensation plan in transactions exempt from, or not subject to, the registration requirements of section 5 of the Securities Act of 1933 (15 U.S.C. 77e); and

(B) Held by persons who received the securities in a transaction exempt from, or not subject to, the registration requirements of section 5 of the Securities Act (15 U.S.C. 77e) from the issuer, a predecessor of the issuer or an acquired company in substitution or exchange for excludable securities under paragraph (a)(8)(i)(A) of this section, as long as the persons were eligible to receive securities pursuant to § 230.701(c) of this chapter at the time the excludable securities were originally issued to them.

(ii) As a non-exclusive safe harbor under this paragraph (a)(8):

(A) An issuer may deem a person to have received the securities pursuant to an employee compensation plan if such plan and the person who received the securities pursuant to the plan met the plan and participant conditions of § 230.701(c) of this chapter; and

(B) An issuer may, solely for the purposes of Section 12(g) of the Act (15 U.S.C. 78*l*(g)(1)), deem the securities to have been issued in a transaction exempt from, or not subject to, the registration requirements of Section 5 of the Securities Act (15 U.S.C. 77e) if the issuer had a reasonable belief at the time of the issuance that the securities were issued in such a transaction.

(b) Notwithstanding paragraph (a) of this section:

(1) Securities held, to the knowledge of the issuer, subject to a voting trust, deposit agreement or similar arrangement shall be included as held of record by the record holders of the voting trust certificates, certificates of deposit, receipts or similar evidences of interest in such securities; *Provided however,* That the issuer may rely in good faith on such information as is received in response to its request from a non-affiliated issuer of the certificates or evidences of interest.

(2) Whole or fractional securities issued by a savings and loan association, building and loan association, cooperative bank, homestead association, or similar institution for the sole purpose of qualifying a borrower for membership in the issuer, and which are to be redeemed or repurchased by the issuer when the borrower's loan is terminated, shall not be included as held of record by any person.

(3) If the issuer knows or has reason to know that the form of holding securities of record is used primarily to circumvent the provisions of Section 12(g) or 15(d) of the Act, the beneficial owners of such securities shall be deemed to be the record owners thereof.

Rule 12g5-2. Definition of "Total Assets"

For the purpose of Section 12(g)(1) of the Act, the term "total assets"shall mean the total assets as shown on the issuer's balance sheet or the balance sheet of the issuer and its subsidiaries consolidated, whichever is larger, as required to be filed on the form prescribed for registration under this section and prepared in accordance with the pertinent provisions of Regulation S-X. Where the security is a certificate of deposit, voting trust certificate, or certificate or other evidence of interest in a similar trust or agreement, the "total assets"of the issuer of the security held under the trust or agreement shall be deemed to be the "total assets" of the issuer of such certificate or evidence of interest.

Rule 12h-1. Exemptions From Registration Under Section 12(g) of the Act.

Issuers shall be exempt from the provisions of Section 12(g) of the Act with respect to the following securities:

(a) Any interest or participation in an employee stock bonus, stock purchase, profit sharing, pension, retirement, incentive, thrift, savings or similar plan which is not transferable by the holder except in the event of death or mental incompetency, or any security issued solely to fund such plans;

(b) Any interest or participation in any common trust fund or similar fund maintained by a bank exclusively for the collective investment and reinvestment of monies contributed thereto by the bank in its capacity as a trustee, executor, administrator, or guardian. For purposes of this paragraph (b), the term "common trust fund" shall include a common trust fund which is maintained by a bank which is a member of an affiliated group, as defined in Section 1504(a) of the Internal Revenue Code of 1954, and which is maintained exclusively for the investment and reinvestment of monies contributed thereto by one or more bank members of such affiliated group in the capacity of trustee, executor, administrator, or guardian, *provided* that:

(1) The common trust fund is operated in compliance with the same state and federal regulatory requirements as would apply if the bank maintaining such fund and any other contributing banks were the same entity; and

(2) The rights of persons for whose benefit a contributing bank acts as trustee, executor, administrator or guardian would not be diminished by reason of the maintenance of such common trust fund by another bank member of the affiliated group;

(c) Any class of equity security which would not be outstanding 60 days after a registration statement would be required to be filed with respect thereto;

(d) Any standardized option, as that term is defined in Rule 9b-1(a)(4), that is issued by a clearing agency registered under section 17A of the Act (15 U.S.C. 78q-1) and traded on a national securities exchange registered pursuant to section 6(a) of the Act (15 U.S.C. 78f(a)) or on a national securities association registered pursuant to section 15A(a) of the Act (15 U.S.C. 78*o*-3(a));

(e) Any security futures product that is traded on a national securities exchange registered pursuant to section 6 of the Act (15 U.S.C. 78f) or on a national securities association registered pursuant to section 15A(a) of the Act (15 U.S.C. 78*o*-3(a)) and cleared by a clearing agency that is registered pursuant to section 17A of the Act (15 U.S.C. 78q-1) or is exempt from registration under section 17A(b)(7) of the Act (15 U.S.C. 78q-1(b)(7)).

(f)(1) Stock options issued under written compensatory stock option plans under the following conditions:

(i) The issuer of the equity security underlying the stock options does not have a class of security registered under section 12 of the Act and is not required to file reports pursuant to section 15(d) of the Act;

(ii) The stock options have been issued pursuant to one or more written compensatory stock option plans established by the issuer, its parents, its majority-owned subsidiaries or majority-owned subsidiaries of the issuer's parents;

Note to Paragraph (f)(1)(ii): All stock options issued under all written compensatory stock option plans on the same class of equity security of the issuer will be considered part of the same class of equity security for purposes of the provisions of paragraph (f) of this section.

(iii) The stock options are held only by those persons described in Rule 701(c) under the Securities Act (17 CFR 230.701(c)) or their permitted transferees as provided in paragraph (f)(1)(iv) of this section;

(iv) The stock options and, prior to exercise, the shares to be issued on exercise of the stock options are restricted as to transfer by the optionholder other than to persons who are family members (as defined in Rule 701(c)(3) under the Securities Act (17 CFR 230.701(c)(3))) through gifts or domestic relations orders, or to an executor or guardian of the optionholder upon the death or disability of the optionholder until the issuer becomes subject to the reporting requirements of section 13 or 15(d) of the Act or is no longer relying on the exemption pursuant to this section; provided that the optionholder may transfer the stock options to the issuer, or in connection with a change of control or other acquisition transaction involving the issuer, if after such transaction the stock options no longer will be outstanding and the issuer no longer will be relying on the exemption pursuant to this section;

Note to Paragraph (f)(1)(iv): For purposes of this section, optionholders may include any permitted transferee under paragraph (f)(1)(iv) of this section; provided that such permitted transferees may not further transfer the stock options;

(v) The stock options and the shares issuable upon exercise of such stock options are restricted as to any pledge, hypothecation, or other transfer, including any short position, any "put equivalent position" (as defined in § 240.16a-1(h) of this chapter), or any "call equivalent position" (as defined in § 240.16a-1(b) of this chapter) by the optionholder prior to exercise of an option, except in the circumstances permitted in paragraph (f)(1)(iv) of this section, until the issuer becomes subject to the reporting requirements of section 13 or 15(d) of the Act or is no longer relying on the exemption pursuant paragraph [*sic*] (f)(1) of this section; and

Note to Paragraphs (f)(1)(iv) and (f)(1)(v): The transferability restrictions in paragraphs (f)(1)(iv) and (f)(1)(v) of this section must be contained in a written compensatory stock option plan, individual written compensatory stock option agreement, other stock purchase or stockholder agreement to which the issuer and the optionholder are a signatory or party, other enforceable agreement by or against the issuer and the optionholder, or in the issuer's by-laws or certificate or articles of incorporation; and

(vi) The issuer has agreed in the written compensatory stock option plan, the individual written compensatory stock option agreement, or another agreement enforceable against the issuer to provide the following information to optionholders once the issuer is relying on the exemption pursuant to paragraph (f)(1) of this section until the issuer becomes subject to the reporting requirements of section 13 or 15(d) of the Act or is no longer relying on the exemption pursuant paragraph (f)(1) of this section:

The information described in Rules 701(e)(3), (4), and (5) under the Securities Act (17 CFR 230.701(e)(3), (4), and (5)), every six months with the financial statements being not more than 180 days old and with such information provided either by physical or electronic delivery to the optionholders or by written notice to the optionholders of the availability of the information on an Internet site that may be password-protected and of any password needed to access the information.

Note to Paragraph (f)(1)(vi): The issuer may request that the optionholder agree to keep the information to be provided pursuant to this section confidential. If an optionholder does not agree to keep the information to be provided pursuant to this section confidential, then the issuer is not required to provide the information.

(2) If the exemption provided by paragraph (f)(1) of this section ceases to be available, the issuer of the stock options that is relying on the exemption provided by this section must file a registration statement to register the class of stock options under section 12 of the Act within 120 calendar days after the exemption provided by paragraph (f)(1) of this section ceases to be available; and

(g)(1) Stock options issued under written compensatory stock option plans under the following conditions:

(i) The issuer of the equity security underlying the stock options has registered a class of security under section 12 of the Act or is required to file periodic reports pursuant to section 15(d) of the Act;

(ii) The stock options have been issued pursuant to one or more written compensatory stock option plans established by the issuer, its parents, its majority-owned subsidiaries or majority-owned subsidiaries of the issuer's parents;

Note to Paragraph (g)(1)(ii): All stock options issued under all of the written compensatory stock option plans on the same class of equity security of the issuer will be considered part of the same class of equity security of the issuer for purposes of the provisions of paragraph (g) of this section; and

(iii) The stock options are held only by those persons described in Rule 701(c) under the Securities Act (17 CFR 230.701(c)) or those persons specified in General Instruction A.1(a) of Form S-8 (17 CFR 239.16b); provided that an issuer can still rely on this exemption if there is an insignificant deviation from satisfaction of the condition in this paragraph (g)(1)(iii) and after December 7, 2007, the issuer has made a good faith and reasonable attempt to comply with the conditions of this paragraph (g)(1)(iii). For purposes of this paragraph (g)(1)(iii), an insignificant deviation exists if the number of optionholders that do not meet the condition in this paragraph (g)(1)(iii) are insignificant both as to the aggregate number of optionholders and number of outstanding stock options.

(2) If the exemption provided by paragraph (g)(1) of this section ceases to be available, the issuer of the stock options that is relying on the exemption provided by this section must file a registration statement to register the class of stock options or a class of security under section 12 of the Act within 60 calendar days after the exemption provided in paragraph (g)(1) of this section ceases to be available.

(h) Any security-based swap that is issued by a clearing agency registered as a clearing agency under Section 17A of the Act (15 U.S.C. 78q-1) or exempt from registration under Section 17A of the Act pursuant to a rule, regulation, or order of the Commission in its function as a central counterparty that the Commission has determined must be cleared or that is permitted to be cleared pursuant to the clearing agency's rules, and that was sold to an eligible contract participant (as defined in Section 1a(18) of the Commodity Exchange Act (7 U.S.C. 1a(18))) in reliance on Rule 239 under the Securities Act of 1933 (17 CFR 230.239).

Rule 12h-3. Suspension of Duty to File Reports under Section 15(d)

(a) Subject to paragraphs (c) and (d) of this section, the duty under section 15(d) to file reports required by section 13(a) of the Act with respect to a class of securities specified in paragraph (b) of this section shall be suspended for such class of securities immediately upon filing with the Commission a certification on Form 15 [17 CFR 249.323] if the issuer of such class has filed all reports required by Section 13(a), without regard to Rule 12b-25 [17 CFR 249.322], for the shorter of its most recent three fiscal years and the portion of the current year preceding the date of filing Form 15, or the period since the issuer became subject to such reporting obligation. If the certification on Form 15 is subsequently withdrawn or denied, the issuer shall, within 60 days, file with the Commission all reports which would have been required if such certification had not been filed.

(b) The classes of securities eligible for the suspension provided in paragraph (a) of this section are:

(1) Any class of securities, other than any class of asset-backed securities, held of record by:

(i) Fewer than 300 persons, or in the case of a bank; a savings and loan holding company, as such term is defined in section 10 of the Home Owners' Loan Act (12 U.S.C. 1461); or a bank holding company, as such term is defined in section 2 of the Bank Holding Company Act of 1956 (12 U.S.C. 1841), 1,200 persons; or

(ii) Fewer than 500 persons, where the total assets of the issuer have not exceeded $10 million on the last day of each of the issuer's three most recent fiscal years; and

(2) Any class of securities de-registered pursuant to Section 12(d) of the Act if such class would not thereupon be deemed registered under Section 12(g) of the Act or the rules thereunder.

Note to Paragraph (b): The suspension of classes of asset-backed securities is addressed in § 240.15d-22.

(c) This section shall not be available for any class of securities for a fiscal year in which a registration statement relating to that class becomes effective under the Securities Act of 1933, or is required to be updated pursuant to Section 10(a)(3) of the Act, and, in the case of paragraph (b)(1)(ii), the two succeeding fiscal years.

Provided, however, that this paragraph shall not apply to the duty to file reports which arises solely from a registration statement filed by an issuer with no significant assets, for the reorganization of a non-reporting issuer into a one-subsidiary holding company in which equity security holders receive the same proportional interest in the holding company as they held in the non-reporting issuer, except for changes resulting from the exercise of dissenting shareholder rights under state law.

(d) The suspension provided by this rule relates only to the reporting obligation under Section 15(d) with respect to a class of securities, does not affect any other duties imposed on that class of securities, and shall continue as long as either criteria (i) or (ii) of paragraph (b)(i)] is met on the first day of any subsequent fiscal year. *Provided, however*, that such criterion need not be met if the duty to file reports arises solely from a registration statement filed by an issuer with no significant assets in a reorganization of a nonreporting company into a one-subsidiary holding company in which equity security holders receive the same proportional interest in the holding company as they held in the non-reporting issuer, except for changes resulting from the exercise of dissenting shareholder rights under state law.

(e) If the suspension provided by this rule is discontinued because a class of securities does not meet the eligibility criteria of paragraph (b) on the first day of an issuer's fiscal year, then the issuer shall resume periodic reporting pursuant to section 15(d) by filing an annual report on Form 10-K for its preceding fiscal year, not later than 120 days after the end of such fiscal year.

Rule 12h-6. Certification by a Foreign Private Issuer Regarding the Termination of Registration of a Class of Securities Under Section 12(g) or the Duty to File Reports Under Section 13(a) or Section 15(d).

(a) A foreign private issuer may terminate the registration of a class of securities under section 12(g) of the Act (15 U.S.C. 78*l* (g)), or terminate the obligation under section 15(d) of the Act (15 U.S.C. 78o(d)) to file or furnish reports required by section 13(a) of the Act (15 U.S.C. 78m(a)) with respect to a class of equity securities, or both, after certifying to the Commission on Form 15F (17 CFR 249.324) that:

(1) The foreign private issuer has had reporting obligations under section 13(a) or section 15(d) of the Act for at least the 12 months preceding the filing of the Form 15F, has filed or furnished all reports required for this period, and has filed at least one annual report pursuant to section 13(a) of the Act;

(2) The foreign private issuer's securities have not been sold in the United States in a registered offering under the Securities Act of 1933 (15 U.S.C. 77a *et seq.*) during the 12 months preceding the filing of the Form 15F, other than securities issued:

(i) To the issuer's employees;

(ii) By selling security holders in non-underwritten offerings;

(iii) Upon the exercise of outstanding rights granted by the issuer if the rights are granted pro rata to all existing security holders of the class of the issuer's securities to which the rights attach;

(iv) Pursuant to a dividend or interest reinvestment plan; or

(v) Upon the conversion of outstanding convertible securities or upon the exercise of outstanding transferable warrants issued by the issuer;

Note to Paragraph (a)(2): The exceptions in paragraphs (a)(2)(iii)-(v) do not apply to securities issued pursuant to a standby underwritten offering or other similar arrangement in the United States;

(3) The foreign private issuer has maintained a listing of the subject class of securities for at least the 12 months preceding the filing of the Form 15F on one or more exchanges in a foreign jurisdiction that, either singly or together with the trading of the same class of the issuer's securities in another foreign jurisdiction, constitutes the primary trading market for those securities; and

(4) (i) The average daily trading volume of the subject class of securities in the United States for a recent 12-month period has been no greater than 5 percent of the average daily trading volume of that class of securities on a worldwide basis for the same period; or

(ii) On a date within 120 days before the filing date of the Form 15F, a foreign private issuer's subject class of equity securities is either held of record by:

(A) Less than 300 persons on a worldwide basis; or

(B) Less than 300 persons resident in the United States.

Note to Paragraph (a)(4): If an issuer's equity securities trade in the form of American Depositary Receipts in the United States, for purposes of paragraph (a)(4)(i), it must calculate the trading volume of its American Depositary Receipts in terms of the number of securities represented by those American Depositary Receipts.

(b) A foreign private issuer must wait at least 12 months before it may file a Form 15F to terminate its section 13(a) or 15(d) reporting obligations in reliance on paragraph (a)(4)(i) of this section if:

(1) The issuer has delisted a class of equity securities from a national securities exchange or inter-dealer quotation system in the United States, and at the time of delisting, the average daily trading volume of that class of securities in the United States exceeded 5 percent of the average daily trading volume of that class of securities on a worldwide basis for the preceding 12 months; or

(2) The issuer has terminated a sponsored American Depositary Receipts facility, and at the time of termination the average daily trading volume in the United States of the

American Depositary Receipts exceeded 5 percent of the average daily trading volume of the underlying class of securities on a worldwide basis for the preceding 12 months.

(c) A foreign private issuer may terminate its duty to file or furnish reports pursuant to section 13(a) or section 15(d) of the Act with respect to a class of debt securities after certifying to the Commission on Form 15F that:

(1) The foreign private issuer has filed or furnished all reports required by section 13(a) or section 15(d) of the Act, including at least one annual report pursuant to section 13(a) of the Act; and

(2) On a date within 120 days before the filing date of the Form 15F, the class of debt securities is either held of record by:

(i) Less than 300 persons on a worldwide basis; or

(ii) Less than 300 persons resident in the United States.

(d)(1) Following a merger, consolidation, exchange of securities, acquisition of assets or otherwise, a foreign private issuer that has succeeded to the registration of a class of securities under section 12(g) of the Act of another issuer pursuant to § 240.12g-3, or to the reporting obligations of another issuer under section 15(d) of the Act pursuant to § 240.15d-5, may file a Form 15F to terminate that registration or those reporting obligations if:

(i) Regarding a class of equity securities, the successor issuer meets the conditions under paragraph (a) of this section; or

(ii) Regarding a class of debt securities, the successor issuer meets the conditions under paragraph (c) of this section.

(2) When determining whether it meets the prior reporting requirement under paragraph (a)(1) or paragraph (c)(1) of this section, a successor issuer may take into account the reporting history of the issuer whose reporting obligations it has assumed pursuant to § 240.12g-3 or § 240.15d-5.

(e) *Counting Method*. When determining under this section the number of United States residents holding a foreign private issuer's equity or debt securities:

(1)(i) Use the method for calculating record ownership § 240.12g3-2(a), except that you may limit your inquiry regarding the amount of securities represented by accounts of customers resident in the United States to brokers, dealers, banks and other nominees located in:

(A) The United States;

(B) The foreign private issuer's jurisdiction of incorporation, legal organization or establishment; and

(C) The foreign private issuer's primary trading market, if different from the issuer's jurisdiction of incorporation, legal organization or establishment.

(ii) If you aggregate the trading volume of the issuer's securities in two foreign jurisdictions for the purpose of complying with paragraph (a)(3) of this section, you must include both of those foreign jurisdictions when conducting your inquiry under paragraph (e)(1)(i) of this section.

(2) If, after reasonable inquiry, you are unable without unreasonable effort to obtain information about the amount of securities represented by accounts of customers resident in the United States, for purposes of this section, you may assume that the customers are the residents of the jurisdiction in which the nominee has its principal place of business.

(3) You must count securities as owned by United States holders when publicly filed reports of beneficial ownership or other reliable information that is provided to you indicates that the securities are held by United States residents.

(4) When calculating under this section the number of your United States resident security holders, you may rely in good faith on the assistance of an independent information services provider that in the regular course of its business assists issuers in determining the number of, and collecting other information concerning, their security holders.

535

(f) *Definitions*. For the purpose of this section:

(1) *Debt security* means any security other than an equity security as defined under § 240.3a11-1, including:

(i) Non-participatory preferred stock, which is defined as non-convertible capital stock, the holders of which are entitled to a preference in payment of dividends and in distribution of assets on liquidation, dissolution, or winding up of the issuer, but are not entitled to participate in residual earnings or assets of the issuer; and

(ii) Notwithstanding § 240.3a11-1, any debt security described in paragraph (f)(3)(i) and (ii) of this section;

(2) *Employee* has the same meaning as the definition of employee provided in Form S-8 (§ 239.16b).

(3) *Equity security* means the same as under § 240.3a11-1, but, for purposes of paragraphs (a)(3) and (a)(4)(i) of this section, does not include:

(i) Any debt security that is convertible into an equity security, with or without consideration;

(ii) Any debt security that includes a warrant or right to subscribe to or purchase an equity security;

(iii) Any such warrant or right; or

(iv) Any put, call, straddle, or other option or privilege that gives the holder the option of buying or selling a security but does not require the holder to do so.

(4) *Foreign private issuer* has the same meaning as under § 240.3b-4.

(5) *Primary trading market* means that:

(i) At least 55 percent of the trading in a foreign private issuer's class of securities that is the subject of Form 15F took place in, on or through the facilities of a securities market or markets in a single foreign jurisdiction or in no more than two foreign jurisdictions during a recent 12-month period; and

(ii) If a foreign private issuer aggregates the trading of its subject class of securities in two foreign jurisdictions for the purpose of paragraph (a)(3) of this section, the trading for the issuer's securities in at least one of the two foreign jurisdictions must be larger than the trading in the United States for the same class of the issuer's securities.

(6) *Recent 12-month period* means a 12-calendar-month period that ended no more than 60 days before the filing date of the Form 15F.

(g)(1) Suspension of a foreign private issuer's duty to file reports under section 13(a) or section 15(d) of the Act shall occur immediately upon filing the Form 15F with the Commission if filing pursuant to paragraph (a), (c) or (d) of this section. If there are no objections from the Commission, 90 days, or such shorter period as the Commission may determine, after the issuer has filed its Form 15F, the effectiveness of any of the following shall occur:

(i) The termination of registration of a class of securities under section 12(g); and

(ii) The termination of a foreign private issuer's duty to file reports under section 13(a) or section 15(d) of the Act.

(2) If the Form 15F is subsequently withdrawn or denied, the issuer shall, within 60 days after the date of the withdrawal or denial, file with or submit to the Commission all reports that would have been required had the issuer not filed the Form 15F.

(h) As a condition to termination of registration or reporting under paragraph (a), (c) or (d) of this section, a foreign private issuer must, either before or on the date that it files its Form 15F, publish a notice in the United States that discloses its intent to terminate its registration of a class of securities under section 12(g) of the Act, or its reporting obligations under section 13(a) or section 15(d) of the Act, or both. The issuer must publish the notice through a means reasonably designed to provide broad dissemination of the information to the public in the United States. The issuer must also submit a copy of the notice to the

Commission, either under cover of a Form 6-K (17 CFR 249.306) before or at the time of filing of the Form 15F, or as an exhibit to the Form 15F.

(i) (1) A foreign private issuer that, before the effective date of this section, terminated the registration of a class of securities under section 12(g) of the Act or suspended its reporting obligations regarding a class of equity or debt securities under section 15(d) of the Act may file a Form 15F in order to:

(i) Terminate under this section the registration of a class of equity securities that was the subject of a Form 15 (§ 249.323 of this chapter) filed by the issuer pursuant to § 240.12g-4; or

(ii) Terminate its reporting obligations under section 15(d) of the Act, which had been suspended by the terms of that section or by the issuer's filing of a Form 15 pursuant to § 240.12h-3, regarding a class of equity or debt securities.

(2) In order to be eligible to file a Form 15F under this paragraph:

(i) If a foreign private issuer terminated the registration of a class of securities pursuant to § 240.12g-4 or suspended its reporting obligations pursuant to § 240.12h-3 or section 15(d) of the Act regarding a class of equity securities, the issuer must meet the requirements under paragraph (a)(3) and paragraph (a)(4)(i) or (a)(4)(ii) of this section; or

(ii) If a foreign private issuer suspended its reporting obligations pursuant to § 240.12h-3 or section 15(d) of the Act regarding a class of debt securities, the issuer must meet the requirements under paragraph (c)(2) of this section.

(3) (i) If the Commission does not object, 90 days after the filing of a Form 15F under this paragraph, or such shorter period as the Commission may determine, the effectiveness of any of the following shall occur:

(A) The termination under this section of the registration of a class of equity securities, which was the subject of a Form 15 filed pursuant to § 240.12g-4, and the duty to file reports required by section 13(a) of the Act regarding that class of securities; or

(B) The termination of a foreign private issuer's reporting obligations under section 15(d) of the Act, which had previously been suspended by the terms of that section or by the issuer's filing of a Form 15 pursuant to § 240.12h-3, regarding a class of equity or debt securities.

(ii) If the Form 15F is subsequently withdrawn or denied, the foreign private issuer shall, within 60 days after the date of the withdrawal or denial, file with or submit to the Commission all reports that would have been required had the issuer not filed the Form 15F.

Note to § 240.12h-6: The suspension of classes of asset-backed securities is addressed in § 240.15d-22.

REGULATION 13A—REPORTS OF ISSUERS OF SECURITIES REGISTERED PURSUANT TO SECTION 12

Annual Reports

Rule 13a-1. Requirements of Annual Reports

Every issuer having securities registered pursuant to section 12 of the Act (15 U.S.C. 78*l*) shall file an annual report on the appropriate form authorized or prescribed therefor for each fiscal year after the last full fiscal year for which financial statements were filed in its registration statement. Annual reports shall be filed within the period specified in the appropriate form.

Other Reports

Rule 13a-11. Current Reports on Form 8-K

(a) Except as provided in paragraph (b) of this section, every registrant subject to § 240.13a-1 shall file a current report on Form 8-K within the period specified in that form, unless substantially the same information as that required by Form 8-K has been previously reported by the registrant.

(b) This section shall not apply to foreign governments, foreign private issuers required to make reports on Form 6-K (17 CFR 249.306) pursuant to § 240.13a-16, issuers of American Depositary Receipts for securities of any foreign issuer, or investment companies required to file reports pursuant to § 270.30a-1 of this chapter under the Investment Company Act of 1940, except where such an investment company is required to file:

(1) Notice of a blackout period pursuant to § 245.104 of this chapter;

(2) Disclosure pursuant to Instruction 2 to § 240.14a-11(b)(1) of information concerning outstanding shares and voting; or

(3) Disclosure pursuant to Instruction 2 to § 240.14a-11(b)(10) of the date by which a nominating shareholder or nominating shareholder group must submit the notice required pursuant to § 240.14a-11(b)(10).

(c) No failure to file a report on Form 8-K that is required solely pursuant to Item 1.01, 1.02, 2.03, 2.04, 2.05, 2.06, 4.02(a), 5.02(e) or 6.03 of Form 8-K shall be deemed to be a violation of 15 U.S.C. 78j(b) and § 240.10b-5.

Rule 13a-13. Quarterly Reports on Form 10-Q (§ 249.308a of this Chapter)

(a) Except as provided in paragraphs (b) and (c) of this section, every issuer that has securities registered pursuant to section 12 of the Act and is required to file annual reports pursuant to section 13 of the Act, and has filed or intends to file such reports on Form 10-K (§ 249.310 of this chapter), shall file a quarterly report on Form 10-Q (§ 249.308a of this chapter) within the period specified in General Instruction A.1. to that form for each of the first three quarters of each fiscal year of the issuer, commencing with the first fiscal quarter following the most recent fiscal year for which full financial statements were included in the registration statement, or, if the registration statement included financial statements for an interim period subsequent to the most recent fiscal year end meeting the requirements of Article 10 of Regulation S-X and Rule 8-03 of Regulation S-X for smaller reporting companies, for the first fiscal quarter subsequent to the quarter reported upon in the registration statement. The first quarterly report of the issuer shall be filed either within 45 days after the effective date of the registration statement or on or before the date on which such report would have been required to be filed if the issuer has been required to file reports on Form 10-Q as of its last fiscal quarter, whichever is later.

(b) The provisions of this rule shall not apply to the following issuers:

(1) Investment companies required to file reports pursuant to § 270.30a-1;

(2) Foreign private issuers required to file reports pursuant to § 240.13a-16; and

(3) Asset-backed issuers required to file reports pursuant to § 240.13a-17.

(c) Part I of the quarterly reports on Form 10-Q need not be filed by:

(1) Mutual life insurance companies; or exploration for the development of mineral deposits other than oil, gas or coal, if all of the following conditions are met:

(i) The registrant has not been in production during the current fiscal year or the two years immediately prior thereto; except that being in production for an aggregate period of not more than eight months over the three-year period shall not be a violation of this condition.

(ii) Receipts from the sale of mineral products or from the operations of mineral producing properties by the registrant and its subsidiaries combined have not exceeded $500,000 in any of the most recent six years and have not aggregated more than $1,500,000 in the most recent six fiscal years.

(d) Notwithstanding the foregoing provisions of this section, the financial information required by Part I of Form 10-Q shall not be deemed to be "filed" for the purpose of Section 18 of the Act or otherwise subject to the liabilities of that section of the Act, but shall be subject to all other provisions of the Act.

Rule 13a-14. Certification of Disclosure in Annual and Quarterly Reports

(a) Each report, including transition reports, filed on Form 10-Q, Form 10-K, Form 20-F or Form 40-F (§ § 249.308a, 249.310, 249.220f or 249.240f of this chapter) under section 13(a) of the Act (15 U.S.C. 78m(a)), other than a report filed by an Asset-Backed Issuer (as defined in § 229.1101 of this chapter) or a report on Form 20-F filed under § 240.13a-19, must include certifications in the form specified in the applicable exhibit filing requirements of such report and such certifications must be filed as an exhibit to such report. Each principal executive and principal financial officer of the issuer, or persons performing similar functions, at the time of filing of the report must sign a certification. The principal executive and principal financial officers of an issuer may omit the portion of the introductory language in paragraph 4 as well as language in paragraph 4(b) of the certification that refers to the certifying officers' responsibility for designing, establishing and maintaining internal control over financial reporting for the issuer until the issuer becomes subject to the internal control over financial reporting requirements in § 240.13a-15 or 240.15d-15.

(b) Each periodic report containing financial statements filed by an issuer pursuant to section 13(a) of the Act (15 U.S.C. 78m(a)) must be accompanied by the certifications required by Section 1350 of Chapter 63 of Title 18 of the United States Code (18 U.S.C. 1350) and such certifications must be furnished as an exhibit to such report as specified in the applicable exhibit requirements for such report. Each principal executive and principal financial officer of the issuer (or equivalent thereof) must sign a certification. This requirement may be satisfied by a single certification signed by an issuer's principal executive and principal financial officers.

(c) A person required to provide a certification specified in paragraph (a), (b) or (d) of this section may not have the certification signed on his or her behalf pursuant to a power of attorney or other form of confirming authority.

(d) Each annual report and transition report filed on Form 10-K (§ 249.310 of this chapter) by an asset-backed issuer under section 13(a) of the Act (15 U.S.C. 78m(a)) must include a certification in the form specified in the applicable exhibit filing requirements of such report and such certification must be filed as an exhibit to such report. Terms used in paragraphs (d) and (e) of this section have the same meaning as in Item 1101 of Regulation AB (§ 229.1101 of this chapter).

(e) With respect to asset-backed issuers, the certification required by paragraph (d) of this section must be signed by either:

(1) The senior officer in charge of securitization of the depositor if the depositor is signing the report; or

(2) The senior officer in charge of the servicing function of the servicer if the servicer is signing the report on behalf of the issuing entity. If multiple servicers are involved in servicing the pool assets, the senior officer in charge of the servicing function of the master servicer (or entity performing the equivalent function) must sign if a representative of the servicer is to sign the report on behalf of the issuing entity.

(f) The certification requirements of this section do not apply to an Interactive Data File, as defined in § 232.11 of this chapter (Rule 11 of Regulation S-T).

Rule 13a-15. Controls and Procedure

(a) Every issuer that has a class of securities registered pursuant to section 12 of the Act (15 U.S.C. 78*l*), other than an Asset-Backed Issuer (as defined in § 229.1101 of this chapter), a small business investment company registered on Form N-5 (§ § 239.24 and 274.5 of this chapter), or a unit investment trust as defined in section 4(2) of the Investment Company Act of 1940 (15 U.S.C. 80a-4(2)), must maintain disclosure controls and procedures (as defined in paragraph (e) of this section) and, if the issuer either had been required to file an annual report pursuant to section 13(a) or 15(d) of the Act (15 U.S.C. 78m(a) or 78o(d)) for the prior fiscal year or had filed an annual report with the Commission for the prior fiscal year, internal control over financial reporting (as defined in paragraph (f) of this section).

(b) Each such issuer's management must evaluate, with the participation of the issuer's principal executive and principal financial officers, or persons performing similar functions, the effectiveness of the issuer's disclosure controls and procedures, as of the end of each fiscal quarter, except that management must perform this evaluation:

(1) In the case of a foreign private issuer (as defined in § 240.3b-4) as of the end of each fiscal year; and

(2) In the case of an investment company registered under section 8 of the Investment Company Act of 1940 (15 U.S.C. 80a-8), within the 90-day period prior to the filing date of each report requiring certification under § 270.30a-2 of this chapter.

(c) The management of each such issuer, that either had been required to file an annual report pursuant to section 13(a) or 15(d) of the Act (15 U.S.C. 78m(a) or 78o(d)) for the prior fiscal year or previously had filed an annual report with the Commission for the prior fiscal year, other than an investment company registered under section 8 of the Investment Company Act of 1940, must evaluate, with the participation of the issuer's principal executive and principal financial officers, or persons performing similar functions, the effectiveness, as of the end of each fiscal year, of the issuer's internal control over financial reporting. The framework on which management's evaluation of the issuer's internal control over financial reporting is based must be a suitable, recognized control framework that is established by a body or group that has followed due-process procedures, including the broad distribution of the framework for public comment. Although there are many different ways to conduct an evaluation of the effectiveness of internal control over financial reporting to meet the requirements of this paragraph, an evaluation that is conducted in accordance with the interpretive guidance issued by the Commission in Release No. 34-55929 will satisfy the evaluation required by this paragraph.

(d) The management of each such issuer, other than an investment company registered under section 8 of the Investment Company Act of 1940, must evaluate, with the participation of the issuer's principal executive and principal financial officers, or persons performing similar functions, any change in the issuer's internal control over financial reporting, that occurred during each of the issuer's fiscal quarters, or fiscal year in the case of a foreign private issuer, that has materially affected, or is reasonably likely to materially affect, the issuer's internal control over financial reporting.

(e) For purposes of this section, the term *disclosure controls and procedures* means controls and other procedures of an issuer that are designed to ensure that information required to be disclosed by the issuer in the reports that it files or submits under the Act (15 U.S.C. 78a *et seq.*) is recorded, processed, summarized and reported, within the time periods specified in the Commission's rules and forms. Disclosure controls and procedures include, without limitation, controls and procedures designed to ensure that information required to be disclosed by an issuer in the reports that it files or submits under the Act is accumulated and communicated to the issuer's management, including its principal executive and principal financial officers, or persons performing similar functions, as appropriate to allow timely decisions regarding required disclosure.

(f) The term *internal control over financial reporting* is defined as a process designed by, or under the supervision of, the issuer's principal executive and principal financial officers, or persons performing similar functions, and effected by the issuer's board of directors, management and other personnel, to provide reasonable assurance regarding the reliability of financial reporting and the preparation of financial statements for external purposes in accordance with generally accepted accounting principles and includes those policies and procedures that:

(1) Pertain to the maintenance of records that in reasonable detail accurately and fairly reflect the transactions and dispositions of the assets of the issuer;

(2) Provide reasonable assurance that transactions are recorded as necessary to permit preparation of financial statements in accordance with generally accepted accounting principles, and that receipts and expenditures of the issuer are being made only in accordance with authorizations of management and directors of the issuer; and

(3) Provide reasonable assurance regarding prevention or timely detection of unauthorized acquisition, use or disposition of the issuer's assets that could have a material effect on the financial statements.

REGULATION 13B-2: MAINTENANCE OF RECORDS AND PREPARATION OF REQUIRED REPORTS

Rule 13b2-1. Falsification of Accounting Records

No person shall, directly or indirectly, falsify or cause to be falsified, any book, record or account subject to Section 13(b)(2)(A) of the Securities Exchange Act

Rule 13b2-2. Representations and conduct in connection with the preparation of required reports and documents

(a) No director or officer of an issuer shall, directly or indirectly:

(1) Make or cause to be made a materially false or misleading statement to an accountant in connection with; or

(2) Omit to state, or cause another person to omit to state, any material fact necessary in order to make statements made, in light of the circumstances under which such statements were made, not misleading, to an accountant in connection with:

(i) Any audit, review or examination of the financial statements of the issuer required to be made pursuant to this subpart; or

(ii) The preparation or filing of any document or report required to be filed with the Commission pursuant to this subpart or otherwise.

(b)(1) No officer or director of an issuer, or any other person acting under the direction thereof, shall directly or indirectly take any action to coerce, manipulate, mislead, or fraudulently influence any independent public or certified public accountant engaged in the performance of an audit or review of the financial statements of that issuer that are required to be filed with the Commission pursuant to this subpart or otherwise if that person knew or should have known that such action, if successful, could result in rendering the issuer's financial statements materially misleading.

(2) For purposes of paragraphs (b)(1) and (c)(2) of this section, actions that,"if successful, could result in rendering the issuer's financial statements materially misleading" include, but are not limited to, actions taken at any time with respect to the professional engagement period to coerce, manipulate, mislead, or fraudulently influence an auditor:

(i) To issue or reissue a report on an issuer's financial statements that is not warranted in the circumstances (due to material violations of generally accepted accounting principles, generally accepted auditing standards, the standards of the PCAOB, or other professional or regulatory standards);

(ii) Not to perform audit, review or other procedures required by the standards of the PCAOB, or other professional or regulatory standards;

(iii) Not to withdraw an issued report; or

(iv) Not to communicate matters to an issuer's audit committee.

(c) In addition, in the case of an investment company registered under section 8 of the Investment Company Act of 1940 (15 U.S.C. 80a-8), or a business development company as defined in section 2(a)(48) of the Investment Company Act of 1940 (15 U.S.C. 80a-2(a)(48)), no officer or director of the company's investment adviser, sponsor, depositor, trustee, or administrator (or, in the case of paragraph (c)(2) of this section, any other person acting under the direction thereof) shall, directly or indirectly:

(1)(i) Make or cause to be made a materially false or misleading statement to an accountant in connection with; or

(ii) Omit to state, or cause another person to omit to state, any material fact necessary in order to make statements made, in light of the circumstances under which such statements were made, not misleading to an accountant in connection with:

(A) Any audit, review, or examination of the financial statements of the investment company required to be made pursuant to this subpart; or

(B) The preparation or filing of any document or report required to be filed with the Commission pursuant to this subpart or otherwise; or

(2) Take any action to coerce, manipulate, mislead, or fraudulently influence any independent public or certified public accountant engaged in the performance of an audit or review of the financial statements of that investment company that are required to be filed with the Commission pursuant to this subpart or otherwise if that person knew or should have known that such action, if successful, could result in rendering the investment company's financial statements materially misleading.

REGULATION 13D-G

Rule 13d-1. Filing of Schedules 13D and 13G

(a) Any person who, after acquiring directly or indirectly the beneficial ownership of any equity security of a class which is specified in paragraph (i) of this section, is directly or indirectly the beneficial owner of more than five percent of the class shall, within 10 days after the acquisition, file with the Commission, a statement containing the information required by Schedule 13D (§ 240.13d-101).

(b) (1) A person who would otherwise be obligated under paragraph (a) of this section to file a statement on Schedule 13D (§ 240.13d-101) may, in lieu thereof, file with the Commission, a short-form statement on Schedule 13G (§ 240.13d-102), *Provided*, That:

(i) Such person has acquired such securities in the ordinary course of his business and not with the purpose nor with the effect of changing or influencing the control of the issuer, nor in connection with or as a participant in any transaction having such purpose or effect, including any transaction subject § 240.13d-3(b), other than activities solely in connection with a nomination under § 240.14a-11; and

(ii) Such person is:

(A) A broker or dealer registered under section 15 of the Act;

(B) A bank as defined in section 3(a)(6) of the Act;

(C) An insurance company as defined in section 3(a)(19) of the Act;

(D) An investment company registered under section 8 of the Investment Company Act;

(E) Any person registered as an investment adviser under Section 203 of the Investment Advisers Act of 1940 (15 U.S.C. 80b-3) or under the laws of any state;

(F) An employee benefit plan as defined in Section 3(3) of the Employee Retirement Income Security Act of 1974, as amended, 29 U.S.C. 1001 et seq. ("ERISA") that is subject to the provisions of ERISA, or any such plan that is not subject to ERISA that is maintained primarily for the benefit of the employees of a state or local government or instrumentality, or an endowment fund;

(G) A parent holding company or control person, provided the aggregate amount held directly by the parent or control person, and directly and indirectly by their subsidiaries or affiliates that are not persons specified in § 240.13d-1(b)(1)(ii)(A) through (J), does not exceed one percent of the securities of the subject class;

(H) A savings association as defined in Section 3(b) of the Federal Deposit Insurance Act (12 U.S.C. 1813);

(I) A church plan that is excluded from the definition of an investment company under Section 3(c)(14) of the Investment Company Act;

(J) A non-U.S. institution that is the functional equivalent of any of the institutions listed in paragraphs (b)(1)(ii)(A) through (I) of this section, so long as the non-U.S. institution is subject to a regulatory scheme that is substantially comparable to the regulatory scheme applicable to the equivalent U.S. institution; and

(K) A group, provided that all the members are persons specified in § 240.13d-1(b)(1)(ii)(A) through (J).

(iii) Such person has promptly notified any other person (or group within the meaning of Section 13(d)(3) of the Act) on whose behalf it holds, on a discretionary basis, securities exceeding five percent of the class, of any acquisition or transaction on behalf of such other person which might be reportable by that person under Section 13(d) of the Act. This paragraph only requires notice to the account owner of information which the filing person reasonably should be expected to know and which would advise the account owner of an obligation he may have to file a statement pursuant to Section 13(d) of the Act or an amendment thereto.

Instruction 1 to Paragraph (b)(1). For purposes of paragraph (b)(1)(i) of this section, the exception for activities solely in connection with a nomination under§ 240.14a-11 will not be available after the election of directors.

(2) The Schedule 13G filed pursuant to paragraph (b)(1) of this section shall be filed within 45 days after the end of the calendar year in which the person became obligated under paragraph (b)(1) of this section to report the person's beneficial ownership as of the last day of the calendar year, *Provided, That* it shall not be necessary to file a Schedule 13G unless the percentage of the class of equity security specified in paragraph (i) of this section beneficially owned as of the end of the calendar year is more than five percent; However, if the person's direct or indirect beneficial ownership exceeds 10 percent of the class of equity securities prior to the end of the calendar year, the initial Schedule 13G shall be filed within 10 days after the end of the first month in which the person's direct or indirect beneficial ownership exceeds 10 percent of the class of equity securities, computed as of the last day of the month.

(c) A person who would otherwise be obligated under paragraph (a) of this section to file a statement on Schedule 13D (§ 240.13d-101) may, in lieu thereof, file with the Commission, within 10 days after an acquisition described in paragraph (a) of this section, a short-form statement on Schedule 13G (§ 240.13d-102). *Provided,* That the person:

(1) Has not acquired the securities with any purpose, or with the effect of, changing or influencing the control of the issuer, or in connection with or as a participant in any transaction having that purpose or effect, including any transaction subject to § 240.13d-3(b), other than activities solely in connection with a nomination under§ 240.14a-11;

Instruction 1 to Paragraph (c)(1). For purposes of paragraph (c)(1) of this section, the exception for activities solely in connection with a nomination under§ 240.14a-11 will not be available after the election of directors.

(2) Is not a person reporting pursuant to paragraph (b)(1) of this section; and

(3) Is not directly or indirectly the beneficial owner of 20 percent or more of the class.

(d) Any person who, as of the end of any calendar year, is or becomes directly or indirectly the beneficial owner of more than five percent of any equity security of a class specified in paragraph (i) of this section and who is not required to file a statement under paragraph (a) of this section by virtue of the exemption provided by Section 13(d)(6)(A) or (B) of the Act (15 U.S.C. 78m(d)(6)(A) or 78m(d)(6)(B)), or because the beneficial ownership was acquired prior to December 22, 1970, or because the person otherwise (except for the exemption provided by Section 13(d)(6)(C) of the Act (15 U.S.C. 78m(d)(6)(C))) is not required to file a statement, shall file with the Commission, within 45 days after the end of the calendar year in which the person became obligated to report under this paragraph (d), a statement containing the information required by Schedule 13G (§ 240.13d-102).

(e)(1) Notwithstanding paragraphs (b) and (c) of this section and § 240.13d-2(b), a person that has reported that it is the beneficial owner of more than five percent of a class of equity securities in a statement on Schedule 13G (§ 240.13d-102) pursuant to paragraph (b) or (c) of this section, or is required to report the acquisition but has not yet filed the schedule, shall immediately become subject to §§ 240.13d-1(a) and 240.13d-2(a) and shall file a statement on Schedule 13D (§ 240.13d-101) within 10 days if, and shall remain subject to those requirements for so long as, the person:

(i) Has acquired or holds the securities with a purpose or effect of changing or influencing control of the issuer, or in connection with or as a participant in any transaction having that purpose or effect, including any transaction subject to § 240.13d-3(b); and

(ii) Is at that time the beneficial owner of more than five percent of a class of equity securities described in § 240.13d-1(i).

(2) From the time the person has acquired or holds the securities with a purpose or effect of changing or influencing control of the issuer, or in connection with or as a participant in any transaction having that purpose or effect until the expiration of the tenth day from the date of the filing of the Schedule 13D (§ 240.13d-101) pursuant to this section, that person shall not:

(i) Vote or direct the voting of the securities described therein; or

(ii) Acquire an additional beneficial ownership interest in any equity securities of the issuer of the securities, nor of any person controlling the issuer.

(f)(1) Notwithstanding paragraph (c) of this section and § 240.13d-2(b), persons reporting on Schedule 13G (§ 240.13d-102) pursuant to paragraph (c) of this section shall immediately become subject to §§ 240.13d-1(a) and 240.13d-2(a) and shall remain subject to those requirements for so long as, and shall file a statement on Schedule 13D (§ 240.13d-101) within 10 days of the date on which, the person's beneficial ownership equals or exceeds 20 percent of the class of equity securities.

(2) From the time of the acquisition of 20 percent or more of the class of equity securities until the expiration of the tenth day from the date of the filing of the Schedule 13D (§ 240.13d-101) pursuant to this section, the person shall not:

(i) Vote or direct the voting of the securities described therein, or

(ii) Acquire an additional beneficial ownership interest in any equity securities of the issuer of the securities, nor of any person controlling the issuer.

(g) Any person who has reported an acquisition of securities in a statement on Schedule 13G (§ 240.13d-102) pursuant to paragraph (b) of this section, or has become obligated to report on the Schedule 13G (§ 240.13d-102) but has not yet filed the Schedule, and thereafter ceases to be a person specified in paragraph (b)(1)(ii) of this section or determines that it no longer has acquired or holds the securities in the ordinary course of business shall immediately become subject to § 240.13d-1(a) or § 240.13d-1(c) (if the person satisfies the requirements specified in § 240.13d-1(c)), and §§ 240.13d-2(a), (b) or (d), and shall file, within 10 days thereafter, a statement on Schedule 13D (§ 240.13d-101) or amendment to Schedule 13G, as applicable, if the person is a beneficial owner at that time of more than five percent of the class of equity securities.

(h) Any person who has filed a Schedule 13D (§ 240.13d-101) pursuant to paragraph (e), (f) or (g) of this section may again report its beneficial ownership on Schedule 13G (§ 240.13d-102) pursuant to paragraphs (b) or (c) of this section provided the person qualifies thereunder, as applicable, by filing a Schedule 13G (§ 240.13d-102) once the person determines that the provisions of paragraph (e), (f) or (g) of this section no longer apply.

(i) For the purpose of this regulation, the term "equity security" means any equity security of a class which is registered pursuant to Section 12 of that Act, or any equity security of any insurance company which would have been required to be so registered except for the exemption contained in Section 12(g)(2)(G) of the Act, or any equity security issued by a closed-end investment company registered under the Investment Company Act of 1940: provided, such term shall not include securities of a class of non-voting securities.

(j) For the purposes of Sections 13(d) and 13(g), any person, in determining the amount of outstanding securities of a class of equity securities, may rely upon information set forth in the issuer's most recent quarterly or annual report, and any current report subsequent thereto, filed with the Commission pursuant to this Act, unless he knows or has reason to believe that the information contained therein is inaccurate.

(k)(1) Whenever two or more persons are required to file a statement containing the information required by Schedule 13D or Schedule 13G with respect to the same securities, only one statement need be filed, provided that:

(i) Each person on whose behalf the statement is filed is individually eligible to use the Schedule on which the information is filed;

(ii) Each person on whose behalf the statement is filed is responsible for the timely filing of such statement and any amendments thereto, and for the completeness and accuracy of the information concerning such person contained therein; such person is not responsible for the completeness or accuracy of the information concerning the other persons making the filing, unless such person knows or has reason to believe that such information is inaccurate; and

(iii) Such statement identifies all such persons, contains the required information with regard to each such person, indicates that such statement is filed on behalf of all such persons, and includes, as an exhibit, their agreement in writing that such a statement is filed on behalf of each of them.

(2) A group's filing obligation may be satisfied either by a single joint filing or by each of the group's members making an individual filing. If the group's members elect to make their own filings, each such filing should identify all members of the group but the information provided concerning the other persons making the filing need only reflect information which the filing person knows or has reason to know.

Rule 13d-2. Filing of Amendments to Schedules 13D or 13G

(a) If any material change occurs in the facts set forth in the Schedule 13D (§ 240.13d-101) required by § 240.13d-1(a), including, but not limited to, any material increase or decrease in the percentage of the class beneficially owned, the person or persons who were required to file the statement shall promptly file or cause to be filed with the Commission an amendment disclosing that change. An acquisition or disposition of beneficial ownership of securities in an amount equal to one percent or more of the class of securities shall be deemed "material" for purposes of this section; acquisitions or dispositions of less than those amounts may be material, depending upon the facts and circumstances.

(b) Notwithstanding paragraph (a) of this section, and provided that the person filing a Schedule 13G (§ 240.13d-102) pursuant to § 240.13d-1(b) or § 240.13d-1(c) continues to meet the requirements set forth therein, any person who has filed a Schedule 13G (§ 240.13d-102) pursuant to § 240.13d-1(b), § 240.13d-1(c) or § 240.13d-1(d) shall amend the statement within forty-five days after the end of each calendar year if, as of the end of the calendar year, there are any changes in the information reported in the previous filing on that Schedule; *Provided, however,* That an amendment need not be filed with respect to a change in the percent of class outstanding previously reported if the change results solely from a change in the aggregate number of securities outstanding. Once an amendment has been filed reflecting beneficial ownership of five percent or less of the class of securities, no additional filings are required unless the person thereafter becomes the beneficial owner of more than five percent of the class and is required to file pursuant to § 240.13d-1.

(c) Any person relying on § 240.13d-1(b) that has filed its initial Schedule 13G (§ 240.13d-102) pursuant to that paragraph shall, in addition to filing any amendments pursuant to § 240.13d-2(b), file an amendment on Schedule 13G (§ 240.13d-102) within 10 days after the end of the first month in which the person's direct or indirect beneficial ownership, computed as of the last day of the month, exceeds 10 percent of the class of equity securities. Thereafter, that person shall, in addition to filing any amendments pursuant to § 240.13d-2(b), file an amendment on Schedule 13G (§ 240.13d-102) within 10 days after the end of the first month in which the person's direct or indirect beneficial ownership, computed as of the last day of the month, increases or decreases by more than five percent of the class of equity securities. Once an amendment has been filed reflecting beneficial ownership of five percent or less of the class of securities, no additional filings are required by this paragraph (c).

(d) Any person relying on § 240.13d-1(c) and has filed its initial Schedule 13G (§ 240.13d-102) pursuant to that paragraph shall, in addition to filing any amendments pursuant to § 240.13d-2(b), file an amendment on Schedule 13G (§ 240.13d-102) promptly upon acquiring, directly or indirectly, greater than 10 percent of a class of equity securities specified in § 240.13d-1(d), and thereafter promptly upon increasing or decreasing its beneficial ownership by more than five percent of the class of equity securities. Once an amendment has been filed reflecting beneficial ownership of five percent or less of the class of securities, no additional filings are required by this paragraph (d).

(e) The first electronic amendment to a paper format Schedule 13D (§ 240.13d-101 of this chapter) or Schedule 13G (§ 240.13d-102 of this chapter) shall restate the entire text of the Schedule 13D or 13G, but previously filed paper exhibits to such Schedules are not required to be restated electronically. See Rule 102 of Regulation S-T (§ 232.102 of this chapter) regarding amendments to exhibits previously filed in paper format. Notwithstanding the foregoing, if the sole purpose of filing the first electronic Schedule 13D or 13G amendment is to report a change in beneficial ownership that would terminate the filer's obligation to report, the amendment need not include a restatement of the entire text of the Schedule being amended.

Note to § 240.13d-2: For persons filing a short-form statement pursuant to Rule 13d-1(b) or (c), see also Rules 13d-1(e), (f), and (g).

Rule 13d-3. Determination of Beneficial Ownership

(a) For the purposes of Sections 13(d) and 13(g) of the Act a beneficial owner of a security includes any person who, directly or indirectly, through any contract, arrangement, understanding, relationship, or otherwise has or shares:

(1) Voting power which includes the power to vote, or to direct the voting of, such security; and/or

(2) Investment power which includes the power to dispose, or to direct the disposition of, such security.

(b) Any person who, directly or indirectly, creates or uses a trust, proxy, power of attorney, pooling arrangement or any other contract, arrangement, or device with the purpose or effect of divesting such person of beneficial ownership of a security or preventing the vesting of such beneficial ownership as part of a plan or scheme to evade the reporting requirements of Section 13(d) or 13(g) of the Act shall be deemed for purposes of such sections to be the beneficial owner of such security.

(c) All securities of the same class beneficially owned by a person, regardless of the form which such beneficial ownership takes, shall be aggregated in calculating the number of shares beneficially owned by such person.

(d) Notwithstanding the provisions of paragraphs (a) and (c) of this rule:

(1)(i) A person shall be deemed to be the beneficial owner of a security, subject to the provisions of paragraph (b) of this rule, if that person has the right to acquire beneficial ownership of such security, as defined in Rule 13d-3(a) (§ 240.13d-3(a)) within sixty days, including but not limited to any right to acquired: (A) through the exercise of any option, warrant or right; (B) through the conversion of a security; (C) pursuant to the power to revoke a trust, discretionary account, or similar arrangement; or (D) pursuant to the automatic termination of a trust, discretionary account or similar arrangement; provided, however, any person who acquires a security or power specified in paragraphs (A), (B) or (C), above, with the purpose or effect of changing or influencing the control of the issuer, or in connection with or as a participant in any transaction having such purpose or effect, immediately upon such acquisition shall be deemed to be the beneficial owner of the securities which may be acquired through the exercise or conversion of such security or power. Any securities not outstanding which are subject to such options, warrants, rights or conversion privileges shall be deemed to be outstanding for the purpose of computing the percentage of outstanding securities of the class owned by such person but shall not be deemed to be outstanding for the purpose of computing the percentage of the class by any other person.

(ii) Paragraph (d)(1)(i) of this section remains applicable for the purpose of determining the obligation to file with respect to the underlying security even though the option, warrant, right or convertible security is of a class of equity security, as defined in § 240.13d-1(i), and may therefore give rise to a separate obligation to file.

(2) A member of a national securities exchange shall not be deemed to be a beneficial owner of securities held directly or indirectly by it on behalf of another person solely because such member is the record holder of such securities and, pursuant to the rules

of such exchange, may direct the vote of such securities, without instruction, on other than contested matters or matters that may affect substantially the rights or privileges of the holders of the securities to be voted, but is otherwise precluded by the rules of such exchange from voting without instruction.

(3) A person who in the ordinary course of business is a pledgee of securities under a written pledge agreement shall not be deemed to be the beneficial owner of such pledged securities until the pledgee has taken all formal steps necessary which are required to declare a default and determines that the power to vote or to direct to vote or to dispose or to direct the disposition of such pledged securities will be exercised, provided that:

(i) The pledgee agreement is bona fide and was not entered into with the purpose nor with the effect of changing or influencing the control of the issuer, nor in connection with any transaction having such purpose or effect, including any transaction subject to Rule 13d-3(b);

(ii) The pledgee is a person specified in Rule 13d-1(b)(ii), including persons meeting the conditions set forth in paragraph (G) thereof; and

(iii) The pledgee agreement, prior to default, does not grant to the pledgee:

(A) The power to vote or to direct the vote of the pledged securities; or

(B) The power to dispose or direct the disposition of the pledged securities, other than the grant of such power(s) pursuant to a pledge agreement under which credit is extended subject to Regulation T (12 CFR 220.1 to 220.8) and in which the pledgee is a broker or dealer registered under section 15 of the Act.

(4) A person engaged in business as an underwriter of securities who acquires securities through his participation in good faith in a firm commitment underwriting registered under the Securities Act of 1933 shall not be deemed to be the beneficial owner of such securities until the expiration of forty days after the date of such acquisition.

Rule 13d-4. Disclaimer of Beneficial Ownership

Any person may expressly declare in any statement filed that the filing of such statement shall not be construed as an admission that such person is, for the purposes of section 13(d), or 13(g) of the Act, the beneficial owner of any securities covered by the statement.

Rule 13d-5. Acquisition of Securities

(a) A person who becomes a beneficial owner of securities shall be deemed to have acquired such securities for purposes of Section 13(d)(1) of the Act, whether such acquisition was through purchase or otherwise. However, executors or administrators of a decedent's estate generally will be presumed not to have acquired beneficial ownership of the securities in the decedent's estate until such time as such executors or administrators are qualified under local law to perform their duties.

(b)(1) When two or more persons agree to act together for the purpose of acquiring, holding, voting or disposing of equity securities of an issuer, the group formed thereby shall be deemed to have acquired beneficial ownership, for purposes of Sections 13(d) and 13(g) of the Act, as of the date of such agreement, of all equity securities of that issuer beneficially owned by any such persons.

(2) Notwithstanding the previous paragraph, a group shall be deemed not to have acquired any equity securities beneficially owned by the other members of the group solely by virtue of their concerted actions relating to the purchase of equity securities directly from an issuer in a transaction not involving a public offering, provided that:

(i) All the members of the group are persons specified in Rule 13d-1(b)(1)(ii);

(ii) The purchase is in the ordinary course of each member's business and not with the purpose nor with the effect of changing or influencing control of the issuer, nor in connection with or as a participant in any transaction having such purpose or effect, including any transaction subject to Rule 13d-3(b);

(iii) There is no agreement among, or between any members of the group to act together with respect to the issuer or its securities except for the purpose of facilitating the specific purchase involved; and

(iv) The only actions among or between any members of the group with respect to the issuer or its securities subsequent to the closing date of the non-public offering are those which are necessary to conclude ministerial matters directly related to the completion of the offer or sale of the securities.

Rule 13d-6. Exemption of Certain Acquisitions

The acquisition of securities of an issuer by a person who, prior to such acquisition, was a beneficial owner of more than five percent of the outstanding securities of the same class as those acquired shall be exempt from section 13(d) of the Act, provided that:

(a) The acquisition is made pursuant to preemptive subscription rights in an offering made to all holders of securities of the class to which the preemptive subscription rights pertain;

(b) Such person does not acquire additional securities except through the exercise of his pro rata share of the preemptive subscription rights; and

(c) The acquisition is duly reported, if required, pursuant to section 16(a) of the Act and the rules and regulations thereunder.

Rule 13d-7. Dissemination

One copy of the Schedule filed pursuant to §§ 240.13d-1 and 240.13d-2 shall be sent to the issuer of the security at its principal executive office, by registered or certified mail. A copy of Schedules filed pursuant to §§ 240.13d-1(a) and 240.13d-2(a) shall also be sent to each national securities exchange where the security is traded.

Rule 13e-1. Purchase of Securities by the Issuer During a Third-Party Tender Offer

An issuer that has received notice that it is the subject of a tender offer made under Section 14(d)(1) of the Act (15 U.S.C. 78n), that has commenced under § 240.14d-2 must not purchase any of its equity securities during the tender offer unless the issuer first:

(a) Files a statement with the Commission containing the following information:

(1) The title and number of securities to be purchased;

(2) The names of the persons or classes of persons from whom the issuer will purchase the securities;

(3) The name of any exchange, inter-dealer quotation system or any other market on or through which the securities will be purchased;

(4) The purpose of the purchase;

(5) Whether the issuer will retire the securities, hold the securities in its treasury, or dispose of the securities. If the issuer intends to dispose of the securities, describe how it intends to do so; and

(6) The source and amount of funds or other consideration to be used to make the purchase. If the issuer borrows any funds or other consideration to make the purchase or enters any agreement for the purpose of acquiring, holding, or trading the securities, describe the transaction and agreement and identify the parties; and

(b) Pays the fee required by § 240.0-11 when it files the initial statement.

(c) This section does not apply to periodic repurchases in connection with an employee benefit plan or other similar plan of the issuer so long as the purchases are made in the ordinary course and not in response to the tender offer.

Instruction to § 240.13e-1: File eight copies if paper filing is permitted.

Rule 13e-3. Going Private Transactions by Certain Issuers or Their Affiliates

(a) *Definitions.* Unless indicated otherwise or the context requires, all terms used in this section and in Schedule 13E-3 [§ 240.13e-100] shall have the same meaning as in the Act or elsewhere in the General Rules and Regulations thereunder. In addition, the following definitions apply:

(1) An "affiliate" of an issuer is a person that directly or indirectly through one or more intermediaries controls, is controlled by, or is under common control with such issuer. For the purposes of this section only, a person who is not an affiliate of an issuer at the commencement of such person's tender offer for a class of equity securities of such issuer will not be deemed an affiliate of such issuer prior to the stated termination of such tender offer and any extensions thereof;

(2) The term "purchase" means any acquisition for value including, but not limited to, (i) any acquisition pursuant to the dissolution of an issuer subsequent to the sale or other disposition of substantially all the assets of such issuer to its affiliate, (ii) any acquisition pursuant to a merger, (iii) any acquisition of fractional interests in connection with a reverse stock split, and (iv) any acquisition subject to the control of an issuer or an affiliate of such issuer;

(3) A "Rule 13e-3 transaction" is any transaction or series of transactions involving one or more of the transactions described in paragraph (a)(3)(i) of this section which has either a reasonable likelihood or a purpose of producing, either directly or indirectly, any of the effects described in paragraph (a)(3)(ii) of this section;

(i) The transactions referred to in paragraph (a)(3) of this section are:

(A) A purchase of any equity security by the issuer of such security or by an affiliate of such issuer;

(B) A tender offer for or request or invitation for tenders of any equity security made by the issuer of such class of securities or by an affiliate of such issuer; or

(C) A solicitation subject to Regulation 14A [§§ 240.14a-1 to 240.14b-1] of any proxy, consent or authorization of, or a distribution subject to Regulation 14C [§§ 240.14c-1 to 240.14c-101] of information statements to, any equity security holder by the issuer of the class of securities or by an affiliate of such issuer, in connection with: a merger, consolidation, reclassification, recapitalization, reorganization or similar corporate transaction of an issuer or between an issuer (or its subsidiaries) and its affiliate; a sale of substantially all the assets of an issuer to its affiliate or group of affiliates; or a reverse stock split of any class of equity securities of the issuer involving the purchase of fractional interests.

(ii) The effects referred to in paragraph (a)(3) of this section are:

(A) Causing any class of equity securities of the issuer which is subject to section 12(g) or section 15(d) of the Act to become eligible for termination of registration under Rule 12g-4 (§ 240.12g-4) or Rule 12h-6 (§ 240.12h-6), or causing the reporting obligations with respect to such class to become eligible for termination under Rule 12h-6 (§ 240.12h-6); or suspension under Rule 12h-3 (§ 240.12h-3) or section 15(d); or

(B) Causing any class of equity securities of the issuer which is either listed on a national securities exchange or authorized to be quoted in an inter-dealer quotation system of a registered national securities association to be neither listed on any national securities exchange nor authorized to be quoted on an inter-dealer quotation system of any registered national securities association.

(4) An "unaffiliated security holder" is any security holder of an equity security subject to a Rule 13e-3 transaction who is not an affiliate of the issuer of such security.

(b) *Application of section to an issuer (or an affiliate of such issuer) subject to section 12 of the Act.*

(1) It shall be a fraudulent, deceptive or manipulative act or practice, in connection with a Rule 13e-3 transaction, for an issuer which has a class of equity securities registered pursuant to Section 12 of the Act or which is a closed-end investment company registered under the Investment Company Act of 1940, or an affiliate of such issuer, directly or indirectly.

(i) To employ any device, scheme or artifice to defraud any person;

(ii) To make any untrue statement of a material fact or to omit to state a material fact necessary in order to make the statements made, in light of the circumstances under which they were made, not misleading; or

(iii) To engage in any act, practice or course of business which operates or would operate as a fraud or deceit upon any person.

(2) As a means reasonably designed to prevent fraudulent, deceptive or manipulative acts or practices in connection with any Rule 13e-3 transaction, it shall be unlawful for an issuer which has a class of equity securities registered pursuant to Section 12 of the Act, or an affiliate of such issuer, to engage, directly or indirectly, in a Rule 13e-3 transaction unless:

(i) Such issuer or affiliate complies with the requirements of paragraphs (d), (e) and (f) of this Section; and

(ii) The Rule 13e-3 transaction is not in violation of paragraph (b)(1) of this section.

(c) *Application of section to an issuer (or an affiliate of such issuer) subject to Section 15(d) of the Act.*

(1) It shall be unlawful as a fraudulent, deceptive or manipulative act or practice for an issuer which is required to file periodic reports pursuant to Section 15(d) of the Act, or an affiliate of such issuer, to engage, directly or indirectly, in a Rule 13e-3 transaction unless such issuer or affiliate complies with the requirements of paragraphs (d), (e) and (f) of this section.

(2) An issuer or affiliate which is subject to paragraph (c)(1) of this section and which is soliciting proxies or distributing information statements in connection with a transaction described in paragraph (a)(3)(i)(A) of this section may elect to use the timing procedures for conducting a solicitation subject to Regulation 14A (§§ 240.14a-1 to 240.14b-1) or a distribution subject to Regulation 14C (§§ 240.14c-1 to 240.14c-101) in complying with paragraphs (d), (e) and (f) of this section, provided that if an election is made, such solicitation or distribution is conducted in accordance with the requirements of the respective regulations, including the filing of preliminary copies of soliciting materials or an information statement at the time specified in Regulation 14A or 14C, respectively.

(d) *Material required to be filed.* The issuer or affiliate engaging in a Rule 13e-3 transaction must file with the Commission:

(1) A Schedule 13E-3 (§ 240.13e-100), including all exhibits;

(2) An amendment to Schedule 13E-3 reporting promptly any material changes in the information set forth in the schedule previously filed; and

(3) A final amendment to Schedule 13E-3 reporting promptly the results of the Rule 13e-3 transaction.

(e) *Disclosure of information to security holders.*

(1) In addition to disclosing the information required by any other applicable rule or regulation under the federal securities laws, the issuer or affiliate engaging in a § 240.13e-3 transaction must disclose to security holders of the class that is the subject of the transaction, as specified in paragraph (f) of this section, the following:

(i) The information required by Item 1 of Schedule 13E-3 (§ 240.13e-100) (Summary Term Sheet);

(ii) The information required by Items 7, 8 and 9 of Schedule 13E-3, which must be prominently disclosed in a "Special Factors" section in the front of the disclosure document;

(iii) A prominent legend on the outside front cover page that indicates that neither the Securities and Exchange Commission nor any state securities commission has: approved or disapproved of the transaction; passed upon the merits or fairness of the transaction; or passed upon the adequacy or accuracy of the disclosure in the document. The legend also must make it clear that any representation to the contrary is a criminal offense;

(iv) The information concerning appraisal rights required by § 229.1016(f) of this chapter; and

(v) The information required by the remaining items of Schedule 13E-3, except for § 229.1016 of this chapter (exhibits), or a fair and adequate summary of the information.

Instructions to paragraph (e)(1):

1. If the Rule 13e-3 transaction also is subject to Regulation 14A (§§ 240.14a-1 through 240.14b-2) or 14C (§§ 240.14c-1 through 240.14c-101), the registration provisions and rules of the Securities Act of 1933, Regulation 14D or § 240.13e-4, the information required by paragraph (e) (1) of this section must be combined with the proxy statement, information statement, prospectus or tender offer material sent or given to security holders.

2. If the Rule 13e-3 transaction involves a registered securities offering, the legend required by § 229.501(b)(7) of this chapter must be combined with the legend required by paragraph (e)(1)(iii) of this section.

3. The required legend must be written in clear, plain language.

(2) If there is any material change in the information previously disclosed to security holders, the issuer or affiliate must disclose the change promptly to security holders as specified in paragraph (f)(1)(iii) of this section.

(f) *Dissemination of information to security holders.* (1) If the Rule 13e-3 transaction involves a purchase as described in paragraph (a)(3)(i)(A) of this section or a vote, consent, authorization, or distribution of information statements as described in paragraph (a)(3)(i)(C) of this section, the issuer or affiliate engaging in the Rule 13e-3 transaction shall:

(i) Provide the information required by paragraph (e) of this section: (A) in accordance with the provisions of any applicable federal or state law, but in no event later than 20 days prior to; any such purchase; any such vote, consent or authorization; or with respect to the distribution of information statements, the meeting date, or if corporate action is to be taken by means of the written authorization or consent of security holders, the earliest date on which corporate action may be taken: *Provided, however,* That if the purchase subject to this section is pursuant to a tender offer excepted from Rule 13e-4 by paragraph (g)(5) of Rule 13e-4, the information required by paragraph (e) of this section shall be disseminated in accordance with paragraph (e) of Rule 13e-4 no later than 10 business days prior to any purchase pursuant to such tender offer, (B) to each person who is a record holder of a class of equity security subject to the Rule 13e-3 transaction as of a date not more than 20 days prior to the date of dissemination of such information.

(ii) If the issuer or affiliate knows that securities of the class of securities subject to the Rule 13e-3 transaction are held of record by a broker, dealer, bank or voting trustee or their nominees, such issuer or affiliate shall (unless Rule 14a-13(a) [§ 240.14a-13(a)] or 14c-7 [§ 240.14c-7] is applicable) furnish the number of copies of the information required by paragraph (e) of this section that are requested by such persons (pursuant to inquiries by or on behalf of the issuer or affiliate), instruct such persons to forward such information to the beneficial owners of such securities in a timely manner and undertake to pay the reasonable expenses incurred by such persons in forwarding such information; and

(iii) Promptly disseminate disclosure of material changes to the information required by paragraph (d) of this section in a manner reasonably calculated to inform security holders.

(2) If the Rule 13e-3 transaction is a tender offer or a request or invitation for tenders of equity securities which is subject to Regulation 14D [§§ 240.14d-1 to 240.14d-101] or Rule 13e-4 [§ 240.13e-4], the tender offer containing the information required by paragraph (e) of this section, and any material change with respect thereto, shall be published, sent or given in accordance with Regulation 14D or Rule 13e-4, respectively, to security holders of the class of securities being sought by the issuer or affiliate.

(g) *Exceptions.* This section shall not apply to:

(1) Any Rule 13e-3 transaction by or on behalf of a person which occurs within one year of the date of termination of a tender offer in which such person was the bidder and became an affiliate of the issuer as a result of such tender offer *provided* that the consideration offered to unaffiliated security holders in such Rule 13e-3 transaction is at least equal to the highest consideration offered during such tender offer and *provided further* that:

(i) If such tender offer was made for any or all securities of a class of the issuer:

(A) Such tender offer fully disclosed such person's intention to engage in a Rule 13e-3 transaction, the form and effect of such transaction and, to the extent known, the proposed terms thereof; and

(B) Such Rule 13e-3 transaction is substantially similar to that described in such tender offer; or

(ii) If such tender offer was made for less than all the securities of a class of the issuer:

(A) Such tender offer fully disclosed a plan of merger, a plan of liquidation or a similar binding agreement between such person and the issuer with respect to a Rule 13e-3 transaction; and

(B) Such Rule 13e-3 transaction occurs pursuant to the plan of merger, plan of liquidation or similar binding agreement disclosed in the bidder's tender offer.

(2) Any Rule 13e-3 transaction in which the security holders are offered or receive only an equity security *provided* That:

(i) such equity security has substantially the same rights as the equity security which is the subject of the Rule 13e-3 transaction including, but not limited to, voting, dividends, redemption and liquidation rights except that this requirement shall be deemed to be satisfied if unaffiliated security holders are offered common stock;

(ii) such equity security is registered pursuant to section 12 of the Act or reports are required to be filed by the issuer thereof pursuant to section 15(d) of the Act; and

(iii) if the security which is the subject of the Rule 13e-3 transaction was either listed on a national securities exchange or authorized to be quoted in an inter-dealer quotation system of a registered national securities association, such equity security is either listed on a national securities exchange or authorized to be quoted in an inter-dealer quotation system of a registered national securities association.

(3) [Reserved.]

(4) Redemptions, calls or similar purchases of an equity security by an issuer pursuant to specific provisions set forth in the instrument(s) creating or governing that class of equity securities; or

(5) Any solicitation by an issuer with respect to a plan of reorganization under Chapter XI of the Bankruptcy Act, as amended, if made after the entry of an order approving such plan pursuant to section 1125(b) of that Act and after, or concurrently with, the transmittal of information concerning such plan as required by section 1125(b) of that Act.

(6) Any tender offer or business combination made in compliance with § 230.802 of this chapter, § 240.13e-4(h)(8) or § 240.14d-1(c) or any other kind of transaction that otherwise meets the conditions for reliance on the cross-border exemptions set forth in § 240.13e-4(h)(8), 240.14d-1(c) or 230.802 of this chapter except for the fact that it is not technically subject to those rules.

Instruction to § 240.13e-3(g)(6): To the extent applicable, the acquiror must comply with the conditions set forth in § 230.802 of this chapter, and §§ 240.13e-4(h)(8) and 14d-1(c). If the acquiror publishes or otherwise disseminates an informational document to the holders of the subject securities in connection with the transaction, the acquiror must furnish an English translation of that informational document, including any amendments thereto, to the Commission under cover of Form CB (§ 239.800 of this chapter) by the first business day after publication or dissemination. If the acquiror is a foreign entity, it must also file a Form F-X (§ 239.42 of this chapter) with the Commission at the same time as the submission of the Form CB to appoint an agent for service in the United States.

Rule 13p-1. Requirement of Report Regarding Disclosure of Registrant's Supply Chain Information Regarding Conflict Minerals.

Every registrant that files reports with the Commission under Sections 13(a) (15 U.S.C. 78m(a)) or 15(d) (15 U.S.C. 78o(d)) of the Exchange Act, having conflict minerals that are necessary to the functionality or production of a product manufactured or contracted by that registrant to be manufactured, shall file a report on Form SD within the period specified in that Form disclosing the information required by the applicable items of Form SD as specified in that Form (17 CFR 249b.400).

Rule 13q-1. Disclosure of Payments Made By Resource Extraction Issuers.

(a) *Resource Extraction Issuers.* Every issuer that is required to file an annual report with the Commission pursuant to Section 13 or 15(d) of the Exchange Act (15 U.S.C. 78m or 78*o*(d)) and engages in the commercial development of oil, natural gas, or minerals must file a report on Form SD (17 CFR 249b.400) within the period specified in that Form disclosing the information required by the applicable items of Form SD as specified in that Form.

(b) *Anti-Evasion.* Disclosure is required under this section in circumstances in which an activity related to the commercial development of oil, natural gas, or minerals, or a payment or series of payments made by a resource extraction issuer to a foreign government or the Federal Government for the purpose of commercial development of oil, natural gas, or minerals is not, in form or characterization, within one of the categories of activities or payments specified in Form SD, but is part of a plan or scheme to evade the disclosure required under this section.

(c) *Alternative Reporting.* An application for recognition of a regime as substantially similar for purposes of alternative reporting must be filed in accordance with the procedures set forth in Rule 0-13 (§ 240.0-13), except that, for purposes of this paragraph (c), applications may be submitted by resource extraction issuers, governments, industry groups, or trade associations.

(d) *Exemptive Relief.* An application for exemptive relief under this section may be filed in accordance with the procedures set forth in Rule 0-12 (§ 240.0-12).

(e) *Public Compilation.* To the extent practicable, the staff will periodically make a compilation of the information required to be filed under this section publicly available online. The staff may determine the form, manner and timing of the compilation, except that no information included therein may be anonymized (whether by redacting the names of the resource extraction issuer or otherwise).

PROXY RULES

REGULATION 14A—SOLICITATION OF PROXIES

Rule 14a-1. Definitions

Unless the context otherwise requires, all terms used in this regulation have the same meanings as in the Act or elsewhere in the general rules and regulations thereunder. In addition, the following definitions apply unless the context otherwise requires:

(a) *Associate.* The term "associate," used to indicate a relationship with any person, means (1) any corporation or organization (other than the registrant or a majority owned subsidiary of the registrant) of which such person is an officer or partner or is, directly or indirectly, the beneficial owner of 10 percent or more of any class of equity securities; (2) any trust or other estate in which such person has a substantial beneficial interest or as to which such person serves as trustee or in a similar fiduciary capacity; and (3) any relative or spouse of such person, or any relative of such spouse, who has the same home as such person or who is a director or officer of the registrant or any of its parents or subsidiaries.

(b) *Employee benefit plan.* For purposes of § § 240.14a-13, 240.14b-1 and 240.14b-2, the term "employee benefit plan" means any purchase, savings, option, bonus, appreciation, profit sharing, thrift, incentive, pension or similar plan primarily for employees, directors, trustees or officers.

(c) *Entity that exercises fiduciary powers.* The term "entity that exercises fiduciary powers" means any entity that holds securities in nominee name or otherwise on behalf of a beneficial owner but does not include a clearing agency registered pursuant to section 17A of the Act or a broker or a dealer.

(d) *Exempt employee benefit plan securities.* For purposes of § § 240.14a-13, 240.14b-1 and 240.14b-2, the term "exempt employee benefit plan securities" means: (1) securities of the registrant held by an employee benefit plan, as defined in paragraph (b) of this section, where such plan is established by the registrant; or (2) if notice regarding the current solicitation has been given pursuant to § 240.14a-13(a)(1)(ii)(C) or if notice regarding the current request for a list of names, addresses and securities positions of beneficial owners has been given pursuant to § 240.14a-13(b)(3), securities of the registrant held by an employee benefit plan, as defined in paragraph (b) of this section, where such plan is established by an affiliate of the registrant.

(e) *Last fiscal year.* The term "last fiscal year" of the registrant means the last fiscal year of the registrant ending prior to the date of the meeting for which proxies are to be solicited or if the solicitation involves written authorizations or consents in lieu of a meeting, the earliest date they may be used to effect corporate action.

(f) *Proxy.* The term "proxy" includes every proxy, consent or authorization within the meaning of section 14(a) of the Act. The consent or authorization may take the form of failure to object or to dissent.

(g) *Proxy statement.* The term "proxy statement" means the statement required by § 240.14a-3(a) whether or not contained in a single document.

(h) *Record date.* The term "record date" means the date as of which the record holders of securities entitled to vote at a meeting or by written consent or authorization shall be determined.

(i) *Record holder.* For purposes of §§ 240.14a-13, 240.14b-1 and 240.14b-2, the term "record holder" means any broker, dealer, voting trustee, bank, association or other entity that exercises fiduciary powers which holds securities of record in nominee name or otherwise or as a participant in a clearing agency registered pursuant to section 17A of the Act.

(j) *Registrant.* The term "registrant" means the issuer of the securities in respect of which proxies are to be solicited.

(k) *Respondent bank.* For purposes of §§ 240.14a-13, 240.14b-1 and 240.14b-2, the term "respondent bank" means any bank, association or other entity that exercises fiduciary powers which holds securities on behalf of beneficial owners and deposits such securities for safekeeping with another bank, association or other entity that exercises fiduciary powers.

(l) *Solicitation.* (1) The terms "solicit" and "solicitation" include:

(i) Any request for a proxy whether or not accompanied by or included in a form of proxy;

(ii) Any request to execute or not to execute, or to revoke, a proxy; or

(iii) The furnishing of a form of proxy or other communication to security holders under circumstances reasonably calculated to result in the procurement, withholding or revocation of a proxy.

(2) The terms do not apply, however, to:

(i) The furnishing of a form of proxy to a security holder upon the unsolicited request of such security holder;

(ii) The performance by the registrant of acts required by § 240.14a-7;

(iii) The performance by any person of ministerial acts on behalf of a person soliciting a proxy; or

(iv) A communication by a security holder who does not otherwise engage in a proxy solicitation (other than a solicitation exempt under § 240.14a-2) starting how the security holder intends to vote and the reasons therefor, provided that the communication:

(A) is made by means of speeches in public forums, press releases, published or broadcast opinions, statements, or advertisements appearing in a broadcast media, or newspaper, magazine or other bona fide publication disseminated on a regular basis,

(B) is directed to persons to whom the security holder owes a fiduciary duty in connection with the voting of securities of a registrant held by the security holder, or

(C) is made in response to unsolicited requests for additional information with respect to a prior communication by the security holder made pursuant to this paragraph (*l*)(2)(iv).

Rule 14a-2. Solicitations to Which §240.14a-3 to §240.14a-15 Apply

Sections 240.14a-3 to 240.14a-15, except as specified below, apply to every solicitation of a proxy with respect to securities registered pursuant to Section 12 of the Act (15 U.S.C. 78*l*), whether or not trading in such securities has been suspended. To the extent specified below, certain of these sections also apply to roll-up transactions that do not involve an entity with securities registered pursuant to Section 12 of the Act.

(a) Sections 240.14a-3 to 240.14a-15 do not apply to the following:

(1) Any solicitation by a person in respect to securities carried in his name or in the name of his nominee (otherwise than as voting trustee) or held in his custody, if such person—

(i) Receives no commission or remuneration for such solicitation, directly or indirectly, other than reimbursement of reasonable expenses,

(ii) Furnishes promptly to the person solicited (or such person's household in accordance with §240.14a-3(e)(1)) a copy of all soliciting material with respect to the same subject matter or meeting received from all persons who shall furnish copies thereof for such purpose and who shall, if requested, defray the reasonable expenses to be incurred in forwarding such material, and

(iii) In addition, does no more than impartially instruct the person solicited to forward a proxy to the person, if any, to whom the person solicited desires to give a proxy, or impartially request from the person solicited instructions as to the authority to be conferred by the proxy and state that a proxy will be given if no instructions are received by a certain date.

(2) Any solicitation by a person in respect of securities of which he is the beneficial owner;

(3) Any solicitation involved in the offer and sale of securities registered under the Securities Act of 1933: *Provided,* That this paragraph shall not apply to securities to be issued in any transaction of the character specified in paragraph (a) of Rule 145 under that Act;

(4) Any solicitation with respect to a plan of reorganization under Chapter 11 of the Bankruptcy Reform Act of 1978, as amended, if made after the entry of an order approving the written disclosure statement concerning a plan of reorganization pursuant to section 1125 of said Act and after, or concurrently with, the transmittal of such disclosure statement as required by section 1125 of said Act;

(5) [Reserved.]

(6) Any solicitation through the medium of a newspaper advertisement which informs security holders of a source from which they may obtain copies of a proxy statement, form of proxy and any other soliciting material and does no more than (i) name the registrant, (ii) state the reason for the advertisement, and (iii) identify the proposal or proposals to be acted upon by security holders.

(b) Sections 240.14a-3 to 240.14a-6 (other than paragraphs 14a-6(g) and 14a-6(p)), §240.14a-8, §240.14a-10, and §§240.14a-12 to 240.14a-15 do not apply to the following:

(1) Any solicitation by or on behalf of any person who does not, at any time during such solicitation, seek directly or indirectly, either on its own or another's behalf, the power to act as proxy for a security holder and does not furnish or otherwise request, or act on behalf of a person who furnishes or requests, a form of revocation, abstention, consent or authorization. *Provided, however,* that the exemption set forth in this paragraph shall not apply to:

(i) the registrant or an affiliate or associate of the registrant (other than an officer or director or any person serving in a similar capacity);

(ii) an officer or director of the registrant or any person serving in a similar capacity engaging in a solicitation financed directly or indirectly by the registrant;

(iii) an officer, director, affiliate or associate of a person that is ineligible to rely on the exemption set forth in this paragraph (other than persons specified in paragraph (b)(1)(i) of this section), or any person serving in a similar capacity;

(iv) any nominee for whose election as a director proxies are solicited;

(v) any person soliciting in opposition to a merger, recapitalization, reorganization, sale of assets or other extraordinary transaction recommended or approved by the board of directors of the registrant who is proposing or intends to propose an alternative transaction to which such person or one of its affiliates is a party;

(vi) any person who is required to report beneficial ownership of the registrant's equity securities on a Schedule 13D [§ 240.13d-101], unless such person has filed a Schedule 13D and has not disclosed pursuant to Item 4 thereto an intent, or reserved the right, to engage in a control transaction, or any contested solicitation for the election of directors;

(vii) any person who receives compensation from an ineligible person directly related to the solicitation of proxies, other than pursuant to § 240.14a-13;

(viii) where the registrant is an investment company registered under the Investment Company Act of 1940 [15 U.S.C. 80a-1 et seq.], an "interested person" of that investment company, as that term is defined in Section 2(a)(19) of the investment Company Act [15 U.S.C. 80a-2];

(ix) any person who, because of a substantial interest in the subject matter of the solicitation, is likely to receive a benefit from a successful solicitation that would not be shared pro rata by all other holders of the same class of securities, other than a benefit arising from the person's employment with the registrant; and

(x) any person acting on behalf of any of the foregoing.

(2) Any solicitation made otherwise than on behalf of the registrant where the total number of persons solicited is not more than ten; and

(3) The furnishing of proxy voting advice by any person (the "advisor") to any other person with whom the advisor has a business relationship, if:

(i) The advisor renders financial advice in the ordinary course of his business;

(ii) The advisor discloses to the recipient of the advice any significant relationship with the registrant or any of its affiliates, or a security holder proponent of the matter on which advice is given, as well as any material interest of the advisor in such matter.

(iii) The advisor receives no special commission or remuneration for furnishing the proxy voting advice from any person other than a recipient of the advice and other persons who receive similar advice under this subsection; and

(iv) The proxy voting advice is not furnished on behalf of any person soliciting proxies or on behalf of a participant in an election subject to the provisions of § 240.14a-12(c); and.

(4) Any solicitation in connection with a roll-up transaction as defined in Item 901(c) of Regulation S-K (§ 229.901 of this chapter) in which the holder of a security that is the subject of a proposed roll-up transaction engages in preliminary communications with other holders of securities that are the subject of the same limited partnership roll-up transaction for the purpose of determining whether to solicit proxies, consents, or authorizations in opposition to the proposed limited partnership roll-up transaction; *provided, however,* that:

(i) This exemption shall not apply to a security holder who is an affiliate of the registrant or general partner or sponsor; and

(ii) This exemption shall not apply to a holder of five percent (5%) or more of the outstanding securities of a class that is the subject of the proposed roll-up transaction who engages in the business of buying and selling limited partnership interests in the secondary market unless that holder discloses to the persons to whom the communications are made such ownership interest and any relations of the holder to the parties of the transaction or to the transaction itself, as required by § 240.14a-6(n)(1) and specified in the Notice of Exempt Preliminary Roll-up Communication (§ 240.14a-104). If the communication is oral, this disclosure may be provided to the security holder orally. Whether the communication is written or oral, the notice required by § 240.14a-6(n) and § 240.14a-104 shall be furnished to the Commission.

(5) Publication or distribution by a broker or a dealer of a research report in accordance with Rule 138 (§ 230.138 of this chapter) or Rule 139 (§ 230.139 of this chapter) during a transaction in which the broker or dealer or its affiliate participates or acts in an advisory role.

(6) Any solicitation by or on behalf of any person who does not seek directly or indirectly, either on its own or another's behalf, the power to act as proxy for a shareholder and does not furnish or otherwise request, or act on behalf of a person who furnishes or requests, a form of revocation, abstention, consent, or authorization in an electronic shareholder forum that is established, maintained or operated pursuant to the provisions of § 240.14a-17, provided that the solicitation is made more than 60 days prior to the date announced by a registrant for its next annual or special meeting of shareholders. If the registrant announces the date of its next annual or special meeting of shareholders less than 60 days before the meeting date, then the solicitation may not be made more than two days following the date of the registrant's announcement of the meeting date. Participation in an electronic shareholder forum does not eliminate a person's eligibility to solicit proxies after the date that this exemption is no longer available, or is no longer being relied upon, provided that any such solicitation is conducted in accordance with this regulation.

(7) Any solicitation by or on behalf of any shareholder in connection with the formation of a nominating shareholder group pursuant to § 240.14a-11, provided that:

(i) The soliciting shareholder is not holding the registrant's securities with the purpose, or with the effect, of changing control of the registrant or to gain a number of seats on the board of directors that exceeds the maximum number of nominees that the registrant could be required to include under § 240.14a-11(d);

(ii) Each written communication includes no more than:

(A) A statement of each soliciting shareholder's intent to form a nominating shareholder group in order to nominate one or more directors under § 240.14a-11;

(B) Identification of, and a brief statement regarding, the potential nominee or nominees or, where no nominee or nominees have been identified, the characteristics of the nominee or nominees that the shareholder intends to nominate, if any;

(C) The percentage of voting power of the registrant's securities that are entitled to be voted on the election of directors that each soliciting shareholder holds or the aggregate percentage held by any group to which the shareholder belongs; and

(D) The means by which shareholders may contact the soliciting party.

(iii) Any written soliciting material published, sent or given to shareholders in accordance with this paragraph must be filed by the shareholder with the Commission, under the registrant's Exchange Act file number, or, in the case of a registrant that is an investment company registered under the Investment Company Act of 1940 (15 U.S.C. 80a-1 et seq.),under the registrant's Investment Company Act file number, no later than the date the material is first published, sent or given to shareholders. Three copies of the material must at the same time be filed with, or mailed for filing to, each national securities exchange upon which any class of securities of the registrant is listed and registered. The soliciting material must include a cover page in the form set forth in Schedule 14N (§ 240.14n-101) and the appropriate box on the cover page must be marked.

(iv) In the case of an oral solicitation made in accordance with the terms of this section, the nominating shareholder must file a cover page in the form set forth in Schedule 14N (§ 240.14n-101), with the appropriate box on the cover page marked, under the registrant's Exchange Act file number (or in the case of an investment company registered under the Investment Company Act of 1940 (15 U.S.C. 80a-1 *et seq.*), under the registrant's Investment Company Act file number), no later than the date of the first such communication.

Instruction to Paragraph (b)(7). The exemption provided in paragraph (b)(7) of this section shall not apply to a shareholder that subsequently engages in soliciting or other nominating activities outside the scope of § 240.14a-2(b)(8) and § 240.14a-11 in connection with the subject election of directors or is or becomes a member of any other group, as determined under section 13(d)(3) of the Act (15 U.S.C. 78m(d)(3) and § 240.13d-5(b)), or otherwise, with persons engaged in soliciting or other nominating activities in connection with the subject election of directors.

(8) Any solicitation by or on behalf of a nominating shareholder or nominating shareholder group in support of its nominee that is included or that will be included on the registrant's form of proxy in accordance with § 240.14a-11 or for or against the registrant's nominee or nominees, provided that:

(i) The soliciting party does not, at any time during such solicitation, seek directly or indirectly, either on its own or another's behalf, the power to act as proxy for a shareholder and does not furnish or otherwise request, or act on behalf of a person who furnishes or requests, a form of revocation, abstention, consent or authorization;

(ii) Any written communication includes:

(A) The identity of each nominating shareholder and a description of his or her direct or indirect interests, by security holdings or otherwise;

(B) A prominent legend in clear, plain language advising shareholders that a shareholder nominee is or will be included in the registrant's proxy statement and that they should read the registrant's proxy statement when available because it includes important information (or, if the registrant's proxy statement is publicly available, advising shareholders of that fact and encouraging shareholders to read the registrant's proxy statement because it includes important information). The legend also must explain to shareholders that they can find the registrant's proxy statement, other soliciting material, and any other relevant documents at no charge on the Commission's Web site; and

(iii) Any written soliciting material published, sent or given to shareholders in accordance with this paragraph must be filed by the nominating shareholder or nominating shareholder group with the Commission, under the registrant's Exchange Act file number, or, in the case of a registrant that is an investment company registered under the Investment Company Act of 1940 (15 U.S.C. 80a-1 *et seq.*), under the registrant's Investment Company Act file number, no later than the date the material is first published, sent or given to shareholders. Three copies of the material must at the same time be filed with, or mailed for filing to, each national securities exchange upon which any class of securities of the registrant is listed and registered. The soliciting material must include a cover page in the form set forth in Schedule 14N (§ 240.14n-101) and the appropriate box on the cover page must be marked.

Instruction 1 to Paragraph (b)(8). A nominating shareholder or nominating shareholder group may rely on the exemption provided in paragraph (b)(8) of this section only after receiving notice from the registrant in accordance with § 240.14a-11(g)(1) or § 240.14a-11(g)(3)(iv) that the registrant will include the nominating shareholder's or nominating shareholder group's nominee or nominees in its form of proxy.

Instruction 2 to Paragraph (b)(8). Any solicitation by or on behalf of a nominating shareholder or nominating shareholder group in support of its nominee included or to be included on the registrant's form of proxy in accordance with § 240.14a-11 or for or against the registrant's nominee or nominees must be made in reliance on the exemption provided in paragraph (b)(8) of this section and not on any other exemption.

Instruction 3 to Paragraph (b)(8). The exemption provided in paragraph (b)(8) of this section shall not apply to a person that subsequently engages in soliciting or other nominating activities outside the scope of § 240.14a-11 in connection with the subject election of directors or is or becomes a member of any other group, as determined under section 13(d)(3) of the

Act (15 U.S.C. 78m(d)(3) and § 240.13d-5(b)), or otherwise, with persons engaged in soliciting or other nominating activities in connection with the subject election of directors.

Rule 14a-3. Information to Be Furnished Security Holders

(a) No solicitation subject to this regulation shall be made unless each person solicited is concurrently furnished or has previously been furnished with:

(1) A publicly-filed preliminary or definitive proxy statement, in the form and manner described in § 240.14a-16, containing the information specified in Schedule 14A (§ 240.14a-101);

(2) A preliminary or definitive written proxy statement included in a registration statement filed under the Securities Act of 1933 on Form S-4 or F-4 (§ 239.25 or § 239.34 of this chapter) or Form N-14 (§ 239.23 of this chapter) and containing the information specified in such Form; or

(3) A publicly-filed preliminary or definitive proxy statement, not in the form and manner described in § 240.14a-16, containing the information specified in Schedule 14A (§ 240.14a-01), if:

(i) The solicitation relates to a business combination transaction as defined in § 230.165 of this chapter, as well as transactions for cash consideration requiring disclosure under Item 14 of § 240.14a-101.

(ii) The solicitation may not follow the form and manner described in § 240.14a-16 pursuant to the laws of the state of incorporation of the registrant;

(b) If the solicitation is made on behalf of the registrant, other than an investment company registered under the Investment Company Act of 1940, and relates to an annual (or special meeting in lieu of the annual) meeting of security holders, or written consent in lieu of such meeting, at which directors are to be elected, each proxy statement furnished pursuant to paragraph (a) of this section shall be accompanied or preceded by an annual report to security holders as follows:

(1) The report shall include, for the registrant and its subsidiaries, consolidated and audited balance sheets as of the end of the two most recent fiscal years and audited statements of income and cash flows for each of the three most recent fiscal years prepared in accordance with Regulation S-X (part 210 of this chapter), except that the provisions of Article 3 (other than §§ 210.3-03(e), 210.3-04 and 210.3-20) and Article 11 shall not apply. Any financial statement schedules or exhibits or separate financial statements which may otherwise be required in filings with the Commission may be omitted. If the financial statements of the registrant and its subsidiaries consolidated in the annual report filed or to be filed with the Commission are not required to be audited, the financial statements required by this paragraph may be unaudited. A smaller reporting company may provide the information in Article 8 of Regulation S-X (§ 210.8 of this chapter) in lieu of the financial information required by this paragraph 9(b)(1).

Note 1 to Paragraph (b)(1): If the financial statements for a period prior to the most recently completed fiscal year have been examined by a predecessor accountant, the separate report of the predecessor accountant may be omitted in the report to security holders, provided the registrant has obtained from the predecessor accountant a reissued report covering the prior period presented and the successor accountant clearly indicates in the scope paragraph of his or her report (a) that the financial statements of the prior period were examined by other accountants, (b) the date of their report, (c) the type of opinion expressed by the predecessor accountant and (d) the substantive reasons therefore, if it was other than unqualified. It should be noted, however, that the separate report of any predecessor accountant is required in filings with the Commission. If, for instance, the financial statements in the annual report to security holders are incorporated by reference in a Form 10-K, the separate report of a predecessor accountant shall be filed in Part II or in Part IV as a financial statement schedule.

Note 2 to Paragraph (b)(i): For purposes of complying with Rule 14a-3, if the registrant, has changed its fiscal closing date, financial statements covering two years and one period of nine to 12 months shall be deemed to satisfy the requirements for statements of income and cash flows for the three most recent fiscal years. (2)(i) Financial statements and notes thereto shall be presented in roman type at least as large and as legible as 10-point modern type. If necessary for convenient presentation, the financial statements may be in roman type as large and as legible as eight-point modern type. All type shall be leaded at least two points.

(ii) Where the annual report to security holders is delivered through an electronic medium, issuers may satisfy legibility requirements applicable to printed documents, such as type size and font, by presenting all required information in a format readily communicated to investors.

(3) The report shall contain the supplementary financial information required by Item 302 of Regulation S-K or, if applicable, a plan of operation required by Item 303(a) of Regulation S-B.

(4) The report shall contain information concerning changes in and disagreements with accountants on accounting and financial disclosure required by Item 304 of Regulation S-K.

(5)(i) The report shall contain the selected financial data required by Item 301 of Regulation S-K.

(ii) The report shall contain management's discussion and analysis of financial condition and results of operations required by Item 303 of Regulation S-K (§ 229.303 of this chapter).

(iii) The report shall contain the quantitative and qualitative disclosures about market risk required by Item 305 of Regulation S-K.

(6) The report shall contain a brief description of the business done by the registrant and its subsidiaries during the most recent fiscal year which will, in the opinion of management, indicate the general nature and scope of the business of the registrant and its subsidiaries.

(7) The report shall contain information relating to the registrant's industry segments, classes of similar products or services, foreign and domestic operations and export sales required by paragraphs (b), (c)(1)(i) and (d) of Item 101 of Regulation S-K.

(8) The report shall identify each of the registrant's directors and executive officers, and shall indicate the principal occupation or employment of each such person and the name and principal business of any organization by which such person is employed.

(9) The report shall contain the market price of and dividends on the registrant's common equity and related security holder matters required by Items 201(a), (b) and (c) of Regulation S-K (§ 229.201(a), (b) and (c) of this chapter). If the report precedes or accompanies a proxy statement or information statement relating to an annual meeting of security holders at which directors are to be elected (or special meeting or written consents in lieu of such meeting), furnish the performance graph required by Item 201(e) (§ 229.201(e) of this chapter).

(10) The registrant's proxy statement, or the report, shall contain an undertaking in bold face or otherwise reasonably prominent type to provide without charge to each person solicited upon the written request of any such person, a copy of the registrant's annual report on Form 10-K, including the financial statements and the financial statement schedules, required to be filed with the Commission pursuant to Rule 13a-1 (§ 240.13a-1 of this chapter) under the Act for the registrant's most recent fiscal year, and shall indicate the name and address (including title or department) of the person to whom such a written request is to be directed. In the discretion of management, a registrant need not undertake to furnish without charge copies of all exhibits to its Form 10-K, provided that the copy of the annual report on Form 10-K furnished without charge to requesting security holders is accompanied by a list briefly describing all the exhibits not contained therein and indicating that the registrant will furnish any exhibit upon the payment of a specified reasonable fee, which fee shall be limited to the registrant's reasonable expenses in furnishing such exhibit. If the registrant's annual report to security holders complies with all of the disclosure requirements of Form 10-K and is filed with the Commission in satisfaction of its Form 10-K filing requirements, such registrant need not furnish a separate Form 10-K to security holders who receive a copy of such annual report.

Note to Paragraph (b)(10): Pursuant to the undertaking required by paragraph (b)(10) of this section, a registrant shall furnish a copy of its annual report on Form 10-K (§ 249.310 of this chapter) to a beneficial owner of its securities upon receipt of a written request from such person. Each request must set forth a good faith representation that, as of the record date for the solicitation requiring the furnishing of the annual report to security holders pursuant to paragraph (b) of this section, the person making the request was a beneficial owner of securities entitled to vote.

(11) Subject to the foregoing requirements, the report may be in any form deemed suitable by management and the information required by subparagraphs (b)(5) to (10) may be presented in an appendix or other separate section of the report, provided that the attention of security holders is called to such presentation.

Note. Registrants are encouraged to utilize tables, schedules, charts, and graphic illustrations of present financial information in an understandable manner. Any presentation of financial information must be consistent with the data in the financial statements contained in the report and, if appropriate, should refer to relevant portions of the financial statements and notes thereto.

(12) [Reserved.]

(13) Paragraph (b) of this rule shall not apply, however, to solicitations made on behalf of the registrant before the financial statements are available if a solicitation is being made at the same time in opposition to the registrant and if the registrant's proxy statement includes an undertaking in boldface type to furnish such annual report to security holders to all persons being solicited at least 20 calendar days before the date of the meeting or, if the solicitation refers to a written consent or authorization in lieu of a meeting, at least 20 calendar days prior to the earliest date on which it may be used to effect corporate action.

(c) Seven copies of the report sent to security holders pursuant to this rule shall be mailed to the Commission, solely for its information, not later than the date on which such report is first sent or given to security holders or the date on which preliminary copies, or definitive copies, if preliminary filing was not required, of solicitation material are filed with the Commission pursuant to Rule 14a-6(a), whichever date is later. The report is not deemed to be "soliciting material" or to be "filed" with the Commission or subject to this regulation otherwise than as provided in this rule, or to the liabilities of Section 18 of the Act, except to the extent that the registrant specifically requests that it be treated as a part of the proxy soliciting material or incorporates it in the proxy statement or other filed report by reference.

(d) An annual report to security holders prepared on an integrated basis pursuant to General Instruction H to Form 10-K (§ 249.310 of this chapter) may also be submitted in satisfaction of this section. When filed as the annual report on Form 10-K, responses to the Items of that form are subject to section 18 of the Act notwithstanding paragraph (c) of this section.

(e)(1)(i) A registrant will be considered to have delivered an annual report to security holders, proxy statement or Notice of Internet Availability of Proxy Materials, as described in § 240.14a-16, to all security holders of record who share an address if:

(A) The registrant delivers one annual report to security holders, proxy statement or Notice of Internet Availability of Proxy Materials, as applicable, to the shared address; (B) The registrant addresses the annual report to security holders, proxy statement or Notice of Internet Availability of Proxy Materials, as applicable, to the security holders as a group (for example, "ABC Fund [or Corporation] Security Holders," "Jane Doe and Household," "The Smith Family"), to each of the security holders individually (for example, "John Doe and Richard Jones") or to the security holders in a form to which each of the security holders has consented in writing;

Note to paragraph (e)(1)(i)(B): Unless the registrant addresses the annual report to security holders, proxy statement or Notice of Internet Availability of Proxy Materials to the security holders as a group or to each of the security holders individually, it must obtain, from each security holder to be included in the householded group, a separate affirmative written consent to the specific form of address the registrant will use.

(C) The security holders consent, in accordance with paragraph (e)(1)(ii) of this section, to delivery of one annual report to security holders or proxy statement, as applicable;

(D) With respect to delivery of the proxy statement or Notice of Internet Availability of Proxy Materials, the registrant delivers, together with or subsequent to delivery of the proxy statement, a separate proxy card for each security holder at the shared address; and

(E) The registrant includes an undertaking in the proxy statement to deliver promptly upon written or oral request a separate copy of the annual report to security holders, proxy statement or Notice of Internet Availability of Proxy Materials, as applicable, to a security holder at a shared address to which a single copy of the document was delivered.

(ii) *Consent.*

(A) *Affirmative Written Consent.* Each security holder must affirmatively consent, in writing, to delivery of one annual report to security holders or proxy statement, as applicable. A security holder's affirmative written consent will be considered valid only if the security holder has been informed of:

(*1*) The duration of the consent;

(*2*) The specific types of documents to which the consent will apply;

(*3*) The procedures the security holder must follow to revoke consent; and

(*4*) The registrant's obligation to begin sending individual copies to a security holder within thirty days after the security holder revokes consent.

(B) *Implied Consent.* The registrant need not obtain affirmative written consent from a security holder for purposes of paragraph (e)(1)(ii)(A) of this Rule 14a-3 if all of the following conditions are met:

(*1*) The security holder has the same last name as the other security holders at the shared address or the registrant reasonably believes that the security holders are members of the same family;

(*2*) The registrant has sent the security holder a notice at least 60 days before the registrant begins to rely on this section concerning delivery of annual reports to security holders, proxy statements or Notices of Internet Availability of Proxy Materials to that security holder. The notice must:

(*i*) Be a separate written document;

(*ii*) State that only one annual report to security holders, proxy statement or Notice of Internet Availability of Proxy Materials, as applicable, will be delivered to the shared address unless the registrant receives contrary instructions;

(*iii*) Include a toll-free telephone number, or be accompanied by a reply form that is pre-addressed with postage provided, that the security holder can use to notify the registrant that the security holder wishes to receive a separate annual report to security holders, proxy statement or Notice of Internet Availability of Proxy Materials;

(*iv*) State the duration of the consent;

(*v*) Explain how a security holder can revoke consent;

(*vi*) State that the registrant will begin sending individual copies to a security holder within thirty days after the security holder revokes consent; and

(*vii*) Contain the following prominent statement, or similar clear and understandable statement, in bold-face type: "Important Notice Regarding Delivery of Security Holder Documents." This statement also must appear on the envelope in which the notice is delivered. Alternatively, if the notice is delivered separately from other communications to security holders, this statement may appear either on the notice or on the envelope in which the notice is delivered.

Note to paragraph (e)(1)(ii)(B)(2): The notice should be written in plain English. See Securities Act Rule 421(d)(2) for a discussion of plain English principles.

(*3*) The registrant has not received the reply form or other notification indicating that the security holder wishes to continue to receive an individual copy of the annual report to security holders, proxy statement or Notice of Internet Availability of Proxy Materials, as applicable, within 60 days after the registrant sent the notice required by paragraph (e)(1)(ii)(B)(2) of this section; and

(*4*) The registrant delivers the document to a post office box or residential street address.

Note to paragraph (e)(1)(ii)(B)(4): The registrant can assume that a street address is residential unless the registrant has information that indicates the street address is a business.

(iii) *Revocation of Consent.* If a security holder, orally or in writing, revokes consent to delivery of one annual report to security holders, proxy statement or Notice of Internet Availability of Proxy Materials to a shared address, the registrant must begin sending individual copies to that security holder within 30 days after the registrant receives revocation of the security holder's consent.

(iv) *Definition of Address.* Unless otherwise indicated, for purposes of this rule 14a-3, *address* means a street address, a post office box number, an electronic mail address, a facsimile telephone number or other similar destination to which paper or electronic documents are delivered, unless otherwise provided in this Rule 14a-3. If the registrant has reason to believe that the address is a street address of a multi-unit building, the address must include the unit number.

Note to paragraph (e)(1): A person other than the registrant making a proxy solicitation may deliver a single proxy statement to security holders of record or beneficial owners who have separate accounts and share an address if:

(a) the registrant or intermediary has followed the procedures in this Rule 14a-3; and

(b) the registrant or intermediary makes available the shared address information to the person in accordance with Exchange Act Rule 14a-7(a)(2)(i) and (ii).

(2) Notwithstanding paragraphs (a) and (b) of this section, unless state law requires otherwise, a registrant is not required to send an annual report to security holders, proxy statement or Notice of Internet Availability of Proxy Materials to a security holder if:

(i) An annual report to security holders and a proxy statement, or a Notice of Internet of Availability of Proxy Materials, for two consecutive annual meetings; or

(ii) All, and at least two, payments (if sent by first class mail) of dividends or interest on securities, or dividend reinvestment confirmations, during a twelve month period, have been mailed to such security holder's address and have been returned as undeliverable. If any such security holder delivers or causes to be delivered to the registrant written notice setting forth his then current address for security holder communications purposes, the registrant's obligation to deliver an annual report to security holders, a proxy statement or a Notice of Internet Availability of Proxy Materials under this section is reinstated.

(f) The provisions of paragraph (a) of this section shall not apply to a communication made by means of speeches in public forums, press releases, published or broadcast opinions, statements or advertisements appearing in a broadcast media, newspaper, magazine or other *bona fide* publication disseminated on a regular basis, *provided* that:

(1) No form of proxy, consent or authorization or means to execute the same is provided to a security holder in connection with the communication; and

(2) At the time the communication is made, a definitive proxy statement is on file with the Commission pursuant to Rule 14a-6(b).

Rule 14a-4. Requirements as to Proxy

(a) The form of proxy (1) shall indicate in bold-face type whether or not the proxy is solicited on behalf of the registrant's board of directors or, if provided other than by a majority of the board of directors, shall indicate in bold-face type on whose behalf the solicitation is made; (2) shall provide a specifically designated blank space for dating the proxy card; and (3) shall identify clearly and impartially each separate matter intended to be acted upon, whether or not related to or conditioned on the approval of other matters, and whether proposed by the registrant or by security holders. No reference need be made, however, to proposals as to which discretionary authority is conferred pursuant to paragraph (c) of this section.

Note to paragraph (a) (3) (electronic filers): Electronic filers shall satisfy the filing requirements of Rule 14a-6(a) or (b) (§ 240.14a-6(a) or (b)) with respect to the form of proxy by filing the form of proxy as an appendix at the end of the proxy statement. Forms of proxy shall not be filed as exhibits or separate documents within an electronic submission.

(b) (1) Means shall be provided in the form of proxy whereby the person solicited is afforded an opportunity to specify by boxes a choice between approval or disapproval of, or abstention with respect to each separate matter referred to therein as intended to be acted upon, other than elections to office and votes to determine the frequency of shareholder votes on executive compensation pursuant to § 240.14a-21(b) of this chapter. A proxy may confer discretionary authority with respect to matters as to which a choice is not specified by the security holder provided that the form of proxy states in bold-face type how it is intended to vote the shares represented by the proxy in each such case.

(2) A form of proxy which provides for the election of directors shall set forth the names of persons nominated for election as directors. A form of proxy that provides for the election of directors shall set forth the names of persons nominated for election as directors, including any person whose nomination by a shareholder or shareholder group satisfies the requirements of § 240.14a-11, an applicable state or foreign law provision, or a registrant's governing documents as they relate to the inclusion of shareholder director nominees in the registrant's proxy materials. Such form of proxy shall clearly provide any of the following means for security holders to withhold authority to vote for each nominee:

(i) a box opposite the name of each nominee which may be marked to indicate that authority to vote for such nominee is withheld; or

(ii) an instruction in bold-face type which indicates that the security holder may withhold authority to vote for any nominee by lining through or otherwise striking out the name of any nominee; or

(iii) designated blank spaces in which the security holder may enter the names of nominees with respect to whom the shareholder chooses to withhold authority to vote; or

(iv) any other similar means, provided that clear instructions are furnished indicating how the security holder may withhold authority to vote for any nominee.

Such form of proxy also may provide a means for the security holder to grant authority to vote for the nominees set forth, as a group, *provided* that there is a similar means for the security holder to withhold authority to vote for such group of nominees. Any such form of proxy which is executed by the security holder in such manner as not to withhold authority to vote for the election of any nominee shall be deemed to grant such authority, *provided* that the form of proxy so states in bold-face type. Means to grant authority to vote for any nominees as a group or to withhold authority for any nominees as a group may not be provided if the form of proxy includes one or more shareholder nominees in accordance with § 240.14a-11, an applicable state or foreign law provision, or a registrant's governing documents as they relate to the inclusion of shareholder director nominees in the registrant's proxy materials.

Instructions. 1. Paragraph (2) does not apply in the case of a merger, consolidation or other plan if the election of directors is an integral part of the plan.

2. If applicable state law gives legal effect to votes cast against a nominee, then in lieu of, or in addition to, providing a means for security holders to withhold authority to vote, the issuer should provide a similar means for security holders to vote against each nominee.

(3) A form of proxy which provides for a shareholder vote on the frequency of shareholder votes to approve the compensation of executives required by section 14A(a) (2) of the Securities Exchange Act of 1934 (15 U.S.C. 78n-1(a) (2)) shall provide means whereby the

person solicited is afforded an opportunity to specify by boxes a choice among 1, 2 or 3 years, or abstain.

(c) A proxy may confer discretionary authority to vote on any of the following matters:

(1) For an annual meeting of shareholders, if the registrant did not have notice of the matter at least 45 days before the date on which the registrant first sent its proxy materials for the prior year's annual meeting of shareholders (or date specified by an advance notice provision), and a specific statement to that effect is made in the proxy statement or form of proxy. If during the prior year the registrant did not hold an annual meeting, or if the date of the meeting has changed more than 30 days from the prior year, then notice must not have been received a reasonable time before the registrant sends its proxy materials for the current year.

(2) In the case in which the registrant has received timely notice in connection with an annual meeting of shareholders (as determined under paragraph (c)(1) of this section), if the registrant includes, in the proxy statement, advice on the nature of the matter and how the registrant intends to exercise its discretion to vote on each matter. However, even if the registrant includes this information in its proxy statement, it may not exercise discretionary voting authority on a particular proposal if the proponent:

(i) Provides the registrant with a written statement, within the time-frame determined under paragraph (c)(1) of this section, that the proponent intends to deliver a proxy statement and form of proxy to holders of at least the percentage of the company's voting shares required under applicable law to carry the proposal;

(ii) Includes the same statement in its proxy materials filed under § 240.14a-6; and

(iii) Immediately after soliciting the percentage of shareholders required to carry the proposal, provides the registrant with a statement from any solicitor or other person with knowledge that the necessary steps have been taken to deliver a proxy statement and form of proxy to holders of at least the percentage of the company's voting shares required under applicable law to carry the proposal.

(3) For solicitations other than for annual meetings or for solicitations by persons other than the registrant, matters which the persons making the solicitation do not know, a reasonable time before the solicitation, are to be presented at the meeting, if a specific statement to that effect is made in the proxy statement or form of proxy.

(4) Approval of the minutes of the prior meeting if such approval does not amount to ratification of the action taken at that meeting;

(5) The election of any person to any office for which a bona fide nominee is named in the proxy statement and such nominee is unable to serve or for good cause will not serve.

(6) Any proposal omitted from the proxy statement and form of proxy pursuant to § 240.14a-8 or § 240.14a-9 of this chapter.

(7) Matters incident to the conduct of the meeting.

(d) No proxy shall confer authority (1) to vote for the election of any person to any office for which a bona fide nominee is not named in the proxy statement, (2) to vote at any annual meeting other than the next annual meeting (or any adjournment thereof) to be held after the date on which the proxy statement and form of proxy are first sent or given to security holders, (3) to vote with respect to more than one meeting (and any adjournment thereof) or more than one consent solicitation or (4) to consent to or authorize any action other than the action proposed to be taken in the proxy statement, or matters referred to in paragraph (c) of this rule. A person shall not be deemed to be a bona fide nominee and he shall not be named as such unless he has consented to being named in the proxy statement and to serve if elected. *Provided, however,* that nothing in this section 240.14a-4 shall prevent any person soliciting in support of nominees who, if elected, would constitute a minority of the board of directors, from seeking authority to vote for nominees named in the registrant's proxy statement, so long as the soliciting party:

(i) seeks authority to vote in the aggregate for the number of director positions then subject to election;

(ii) represents that it will vote for all the registrant nominees, other than those registrant nominees specified by the soliciting party;

(iii) provides the security holder an opportunity to withhold authority with respect to any other registrant nominee by writing the name of that nominee on the form of proxy; and

(iv) states on the form of proxy and in the proxy statement that there is no assurance that the registrant's nominees will serve if elected with any of the soliciting party's nominees.

(e) The proxy statement or form of proxy shall provide, subject to reasonable specified conditions, that the shares represented by the proxy will be voted and that where the person solicited specifies by means of a ballot provided pursuant to paragraph (b) a choice with respect to any matter to be acted upon, the shares will be voted in accordance with the specifications so made.

(f) No person conducting a solicitation subject to this regulation shall deliver a form of proxy, consent or authorization to any security holder unless the security holder concurrently receives, or has previously received, a definitive proxy statement that has been filed with the Commission pursuant to § 240.14a-6(b).

Rule 14a-5. Presentation of Information in Proxy Statement

(a) The information included in the proxy statement shall be clearly presented and the statements made shall be divided into groups according to subject matter and the various groups of statements shall be preceded by appropriate headings. The order of items and sub-items in the schedule need not be followed. Where practicable and appropriate, the information shall be presented in tabular form. All amounts shall be stated in figures. Information required by more than one applicable item need not be repeated. No statement need be made in response to any item or sub-item which is inapplicable.

(b) Any information required to be included in the proxy statement as to terms of securities or other subject matter which from a standpoint of practical necessity must be determined in the future may be stated in terms of present knowledge and intention. To the extent practicable, the authority to be conferred concerning each such matter shall be confined within limits reasonably related to the need for discretionary authority. Subject to the foregoing, information which is not known to the persons on whose behalf the solicitation is to be made and which it is not reasonably within the power of such persons to ascertain or procure may be omitted, if a brief statement of the circumstances rendering such information unavailable is made.

(c) Any information contained in any other proxy soliciting material which has been furnished to each person solicited in connection with the same meeting or subject matter may be omitted from the proxy statement, if a clear reference is made to the particular document containing such information.

(d) (1) All printed proxy statements shall be in roman type at least as large and as legible as 10-point modern type, except that to the extent necessary for convenient presentation financial statements and other tabular data, but not the notes thereto, may be in roman type at least as large and as legible as 8-point modern type. All such type shall be leaded at least 2 points.

(2) Where a proxy statement is delivered through an electronic medium, issuers may satisfy legibility requirements applicable to printed documents, such as type size and font, by presenting all required information in a format readily communicated to investors.

(e) All proxy statements shall disclose, under an appropriate caption, the following dates:

(1) The deadline for submitting shareholder proposals for inclusion in the registrant's proxy statement and form of proxy for the registrant's next annual meeting, calculated in the manner provided in § 240.14a-8(e) (Question 5); and

(2) The date after which notice of a shareholder proposal submitted outside the processes of § 240.14a-8 is considered untimely, either calculated in the manner provided by § 240.14a-4(c) (1) or as established by the registrant's advance notice provision, if any, authorized by applicable state law.

(f) If the date of the next annual meeting is subsequently advanced or delayed by more than 30 calendar days from the date of the annual meeting to which the proxy statement relates, the registrant shall, in a timely manner, inform shareholders of such change, and the new dates referred to in paragraphs (e)(1) and (e)(2) of this section, by including a notice, under Item 5, in its earliest possible quarterly report on Form 10-Q (§ 249.308a of this chapter) or, in the case of investment companies, in a shareholder report under § 270.30d-1 of this chapter under the Investment Company Act of 1940, or, if impracticable, any means reasonably calculated to inform shareholders.

Rule 14a-6. Filing Requirements

(a) *Preliminary proxy statement.* Five preliminary copies of the proxy statement and form of proxy shall be filed with the Commission at least 10 calendar days prior to the date definitive copies of such material are first sent or given to security holders, or such shorter period prior to that date as the Commission may authorize upon a showing of good cause thereunder. A registrant, however, shall not file with the Commission a preliminary proxy statement, form of proxy or other soliciting material to be furnished to security holders concurrently therewith if the solicitation relates to an annual (or special meeting in lieu of the annual) meeting, or for an investment company registered under the Investment Company Act of 1940 (15 U.S.C. 80a-1 *et seq.*) or a business development company, if the solicitation relates to any meeting of security holders at which the only matters to be acted upon are:

(1) The election of directors;

(2) The election, approval or ratification of accountant(s);

(3) A security holder proposal included pursuant to Rule 14a-8;

(4) A shareholder nominee for director included pursuant to § 240.14a-11, an applicable state or foreign law provision, or a registrant's governing documents as they relate to the inclusion of shareholder director nominees in the registrant's proxy materials.

(5) The approval or ratification of a plan as defined in paragraph (a)(6)(ii) of Item 402 of Regulation S-K (§ 229.402(a)(6)(ii) of this chapter) or amendments to such a plan;

(6) With respect to an investment company registered under the Investment Company Act of 1940 or a business development company, a proposal to continue, without change, any advisory or other contract or agreement that previously has been the subject of a proxy solicitation for which proxy material was filed with the Commission pursuant to this section;

(7) With respect to an open-end investment company registered under the Investment Company Act of 1940, a proposal to increase the number of shares authorized to be issued;

(8) A vote to approve the compensation of executives as required pursuant to section 14A(a)(1) of the Securities Exchange Act of 1934 (15 U.S.C. 78n-1(a)(1)) and § 240.14a-21(a) of this chapter, or pursuant to section 111(e)(1) of the Emergency Economic Stabilization Act of 2008 (12 U.S.C. 5221(e)(1)) and § 240.14a-20 of this chapter, a vote to determine the frequency of shareholder votes to approve the compensation of executives as required pursuant to Section 14A(a)(2) of the Securities Exchange Act of 1934 (15 U.S.C. 78n-1(a)(2)) and § 240.14a-21(b) of this chapter, or any other shareholder advisory vote on executive compensation.

This exclusion from filing preliminary proxy material does not apply if the registrant comments upon or refers to a solicitation in opposition in connection with the meeting in its proxy material.

Note 1 to Paragraph (a): The filing of revised material does not recommence the ten day time period unless the revised material contains material revisions or material new proposal(s) that constitute a fundamental change in the proxy material.

Note 2 to Paragraph (a): The official responsible for the preparation of the proxy material should make every effort to verify the accuracy and completeness of the information required by the applicable rules. The preliminary material should be filed with the Commission at the earliest practicable date.

Note 3 to Paragraph (a): Solicitation in Opposition. For purposes of the exclusion from filing preliminary proxy material, a "solicitation in opposition" includes: (a) any solicitation opposing a proposal supported by the registrant; and (b) any solicitation supporting a proposal that the registrant does not expressly support, other than a security holder proposal included in the registrant's proxy material pursuant to Rule 14a-8 (§ 240.14a-8 of this chapter). The inclusion of a security holder proposal in the registrant's proxy material pursuant to Rule 14a-8 does not constitute a "solicitation in opposition," even if the registrant opposes the proposal and/or includes a statement in opposition to the proposal.

Note 4 to Paragraph (a): A registrant that is filing proxy material in preliminary form only because the registrant has commented on or referred to a solicitation in opposition should indicate that fact in a transmittal letter when filing the preliminary material with the Commission.

(b) *Definitive proxy statement and other soliciting material.* Eight definitive copies of the proxy statement, form of proxy and all other soliciting materials, in the same form as the materials sent to security holders, must be filed with the Commission no later than the date they are first sent or given to security holders. Three copies of these materials also must be filed with, or mailed for filing to, each national securities exchange on which the registrant has a class of securities listed and registered.

(c) *Personal solicitation materials.* If part or all of the solicitation involves personal solicitation, then eight copies of all written instructions or other materials that discuss, review or comment on the merits of any matter to be acted on, that are furnished to persons making the actual solicitation for their use directly or indirectly in connection with the solicitation, must be filed with the Commission no later than the date the materials are first sent or given to these persons.

(d) *Release dates.* All preliminary proxy statements and forms of proxy filed pursuant to paragraph (a) of this section shall be accompanied by a statement of the date on which definitive copies thereof filed pursuant to paragraph (b) of this section are intended to be released to security holders. All definitive material filed pursuant to paragraph (b) of this section shall be accompanied by a statement of the date on which copies of such material were released to security holders, or, if not released, the date on which copies thereof are intended to be released. All material filed pursuant to paragraph (c) of this section shall be accompanied by a statement of the date on which copies thereof are released to the individual who will make the actual solicitation or if not released, the date on which copies thereof are intended to be released.

(e)(1) *Public availability of information.* All copies of preliminary proxy statements and forms of proxy filed pursuant to paragraph (a) of this section shall be clearly marked "Preliminary Copies," and shall be deemed available for public inspection unless confidential treatment is obtained pursuant to paragraph (e)(2) of this section.

(2) *Confidential treatment.* If action will be taken on any matter specified in Item 14 of Schedule 14A (§ 240.14a-101), all copies of the preliminary proxy statement and form of proxy filed under paragraph (a) of this section will be for the information of the Commission only and will not be deemed available for public inspection until filed with the Commission in definitive form so long as:

(i) The proxy statement does not relate to a matter or proposal subject to § 240.13e-3 or a roll-up transaction as defined in Item 901(c) of Regulation S-K (§ 229.901(c) of this chapter);

(ii) Neither the parties to the transaction nor any persons authorized to act on their behalf have made any public communications relating to the transaction except for statements where the content is limited to the information specified in § 230.135 of this chapter; and

(iii) The materials are filed in paper and marked "Confidential, For Use of the Commission Only." In all cases, the materials may be disclosed to any department or agency of the United States Government and to the Congress, and the Commission may make any inquiries or investigation into the materials as may be necessary to conduct an adequate review by the Commission.

Instruction to paragraph (e)(2): If communications are made publicly that go beyond the information specified in § 230.135 of this chapter, the preliminary proxy materials must be re-filed promptly with the Commission as public materials.

(f) *Communications not required to be filed.* Copies of replies to inquiries from security holders requesting further information and copies of communications which do no more than request that forms of proxy theretofore solicited be signed and returned need not be filed pursuant to this rule.

(g) *Solicitations subject to § 240.14a-2(b)(1).*

(1) Any person who:

(i) engages in a solicitation pursuant to § 240.14a-2(b)(1), and

(ii) at the commencement of that solicitation owns beneficially securities of the class which is the subject of the solicitation with a market value of over $5 million, shall furnish or mail to the Commission, not later than three days after the date the written solicitation is first sent or given to any security holder, five copies of a statement containing the information specified in the Notice of Exempt Solicitation [§ 240.14a-103] which statement shall attach as an exhibit all written soliciting materials. Five copies of an amendment to such statement shall be furnished or mailed to the Commission, in connection with dissemination of any additional communications, not later than three days after the date the additional material is first sent or given to any security holder. Three copies of the Notice of Exempt Solicitation and amendments thereto shall, at the same time the materials are furnished or mailed to the Commission, be furnished or mailed to each national securities exchange upon which any class of securities of the registrant is listed and registered.

(2) Notwithstanding paragraph (g)(1) of this section, no such submission need be made with respect to oral solicitations (other than with respect to scripts used in connection with such oral solicitations), speeches delivered in a public forum, press releases, published or broadcast opinions, statements, and advertisements appearing in a broadcast media, or a newspaper, magazine or other bona fide publication disseminated on a regular basis.

(h) *Revised material.* Where any proxy statement, form of proxy or other material filed pursuant to this rule is amended or revised, two of the copies of such amended or revised material filed pursuant to this rule (or in the case of investment companies registered under the Investment Company Act of 1940, three of such copies) shall be marked to indicate clearly and precisely the changes effected therein. If the amendment or revision alters the text of the material the change in such text shall be indicated by means of underscoring or in some other appropriate manner.

(i) *Fees.* At the time of filing the proxy solicitation material, the persons upon whose behalf the solicitation is made, other than investment companies registered under the Investment Company Act of 1940, shall pay to the Commission the following applicable fee:

(1) For preliminary proxy material involving acquisitions, mergers, spinoffs, consolidations or proposed sales or other dispositions of substantially all the assets of the company, a fee established in accordance with Rule 0-11 (§ 240.0-11 of this chapter) shall be paid. No refund shall be given.

(2) For all other proxy submissions and submissions made pursuant to § 240.14a-6(g), no fee shall be required.

(j) *Merger proxy materials.* Any proxy statement, form of proxy or other soliciting material required to be filed by this section that also is either: (i) included in a registration statement filed under the Securities Act of 1933 on Forms S-4 (§ 239.25 of this chapter), F-4 (§ 239.34 of this chapter) or N-14 (§ 239.23 of this chapter); or (ii) filed under § 230.424, § 230.425 or § 230.497 of this chapter is required to be filed only under the Securities Act, and is deemed filed under this section. In that case, the fee required under paragraph (i) of this section need not be paid.

(k) *Computing time periods.* In computing time periods beginning with the filing date specified in Regulation 14A (§§ 240.14a-1 to 240.14b-1 of this chapter), the filing date shall be counted as the first day of the time period and midnight of the last day shall constitute the end of the specified time period.

(l) *Roll-up transactions.* If a transaction is a roll-up transaction as defined in Item 901(c) of Regulation S-K (17 CFR 229.901(c)) and is registered (or authorized to be registered) on Form S-4 (17 CFR 229.25) or Form F-4 (17 CFR 229.34), the proxy statement of the sponsor or the general partner as defined in Item 901(d) and Item 901(a), respectively, of Regulation S-K (17 CFR 229.901) must be distributed to security holders no later than the lesser of 60 calendar days prior to the date on which the meeting of security holders no later than the lesser of 60 calendar days prior to the date on which the meeting of security holders is held or action is taken, or the maximum number of days permitted for giving notice under applicable state law.

(m) *Cover Page.* Proxy materials filed with the Commission shall include a cover page in the form set in Schedule 14A (§ 240.14a-101 of this chapter). The cover page required by this paragraph need not be distributed to security holders.

(n) *Solicitations subject to § 240.14a-2(b)(4).* Any person who:

(1) Engages in a solicitation pursuant to § 240.14a-2(b)(4), and

(2) At the commencement of that solicitation both owns five percent (5%) or more of the outstanding securities of a class that is the subject of the proposed roll-up transaction, and engages in the business of buying and selling limited partnership interests in the secondary market, shall furnish or mail to the Commission, not later than three days after the date an oral or written solicitation by that person is first made, sent or provided to any security holder, five copies of a statement containing the information specified in the Notice of Exempt Preliminary Roll-up Communication (§ 240.14a-104). Five copies of any amendment to such statement shall be furnished or mailed to the Commission not later than three days after a communication containing revised material is first made, sent or provided to any security holder.

(o) *Solicitations before furnishing a definitive proxy statement.* Solicitations that are published, sent or given to security holders before they have been furnished a definitive proxy statement must be made in accordance with § 240.14a-12 unless there is an exemption available under § 240.14a-2.

(p) *Solicitations Subject to § 240.14a-11.* Any soliciting material that is published, sent or given to shareholders in connection with § 240.14a-2(b)(7) or (b)(8) must be filed with the Commission as specified in that section.

Rule 14a-7. Obligations of Registrants to Provide a List of, or Mail Soliciting Material to, Security Holders

(a) If the registrant has made or intends to make a proxy solicitation in connection with a security holder meeting or action by consent or authorization, upon the written request by any record or beneficial holder of securities of the class entitled to vote at the meeting or to execute a consent or authorization to provide a list of security holders or to mail the requesting security holder's materials, regardless of whether the request references this section, the registrant shall:

(1) deliver to the requesting security holder within five business days after receipt of the request:

(i) notification as to whether the registrant has elected to mail the security holder's soliciting materials or provide a security holder list if the election under paragraph (b) is to be made by the registrant;

(ii) a statement of the approximate number of record holders and beneficial holders, separated by type of holder and class, owning securities in the same class or classes as holders which have been or are to be solicited on management's behalf, or any more limited group of such holders designated by the security holder if available or retrievable under the registrant's or its transfer agent's security holder data systems; and

(iii) the estimated cost of mailing a proxy statement, form of proxy or other communication to such holders, including to the extent known or reasonably available, the estimated costs of any bank, broker, and similar person through whom the registrant has solicited or intends to solicit beneficial owners in connection with the security holder meeting or action.

(2) perform the acts set forth in either paragraphs (a)(2)(i) or (a)(2)(ii) of this section, at the registrant's or requesting security holder's option, as specified in paragraph (b) of this section:

(i) Send copies of any proxy statement, form of proxy, or other soliciting material, including a Notice of Internet Availability of Proxy Materials (as described in § 240.14a-16), furnished by the security holder to the record holders, including banks, brokers, and similar entities, designated by the security holder. A sufficient number of copies must be sent to the banks, brokers, and similar entities for distribution to all beneficial owners designated by the security holder. The security holder may designate only record holders and/or beneficial owners who have not requested paper and/or e-mail copies of the proxy statement. If the registrant has received affirmative written or implied consent to deliver a single proxy statement to security holders at a shared address in accordance with the procedures in § 240.14a-3(e)(1), a single copy of the proxy statement or Notice of Internet Availability of Proxy Materials furnished by the security holder shall be sent to that address, provided that if multiple copies of the Notice of Internet Availability of Proxy Materials are furnished by the security holder for that address, the registrant shall deliver those copies in a single envelope to that address. The registrant shall send the security holder material with reasonable promptness after tender of the material to be sent, envelopes or other containers therefore, postage or payment for postage and other reasonable expenses of effecting such distribution. The registrant shall not be responsible for the content of the material; or

(ii) Deliver the following information to the requesting security holder within five business days of receipt of the request:

(A) A reasonably current list of the names, addresses and security positions of the record holders, including banks, brokers and similar entities holding securities in the same class or classes as holders which have been or are to be solicited on management's behalf, or any more limited group of such holders designated by the security holder if available or retrievable under the registrant's or its transfer agent's security holder data systems;

(B) The most recent list of names, addresses and security positions of beneficial owners as specified in § 240.14a-13(b), in the possession, or which subsequently comes into the possession, of the registrant;

(C) The names of security holders at a shared address that have consented to delivery of a single copy of proxy materials to a shared address, if the registrant has received written or implied consent in accordance with § 240.14a-3(e)(1); and

(D) If the registrant has relied on § 240.14a-16, the names of security holders who have requested paper copies of the proxy materials for all meetings and the names of security holders who, as of the date that the registrant receives the request, have requested paper copies of the proxy materials only for the meeting to which the solicitation relates.

(iii) All security holder list information shall be in the form requested by the security holder to the extent that such form is available to the registrant without undue burden or expense. The registrant shall furnish the security holder with updated record holder information on a daily basis or, if not available on a daily basis, at the shortest reasonable intervals; provided, however, the registrant need not provide beneficial or record holder information more current than the record date for the meeting or action.

(b) (1) The requesting security holder shall have the options set forth in paragraph (a) (2) of this section, and the registrant shall have corresponding obligations, if the registrant or general partner or sponsor is soliciting or intends to solicit with respect to:

(i) A proposal that is subject to § 240.13e-3;

(ii) A roll-up transaction as defined in Item 901 (c) of Regulation S-K (§ 229.901 (c) of this chapter) that involves an entity with securities registered pursuant to Section 12 of the Act (15 U.S.C. 78*l*); or

(iii) A roll-up transaction as defined in Item 901 (c) of Regulation S-K (§ 229.901 (c) of this chapter) that involves a limited partnership, unless the transaction involves only:

(A) Partnership whose investors will receive new securities or securities in another entity that are not reported under a transaction reporting plan declared effective before December 17, 1993 by the Commission under Section 11A of the Act (15 U.S.C. 78k-1); or

(B) Partnerships whose investors' securities are reported under a transaction reporting plan declared effective before December 17, 1993 by the Commission under Section 11A of the Act (15 U.S.C. 78k-1).

(2) With respect to all other requests pursuant to this section, the registrant shall have the option to either mail the security holder's material or furnish the security holder list as set forth in this section.

(c) At the time of a list request, the security holder making the request shall:

(1) if holding the registrant's securities through a nominee, provide the registrant with a statement by the nominee or other independent third party, or a copy of a current filing made with the Commission and furnished to the registrant, confirming such holder's beneficial ownership; and

(2) provide the registrant with an affidavit, declaration, affirmation or other similar document provided for under applicable state law identifying the proposal or other corporate action that will be the subject of the security holder's solicitation or communication and attesting that:

(i) the security holder will not use the list information for any purpose other than to solicit security holders with respect to the same meeting or action by consent or authorization for which the registrant is soliciting or intends to solicit or to communicate with security holders with respect to a solicitation commenced by the registrant; and

(ii) the security holder will not disclose such information to any person other than a beneficial owner for whom the request was made and an employee or agent to the extent necessary to effectuate the communication or solicitation.

(d) The security holder shall not use the information furnished by the registrant pursuant to paragraph (a) (2) (ii) of this section for any purpose other than to solicit security holders with respect to the same meeting or action by consent or authorization for which the registrant is soliciting or intends to solicit or to communicate with security holders with respect to a solicitation commenced by the registrant; or disclose such information to any person other than an employee, agent, or beneficial owner for whom a request was made to the extent necessary to effectuate the communication or solicitation. The security holder shall return the information provided pursuant to paragraph (a) (2) (ii) of this section and shall not retain any copies thereof or of any information derived from such information after the termination of the solicitation.

(e) The security holder shall reimburse the reasonable expenses incurred by the registrant in performing the acts requested pursuant to paragraph (a) of this section.

Note 1 to § 240.14a-7. Reasonably prompt methods of distribution to security holders may be used instead of mailing. If an alternative distribution method is chosen, the costs of that method should be considered where necessary rather than the costs of mailing.

Note 2 to § 240.14a-7. When providing the information required by Exchange Act Rule 14a-7(a)(1)(ii), if the registrant has received affirmative written or implied consent to delivery of a single copy of proxy materials to a shared address in accordance with Exchange Act Rule 14a-3(e)(1), it shall exclude from the number of record holders those to whom it does not have to deliver a separate proxy statement.

Rule 14a-8. Shareholder Proposals

This section addresses when a company must include a shareholder's proposal in its proxy statement and identify the proposal in its form of proxy when the company holds an annual or special meeting of shareholders. In summary, in order to have your shareholder proposal included on a company's proxy card, and included along with any supporting statement in its proxy statement, you must be eligible and follow certain procedures. Under a few specific circumstances, the company is permitted to exclude your proposal, but only after submitting its reasons to the Commission. We structured this section in a question-and-answer format so that it is easier to understand. The references to "you" are to a shareholder seeking to submit the proposal.

(a) **Question 1: What is a proposal?**

A shareholder proposal is your recommendation or requirement that the company and/or its board of directors take action, which you intend to present at a meeting of the company's shareholders. Your proposal should state as clearly as possible the course of action that you believe the company should follow. If your proposal is placed on the company's proxy card, the company must also provide in the form of proxy means for shareholders to specify by boxes a choice between approval or disapproval, or abstention. Unless otherwise indicated, the word "proposal" as used in this section refers both to your proposal, and to your corresponding statement in support of your proposal (if any).

(b) **Question 2: Who is eligible to submit a proposal, and how do I demonstrate to the company that I am eligible?**

(1) In order to be eligible to submit a proposal, you must have continuously held at least $2,000 in market value, or 1%, of the company's securities entitled to be voted on the proposal at the meeting for at least one year by the date you submit the proposal. You must continue to hold those securities through the date of the meeting.

(2) If you are the registered holder of your securities, which means that your name appears in the company's records as a shareholder, the company can verify your eligibility on its own, although you will still have to provide the company with a written statement that you intend to continue to hold the securities through the date of the meeting of shareholders. However, if like many shareholders you are not a registered holder, the company likely does not know that you are a shareholder, or how many shares you own. In this case, at the time you submit your proposal, you must prove your eligibility to the company in one of two ways:

(i) The first way is to submit to the company a written statement from the "record" holder of your securities (usually a broker or bank) verifying that, at the time you submitted your proposal, you continuously held the securities for at least one year. You must also include your own written statement that you intend to continue to hold the securities through the date of the meeting of shareholders; or

(ii) The second way to prove ownership applies only if you have filed a Schedule 13D (§ 240.13d-101), Schedule 13G (§ 240.13d-102), Form 3 (§ 249.103 of this chapter), Form 4 (§ 249.104 of this chapter) and/or Form 5 (§ 249.105 of this chapter), or amendments to those documents or updated forms, reflecting your ownership of the shares as of or before the date on which the one-year eligibility period begins. If you have filed one of these documents with the SEC, you may demonstrate your eligibility by submitting to the company:

(A) A copy of the schedule and/or form, and any subsequent amendments reporting a change in your ownership level;

(B) Your written statement that you continuously held the required number of shares for the one-year period as of the date of the statement; and

(C) Your written statement that you intend to continue ownership of the shares through the date of the company's annual or special meeting.

(c) **Question 3: How many proposals may I submit?**

Each shareholder may submit no more than one proposal to a company for a particular shareholders' meeting.

(d) **Question 4: How long can my proposal be?**

The proposal, including any accompanying supporting statement, may not exceed 500 words.

(e) **Question 5: What is the deadline for submitting a proposal?**

(1) If you are submitting your proposal for the company's annual meeting, you can in most cases find the deadline in last year's proxy statement. However, if the company did not hold an annual meeting last year, or has changed the date of its meeting for this year more than 30 days from last year's meeting, you can usually find the deadline in one of the company's quarterly reports on Form 10-Q (§ 249.308a of this chapter) or in shareholder reports of investment companies under § 270.30d-1 of this chapter of the Investment Company Act of 1940. In order to avoid controversy, shareholders should submit their proposals by means, including electronic means, that permit them to prove the date of delivery.

(2) The deadline is calculated in the following manner if the proposal is submitted for a regularly scheduled annual meeting. The proposal must be received at the company's principal executive offices not less than 120 calendar days before the date of the company's proxy statement released to shareholders in connection with the previous year's annual meeting. However, if the company did not hold an annual meeting the previous year, or if the date of this year's annual meeting has been changed by more than 30 days from the date of the previous year's meeting, then the deadline is a reasonable time before the company begins to print and send its proxy materials.

(3) If you are submitting your proposal for a meeting of shareholders other than a regularly scheduled annual meeting, the deadline is a reasonable time before the company begins to print and send its proxy materials.

(f) **Question 6: What if I fail to follow one of the eligibility or procedural requirements explained in answers to Questions 1 through 4 of this section?**

(1) The company may exclude your proposal, but only after it has notified you of the problem, and you have failed adequately to correct it. Within 14 calendar days of receiving your proposal, the company must notify you in writing of any procedural or eligibility deficiencies, as well as of the time frame for your response. Your response must be postmarked, or transmitted electronically, no later than 14 days from the date you received the company's notification. A company need not provide you such notice of a deficiency if the deficiency cannot be remedied, such as if you fail to submit a proposal by the company's properly determined deadline. If the company intends to exclude the proposal, it will later have to make a submission under § 240.14a-8 and provide you with a copy under Question 10 below, § 240.14a-8(j).

(2) If you fail in your promise to hold the required number of securities through the date of the meeting of shareholders, then the company will be permitted to exclude all of your proposals from its proxy materials for any meeting held in the following two calendar years.

(g) **Question 7: Who has the burden of persuading the Commission or its staff that my proposal can be excluded?**

Except as otherwise noted, the burden is on the company to demonstrate that it is entitled to exclude a proposal.

(h) **Question 8: Must I appear personally at the shareholders' meeting to present the proposal?**

(1) Either you, or your representative who is qualified under state law to present the proposal on your behalf, must attend the meeting to present the proposal. Whether you

attend the meeting yourself or send a qualified representative to the meeting in your place, you should make sure that you, or your representative, follow the proper state law procedures for attending the meeting and/or presenting your proposal.

(2) If the company holds its shareholder meeting in whole or in part via electronic media, and the company permits you or your representative to present your proposal via such media, then you may appear through electronic media rather than traveling to the meeting to appear in person.

(3) If you or your qualified representative fail to appear and present the proposal, without good cause, the company will be permitted to exclude all of your proposals from its proxy materials for any meetings held in the following two calendar years.

(i) **Question 9: If I have complied with the procedural requirements, on what other bases may a company rely to exclude my proposal?**

(1) *Improper under state law:* If the proposal is not a proper subject for action by shareholders under the laws of the jurisdiction of the company's organization;

Note to paragraph (i) (1): Depending on the subject matter, some proposals are not considered proper under state law if they would be binding on the company if approved by shareholders. In our experience, most proposals that are cast as recommendations or requests that the board of directors take specified action are proper under state law. Accordingly, we will assume that a proposal drafted as a recommendation or suggestion is proper unless the company demonstrates otherwise.

(2) *Violation of law:* If the proposal would, if implemented, cause the company to violate any state, federal, or foreign law to which it is subject;

Note to paragraph (i) (2): We will not apply this basis for exclusion to permit exclusion of a proposal on grounds that it would violate foreign law if compliance with the foreign law would result in a violation of any state or federal law.

(3) *Violation of proxy rules:* If the proposal or supporting statement is contrary to any of the Commission's proxy rules, including § 240.14a-9, which prohibits materially false or misleading statements in proxy soliciting materials;

(4) *Personal grievance; special interest:* If the proposal relates to the redress of a personal claim or grievance against the company or any other person, or if it is designed to result in a benefit to you, or to further a personal interest, which is not shared by the other shareholders at large;

(5) *Relevance:* If the proposal relates to operations which account for less than 5 percent of the company's total assets at the end of its most recent fiscal year, and for less than 5 percent of its net earnings and gross sales for its most recent fiscal year, and is not otherwise significantly related to the company's business;

(6) *Absence of power/authority:* If the company would lack the power or authority to implement the proposal;

(7) *Management functions:* If the proposal deals with a matter relating to the company's ordinary business operations;

(8) *Director Elections*: If the proposal:

(i) Would disqualify a nominee who is standing for election;

(ii) Would remove a director from office before his or her term expired;

(iii) Questions the competence, business judgment, or character of one or more nominees or directors;

(iv) Seeks to include a specific individual in the company's proxy materials for election to the board of directors; or

(v) Otherwise could affect the outcome of the upcoming election of directors.

(9) *Conflicts with company's proposal:* If the proposal directly conflicts with one of the company's own proposals to be submitted to shareholders at the same meeting;

Note to paragraph (i) (9): A company's submission to the Commission under this section should specify the points of conflict with the company's proposal.

(10) *Substantially implemented:* If the company has already substantially implemented the proposal

Note to Paragraph (i)(10): A company may exclude a shareholder proposal that would provide an advisory vote or seek future advisory votes to approve the compensation of executives as disclosed pursuant to Item 402 of Regulation S-K (§ 229.402 of this chapter) or any successor to Item 402 (a "say-on-pay vote") or that relates to the frequency of say-on-pay votes, provided that in the most recent shareholder vote required by § 240.14a-21(b) of this chapter a single year (i.e., one, two, or three years) received approval of a majority of votes cast on the matter and the company has adopted a policy on the frequency of say-on-pay votes that is consistent with the choice of the majority of votes cast in the most recent shareholder vote required by § 240.14a-21(b) of this chapter.

(11) *Duplication:* If the proposal substantially duplicates another proposal previously submitted to the company by another proponent that will be included in the company's proxy materials for the same meeting;

(12) *Resubmissions:* If the proposal deals with substantially the same subject matter as another proposal or proposals that has or have been previously included in the company's proxy materials within the preceding 5 calendar years, a company may exclude it from its proxy materials for any meeting held within 3 calendar years of the last time it was included if the proposal received:

(i) Less than 3% of the vote if proposed once within the preceding 5 calendar years;

(ii) Less than 6% of the vote on its last submission to shareholders if proposed twice previously within the preceding 5 calendar years; or

(iii) Less than 10% of the vote on its last submission to shareholders if proposed three times or more previously within the preceding 5 calendar years; and

(13) *Specific amount of dividends:* If the proposal relates to specific amounts of cash or stock dividends.

(j) **Question 10: What procedures must the company follow if it intends to exclude my proposal?**

(1) If the company intends to exclude a proposal from its proxy materials, it must file its reasons with the Commission no later than 80 calendar days before it files its definitive proxy statement and form of proxy with the Commission. The company must simultaneously provide you with a copy of its submission. The Commission staff may permit the company to make its submission later than 80 days before the company files its definitive proxy statement and form of proxy, if the company demonstrates good cause for missing the deadline.

(2) The company must file six paper copies of the following:

(i) The proposal;

(ii) An explanation of why the company believes that it may exclude the proposal, which should, if possible, refer to the most recent applicable authority, such as prior Division letters issued under the rule; and

(iii) A supporting opinion of counsel when such reasons are based on matters of state or foreign law.

(k) **Question 11: May I submit my own statement to the Commission responding to the company's arguments?**

Yes, you may submit a response, but it is not required. You should try to submit any response to us, with a copy to the company, as soon as possible after the company makes its submission. This way, the Commission staff will have time to consider fully your submission before it issues its response. You should submit six paper copies of your response.

(l) **Question 12: If the company includes my shareholder proposal in its proxy materials, what information about me must it include along with the proposal itself?**

(1) The company's proxy statement must include your name and address, as well as the number of the company's voting securities that you hold. However, instead of provid-

ing that information, the company may instead include a statement that it will provide the information to shareholders promptly upon receiving an oral or written request.

(2) The company is not responsible for the contents of your proposal or supporting statement.

(m) **Question 13: What can I do if the company includes in its proxy statement reasons why it believes shareholders should not vote in favor of my proposal, and I disagree with some of its statements?**

(1) The company may elect to include in its proxy statement reasons why it believes shareholders should vote against your proposal. The company is allowed to make arguments reflecting its own point of view, just as you may express your own point of view in your proposal's supporting statement.

(2) However, if you believe that the company's opposition to your proposal contains materially false or misleading statements that may violate our anti-fraud rule, § 240.14a-9, you should promptly send to the Commission staff and the company a letter explaining the reasons for your view, along with a copy of the company's statements opposing your proposal. To the extent possible, your letter should include specific factual information demonstrating the inaccuracy of the company's claims. Time permitting, you may wish to try to work out your differences with the company by yourself before contacting the Commission staff.

(3) We require the company to send you a copy of its statements opposing your proposal before it sends its proxy materials, so that you may bring to our attention any materially false or misleading statements, under the following timeframes:

(i) If our no-action response requires that you make revisions to your proposal or supporting statement as a condition to requiring the company to include it in its proxy materials, then the company must provide you with a copy of its opposition statements no later than 5 calendar days after the company receives a copy of your revised proposal; or

(ii) In all other cases, the company must provide you with a copy of its opposition statements no later than 30 calendar days before its files definitive copies of its proxy statement and form of proxy under § 240.14a-6.

Rule 14a-9. False or Misleading Statements

(a) No solicitation subject to this regulation shall be made by means of any proxy statement, form of proxy, notice of meeting or other communication, written or oral, containing any statement which, at the time and in the light of the circumstances under which it is made, is false or misleading with respect to any material fact, or which omits to state any material fact necessary in order to make the statements therein not false or misleading or necessary to correct any statement in any earlier communication with respect to the solicitation of a proxy for the same meeting or subject matter which has become false or misleading.

(b) The fact that a proxy statement, form of proxy or other soliciting material has been filed with or examined by the Commission shall not be deemed a finding by the Commission that such material is accurate or complete or not false or misleading, or that the Commission has passed upon the merits of or approved any statement contained therein or any matter to be acted upon by security holders. No representation contrary to the foregoing shall be made.

(c) No nominee, nominating shareholder or nominating shareholder group, or any member thereof, shall cause to be included in a registrant's proxy materials, either pursuant to the Federal proxy rules, an applicable state or foreign law provision, or a registrant's governing documents as they relate to including shareholder nominees for director in a registrant's proxy materials, include in a notice on Schedule 14N (§ 240.14n-101), or include in any other related communication, any statement which, at the time and in the light of the circumstances under which it is made, is false or misleading with respect to any material fact, or which omits to state any material fact necessary in order to make the statements therein not false or misleading or necessary to correct any statement in any earlier communication with respect to a solicitation for the same meeting or subject matter which has become false or misleading.

Note: The following are some examples of what, depending upon particular facts and circumstances, may be misleading within the meaning of this section.

a. Predictions as to specific future market values.

b. Material which directly or indirectly impugns character, integrity or personal reputation, or directly or indirectly makes charges concerning improper, illegal or immoral conduct or associations, without factual foundation.

c. Failure to so identify a proxy statement, form of proxy and other soliciting material as to clearly distinguish it from the soliciting material of any other person or persons soliciting for the same meeting or subject matter.

d. Claims made prior to a meeting regarding the results of a solicitation.

Rule 14a-10. Prohibition of Certain Solicitations

No person making a solicitation which is subject to §§ 240.14a-1 to 240.14a-10 shall solicit:

(a) any undated or post-dated proxy, or

(b) any proxy which provides that it shall be deemed to be dated as of any date subsequent to the date on which it is signed by the security holder.

Rule 14a-11. Shareholder Nominations [*Vacated.*]

Rule 14a-12. Solicitation Before Furnishing a Proxy Statement

(a) Notwithstanding the provisions of § 240.14a-3(a), a solicitation may be made before furnishing security holders with a proxy statement meeting the requirements of Reg. 240.14a-3(a) if:

(1) Each written communication includes:

(i) The identity of the participants in the solicitation (as defined in Instruction 3 to Item 4 of Schedule 14A (§ 240.14a-101)) and a description of their direct or indirect interests, by security holdings or otherwise, or a prominent legend in clear, plain language advising security holders where they can obtain that information; and

(ii) A prominent legend in clear, plain language advising security holders to read the proxy statement when it is available because it contains important information. The legend also must explain to investors that they can get the proxy statement, and any other relevant documents, for free at the Commission's web site and describe which documents are available free from the participants; and

(2) A definitive proxy statement meeting the requirements of § 240.14a-3(a) is sent or given to security holders solicited in reliance on this section before or at the same time as the forms of proxy, consent or authorization are furnished to or requested from security holders.

(b) Any soliciting material published, sent or given to security holders in accordance with paragraph (a) of this section must be filed with the Commission no later than the date the material is first published, sent or given to security holders. Three copies of the material must at the same time be filed with, or mailed for filing to, each national securities exchange upon which any class of securities of the registrant is listed and registered. The soliciting material must include a cover page in the form set forth in Schedule 14A (§ 240.14a-101) and the appropriate box on the cover page must be marked. Soliciting material in connection with a registered offering is required to be filed only under § 230.424 or § 230.425 of this chapter, and will be deemed filed under this section.

(c) Solicitations by any person or group of persons for the purpose of opposing a solicitation subject to this regulation by any other person or group of persons with respect to the election or removal of directors at any annual or special meeting of security holders also are subject to the following provisions:

(1) *Application of this rule to annual report to security holders.* Notwithstanding the provisions of § 240.14a-3(b) and (c), any portion of the annual report to security holders referred to in § 240.14a-3(b) that comments upon or refers to any solicitation subject to this rule, or to any participant in the solicitation, other than the solicitation by the management, must be filed with the Commission as proxy material subject to this regulation. This must be filed in electronic format unless an exemption is available under Rules 201 or 202 of Regulation S-T (§ 232.201 or § 232.202 of this chapter).

(2) *Use of reprints or reproductions.* In any solicitation subject to this § 240.14a-12(c), soliciting material that includes, in whole or part, any reprints or reproductions of any previously published material must:

(i) State the name of the author and publication, the date of prior publication, and identify any person who is quoted without being named in the previously published material.

(ii) Except in the case of a public or official document or statement, state whether or not the consent of the author and publication has been obtained to the use of the previously published material as proxy soliciting material.

(iii) If any participant using the previously published material, or anyone on his or her behalf, paid, directly or indirectly, for the preparation or prior publication of the previously published material, or has made or proposes to make any payments or give any other consideration in connection with the publication or republication of the material, state the circumstances.

Instruction 1 to § 240.14a-12. If paper filing is permitted, file eight copies of the soliciting material with the Commission, except that only three copies of the material specified by § 240.14a-12(c)(1) need be filed.

Instruction 2 to § 240.14a-12. Any communications made under this section after the definitive proxy statement is on file but before it is disseminated also must specify that the proxy statement is publicly available and the anticipated date of dissemination.

Instruction 3 to § 240.14a-12. Inclusion of a nominee pursuant to § 240.14a-11, an applicable state or foreign law provision, or a registrant's governing documents as they relate to the inclusion of shareholder director nominees in the registrant's proxy materials, or solicitations by a nominating shareholder or nominating shareholder group that are made in connection with that nomination constitute solicitations in opposition subject to § 240.14a-12(c), except for purposes of § 240.14a-6(a).

Rule 14a-13. Obligation of Registrants in Communicating with Beneficial Owners

(a) If the registrant knows that securities of any class entitled to vote at a meeting (or by written consents or authorizations if no meeting is held) with respect to which the registrant intends to solicit proxies, consents or authorizations are held of record by a broker, dealer, voting trustee, bank, association, or other entity that exercises fiduciary powers in nominee name or otherwise, the registrant shall:

(1) By first class mail or other equally prompt means: (i) inquire of each such record holder: (A) whether other persons are the beneficial owners of such securities and if so, the number of copies of the proxy and other soliciting material necessary to supply such material to such beneficial owners; (B) in the case of an annual (or special meeting in lieu of the annual) meeting, or written consents in lieu of such meeting, at which directors are to be elected, the number of copies of the annual report to security holders necessary to supply such report to beneficial owners to whom such reports are to be distributed by such record holder or its nominee and not by the registrant; and (C) if the record holder has an obligation under § 240.14b-1(b)(3) or § 240.14b-2(b)(4)(ii) and (iii), whether an agent has been designated to act on its behalf in fulfilling such obligation and, if so, the name and address of such agent; and (D) whether it holds the registrant's securities on behalf of any respondent bank and, if so, the name and address of each such respondent bank; and (ii) indicate to each such record holder: (A) whether the registrant, pursuant to paragraph (c) of this section, intends

to distribute the annual report to security holders to beneficial owners of its securities whose names, addresses and securities positions are disclosed pursuant to §240.14b-1(c) and §240.14b-2(e)(2) and (3); (B) the record date; and (C) at the option of the registrant, any employee benefit plan established by an affiliate of the registrant that holds securities of the registrant that the registrant elects to treat as exempt employee benefit plan securities;

(2) Upon receipt of a record holder's or respondent bank's response indicating, pursuant to §240.14b-2(b)(1)(i), the names and addresses of its respondent banks, within one business day after the date such response is received, make an inquiry of and give notification to each such respondent bank in the same manner required by paragraph (a)(1) of this section; *Provided, however,* the inquiry required by paragraphs (a)(1) and (a)(2) of this section shall not cover beneficial owners of exempt employee benefit plan securities;

(3) Make the inquiry required by paragraph (a)(1) of this section at least 20 business days prior to the record date of the meeting of security holders, or (i) if such inquiry is impracticable 20 business days prior to the record date of a special meeting, as many days before the record date of such meeting as is practicable or, (ii) if consents or authorizations are solicited, and such inquiry is impracticable 20 business days before the earliest date on which they may be used to effect corporate action, as many days before that date as is practicable, or (iii) at such later time as the rules of a national securities exchange on which the class of securities in question is listed may permit for good cause shown; *Provided, however,* that if a record holder or respondent bank has informed the registrant that a designated office(s) or department(s) is to receive such inquiries, the inquiry shall be made to such designated office(s) or department(s); and

(4) Supply, in a timely manner, each record holder and respondent bank of whom the inquiries required by paragraphs (a)(1) and (a)(2) of this section are made with copies of the proxy, other proxy soliciting material, and/or the annual report to security holders, in such quantities, assembled in such form and at such place(s), as the record holder or respondent bank may reasonably request in order to send such material to each beneficial owner of securities who is to be furnished with such material by the record holder or respondent bank; and

(5) Upon the request of any record holder or respondent bank that is supplied with proxy soliciting material and/or annual reports to security holders pursuant to paragraph (a)(4) of this section, pay its reasonable expenses for completing the sending of such material to beneficial owners.

Note 1.—If the registrant's list of security holders indicates that some of its securities are registered in the name of a clearing agency registered pursuant to section 17A of the Act (*e.g.,* "Cede & Co.," nominee for the Depository Trust Company), the registrant shall make appropriate inquiry of the clearing agency and thereafter of the participants in such clearing agency who may hold on behalf of a beneficial owner or respondent bank, and shall comply with the above paragraph with respect to any such participant (see §240.14a-1(i)).

Note 2.—The attention of registrants is called to the fact that each broker, dealer, bank, association, and other entity that exercises fiduciary powers has an obligation pursuant to §240.14b-1 and §240.14b-2 (except as provided therein with respect to exempt employee benefit plan securities held in nominee name) and, with respect to brokers and dealers, applicable self-regulatory organization requirements to obtain and forward, within the time periods prescribed therein, (a) proxies (or in lieu thereof requests for voting instructions) and proxy soliciting materials to beneficial owners on whose behalf it holds securities, and (b) annual reports to security holders to beneficial owners on whose behalf it holds securities, unless the registrant has notified the record holder or respondent bank that it has assumed responsibility to send such material to beneficial owners whose names, addresses, and securities positions are disclosed pursuant to §240.14b-1(b)(3) and §240.14b-2(b)(4)(ii) and (iii).

Note 3.—The attention of registrants is called to the fact that registrants have an obligation, pursuant to paragraph (d) of this section, to cause proxies (or in lieu thereof requests for voting instructions), proxy soliciting material and annual reports to security holders to be furnished, in a timely manner, to beneficial owners of exempt employee benefit plan securities.

(b) Any registrant requesting pursuant to §240.14b-1(c) and §240.14b-2(e)(2) and (3) a list of names, addresses and securities positions of beneficial owners of its securities who either have consented or have not objected to disclosure of such information shall:

(1) By first class mail or other equally prompt means, inquire of each record holder and each respondent bank identified to the registrant pursuant to §240.14b-2(b)(4)(i) whether such record holder or respondent bank holds the registrant's securities on behalf of any respondent banks and, if so, the name and address of each such respondent bank.

(2) Request such list to be compiled as of a date no earlier than five business days after the date the registrant's request is received by the record holder or respondent bank; *Provided, however,* that if the record holder or respondent bank has informed the registrant that a designated office(s) or department(s) is to receive such requests, the request shall be made to such designated office(s) or department(s);

(3) Make such request to the following persons that hold the registrant's securities on behalf of beneficial owners: all brokers, dealers, banks, associations and other entities that exercise fiduciary powers; *Provided, however,* such request shall not cover beneficial owners of exempt employee benefit plan securities as defined in §240.14a-1(d)(1); and, at the option of the registrant, such request may give notice of any employee benefit plan established by an affiliate of the registrant that holds securities of the registrant that the registrant elects to treat as exempt employee benefit plan securities;

(4) Use the information furnished in response to such request exclusively for purposes of corporate communications; and

(5) Upon the request of any record holder or respondent bank to whom such request is made, pay the reasonable expenses, both direct and indirect, of providing beneficial owner information.

Note.—A registrant will be deemed to have satisfied its obligations under paragraph (b) of this section by requesting consenting and non-objecting beneficial owner lists from a designated agent acting on behalf of the record holder or respondent bank and paying to that designated agent the reasonable expenses of providing the beneficial owner information.

(c) A registrant, at its option, may send its annual report to security holders to the beneficial owners whose identifying information is provided by record holders and respondent banks, pursuant to §240.14b-1(c) and §240.14b-2(e)(2) and (3), provided that such registrant notifies the record holders and respondent banks, at the time it makes the inquiry required by paragraph (a) of this section, that the registrant will send the annual report to security holders to the beneficial owners so identified.

(d) If a registrant solicits proxies, consents or authorizations from record holders and respondent banks who hold securities on behalf of beneficial owners, the registrant shall cause proxies (or in lieu thereof requests for voting instructions), proxy soliciting material and annual reports to security holders to be furnished, in a timely manner, to beneficial owners of exempt employee benefit plan securities.

Rule 14a-16. Internet Availability of Proxy Materials.

(a)(1) A registrant shall furnish a proxy statement pursuant to §240.14a-3(a), or an annual report to security holders pursuant to §240.14a-3(b), to a security holder by sending the security holder a Notice of Internet Availability of Proxy Materials, as described in this section, 40 calendar days or more prior to the security holder meeting date, or if no meeting is to be held, 40 calendar days or more prior to the date the votes, consents or authorizations may be used to effect the corporate action, and complying with all other requirements of this section.

(2) Unless the registrant chooses to follow the full set delivery option set forth in paragraph (n) of this section, it must provide the record holder or respondent bank with all information listed in paragraph (d) of this section in sufficient time for the record holder or respondent bank to prepare, print and send a Notice of Internet Availability of Proxy Materials to beneficial owners at least 40 calendar days before the meeting date.

(b) (1) All materials identified in the Notice of Internet Availability of Proxy Materials must be publicly accessible, free of charge, at the Web site address specified in the notice on or before the time that the notice is sent to the security holder and such materials must remain available on that Web site through the conclusion of the meeting of security holders.

(2) All additional soliciting materials sent to security holders or made public after the Notice of Internet Availability of Proxy Materials has been sent must be made publicly accessible at the specified Web site address no later than the day on which such materials are first sent to security holders or made public.

(3) The Web site address relied upon for compliance under this section may not be the address of the Commission's electronic filing system.

(4) The registrant must provide security holders with a means to execute a proxy as of the time the Notice of Internet Availability of Proxy Materials is first sent to security holders.

(c) The materials must be presented on the Web site in a format, or formats, convenient for both reading online and printing on paper.

(d) The Notice of Internet Availability of Proxy Materials must contain the following:

(1) A prominent legend in bold-face type that states **"Important Notice Regarding the Availability of Proxy Materials for the Shareholder Meeting to Be Held on [insert meeting date]"**;

(2) An indication that the communication is not a form for voting and presents only an overview of the more complete proxy materials, which contain important information and are available on the Internet or by mail, and encouraging a security holder to access and review the proxy materials before voting;

(3) The Internet Web site address where the proxy materials are available;

(4) Instructions regarding how a security holder may request a paper or email copy of the proxy materials at no charge, including the date by which they should make the request to facilitate timely delivery, and an indication that they will not otherwise receive a paper or email copy;

(5) The date, time, and location of the meeting, or if corporate action is to be taken by written consent, the earliest date on which the corporate action may be effected;

(6) A clear and impartial identification of each separate matter intended to be acted on and the soliciting person's recommendations, if any, regarding those matters, but no supporting statements;

(7) A list of the materials being made available at the specified Web site;

(8) A toll-free telephone number, an e-mail address, and an Internet Web site where the security holder can request a copy of the proxy statement, annual report to security holders, and form of proxy, relating to all of the registrant's future security holder meetings and for the particular meeting to which the proxy materials being furnished relate;

(9) Any control/identification numbers that the security holder needs to access his or her form of proxy;

(10) Instructions on how to access the form of proxy, provided that such instructions do not enable a security holder to execute a proxy without having access to the proxy statement and, if required by § 240.14a-3(b), the annual report to security holders; and

(11) Information on how to obtain directions to be able to attend the meeting and vote in person.

(e) (1) The Notice of Internet Availability of Proxy Materials may not be incorporated into, or combined with, another document, except that it may be incorporated into, or combined with, a notice of security holder meeting required under state law, unless state law prohibits such incorporation or combination.

(2) The Notice of Internet Availability of Proxy Materials may contain only the information required by paragraph (d) of this section and any additional information required to be included in a notice of security holders meeting under state law; provided that:

(i) The registrant must revise the information on the Notice of Internet Availability of Proxy Materials, including any title to the document, to reflect the fact that:

(A) The registrant is conducting a consent solicitation rather than a proxy solicitation; or

(B) The registrant is not soliciting proxy or consent authority, but is furnishing an information statement pursuant to § 240.14c-2; and

(ii) The registrant may include a statement on the Notice to educate security holders that no personal information other than the identification or control number is necessary to execute a proxy.

(f) (1) Except as provided in paragraph (h) of this section, the Notice of Internet Availability of Proxy Materials must be sent separately from other types of security holder communications and may not accompany any other document or materials, including the form of proxy.

(2) Notwithstanding paragraph (f) (1) of this section, the registrant may accompany the Notice of Internet Availability of Proxy Materials with:

(i) A pre-addressed, postage-paid reply card for requesting a copy of the proxy materials;

(ii) A copy of any notice of security holder meeting required under state law if that notice is not combined with the Notice of Internet Availability of Proxy Materials;

(iii) In the case of an investment company registered under the Investment Company Act of 1940, the company's prospectus, a summary prospectus that satisfies the requirements of § 230.498(b), § 230.498A(b) or (c) of this chapter, a Notice under § 270.30e-3 of this chapter, or a report that is required to be transmitted to stockholders by section 30(e) of the Investment Company Act (15 U.S.C. 80a-29(e)) and its implementing regulations (*e.g.*, § § 270.30e-1 and 270.30e-2 of this chapter); and

(iv) An explanation of the reasons for a registrant's use of the rules detailed in this section and the process of receiving and reviewing the proxy materials and voting as detailed in this section.

(g) *Plain English.*

(1) To enhance the readability of the Notice of Internet Availability of Proxy Materials, the registrant must use plain English principles in the organization, language, and design of the notice.

(2) The registrant must draft the language in the Notice of Internet Availability of Proxy Materials so that, at a minimum, it substantially complies with each of the following plain English writing principles:

(i) Short sentences;

(ii) Definite, concrete, everyday words;

(iii) Active voice;

(iv) Tabular presentation or bullet lists for complex material, whenever possible;

(v) No legal jargon or highly technical business terms; and

(vi) No multiple negatives.

(3) In designing the Notice of Internet Availability of Proxy Materials, the registrant may include pictures, logos, or similar design elements so long as the design is not misleading and the required information is clear.

(h) The registrant may send a form of proxy to security holders if:

(1) At least 10 calendar days or more have passed since the date it first sent the Notice of Internet Availability of Proxy Materials to security holders and the form of proxy is accompanied by a copy of the Notice of Internet Availability of Proxy Materials; or

(2) The form of proxy is accompanied or preceded by a copy, via the same medium, of the proxy statement and any annual report to security holders that is required by § 240.14a-3(b).

(i) The registrant must file a form of the Notice of Internet Availability of Proxy Materials with the Commission pursuant to § 240.14a-6(b) no later than the date that the registrant first sends the notice to security holders.

(j) *Obligation to Provide Copies.*

(1) The registrant must send, at no cost to the record holder or respondent bank and by U.S. first class mail or other reasonably prompt means, a paper copy of the proxy statement, information statement, annual report to security holders, and form of proxy (to the extent each of those documents is applicable) to any record holder or respondent bank requesting such a copy within three business days after receiving a request for a paper copy.

(2) The registrant must send, at no cost to the record holder or respondent bank and via e-mail, an electronic copy of the proxy statement, information statement, annual report to security holders, and form of proxy (to the extent each of those documents is applicable) to any record holder or respondent bank requesting such a copy within three business days after receiving a request for an electronic copy via e-mail.

(3) The registrant must provide copies of the proxy materials for one year after the conclusion of the meeting or corporate action to which the proxy materials relate, provided that, if the registrant receives the request after the conclusion of the meeting or corporate action to which the proxy materials relate, the registrant need not send copies via First Class mail and need not respond to such request within three business days.

(4) The registrant must maintain records of security holder requests to receive materials in paper or via e-mail for future solicitations and must continue to provide copies of the materials to a security holder who has made such a request until the security holder revokes such request.

(k) *Security Holder Information.*

(1) A registrant or its agent shall maintain the Internet Web site on which it posts its proxy materials in a manner that does not infringe on the anonymity of a person accessing such Web site.

(2) The registrant and its agents shall not use any e-mail address obtained from a security holder solely for the purpose of requesting a copy of proxy materials pursuant to paragraph (j) for any purpose other than to send a copy of those materials to that security holder. The registrant shall not disclose such information to any person other than an employee or agent to the extent necessary to send a copy of the proxy materials pursuant to paragraph (j).

(l) A person other than the registrant may solicit proxies pursuant to the conditions imposed on registrants by this section, provided that:

(1) A soliciting person other than the registrant is required to provide copies of its proxy materials only to security holders to whom it has sent a Notice of Internet Availability of Proxy Materials; and

(2) A soliciting person other than the registrant must send its Notice of Internet Availability of Proxy Materials by the later of:

(i) 40 calendar days prior to the security holder meeting date or, if no meeting is to be held, 40 calendar days prior to the date the votes, consents, or authorizations may be used to effect the corporate action; or

(ii) The date on which it files its definitive proxy statement with the Commission, provided its preliminary proxy statement is filed no later than 10 calendar days after the date that the registrant files its definitive proxy statement.

(3) *Content of the Soliciting Person's Notice of Internet Availability of Proxy Materials.*

(i) If, at the time a soliciting person other than the registrant sends its Notice of Internet Availability of Proxy Materials, the soliciting person is not aware of all matters on the registrant's agenda for the meeting of security holders, the soliciting person's Notice on Internet Availability of Proxy Materials must provide a clear and impartial identification of each separate matter on the agenda to the extent known by the soliciting person at that time. The soliciting person's notice also must include a clear statement indicating that there may be additional agenda items of which the soliciting person is not aware and that the security holder cannot direct a vote for those items on the soliciting person's proxy card provided at that time.

(ii) If a soliciting person other than the registrant sends a form of proxy not containing all matters intended to be acted upon, the Notice of Internet Availability of Proxy Materials must clearly state whether execution of the form of proxy will invalidate a security holder's prior vote on matters not presented on the form of proxy.

(m) This section shall not apply to a proxy solicitation in connection with a business combination transaction, as defined in § 230.165 of this chapter.

(n) *Full Set Delivery Option.*

(1) For purposes of this paragraph (n), the term full set of proxy materials shall include all of the following documents:

(i) A copy of the proxy statement;

(ii) A copy of the annual report to security holders if required by § 240.14a-3(b); and

(iii) A form of proxy.

(2) Notwithstanding paragraphs (e) and (f)(2) of this section, a registrant or other soliciting person may:

(i) Accompany the Notice of Internet Availability of Proxy Materials with a full set of proxy materials; or

(ii) Send a full set of proxy materials without a Notice of Internet Availability of Proxy Materials if all of the information required in a Notice of Internet Availability of Proxy Materials pursuant to paragraphs (d) and (n)(4) is incorporated in the proxy statement and the form of proxy.

(3) A registrant or other soliciting person that sends a full set of proxy materials to a security holder pursuant to this paragraph (n) need not comply with

(i) The timing provisions of paragraphs (a) and (l)(2); and

(ii) The obligation to provide copies pursuant to paragraph (j).

(4) A registrant or other soliciting person that sends a full set of proxy materials to a security holder pursuant to this paragraph (n) need not include in its Notice of Internet Availability of Proxy Materials, proxy statement, or form of proxy the following disclosures:

(i) Instructions regarding the nature of the communication pursuant to paragraph (d)(2) of this section;

(ii) Instructions on how to request a copy of the proxy materials; and

(iii) Instructions on how to access the form of proxy pursuant to paragraph (d)(10).

Rule 14a-17. Electronic Shareholder Forums.

(a) A shareholder, registrant, or third party acting on behalf of a shareholder or registrant may establish, maintain, or operate an electronic shareholder forum to facilitate interaction among the registrant's shareholders and between the registrant and its shareholders as the shareholder or registrant deems appropriate. Subject to paragraphs (b) and (c) of this section, the forum must comply with the federal securities laws, including Section 14(a) of the Act and its associated regulations, other applicable federal laws, applicable state laws, and the registrant's governing documents.

(b) No shareholder, registrant, or third party acting on behalf of a shareholder or registrant, by reason of establishing, maintaining, or operating an electronic shareholder forum, will be liable under the federal securities laws for any statement or information provided by another person to the electronic shareholder forum. Nothing in this section prevents or alters the application of the federal securities laws, including the provisions for liability for fraud, deception, or manipulation, or other applicable federal and state laws to the person or persons that provide a statement or information to an electronic shareholder forum.

(c) Reliance on the exemption in § 240.14a-2(b)(6) to participate in an electronic share-holder forum does not eliminate a person's eligibility to solicit proxies after the date that the exemption in § 240.14a-2(b)(6) is no longer available, or is no longer being relied upon, provided that any such solicitation is conducted in accordance with this regulation.

Rule 14a-21. Shareholder Approval of Executive Compensation, Frequency of Votes For Approval of Executive Compensation and Shareholder Approval of Golden Parachute Compensation.

(a) If a solicitation is made by a registrant, other than an emerging growth company as defined in Rule 12b-2 (§ 240.12b-2), and the solicitation relates to an annual or other meeting of shareholders at which directors will be elected and for which the rules of the Commission require executive compensation disclosure pursuant to Item 402 of Regulation S-K (§ 229.402 of this chapter), the registrant shall, for the first annual or other meeting of shareholders on or after January 21, 2011, or for the first annual or other meeting of shareholders on or after January 21, 2013 if the registrant is a smaller reporting company, and thereafter no later than the annual or other meeting of shareholders held in the third calendar year after the imme-diately preceding vote under this subsection, include a separate resolution subject to share-holder advisory vote to approve the compensation of its named executive officers, as disclosed pursuant to Item 402 of Regulation S-K.

Instruction to Paragraph (a): The registrant's resolution shall indicate that the shareholder advisory vote under this subsection is to approve the compensation of the registrant's named executive officers as disclosed pursuant to Item 402 of Regulation S-K (§ 229.402 of this chapter). The following is a non-exclusive example of a resolution that would satisfy the requirements of this subsection: "RESOLVED, that the compensation paid to the company's named executive officers, as disclosed pursuant to Item 402 of Regulation S-K, including the Compensation Discussion and Analysis, compensation tables and narrative discussion is hereby APPROVED."

(b) If a solicitation is made by a registrant, other than an emerging growth company as defined in Rule 12b-2 (§ 240.12b-2), and the solicitation relates to an annual or other meeting of shareholders at which directors will be elected and for which the rules of the Commission require executive compensation disclosure pursuant to Item 402 of Regulation S-K (§ 229.402 of this chapter), the registrant shall, for the first annual or other meeting of shareholders on or after January 21, 2011, or for the first annual or other meeting of shareholders on or after January 21, 2013 if the registrant is a smaller reporting company, and thereafter no later than the annual or other meeting of shareholders held in the sixth calendar year after the imme-diately preceding vote under this subsection, include a separate resolution subject to share-holder advisory vote as to whether the shareholder vote required by paragraph (a) of this section should occur every 1, 2 or 3 years. Registrants required to provide a separate share-holder vote pursuant to § 240.14a-20 of this chapter shall include the separate resolution required by this section for the first annual or other meeting of shareholders after the regis-trant has repaid all obligations arising from financial assistance provided under the TARP, as defined in section 3(8) of the Emergency Economic Stabilization Act of 2008 (12 U.S.C. 5202(8)), and thereafter no later than the annual or other meeting of shareholders held in the sixth calendar year after the immediately preceding vote under this subsection.

(c) If a solicitation is made by a registrant, other than an emerging growth company as defined in Rule 12b-2 (§ 240.12b-2), for a meeting of shareholders at which shareholders are asked to approve an acquisition, merger, consolidation or proposed sale or other disposition of all or substantially all the assets of the registrant, the registrant shall include a separate resolution subject to shareholder advisory vote to approve any agreements or understandings and compensation disclosed pursuant to Item 402(t) of Regulation S-K (§ 229.402(t) of this chapter), unless such agreements or understandings have been subject to a shareholder advisory vote under paragraph (a) of this section. Consistent with section 14A(b) of the Exchange Act (15 U.S.C. 78n-1(b)), any agreements or understandings between an acquiring company and the named executive officers of the registrant, where the registrant is not the acquiring company, are not required to be subject to the separate shareholder advisory vote under this paragraph.

Instructions to § 240.14a-21:

1. Disclosure relating to the compensation of directors required by Item 402(k) (§ 229.402(k) of this chapter) and Item 402(r) of Regulation S-K (§ 229.402(r) of this chapter) is not subject to the shareholder vote required by paragraph (a) of this section. If a registrant includes disclosure pursuant to Item 402(s) of Regulation S-K (§ 229.402(s) of this chapter) about the registrant's compensation policies and practices as they relate to risk management and risk-taking incentives, these policies and practices would not be subject to the shareholder vote required by paragraph (a) of this section. To the extent that risk considerations are a material aspect of the registrant's compensation policies or decisions for named executive officers, the registrant is required to discuss them as part of its Compensation Discussion and Analysis under § 229.402(b) of this chapter, and therefore such disclosure would be considered by shareholders when voting on executive compensation.

2. If a registrant includes disclosure of golden parachute compensation arrangements pursuant to Item 402(t) (§ 229.402(t) of this chapter) in an annual meeting proxy statement, such disclosure would be subject to the shareholder advisory vote required by paragraph (a) of this section.

3. Registrants that are smaller reporting companies entitled to provide scaled disclosure in accordance with Item 402(l) of Regulation S-K (§ 229.402(l) of this chapter) are not required to include a Compensation Discussion and Analysis in their proxy statements in order to comply with this section. For smaller reporting companies, the vote required by paragraph (a) of this section must be to approve the compensation of the named executive officers as disclosed pursuant to Item 402(m) through (q) of Regulation S-K (§ 229.402(m) through (q) of this chapter).

4. A registrant that has ceased being an emerging growth company shall include the first separate resolution described under § 240.14a-21(a) not later than the end of (i) in the case of a registrant that was an emerging growth company for less than two years after the date of first sale of common equity securities of the registrant pursuant to an effective registration statement under the Securities Act of 1933 (15 U.S.C 77a *et seq*.), the three-year period beginning on such date; and (ii) in the case of any other registrant, the one-year period beginning on the date the registrant is no longer an emerging growth company.

REGULATION 14D

Disclosure Requirements and Minimum Time for Tender Offers

Rule 14d-1. Scope of and Definitions Applicable to Regulations 14D and 14E

(a) *Scope*. Regulation 14D (§§ 240.14d-1 through 240.14d-101) shall apply to any tender offer that is subject to section 14(d)(1) of the Act (15 U.S.C. 78n(d)(1)), including, but not limited to, any tender offer for securities of a class described in that section that is made by an affiliate of the issuer of such class. Regulation 14E (§§ 240.14e-1 through 240.14e-8) shall apply to any tender offer for securities (other than exempted securities) unless otherwise noted therein.

(b) The requirements imposed by sections 14(d)(1) through 14(d)(7) of the Act, Regulation 14D and Schedules TO and 14D-9 thereunder, and Rule 14e-1 of Regulation 14E under the Act, shall be deemed satisfied with respect to any tender offer, including any exchange offer, for the securities of an issuer incorporated or organized under the laws of Canada or any Canadian province or territory, if such issuer is a foreign private issuer and is not an investment company registered or required to be registered under the Investment Company Act of 1940, if less than 40 percent of the class of securities outstanding that is the subject of the tender offer is held by U.S. holders, and the tender offer is subject to, and the bidder complies with, the laws, regulations and policies of Canada and/or any of its provinces or territories governing the conduct of the offer (unless the bidder has received an exemption(s) from, and the tender offer does not comply with, requirements that otherwise would be prescribed by Regulation 14D or 14E), *provided that:*

(1) In the case of tender offers subject to section 14(d)(1) of the Act, where the consideration for a tender offer subject to this section consists solely of cash, the entire disclosure document or documents required to be furnished to holders of the class of securities to be acquired shall be filed with the Commission on Schedule 14D-1F (§ 240.14d-102) and disseminated to shareholders of the subject company residing in the United States in accordance with such Canadian laws, regulations and policies; or

(2) Where the consideration for a tender offer subject to this section includes securities of the bidder to be issued pursuant to the offer, any registration statement and/or prospectus relating thereto shall be filed with the Commission along with the Schedule 14D-1F referred to in paragraph (b)(1) of this section, and shall be disseminated, together with the home jurisdiction document(s) accompanying such Schedule, to shareholders of the subject company residing in the United States in accordance with such Canadian laws, regulations and policies.

NOTES: 1. For purposes of any tender offer, including any exchange offer, otherwise eligible to proceed in accordance with Rule 14d-1(b) under the Act, the issuer of the subject securities will be presumed to be a foreign private issuer and U.S. holders will be presumed to hold less than 40 percent of such outstanding securities, *unless* (a) the aggregate trading volume of that class on national securities exchanges in the United States and on NASDAQ exceeded its aggregate trading volume on securities exchanges in Canada and on the Canadian Dealing Network, Inc. ("CDN") over the 12 calendar month period prior to commencement of this offer, or if commenced in response to a prior offer, over the 12 calendar month period prior to the commencement of the initial offer (based on volume figures published by such exchanges and NASDAQ and CDN); (b) the most recent annual report or annual information form filed or submitted by the issuer with securities regulators of Ontario, Quebec, British Columbia or Alberta (or, if the issuer of the subject securities is not a reporting issuer in any of such provinces, with any other Canadian securities regulator) or with the Commission indicates that U.S. holders hold 40 percent or more of the outstanding subject class of securities; or (c) the offeror has actual knowledge that the level of U.S. ownership equals or exceeds 40 percent of such securities.

2. Notwithstanding the grant of an exemption from one or more of the applicable Canadian regulatory provisions imposing requirements that otherwise would be prescribed by Regulation 14D or 14E, the tender offer will be eligible to proceed in accordance with the requirements of this section if the Commission by order determines that the applicable Canadian regulatory provisions are adequate to protect the interest of investors.

(c) *Tier I.* Any tender offer for the securities of a foreign private issuer as defined in § 240.3b-4 is exempt from the requirements of Sections 14(d)(1) through 14(d)(7) of the Act (15 U.S.C. 78n(d)(1) through 78n(d)(7)), Regulation 14D (§ 240.14d-1 through § 240.14d-10) and Schedules TO (§ 240.14d-100) and 14D-9 (§ 240.14d-101) thereunder, and § 240.14e-1 and § 240.14e-2 of Regulation 14E under the Act if the following conditions are satisfied:

(1) *U.S. Ownership Limitation.* Except the in case of a tender offer that is commenced during the pendency of a tender offer made by a prior bidder in reliance on this paragraph or § 240.13e-4(h)(8), U.S. holders do not hold more than 10 percent of the class of securities sought in the offer (as determined under Instructions 2 or 3 to paragraphs (c) and (d) of this section).

(2) *Equal treatment.* The bidder must permit U.S. holders to participate in the offer on terms at least as favorable as those offered any other holder of the same class of securities that is the subject of the tender offer; however:

(i) *Registered exchange offers.* If the bidder offers securities registered under the Securities Act of 1933 (15 U.S.C. 77a *et seq.*), the bidder need not extend the offer to security holders in those states or jurisdictions that prohibit the offer or sale of the securities after the bidder has made a good faith effort to register or qualify the offer and sale of securities in that state or jurisdiction, except that the bidder must offer the same cash alternative to security holders in any such state or jurisdiction that it has offered to security holders in any other state or jurisdiction.

(ii) *Exempt exchange offers.* If the bidder offers securities exempt from registration under § 230.802 of this chapter, the bidder need not extend the offer to security holders in those states or jurisdictions that require registration or qualification, except that the bidder must offer the same cash alternative to security holders in any such state or jurisdiction that it has offered to security holders in any other state or jurisdiction.

(iii) *Cash only consideration.* The bidder may offer U.S. holders only a cash consideration for the tender of the subject securities, notwithstanding the fact that the bidder is offering security holders outside the United States a consideration that consists in whole or in part of securities of the bidder, so long as the bidder has a reasonable basis for believing that the amount of cash is substantially equivalent to the value of the consideration offered to non-U.S. holders, and either of the following conditions are satisfied:

(A) The offered security is a "margin security" within the meaning of Regulation T (12 CFR 220.2) and the issuer undertakes to provide, upon the request of any U.S. holder or the Commission staff, the closing price and daily trading volume of the security on the principal trading market for the security as of the last trading day of each of the six months preceding the announcement of the offer and each of the trading days thereafter; or

(B) If the offered security is not a "margin security" within the meaning of Regulation T (12 CFR 220.2) the issuer undertakes to provide, upon the request of any U.S. holder or the Commission staff, an opinion of an independent expert stating that the cash consideration offered to U.S. holders is substantially equivalent to the value of the consideration offered security holders outside the United States.

(iv) *Disparate tax treatment.* If the bidder offers loan notes solely to offer sellers tax advantages not available in the United States and these notes are neither listed on any organized securities market nor registered under the Securities Act of 1933 (15 U.S.C. 77a *et seq.*), the loan notes need not be offered to U.S. holders.

(3) *Informational documents.* (i) The bidder must disseminate any informational document to U.S. holders, including any amendments thereto, in English, on a comparable basis to that provided to security holders in the home jurisdiction.

(ii) If the bidder disseminates by publication in its home jurisdiction, the bidder must publish the information in the United States in a manner reasonably calculated to inform U.S. holders of the offer.

(iii) In the case of tender offers for securities described in Section 14(d)(1) of the Act (15 U.S.C. 78n(d)(1)), if the bidder publishes or otherwise disseminates an informational document to the holders of the securities in connection with the tender offer, the bidder must furnish that informational document, including any amendments thereto, in English, to the Commission on Form CB (§ 249.480 of this chapter) by the first business day after publication or dissemination. If the bidder is a foreign company, it must also file a Form F-X (§ 239.42 of this chapter) with the Commission at the same time as the submission of Form CB to appoint an agent for service in the United States.

(4) *Investment companies.* The issuer of the securities that are the subject of the tender offer is not an investment company registered or required to be registered under the Investment Company Act of 1940 (15 U.S.C. 80a-1 *et seq.*), other than a registered closed-end investment company.

(d) *Tier II.* A person conducting a tender offer (including any exchange offer) that meets the conditions in paragraph (d)(1) of this section shall be entitled to the exemptive relief specified in paragraph (d)(2) of this section, provided that such tender offer complies with all the requirements of this section other than those for which an exemption has been specifically provided in paragraph (d)(2) of this section. In addition, a person conducting a tender offer subject only to the requirements of section 14(e) of the Act (15 U.S.C. 78n(e)) and Regulation 14E thereunder that meets the conditions in paragraph (d)(1) of the section also shall be entitled to the exemptive relief specified in paragraph (d)(2) of this section, to the extent needed under the requirements of Regulation 14E, so long as the tender offer complies with all requirements of Regulation 14E other than those for which an exemption has been specifically provided in paragraph (d)(2) of this section:

(1) *Conditions.* (i) The subject company is a foreign private issuer as defined in § 240.3b-4 and is not an investment company registered or required to be registered under the Investment Company Act of 1940 (15 U.S.C. 80a-1 *et seq.*), other than a registered closed-end investment company;

(ii) Except in the case of a tender offer that is commenced during the pendency of a tender offer made by a prior bidder in reliance on this paragraph or § 240.13e-4(i), U.S. holders do not hold more than 40 percent of the class of securities sought in the offer (as determined under Instructions 2 or 3 to paragraphs (c) and (d) of this section); and

(iii) The bidder complies with all applicable U.S. tender offer laws and regulations, other than those for which an exemption has been provided for in paragraph (d)(2) of this section.

(2) *Exemptions.* (i) *Equal treatment—loan notes.* If the bidder offers loan notes solely to offer sellers tax advantages not available in the United States and these notes are neither listed on any organized securities market nor registered under the Securities Act of 1933 (15 U.S.C. 77a *et seq.*), the loan notes need not be offered to U.S. holders, notwithstanding § 240.14d-10.

(ii) *Equal Treatment—Separate U.S. and Foreign Offers.* Notwithstanding the provisions of § 240.14d-10, a bidder conducting a tender offer meeting the conditions of paragraph (d)(1) of this section may separate the offer into multiple offers: one offer made to U.S. holders, which also may include all holders of American Depositary Shares representing interests in the subject securities, and one or more offers made to non-U.S. holders. The U.S. offer must be made on terms at least as favorable as those offered any other holder of the same class of securities that is the subject of the tender offers. U.S. holders may be included in the foreign offer(s) only where the laws of the jurisdiction governing such foreign offer(s) expressly preclude the exclusion of U.S. holders from the foreign offer(s) and where the offer materials distributed to U.S. holders fully and adequately disclose the risks of participating in the foreign offer(s).

(iii) *Notice of extensions.* Notice of extensions made in accordance with the requirements of the home jurisdiction law or practice will satisfy the requirements of § 240.14e-1(d).

(iv) *Prompt Payment.* Payment made in accordance with the requirements of the home jurisdiction law or practice will satisfy the requirements of § 240.14e-1(c). Where payment may not be made on a more expedited basis under home jurisdiction law or practice, payment for securities tendered during any subsequent offering period within 20 business days of the date of tender will satisfy the prompt payment requirements of § 240.14d-11(e). For purposes of this paragraph, a business day is determined with reference to the target's home jurisdiction.

(v) *Subsequent offering period/Withdrawal rights.* A bidder will satisfy the announcement and prompt payment requirements of § 240.14d-11(d), if the bidder announces the results of the tender offer, including the approximate number of securities deposited to date, and pays for tendered securities in accordance with the requirements of the home jurisdiction law or practice and the subsequent offering period commences immediately following such announcement. Notwithstanding Section 14(d)(5) of the Act (15 U.S.C. 78n(d)(5)), the bidder need not extend withdrawal rights following the close of the offer and prior to the commencement of the subsequent offering period.

(vi) *Payment of Interest on Securities Tendered During Subsequent Offering Period.* Notwithstanding the requirements of § 240.14d-11(f), the bidder may pay interest on securities tendered during a subsequent offering period, if required under applicable foreign law. Paying interest on securities tendered during a subsequent offering period in accordance with this section will not be deemed to violate § 240.14d-10(a)(2).

(vii) *Suspension of Withdrawal Rights During Counting of Tendered Securities.* The bidder may suspend withdrawal rights required under section 14(d)(5) of the Act (15 U.S.C.

78n(d)(5)) at the end of the offer and during the period that securities tendered into the offer are being counted, provided that:

(A) The bidder has provided an offer period including withdrawal rights for a period of at least 20 U.S. business days;

(B) At the time withdrawal rights are suspended, all offer conditions have been satisfied or waived, except to the extent that the bidder is in the process of determining whether a minimum acceptance condition included in the terms of the offer has been satisfied by counting tendered securities; and

(C) Withdrawal rights are suspended only during the counting process and are reinstated immediately thereafter, except to the extent that they are terminated through the acceptance of tendered securities.

(viii) *Mix and Match Elections and the Subsequent Offering Period.* Notwithstanding the requirements of § 240.14d-11(b), where the bidder offers target security holders a choice between different forms of consideration, it may establish a ceiling on one or more forms of consideration offered. Notwithstanding the requirements of § 240.14d-11(f), a bidder that establishes a ceiling on one or more forms of consideration offered pursuant to this subsection may offset elections of tendering security holders against one another, subject to proration, so that elections are satisfied to the greatest extent possible and pro rated to the extent that they cannot be satisfied in full. Such a bidder also may separately offset and pro rate securities tendered during the initial offering period and those tendered during any subsequent offering period, notwithstanding the requirements of § 240.14d-10(c).

(ix) *Early Termination of an Initial Offering Period.* A bidder may terminate an initial offering period, including a voluntary extension of that period, if at the time the initial offering period and withdrawal rights terminate, the following conditions are met:

(A) The initial offering period has been open for at least 20 U.S. business days;

(B) The bidder has adequately discussed the possibility of and the impact of the early termination in the original offer materials;

(C) The bidder provides a subsequent offering period after the termination of the initial offering period;

(D) All offer conditions are satisfied as of the time when the initial offering period ends; and

(E) The bidder does not terminate the initial offering period or any extension of that period during any mandatory extension required under U.S. tender offer rules.

Instructions to paragraphs (c) and (d):

1. Home jurisdiction means both the jurisdiction of the subject company's incorporation, organization or chartering and the principal foreign market where the subject company's securities are listed or quoted.

2. *U.S. holder* means any security holder resident in the United States. Except as otherwise provided in Instruction 3 below, to determine the percentage of outstanding securities held by U.S. holders:

i. Calculate the U.S. ownership as of a date no more than 60 before and no more than 30 days after public announcement of the tender offer. If you are unable to calculate as of a date within these time frames, the calculation may be made as of the most recent practicable date before public announcement, but in no event earlier than 120 days before announcement;

ii. Include securities underlying American Depositary Shares convertible or exchangeable into the securities that are the subject of the tender offer when calculating the number of subject securities outstanding, as well as the number held by U.S. holders. Exclude from the calculations other types of securities that are convertible or exchangeable into the securities that are the subject of the tender offer, such as warrants, options and convertible securities. Exclude from those calculations securities held by the bidder;

iii. Use the method of calculating record ownership in Rule 12g3-2(a) under the Act (§ 240.12g3-2(a) of this chapter), except that your inquiry as to the amount of securities represented by accounts of customers resident in the United States may be limited to brokers, dealers, banks and other nominees located in the United States, the subject company's jurisdiction of incorporation or that of each participant in a business combination, and the jurisdiction that is the primary trading market for the subject securities, if different than the subject company's jurisdiction of incorporation;

iv. If, after reasonable inquiry, you are unable to obtain information about the amount of securities represented by accounts of customers resident in the United States, you may assume, for purposes of this definition, that the customers are residents of the jurisdiction in which the nominee has its principal place of business; and

v. Count securities as beneficially owned by residents of the United States as reported on reports of beneficial ownership that are provided to you or publicly filed and based on information otherwise provided to you.

3. In a tender offer by a bidder other than an affiliate of the issuer of the subject securities that is not made pursuant to an agreement with the issuer of the subject securities, the issuer of the subject securities will be presumed to be a foreign private issuer and U.S. holders will be presumed to hold less than 10 percent (40 percent in the case of paragraph (d) of this section) of such outstanding securities, unless paragraphs i., ii., or iii. of this section indicate otherwise. In addition, where the bidder is unable to conduct the analysis of U.S. ownership set forth in Instruction 2 above, the bidder may presume that the percentage of securities held by U.S. holders is less than 10 percent (40 percent in the case of paragraph (d) of this section) of the outstanding securities so long as there is a primary trading market for the subject securities outside the U.S., as defined in Rule 12h-6(f)(5), unless:

i. Average daily trading volume of the subject securities in the United States for a recent twelve-month period ending on a date no more than 60 days before the public announcement of the offer exceeds 10 percent (40 percent in the case of paragraph (d) of this section) of the average daily trading volume of that class of securities on a worldwide basis for the same period; or

ii. The most recent annual report or annual information filed or submitted by the issuer with securities regulators of the home jurisdiction or with the Commission or any jurisdiction in which the subject securities trade before the public announcement of the offer indicates that U.S. holders hold more than 10 percent (40 percent in the case of paragraph (d) of this section) of the outstanding subject class of securities; or

iii. The bidder knows or has reason to know, before the public announcement of the offer, that the level of U.S. ownership exceeds 10 percent (40 percent in the case of paragraph (d) of this section) of such securities. As an example, a bidder is deemed to know information about U.S. ownership of the subject class of securities that is publicly available and that appears in any filing with the Commission or any regulatory body in the issuer's jurisdiction of incorporation or (if different) the non-U.S. jurisdiction in which the primary trading market for the subject securities is located. The bidder is deemed to know information about U.S. ownership available from the issuer or obtained or readily available from any other source that is reasonably reliable, including from persons it has retained to advise it about the transaction, as well as from third-party information providers. These examples are not intended to be exclusive.

iv. The bidder knows or has reason to know that the level of U.S. ownership exceeds 10 percent (40 percent in the case of 14d-1(d)) of such securities.

4. *United States* means the United States of America, its territories and possessions, any State of the United States, and the District of Columbia.

5. The exemptions provided by paragraphs (c) and (d) of this section are not available for any securities transaction or series of transactions that technically complies with para-

graph (c) or (d) of this section but are part of a plan or scheme to evade the provisions of Regulations 14D or 14E.

(e) Notwithstanding paragraph (a) of this section, the requirements imposed by sections 14(d)(1) through 14(d)(7) of the Act [15 U.S.C. 78n(d)(1) through 78n(d)(7)], Regulation 14D promulgated thereunder (§§ 240.14d-1 through 240.14d-10), and §§ 240.14e-1 and 240.14e-2 shall not apply by virtue of the fact that a bidder for the securities of a foreign private issuer, as defined in § 240.3b-4, the subject company of such a tender offer, their representatives, or any other person specified in § 240.14d-9(d), provides any journalist with access to its press conferences held outside of the United States, to meetings with its representatives conducted outside of the United States, or to written press-related materials released outside the United States, at or in which a present or proposed tender offer is discussed, if:

(1) Access is provided to both U.S. and foreign journalists; and

(2) With respect to any written press-related materials released by the bidder or its representatives that discuss a present or proposed tender offer for equity securities registered under Section 12 of the Act [15 U.S.C. 78l], the written press-related materials must state that these written press-related materials are not an extension of a tender offer in the United States for a class of equity securities of the subject company. If the bidder intends to extend the tender offer in the United States at some future time, a statement regarding this intention, and that the procedural and filing requirements of the Williams Act will be satisfied at that time, also must be included in these written press-related materials. No means to tender securities, or coupons that could be returned to indicate interest in the tender offer, may be provided as part of, or attached to, these written press-related materials.

(f) For the purpose of § 240.14d-1(e), a bidder may presume that a target company qualifies as a foreign private issuer if the target company is a foreign issuer and files registration statements or reports on the disclosure forms specifically designated for foreign private issuers, claims the exemption from registration under the Act pursuant to § 240.12g3-2(b), or is not reporting in the United States.

(g) *Definitions.* Unless the context otherwise requires, all terms used in Regulation 14D and Regulation 14E have the same meaning as in the Act and in Rule 12b-2 (§ 240.12b-2) promulgated thereunder. In addition, for purposes of section 14(d) and 14(e) of the Act and Regulations 14D and 14E, the following definitions apply:

(1) The term "beneficial owner" shall have the same meaning as that set forth in Rule 13d-3: *Provided, however,* That, except with respect to Rule 14d-3 and Rule 14d-9(d), the term shall not include a person who does not have or share investment power or who is deemed to be a beneficial owner by virtue of Rule 13d-3(d)(1) (§ 240.13d-3(d)(1));

(2) The term "bidder" means any person who makes a tender offer or on whose behalf a tender offer is made: *Provided, however,* That the term does not include an issuer which makes a tender offer for securities of any class of which it is the issuer;

(3) The term "business day" means any day, other than Saturday, Sunday or a federal holiday, and shall consist of the time period from 12:01 a.m. through 12:00 midnight Eastern time. In computing any time period under section 14(d)(5) or section 14(d)(6) of the Act or under Regulation 14D or Regulation 14E, the date of the event which begins the running of such time period shall be included *except that* if such event occurs on other than a business day such period shall begin to run on and shall include the first business day thereafter; and

(4) The term *initial offering period* means the period from the time the offer commences until all minimum time periods, including extensions, required by Regulations 14D (§§ 240.14d-1 through 240.14d-103) and 14E (§§ 240.14e-1 through 240.14e-8) have been satisfied and all conditions to the offer have been satisfied or waived within these time periods.

(5) The term "security holders" means holders of record and beneficial owners of securities which are the subject of a tender offer;

(6) The term "security position listing" means, with respect to securities of any issuer held by a registered clearing agency in the name of the clearing agency or its nominee, a list of those participants in the clearing agency on whose behalf the clearing agency holds the

issuer's securities and of the participants' respective positions in such securities as of a specified date.

(7) The term "subject company" means any issuer of securities which are sought by a bidder pursuant to a tender offer;

(8) The term *subsequent offering period* means the period immediately following the initial offering period meeting the conditions specified in § 240.14d-11.

(9) The term "tender offer material" means:

(i) The bidder's formal offer, including all the material terms and conditions of the tender offer and all amendments thereto;

(ii) The related transmittal letter (whereby securities of the subject company which are sought in the tender offer may be transmitted to the bidder or its depositary) and all amendments thereto; and

(iii) Press releases, advertisements, letters and other documents published by the bidder or sent or given by the bidder to security holders which, directly or indirectly, solicit, invite or request tenders of the securities being sought in the tender offer;

(h) *Signatures.* Where the Act or the rules, forms, reports or schedules thereunder require a document filed with or furnished to the Commission to be signed, such document shall be manually signed, or signed using either typed signatures or duplicated or facsimile versions of manual signatures. Where typed, duplicated or facsimile signatures are used, each signatory to the filing shall manually sign a signature page or other document authenticating, acknowledging or otherwise adopting his or her signature that appears in the filing. Such document shall be executed before or at the time the filing is made and shall be retained by the filer for a period of five years. Upon request, the filer shall furnish to the Commission or its staff a copy of any or all documents retained pursuant to this section.

Rule 14d-2. Commencement of a Tender Offer

(a) *Date of commencement.* A bidder will have commenced its tender offer for purposes of section 14(d) of the Act (15 U.S.C. 78n) and the rules under that section at 12:01 a.m. on the date when the bidder has first published, sent or given the means to tender to security holders. For purposes of this section, the means to tender includes the transmittal form or a statement regarding how the transmittal form may be obtained.

(b) *Pre-commencement communications.* A communication by the bidder will not be deemed to constitute commencement of a tender offer if:

(1) It does not include the means for security holders to tender their shares into the offer; and

(2) All written communications relating to the tender offer, from and including the first public announcement, are filed under cover of Schedule TO (§ 240.14d-100) with the Commission no later than the date of the communication. The bidder also must deliver to the subject company and any other bidder for the same class of securities the first communication relating to the transaction that is filed, or required to be filed, with the Commission.

Instructions to paragraph (b)(2): 1. The box on the front of Schedule TO indicating that the filing contains pre-commencement communications must be checked.

2. Any communications made in connection with an exchange offer registered under the Securities Act of 1933 need only be filed under § 230.425 of this chapter and will be deemed filed under this section.

3. Each pre-commencement written communication must include a prominent legend in clear, plain language advising security holders to read the tender offer statement when it is available because it contains important information. The legend also must advise investors that they can get the tender offer statement and other filed documents for free at the Commission's web site and explain which documents are free from the offeror.

4. See Regs. 230.135, 230.165 and 230.166 of this chapter for pre-commencement communications made in connection with registered exchange offers.

5. "Public announcement" is any oral or written communication by the bidder, or any person authorized to act on the bidder's behalf, that is reasonably designed to, or has the effect of, informing the public or security holders in general about the tender offer.

(c) *Filing and other obligations triggered by commencement.* As soon as practicable on the date of commencement, a bidder must comply with the filing requirements of § 240.14d-3(a), the dissemination requirements of § 240.14d-4(a) or (b), and the disclosure requirements of § 240.14d-6(a).

Rule 14d-3. Filing and Transmission of Tender Offer Statement

(a) *Filing and transmittal.* No bidder shall make a tender offer if, after consummation thereof, such bidder would be the beneficial owner of more than 5 percent of the class of the subject company's securities for which the tender offer is made, unless as soon as practicable on the date of the commencement of the tender offer such bidder:

(1) Files with the Commission a Tender Offer Statement on Schedule TO (§ 240.14d-100), including all exhibits thereto;

(2) Delivers a copy of such Schedule TO, including all exhibits thereto:

(i) To the subject company at its principal executive office; and

(ii) To any other bidder, which has filed a Schedule TO with the Commission relating to a tender offer which has not yet terminated for the same class of securities of the subject company, at such bidder's principal executive office or at the address of the person authorized to receive notices and communications (which is disclosed on the cover sheet of such other bidder's Schedule TO);

(3) Gives telephonic notice of the information required by Rule 14d-6(d)(2)(i) and (ii) (§ 240.14d-6(d)(2)(i) and (ii)) and mails by means of first class mail a copy of such Schedule TO, including all exhibits thereto:

(i) To each national securities exchange where such class of the subject company's securities is registered and listed for trading (which may be based upon information contained in the subject company's most recent Annual Report on Form 10-K (§ 249.310 of this chapter) filed with the Commission unless the bidder has reason to believe that such information is not current), which telephonic notice shall be made when practicable prior to the opening of each such exchange; and

(ii) To the National Association of Securities Dealers, Inc. ("NASD") if such class of the subject company's securities is authorized for quotation in the NASDAQ interdealer quotation system.

(b) *Post-commencement amendments and additional materials.* The bidder making the tender offer must file with the Commission:

(1) An amendment to Schedule TO (§ 240.14d-100) reporting promptly any material changes in the information set forth in the schedule previously filed and including copies of any additional tender offer materials as exhibits; and

(2) A final amendment to Schedule TO (§ 240.14d-100) reporting promptly the results of the tender offer.

Instruction to paragraph (b): A copy of any additional tender offer materials or amendment filed under this section must be sent promptly to the subject company and to any exchange and/or NASD, as required by paragraph (a) of this section, but in no event later than the date the materials are first published, sent or given to security holders.

(c) *Certain announcements.* Notwithstanding the provisions of paragraph (b) of this section, if the additional tender offer material or an amendment to Schedule TO discloses only the number of shares deposited to date, and/or announces an extension of the time during which shares may be tendered, then the bidder may file such tender offer material or amendment and send a copy of such tender offer material or amendment to the subject company, any exchange and/or the NASD, as required by paragraph (a) of this section, promptly after the date such tender offer material is first published or sent or given to security holders.

Rule 14d-4. Dissemination of Tender Offers to Security Holders

As soon as practicable on the date of commencement of a tender offer, the bidder must publish, send or give the disclosure required by § 240.14d-6 to security holders of the class of securities that is the subject of the offer, by complying with all of the requirements of any of the following:

(a) *Cash tender offers and exempt securities offers.* For tender offers in which the consideration consists solely of cash and/or securities exempt from registration under section 3 of the Securities Act of 1933 (15 U.S.C. 77c):

(1) *Long-form publication.* The bidder makes adequate publication in a newspaper or newspapers of long-form publication of the tender offer.

(2) *Summary publication.*

(i) If the tender offer is not subject to Rule 13e-3 (§ 240.13e-3), the bidder makes adequate publication in a newspaper or newspaper of a summary advertisement of the tender offer; and

(ii) Mails by first class mail or otherwise furnishes with reasonable promptness the bidder's tender offer materials to any security holder who requests such tender offer materials pursuant to the summary advertisement or otherwise.

(3) *Use of stockholder lists and security position listings.* Any bidder using stockholder lists and security position listings under § 240.14d-5 must comply with paragraph (a)(1) or (2) of this section on or before the date of the bidder's request under § 240.14d-5(a).

Instruction to paragraph (a): Tender offers may be published or sent or given to security holders by other methods, but with respect to summary publication and the use of stockholder lists and security position listings under § 240.14d-5, paragraphs (a)(2) and (a)(3) of this section are exclusive.

(b) *Registered securities offers.* For tender offers in which the consideration consists solely or partially of securities registered under the Securities Act of 1933, a registration statement containing all of the required information, including pricing information, has been filed and a preliminary prospectus or a prospectus that meets the requirements of Section 10(a) of the Securities Act (15 U.S.C. 77j(a)), including a letter of transmittal, is delivered to security holders. However, for going-private transactions (as defined by § 240.13e-3) and roll-up transactions (as described by Item 901 of Regulation S-K (§ 229.901 of this chapter)), a registration statement registering the securities to be offered must have become effective and only a prospectus that meets the requirements of Section 10(a) of the Securities Act may be delivered to security holders on the date of commencement.

Instructions to paragraph (b): 1. If the prospectus is being delivered by mail, mailing on the date of commencement is sufficient.

2. A preliminary prospectus used under this section may not omit information under § 230.430 or § 230.430A of this chapter.

3. If a preliminary prospectus is used under this section and the bidder must disseminate material changes, the tender offer must remain open for the period specified in paragraph (d)(2) of this section.

4. If a preliminary prospectus is used under this section, tenders may be requested in accordance with § 230.162(a) of this chapter.

(c) *Adequate publication.* Depending on the facts and circumstances involved, adequate publication of a tender offer pursuant to this section may require publication in a newspaper with a national circulation or may only require publication in a newspaper with metropolitan or regional circulation or may require publication in a combination thereof: *Provided, however*, That publication in all editions of a daily newspaper with a national circulation shall be deemed to constitute adequate publication.

(d)(1) *Publication of changes and extension of the offer.* If a tender offer has been published or sent or given to security holders by one or more of the methods enumerated in this section, a material change in the information published, sent or given to security holders shall be promptly disseminated to security holders in a manner reasonably designed to inform security holders of such change; *Provided, however,* That if the bidder has elected pursuant to Rule 14d-5(f)(1) of this section to require the subject company to disseminate amendments disclosing material changes to the tender offer materials pursuant to Rule 14d-5, the bidder shall disseminate material changes in the information published or sent or given to security holders at least pursuant to Rule 14d-5.

(2) In a registered securities offer where the bidder disseminates the preliminary prospectus as permitted by paragraph (b) of this section, the offer must remain open from the date that material changes to the tender offer materials are disseminated to security holders, as follows:

(i) Five business days for a prospectus supplement containing a material change other than price or share levels;

(ii) Ten business days for a prospectus supplement containing a change in price, the amount of securities sought, the dealer's soliciting fee, or other similarly significant change;

(iii) Ten business days for a prospectus supplement included as part of a post-effective amendment; and

(iv) Twenty business days for a revised prospectus when the initial prospectus was materially deficient.

Rule 14d-5. Dissemination of Certain Tender Offers by the Use of Stockholder Lists and Security Position Listings

(a) *Obligations of the subject company.* Upon receipt by a subject company at its principal executive offices of a bidder's written request, meeting the requirements of paragraph (e) of this section, the subject company shall comply with the following sub-paragraphs.

(1) The subject company shall notify promptly transfer agents and any other person who will assist the subject company in complying with the requirements of this section of the receipt by the subject company of a request by a bidder pursuant to this section.

(2) The subject company shall promptly ascertain whether the most recently prepared stockholder list, written or otherwise, within the access of the subject company was prepared as of a date earlier than ten business days before the date of the bidder's request and, if so, the subject company shall promptly prepare or cause to be prepared a stockholder list as of the most recent practicable date which shall not be more than ten business days before the date of the bidder's request.

(3) The suject company shall make an election to comply and shall comply with all of the provisions of either paragraph (b) or paragraph (c) of this section. The subject company's election once made shall not be modified or revoked during the bidder's tender offer and extensions thereof.

(4) No later than the second business day after the date of the bidder's request, the subject company shall orally notify the bidder, which notification shall be confirmed in writing, of the subject company's election made pursuant to paragraph (a)(3) of this section. Such notification shall indicate (i) the approximate number of security holders of the class of securities being sought by the bidder and, (ii) if the subject company elects to comply with paragraph (b) of this section, appropriate information concerning the location for delivery of the bidder's tender offer materials and the approximate direct costs incidental to the mailing to security holders of the bidder's tender offer materials computed in accordance with paragraph (g)(2) of this section.

(b) *Mailing of tender offer materials by the subject company.* A subject company which elects pursuant to paragraph (a)(3) of this section to comply with the provisions of this paragraph shall perform the acts prescribed by the following subparagraphs.

(1) The subject company shall promptly contact each participant named on the most recent security position listing of any clearing agency within the access of the subject company and make inquiry of each such participant as to the approximate number of beneficial owners of the subject company securities being sought in the tender offer held by each such participant.

(2) No later than the third business day after delivery of the bidder's tender offer materials pursuant to paragraph (g)(1) of this section, the subject company shall begin to mail or cause to be mailed by means of first class mail a copy of the bidder's tender offer materials to each person whose name appears as a record holder of the class of securities for which the offer is made on the most recent stockholder list referred to in paragraph (a)(2) of this section. The subject company shall use its best efforts to complete the mailing in a timely manner but in no event shall such mailing be completed in a substantially greater period of time than the subject company would complete a mailing to security holders of its own materials relating to the tender offer.

(3) No later than the third business day after the delivery of the bidder's tender offer materials pursuant to paragraph (g)(1) of this section, the subject company shall begin to transmit or cause to be transmitted a sufficient number of sets of the bidder's tender offer materials to the participants named on the security position listings described in paragraph (b)(1) of this section. The subject company shall use its best efforts to complete the transmittal in a timely manner but in no event shall such transmittal be completed in a substantially greater period of time than the subject company would complete a transmittal to such participants pursuant to security position listings of clearing agencies of its own material relating to the tender offer.

(4) The subject company shall promptly give oral notification to the bidder, which notification shall be confirmed in writing, of the commencement of the mailing pursuant to paragraph (b)(2) of this section and of the transmittal pursuant to paragraph (b)(3) of this section.

(5) During the tender offer and any extension thereof the subject company shall use reasonable efforts to update the stockholder list and shall mail or cause to be mailed promptly following each update a copy of the bidder's tender offer materials (to the extent sufficient sets of such materials have been furnished by the bidder) to each person who has become a record holder since the later of (i) the date of preparation of the most recent stockholder list referred to in paragraph (a)(2) of this section or (ii) the last preceding update.

(6) If the bidder has elected pursuant to paragraph (f)(1) of this section to require the subject company to disseminate amendments disclosing material changes to the tender offer materials pursuant to this section, the subject company, promptly following delivery of each such amendment, shall mail or cause to be mailed a copy of each such amendment to each record holder whose name appears on the shareholder list described in paragraphs (a)(2) and (b)(5) of this section and shall transmit or cause to be transmitted sufficient copies of such amendment to each participant named on security position listings who received sets of the bidder's tender offer materials pursuant to paragraph (b)(3) of this section.

(7) The subject company shall not include any communication other than the bidder's tender offer materials or amendments thereto in the envelopes or other containers furnished by the bidder.

(8) Promptly following the termination of the tender offer, the subject company shall reimburse the bidder the excess, if any, of the amounts advanced pursuant to paragraph (f)(3)(iii) over the direct costs incidental to compliance by the subject company and its agents in performing the acts required by this section computed in accordance with paragraph (g)(2) of this section.

(c) *Delivery of stockholder lists and security position listings.* A subject company which elects pursuant to paragraph (a)(3) of this section to comply with the provisions of this paragraph shall perform the acts prescribed by the following subparagraphs.

(1) No later than the third business day after the date of the bidder's request, the subject company must furnish to the bidder at the subject company's principal executive office a copy of the names and addresses of the record holders on the most recent stockholder list referred to in paragraph (a)(2) of this section; the names and addresses of participants identified on the most recent security position listing of any clearing agency that is within the access of the subject company; and the most recent list of names, addresses and security positions of beneficial owners as specified in § 240.14a-13(b), in the possession of the subject company, or that subsequently comes into its possession.

All security holder list information must be in the format requested by the bidder to the extent the format is available to the subject company without undue burden or expense.

(2) If the bidder has elected pursuant to paragraph (f)(1) of this section to require the subject company to disseminate amendments disclosing material changes to the tender offer materials, the subject company shall update the stockholder list by furnishing the bidder with the name and address of each record holder named on the stockholder list, and not previously furnished to the bidder, promptly after such information becomes available to the subject company during the tender offer and any extensions thereof.

(d) *Liability of subject company and others.* Neither the subject company nor any affiliate or agent of the subject company nor any clearing agency shall be:

(1) Deemed to have made a solicitation or recommendation respecting the tender offer within the meaning of section 14(d)(4) based solely upon the compliance or noncompliance by the subject company or any affiliate or agent of the subject company with one or more requirements of this section;

(2) Liable under any provision of the Federal securities laws to the bidder or to any security holder based solely upon the inaccuracy of the current names or addresses on the stockholder list or security position listing, unless such inaccuracy results from a lack of reasonable care on the part of the subject company or any affiliate or agent of the subject company;

(3) Deemed to be an "underwriter" within the meaning of section (2)(11) of the Securities Act of 1933 for any purpose of that Act or any rule or regulation promulgated thereunder based solely upon the compliance or noncompliance by the subject company or any affiliate or agent of the subject company with one or more of the requirements of this section;

(4) Liable under any provision of the Federal securities laws for the disclosure in the bidder's tender offer materials, including any amendment thereto, based solely upon the compliance or noncompliance by the subject company or any affiliate or agent of the subject company with one or more of the requirements of this section.

(e) *Content of the bidder's request.* The bidder's written request referred to in paragraph (a) of this section shall include the following:

(1) The identity of the bidder;

(2) The title of the class of securities which is the subject of the bidder's tender offer;

(3) A statement that the bidder is making a request to the subject company pursuant to paragraph (a) of this section for the use of the stockholder list and security position listings for the purpose of disseminating a tender offer to security holders;

(4) A statement that the bidder is aware of and will comply with the provisions of paragraph (f) of this section;

(5) A statement as to whether or not it has elected pursuant to paragraph (f)(1) of this section to disseminate amendments disclosing material changes to the tender offer materials pursuant to this section; and

(6) The name, address and telephone number of the person whom the subject company shall contact pursuant to paragraph (a)(4) of this section.

(f) *Obligations of the bidder.* Any bidder who requests that a subject company comply with the provisions of paragraph (a) of this section shall comply with the following subparagraphs.

(1) The bidder shall make an election whether or not to require the subject company to disseminate amendments disclosing material changes to the tender offer materials pursuant to this section, which election shall be included in the request referred to in paragraph (a) of this section and shall not be revocable by the bidder during the tender offer and extensions thereof.

(2) With respect to a tender offer subject to section 14(d)(1) of the Act in which the consideration consists solely of cash and/or securities exempt from registration under section 3 of the Securities Act of 1933, the bidder shall comply with the requirements of Rule 14d-4(a)(3).

(3) If the subject company elects to comply with paragraph (b) of this section,

(i) The bidder shall promptly deliver the tender offer materials after receipt of the notification from the subject company as provided in paragraph (a)(4) of this section;

(ii) The bidder shall promptly notify the subject company of any amendment to the bidder's tender offer materials requiring compliance by the subject company with paragraph (b)(6) of this section and shall promptly deliver such amendment to the subject company pursuant to paragraph (g)(1) of this section;

(iii) The bidder shall advance to the subject company an amount equal to the approximate cost of conducting mailings to security holders computed in accordance with paragraph (g)(2) of this section;

(iv) The bidder shall promptly reimburse the subject company for the direct costs incidental to compliance by the subject company and its agents in performing the acts required by this section computed in accordance with paragraph (g)(2) of this section which are in excess of the amount advanced pursuant to paragraph (f)(2)(iii) of this section; and

(v) The bidder shall mail by means of first class mail or otherwise furnish with reasonable promptness the tender offer materials to any security holder who requests such materials.

(4) If the subject company elects to comply with paragraph (c) of this section,

(i) The subject company shall use the stockholder list and security position listings furnished to the bidder pursuant to paragraph (c) of this section exclusively in the dissemination of tender offer materials to security holders in connection with the bidder's tender offer and extensions thereof;

(ii) The bidder shall return the stockholder lists and security position listings furnished to the bidder pursuant to paragraph (c) of this section promptly after the termination of the bidder's tender offer;

(iii) The bidder shall accept, handle and return the stockholder lists and security position listings furnished to the bidder pursuant to paragraph (c) of this section to the subject company on a confidential basis;

(iv) The bidder shall not retain any stockholder list or security position listing furnished by the subject company pursuant to paragraph (c) of this section, or any copy thereof, nor retain any information derived from any such list or listing or copy thereof after the termination of the bidder's tender offer;

(v) The bidder shall mail by means of first class mail, at its own expense, a copy of its tender offer materials to each person whose identity appears on the stockholder list as furnished and updated by the subject company pursuant to paragraphs (c)(1) and (c)(2) of this section;

(vi) The bidder shall contact the participants named on the security position listing of any clearing agency, make inquiry of each participant as to the approximate number of sets of tender offer materials required by each such participant, and furnish, at its own expense, sufficient sets of tender offer materials and any amendment thereto to each such participant for subsequent transmission to the beneficial owners of the securities being sought by the bidder;

(vii) The bidder shall mail by means of first class mail or otherwise furnish with reasonable promptness the tender offer materials to any security holder who requests such materials; and

(viii) The bidder shall promptly reimburse the subject company for direct costs incidental to compliance by the subject company and its agents in performing the acts required by this section computed in accordance with paragraph (g)(2) of this section.

(g) *Delivery of materials, computation of direct costs.*

(1) Whenever the bidder is required to deliver tender offer materials or amendments to tender offer materials, the bidder shall deliver to the subject company at the location specified by the subject company in its notice given pursuant to paragraph (a)(4) of this section a number of sets of the materials or of the amendment, as the case may be, at least equal to the approximate number of security holders specified by the subject company in such notice, together with appropriate envelopes or other containers therefor: *Provided, however,* That such delivery shall be deemed not to have been made unless the bidder has complied with paragraph (f)(3)(iii) of this section at the time the materials or amendments, as the case may be, are delivered.

(2) The approximate direct cost of mailing the bidder's tender offer materials shall be computed by adding (i) the direct cost incidental to the mailing of the subject company's last annual report to shareholders (excluding employee time), less the cost of preparation and printing of the report, and postage, plus (ii) the amount of first class postage required to mail the bidder's tender offer materials. The approximate direct costs incidental to the mailing of the amendments to the bidder's tender offer materials shall be computed by adding (iii) the estimated direct costs of preparing mailing labels, of updating shareholder lists and of third party handling charges plus (iv) the amount of first class postage required to mail the bidder's amendment. Direct costs incidental to the mailing of the bidder's tender offer materials and amendments thereto when finally computed may include all reasonable charges paid by the subject company to third parties for supplies or services, including costs attendant to preparing shareholder lists, mailing labels, handling the bidder's materials, contacting participants named on security position listings and for postage, but shall exclude indirect costs, such as employee time which is devoted to either contesting or supporting the tender offer on behalf of the subject company. The final billing for direct costs shall be accompanied by an appropriate accounting in reasonable detail.

Note to § 240.14d-5. Reasonably prompt methods of distribution to security holders may be used instead of mailing. If alternative methods are chosen, the approximate direct costs of distribution shall be computed by adding the estimated direct costs of preparing the document for distribution through the chosen medium (including updating of shareholder lists) plus the estimated reasonable cost of distribution through that medium. Direct costs incidental to the distribution of tender offer materials and amendments thereto may include all reasonable charges paid by the subject company to third parties for supplies or services, including costs attendant to preparing shareholder lists, handling the bidder's materials, and contacting participants named on security position listings, but shall not include indirect costs, such as employee time which is devoted to either contesting or supporting the tender offer on behalf of the subject company.

Rule 14d-6. Disclosure of Tender Offer Information to Security Holders

(a) *Information required on date of commencement.*

(1) *Long-form publication.* If a tender offer is published, sent or given to security holders on the date of commencement by means of long-form publication under § 240.14d-4(a)(1), the long-form publication must include the information required by paragraph (d)(1) of this section.

(2) *Summary publication.* If a tender offer is published, sent or given to security holders on the date of commencement by means of summary publication under § 240.14d-4(a)(2):

(i) The summary advertisement must contain at least the information required by paragraph (d)(2) of this section; and

(ii) The tender offer materials furnished by the bidder upon request of any security holder must include the information required by paragraph (d)(1) of this section.

(3) *Use of stockholder lists and security position listings.* If a tender offer is published, sent or given to security holders on the date of commencement by the use of stockholder lists and security position listings under § 240.14d-4(a)(3):

(i) The summary advertisement must contain at least the information required by paragraph (d)(2) of this section; and

(ii) The tender offer materials transmitted to security holders pursuant to such lists and security position listings and furnished by the bidder upon the request of any security holder must include the information required by paragraph (d)(1) of this section.

(4) *Other tender offers.* If a tender offer is published or sent or given to security holders other than pursuant to § 240.14d-4(a), the tender offer materials that are published or sent or given to security holders on the date of commencement of such offer must include the information required by paragraph (d)(1) of this section.

(b) *Information required in other tender offer materials published after commencement.* Except for tender offer materials described in paragraphs (a)(2)(ii) and (a)(3)(ii) of this section, additional tender offer materials published, sent or given to security holders after commencement must include:

(1) The identities of the bidder and subject company;

(2) The amount and class of securities being sought;

(3) The type and amount of consideration being offered; and

(4) The scheduled expiration date of the tender offer, whether the tender offer may be extended and, if so, the procedures for extension of the tender offer.

Instruction to paragraph (b): If the additional tender offer materials are summary advertisements, they also must include the information required by paragraphs (d) (2) (v) of this section.

(c) *Material changes.* A material change in the information published or sent or given to security holders must be promptly disclosed to security holders in additional tender offer materials.

(d) *Information to be included.*

(1) *Tender offer materials other than summary publication.* The following information is required by paragraphs (a) (1), (a) (2) (ii), (a) (3) (ii) and (a) (4) of this section:

(i) The information required by Item 1 of Schedule TO (§ 240.14d-100) (Summary Term Sheet); and

(ii) The information required by the remaining items of Schedule TO (§ 240.14d-100) for third-party tender offers, except for Item 12 (exhibits) of Schedule TO (§ 240.14d-100), or a fair and adequate summary of the information.

(2) *Summary Publication.* The following information is required in a summary advertisement under paragraphs (a) (2) (i) and (a) (3) (i) of this section:

(i) The identity of the bidder and the subject company;

(ii) The information required by Item 1004 (a) (1) of Regulation M-A (§ 229.1004 (a) (1) of this chapter);

(iii) If the tender offer is for less than all of the outstanding securities of a class of equity securities, a statement as to whether the purpose or one of the purposes of the tender offer is to acquire or influence control of the business of the subject company;

(iv) A statement that the information required by paragraph (d) (1) of this section is incorporated by reference into the summary advertisement;

(v) Appropriate instructions as to how security holders may obtain promptly, at the bidder's expense, the bidder's tender offer materials; and

(vi) In a tender offer published or sent or given to security holders by use of stockholder lists and security position listings under § 240.14d-4 (a) (3), a statement that a request is being made for such lists and listings. The summary publication also must state that tender offer materials will be mailed to record holders and will be furnished to brokers, banks and similar persons whose name appears or whose nominee appears on the list of security holders or, if applicable, who are listed as participants in a clearing agency's security position listing for subsequent transmittal to beneficial owners of such securities. If the list furnished to the bidder also included beneficial owners pursuant to § 240.14d-5 (c) (1) and tender offer materials will be mailed directly to beneficial holders, include a statement to that effect.

(3) *No transmittal letter.* Neither the initial summary advertisement nor any subsequent summary advertisement may include a transmittal letter (the letter furnished to security holders for transmission of securities sought in the tender offer) or any amendment to the transmittal letter.

Rule 14d-7. Additional Withdrawal Rights

(a) (1) *Rights.* In addition to the provisions of section 14 (d) (5) of the Act, any person who has deposited securities pursuant to a tender offer has the right to withdraw any such securities during the period such offer request or invitation remains open.

(2) *Exemption during subsequent offering period.* Notwithstanding the provisions of Section 14 (d) (5) of the Act (15 U.S.C. 78n(d) (5)) and paragraph (a) of this section, the bidder need not offer withdrawal rights during a subsequent offering period.

(b) *Notice of withdrawal.* Notice of withdrawal pursuant to this section shall be deemed to be timely upon the receipt by the bidder's depositary of a written notice of withdrawal specifying the name(s) of the tendering stockholder(s), the number or amount of the securities to be withdrawn and the name(s) in which the certificate(s) is (are) registered, if different from that of the tendering security holder(s). A bidder may impose other reasonable requirements, including certificate numbers and a signed request for withdrawal accompanied by a signature guarantee, as conditions precedent to the physical release of withdrawn securities.

Rule 14d-8. Exemption from Statutory Pro Rata Requirement

Notwithstanding the pro rata provisions of Section 14(d) (6) of the Act, if any person makes a tender offer or request or invitation for tenders, for less than all of the outstanding equity securities of a class, and if a greater number of securities are deposited pursuant thereto than such person is bound or willing to take up and pay for, the securities taken up and paid for shall be taken up and paid for as nearly as may be pro rata, disregarding fractions, according to the number of securities deposited by each depositor during the period such offer, request or invitation remains open.

Rule 14d-9. Recommendation or Solicitation by the Subject Company and Others

(a) *Pre-commencement communications.*

A communication by a person described in paragraph (e) of this section with respect to a tender offer will not be deemed to constitute a recommendation or solicitation under this section if:

(1) The tender offer has not commenced under § 240.14d-2; and

(2) The communication is filed under cover of Schedule 14D-9 (§ 240.14d-101) with the Commission no later than the date of the communication.

Instructions to paragraph (a)(2):

1. The box on the front of Schedule 14D-9 (§ 240.14d-101) indicating that the filing contains pre-commencement communications must be checked.

2. Any communications made in connection with an exchange offer registered under the Securities Act of 1933 need only be filed under § 230.425 of this chapter and will be deemed filed under this section.

3. Each pre-commencement written communication must include a prominent legend in clear, plain language advising security holders to read the company's solicitation/ recommendation statement when it is available because it contains important information. The legend also must advise investors that they can get the recommendation and other filed documents for free at the Commission's web site and explain which documents are free from the filer.

4. See Sections 230.135, 230.165 and 230.166 of this chapter for pre-commencement communications made in connection with registered exchange offers.

(b) *Post-commencement communications.*

After commencement by a bidder under § 240.14d-2, no solicitation or recommendation to security holders may be made by any person described in paragraph (e) of this section with respect to a tender offer for such securities unless as soon as practicable on the date such solicitation or recommendation is first published or sent or given to security holders such person complies with the following:

(1) Such person shall file with the Commission a Tender Offer Solicitation/Recommendation Statement on Schedule 14D-9 (240.14d-101), including all exhibits thereto; and

(2) If such person is either the subject company or an affiliate of the subject company,

(i) Such person shall hand deliver a copy of the Schedule 14D-9 to the bidder at its principal office or at the address of the person authorized to receive notices and communications (which is set forth on the cover sheet of the bidder's Schedule TO (§ 240.14d-100) filed with the Commission; and

(ii) Such person shall give telephonic notice (which notice to the extent possible shall be given prior to the opening of the market) of the information required by Items 1003(d) and 1012(a) of Regulation M-A (§ 229.1005(d) and § 229.1012(a)) and shall mail a copy of the Schedule to each national securities exchange where the class of securities is registered and listed for trading and, if the class is authorized for quotation in the NASDAQ interdealer quotation system, to the National Association of Securities Dealers, Inc. ("NASD").

(3) If such person is neither the subject company nor an affiliate of the subject company,

(i) Such person shall mail a copy of the schedule to the bidder at its principal office or at the address of the person authorized to receive notices and communications (which is set forth on the cover sheet of the bidder's Schedule TO (§ 240.14d-100) filed with the Commission); and

(ii) Such person shall mail a copy of the Schedule to the subject company at its principal office.

(c) *Amendments.* If any material change occurs in the information set forth in the Schedule 14D-9 (§ 240.14d-101) required by this section, the person who filed such Schedule 14D-9 shall:

(1) File with the Commission an amendment on Schedule 14D-9 (§ 240.14d-101) disclosing such change promptly, but not later than the date such material is first published, sent or given to security holders; and

(2) Promptly deliver copies and give notice of the amendment in the same manner as that specified in paragraph (b)(2) or (3) of this section, whichever is applicable; and

(3) Promptly disclose and disseminate such change in a manner reasonably designed to inform security holders of such change.

(d) *Information required in solicitation or recommendation.*

Any solicitation or recommendation to holders of a class of securities referred to in section 14(d)(1) of the Act with respect to a tender offer for such securities shall include the name of the person making such solicitation or recommendation and the information required by Items 1 through 8 of Schedule 14D-9 (§ 240.14d-101) or a fair and adequate summary thereof: *Provided, however,* That such solicitation or recommendation may omit any of such information previously furnished to security holders of such class of securities by such person with respect to such tender offer.

(e) *Applicability.*

(1) Except as is provided in paragraphs (e)(2) and (f) of this section, this section shall only apply to the following persons:

(i) The subject company, any director, officer, employee, affiliate or subsidiary of the subject company;

(ii) Any record holder or beneficial owner of any security issued by the subject company, by the bidder, or by any affiliate of either the subject company or the bidder; and

(iii) Any person who makes a solicitation or recommendation to security holders on behalf of any of the foregoing or on behalf of the bidder other than by means of a solicitation or recommendation to security holders which has been filed with the Commission pursuant to this section or Rule 14d-3 (§ 240.14d-3).

(2) Notwithstanding paragraph (e)(1) of this section, this section shall not apply to the following persons:

(i) A bidder who has filed a Schedule TO (§ 240.14d-100) pursuant to Rule 14d-3 (§ 240.14d-3);

(ii) Attorneys, banks, brokers, fiduciaries or investment advisers who are not participating in a tender offer in more than a ministerial capacity and who furnish information and/or advice regarding such tender offer to their customers or clients on the unsolicited request of such customers or clients or solely pursuant to a contract or a relationship providing for advice to the customer or client to whom the information and/or advice is given.

(iii) Any person specified in paragraph (e)(1) of this section if:

(A) The subject company is the subject of a tender offer conducted under §240.14d-1(c);

(B) Any person specified in paragraph (e)(1) of this section furnishes to the Commission on Form CB (§249.480 of this chapter) the entire informational document it publishes or otherwise disseminates to holders of the class of securities in connection with the tender offer no later than the next business day after publication or dissemination;

(C) Any person specified in paragraph (e)(1) of this section disseminates any informational document to U.S. holders, including any amendments thereto, in English, on a comparable basis to that provided to security holders in the issuer's home jurisdiction; and

(D) Any person specified in paragraph (e)(1) of this section disseminates by publication in its home jurisdiction, such person must publish the information in the United States in a manner reasonably calculated to inform U.S. security holders of the offer.

(f) *Stop-look-and-listen communication.* This section shall not apply to the subject company with respect to a communication by the subject company to its security holders which only:

(1) Identifies the tender offer by the bidder;

(2) States that such tender offer is under consideration by the subject company's board of directors and/or management;

(3) States that on or before a specified date (which shall be no later than 10 business days from the date of commencement of such tender offer) the subject company will advise such security holders of (i) whether the subject company recommends acceptance or rejection of such tender offer; expresses no opinion and remains neutral toward such tender offer; or is unable to take a position with respect to such tender offer and (ii) the reason(s) for the position taken by the subject company with respect to the tender offer (including the inability to take a position); and

(4) Requests such security holders to defer making a determination whether to accept or reject such tender offer until they have been advised of the subject company's position with respect thereto pursuant to paragraph (f)(3) of this section.

(g) *Statement of management's position.* A statement by the subject company of its position with respect to a tender offer which is required to be published or sent or given to security holders pursuant to Rule 14e-2 shall be deemed to constitute a solicitation or recommendation within the meaning of this section and section 14(d)(4) of the Act.

Rule 14d-10. Equal Treatment of Security Holders

(a) No bidder shall make a tender offer unless:

(1) The tender offer is open to all security holders of the class of securities subject to the tender offer; and

(2) The consideration paid to any security holder for securities tendered in the tender offer is the highest consideration paid to any other security holder for securities tendered in the tender offer.

(b) Paragraph (a)(1) of this section shall not:

(1) Affect dissemination under Rule 14d-4 (§240.14d-4); or

(2) Prohibit a bidder from making a tender offer excluding all security holders in a state where the bidder is prohibited from making the tender offer by administrative or judicial action pursuant to a state statute after a good faith effort by the bidder to comply with such statute.

(c) Paragraph (a)(2) of this section shall not prohibit the offer of more than one type of consideration in a tender offer, provided that:

(1) Security holders are afforded equal right to elect among each of the types of consideration offered; and

(2) The highest consideration of each type paid to any security holder is paid to any other security holder receiving that type of consideration.

(d)(1) Paragraph (a)(2) of this section shall not prohibit the negotiation, execution or amendment of an employment compensation, severance or other employee benefit arrangement, or payments made or to be made or benefits granted or to be granted according to such an arrangement, with respect to any security holder of the subject company, where the amount payable under the arrangement:

(i) Is being paid or granted as compensation for past services performed, future services to be performed, or future services to be refrained from performing, by the security holder (and matters incidental thereto); and

(ii) Is not calculated based on the number of securities tendered or to be tendered in the tender offer by the security holder.

(2) The provisions of paragraph (d)(1) of this section shall be satisfied and, therefore, pursuant to this non-exclusive safe harbor, the negotiation, execution or amendment of an arrangement and any payments made or to be made or benefits granted or to be granted according to that arrangement shall not be prohibited by paragraph (a)(2) of this section, if the arrangement is approved as an employment compensation, severance or other employee benefit arrangement solely by independent directors as follows:

(i) The compensation committee or a committee of the board of directors that performs functions similar to a compensation committee of the subject company approves the arrangement, regardless of whether the subject company is a party to the arrangement, or, if the bidder is a party to the arrangement, the compensation committee or a committee of the board of directors that performs functions similar to a compensation committee of the bidder approves the arrangement; or

(ii) If the subject company's or bidder's board of directors, as applicable, does not have a compensation committee or a committee of the board of directors that performs functions similar to a compensation committee or if none of the members of the subject company's or bidder's compensation committee or committee that performs functions similar to a compensation committee is independent, a special committee of the board of directors formed to consider and approve the arrangement approves the arrangement; or

(iii) If the subject company or bidder, as applicable, is a foreign private issuer, any or all members of the board of directors or any committee of the board of directors authorized to approve employment compensation, severance or other employee benefit arrangements under the laws or regulations of the home country approves the arrangement.

Instructions to paragraph (d)(2):

For purposes of determining whether the members of the committee approving an arrangement in accordance with the provisionsof paragraph (d)(2) of this section are independent, the following provisions shall apply:

1. If the bidder or subject company, as applicable, is a listed issuer (as defined in § 240.10A-3 of this chapter) whose securities are listed either on a national securities exchange registered pursuant to section 6(a) of the Exchange Act (15 U.S.C. 78f(a)) or in an inter-dealer quotation system of a national securities association registered pursuant to section 15A(a) of the Exchange Act (15 U.S.C. 78o-3(a)) that has independence requirements for compensation committee members that have been approved by the Commission (as those requirements may be modified or supplemented), apply the bidder's or subject company's definition of independence that it uses for determining that the members of the compensation committee are independent in compliance with the listing standards applicable to compensation committee members of the listed issuer.

2. If the bidder or subject company, as applicable, is not a listed issuer (as defined in §240.10A-3 of this chapter), apply the independence requirements for compensation committee members of a national securities exchange registered pursuant to section 6(a) of the Exchange Act (15 U.S.C. 78f(a)) or an inter-dealer quotation system of a national securities association registered pursuant to section 15A(a) of the Exchange Act (15 U.S.C. 78o-3(a)) that have been approved by the Commission (as those requirements may be modified or supplemented). Whatever definition the bidder or subject company, as applicable, chooses, it must apply that definition consistently to all members of the committee approving the arrangement.

3. Notwithstanding Instructions 1 and 2 to paragraph (d)(2), if the bidder or subject company, as applicable, is a closed-end investment company registered under the Investment Company Act of 1940, a director is considered to be independent if the director is not, other than in his or her capacity as a member of the board of directors or any board committee, an "interested person" of the investment company, as defined in section 2(a)(19) of the Investment Company Act of 1940 (15 U.S.C. 80a-2(a)(19)).

4. If the bidder or the subject company, as applicable, is a foreign private issuer, apply either the independence standards set forth in Instructions 1 and 2 to paragraph (d)(2) or the independence requirements of the laws, regulations, codes or standards of the home country of the bidder or subject company, as applicable, for members of the board of directors or the committee of the board of directors approving the arrangement.

5. A determination by the bidder's or the subject company's board of directors, as applicable, that the members of the board of directors or the committee of the board of directors, as applicable, approving an arrangement in accordance with the provisions of paragraph (d)(2) are independent in accordance with the provisions of this instruction to paragraph (d)(2) shall satisfy the independence requirements of paragraph (d)(2).

Instruction to paragraph (d): The fact that the provisions of paragraph (d) of this section extend only to employment compensation, severance and other employee benefit arrangements and not to other arrangements, such as commercial arrangements, does not raise any inference that a payment under any such other arrangement constitutes consideration paid for securities in a tender offer.

(e) If the offer and sale of securities constituting consideration offered in a tender offer is prohibited by the appropriate authority of a state after a good faith effort by the bidder to register or qualify the offer and sale of such securities in such state:

(1) The bidder may offer security holders in such state an alternative form of consideration; and

(2) Paragraph (c) of this rule shall not operate to require the bidder to offer or pay the alternative form of consideration to security holders in any other state.

(f) This section shall not apply to any tender offer with respect to which the Commission, upon written request or upon its own motion, either unconditionally or on specified terms and conditions, determines that compliance with this rule is not necessary or appropriate in the public interest or for the protection of investors.

Rule 14d-11. Subsequent Offering Period

A bidder may elect to provide a subsequent offering period of at least three business days during which tenders will be accepted if:

(a) The initial offering period of at least 20 business days has expired;

(b) The offer is for all outstanding securities of the class that is the subject of the tender offer, and if the bidder is offering security holders a choice of different forms of consideration, there is no ceiling on any form of consideration offered;

(c) The bidder immediately accepts and promptly pays for all securities tendered during the initial offering period;

(d) The bidder announces the results of the tender offer, including the approximate number and percentage of securities deposited to date, no later than 9:00 a.m. Eastern time on the next business day after the expiration date of the initial offering period and immediately begins the subsequent offering period;

(e) The bidder immediately accepts and promptly pays for all securities as they are tendered during the subsequent offering period; and

(f) The bidder offers the same form and amount of consideration to security holders in both the initial and the subsequent offering period.

Note § 240.14d-11: No withdrawal rights apply during the subsequent offering period in accordance with § 240.14d-7(a)(2).

REGULATION 14E

Note: For the scope of and definitions applicable to Regulation 14E refer to § 240.14d-1.

Rule 14e-1. Unlawful Tender Offer Practices

As a means reasonably designed to prevent fraudulent, deceptive or manipulative acts or practices within the meaning of section 14(e) of the Act, no person who makes a tender offer shall:

(a) Hold such tender offer open for less than twenty business days from the date such tender offer is first published or sent to security holders; provided, however, that if the tender offer involves a roll-up transaction as defined in Item 901(c) of Regulation S-K (17 CFR 229.901(c)) and the securities being offered are registered (or authorized to be registered) on Form S-4 (17 CFR 229.25) or Form F-4 (17 CFR 229.34), the offer shall not be open for less than sixty calendar days from the date the tender offer is first published or sent to security holders;

(b) Increase or decrease the percentage of the class of securities being sought or the consideration offered or the dealer's soliciting fee to be given in a tender offer unless such tender offer remains open for at least ten business days from the date that notice of such increase or decrease is first published or sent or given to security holders;

Provided, however, That, for purposes of this paragraph, the acceptance for payment of an additional amount of securities not to exceed two percent of the class of securities that is the subject of the tender offer shall not be deemed to be an increase. For purposes of this paragraph, the percentage of a class of securities shall be calculated in accordance with section 14(d)(3) of the Act.

(c) Fail to pay the consideration offered or return the securities deposited by or on behalf of security holders promptly after the termination or withdrawal of a tender offer. This paragraph does not prohibit a bidder electing to offer a subsequent offering period under § 240.14d-11 from paying for securities during the subsequent offering period in accordance with that section.

(d) Extend the length of a tender offer without issuing a notice of such extension by press release or other public announcement, which notice shall include disclosure of the approximate number of securities deposited to date and shall be issued no later than the earlier of (i) 9:00 a.m. Eastern time, on the next business day after the scheduled expiration date of the offer or (ii), if the class of securities which is the subject of the tender offer is registered on one or more national securities exchanges, the first opening of any one of such exchanges on the next business day after the scheduled expiration date of the offer.

(e) The periods of time required by paragraphs (a) and (b) of this section shall be tolled for any period during which the bidder has failed to file in electronic format, absent a hardship exemption (§§ 232.201 and 232.202 of this chapter), the Schedule TO Tender Offer Statement (§ 240.14d-100), any tender offer material required to be filed by Item 12 of that Schedule pursuant to paragraph (a) of Item 1016 of Regulation M-A (§ 229.1016(a) of this chapter), and any amendments thereto. If such documents were filed in paper pursuant to a hardship exemption (*see* § 232.201 and § 232.202(d)), the minimum offering periods shall be tolled for any period during which a required confirming electronic copy of such Schedule and tender offer material is delinquent.

Rule 14e-2. Position of a Subject Company with Respect to a Tender Offer

(a) *Position of subject company.* As a means reasonably designed to prevent fraudulent, deceptive or manipulative acts or practices within the meaning of section 14(e) of the Act, the subject company, no later than 10 business days from the date the tender offer is first published or sent or given, shall publish, send or give to security holders a statement disclosing that the subject company:

(1) Recommends acceptance or rejection of the bidder's tender offer;

(2) Expresses no opinion and is remaining neutral toward the bidder's tender offer; or

(3) Is unable to take a position with respect to the bidder's tender offer.

Such statement shall also include the reason(s) for the position (including the inability to take a position) disclosed therein.

(b) *Material change.* If any material change occurs in the disclosure required by paragraph (a) of this section, the subject company shall promptly publish, send or give a statement disclosing such material change to security holders.

(c) Any issuer, a class of the securities of which is the subject of a tender offer filed with the Commission on Schedule 14D-1F and conducted in reliance upon and in conformity with Rule 14d-1(b) under the Act, and any director or officer of such issuer where so required by the laws, regulations and policies of Canada and/or any of its provinces or territories, in lieu of the statements called for by paragraph (a) of this section and Rule 14d-9 under the Act, shall file with the Commission on Schedule 14D-9F the entire disclosure document(s) required to be furnished to holders of securities of the subject issuer by the laws, regulations and policies of Canada and/or any of its provinces or territories governing the conduct of the tender offer, and shall disseminate such document(s) in the United States in accordance with such laws, regulations and policies.

(d) *Exemption for cross-border tender offers.* The subject company shall be exempt from this section with respect to a tender offer conducted under § 240.14d-1(c).

Rule 14e-3. Transactions in Securities on the Basis of Material, Nonpublic Information in the Context of Tender Offers

(a) If any person has taken a substantial step or steps to commence, or has commenced, a tender offer (the "offering person"), it shall constitute a fraudulent, deceptive or manipulative act or practice within the meaning of section 14(e) of the Act for any other person who is in possession of material information relating to such tender offer which information he knows or has reason to know is nonpublic and which he knows or has reason to know has been acquired directly or indirectly from (1) the offering person, (2) the issuer of the securities sought or to be sought by such tender offer, or (3) any officer, director, partner or employee or any other person acting on behalf of the offering person or such issuer, to purchase or sell or cause to be purchased or sold any of such securities or any securities convertible into or exchangeable for any such securities or any option or right to obtain or to dispose of any of the foregoing securities, unless within a reasonable time prior to any purchase or sale such information and its source are publicly disclosed by press release or otherwise.

(b) A person other than a natural person shall not violate paragraph (a) of this section if such persons shows that:

(1) The individual(s) making the investment decision on behalf of such person to purchase or sell any security described in paragraph (a) or to cause any such security to be purchased or sold by or on behalf of others did not know the material, nonpublic information; and

(2) Such person had implemented one or a combination of policies and procedures, reasonable under the circumstances, taking into consideration the nature of the person's business, to ensure that individual(s) making investment decision(s) would not violate paragraph (a), which policies and procedures may include, but are not limited to, (i) those which restrict any purchase, sale and causing any purchase and sale of any such security or (ii) those which prevent such individual(s) from knowing such information.

(c) Notwithstanding anything in paragraph (a) to the contrary, the following transactions shall not be violations of paragraph (a) of this section:

(1) Purchase(s) of any security described in paragraph (a) by a broker or by another agent on behalf of an offering person; or

(2) Sale(s) by any person of any security described in paragraph (a) to the offering person.

(d) (1) As a means reasonably designed to prevent fraudulent, deceptive or manipulative acts or practices within the meaning of section 14(e) of the Act, it shall be unlawful for any person described in paragraph (d)(2) of this section to communicate material, nonpublic information relating to a tender offer to any other person under circumstances in which it is reasonably foreseeable that such communication is likely to result in a violation of this section *except* that this paragraph shall not apply to a communication made in good faith,

(i) To the officers, directors, partners or employees of the offering person, to its advisors or to other persons, involved in the planning, financing, preparation or execution of such tender offer;

(ii) To the issuer whose securities are sought or to be sought by such tender offer, to its officers, directors, partners, employees or advisors or to other persons, involved in the planning, financing, preparation or execution of the activities of the issuer with respect to such tender offer; or

(iii) To any person pursuant to a requirement of any statute or rule or regulation promulgated thereunder.

(2) The persons referred to in paragraph (d)(1) of this section are:

(i) The offering person or its officers, directors, partners, employees or advisers;

(ii) The issuer of the securities sought or to be sought by such tender offer or its officers, directors, partners, employees or advisors;

(iii) Anyone acting on behalf of the persons in paragraph (d)(2)(i) or the issuer or persons in paragraph (d)(2)(ii); and

(iv) Any person in possession of material information relating to a tender offer which information he knows or has reason to know is nonpublic and which he knows or has reason to know has been acquired directly or indirectly from any of the above.

Rule 14e-4. Prohibited Transactions In Connection With Partial Tender Offers

(a) Definitions. For purposes of this section:

(1) The amount of a person's "net long position" in a subject security shall equal the excess, if any, of such person's "long position" over such person's "short position." For the purposes of determining the net long position as of the end of the proration period and for tendering concurrently to two or more partial tender offers, securities that have been tendered in accordance with the Rule and not withdrawn are deemed to be part of the person's long position.

(i) Such person's "long position," is the amount of subject securities that such person:

(A) or his agent has title to or would have title to but for having lent such securities; or

(B) has purchased, or has entered into an unconditional contract, binding on both parties thereto, to purchase but has not yet received; or

(C) has exercised a standardized call option for; or

(D) has converted, exchanged, or exercised an equivalent security for; or

(E) is entitled to receive upon conversion, exchange, or exercise of an equivalent security.

(ii) Such person's "short position," is the amount of subject securities or subject securities underlying equivalent securities that such person:

(A) has sold, or has entered into an unconditional contract, binding on both parties thereto, to sell; or

(B) has borrowed; or

(C) has written a non-standardized call option, or granted any other right pursuant to which his shares may be tendered by another person; or

(D) is obligated to deliver upon exercise of a standardized call option sold on or after the date that a tender offer is first publicly announced or otherwise made known by the bidder to holders of the security to be acquired, if the exercise price of such option is lower than the highest tender offer price or stated amount of the consideration offered for the subject security. For the purpose of this paragraph, if one or more tender offers for the same security are ongoing on such date, the announcement date shall be that of the first announced offer.

(2) The term "equivalent security" means (i) any security (including any option, warrant, or other right to purchase the subject security), issued by the person whose securities are the subject of the offer, that is immediately convertible into, or exchangeable or exercisable for, a subject security, or (ii) any other right or option (other than a standardized call option) that entitles the holder thereof to acquire a subject security, but only if the holder thereof reasonably believes that the maker or writer of the right or option has title to and possession of the subject security and upon exercise will promptly deliver the subject security.

(3) The term "subject security" means a security that is the subject of any tender offer or request or invitation for tenders.

(4) For purposes of this rule, a person shall be deemed to "tender" a security if he (i) delivers a subject security pursuant to an offer, (ii) causes such delivery to be made, (iii) guarantees delivery of a subject security pursuant to a tender offer, (iv) causes a guarantee of such delivery to be given by another person, or (v) uses any other method by which acceptance of a tender offer may be made.

(5) The term "partial tender offer" means a tender offer or request or invitation for tenders for less than all of the outstanding securities subject to the offer in which tenders are accepted either by lot or on a *pro rata* basis for a specified period, or a tender offer for all of the outstanding shares that offers a choice of consideration in which tenders for different forms of consideration may be accepted either by lot or on a *pro rata* basis for a specified period.

(6) The term "standardized call option" means any call option that is traded on an exchange, or for which quotation information is disseminated in an electronic interdealer quotation system of a registered national securities association.

(b) It shall be unlawful for any person acting alone or in concert with others, directly or indirectly, to tender any subject security in a partial tender offer:

(1) For his own account unless at the time of tender, and at the end of the proration period or period during which securities are accepted by lot (including any extensions thereof), he has a net long position equal to or greater than the amount tendered in:

(i) the subject security and will deliver or cause to be delivered such security for the purpose of tender to the person making the offer within the period specified in the offer; or

(ii) an equivalent security and, upon the acceptance of his tender will acquire the subject security by conversion, exchange, or exercise of such equivalent security to the extent required by the terms of the offer, and will deliver or cause to be delivered the subject security so acquired for the purpose of tender to the person making the offer within the period specified in the offer; or

(2) For the account of another person unless the person making the tender (i) possesses the subject security or an equivalent security, or (ii) has a reasonable belief that, upon information furnished by the person on whose behalf the tender is made, such person owns the subject security or an equivalent security and will promptly deliver the subject security or such equivalent security for the purpose of tender to the person making the tender.

(c) This rule shall not prohibit any transaction or transactions which the Commission, upon written request or upon its own motion, exempts, either unconditionally or on specified terms and conditions.

Rule 14e-5. Prohibiting Purchases Outside of a Tender Offer

(a) *Unlawful activity.* As a means reasonably designed to prevent fraudulent, deceptive or manipulative acts or practices in connection with a tender offer for equity securities, no covered person may directly or indirectly purchase or arrange to purchase any subject securities or any related securities except as part of the tender offer. This prohibition applies from the time of public announcement of the tender offer until the tender offer expires. This prohibition does not apply to any purchases or arrangements to purchase made during the time of any subsequent offering period as provided for in § 240.14d-11 if the consideration paid or to be paid for the purchases or arrangements to purchase is the same in form and amount as the consideration offered in the tender offer.

(b) *Excepted activity.* The following transactions in subject securities or related securities are not prohibited by paragraph (a) of this section:

(1) *Exercises of securities.* Transactions by covered persons to convert, exchange, or exercise related securities into subject securities, if the covered person owned the related securities before public announcement;

(2) *Purchases for plans.* Purchases or arrangements to purchase by or for a plan that are made by an agent independent of the issuer;

(3) *Purchases during odd-lot offers.* Purchases or arrangements to purchase if the tender offer is excepted under § 240.13e-4(h)(5);

(4) *Purchases as intermediary.* Purchases by or through a dealer-manager or its affiliates that are made in the ordinary course of business and made either:

(i) On an agency basis not for a covered person; or

(ii) As principal for its own account if the dealer-manager or its affiliate is not a market maker, and the purchase is made to offset a contemporaneous sale after having received an unsolicited order to buy from a customer who is not a covered person;

(5) *Basket transactions.* Purchases or arrangements to purchase a basket of securities containing a subject security or a related security if the following conditions are satisfied:

(i) The purchase or arrangement to purchase is made in the ordinary course of business and not to facilitate the tender offer;

(ii) The basket contains 20 or more securities; and

(iii) Covered securities and related securities do not comprise more than 5% of the value of the basket;

(6) *Covering transactions.* Purchases or arrangements to purchase that are made to satisfy an obligation to deliver a subject security or a related security arising from a short sale or from the exercise of an option by a non-covered person if:

(i) The short sale or option transaction was made in the ordinary course of business and not to facilitate the offer;

(ii) In the case of a short sale, the short sale was entered into before public announcement of the tender offer; and

(iii) In the case of an exercise of an option, the covered person wrote the option before public announcement of the tender offer;

(7) *Purchases pursuant to contractual obligations.* Purchases or arrangements to purchase pursuant to a contract if the following conditions are satisfied:

(i) The contract was entered into before public announcement of the tender offer;

(ii) The contract is unconditional and binding on both parties; and

(iii) The existence of the contract and all material terms including quantity, price and parties are disclosed in the offering materials;

(8) *Purchases or arrangements to purchase by an affiliate of the dealer-manager.* Purchases or arrangements to purchase by an affiliate of a dealer-manager if the following conditions are satisfied:

(i) The dealer-manager maintains and enforces written policies and procedures reasonably designed to prevent the flow of information to or from the affiliate that might result in a violation of the federal securities laws and regulations;

(ii) The dealer-manager is registered as a broker or dealer under Section 15(a) of the Act;

(iii) The affiliate has no officers (or persons performing similar functions) or employees (other than clerical, ministerial, or support personnel) in common with the dealer-manager that direct, effect, or recommend transactions in securities; and

(iv) The purchases or arrangements to purchase are not made to facilitate the tender offer;

(9) *Purchases by connected exempt market makers or connected exempt principal traders.* Purchases or arrangements to purchase if the following conditions are satisfied:

(i) The issuer of the subject security is a foreign private issuer, as defined in § 240.3b-4(c);

(ii) The tender offer is subject to the United Kingdom's City Code on Takeovers and Mergers;

(iii) The purchase or arrangement to purchase is effected by a connected exempt market maker or a connected exempt principal trader, as those terms are used in the United Kingdom's City Code on Takeovers and Mergers;

(iv) The connected exempt market maker or the connected exempt principal trader complies with the applicable provisions of the United Kingdom's City Code on Takeovers and Mergers; and

(v) The tender offer documents disclose the identity of the connected exempt market maker or the connected exempt principal trader and disclose, or describe how U.S. security holders can obtain, information regarding market making or principal purchases by such market maker or principal trader to the extent that this information is required to be made public in the United Kingdom;

(10) *Purchases during cross-border tender offers.* Purchases or arrangements to purchase if the following conditions are satisfied:

(i) The tender offer is excepted under § 240.13e-4(h)(8) or § 240.14d-1(c);

(ii) The offering documents furnished to U.S. holders prominently disclose the possibility of any purchases, or arrangements to purchase, or the intent to make such purchases;

(iii) The offering documents disclose the manner in which any information about any such purchases or arrangements to purchase will be disclosed;

(iv) The offeror discloses information in the United States about any such purchases or arrangements to purchase in a manner comparable to the disclosure made in the home jurisdiction, as defined in § 240.13e-4(i)(3); and

(v) The purchases comply with the applicable tender offer laws and regulations of the home jurisdiction; and

(11) *Purchases or Arrangements to Purchase Pursuant to a Foreign Tender Offer(s).* Purchases or arrangements to purchase pursuant to a foreign offer(s) where the offeror seeks to acquire subject securities through a U.S. tender offer and a concurrent or substantially concurrent foreign offer(s), if the following conditions are satisfied:

(i) The U.S. and foreign tender offer(s) meet the conditions for reliance on the Tier II cross-border exemptions set forth in § 240.14d-1(d);

(ii) The economic terms and consideration in the U.S. tender offer and foreign tender offer(s) are the same, provided that any cash consideration to be paid to U.S. security holders may be converted from the currency to be paid in the foreign tender offer(s) to U.S. dollars at an exchange rate disclosed in the U.S. offering documents;

(iii) The procedural terms of the U.S. tender offer are at least as favorable as the terms of the foreign tender offer(s);

(iv) The intention of the offeror to make purchases pursuant to the foreign tender offer(s) is disclosed in the U.S. offering documents; and

(v) Purchases by the offeror in the foreign tender offer(s) are made solely pursuant to the foreign tender offer(s) and not pursuant to an open market transaction(s), a private transaction(s), or other transaction(s); and

(12) *Purchases or Arrangements to Purchase by an Affiliate of the Financial Advisor and an Offeror and its Affiliates.*

(i) Purchases or arrangements to purchase by an affiliate of a financial advisor and an offeror and its affiliates that are permissible under and will be conducted in accordance with the applicable laws of the subject company's home jurisdiction, if the following conditions are satisfied:

(A) The subject company is a foreign private issuer as defined in § 240.3b-4(c);

(B) The covered person reasonably expects that the tender offer meets the conditions for reliance on the Tier II cross-border exemptions set forth in § 240.14d-1(d);

(C) No purchases or arrangements to purchase otherwise than pursuant to the tender offer are made in the United States;

(D) The United States offering materials disclose prominently the possibility of, or the intention to make, purchases or arrangements to purchase subject securities or related securities outside of the tender offer, and if there will be public disclosure of purchases of subject or related securities, the manner in which information regarding such purchases will be disseminated;

(E) There is public disclosure in the United States, to the extent that such information is made public in the subject company's home jurisdiction, of information regarding all purchases of subject securities and related securities otherwise than pursuant to the tender offer from the time of public announcement of the tender offer until the tender offer expires;

(F) Purchases or arrangements to purchase by an offeror and its affiliates must satisfy the following additional condition: the tender offer price will be increased to match any consideration paid outside of the tender offer that is greater than the tender offer price; and

(G) Purchases or arrangements to purchase by an affiliate of a financial advisor must satisfy the following additional conditions:

(1) The financial advisor and the affiliate maintain and enforce written policies and procedures reasonably designed to prevent the transfer of information among the financial advisor and affiliate that might result in a violation of U.S. federal securities laws and regulations through the establishment of information barriers;

(2) The financial advisor has an affiliate that is registered as a broker or dealer under section 15(a) of the Act (15 U.S.C. 78o(a));

(3) The affiliate has no officers (or persons performing similar functions) or employees (other than clerical, ministerial, or support personnel) in common with the financial advisor that direct, effect, or recommend transactions in the subject securities or related securities who also will be involved in providing the offeror or subject company with financial advisory services or dealer-manager services; and

(4) The purchases or arrangements to purchase are not made to facilitate the tender offer.

(ii) Reserved.

(c) *Definitions.* For purposes of this section, the term:

(1) *Affiliate* has the same meaning as in § 240.12b-2;

(2) *Agent independent of the issuer* has the same meaning as in § 242.100(b) of this chapter;

(3) *Covered person* means:

(i) The offeror and its affiliates;

(ii) The offeror's dealer-manager and its affiliates;

(iii) Any advisor to any of the persons specified in paragraph (c)(3)(i) and (ii) of this section, whose compensation is dependent on the completion of the offer; and

(iv) Any person acting, directly or indirectly, in concert with any of the persons specified in this paragraph (c)(3) in connection with any purchase or arrangement to purchase any subject securities or any related securities;

(4) *Plan* has the same meaning as in § 242.100(b) of this chapter;

(5) *Public announcement* is any oral or written communication by the offeror or any person authorized to act on the offeror's behalf that is reasonably designed to, or has the effect of, informing the public or security holders in general about the tender offer;

(6) *Related securities* means securities that are immediately convertible into, exchangeable for, or exercisable for subject securities;

(7) *Subject securities* has the same meaning as in § 229.1000 of this chapter; and

(8) *Subject company* has the same meaning as in § 229.1000 of this chapter; and

(9) *Home jurisdiction* has the same meaning as in the Instructions to paragraphs (c) and (d) of § 240.14d-1.

(d) *Exemptive authority.* Upon written application or upon its own motion, the Commission may grant an exemption from the provisions of this section, either unconditionally or on specified terms or conditions, to any transaction or class of transactions or any security or class of security, or any person or class of persons.

RULES RELATING TO OVER-THE-COUNTER MARKETS

Rule 15c1-1. Definitions

As used in any rule adopted pursuant to Section 15(c)(1) of the Act:

(a) The term "customer" shall not include a broker or dealer or a municipal securities dealer; provided, however, that the term "customer" shall include a municipal securities dealer (other than a broker or dealer) with respect to transactions in securities other than municipal securities.

(b) The term "the completion of the transaction" means:

(1) In the case of a customer who purchases a security through or from a broker, dealer or municipal securities dealer, except as provided in subparagraph (2) of this paragraph, the time when such customer pays the broker, dealer or municipal securities dealer any part of the purchase price, or, if payment is effected by a bookkeeping entry, the time when such bookkeeping entry is made by the broker, dealer or municipal securities dealer for any part of the purchase price;

(2) In the case of a customer who purchases a security through or from a broker, dealer or municipal securities dealer and who makes payment therefor prior to the time when paymet is requested or notification is given that payment is due, the time when such broker, dealer or municipal securities dealer delivers the security to or into the account of such customer;

(3) In the case of a customer who sells a security through or to a broker, dealer or municipal securities dealer except as provided in subparagraph (4) of this paragraph, if the security is not in the custody of the broker, dealer or municipal securities dealer at the time of sale, the time when the security is delivered to the broker, dealer or municipal securities dealer, and if the security is in the custody of the broker, dealer or municipal securities dealer at the time of sale, the time when the broker, dealer or municipal securities dealer transfers the security from the account of such customer;

(4) In the case of a customer who sells a security through or to a broker, dealer or municipal securities dealer and who delivers such security to such broker, dealer or municipal securities dealer prior to the time when delivery is requested or notification is given that delivery is due, the time when such broker, dealer or municipal securities dealer makes payment to or into the account of such customer.

Rule 15c1-2. Fraud and Misrepresentation

(a) The term "manipulative, deceptive, or other fraudulent device or contrivance," as used in Section 15(c)(1) of the Act, is hereby defined to include any act, practice, or course of business which operates or would operate as a fraud or deceit upon any person.

(b) The term "manipulative, deceptive, or other fraudulent device or contrivance," as used in Section 15(c)(1) of the Act, is hereby defined to include any untrue statement of a material fact and any omission to state a material fact necessary in order to make the statements made, in the light of the circumstances under which they are made, not misleading, which statement or omission is made with knowledge or reasonable grounds to believe that it is untrue or misleading.

(c) The scope of this rule shall not be limited by any specific definitions of the term "manipulative, deceptive, or other fraudulent device or contrivance" contained in other rules adopted pursuant to Section 15(c)(1) of the Act.

Rule 15c1-6. Disclosure of Interest in Distribution

The term "manipulative, deceptive, or other fraudulent device or contrivance," as used in Section 15(c)(1) of the Act, is hereby defined to include any act of any broker who is acting for a customer or for both such customer and some other person, or of any dealer or municipal securities dealer who receives or has promise of receiving a fee from a customer for advising such customer with respect to securities, designed to effect with or for the account of such customer any transaction in, or to induce the purchase or sale by such customer of, any security in the primary or secondary distribution of which such broker, dealer or municipal securities dealer is participating or is otherwise financially interested unless such broker, dealer or municipal securities dealer, at or before the completion of each such transaction gives or sends to such customer written notification of the existence of such participation or interest.

Rule 15c2-1. Hypothecation of Customers' Securities

(a) *General Provisions.* The term "fraudulent, deceptive, or manipulative act or practice," as used in section 15(c)(2) of the Act, is hereby defined to include the direct or indirect hypothecation by a broker or dealer, or his arranging for or permitting, directly, or indirectly, the continued hypothecation of any securities carried for the account of any customer under circumstances—

(1) that will permit the commingling of securities carried for the account of any such customer with securities carried for the account of any other customer, without first obtaining the written consent of each such customer to such hypothecation;

(2) that will permit such securities to be commingled with securities carried for the account of any person other than a bona fide customer of such broker or dealer under a lien for a loan made to such broker or dealer; or

(3) that will permit securities carried for the account of customers to be hypothecated, or subjected to any lien or liens or claim or claims of the pledgee or pledgees, for a sum which exceeds the aggregate indebtedness of all customers in respect of securities carried for their accounts; except that this clause shall not be deemed to be violated by reason of an excess arising on any day through the reduction of the aggregate indebtedness of customers on such day, provided that funds or securities in an amount sufficient to eliminate such excess are paid or placed in transfer to pledgees for the purpose of reducing the sum of the liens or claims to which securities carried for the account of customers are subjected as promptly as practicable after such reduction occurs, but before the lapse of one-half hour after the commencement of banking hours on the next banking day at the place where the largest principal amount of loans of such broker or dealer are payable and, in any event, before such broker or dealer on such day has obtained or increased any bank loan collateralized by securities carried for the account of customers.

(b) *Definitions.* For the purposes of this rule—

(1) The term *customer* shall not include any general or special partner or any director or officer of such broker or dealer, or any participant, as such, in any joint, group or syndicate account with such broker or dealer or with any partner, officer or director thereof. The term also shall not include a counterparty who has delivered collateral to an OTC derivatives dealer pursuant to a transaction in an eligible OTC derivative instrument, or pursuant to the

OTC derivatives dealer's cash management securities activities or ancillary portfolio management securities activities, and who has received a prominent written notice from the OTC derivatives dealer that:

(i) Except as otherwise agreed in writing by the OTC derivatives dealer and the counterparty, the dealer may repledge or otherwise use the collateral in its business;

(ii) In the event of the OTC derivatives dealer's failure, the counterparty will likely be considered an unsecured creditor of the dealer as to that collateral;

(iii) The Securities Investor Protection Act of 1970 (15 U.S.C 78aaa through 78lll) does not protect the counterparty; and

(iv) The collateral will not be subject to the requirements of § 240.8c-1, § 240.15c2-1, § 240.15c3-2, or § 240.15c3-3;

(2) the term "securities carried for the account of any customer" shall be deemed to mean:

(i) securities received by or on behalf of such broker or dealer for the account of any customer;

(ii) securities sold and appropriated by such broker or dealer to a customer, except that if such securities were subject to a lien when appropriated to a customer they shall not be deemed to be "securities carried for the account of any customer" pending their release from such lien as promptly as practicable;

(iii) securities sold, but not appropriated, by such broker or dealer to a customer who has made any payment therefor, to the extent that such broker or dealer owns and has received delivery of securities of like kind, except that if such securities were subject to a lien when such payment was made they shall not be deemed to be "securities carried for the account of any customer" pending their release from such lien as promptly as practicable;

(3) "aggregate indebtedness" shall not be deemed to be reduced by reason of uncollected items. In computing aggregate indebtedness, related guaranteed and guarantor accounts shall be treated as a single account and considered on a consolidated basis, and balances in accounts carrying both long and short positions shall be adjusted by treating the market value of the securities required to cover such short positions as though such market value were a debit; and

(4) in computing the sum of the liens or claims to which securities carried for the account of customers of a broker or dealer are subject, any rehypothecation of such securities by another broker or dealer who is subject to this section or to § 240.8c-1 shall be disregarded.

(c) *Exemption for Cash Accounts.* The provisions of paragraph (a)(1) hereof shall not apply to any hypothecation of securities carried for the account of a customer in a special cash account within the meaning of Section 4(c) of Regulation T of the Board of Governors of the Federal Reserve System, provided that at or before the completion of the transaction of purchase of such securities for, or of sale of such securities to, such customer, written notice is given or sent to such customer disclosing that such securities are or may be hypothecated under circumstances which will permit the commingling thereof with securities carried for the account of other customers. The term "the completion of the transaction" shall have the meaning given to such term by § 240.15c1-1(b).

(d) *Exemption for Clearing House Liens.* The provisions of paragraphs (a)(2), (a)(3), and (f) hereof shall not apply to any lien or claim of the clearing corporation, or similar department or association, of a national securities exchange or a registered national securities association, for a loan made and to be repaid on the same calendar day, which is incidental to the clearing of transactions in securities or loans through such corporation, department or association: Provided, however, that for the purpose of paragraph (a)(3) hereof, "aggregate indebtedness of all customers in respect of securities carried for their accounts" shall not include indebtedness in respect of any securities subject to any lien or claim exempted by this paragraph.

(e) *Exemption for Certain Liens on Securities of Noncustomers.* The provisions of paragraph (a)(2) hereof shall not be deemed to prevent such broker or dealer from permitting securities not carried for the account of a customer to be subjected (i) to a lien for a loan made against securities carried for the account of customers, or (ii) to a lien for a loan made and to be repaid on the same calendar day. For the purpose of this exemption, a loan shall be deemed to be "made against securities carried for the account of customers" if only securities carried for the account of customers are used to obtain or to increase such loan or as substitute for other securities carried for the account of customers.

(f) *Notice and Certification Requirements.* No person subject to this rule shall hypothecate any security carried for the account of a customer unless, at or prior to the time of each such hypothecation, he gives written notice to the pledgee that the security pledged is carried for the account of a customer and that such hypothecation does not contravene any provision of this rule, except that in the case of an omnibus account the broker or dealer for whom such account is carried may furnish a signed statement to the person carrying such account that all securities carried therein by such broker or dealer will be securities carried for the account of his customers and that the hypothecation thereof by such broker or dealer will not contravene any provision of this rule. The provisions of this clause shall not apply to any hypothecation of securities under any lien or claim of a pledgee securing a loan made and to be repaid on the same calendar day.

(g) The fact that securities carried for the accounts of customers and securities carried for the accounts of others are represented by one or more certificates in the custody of a clearing corporation or other subsidiary organization of either a national securities exchange or of a registered national securities association, or of a custodian bank, in accordance with a system for the central handling of securities established by a national securities exchange or a registered national securities association, pursuant to which system the hypothecation of such securities is effected by bookkeeping entries without physical delivery of such securities, shall not, in and of itself, result in a commingling of securities prohibited by paragraph (a)(1) or (a)(2) hereof, whenever a participating member, broker or dealer hypothecates securities in accordance with such system, *provided, however,* that (i) any such custodian of any securities held by or for such system shall agree that it will not for any reason, including the assertion of any claim, right or lien of any kind, refuse or refrain from promptly delivering any such securities (other than securities then hypothecated in accordance with such system) to such clearing corporation or other subsidiary organization or as directed by it, except that nothing in such agreement shall be deemed to require the custodian to deliver any securities in contravention of any notice of levy, seizure or similar notice, or order, or judgment, issued or directed by a governmental agency or court, or officer thereof, having jurisdiction over such custodian, which on its face affects such securities; (ii) such system shall have safeguards in the handling, transfer and delivery of securities and provisions for fidelity bond coverage of the employees and agents of the clearing corporation or other subsidiary organization and for periodic examinations by independent public accountants; and (iii) the pro visi ons of this subparagraph (g) shall not be effective with respect to any particular system unless the agreement required by (i) and the safeguards and provisions required by (ii) shall have been deemed adequate by the Commission for the protection of investors, and unless any subsequent amendments to such agreement, safeguards or provisions shall have been deemed adequate by the Commission for the protection of investors.

Rule 15c2-8. Delivery of Prospectus

(a) It shall constitute a deceptive act or practice, as those terms are used in section 15(c)(2) of the Act, for a broker or dealer to participate in a distribution of securities with respect to which a registration statement has been filed under the Securities Act of 1933 unless he complies with the requirements set forth in paragraphs (b) through (h) of this section. For the purposes of this section, a broker or dealer participating in the distribution shall mean any underwriter and any member or proposed member of the selling group.

(b) In connection with an issue of securities, the issuer of which has not previously been required to file reports pursuant to sections 13(a) or 15(d) of the Securities Exchange Act of 1934, unless such issuer has been exempted from the requirement to file reports thereunder pursuant to section 12(h) of the Act, such broker or dealer shall deliver a copy of the preliminary prospectus to any person who is expected to receive a confirmation of sale at least 48 hours prior to the sending of such confirmation. Provided, however, this paragraph (b) shall apply to all issuances of asset-backed securities (as defined in § 229.1101(c) of this chapter) regardless of whether the issuer has previously been required to file reports pursuant to sections 13(a) or 15(d) of the Securities Exchange Act of 1934, or exempted from the requirement to file reports thereunder pursuant to section 12(h) of the Act (15 U.S.C. 78*l*).

(c) Such broker or dealer shall take reasonable steps to furnish to any person who makes written request for a preliminary prospectus between the filing date and a reasonable time prior to the effective date of the registration statement to which such prospectus relates, a copy of the latest preliminary prospectus on file with the Commission. Reasonable steps shall include receiving an undertaking by the managing underwriter or underwriters to send such copy to the address given in the requests.

(d) Such broker or dealer shall take reasonable steps to comply promptly with the written request of any person for a copy of the final prospectus relating to such securities during the period between the effective date of the registration statement and the later of either the termination of such distribution, or the expiration of the applicable 40 or 90 day period under Section 4(3) of the Securities Act of 1933. Reasonable steps shall include receiving an undertaking by the managing underwriter or underwriters to send such copy to the address given in the requests. (The 40-day and 90-day periods referred to above shall be deemed to apply for purposes of this rule irrespective of the provisions of paragraphs (b) and (d) of Rule 174 under the Securities Act of 1933).

(e) Such broker or dealer shall take reasonable steps (i) to make available a copy of the preliminary prospectus relating to such securities to each of his associated persons who is expected, prior to the effective date, to solicit customers' orders for such securities before the making of any such solicitation by such associated persons and (ii) to make available to each such associated person a copy of any amended preliminary prospectus promptly after the filing thereof.

(f) Such broker or dealer shall take reasonable steps to make available a copy of the final prospectus relating to such securities to each of his associated persons who is expected, after the effective date, to solicit customers orders for such securities prior to the making of any such solicitation by such associated persons, unless a preliminary prospectus which is substantially the same as the final prospectus except for matters relating to the price of the stock has been so made available.

(g) If the broker or dealer is a managing underwriter of such distribution, he shall take reasonable steps to see to it that all other brokers or dealers participating in such distribution are promptly furnished with sufficient copies, as requested by them, of each preliminary prospectus, each amended preliminary prospectus and the final prospectus to enable them to comply with paragraphs (b), (c), (d) and (e) above.

(h) If the broker or dealer is a managing underwriter of such distribution, he shall take reasonable steps to see that any broker or dealer participating in the distribution or trading in the registered security is furnished reasonable quantities of the final prospectus relating to such securities, as requested by him, in order to enable him to comply with the prospectus delivery requirements of Section 5(b)(1) and (2) of the Securities Act of 1933.

(i) This rule shall not require the furnishing of prospectuses in any state where such furnishing would be unlawful under the laws of such state; provided, however, that this provisions is not to be construed to relieve a broker-dealer from complying with the requirements of Section 5(b)(1) and (2) of the Securities Act of 1933. Prospectuses shall not be furnished pursuant to this rule while the registration statement is subject to an examination, proceeding, or stop order pursuant to Section 8 of the Securities Act of 1933.

Rule 15c2-11. Initiation or Resumption of Quotations without Specified Information

Preliminary Note: Brokers and dealers may wish to refer to Securities Exchange Act Release No. 29094 (April 17, 1991), for a discussion of procedures for gathering and reviewing the information required by this rule and the requirement that a broker or dealer have a reasonable basis for believing that the information is accurate and obtained from reliable sources.

(a) As a means reasonably designed to prevent fraudulent, deceptive, or manipulative acts or practices, it shall be unlawful for a broker or dealer to publish any quotation for a security or, directly or indirectly, to submit any such quotation for publication, in any quotation medium (as defined in this section) unless such broker or dealer has in its records the documents and information required by this paragraph (for purposes of this section, "paragraph (a) information"), and, based upon a review of the paragraph (a) information together with any other documents and information required by paragraph (b) of this section, has a reasonable basis under the circumstances for believing that the paragraph (a) information is accurate in all material respects, and that the sources of the paragraph (a) information are reliable. The information required pursuant to this paragraph is:

(1) A copy of the prospectus specified by section 10(a) of the Securities Act of 1933 for an issuer that has filed a registration statement under the Securities Act of 1933, other than a registration statement on Form F-6, which became effective less than 90 calendar days prior to the day on which such broker or dealer publishes or submits the quotation to the quotation medium, *Provided* That such registration statement has not thereafter been the subject of a stop order which is still in effect when the quotation is published or submitted; or

(2) A copy of the offering circular provided for under Regulation A under the Securities Act of 1933 for an issuer that has filed a notification under Regulation A which became effective less than 40 calendar days prior to the day on which such broker or dealer publishes or submits the quotation to the quotation medium, *Provided* That the offering circular provided for under Regulation A has not thereafter become the subject of a suspension order which is still in effect when the quotation is published or submitted; or

(3) A copy of the issuer's most recent annual report filed pursuant to section 13 or 15(d) of the Act or pursuant to Regulation A ((§§ 230.251 through 230.263 of this chapter), or a copy of the annual statement referred to in section 12(g)(2)(G)(i) of the Act in the case of an issuer required to file reports pursuant to section 13 or 15(d) of the Act or an issuer of a security covered by section 12(g)(2)(B) or (G) of the Act, together with any semiannual, quarterly and current reports that have been filed under the provisions of the Act or Regulation A by the issuer after such annual report or annual statement; *provided, however,* that until such issuer has filed its first annual report pursuant to section 13 or 15(d) of the Act or pursuant to Regulation A, or annual statement referred to in section 12(g)(2)(G)(i) of the Act, the broker or dealer has in its records a copy of the prospectus specified by section 10(a) of the Securities Act of 1933 included in a registration statement filed by the issuer under the Securities Act of 1933, other than a registration statement on Form F-6, or a copy of the offering circular specified by Regulation A included in an offering statement filed by the issuer under Regulation A, that became effective or was qualified within the prior 16 months, or a copy of any registration statement filed by the issuer under section 12 of the Act that became effective within the prior 16 months, together with any semiannual, quarterly and current reports filed thereafter under section 13 or 15(d) of the Act or Regulation A; and *provided further,* that the broker or dealer has a reasonable basis under the circumstances for believing that the issuer is current in filing annual, semiannual, quarterly, and current reports filed pursuant to section 13 or 15(d) of the Act or Regulation A, or, in the case of an insurance company exempted from section 12(g) of the Act by reason of section 12(g)(2)(G) thereof, the annual statement referred to in section 12(g)(2)(G)(i) of the Act; or

(4) The information that, since the beginning of its last fiscal year, the issuer has published pursuant to § 240.12g3-2(b), and which the broker or dealer shall make reasonably available upon the request of a person expressing an interest in a proposed transaction in the issuer's security with the broker or dealer, such as by providing the requesting person with appropriate instructions regarding how to obtain the information electronically; or

(5) The following information, which shall be reasonably current in relation to the day the quotation is submitted and which the broker or dealer shall make reasonably available upon request to any person expressing an interest in a proposed transaction in the security with such broker or dealer:

(i) the exact name of the issuer and its predecessor (if any);

(ii) the address of its principal executive offices;

(iii) the state of incorporation, if it is a corporation;

(iv) the exact title and class of the security;

(v) the par or stated value of the security;

(vi) the number of shares or total amount of the securities outstanding as of the end of the issuer's most recent fiscal year;

(vii) the name and address of the transfer agent;

(viii) the nature of the issuer's business;

(ix) the nature of products or services offered;

(x) the nature and extent of the issuer's facilities;

(xi) the name of the chief executive officer and members of the board of directors;

(xii) the issuer's most recent balance sheet and profit and loss and retained earnings statements;

(xiii) similar financial information for such part of the two preceding fiscal years as the issuer or its predecessor has been in existence;

(xiv) whether the broker or dealer or any associated person is affiliated, directly or indirectly with the issuer;

(xv) whether the quotation is being published or submitted on behalf of any other broker or dealer, and, if so, the name of such broker or dealer; and,

(xvi) whether the quotation is being submitted or published directly or indirectly on behalf of the issuer, or any director, officer or any person, directly or indirectly the beneficial owner of more than 10 per cent of the outstanding units or shares of any equity security of the issuer, and, if so, the name of such person, and the basis for any exemption under the federal securities laws for any sales of such securities on behalf of such person. If such information is made available to others upon request pursuant to this paragraph, such delivery, unless otherwise represented, shall not constitute a representation by such broker or dealer that such information is accurate, but shall constitute a representation by such broker or dealer that the information is reasonably current in relation to the day the quotation is submitted, that the broker or dealer has a reasonable basis under the circumstances for believing the information is accurate in all material respects, and that the information was obtained from sources which the broker or dealer has a reasonable basis for believing are reliable. This paragraph (a)(5) shall not apply to any security of an issuer included in paragraph (a)(3) of this section unless a report or statement of such issuer described in paragraph (a)(3) of this section is not reasonably available to the broker or dealer. A report or statement of an issuer described in paragraph (a)(3) of this section shall be "reasonably available" when such report or statement is filed with the Commission.

(b) With respect to any security the quotation of which is within the provisions of this section, the broker or dealer submitting or publishing such quotation shall have in its records the following documents and information:

(1) A record of the circumstances involved in the submission of publication of such quotation, including the identity of the person or persons for whom the quotation is being submitted or published and any information regarding the transactions provided to the broker or dealer by such person or persons;

(2) A copy of any trading suspension order issued by the Commission pursuant to Section 12(k) of the Act respecting any securities of the issuer or its predecessor (if any) during the 12 months preceding the date of the publication or submission of the quotation, or a copy of the public release issued by the Commission announcing such trading suspension order; and

(3) A copy or a written record of any other material information (including adverse information) regarding the issuer which comes to the broker's or dealer's knowledge or possession before the publication or submission of the quotation.

(c) The broker or dealer shall preserve the documents and information required under paragraphs (a) and (b) of this section for a period of not less than three years, the first two years in an easily accessible place.

(d) (1) For any security of an issuer included in paragraph (a) (5) of this section, the broker or dealer submitting the quotation shall furnish to the interdealer quotation system (as defined in paragraph (e) (2) of this section), in such form as such system shall prescribe, at least 3 business days before the quotation is published or submitted, the information regarding the security and the issuer which such broker or dealer is required to maintain pursuant to said paragraph (a) (5) of this section.

(2) For any security of an issuer included in paragraph (a) (3) of this section:

(i) A broker-dealer shall be in compliance with the requirement to obtain current reports filed by the issuer if the broker-dealer obtains all current reports filed with the Commission by the issuer as of a date up to five business days in advance of the earlier of the date of submission of the quotation to the quotation medium and the date of submission of the information in paragraph (a) of this section pursuant to the applicable rule of the Financial Industry Regulatory Authority, Inc. or its successor organization; and

(ii) a broker-dealer shall be in compliance with the requirements to obtain the annual, quarterly, and current reports filed by the issuer, if the broker-dealer has made arrangements to receive all such reports when filed by the issuer and it has regularly received reports from the issuer on a timely basis, unless the broker-dealer has a reasonable basis under the circumstances for believing that the issuer has failed to file a required report or has filed a report but has not sent it to the broker-dealer.

(e) For purposes of this rule:

(1) "Quotation medium" shall mean any "inter-dealer quotation system" or any publication or electronic communications network or other device which is used by brokers or dealers to make known to others their interest in transactions in any security, including offers to buy or sell at a stated price or otherwise, or invitations of offers to buy or sell.

(2) "inter-dealer quotation system" shall mean any system of general circulation to brokers or dealers which regularly disseminates quotations of identified brokers or dealers.

(3) Except as otherwise specified in this rule, "quotation" shall mean any bid or offer at a specified price with respect to a security, or any indication of interest by a broker or dealer in receiving bids or offers from others for a security, or any indication by a broker or dealer that he wishes to advertise his general interest in buying or selling a particular security.

(4) "Issuer," in the case of quotations represented by American Depositary Receipts, shall mean the issuer of the deposited shares represented by such American Depositary Receipts.

(f) The provisions of this rule shall not apply to:

(1) The publication or submission of a quotation respecting a security admitted to trading on a national securities exchange and which is traded on such an exchange on the same day as, or on the business day next preceding, the day the quotation is published or submitted.

(2) The publication or submission by a broker or dealer, solely on behalf of a customer (other than a person acting as or for a dealer), of a quotation that represents the customer's indication of interest and does not involve the solicitation of the customer's interest; *Provided, however,* That this paragraph (f) (2) shall not apply to a quotation consisting of both a bid and an offer, each of which is at a specified price, unless the quotation medium specifically identifies the quotation as representing such an unsolicited customer interest.

(3) (i) The publication or submission, in an interdealer quotation system that specifically identifies as such unsolicited customer indications of interest of the kind described in paragraph (f) (2) of this section, of a quotation respecting a security which has been the subject of quotations (exclusive of any identified customer interests) in such a system on each of at least 12 days within the previous 30 calendar days, with no more than 4 business days in succession without a quotation; or

(ii) The publication or submission, in an interdealer quotation system that does not so identify any such unsolicited customer indications of interest, of a quotation respecting a security which has been the subject of both bid and ask quotations in an interdealer quotation system at specified prices on each of at least 12 days within the previous 30 calendar days, with no more than 4 business days in succession without such a two-way quotation;

(iii) A dealer acting in the capacity of market maker, as defined in section 3(a)(38) of the Act, that has published or submitted a quotation respecting a security in an interdealer quotation system and such quotation has qualified for an exception provided in this paragraph (f)(3), may continue to publish or submit quotations for such security in the interdealer quotation system without compliance with this section unless and until such dealer ceases to submit or publish a quotation or ceases to act in the capacity of market maker respecting such security.

(4) The publication or submission of a quotation respecting a municipal security.

(5) The publication or submission of a quotation respecting a Nasdaq security (as defined in § 242.600 of this chapter), and such security's listing is not suspended, terminated, or prohibited.

(g) The requirement in subparagraph (a)(5) that the information with respect to the issuer be "reasonably current" will be presumed to be satisfied, unless the broker or dealer has information to the contrary, if:

(1) the balance sheet is as of a date less than 16 months before the publication or submission of the quotation, the statements of profit and loss and retained earnings are for the 12 months preceding the date of such balance sheet, and if such balance sheet is not as of a date less than 6 months before the publication or submission of the quotation, it shall be accompanied by additional statements of profit and loss and retained earnings for the period from the date of such balance sheet to a date less than 6 months before the publication or submission of the quotation.

(2) other information regarding the issuer specified in subparagraph (a)(5) is as of a date within 12 months prior to the publication or submission of the quotation.

(h) This rule shall not prohibit any publication or submission of any quotation if the Commission, upon written request or upon its own motion, exempts such quotation either unconditionally or on specific terms and conditions, as not constituting a fraudulent, manipulative or deceptive practice comprehended within the purpose of this rule.

Rule 15c2-12. Municipal Securities Disclosure

Preliminary Note: For a discussion of disclosure obligations relating to municipal securities, issuers, brokers, dealers, and municipal securities dealers should refer to Securities Act Release No. 7049, Securities Exchange Act Release No. 33741, FR-42 (March 9, 1994). For a discussion of the obligations of underwriters to have a reasonable basis for recommending municipal securities, brokers, dealers, and municipal securities dealers should refer to Securities Exchange Act Release No. 26100 (Sept. 22, 1988) and Securities Exchange Act Release No. 26985 (June 28, 1989).

(a) *General.* As a means reasonably designed to prevent fraudulent, deceptive, or manipulative acts or practices, it shall be unlawful for any broker, dealer, or municipal securities dealer (a "Participating Underwriter" when used in connection with an Offering) to act as an underwriter in a primary offering of municipal securities with an aggregate principal amount of $1,000,000 or more (an "Offering") unless the Participating Underwriter complies with the requirements of this section or is exempted from the provisions of this section.

(b) *Requirements.*

(1) Prior to the time the Participating Underwriter bids for, purchases, offers, or sells municipal securities in an Offering, the Participating Underwriter shall obtain and review an official statement that an issuer of such securities deems final as of its date, except for the omission of no more than the following information: the offering price(s), interest

rate(s), selling compensation, aggregate principal amount, principal amount per maturity, delivery dates, any other terms or provisions required by an issuer of such securities to be specified in a competitive bid, ratings, other terms of the securities depending on such matters, and the identity of the underwriter(s).

(2) Except in competitively bid offerings, from the time the Participating Underwriter has reached an understanding with an issuer of municipal securities that it will become a Participating Underwriter in an Offering until a final official statement is available, the Participating Underwriter shall send no later than the next business day, by first class mail or other equally prompt means, to any potential customer, on request, a single copy of the most recent preliminary official statement, if any.

(3) The Participating Underwriter shall contract with an issuer of municipal securities or its designated agent to receive, within seven business days after any final agreement to purchase, offer, or sell the municipal securities in an Offering and in sufficient time to accompany any confirmation that requests payment from any customer, copies of a final official statement in sufficient quantity to comply with paragraph (b)(4) of this rule and the rules of the Municipal Securities Rulemaking Board.

(4) From the time the final official statement becomes available until the earlier of

(i) ninety days from the end of the underwriting period or

(ii) The time when the official statement is available to any person from the Municipal Securities Rulemaking Board, but in no case less than twenty-five days following the end of the underwriting period, the Participating Underwriter in an Offering shall send no later than the next business day, by first-class mail or other equally prompt means, to any potential customer, on request, a single copy of the final official statement.

(5)(i) A Participating Underwriter shall not purchase or sell municipal securities in connection with an Offering unless the Participating Underwriter has reasonably determined that an issuer of municipal securities, or an obligated person for whom financial or operating data is presented in the final official statement has undertaken, either individually or in combination with other issuers of such municipal securities or obligated persons, in a written agreement or contract for the benefit of holders of such securities, to provide the following to the Municipal Securities Rulemaking Board in an electronic format as prescribed by the Municipal Securities Rulemaking Board, either directly or indirectly through an indenture trustee or a designated agent:

(A) Annual financial information for each obligated person for whom financial information or operating data is presented in the final official statement, or, for each obligated person meeting the objective criteria specified in the undertaking and used to select the obligated persons for whom financial information or operating data is presented in the final official statement, except that, in the case of pooled obligations, the undertaking shall specify such objective criteria;

(B) If not submitted as part of the annual financial information, then when and if available, audited financial statements for each obligated person covered by paragraph (b)(5)(i)(A) of this section;

(C) In a timely manner not in excess of ten business days after the occurrence of the event, notice of any of the following events with respect to the securities being offered in the Offering:

(1) Principal and interest payment delinquencies;

(2) Non-payment related defaults, if material;

(3) Unscheduled draws on debt service reserves reflecting financial difficulties;

(4) Unscheduled draws on credit enhancements reflecting financial difficulties;

(5) Substitution of credit or liquidity providers, or their failure to perform;

(6) Adverse tax opinions, the issuance by the Internal Revenue Service of proposed or final determinations of taxability, Notices of Proposed Issue (IRS

Form 5701-TEB) or other material notices or determinations with respect to the tax status of the security, or other material events affecting the tax status of the security;

(7) Modifications to rights of security holders, if material;

(8) Bond calls, if material, and tender offers;

(9) Defeasances;

(10) Release, substitution, or sale of property securing repayment of the securities, if material;

(11) Rating changes;

(12) Bankruptcy, insolvency, receivership or similar event of the obligated person;

Note to Paragraph (b)(5)(i)(C)(12): For the purposes of the event identified in paragraph (b)(5)(i)(C)(12) of this section, the event is considered to occur when any of the following occur: The appointment of a receiver, fiscal agent or similar officer for an obligated person in a proceeding under the U.S. Bankruptcy Code or in any other proceeding under state or federal law in which a court or governmental authority has assumed jurisdiction over substantially all of the assets or business of the obligated person, or if such jurisdiction has been assumed by leaving the existing governing body and officials or officers in possession but subject to the supervision and orders of a court or governmental authority, or the entry of an order confirming a plan of reorganization, arrangement or liquidation by a court or governmental authority having supervision or jurisdiction over substantially all of the assets or business of the obligated person;

(13) The consummation of a merger, consolidation, or acquisition involving an obligated person or the sale of all or substantially all of the assets of the obligated person, other than in the ordinary course of business, the entry into a definitive agreement to undertake such an action or the termination of a definitive agreement relating to any such actions, other than pursuant to its terms, if material;

(14) Appointment of a successor or additional trustee or the change of name of a trustee, if material;

(*15*) Incurrence of a financial obligation of the obligated person, if material, or agreement to covenants, events of default, remedies, priority rights, or other similar terms of a financial obligation of the obligated person, any of which affect security holders, if material; and

(*16*) Default, event of acceleration, termination event, modification of terms, or other similar events under the terms of a financial obligation of the obligated person, any of which reflect financial difficulties.

(D) In a timely manner, notice of a failure of any person specified in paragraph (b)(5)(i)(A) of this section to provide required annual financial information, on or before the date specified in the written agreement or contract.

(ii) The written agreement or contract for the benefit of holders of such securities also shall identify each person for whom annual financial information and notices of material events will be provided, either by name or by the objective criteria used to select such persons, and, for each such person shall:

(A) Specify, in reasonable detail, the type of financial information and operating data to be provided as part of annual financial information;

(B) Specify, in reasonable detail, the accounting principles pursuant to which financial statements will be prepared, and whether the financial statements will be audited; and

(C) Specify the date on which the annual financial information for the preceding fiscal year will be provided.

(iii) Such written agreement or contract for the benefit of holders of such securities also may provide that the continuing obligation to provide annual financial information and notices of events may be terminated with respect to any obligated person, if and when such obligated person no longer remains an obligated person with respect to such municipal securities.

(iv) Such written agreement or contract for the benefit of holders of such securities also shall provide that all documents provided to the Municipal Securities Rulemaking Board shall be accompanied by identifying information as prescribed by the Municipal Securities Rulemaking Board.

(c) *Recommendations.* As a means reasonably designed to prevent fraudulent, deceptive, or manipulative acts or practices, it shall be unlawful for any broker, dealer, or municipal securities dealer to recommend the purchase or sale of a municipal security unless such broker, dealer, or municipal securities dealer has procedures in place that provide reasonable assurance that it will receive prompt notice of any event disclosed pursuant to paragraph (b)(5)(i)(C), paragraph (b)(5)(i)(D), and paragraph (d)(2)(ii)(B) of this section with respect to that security.

(d) *Exemptions.* (1) This section shall not apply to a primary offering of municipal securities in authorized denominations of $100,000 or more, if such securities:

(i) Are sold to no more than thirty-five persons each of whom the Participating Underwriter reasonably believes:

(A) Has such knowledge and experience in financial and business matters that it is capable of evaluating the merits and risks of the prospective investment; and

(B) Is not purchasing for more than one account or with a view to distributing the securities; or

(ii) Have a maturity of nine months or less.

(2) Paragraph (b)(5) of this section shall not apply to an Offering of municipal securities if, at such time as an issuer of such municipal securities delivers the securities to the Participating Underwriters:

(i) No obligated person will be an obligated person with respect to more than $10,000,000 in aggregate amount of outstanding municipal securities, including the offered securities and excluding municipal securities that were offered in a transaction exempt from this section pursuant to paragraph (d)(1) of this section;

(ii) An issuer of municipal securities or obligated person has undertaken, either individually or in combination with other issuers of municipal securities or obligated persons, in a written agreement or contract for the benefit of holders of such municipal securities, to provide the following to the Municipal Securities Rulemaking Board in an electronic format as prescribed by the Municipal Securities Rulemaking Board:

(A) At least annually, financial information or operating data regarding each obligated person for which information or operating data is presented in the final official statement, as specified in the undertaking, which financial information and operating data shall include, at a minimum, that financial information and operating data which is customarily prepared by such obligated person and is publicly available; and

(B) In a timely manner not in excess of ten business days after the occurrence of the event, notice of events specified in paragraph (b)(5)(i)(C) of this section with respect to the securities that are the subject of the Offering; and

(C) Such written agreement or contract for the benefit of holders of such securities also shall provide that all documents provided to the Municipal Securities Rulemaking Board shall be accompanied by identifying information as prescribed by the Municipal Securities Rulemaking Board; and

(iii) the final official statement identifies by name, address, and telephone number the persons from which the foregoing information, data, and notices can be obtained.

(3) The provisions of paragraph (b)(5) of this section, other than paragraph (b)(5)(i)(C) of this section, shall not apply to an Offering of municipal securities, if such municipal securities have a stated maturity of 18 months or less.

(4) The provisions of paragraph (c) of this section shall not apply to municipal securities:

(i) Sold in an Offering to which paragraph (b)(5) of this section did not apply, other than Offerings exempt under paragraph (d)(2)(ii) of this section; or

(ii) Sold in an Offering exempt from this section under paragraph (d)(1) of this section.

(5) With the exception of paragraphs (b)(1) through (b)(4), this section shall apply to a primary offering of municipal securities in authorized denominations of $100,000 or more if such securities may, at the option of the holder thereof, be tendered to an issuer of such securities or its designated agent for redemption or purchase at par value or more at least as frequently as every nine months until maturity, earlier redemption, or purchase by an issuer or its designated agent; provided, however, that paragraphs (b)(5) and (c) of this section shall not apply to such securities outstanding on November 30, 2010 for so long as they continuously remain in authorized denominations of $100,000 or more and may, at the option of the holder thereof, be tendered to an issuer of such securities or its designated agent for redemption or purchase at par value or more at least as frequently as every nine months until maturity, earlier redemption, or purchase by an issuer or its designated agent.

(e) *Exemptive Authority.* The Commission, upon written request, or upon its own motion, may exempt any broker, dealer, or municipal securities dealer, whether acting in the capacity of a Participating Underwriter or otherwise, that is a participant in a transaction or class of transactions from any requirement of this section, either unconditionally or on specified terms and conditions, if the Commission determines that such an exemption is consistent with the public interest and the protection of investors.

(f) *Definitions.* For the purposes of this rule—

(1) The term *authorized denominations of $100,000 or more* means municipal securities with a principal amount of $100,000 or more and with restrictions that prevent the sale or transfer of such securities in principal amounts of less than $100,000 other than through a primary offering; except that, for municipal securities with an original issue discount of 10 percent or more, the term means municipal securities with a minimum purchase price of $100,000 or more and with restrictions that prevent the sale or transfer of such securities, in principal amounts that are less than the original principal amount at the time of the primary offering, other than through a primary offering.

(2) The term *end of the underwriting period* means the later of such time as (i) the issuer of municipal securities delivers the securities to the Participating Underwriters or (ii) the Participating Underwriter does not retain, directly or as a member or an underwriting syndicate, an unsold balance of the securities for sale to the public.

(3) The term *final official statement* means a document or set of documents prepared by an issuer of municipal securities or its representatives that is complete as of the date delivered to the Participating Underwriter(s) and that sets forth information concerning the terms of the proposed issue of securities; information, including financial information or operating data, concerning such issuers of municipal securities and those other entities, enterprises, funds, accounts, and other persons material to an evaluation of the Offering; and a description of the undertakings be provided pursuant to paragraph (b)(5)(i), paragraph (d)(2)(ii), and paragraph (d)(2)(iii) of this section, if applicable, and of any instances in the previous five years in which each person specified pursuant to paragraph (b)(5)(ii) of this section failed to comply, in all material respects, with any previous undertakings in a written contract or agreement specified in paragraph (b)(5)(i) of this section. Financial information or operating data may be set forth in the document or set of documents, or may be included by specific reference to documents available to the public on the Municipal Securities Rulemaking Board's Internet Web site or filed with the Commission.

(4) The term *issuer of municipal securities* means the governmental issuer specified in section 3(a)(29) of the Act and the issuer of any separate security, including a separate security as defined in rule 3b-5(a) under the Act.

(5) The term *potential customer* means (i) any person contacted by the Participating Underwriter concerning the purchase of municipal securities that are intended to be offered or have been sold in an Offering, (ii) any person who has expressed an interest to the Participating Underwriter in possibly purchasing such municipal securities, and (iii) any person who has a customer account with the Participating Underwriter.

(6) The term *preliminary official statement* means an official statement prepared by or for an issuer of municipal securities for dissemination to potential customers prior to the availability of the final official statement.

(7) The term *primary offering* means an offering of municipal securities directly or indirectly by or on behalf of an issuer of such securities, including any remarketing of municipal securities (i) that is accompanied by a change in the authorized denomination of such securities from $100,000 or more to less than $100,000, or (ii) that is accompanied by a change in the period during which such securities may be tendered to an issuer of such securities or its designated agent for redemption or purchase from a period of nine months or less to a period of more than nine months.

(8) The term *underwriter* means any person who has purchased from an issuer of municipal securities with a view to, or offers or sells for an issuer of municipal securities in connection with, the offering of any municipal security, or participates or has a direct or indirect participating in any such undertaking, or participates or has a participation in the direct or indirect underwriting of any such undertaking; except, that such term shall not include a person whose interest is limited to a commission, concession, or allowance from an underwriter, broker, dealer, or municipal securities dealer not in excess of the usual and customary distributors' or sellers' commission, concession, or allowance.

(9) The term *annual financial information* means financial information or operating data, provided at least annually, of the type included in the final official statement with respect to an obligated person, or in the case where no financial information or operating data was provided in the final official statement with respect to such obligated person, of the type included in the final official statement with respect to those obligated persons that meet the objective criteria applied to select the persons for which financial information or operating data will be provided on an annual basis. Financial information or operating data may be set forth in the document or set of documents, or may be included by specific reference to documents available to the public on the Municipal Securities Rulemaking Board's Internet Web site or filed with the Commission.

(10) The term *obligated person* means any person, including an issuer of municipal securities, who is either generally or through an enterprise, fund, or account of such person committed by contract or other arrangement to support payment of all, or part of the obligations on the municipal securities to be sold in the Offering (other than providers of municipal bond insurance, letters of credit, or other liquidity facilities).

(g) *Transitional Provision.* If on July 28, 1989 a Participating Underwriter was contractually committed to act as underwriter in an Offering of municipal securities originally issued before July 29, 1989, and requirements of paragraphs (b)(3) and (b)(4) shall not apply to the Participating Underwriter in connection with such an Offering. Paragraph (b)(5) of this section shall not apply to a Participating Underwriter that has contractually committed to act as an underwriter in an Offering of municipal securities before July 3, 1995; *except that* paragraph (b)(5)(i)(A) and paragraph (b)(5)(i)(B) shall not apply with respect to fiscal years ending prior to January 1, 1996. Paragraph (c) shall become effective on January 1, 1996. Paragraph (d)(2)(ii) and paragraph (d)(2)(iii) of this section shall not apply to an Offering of municipal securities commencing prior to January 1, 1996.

Rule 15c3-5. Risk Management Controls For Brokers or Dealers With Market Access.

(a) For the purpose of this section:

(1) The term market access shall mean (i) access to trading in securities on an exchange or alternative trading system as a result of being a member or subscriber of

the exchange or alternative trading system, respectively; or (ii) access to trading in securities on an alternative trading system provided by a broker-dealer operator of an alternative trading system to a non-broker-dealer.

(2) The term *regulatory requirements* shall mean all federal securities laws, rules and regulations, and rules of self-regulatory organizations, that are applicable in connection with market access.

(b) A broker or dealer with market access, or that provides a customer or any other person with access to an exchange or alternative trading system through use of its market participant identifier or otherwise, shall establish, document, and maintain a system of risk management controls and supervisory procedures reasonably designed to manage the financial, regulatory, and other risks of this business activity. Such broker or dealer shall preserve a copy of its supervisory procedures and a written description of its risk management controls as part of its books and records in a manner consistent with § 240.17a-4 (e) (7). A broker-dealer that routes orders on behalf of an exchange or alternative trading system for the purpose of accessing other trading centers with protected quotations in compliance with Rule 611 of Regulation NMS (§ 242.611) for NMS stocks, or in compliance with a national market system plan for listed options, shall not be required to comply with this rule with regard to such routing services, except with regard to paragraph (c) (1) (ii) of this section.

(c) The risk management controls and supervisory procedures required by paragraph (b) of this section shall include the following elements:

(1) *Financial Risk Management Controls and Supervisory Procedures.* The risk management controls and supervisory procedures shall be reasonably designed to systematically limit the financial exposure of the broker or dealer that could arise as a result of market access, including being reasonably designed to:

(i) Prevent the entry of orders that exceed appropriate pre-set credit or capital thresholds in the aggregate for each customer and the broker or dealer and, where appropriate, more finely-tuned by sector, security, or otherwise by rejecting orders if such orders would exceed the applicable credit or capital thresholds; and

(ii) Prevent the entry of erroneous orders, by rejecting orders that exceed appropriate price or size parameters, on an order-by-order basis or over a short period of time, or that indicate duplicative orders.

(2) *Regulatory Risk Management Controls and Supervisory Procedures.* The risk management controls and supervisory procedures shall be reasonably designed to ensure compliance with all regulatory requirements, including being reasonably designed to:

(i) Prevent the entry of orders unless there has been compliance with all regulatory requirements that must be satisfied on a pre-order entry basis;

(ii) Prevent the entry of orders for securities for a broker or dealer, customer, or other person if such person is restricted from trading those securities;

(iii) Restrict access to trading systems and technology that provide market access to persons and accounts pre-approved and authorized by the broker or dealer; and

(iv) Assure that appropriate surveillance personnel receive immediate post-trade execution reports that result from market access.

(d) The financial and regulatory risk management controls and supervisory procedures described in paragraph (c) of this section shall be under the direct and exclusive control of the broker or dealer that is subject to paragraph (b) of this section.

(1) Notwithstanding the foregoing, a broker or dealer that is subject to paragraph (b) of this section may reasonably allocate, by written contract, after a thorough due diligence review, control over specific regulatory risk management controls and supervisory procedures described in paragraph (c) (2) of this section to a customer that is a registered broker or dealer, provided that such broker or dealer subject to paragraph (b) of this section has a reasonable basis for determining that such customer, based on its position in the transaction and relationship with an ultimate customer, has better access than the broker or dealer to that ultimate customer and its trading information such that it can more effectively implement the specified controls or procedures.

(2) Any allocation of control pursuant to paragraph (d) (1) of this section shall not relieve a broker or dealer that is subject to paragraph (b) of this section from any obligation

under this section, including the overall responsibility to establish, document, and maintain a system of risk management controls and supervisory procedures reasonably designed to manage the financial, regulatory, and other risks of market access.

(e) A broker or dealer that is subject to paragraph (b) of this section shall establish, document, and maintain a system for regularly reviewing the effectiveness of the risk management controls and supervisory procedures required by paragraphs (b) and (c) of this section and for promptly addressing any issues.

(1) Among other things, the broker or dealer shall review, no less frequently than annually, the business activity of the broker or dealer in connection with market access to assure the overall effectiveness of such risk management controls and supervisory procedures. Such review shall be conducted in accordance with written procedures and shall be documented. The broker or dealer shall preserve a copy of such written procedures, and documentation of each such review, as part of its books and records in a manner consistent with § 240.17a-4(e)(7) and § 240.17a-4(b), respectively.

(2) The Chief Executive Officer (or equivalent officer) of the broker or dealer shall, on an annual basis, certify that such risk management controls and supervisory procedures comply with paragraphs (b) and (c) of this section, and that the broker or dealer conducted such review, and such certifications shall be preserved by the broker or dealer as part of its books and records in a manner consistent with § 240.17a-4(b).

(f) The Commission, by order, may exempt from the provisions of this section, either unconditionally or on specified terms and conditions, any broker or dealer, if the Commission determines that such exemption is necessary or appropriate in the public interest consistent with the protection of investors.

PENNY STOCK DISCLOSURES

Rule 15g-1. Exemptions for Certain Transactions

The following transactions shall be exempt from 17 CFR 240.15g-2, 17 CFR 240.15g-3, 17 CFR 240.15g-4, 17 CFR 240.15g-5, and 17 CFR 240.15g-6:

(a) Transactions by a broker or dealer:

(1) whose commissions, commission equivalents, mark-ups, and mark-downs from transactions in penny stocks during each of the immediately preceding three months and during eleven or more of the preceding twelve months, or during the immediately preceding six months, did not exceed five percent of its total commissions, commission equivalents, mark-ups, and mark-downs from transactions in securities during those months; and

(2) who has not been a market maker in the penny stock that is the subject of the transaction in the immediately preceding twelve months.

Note: Prior to April 28, 1993, commissions, commission equivalents, mark-ups, and mark-downs from transactions in designated securities, as defined in 17 CFR 240.15c2-6(d)(2) as of April 15, 1992, may be considered to be commissions, commission equivalents, mark-ups, mark-downs from transactions in penny stocks for purposes of paragraph (a)(1) of this section.

(b) Transactions in which the customer is an institutional accredited investor, as defined in 17 CFR 230.501(a)(1), (2), (3), (7) or (8) of this chapter.

(c) Transactions that meet the requirements of Regulation D (17 CFR 230.501—230.508 of this chapter), or transactions with an issuer not involving any public offering pursuant to Section 4(2) of the Securities Act of 1933.

(d) Transactions in which the customer is the issuer, or a director, officer, general partner, or direct or indirect beneficial owner of more than five percent of any class of equity security of the issuer, of the penny stock that is the subject of the transaction.

(e) Transactions that are not recommended by the broker or dealer.

(f) Any other transaction or class of transactions or persons or class of persons that, upon prior written request or upon its own motion, the Commission conditionally or unconditionally exempts by order as consistent with the public interest and the protection of investors.

Rule 15g-2. Penny Stock Disclosure Document Relating to the Penny Stock Market

(a) It shall be unlawful for a broker or dealer to effect a transaction in any penny stock for or with the account of a customer unless, prior to effecting such transaction, the broker or dealer has furnished to the customer a document containing the information set forth in Schedule 15G, § 240.15g-100, and has obtained from the customer a signed and dated acknowledgement of receipt of the document.

(b) Regardless of the form of acknowledgement used to satisfy the requirements of paragraph (a) of this section, it shall be unlawful for a broker or dealer to effect a transaction in any penny stock for or with the account of a customer less than two business days after the broker or dealer sends such document.

(c) The broker or dealer shall preserve, as part of its records, a copy of the written acknowledgment required by paragraph (a) of this section for the period specified in 17 CFR 240.17a-4(b) of this chapter.

(d) Upon request of the customer, the broker or dealer shall furnish the customer with a copy of the information set forth on the Commission's Web site at *http://www.sec.gov/investor/ pubs/microcapstock.htm*.

Rule 15g-3. Broker or Dealer Disclosure of Quotations and Other Information Relating to the Penny Stock Market

(a) *Requirement*. It shall be unlawful for a broker or dealer to effect a transaction in any penny stock with or for the account of a customer unless such broker or dealer discloses to such customer, within the time periods and in the manner required by paragraph (b) of this section, the following information:

(1) The inside bid quotation and the inside offer quotation for the penny stock.

(2) If paragraph (a)(1) of this section does not apply because of the absence of an inside bid quotation and an inside offer quotation:

(i) With respect to a transaction effected with or for a customer on a principal basis (other than as provided in paragraph (a)(2)(ii) of this section):

(A) The dealer shall disclose its offer price for the security:

(1) if during the previous five days the dealer has effected no fewer than three *bona fide* sales to other dealers consistently at its offer price for the security current at the time of those sales, and

(2) if the dealer reasonably believes in good faith at the time of the transaction with the customer that its offer price accurately reflects the price at which it is willing to sell one or more round lots to another dealer.

For purposes of this paragraph (a)(2)(i)(A), "consistently" shall constitute, at a minimum, seventy-five percent of the dealer's *bona fide* interdealer sales during the previous five-day period, and, if the dealer has effected only three *bona fide* inter-dealer sales during such period, all three of such sales.

(B) The dealer shall disclose its bid price for the security:

(1) if during the previous five days the dealer has effected no fewer than three *bona fide* purchases from other dealers consistently at its bid price for the security current at the time of those purchases, and

(2) if the dealer reasonably believes in good faith at the time of the transaction with the customer that its bid price accurately reflects the price at which it is willing to buy one or more round lots from another dealer.

For purposes of this paragraph (a)(2)(i)(B), "consistently" shall constitute, at a minimum, seventy-five percent of the dealer's *bona fide* interdealer purchases during the previous five-day period, and, if the dealer has effected only three *bona fide* inter-dealer purchases during such period, all three of such purchases.

(C) If the dealer's bid or offer prices to the customer do not satisfy the criteria of paragraphs (a)(2)(i)(A) or (a)(2)(i)(B) of this section, the dealer shall disclose to the customer:

(*1*) that it has not effected inter-dealer purchases or sales of the penny stock consistently at its bid or offer price, and

(*2*) the price at which it last purchased the penny stock from, or sold the penny stock to, respectively, another dealer in a *bona fide* transaction.

(ii) With respect to transactions effected by a broker or dealer with or for the account of the customer:

(A) on an agency basis or

(B) on a basis other than as a market maker in the security, where, after having received an order from the customer to purchase a penny stock, the dealer effects the purchase from another person to offset a contemporaneous sale of the penny stock to such customer, or, after having received an order from the customer to sell the penny stock, the dealer effects the sale to another person to offset a contemporaneous purchase from such customer, the broker or dealer shall disclose the best independent interdealer bid and offer prices for the penny stock that the broker or dealer obtains through reasonable diligence. A broker-dealer shall be deemed to have exercised reasonable diligence if it obtains quotations from three market makers in the security (or all known market makers if there are fewer than three).

(3) With respect to bid or offer prices and transaction prices disclosed pursuant to paragraph (a) of this section, the broker or dealer shall disclose the number of shares to which the bid and offer prices apply.

(b) *Timing*. (1) The information described in paragraph (a) of this section:

(i) shall be provided to the customer orally or in writing prior to effecting any transaction with or for the customer for the purchase or sale of such penny stock; and

(ii) shall be given or sent to the customer in writing, at or prior to the time that any written confirmation of the transaction is given or sent to the customer pursuant to 17 CFR 240.10b-10 of this chapter.

(2) A broker or dealer, at the time of making the disclosure pursuant to paragraph (b)(1)(i) of this section, shall make and preserve as part of its records, a record of such disclosure for the period specified in 17 CFR 240.17a-4(b) of this chapter.

(c) *Definitions*. For purposes of this section:

(1) The term "bid price" shall mean the price most recently communicated by the dealer to another broker or dealer at which the dealer is willing to purchase one or more round lots of the penny stock, and shall not include indications of interest.

(2) The term "offer price" shall mean the price most recently communicated by the dealer to another broker or dealer at which the dealer is willing to sell one or more round lots of the penny stock, and shall not include indications of interest.

(3) The term "inside bid quotation" for a security shall mean the highest bid quotation for the security displayed by a market maker in the security on a Qualifying Electronic Quotation System, at any time in which at least two market makers are contemporaneously displaying on such system bid and offer quotations for the security at specified prices.

(4) The term "inside offer quotation" for a security shall mean the lowest offer quotation for the security displayed by a market maker in the security on a Qualifying Electronic Quotation System, at any time in which at least two market makers are contemporaneously displaying on such system bid and offer quotations for the security at specified prices.

(5) The term "Qualifying Electronic Quotation System" shall mean an automated inter-dealer quotation system that has the characteristics set forth in Section 17B(b)(2) of the Act, or such other automated interdealer quotation system designated by the Commission for purposes of this section.

Rule 15g-4. Disclosure of Compensation to Brokers or Dealers

Preliminary Note: Brokers and dealers may wish to refer to Securities Exchange Act Release No. 30608 (April 20, 1992) for a discussion of the procedures for computing compensation in active and competitive markets, inactive and competitive markets, and dominated and controlled markets.

(a) *Disclosure Requirement.* It shall be unlawful for any broker or dealer to effect a transaction in any penny stock for or with the account of a customer unless such broker or dealer discloses to such customer, within the time periods and in the manner required by paragraph (b) of this section, the aggregate amount of any compensation received by such broker or dealer in connection with such transaction.

(b) *Timing.* (1) The information described in paragraph (a) of this section:

(i) shall be provided to the customer orally or in writing prior to effecting any transaction with or for the customer for the purchase or sale of such penny stock; and

(ii) shall be given or sent to the customer in writing, at or prior to the time that any written confirmation of the transaction is given or sent to the customer pursuant to 17 CFR 240.10b-10 of this chapter.

(2) A broker or dealer, at the time of making the disclosure pursuant to paragraph (b)(1)(i) of this section, shall make and preserve as part of its records, a record of such disclosure for the period specified in 17 CFR 240.17a-4(b) of this chapter.

(c) *Definition of Compensation.* For purposes of this section, "compensation" means, with respect to a transaction in a penny stock:

(1) if a broker is acting as agent for a customer, the amount of any remuneration received or to be received by it from such customer in connection with such transaction;

(2) if, after having received a buy order from a customer, a dealer other than a market maker purchased the penny stock as principal from another person to offset a contemporaneous sale to such customer or, after having received a sell order from a customer, sold the penny stock as principal to another person to offset a contemporaneous purchase from such customer, the difference between the price to the customer and such contemporaneous purchase or sale price; or

(3) if the dealer otherwise is acting as principal for its own account, the difference between the price to the customer and the prevailing market price.

(d) *"Active and competitive" market.* For purposes of this section only, a market may be deemed to be "active and competitive" in determining the prevailing market price with respect to a transaction by a market maker in a penny stock if the aggregate number of transactions effected by such market maker in the penny stock in the five business days preceding such transaction is less than twenty percent of the aggregate number of all transactions in the penny stock reported on a Qualifying Electronic Quotation System (as defined in 17 CFR 240.15g-3(c)(5)) during such five-day period. No presumption shall arise that a market is not "active and competitive" solely by reason of a market maker not meeting the conditions specified in this paragraph.

Rule 15g-5. Disclosure of Compensation of Associated Persons in Connection with Penny Stock Transactions

(a) *General.* (1) It shall be unlawful for a broker or dealer to effect a transaction in any penny stock for or with the account of a customer unless the broker or dealer discloses to such customer, within the time periods and in the manner required by paragraph (b) of this section, the aggregate amount of cash compensation that any associated person of the broker or dealer who is a natural person and has communicated with the customer concerning the transaction at or prior to receipt of the customer's transaction order, other than any person whose function is solely clerical or ministerial, has received or will receive from any source in connection with the transaction and that is determined at or prior to the time of the transaction, including separate disclosure, if applicable, of the source and amount of such compensation that is not paid by the broker or dealer.

(b) *Timing.* (1) The information described in paragraph (a) of this section:

(i) shall be provided to the customer orally or in writing prior to effecting any transaction with or for the customer for the purchase or sale of such penny stock; and

(ii) shall be given or sent to the customer in writing, at or prior to the time that any written confirmation of the transaction is given or sent to the customer pursuant to 17 CFR 240.10b-10 of this chapter.

(2) A broker or dealer, at the time of making the disclosure pursuant to paragraph (b)(1)(i) of this section, shall make and preserve as part of its records, a record of such disclosure for the period specified in 17 CFR 240.17a-4(b) of this chapter.

(c) *Contingent Compensation Arrangements.* Where a portion or all of the cash or other compensation that the associated person may receive in connection with the transaction may be determined and paid following the transaction based on aggregate sales volume levels or other contingencies, the written disclosure required by paragraph (b)(1)(ii) of this section shall state that fact and describe the basis upon which such compensation is determined.

Rule 15g-6. Account Statements for Penny Stock Customers

(a) *Requirement.* It shall be unlawful for any broker or dealer that has effected the sale to any customer, other than in a transaction that is exempt pursuant to 17 CFR 240.15g-1 of this chapter, of any security that is a penny stock on the last trading day of any calendar month, or any successor of such broker or dealer, to fail to give or send to such customer a written statement containing the information described in paragraphs (c) and (d) of this section with respect to each such month in which such security is held for the customer's account with the broker or dealer, within ten days following the end of such month.

(b) *Exemptions.* A broker or dealer shall be exempted from the requirement of paragraph (a) of this section under either of the following circumstances:

(1) If the broker or dealer does not effect any transactions in penny stocks for or with the account of the customer during a period of six consecutive calendar months, then the broker or dealer shall not be required to provide monthly statements for each quarterly period that is immediately subsequent to such six-month period and in which the broker or dealer does not effect any transaction in penny stocks for or with the account of the customer, *provided* that the broker or dealer gives or sends to the customer written statements containing the information described in paragraphs (d) and (e) of this section on a quarterly basis, within ten days following the end of each such quarterly period.

(2) If, on all but five or fewer trading days of any quarterly period, a security has a price of five dollars or more, the broker or dealer shall not be required to provide a monthly statement covering the security for subsequent quarterly periods, until the end of any such subsequent quarterly period on the last trading day of which the price of the security is less than five dollars.

(c) *Price Determinations.* For purposes of paragraphs (a) and (b) of this section, the price of a security on any trading day shall be determined at the close of business in accordance with the provisions of 17 CFR 240.3a51-1(d)(1) of this chapter.

(d) *Market and Price Information.* The statement required by paragraph (a) of this section shall contain at least the following information with respect to each penny stock covered by paragraph (a) of this section, as of the last trading day of the period to which the statement relates:

(1) The identity and number of shares or units of each such security held for the customer's account; and

(2) The estimated market value of the security, to the extent that such estimated market value can be determined in accordance with the following provisions:

(i) The highest inside bid quotation for the security on the last trading day of the period to which the statement relates, multiplied by the number of shares or units of the security held for the customer's account; or

(ii) If paragraph (d)(2)(i) of this section is not applicable because of the absence of an inside bid quotation, and if the broker or dealer furnishing the statement has effected at least ten separate Qualifying Purchases in the security during the last five trading days of the period to which the statement relates, the weighted average price per share paid by the broker or dealer in all Qualifying Purchases effected during such five-day period, multiplied by the number of shares or units of the security held for the customer's account; or

(iii) If neither of paragraphs (d)(2)(i) nor (d)(2)(ii) of this section is applicable, a statement that there is "no estimated market value" with respect to the security.

(e) *Legend*. In addition to the information required by paragraph (d) of this section, the written statement required by paragraph (a) of this section shall include a conspicuous legend that is identified with the penny stocks described in the statement and that contains the following language:

IF THIS STATEMENT CONTAINS AN ESTIMATED VALUE, YOU SHOULD BE AWARE THAT THIS VALUE MAY BE BASED ON A LIMITED NUMBER OF TRADES OR QUOTES. THEREFORE, YOU MAY NOT BE ABLE TO SELL THESE SECURITIES AT A PRICE EQUAL OR NEAR TO THE VALUE SHOWN. HOWEVER, THE BROKER-DEALER FURNISHING THIS STATEMENT MAY NOT REFUSE TO ACCEPT YOUR ORDER TO SELL THESE SECURITIES. ALSO, THE AMOUNT YOU RECEIVE FROM A SALE GENERALLY WILL BE REDUCED BY THE AMOUNT OF ANY COMMISSIONS OR SIMILAR CHARGES. IF AN ESTIMATED VALUE IS NOT SHOWN FOR A SECURITY, A VALUE COULD NOT BE DETERMINED BECAUSE OF A LACK OF INFORMATION.

(f) *Preservation of Records*. Any broker or dealer subject to this section shall preserve, as part of its records, copies of the written statements required by paragraph (a) of this section and keep such records for the periods specified in 17 CFR 240.17a-4(b) of this chapter.

(g) *Definitions*. For purposes of this section:

(1) The term "Quarterly period" shall mean any period of three consecutive full calendar months.

(2) The "inside bid quotation" for a security shall mean the highest bid quotation for the security displayed by a market maker in the security on a Qualifying Electronic Quotation System, at any time in which at least two market makers are contemporaneously displaying on such system bid and offer quotations for the security at specified prices.

(3) The term "Qualifying Electronic Quotation System" shall mean an automated interdealer quotation system that has the characteristics set forth in Section 17B(b)(2) of the Act, or such other automated interdealer quotation system designated by the Commission for purposes of this section.

(4) The term "Qualifying Purchases" shall mean *bona fide* purchases by a broker or dealer of a penny stock for its own account, each of which involves at least 100 shares, but excluding any block purchase involving more than one percent of the outstanding shares or units of the security.

Rule 15g-8. Sales of Escrowed Securities of Blank Check Companies

As a means reasonably designed to prevent fraudulent, deceptive, or manipulative acts or practices, it shall be unlawful for any person to sell or offer to sell any security that is deposited and held in an escrow or trust account pursuant to Rule 419 under the Securities Act of 1933 [17 CFR 230.419], or any interest in or related to such security, other than pursuant to a qualified domestic relations order as defined by the Internal Revenue Code of 1986, as amended [26 U.S.C. 1 *et seq.*], or Title I of the Employee Retirement Income Security Act [29 U.S.C. 1001 *et seq.*], or the rules thereunder.

Rule 15g-9. Sales Practice Requirements for Certain Low-Priced Securities

(a) As a means reasonably designed to prevent fraudulent, deceptive, or manipulative acts or practices, it shall be unlawful for a broker or dealer to sell a penny stock to, or to effect the purchase of a penny stock by, any person unless:

(1) the transaction is exempt under paragraph (c) of this section; or

(2) prior to the transaction:

(i) the broker or dealer has approved the person's account for transactions in penny stocks in accordance with the procedures set forth in paragraph (b) of this section; and

(ii) (A) The broker or dealer has received from the person an agreement to the transaction setting forth the identity and quantity of the penny stock to be purchased; and

(B) Regardless of the form of agreement used to satisfy the requirements of paragraph (a) (2) (ii) (A) of this section, it shall be unlawful for such broker or dealer to sell a penny stock to, or to effect the purchase of a penny stock by, for or with the account of a customer less than two business days after the broker or dealer sends such agreement.

(b) In order to approve a person's account for transactions in penny stocks, the broker or dealer must:

(1) obtain from the person information concerning the person's financial situation, investment experience, and investment objectives;

(2) reasonably determine, based on the information required by paragraph (b) (1) of this section and any other information known by the broker-dealer, that transactions in penny stocks are suitable for the person, and that the person (or the person's independent adviser in these transactions) has sufficient knowledge and experience in financial matters that the person (or the person's independent adviser in these transactions) reasonably may be expected to be capable of evaluating the risks of transactions in penny stocks;

(3) deliver to the person a written statement:

(i) setting forth the basis on which the broker or dealer made the determination required by paragraph (b) (2) of this section;

(ii) stating in a highlighted format that it is unlawful for the broker or dealer to effect a transaction in a penny stock subject to the provisions of paragraph (a) (2) of this section unless the broker or dealer has received, prior to the transaction, a written agreement to the transaction from the person; and

(iii) stating in a highlighted format immediately preceding the customer signature line that:

(A) the broker or dealer is required by this section to provide the person with the written statement; and

(B) the person should not sign and return the written statement to the broker or dealer if it does not accurately reflect the person's financial situation, investment experience, and investment objectives; and

(4) (i) Obtain from the person a signed and dated copy of the statement required by paragraph (b) (3) of this section; and

(ii) Regardless of the form of statement used to satisfy the requirements of paragraph (b) (4) (i) of this section, it shall be unlawful for such broker or dealer to sell a penny stock to, or to effect the purchase of a penny stock by, for or with the account of a customer less than two business days after the broker or dealer sends such statement.

(c) For purposes of this section, the following transactions shall be exempt:

(1) Transactions that are exempt under 17 CFR 240.15g-1 (a), (b), (d), (e), and (f).

(2) Transactions that meet the requirements of 17 CFR 230.506 (including, where applicable, the requirements of 17 CFR 230.501 through 230.503, and 230.507 through 230.508), or transactions with an issuer not involving any public offering pursuant to Section 4(a)2 of the Securities Act of 1933.

(3) Transactions in which the purchaser is an established customer of the broker or dealer.

(d) For purposes of this section:

(1) The term "penny stock" shall have the same meaning as in 17 CFR 240.3a51-1.

(2) The term "established customer" shall mean any person for whom the broker or dealer, or a clearing broker on behalf of such broker or dealer, carries an account, and who in such account:

(i) has effected a securities transaction, or made a deposit of funds or securities, more than one year previously; or

(ii) has made three purchases of penny stocks that occurred on separate days and involved different issuers.

Rule 15l-1. Regulation Best Interest

(a) Best Interest Obligation.

(1) A broker, dealer, or a natural person who is an associated person of a broker or dealer, when making a recommendation of any securities transaction or investment strategy involving securities (including account recommendations) to a retail customer, shall act in the best interest of the retail customer at the time the recommendation is made, without placing the financial or other interest of the broker, dealer, or natural person who is an associated person of a broker or dealer making the recommendation ahead of the interest of the retail customer.

(2) The best interest obligation in paragraph (a)(1) shall be satisfied if:

(i) Disclosure Obligation. The broker, dealer, or natural person who is an associated person of a broker or dealer, prior to or at the time of the recommendation, provides the retail customer, in writing, full and fair disclosure of:

(A) All material facts relating to the scope and terms of the relationship with the retail customer, including: (i) that the broker, dealer, or such natural person is acting as a broker, dealer, or an associated person of a broker or dealer with respect to the recommendation; (ii) The material fees and costs that apply to the retail customer's transactions, holdings, and accounts; and (iii) The type and scope of services provided to the retail customer, including any material limitations on the securities or investment strategies involving securities that may be recommended to the retail customer; and

(B) All material facts relating to conflicts of interest that are associated with the recommendation.

(ii) Care Obligation. The broker, dealer, or natural person who is an associated person of a broker or dealer, in making the recommendation, exercises reasonable diligence, care, and skill to:

(A) Understand the potential risks, rewards, and costs associated with the recommendation, and have a reasonable basis to believe that the recommendation could be in the best interest of at least some retail customers;

(B) Have a reasonable basis to believe that the recommendation is in the best interest of a particular retail customer based on that retail customer's investment profile and the potential risks, rewards, and costs associated with the recommendation and does not place the financial or other interest of the broker, dealer, or such natural person ahead of the interest of the retail customer;

(C) Have a reasonable basis to believe that a series of recommended transactions, even if in the retail customer's best interest when viewed in isolation, is not excessive and is in the retail customer's best interest when taken together in light of the retail customer's investment profile and does not place the financial or other interest of the broker, dealer, or such natural person making the series of recommendations ahead of the interest of the retail customer.

(iii) Conflict of Interest Obligation. The broker or dealer establishes, maintains, and enforces written policies and procedures reasonably designed to:

(A) Identify and at a minimum disclose, in accordance with subparagraph (a)(2)(i), or eliminate, all conflicts of interest associated with such recommendations;

(B) Identify and mitigate any conflicts of interest associated with such recommendations that create an incentive for a natural person who is an associated person of a broker or dealer to place the interest of the broker, dealer, or such natural person ahead of the interest of the retail customer;

(C) (i) Identify and disclose any material limitations placed on the securities or investment strategies involving securities that may be recommended to a retail customer and any conflicts of interest associated with such limitations, in accordance with subparagraph (a)(2)(i), and (ii) Prevent such limitations and associated conflicts of interest from causing the broker, dealer, or a natural person who is an associated person of the broker or dealer to make recommendations that place the interest of the broker, dealer, or such natural person ahead of the interest of the retail customer; and

(D) Identify and eliminate any sales contests, sales quotas, bonuses, and non-cash compensation that are based on the sales of specific securities or specific types of securities within a limited period of time.

(iv) Compliance Obligation. In addition to the policies and procedures required by paragraph (iii), the broker or dealer establishes, maintains, and enforces written policies and procedures reasonably designed to achieve compliance with Regulation Best Interest.

(b) Definitions. Unless otherwise provided, all terms used in this rule shall have the same meaning as in the [Securities Exchange Act of 1934]. In addition, the following definitions shall apply for purposes of this section:

(1) Retail Customer means a natural person, or the legal representative of such natural person, who:

(A) Receives a recommendation of any securities transaction or investment strategy involving securities from a broker, dealer, or a natural person who is an associated person of a broker or dealer; and

(B) Uses the recommendation primarily for personal, family, or household purposes.

(2) Retail Customer Investment Profile includes, but is not limited to, the retail customer's age, other investments, financial situation and needs, tax status, investment objectives, investment experience, investment time horizon, liquidity needs, risk tolerance, and any other information the retail customer may disclose to the broker, dealer, or a natural person who is an associated person of a broker or dealer in connection with a recommendation.

(3) Conflict of Interest means an interest that might incline a broker, dealer, or a natural person who is an associated person of a broker or dealer—consciously or unconsciously— to make a recommendation that is not disinterested.

REPORTS OF DIRECTORS, OFFICERS, AND PRINCIPAL STOCKHOLDERS

Rule 16a-1. Definition of Terms

Terms defined in this Rule shall apply solely to Section 16 of the Act and the rules thereunder. These terms shall not be limited to Section 16(a) of the Act but also shall apply to all other subsections under Section 16 of the Act.

(a) The term "beneficial owner" shall have the following applications:

(1) Solely for purposes of determining whether a person is a beneficial owner of more than ten percent of any class of equity securities registered pursuant to Section 12 of the Act, the term "beneficial owner" shall mean any person who is deemed a beneficial owner pursuant to Section 13(d) of the Act and the rules thereunder; *provided, however*, that the following institutions or persons shall not be deemed the beneficial owner of securities of such class held for the benefit of third parties or in customer or fiduciary accounts in the ordinary course of business (or in the case of an employee benefit plan specified in subparagraph (vi) below, of securities of such class allocated to plan participants where participants have voting power) as long as such shares are acquired by such institutions or persons without the purpose or effect of changing or influencing control of the issuer or engaging in any arrangement subject to Rule 13d-3(b) (§ 240.13d-3(b)):

(i) A broker or dealer registered under section 15 of the Act (15 U.S.C. 78o);

(ii) A bank as defined in section 3(a)(6) of the Act (15 U.S.C. 78c);

(iii) An insurance company as defined in section 3(a)(19) of the Act (15 U.S.C. 78c);

(iv) An investment company registered under section 8 of the Investment Company Act of 1940 (15 U.S.C. 80a-8);

(v) Any person registered as an investment adviser under Section 203 of the Investment Advisers Act of 1940 (15 U.S.C. 80b-3) or under the laws of any state;

(vi) An employee benefit plan as defined in Section 3(3) of the Employee Retirement Income Security Act of 1974, as amended, 29 U.S.C. 1001 et seq. ("ERISA") that is subject to the provisions of ERISA, or any such plan that is not subject to ERISA that is maintained primarily for the benefit of the employees of a state or local government or instrumentality, or an endowment fund;

(vii) A parent holding company or control person, provided the aggregate amount held directly by the parent or control person, and directly and indirectly by their subsidiaries or affiliates that are not persons specified in paragraphs (a)(1)(i) through (x), does not exceed one percent of the securities of the subject class;

(viii) A savings association as defined in Section 3(b) of the Federal Deposit Insurance Act (12 U.S.C. 1813);

(ix) A church plan that is excluded from the definition of an investment company under section 3(c)(14) of the Investment Company Act of 1940 (15 U.S.C. 80a-3);

(x) A non-U.S. institution that is the functional equivalent of any of the institutions listed in paragraphs (a)(1)(i) through (ix) of this section, so long as the non-U.S. institution is subject to a regulatory scheme that is substantially comparable to the regulatory scheme applicable to the equivalent U.S. institution and the non-U.S. institution is eligible to file a Schedule 13G pursuant to § 240.13d-1(b)(1)(ii)(J); and

(xi) A group, provided that all the members are persons specified in § 240.16a-1(a)(1)(i) through (x).

Note to paragraph (a). Pursuant to this section, a person deemed a beneficial owner of more than ten percent of any class of equity securities registered under Section 12 of the Act would file a Form 3 (§ 249.103), but the securities holdings disclosed on Form 3, and changes in beneficial ownership reported on subsequent Forms 4 (§ 249.104) or 5 (§ 249.105), would be determined by the definition of "beneficial owner" in paragraph (a)(2) of this section.

(2) Other than for purposes of determining whether a person is a beneficial owner of more than ten percent of any class of equity securities registered under Section 12 of the Act, the term "beneficial owner" shall mean any person who, directly or indirectly, through any contract, arrangement, understanding, relationship or otherwise, has or shares a direct or indirect pecuniary interest in the equity securities, subject to the following:

(i) The term "pecuniary interest" in any class of equity securities shall mean the opportunity, directly or indirectly, to profit or share in any profit derived from a transaction in the subject securities.

(ii) The term "indirect pecuniary interest" in any class of equity securities shall include, but not be limited to:

(A) securities held by members of a person's immediate family sharing the same household *provided, however*, that the presumption of such beneficial ownership may be rebutted; *see* also § 240.16a-1(a)(4);

(B) a general partner's proportionate interest in the portfolio securities held by a general or limited partnership. The general partner's proportionate interest, as evidenced by the partnership agreement in effect at the time of the transaction and the partnership's most recent financial statements, shall be the greater of:

(*1*) the general partner's share of the partnership's profits, including profits attributed to any limited partnership interests held by the general partner and any other interests in profits that arise from the purchase and sale of the partnership's portfolio securities; or

(2) the general partner's share of the partnership capital account, including the share attributable to any limited partnership interest held by the general partner.

(C) a performance-related fee, other than an asset-based fee, received by any broker, dealer, bank, insurance company, investment company, investment adviser, investment manager, trustee or person or entity performing a similar function; *provided, however*, that no pecuniary interest shall be present where:

(1) the performance-related fee, regardless of when payable, is calculated based upon net capital gains and/or net capital appreciation generated from the portfolio or from the fiduciary's overall performance over a period of one year or more; and

(2) equity securities of the issuer do not account for more than ten percent of the market value of the portfolio. A right to a nonperformance-related fee alone shall not represent a pecuniary interest in the securities;

(D) A person's right to dividends that is separated or separable from the underlying securities. Otherwise, a right to dividends alone shall not represent a pecuniary interest in the securities;

(E) A person's interest in securities held by a trust, as specified in § 240.16a-8(b); and

(F) A person's right to acquire equity securities through the exercise or conversion of any derivative security, whether or not presently exercisable.

(iii) A shareholder shall not be deemed to have a pecuniary interest in the portfolio securities held by a corporation or similar entity in which the person owns securities if the shareholder is not a controlling shareholder of the entity and does not have or share investment control over the entity's portfolio.

(3) Where more than one person subject to section 16 of the Act is deemed to be a beneficial owner of the same equity securities, all such persons must report as beneficial owners of the securities, either separately or jointly, as provided in § 240.16a-3(j). In such cases, the amount of short-swing profit recoverable shall not be increased above the amount recoverable if there were only one beneficial owner.

(4) Any person filing a statement pursuant to Section 16(a) of the Act may state that the filing shall not be deemed an admission that such person is, for purposes of Section 16 of the Act or otherwise, the beneficial owner of any equity securities covered by the statement.

(5) The following interests are deemed not to confer beneficial ownership for purposes of Section 16 of the Act:

(i) Interests in portfolio securities held by any investment company registered under the Investment Company Act of 1940; and

(ii) Interests in securities comprising part of a broad-based, publicly traded market basket or index of stocks, approved for trading by the appropriate federal governmental authority.

(b) The term "call equivalent position" shall mean a derivative security position that increases in value as the value of the underlying equity increases, including, but not limited to, a long convertible security, a long call option, and a short put option position.

(c) The term "derivative securities" shall mean any option, warrant, convertible security, stock appreciation right, or similar right with an exercise or conversion privilege at a price related to an equity security, or similar securities with a value derived from the value of an equity security, but shall not include:

(1) rights of a pledgee of securities to sell the pledged securities;

(2) rights of all holders of a class of securities of an issuer to receive securities pro rata, or obligations to dispose of securities, as a result of a merger, exchange offer, or consolidation involving the issuer of the securities;

(3) Rights or obligations to surrender a security, or have a security withheld, upon the receipt or exercise of a derivative security or the receipt or vesting of equity securities, in order to satisfy the exercise price or the tax withholding consequences of receipt, exercise or vesting;

(4) interests in broad-based index options, broad-based index futures, and broad-based publicly traded market baskets of stocks approved for trading by the appropriate federal governmental authority;

(5) interests or rights to participate in employee benefit plans of the issuer; or

(6) rights with an exercise or conversion privilege at a price that is not fixed; or

(7) Options granted to an underwriter in a registered public offering for the purpose of satisfying over-allotments in such offering.

(d) The term "equity security of such issuer" shall mean any equity security or derivative security relating to an issuer, whether or not issued by that issuer.

(e) The term "immediate family" shall mean any child, stepchild, grandchild, parent, stepparent, grandparent, spouse, sibling, mother-in-law, father-in-law, son-in-law, daughter-in-law, brother-in-law, or sister-in-law, and shall include adoptive relationships.

(f) The term "officer" shall mean an issuer's president, principal financial officer, principal accounting officer (or, if there is no such accounting officer, the controller), any vice-president of the issuer in charge of a principal business unit, division or function (such as sales, administration or finance), any other officer who performs a policy-making function, or any other person who performs similar policy-making functions for the issuer. Officers of the issuer's parent(s) or subsidiaries shall be deemed officers of the issuer if they perform such policy-making functions for the issuer. In addition, when the issuer is a limited partnership, officers or employees of the general partner(s) who perform policy-making functions for the limited partnership are deemed officers of the limited partnership. When the issuer is a trust, officers or employees of the trustee(s) who perform policy-making functions for the trust are deemed officers of the trust.

Note: "Policy-making function" is not intended to include policy-making functions that are not significant. If pursuant to Item 401(b) of Regulation S-K (§ 229.401(b)) the issuer identifies a person as an "executive officer," it is presumed that the Board of Directors has made that judgment and that the persons so identified are the officers for purposes of Section 16 of the Act, as are such other persons enumerated in this paragraph (f) but not in Item 401(b).

(g) The term "portfolio securities" shall mean all securities owned by an entity, other than securities issued by the entity.

(h) The term "put equivalent position" shall mean a derivative security position that increases in value as the value of the underlying equity decreases, including, but not limited to, a long put option and a short call option position.

Rule 16a-2. Persons and Transactions Subject to Section 16

Any person who is the beneficial owner, directly or indirectly, of more than ten percent of any class of equity securities ("ten percent beneficial owner") registered pursuant to section 12 of the Exchange Act (15 U.S.C. 78*l*), any director or officer of the issuer of such securities, and any person specified in section 30(h) of the Investment Company Act of 1940 (15 U.S.C. 80a-29(h)), including any person specified in Exchange Act Rule 16a-8, shall be subject to the provisions of section 16 of the Act (15 U.S.C. 78p). The rules under Section 16 of the Act apply to any class of equity securities of an issuer whether or not registered under Section 12 of the Act. The rules under Section 16 of the Act also apply to non-equity securities as provided by the Investment Company Act of 1940. With respect to transactions by persons subject to Section 16 of the Act:

(a) A transaction(s) carried out by a director or officer in the six months prior to the director or officer becoming subject to Section 16 of the Act shall be subject to Section 16 of the Act and reported on the first required Form 4 only if the transaction(s) occurred within six months of the transaction giving rise to the Form 4 filing obligation and the director or officer became subject to Section 16 of the Act solely as a result of the issuer registering a class of equity securities pursuant to Section 12 of the Act.

(b) A transaction(s) following the cessation of director or officer status shall be subject to section 16 of the Act only if:

(1) Executed within a period of less than six months of an opposite transaction subject to section 16(b) of the Act that occurred while that person was a director or officer; and

(2) Not otherwise exempted from section 16(b) of the Act pursuant to the provisions of this chapter.

Note to paragraph (b): For purposes of this paragraph, an acquisition and a disposition each shall be an opposite transaction with respect to the other.

(c) The transaction that results in a person becoming a ten percent beneficial owner is not subject to Section 16 of the Act unless the person otherwise is subject to Section 16 of the Act. A ten percent beneficial owner not otherwise subject to Section 16 of the Act must report only those transactions conducted while the beneficial owner of more than ten percent of a class of equity securities of the issuer registered pursuant to Section 12 of the Act.

(d)(1) Transactions by a person or entity shall be exempt from the provisions of Section 16 of the Act for the 12 months following appointment and qualification, to the extent such person or entity is acting as:

(i) Executor or administrator of the estate of a decedent;

(ii) Guardian or member of a committee for an incompetent;

(iii) Receiver, trustee in bankruptcy, assignee for the benefit of creditors, conservator, liquidating agent, or other similar person duly authorized by law to administer the estate or assets of another person; or

(iv) Fiduciary in a similar capacity.

(2) Transactions by such person or entity acting in a capacity specified in paragraph (d)(1) of this section after the period specified in that paragraph shall be subject to section 16 of the Act only where the estate, trust or other entity is a beneficial owner of more than ten percent of any class of equity security registered pursuant to section 12 of the Act.

Rule 16a-3. Reporting Transactions and Holdings

(a) Initial statements of beneficial ownership of equity securities required by Section 16(a) of the Act shall be filed on Form 3. Statements of changes in beneficial ownership required by that Section shall be filed on Form 4. Annual statements shall be filed on Form 5. At the election of the reporting person, any transaction required to be reported on Form 5 may be reported on an earlier filed Form 4. All such statements shall be prepared and filed in accordance with the requirements of the applicable form.

(b) A person filing statements pursuant to Section 16(a) of the Act with respect to any class of equity securities registered pursuant to Section 12 of the Act need not file an additional statement on Form 3:

(1) When an additional class of equity securities of the same issuer becomes registered pursuant to Section 12 of the Act; or

(2) When such person assumes a different or an additional relationship to the same issuer (for example, when an officer becomes a director).

(c) Any issuer that has equity securities listed on more than one national securities exchange may designate one exchange as the only exchange with which reports pursuant to Section 16(a) of the Act need be filed. Such designation shall be made in writing and shall be filed with the Commission and with each national securities exchange on which any equity security of the issuer is listed at the time of such election. The reporting person's obligation to file reports with each national securities exchange on which any equity security of the issuer is listed shall be satisfied by filing with the exchange so designated.

(d) Any person required to file a statement with respect to securities of a single issuer under both section 16(a) of the Act (15 U.S.C. 78p(a)) and section 30(h) of the Investment Company Act of 1940 (15 U.S.C. 80a-29(h)) may file a single statement containing the required information, which will be deemed to be filed under both Acts.

(e) [Reserved.]

(f)(1) A Form 5 shall be filed by every person who at any time during the issuer's fiscal year was subject to Section 16 of the Act with respect to such issuer, except as provided in paragraph (2) below. The Form shall be filed within 45 days after the issuer's fiscal year end, and shall disclose the following holdings and transactions not reported previously on Forms 3, 4 or 5:

    (i) All transactions during the most recent fiscal year that were exempt from section 16(b) of the Act, except:

        (A) Exercises and conversions of derivative securities exempt under either § 240.16b-3 or § 240.16b-6(b), and any transaction exempt under § 240.16b-3(d), § 240.16b-3(e), or § 240.16b-3(f) (these are required to be reported on Form 4);

        (B) Transactions exempt from section 16(b) of the Act pursuant to § 240.16b-3(c), which shall be exempt from section 16(a) of the Act; and

        (C) Transactions exempt from section 16(a) of the Act pursuant to another rule;

    (ii) Transactions that constituted small acquisitions pursuant to § 240.16a-6(a);

    (iii) all holdings and transactions that should have been reported during the most recent fiscal year, but were not; and

    (iv) with respect to the first Form 5 requirement for a reporting person, all holdings and transactions that should have been reported in each of the issuer's last two fiscal years but were not, based on the reporting person's reasonable belief in good faith in the completeness and accuracy of the information.

(2) Notwithstanding the above, no Form 5 shall be required where all transactions otherwise required to be reported on the Form 5 have been reported before the due date of the Form 5.

Note: Persons no longer subject to Section 16 of the Act, but who were subject to the Section at any time during the issuer's fiscal year, must file a Form 5 unless paragraph (f)(2) is satisfied. *See also* § 240.16a-2(b) regarding the reporting obligations of persons ceasing to be officers or directors.

(g)(1) A Form 4 must be filed to report: all transactions not exempt from section 16(b) of the Act; all transactions exempt from section 16(b) of the Act pursuant to § 240.16b-3(d), § 240.16b-3(e), or § 240.16b-3(f); and all exercises and conversions of derivative securities, regardless of whether exempt from section 16(b) of the Act. Form 4 must be filed before the end of the second business day following the day on which the subject transaction has been executed.

(2) Solely for purposes of section 16(a)(2)(C) of the Act and paragraph (g)(1) of this section, the date on which the executing broker, dealer or plan administrator notifies the reporting person of the execution of the transaction is deemed the date of execution for a transaction where the following conditions are satisfied:

    (i) the transaction is pursuant to a contract, instruction or written plan for the purchase or sale of equity securities of the issuer (as defined in § 16a-1(d)) that satisfies the affirmative defense conditions of § 240.10b5-1(c) of this chapter; and

    (ii) the reporting person does not select the date of execution.

(3) Solely for purposes of section 16(a)(2)(C) of the Act and paragraph (g)(1) of this section, the date on which the plan administrator notifies the reporting person that the transaction has been executed is deemed the date of execution for a discretionary transaction (as defined in § 16b-3(b)(1)) for which the reporting person does not select the date of execution.

(4) In the case of the transactions described in paragraphs (g)(2) and (g)(3) of this section, if the notification date is later than the third business day following the trade date of

the transaction, the date of execution is deemed to be the third business day following the trade date of the transaction.

(5) At the option of the reporting person, transactions that are reportable on Form 5 may be reported on Form 4, so long as the Form 4 is filed no later than the due date of the Form 5 on which the transaction is otherwise required to be reported.

(h) The date of filing with the Commission shall be the date of receipt by the Commission.

(i) *Signatures*. Where Section 16 of the Act, or the rules or forms thereunder, require a document filed with or furnished to the Commission to be signed, such document shall be manually signed, or signed using either typed signatures or duplicated or facsimile versions of manual signatures. Where typed, duplicated or facsimile signatures are used, each signatory to the filing shall manually sign a signature page or other document authenticating, acknowledging or otherwise adopting his or her signature that appears in the filing. Such document shall be executed before or at the time the filing is made and shall be retained by the filer for a period of five years. Upon request, the filer shall furnish to the Commission or its staff a copy of any or all documents retained pursuant to this section.

(j) Where more than one person subject to section 16 of the Act is deemed to be a beneficial owner of the same equity securities, all such persons must report as beneficial owners of the securities, either separately or jointly. Where persons in a group are deemed to be beneficial owners of equity securities pursuant to § 240.16a-1(a)(1) due to the aggregation of holdings, a single Form 3, 4 or 5 may be filed on behalf of all persons in the group. Joint and group filings must include all required information for each beneficial owner, and such filings must be signed by each beneficial owner, or on behalf of such owner by an authorized person.

(k) Any issuer that maintains a corporate website shall post on that website by the end of the business day after filing any Form 3, 4 or 5 filed under section 16(a) of the Act as to the equity securities of that issuer. Each such form shall remain accessible on such issuer's website for at least a 12-month period. In the case of an issuer that is an investment company and that does not maintain its own website, if any of the issuer's investment adviser, sponsor, depositor, trustee, administrator, principal underwriter, or any affiliated person of the investment company maintains a website that includes the name of the issuer, the issuer shall comply with the posting requirements by posting the forms on one such website.

Rule 16a-4. Derivative Securities

(a) For purposes of Section 16 of the Act, both derivative securities and the underlying securities to which they relate shall be deemed to be the same class of equity securities, *except that* the acquisition or disposition of any derivative security shall be separately reported.

(b) The exercise or conversion of a call equivalent position shall be reported on Form 4 and treated for reporting purposes as:

(1) A purchase of the underlying security; and

(2) A closing of the derivative security position.

(c) The exercise or conversion of a put equivalent position shall be reported on Form 4 and treated for reporting purposes as:

(1) A sale of the underlying security; and

(2) A closing of the derivative security position.

(d) The disposition or closing of a long derivative security position, as a result of cancellation or expiration, shall be exempt from section 16(a) of the Act if exempt from section 16(b) of the Act pursuant to § 240.16b-6(d).

Note to § 240.16a-4: A purchase or sale resulting from an exercise or conversion of a derivative security may be exempt from section 16(b) of the Act pursuant to § 240.16b-3 or § 240.16b6(b).

Rule 16a-6. Small Acquisitions

(a) Any acquisition of an equity security or the right to acquire such securities, other than an acquisition from the issuer (including an employee benefit plan sponsored by the issuer), not exceeding $10,000 in market value shall be reported on Form 5, subject to the following conditions:

(1) Such acquisition, when aggregated with other acquisitions of securities of the same class (including securities underlying derivative securities, but excluding acquisitions exempted by rule from section 16(b) or previously reported on Form 4 or Form 5) within the prior six months, does not exceed a total of $10,000 in market value; and

(2) The person making the acquisition does not within six months thereafter make any disposition, other than by a transaction exempt from section 16(b) of the Act.

(b) If an acquisition no longer qualifies for the reporting deferral in paragraph (a) of this section, all such acquisitions that have not yet been reported must be reported on Form 4 before the end of the second business day following the day on which the conditions of paragraph (a) of this section are no longer met.

Rule 16a-8. Trusts

(a) *Persons Subject to Section 16.*

(1) *Trusts.* A trust shall be subject to section 16 of the Act with respect to securities of the issuer if the trust is a beneficial owner, pursuant to § 240.16a-1(a)(1), of more than ten percent of any class of equity securities of the issuer registered pursuant to section 12 of the Act ("ten percent beneficial owner").

(2) *Trustees, Beneficiaries, and Settlors.* In determining whether a trustee, beneficiary, or settlor is a ten percent beneficial owner with respect to the issuer:

(i) such persons shall be deemed the beneficial owner of the issuer's securities held by the trust, to the extent specified by § 240.16a-1(a)(1); and

(ii) settlors shall be deemed the beneficial owner of the issuer's securities held by the trust where they have the power to revoke the trust without the consent of another person.

(b) *Trust Holdings and Transactions.* Holdings and transactions in the issuer's securities held by a trust shall be reported by the trustee on behalf of the trust, if the trust is subject to Section 16 of the Act, except as provided below. Holdings and transactions in the issuer's securities held by a trust (whether or not subject to Section 16 of the Act) may be reportable by other parties as follows:

(1) *Trusts.* The trust need not report holdings and transactions in the issuer's securities held by the trust in an employee benefit plan subject to the Employee Retirement Income Security Act over which no trustee exercises investment control.

(2) *Trustees.* If, as provided by § 240.16a-1(a)(2), a trustee subject to Section 16 of the Act has a pecuniary interest in any holding or transaction in the issuer's securities held by the trust, such holding or transaction shall be attributed to the trustee and shall be reported by the trustee in the trustee's individual capacity, as well as on behalf of the trust. With respect to performance fees and holdings of the trustee's immediate family, trustees shall be deemed to have a pecuniary interest in the trust holdings and transactions in the following circumstances:

(i) a performance fee is received that does not meet the proviso of § 240.16a-1(a)(2)(ii)(C); or

(ii) at least one beneficiary of the trust is a member of the trustee's immediate family. The pecuniary interest of the immediate family member(s) shall be attributed to and reported by the trustee.

(3) *Beneficiaries.* A beneficiary subject to Section 16 of the Act shall have or share reporting obligations with respect to transactions in the issuer's securities held by the trust, if the beneficiary is a beneficial owner of the securities pursuant to § 240.16a-1(a)(2), as follows:

(i) If a beneficiary shares investment control with the trustee with respect to a trust transaction, the transaction shall be attributed to and reported by both the beneficiary and the trust;

(ii) If a beneficiary has investment control with respect to a trust transaction without consultation with the trustee, the transaction shall be attributed to and reported by the beneficiary only; and

(iii) In making a determination as to whether a beneficiary is the beneficial owner of the securities pursuant to § 240.16a-1(a)(2), beneficiaries shall be deemed to have a pecuniary interest in the issuer's securities held by the trust to the extent of their pro rata interest in the trust where the trustee does not exercise exclusive investment control.

Note to paragraph (b)(3): Transactions and holdings attributed to a trust beneficiary may be reported by the trustee on behalf of the beneficiary, provided that the report is signed by the beneficiary or other authorized person. Where the transactions and holdings are attributed both to the trustee and trust beneficiary, a joint report may be filed in accordance with § 240.16a-3(j).

(4) *Settlors*. If a settlor subject to Section 16 of the Act reserves the right to revoke the trust without the consent of another person, the trust holdings and transactions shall be attributed to and reported by the settlor instead of the trust; *provided, however*, that if the settlor does not exercise or share investment control over the issuer's securities held by the trust, the trust holdings and transactions shall be attributed to and reported by the trust instead of the settlor.

(c) *Remainder interests*. Remainder interests in a trust are deemed not to confer beneficial ownership for purposes of Section 16 of the Act, provided that the persons with the remainder interests have no power, directly or indirectly, to exercise or share investment control over the trust.

(d) A trust, trustee, beneficiary or settlor becoming subject to Section 16(a) of the Act pursuant to this Rule also shall be subject to Sections 16(b) and 16(c) of the Act.

Rule 16a-10. Exemptions Under Section 16(a)

Except as provided in § 240.16a-6, any transaction exempted from the requirements of Section 16(a) of the Act, insofar as it is otherwise subject to the provisions of Section 16(b), shall be likewise exempt from Section 16(b) of the Act.

EXEMPTION OF CERTAIN TRANSACTIONS FROM SECTION 16(b)

Rule 16b-3. Transactions between an issuer and its officers or directors

(a) *General*. A transaction between the issuer (including an employee benefit plan sponsored by the issuer) and an officer or director of the issuer that involves issuer equity securities shall be exempt from section 16(b) of the Act if the transaction satisfies the applicable conditions set forth in this section.

(b) *Definitions*. (1) A Discretionary Transaction shall mean a transaction pursuant to an employee benefit plan that:

(i) Is at the volition of a plan participant;

(ii) Is not made in connection with the participant's death, disability, retirement or termination of employment;

(iii) Is not required to be made available to a plan participant pursuant to a provision of the Internal Revenue Code; and

(iv) Results in either an intra-plan transfer involving an issuer equity securities fund, or a cash distribution funded by a volitional disposition of an issuer equity security.

(2) An Excess Benefit Plan shall mean an employee benefit plan that is operated in conjunction with a Qualified Plan, and provides only the benefits or contributions that would be provided under a Qualified Plan but for any benefit or contribution limitations set forth in the Internal Revenue Code of 1986, or any successor provisions thereof.

(3) (i) A Non-Employee Director shall mean a director who:

(A) Is not currently an officer (as defined in § 240.16a-1(f)) of the issuer or a parent or subsidiary of the issuer, or otherwise currently employed by the issuer or a parent or subsidiary of the issuer;

(B) Does not receive compensation, either directly or indirectly, from the issuer or a parent or subsidiary of the issuer, for services rendered as a consultant or in any capacity other than as a director, except for an amount that does not exceed the dollar amount for which disclosure would be required pursuant to § 229.404(a) of this chapter;

(C) Does not possess an interest in any other transaction for which disclosure would be required pursuant to § 229.404(a) of this chapter.

(ii) Notwithstanding paragraph (b)(3)(i) of this section, a Non-Employee Director of a closedend investment company shall mean a director who is not an "interested person" of the issuer, as that term is defined in Section 2(a)(19) of the Investment Company Act of 1940.

(4) A Qualified Plan shall mean an employee benefit plan that satisfies the coverage and participation requirements of sections 410 and 401(a)(26) of the Internal Revenue Code of 1986, or any successor provisions thereof.

(5) A Stock Purchase Plan shall mean an employee benefit plan that satisfies the coverage and participation requirements of sections 423(b)(3) and 423(b)(5), or section 410, of the Internal Revenue Code of 1986, or any successor provisions thereof.

(c) *Tax-conditioned plans.* Any transaction (other than a Discretionary Transaction) pursuant to a Qualified Plan, an Excess Benefit Plan, or a Stock Purchase Plan shall be exempt without condition.

(d) *Acquisitions from the issuer.* Any transaction, other than a Discretionary Transaction, involving an acquisition from the issuer (including without limitation a grant or award), whether or not intended for a compensatory or other particular purpose, shall be exempt if:

(1) The transaction is approved by the board of directors of the issuer, or a committee of the board of directors that is composed solely of two or more Non-Employee Directors;

(2) The transaction is approved or ratified, in compliance with section 14 of the Act, by either: the affirmative votes of the holders of a majority of the securities of the issuer present, or represented, and entitled to vote at a meeting duly held in accordance with the applicable laws of the state or other jurisdiction in which the issuer is incorporated; or the written consent of the holders of a majority of the securities of the issuer entitled to vote; provided that such ratification occurs no later than the date of the next annual meeting of shareholders; or

(3) The issuer equity securities so acquired are held by the officer or director for a period of six months following the date of such acquisition, provided that this condition shall be satisfied with respect to a derivative security if at least six months elapse from the date of acquisition of the derivative security to the date of disposition of the derivative security (other than upon exercise or conversion) or its underlying equity security.

(e) *Dispositions to the issuer.* Any transaction, other than a Discretionary Transaction, involving the disposition to the issuer of issuer equity securities, whether or not intended for a compensatory or other particular purpose, shall be exempt, provided that the terms of such disposition are approved in advance in the manner prescribed by either paragraph (d)(1) or paragraph (d)(2) of this section.

(f) *Discretionary Transactions.* A Discretionary Transaction shall be exempt only if effected pursuant to an election made at least six months following the date of the most recent election, with respect to any plan of the issuer, that effected a Discretionary Transaction that was:

(i) An acquisition, if the transaction to be exempted would be a disposition; or

(ii) A disposition, if the transaction to be exempted would be an acquisition.

Notes to § 240.16b-3:

Note (1): The exercise or conversion of a derivative security that does not satisfy the conditions of this section is eligible for exemption from section 16(b) of the Act to the extent that the conditions of § 240.16b-6(b) are satisfied.

Note (2): Section 16(a) reporting requirements applicable to transactions exempt pursuant to this section are set forth in § 240.16a-3(f) and (g) and § 240.16a-4.

Note (3): The approval conditions of paragraphs (d)(1), (d)(2) and (e) of this section require the approval of each specific transaction, and are not satisfied by approval of a plan in its entirety except for the approval of a plan pursuant to which the terms and conditions of each transaction are fixed in advance, such as a formula plan. Where the terms of a subsequent transaction (such as the exercise price of an option, or the provision of an exercise or tax withholding right) are provided for in a transaction as initially approved pursuant to paragraphs (d)(1), (d)(2) or (e), such subsequent transaction shall not require further specific approval.

Note (4): For purposes of determining a director's status under those portions of paragraph (b)(3)(i) that reference § 229.404(a) of this chapter, an issuer may rely on the disclosure provided under § 229.404(a) of this chapter for the issuer's most recent fiscal year contained in the most recent filing in which disclosure required under § 229.404(a) is presented. Where a transaction disclosed in that filing was terminated before the director's proposed service as a Non-Employee Director, that transaction will not bar such service. The issuer must believe in good faith that any current or contemplated transaction in which the director participates will not be required to be disclosed under § 229.404(a) of this chapter, based on information readily available to the issuer and the director at the time such director proposes to act as a Non-Employee Director. At such time as the issuer believes in good faith, based on readily available information, that a current or contemplated transaction with a director will be required to be disclosed under § 229.404(a) in a future filing, the director no longer is eligible to serve as a Non-Employee Director; provided, however, that this determination does not result in retroactive loss of a Rule 16b-3 exemption for a transaction previously approved by the director while serving as a Non-Employee Director consistent with this note. In making the determinations specified in this Note, the issuer may rely on information it obtains from the director, for example, pursuant to a response to an inquiry.

Rule 16b-5. Bona Fide Gifts and Inheritance

Both the acquisition and the disposition of equity securities shall be exempt from the operation of Section 16(b) of the Act if they are: (a) bona fide gifts; or (b) transfers of securities by will or the laws of descent and distribution.

Rule 16b-6. Derivative Securities

(a) The establishment of or increase in a call equivalent position or liquidation of or decrease in a put equivalent position shall be deemed a purchase of the underlying security for purposes of Section 16(b) of the Act, and the establishment of or increase in a put equivalent position or liquidation of or decrease in a call equivalent position shall be deemed a sale of the underlying securities for purposes of Section 16(b) of the Act; *provided, however*, that if the increase or decrease occurs as a result of the fixing of the exercise price of a right initially issued without a fixed price, where the date the price is fixed is not known in advance and is outside the control of the recipient, the increase or decrease shall be exempt from Section 16(b) of the Act with respect to any offsetting transaction within the six months prior to the date the price is fixed.

(b) The closing of a derivative security position as a result of its exercise or conversion shall be exempt from the operation of Section 16(b) of the Act, and the acquisition of underlying securities at a fixed exercise price due to the exercise or conversion of a call equivalent position or the disposition of underlying securities at a fixed exercise price due to the exercise of a put equivalent position shall be exempt from the operation of Section 16(b) of the Act; *provided, however*, that the acquisition of underlying securities from the exercise of an out-of-the-money option, warrant, or right shall not be exempt unless the exercise is necessary to comport with the sequential exercise provisions of the Internal Revenue Code (26 U.S.C. § 422A).

Note to Paragraph (b): The exercise or conversion of a derivative security that does not satisfy the conditions of this section is eligible for exemption from section 16(b) of the Act to the extent that the conditions of § 240.16b-3 are satisfied.

(c) In determining the short-swing profit recoverable pursuant to Section 16(b) of the Act from transactions involving the purchase and sale or sale and purchase of derivative and other securities, the following rules apply:

(1) Short-swing profits in transactions involving the purchase and sale or sale and purchase of derivative securities that have identical characteristics (*e.g.*, purchases and sales of call options of the same strike price and expiration date, or purchases and sales of the same series of convertible debentures) shall be measured by the actual prices paid or received in the short-swing transactions.

(2) Short-swing profits in transactions involving the purchase and sale or sale and purchase of derivative securities having different characteristics but related to the same underlying security (*e.g.*, the purchase of a call option and the sale of a convertible debenture) or derivative securities and underlying securities shall not exceed the difference in price of the underlying security on the date of purchase or sale and the date of sale or purchase. Such profits may be measured by calculating the short-swing profits that would have been realized had the subject transactions involved purchases and sales solely of the derivative security that was purchased or solely of the derivative security that was sold, valued as of the time of the matching purchase or sale, and calculated for the lesser of the number of underlying securities actually purchased or sold.

(d) Upon cancellation or expiration of an option within six months of the writing of the option, any profit derived from writing the option shall be recoverable under Section 16(b) of the Act. The profit shall not exceed the premium received for writing the option. The disposition or closing of a long derivative security position, as a result of cancellation or expiration, shall be exempt from Section 16(b) of the Act where no value is received from the cancellation or expiration.

Rule 16b-7. Mergers, Reclassifications, and Consolidations

(a) The following transactions shall be exempt from the provisions of Section 16(b) of the Act:

(1) The acquisition of a security of a company, pursuant to a merger, reclassification or consolidation, in exchange for a security of a company that before the merger, reclassification or consolidation, owned 85 percent or more of either:

(i) The equity securities of all other companies involved in the merger, reclassification or consolidation, or in the case of a consolidation, the resulting company; or

(ii) The combined assets of all the companies involved in the merger, reclassification or consolidation, computed according to their book values before the merger, reclassification or consolidation as determined by reference to their most recent available financial statements for a 12 month period before the merger, reclassification or consolidation, or such shorter time as the company has been in existence.

(2) The disposition of a security, pursuant to a merger, reclassification or consolidation, of a company that before the merger, reclassification or consolidation, owned 85 percent or more of either:

(i) The equity securities of all other companies involved in the merger, reclassification or consolidation or, in the case of a consolidation, the resulting company; or

(ii) The combined assets of all the companies undergoing merger, reclassification or consolidation, computed according to their book values before the merger, reclassification or consolidation as determined by reference to their most recent available financial statements for a 12 month period before the merger, reclassification or consolidation.

(b) A merger within the meaning of this section shall include the sale or purchase of substantially all the assets of one company by another in exchange for equity securities which are then distributed to the security holders of the company that sold its assets.

(c) The exemption provided by this section applies to any securities transaction that satisfies the conditions specified in this section and is not conditioned on the transaction satisfying any other conditions.

(d) Notwithstanding the foregoing, if a person subject to section 16 of the Act makes any non-exempt purchase of a security in any company involved in the merger, reclassification or consolidation and any non-exempt sale of a security in any company involved in the merger, reclassification or consolidation within any period of less than six months during which the merger, reclassification or consolidation took place, the exemption provided by this section shall be unavailable to the extent of such purchase and sale.

NATIONALLY RECOGNIZED STATISTICAL RATING ORGANIZATIONS

Rule 17g-1. Application for Registration as a Nationally Recognized Statistical Rating Organization

(a) *Initial Application.* A credit rating agency applying to the Commission to be registered under section 15E of the Act (15 U.S.C. 78o-7) as a nationally recognized statistical rating organization must furnish the Commission with an initial application on Form NRSRO (§ 249b.300 of this chapter) that follows all applicable instructions for the Form.

(b) *Application to Register for an Additional Class of Credit Ratings.* A nationally recognized statistical rating organization applying to register for an additional class of the credit ratings described in section 3(a)(62)(B) of the Act (15 U.S.C. 78c(a)(62)(B)) must furnish the Commission with an application to add a class of credit ratings on Form NRSRO that follows all applicable instructions for the Form. The application will be subject to the requirements of section 15E(a)(2) of the Act (15 U.S.C. 78o-7(a)(2)).

(c) *Supplementing an Application Prior to Final Action by the Commission.* An applicant must promptly furnish the Commission with a written notice if information submitted to the Commission in an initial application to be registered as a nationally recognized statistical rating organization or in an application to register for an additional class of credit ratings is found to be or becomes materially inaccurate prior to the date of a Commission order granting or denying the application. The notice must identify the information that was found to be materially inaccurate. The applicant also must promptly furnish the Commission with an application supplement on Form NRSRO that follows all applicable instructions for the Form.

(d) *Withdrawing an Application.* An applicant may withdraw an initial application to be registered as a nationally recognized statistical rating organization or an application to register for an additional class of credit ratings prior to the date of a Commission order granting or denying the application. To withdraw the application, the applicant must furnish the Commission with a written notice of withdrawal executed by a duly authorized person.

(e) *Update of Registration.* A nationally recognized statistical rating organization amending materially inaccurate information in its application for registration pursuant to section 15E(b)(1) of the Act (15 U.S.C. 78o-7(b)(1)) must promptly furnish the Commission with the update of its registration on Form NRSRO that follows all applicable instructions for the Form.

(f) *Annual Certification.* A nationally recognized statistical rating organization amending its application for registration pursuant to section 15E(b)(2) of the Act (15 U.S.C. 78o-7(b)(2)) must furnish the Commission with the annual certification on Form NRSRO that follows all applicable instructions for the Form not later than 90 days after the end of each calendar year.

(g) *Withdrawal from Registration.* A nationally recognized statistical rating organization withdrawing from registration pursuant to section 15E(e)(1) of the Act (15 U.S.C. 78o-7(e)(1)) must furnish the Commission with a notice of withdrawal from registration on Form NRSRO that follows all applicable instructions for the Form. The withdrawal from registration will become effective 45 calendar days after the notice is furnished to the Commission upon such terms and conditions as the Commission may establish as necessary in the public interest or for the protection of investors.

(h) *Furnishing Form NRSRO.* A Form NRSRO submitted under any paragraph of this section will be considered furnished to the Commission on the date the Commission receives a complete and properly executed Form NRSRO that follows all applicable instructions for the Form. Information submitted on a confidential basis and for which confidential treatment has been requested pursuant to applicable Commission rules will be accorded confidential treatment to the extent permitted by law.

(i) *Public Availability of Form NRSRO.* A nationally recognized statistical rating organization must make its current Form NRSRO and information and documents submitted in Exhibits 1 through 9 to Form NRSRO publicly available on its Web site, or through another comparable, readily accessible means within 10 business days after the date of the Commission order granting an initial application for registration as a nationally recognized statistical rating organization or an application to register for an additional class of credit ratings and within 10 business days after furnishing a Form NRSRO to the Commission under paragraphs (e), (f), or (g) of this section.

Rule 17g-2. Records to Be Made and Retained by Nationally Recognized Statistical Rating Organizations

(a) *Records Required to Be Made and Retained.* A nationally recognized statistical rating organization must make and retain the following books and records, which must be complete and current:

(1) Records of original entry into the accounting system of the nationally recognized statistical rating organization and records reflecting entries to and balances in all general ledger accounts of the nationally recognized statistical rating organization for each fiscal year.

(2) Records with respect to each current credit rating of the nationally recognized statistical rating organization indicating (as applicable):

(i) The identity of any credit analyst(s) that participated in determining the credit rating;

(ii) The identity of the person(s) that approved the credit rating before it was issued.

(iii) If a quantitative model was a substantial component in the process of determining the credit rating of a security or money market instrument issued by an asset pool or as part of any asset-backed or mortgage-backed securities transaction, a record of the rationale for any material difference between the credit rating implied by the model and the final credit rating issued; and

(iv) Whether the credit rating was solicited or unsolicited.

(3) An account record for each person (for example, an obligor, issuer, underwriter, or other user) that has paid the nationally recognized statistical rating organization for the issuance or maintenance of a credit rating indicating:

(i) The identity and address of the person; and

(ii) The credit rating(s) determined or maintained for the person.

(4) An account record for each subscriber to the credit ratings and/or credit analysis reports of the nationally recognized statistical rating organization indicating the identity and address of the subscriber.

(5) A record listing the general types of services and products offered by the nationally recognized statistical rating organization.

(6) A record documenting the established procedures and methodologies used by the nationally recognized statistical rating organization to determine credit ratings.

(7) A record that lists each security and money market instrument and its corresponding credit rating issued by an asset pool or as part of any asset-backed or mortgage backed securities transaction where the nationally recognized statistical rating organization, in determining the credit rating for the security or money market instrument, treats assets within such pool or as a part of such transaction that are not subject to a credit rating of the nationally recognized statistical rating organization by any or a combination of the following methods:

(i) Determining credit ratings for the unrated assets;

(ii) Performing credit assessments or determining private credit ratings for the unrated assets;

(iii) Determining credit ratings or private credit ratings, or performing credit assessments for the unrated assets by taking into consideration the internal credit analysis of another person; or

(iv) Determining credit ratings or private credit ratings, or performing credit assessments for the unrated assets by taking into consideration (but not necessarily adopting) the credit ratings of another nationally recognized statistical rating organization.

(8) For each outstanding credit rating, a record showing all rating actions and the date of such actions from the initial credit rating to the current credit rating identified by the name of the rated security or obligor and, if applicable, the CUSIP of the rated security or the Central Index Key (CIK) number of the rated obligor.

(b) *Records Required to Be Retained.* A nationally recognized statistical rating organization must retain the following books and records (excluding drafts of documents) that relate to its business as a credit rating agency:

(1) Significant records (for example, bank statements, invoices, and trial balances) underlying the information included in the annual financial reports furnished by the nationally recognized statistical rating organization to the Commission pursuant to § 240.17g-3.

(2) Internal records, including nonpublic information and work papers, used to form the basis of a credit rating issued by the nationally recognized statistical rating organization.

(3) Credit analysis reports, credit assessment reports, and private credit rating reports of the nationally recognized statistical rating organization and internal records, including nonpublic information and work papers, used to form the basis for the opinions expressed in these reports.

(4) Compliance reports and compliance exception reports.

(5) Internal audit plans, internal audit reports, documents relating to internal audit follow-up measures, and all records identified by the internal auditors of the nationally recognized statistical rating organization as necessary to perform the audit of an activity that relates to its business as a credit rating agency

(6) Marketing materials of the nationally recognized statistical rating organization that are published or otherwise made available to persons that are not associated with the nationally recognized statistical rating organization.

(7) External and internal communications, including electronic communications, received and sent by the nationally recognized statistical rating organization and its employees that relate to initiating, determining, maintaining, monitoring, changing, or withdrawing a credit rating.

(8) Any written communications received from persons not associated with the nationally recognized statistical rating organization that contain complaints about the performance of a credit analyst in initiating, determining, maintaining, monitoring, changing, or withdrawing a credit rating.

(9) Internal documents that contain information, analysis, or statistics that were used to develop a procedure or methodology to treat the credit ratings of another nationally recognized statistical rating organization for the purpose of determining a credit rating for a security or money market instrument issued by an asset pool or part of any asset-backed or mortgage-backed securities transaction.

(10) For each security or money market instrument identified in the record required to be made and retained under paragraph (a) (7) of this section, any document that contains a description of how assets within such pool or as a part of such transaction not rated by the nationally recognized statistical rating organization but rated by another nationally recognized statistical rating organization were treated for the purpose of determining the credit rating of the security or money market instrument.

(11) Form NRSROs (including Exhibits and accompanying information and documents) submitted to the Commission by the nationally recognized statistical rating organization.

(c) *Record Retention Periods.* The records required to be retained pursuant to paragraphs (a) and (b) of this section must be retained for three years after the date the record is made or received.

(d) (1) *Manner of Retention.* An original, or a true and complete copy of the original, of each record required to be retained pursuant to paragraphs (a) and (b) of this section must be maintained in a manner that, for the applicable retention period specified in paragraph (c) of this section, makes the original record or copy easily accessible to the principal office of the nationally recognized statistical rating organization and to any other office that conducted activities causing the record to be made or received.

(2) A nationally recognized statistical rating organization must make and keep publicly available on its corporate Internet Web site in an XBRL (eXtensible Business Reporting Language) format the ratings action information for ten percent of the outstanding credit ratings required to be retained pursuant to paragraph (a) (8) of this section, selected on a random basis, for each class of credit rating for which it is registered and for which it has issued 500 or more outstanding credit ratings paid for by the obligor being rated or by the issuer, underwriter, or sponsor of the security being rated. Any ratings action required to be disclosed pursuant to this paragraph (d) (2) need not be made public less than six months from the date such ratings action is taken. If a credit rating made public pursuant to this paragraph is withdrawn or the instrument rated matures, the nationally recognized statistical rating organization must randomly select a new outstanding credit rating from that class of credit ratings in order to maintain the 10 percent disclosure threshold. In making the information available on its corporate Internet Web site, the nationally recognized statistical rating organization shall use the List of XBRL Tags for NRSROs as specified on the Commission's Internet Web site.

(3) (i) (A) A nationally recognized statistical rating organization must make publicly available on its corporate Internet Web site in an interactive data file that uses a machine-readable format the ratings action information required to be retained pursuant to paragraph (a) (8) of this section for any credit rating initially determined by the nationally recognized statistical rating organization on or after June 26, 2007.

(B) Any ratings action information required to be made and kept publicly available on a nationally recognized statistical rating organization's corporate Internet Web pursuant to paragraph (d) (3) (i) (A) with respect to credit ratings paid for by the obligor being rated or by the issuer, underwriter, or sponsor of the security being rated need not be made public less than twelve months from the date such ratings action is taken.

(C) Any ratings action information required to be made and kept publicly available on a nationally recognized statistical rating organization's corporate Internet Web pursuant to paragraph (d) (3) (i) (A) with respect to credit ratings other than those ratings described in paragraph (d) (3) (i) (B) need not be made public less than twenty-four months from the date such ratings action is taken.

(ii) In making the information required under paragraph (d) (3) (i) available in an interactive data file on its corporate Internet Web site, the nationally recognized statistical rating organization shall use any machine-readable format, including but not limited to XBRL format, until 60 days after the date on which the Commission publishes a List of XBRL Tags for NRSROs on its Internet Web site, at which point the nationally recognized statistical rating organization shall make this information available in an interactive data file on its corporate Internet Web site in XBRL format using the List of XBRL Tags for NRSROs as published by the Commission on its Internet Web site.

(e) *Third-Party Record Custodian.* The records required to be retained pursuant to paragraphs (a) and (b) of this section may be made or retained by a third-party record custodian, provided the nationally recognized statistical rating organization furnishes the Commission at its principal office in Washington, DC with a written undertaking of the custodian executed by a duly authorized person. The undertaking must be in substantially the following form:

The undersigned acknowledges that books and records it has made or is retaining for [the nationally recognized statistical rating organization] are the exclusive property of [the nationally recognized statistical rating organization]. The undersigned undertakes that upon the request of [the nationally recognized statistical rating organization] it will promptly provide the books and records to [the nationally recognized statistical rating organization] or the U.S. Securities and Exchange Commission ("Commission") or its representatives and that upon the request of the Commission it will promptly permit examination by the Commission or its representatives of the records at any time or from time to time during business hours and promptly furnish to the Commission or its representatives a true and complete copy of any or all or any part of such books and records. A nationally recognized statistical rating organization that engages a third-party record custodian remains responsible for complying with every provision of this section.

(f) A nationally recognized statistical rating organization must promptly furnish the Commission or its representatives with legible, complete, and current copies, and, if specifically requested, English translations of those records of the nationally recognized statistical rating organization required to be retained pursuant to paragraphs (a) and (b) this section, or any other records of the nationally recognized statistical rating organization subject to examination under section 17(b) of the Act (15 U.S.C. 78q(b)) that are requested by the Commission or its representatives.

Rule 17g-3. Annual Financial Reports to Be Furnished by Nationally Recognized Statistical Rating Organizations

(a) A nationally recognized statistical rating organization must annually, not more than 90 calendar days after the end of its fiscal year (as indicated on its current Form NRSRO), furnish the Commission, at the Commission's principal office in Washington, DC, with the following financial reports as of the end of its most recent fiscal year:

(1) Audited financial statements of the nationally recognized statistical rating organization or audited consolidated financial statements of its parent if the nationally recognized statistical rating organization is a separately identifiable division or department of the parent. The audited financial statements must:

(i) Include a balance sheet, an income statement (or a statement of comprehensive income, as defined in § 210.1-02 of Regulation S-X of this chapter, if required by the applicable generally accepted accounting principles noted in paragraph (a)(1)(ii) of this section) and statement of cash flows, and a statement of changes in ownership equity;

(ii) Be prepared in accordance with generally accepted accounting principles in the jurisdiction in which the nationally recognized statistical rating organization or its parent is incorporated, organized, or has its principal office; and

(iii) Be certified by an accountant who is qualified and independent in accordance with paragraphs (a), (b), and (c)(1), (2), (3), (4), (5) and (8) of § 210.2-01 of this chapter. The accountant must give an opinion on the financial statements in accordance with paragraphs (a) through (d) of § 210.2-02 of this chapter.

(2) If applicable, unaudited consolidating financial statements of the parent of the nationally recognized statistical rating organization that include the nationally recognized statistical rating organization.

Note to paragraph (a)(2): This financial report must be furnished only if the audited financial statements provided pursuant to paragraph (a)(1) of this section are consolidated financial statements of the parent of the nationally recognized statistical rating organization.

(3) An unaudited financial report providing information concerning the revenue of the nationally recognized statistical rating organization in each of the following categories (as applicable) for the fiscal year:

(i) Revenue from determining and maintaining credit ratings;

(ii) Revenue from subscribers;

(iii) Revenue from granting licenses or rights to publish credit ratings; and

(iv) Revenue from all other services and products (include descriptions of any major sources of revenue).

(4) An unaudited financial report providing the total aggregate and median annual compensation of the credit analysts of the nationally recognized statistical rating organization for the fiscal year.

Note to paragraph (a)(4): In calculating total and median annual compensation, the nationally recognized statistical rating organization may exclude deferred compensation, provided such exclusion is noted in the report.

(5) An unaudited financial report listing the 20 largest issuers and subscribers that used credit rating services provided by the nationally recognized statistical rating organization by amount of net revenue attributable to the issuer or subscriber during the fiscal year. Additionally, include on the list any obligor or underwriter that used the credit rating services provided by the nationally recognized statistical rating organization if the net revenue attributable to the obligor or underwriter during the fiscal year equaled or exceeded the net revenue attributable to the 20th largest issuer or subscriber. Include the net revenue amount for each person on the list.

Note to paragraph (a)(5): A person is deemed to have "used the credit rating services" of the nationally recognized statistical rating organization if the person is any of the following: an obligor that is rated by the nationally recognized statistical rating organization (regardless of whether the obligor paid for the credit rating); an issuer that has securities or money market instruments subject to a credit rating of the nationally recognized statistical rating organization (regardless of whether the issuer paid for the credit rating); any other person that has paid the nationally recognized statistical rating organization to determine a credit rating with respect to a specific obligor, security, or money market instrument; or a subscriber to the credit ratings, credit ratings data, or credit analysis of the nationally recognized statistical rating organization. In calculating net revenue attributable to a person, the nationally recognized statistical rating organization should include all revenue earned by the nationally recognized statistical rating organization for any type of service or product, regardless of whether related to credit rating services, and net of any rebates and allowances paid or owed to the person by the nationally recognized statistical rating organization.

(6) An unaudited report of the number of credit ratings actions (upgrades, downgrades, placements on credit watch, and withdrawals) taken during the fiscal year in each class of credit ratings identified in section 3(a)(62)(B) of the Act (15 U.S.C. 78c(a)(62)(B)) for which the nationally recognized statistical rating organization is registered with the Commission.

Note to Paragraph (a)(6): A nationally recognized statistical rating organization registered in the class of credit ratings described in section 3(a)(62)(B)(iv) of the Act (15 U.S.C. 78c(a)(62)(B)(iv)) must include credit ratings actions taken on credit ratings of any security or money market instrument issued by an asset pool or as part of any asset-backed or mortgage-backed securities transaction for purposes of reporting the number of credit ratings actions in this class.

(b) The nationally recognized statistical rating organization must attach to the financial reports furnished pursuant to paragraphs (a)(1) through (a)(6) of this section a signed statement by a duly authorized person associated with the nationally recognized statistical rating organization stating that the person has responsibility for the financial reports and, to the best knowledge of the person, the financial reports fairly present, in all material respects, the financial condition, results of operations, cash flows, revenues, analyst compensation, and credit rating actions of the nationally recognized statistical rating organization for the period presented.

(c) The Commission may grant an extension of time or an exemption with respect to any requirements in this section either unconditionally or on specified terms and conditions on the written request of a nationally recognized statistical rating organization if the Commission finds that such extension or exemption is necessary or appropriate in the public interest and consistent with the protection of investors.

Rule 17g-4. Prevention of Misuse of Material Nonpublic Information

(a) The written policies and procedures a nationally recognized statistical rating organization establishes, maintains, and enforces to prevent the misuse of material, nonpublic information pursuant to section 15E(g)(1) of the Act (15 U.S.C. 78o-7(g)(1)) must include policies and procedures reasonably designed to prevent:

(1) The inappropriate dissemination within and outside the nationally recognized statistical rating organization of material nonpublic information obtained in connection with the performance of credit rating services;

(2) A person within the nationally recognized statistical rating organization from purchasing, selling, or otherwise benefiting from any transaction in securities or money market instruments when the person is aware of material nonpublic information obtained in connection with the performance of credit rating services that affects the securities or money market instruments; and

(3) The inappropriate dissemination within and outside the nationally recognized statistical rating organization of a pending credit rating action before issuing the credit rating on the Internet or through another readily accessible means.

(b) For the purposes of this section, the term *person within a nationally recognized statistical rating organization* means a nationally recognized statistical rating organization, its credit rating affiliates identified on Form NRSRO, and any partner, officer, director, branch manager, and employee of the nationally recognized statistical rating organization or its credit rating affiliates (or any person occupying a similar status or performing similar functions).

Rule 17g-5. Conflicts of Interest

(a) A person within a nationally recognized statistical rating organization is prohibited from having a conflict of interest relating to the issuance or maintenance of a credit rating identified in paragraph (b) of this section, unless:

(1) The nationally recognized statistical rating organization has disclosed the type of conflict of interest in Exhibit 6 to Form NRSRO in accordance with section 15E(a)(1)(B)(vi) of the Act (15 U.S.C. 78o-7(a)(1)(B)(vi)) and §240.17g-1;

(2) The nationally recognized statistical rating organization has established and is maintaining and enforcing written policies and procedures to address and manage conflicts of interest in accordance with section 15E(h) of the Act (15 U.S.C. 78o-7(h)); and

(3) In the case of the conflict of interest identified in paragraph (b)(9) of this section relating to issuing or maintaining a credit rating for a security or money market instrument issued by an asset pool or as part of any asset-backed or mortgage-backed securities transaction, the nationally recognized statistical rating organization:

(i) Maintains on a password-protected Internet Web site a list of each such security or money market instrument for which it is currently in the process of determining an initial credit rating in chronological order and identifying the type of security or money market instrument, the name of the issuer, the date the rating process was initiated, and the Internet Web site address where the issuer, sponsor, or underwriter of the security or money market instrument represents that the information described in paragraphs (a)(3)(iii)(C) and (a)(3)(iii)(D) of this section can be accessed;

(ii) Provides free and unlimited access to such password-protected Internet Web site during the applicable calendar year to any nationally recognized statistical rating organization that provides it with a copy of the certification described in paragraph (e) of this section that covers that calendar year, provided that such certification indicates that the nationally recognized statistical rating organization providing the certification either:

(A) Determined and maintained credit ratings for at least 10% of the issued securities and money market instruments for which it accessed information pursuant to 17 CFR §240.17g-5(a)(3)(iii) in the calendar year prior to the year covered by the certification, if it accessed such information for 10 or more issued securities or money market instruments; or

(B) Has not accessed information pursuant to 17 CFR § 240.17g-5 (a) (3) 10 or more times during the most recently ended calendar year; and

(iii) Obtains from the issuer, sponsor, or underwriter of each such security or money market instrument a written representation that can reasonably be relied upon that the issuer, sponsor, or underwriter will:

(A) Maintain the information described in paragraphs (a) (3) (iii) (C) and (a) (3) (iii) (D) of this section available at an identified password-protected Internet Web site that presents the information in a manner indicating which information currently should be relied on to determine or monitor the credit rating;

(B) Provide access to such password-protected Internet Web site during the applicable calendar year to any nationally recognized statistical rating organization that provides it with a copy of the certification described in paragraph (e) of this section that covers that calendar year, provided that such certification indicates that the nationally recognized statistical rating organization providing the certification either:

(1) Determined and maintained credit ratings for at least 10% of the issued securities and money market instruments for which it accessed information pursuant to 17 CFR § 240.17g-5 (a) (3) (iii) in the calendar year prior to the year covered by the certification, if it accessed such information for 10 or more issued securities or money market instruments; or

(2) Has not accessed information pursuant to 17 CFR § 240.17g-5 (a) (3) 10 or more times during the most recently ended calendar year.

(C) Post on such password-protected Internet Web site all information the issuer, sponsor, or underwriter provides to the nationally recognized statistical rating organization, or contracts with a third party to provide to the nationally recognized statistical rating organization, for the purpose of determining the initial credit rating for the security or money market instrument, including information about the characteristics of the assets underlying or referenced by the security or money market instrument, and the legal structure of the security or money market instrument, at the same time such information is provided to the nationally recognized statistical rating organization; and

(D) Post on such password-protected Internet Web site all information the issuer, sponsor, or underwriter provides to the nationally recognized statistical rating organization, or contracts with a third party to provide to the nationally recognized statistical rating organization, for the purpose of undertaking credit rating surveillance on the security or money market instrument, including information about the characteristics and performance of the assets underlying or referenced by the security or money market instrument at the same time such information is provided to the nationally recognized statistical rating organization.

(E) Post on such password-protected Internet Web site, promptly after receipt, any executed Form ABS Due Diligence-15E (§ 249b.500 of this chapter) containing information about the security or money market instrument delivered by a person employed to provide third-party due diligence services with respect to the security or money market instrument.

(iv) The provisions of paragraphs (a) (3) (i) through (iii) of this section will not apply to a nationally recognized statistical rating organization when issuing or maintaining a credit rating for a security or money market instrument issued by an asset pool or as part of any asset-backed securities transaction, if:

(A) The issuer of the security or money market instrument is not a U.S. person (as defined in § 230.902 (k) of this chapter); and

(B) The nationally recognized statistical rating organization has a reasonable basis to conclude that all offers and sales of the security or money market instrument by any issuer, sponsor, or underwriter linked to the security or money market instrument will occur outside the United States (as that phrase is used in §§ 230.901 through 230.905 (Regulation S) of this chapter).

(b) *Conflicts of Interest.* For purposes of this section, each of the following is a conflict of interest:

(1) Being paid by issuers or underwriters to determine credit ratings with respect to securities or money market instruments they issue or underwrite.

(2) Being paid by obligors to determine credit ratings with respect to the obligors.

(3) Being paid for services in addition to determining credit ratings by issuers, underwriters, or obligors that have paid the nationally recognized statistical rating organization to determine a credit rating.

(4) Being paid by persons for subscriptions to receive or access the credit ratings of the nationally recognized statistical rating organization and/or for other services offered by the nationally recognized statistical rating organization where such persons may use the credit ratings of the nationally recognized statistical rating organization to comply with, and obtain benefits or relief under, statutes and regulations using the term *nationally recognized statistical rating organization.*

(5) Being paid by persons for subscriptions to receive or access the credit ratings of the nationally recognized statistical rating organization and/or for other services offered by the nationally recognized statistical rating organization where such persons also may own investments or have entered into transactions that could be favorably or adversely impacted by a credit rating issued by the nationally recognized statistical rating organization.

(6) Allowing persons within the nationally recognized statistical rating organization to directly own securities or money market instruments of, or having other direct ownership interests in, issuers or obligors subject to a credit rating determined by the nationally recognized statistical rating organization.

(7) Allowing persons within the nationally recognized statistical rating organization to have a business relationship that is more than an arms length ordinary course of business relationship with issuers or obligors subject to a credit rating determined by the nationally recognized statistical rating organization.

(8) Having a person associated with the nationally recognized statistical rating organization that is a broker or dealer engaged in the business of underwriting securities or money market instruments.

(9) Issuing or maintaining a credit rating for a security or money market instrument issued by an asset pool or as part of any asset-backed or mortgage-backed securities transaction that was paid for by the issuer, sponsor, or underwriter of the security or money market instrument;

(10) Any other type of conflict of interest relating to the issuance of credit ratings by the nationally recognized statistical rating organization that is material to the nationally recognized statistical rating organization and that is identified by the nationally recognized statistical rating organization in Exhibit 6 to Form NRSRO in accordance with section 15E(a)(1)(B)(vi) of the Act (15 U.S.C. 78o-7(a)(1)(B)(vi)) and § 240.17g-1.

(c) *Prohibited Conflicts.* A nationally recognized statistical rating organization is prohibited from having the following conflicts of interest relating to the issuance or maintenance of a credit rating as a credit rating agency:

(1) The nationally recognized statistical rating organization issues or maintains a credit rating solicited by a person that, in the most recently ended fiscal year, provided the nationally recognized statistical rating organization with net revenue (as reported under § 240.17g-3) equaling or exceeding 10% of the total net revenue of the nationally recognized statistical rating organization for the fiscal year;

(2) The nationally recognized statistical rating organization issues or maintains a credit rating with respect to a person (excluding a sovereign nation or an agency of a sovereign nation) where the nationally recognized statistical rating organization, a credit analyst that

participated in determining the credit rating, or a person responsible for approving the credit rating, directly owns securities of, or has any other direct ownership interest in, the person that is subject to the credit rating;

(3) The nationally recognized statistical rating organization issues or maintains a credit rating with respect to a person associated with the nationally recognized statistical rating organization;

(4) The nationally recognized statistical rating organization issues or maintains a credit rating where a credit analyst who participated in determining the credit rating, or a person responsible for approving the credit rating, is an officer or director of the person that is subject to the credit rating;

(5) The nationally recognized statistical rating organization issues or maintains a credit rating with respect to an obligor or security where the nationally recognized statistical rating organization or a person associated with the nationally recognized statistical rating organization made recommendations to the obligor or the issuer, underwriter, or sponsor of the security about the corporate or legal structure, assets, liabilities, or activities of the obligor or issuer of the security;

(6) The nationally recognized statistical rating organization issues or maintains a credit rating where the fee paid for the rating was negotiated, discussed, or arranged by a person within the nationally recognized statistical rating organization who has responsibility for participating in determining credit ratings or for developing or approving procedures or methodologies used for determining credit ratings, including qualitative and quantitative models;

(7) The nationally recognized statistical rating organization issues or maintains a credit rating where a credit analyst who participated in determining or monitoring the credit rating, or a person responsible for approving the credit rating received gifts, including entertainment, from the obligor being rated, or from the issuer, underwriter, or sponsor of the securities being rated, other than items provided in the context of normal business activities such as meetings that have an aggregate value of no more than $25.

(8) The nationally recognized statistical rating organization issues or maintains a credit rating where a person within the nationally recognized statistical rating organization who participates in determining or monitoring the credit rating, or developing or approving procedures or methodologies used for determining the credit rating, including qualitative and quantitative models, also:

(i) Participates in sales or marketing of a product or service of the nationally recognized statistical rating organization or a product or service of an affiliate of the nationally recognized statistical rating organization; or

(ii) Is influenced by sales or marketing considerations.

(d) For the purposes of this section, the term *person within a nationally recognized statistical rating organization* means a nationally recognized statistical rating organization, its credit rating affiliates identified on Form NRSRO, and any partner, officer, director, branch manager, and employee of the nationally recognized statistical rating organization or its credit rating affiliates (or any person occupying a similar status or performing similar functions).

(e) Certification. In order to access a password-protected Internet Web site described in paragraph (a)(3) of this section, a nationally recognized statistical rating organization must furnish to the Commission, for each calendar year for which it is requesting a password, the following certification, signed by a person duly authorized by the certifying entity:

The undersigned hereby certifies that it will access the Internet Web sites described in 17 CFR § 240.17g-5(a)(3) solely for the purpose of determining or monitoring credit ratings. Further, the undersigned certifies that it will keep the information it accesses pursuant to 17 CFR § 240.17g-5(a)(3) confidential and treat it as material nonpublic information subject to its written policies and procedures established, maintained, and enforced pursuant to section 15E(g)(1) of the Act (15 U.S.C. 78o-7(g)(1)) and 17 CFR § 240.17g-4. Further, the undersigned certifies that it will determine and maintain credit ratings for at least 10% of the issued securities and money market instruments for which it accesses information pursuant to 17 CFR § 240.17g-5(a)(3)(iii), if it accesses such information for 10 or more issued securities or money market instruments in the calendar year covered by the certification. Further, the undersigned certifies one of the following as applicable: (1) In the most recent calendar year during which it accessed information pursuant to 17 CFR § 240.17g-5(a)(3), the undersigned accessed information for [Insert Number] issued securities and money market instruments through Internet Web sites described in 17 CFR § 240.17g-5(a)(3) and determined and maintained credit ratings for [Insert Number] of such securities and money market instruments; or (2) The undersigned previously has not accessed information pursuant to 17 CFR § 240.17g-5(a)(3) 10 or more times during the most recently ended calendar year.

Rule 17g-6. Prohibited Acts and Practices

(a) *Prohibitions.* A nationally recognized statistical rating organization is prohibited from engaging in any of the following unfair, coercive, or abusive practices:

(1) Conditioning or threatening to condition the issuance of a credit rating on the purchase by an obligor or issuer, or an affiliate of the obligor or issuer, of any other services or products, including pre-credit rating assessment products, of the nationally recognized statistical rating organization or any person associated with the nationally recognized statistical rating organization.

(2) Issuing, or offering or threatening to issue, a credit rating that is not determined in accordance with the nationally recognized statistical rating organization's established procedures and methodologies for determining credit ratings, based on whether the rated person, or an affiliate of the rated person, purchases or will purchase the credit rating or any other service or product of the nationally recognized statistical rating organization or any person associated with the nationally recognized statistical rating organization.

(3) Modifying, or offering or threatening to modify, a credit rating in a manner that is contrary to the nationally recognized statistical rating organization's established procedures and methodologies for modifying credit ratings based on whether the rated person, or an affiliate of the rated person, purchases or will purchase the credit rating or any other service or product of the nationally recognized statistical rating organization or any person associated with the nationally recognized statistical rating organization.

(4) Issuing or threatening to issue a lower credit rating, lowering or threatening to lower an existing credit rating, refusing to issue a credit rating, or withdrawing or threatening to withdraw a credit rating, with respect to securities or money market instruments issued by an asset pool or as part of any asset-backed or mortgage-backed securities transaction, unless all or a portion of the assets within such pool or part of such transaction also are rated by the nationally recognized statistical rating organization, where such practice is engaged in by the nationally recognized statistical rating organization for an anticompetitive purpose.

Rule 17g-7. Disclosure Requirements

(a) *Disclosures to Be Made When Taking a Rating Action.* Except as provided in paragraph (a)(3) of this section, a nationally recognized statistical rating organization must publish the items described in paragraphs (a)(1) and (2) of this section, as applicable, when taking a rating action with respect to a credit rating assigned to an obligor, security, or money market instrument in a class of credit ratings for which the nationally recognized statistical rating organization is registered. For purposes of this section, the term *rating action* means any of the following: the publication of an expected or preliminary credit rating assigned to an obligor, security, or money market instrument before the publication of an initial credit rating; an initial credit rating; an upgrade or downgrade of an existing credit rating (including a downgrade to, or assignment of, default); and an affirmation or withdrawal of an existing credit rating if the affirmation or withdrawal is the result of a review of the credit rating assigned to the obligor, security, or money market instrument by the nationally recognized statistical rating organization using applicable procedures and methodologies for determining credit ratings. The items described in paragraphs (a) (1) and (2) of this section must be published in the same manner as the credit rating that is the result or subject of the rating action and made available to the same persons who can receive or access the credit rating that is the result or subject of the rating action.

(1) *Information Disclosure Form.* A form generated by the nationally recognized statistical rating organization that meets the requirements of paragraphs (a) (1) (i) through (iii) of this section.

(i) *Format.* The form generated by the nationally recognized statistical rating organization must be in a format that:

(A) Organizes the information into numbered items that are identified by the type of information being disclosed and a reference to the paragraph in this section that specifies the disclosure of the information, and are in the order that the paragraphs specifying the information to be disclosed are codified in this section;

Note to Paragraph (a)(1)(i)(A): A given item in the form should be identified by a title that identifies the type of information and references paragraph (a) (1) (ii) (A), (B), (C), (D), (E), (F), (G), (H), (I), (J), (K), (L), (M), (N), or (a) (2) of this section based on the information being disclosed in the item. For example, the information specified in paragraph (a) (1) (ii) (C) of this section should be identified with the caption "Main Assumptions and Principles Used to Construct the Rating Methodology used to Determine the Credit Rating as required by Paragraph (a) (1) (ii) (C) of Rule 17g-7"). The form must organize the items of information in the following order: items 1 through 14 must contain the information specified in paragraphs (a) (1) (ii) (A) through (N) of this section, respectively, and item 15 must contain the certifications specified in paragraph (a) (2) of this section (the information specified in each paragraph comprising a separate item). For example, item 3 must contain the information specified in paragraph (a) (1) (ii) (C) of this section.

(B) Is easy to use and helpful for users of credit ratings to understand the information contained in the form; and

(C) Provides the content described in paragraphs (a) (1) (ii) (K) through (M) of this section in a manner that is directly comparable across types of obligors, securities, and money market instruments.

(ii) *Content.* The form generated by the nationally recognized statistical rating organization must contain the following information about the credit rating:

(A) The symbol, number, or score in the rating scale used by the nationally recognized statistical rating organization to denote credit rating categories and notches within categories assigned to the obligor, security, or money market instrument that is the subject of the credit rating and, as applicable, the identity of the obligor or the identity and a description of the security or money market instrument;

(B) The version of the procedure or methodology used to determine the credit rating;

(C) The main assumptions and principles used in constructing the procedures and methodologies used to determine the credit rating, including qualitative methodologies and quantitative inputs, and, if the credit rating is for a structured finance product, assumptions about the correlation of defaults across the underlying assets;

(D) The potential limitations of the credit rating, including the types of risks excluded from the credit rating that the nationally recognized statistical rating organization does not comment on, including, as applicable, liquidity, market, and other risks;

(E) Information on the uncertainty of the credit rating including:

(*1*) Information on the reliability, accuracy, and quality of the data relied on in determining the credit rating; and

(*2*) A statement relating to the extent to which data essential to the determination of the credit rating were reliable or limited, including:

(*i*) Any limits on the scope of historical data; and

(*ii*) Any limits on accessibility to certain documents or other types of information that would have better informed the credit rating;

(F) Whether and to what extent the nationally recognized statistical rating organization used due diligence services of a third party in taking the rating action, and, if the nationally recognized statistical rating organization used such services, either:

(*1*) A description of the information that the third party reviewed in conducting the due diligence services and a summary of the findings and conclusions of the third party; or

(*2*) A cross-reference to a Form ABS Due Diligence-15E executed by the third party that is published with the form, provided the cross-referenced Form ABS Due Diligence-15E (§ 249b.500 of this chapter) contains a description of the information that the third party reviewed in conducting the due diligence services and a summary of the findings and conclusions of the third party;

(G) If applicable, how servicer or remittance reports were used, and with what frequency, to conduct surveillance of the credit rating;

(H) A description of the types of data about any obligor, issuer, security, or money market instrument that were relied upon for the purpose of determining the credit rating;

(I) A statement containing an overall assessment of the quality of information available and considered in determining the credit rating for the obligor, security, or money market instrument, in relation to the quality of information available to the nationally recognized statistical rating organization in rating similar obligors, securities, or money market instruments;

(J) Information relating to conflicts of interest of the nationally recognized statistical rating organization, which must include:

(*1*) As applicable, a statement that the nationally recognized statistical rating organization was:

(*i*) Paid to determine the credit rating by the obligor being rated or the issuer, underwriter, depositor, or sponsor of the security or money market instrument being rated;

(*ii*) Paid to determine the credit rating by a person other than the obligor being rated or the issuer, underwriter, depositor, or sponsor of the security or money market instrument being rated; or

(*iii*) Not paid to determine the credit rating;

(2) If applicable, in a statement required under paragraph (a)(1)(ii)(J)(*1*)(*i*) or (*ii*) of this section, a statement that the nationally recognized statistical rating organization also was paid for services other than determining credit ratings during the most recently ended fiscal year by the person that paid the nationally recognized statistical rating organization to determine the credit rating; and

(*3*) If the rating action results from a review conducted pursuant to section 15E(h)(4)(A) of the Act (15 U.S.C. 78*o*-7(h)(4)(A)) and § 240.17g-8(c), the following information (as applicable):

(*i*) If the rating action is a revision of a credit rating pursuant to § 240.17g-8(c)(2)(i)(A), an explanation that the reason for the action is the discovery that a credit rating assigned to the obligor, security, or money market instrument in one or more prior rating actions was influenced by a conflict of interest, including a description of the nature of the conflict, the date and associated credit rating of each prior rating action that the nationally recognized statistical rating organization has determined was influenced by the conflict, and a description of the impact the conflict had on the prior rating action or actions; or (*ii*) If the rating action is an affirmation of a credit rating pursuant to § 240.17g-8(c)(2)(i)(B), an explanation that the reason for the action is the discovery that a credit rating assigned to the obligor, security, or money market instrument in one or more prior rating actions was influenced by a conflict of interest, including a description of the nature of the conflict, an explanation of why no rating action was taken to revise the credit rating notwithstanding the presence of the conflict, the date and associated credit rating of each prior rating action the nationally recognized statistical rating organization has determined was influenced by the conflict, and a description of the impact the conflict had on the prior rating action or actions.

(K) An explanation or measure of the potential volatility of the credit rating, including:

(*1*) Any factors that are reasonably likely to lead to a change in the credit rating; and

(*2*) The magnitude of the change that could occur under different market conditions determined by the nationally recognized statistical rating organization to be relevant to the rating;

(L) Information on the content of the credit rating, including:

(*1*) If applicable, the historical performance of the credit rating; and

(*2*) The expected probability of default and the expected loss in the event of default;

(M) Information on the sensitivity of the credit rating to assumptions made by the nationally recognized statistical rating organization, including:

(*1*) Five assumptions made in the ratings process that, without accounting for any other factor, would have the greatest impact on the credit rating if the assumptions were proven false or inaccurate; provided that, if the nationally recognized statistical rating organization has made fewer than five such assumptions, it need only disclose information on the assumptions that would have an impact on the credit rating; and

(*2*) An analysis, using specific examples, of how each of the assumptions identified in paragraph (a)(1)(ii)(M)(*1*) of this section impacts the credit rating;

(N)(*1*) If the credit rating is assigned to an asset-backed security as defined in section 3(a)(79) of the Act (15 U.S.C. 78c(a)(79)), information on:

(*i*) The representations, warranties, and enforcement mechanisms available to investors which were disclosed in the prospectus, private placement memorandum or other offering documents for the asset-backed security and that relate to the asset pool underlying the asset-backed security; and

(*ii*) How they differ from the representations, warranties, and enforcement mechanisms in issuances of similar securities;

(*2*) A nationally recognized statistical rating organization must include the information required under paragraph (a)(1)(ii)(N)(*1*) of this section only if the rating action is a preliminary credit rating, an initial credit rating, or, in the case of a rating action other than a preliminary credit rating or initial credit rating, the rating action is the first rating action taken after a material change in the representations, warranties, or enforcement mechanisms described in paragraph (a)(1)(ii)(N)(*1*) of this section and the rating action involves an asset-backed security that was initially rated by the nationally recognized statistical rating organization on or after September 26, 2011.

(iii) *Attestation.* The nationally recognized statistical rating organization must attach to the form a signed statement by a person within the nationally recognized statistical rating organization stating that the person has responsibility for the rating action and, to the best knowledge of the person:

(A) No part of the credit rating was influenced by any other business activities;

(B) The credit rating was based solely upon the merits of the obligor, security, or money market instrument being rated; and

(C) The credit rating was an independent evaluation of the credit risk of the obligor, security, or money market instrument.

(2) *Third-Party Due Diligence Certification*. Any executed Form ABS Due Diligence-15E (§ 249b.500 of this chapter) containing information about the security or money market instrument subject to the rating action that is received by the nationally recognized statistical rating organization or obtained by the nationally recognized statistical rating organization through an Internet Web site maintained by the issuer, sponsor, or underwriter of the security or money market instrument pursuant to § 240.17g-5(a)(3).

Exemption. The provisions of paragraphs (a)(1) and (2) of this section do not apply to a rating action if:

(i) The rated obligor or issuer of the rated security or money market instrument is not a U.S. person (as defined in § 230.902(k) of this chapter); and

(ii) The nationally recognized statistical rating organization has a reasonable basis to conclude that:

(A) With respect to any security or money market instrument issued by a rated obligor, all offers and sales by any issuer, sponsor, or underwriter linked to the security or money market instrument will occur outside the United States (as that phrase is used in §§ 230.901 through 230.905 (Regulation S) of this chapter); or

(B) With respect to a rated security or money market instrument, all offers and sales by any issuer, sponsor, or underwriter linked to the security or money market instrument will occur outside the United States (as that phrase is used in §§ 230.901 through 230.905 (Regulation S) of this chapter).

(b) *Disclosure of Credit Rating Histories*—

(1) *Credit Ratings Subject to the Disclosure Requirement*. A nationally recognized statistical rating organization must publicly disclose for free on an easily accessible portion of its corporate Internet Web site:

(i) For a class of credit rating in which the nationally recognized statistical rating organization is registered with the Commission as of the effective date of paragraph (b) of this section, the credit rating assigned to each obligor, security, and money market instrument in the class that was outstanding as of, or initially determined on or after, the date three years prior to the effective date of this rule, and any subsequent upgrade or downgrade of the credit rating (including a downgrade to, or assignment of, default), and a withdrawal of the credit rating; and

(ii) For a class of credit rating in which the nationally recognized statistical rating organization is registered with the Commission after the effective date of paragraph (b) of this section, the credit rating assigned to each obligor, security, and money market instrument in the class that was outstanding as of, or initially determined on or after, the date three years prior to the date the nationally recognized statistical rating organization is registered in the class, and any subsequent upgrade or downgrade of the credit rating (including a downgrade to, or assignment of, default), and a withdrawal of the credit rating.

(2) *Information*. A nationally recognized statistical rating organization must include, at a minimum, the following information with each credit rating disclosed pursuant to paragraph (b)(1) of this section:

(i) The identity of the nationally recognized statistical rating organization disclosing the rating action;

(ii) The date of the rating action;

(iii) If the rating action is taken with respect to a credit rating of an obligor as an entity, the following identifying information about the obligor, as applicable:

(A) The Legal Entity Identifier issued by a utility endorsed or otherwise governed by the Global LEI Regulatory Oversight Committee or the Global LEI Foundation (LEI) of the obligor, if available, or, if an LEI is not available, the Central Index Key (CIK) number of the obligor, if available; and

(B) The name of the obligor.

(iv) If the rating action is taken with respect to a credit rating of a security or money market instrument, as applicable:

(A) The LEI of the issuer of the security or money market instrument, if available, or, if an LEI is not available, the CIK number of the issuer of the security or money market instrument, if available;

(B) The name of the issuer of the security or money market instrument; and

(C) The CUSIP of the security or money market instrument;

(v) A classification of the rating action as either:

(A) An addition to the rating history disclosure because the credit rating was outstanding as of the date three years prior to the effective date of the requirements in paragraph (b) of this section or because the credit rating was outstanding as of the date three years prior to the nationally recognized statistical rating organization becoming registered in the class of credit ratings;

(B) An initial credit rating;

(C) An upgrade of an existing credit rating;

(D) A downgrade of an existing credit rating, which would include classifying the obligor, security, or money market instrument as in default, if applicable; or

(E) A withdrawal of an existing credit rating and, if the classification is withdrawal, the nationally recognized statistical rating organization also must classify the reason for the withdrawal as either:

(1) The obligor defaulted, or the security or money market instrument went into default;

(2) The obligation subject to the credit rating was extinguished by payment in full of all outstanding principal and interest due on the obligation according to the terms of the obligation; or

(3) The credit rating was withdrawn for reasons other than those set forth in paragraph (b)(2)(v)(E)(1) or (2) of this section; and

(vi) The classification of the class or subclass that applies to the credit rating as either:

(A) Financial institutions, brokers, or dealers;

(B) Insurance companies;

(C) Corporate issuers; or

(D) Issuers of structured finance products in one of the following subclasses:

(1) Residential mortgage backed securities ("RMBS") (for purposes of this subclass, RMBS means a securitization primarily of residential mortgages);

(2) Commercial mortgage backed securities ("CMBS") (for purposes of this subclass, CMBS means a securitization primarily of commercial mortgages);

(3) Collateralized loan obligations ("CLOs") (for purposes of this subclass, a CLO means a securitization primarily of commercial loans);

(4) Collateralized debt obligations ("CDOs") (for purposes of this subclass, a CDO means a securitization primarily of other debt instruments such as RMBS, CMBS, CLOs, CDOs, other asset backed securities, and corporate bonds);

(5) Asset-backed commercial paper conduits ("ABCP") (for purposes of this subclass, ABCP means short term notes issued by a structure that securitizes a variety of financial assets, such as trade receivables or credit card receivables, which secure the notes);

(*6*) Other asset-backed securities ("other ABS") (for purposes of this subclass, other ABS means a securitization primarily of auto loans, auto leases, floor plans, credit card receivables, student loans, consumer loans, or equipment leases); or

(*7*) Other structured finance products ("other SFPs") (for purposes of this subclass, other SFPs means any structured finance product not identified in paragraphs (b)(2)(iv)(D)(*1*) through (*6*) [*sic*]) of this section; or

(E) Issuers of government securities, municipal securities, or securities issued by a foreign government in one of the following subclasses:

(*1*) Sovereign issuers;

(*2*) U.S. public finance; or

(*3*) International public finance; and

(vii) The credit rating symbol, number, or score in the applicable rating scale of the nationally recognized statistical rating organization assigned to the obligor, security, or money market instrument as a result of the rating action or, if the credit rating remained unchanged as a result of the action, the credit rating symbol, number, or score in the applicable rating scale of the nationally recognized statistical rating organization assigned to the obligor, security, or money market instrument as of the date of the rating action (in either case, include a credit rating in a default category, if applicable).

(3) *Format and Frequency of Updating*. The information identified in paragraph (b)(2) of this section must be disclosed in an interactive data file that uses an XBRL (eXtensible Business Reporting Language) format and the List of XBRL Tags for nationally recognized statistical rating organizations as published on the Internet Web site of the Commission, and must be updated no less frequently than monthly.

(4) *Timing*. The nationally recognized statistical rating organization must disclose the information required in paragraph (b)(2) of this section:

(i) Within twelve months from the date the rating action is taken, if the credit rating subject to the action was paid for by the obligor being rated or by the issuer, underwriter, depositor, or sponsor of the security being rated; or

(ii) Within twenty-four months from the date the rating action is taken, if the credit rating subject to the action is not a credit rating described in paragraph (b)(4)(i) of this section.

(5) *Removal of a Credit Rating History*. The nationally recognized statistical rating organization may cease disclosing a rating history of an obligor, security, or money market instrument if at least 15 years have elapsed since a rating action classified as a withdrawal of a credit rating pursuant to paragraph (b)(2)(v)(E) of this section was disclosed in the rating history of the obligor, security, or money market instrument.

MEMBERSHIP ON NATIONAL SECURITIES EXCHANGES

Rule 19b-4. Filings with Respect to Proposed Rule Changes by Self-Regulatory Organizations

A self-regulatory organization also must refer to Form 19b-4 (17 CFR 249.819) for further requirements with respect to the filing of proposed rule changes.

(a) Definitions. As used in this section:

(1) The term advance notice means a notice required to be made by a designated clearing agency pursuant to Section 806(e) of the Payment, Clearing and Settlement Supervision Act (12 U.S.C. 5465(e));

(2) The term designated clearing agency means a clearing agency that is registered with the Commission, and for which the Commission is the Supervisory Agency (as determined in accordance with section 803(8) of the Payment, Clearing and Settlement Supervision Act (12 U.S.C. 5462(8)), that has been designated by the Financial Stability Oversight

Council pursuant to section 804 of the Payment, Clearing and Settlement Supervision Act (12 U.S.C. 5463) as systemically important or likely to become systemically important;

(3) The term Payment, Clearing and Settlement Supervision Act means Title VIII of the Dodd-Frank Wall Street Reform and Consumer Protection Act (124 Stat. 1802, 1803, 1807, 1809, 1811, 1814, 1816, 1818, 1820, 1821; 12 U.S.C. 5461 et seq.);

(4) The term proposed rule change has the meaning set forth in Section 19(b)(1) of the Act (15 U.S.C. 78s(b)(1));

(5) The term security-based swap submission means a submission of identifying information required to be made by a clearing agency pursuant to section 3C(b)(2) of the Act (15 U.S.C. 78c-3(b)(2)) for each security-based swap, or any group, category, type or class of security-based swaps, that such clearing agency plans to accept for clearing;

(6) The term stated policy, practice, or interpretation means:

(i) Any material aspect of the operation of the facilities of the self-regulatory organization; or

(ii) Any statement made generally available to the membership of, to all participants in, or to persons having or seeking access (including, in the case of national securities exchanges or registered securities associations, through a member) to facilities of, the self-regulatory organization ("specified persons"), or to a group or category of specified persons, that establishes or changes any standard, limit, or guideline with respect to:

(A) The rights, obligations, or privileges of specified persons or, in the case of national securities exchanges or registered securities associations, persons associated with specified persons; or

(B) The meaning, administration, or enforcement of an existing rule.

(b)(1) Filings with respect to proposed rule changes by a self-regulatory organization, except filings with respect to proposed rules changes by self-regulatory organizations submitted pursuant to section 19(b)(7) of the Act (15 U.S.C. 78s(b)(7)), shall be made electronically on Form 19b-4 (17 CFR 249.819).

(2) For purposes of Section 19(b) of the Act and this rule, a "business day" is any day other than a Saturday, Sunday, Federal holiday, a day that the Office of Personnel Management has announced that Federal agencies in the Washington, DC area are closed to the public, a day on which the Commission is subject to a Federal government shutdown or a day on which the Commission's Washington, DC office is otherwise not open for regular business.

(c) A stated policy, practice, or interpretation of the self-regulatory organization shall be deemed to be a proposed rule change unless (1) it is reasonably and fairly implied by an existing rule of the self-regulatory organization or (2) it is concerned solely with the administration of the self-regulatory organization and is not a stated policy, practice, or interpretation with respect to the meaning, administration, or enforcement of an existing rule of the self-regulatory organization.

(d) Regardless of whether it is made generally available, an interpretation of an existing rule of the self-regulatory organization shall be deemed to be a proposed rule change if

(1) it is approved or ratified by the governing body of the self-regulatory organization and

(2) it is not reasonably and fairly implied by that rule.

(e) For the purposes of this paragraph, *new derivative securities product* means any type of option, warrant, hybrid securities product or any other security whose value is based, in whole or in part, upon the performance of, or interest in, an underlying instrument.

(1) The listing and trading of a new derivative securities product by a self-regulatory organization shall not be deemed a proposed rule change, pursuant to paragraph (c)(1) of this section, if the Commission has approved, pursuant to Section 19(b) of the Act (15 U.S.C. 78s(b)), the self-regulatory organization's trading rules, procedures and listing standards for

the product class that would include the new derivative securities product and the self-regulatory organization has a surveillance program for the product class.

(2) *Recordkeeping and Reporting.*

(i) Self-regulatory organizations shall retain at their principal place of business a file, available to Commission staff for inspection, of all relevant records and information pertaining to each new derivative securities product traded pursuant to this paragraph (e) for a period of not less than five years, the first two years in an easily accessible place, as prescribed in § 240.17a-1.

(ii) When relying on this paragraph (e), a self-regulatory organization shall submit Form 19b-4(e) (17 CFR 249.820) to the Commission within five business days after commencement of trading a new derivative securities product.

(f) A proposed rule change may take effect upon filing with the Commission pursuant to Section 19(b)(3)(A) of the Act, 15 U.S.C. 78s(b)(3)(A), if properly designated by the self-regulatory organization as:

(1) Constituting a stated policy, practice, or interpretation with respect to the meaning, administration, or enforcement of an existing rule;

(2) Establishing or changing a due, fee, or other charge;

(3) Concerned solely with the administration of the self-regulatory organization;

(4) Affecting a change in an existing service of a registered clearing agency that either:

(i)(A) Does not adversely affect the safeguarding of securities or funds in the custody or control of the clearing agency or for which it is responsible; and

(B) Does not significantly affect the respective rights or obligations of the clearing agency or persons using the service; or

(ii)(A) Primarily affects the clearing operations of the clearing agency with respect to products that are not securities, including futures that are not security futures, swaps that are not security-based swaps or mixed swaps, and forwards that are not security forwards; and

(B) Either

(1) Does not significantly affect any securities clearing operations of the clearing agency or any rights or obligations of the clearing agency with respect to securities clearing or persons using such securities-clearing service, or (2) Does significantly affect any securities clearing operations of the clearing agency or the rights or obligations of the clearing agency with respect to securities clearing or persons using such securities-clearing service, but is necessary to maintain fair and orderly markets for products that are not securities, including futures that are not security futures, swaps that are not security-based swaps or mixed swaps, and forwards that are not security forwards. Proposed rule changes filed pursuant to this subparagraph II must also be filed in accordance with the procedures of Section 19(b)(1) for approval pursuant to Section 19(b)(2) and the regulations thereunder within fifteen days of being filed under Section 19(b)(3)(A).

(5) Effecting a change in an existing order-entry or trading system of a self-regulatory organization that:

(i) Does not significantly affect the protection of investors or the public interest;

(ii) Does not impose any significant burden on competition; and

(iii) Does not have the effect of limiting the access to or availability of the system; or

(6) Effecting a change that:

(i) Does not significantly affect the protection of investors or the public interest;

(ii) Does not impose any significant burden on competition; and

(iii) By its terms, does not become operative for 30 days after the date of the filing, or such shorter time as the Commission may designate if consistent with the protection of investors and the public interest; provided that the self-regulatory organization has given the Commission written notice of its intent to file the proposed rule change, along with a brief description and text of the proposed rule change, at least five business days prior to the date of filing of the proposed rule change, or such shorter time as designated by the Commission.

(g) Proceedings to determine whether a proposed rule change should be disapproved will be conducted pursuant to 17 CFR 201.700–701 (Initiation of Proceedings for SRO Proposed Rule Changes).

(h) Notice of orders issued pursuant to Section 19(b) of the Act will be given by prompt publication thereof, together with a statement of written reasons therefor.

(i) Self-regulatory organizations shall retain at their principal place of business a file, available to interested persons for public inspection and copying, of all filings, notices and submissions made pursuant to this rule and all correspondence and other communications reduced to writing (including comment letters) to and from such selfregulatory organization concerning any such filing, notice or submission, whether such correspondence and communications are received or prepared before or after the filing, notice or submission of the proposed rule change, advance notice or security-based swap submission, as applicable.

SECURITIES WHISTLEBLOWER INCENTIVES AND PROTECTION

Rule 21F-1. General

Section 21F of the Securities Exchange Act of 1934 ("Exchange Act") (15 U.S.C.78u-6), entitled "Securities Whistleblower Incentives and Protection," requires the Securities and Exchange Commission ("Commission") to pay awards, subject to certain limitations and conditions, to whistleblowers who provide the Commission with original information about violations of the Federal securities laws. These rules describe the whistleblower program that the Commission has established to implement the provisions of Section 21F, and explain the procedures you will need to follow in order to be eligible for an award. You should read these procedures carefully because the failure to take certain required steps within the time frames described in these rules may disqualify you from receiving an award for which you otherwise may be eligible. Unless expressly provided for in these rules, no person is authorized to make any offer or promise, or otherwise to bind the Commission with respect to the payment of any award or the amount thereof. The Securities and Exchange Commission's Office of the Whistleblower administers our whistleblower program. Questions about the program or these rules should be directed to the SEC Office of the Whistleblower, 100 F Street, NE., Washington, DC 20549-5631.

Rule 21F-2. Whistleblower Status and Retaliation Protection

(a) Definition of a Whistleblower.

(1) You are a whistleblower if, alone or jointly with others, you provide the Commission with information pursuant to the procedures set forth in § 240.21F-9(a) of this chapter, and the information relates to a possible violation of the Federal securities laws (including any rules or regulations there under)that has occurred, is ongoing, or is about to occur. A whistleblower must be an individual. A company or another entity is not eligible to be a whistleblower.

(2) To be eligible for an award, you must submit original information to the Commission in accordance with the procedures and conditions described in§ § 240.21F-4, 240.21F-8, and 240.21F-9 of this chapter.

(b) Prohibition Against Retaliation.

(1) For purposes of the anti-retaliation protections afforded by Section 21F(h)(1) of the Exchange Act (15 U.S.C. 78u-6(h)(1)),you are a whistleblower if:

(i) You possess a reasonable belief that the information you are providing relates to a possible securities law violation (or, where applicable, to a possible violation of the provisions set forth in 18 U.S.C. 1514A(a)) that has occurred, is ongoing, or is about to occur, and;

(ii) You provide that information in a manner described in Section 21F(h)(1)(A) of the Exchange Act (15 U.S.C. 78u-6(h)(1)(A)).

(iii) The anti-retaliation protections apply whether or not you satisfy the requirements, procedures and conditions to qualify for an award.

(2) Section 21F(h)(1) of the Exchange Act (15 U.S.C. 78u-6(h)(1)), including any rules promulgated there under, shall be enforceable in an action or proceeding brought by the Commission.

Rule 21F-3. Payment of Awards

(a) Commission Actions: Subject to the eligibility requirements described in §§ 240.21F-2, 240.21F-8, and 240.21F-16 of this chapter, the Commission will pay an award or awards to one or more whistleblowers who:

(1) Voluntarily provide the Commission

(2) With original information

(3) That leads to the successful enforcement by the Commission of a Federal court or administrative action

(4) In which the Commission obtains monetary sanctions totaling more than $1,000,000.

Note to Paragraph (a): The terms voluntarily, original information, leads to successful enforcement, action, and monetary sanctions are defined in § 240.21F-4of this chapter.

(b) Related Actions: The Commission will also pay an award based on amounts collected in certain related actions.

(1) A related action is a judicial or administrative action that is brought by:

(i) The Attorney General of the United States;

(ii) An appropriate regulatory authority;

(iii) A self-regulatory organization; or

(iv) A state attorney general in a criminal case, and is based on the same original information that the whistleblower voluntarily provided to the Commission, and that led the Commission to obtain monetary sanctions totaling more than $1,000,000.

Note to Paragraph (b)(1): The terms appropriate regulatory authority and self-regulatory organization are defined in § 240.21F-4 of this chapter.

(2) In order for the Commission to make an award in connection with a related action, the Commission must determine that the same original information that the whistleblower gave to the Commission also led to the successful enforcement of there lated action under the same criteria described in these rules for awards made in connection with Commission actions. The Commission may seek assistance and confirmation from the authority bringing the related action in making this determination. The Commission will deny an award in connection with the related action if:

(i) The Commission determines that the criteria for an award are not satisfied; or

(ii) The Commission is unable to make a determination because the Office of the Whistleblower could not obtain sufficient and reliable information that could be used as the basis for an award determination pursuant to § 240.21F-12(a) of this chapter. Additional procedures apply to the payment of awards in related actions. These procedures are described in §§ 240.21F-11 and 240.21F-14 of this chapter.

(3) The Commission will not make an award to you for a related action if you have already been granted an award by the Commodity Futures Trading Commission ("CFTC") for that same action pursuant to its whistleblower award program under Section 23 of the Commodity Exchange Act (7 U.S.C. 26). Similarly, if the CFTC has previously denied an award to you in a related action, you will be precluded from relitigating any issues before the Commission that the CFTC resolved against you as part of the award denial.

Rule 21F-4. Other Definitions

(a) Voluntary Submission of Information. (1) Your submission of information is made voluntarily within the meaning of §§ 240.21F-1 through 240.21F-17 of this chapter if you provide your submission before a request, inquiry, or demand that relates to the subject matter of your submission is directed to you or anyone representing you (such as an attorney):

(i) By the Commission;

(ii) In connection with an investigation, inspection, or examination by the Public Company Accounting Oversight Board, or any self-regulatory organization; or

(iii) In connection with an investigation by Congress, any other authority of the Federal government, or a state Attorney General or securities regulatory authority.

(2) If the Commission or any of these other authorities direct a request, inquiry, or demand as described in paragraph (a) (1) of this section to you or your representative first, your submission will not be considered voluntary, and you will not be eligible for an award, even if your response is not compelled by subpoena or other applicable law. However, your submission of information to the Commission will be considered voluntary if you voluntarily provided the same information to one of the other authorities identified above prior to receiving a request, inquiry, or demand from the Commission.

(3) In addition, your submission will not be considered voluntary if you are required to report your original information to the Commission as a result of a pre-existing legal duty, a contractual duty that is owed to the Commission or to one of the other authorities set forth in paragraph (a) (1) of this section, or a duty that arises out of a judicial or administrative order.

(b) Original Information. (1) In order for your whistleblower submission to be considered original information, it must be:

(i) Derived from your independent knowledge or independent analysis;

(ii) Not already known to the Commission from any other source, unless you are the original source of the information;

(iii) Not exclusively derived from an allegation made in a judicial or administrative hearing, in a governmental report, hearing, audit, or investigation, or from the news media, unless you are a source of the information; and

(iv) Provided to the Commission for the first time after July 21, 2010 (the date of enactment of the Dodd-Frank Wall Street Reform and Consumer Protection Act).

(2) Independent knowledge means factual information in your possession that is not derived from publicly available sources. You may gain independent knowledge from your experiences, communications and observations in your business or social interactions.

(3) Independent analysis means your own analysis, whether done alone or in combination with others. Analysis means your examination and evaluation of information that may be publicly available, but which reveals information that is not generally known or available to the public.

(4) The Commission will not consider information to be derived from your independent knowledge or independent analysis in any of the following circumstances:

(i) If you obtained the information through a communication that was subject to the attorney-client privilege, unless disclosure of that information would otherwise be permitted by an attorney pursuant to § 205.3 (d) (2) of this chapter, the applicable state attorney conduct rules, or otherwise;

(ii) If you obtained the information in connection with the legal representation of a client on whose behalf you or your employer or firm are providing services, and you seek to use the information to make a whistleblower submission for your own benefit, unless disclosure would otherwise be permitted by an attorney pursuant to § 205.3 (d) (2) of this chapter, the applicable state attorney conduct rules, or otherwise; or

(iii) In circumstances not covered by paragraphs (b) (4) (i) or (b) (4) (ii) of this section, if you obtained the information because you were:

(A) An officer, director, trustee, or partner of an entity and another person informed you of allegations of misconduct, or you learned the information in connection with the entity's processes for identifying, reporting, and addressing possible violations of law;

(B) An employee whose principal duties involve compliance or internal audit responsibilities, or you were employed by or otherwise associated with a firm retained to perform compliance or internal audit functions for an entity;

(C) Employed by or otherwise associated with a firm retained to conduct an inquiry or investigation into possible violations of law; or

(D) An employee of, or other person associated with, a public accounting firm, if you obtained the information through the performance of an engagement required of an independent public accountant under the Federal securities laws (other than an audit subject to § 240.21F-8(c)(4) of this chapter), and that information related to a violation by the engagement client or the client's directors, officers or other employees.

(iv) If you obtained the information by a means or in a manner that is determined by a United States court to violate applicable Federal or state criminal law; or

(v) Exceptions. Paragraph (b)(4)(iii) of this section shall not apply if:

(A) You have a reasonable basis to believe that disclosure of the information to the Commission is necessary to prevent the relevant entity from engaging in conduct that is likely to cause substantial injury to the financial interest or property of the entity or investors;

(B) You have a reasonable basis to believe that the relevant entity is engaging in conduct that will impede an investigation of the misconduct; or

(C) At least 120 days have elapsed since you provided the information to the relevant entity's audit committee, chief legal officer, chief compliance officer (or their equivalents), or your supervisor, or since you received the information, if you received it under circumstances indicating that the entity's audit committee, chief legal officer, chief compliance officer (or their equivalents), or your supervisor was already aware of the information.

(vi) If you obtained the information from a person who is subject to this section, unless the information is not excluded from that person's use pursuant to this section, or you are providing the Commission with information about possible violations involving that person.

(5) The Commission will consider you to be an original source of the same information that we obtain from another source if the information satisfies the definition of original information and the other source obtained the information from you or your representative. In order to be considered an original source of information that the Commission receives from Congress, any other authority of the Federal government, a state Attorney General or securities regulatory authority, any self-regulatory organization, or the Public Company Accounting Oversight Board, you must have voluntarily given such authorities the information within the meaning of these rules. You must establish your status as the original source of information to the Commission's satisfaction. In determining whether you are the original source of information, the Commission may seek assistance and confirmation from one of the other authorities described above, or from another entity (including your employer), in the event that you claim to be the original source of information that an authority or another entity provided to the Commission.

(6) If the Commission already knows some information about a matter from other sources at the time you make your submission, and you are not an original source of that information under paragraph (b)(5) of this section, the Commission will consider you an original source of any information you provide that is derived from your independent knowledge or analysis and that materially adds to the information that the Commission already possesses.

(7) If you provide information to the Congress, any other authority of the Federal government, a state Attorney General or securities regulatory authority, any self-regulatory organization, or the Public Company Accounting Oversight Board, or to an entity's internal whistleblower, legal, or compliance procedures for reporting allegations of possible violations of law, and you, within 120 days, submit the same information to the Commission pursuant to § 240.21F-9 of this chapter, as you must do in order for you to be eligible to be

considered for an award, then, for purposes of evaluating your claim to an award under §§ 240.21F-10 and 240.21F-11 of this chapter, the Commission will consider that you provided information as of the date of your original disclosure, report or submission to one of these other authorities or persons. You must establish the effective date of any prior disclosure, report, or submission, to the Commission's satisfaction. The Commission may seek assistance and confirmation from the other authority or person in making this determination.

(c) Information that Leads to Successful Enforcement. The Commission will consider that you provided original information that led to the successful enforcement of a judicial or administrative action in any of the following circumstances:

(1) You gave the Commission original information that was sufficiently specific, credible, and timely to cause the staff to commence an examination, open an investigation, reopen an investigation that the Commission had closed, or to inquire concerning different conduct as part of a current examination or investigation, and the Commission brought a successful judicial or administrative action based in whole or in part on conduct that was the subject of your original information; or

(2) You gave the Commission original information about conduct that was already under examination or investigation by the Commission, the Congress, any other authority of the Federal government, a state Attorney General or securities regulatory authority, any self-regulatory organization, or the PCAOB (except in cases where you were an original source of this information as defined in paragraph (b)(4) of this section), and your submission significantly contributed to the success of the action.

(3) You reported original information through an entity's internal whistleblower, legal, or compliance procedures for reporting allegations of possible violations of law before or at the same time you reported them to the Commission; the entity later provided your information to the Commission, or provided results of an audit or investigation initiated in whole or in part in response to information you reported to the entity; and the information the entity provided to the Commission satisfies either paragraph (c)(1) or (c)(2) of this section. Under this paragraph (c)(3), you must also submit the same information to the Commission in accordance with the procedures set forth in § 240.21F-9 within 120 days of providing it to the entity.

(d) An action generally means a single captioned judicial or administrative proceeding brought by the Commission. Notwithstanding the foregoing:

(1) For purposes of making an award under § 240.21F-10 of this chapter, the Commission will treat as a Commission action two or more administrative or judicial proceedings brought by the Commission if these proceedings arise out of the same nucleus of operative facts; or

(2) For purposes of determining the payment on an award under § 240.21F-14 of this chapter, the Commission will deem as part of the Commission action upon which the award was based any subsequent Commission proceeding that, individually, results in a monetary sanction of $1,000,000 or less, and that arises out of the same nucleus of operative facts.

(e) Monetary sanctions means any money, including penalties, disgorgement, and interest, ordered to be paid and any money deposited into a disgorgement fund or other fund pursuant to Section 308(b) of the Sarbanes-Oxley Act of 2002 (15 U.S.C. 7246(b)) as a result of a Commission action or a related action.

(f) Appropriate regulatory agency means the Commission, the Comptroller of the Currency, the Board of Governors of the Federal Reserve System, the Federal Deposit Insurance Corporation, the Office of Thrift Supervision, and any other agencies that may be defined as appropriate regulatory agencies under Section 3(a)(34) of the Exchange Act (15 U.S.C. 78c(a)(34)).

(g) Appropriate regulatory authority means an appropriate regulatory agency other than the Commission.

(h) Self-regulatory organization means any national securities exchange, registered securities association, registered clearing agency, the Municipal Securities Rule making Board, and any other organizations that may be defined as self-regulatory organizations under Section 3(a)(26) of the Exchange Act (15 U.S.C. 78c(a)(26)).

Rule 21F-5. Amount of Award

(a) The determination of the amount of an award is in the discretion of the Commission.

(b) If all of the conditions are met for a whistleblower award in connection with a Commission action or a related action, the Commission will then decide the percentage amount of the award applying the criteria set forth in § 240.21F-6 of this chapter and pursuant to the procedures set forth in §§ 240.21F-10 and 240.21F-11 of this chapter. The amount will be at least 10 percent and no more than 30 percent of the monetary sanctions that the Commission and the other authorities are able to collect. The percentage awarded in connection with a Commission action may differ from the percentage awarded in connection with a related action.

(c) If the Commission makes awards to more than one whistleblower in connection with the same action or related action, the Commission will determine an individual percentage award for each whistleblower, but in no event will the total amount awarded to all whistleblowers in the aggregate be less than 10 percent or greater than 30 percent of the amount the Commission or the other authorities collect.

Rule 21F-6. Criteria For Determining Amount of Award

In exercising its discretion to determine the appropriate award percentage, the Commission may consider the following factors in relation to the unique facts and circumstances of each case, and may increase or decrease the award percentage based on its analysis of these factors. In the event that awards are determined for multiple whistleblowers in connection an [sic] action, these factors will be used to determine the relative allocation of awards among the whistleblowers.

(a) *Factors that May Increase the Amount of a Whistleblower's Award.* In determining whether to increase the amount of an award, the Commission will consider the following factors, which are not listed in order of importance.(1) Significance of the Information Provided By the Whistleblower. The Commission will assess the significance of the information provided by a whistleblower to the success of the Commission action or related action. In considering this factor, the Commission may take into account, among other things:

(i) The nature of the information provided by the whistleblower and how it related to the successful enforcement action, including whether the reliability and completeness of the information provided to the Commission by the whistleblower resulted in the conservation of Commission resources;

(ii) The degree to which the information provided by the whistleblower supported one or more successful claims brought in the Commission or related action.

(2) *Assistance Provided By the Whistleblower.* The Commission will assess the degree of assistance provided by the whistleblower and any legal representative of the whistleblower in the Commission action or related action. In considering this factor, the Commission may take into account, among other things:

(i) Whether the whistleblower provided ongoing, extensive, and timely cooperation and assistance by, for example, helping to explain complex transactions, interpreting key evidence, or identifying new and productive lines of inquiry;

(ii) The timeliness of the whistleblower's initial report to the Commission or to an internal compliance or reporting system of business organizations committing, or impacted by, the securities violations, where appropriate;

(iii) The resources conserved as a result of the whistleblower's assistance;

(iv) Whether the whistleblower appropriately encouraged or authorized others to assist the staff of the Commission who might otherwise not have participated in the investigation or related action;

(v) The efforts undertaken by the whistleblower to remediate the harm caused by the violations, including assisting the authorities in the recovery of the fruits and instrumentalities of the violations; and (vi) Any unique hardships experienced by the whistleblower as a result of his or her reporting and assisting in the enforcement action.

(3) *Law Enforcement Interest.* The Commission will assess its programmatic interest in deterring violations of the securities laws by making awards to whistleblowers who provide information that leads to the successful enforcement of such laws. In considering this factor, the Commission may take into account, among other things:

(i) The degree to which an award enhances the Commission's ability to enforce the Federal securities laws and protect investors; and

(ii) The degree to which an award encourages the submission of high quality information from whistleblowers by appropriately rewarding whistleblowers' submission of significant information and assistance, even in cases where the monetary sanctions available for collection are limited or potential monetary sanctions were reduced or eliminated by the Commission because an entity self-reported a securities violation following the whistleblower's related internal disclosure, report, or submission.

(iii) Whether the subject matter of the action is a Commission priority, whether the reported misconduct involves regulated entities or fiduciaries, whether the whistleblower exposed an industry-wide practice, the type and severity of the securities violations, the age and duration of misconduct, the number of violations, and the isolated, repetitive, or ongoing nature of the violations; and

(iv) The dangers to investors or others presented by the underlying violations involved in the enforcement action, including the amount of harm or potential harm caused by the underlying violations, the type of harm resulting from or threatened by the underlying violations, and the number of individuals or entities harmed.

(4) *Participation in Internal Compliance Systems.* The Commission will assess whether, and the extent to which, the whistleblower and any legal representative of the whistleblower participated in internal compliance systems. In considering this factor, the Commission may take into account, among other things:

(i) Whether, and the extent to which, a whistleblower reported the possible securities violations through internal whistleblower, legal or compliance procedures before, or at the same time as, reporting them to the Commission; and

(ii) Whether, and the extent to which, a whistleblower assisted any internal investigation or inquiry concerning the reported securities violations.

(b) *Factors that May Decrease the Amount of a Whistleblower's Award.* In determining whether to decrease the amount of an award, the Commission will consider the following factors, which are not listed in order of importance.

(1) *Culpability.* The Commission will assess the culpability or involvement of the whistleblower in matters associated with the Commission's action or related actions. In considering this factor, the Commission may take into account, among other things:

(i) The whistleblower's role in the securities violations;

(ii) The whistleblower's education, training, experience, and position of responsibility at the time the violations occurred;

(iii) Whether the whistleblower acted with scienter, both generally and in relation to others who participated in the violations;

(iv) Whether the whistleblower financially benefitted from the violations;

(v) Whether the whistleblower is a recidivist;

(vi) The egregiousness of the underlying fraud committed by the whistleblower; and

(vii) Whether the whistleblower knowingly interfered with the Commission's investigation of the violations or related enforcement actions.

(2) *Unreasonable Reporting Delay.* The Commission will assess whether the whistle-blower unreasonably delayed reporting the securities violations. In considering this factor, the Commission may take into account, among other things:

(i) Whether the whistleblower was aware of the relevant facts but failed to take reasonable steps to report or prevent the violations from occurring or continuing;

(ii) Whether the whistleblower was aware of the relevant facts but only reported them after learning about a related inquiry, investigation, or enforcement action; and

(iii) Whether there was a legitimate reason for the whistleblower to delay reporting the violations.

(3) *Interference With Internal Compliance and Reporting Systems.* The Commission will assess, in cases where the whistleblower interacted with his or her entity's internal compliance or reporting system, whether the whistleblower undermined the integrity of such system. In considering this factor, the Commission will take into account whether there is evidence provided to the Commission that the whistleblower knowingly:

(i) Interfered with an entity's established legal, compliance, or audit procedures to prevent or delay detection of the reported securities violation;

(ii) Made any material false, fictitious, or fraudulent statements or representations that hindered an entity's efforts to detect, investigate, or remediate the reported securities violations; and

(iii) Provided any false writing or document knowing the writing or document contained any false, fictitious or fraudulent statements or entries that hindered an entity's efforts to detect, investigate, or remediate the reported securities violations.

Rule 21F-7. Confidentiality of Submissions

(a) Section 21F(h)(2) of the Exchange Act (15 U.S.C. 78u-6(h)(2)) requires that the Commission not disclose information that could reasonably be expected to reveal the identity of a whistleblower, except that the Commission may disclose such information in the following circumstances:

(1) When disclosure is required to a defendant or respondent in connection with a Federal court or administrative action that the Commission files or in another publicaction or proceeding that is filed by an authority to which we provide the information, as described below;

(2) When the Commission determines that it is necessary to accomplish the purposes of the Exchange Act (15 U.S.C. 78a) and to protect investors, it may provide your information to the Department of Justice, an appropriate regulatory authority, a self-regulatory organization, a state attorney general in connection with a criminal investigation, any appropriate state regulatory authority, the Public Company Accounting Oversight Board, or foreign securities and law enforcement authorities. Each of these entities other than foreign securities and law enforcement authorities is subject to the confidentiality requirements set forth in Section 21F(h) of the Exchange Act (15U.S.C. 78u-6(h)). The Commission will determine what assurances of confidentiality it deems appropriate in providing such information to foreign securities and law enforcement authorities.

(3) The Commission may make disclosures in accordance with the Privacy Act of1974 (5 U.S.C. 552a).

(b) You may submit information to the Commission anonymously. If you do so, however, you must also do the following:

(1) You must have an attorney represent you in connection with both your submission of information and your claim for an award, and your attorney's name and contact information must be provided to the Commission at the time you submit your information;

(2) You and your attorney must follow the procedures set forth in § 240.21F-9 of this chapter for submitting original information anonymously; and

(3) Before the Commission will pay any award to you, you must disclose your identity to the Commission and your identity must be verified by the Commission as set forth in § 240.21F-10 of this chapter.

Rule 21F-8. Eligibility

(a) To be eligible for a whistleblower award, you must give the Commission information in the form and manner that the Commission requires. The procedures for submitting information and making a claim for an award are described in § 240.21F-9through § 240.21F-11 of this chapter. You should read these procedures carefully because you need to follow them in order to be eligible for an award, except that the Commission may, in its sole discretion, waive any of these procedures based upon as howing of extraordinary circumstances.

(b) In addition to any forms required by these rules, the Commission may also require that you provide certain additional information. You may be required to:

(1) Provide explanations and other assistance in order that the staff may evaluate and use the information that you submitted;

(2) Provide all additional information in your possession that is related to the subject matter of your submission in a complete and truthful manner, through follow-up meetings, or in other forms that our staff may agree to;

(3) Provide testimony or other evidence acceptable to the staff relating to whether you are eligible, or otherwise satisfy any of the conditions, for an award; and

(4) Enter into a confidentiality agreement in a form acceptable to the Office of the Whistleblower, covering any non-public information that the Commission provides to you, and including a provision that a violation of the agreement may lead to your ineligibility to receive an award.

(c) You are not eligible to be considered for an award if you do not satisfy the requirements of paragraphs (a) and (b) of this section. In addition, you are not eligible if:

(1) You are, or were at the time you acquired the original information provided to the Commission, a member, officer, or employee of the Commission, the Department of Justice, an appropriate regulatory agency, a self-regulatory organization, the Public Company Accounting Oversight Board, or any law enforcement organization;

(2) You are, or were at the time you acquired the original information provided to the Commission, a member, officer, or employee of a foreign government, any political subdivision, department, agency, or instrumentality of a foreign government, or any other foreign financial regulatory authority as that term is defined in Section 3(a)(52) of the Exchange Act (15 U.S.C. 78c(a)(52));

(3) You are convicted of a criminal violation that is related to the Commission action or to a related action (as defined in § 240.21F-4 of this chapter) for which you otherwise could receive an award;

(4) You obtained the original information that you gave the Commission through an audit of a company's financial statements, and making a whistleblower submission would be contrary to requirements of Section 10A of the Exchange Act (15 U.S.C.78j-a).

(5) You are the spouse, parent, child, or sibling of a member or employee of the Commission, or you reside in the same household as a member or employee of the Commission;

(6) You acquired the original information you gave the Commission from a person:

(i) Who is subject to paragraph (c)(4) of this section, unless the information is not excluded from that person's use, or you are providing the Commission with information about possible violations involving that person; or

(ii) With the intent to evade any provision of these rules; or

(7) In your whistleblower submission, your other dealings with the Commission, or your dealings with another authority in connection with a related action, you knowingly and willfully make any false, fictitious, or fraudulent statement or representation, or use any false

writing or document knowing that it contains any false, fictitious, or fraudulent statement or entry with intent to mislead or otherwise hinder the Commission or another authority.

Rule 21F-9. Procedures for Submitting Original Information

(a) To be considered a whistleblower under Section 21F of the Exchange Act (15U.S.C. 78u-6(h)), you must submit your information about a possible securities law violation by either of these methods:

(1) Online, through the Commission's Web site located at http://www.sec.gov; or

(2) By mailing or faxing a Form TCR (Tip, Complaint or Referral) (referenced in§ 249.1800 of this chapter) to the SEC Office of the Whistleblower, 100 F Street NE., Washington, DC 20549-5631, Fax (703) 813–9322.

(b) Further, to be eligible for an award, you must declare under penalty of perjury at the time you submit your information pursuant to paragraph (a)(1) or (2) of this section that your information is true and correct to the best of your knowledge and belief.

(c) Notwithstanding paragraphs (a) and (b) of this section, if you are providing your original information to the Commission anonymously, then your attorney must submit your information on your behalf pursuant to the procedures specified in paragraph (a)of this section. Prior to your attorney's submission, you must provide your attorney with a completed Form TCR (referenced in § 249.1800 of this chapter) that you have signed under penalty of perjury. When your attorney makes her submission on your behalf, your attorney will be required to certify that he or she:

(1) Has verified your identity;

(2) Has reviewed your completed and signed Form TCR (referenced in § 249.1800of this chapter) for completeness and accuracy and that the information contained therein is true, correct and complete to the best of the attorney's knowledge, information and belief;

(3) Has obtained your non-waivable consent to provide the Commission with your original completed and signed Form TCR (referenced in § 249.1800 of this chapter) in the event that the Commission requests it due to concerns that you may have knowingly and willfully made false, fictitious, or fraudulent statements or representations, or used any false writing or document knowing that the writing or document contains any false fictitious or fraudulent statement or entry; and

(4) Consents to be legally obligated to provide the signed Form TCR (referenced in§ 249.1800 of this chapter) within seven (7) calendar days of receiving such request from the Commission.

(d) If you submitted original information in writing to the Commission after July 21,2010 (the date of enactment of the Dodd-Frank Wall Street Reform and Consumer Protection Act) but before the effective date of these rules, your submission will be deemed to satisfy the requirements set forth in paragraphs (a) and (b) of this section. If you were an anonymous whistleblower, however, you must provide your attorney with a completed and signed copy of Form TCR (referenced in § 249.1800 of this chapter)within 60 days of the effective date of these rules, your attorney must retain the signed form in his or her records, and you must provide of [sic] copy of the signed form to the Commission staff upon request by Commission staff prior to any payment of an award to you in connection with your submission. Notwithstanding the foregoing, you must follow the procedures and conditions for making a claim for a whistleblower award described in § § 240.21F-10 and 240.21F-11 of this chapter.

Rule 21F-10. Procedures for Making a Claim For a Whistleblower Award in SEC Actions that Result in Monetary Sanctions in Excess of$1,000,000

(a) Whenever a Commission action results in monetary sanctions totaling more than$1,000,000, the Office of the Whistleblower will cause to be published on the Commission's Web site a "Notice of Covered Action." Such Notice will be published subsequent to the entry of a final judgment or order that alone, or collectively with other judgments or orders previously entered in the Commission action, exceeds$1,000,000; or, in the absence of such judgment or order subsequent to the deposit of monetary sanctions exceeding $1,000,000 into a disgorgement or other fund pursuant to Section 308(b) of the Sarbanes-Oxley Act of 2002. A claimant will have ninety (90) days from the date of the Notice of Covered Action to file a claim for an award based on that action, or the claim will be barred.

(b) To file a claim for a whistleblower award, you must file Form WB-APP, Application for Award for Original Information Provided Pursuant to Section 21F of the Securities Exchange Act of 1934 (referenced in § 249.1801 of this chapter). You must sign this form as the claimant and submit it to the Office of the Whistleblower by mail or fax. All claim forms, including any attachments, must be received by the Office of the Whistleblower within ninety (90) calendar days of the date of the Notice of Covered Action in order to be considered for an award.

(c) If you provided your original information to the Commission anonymously, you must disclose your identity on the Form WB-APP (referenced in § 249.1801 of this chapter), and your identity must be verified in a form and manner that is acceptable to the Office of the Whistleblower prior to the payment of any award.

(d) Once the time for filing any appeals of the Commission's judicial or administrative action has expired, or where an appeal has been filed, after all appeals in the action have been concluded, the staff designated by the Director of the Division of Enforcement ("Claims Review Staff") will evaluate all timely whistleblower award claims submitted on Form WB-APP (referenced in § 249.1801 of this chapter) in accordance with the criteria set forth in these rules. In connection with this process, the Office of the Whistleblower may require that you provide additional information relating to your eligibility for an award or satisfaction of any of the conditions for an award, as set forth in § 240.21F-(8)(b) [sic] of this chapter. Following that evaluation, the Office of the Whistleblower will send you a Preliminary Determination setting forth a preliminary assessment as to whether the claim should be allowed or denied and, if allowed, setting forth the proposed award percentage amount.

(e) You may contest the Preliminary Determination made by the Claims Review Staff by submitting a written response to the Office of the Whistleblower setting forth the grounds for your objection to either the denial of an award or the proposed amount of an award. The response must be in the form and manner that the Office of the Whistleblower shall require. You may also include documentation or other evidentiary support for the grounds advanced in your response.

(1) Before determining whether to contest a Preliminary Determination, you may:

(i) Within thirty (30) days of the date of the Preliminary Determination, request that the Office of the Whistleblower make available for your review the materials from among those set forth in § 240.21F-12(a) of this chapter that formed the basis of the Claims Review Staff's Preliminary Determination.

(ii) Within thirty (30) calendar days of the date of the Preliminary Determination, request a meeting with the Office of the Whistleblower; however, such meetings are not required and the office may in its sole discretion decline the request.

(2) If you decide to contest the Preliminary Determination, you must submit your written response and supporting materials within sixty (60) calendar days of the date of the Preliminary Determination, or if a request to review materials is made pursuant to paragraph (e)(1) of this section, then within sixty (60) calendar days of the Office of the Whistleblower making those materials available for your review.

(f) If you fail to submit a timely response pursuant to paragraph (e) of this section, then the Preliminary Determination will become the Final Order of the Commission (except where the Preliminary Determination recommended an award, in which case the Preliminary Determination will be deemed a Proposed Final Determination for purposes of paragraph (h) of this section). Your failure to submit a timely response contesting a Preliminary Determination will constitute a failure to exhaust administrative remedies, and you will be prohibited from pursuing an appeal pursuant to § 240.21F-13 of this chapter.

(g) If you submit a timely response pursuant to paragraph (e) of this section, then the Claims Review Staff will consider the issues and grounds advanced in your response, along with any supporting documentation you provided, and will make its Proposed Final Determination.

(h) The Office of the Whistleblower will then notify the Commission of each Proposed Final Determination. Within thirty (30) days thereafter, any Commissioner may request that the Proposed Final Determination be reviewed by the Commission. If no Commissioner requests such a review within the 30-day period, then the Proposed Final Determination will become the Final Order of the Commission. In the event a Commissioner requests a review, the Commission will review the record that the staff relied upon in making its determinations, including your previous submissions to the Office of the Whistleblower, and issue its Final Order.

(i) The Office of the Whistleblower will provide you with the Final Order of the Commission.

Rule 21F-11. Procedures for Determining Awards Based upon a Related Action

(a) If you are eligible to receive an award following a Commission action that results in monetary sanctions totaling more than $1,000,000, you also may be eligible to receive an award based on the monetary sanctions that are collected from a related action (as defined in § 240.21F-3 of this chapter).

(b) You must also use Form WB-APP (referenced in § 249.1801 of this chapter) to submit a claim for an award in a related action. You must sign this form as the claimant and submit it to the Office of the Whistleblower by mail or fax as follows:

(1) If a final order imposing monetary sanctions has been entered in a related action at the time you submit your claim for an award in connection with a Commission action, you must submit your claim for an award in that related action on the same Form WB-APP (referenced in § 249.1801 of this chapter) that you use for the Commission action.

(2) If a final order imposing monetary sanctions in a related action has not been entered at the time you submit your claim for an award in connection with a Commission action, you must submit your claim on Form WB-APP (referenced in§ 249.1801 of this chapter) within ninety (90) days of the issuance of a final order imposing sanctions in the related action.

(c) The Office of the Whistleblower may request additional information from you in connection with your claim for an award in a related action to demonstrate that you directly (or through the Commission) voluntarily provided the governmental agency, regulatory authority or self-regulatory organization the same original information that led to the Commission's successful covered action, and that this information led to the successful enforcement of the related action. The Office of the Whistleblower may, in its discretion, seek assistance and confirmation from the other agency in making this determination.

(d) Once the time for filing any appeals of the final judgment or order in a related action has expired, or if an appeal has been filed, after all appeals in the action have been concluded, the Claims Review Staff will evaluate all timely whistleblower award claims submitted on Form WB-APP (referenced in § 249.1801 of this chapter) in connection with the related action. The evaluation will be undertaken pursuant to the criteria set forth in these rules. In connection with this process, the Office of the Whistleblower may require that you provide additional information relating to you religibility for an award or satisfaction of any of the conditions for an award, as set forth in § 240.21F-(8)(b) [sic] of this chapter. Following this evaluation, the Office of the Whistleblower will send you a Preliminary Determination setting forth a preliminary assessment as to whether the claim should be allowed or denied and, if allowed, setting forth the proposed award percentage amount.

(e) You may contest the Preliminary Determination made by the Claims Review Staff by submitting a written response to the Office of the Whistleblower setting forth the grounds for your objection to either the denial of an award or the proposed amount of an award. The response must be in the form and manner that the Office of the Whistleblower shall require.

You may also include documentation or other evidentiary support for the grounds advanced in your response.

(1) Before determining whether to contest a Preliminary Determination, you may:

(i) Within thirty (30) days of the date of the Preliminary Determination, request that the Office of the Whistleblower make available for your review the materials from among those set forth in § 240.21F-12(a) of this chapter that formed the basis of the Claims Review Staff's Preliminary Determination.

(ii) Within thirty (30) days of the date of the Preliminary Determination, request a meeting with the Office of the Whistleblower; however, such meetings are not required and the office may in its sole discretion decline the request.

(2) If you decide to contest the Preliminary Determination, you must submit your written response and supporting materials within sixty (60) calendar days of the date of the Preliminary Determination, or if a request to review materials is made pursuant to paragraph (e)(1)(i) of this section, then within sixty (60) calendar days of the Office of the Whistleblower making those materials available for your review.

(f) If you fail to submit a timely response pursuant to paragraph (e) of this section, then the Preliminary Determination will become the Final Order of the Commission (except where the Preliminary Determination recommended an award, in which case the Preliminary Determination will be deemed a Proposed Final Determination for purposes of paragraph (h) of this section). Your failure to submit a timely response contesting a Preliminary Determination will constitute a failure to exhaust administrative remedies, and you will be prohibited from pursuing an appeal pursuant to§ 240.21F-13 of this chapter.

(g) If you submit a timely response pursuant to paragraph (e) of this section, then the Claims Review Staff will consider the issues and grounds that you advanced in your response, along with any supporting documentation you provided, and will make its Proposed Final Determination.

(h) The Office of the Whistleblower will notify the Commission of each Proposed Final Determination. Within thirty (30) days thereafter, any Commissioner may request that the Proposed Final Determination be reviewed by the Commission. If no Commissioner requests such a review within the 30-day period, then the Proposed Final Determination will become the Final Order of the Commission. In the event a Commissioner requests a review, the Commission will review the record that the staff relied upon in making its determinations, including your previous submissions to the Office of the Whistleblower, and issue its Final Order.

(i) The Office of the Whistleblower will provide you with the Final Order of the Commission.

Rule 21F-12. Materials that May Form the Basis of an Award Determination and that May Comprise the Record on Appeal

(a) The following items constitute the materials that the Commission and the Claims Review Staff may rely upon to make an award determination pursuant to § § 240.21F-10and 240.21F-11 of this chapter:

(1) Any publicly available materials from the covered action or related action, including:

(i) The complaint, notice of hearing, answers and any amendments thereto;

(ii) The final judgment, consent order, or final administrative order;

(iii) Any transcripts of the proceedings, including any exhibits;

(iv) Any items that appear on the docket; and

(v) Any appellate decisions or orders.

(2) The whistleblower's Form TCR (referenced in § 249.1800 of this chapter),including attachments, and other related materials provided by the whistleblower to assist the Commission with the investigation or examination;

(3) The whistleblower's Form WB-APP (referenced in §249.1800 of this chapter),including attachments, and any other filings or submissions from the whistleblower in support of the award application;

(4) Sworn declarations (including attachments) from the Commission staff regarding any matters relevant to the award determination;

(5) With respect to an award claim involving a related action, any statements or other information that the entity provides or identifies in connection with an award determination, provided the entity has authorized the Commission to share the information with the claimant. (Neither the Commission nor the Claims Review Staff may rely upon information that the entity has not authorized the Commission to share with the claimant); and

(6) Any other documents or materials including sworn declarations from third parties that are received or obtained by the Office of the Whistleblower to assist the Commission resolve the claimant's award application, including information related to the claimant's eligibility. (Neither the Commission nor the Claims Review Staff may rely upon information that the entity has not authorized the Commission to share with the claimant).

(b) These rules do not entitle claimants to obtain from the Commission any materials (including any pre-decisional or internal deliberative process materials that are prepared exclusively to assist the Commission in deciding the claim) other than those listed in paragraph (a) of this section. Moreover, the Office of the Whistleblower may make redactions as necessary to comply with any statutory restrictions, to protect the Commission's law enforcement and regulatory functions, and to comply with requests for confidential treatment from other law enforcement and regulatory authorities. The Office of the Whistleblower may also require you to sign a confidentiality agreement, as set forth in §240.21F-(8)(b)(4) [sic] of this chapter, before providing these materials.

Rule 21F-13. Appeals

(a) Section 21F of the Exchange Act (15 U.S.C. 78u-6) commits determinations of whether, to whom, and in what amount to make awards to the Commission's discretion. A determination of whether or to whom to make an award may be appealed within 30days after the Commission issues its final decision to the United States Court of Appeals for the District of Columbia Circuit, or to the circuit where the aggrieved person resides or has his principal place of business. Where the Commission makes an award based on the factors set forth in §240.21F-6 of this chapter of not less than 10percent and not more than 30 percent of the monetary sanctions collected in the Commission or related action, the Commission's determination regarding the amount of an award (including the allocation of an award as between multiple whistleblowers, and any factual findings, legal conclusions, policy judgments, or discretionary assessments involving the Commission's consideration of the factors in §240.21F-6 of this chapter) is not appeal able.

(b) The record on appeal shall consist of the Preliminary Determination, the Final Order of the Commission, and any other items from those set forth in §240.21F-12(a)of this chapter that either the claimant or the Commission identifies for inclusion in the record. The record on appeal shall not include any pre-decisional or internal deliberative process materials that are prepared exclusively to assist the Commission in deciding the claim (including the staff's Draft Final Determination in the event that the Commissioners reviewed the claim and issued the Final Order).

Rule 21F-14. Procedures Applicable to the Payment of Awards

(a) Any award made pursuant to these rules will be paid from the Securities and Exchange Commission Investor Protection Fund (the "Fund").

(b) A recipient of a whistleblower award is entitled to payment on the award only to the extent that a monetary sanction is collected in the Commission action or in a related action upon which the award is based.

(c) Payment of a whistleblower award for a monetary sanction collected in a Commission action or related action shall be made following the later of:

(1) The date on which the monetary sanction is collected; or

(2) The completion of the appeals process for all whistleblower award claims arising from:

(i) The Notice of Covered Action, in the case of any payment of an award for a monetary sanction collected in a Commission action; or

(ii) The related action, in the case of any payment of an award for a monetary sanction collected in a related action.

(d) If there are insufficient amounts available in the Fund to pay the entire amount of an award payment within a reasonable period of time from the time for payment specified by paragraph (c) of this section, then subject to the following terms, the balance of the payment shall be paid when amounts become available in the Fund, as follows:

(1) Where multiple whistleblowers are owed payments from the Fund based on awards that do not arise from the same Notice of Covered Action (or related action), priority in making these payments will be determined based upon the date that the collections for which the whistleblowers are owed payments occurred. If two or more of these collections occur on the same date, those whistleblowers owed payments based on these collections will be paid on a pro rata basis until sufficient amounts become available in the Fund to pay their entire payments.

(2) Where multiple whistleblowers are owed payments from the Fund based on awards that arise from the same Notice of Covered Action (or related action), they will share the same payment priority and will be paid on a pro rata basis until sufficient amounts become available in the Fund to pay their entire payments.

Rule 21F-15. No Amnesty

The Securities Whistleblower Incentives and Protection provisions do not provide amnesty to individuals who provide information to the Commission. The fact that you may become a whistleblower and assist in Commission investigations and enforcement actions does not preclude the Commission from bringing an action against you based upon your own conduct in connection with violations of the Federal securities laws. If such an action is determined to be appropriate, however, the Commission will take your cooperation into consideration in accordance with its Policy Statement Concerning Cooperation by Individuals in Investigations and Related Enforcement Actions (17 CFR§ 202.12).

Rule 21F-16. Awards to Whistleblowers Who Engage in Culpable Conduct

In determining whether the required $1,000,000 threshold has been satisfied (this threshold is further explained in § 240.21F-10 of this chapter) for purposes of making any award, the Commission will not take into account any monetary sanctions that the whistleblower is ordered to pay, or that are ordered against any entity whose liability is based substantially on conduct that the whistleblower directed, planned, or initiated. Similarly, if the Commission determines that a whistleblower is eligible for an award, any amounts that the whistleblower or such an entity pay in sanctions as a result of the action or related actions will not be included within the calculation of the amounts collected for purposes of making payments.

Rule 21F-17. Staff Communications with Individuals Reporting Possible Securities Law Violations

(a) No person may take any action to impede an individual from communicating directly with the Commission staff about a possible securities law violation, including enforcing, or threatening to enforce, a confidentiality agreement (other than agreements dealing with information covered by § 240.21F-4(b)(4)(i) and § 240.21F-4(b)(4)(ii) of this chapter related to the legal representation of a client) with respect to such communications.

(b) If you are a director, officer, member, agent, or employee of an entity that has counsel, and you have initiated communication with the Commission relating to a possible securities law violation, the staff is authorized to communicate directly with you regarding the possible securities law violation without seeking the consent of the entity's counsel.

SECURITIES EXCHANGE ACT OF 1934—SELECTED FORMS

Selected Forms and Schedules

Form	Subject
10-Q	Quarterly reports pursuant to Section 13 or 15(d) of the Securities and Exchange Act of 1934
8-K	Current report pursuant to Section 13 or 15(d) of the Securities and Exchange Act of 1934
10-K	Annual report pursuant to Section 13 or 15(d) of the Securities and Exchange Act of 1934
Schedule 13D	Schedule 13D Information to be Included in Statements Filed Pursuant to §240.13d-1(a) and Amendments Thereto Filed Pursuant to §240.13d-2(a)
Schedule 13E-3	Transaction statement under Section 13(e) of the Securities and Exchange Act of 1934 and Rule 13E-3
Schedule 14A	Information required in proxy statement
Schedule TO	Tender offer statement pursuant to section 14(d)(1) of the Securities Exchange Act of 1934
Schedule 14D-9	Solicitation/recommendation statement under Section 14(d)(4) of the Securities and Exchange Act of 1934
Schedule 15G	Information to be included in the document distributed pursuant to 17 CFR 240.15g-2
Form 4	Statement of changes of beneficial ownership of securities

SECURITIES AND EXCHANGE COMMISSION
Washington, D.C. 20549

FORM 10-Q

GENERAL INSTRUCTIONS

A. Rule as to Use of Form 10-Q.

1. Form 10-Q shall be used for quarterly reports under Section 13 or 15(d) of the Securities Exchange Act of 1934 (15 U.S.C. 78m or 78o(d)), filed pursuant to Rule 13a-13 (17 CFR 240.13a-13) or Rule 15d-13 (17 CFR 240.15d-13). A quarterly report on this form pursuant to Rule 13a-13 or Rule 15d-13 shall be filed within the following period after the end of each of the first three fiscal quarters of each fiscal year, but no report need be filed for the fourth quarter of any fiscal year:

a. 40 days after the end of the fiscal quarter for large accelerated filers and accelerated filers (as defined in 17 CFR 240.12b-2); and

b. 45 days after the end of the fiscal quarter for all other registrants.

2. Form 10-Q also shall be used for transition and quarterly reports under Section 13 or 15(d) of the Securities Exchange Act of 1934, filed pursuant to Rule 13a-10 (17 CFR 240.13a-10) or Rule 15d-10 (17 CFR 240.15d-10). Such transition or quarterly reports shall be filed in accordance with the requirements set forth in Rule 13a-10 or Rule 15d-10 applicable when the registrant changes its fiscal year end.

B. Application of General Rules and Regulations.

1. The General Rules and Regulations under the Act contain certain general requirements which are applicable to reports on any form. These general requirements should be carefully read and observed in the preparation and filing of reports on this form.

2. Particular attention is directed to Regulation 12B which contains general requirements regarding matters such as the kind and size of paper to be used, the legibility of the report, the information to be given whenever the title of securities is required to be stated, and the filing of the report. The definitions contained in Rule 12b-2 (17 CFR 240.12b-2) should be especially noted. See also Regulations 13A and 15D.

C. Preparation of Report.

1. This is not a blank form to be filled in. It is a guide copy to be used in preparing the report in accordance with Rules 12b-11 (17 CFR 240.12b-11) and 12b-12 (17 CFR 240.12b-12). The Commission does not furnish blank copies of this form to be filled in for filing.

2. These general instructions are not to be filed with the report. The instructions to the various captions of the form are also to be omitted from the report as filed.

D. Incorporation by Reference.

1. If the registrant makes available to its stockholders or otherwise publishes, within the period prescribed for filing the report, a document or statement containing information meeting some or all of the requirements of Part I of this form, the information called for may be incorporated by reference from such published document or statement, in answer or partial answer to any item or items of Part I of this form, provided copies thereof are filed as an exhibit to Part I of the report on this form.

2. Other information may be incorporated by reference in answer or partial answer to any item or items of Part II of this form in accordance with the provisions of Rule 12b-23 (17 CFR 240.12b-23).

3. If any information required by Part I or Part II is incorporated by reference into an electronic format document from the quarterly report to security holders as provided in General Instruction D, any portion of the quarterly report to security holders incorporated by reference shall be filed as an exhibit in electronic format, as required by Item 601(b)(13) of Regulation S-K.

E. Integrated Reports to Security Holders.

Quarterly reports to security holders may be combined with the required information of Form 10-Q and will be suitable for filing with the Commission if the following conditions are satisfied:

1. The combined report contains full and complete answers to all items required by Part I of this form. When responses to a certain item of required disclosure are separated within the combined report, an appropriate cross-reference should be made.

2. If not included in the combined report, the cover page, appropriate responses to Part II, and the required signatures shall be included in the Form 10-Q. Additionally, as appropriate, a cross-reference sheet should be filed indicating the location of information required by the items of the form.

3. If an electronic filer files any portion of a quarterly report to security holders in combination with the required information of Form 10-Q, as provided in this instruction, only such portions filed in satisfaction of the Form 10-Q requirements shall be filed in electronic format.

F. Filed Status of Information Presented.

1. Pursuant to Rule 13a-13(d) and Rule 15d-13(d), the information presented in satisfaction of the requirements of Items 1, 2, and 3 of Part I of this form, whether included directly in a report on this form, incorporated therein by reference from a report, document or statement filed as an exhibit to Part I of this form pursuant to Instruction D(1) above, included in an integrated report pursuant to Instruction E above, or contained in a statement regarding computation of per share earnings or a letter regarding a change in accounting principles filed as an exhibit to Part I pursuant to Item 601 of Regulation S-K (§ 229.601 of this chapter), except as provided by Instruction F(2) below, shall not be deemed filed for the purpose of Section 18 of the Act or otherwise subject to the liabilities of that section of the Act but shall be subject to the other provisions of the Act.

2. Information presented in satisfaction of the requirements of this form other than those of Items 1, 2, and 3 of Part I of this form shall be deemed filed for the purpose of Section 18 of the Act; except that, where information presented in response to Item 1 or 2 of Part I of this form (or as an exhibit thereto) is also used to satisfy Part II requirements through incorporation by reference, only that portion of Part I (or exhibit thereto) consisting of the information required by Part II shall be deemed so filed.

G. Signature and Filing of Report.

If the report is filed in paper pursuant to a hardship exemption from electronic filing (see Item 201 *et seq.* of Regulation S-T (17 CFR 232.201 *et seq.*), three complete copies of the report, including any financial statements, exhibits or other papers or documents filed as a part thereof, and five additional copies which need not include exhibits must be filed with the Commission. At least one complete copy of the report, including any financial statements, exhibits or other papers or documents filed as a part thereof, must be filed with each exchange on which any class of securities of the registrant is registered. At least one complete copy of the report filed with the Commission and one such copy filed with each exchange must be manually signed on the registrant's behalf by a duly authorized officer of the registrant and by the principal financial or chief accounting officer of the registrant. (See Rule 12b-11(d) (17 CFR 240.12b-11(d).) Copies not manually signed must bear typed or printed signatures. In the case where the principal executive officer, principal financial officer or chief accounting officer is also duly authorized to sign on behalf of the registrant, one signature is acceptable provided that the registrant clearly indicates the dual responsibilities of the signatory.

H. Omission of Information by Certain Wholly-Owned Subsidiaries.

If on the date of the filing of its report on Form 10-Q, the registrant meets the conditions specified in paragraph (1) below, then such registrant may omit the information called for in the items specified in paragraph (2) below.

1. Conditions for availability of the relief specified in paragraph (2) below:

a. All of the registrant's equity securities are owned, either directly or indirectly, by a single person which is a reporting company under the Act and which has filed all the material required to be filed pursuant to section 13, 14 or 15(d) thereof, as applicable;

b. During the preceding thirty-six calendar months and any subsequent period of days, there has not been any material default in the payment of principal, interest, a sinking or purchase fund installment, or any other material default not cured within thirty days, with respect to any indebtedness of the registrant or its subsidiaries, and there has not been any material default in the payment of rentals under material long-term leases; and

c. There is prominently set forth, on the cover page of the Form 10-Q, a statement that the registrant meets the conditions set forth in General Instruction H(1)(a) and (b) of Form 10-Q and is therefore filing this form with the reduced disclosure format.

2. Registrants meeting the conditions specified in paragraph (1) above are entitled to the following relief:

a. Such registrants may omit the information called for by Item 2 of Part I, Management's Discussion and Analysis of Financial Condition and Results of Operations, provided that the registrant includes in the Form 10-Q a management's narrative analysis of the results of operations explaining the reasons for material changes in the amount of revenue and expense items between the most recent fiscal year-to-date period presented and the corresponding year-to-date period in the preceding fiscal year. Explanations of material changes should include, but not be limited to, changes in the various elements which determine revenue and expense levels such as unit sales volume, prices charged and paid, production levels, production cost variances, labor costs and discretionary spending programs. In addition, the analysis should include an explanation of the effect of any changes in accounting principles and practices or method of application that have a material effect on net income as reported.

b. Such registrants may omit the information called for in the following Part II Items: Item 2, Changes in Securities; Item 3, Defaults Upon Senior Securities; and Item 4, Submission of Matters to a Vote of Security Holders.

c. Such registrants may omit the information called for by Item 3 of Part I, Quantitative and Qualitative Disclosures About Market Risk.

FORM 10-Q

SECURITIES AND EXCHANGE COMMISSION
WASHINGTON, D.C. 20549

(Mark One)

[ ] QUARTERLY REPORT PURSUANT TO SECTION 13 OR 15(d) OF THE SECURITIES EXCHANGE ACT OF 1934

For the quarterly period ended _____

OR

[ ] TRANSITION REPORT PURSUANT TO SECTION 13 OR 15(d) OF THE SECURITIES EXCHANGE ACT OF 1934

For the transition period from _____ to _____

Commission file number _____

_____
(Exact name of registrant as specified in its charter)

_____   _____
(State or other jurisdiction of incorporation or   (I.R.S. Employer Identification No.)
organization)

_____
(Address of principal executive offices)
(Zip Code)

_____
(Registrant's telephone number, including area code)

_____
(Former name, former address and former fiscal year, if changed since last report)

Securities registered pursuant to Section 12(b) of the Act:

Title of each class	Trading Symbol(s)	Name of each exchange on which registered

Indicate by check mark whether the registrant (1) has filed all reports required to be filed by Section 13 or 15(d) of the Securities Exchange Act of 1934 during the preceding 12 months (or for such shorter period that the registrant was required to file such reports), and (2) has been subject to such filing requirements for the past 90 days. Yes__ No__

Indicate by check mark whether the registrant has submitted electronically every Interactive Data File required to be submitted pursuant to Rule 405 of Regulation S-T (§ 232.405 of this chapter) during the preceding 12 months (or for such shorter period that the registrant was required to submit such files). Yes__ No__

Indicate by check mark whether the registrant is a large accelerated filer, an accelerated filer, a non-accelerated filer, or a smaller reporting company. See the definitions of "large accelerated filer," "accelerated filer" and "smaller reporting company" in Rule 12b-2 of the Exchange Act.

Large accelerated filer ☐   Accelerated filer ☐
Non-accelerated filer ☐   Smaller reporting company ☐
                                              Emerging growth company ☐

If an emerging growth company, indicate by check mark if the registrant has elected not to use the extended transition period for complying with any new or revised financial accounting standards provided pursuant to Section 13(a) of the Exchange.

Indicate by check mark whether the registrant is a shell company (as defined in Rule 12b-2 of the Exchange Act).
Yes__ No__
APPLICABLE ONLY TO ISSUERS INVOLVED IN BANKRUPTCY PROCEEDINGS DURING THE PRECEDING FIVE YEARS:
Indicate by check mark whether the registrant has filed all documents and reports required to be filed by Sections 12, 13 or 15(d) of the Securities Exchange Act of 1934 subsequent to the distribution of securities under a plan confirmed by a court.
Yes__ No__
APPLICABLE ONLY TO CORPORATE ISSUERS:
Indicate the number of shares outstanding of each of the issuer's classes of common stock, as of the latest practicable date.

PART I—FINANCIAL INFORMATION

Item 1. Financial Statements.

Provide the information required by Rule 10-01 of Regulation S-X (17 CFR 210). A smaller reporting company, defined in Rule 12b-2 (§ 240.12b-2 of this chapter) may provide the information required by Article 8-03 of Regulation S-X (§ 210.8-03 of this chapter).

Item 2. Management's Discussion and Analysis of Financial Condition and Results of Operations.

Furnish the information required by Item 303 of Regulation S-K (§ 229.303 of this chapter).

Item 3. Quantitative and Qualitative Disclosures About Market Risk.

Furnish the information required by Item 305 of Regulation S-K (§ 229.305 of this chapter).

Item 4. Controls and Procedures.

Furnish the information required by Items 307 of Regulation S-K (17 CFR 229.307) and 308(c) of Regulation S-K (17 CFR 229.308(c)).

Item 4T. Controls and Procedures.

(a) If the registrant is neither a large accelerated filer nor an accelerated filer as those terms are defined in § 240.12b-2 of this chapter, furnish the information required by Items 307 and 308T of Regulation S-K (17 CFR 229.307 and 229.308T) with respect to a quarterly report that the registrant is required to file for a fiscal year ending on or after December 15, 2007 but before June 15, 2010.

(b) This temporary Item 4T will expire on December 15, 2010.

PART II—OTHER INFORMATION

Instruction. The report shall contain the item numbers and captions of all applicable items of Part II, but the text of such items may be omitted provided the responses clearly indicate the coverage of the item. Any item which is inapplicable or to which the answer is negative may be omitted and no reference thereto need be made in the report. If substantially the same information has been previously reported by the registrant, an additional report of the information on this form need not be made. The term "previously reported" is defined in Rule 12b-2 (17 CFR 240.12b-2). A separate response need not be presented in Part II where information called for is already disclosed in the financial information provided in Part I and is incorporated by reference into Part II of the report by means of a statement to that effect in Part II which specifically identifies the incorporated information.

Item 1. Legal Proceedings.

Furnish the information required by Item 103 of Regulation S-K (§ 229.103 of this chapter). As to such proceedings which have been terminated during the period covered by the report, provide similar information, including the date of termination and a description of the disposition thereof with respect to the registrant and its subsidiaries.

Instruction. A legal proceeding need only be reported in the 10-Q filed for the quarter in which it first became a reportable event and in subsequent quarters in which there have been material developments. Subsequent Form 10-Q filings in the same fiscal year in which a legal proceeding or a material development is reported should reference any previous reports in that year.

Item 1A. Risk Factors.

Set forth any material changes from risk factors as previously disclosed in the registrant's Form 10-K (§ 249.310) in response to Item 1A. to Part 1 of Form 10-K. Smaller reporting companies are not required to provide the information required by this item.

Item 2. Unregistered Sales of Equity Securities and Use of Proceeds.

(a) Furnish the information required by Item 701 of Regulation S-K (17 CFR 229.701) as to all equity securities of the registrant sold by the registrant during the period covered by the report that were not registered under the Securities Act. If the Item 701 information previously has been included in a Current Report on Form 8-K (17 CFR 249.308), however, it need not be furnished.

(b) If required pursuant to Rule 463 (17 CFR 230.463) of the Securities Act of 1933, furnish the information required by Item 701(f) of Regulation S-K (229.701(f) of this chapter).

(c) Furnish the information required by Item 703 of Regulation S-K (§ 229.703 of this chapter) for any repurchase made in the quarter covered by the report. Provide disclosures covering repurchases made on a monthly basis. For example, if the quarter began on January 16 and ended on April 15, the chart would show repurchases for the months from January 16 through February 15, February 16 through March 15, and March 16 through April 15.

Instruction. Working capital restrictions and other limitations upon the payment of dividends are to be reported hereunder.

Item 3. Defaults Upon Senior Securities.

(a) If there has been any material default in the payment of principal, interest, a sinking or purchase fund installment, or any other material default not cured within 30 days, with respect to any indebtedness of the registrant or any of its significant subsidiaries exceeding 5 percent of the total assets of the registrant and its consolidated subsidiaries, identify the indebtedness and state the nature of the default. In the case of such a default in the payment of principal, interest, or a sinking or purchase fund installment, state the amount of the default and the total arrearage on the date of filing this report.

Instruction. This paragraph refers only to events which have become defaults under the governing instruments, i.e., after the expiration of any period of grace and compliance with any notice requirements.

(b) If any material arrearage in the payment of dividends has occurred or if there has been any other material delinquency not cured within 30 days, with respect to any class of preferred stock of the registrant which is registered or which ranks prior to any class of registered securities, or with respect to any class of preferred stock of any significant subsidiary of the registrant, give the title of the class and state the nature of the arrearage or delinquency. In the case of an arrearage in the payment of dividends, state the amount and the total arrearage on the date of filing this report.

Instructions to Item 3

1. Item 3 need not be answered as to any default or arrearage with respect to any class of securities all of which is held by or for the account of the registrant or its totally held subsidiaries.

2. The information required by Item 3 need not be made if previously disclosed on a report on Form 8-K (17 CFR 249.308).

Item 4. Submission of Matters to a Vote of Security Holders.

If any matter has been submitted to a vote of security holders during the period covered by this report, through the solicitation of proxies or otherwise, furnish the following information:

(a) The date of the meeting and whether it was an annual or special meeting.

(b) If the meeting involved the election of directors, the name of each director elected at the meeting and the name of each other director whose term of office as a director continued after the meeting.

(c) A brief description of each matter voted upon at the meeting and state the number of votes cast for, against or withheld, as well as the number of abstentions and broker nonvotes, as to each such matter, including a separate tabulation with respect to each nominee for office.

(d) A description of the terms of any settlement between the registrant and any other participant (as defined in Instruction 3 to Item 4 of Schedule 14A (§ 240.14a-101)) terminating any solicitation subject to § 240.14a-12(c), including the cost or anticipated cost to the registrant.

Instructions:

1. If any matter has been submitted to a vote of security holders otherwise than at a meeting of such security holders, corresponding information with respect to such submission shall be furnished. The solicitation of any authorization or consent (other than a proxy to vote at a stockholders' meeting) with respect to any matter shall be deemed a submission of such matter to a vote of security holders within the meaning of this item.

2. Paragraph (a) need be answered only if paragraph (b) or (c) is required to be answered.

3. Paragraph (b) need not be answered if (i) proxies for the meeting were solicited pursuant to Regulation 14 under the Act, (ii) there was no solicitation in opposition to the management's nominees as listed in the proxy statement, and (iii) all of such nominees were elected. If the registrant did not solicit proxies and the board of directors as previously reported to the Commission was re-elected in its entirety, a statement to that effect in answer to paragraph (b) will suffice as an answer thereto.

4. Paragraph (c) must be answered for all matters voted upon at the meeting, including both contested and uncontested elections of directors.

5. If the registrant has furnished to its security holders proxy soliciting material containing the information called for by paragraph (d), the paragraph may be answered by reference to the information contained in such material.

6. If the registrant has published a report containing all of the information called for by this item, the item may be answered by a reference to the information contained in such report.

Item 5. Other Information.

(a) The registrant must disclose under this item any information required to be disclosed in a report on Form 8-K during the period covered by this Form 10-Q, but not reported, whether or not otherwise required by this Form 10-Q. If disclosure of such information is made under this item, it need not be repeated in a report on Form 8-K which would otherwise be required to be filed with respect to such information or in a subsequent report on Form 10-Q.

(b) Furnish the information required by Item 407(c)(3) of Regulation S-K (§ 229.407 of this chapter).

Item 6. Exhibits.

Furnish the exhibits required by Item 601 of Regulation S-K (§ 229.601 of this chapter).

SIGNATURES*

Pursuant to the requirements of the Securities Exchange Act of 1934, the registrant has duly caused this report to be signed on its behalf by the undersigned thereunto duly authorized.

_____

(Registrant) _____

Date _____   _____

(Signature)**

Date _____   _____

(Signature)** _____

* See General Instruction E.

** Print name and title of the signing officer under his signature.

FORM 8-K

UNITED STATES
SECURITIES AND EXCHANGE COMMISSION
Washington, D.C. 20549

FORM 8-K

CURRENT REPORT

Pursuant to Section 13 or 15(d) of the Securities Exchange Act of 1934

Date of Report (Date of earliest event reported) ....

....

(Exact name of registrant as specified in its charter)

....

| (State or other jurisdiction of incorporation) | (Commission File Number) | (IRS Employer, Identification No.) |

....

(Address of principal executive offices)   (Zip Code)

Registrant's telephone number, including area code

....

(Former name or former address, if changed since last report.)

Securities registered pursuant to Section 12(b) of the Act:

Title of each class	Trading Symbol(s)	Name of each exchange on which registered

Check the appropriate box below if the Form 8-K filing is intended to simultaneously satisfy the filing obligation of the registrant under any of the following provisions (see General Instruction A.2. below):

[ ] Written communications pursuant to Rule 425 under the Securities Act (17 CFR 230.425)

[ ] Soliciting material pursuant to Rule 14a-12 under the Exchange Act (17 CFR 240.14a-12)

[ ] Pre-commencement communications pursuant to Rule 14d-2(b) under the Exchange Act (17 CFR 240.14d-2(b))

[ ] Pre-commencement communications pursuant to Rule 13e-4(c) under the Exchange Act (17 CFR 240.13e-4(c))

Indicate by check mark whether the registrant is an emerging growth company as defined in as defined in Rule 405 of the Securities Act of 1933 (§ 230.405 of this chapter) or Rule 12b-2 of the Securities Exchange Act of 1934 (§ 240.12b-2 of this chapter).

Emerging growth company ☐

If an emerging growth company, indicate by check mark if the registrant has elected not to use the extended transition period for complying with any new or revised financial accounting standards provided pursuant to Section 13(a) of the Exchange Act. ☐

GENERAL INSTRUCTIONS

A. Rule as to Use of Form 8-K.

1. Form 8-K shall be used for current reports under Section 13 or 15(d) of the Securities Exchange Act of 1934, filed pursuant to Rule 13a-11 or Rule 15d-11, and for reports of nonpublic information required to be disclosed by Regulation FD (17 CFR 243.100 and 243.101).

2. Form 8-K may be used by a registrant to satisfy its filing obligations pursuant to Rule 425 under the Securities Act, regarding written communications related to business combination transactions, or Rules 14a-12(b) or Rule 14d-2(b) under the Exchange Act, relating to soliciting materials and pre-commencement communications pursuant to tender offers, respectively, provided that the Form 8-K filing satisfies all the substantive requirements of those rules (other than the Rule 425(c) requirement to include certain specified information in any prospectus filed pursuant to such rule). Such filing is also deemed to be filed pursuant to any rule for which the box is checked. A registrant is not required to check the box in connection with Rule 14a-12(b) or Rule 14d-2(b) if the communication is filed pursuant to Rule 425. Communications filed pursuant to Rule 425 are deemed filed under the other applicable sections. See Note 2 to Rule 425, Rule 14a-12(b) and Instruction 2 to Rule 14d-2(b)(2).

B. Events to be Reported and Time for Filing of Reports

1. A report on this form is required to be filed or furnished, as applicable, upon the occurrence of any one or more of the events specified in the items in Sections 1-6 and 9 of this form. Unless otherwise specified, a report is to be filed or furnished within four business days after occurrence of the event. If the event occurs on a Saturday, Sunday or holiday on which the Commission is not open for business, then the four business day period shall begin to run on, and include, the first business day thereafter. A registrant either furnishing a report on this form under Item 7.01 (Regulation FD Disclosure) or electing to file a report on this form under Item 8.01 (Other Events) solely to satisfy its obligations under Regulation FD (17 CFR 243.100 and 243.101) must furnish such report or make such filing, as applicable, in accordance with the requirements of Rule 100(a) of Regulation FD (17 CFR 243.100(a)), including the deadline for furnishing or filing such report. A report pursuant to Item 5.08 is to be filed within four business days after the registrant determines the anticipated meeting date.

2. The information in a report furnished pursuant to Item 2.02 (Results of Operations and Financial Condition) or Item 7.01 (Regulation FD Disclosure) shall not be deemed to be "filed" for purposes of Section 18 of the Exchange Act or otherwise subject to the liabilities of that section, unless the registrant specifically states that the information is to be considered "filed" under the Exchange Act or incorporates it by reference into a filing under the Securities Act or the Exchange Act. If a report on Form 8-K contains disclosures under Item 2.02 or Item 7.01, whether or not the report contains disclosures regarding other items, all exhibits to such report relating to Item 2.02 or Item 7.01 will be deemed furnished, and not filed, unless the registrant specifies, under Item 9.01 (Financial Statements and Exhibits), which exhibits, or portions of exhibits, are intended to be deemed filed rather than furnished pursuant to this instruction.

3. If the registrant previously has reported substantially the same information as required by this form, the registrant need not make an additional report of the information on this form. To the extent that an item calls for disclosure of developments concerning a previously reported event or transaction, any information required in the new report or amendment about the previously reported event or transaction may be provided by incorporation by reference to the previously filed report. The term *previously reported* is defined in Rule 12b-2 (17 CFR 240.12b-2).

4. Copies of agreements, amendments or other documents or instruments required to be filed pursuant to Form 8-K are not required to be filed or furnished as exhibits to the Form 8-K unless specifically required to be filed or furnished by the applicable Item. This instruction does not affect the requirement to otherwise file such agreements, amendments or other documents or instruments, including as exhibits to registration statements and periodic reports pursuant to the requirements of Item 601 of Regulation S-K.

5. When considering current reporting on this form, particularly of other events of material importance pursuant to Item 7.01 (Regulation FD Disclosure) and Item 8.01(Other Events), registrants should have due regard for the accuracy, completeness and currency of the information in registration statements filed under the Securities Act which incorporate by reference information in reports filed pursuant to the Exchange Act, including reports on this form.

6. A registrant's report under Item 7.01 (Regulation FD Disclosure) or Item 8.01 (Other Events) will not be deemed an admission as to the materiality of any information in the report that is required to be disclosed solely by Regulation FD.

C. Application of General Rules and Regulations.

1. The General Rules and Regulations under the Act (17 CFR Part 240) contain certain general requirements which are applicable to reports on any form. These general requirements should be carefully read and observed in the preparation and filing of reports on this form.

2. Particular attention is directed to Regulation 12B (17 CFR 240.12b-1 *et seq.*) which contains general requirements regarding matters such as the kind and size of paper to be used, the legibility of the report, the information to be given whenever the title of securities is required to be stated, and the filing of the report. The definitions contained in Rule 12b-2 should be especially noted. See also Regulations 13A (17 CFR 240.13a-1 *et seq.*) and 15D (17 CFR 240.15d-1 *et seq.*).

D. Preparation of Report.

This form is not to be used as a blank form to be filled in, but only as a guide in the preparation of the report on paper meeting the requirements of Rule 12b-12 (17 CFR 240.12b-12). The report shall contain the number and caption of the applicable item, but the text of such item may be omitted, provided the answers thereto are prepared in the manner specified in Rule 12b-13 (17 CFR 240.12b-13). To the extent that Item 1.01 and one or more other items of the form are applicable, registrants need not provide the number and caption of Item 1.01 so long as the substantive disclosure required by Item 1.01 is disclosed in the report and the number and caption of the other applicable item(s) are provided. All items that are not required to be answered in a particular report may be omitted and no reference thereto need be made in the report. All instructions should also be omitted.

E. Signature and Filing of Report.

Three complete copies of the report, including any financial statements, exhibits or other papers or documents filed as a part thereof, and five additional copies which need not include exhibits, shall be filed with the Commission. At least one complete copy of the report, including any financial statements, exhibits or other papers or documents filed as a part thereof, shall be filed, with each exchange on which any class of securities of the registrant is registered. At least one complete copy of the report filed with the Commission and one such copy filed with each exchange shall be manually signed. Copies not manually signed shall bear typed or printed signatures.

F. Incorporation by Reference.

If the registrant makes available to its stockholders or otherwise publishes, within the period prescribed for filing the report, a press release or other document or statement containing information meeting some or all of the requirements of this form, the information called for may be incorporated by reference to such published document or statement, in answer or partial answer to any item or items of this form, provided copies thereof are filed as an exhibit to the report on this form.

G. Use of this Form by Asset-Backed Issuers.

The following applies to registrants that are asset-backed issuers. Terms used in this General Instruction G. have the same meaning as in Item 1101 of Regulation AB (17 CFR 229.1101).

1. *Reportable Events That May Be Omitted.*

The registrant need not file a report on this Form upon the occurrence of any one or more of the events specified in the following:

(a) Item 2.01, Completion of Acquisition or Disposition of Assets;

(b) Item 2.02, Results of Operations and Financial Condition;

(c) Item 2.03, Creation of a Direct Financial Obligation or an Obligation under an Off-Balance Sheet Arrangement of a Registrant;

(d) Item 2.05, Costs Associated with Exit or Disposal Activities;

(e) Item 2.06, Material Impairments;

(f) Item 3.01, Notice of Delisting or Failure to Satisfy a Continued Listing Rule or Standard; Transfer of Listing;

(g) Item 3.02, Unregistered Sales of Equity Securities;

(h) Item 4.01, Changes in Registrant's Certifying Accountant;

(i) Item 4.02, Non-Reliance on Previously Issued Financial Statements or a Related Audit Report or Completed Interim Review;

(j) Item 5.01, Changes in Control of Registrant;

(k) Item 5.02, Departure of Directors or Principal Officers; Election of Directors; Appointment of Principal Officers;

(l) Item 5.04, Temporary Suspension of Trading Under Registrant's Employee Benefit Plans; and

(m) Item 5.05, Amendments to the Registrant's Code of Ethics, or Waiver of a Provision of the Code of Ethics.

2. *Additional Disclosure for the Form 8-K Cover Page.*

Immediately after the name of the issuing entity on the cover page of the Form 8-K, as separate line items, identify the exact name of the depositor as specified in its charter and the exact name of the sponsor as specified in its charter. Include a Central Index Key number for the depositor and the issuing entity, and if available, the sponsor.

3. *Signatures.*

The Form 8-K must be signed by the depositor. In the alternative, the Form 8-K may be signed on behalf of the issuing entity by a duly authorized representative of the servicer. If multiple servicers are involved in servicing the pool assets, a duly authorized representative of the master servicer (or entity performing the equivalent function) must sign if a representative of the servicer is to sign the report on behalf of the issuing entity.

INFORMATION TO BE INCLUDED IN THE REPORT

Section 1—Registrant's Business and Operations

Item 1.01. Entry into a Material Definitive Agreement.

(a) If the registrant has entered into a material definitive agreement not made in the ordinary course of business of the registrant, or into any amendment of such agreement that is material to the registrant, disclose the following information:

(1) the date on which the agreement was entered into or amended, the identity of the parties to the agreement or amendment and a brief description of any material relationship between the registrant or its affiliates and any of the parties, other than in respect of the material definitive agreement or amendment; and

(2) a brief description of the terms and conditions of the agreement or amendment that are material to the registrant.

(b) For purposes of this Item 1.01, a *material definitive agreement* means an agreement that provides for obligations that are material to and enforceable against the registrant, or rights that are material to the registrant and enforceable by the registrant against one or more other parties to the agreement, in each case whether or not subject to conditions.

Instructions.

1. Any material definitive agreement of the registrant not made in the ordinary course of the registrant's business must be disclosed under this Item 1.01. An agreement is deemed to be not made in the ordinary course of a registrant's business even if the agreement is such as ordinarily accompanies the kind of business conducted by the registrant if it involves the subject matter identified in Item 601(b)(10)(ii)(A)–(D) of Regulation S-K (17 CFR 229.601(b)(10)(ii)(A)–(D)). An agreement involving the subject matter identified in Item 601(b)(10)(iii)(A) or (B) need not be disclosed under this Item.

2. A registrant must provide disclosure under this Item 1.01 if the registrant succeeds as a party to the agreement or amendment to the agreement by assumption or assignment (other than in connection with a merger or acquisition or similar transaction).

3. With respect to asset-backed securities, as defined in Item 1101 of Regulation AB (17 CFR 229.1101), disclosure is required under this Item 1.01 regarding the entry into or an amendment to a definitive agreement that is material to the asset-backed securities transaction, even if the registrant is not a party to such agreement (*e.g.*, a servicing agreement with a servicer contemplated by Item 1108(a)(3) of Regulation AB (17 CFR 229.1108(a)(3)).

4. To the extent a material definitive agreement is filed as an exhibit under this Item 1.01, schedules (or similar attachments) to the exhibits are not required to be filed unless they contain information material to an investment or voting decision and that information is not otherwise disclosed in the exhibit or the disclosure document. Each exhibit filed must contain a list briefly identifying the contents of all omitted schedules. Registrants need not prepare a separate list of omitted information if such information is already included within the exhibit in a manner that conveys the subject matter of the omitted schedules and attachments. In addition, the registrant must provide a copy of any omitted schedule to the Commission or its staff upon request.

5. To the extent a material definitive agreement is filed as an exhibit under this Item 1.01, the registrant may redact information from the exhibit if disclosure of such information would constitute a clearly unwarranted invasion of personal privacy (*e.g.*, disclosure of bank account numbers, social security numbers, home addresses and similar information).

6. To the extent a material definitive agreement is filed as an exhibit under this Item 1.01, the registrant may redact provisions or terms of the exhibit if those provisions or terms are both (i) not material and (ii) would likely cause competitive harm to the registrant if publicly disclosed, provided that the registrant intends to incorporate by reference this filing into its future periodic reports or registration statements, as applicable, in satisfaction of Item 601(b)(10) of Regulation S-K. If it chooses to redact information pursuant to this instruction, the registrant should mark the exhibit index to indicate that portions of the exhibit or exhibits have been omitted and include a prominent statement on the first page of the redacted exhibit that certain identified information has been excluded from the exhibit because it is both (i) not material and (ii) would likely cause competitive harm to the registrant if publicly disclosed. The registrant also must indicate by brackets where the information is omitted from the filed version of the exhibit.

If requested by the Commission or its staff, the registrant must promptly provide an unredacted copy of the exhibit on a supplemental basis. The Commission or its staff also may request the registrant to provide its materiality and competitive harm analyses on a supplemental basis. Upon evaluation of the registrant's supplemental materials, the Commission or its staff may request the registrant to amend its filing to include in the exhibit any previously redacted information that is not adequately supported by the registrant's materiality and competitive harm analyses.

The registrant may request confidential treatment of the supplemental material submitted under Instruction 6 of this Item pursuant to Rule 83 (§ 200.83 of this chapter) while it is in the possession of the Commission or its staff. After completing its review of the supplemental information, the Commission or its staff will return or destroy it at the request of the registrant, if the registrant complies with the procedures outlined in Rules 418 or 12b-4 (§ 230.418 or 240.12b-4 of this chapter).

Item 1.02. Termination of a Material Definitive Agreement.

(a) If a material definitive agreement which was not made in the ordinary course of business of the registrant and to which the registrant is a party is terminated otherwise than by expiration of the agreement on its stated termination date, or as a result of all parties completing their obligations under such agreement, and such termination of the agreement is material to the registrant, disclose the following information:

(1) the date of the termination of the material definitive agreement, the identity of the parties to the agreement and a brief description of any material relationship between the registrant or its affiliates and any of the parties other than in respect of the material definitive agreement;

(2) a brief description of the terms and conditions of the agreement that are material to the registrant;

(3) a brief description of the material circumstances surrounding the termination; and

(4) any material early termination penalties incurred by the registrant.

(b) For purposes of this Item 1.02, the term *material definitive agreement* shall have the same meaning as set forth in Item 1.01(b).

Instructions.

1. No disclosure is required solely by reason of this Item 1.02 during negotiations or discussions regarding termination of a material definitive agreement unless and until the agreement has been terminated.

2. No disclosure is required solely by reason of this Item 1.02 if the registrant believes in good faith that the material definitive agreement has not been terminated, unless the registrant has received a notice of termination pursuant to the terms of agreement.

3. With respect to asset-backed securities, as defined in Item 1101 of Regulation AB (17 CFR 229.1101), disclosure is required under this Item 1.02 regarding the termination of a definitive agreement that is material to the asset-backed securities transaction (otherwise than by expiration of the agreement on its stated termination date or as a result of all parties completing their obligations under such agreement), even if the registrant is not a party to such agreement (*e.g.*, a servicing agreement with a servicer contemplated by Item 1108(a)(3) of Regulation AB (17 CFR 229.1108(a)(3)).

Item 1.03. Bankruptcy or Receivership.

(a) If a receiver, fiscal agent or similar officer has been appointed for a registrant or its parent, in a proceeding under the U.S. Bankruptcy Code or in any other proceeding under state or federal law in which a court or governmental authority has assumed jurisdiction over substantially all of the assets or business of the registrant or its parent, or if such jurisdiction has been assumed by leaving the existing directors and officers in possession but subject to the supervision and orders of a court or governmental authority, disclose the following information:

(1) the name or other identification of the proceeding;

(2) the identity of the court or governmental authority;

(3) the date that jurisdiction was assumed; and

(4) the identity of the receiver, fiscal agent or similar officer and the date of his or her appointment.

(b) If an order confirming a plan of reorganization, arrangement or liquidation has been entered by a court or governmental authority having supervision or jurisdiction over substantially all of the assets or business of the registrant or its parent, disclose the following:

(1) the identity of the court or governmental authority;

(2) the date that the order confirming the plan was entered by the court or governmental authority;

(3) a summary of the material features of the plan and, pursuant to Item 9.01 (Financial Statements and Exhibits), a copy of the plan as confirmed;

(4) the number of shares or other units of the registrant or its parent issued and outstanding, the number reserved for future issuance in respect of claims and interests filed and allowed under the plan, and the aggregate total of such numbers; and

(5) information as to the assets and liabilities of the registrant or its parent as of the date that the order confirming the plan was entered, or a date as close thereto as practicable.

Instructions.

1. The information called for in paragraph (b)(5) of this Item 1.03 may be presented in the form in which it was furnished to the court or governmental authority.

2. With respect to asset-backed securities, disclosure also is required under this Item 1.03 if the depositor (or servicer if the servicer signs the report on Form 10-K (17 CFR 249.310) of the issuing entity) becomes aware of any instances described in paragraph (a) or (b) of this Item with respect to the sponsor, depositor, servicer contemplated by Item 1108(a)(3) of Regulation AB (17 CFR 229.1108(a)(3)), trustee, significant obligor, enhancement or support provider contemplated by Items 1114(b) or 1115 of Regulation AB (17 CFR 229.1114(b) or 229.1115) or other material party contemplated by Item 1101(d)(1) of Regulation AB (17 CFR 1101(d)(1)). Terms used in this Instruction 2 have the same meaning as in Item 1101 of Regulation AB (17 CFR 229.1101).

Item 1.04. Mine Safety—Reporting of Shutdowns and Patterns of Violations.

(a) If the registrant or a subsidiary of the registrant has received, with respect to a coal or other mine of which the registrant or a subsidiary of the registrant is an operator

- an imminent danger order issued under section 107(a) of the Federal Mine Safety and Health Act of 1977 (30 U.S.C. 817(a));
- a written notice from the Mine Safety and Health Administration that the coal or other mine has a pattern of violations of mandatory health or safety standards that are of such nature as could have significantly and substantially contributed to the cause and effect of coal or other mine health or safety hazards under section 104(e) of such Act (30 U.S.C. 814(e)); or
- a written notice from the Mine Safety and Health Administration that the coal or other mine has the potential to have such a pattern, disclose the following information:

(1) The date of receipt by the issuer or a subsidiary of such order or notice.

(2) The category of the order or notice.

(3) The name and location of the mine involved.

Instructions to Item 1.04.

1. The term "*coal or other mine*" means a coal or other mine, as defined in section 3 of the Federal Mine Safety and Health Act of 1977 (30 U.S.C. 802), that is subject to the provisions of such Act (30 U.S.C. 801 *et seq.*).

2. The term "*operator*" has the meaning given the term in section 3 of the Federal Mine Safety and Health Act of 1977 (30 U.S.C. 802).

Section 2—Financial Information

Item 2.01. Completion of Acquisition or Disposition of Assets.

If the registrant or any of its majority-owned subsidiaries has completed the acquisition or disposition of a significant amount of assets, otherwise than in the ordinary course of business, disclose the following information:

(a) the date of completion of the transaction;

(b) a brief description of the assets involved;

(c) the identity of the person(s) from whom the assets were acquired or to whom they were sold and the nature of any material relationship, other than in respect of the transaction, between such person(s) and the registrant or any of its affiliates, or any director or officer of the registrant, or any associate of any such director or officer;

(d) the nature and amount of consideration given or received for the assets and, if any material relationship is disclosed pursuant to paragraph (c) of this Item 2.01, the formula or principle followed in determining the amount of such consideration; and

(e) if the transaction being reported is an acquisition and if a material relationship exists between the registrant or any of its affiliates and the source(s) of the funds used in the acquisition, the identity of the source(s) of the funds unless all or any part of the consideration used is a loan made in the ordinary course of business by a bank as defined by Section 3(a)(6) of the Act, in which case the identity of such bank may be omitted provided the registrant:

(1) has made a request for confidentiality pursuant to Section 13(d)(1)(B) of the Act; and

(2) states in the report that the identity of the bank has been so omitted and filed separately with the Commission.

Instructions.

1. No information need be given as to:

(i) any transaction between any person and any wholly-owned subsidiary of such person;

(ii) any transaction between two or more wholly-owned subsidiaries of any person; or

(iii) the redemption or other acquisition of securities from the public, or the sale or other disposition of securities to the public, by the issuer of such securities or by a wholly-owned subsidiary of that issuer.

2. The term *acquisition* includes every purchase, acquisition by lease, exchange, merger, consolidation, succession or other acquisition, except that the term does not include the construction or development of property by or for the registrant or its subsidiaries or the acquisition of materials for such purpose. The term *disposition* includes every sale, disposition by lease, exchange, merger, consolidation, mortgage, assignment or hypothecation of assets, whether for the benefit of creditors or otherwise, abandonment, destruction, or other disposition.

3. The information called for by this Item 2.01 is to be given as to each transaction or series of related transactions of the size indicated. The acquisition or disposition of securities is deemed the indirect acquisition or disposition of the assets represented by such securities if it results in the acquisition or disposition of control of such assets.

4. An acquisition or disposition shall be deemed to involve a significant amount of assets:

(i) if the registrant's and its other subsidiaries' equity in the net book value of such assets or the amount paid or received for the assets upon such acquisition or disposition exceeded 10% of the total assets of the registrant and its consolidated subsidiaries; or

(ii) if it involved a business (see 17 CFR 210.11-01(d)) that is significant (see 17 CFR 210.11-01(b)).

Acquisitions of individually insignificant businesses are not required to be reported pursuant to this Item 2.01 unless they are related businesses (see 17 CFR 210.3-05(a)(3)) and are significant in the aggregate.

5. Attention is directed to the requirements in Item 9.01 (Financial Statements and Exhibits) with respect to the filing of:

           (i) financial statements of businesses acquired;

           (ii) pro forma financial information; and

           (iii) copies of the plans of acquisition or disposition as exhibits to the report.

(f) If the registrant was a shell company, other than a business combination related shell company, as those terms are defined in Rule 12b-2 under the Exchange Act (17 CFR 240.12b-2), immediately before the transaction, the information that would be required if the registrant were filing a general form for registration of securities on Form 10 under the Exchange Act reflecting all classes of the registrant's securities subject to the reporting requirements of Section 13 (15 U.S.C. 78m) or Section 15(d) (15 U.S.C. 78o(d)) of such Act upon consummation of the transaction, with such information reflecting the registrant and its securities upon con-summation of the transaction. Notwithstanding General Instruction B.3. to Form 8-K, if any disclosure required by this Item 2.01(f) is previously reported, as that term is defined in Rule 12b-2 under the Exchange Act (17 CFR 240.12b-2), the registrant may identify the filing in which that disclosure is included instead of including that disclosure in this report.

Item 2.02. Results of Operations and Financial Condition.

(a) If a registrant, or any person acting on its behalf, makes any public announcement or release (including any update of an earlier announcement or release) disclosing material non-public information regarding the registrant's results of operations or financial condition for a completed quarterly or annual fiscal period, the registrant shall disclose the date of the announcement or release, briefly identify the announcement or release and include the text of that announcement or release as an exhibit.

(b) A Form 8-K is not required to be furnished to the Commission under this Item 2.02 in the case of disclosure of material non-public information that is disclosed orally, telephonically, by webcast, by broadcast, or by similar means if:

(1) the information is provided as part of a presentation that is complementary to, and initially occurs within 48 hours after, a related, written announcement or release that has been furnished on Form 8-K pursuant to this Item 2.02 prior to the presentation;

(2) the presentation is broadly accessible to the public by dial-in conference call, by webcast, by broadcast or by similar means;

(3) the financial and other statistical information contained in the presentation is pro-vided on the registrant's website, together with any information that would be required under 17 CFR 244.100; and

(4) the presentation was announced by a widely disseminated press release, that included instructions as to when and how to access the presentation and the location on the registrant's website where the information would be available.

Instructions.

1. The requirements of this Item 2.02 are triggered by the disclosure of material non-public information regarding a completed fiscal year or quarter. Release of additional or updated material non-public information regarding a completed fiscal year or quarter would trigger an additional Item 2.02 requirement.

2. The requirements of paragraph (e)(1)(i) of Item 10 of Regulation S-K (17 CFR 229.10(e)(1)(i)) shall apply to disclosures under this Item 2.02.

3. Issuers that make earnings announcements or other disclosures of material non-public information regarding a completed fiscal year or quarter in an interim or annual report to shareholders are permitted to specify which portion of the report contains the information required to be furnished under this Item 2.02.

4. This Item 2.02 does not apply in the case of a disclosure that is made in a quarterly report filed with the Commission on Form 10-Q (17 CFR 249.308a) or an annual report filed with the Commission on Form 10-K (17 CFR 249.310).

Item 2.03. Creation of a Direct Financial Obligation or an Obligation under an Off-Balance Sheet Arrangement of a Registrant.

(a) If the registrant becomes obligated on a direct financial obligation that is material to the registrant, disclose the following information:

(1) the date on which the registrant becomes obligated on the direct financial obligation and a brief description of the transaction or agreement creating the obligation;

(2) the amount of the obligation, including the terms of its payment and, if applicable, a brief description of the material terms under which it may be accelerated or increased and the nature of any recourse provisions that would enable the registrant to recover from third parties; and

(3) a brief description of the other terms and conditions of the transaction or agreement that are material to the registrant.

(b) If the registrant becomes directly or contingently liable for an obligation that is material to the registrant arising out of an off-balance sheet arrangement, disclose the following information:

(1) the date on which the registrant becomes directly or contingently liable on the obligation and a brief description of the transaction or agreement creating the arrangement and obligation;

(2) a brief description of the nature and amount of the obligation of the registrant under the arrangement, including the material terms whereby it may become a direct obligation, if applicable, or may be accelerated or increased and the nature of any recourse provisions that would enable the registrant to recover from third parties;

(3) the maximum potential amount of future payments (undiscounted) that the registrant may be required to make, if different; and

(4) a brief description of the other terms and conditions of the obligation or arrangement that are material to the registrant.

(c) For purposes of this Item 2.03, *direct financial obligation* means any of the following:

(1) a long-term debt obligation, as defined in Item 303(a)(5)(ii)(A) of Regulation S-K (17 CFR 229.303(a)(5)(ii)(A));

(2) a capital lease obligation, as defined in Item 303(a)(5)(ii)(B) of Regulation S-K (17 CFR 229.303(a)(5)(ii)(B));

(3) an operating lease obligation, as defined in Item 303(a)(5)(ii)(C) of Regulation S-K (17 CFR 229.303(a)(5)(ii)(C)); or

(4) a short-term debt obligation that arises other than in the ordinary course of business.

(d) For purposes of this Item 2.03, *off-balance sheet arrangement* has the meaning set forth in Item 303(a)(4)(ii) of Regulation S-K (17 CFR 229.303(a)(4)(ii)).

(e) For purposes of this Item 2.03, *short-term debt obligation* means a payment obligation under a borrowing arrangement that is scheduled to mature within one year, or, for those registrants that use the operating cycle concept of working capital, within a registrant's operating cycle that is longer than one year, as discussed in FASB ASC paragraph 210-10-45-3 (Balance Sheet Topic).

Instructions.

1. A registrant has no obligation to disclose information under this Item 2.03 until the registrant enters into an agreement enforceable against the registrant, whether or not subject to conditions, under which the direct financial obligation will arise or be created or issued. If there is no such agreement, the registrant must provide the disclosure within four business days after the occurrence of the closing or settlement of the transaction or arrangement under which the direct financial obligation arises or is created.

2. A registrant must provide the disclosure required by paragraph (b) of this Item 2.03 whether or not the registrant is also a party to the transaction or agreement creating the contingent obligation arising under the off-balance sheet arrangement. In the event that neither the registrant nor any affiliate of the registrant is also a party to the transaction or agreement creating the contingent obligation arising under the off-balance sheet arrangement in question, the four business day period for reporting the event under this Item 2.03 shall begin on the earlier of (i) the fourth business day after the contingent obligation is

created or arises, and (ii) the day on which an executive officer, as defined in 17 CFR 240.3b-7, of the registrant becomes aware of the contingent obligation.

3. In the event that an agreement, transaction or arrangement requiring disclosure under this Item 2.03 comprises a facility, program or similar arrangement that creates or may give rise to direct financial obligations of the registrant in connection with multiple transactions, the registrant shall:

(i) disclose the entering into of the facility, program or similar arrangement if the entering into of the facility is material to the registrant; and

(ii) as direct financial obligations arise or are created under the facility or program, disclose the required information under this Item 2.03 to the extent that the obligations are material to the registrant (including when a series of previously undisclosed individually immaterial obligations become material in the aggregate).

4. For purposes of Item 2.03(b)(3), the maximum amount of future payments shall not be reduced by the effect of any amounts that may possibly be recovered by the registrant under recourse or collateralization provisions in any guarantee agreement, transaction or arrangement.

5. If the obligation required to be disclosed under this Item 2.03 is a security, or a term of a security, that has been or will be sold pursuant to an effective registration statement of the registrant, the registrant is not required to file a Form 8-K pursuant to this Item 2.03, *provided* that the prospectus relating to that sale contains the information required by this Item 2.03 and is filed within the required time period under Securities Act Rule 424 (§ 230.424 of this chapter).

Item 2.04. Triggering Events That Accelerate or Increase a Direct Financial Obligation or an Obligation under an Off-Balance Sheet Arrangement.

(a) If a triggering event causing the increase or acceleration of a direct financial obligation of the registrant occurs and the consequences of the event, taking into account those described in paragraph (a)(4) of this Item 2.04, are material to the registrant, disclose the following information:

(1) the date of the triggering event and a brief description of the agreement or transaction under which the direct financial obligation was created and is increased or accelerated;

(2) a brief description of the triggering event;

(3) the amount of the direct financial obligation, as increased if applicable, and the terms of payment or acceleration that apply; and

(4) any other material obligations of the registrant that may arise, increase, be accelerated or become direct financial obligations as a result of the triggering event or the increase or acceleration of the direct financial obligation.

(b) If a triggering event occurs causing an obligation of the registrant under an off-balance sheet arrangement to increase or be accelerated, or causing a contingent obligation of the registrant under an off-balance sheet arrangement to become a direct financial obligation of the registrant, and the consequences of the event, taking into account those described in paragraph (b)(4) of this Item 2.04, are material to the registrant, disclose the following information:

(1) the date of the triggering event and a brief description of the off-balance sheet arrangement;

(2) a brief description of the triggering event;

(3) the nature and amount of the obligation, as increased if applicable, and the terms of payment or acceleration that apply; and

(4) any other material obligations of the registrant that may arise, increase, be accelerated or become direct financial obligations as a result of the triggering event or the increase or acceleration of the obligation under the off-balance sheet arrangement or its becoming a direct financial obligation of the registrant.

(c) For purposes of this Item 2.04, the term *direct financial obligation* has the meaning provided in Item 2.03 of this form, but shall also include an obligation arising out of an off-balance sheet arrangement that is accrued under FASB ASC Section 450-20-25, Contingencies—Loss Contingencies—Recognition, as a probable loss contingency.

(d) For purposes of this Item 2.04, the term *off-balance sheet arrangement* has the meaning provided in Item 2.03 of this form.

(e) For purposes of this Item 2.04, a *triggering event* is an event, including an event of default, event of acceleration or similar event, as a result of which a direct financial obligation of the registrant or an obligation of the registrant arising under an off-balance sheet arrangement is increased or becomes accelerated or as a result of which a contingent obligation of the registrant arising out of an off-balance sheet arrangement becomes a direct financial obligation of the registrant.

Instructions.

1. Disclosure is required if a triggering event occurs in respect of an obligation of the registrant under an off-balance sheet arrangement and the consequences are material to the registrant, whether or not the registrant is also a party to the transaction or agreement under which the triggering event occurs.

2. No disclosure is required under this Item 2.04 unless and until a triggering event has occurred in accordance with the terms of the relevant agreement, transaction or arrangement, including, if required, the sending to the registrant of notice of the occurrence of a triggering event pursuant to the terms of the agreement, transaction or arrangement and the satisfaction of all conditions to such occurrence, except the passage of time.

3. No disclosure is required solely by reason of this Item 2.04 if the registrant believes in good faith that no triggering event has occurred, unless the registrant has received a notice described in Instruction 2 to this Item 2.04.

4. Where a registrant is subject to an obligation arising out of an off-balance sheet arrangement, whether or not disclosed pursuant to Item 2.03 of this form, if a triggering event occurs as a result of which under that obligation an accrual for a probable loss is required under FASB ASC Section 450-20-25, the obligation arising out of the off-balance sheet arrangement becomes a direct financial obligation as defined in this Item 2.04. In that situation, if the consequences as determined under Item 2.04(b) are material to the registrant, disclosure is required under this Item 2.04.

5. With respect to asset-backed securities, as defined in 17 CFR 229.1101, disclosure also is required under this Item 2.04 if an early amortization, performance trigger or other event, including an event of default, has occurred under the transaction agreements for the asset-backed securities that would materially alter the payment priority or distribution of cash flows regarding the asset-backed securities or the amortization schedule for the asset-backed securities. In providing the disclosure required by this Item, identify the changes to the payment priorities, flow of funds or asset-backed securities as a result. Disclosure is required under this Item whether or not the registrant is a party to the transaction agreement that results in the occurrence identified.

Item 2.05. Costs Associated with Exit or Disposal Activities.

If the registrant's board of directors, a committee of the board of directors or the officer or officers of the registrant authorized to take such action if board action is not required, commits the registrant to an exit or disposal plan, or otherwise disposes of a long-lived asset or terminates employees under a plan of termination described in FASB ASC paragraph 420-10-25-4 (Exit or Disposal Cost Obligations Topic), under which material charges will be incurred under generally accepted accounting principles applicable to the registrant, disclose the following information:

(a) the date of the commitment to the course of action and a description of the course of action, including the facts and circumstances leading to the expected action and the expected completion date;

(b) for each major type of cost associated with the course of action (for example, one-time termination benefits, contract termination costs and other associated costs), an estimate of the total amount or range of amounts expected to be incurred in connection with the action;

(c) an estimate of the total amount or range of amounts expected to be incurred in connection with the action; and

(d) the registrant's estimate of the amount or range of amounts of the charge that will result in future cash expenditures, *provided, however*, that if the registrant determines that at the time of filing it is unable in good faith to make a determination of an estimate required by paragraphs (b), (c) or (d) of this Item 2.05, no disclosure of such estimate shall be required; *provided further, however*, that in any such event, the registrant shall file an amended report on Form 8-K under this Item 2.05 within four business days after it makes a determination of such an estimate or range of estimates.

Item 2.06. Material Impairments.

If the registrant's board of directors, a committee of the board of directors or the officer or officers of the registrant authorized to take such action if board action is not required, concludes that a material charge for impairment to one or more of its assets, including, without limitation, impairments of securities or goodwill, is required under generally accepted accounting principles applicable to the registrant, disclose the following information:

(a) the date of the conclusion that a material charge is required and a description of the impaired asset or assets and the facts and circumstances leading to the conclusion that the charge for impairment is required;

(b) the registrant's estimate of the amount or range of amounts of the impairment charge; and

(c) the registrant's estimate of the amount or range of amounts of the impairment charge that will result in future cash expenditures, *provided, however*, that if the registrant determines that at the time of filing it is unable in good faith to make a determination of an estimate required by paragraphs (b) or (c) of this Item 2.06, no disclosure of such estimate shall be required; *provided further, however*, that in any such event, the registrant shall file an amended report on Form 8-K under this Item 2.06 within four business days after it makes a determination of such an estimate or range of estimates.

Instruction. No filing is required under this Item 2.06 if the conclusion is made in connection with the preparation, review or audit of financial statements required to be included in the next periodic report due to be filed under the Exchange Act, the periodic report is filed on a timely basis and such conclusion is disclosed in the report.

Section 3—Securities and Trading Markets

Item 3.01. Notice of Delisting or Failure to Satisfy a Continued Listing Rule or Standard; Transfer of Listing.

(a) If the registrant has received notice from the national securities exchange or national securities association (or a facility thereof) that maintains the principal listing for any class of the registrant's common equity (as defined in Exchange Act Rule 12b-2 (17 CFR 240.12b-2)) that:

- the registrant or such class of the registrant's securities does not satisfy a rule or standard for continued listing on the exchange or association;
- the exchange has submitted an application under Exchange Act Rule 12d2-2 (17 CFR 240.12d2-2) to the Commission to delist such class of the registrant's securities; or
- the association has taken all necessary steps under its rules to delist the security from its automated inter-dealer quotation system,

the registrant must disclose:

(i) the date that the registrant received the notice;

(ii) the [a] rule or standard for continued listing on the national securities exchange or national securities association that the registrant fails, or has failed to, satisfy; and

(iii) any action or response that, at the time of filing, the registrant has determined to take in response to the notice.

(b) If the registrant has notified the national securities exchange or national securities association (or a facility thereof) that maintains the principal listing for any class of the registrant's common equity (as defined in Exchange Act Rule 12b-2 (17 CFR 240.12b-2) that the registrant is aware of any material noncompliance with a rule or standard for continued listing on the exchange or association, the registrant must disclose:

(i) the date that the registrant provided such notice to the exchange or association;

(ii) the rule or standard for continued listing on the exchange or association that the registrant fails, or has failed, to satisfy; and

(iii) any action or response that, at the time of filing, the registrant has determined to take regarding its noncompliance.

(c) If the national securities exchange or national securities association (or a facility thereof) that maintains the principal listing for any class of the registrant's common equity (as defined in Exchange Act Rule 12b-2 (17 CFR 240.12b-2)), in lieu of suspending trading in or delisting such class of the registrant's securities, issues a public reprimand letter or similar communication indicating that the registrant has violated a rule or standard for continued listing on the exchange or association, the registrant must state the date, and summarize the contents of the letter or communication.

(d) If the registrant's board of directors, a committee of the board of directors or the officer or officers of the registrant authorized to take such action if board action is not required, has taken definitive action to cause the listing of a class of its common equity to be withdrawn from the national securities exchange, or terminated from the automated inter-dealer quotation system of a registered national securities association, where such exchange or association maintains the principal listing for such class of securities, including by reason of a transfer of the listing or quotation to another securities exchange or quotation system, describe the action taken and state the date of the action.

Instructions.

1. The registrant is not required to disclose any information required by paragraph (a) of this Item 3.01 where the delisting is a result of one of the following:

- the entire class of the security has been called for redemption, maturity or retirement; appropriate notice thereof has been given; if required by the terms of the securities, funds sufficient for the payment of all such securities have been deposited with an agency authorized to make such payments; and such funds have been made available to security holders;

- the entire class of the security has been redeemed or paid at maturity or retirement;

- the instruments representing the entire class of securities have come to evidence, by operation of law or otherwise, other securities in substitution therefor and represent no other right, except, if true, the right to receive an immediate cash payment (the right of dissenters to receive the appraised or fair value of their holdings shall not prevent the application of this provision); or

- all rights pertaining to the entire class of the security have been extinguished; provided, however, that where such an event occurs as the result of an order of a court or other governmental authority, the order shall be final, all applicable appeal periods shall have expired and no appeals shall be pending.

2. A registrant must provide the disclosure required by paragraph (a) or (b) of this Item 3.01, as applicable, regarding any failure to satisfy a rule or standard for continued listing on the national securities exchange or national securities association (or a facility thereof) that maintains the principal listing for any class of the registrant's common equity (as defined in Exchange Act Rule 12b-2 (17 CFR 240.12b-2)) even if the registrant has the benefit of a grace period or similar extension period during which it may cure the deficiency that triggers the disclosure requirement.

3. Notices or other communications subsequent to an initial notice sent to, or by, a registrant under Item 3.01(a), (b) or (c) that continue to indicate that the registrant does not comply with the same rule or standard for continued listing that was the subject of the initial notice are not required to be filed, but may be filed voluntarily.

4. Registrants whose securities are quoted exclusively (i.e., the securities are not otherwise listed on an exchange or association) on automated inter-dealer quotation systems are not subject to this Item 3.01 and such registrants are thus not required to file a Form 8-K pursuant to this Item 3.01 if the securities are no longer quoted on such quotation system. If a security is listed on an exchange or association and is also quoted on an automated inter-dealer quotation system, the registrant is subject to the disclosure obligations of Item 3.01 if any of the events specified in Item 3.01 occur.

Item 3.02. Unregistered Sales of Equity Securities.

(a) If the registrant sells equity securities in a transaction that is not registered under the Securities Act, furnish the information set forth in paragraphs (a) and (c) through (e) of Item 701 of Regulation S-K (17 CFR 229.701(a) and (c) through (e)). For purposes of determining the required filing date for the Form 8-K under this Item 3.02(a), the registrant has no obligation to disclose information under this Item 3.02 until the registrant enters into an agreement enforceable against the registrant, whether or not subject to conditions, under which the equity securities are to be sold. If there is no such agreement, the registrant must provide the disclosure within four business days after the occurrence of the closing or settlement of the transaction or arrangement under which the equity securities are to be sold.

(b) No report need be filed under this Item 3.02 if the equity securities sold, in the aggregate since its last report filed under this Item 3.02 or its last periodic report, whichever is more recent, constitute less than 1% of the number of shares outstanding of the class of equity securities sold. In the case of a smaller reporting company, no report need be filed if the equity securities sold, in the aggregate since its last report filed under this Item 3.02 or its last periodic report, whichever is more recent, constitute less than 5% of the number of shares outstanding of the class of equity securities sold.

Instructions.

1. For purposes of this Item 3.02, "the number of shares outstanding" refers to the actual number of shares of equity securities of the class outstanding and does not include outstanding securities convertible into or exchangeable for such equity securities.

2. A smaller reporting company is defined under Item 10(f)(1) of Regulation S-K (17 CFR 229.10(f)(1)).

Item 3.03. Material Modification to Rights of Security Holders.

(a) If the constituent instruments defining the rights of the holders of any class of registered securities of the registrant have been materially modified, disclose the date of the modification, the title of the class of securities involved and briefly describe the general effect of such modification upon the rights of holders of such securities.

(b) If the rights evidenced by any class of registered securities have been materially limited or qualified by the issuance or modification of any other class of securities by the registrant, briefly disclose the date of the issuance or modification, the general effect of the issuance or modification of such other class of securities upon the rights of the holders of the registered securities.

Instruction. Working capital restrictions and other limitations upon the payment of dividends must be reported pursuant to this Item 3.03.

Section 4—Matters Related to Accountants and Financial Statements

Item 4.01. Changes in Registrant's Certifying Accountant.

(a) If an independent accountant who was previously engaged as the principal accountant to audit the registrant's financial statements, or an independent accountant upon whom the principal accountant expressed reliance in its report regarding a significant subsidiary, resigns (or indicates that it declines to stand for re-appointment after completion of the current audit) or is dismissed, disclose the information required by Item 304(a)(1) of Regulation S-K (§ 229.304(a)(1) of this chapter), including compliance with Item 304(a)(3) of Regulation S-K (§ 229.304(a)(3) of this chapter).

(b) If a new independent accountant has been engaged as either the principal accountant to audit the registrant's financial statements or as an independent accountant on whom the principal accountant is expected to express reliance in its report regarding a significant subsidiary, the registrant must disclose the information required by Item 304(a)(2) of Regulation S-K (17 CFR 229.302(a)(2)).

Instruction. The resignation or dismissal of an independent accountant, or its refusal to stand for re-appointment, is a reportable event separate from the engagement of a new independent accountant. On some occasions, two reports on Form 8-K are required for a single change in accountants, the first on the resignation (or refusal to stand for re-appointment) or dismissal of the former accountant and the second when the new accountant is engaged. Information required in the second Form 8-K in such situations need not be provided to the extent that it has been reported previously in the first Form 8-K.

Item 4.02. Non-Reliance on Previously Issued Financial Statements or a Related Audit Report or Completed Interim Review.

(a) If the registrant's board of directors, a committee of the board of directors or the officer or officers of the registrant authorized to take such action if board action is not required, concludes that any previously issued financial statements, covering one or more years or interim periods for which the registrant is required to provide financial statements under Regulation S-X (17 CFR 210) should no longer be relied upon because of an error in such financial statements as addressed in FASB ASC Topic 250, Accounting Changes and Error Corrections, as may be modified, supplemented or succeeded, disclose the following information:

(1) the date of the conclusion regarding the non-reliance and an identification of the financial statements and years or periods covered that should no longer be relied upon;

(2) a brief description of the facts underlying the conclusion to the extent known to the registrant at the time of filing; and

(3) a statement of whether the audit committee, or the board of directors in the absence of an audit committee, or authorized officer or officers, discussed with the registrant's independent accountant the matters disclosed in the filing pursuant to this Item 4.02(a).

(b) If the registrant is advised by, or receives notice from, its independent accountant that disclosure should be made or action should be taken to prevent future reliance on a previously issued audit report or completed interim review related to previously issued financial statements, disclose the following information:

(1) the date on which the registrant was so advised or notified;

(2) identification of the financial statements that should no longer be relied upon;

(3) a brief description of the information provided by the accountant; and

(4) a statement of whether the audit committee, or the board of directors in the absence of an audit committee, or authorized officer or officers, discussed with the independent accountant the matters disclosed in the filing pursuant to this Item 4.02(b).

(c) If the registrant receives advisement or notice from its independent accountant requiring disclosure under paragraph (b) of this Item 4.02, the registrant must:

(1) provide the independent accountant with a copy of the disclosures it is making in response to this Item 4.02 that the independent accountant shall receive no later than the day that the disclosures are filed with the Commission;

(2) request the independent accountant to furnish to the registrant as promptly as possible a letter addressed to the Commission stating whether the independent accountant agrees with the statements made by the registrant in response to this Item 4.02 and, if not, stating the respects in which it does not agree; and

(3) amend the registrant's previously filed Form 8-K by filing the independent accountant's letter as an exhibit to the filed Form 8-K no later than two business days after the registrant's receipt of the letter.

Section 5—Corporate Governance and Management

Item 5.01. Changes in Control of Registrant.

(a) If, to the knowledge of the registrant's board of directors, a committee of the board of directors or authorized officer or officers of the registrant, a change in control of the registrant has occurred, furnish the following information:

(1) the identity of the person(s) who acquired such control;

(2) the date and a description of the transaction(s) which resulted in the change in control;

(3) the basis of the control, including the percentage of voting securities of the registrant now beneficially owned directly or indirectly by the person(s) who acquired control;

(4) the amount of the consideration used by such person(s);

(5) the source(s) of funds used by the person(s), *unless* all or any part of the consideration used is a loan made in the ordinary course of business by a bank as defined by Section 3(a)(6) of the Act, in which case the identity of such bank may be omitted provided the person who acquired control:

(i) has made a request for confidentiality pursuant to Section 13(d)(1)(B) of the Act; and

(ii) states in the report that the identity of the bank has been so omitted and filed separately with the Commission.

(6) the identity of the person(s) from whom control was assumed; and

(7) any arrangements or understandings among members of both the former and new control groups and their associates with respect to election of directors or other matters.

(8) if the registrant was a shell company, other than a business combination related shell company, as those terms are defined in Rule 12b-2 under the Exchange Act (17 CFR 240.12b-2), immediately before the change in control, the information that would be required if the registrant were filing a general form for registration of securities on Form 10 under the Exchange Act reflecting all classes of the registrant's securities subject to the reporting requirements of Section 13 (15 U.S.C. 78m) or Section 15(d) (15 U.S.C. 78o(d)) of such Act upon consummation of the change in control, with such information reflecting the registrant and its securities upon consummation of the transaction. Notwithstanding General Instruction B.3. to Form 8-K, if any disclosure required by this Item 5.01(a)(8) is previously reported, as that term is defined in Rule 12b-2 under the Exchange Act (17 CFR 240.12b-2), the registrant may identify the filing in which that disclosure is included instead of including that disclosure in this report.

(b) Furnish the information required by Item 403(c) of Regulation S-K (17 CFR 229.403(c)).

Item 5.02. Departure of Directors or Certain Officers; Election of Directors; Appointment of Certain Officers; Compensatory Arrangements of Certain Officers.

(a)(1) If a director has resigned or refuses to stand for re-election to the board of directors since the date of the last annual meeting of shareholders because of a disagreement with the registrant, known to an executive officer of the registrant, as defined in 17 CFR 240.3b-7, on any matter relating to the registrant's operations, policies or practices, or if a director has been removed for cause from the board of directors, disclose the following information:

(i) the date of such resignation, refusal to stand for re-election or removal;

(ii) any positions held by the director on any committee of the board of directors at the time of the director's resignation, refusal to stand for re-election or removal; and

(iii) a brief description of the circumstances representing the disagreement that the registrant believes caused, in whole or in part, the director's resignation, refusal to stand for re-election or removal.

(2) If the director has furnished the registrant with any written correspondence concerning the circumstances surrounding his or her resignation, refusal or removal, the registrant shall file a copy of the document as an exhibit to the report on Form 8-K.

(3) The registrant also must:

(i) provide the director with a copy of the disclosures it is making in response to this Item 5.02 no later than the day the registrant file the disclosures with the Commission;

(ii) provide the director with the opportunity to furnish the registrant as promptly as possible with a letter addressed to the registrant stating whether he or she agrees with the statements made by the registrant in response to this Item 5.02 and, if not, stating the respects in which he or she does not agree; and

(iii) file any letter received by the registrant from the director with the Commission as an exhibit by an amendment to the previously filed Form 8-K within two business days after receipt by the registrant.

(b) If the registrant's principal executive officer, president, principal financial officer, principal accounting officer, principal operating officer, or any person performing similar functions, or any named executive officer, retires, resigns or is terminated from that position, or if a director retires, resigns, is removed, or refuses to stand for re-election (except in circumstances described in paragraph (a) of this Item 5.02), disclose the fact that the event has occurred and the date of the event.

(c) If the registrant appoints a new principal executive officer, president, principal financial officer, principal accounting officer, principal operating officer, or person performing similar functions, disclose the following information with respect to the newly appointed officer:

(1) the name and position of the newly appointed officer and the date of the appointment;

(2) the information required by Items 401(b), (d), (e) and Item 404(a) of Regulation S-K (17 CFR 229.401(b), (d), (e) and 229.404(a)), and

(3) a brief description of any material plan, contract or arrangement (whether or not written) to which a covered officer is a party or in which he or she participates that is entered into or material amendment in connection with the triggering event or any grant or award to any such covered person or modification thereto, under any such plan, contract or arrangement in connection with any such event.

Instruction to paragraph (c). If the registrant intends to make a public announcement of the appointment other than by means of a report on Form 8-K, the registrant may delay filing the Form 8-K containing the disclosures required by this Item 5.02(c) until the day on which the registrant otherwise makes public announcement of the appointment of such officer.

(d) If the registrant elects a new director, except by a vote of security holders at an annual meeting or special meeting convened for such purpose, disclose the following information:

(1) the name of the newly elected director and the date of election;

(2) a brief description of any arrangement or understanding between the new director and any other persons, naming such persons, pursuant to which such director was selected as a director;

(3) the committees of the board of directors to which the new director has been, or at the time of this disclosure is expected to be, named; and

(4) the information required by Item 404(a) of Regulation S-K (17 CFR 229.404(a)).

(5) a brief description of any material plan, contract or arrangement (whether or not written) to which the director is a party or in which he or she participates that is entered into

or material amendment in connection with the triggering event or any grant or award to any such covered person or modification thereto, under any such plan, contract or arrangement in connection with any such event.

(e) If the registrant enters into, adopts, or otherwise commences a material compensatory plan, contract or arrangement (whether or not written), as to which the registrant's principal executive officer, principal financial officer, or a named executive officer participates or is a party, or such compensatory plan, contract or arrangement is materially amended or modified, or a material grant or award under any such plan, contract or arrangement to any such person is made or materially modified, then the registrant shall provide a brief description of the terms and conditions of the plan, contract or arrangement and the amounts payable to the officer thereunder.

Instructions to paragraph (e).

1. Disclosure under this Item 5.02(e) shall be required whether or not the specified event is in connection with events otherwise triggering disclosure pursuant to this Item 5.02.

2. Grants or awards (or modifications thereto) made pursuant to a plan, contract or arrangement (whether involving cash or equity), that are materially consistent with the previously disclosed terms of such plan, contract or arrangement, need not be disclosed under this Item 5.02(e), provided the registrant has previously disclosed such terms and the grant, award or modification is disclosed when Item 402 of Regulation S-K (17 CFR 229.402) requires such disclosure.

(f)(1) If the salary or bonus of a named executive officer cannot be calculated as of the most recent practicable date and is omitted from the Summary Compensation Table as specified in Instruction 1 to Item 402(c)(2)(iii) and (iv) of Regulation S-K, disclose the appropriate information under this Item 5.02(f) when there is a payment, grant, award, decision or other occurrence as a result of which such amounts become calculable in whole or part. Disclosure under this Item 5.02(f) shall include a new total compensation figure for the named executive officer, using the new salary or bonus information to recalculate the information that was previously provided with respect to the named executive officer in the registrant's Summary Compensation Table for which the salary and bonus information was omitted in reliance on Instruction 1 to Item 402(c)(2)(iii) and (iv) of Regulation S-K (17 CFR 229.402(c)(2)(iii) and (iv)).

(2) As specified in Instruction 6 to Item 402(u) of Regulation S-K (17 CFR 229.402(u)), disclosure under this Item 5.02(f) with respect to the salary or bonus of a principal executive officer shall include pay ratio disclosure pursuant to Item 402(u) of Regulation S-K calculated using the new total compensation figure for the principal executive officer. Pay ratio disclosure is not required under this Item 5.02(f) until the omitted salary or bonus amounts for such principal executive officer become calculable in whole.

Instructions to Item 5.02.

1. The disclosure requirements of this Item 5.02 do not apply to a registrant that is a wholly-owned subsidiary of an issuer with a class of securities registered under Section 12 of the Exchange Act (15 U.S.C. 78l), or that is required to file reports under Section 15(d) of the Exchange Act (15 U.S.C. 78o(d)).

2. To the extent that any information called for in Item 5.02(c)(3) or Item 5.02(d)(3) or Item 5.02(d)(4) is not determined or is unavailable at the time of the required filing, the registrant shall include a statement [to] this effect in the filing and then must file an amendment to its Form 8-K filing under this Item 5.02 containing such information within four business days after the information is determined or becomes available.

3. The registrant need not provide information with respect to plans, contracts, and arrangements to the extent they do not discriminate in scope, terms or operation, in favor of executive officers or directors of the registrant and that are available generally to all salaried employees.

4. For purposes of this Item, the term "named executive officer" shall refer to those executive officers for whom disclosure was required in the registrant's most recent filing with the Commission under the Securities Act (15 U.S.C. 77a *et seq.*) or Exchange Act (15 U.S.C. 78a *et seq.*) that required disclosure pursuant to Item 402(c).

Item 5.03. Amendments to Articles of Incorporation or Bylaws; Change in Fiscal Year.

(a) If a registrant with a class of equity securities registered under Section 12 of the Exchange Act (15 U.S.C. 78l) amends its articles of incorporation or bylaws and a proposal for the amendment was not disclosed in a proxy statement or information statement filed by the registrant, disclose the following information:

(1) the effective date of the amendment; and

(2) a description of the provision adopted or changed by amendment and, if applicable, the previous provision.

(b) If the registrant determines to change the fiscal year from that used in its most recent filing with the Commission other than by means of:

(1) a submission to a vote of security holders through the solicitation of proxies or otherwise; or

(2) an amendment to its articles of incorporation or bylaws,

disclose the date of such determination, the date of the new fiscal year end and the form (for example, Form 10-K or Form 10-Q) on which the report covering the transition period will be filed.

Instructions to Item 5.03.

1. Refer to Item 601(b)(3) of Regulation S-K (17 CFR 229.601(b)(3)) regarding the filing of exhibits to this Item 5.03.

2. With respect to asset-backed securities, as defined in 17 CFR 229.1101, disclosure is required under this Item 5.03 regarding any amendment to the governing documents of the issuing entity, regardless of whether the class of asset-backed securities is reporting under Section 13 or 15(d) of the Exchange Act.

Item 5.04. Temporary Suspension of Trading Under Registrant's Employee Benefit Plans.

(a) No later than the fourth business day after which the registrant receives the notice required by section 101(i)(2)(E) of the Employment Retirement Income Security Act of 1974 (29 U.S.C. 1021(i)(2)(E)), or, if such notice is not received by the registrant, on the same date by which the registrant transmits a timely notice to an affected officer or director within the time period prescribed by Rule 104(b)(2)(i)(B) or 104(b)(2)(ii) of Regulation BTR (17 CFR 245.104(b)(2)(i)(B) or 17 CFR 245.104(b)(2)(ii)), provide the information specified in Rule 104(b) (17 CFR 245.104(b)) and the date the registrant received the notice required by section 101(i)(2)(E) of the Employment Retirement Income Security Act of 1974 (29 U.S.C. 1021(i)(2)(E)), if applicable.

(b) On the same date by which the registrant transmits a timely updated notice to an affected officer or director, as required by the time period under Rule 104(b)(2)(iii) of Regulation BTR (17 CFR 245.104(b)(2)(iii)), provide the information specified in Rule 104(b)(3)(iii) (17 CFR 245.104(b)(2)(iii)).

Item 5.05. Amendments to the Registrant's Code of Ethics, or Waiver of a Provision of the Code of Ethics.

(a) Briefly describe the date and nature of any amendment to a provision of the registrant's code of ethics that applies to the registrant's principal executive officer, principal financial officer, principal accounting officer or controller or persons performing similar functions and that relates to any element of the code of ethics definition enumerated in Item 406(b) of Regulation S-K (17 CFR 229.406(b)).

(b) If the registrant has granted a waiver, including an implicit waiver, from a provision of the code of ethics to an officer or person described in paragraph (a) of this Item 5.05, and the waiver relates to one or more of the elements of the code of ethics definition referred to in paragraph (a) of this Item 5.05, briefly describe the nature of the waiver, the name of the person to whom the waiver was granted, and the date of the waiver.

(c) The registrant does not need to provide any information pursuant to this Item 5.05 if it discloses the required information on its Internet website within four business days following the date of the amendment or waiver and the registrant has disclosed in its most recently filed annual report its Internet address and intention to provide disclosure in this manner. If the registrant elects to disclose the information required by this Item 5.05 through its website, such information must remain available on the website for at least a 12-month period. Following the 12-month period, the registrant must retain the information for a period of not less than five years. Upon request, the registrant must furnish to the Commission or its staff a copy of any or all information retained pursuant to this requirement.

Instructions.

1. The registrant does not need to disclose technical, administrative or other non-substantive amendments to its code of ethics.

2. For purposes of this Item 5.05:

(i) The term *waiver* means the approval by the registrant of a material departure from a provision of the code of ethics; and

(ii) The term *implicit waiver* means the registrant's failure to take action within a reasonable period of time regarding a material departure from a provision of the code of ethics that has been made known to an executive officer, as defined in Rule 3b-7 (17 CFR 240.3b-7) of the registrant.

Item 5.06. Change in Shell Company Status.

If a registrant that was a shell company, other than a business combination related shell company, as those terms are defined in Rule 12b-2 under the Exchange Act (17 CFR 240.12b-2), has completed a transaction that has the effect of causing it to cease being a shell company, as defined in Rule 12b-2, disclose the material terms of the transaction. Notwithstanding General Instruction B.3. to Form 8-K, if any disclosure required by this Item 5.06 is previously reported, as that term is defined in Rule 12b-2 under the Exchange Act (17 CFR 240.12b-2), the registrant may identify the filing in which that disclosure is included instead of including that disclosure in this report.

Item 5.07. Submission of Matters to a Vote of Security Holders

If any matter was submitted to a vote of security holders, through the solicitation of proxies or otherwise, provide the following information:

(a) The date of the meeting and whether it was an annual or special meeting. This information must be provided only if a meeting of security holders was held.

(b) If the meeting involved the election of directors, the name of each director elected at the meeting, as well as a brief description of each other matter voted upon at the meeting; and state the number of votes cast for, against or withheld, as well as the number of abstentions and broker non-votes as to each such matter, including a separate tabulation with respect to each nominee for office. For the vote on the frequency of shareholder advisory votes on executive compensation required by section 14A(a)(2) of the Securities Exchange Act of 1934 (15 U.S.C. 78n-1) and § 240.14a-21(b), state the number of votes cast for each of 1 year, 2 years, and 3 years, as well as the number of abstentions.

(c) A description of the terms of any settlement between the registrant and any other participant (as defined in Instruction 3 to Item 4 of Schedule 14A (17 CFR 240.14a-101)) terminating any solicitation subject to Rule 14a-12(c), including the cost or anticipated cost to the registrant.

(d) No later than one hundred fifty calendar days after the end of the annual or other meeting of shareholders at which shareholders voted on the frequency of shareholder votes on the compensation of executives as required by section 14A(a)(2) of the Securities Exchange Act of 1934 (15 U.S.C. 78n-1), but in no event later than sixty calendar days prior to the deadline for submission of shareholder proposals under § 240.14a-8, as disclosed in the registrant's most recent proxy statement for an annual or other meeting of shareholders relating to the election of directors at which shareholders voted on the frequency of shareholder votes on the compensation of executives as required by section 14A(a)(2) of the Securities Exchange Act of 1934 (15 U.S.C. 78n-1(a)(2)), by amendment to the most recent Form 8-K filed pursuant to (b) of this Item, disclose the company's decision in light of such vote as to how frequently the company will include a shareholder vote on the compensation of executives in its proxy materials until the next required vote on the frequency of shareholder votes on the compensation of executives.

Instruction 1 to Item 5.07. The four business day period for reporting the event under this Item 5.07, other than with respect to Item 5.07(d), shall begin to run on the day on which the meeting ended. The registrant shall disclose on Form 8-K under this Item 5.07 the preliminary voting results. The registrant shall file an amended report on Form 8-K under this Item 5.07 to disclose the final voting results within four business days after the final voting results are known. However, no preliminary voting results need be disclosed under this Item 5.07 if the registrant has disclosed final voting results on Form 8-K under this Item.

Instruction 2 to Item 5.07. If any matter has been submitted to a vote of security holders otherwise than at a meeting of such security holders, corresponding information with respect to such submission shall be provided. The solicitation of any authorization or consent (other than a proxy to vote at a stockholders' meeting) with respect to any matter shall be deemed a submission of such matter to a vote of security holders within the meaning of this item.

Instruction 3 to Item 5.07. If the registrant did not solicit proxies and the board of directors as previously reported to the Commission was re-elected in its entirety, a statement to that effect in answer to paragraph (b) will suffice as an answer thereto regarding the election of directors.

Instruction 4 to Item 5.07. If the registrant has furnished to its security holders proxy soliciting material containing the information called for by paragraph (c), the paragraph may be answered by reference to the information contained in such material.

Instruction 5 to Item 5.07. A registrant may omit the information called for by this Item 5.07 if, on the date of the filing of its report on Form 8-K, the registrant meets the following conditions:

1. All of the registrant's equity securities are owned, either directly or indirectly, by a single person which is a reporting company under the Exchange Act and which has filed all the material required to be filed pursuant to Section 13, 14 or 15(d) thereof, as applicable; and

2. During the preceding thirty-six calendar months and any subsequent period of days, there has not been any material default in the payment of principal, interest, a sinking or purchase fund installment, or any other material default not cured within thirty days, with respect to any indebtedness of the registrant or its subsidiaries, and there has not been any material default in the payment of rentals under material long-term leases.

Item 5.08. Shareholder Director Nominations.

(a) If the registrant did not hold an annual meeting the previous year, or if the date of this year's annual meeting has been changed by more than 30 calendar days from the date of the previous year's meeting, then the registrant is required to disclose the date by which a nominating shareholder or nominating shareholder group must submit the notice on Schedule14N (§240.14n-101) required pursuant to §240.14a-11(b)(10), which date shall be a reasonable time before the registrant mails its proxy materials for the meeting. Where a registrant is required to include shareholder director nominees in the registrant's proxy materials pursuant to either an applicable state or foreign law provision, or a provision in the registrant's governing documents, then the registrant is required to disclose the date by which a nominating shareholder or nominating shareholder group must submit the notice on Schedule 14Nrequired pursuant to §240.14a-18.

(b) If the registrant is a series company as defined in Rule 18f-2(a) under the Investment Company Act of 1940 (§270.18f-2 of this chapter), then the registrant is required to disclose in connection with the election of directors at an annual meeting of shareholders (or, in lieu of such an annual meeting, a special meeting of shareholders) the total number of shares of the registrant outstanding and entitled to be voted (or if the votes are to be cast on a basis other than one vote per share, then the total number of votes entitled to be voted and the basis for allocating such votes) on the election of directors at such meeting of shareholders as of the end of the most recent calendar quarter.

Section 6—Asset-Backed Securities

The Items in this Section 6 apply only to asset-backed securities. Terms used in this Section 6 have the same meaning as in Item 1101 of Regulation AB (17 CFR 229.1101).

Item 6.01. ABS Informational and Computational Material.

Report under this Item any ABS informational and computational material filed in, or as an exhibit to, this report.

Item 6.02. Change of Servicer or Trustee.

If a servicer contemplated by Item 1108(a)(2) of Regulation AB (17 CFR 229.1108(a)(2)) or a trustee has resigned or has been removed, replaced or substituted, or if a new servicer contemplated by Item 1108(a)(2) of Regulation AB or trustee has been appointed, state the date the event occurred and the circumstances surrounding the change. In addition, provide the disclosure required by Item 1108(d) of Regulation AB (17 CFR 229.1108(c)), as applicable, regarding the servicer or trustee change. If a new servicer contemplated by Item 1108(a)(3) of this Regulation AB or a new trustee has been appointed, provide the information required by Item 1108(b) through (d) of Regulation AB regarding such servicer or Item 1109 of Regulation AB (17 CFR 229.1109) regarding such trustee, as applicable.

Instruction. To the extent that any information called for by this Item regarding such servicer or trustee is not determined or is unavailable at the time of the required filing, the registrant shall include a statement to this effect in the filing and then must file an amendment to its Form 8-K filing under this Item 6.02 containing such information within four business days after the information is determined or becomes available.

Item 6.03. Change in Credit Enhancement or Other External Support.

(a) *Loss of existing enhancement or support*. If the depositor (or servicer if the servicer signs the report on Form 10-K (17 CFR 249.310) of the issuing entity) becomes aware that any material enhancement or support specified in Item 1114(a)(1) through (3) of Regulation AB (17 CFR 229.1114(a)(1) through (3)) or Item 1115 of Regulation AB (17 CFR 229.1115) that was previously applicable regarding one or more classes of the asset-backed securities has terminated other than by expiration of the contract on its stated termination date or as a result of all parties completing their obligations under such agreement, then disclose:

(1) the date of the termination of the enhancement;

(2) the identity of the parties to the agreement relating to the enhancement or support;

(3) a brief description of the terms and conditions of the enhancement or support that are material to security holders;

(4) a brief description of the material circumstances surrounding the termination; and

(5) any material early termination penalties paid or to be paid out of the cash flows backing the asset-backed securities.

(b) *Addition of new enhancement or support*. If the depositor (or servicer if the servicer signs the report on Form 10-K (17 CFR 249.310) of the issuing entity) becomes aware that any material enhancement specified in Item 1114(a)(1) through (3) of Regulation AB (17 CFR 229.1114(a)(1) through (3)) or Item 1115 of Regulation AB (17 CFR 229.1115) has been added with respect to one or more classes of the asset-backed securities, then provide the date of addition of the new enhancement or support and the disclosure required by Items 1114 or 1115 of Regulation AB, as applicable, with respect to such new enhancement or support.

(c) *Material change to enhancement or support.* If the depositor (or servicer if the servicer signs the report on Form 10-K (17 CFR 249.310) of the issuing entity) becomes aware that any existing material enhancement or support specified in Item 1114(a)(1) through (3) of Regulation AB or Item 1115 of Regulation AB with respect to one or more classes of the asset-backed securities has been materially amended or modified, disclose:

(1) the date on which the agreement or agreements relating to the enhancement or support was amended or modified;

(2) the identity of the parties to the agreement or agreements relating to the amendment or modification; and

(3) a brief description of the material terms and conditions of the amendment or modification.

Instructions.

1. Disclosure is required under this Item whether or not the registrant is a party to any agreement regarding the enhancement or support if the loss, addition or modification of such enhancement or support materially affects, directly or indirectly, the asset-backed securities, the pool assets or the cash flow underlying the asset-backed securities.

2. To the extent that any information called for by this Item regarding the enhancement or support is not determined or is unavailable at the time of the required filing, the registrant shall include a statement to this effect in the filing and then must file an amendment to its Form 8-K filing under this Item 6.03 containing such information within four business days after the information is determined or becomes available.

3. The instructions to Items 1.01 and 1.02 of this Form apply to this Item.

4. Notwithstanding Items 1.01 and 1.02 of this Form, disclosure regarding changes to material enhancement or support is to be reported under this Item 6.03 in lieu of those Items.

Item 6.04. Failure to Make a Required Distribution.

If a required distribution to holders of the asset-backed securities is not made as of the required distribution date under the transaction documents, and such failure is material, identify the failure and state the nature of the failure to make the timely distribution.

Item 6.05. Securities Act Updating Disclosure.

Regarding an offering of asset-backed securities registered on Form SF-3 (17 CFR 239.45), if any material pool characteristic of the actual asset pool at the time of issuance of the asset-backed securities differs by 5% or more (other than as a result of the pool assets converting into cash in accordance with their terms) from the description of the asset pool in the prospectus filed for the offering pursuant to Securities Act Rule 424 (17 CFR 230.424), disclose the information required by Items 1111 and 1112 of Regulation AB (17 CFR 229.1111 and 17 CFR 229.1112) regarding the characteristics of the actual asset pool. If applicable, also provide information required by Items 1108 and 1110 of Regulation AB (17 CFR 229.1108 and 17 CFR 229.1110) regarding any new servicers or originators that would be required to be disclosed under those items regarding the pool assets.

Instruction. No report is required under this Item if substantially the same information is provided in a post-effective amendment to the Securities Act registration statement or in a subsequent prospectus filed pursuant to Securities Act Rule 424 (17 CFR 230.424).

Item 6.06. Static Pool.

Regarding an offering of asset-backed securities registered on Form SF-1 (17 CFR 239.44) or Form SF-3 (17 CFR 239.45), in lieu of providing the static pool information as required by Item 1105 of Regulation AB (17 CFR 229.1105) in a form of prospectus or prospectus, an issuer may file the required information in this report or as an exhibit to this report. The static pool disclosure must be filed by the time of effectiveness of a registration statement on Form SF-1, by the same date of the filing of a form of prospectus, as required by Rule 424(h) (17 CFR 230.424(h)), and by the same date of the filing of a final prospectus meeting the requirements of section 10(a) of the Securities Act (15 U.S.C. 77j(a)) filed in accordance with Rule 424(b) (17 CFR 230.424(b)).

Instructions.

1. Refer to Item 601(b)(106) of Regulation S-K (17 CFR 229.601(b)(106)) regarding the filing of exhibits to this Item 6.06.

2. Refer to Item 10 of Form SF-1 (17 CFR 239.44) or Item 10 of Form SF-3 (17 CFR 239.45) regarding incorporation by reference.

Section 7—Regulation FD

Item 7.01. Regulation FD Disclosure.

Unless filed under Item 8.01, disclose under this item only information that the registrant elects to disclose through Form 8-K pursuant to Regulation FD (17 CFR 243.100 through 243.103).

Section 8—Other Events

Item 8.01. Other Events.

The registrant may, at its option, disclose under this Item 8.01 any events, with respect to which information is not otherwise called for by this form, that the registrant deems of importance to security holders. The registrant may, at its option, file a report under this Item 8.01 disclosing the nonpublic information required to be disclosed by Regulation FD (17 CFR 243.100 through 243.103).

Section 9—Financial Statements and Exhibits

Item 9.01. Financial Statements and Exhibits.

List below the financial statements, pro forma financial information and exhibits, if any, filed as a part of this report.

(a) *Financial statements of businesses acquired.*

(1) For any business acquisition required to be described in answer to Item 2.01 of this form, financial statements of the business acquired shall be filed for the periods specified in Rule 3-05(b) of Regulation S-X (17 CFR 210.3-05(b)) or Rule 8-04(b) of Regulation S-X (17 CFR 210.8-04(b) for smaller reporting companies.

(2) The financial statements shall be prepared pursuant to Regulation S-X except that supporting schedules need not be filed. A manually signed accountant's report should be provided pursuant to Rule 2-02 of Regulation S-X (17 CFR 210.2-02).

(3) With regard to the acquisition of one or more real estate properties, the financial statements and any additional information specified by Rules 3-14 of Regulation S-X (17 CFR 210.3-14) or Rule 8-06 of Regulation S-X (17 CFR 210.8-06) for smaller reporting companies.

(4) Financial statements required by this item may be filed with the initial report, or by amendment not later than 71 calendar days after the date that the initial report on Form 8-K must be filed. If the financial statements are not included in the initial report, the registrant should so indicate in the Form 8-K report and state when the required financial statements will be filed. The registrant may, at its option, include unaudited financial statements in the initial report on Form 8-K.

(b) *Pro forma financial information.*

(1) For any transaction required to be described in answer to Item 2.01 of this form, furnish any pro forma financial information that would be required pursuant to Article 11 of Regulation S-X (§ 210.11 of this chapter) or Rule 8-05 of Regulation S-X (§ 210.8-05 of this chapter) for smaller reporting companies.

(2) The provisions of paragraph (a)(4) of this Item 9.01 shall also apply to pro forma financial information relative to the acquired business.

(c) *Shell company transactions*. The provisions of paragraph (a)(4) and (b)(2) of this Item shall not apply to the financial statements or *pro forma* financial information required to be filed under this Item with regard to any transaction required to be described in answer to Item 2.01 of this Form by a registrant that was a shell company, other than a business combination related shell company, as those terms are defined in Rule 12b-2 under the Exchange Act (17 CFR 240.12b-2), immediately before that transaction. Accordingly, with regard to any transaction required to be described in answer to Item 2.01 of this Form by a registrant that was a shell company, other than a business combination related shell company, immediately before that transaction, the financial statements and *pro forma* financial information required by this Item must be filed in the initial report. Notwithstanding General Instruction B.3. to Form 8-K, if any financial statement or any financial information required to be filed in the initial report by this Item 9.01(c) is previously reported, as that term is defined in Rule 12b-2 under the Exchange Act (17 CFR 240.12b-2), the registrant may identify the filing in which that disclosure is included instead of including that disclosure in the initial report.

(d) *Exhibits*. The exhibits shall be deemed to be filed or furnished, depending upon the relevant item requiring such exhibit, in accordance with the provisions of Item 601 of Regulation S-K (17 CFR 229.601) and Instruction B.2 to this form.

Instruction. During the period after a registrant has reported a business combination pursuant to Item 2.01 of this form, until the date on which the financial statements specified by this Item 9.01 must be filed, the registrant will be deemed current for purposes of its reporting obligations under Section 13(a) or 15(d) of the Exchange Act (15 U.S.C. 78m or 78o(d)). With respect to filings under the Securities Act, however, registration statements will not be declared effective and post-effective amendments to registrations statements will not be declared effective unless financial statements meeting the requirements of Rule 3-05 of Regulation S-X (17 CFR 210.3-05) are provided. In addition, offerings should not be made pursuant to effective registration statements, or pursuant to Rule 506 of Regulation D (17 CFR 230.506) where any purchasers are not accredited investors under Rule 501(a) of that Regulation, until the audited financial statements required by Rule 3-05 of Regulation S-X (17 CFR 210.3-05) are filed; *provided*, *however*, that the following offerings or sales of securities may proceed notwithstanding that financial statements of the acquired business have not been filed:

(a) offerings or sales of securities upon the conversion of outstanding convertible securities or upon the exercise of outstanding warrants or rights;

(b) dividend or interest reinvestment plans;

(c) employee benefit plans;

(d) transactions involving secondary offerings; or

(e) sales of securities pursuant to Rule 144 (17 CFR 230.144).

SIGNATURES

Pursuant to the requirements of the Securities Exchange Act of 1934, the registrant has duly caused this report to be signed on its behalf by the undersigned hereunto duly authorized.

....
(Registrant)

Date ....
(Signature)[*]

---

[*] Print name and title of the signing officer under his signature.

SECURITIES AND EXCHANGE COMMISSION
Washington, D.C. 20549

Form 10-K
Annual Report Pursuant to Section 13 or 15(d) of
the Securities Exchange Act of 1934
GENERAL INSTRUCTIONS

A. Rule as to Use of Form 10-K.

(1) This Form shall be used for annual reports pursuant to Section 13 or 15(d) of the Securities Exchange Act of 1934 (15 U.S.C. 78m or 78o(d)) (the "Act") for which no other form is prescribed. This Form also shall be used for transition reports filed pursuant to Section 13 or 15(d) of the Act.

(2) Annual reports on this Form shall be filed within the following period:

(a) 60 days after the end of the fiscal year covered by the report (75 days for fiscal years ending before December 15, 2006) for large accelerated filers (as defined in 17 CFR 240.12b-2):

(b) 75 days after the end of the fiscal year covered by the report for accelerated filers (as defined in 17 CFR 240.12b-2); and

(c) 90 days after the end of the fiscal year covered by the report for all other registrants.

(3) Transition reports on this Form shall be filed in accordance with the requirements set forth in Rule 13a-10 (17 CFR 240.13a-10) or Rule 15d-10 (17 CFR 240.15d-10) applicable when the registrant changes its fiscal year end.

(4) Notwithstanding paragraphs (2) and (3) of this General Instruction A., all schedules required by Article 12 of Regulation S-X (17 CFR 210.12-01 - 210.12-29) may, at the option of the registrant, be filed as an amendment to the report not later than 30 days after the applicable due date of the report.

B. Application of General Rules and Regulations.

(1) The General Rules and Regulations under the Act (17 CFR 240) contain certain general requirements which are applicable to reports on any form. These general requirements should be carefully read and observed in the preparation and filing of reports on this Form.

(2) Particular attention is directed to Regulation 12B which contains general requirements regarding matters such as the kind and size of paper to be used, the legibility of the report, the information to be given whenever the title of securities is required to be stated, and the filing of the report. The definitions contained in Rule 12b-2 should be especially noted. *See also* Regulations 13A and 15D.

C. Preparation of Report.

(1) This Form is not to be used as a blank form to be filled in, but only as a guide in the preparation of the report on paper meeting the requirements of Rule 12b-12. Except as provided in General Instruction G, the answers to the items shall be prepared in the manner specified in Rule 12b-13.

(2) Except where information is required to be given for the fiscal year or as of a specified date, it shall be given as of the latest practicable date.

(3) Attention is directed to Rule 12b-20, which states: "In addition to the information expressly required to be included in a statement or report, there shall be added such further

material information, if any, as may be necessary to make the required statements, in the light of the circumstances under which they are made, not misleading."

D. Signature and Filing of Report.

(1) Three complete copies of the report, including financial statements, financial statement schedules, exhibits, and all other papers and documents filed as a part thereof, and five additional copies which need not include exhibits, shall be filed with the Commission. At least one complete copy of the report, including financial statements, financial statement schedules, exhibits, and all other papers and documents filed as a part thereof, shall be filed with each exchange on which any class of securities of the registrant is registered. At least one complete copy of the report filed with the Commission and one such copy filed with each exchange shall be manually signed. Copies not manually signed shall bear typed or printed signatures.

(2) (a) The report must be signed by the registrant, and on behalf of the registrant by its principal executive officer or officers, its principal financial officer or officers, its controller or principal accounting officer, and by at least the majority of the board of directors or persons performing similar functions. Where the registrant is a limited partnership, the report must be signed by the majority of the board of directors of any corporate general partner who signs the report.

(b) The name of each person who signs the report shall be typed or printed beneath his signature. Any person who occupies more than one of the specified positions shall indicate each capacity in which he signs the report. Attention is directed to Rule 12b-11 (17 CFR 240.12b-11) concerning manual signatures and signatures pursuant to powers of attorney.

(3) Registrants are requested to indicate in a transmittal letter with the Form 10-K whether the financial statements in the report reflect a change from the preceding year in any accounting principles or practices, or in the method of applying any such principles or practices.

E. Disclosure With Respect to Foreign Subsidiaries.

Information required by any item or other requirement of this form with respect to any foreign subsidiary may be omitted to the extent that the required disclosure would be detrimental to the registrant. However, financial statements and financial statement schedules, otherwise required, shall not be omitted pursuant to this Instruction. Where information is omitted pursuant to this Instruction, a statement shall be made that such information has been omitted and the names of the subsidiaries involved shall be separately furnished to the Commission. The Commission may, in its discretion, call for justification that the required disclosure would be detrimental.

F. Information as to Employee Stock Purchase, Savings and Similar Plans.

Attention is directed to Rule 15d-21 which provides that separate annual and other reports need not be filed pursuant to Section 15(d) of the Act with respect to any employee stock purchase, savings or similar plan if the issuer of the stock or other securities offered to employees pursuant to the plan furnishes to the Commission the information and documents specified in the Rule.

G. Information to be Incorporated by Reference.

(1) Attention is directed to Rule 12b-23 which provides for the incorporation by reference of information contained in certain documents in answer or partial answer to any item of a report.

(2) The information called for by Parts I and II of this Form (Items 1 through 9A or any portion thereof) may, at the registrant's option, be incorporated by reference from the registrant's annual report to security holders furnished to the Commission pursuant to Rule 14a-3(b) or Rule 14c-3(a) or from the registrant's annual report to security holders, even if not furnished to the Commission pursuant to Rule 14a-3(b) or Rule 14c-3(a), provided such annual report contains the information required by Rule 14a-3.

Note 1.—In order to fulfill the requirements of Part 1 of Form 10-K, the incorporated portion of the annual report to security holders must contain the information required by Items 1-3 of Form 10-K, to the extent applicable.

Note 2.—If any information required by Part I or Part II is incorporated by reference into an electronic format document from the annual report to security holders as provided in General Instruction G, any portion of the annual report to security holders incorporated by reference shall be filed as [a]n exhibit in electronic format, as required by Item 601(b)(13) of Regulation S-K.

(3) The information required by Part III (Items 10, 11, 12, 13 and 14) may be incorporated by reference from the registrant's definitive proxy statement (filed or to be filed pursuant to Regulation 14A) or definitive information statement (filed or to be filed pursuant to Regulation 14C) which involves the election of directors, if such definitive proxy statement or information statement is filed with the Commission not later than 120 days after the end of the fiscal year covered by the Form 10-K. However, if such definitive proxy statement or information statement is not filed with the Commission in the 120-day period or is not required to be filed with the Commission by virtue of Rule 3a12-3(b) under the Exchange Act, the Items comprising the Part III information must be filed as part of the Form 10-K, or as an amendment to the Form 10-K, not later than the end of the 120-day period. It should be noted that the information regarding executive officers required by Item 401 of Regulation S-K (§ 229.401 of this chapter) may be included in Part I of Form 10-K under an appropriate caption. See Item 401(b) of Regulation S-K (§ 229.401(b) of this chapter).

(4) No item numbers of captions of items need be contained in the material incorporated by reference into the report. When the registrant combines all of the information in Parts I and II of this Form (Items 1 through 9A) by incorporation by reference from the registrant's annual report to security holders and all of the information in Part III of this Form (Items 10 through 14) by incorporating by reference from a definitive proxy statement or information statement involving the election of directors, then, notwithstanding General Instruction C(1), this Form shall consist of the facing or cover page, those sections incorporated from the annual report to security holders, the proxy or information statement, and the information, if any, required by Part IV of this Form, signatures, and a cross-reference sheet setting forth the item numbers and captions in Parts I, II and III of this Form and the page and/or pages in the referenced materials where the corresponding information appears.

H. Integrated Reports to Security Holders.

Annual reports to security holders may be combined with the required information of Form 10-K and will be suitable for filing with the Commission if the following conditions are satisfied:

(1) The combined report contains full and complete answers to all items required by Form 10-K. When responses to a certain item of required disclosure are separated within the combined report, an appropriate cross-reference should be made. If the information required by Part III of Form 10-K is omitted by virtue of General Instruction G, a definitive proxy or information statement shall be filed.

(2) The cover page and the required signatures are included. As appropriate, a cross-reference sheet should be filed indicating the location of information required by the items of the Form.

(3) If an electronic filer files any portion of an annual report to security holders in combination with the required information of Form 10-K, as provided in this instruction,

only such portions filed in satisfaction of the Form 10-K requirements shall be filed in electronic format.

I. Omission of Information by Certain Wholly-Owned Subsidiaries.

If, on the date of the filing of its report on Form 10-K, the registrant meets the conditions specified in paragraph (1) below, then such registrant may furnish the abbreviated narrative disclosure specified in paragraph (2) below.

(1) Conditions for availability of the relief specified in paragraph (2) below.

(a) All of the registrant's equity securities are owned, either directly or indirectly, by a single person which is a reporting company under the Act and which has filed all the material required to be filed pursuant to section 13, 14, or 15(d) thereof, as applicable, and which is named in conjunction with the registrant's description of its business;

(b) During the preceding thirty-six calendar months and any subsequent period of days, there has not been any material default in the payment of principal, interest, a sinking or purchase fund installment, or any other material default not cured within thirty days, with respect to any indebtedness of the registrant or its subsidiaries, and there has not been any material default in the payment of rentals under material long-term leases;

(c) There is prominently set forth, on the cover page of the Form 10-K, a statement that the registrant meets the conditions set forth in General Instruction (I)(1)(a) and (b) of Form 10-K and is therefore filing this Form with the reduced disclosure format; and

(d) The registrant is not an asset-backed issuer, as defined in Item 1101 or Regulation AB (17 CFR 229.1101).

(2) Registrants meeting the conditions specified in paragraph (1) above are entitled to the following relief:

(a) Such registrants may omit the information called for by Item 6, Selected Financial Data, and Item 7, Management's Discussion and Analysis of Financial Condition and Results of Operations provided that the registrant includes in the Form 10-K a management's narrative analysis of the results of operations explaining the reasons for material changes in the amount of revenue and expense items between the most recent fiscal year presented and the fiscal year immediately preceding it. Explanations of material changes should include, but not be limited to, changes in the various elements which determine revenue and expense levels such as unit sales volume, prices charged and paid, production levels, production cost variances, labor costs and discretionary spending programs. In addition, the analysis should include an explanation of the effect of any changes in accounting principles and practices or method of application that have a material effect on net income as reported.

(b) Such registrants may omit the list of subsidiaries exhibit required by Item 601 of Regulation S-K (§ 229.601 of this chapter).

(c) Such registrants may omit the information called for by the following otherwise required Items: Item 4, Submission of Matters to a Vote of Security Holders; Item 10, Directors and Executive Officers of the Registrant; Item 11, Executive Compensation; Item 12, Security Ownership of Certain Beneficial Owners and Management; and Item 13, Certain Relationships and Related Transactions.

(d) In response to Item 1, Business, such registrant only need furnish a brief description of the business done by the registrant and its subsidiaries during the most recent fiscal year which will, in the opinion of management, indicate the general nature and scope of the business of the registrant and its subsidiaries, and in response to Item 2, Properties, such registrant only need furnish a brief description of the material properties of the registrant and its subsidiaries to the extent, in the opinion of the management, necessary to an understanding of the business done by the registrant and its subsidiaries.

J. Use of this Form by Asset-Backed Issuers.

The following applies to registrants that are asset-backed issuers. Terms used in this General Instruction J. have the same meaning as in Item 1101 of Regulation AB (17 CFR 229.1101).

(1) *Items that May be Omitted.* Such registrants may omit the information called for by the following otherwise required Items:

(a) Item 1, Business;

(b) Item 1A. Risk Factors;

(c) Item 2, Properties;

(d) Item 3, Legal Proceedings;

(e) [Reserved.]

(f) Item 5, Market for Registrant's Common Equity, Related Stockholder Matters and Issuer Purchases of Equity Securities;

(g) Item 6, Selected Financial Data;

(h) Item 7, Management's Discussion and Analysis of Financial Condition and Results of Operations;

(i) Item 7A, Quantitative and Qualitative Disclosures About Market Risk;

(j) Item 8, Financial Statements and Supplementary Data;

(k) Item 9, Changes in and Disagreements With Accountants on Accounting and Financial Disclosure;

(l) Item 9A, Controls and Procedures;

(m) If the issuing entity does not have any executive officers or directors, Item 10, Directors and Executive Officers of the Registrant, Item 11, Executive Compensation, Item 12, Security Ownership of Certain Beneficial Owners and Management, and Item 13, Certain Relationships and Related Transactions; and

(n) Item 14, Principal Accountant Fees and Services.

(2) *Substitute Information to be Included.* In addition to the Items that are otherwise required by this Form, the registrant must furnish in the Form 10-K the following information:

(a) Immediately after the name of the issuing entity on the cover page of the Form 10-K, as separate line items, the exact name of the depositor as specified in its charter and the exact name of the sponsor as specified in its charter.

(b) Item 1112(b) of Regulation AB;

(c) Items 1114(b)(2) and 1115(b) of Regulation AB;

(d) Item 1117 of Regulation AB;

(e) Item 1119 of Regulation AB;

(f) Item 1122 of Regulation AB; and

(g) Item 1123 of Regulation AB.

(3) *Signatures.*

The Form 10-K must be signed either:

(a) On behalf of the depositor by the senior officer in charge of securitization of the depositor; or

(b) On behalf of the issuing entity by the senior officer in charge of the servicing function of the servicer. If multiple servicers are involved in servicing the pool assets, the senior officer in charge of the servicing function of the master servicer (or entity performing the equivalent function) must sign if a representative of the servicer is to sign the report on behalf of the issuing entity.

UNITED STATES
SECURITIES AND EXCHANGE COMMISSION
Washington, D.C. 20549

FORM 10-K

(Mark One)

[ ]   ANNUAL REPORT PURSUANT TO SECTION 13 OR 15(d) OF THE SECURITIES EXCHANGE ACT
       OF 1934

For the fiscal year ended ....

OR

[ ]   TRANSITION REPORT PURSUANT TO SECTION 13 OR 15(d) OF THE SECURITIES EXCHANGE
       ACT OF 1934

For the transition period from .... **to** ....

Commission file number...

....

(Exact name of registrant as specified in its charter)

....

..................................State or other jurisdiction of   (I.R.S. Employer.......................
..................................incorporation or organization   Identification No.) ....

....
(Address of principal executive offices) ....   (Zip Code) ....

Registrant's telephone number, including area code ....
Securities registered pursuant to Section 12(b) of the Act:

Title of each class	Trading Symbol(s)	Name of each exchange on which registered

Securities registered pursuant to section 12(g) of the Act:
....
(Title of class)
....
(Title of class)

Indicate by check mark if the registrant is a well-known seasoned issuer, as defined in Rule 405 of the Securities Act. Yes .... No ....

Indicate by check mark if the registrant is not required to file reports pursuant to Section 13 or Section 15(d) of the Act. Yes .... No ....

Note—Checking the box above will not relieve any registrant required to file reports pursuant to Section 13 or 15(d) of the Exchange Act from their obligations under those Sections.

Indicate by check mark whether the registrant (1) has filed all reports required to be filed by Section 13 or 15(d) of the Securities Exchange Act of 1934 during the preceding 12 months (or for such shorter period that the registrant was required to file such reports), and (2) has been subject to such filing requirements for the past 90 days. Yes .... No ....

Indicate by check mark whether the registrant has submitted electronically every Interactive Data File required to be submitted pursuant to Rule 405 of Regulation S-T (§ 232.405 of this chapter) during the preceding 12 months (or for such shorter period that the registrant was required to submit such files).
Yes__ No__

Indicate by check mark whether the registrant is a large accelerated filer, an accelerated filer, a non-accelerated filer, smaller reporting company, or an emerging growth company. See the definitions of "large accelerated filer," "accelerated filer," "smaller reporting company," and "emerging growth company" in Rule 12b-2 of the Exchange Act.

Large accelerated filer ☐   Accelerated filer   ☐
Non-accelerated filer   ☐   Smaller reporting company ☐
                                               Emerging growth company ☐

If an emerging growth company, indicate by check mark if the registrant has elected not to use the extended transition period for complying with any new or revised financial accounting standards provided pursuant to Section 13(a) of the Exchange.

Indicate by check mark whether the registrant has filed a report on and attestation to its management's assessment of the effectiveness of its internal control over financial reporting under Section 404(b) of the Sarbanes-Oxley Act (15 U.S.C. 7262(b)) by the registered public accounting firm that prepared or issued its audit report.

Indicate by check mark whether the registrant is a shell company (as defined in Rule 12b-2 of the Exchange Act). Yes . . . . No . . . .

State the aggregate market value of the voting and non-voting common equity held by non-affiliates computed by reference to the price at which the common equity was last sold, or the average bid and asked price of such common equity, as of the last business day of the registrant's most recently completed second fiscal quarter.

Note.—If a determination as to whether a particular person or entity is an affiliate cannot be made without involving unreasonable effort and expense, the aggregate market value of the common stock held by non-affiliates may be calculated on the basis of assumptions reasonable under the circumstances, provided that the assumptions are set forth in this Form.

APPLICABLE ONLY TO REGISTRANTS INVOLVED IN BANKRUPTCY PROCEEDINGS DURING THE PRECEDING FIVE YEARS:

Indicate by check mark whether the registrant has filed all documents and reports required to be filed by Section 12, 13 or 15(d) of the Securities Exchange Act of 1934 subsequent to the distribution of securities under a plan confirmed by a court.

YES . . . . NO . . . .

(APPLICABLE ONLY TO CORPORATE REGISTRANTS)

Indicate the number of shares outstanding of each of the registrant's classes of common stock, as of the latest practicable date.

DOCUMENTS INCORPORATED BY REFERENCE

List hereunder the following documents if incorporated by reference and the Part of the Form 10-K (e.g., Part I, Part II, etc.) into which the document is incorporated: (1) Any annual report to security holders; (2) Any proxy or information statement; and (3) Any prospectus filed pursuant to Rule 424(b) or (c) under the Securities Act of 1933. The listed documents should be clearly described for identification purposes (e.g., annual report to security holders for fiscal year ended December 24, 1980).

PART I
[See General Instruction G(2)]

Item 1. Business.

Furnish the information required by Item 101 of Regulation S-K (§ 229.101 of this chapter) except that the discussion of the development of the registrant's business need only include developments since the beginning of the fiscal year for which this report is filed.

Item 1A. Risk Factors.

Set forth, under the caption "Risk Factors," where appropriate, the risk factors described in Item 105 of Regulation S-K (§ 229.105 of this chapter) applicable to the registrant. Provide any discussion of risk factors in plain English in accordance with Rule 421(d) of the Securities Act of 1933 (§ 230.421(d) of this chapter). Smaller reporting companies are not required to provide the information required by this item.

Item 1B. Unresolved Staff Comments.

If the registrant is an accelerated filer as defined in Rule 12b-2 of the Exchange Act (§ 240.12b-2 of this chapter) or is a well-known seasoned issuer as defined in Rule 405 of the Securities Act (§ 230.405 of this chapter) and has received written comments from the Commission staff regarding its periodic or current reports under the Act not less than 180 days before the end of its fiscal year to which the annual report relates, and such comments remain unresolved, disclose the substance of any such unresolved comments that the registrant believes are material. Such disclosure may provide other information including the position of the registrant with respect to any such comment.

Item 2. Properties.

Furnish the information required by Item 102 of Regulation S-K (§ 229.102 of this chapter).

Item 3. Legal Proceedings.

(a) Furnish the information required by Item 103 of Regulation S-K (§ 229.103 of this chapter).

(b) As to any proceeding that was terminated during the fourth quarter of the fiscal year covered by this report, furnish information similar to that required by Item 103 of Regulation S-K (§ 229.103 of this chapter), including the date of termination and a description of the disposition thereof with respect to the registrant and its subsidiaries.

Item 4. Mine Safety Disclosures.

If applicable, provide a statement that the information concerning mine safety violations or other regulatory matters required by Section 1503(a) of the Dodd-Frank Wall Street Reform and Consumer Protection Act and Item 104 of Regulation S-K (17 CFR 229.104) is included in exhibit 95 to the annual report.

PART II
[See General Instruction G(2)]

Item 5. Market for Registrant's Common Equity, Related Stockholder Matters and Issuer Purchases of Equity Securities.

(a) Furnish the information required by Item 201 of Regulation S-K (17 CFR 229.201) and Item 701 of Regulation S-K (17 CFR 229.701) as to all equity securities of the registrant sold by the registrant during the period covered by the report that were not registered under the Securities Act. If the Item 701 information previously has been included in a Quarterly Report on Form 10-Q (17 CFR 249.308a), or in a Current Report on Form 8-K (17 CFR 249.308), it need not be furnished.

(b) If required pursuant to Rule 463 (17 CFR 230.463) of the Securities Act of 1933, furnish the information required by Item 701(f) of Regulation S-K (229.701(f) of this chapter).

(c) Furnish the information required by Item 703 of Regulation S-K (§ 229.703 of this chapter) for any repurchase made in a month within the fourth quarter of the fiscal year covered by the report. Provide disclosures covering repurchases made on a monthly basis. For example, if the fourth quarter began on January 16 and ended on April 15, the chart would show repurchases for the months from January 16 through February 15, February 16 through March 15, and March 16 through April 15.

Item 6. Selected Financial Data.

Furnish the information required by Item 301 of Regulation S-K (§ 229.301 of this chapter).

Item 7. Management's Discussion and Analysis of Financial Condition and Results of Operation.

Furnish the information required by Item 303 of Regulation S-K (§ 229.303 of this chapter).

Item 7A. Quantitative and Qualitative Disclosures About Market Risk.

Furnish the information required by Item 305 of Regulation S-K (§ 229.305 of this chapter).

Item 8. Financial Statements and Supplementary Data.

(a) Furnish financial statements meeting the requirements of Regulation S-X (§ 210 of this chapter), except § 210.3-05 and Article 11 thereof, and the supplementary financial information required by Item 302 of Regulation S-K (§ 229.302 of this chapter). Financial statements of the registrant and its subsidiaries consolidated (as required by Rule 14a-3(b)) shall be filed under this item. Other financial statements and schedules required under Regulation S-X may be filed as "Financial Statement Schedules" pursuant to Item 15, Exhibits, Financial Statement Schedules, and Reports on Form 8-K, of this Form.

(b) A smaller reporting company may provide the information required by Article 8 of Regulation S-X in lieu of any financial statements required by Item 8 of this Form.

Item 9. Changes in and Disagreements With Accountants on Accounting and Financial Disclosure.

Furnish the information required by Item 304(b) of Regulation S-K (§ 229.304(b) of this chapter).

Item 9A. Controls and Procedures.

Furnish the information required by Items 307 and 308 of Regulation S-K (17 CFR 229.307 and 229.308).

Item 9B. Other Information.

The registrant must disclose under this item any information required to be disclosed in a report on Form 8-K during the fourth quarter of the year covered by this Form 10-K, but not reported, whether or not otherwise required by this Form 10-K. If disclosure of such information is made under this item, it need not be repeated in a report on Form 8-K which would otherwise be required to be filed with respect to such information or in a subsequent report on Form 10-K.

PART III
[See General Instruction G(3)]

Item 10. Directors, and Executive Officers and Corporate Governance.

Furnish the information required by Items 401, 405, 406, and 407(c)(3), (d)(4) and (d)(5) of Regulation S-K (§§ 229.401, 229.405, 229.406, and 229.407(c)(3), (d)(4) and (d)(5) of this chapter).

Item 11. Executive Compensation.

Furnish the information required by Item 402 of Regulation S-K (§ 229.402 of this chapter) and paragraphs (e)(4) and (e)(5) of Item 407 of Regulation S-K (§ 229.407(e)(4) and (e)(5) of this chapter).

Item 12. Security Ownership of Certain Beneficial Owners and Management and Related Stockholder Matters.

Furnish the information required by Item 201(d) of Regulation S-K (§ 229.201(d) of this chapter) and by Item 403 of Regulation S-K (§ 229.403 of this chapter).

Item 13. Certain Relationships and Related Transactions, and Director Independence.

Furnish the information required by Item 404 of Regulation S-K (§ 229.404 of this chapter) and Item 407(a) of Regulation S-K (§ 229.407(a) of this chapter)

Item 14. Principal Accountant Fees and Services.

Furnish the information required by Item 9(e) of Schedule 14A (§ 240.14a-101 of this chapter).

(1) Disclose, under the caption *Audit Fees*, the aggregate fees billed for each of the last two fiscal years for professional services rendered by the principal accountant for the audit of the registrant's annual financial statements and review of financial statements included in the registrant's Form 10-Q (17 CFR 249.308a) or services that are normally provided by the accountant in connection with statutory and regulatory filings or engagements for those fiscal years.

(2) Disclose, under the caption *Audit-Related Fees*, the aggregate fees billed in each of the last two fiscal years for assurance and related services by the principal accountant that are reasonably related to the performance of the audit or review of the registrant's financial statements and are not reported under Item 9(e)(1) of Schedule 14A. Registrants shall describe the nature of the services comprising the fees disclosed under this category.

(3) Disclose, under the caption *Tax Fees*, the aggregate fees billed in each of the last two fiscal years for professional services rendered by the principal accountant for tax compliance, tax advice, and tax planning. Registrants shall describe the nature of the services comprising the fees disclosed under this category.

(4) Disclose, under the caption *All Other Fees*, the aggregate fees billed in each of the last two fiscal years for products and services provided by the principal accountant, other than the services reported in Items 9(e)(1) through 9(e)(3) of Schedule 14A. Registrants shall describe the nature of the services comprising the fees disclosed under this category.

(5)(i) Disclose the audit committee's pre-approval policies and procedures described in paragraph (c)(7)(i) of Rule 2-01 of Regulation S-X.

(ii) Disclose the percentage of services described in each of Items 9(e)(2) through 9(e)(4) of Schedule 14A that were approved by the audit committee pursuant to paragraph (c)(7)(i)(C) of Rule 2-01 of Regulation S-X.

(6) If greater than 50 percent, disclose the percentage of hours expended on the principal accountant's engagement to audit the registrant's financial statements for the most recent fiscal year that were attributed to work performed by persons other than the principal accountant's full-time, permanent employees.

PART IV

Item 15. Exhibits and Financial Statement Schedules.

(a) List the following documents filed as a part of the report:

1. All financial statements;

2. Those financial statement schedules required to be filed by Item 8 of this form, and by paragraph (b) below.

3. Those exhibits required by Item 601 of Regulation S-K (17 CFR 229.601 of this chapter) and by paragraph (b) below. Identify in the list each management contract or compensatory plan or arrangement required to be filed as an exhibit to this form pursuant to Item 15(b) of this report.

(b) Registrants shall file, as exhibits to this Form, the exhibits required by Item 601 of Regulation S-K (§ 229.601 of this chapter).

(c) Registrants shall file, as financial statement schedules to this Form, the financial statements required by Regulation S-X (17 CFR 210) which are excluded from the annual report to shareholders by Rule 14a-3(b) including (1) separate financial statements of subsidiaries not consolidated and fifty percent or less owned persons; (2) separate financial statements of affiliates whose securities are pledged as collateral; and (3) schedules.

Item 16. Form 10-K Summary

Registrants may, at their option, include a summary of information required by this form, but only if each item in the summary is presented fairly and accurately and includes a hyperlink to the material contained in this form to which such item relates, including to materials contained in any exhibits filed with the form.

Instruction: The summary shall refer only to Form 10-K disclosure that is included in the form at the time it is filed. A registrant need not update the summary to reflect information required by Part III of Form 10-K that the registrant incorporates by reference from a proxy or information statement filed after the Form 10-K, but must state in the summary that the summary does not include Part III information because that information will be incorporated by reference from a later filed proxy or information statement involving the election of directors

SIGNATURES
[See General Instruction D]

Pursuant to the requirements of Section 13 or 15(d) of the Securities Exchange Act of 1934, the registrant has duly caused this report to be signed on its behalf by the undersigned, thereunto duly authorized.

(Registrant) . . . .

By (Signature and Title)* . . . .

Date . . . .

Pursuant to the requirements of the Securities Exchange Act of 1934, this report has been signed below by the following persons on behalf of the registrant and in the capacities and on the dates indicated.

By (Signature and Title)* . . . .

Date . . . .

By (Signature and Title)* . . . .

Date . . . .

---

*Print the name and title of each signing officer under his signature.

Supplemental Information to be Furnished With Reports Filed Pursuant to Section 15(d) of the Act by Registrants Which Have Not Registered Securities Pursuant to Section 12 of the Act

(a) Except to the extent that the materials enumerated in (1) and/or (2) below are specifically incorporated into this Form by reference, every registrant which files an annual report on this Form pursuant to Section 15(d) of the Act shall furnish to the Commission for its information, at the time of filing its report on this Form, four copies of the following:

(1) Any annual report to security holders covering the registrant's last fiscal year; and

(2) Every proxy statement, form of proxy or other proxy soliciting material sent to more than ten of the registrant's security holders with respect to any annual or other meeting of security holders.

(b) The foregoing material shall not be deemed to be "filed" with the Commission or otherwise subject to the liabilities of Section 18 of the Act, except to the extent that the registrant specifically incorporates it in its annual report on this Form by reference.

(c) If no such annual report or proxy material has been sent to security holders, a statement to that effect shall be included under this caption. If such report or proxy material is to be furnished to security holders subsequent to the filing of the annual report of this Form, the registrant shall so state under this caption and shall furnish copies of such material to the Commission when it is sent to security holders.

SCHEDULE 13D
Schedule 13D Information to be Included in Statements Filed Pursuant to § 240.13d-1(a) and Amendments Thereto Filed Pursuant to § 240.13d-2(a).
SECURITIES AND EXCHANGE COMMISSION
Washington, D.C. 20549
SCHEDULE 13D
Under the Securities Exchange Act of 1934 (Amendment No.)*

....
(Name of Issuer)

....
(Title of Class of Securities)

....
(CUSIP Number)

....
(Name, Address and Telephone Number of Person Authorized to Receive Notices and Communications)

....
(Date of Event which Requires Filing of this Statement)

If the filing person has previously filed a statement on Schedule 13G to report the acquisition that is the subject of this Schedule 13D, and is filing this schedule because of § § 240.13d-1(e), 240.13d-1(f) or 240.13d-1(g), check the following box. [ ]

NOTE: Schedules filed in paper format shall include a signed original and five copies of the schedule, including all exhibits. See Rule 13d-7 for other parties to whom copies are to be sent.

*The remainder of this cover page shall be filled out for a reporting person's initial filing on this form with respect to the subject class of securities, and for any subsequent amendment containing information which would alter disclosures provided in a prior cover page.

The information required on the remainder of this cover page shall not be deemed to be "filed" for the purpose of Section 18 of the Securities Exchange Act of 1934 ("Act") or otherwise subject to the liabilities of that section of the Act but shall be subject to all other provisions of the Act (however, see the Notes).

CUSIP No. ....

1)	Names of Reporting Persons...	
2)	Check the Appropriate Box if a Member of a Group (See Instructions) .... (a) .... (b)	
3)	SEC Use Only	
4)	Source of Funds (See Instructions)	
5)	Check if Disclosure of Legal Proceedings is Required Pursuant to Items 2(d) or 2(e)	
6)	Citizenship or Place of Organization	

Number of Shares Beneficially Owned by Each Reporting Person With	(7) Sole Voting Power ....
	(8) Shared Voting Power ....
	(9) Sole Dispositive Power..
	(10) Shared Dispositive Power...

11)	Aggregate Amount Beneficially Owned by Each Reporting Person............
12)	Check if the Aggregate Amount in Row (11) Excludes Certain Shares (See Instructions) ....
13)	Percent of Class Represented by Amount in Row (11) ....
14)	Type of Reporting Person (See Instructions) ....

....
....
....
....
....
....
....
....
....
....

Instructions for Cover Page

(1) Names of Reporting Persons. Furnish the full legal name of each person for whom the report is filed—i.e., each person required to sign the schedule itself—including each member of a group. Do not include the name of a person required to be identified in the report but who is not a reporting person.

(2) If any of the shares beneficially owned by a reporting person are held as a member of a group and the membership is expressly affirmed, please check row 2(a). If the reporting person disclaims membership in a group or describes a relationship with other person but does not affirm the existence of a group, please check row 2(b) [unless it is a joint filing pursuant to Rule 13d-1(k)(1) in which case it may not be necessary to check row 2 (b)].

(3) The 3rd row is for SEC internal use; please leave blank.

(4) Classify the source of funds or other consideration used or to be used in making the purchases as required to be disclosed pursuant to Item 3 of Schedule 13D and insert the appropriate symbol (or symbols if more than one is necessary in row (4):

Category of Source	Symbol
Subject Company (Company whose securities are being acquired)	SC
Bank	BK
Affiliate (of reporting person)	AF
Working Capital (of reporting person)	WC
Personal Funds (of reporting person)	PF
Other	OO

(5) If disclosure of legal proceedings or actions is required pursuant to either Items 2(d) or 2(e) of Schedule 13D, row 5 should be checked.

(6) *Citizenship or Place of Organization*—Furnish citizenship if the named reporting person is a natural person. Otherwise, furnish place of organization. (See Item 2 of Schedule 13D).

(7)-(11) [Reserved]

(12) Check if the aggregate amount reported as beneficially owned in row (11) does not include shares which the reporting person discloses in the report but as to which beneficial ownership is disclaimed pursuant to Rule 13d-4 [17 CFR 240.13d-4] under the Securities Exchange Act of 1934.

(13) *Aggregate Amount Beneficially Owned by Each Reporting Person, Etc.* - Rows (7) through (11), inclusive, and (13) are to be completed in accordance with the provisions of Item 5 of Schedule 13D. All percentages are to be rounded off to nearest tenth (one place after decimal point).

(14) *Type of Reporting Person*—Please classify each "reporting person" according to the following breakdown and place the appropriate symbol (or symbols, i.e., if more than one is applicable, insert all applicable symbols) on the form:

Category	*Symbol*
Broker Dealer	BD
Bank	BK
Insurance Company	IC
Investment Company	IV
Investment Adviser	IA
Employee Benefit Plan or Endowment Fund	EP
Parent Holding Company/Control Person	HC
Savings Association	SA
Church Plan	CP
Corporation	CO
Partnership	PN
Individual	IN
Other	OO

Note: Attach additional pages if needed.

Notes: Attach as many copies of the second part of the cover page as are needed, one reporting person per page.

Filing persons may, in order to avoid unnecessary duplication, answer items on the schedules (Schedule 13D, 13G or TO) by appropriate cross references to an item or items on the cover page(s). This approach may only be used where the cover page item or items provide all the disclosure required by the schedule item. Moreover, such a use of a cover page item will result in the item becoming a part of the schedule and accordingly being considered as "filed" for purposes of Section 18 of the Securities Exchange Act or otherwise subject to the liabilities of that section of the Act.

Reporting persons may comply with their cover page filing requirements by filing either completed copies of the blank forms available from the Commission, printed or typed facsimiles, or computer printed facsimiles, provided the documents filed have identical formats to the forms prescribed in the Commission's regulations and meet existing Securities Exchange Act rules as to such matters as clarity and size (Securities Exchange Act Rule 12b-12).

SPECIAL INSTRUCTIONS FOR COMPLYING WITH SCHEDULE 13D

Under Sections 13(d) and 23 of the Securities Exchange Act of 1934 and the rules and regulations thereunder, the Commission is authorized to solicit the information required to be supplied by this schedule by certain security holders of certain issuers.

Disclosure of the information specified in this schedule is mandatory. The information will be used for the primary purpose of determining and disclosing the holdings of certain beneficial owners of certain equity securities. This statement will be made a matter of public record. Therefore, any information given will be available for inspection by any member of the public.

Because of the public nature of the information, the Commission can utilize it for a variety of purposes, including referral to other governmental authorities or securities self-regulatory organizations for investigatory purposes or in connection with litigation involving the Federal securities laws or other civil, criminal or regulatory statutes or provisions. I.R.S. identification numbers, if furnished, will assist the Commission in identifying security holders and, therefore, in promptly processing statements of beneficial ownership of securities.

Failure to disclose the information requested by this schedule, except for I.R.S. identification numbers, may result in civil or criminal action against the persons involved for violation of the Federal securities laws and rules promulgated thereunder.

Instructions

A. The item numbers and captions of the items shall be included but the text of the items is to be omitted. The answers to the items shall be so prepared as to indicate clearly the coverage of the items without referring to the text of the items. Answer every item. If an item is inapplicable or the answer is in the negative, so state.

B. Information contained in exhibits to the statement may be incorporated by reference in answer or partial answer to any item or sub-item of the statement unless it would render such answer misleading, incomplete, unclear or confusing. Matter incorporated by reference shall be clearly identified in the reference by page, paragraph, caption or otherwise. An express statement that the specified matter is incorporated by reference shall be made at the particular place in the statement where the information is required. A copy of any information or a copy of the pertinent pages of a document containing such information which is incorporated by reference shall be submitted with this statement as an exhibit and shall be deemed to be filed with the Commission for all purposes of the Act.

C. If the statement is filed by a general or limited partnership, syndicate, or other group, the information called for by Items 2-6, inclusive, shall be given with respect to (i) each partner of such general partnership; (ii) each partner who is denominated as a general partner or who functions as a general partner of such limited partnership; (ii) each member of such syndicate or group; and (iv) each person controlling such partner or member. If the statement is filed by a corporation or if a person referred to in (i), (ii), (iii) or (iv) of this Instruction is a corporation, the information called for by the above mentioned items shall be given with respect to (a) each executive officer and director of such corporation; (b) each person controlling such corporation; and (c) each executive officer and director of any corporation or other person ultimately in control of such corporation.

Item 1. Security and Issuer

State the title of the class of equity securities to which this statement relates and the name and address of the principal executive offices of the issuer of such securities.

Item 2. Identity and Background

If the person filing this statement or any person enumerated in Instruction C of this statement is a corporation, general partnership, limited partnership, syndicate or other group of persons, state its name, the state or other place of its organization, its principal business, the address of its principal business, the address of its principal office and the information required by (d) and (e) of this Item. If the person filing this statement or any person enumerated in Instruction C is a natural person, provide the information specified in (a) through (f) of this Item with respect to such person(s).

(a) Name;

(b) Residence or business address;

(c) Present principal occupation or employment and the name, principal business and address of any corporation or other organization in which such employment is conducted;

(d) Whether or not, during the last five years, such person has been convicted in a criminal proceeding (excluding traffic violations or similar misdemeanors) and, if so, give the dates, nature of conviction, name and location of court, any penalty imposed, or other disposition of the case;

(e) Whether or not, during the last five years, such person was a party to a civil proceeding of a judicial or administrative body of competent jurisdiction and as a result of such proceeding was or is subject to a judgment, decree or final order enjoining future violations of, or prohibiting or mandating activities subject to, federal or state securities laws or finding any violation with respect to such laws; and, if so, identify and describe such proceedings and summarize the terms of such judgment, decree or final order; and

(f) Citizenship.

Item 3. Source and Amount of Funds or Other Consideration

State the source and the amount of funds or other consideration used or to be used in making the purchases, and if any part of the purchase price is or will be represented by funds or other consideration borrowed or otherwise obtained for the purpose of acquiring, holding, trading or voting the securities, a description of the transaction and the names of the parties thereto. Where material, such information should also be provided with respect to prior acquisitions not previously reported pursuant to this regulation. If the source of all or any part of the funds is a loan made in the ordinary course of business by a bank, as defined in Section 3(a)(6) of the Act, the name of the bank shall not be made available to the public if the person at the time of filing the statement so requests in writing and files such request, naming such bank, with the Secretary of the Commission. If the securities were acquired other than by purchase, describe the method of acquisition.

Item 4. Purpose of Transaction

State the purpose or purposes of the acquisition of securities of the issuer. Describe any plans or proposals which the reporting persons may have which relate to or would result in:

(a) The acquisition by any person of additional securities of the issuer, or the disposition of securities of the issuer;

(b) An extraordinary corporate transaction, such as a merger, reorganization or liquidation, involving the issuer or any of its subsidiaries;

(c) A sale or transfer of a material amount of assets of the issuer or any of its subsidiaries;

(d) Any change in the present board of directors or management of the issuer, including any plans or proposals to change the number of term of directors or to fill any existing vacancies on the board;

(e) Any material change in the present capitalization or dividend policy of the issuer;

(f) Any other material change in the issuer's business or corporate structure including but not limited to, if the issuer is a registered closed-end investment company, any plans or proposals to make any changes in its investment policy for which a vote is required by section 13 of the Investment Company Act of 1940;

(g) Changes in the issuer's charter, bylaws or instruments corresponding thereto or other actions which may impede the acquisition of control of the issuer by any person;

(h) Causing a class of securities of the issuer to be delisted from a national securities exchange or to cease to be authorized to be quoted in an inter-dealer quotation system of a registered national securities association;

(i) A class of equity securities of the issuer becoming eligible for termination of registration pursuant to Section 12(g)(4) of the Act; or

(j) Any action similar to any of those enumerated above.

Item 5. Interest in Securities of the Issuer

(a) State the aggregate number and percentage of the class of securities identified pursuant to Item 1 (which may be based on the number of securities outstanding as contained in the most recently available filing with the Commission by the issuer unless the filing person has reason to believe such information is not current) beneficially owned (identifying those shares which there is a right to acquire) by each person named in Item 2. The above mentioned information should also be furnished with respect to persons who, together with any of the persons named in Item 2, comprise a group within the meaning of Section 13(d)(3) of the Act;

(b) For each person named in response to paragraph (a), indicate the number of shares as to which there is sole power to vote or to direct the vote, shared power to vote or to direct the vote, sole power to dispose or to direct the disposition, or shared power to dispose or to direct the disposition. Provide the applicable information required by Item 2 with respect to each person with whom the power to vote or to direct the vote or to dispose or direct the disposition is shared;

(c) Describe any transactions in the class of securities reported on that were effected during the past sixty days or since the most recent filing on Schedule 13D (§ 240.13d-191), whichever is less, by the persons named in response to paragraph (a).

Instruction. The description of a transaction required by Item 5(c) shall include, but not necessarily be limited to: (1) the identity of the person covered by Item 5(c) who effected the transaction; (2) the date of the transaction; (3) the amount of securities involved; (4) the price per share or unit; and (5) where and how the transaction was effected.

(d) If any other person is known to have the right to receive or the power to direct the receipt of dividends from, or the proceeds from the sale of, such securities, a statement to that effect should be included in response to this item and, if such interest relates to more than five percent of the class, such person should be identified. A listing of the shareholders of an investment company registered under the Investment Company Act of 1940 or the beneficiaries of an employee benefit plan, pension fund or endowment fund is not required.

(e) If applicable, state the date on which the reporting person ceased to be the beneficial owner of more than five percent of the class of securities.

Instruction. For computations regarding securities which represent a right to acquire an underlying security, see Rule 13d-3(d)(1) and the note thereto.

Item 6. Contracts, Arrangements, Understandings or Relationships with Respect to Securities of the Issuer

Describe any contracts, arrangements, understandings or relationships (legal or otherwise) among the persons named in Item 2 and between such persons and any person with respect to any securities of the issuer, including but not limited to transfer or voting of any of the securities, finder's fees, joint ventures, loan or option arrangements, put or calls, guarantees of profits, division of profits or loss, or the giving or withholding of proxies, naming the persons with whom such contracts, arrangements, understandings or relationships have been entered into. Include such information for any of the securities that are pledged or otherwise subject to a contingency the occurrence of which would give another person voting power or investment power over such securities except that disclosure of standard default and similar provisions contained in loan agreements need not be included.

Item 7. Material to Be Filed as Exhibits

The following shall be filed as exhibits: copies of written agreements relating to the filing of joint acquisition statements as required by Rule 13d-1(k) and copies of all written agreements, contracts, arrangements, understandings, plans or proposals relating to (1) the borrowing of funds to finance the acquisition as disclosed in Item 3; (2) the acquisition of issuer control, liquidation, sale of assets, merger, or change in business or corporate structure or any other matter as disclosed in Item 4; and (3) the transfer or voting of the securities, finder's fees, joint ventures, options, puts, calls, guarantees of loans, guarantees against loss or of profit, or the giving or withholding of any proxy as disclosed in Item 6.

Signature.

After reasonable inquiry and to the best of my knowledge and belief, I certify that the information set forth in this statement is true, complete and correct.

Date   ....

Signature   ....

Name/Title

The original statement shall be signed by each person on whose behalf the statement is filed or his authorized representative. If the statement is signed on behalf of a person by his authorized representative (other than an executive officer or general partner of this filing person), evidence of the representative's authority to sign on behalf of such person shall be filed with the statement, provided, however, that a power of attorney for this purpose which is already on file with the Commission may be incorporated by reference. The name and any title of each person who signs the statement shall be typed or printed beneath his signature.

Attention: Intentional misstatements or omissions of fact constitute Federal criminal violations (See 18 U. S. C. 1001).

SCHEDULE 13E-3
Schedule 13E-3 Transaction Statement under Section 13(e) of the Securities Exchange Act of 1934 and Rule 13e-3 (§ 240.13e-3) thereunder.
SECURITIES AND EXCHANGE COMMISSION

Washington, D.C. 20549

Rule 13e-3 Transaction Statement under Section 13(e) of the Securities Exchange Act of 1934

[Amendment No....................]

....

(Name of the Issuer)

....

(Name of Person(s) Filing Statement)

....

(Title of Class of Securities)

....

(CUSIP Number of Class of Securities)

....

(Name, Address and Telephone Numbers of Person Authorized to Receive Notices and Communications on Behalf of Persons Filing Statement)

This statement is filed in connection with (check the appropriate box):

a. [ ] The filing of solicitation materials or an information statement subject to Regulation 14A (§ § 240.14a-1 through 240.14b-2), Regulation 14C (§ § 240.14c-1 through 240.14c-101) or Rule 13e-3(c) (§ 240.13e-3(c)) under the Securities Exchange Act of 1934 ("the Act").

b. [ ] The filing of a registration statement under the Securities Act of 1933.

c. [ ] A tender offer.

d. [ ] None of the above.

Check the following box if the soliciting materials or information statement referred to in checking box (a) are preliminary copies: [ ]

Check the following box if the filing is a final amendment reporting the results of the transaction: [ ]

Calculation of Filing Fee

Transaction valuation*	Amount of filing fee

*Set forth the amount on which the filing fee is calculated and state how it was determined.

[ ] Check the box if any part of the fee is offset as provided by § 240.0-11(a)(2) and identify the filing with which the offsetting fee was previously paid. Identify the previous filing by registration statement number, or the Form or Schedule and the date of its filing.

Amount Previously Paid:_____

Form or Registration No.:_____

Filing Party:_____

Date Filed:_____

General Instructions:

A. File eight copies of the statement, including all exhibits, with the Commission if paper filing is permitted.

739

B. This filing must be accompanied by a fee payable to the Commission as required by § 240.0-11(b)

C. If the statement is filed by a general or limited partnership, syndicate or other group, the information called for by Items 3, 5, 6, 10 and 11 must be given with respect to: (i) each partner of the general partnership; (ii) each partner who is, or functions as, a general partner of the limited partnership; (iii) each member of the syndicate or group; and (iv) each person controlling the partner or member. If the statement is filed by a corporation or if a person referred to in (i), (ii), (iii) or (iv) of this Instruction is a corporation, the information called for by the items specified above must be given with respect to: (a) each executive officer and director of the corporation; (b) each person controlling the corporation; and (c) each executive officer and director of any corporation or other person ultimately in control of the corporation.

D. Depending on the type of Rule 13e-3 transaction (§ 240.13e-3(a)(3)), this statement must be filed with the Commission:

1. At the same time as filing preliminary or definitive soliciting materials or an information statement under Regulations 14A or 14C of the Act;

2. At the same time as filing a registration statement under the Securities Act of 1933;

3. As soon as practicable on the date a tender offer is first published, sent or given to security holders; or

4. At least 30 days before any purchase of securities of the class of securities subject to the Rule 13e-3 transaction, if the transaction does not involve a solicitation, an information statement, the registration of securities or a tender offer, as described in paragraphs 1, 2 or 3 of this Instruction; and

5. If the Rule 13e-3 transaction involves a series of transactions, the issuer or affiliate must file this statement at the time indicated in paragraphs 1 through 4 of this Instruction for the first transaction and must amend the schedule promptly with respect to each subsequent transaction.

E. If an item is inapplicable or the answer is in the negative, so state. The statement published, sent or given to security holders may omit negative and not applicable responses, except that responses to Items 7, 8 and 9 of this schedule must be provided in full. If the schedule includes any information that is not published, sent or given to security holders, provide that information or specifically incorporate it by reference under the appropriate item number and heading in the schedule. Do not recite the text of disclosure requirements in the schedule or any document published, sent or given to security holders. Indicate clearly the coverage of the requirements without referring to the text of the items.

F. Information contained in exhibits to the statement may be incorporated by reference in answer or partial answer to any item unless it would render the answer misleading, incomplete, unclear or confusing. A copy of any information that is incorporated by reference or a copy of the pertinent pages of a document containing the information must be submitted with this statement as an exhibit, unless it was previously filed with the Commission electronically on EDGAR. If an exhibit contains information responding to more than one item in the schedule, all information in that exhibit may be incorporated by reference once in response to the several items in the schedule for which it provides an answer. Information incorporated by reference is deemed filed with the Commission for all purposes of the Act.

G. If the Rule 13e-3 transaction also involves a transaction subject to Regulation 14A (§ § 240.14a-1 through 240.14b-2) or 14C (§ § 240.14c-1 through 240.14c-101) of the Act, the registration of securities under the Securities Act of 1933 and the General Rules and Regulations of that Act, or a tender offer subject to Regulation 14D (§ § 240.14d-1 through 240.14d-101) or § 240.13e-4, this statement must incorporate by reference the information contained in the proxy, information, registration or tender offer statement in answer to the items of this statement.

H. The information required by the items of this statement is intended to be in addition to any disclosure requirements of any other form or schedule that may be filed with the Commission in connection with the Rule 13e-3 transaction. If those forms or schedules require less information on any topic than this statement, the requirements of this statement control.

I. If the Rule 13e-3 transaction involves a tender offer, then a combined statement on Schedules 13E-3 and TO may be filed with the Commission under cover of Schedule TO (§ 240.14d-100). See Instruction J of Schedule TO (§ 240.14d-100).

J. Amendments disclosing a material change in the information set forth in this statement may omit any information previously disclosed in this statement.

Item 1. *Summary Term Sheet*

Furnish the information required by Item 1001 of Regulation M-A (§ 229.1001 of this chapter) unless information is disclosed to security holders in a prospectus that meets the requirements of § 230.421(d) of this chapter.

Item 2. *Subject Company Information*

Furnish the information required by Item 1002 of Regulation M-A (§ 229.1002 of this chapter).

Item 3. *Identity and Background of Filing Person*

Furnish the information required by Item 1003(a) through (c) of Regulation M-A (§ 229.1003 of this chapter).

Item 4. *Terms of the Transaction*

Furnish the information required by Item 1004(a) and (c) through (f) of Regulation M-A (§ 229.1004 of this chapter).

Item 5. *Past Contacts, Transactions, Negotiations and Agreements*

Furnish the information required by Item 1005(a) through (c) and (e) of Regulation M-A (§ 229.1005 of this chapter).

Item 6. *Purposes of the Transaction and Plans or Proposals*

Furnish the information required by Item 1006(b) and (c)(1) through (8) of Regulation M-A (§ 229.1006 of this chapter).

Instruction to Item 6: In providing the information specified in Item 1006(c) for this item, discuss any activities or transactions that would occur after the Rule 13e-3 transaction.

Item 7. *Purposes, Alternatives, Reasons and Effects*

Furnish the information required by Item 1013 of Regulation M-A (§ 229.1013 of this chapter).

Item 8. *Fairness of the Transaction*

Furnish the information required by Item 1014 of Regulation M-A (§ 229.1014 of this chapter).

Item 9. *Reports, Opinions, Appraisals and Negotiations*

Furnish the information required by Item 1015 of Regulation M-A (§ 229.1015 of this chapter).

Item 10.　*Source and Amounts of Funds or Other Consideration*

Furnish the information required by Item 1007 of Regulation M-A (§ 229.1007 of this chapter).

Item 11.　*Interest in Securities of the Subject Company*

Furnish the information required by Item 1008 of Regulation M-A (§ 229.1008 of this chapter).

Item 12.　*The Solicitation or Recommendation*

Furnish the information required by Item 1012(d) and (e) of Regulation M-A (§ 229.1012 of this chapter).

Item 13.　*Financial Statements*

Furnish the information required by Item 1010(a) through (b) of Regulation M-A (§ 229.1010 of this chapter) for the issuer of the subject class of securities.

Instructions to Item 13:

1. The disclosure materials disseminated to security holders may contain the summarized financial information required by Item 1010(c) of Regulation M-A (§ 229.1010 of this chapter) instead of the financial information required by Item 1010(a) and (b). In that case, the financial information required by Item 1010(a) and (b) of Regulation M-A must be disclosed directly or incorporated by reference in the statement. If summarized financial information is disseminated to security holders, include appropriate instructions on how more complete financial information can be obtained. If the summarized financial information is prepared on the basis of a comprehensive body of accounting principles other than U.S. GAAP, the summarized financial information must be accompanied by a reconciliation as described in Instruction 2.

2. If the financial statements required by this Item are prepared on the basis of a comprehensive body of accounting principles other than U.S. GAAP, provide a reconciliation to U.S. GAAP in accordance with Item 17 of Form 20-F (§ 249.220f of this chapter).

3. The filing person may incorporate by reference financial statements contained in any document filed with the Commission, solely for the purposes of this schedule, if: (a) the financial statements substantially meet the requirements of this Item; (b) an express statement is made that the financial statements are incorporated by reference; (c) the matter incorporated by reference is clearly identified by page, paragraph, caption or otherwise; and (d) if the matter incorporated by reference is not filed with this Schedule, an indication is made where the information may be inspected and copies obtained. Financial statements that are required to be presented in comparative form for two or more fiscal years or periods may not be incorporated by reference unless the material incorporated by reference includes the entire period for which the comparative data is required to be given. *See* General Instruction F to this Schedule.

Item 14.　*Persons/Assets, Retained, Employed, Compensated or Used*

Furnish the information required by Item 1009 of Regulation M-A (§ 229.1009 of this chapter).

Item 15.　*Additional Information*

Furnish the information required by Item 1011(b) and (c) of Regulation M-A (§ 229.1011(b) and (c) of this chapter).

Item 16. *Exhibits*

File as an exhibit to the Schedule all documents specified in Item 1016(a) through (d), (f) and (g) of Regulation M-A (§ 229.1016 of this chapter).

Signature. After due inquiry and to the best of my knowledge and belief, I certify that the information set forth in this statement is true, complete and correct.

_____

(Signature)

_____

(Name and title)

_____

(Date)

Instruction to Signature:

The statement must be signed by the filing person or that person's authorized representative. If the statement is signed on behalf of a person by an authorized representative (other than an executive officer of a corporation or general partner of a partnership), evidence of the representative's authority to sign on behalf of the person must be filed with the statement. The name and any title of each person who signs the statement must be typed or printed beneath the signature. See § 240.12b-11 with respect to signature requirements.

Schedule 14A
Information Required in Proxy Statement
SCHEDULE 14A INFORMATION

Proxy Statement Pursuant to Section 14(a) of the Securities Exchange Act of 1934 (Amendment No.)

Filed by the Registrant [ ]

Filed by a Party other than the Registrant [ ]

Check the appropriate box:

[ ] Preliminary Proxy Statement

[ ] Confidential, for Use of the Commission Only (as permitted by Rule 14a-6(e)(2))

[ ] Definitive Proxy Statement

[ ] Definitive Additional Materials

[ ] Soliciting Material Pursuant to § 240.14a-12

....
(Name of Registrant as Specified In Its Charter)

....
(Name of Person(s) Filing Proxy Statement, if other than the Registrant)

Payment of Filing Fee (Check the appropriate box):

[ ] No fee required.

[ ] Fee computed on table below per Exchange Act Rules 14a-6(i)(1) and 0-11.

1) Title of each class of securities to which transaction applies:

....

2) Aggregate number of securities to which transaction applies:

....

3) Per unit price or other underlying value of transaction computed pursuant to Exchange Act Rule 0-11 (set forth the amount on which the filing fee is calculated and state how it was determined):

....

4) Proposed maximum aggregate value of transaction:

....

5) Total fee paid:

....

[ ] Fee paid previously with preliminary materials.

[ ] Check box if any part of the fee is offset as provided by Exchange Act Rule 0-11(a)(2) and identify the filing for which the offsetting fee was paid previously. Identify the previous filing by registration statement number, or the Form or Schedule and the date of its filing.

1) Amount Previously Paid:

....

2) Form, Schedule or Registration Statement No.:

....

3) Filing Party:

....

4) Date Filed:

....

Notes.—A. Where any item calls for information with respect to any matter to be acted upon and such matter involves other matters with respect to which information is called for by other items of this schedule, the information called for by such other items also shall be given. For example, where a solicitation of security holders is for the purpose of approving the authorization of additional securities which are to be used to acquire another specified company, and the registrants' security holders will not have a separate opportunity to vote upon the transaction, the solicitation to authorize the securities is also a solicitation with respect to the acquisition. Under those facts, information required by Items 11, 13 and 14 shall be furnished.

B. Where any item calls for information with respect to any matter to be acted upon at the meeting, such item need be answered in the registrant's soliciting material only with respect to proposals to be made by or on behalf of the registrant.

C. Except as otherwise specifically provided, where any item calls for information for a specified period with regard to directors, executive officers, officers or other persons holding specified positions or relationships, the information shall be given with regard to any person who held any of the specified positions or relationship at any time during the period. Information, other than information required by Item 404 of Regulation S-K (§ 229.404 of this chapter), need not be included for any portion of the period during which such person did not hold any such position or relationship, provided a statement to that effect is made.

D. Information may be incorporated by reference only in the manner and to the extent specifically permitted in the items of this schedule. Where incorporation by reference is used, the following shall apply:

1. Disclosure must not be incorporated by reference from a second document if that second document incorporates information pertinent to such disclosure by reference to a third document. A registrant incorporating any documents, or portions of documents, shall include a statement on the last page(s) of the proxy statement as to which documents, or portions of documents, are incorporated by reference. Information shall not be incorporated by reference in any case where such incorporation would render the statement incomplete, unclear or confusing.

2. If a document is incorporated by reference but not delivered to security holders, include an undertaking to provide, without charge, to each person to whom a proxy statement is delivered, upon written or oral request of such person and by first class mail or other equally prompt means within one business day of receipt of such request, a copy of any and all of the information that has been incorporated by reference in the proxy statement (not including exhibits to the information that is incorporated by reference unless such exhibits are specifically incorporated by reference into the information that the proxy statement incorporates), and the address (including title or department) and telephone numbers to which such a request is to be directed. This includes information contained in documents filed subsequent to the date on which definitive copies of the proxy statement are sent or given to security holders, up to the date of responding to the request.

3. If a document or portion of a document other than an annual report sent to security holders pursuant to the requirements of Rule 14a-3 (§ 240.14a-3 of this chapter) with respect to the same meeting or solicitation of consents or authorizations as that to which the proxy statement relates is incorporated by reference in the manner permitted by Item 13(b) or 14(e)(1) of this schedule, the proxy statement must be sent to security holders no later than 20 business days prior to the date on which the meeting of such security holders is held or, if no meeting is held, at least 20 business days prior to the date the votes, consents or authorizations may be used to effect the corporate action.

4. *Electronic filings.* If any of the information required by Items 13 or 14 of this Schedule is incorporated by reference from an annual or quarterly report to security holders, such report, or any portion thereof incorporated by reference, shall be filed in electronic format with the proxy statement. This provision shall not apply to registered investment companies.

E. In Item 13 of this Schedule, the reference to "meets the requirement of Form S-3" or "meets the requirements of General Instruction A.2 of Form N-2" shall refer to a registrant who meets the following requirements:

(a) A registrant meets the requirements of Form S-3 if:

(1) The registrant meets the requirements of General Instruction I.A. of Form S-3 (§ 239.13 of this chapter); and

(2) One of the following is met:

(i) The registrant meets the aggregate market value requirement of General Instruction I.B.1 of Form S-3; or

(ii) Action is to be taken as described in Items 11, 12, and 14 of this schedule which concerns non-convertible debt or preferred securities issued by a registrant meeting the requirements of General Instruction I.B.2. of Form S-3 (referenced in 17 CFR 239.13 of this chapter); or

(iii) The registrant is a majority-owned subsidiary and one of the conditions of General Instruction I.C. of Form S-3 is met.

(b) A registrant meets the requirements of General Instruction A.2 of Form N-2 (§ 239.14 and § 274.11a-1 of this chapter) if the registrant meets the conditions included in such General Instruction, provided that General Instruction A.2.c of Form N-2 is subject to the same limitations described in paragraph (a)(2) of this Note E.

Item 1. Date, time and place information

(a) State the date, time and place of the meeting of security holders, and the complete mailing address, including ZIP Code, of the principal executive offices of the registrant, unless such information is otherwise disclosed in material furnished to security holders with or preceding the proxy statement. If action is to be taken by written consent, state the date by which consents are to be submitted if state law requires that such a date be specified or if the person soliciting intends to set a date.

(b) On the first page of the proxy statement, as delivered to security holders, state the approximate date on which the proxy statement and form of proxy are first sent or given to security holders.

(c) Furnish the information required to be in the proxy statement by Rule 14a-5(e) (§ 240.14a-5(e) of this chapter).

Item 2. Revocability of Proxy

State whether or not the person giving the proxy has the power to revoke it. If the right of revocation before the proxy is exercised is limited or is subject to compliance with any formal procedure, briefly describe such limitation or procedure.

Item 3. Dissenters' Right of Appraisal

Outline briefly the rights of appraisal or similar rights of dissenters with respect to any matter to be acted upon and indicate any statutory procedure required to be followed by dissenting security holders in order to perfect such rights. Where such rights may be exercised only within a limited time after the date of adoption of a proposal, the filing of a charter amendment or other similar act, state whether the persons solicited will be notifed of such date.

Instructions. 1. Indicate whether a security holder's failure to vote against a proposal will constitute a waiver of his appraisal or similar rights and whether a vote against a proposal will be deemed to satisfy any notice requirements under State law with respect to appraisal rights. If the State law is unclear, state what position will be taken in regard to these matters.

2. Open-end investment companies registered under the Investment Company Act of 1940 are not required to respond to this item.

Item 4. Persons Making the Solicitation

(a) *Solicitations not subject to Rule 14a-12(c) (§ 240.14a-12(c) of this chapter.)* (1) If the solicitation is made by the registrant, so state. Give the name of any director of the registrant who has informed the registrant in writing that he intends to oppose any action intended to be taken by the registrant and indicate the action which he intends to oppose.

(2) If the solicitation is made otherwise than by the registrant, so state and give the names of the participants in the solicitation, as defined in paragraphs (a)(iii), (iv), (v) and (vi) of Instruction 3 to this Item.

(3) If the solicitation is to be made otherwise than by the use of the mails or pursuant to § 240.14a-16, describe the methods to be employed. If the solicitation is to be made by specially engaged employees or paid solicitors, state (i) the material features of any contract or arrangement for such solicitation and identify the parties, and (ii) the cost or anticipated cost thereof.

(4) State the names of the persons by whom the cost of solicitation has been or will be borne, directly or indirectly.

(b) *Solicitations subject to Rule 14a-12(c) (§ 240.14a-12(c)).* (1) State by whom the solicitation is made and describe the methods employed and to be employed to solicit security holders.

(2) If regular employees of the registrant or any other participant in a solicitation have been or are to be employed to solicit security holders, describe the class or classes of employees to be so employed, and the manner and nature of their employment for such purpose.

(3) If specially engaged employees, representatives or other persons have been or are to be employed to solicit security holders, state (i) the material features of any contract or arrangement for such solicitation and the identity of the parties, (ii) the cost or anticipated cost thereof, and (iii) the approximate number of such employees or employees of any other person (naming such other person) who will solicit security holders).

(4) State the total amount estimated to be spent and the total expenditures to date for, in furtherance of, or in connection with the solicitation of security holders.

(5) State by whom the cost of the solicitation will be borne. If such cost is to be borne initially by any person other than the registrant, state whether reimbursement will be sought from the registrant, and, if so, whether the question of such reimbursement will be submitted to a vote of security holders.

(6) If any such solicitation is terminated pursuant to a settlement between the registrant and any other participant in such solicitation, describe the terms of such settlement, including the cost or anticipated cost thereof to the registrant.

Instructions. 1. With respect to solicitations subject to Rule 14a-12(c) (§ 240.14a-12(c)), costs and expenditures within the meaning of this Item 4 shall include fees for attorneys, accountants, public relations or financial advisers, solicitors, advertising, printing, transportation, litigation and other costs incidental to the solicitation, except that the registrant may exclude the amount of such costs represented by the amount normally expended for a solicitation for an election of directors in the absence of a contest, and costs represented by salaries and wages of regular employees and officers, provided a statement to that effect is included in the proxy statement.

2. The information required pursuant to paragraph (b)(6) of this Item should be included in any amended or revised proxy statement or other soliciting materials relating to the same meeting or subject matter furnished to security holders by the registrant subsequent to the date of settlement.

3. For purposes of this Item 4 and Item 5 of this Schedule 14A: (a) The terms "participant" and "participant in a solicitation" include the following:

(i) the registrant;

(ii) any director of the registrant, and any nominee for whose election as a director proxies are solicited;

(iii) any committee or group which solicits proxies, any member of such committee or group, and any person whether or not named as a member who, acting alone or with one or more other persons, directly or indirectly takes the initiative, or engages, in organizing, directing, or arranging for the financing of any such committee or group;

(iv) any person who finances or joins with another to finance the solicitation of proxies, except persons who contribute not more than $500 and who are not otherwise participants;

(v) any person who lends money or furnishes credit or enters into any other arrangements, pursuant to any contract or understanding with a participant, for the purpose of financing or otherwise inducing the purchase, sale, holding or voting of securities of the registrant by any participant or other persons, in support of or in opposition to a participant; except that such terms do not include a bank, broker or dealer who, in the ordinary course of business, lends money or executes orders for the purchase or sale of securities and who is not otherwise a participant; and

(vi) any person who solicits proxies.

(b) The terms "participant" and "participant in a solicitation" do not include:

(i) any person or organization retained or employed by a participant to solicit security holders and whose activities are limited to the duties required to be performed in the course of such employment;

(ii) any person who merely transmits proxy soliciting material or performs other ministerial or clerical duties;

(iii) any person employed by a participant in the capacity of attorney, accountant, or advertising, public relations or financial adviser, and whose activities are limited to the duties required to be performed in the course of such employment;

(iv) any person regularly employed as an officer or employee of the registrant or any of its subsidiaries who is not otherwise a participant; or

(v) any officer or director of, or any person regularly employed by, any other participant, if such officer, director or employee is not otherwise a participant.

Item 5. Interest of Certain Persons in Matters to Be Acted Upon

(a) *Solicitations not subject to Rule 14a-12(c) (§ 240.14a-12(c) of this chapter).* Describe briefly any substantial interest, direct or indirect, by security holdings or otherwise, of each of the following persons in any matter to be acted upon, other than elections to office:

(1) If the solicitation is made on behalf of the registrant, each person who has been a director or executive officer of the registrant at any time since the beginning of the last fiscal year.

(2) If the solicitation is made otherwise than on behalf of the registrant, each participation in the solicitation, as defined in paragraphs in the solicitation, as defined in paragraphs (a)(iii), (iv), (v), and (vi) of Instruction 3 to Item 4 of This Schedule 14A.

(3) Each nominee for election as a director of the registrant.

(4) Each associate of any of the foregoing persons.

(5) If the solicitation is made on behalf of the registrant, furnish the information required by Item 402(t) of Regulation S-K (§ 229.402(t) of this chapter).

Instruction to Paragraph (a). Except in the case of a solicitation subject to this regulation made in opposition to another solicitation subject to this regulation, the sub-item (a) shall not apply to any interest arising from the ownership of securities of the registrant where the security holder receives no extra or special benefit not shared on a pro rata basis by all other holders of the same class.

(b) *Solicitation subject to Rule 14a-12(c) (§ 240.14a-12(c) of this chapter).* With respect to any solicitation subject to Rule 14a-12(c) (§ 240.14a-12(c)):

(1) Describe briefly any substantial interest, direct or indirect, by security holdings or otherwise, of each participant as defined in paragraphs (a)(ii), (iii), (iv), (v) and (vi) of Instruction 3 to Item 4 of this Schedule 14A, in any matter to be acted upon at the meeting, and include with respect to each participant the following information, or a fair and accurate summary thereof:

(i) Name and business address of the participant.

(ii) The participant's present principal occupation or employment and the name, principal business and address of any corporation or other organization in which such employment is carried on.

(iii) State whether or not, during the past ten years, the participant has been convicted in a criminal proceeding (excluding traffic violations or similar misdemeanors) and, if so, give dates, nature of conviction, name and location of court, and penalty imposed or other disposition of the case. A negative answer need not be included in the proxy statement or other soliciting material.

(iv) State the amount of each class of securities of the registrant which the participant owns beneficially, directly or indirectly.

(v) State the amount of each class of securities of the registrant which the participant owns of record but not beneficially.

(vi) State with respect to all securities of the registrant purchased or sold within the past two years, the dates on which they were purchased or sold and the amount purchased or sold on each such date.

(vii) If any part of the purchase price or market value of any of the shares specified in paragraph (b)(1)(vi) of this Item is represented by funds borrowed or otherwise obtained for the purpose of acquiring or holding such securities, so state and indicate the amount of the indebtedness as of the latest practicable date. If such funds were borrowed or obtained otherwise than pursuant to a margin account or bank loan in the regular course of business of a bank, broker or dealer, briefly describe the transaction, and state the names of the parties.

(viii) State whether or not the participant is, or was within the past year, a party to any contract, arrangements or understandings with any person with respect to any securities of the registrant, including, but not limited to joint ventures, loan or option arrangements, puts or calls, guarantees against loss or guarantees of profit, division of losses or profits, or the giving or withholding of proxies. If so, name the parties to such contracts, arrangements or understandings and give the details thereof.

(ix) State the amount of securities of the registrant owned beneficially, directly or indirectly, by each of the participant's associates and the name and address of each such associate.

(x) State the amount of each class of securities of any parent or subsidiary of the registrant which the participant owns beneficially, directly or indirectly.

(xi) Furnish for the participant and associates of the participant the information required by Item 404(a) of Regulation S-K (§ 229.404(a) of this chapter).

(xii) State whether or not the participant or any associates of the participant have any arrangement or understanding with any person—

(A) with respect to any future employment by the registrant or its affiliates; or

(B) with respect to any future transactions to which the registrant or any of its affiliates will or may be a party.

If so, describe such arrangement or understanding and state the names of the parties thereto.

(2) With respect to any person, other than a director or executive officer of the registrant acting solely in that capacity, who is a party to an arrangement or understanding pursuant to which a nominee for election as director is proposed to be elected, describe any substantial interest, direct or indirect, by security holdings or otherwise, that such person has in any matter to be acted upon at the meeting, and furnish the information called for by paragraphs (b)(1)(xi) and (xii) of this Item.

(3) If the solicitation is made on behalf of the registrant, furnish the information required by Item 402(t) of Regulation S-K (§ 229.402(t) of this chapter).

Instruction to Paragraph (b). For purposes of this Item 5, beneficial ownership shall be determined in accordance with Rule 13d-3 under the Act (Section 240.13d-3 of this chapter).

Item 6. Voting Securities and Principal Holders Thereof

(a) As to each class of voting securities of the registrant entitled to be voted at the meeting (or by written consents or authorizations if no meeting is held), state the number of shares outstanding and the number of votes to which each class is entitled.

(b) State the record date, if any, with respect to this solicitation. If the right to vote or give consent is not to be determined, in whole or in part, by reference to a record date, indicate the criteria for the determination of security holders entitled to vote or give consent.

(c) If action is to be taken with respect to the election of directors and if the persons solicited have cumulative voting rights: (1) Make a statement that they have such rights, (2) briefly describe such rights, (3) state briefly the conditions precedent to the exercise thereof, and (4) if discretionary authority to cumulate votes is solicited, so indicate.

(d) Furnish the information required by Item 403 of Regulation S-K (§ 229.403 of this chapter) to the extent known by the persons on whose behalf the solicitation if made.

(e) If, to the knowledge of the persons on whose behalf the solicitation is made, a change in control of the registrant has occurred since the beginning of its last fiscal year, state the name of the person(s) who acquired such control, the amount and the source of the consideration used by such person or persons; the basis of the control, the date and a description of the transaction(s) which resulted in the change of control and the percentage of voting securities of the registrant now beneficially owned directly or indirectly by the person(s) who acquired control; and the identity of the person(s) from whom control was assumed. If the source of all or any part of the consideration used is a loan made in the ordinary course of business by a bank as defined by section 3(a)(6) of the Act, the identity of such bank shall be omitted provided a request for confidentiality has been made pursuant to section 13(d)(1)(B) of the Act by the person(s) who acquired control. In lieu thereof, the material shall indicate that the identity of the bank has been so omitted and filed separately with the Commission.

Instruction. 1. State the terms of any loans or pledges obtained by the new control group for the purposes of acquiring control, and the names of the lenders or pledgees.

2. Any arrangements or understandings among members of both the former and new control groups and their associates with respect to election of directors or other matters should be described.

Item 7. Directors and Executive Officers

If action is to be taken with respect to the election of directors, furnish the following information in tabular form to the extent practicable. If, however, the solicitation is made on behalf of persons other than the registrant, the information required need be furnished only as to nominees of the persons making the solicitation.

(a) The information required by Instruction 4 to Item 103 of Regulation S-K (§ 229.103 of this chapter) with respect to directors and executive officers.

(b) The information required by Items 401, 404(a) and (b), 405 and 407 of Regulation S-K (§§ 229.401, 229.404(a) and (b), 229.405 and 229.407 of this chapter), other than the information required by:

(i) Paragraph (c)(3) of Item 407 of Regulation S-K (§ 229.407(c)(3) of this chapter); and

(ii) Paragraphs (e)(4) and (e)(5) of Item 407 of Regulation S-K (§§ 229.407(e)(4) and 229.407(e)(5) of this chapter) (which are required by Item 8 of this Schedule 14A).

(c) If a shareholder nominee or nominees are submitted to the registrant for inclusion in the registrant's proxy materials pursuant to § 240.14a-11 and the registrant is not permitted to exclude the nominee or nominees pursuant to the provisions of § 240.14a-11, the registrant must include in its proxy statement the disclosure required from the nominating shareholder or nominating shareholder group under Item 5 of § 240.14n-101 with regard to the nominee or nominees and the nominating shareholder or nominating shareholder group.

(d) If a registrant is required to include a shareholder nominee or nominees submitted to the registrant for inclusion in the registrant's proxy materials pursuant to a procedure set forth under applicable state or foreign law, or the registrant's governing documents providing for the inclusion of shareholder director nominees in the registrant's proxy materials, the registrant must include in its proxy statement the disclosure required from the nominating shareholder or nominating shareholder group under Item 6 of § 240.14n-101 with regard to the nominee or nominees and the nominating shareholder or nominating shareholder group.

Instruction to Item 7. The information disclosed pursuant to paragraph (c) and (d) of this Item will not be deemed incorporated by reference into any filing under the Securities Act of 1933 (15 U.S.C. 77a *et seq.*), the Securities Exchange Act of 1934 (15 U.S.C. 78a *et seq.*), or the

Investment Company Act of 1940 (15 U.S.C. 80a-1 *et seq.*), except to the extent that the registrant specifically incorporates that information by reference.

(e) In lieu of the information required by this Item 7, investment companies registered under the Investment Company Act of 1940 (15 U.S.C. 80a) must furnish the information required by Item 22(b) of this Schedule 14A.

Item 8. Compensation of Directors and Executive Officers

Furnish the information required by Item 402 of Regulation S-K (§ 229.402 of this chapter) and paragraphs (e)(4) and (e)(5) of Item 407 of Regulation S-K (§ 229.407(e)(4) and (e)(5) of this chapter) if action is to be taken with regard to:

(a) the election of directors;

(b) any bonus, profit sharing or other compensation plan, contract or arrangement in which any director, nominee for election as a director, or executive officer of the registrant will participate;

(c) any pension or retirement plan in which any such person will participate; or

(d) the granting or extension to any such person of any options, warrants or rights to purchase any securities, other than warrants or rights issued to security holders as such, on a pro rata basis.

However, if the solicitation is made on behalf of persons other than the registrant, the information required need be furnished only as to nominees of the persons making the solicitation and associates of such nominees. In the case of investment companies registered under the Investment Company Act of 1940 (15 U.S.C. 80a), furnish the information required by Item 22(b)(13) of this Schedule 14A.

Instruction. If an otherwise reportable compensation plan became subject to such requirements because of an acquisition or merger and, within one year of the acquisition or merger, such plan was terminated for purposes of prospective eligibility, the registrant may furnish a description of its obligation to the designated individuals pursuant to the compenation plan. Such description may be furnished in lieu of a description of the compensation plan in the proxy statement.

Item 9. Independent Public Accountants

If the solicitation is made on behalf of the registrant and relates to (1) the annual (or special meeting in lieu of annual) meeting of security holders at which directors are to be elected, or a solicitation of consents or authorizations in lieu of such meeting or (2) the election, approval or ratification of the registrant's accountant, furnish the following information describing the registrant's relationship with its independent public accountant:

(a) The name of the principal accountant selected or being recommended to security holders for election, approval or ratification for the current year. If no accountant has been selected or recommended, so state and briefly describe the reasons therefor.

(b) The name of the principal accountant for the fiscal year most recently completed if different from the accountant selected or recommended for the current year of if no accountant has yet been selected or recommended for the current year.

(c) The proxy statement shall indicate (1) whether or not representatives of the principal accountant for the current year and for the most recently completed fiscal year are expected to be present at the security holders' meeting, (2) whether or not they will have the opportunity to make a statement if they desire to do so and (3) whether or not such representatives are expected to be available to respond to appropriate questions.

(d) If during the registrant's two most recent fiscal years or any subsequent interim period, (1) an independent accountant who was previously engaged as the principal accountant to audit the registrant's financial statements, or an independent accountant on whom the principal accountant expressed reliance in its report regarding a significant subsidiary, has resigned (or indicated it has declined to stand for re-election after the completion of the current audit) or was dismissed, or (2) a new independent accountant has been engaged as either the principal accountant to audit the registrant's financial statements or as an independent accountant on whom the principal accountant has expressed or is expected to express reliance in its report regarding a significant subsidiary, then, notwithstanding any previous disclosure, provide the information required by Item 304(a) of Regulation S-K (§ 229.304 of this chapter).

(e)(1) Disclose, under the caption *Audit Fees*, the aggregate fees billed for each of the last two fiscal years for professional services rendered by the principal accountant for the audit of the registrant's annual financial statements and review of financial statements included in the registrant's Form 10-Q (17 CFR 249.308a) or services that are normally provided by the accountant in connection with statutory and regulatory filings or engagements for those fiscal years.

(2) Disclose, under the caption *Audit-Related Fees*, the aggregate fees billed in each of the last two fiscal years for assurance and related services by the principal accountant that are reasonably related to the performance of the audit or review of the registrant's financial statements and are not reported under paragraph (e)(1) of this section. Registrants shall describe the nature of the services comprising the fees disclosed under this category.

(3) Disclose, under the caption *Tax Fees*, the aggregate fees billed in each of the last two fiscal years for professional services rendered by the principal accountant for tax compliance, tax advice, and tax planning. Registrants shall describe the nature of the services comprising the fees disclosed under this category.

(4) Disclose, under the caption *All Other Fees*, the aggregate fees billed in each of the last two fiscal years for products and services provided by the principal accountant, other than the services reported in paragraphs (e)(1) through (e)(3) of this section. Registrants shall describe the nature of the services comprising the fees disclosed under this category.

(5)(i) Disclose the audit committee's pre-approval policies and procedures described in 17 CFR 210.2-01(c)(7)(i).

(ii) Disclose the percentage of services described in each of paragraphs (e)(2) through (e)(4) of this section that were approved by the audit committee pursuant to 17 CFR 210.2-01(c)(7)(i)(C).

(6) If greater than 50 percent, disclose the percentage of hours expended on the principal accountant's engagement to audit the registrant's financial statements for the most recent fiscal year that were attributed to work performed by persons other than the principal accountant's full-time, permanent employees.

(7) If the registrant is an investment company, disclose the aggregate non-audit fees billed by the registrant's accountant for services rendered to the registrant, and to the registrant's investment adviser (not including any subadviser whose role is primarily portfolio management and is subcontracted with or overseen by another investment adviser), and any entity controlling, controlled by, or under common control with the adviser that provides ongoing services to the registrant for each of the last two fiscal years of the registrant.

(8) If the registrant is an investment company, disclose whether the audit committee of the board of directors has considered whether the provision of non-audit services that were rendered to the registrant's investment adviser (not including any subadviser whose role is primarily portfolio management and is subcontracted with or overseen by another investment adviser), and any entity controlling, controlled by, or under common control with the investment adviser that provides ongoing services to the registrant that were not pre-approved pursuant to 17 CFR 210.2-01(c)(7)(ii) is compatible with maintaining the principal accountant's independence.

Instruction to Item 9(e). For purposes of Item 9(e)(2), (3), and (4), registrants that are investment companies must disclose fees billed for services rendered to the registrant and separately, disclose fees required to be approved by the investment company registrant's audit committee pursuant to 17 CFR 210.2-01(c)(7)(ii). Registered investment companies must also disclose the fee percentages as required by item 9(e)(5)(ii) for the registrant and separately, disclose the fee percentages as required by item 9(e)(5)(ii) for the fees required to be approved by the investment company registrant's audit committee pursuant to 17 CFR 210.2-01(c)(7)(ii).

Item 10. Compensation Plans

If action is to be taken with respect to any plan pursuant to which cash or noncash compensation may be paid or distributed, furnish the following information:

(a) *Plans Subject to Securityholder Action.*

(1) Describe briefly the material features of the plan being acted upon, identify each class of persons who will be eligible to participate therein, indicate the approximate number of persons in each such class and state the basis of such participation.

(2) (i) In the tabular format specified below, disclose the benefits or amounts that will be received by or allocated to each of the following under the plan being acted upon, if such benefits or amounts are determinable:

NEW PLAN BENEFITS

Plan Name

Name and Position	Dollar Value ($)	Number of Units
CEO		
A		
B		
C		
D		
Executive Group		
Non-Executive Director Group		

(ii) The table required by paragraph (a)(2)(i) of this Item shall provide information as to the following persons:

(A) Each person (stating name and position) specified in paragraph (a)(3) of Item 402 of Regulation S-K (§ 229.402(a)(3) of this chapter);

Instruction: In the case of investment companies registered under the Investment Company Act of 1940, furnish the information for Compensated Persons as defined in Item 22(b)(13) of this Schedule in lieu of the persons specified in paragraph (a)(3) of Item 402 of Regulation S-K (§ 229.402(a)(3) of this chapter).

(B) All current executive officers as a group;

(C) All current directors who are not executive officers as a group; and

(D) All employees, including all current officers who are not executive officers, as a group.

Instruction to New Plan Benefits Table. Additional columns should be added for each plan with respect to which securityholder action is to be taken.

(iii) If the benefits or amounts specified in paragraph (a)(2)(i) of this Item are not determinable, state the benefits or amounts which would have been received by or allocated to each of the following for the last completed fiscal year if the plan had been in effect, if such benefits or amounts may be determined in the table specified in paragraph (a)(2)(i) of this Item:

(A) Each person (stating name and position) specified in paragraph (a)(3) of Item 402 of Regulation S-K (§ 229.402 (a)(3) of this chapter);

(B) All current executive officers as a group;

(C) All current directors who are not executive officers as a group; and

(D) All employees, including all current officers who are not executive officers, as a group.

(3) If the plan to be acted upon can be amended, otherwise than by a vote of securityholders, to increase the cost thereof to the registrant or to alter the allocation of the benefits as between the persons and groups specified in paragraph (2)(a) of this item, state the nature of the amendments which can be so made.

(b) *Additional Information Regarding Specific Plans Subject to Securityholder Action*.

(1) With respect to any pension or retirement plan submitted for securityholder action, state:

(i) The approximate total amount necessary to fund the plan with respect to past services, the period over which such amount is to be paid and the estimated annual payments necessary to pay the total amount over such period; and

(ii) The estimated annual payment to be made with respect to current services. In the case of a pension or retirement plan, information called for by paragraph (a)(2) of this Item may be furnished in the format specified by paragraph (h)(2) of Item 402 of Regulation S-K (§ 229.402(f)(1) of this chapter).

Instruction to Paragraph (b)(1)(ii). In the case of investment companies registered under the Investment Company Act of 1940 (15 U.S.C. 80a), refer to Instruction 4 in Item 22(b)(13)(i) of this Schedule in lieu of paragraph (h)(2) of Item 402 of Regulation S-K (§ 229.402(h)(2) of this chapter).

(2)(i) With respect to any specific grant of or any plan containing options, warrants or rights submitted for security holder action, state:

(A) The title and amount of securities underlying such options, warrants or rights;

(B) The prices, expiration dates and other material conditions upon which the options, warrants or rights may be exercised;

(C) The consideration received or to be received by the registrant or subsidiary for the granting or extension of the options, warrants or rights;

(D) The market value of the securities underlying the options, warrants or rights as of the latest practicable date; and

(E) In the case of options, the federal income tax consequences of the issuance and exercise of such options to the recipient and the registrant; and

(ii) State separately the amount of such options received or to be received by the following persons if such benefits or amounts are determinable:

(A) Each person (stating name and position) specified in paragraph (a)(3) of Item 402 of Regulation S-K (§ 229.402(a)(3) of this chapter);

(B) All current executive officers as a group;

(C) All current directors who are not executive officers as a group;

(D) Each nominee for election as a director;

(E) Each associate of any of such directors, executive officer or nominees;

(F) Each other person who received or is to receive 5 percent of such options, warrants or rights; and

(G) All employees, including all current officers who are not executive officers, as a group.

(c) *Information regarding plans and other arrangements not subject to security holder action.* Furnish the information required by Item 201(d) of Regulation S-K (§ 229.201(d) of this chapter).

Instructions to paragraph (c).

1. If action is to be taken as described in paragraph (a) of this Item with respect to the approval of a new compensation plan under which equity securities of the registrant are authorized for issuance, information about the plan shall be disclosed as required under paragraphs (a) and (b) of this Item and shall not be included in the disclosure required by Item 201(d) of Regulation S-K (§ 229.201(d) of this chapter). If action is to be taken as described in paragraph (a) of this Item with respect to the amendment or modification of an existing plan under which equity securities of the registrant are authorized for issuance, the registrant shall include information about securities previously authorized for issuance under the plan (including any outstanding options, warrants and rights previously granted pursuant to the plan and any securities remaining available for future issuance under the plan) in the disclosure required by Item 201(d) of Regulation S-K (§ 229.201(d) of this chapter). Any additional securities that are the subject of the amendments or modification of the existing plan shall be disclosed as required under paragraphs (a) and (b) of this Item and shall not be included in the Item 201(d) disclosure.

Instructions

1. The term plan as used in this Item means any plan as defined in paragraph (a)(6)(ii) of Item 402 of Regulation S-K (§ 229.402(a)(6)(ii) of this chapter).

2. If action is to be taken with respect to a material amendment or modification of an existing plan, the item shall be answered with respect to the plan as proposed to be amended or modified and shall indicate any material differences from the existing plan.

3. If the plan to be acted upon is set forth in a written document, three copies thereof shall be filed with the Commission at the time copies of the proxy statement and form of proxy are first filed pursuant to paragraph (a) or (b) of § 240.14a-6. Electronic filers shall file with the Commission a copy of such written plan document in electronic format as an appendix to the proxy statement. It need not be provided to security holders unless it is a part of the proxy statement.

4. Paragraphs (b)(2)(ii) does not apply to warrants or rights to be issued to security holders as such on a pro rata basis.

5. The Commission should be informed, as supplemental information, when the proxy statement is first filed, as to when the options, warrants, or rights and the shares called for thereby will be registered under the Securities Act or, if such registration is not contemplated, the section of the Securities Act or rule of the Commission under which exemption from such registration is claimed and the facts relied upon to make the exemption available.

Item 11. Authorization or Issuance of Securities Otherwise than for Exchange

If action is to be taken with respect to the authorization or issuance of any securities otherwise than for exchange for outstanding securities of the registrant, furnish the following information:

(a) State the title and amount of securities to be authorized or issued.

(b) Furnish the information required by Item 202 of Regulation S-K (§ 229.202 of this chapter). If the terms of the securities cannot be stated or estimated with respect to any or all of the securities to be authorized, because no offering thereof is contemplated in the proximate future, and if no further authorization by security holders for the issuance thereof is to be obtained, it should be stated that the terms of the securities to be authorized, including dividend or interest rates, conversion prices, voting rights, redemption prices, maturity dates, and similar matters will be determined by the board of directors. If the securities are additional shares of common stock of a class outstanding, the description may be omitted except for a statement of the preemptive rights, if any. Where the statutory provisions with respect to preemptive rights are so indefinite or complex that they cannot be stated in summarized form, it will suffice to make a statement in the form of an opinion of counsel as to the existence and extent of such rights.

(c) Describe briefly the transaction in which the securities are to be issued including a statement as to (1) the nature and approximate amount of consideration received or to be received by the registrant and (2) the approximate amount devoted to each purpose so far as determinable for which the net proceeds have been or are to be used. If it is impracticable to describe the transaction in which the securities are to be issued, state the reason, indicate the purpose of the authorization of the securities, and state whether further authorization for the issuance of the securities by a vote of security holders will be solicited prior to such issuance.

(d) If the securities are to be issued otherwise than in a public offering for cash, state the reasons for the proposed authorization or issuance and the general effect thereof upon the rights of existing security holders.

(e) Furnish the information required by Item 13(a) of this schedule.

Item 12. Modification or Exchange of Securities

If action is to be taken with respect to the modification of any class of securities of the registrant, or the issuance or authorization for issuance of securities of the registrant in exchange for outstanding securities of the registrant furnish the following information:

(a) If outstanding securities are to be modified, state the title and amount thereof. If securities are to be issued in exchange for outstanding securities, state the title and amount of securities to be so issued, the title and amount of outstanding securities to be exchanged therefor and the basis of the exchange.

(b) Describe any material differences between the outstanding securities and the modified or new securities in respect of any of the matters concerning which information would be required in the description of the securities in Item 202 of Regulation S-K (§ 229.202 of this chapter).

(c) State the reasons for the proposed modification or exchange and the general effect thereof upon the rights of existing security holders.

(d) Furnish a brief statement as to arrears in dividends or as to defaults in principal or interest in respect to the outstanding securities which are to be modified or exchanged and such other information as may be appropriate in the particular case to disclose adequately the nature and effect of the proposed action.

(e) Outline briefly any other material features of the proposed modification or exchange. If the plan of proposed action is set forth in a written document, file copies thereof with the Commission in accordance with § 240.14a-8.

(f) Furnish the information required by Item 13(a) of this Schedule.

Instruction. If the existing security is presently listed and registered on a national securities exchange, state whether the registrant intends to apply for listing and registration of the new or reclassified security on such exchange or any other exchange. If the registrant does not intend to make such application, state the effect of the termination of such listing and registration.

Item 13. Financial and Other Information

(*See* Notes D and E at the beginning of this Schedule.)

(a) Information required. If action is to be taken with respect to any matter specified in Item 11 or 12, furnish the following information:

(1) Financial statements meeting the requirements of Regulation S-X, including financial information required by Rule 3-05 and Article 11 of Regulation S-X with respect to transactions other than that pursuant to which action is to be taken as described in this proxy statement (A smaller reporting company may provide the information in Rules 8-04

and 8-05 of Regulation S-X (§ 210.8-04 and § 210.8-05 of this chapter) in lieu of the financial information required by Rule 3-05 and Article 11 of Regulation S-X);

(2) Item 302 of Regulation S-K, supplementary financial information;

(3) Item 303 of Regulation S-K, management's discussion and analysis of financial condition and results of operations;

(4) Item 304 of Regulation S-K, changes in and disagreements with accountants on accounting and financial disclosure;

(5) Item 305 of Regulation S-K, quantitative and qualitative disclosures about market risk; and

(6) A statement as to whether or not representatives of the principal accountants for the current year and for the most recently completed fiscal year:

(i) are expected to be present at the security holders' meeting;

(ii) will have the opportunity to make a statement if they desire to do so; and

(iii) are expected to be available to respond to appropriate questions.

(b) Incorporation by reference. The information required pursuant to paragraph (a) of this Item may be incorporated by reference into the proxy statement as follows:

(1) S-3 Registrants and Certain N-2 Registrants. If the registrant meets the requirements of Form S-3 or General Instruction A.2 of Form N-2 (see Note E to this Schedule), it may incorporate by reference to previously-filed documents any of the information required by paragraph (a) of this Item, provided that the requirements of paragraph (c) are met. Where the registrant meets the requirements of Form S-3 or General Instruction A.2 of Form N-2 and has elected to furnish the required information by incorporation by reference, the registrant may elect to update the information so incorporated by reference to information in subsequently-filed documents.

(2) All registrants. The registrant may incorporate by reference any of the information required by paragraph (a) of this Item, provided that the information is contained in an annual report to security holders or a previously-filed statement or report, such report or statement is delivered to security holders with the proxy statement and the requirements of paragraph (c) are met.

(c) *Certain conditions applicable to incorporation by reference.* Registrants eligible to incorporate by reference into the proxy statement the information required by paragraph (a) of this Item in the manner specified by paragraphs (b)(1) and (b)(2) may do so only if:

(1) the information is not required to be included in the proxy statement pursuant to the requirement of another Item;

(2) the proxy statement identifies on the last page(s) the information incorporated by reference; and

(3) the material incorporated by reference substantially meets the requirements of this Item or the appropriate portions of this Item.

Instructions to Item 13. 1. Notwithstanding the provisions of this Item, any or all of the information required by paragraph (a) of this Item, not material for the exercise of prudent judgment in regard to the matter to be acted upon may be omitted. In the usual case the information is deemed material to the exercise of prudent judgment where the matter to be acted upon is the authorization or issuance of a material amount of senior securities, but the information is not deemed material where the matter to be acted upon is the authorization or issuance of common stock, otherwise than in an exchange, merger, consolidation, acquisition or similar transaction, the authorization of preferred stock without present intent to issue or the authorization of preferred stock for issuance for cash in an amount constituting fair value.

2. In order to facilitate compliance with Rule 2-02(a) of Regulation S-X, one copy of the definitive proxy statement filed with the Commission shall include a manually signed copy of the accountant's report. If the financial statements are incorporated by reference, a manually signed copy of the accountant's report shall be filed with the definitive proxy statement.

3. Notwithstanding the provisions of Regulation S-X, no schedules other than those prepared in accordance with Rules 12-15, 12-28 and 12-29 (or, for management investment companies, Rules 12-12 through 12-14) of that regulation need be furnished in the proxy statement.

4. Unless registered on a national securities exchange or otherwise required to furnish such information, registered investment companies need not furnish the information required by paragraphs (a)(2) or (3) of this Item.

5. If the registrant submits preliminary proxy material incorporating by reference financial statements required by this Item, the registrant should furnish a draft of the financial statements if the document from which they are incorporated has not been filed with or furnished to the Commission.

6. A registered investment company need not comply with items (a)(2), (a)(3), and (a)(5) of this Item 13.

Item 14. Mergers, Consolidations, Acquisitions and Similar Matters

(*See* Notes A and D at the beginning of this Schedule.)

Instructions to Item 14.

1. In transactions in which the consideration offered to security holders consists wholly or in part of securities registered under the Securities Act of 1933, furnish the information required by Form S-4 (§ 239.25 of this chapter), Form F-4 (§ 239.34 of this chapter), or Form N-14 (§ 239.23 of this chapter), as applicable, instead of this Item. Only a Form S-4, Form F-4, or Form N-14 must be filed in accordance with § 240.14a-6(j).

2. (a) In transactions in which the consideration offered to security holders consists wholly of cash, the information required by paragraph (c)(1) of this Item for the acquiring company need not be provided unless the information is material to an informed voting decision (*e.g.*, the security holders of the target company are voting and financing is not assured).

(b) Additionally, if only the security holders of the target company are voting:

i. The financial information in paragraphs (b)(8)—(11) of this Item for the acquiring company and the target need not be provided; and

ii. The information in paragraph (c)(2) of this Item for the target company need not be provided.

If, however, the transaction is a going-private transaction (as defined by § 240.13e-3), then the information required by paragraph (c)(2) of this Item must be provided and to the extent that the going-private rules require the information specified in paragraph (b)(8)-(b)(11) of this Item, that information must be provided as well.

3. In transactions in which the consideration offered to security holders consists wholly of securities exempt from registration under the Securities Act of 1933 or a combination of exempt securities and cash, information about the acquiring company required by paragraph (c)(1) of this Item need not be provided if only the security holders of the acquiring company are voting, unless the information is material to an informed voting decision. If only the security holders of the target company are voting, information about the target company in paragraph (c)(2) of this Item need not be provided. However, the information required by paragraph (c)(2) of this Item must be provided if the transaction is a going-private (as defined by § 240.13e-3) or roll-up (as described by Item 901 of Regulation S-K (§ 229.901 of this chapter)) transaction.

4. The information required by paragraphs (b)(8)-(11) and (c) need not be provided if the plan being voted on involves only the acquiring company and one or more of its totally held subsidiaries and does not involve a liquidation or a spin-off.

5. To facilitate compliance with Rule 2-02(a) of Regulation S-X (§ 210.2-02(a) of this chapter) (technical requirements relating to accountants' reports), one copy of the definitive proxy statement filed with the Commission must include a signed copy of the accountant's report. If the financial statements are incorporated by reference, a signed copy of the accountant's report

must be filed with the definitive proxy statement. Signatures may be typed if the document is filed electronically on EDGAR. *See* Rule 302 of Regulation S-T (§ 232.302 of this chapter).

6. Notwithstanding the provisions of Regulation S-X, no schedules other than those prepared in accordance with § 210.12-15, § 210.12-28 and § 210.12-29 of this chapter (or, for management investment companies, § § 210.12-12 through 210.12-14 of this chapter) of that regulation need be furnished in the proxy statement.

7. If the preliminary proxy material incorporates by reference financial statements required by this Item, a draft of the financial statements must be furnished to the Commission staff upon request if the document from which they are incorporated has not been filed with or furnished to the Commission.

(a) *Applicability.* If action is to be taken with respect to any of the following transactions, provide the information required by this Item:

(1) A merger or consolidation;

(2) An acquisition of securities of another person;

(3) An acquisition of any other going business or the assets of a going business;

(4) A sale or other transfer of all or any substantial part of assets;or

(5) A liquidation or dissolution.

(b) *Transaction information.* Provide the following information for each of the parties to the transaction unless otherwise specified:

(1) *Summary term sheet.* The information required by Item 1001 of Regulation M-A (§ 229.1001 of this chapter).

(2) *Contact information.* The name, complete mailing address and telephone number of the principal executive offices.

(3) *Business conducted.* A brief description of the general nature of the business conducted.

(4) *Terms of the transaction.* The information required by Item 1004(a)(2) of Regulation M-A (§ 229.1004 of this chapter).

(5) *Regulatory approvals.* A statement as to whether any federal or state regulatory requirements must be complied with or approval must be obtained in connection with the transaction and, if so, the status of the compliance or approval.

(6) *Reports, opinions, appraisals.* If a report, opinion or appraisal materially relating to the transaction has been received from an outside party, and is referred to in the proxy statement, furnish the information required by Item 1015(b) of Regulation M-A (§ 229.1015 of this chapter).

(7) *Past contacts, transactions or negotiations.* The information required by Items 1005(b) and 1011(a)(1) of Regulation M-A (§ 229.1005 of this chapter and § 229.1011 of this chapter), for the parties to the transaction and their affiliates during the periods for which financial statements are presented or incorporated by reference under this Item.

(8) *Selected financial data.* The selected financial data required by Item 301 of Regulation S-K (§ 229.301 of this chapter).

(9) *Pro forma selected financial data.* If material, the information required by Item 301 of Regulation S-K (§ 229.301 of this chapter) for the acquiring company, showing the pro forma effect of the transaction.

(10) *Pro forma information.* In a table designed to facilitate comparison, historical and pro forma per share data of the acquiring company and historical and equivalent pro forma per share data of the target company for the following Items:

(i) Book value per share as of the date financial data is presented pursuant to Item 301 of Regulation S-K (§ 229.301 of this chapter);

(ii) Cash dividends declared per share for the periods for which financial data is presented pursuant to Item 301 of Regulation S-K (§ 229.301 of this chapter); and

(iii) Income (loss) per share from continuing operations for the periods for which financial data is presented pursuant to Item 301 of Regulation S-K (§ 229.301 of this chapter).

Instructions to paragraphs (b)(8), (b)(9) and (b)(10):

1. For a business combination accounted for as a purchase, present the financial information required by paragraphs (b)(9) and (b)(10) only for the most recent fiscal year and interim period. For a combination under common control, present the financial information required by paragraphs (b)(9) and (b)(10) (except for information with regard to book value) for the most recent three fiscal years and interim period. For purposes of these paragraphs, book value information need only be provided for the most recent balance sheet date.

2. Calculate the equivalent pro forma per share amounts for one share of the company being acquired by multiplying the exchange ratio times each of:

(i) The pro forma income (loss) per share before non-recurring charges or credits directly attributable to the transaction;

(ii) The pro forma book value per share; and

(iii) The pro forma dividends per share of the acquiring company.

3. Unless registered on a national securities exchange or otherwise required to furnish such information, registered investment companies need not furnish the information required by paragraphs (b)(8) and (b)(9) of this Item.

(11) *Financial information.* If material, financial information required by Article 11 of Regulation S-X (§§ 210.10-01 through 229.11-03 of this chapter) with respect to this transaction.

Instructions to paragraph (b)(11):

1. Present any Article 11 information required with respect to transactions other than those being voted upon (where not incorporated by reference) together with the pro forma information relating to the transaction being voted upon. In presenting this information, you must clearly distinguish between the transaction being voted upon and any other transaction.

2. If current pro forma financial information with respect to all other transactions is incorporated by reference, you need only present the pro forma effect of this transaction.

(c) *Information about the parties to the transaction.*

(1) *Acquiring company.* Furnish the information required by Part B (Registrant Information) of Form S-4 (§ 239.25 of this chapter) or Form F-4 (§ 239.34 of this chapter), as applicable, for the acquiring company. However, financial statements need only be presented for the latest two fiscal years and interim periods.

(2) *Acquired company.* Furnish the information required by Part C (Information with Respect to the Company Being Acquired) of Form S-4 (§ 239.25 of this chapter) or Form F-4 (§ 239.34 of this chapter), as applicable.

(d) *Information about parties to the transaction: registered investment companies and business development companies.*

If the acquiring company or the acquired company is an investment company registered under the Investment Company Act of 1940 or a business development company as defined by Section 2(a) (48) of the Investment Company Act of 1940, provide the following information for that company instead of the information specified by paragraph (c) of this Item:

(1) Information required by Item 101 of Regulation S-K (§ 229.101 of this chapter), description of business;

(2) Information required by Item 102 of Regulation S-K (§ 229.102 of this chapter), description of property;

(3) Information required by Item 103 of Regulation S-K (§ 229.103 of this chapter), legal proceedings;

(4) Information required by Item 201(a), (b) and (c) of Regulation S-K (§ 229.201(a), (b) and (c) of this chapter), market price of and dividends on the registrant's common equity and related stockholder matters;

(5) Financial statements meeting the requirements of Regulation S-X, including financial information required by Rule 3-05 and Article 11 of Regulation S-X (§ 210.3-05 and § 210.11-01 through § 210.11-03 of this chapter) with respect to transactions other than that as to which action is to be taken as described in this proxy statement;

(6) Information required by Item 301 of Regulation S-K (§ 229.301 of this chapter), selected financial data;

(7) Information required by Item 302 of Regulation S-K (§ 229.302 of this chapter), supplementary financial information;

(8) Information required by Item 303 of Regulation S-K (§ 229.303 of this chapter), management's discussion and analysis of financial condition and results of operations; and

(9) Information required by Item 304 of Regulation S-K (§ 229.304 of this chapter), changes in and disagreements with accountants on accounting and financial disclosure.

Instruction to paragraph (d) of Item 14: Unless registered on a national securities exchange or otherwise required to furnish such information, registered investment companies need not furnish the information required by paragraphs (d)(6), (d)(7) and (d)(8) of this Item.

(e) *Incorporation by reference.*

(1) The information required by paragraph (c) of this section may be incorporated by reference into the proxy statement to the same extent as would be permitted by Form S-4 (§ 239.25 of this chapter) or Form F-4 (§ 239.34 of this chapter), as applicable.

(2) Alternatively, the registrant may incorporate by reference into the proxy statement the information required by paragraph (c) of this Item if it is contained in an annual report sent to security holders in accordance with § 240.14a-3 of this chapter with respect to the same meeting or solicitation of consents or authorizations that the proxy statement relates to and the information substantially meets the disclosure requirements of Item 14 or Item 17 of Form S-4 (§ 239.25 of this chapter) or Form F-4 (§ 239.34 of this chapter), as applicable.

Item 15. Acquisition or Disposition of Property

If action is to be taken with respect to the acquisition or disposition of any property, furnish the following information:

(a) Describe briefly the general character and location of the property.

(b) State the nature and amount of consideration to be paid or received by the registrant or any subsidiary. To the extent practicable, outline briefly the facts bearing upon the question of the fairness of the consideration.

(c) State the name and address of the transferer or transferee, as the case may be and the nature of any material relationship of such person to the registrant or any affiliate of the registrant.

(d) Outline briefly any other material features of the contract or transaction.

Item 16. Restatement of Accounts

If action is to be taken with respect to the restatement of any asset, capital, or surplus account of the registrant, furnish the following information:

(a) State the nature of the restatement and the date as of which it is to be effective.

(b) Outline briefly the reasons for the restatement and for the selection of the particular effective date.

(c) State the name and amount of each account (including any reserve accounts) affected by the restatement and the effect of the restatement thereon. Tabular presentation of the amounts shall be made when appropriate, particularly in the case of recapitalizations.

(d) To the extent practicable, state whether and the extent, if any, to which the restatement will, as of the date thereof, alter the amount available for distribution to the holders of equity securities.

Item 17. Action with Respect to Reports

If action is to be taken with respect to any report of the registrant or of its directors, officers or committees or any minutes of a meeting of its security holders furnish the following information:

(a) State whether or not such action is to constitute approval or disapproval of any of the matters referred to in such reports or minutes.

(b) Identify each of such matters which it is intended will be approved or disapproved, and furnish the information required by the appropriate item or items of this schedule with respect to each such matter.

Item 18. Matters Not Required to Be Submitted

If action is to be taken with respect to any matter which is not required to be submitted to a vote of security holders, state the nature of such matter, the reasons for submitting it to a vote of security holders and what action is intended to be taken by the registrant in the event of a negative vote on the matter by the security holders.

Item 19. Amendment of Charter, bylaws or Other Documents

If action is to be taken with respect to any amendment of the registrant's charter, bylaws or other documents as to which information is not required above, state briefly the reasons for and the general effect of such amendment.

Instructions. 1. Where the matter to be acted upon is the classification of directors, state whether vacancies which occur during the year may be filled by the board of directors to serve only until the next annual meeting or may be so filled for the remainder of the full term.

2. Attention is directed to the discussion of disclosure regarding anti-takeover and similar proposals in Release No. 34-15230 (October 13, 1978).

Item 20. Other Proposed Action

If action is to be taken on any matter not specifically referred to in this Schedule 14A, describe briefly the substance of each such matter in substantially the same degree of detail as is required by Items 5 to 19, inclusive, of this Schedule, and, with respect to investment companies registered under the Investment Company Act of 1940, Item 22 of this Schedule. Registrants required to provide a separate shareholder vote pursuant to section 111(e)(1) of the Emergency Economic Stabilization Act of 2008 (12 U.S.C. 5221(e)(1)) and § 240.14a-20 shall disclose that they are providing such a vote as required pursuant to the Emergency Economic Stabilization Act of 2008, and briefly explain the general effect of the vote, such as whether the vote is nonbinding.

Item 21. Voting procedures

As to each matter which is to be submitted to a vote of security holders, furnish the following information:

(a) State the vote required for approval or election, other than for the approval of auditors.

(b) Disclose the method by which votes will be counted, including the treatment and effect of abstentions and broker non-votes under applicable state law as well as registrant charter and by-law provisions.

Item 22. Information Required in Investment Company Proxy Statement

(a) *General*.

(1) *Definitions*. Unless the context otherwise requires, terms used in this Item that are defined in § 240.14a-1 (with respect to proxy soliciting material), in § 240.14c-1 (with respect to information statements), and in the Investment Company Act of 1940 shall have the same meanings provided therein and the following terms shall also apply:

(i) *Administrator*. The term "Administrator" shall mean any person who provides significant administrative or business affairs management services to a Fund.

(ii) *Affiliated Broker*. The term "Affiliated Broker" shall mean any broker:

(A) That is an affiliated person of the Fund;

(B) That is an affiliated person of such person; or

(C) An affiliated person of which is an affiliated person of the Fund, its investment adviser, principal underwriter, or Administrator.

(iii) *Distribution Plan*. The term "Distribution Plan" shall mean a plan adopted pursuant to Rule 12b-1 under the Investment Company Act of 1940 (§ 270.12b-1 of this chapter).

(iv) *Family of Investment Companies*. The term "Family of Investment Companies" shall mean any two or more registered investment companies that:

(A) Share the same investment adviser or principal underwriter; and

(B) Hold themselves out to investors as related companies for purposes of investment and investor services.

(v) *Fund*. The term "Fund" shall mean a Registrant or, where the Registrant is a series company, a separate portfolio of the Registrant.

(vi) *Fund Complex*. The term "Fund Complex" shall mean two or more Funds that:

(A) Hold themselves out to investors as related companies for purposes of investment and investor services; or

(B) Have a common investment adviser or have an investment adviser that is an affiliated person of the investment adviser of any of the other Funds.

(vii) *Immediate Family Member*. The term "Immediate Family Member" shall mean a person's spouse; child residing in the person's household (including step and adoptive children); and any dependent of the person, as defined in section 152 of the Internal Revenue Code (26 U.S.C. 152).

(viii) *Officer*. The term "Officer" shall mean the president, vice-president, secretary, treasurer, controller, or any other officer who performs policy-making functions.

(ix) *Parent*. The term "Parent" shall mean the affiliated person of a specified person who controls the specified person directly or indirectly through one or more intermediaries.

(x) *Registrant*. The term "Registrant" shall mean an investment company registered under the Investment Company Act of 1940 (15 U.S.C. 80a) or a business development company as defined by section 2(a)(48) of the Investment Company Act of 1940 (15 U.S.C. 80a-2(a)(48)).

(xi) *Sponsoring Insurance Company*. The term "Sponsoring Insurance Company" of a Fund that is a separate account shall mean the insurance company that establishes and maintains the separate account and that owns the assets of the separate account.

(xii) *Subsidiary*. The term "Subsidiary" shall mean an affiliated person of a specified person who is controlled by the specified person directly, or indirectly through one or more intermediaries.

(2) [Removed and reserved in Release No. 34-37692, effective October 7, 1996, 61 F.R. 49957.]

(3) *General Disclosure*. Furnish the following information in the proxy statement of a Fund or Funds:

(i) State the name and address of the Fund's investment adviser, principal underwriter, and Administrator.

(ii) When a Fund proxy statement solicits a vote on proposals affecting more than one Fund or class of securities of a Fund (unless the proposal or proposals are the same and affect all Fund or class shareholders), present a summary of all of the proposals in tabular form on one of the first three pages of the proxy statement and indicate which Fund or class shareholders are solicited with respect to each proposal.

(iii) Unless the proxy statement is accompanied by a copy of the Fund's most recent annual report, state prominently in the proxy statement that the Fund will furnish, without charge, a copy of the annual report and the most recent semi-annual report succeeding the annual report, if any, to a shareholder upon request providing the name, address, and toll-free telephone number of the person to whom such request shall be directed (or, if no toll-free telephone number is provided, a self-addressed postage paid card for requesting the annual report). The Fund should provide a copy of the annual report and the most recent semi-annual report succeeding the annual report, if any, to the requesting shareholder by first class mail, or other means designed to assure prompt delivery, within three business days of the request.

(iv) If the action to be taken would, directly or indirectly, establish a new fee or expense or increase any existing fee or expense to be paid by the Fund or its shareholders, provide a table showing the current and pro forma fees (with the required examples) using the format prescribed in the appropriate registration statement form under the Investment Company Act of 1940 (for open-end management investment companies, Item 2 of Form N-1A (§ 239.15A);for closed-end management investment companies, Item 3 of Form N-2 (§ 239.14);and for separate accounts that offer variable annuity contracts, Item 4 of Form N-3 (§ 239.17a)).

Instructions. 1. Where approval is sought only for a change in asset breakpoints for a pre-existing fee that would not have increased the fee for the previous year (or have the effect of increasing fees or expenses, but for any other reason would not be reflected in a pro forma fee table), describe the likely effect of the change in lieu of providing pro forma fee information.

2. An action would indirectly establish or increase a fee or expense where, for example, the approval of a new investment advisory contract would result in higher custodial or transfer agency fees.

3. The tables should be prepared in a manner designed to facilitate understanding of the impact of any change in fees or expenses.

4. A Fund that offers its shares exclusively to one or more separate accounts and thus is not required to include a fee table in its prospectus (*see* Item 2(a)(ii) of Form N-1A (§ 239.15A)) should nonetheless prepare a table showing current and pro forma expenses and disclose that the table does not reflect separate account expenses, including sales load.

(v) If action is to be taken with respect to the election of directors or the approval of an advisory contract, describe any purchases or sales of securities of the investment adviser or its Parents, or Subsidiaries of either, since the beginning of the most recently completed fiscal year by any director or any nominee for election as a director of the Fund.

Instructions. 1. Identify the parties, state the consideration, the terms of payment and describe any arrangement or understanding with respect to the composition of the board of directors of the Fund or of the investment adviser, or with respect to the selection of appointment of any person to any office with either such company.

2. Transactions involving securities in an amount not exceeding one percent of the outstanding securities of any class of the investment adviser or any of its Parents or Subsidiaries may be omitted.

(b) *Election of Directors*. If action is to be taken with respect to the election of directors of a Fund, furnish the following information in the proxy statement in addition to, in the case of business development companies, the information (and in the format) required by Item 7 and Item 8 of this Schedule 14A.

Instructions to introductory text of paragraph (b). 1. Furnish information with respect to a prospective investment adviser to the extent applicable.

2. If the solicitation is made by or on behalf of a person other than the Fund or an investment adviser of the Fund, provide information only as to nominees of the person making the solicitation.

3. When providing information about directors and nominees for election as directors in response to this Item 22(b), furnish information for directors or nominees who are or would be "interested persons" of the Fund within the meaning of section 2(a)(19) of the Investment Company Act of 1940 (15 U.S.C. 80a-2(a)(19)) separately from the information for directors or nominees who are not or would not be interested persons of the Fund. For example, when furnishing information in a table, you should provide separate tables (or separate sections of a single table) for directors and nominees who are or would be interested persons and for directors or nominees who are not or would not be interested persons. When furnishing information in narrative form, indicate by heading or otherwise the directors or nominees who are or would be interested persons and the directors or nominees who are not or would not be interested persons.

4. No information need be given about any director whose term of office as a director will not continue after the meeting to which the proxy statement relates.

(1) Provide the information required by the following table for each director, nominee for election as director, Officer of the Fund, person chosen to become an Officer of the Fund, and, if the Fund has an advisory board, member of the board. Explain in a footnote to the table any family relationship between the persons listed.

(1)	(2)	(3)	(4)	(5)	(6)
Name, Addres, and Age	Position(s) Held with Fund	Term of Office and Length of Time Served	Principal Occupation(s) During Past 5 Years	Number of Portfolios in Fund Complex Overseen by Director or Nominee for Director	Other Directorships Held by Director or Nominee for Director

Instructions to paragraph (b)(1). 1. For purposes of this paragraph, the term "family relationship" means any relationship by blood, marriage, or adoption, not more remote than first cousin.

2. No nominee or person chosen to become a director or Officer who has not consented to act as such may be named in response to this Item. In this regard, see Rule 14a-4(d) under the Exchange Act (§ 240.14a-4(d)).

3. If fewer nominees are named than the number fixed by or pursuant to the governing instruments, state the reasons for this procedure and that the proxies cannot be voted for a greater number of persons than the number of nominees named.

4. For each director or nominee for election as director who is or would be an "interested person" of the Fund within the meaning of section 2(a)(19) of the Investment Company Act of 1940 (15 U.S.C. 80a-2(a)(19)), describe, in a footnote or otherwise, the relationship, events, or transactions by reason of which the director or nominee is or would be an interested person.

5. State the principal business of any company listed under column (4) unless the principal business is implicit in its name.

6. Include in column (5) the total number of separate portfolios that a nominee for election as director would oversee if he were elected.

7. Indicate in column (6) directorships not included in column (5) that are held by a director or nominee for election as director in any company with a class of securities

registered pursuant to section 12 of the Exchange Act (15 U.S.C. 78*l*), or subject to the requirements of section 15(d) of the Exchange Act (15 U.S.C. 78o(d)), or any company registered as an investment company under the Investment Company Act of 1940 (15 U.S.C. 80a), as amended, and name the companies in which the directorships are held.

Where the other directorships include directorships overseeing two or more portfolios in the same Fund Complex, identify the Fund Complex and provide the number of portfolios overseen as a director in the Fund Complex rather than listing each portfolio separately.

(2) For each individual listed in column (1) of the table required by paragraph (b)(1) of this Item, except for any director or nominee for election as director who is not or would not be an "interested person" of the Fund within the meaning of section 2(a)(19) of the Investment Company Act of 1940 (15 U.S.C. 80a-2(a)(19)), describe any positions, including as an officer, employee, director, or general partner, held with affiliated persons or principal underwriters of the Fund.

Instruction to paragraph (b)(2). When an individual holds the same position(s) with two or more registered investment companies that are part of the same Fund Complex, identify the Fund Complex and provide the number of registered investment companies for which the position(s) are held rather than listing each registered investment company separately.

(3) (i) For each director or nominee for election as director, briefly discuss the specific experience, qualifications, attributes, or skills that led to the conclusion that the person should serve as a director for the Fund at the time that the disclosure is made in light of the Fund's business and structure. If material, this disclosure should cover more than the past five years, including information about the person's particular areas of expertise or other relevant qualifications.

(ii) Describe briefly any arrangement or understanding between any director, nominee for election as director, Officer, or person chosen to become an Officer, and any other person(s) (naming the person(s)) pursuant to which he was or is to be selected as a director, nominee, or Officer.

Instruction to paragraph (b)(3)(ii). Do not include arrangements or understandings with directors or Officers acting solely in their capacities as such.

(4) (i) Unless disclosed in the table required by paragraph (b)(1) of this Item, describe any positions, including as an officer, employee, director, or general partner, held by any director or nominee for election as director, who is not or would not be an "interested person" of the Fund within the meaning of section 2(a)(19) of the Investment Company Act of 1940 (15 U.S.C. 80a-2(a)(19)), or Immediate Family Member of the director or nominee, during the past five years, with:

(A) The Fund;

(B) An investment company, or a person that would be an investment company but for the exclusions provided by sections 3(c)(1) and 3(c)(7) of the Investment Company Act of 1940 (15 U.S.C. 80a-3(c)(1) and (c)(7)), having the same investment adviser, principal underwriter, or Sponsoring Insurance Company as the Fund or having an investment adviser, principal underwriter, or Sponsoring Insurance Company that directly or indirectly controls, is controlled by, or is under common control with an investment adviser, principal underwriter, or Sponsoring Insurance Company of the Fund;

(C) An investment adviser, principal underwriter, Sponsoring Insurance Company, or affiliated person of the Fund; or

(D) Any person directly or indirectly controlling, controlled by, or under common control with an investment adviser, principal underwriter, or Sponsoring Insurance Company of the Fund.

(ii) Unless disclosed in the table required by paragraph (b)(1) of this Item or in response to paragraph (b)(4)(i) of this Item, indicate any directorships held during the past five years by each director or nominee for election as director in any company with a class of securities registered pursuant to section 12 of the Exchange Act (15 U.S.C. 78l) or subject to the requirements of section 15(d) of the Exchange Act (15 U.S.C. 78o(d)) or any company registered as an investment company under the Investment Company Act of 1940 (15 U.S.C. 80a-1 et seq.), as amended, and name the companies in which the directorships were held.

Instruction to paragraph (b)(4). When an individual holds the same position(s) with two or more portfolios that are part of the same Fund Complex, identify the Fund Complex and provide the number of portfolios for which the position(s) are held rather than listing each portfolio separately.

(5) For each director or nominee for election as director, state the dollar range of equity securities beneficially owned by the director or nominee as required by the following table:

(i) In the Fund; and

(ii) On an aggregate basis, in any registered investment companies overseen or to be overseen by the director or nominee within the same Family of Investment Companies as the Fund.

(1)	*(2)*	*(3)*
Name of Director or Nominee	*Dollar Range of Equity Securities in the Fund*	*Aggregate Dollar Range of Equity Securities in All Funds Overseen or to be Overseen by Director or Nominee in Family of Investment Companies*

Instructions to paragraph (b)(5). 1. Information should be provided as of the most recent practicable date. Specify the valuation date by footnote or otherwise.

2. Determine "beneficial ownership" in accordance with rule 16a-1(a)(2) under the Exchange Act (§ 240.16a-1(a)(2)).

3. If action is to be taken with respect to more than one Fund, disclose in column (2) the dollar range of equity securities beneficially owned by a director or nominee in each such Fund overseen or to be overseen by the director or nominee.

4. In disclosing the dollar range of equity securities beneficially owned by a director or nominee in columns (2) and (3), use the following ranges: none, $1-$10,000, $10,001-$50,000, $50,001-$100,000, or over $100,000.

(6) For each director or nominee for election as director who is not or would not be an "interested person" of the Fund within the meaning of section 2(a)(19) of the Investment Company Act of 1940 (15 U.S.C. 80a-2(a)(19), and his Immediate Family Members, furnish the information required by the following table as to each class of securities owned beneficially or of record in:

(i) An investment adviser, principal underwriter, or Sponsoring Insurance Company of the Fund; or

(ii) A person (other than a registered investment company) directly or indirectly controlling, controlled by, or under common control with an investment adviser, principal underwriter, or Sponsoring Insurance Company of the Fund:

(1)	*(2)*	*(3)*	*(4)*	*(5)*	*(6)*
Name of Director or Nominee	*Name of Owners and Relationships to Director or Nominee*	*Company*	*Title of Class*	*Value of Securities*	*Percent of Class*

Instructions to paragraph (b)(6). 1. Information should be provided as of the most recent practicable date. Specify the valuation date by footnote or otherwise.

2. An individual is a "beneficial owner" of a security if he is a "beneficial owner" under either rule 13d-3 or rule 16a-1(a)(2) under the Exchange Act (§§ 240.13d-3 or 240.16a-1(a)(2)).

3. Identify the company in which the director, nominee, or Immediate Family Member of the director or nominee owns securities in column (3). When the company is a person directly or indirectly controlling, controlled by, or under common control with an investment adviser, principal underwriter, or Sponsoring Insurance Company, describe the company's relationship with the investment adviser, principal underwriter, or Sponsoring Insurance Company.

4. Provide the information required by columns (5) and (6) on an aggregate basis for each director (or nominee) and his Immediate Family Members.

(7) Unless disclosed in response to paragraph (b)(6) of this Item, describe any direct or indirect interest, the value of which exceeds $120,000, of each director or nominee for election as director who is not or would not be an "interested person" of the Fund within the meaning of section 2(a)(19) of the Investment Company Act of 1940 (15 U.S.C. 80a-2(a)(19)), or Immediate Family Member of the director or nominee, during the past five years, in:

(i) An investment adviser, principal underwriter, or Sponsoring Insurance Company of the Fund; or

(ii) A person (other than a registered investment company) directly or indirectly controlling, controlled by, or under common control with an investment adviser, principal underwriter, or Sponsoring Insurance Company of the Fund.

Instructions to paragraph (b)(7). 1. A director, nominee, or Immediate Family Member has an interest in a company if he is a party to a contract, arrangement, or understanding with respect to any securities of, or interest in, the company.

2. The interest of the director (or nominee) and the interests of his Immediate Family Members should be aggregated in determining whether the value exceeds $120,000.

(8) Describe briefly any material interest, direct or indirect, of any director or nominee for election as director who is not or would not be an "interested person" of the Fund within the meaning of section 2(a)(19) of the Investment Company Act of 1940 (15 U.S.C. 80a-2(a)(19)), or Immediate Family Member of the director or nominee, in any transaction, or series of similar transactions, since the beginning of the last two completed fiscal years of the Fund, or in any currently proposed transaction, or series of similar transactions, in which the amount involved exceeds $120,000 and to which any of the following persons was or is to be a party:

(i) The Fund;

(ii) An Officer of the Fund;

(iii) An investment company, or a person that would be an investment company but for the exclusions provided by sections 3(c)(1) and 3(c)(7) of the Investment Company Act of 1940 (15 U.S.C. 80a-3(c)(1) and (c)(7)), having the same investment adviser, principal underwriter, or Sponsoring Insurance Company as the Fund or having an investment adviser, principal underwriter, or Sponsoring Insurance Company that directly or indirectly controls, is controlled by, or is under common control with an investment adviser, principal underwriter, or Sponsoring Insurance Company of the Fund;

(iv) An Officer of an investment company, or a person that would be an investment company but for the exclusions provided by sections 3(c)(1) and 3(c)(7) of the Investment Company Act of 1940 (15 U.S.C. 80a-3(c)(1) and (c)(7)), having the same investment adviser, principal underwriter, or Sponsoring Insurance Company as the Fund or having an investment adviser, principal underwriter, or Sponsoring Insurance Company that directly or indirectly controls, is controlled by, or is under common control with an investment adviser, principal underwriter, or Sponsoring Insurance Company of the Fund;

(v) An investment adviser, principal underwriter, or Sponsoring Insurance Company of the Fund;

(vi) An Officer of an investment adviser, principal underwriter, or Sponsoring Insurance Company of the Fund;

(vii) A person directly or indirectly controlling, controlled by, or under common control with an investment adviser, principal underwriter, or Sponsoring Insurance Company of the Fund; or

(viii) An Officer of a person directly or indirectly controlling, controlled by, or under common control with an investment adviser, principal underwriter, or Sponsoring Insurance Company of the Fund.

Instructions to paragraph (b)(8). 1. Include the name of each director, nominee, or Immediate Family Member whose interest in any transaction or series of similar transactions is described and the nature of the circumstances by reason of which the interest is required to be described.

2. State the nature of the interest, the approximate dollar amount involved in the transaction, and, where practicable, the approximate dollar amount of the interest.

3. In computing the amount involved in the transaction or series of similar transactions, include all periodic payments in the case of any lease or other agreement providing for periodic payments.

4. Compute the amount of the interest of any director, nominee, or Immediate Family Member of the director or nominee without regard to the amount of profit or loss involved in the transaction(s).

5. As to any transaction involving the purchase or sale of assets, state the cost of the assets to the purchaser and, if acquired by the seller within two years prior to the transaction, the cost to the seller. Describe the method used in determining the purchase or sale price and the name of the person making the determination.

6. If the proxy statement relates to multiple portfolios of a series Fund with different fiscal years, then, in determining the date that is the beginning of the last two completed fiscal years of the Fund, use the earliest date of any series covered by the proxy statement.

7. Disclose indirect, as well as direct, material interests in transactions. A person who has a position or relationship with, or interest in, a company that engages in a transaction with one of the persons listed in paragraphs (b)(8)(i) through (b)(8)(viii) of this Item may have an indirect interest in the transaction by reason of the position, relationship, or interest. The interest in the transaction, however, will not be deemed "material" within the meaning of paragraph (b)(8) of this Item where the interest of the director, nominee, or Immediate Family Member arises solely from the holding of an equity interest (including a limited partnership interest, but excluding a general partnership interest) or a creditor interest in a company that is a party to the transaction with one of the persons specified in paragraphs (b)(8)(i) through (b)(8)(viii) of this Item, and the transaction is not material to the company.

8. The materiality of any interest is to be determined on the basis of the significance of the information to investors in light of all the circumstances of the particular case. The importance of the interest to the person having the interest, the relationship of the parties to the transaction with each other, and the amount involved in the transaction are among the factors to be considered in determining the significance of the information to investors.

9. No information need be given as to any transaction where the interest of the director, nominee, or Immediate Family Member arises solely from the ownership of securities of a person specified in paragraphs (b)(8)(i) through (b)(8)(viii) of this Item and the director, nominee, or Immediate Family Member receives no extra or special benefit not shared on a pro rata basis by all holders of the class of securities.

10. Transactions include loans, lines of credit, and other indebtedness. For indebtedness, indicate the largest aggregate amount of indebtedness outstanding at any time during the period, the nature of the indebtedness and the transaction in which it was incurred, the amount outstanding as of the latest practicable date, and the rate of interest paid or charged.

11. No information need be given as to any routine, retail transaction. For example, the Fund need not disclose that a director has a credit card, bank or brokerage account, residential mortgage, or insurance policy with a person specified in paragraphs (b)(8)(i) through (b)(8)(viii) of this Item unless the director is accorded special treatment.

(9) Describe briefly any direct or indirect relationship, in which the amount involved exceeds $120,000, of any director or nominee for election as director who is not or would not be an "interested person" of the Fund within the meaning of section 2(a)(19) of the Investment Company Act of 1940 (15 U.S.C. 80a-2(a)(19)), or Immediate Family Member of the director or nominee, that exists, or has existed at any time since the beginning of the last two completed fiscal years of the Fund, or is currently proposed, with any of the persons specified in paragraphs (b)(8)(i) through (b)(8)(viii) of this Item. Relationships include:

(i) Payments for property or services to or from any person specified in paragraphs (b)(8)(i) through (b)(8)(viii) of this Item;

(ii) Provision of legal services to any person specified in paragraphs (b)(8)(i) through (b)(8)(viii) of this Item;

(iii) Provision of investment banking services to any person specified in paragraphs (b)(8)(i) through (b)(8)(viii) of this Item, other than as a participating underwriter in a syndicate; and

(iv) Any consulting or other relationship that is substantially similar in nature and scope to the relationships listed in paragraphs (b)(9)(i) through (b)(9)(iii) of this Item.

Instructions to paragraph (b)(9). 1. Include the name of each director, nominee, or Immediate Family Member whose relationship is described and the nature of the circumstances by reason of which the relationship is required to be described.

2. State the nature of the relationship and the amount of business conducted between the director, nominee, or Immediate Family Member and the person specified in paragraphs (b)(8)(i) through (b)(8)(viii) of this Item as a result of the relationship since the beginning of the last two completed fiscal years of the Fund or proposed to be done during the Fund's current fiscal year.

3. In computing the amount involved in a relationship, include all periodic payments in the case of any agreement providing for periodic payments.

4. If the proxy statement relates to multiple portfolios of a series Fund with different fiscal years, then, in determining the date that is the beginning of the last two completed fiscal years of the Fund, use the earliest date of any series covered by the proxy statement.

5. Disclose indirect, as well as direct, relationships. A person who has a position or relationship with, or interest in, a company that has a relationship with one of the persons listed in paragraphs (b)(8)(i) through (b)(8)(viii) of this Item may have an indirect relationship by reason of the position, relationship, or interest.

6. In determining whether the amount involved in a relationship exceeds $120,000, amounts involved in a relationship of the director (or nominee) should be aggregated with those of his Immediate Family Members.

7. In the case of an indirect interest, identify the company with which a person specified in paragraphs (b)(8)(i) through (b)(8)(viii) of this Item has a relationship; the name of the director, nominee, or Immediate Family Member affiliated with the company and the nature of the affiliation; and the amount of business conducted between the company and the person specified in paragraphs (b)(8)(i) through (b)(8)(viii) of this Item since the beginning of the last two completed fiscal years of the Fund or proposed to be done during the Fund's current fiscal year.

8. In calculating payments for property and services for purposes of paragraph (b)(9)(i) of this Item, the following may be excluded:

A. Payments where the transaction involves the rendering of services as a common contract carrier, or public utility, at rates or charges fixed in conformity with law or governmental authority; or

B. Payments that arise solely from the ownership of securities of a person specified in paragraphs (b)(8)(i) through (b)(8)(viii) of this Item and no extra or special benefit not shared on a pro rata basis by all holders of the class of securities is received.

9. No information need be given as to any routine, retail relationship. For example, the Fund need not disclose that a director has a credit card, bank or brokerage account,

residential mortgage, or insurance policy with a person specified in paragraphs (b)(8)(i) through (b)(8)(viii) of this Item unless the director is accorded special treatment.

(10) If an Officer of an investment adviser, principal underwriter, or Sponsoring Insurance Company of the Fund, or an Officer of a person directly or indirectly controlling, controlled by, or under common control with an investment adviser, principal underwriter, or Sponsoring Insurance Company of the Fund, serves, or has served since the beginning of the last two completed fiscal years of the Fund, on the board of directors of a company where a director of the Fund or nominee for election as director who is not or would not be an "interested person" of the Fund within the meaning of section 2(a)(19) of the Investment Company Act of 1940 (15 U.S.C. 80a-2(a)(19)), or Immediate Family Member of the director or nominee, is, or was since the beginning of the last two completed fiscal years of the Fund, an Officer, identify:

(i) The company;

(ii) The individual who serves or has served as a director of the company and the period of service as director;

(iii) The investment adviser, principal underwriter, or Sponsoring Insurance Company or person controlling, controlled by, or under common control with the investment adviser, principal underwriter, or Sponsoring Insurance Company where the individual named in paragraph (b)(10)(ii) of this Item holds or held office and the office held; and

(iv) The director of the Fund, nominee for election as director, or Immediate Family Member who is or was an Officer of the company; the office held; and the period of holding the office.

Instruction to paragraph (b)(10). If the proxy statement relates to multiple portfolios of a series Fund with different fiscal years, then, in determining the date that is the beginning of the last two completed fiscal years of the Fund, use the earliest date of any series covered by the proxy statement.

(11) Provide in tabular form, to the extent practicable, the information required by Items 401(f) and (g), 404(a), 405, and 407(h) of Regulation S-K (§§ 229.401(f) and (g), 229.404(a), and 229.405 of this chapter).

Instruction to paragraph (b)(11). Information provided under paragraph (b)(8) of this Item 22 is deemed to satisfy the requirements of Item 404(a) of Regulation S-K for information about directors, nominees for election as directors, and Immediate Family Members of directors and nominees, and need not be provided under this paragraph (b)(11).

(12) Describe briefly any material pending legal proceedings, other than ordinary routine litigation incidental to the Fund's business, to which any director or nominee for director or affiliated person of such director or nominee is a party adverse to the Fund or any of its affiliated persons or has a material interest adverse to the Fund or any of its affiliated persons. Include the name of the court where the case is pending, the date instituted, the principal parties, a description of the factual basis alleged to underlie the proceeding, and the relief sought.

(13) In the case of a Fund that is an investment company registered under the Investment Company Act of 1940 (15 U.S.C. 80a), for all directors, and for each of the three highest-paid Officers that have aggregate compensation from the Fund for the most recently completed fiscal year in excess of $60,000 ("Compensated Persons"):

(i) Furnish the information required by the following table for the last fiscal year:

Compensation Table

(1)	(2)	(3)	(4)	(5)
Name of Person, Position	Aggregate Compensation From Fund	Pension or Retirement Benefits Accrued as Part of Fund Expenses	Estimated Annual Benefits Upon Retirement	Total Compensation From Fund and Fund Complex Paid to Directors

Instructions to paragraph (b)(13)(i). 1. For column (1), indicate, if necessary, the capacity in which the remuneration is received. For Compensated Persons that are directors of the Fund, compensation is amounts received for service as a director.

2. If the Fund has not completed its first full year since its organization, furnish the information for the current fiscal year, estimating future payments that would be made pursuant to an existing agreement or understanding. Disclose in a footnote to the Compensation Table the period for which the information is furnished.

3. Include in column (2) amounts deferred at the election of the Compensated Person, whether pursuant to a plan established under Section 401(k) of the Internal Revenue Code (26 U.S.C. 401(k)) or otherwise, for the fiscal year in which earned. Disclose in a footnote to the Compensation Table the total amount of deferred compensation (including interest) payable to or accrued for any Compensated Person.

4. Include in columns (3) and (4) all pension or retirement benefits proposed to be paid under any existing plan in the event of retirement at normal retirement date, directly or indirectly, by the Fund or any of its Subsidiaries, or by other companies in the Fund Complex. Omit column (4) where retirement benefits are not determinable.

5. For any defined benefit or actuarial plan under which benefits are determined primarily by final compensation (or average final compensation) and years of service, provide the information required in column (4) in a separate table showing estimated annual benefits payable upon retirement (including amounts attributable to any defined benefit supplementary or excess pension award plans) in specified compensation and years of service classifications. Also provide the estimated credited years of service for each Compensated Person.

6. Include in column (5) only aggregate compensation paid to a director for service on the board and other boards of investment companies in a Fund Complex specifying the number of such other investment companies.

(ii) Describe briefly the material provisions of any pension, retirement, or other plan or any arrangement other than fee arrangements disclosed in paragraph (b)(13)(i) of this Item pursuant to which Compensated Persons are or may be compensated for any services provided, including amounts paid, if any, to the Compensated Person under any such arrangements during the most recently completed fiscal year.

Specifically include the criteria used to determine amounts payable under any plan, the length of service or vesting period required by the plan, the retirement age or other event that gives rise to payments under the plan, and whether the payment of benefits is secured or funded by the Fund.

(14) State whether or not the Fund has a separately designated audit committee established in accordance with section 3(a)(58)(A) of the Act (15 U.S.C. 78c(a)(58)(A)). If the entire board of directors is acting as the Fund's audit committee as specified in section 3(a)(58)(B) of the Act (15 U.S.C. 78c(a)(58)(B)), so state. If applicable, provide the disclosure required by § 240.10A-3(d) regarding an exemption from the listing standards for audit committees. Identify the other standing committees of the Fund's board of directors, and provide the following information about each committee, including any separately designated audit committee:

(i) A concise statement of the functions of the committee;

(ii) The members of the committee;

(ii) The members of the committee and, in the case of a nominating committee, whether or not the members of the committee are "interested persons" of the Fund as defined in section 2(a)(19) of the Investment Company Act of 1940 (15 U.S.C. 80a-2(a)(19)); and

(iii) The number of committee meetings held during the last fiscal year.

Instruction to paragraph (b)(14): For purposes of Item 22(b)(14), the term "nominating committee" refers not only to nominating committees and committees performing similar functions, but also to groups of directors fulfilling the role of a nominating committee, including the entire board of directors.

(15) (i) Provide the information (and in the format) required by Items 407(b)(1), (b)(2) and (f) of Regulation S-K (§ 229.407(b)(1), (b)(2) and (f) of this chapter); and

(ii) Provide the following regarding the requirements for the director nomination process:

(A) The information (and in the format) required by Items 407(c)(1) and (c)(2) of Regulation S-K (§ 229.407(c)(1) and (c)(2) of this chapter); and

(B) If the Fund is a listed issuer (as defined in § 240.10A-3 of this chapter) whose securities are listed on a national securities exchange registered pursuant to section 6(a) of the Act (15 U.S.C. 78f(a)) or in an automated inter-dealer quotation system of a national securities association registered pursuant to section 15A of the Act (15 U.S.C. 78o-3(a)) that has independence requirements for nominating committee members, identify each director that is a member of the nominating committee that is not independent under the independence standards described in this paragraph. In determining whether the nominating committee members are independent, use the Fund's definition of independence that it uses for determining if the members of the nominating committee are independent in compliance with the independence standards applicable for the members of the nominating committee in the listing standards applicable to the Fund. If the Fund does not have independence standards for the nominating committee, use the independence standards for the nominating committee in the listing standards applicable to the Fund.

Instruction to paragraph (b)(15)(ii)(B). If the national securities exchange or inter-dealer quotation system on which the Fund's securities are listed has exemptions to the independence requirements for nominating committee members upon which the Fund relied, disclose the exemption relied upon and explain the basis for the Fund's conclusion that such exemption is applicable.

(16) In the case of a Fund that is a closed-end investment company:

(i) Provide the information (and in the format) required by Item 407(d)(1), (d)(2) and (d)(3) of Regulation S-K (§ 229.407(d)(1), (d)(2) and (d)(3) of this chapter); and

(ii) Identify each director that is a member of the Fund's audit committee that is not independent under the independence standards described in this paragraph. If the Fund does not have a separately designated audit committee, or committee performing similar functions, the Fund must provide the disclosure with respect to all members of its board of directors.

(A) If the Fund is a listed issuer (as defined in § 240.10A-3 of this chapter) whose securities are listed on a national securities exchange registered pursuant to section 6(a) of the Act (15 U.S.C. 78f(a)) or in an automated inter-dealer quotation system of a national securities association registered pursuant to section 15A of the Act (15 U.S.C. 78o-3(a)) that has independence requirements for audit committee members, in determining whether the audit committee members are independent, use the Fund's definition of independence that it uses for determining if the members of the audit committee are independent in compliance with the independence standards applicable for the members of the audit committee in the listing standards applicable to the Fund. If the Fund does not have independence standards for the audit committee, use the independence standards for the audit committee in the listing standards applicable to the Fund.

(B) If the Fund is not a listed issuer whose securities are listed on a national securities exchange registered pursuant to section 6(a) of the Act (15 U.S.C. 78f(a)) or in an automated inter-dealer quotation system of a national securities association registered pursuant to section 15A of the Act (15 U.S.C. 78o-3(a)), in determining whether the audit committee members are independent, use a definition of independence of a national securities exchange registered pursuant to section 6(a) of the Act (15 U.S.C. 78f(a)) or an automated inter-dealer quotation system of a national securities association registered pursuant to section 15A of the Act (15 U.S.C. 780-3(a)) which has requirements that a majority of the board of directors be independent and that has been approved by the Commission, and state which definition is used. Whatever such definition the Fund chooses, it must use the same definition with respect to all directors and nominees for director. If the national securities exchange or national securities association whose standards are used has independence standards for the members of the audit committee, use those specific standards.

Instruction to paragraph (b)(16)(ii). If the national securities exchange or inter-dealer quotation system on which the Fund's securities are listed has exemptions to the independence requirements for nominating committee members upon which the Fund relied, disclose the exemption relied upon and explain the basis for the Fund's conclusion that such exemption is applicable. The same disclosure should be provided if the Fund is not a listed issuer and the national securities exchange or inter-dealer quotation system selected by the Fund has exemptions that are applicable to the Fund.

(17) In the case of a Fund that is an investment company registered under the Investment Company Act of 1940 (15 U.S.C. 80a), if a director has resigned or declined to stand for re-election to the board of directors since the date of the last annual meeting of security holders because of a disagreement with the registrant on any matter relating to the registrant's operations, policies or practices, and if the director has furnished the registrant with a letter describing such disagreement and requesting that the matter be disclosed, the registrant shall state the date of resignation or declination to stand for re-election and summarize the director's description of the disagreement. If the registrant believes that the description provided by the director is incorrect or incomplete, it may include a brief statement presenting its view of the disagreement.

(18) If a shareholder nominee or nominees are submitted to the Fund for inclusion in the Fund's proxy materials pursuant to § 240.14a-11 and the Fund is not permitted to exclude the nominee or nominees pursuant to the provisions of § 240.14a-11, the Fund must include in its proxy statement the disclosure required from the nominating shareholder or nominating shareholder group under Item 5 of § 240.14n-101 with regard to the nominee or nominees and the nominating shareholder or nominating shareholder group.

Instruction to Paragraph (b)(18). The information disclosed pursuant to paragraph (b)(18) of this Item will not be deemed incorporated by reference into any filing under the Securities Act of 1933 (15 U.S.C. 77a), the Securities Exchange Act of 1934 (15 U.S.C. 78a), or the Investment Company Act of 1940 (15 U.S.C. 80a-1), except to the extent that the Fund specifically incorporates that information by reference.

(19) If a Fund is required to include a shareholder nominee or nominees submitted to the Fund for inclusion in the Fund's proxy materials pursuant to a procedure set forth under applicable state or foreign law or the Fund's governing documents providing for the inclusion of shareholder director nominees in the Fund's proxy materials, the Fund must include in its proxy statement the disclosure required from the nominating shareholder or nominating shareholder group under Item 6 of § 240.14n-101 with regard to the nominee or nominees and the nominating shareholder or nominating shareholder group.

Instruction to Paragraph (b)(19). The information disclosed pursuant to paragraph (b)(19) of this Item will not be deemed incorporated by reference into any filing under the Securities Act of 1933 (15 U.S.C. 77a), the Securities Exchange Act of 1934 (15 U.S.C. 78a), or the Investment Company Act of 1940 (15 U.S.C. 80a-1), except to the extent that the Fund specifically incorporates that information by reference.

(c) *Approval of Investment Advisory Contract.* If action is to be taken with respect to an investment advisory contract, include the following information in the proxy statement.

Instruction. Furnish information with respect to a prospective investment adviser to the extent applicable (including the name and address of the prospective adviser).

(1) With respect to the existing investment advisory contract:

(i) State the date of the contract and the date on which it was last submitted to a vote of security holders of the Fund, including the purpose of such submission;

(ii) Briefly describe the terms of the contract, including the rate of compensation of the investment adviser;

(iii) State the aggregate amount of the investment adviser's fee and the amount and purpose of any other material payments by the Fund to the investment adviser, or any affiliated person of the investment adviser, during the last fiscal year of the Fund;

(iv) If any person is acting as an investment adviser of the Fund other than pursuant to a written contract that has been approved by the security holders of the company, identify the person and describe the nature of the services and arrangements;

(v) Describe any action taken with respect to the investment advisory contract since the beginning of the Fund's last fiscal year by the board of directors of the Fund (unless described in response to paragraph (c)(1)(vi)) of this Item 22); and

(vi) If an investment advisory contract was terminated or not renewed for any reason, state the date of such termination or non-renewal, identify the parties involved, and describe the circumstances of such termination or non-renewal.

(2) State the name, address and principal occupation of the principal executive officer and each director or general partner of the investment adviser.

Instruction. If the investment adviser is a partnership with more than ten general partners, name:

(i) the general partners with the five largest economic interests in the partnership, and, if different, those general partners comprising the management or executive committee of the partnership or exercising similar authority;

(ii) the general partners with significant management responsibilities relating to the fund.

(3) State the names and addresses of all Parents of the investment adviser and show the basis of control of the investment adviser and each Parent by its immediate Parent.

Instructions. 1. If any person named is a corporation, include the percentage of its voting securities owned by its immediate Parent.

2. If any person named is a partnership, name the general partners having the three largest partnership interests (computed by whatever method is appropriate in the particular case).

(4) If the investment adviser is a corporation and if, to the knowledge of the persons mailing the solicitation or the persons on whose behalf the solicitation is made, any person not named in answer to paragraph (c)(3) of this Item 22 owns, of record or beneficially, ten percent or more of the outstanding voting securities of the investment adviser, indicate that fact and state the name and address of each such person.

(5) Name each officer or director of the Fund who is an officer, employee, director, general partner or shareholder of the investment adviser. As to any officer or director who is not a director or general partner of the investment adviser and who owns securities or has any other material direct or indirect interest in the investment adviser or any other person controlling, controlled by or under common control with the investment adviser, describe the nature of such interest.

(6) Describe briefly and state the approximate amount of, where practicable, any material interest, direct or indirect, of any director of the Fund in any material transactions since the beginning of the most recently completed fiscal year, or in any material proposed transactions, to which the investment adviser of the Fund, any Parent or Subsidiary of the investment adviser (other than another Fund), or any Subsidiary of the Parent of such entities was or is to be a party.

Instructions. 1. Include the name of each person whose interest in any transaction is described and the nature of the relationship by reason of which such interest is required to be described. Where it is not practicable to state the approximate amount of the interest, indicate the appropriate amount involved in the transaction.

2. As to any transaction involving the purchase or sale of assets by or to the investment adviser, state the cost of the assets to the purchaser and the cost thereof to the seller if acquired by the seller within two years prior to the transaction.

3. If the interest of any person arises from the position of the person as a partner in a partnership, the proportionate interest of such person in transactions to which the partnership is a party need not be set forth, but state the amount involved in the transaction with the partnership.

4. No information need be given in response to this paragraph (c)(6) of Item 22 with respect to any transaction that is not related to the business or operations of the Fund and to which neither the Fund nor any of its Parents or Subsidiaries is a party.

(7) Disclose any financial condition of the investment adviser that is reasonably likely to impair the financial ability of the adviser to fulfil its commitment to the fund under the proposed investment advisory contract.

(8) Describe the nature of the action to be taken on the investment advisory contract and the reasons therefor, the terms of the contract to be acted upon, and, if the action is an amendment to, or a replacement of, an investment advisory contract, the material differences between the current and proposed contract.

(9) If a change in the investment advisory fee is sought, state:

(i) The aggregate amount of the investment adviser's fee during the last year;

(ii) The amount that the adviser would have received had the proposed fee been in effect; and

(iii) The difference between the aggregate amounts stated in response to paragraphs (i) and (ii) this item (c)(9) as a percentage of the amount stated in response to paragraph (i) of this item (c)(9).

(10) If the investment adviser acts as such with respect to any other Fund having a similar investment objective, identify and state the size of such other Fund and the rate of the investment adviser's compensation. Also indicate for any Fund identified whether the investment adviser has waived, reduced, or otherwise agreed to reduce its compensation under any applicable contract.

Instruction. Furnish the information in response to this paragraph (c)(10) of Item 22 in tabular form.

(11) Discuss in reasonable detail the material factors and the conclusions with respect thereto that form the basis for the recommendation of the board of directors that the shareholders approve an investment advisory contract. Include the following in the discussion:

(i) Factors relating to both the board's selection of the investment adviser and approval of the advisory fee and any other amounts to be paid by the Fund under the contract. This would include, but not be limited to, a discussion of the nature, extent, and quality of the services to be provided by the investment adviser; the investment performance of the Fund and the investment adviser; the costs of the services to be provided and profits to be realized by the investment adviser and its affiliates from the relationship with the Fund; the extent to which economies of scale would be realized as the Fund grows; and whether fee levels reflect these economies of scale for the benefit of Fund investors. Also indicate in the discussion whether the board relied upon comparisons of the services to be rendered and the amounts to be paid under the contract with those under other investment advisory contracts, such as contracts of the same and other investment advisers with other registered investment companies or other types of clients (*e.g.*, pension funds and other institutional investors). If the board relied upon such comparisons, describe the comparisons that were relied on and how they assisted the board in determining to recommend that the shareholders approve the advisory contract; and

(ii) If applicable, any benefits derived or to be derived by the investment adviser from the relationship with the Fund such as soft dollar arrangements by which brokers provide research to the Fund or its investment adviser in return for allocating Fund brokerage.

Instructions. 1. Conclusory statements or a list of factors will not be considered sufficient disclosure. Relate the factors to the specific circumstances of the Fund and the investment advisory contract for which approval is sought and state how the board evaluated each factor. For example, it is not sufficient to state that the board considered the amount of the investment advisory fee without stating what the board concluded about the amount of the fee and how that affected its determination to recommend approval of the contract.

2. If any factor enumerated in paragraph (c)(11)(i) of this Item 22 is not relevant to the board's evaluation of the investment advisory contract for which approval is sought, note this and explain the reasons why that factor is not relevant.

(12) Describe any arrangement or understanding made in connection with the proposed investment advisory contract with respect to the composition of the board of directors of the Fund or the investment adviser or with respect to the selection or appointment of any person to any office with either such company.

(13) For the most recently completed fiscal year, state:

(i) The aggregate amount of commissions paid to any Affiliated Broker; and

(ii) The percentage of the Fund's aggregate brokerage commissions paid to any such Affiliated Broker.

Instruction. Identify each Affiliated Broker and the relationships that cause the broker to be an Affiliated Broker.

(14) Disclose the amount of any fees paid by the Fund to the investment adviser, its affiliated persons or any affiliated person of such person during the most recent fiscal year for services provided to the Fund (other than under the investment advisory contract or for brokerage commissions). State whether these services will continue to be provided after the investment advisory contract is approved.

(d) *Approval of Distribution Plan*. If action is to be taken with respect to a Distribution Plan, include the following information in the proxy statement.

Instruction. Furnish information on a prospective basis to the extent applicable.

(1) Describe the nature of the action to be taken on the Distribution Plan and the reason therefor, the terms of the Distribution Plan to be acted upon, and, if the action is an amendment to, or a replacement of, a Distribution Plan, the material differences between the current and proposed Distribution Plan.

(2) If the Fund has a Distribution Plan in effect:

(i) Provide the date that the Distribution Plan was adopted and the date of the last amendment, if any;

(ii) Disclose the persons to whom payments may be made under the Distribution Plan, the rate of the distribution fee and the purposes for which such fee may be used;

(iii) Disclose the amount of distribution fees paid by the Fund pursuant to the plan during its most recent fiscal year, both in the aggregate and as a percentage of the Fund's average net assets during the period;

(iv) Disclose the name of, and the amount of any payments made under the Distribution Plan by the Fund during its most recent fiscal year to, any person who is an affiliated person of the Fund, its investment adviser, principal underwriter, or Administrator, an affiliated person of such person, or a person that during the most recent fiscal year received 10% or more of the aggregate amount paid under the Distribution Plan by the Fund;

(v) Describe any action taken with respect to the Distribution Plan since the beginning of the Fund's most recent fiscal year by the board of directors of the Fund; and

(vi) If a Distribution Plan was or is to be terminated or not renewed for any reason, state the date or prospective date of such termination or non-renewal, identify the parties involved, and describe the circumstances of such termination or non-renewal.

(3) Describe briefly and state the approximate amount of, where practicable, any material interest, direct or indirect, of any director or nominee for election as a director of the Fund in any material transactions since the beginning of the most recently completed fiscal year, or in any material proposed transactions, to which any person identified in response to Item 22(d)(2)(iv) was or is to be a party.

Instructions. 1. Include the name of each person whose interest in any transaction is described and the nature of the relationship by reason of which such interest is required to be described. Where it is not practicable to state the approximate amount of the interest, indicate the approximate amount involved in the transaction.

2. As to any transaction involving the purchase or sale of assets, state the cost of the assets to the purchaser and the cost thereof to the seller if acquired by the seller within two years prior to the transaction.

3. If the interest of any person arises from the position of the person as a partner in a partnership, the proportionate interest of such person in transactions to which the partnership is a party need not be set forth but state the amount involved in the transaction with the partnership.

4. No information need be given in response to this paragraph (d)(3) of Item 22 with respect to any transaction that is not related to the business or operations of the Fund and to which neither the Fund nor any of its Parents or Subsidiaries is a party.

(4) Discuss in reasonable detail the material factors and the conclusions with respect thereto which form the basis for the conclusion of the board of directors that there is a reasonable likelihood that the proposed Distribution Plan (or amendment thereto) will benefit the Fund and its shareholders.

Instruction. Conclusory statements or a list of factors will not be considered sufficient disclosure.

Item 23. Delivery of Documents to Security Holders Sharing an Address

If one annual report to security holders, proxy statement, or Notice of Internet Availability of Proxy Materials is being delivered to two or more security holders who share an address in accordance with § 240.14a-3(e)(1), furnish the following information:

(a) State that only one annual report to security holders, proxy statement, or Notice of Internet Availability of Proxy Materials, as applicable, is being delivered to multiple security holders sharing an address unless the registrant has received contrary instructions from one or more of the security holders;

(b) Undertake to deliver promptly upon written or oral request a separate copy of the annual report to security holders, proxy statement, or Notice of Internet Availability of Proxy Materials, as applicable, to a security holder at a shared address to which a single copy of the documents was delivered and provide instructions as to how a security holder can notify the registrant that the security holder wishes to receive a separate copy of an annual report to security holders, proxy statement, or Notice of Internet Availability of Proxy Materials, as applicable;

(c) Provide the phone number and mailing address to which a security holder can direct a notification to the registrant that the security holder wishes to receive a separate annual report to security holders, proxy statement, or Notice of Internet Availability of Proxy Materials, as applicable, in the future; and

(d) Provide instructions how security holders sharing an address can request delivery of a single copy of annual reports to security holders, proxy statements, or Notices of Internet Availability of Proxy Materials if they are receiving multiple copies of annual reports to security holders, proxy statements, or Notices of Internet Availability of Proxy Materials.

Item 24. Shareholder Approval of Executive Compensation.

Registrants required to provide any of the separate shareholder votes pursuant to § 240.14a-21 of this chapter shall disclose that they are providing each such vote as required pursuant to section 14A of the Securities Exchange Act (15 U.S.C. 78n-1), briefly explain the general effect of each vote, such as whether each such vote is nonbinding, and, when applicable, disclose the current frequency of shareholder advisory votes on executive compensation required by Rule 14a-21(a) and when the next such shareholder advisory vote will occur.

Item 25. Exhibits.

Provide the legal opinion required to be filed by Item 402(u)(4)(i) of Regulation S-K (17 CFR 229.402(u)) in an exhibit to this Schedule 14A.

Schedule TO
Tender offer statement pursuant to section 14(d)(1) of the Securities Exchange Act of 1934.

SECURITIES AND EXCHANGE COMMISSION
Washington, D.C. 20549
SCHEDULE TO

Tender Offer Statement under Section 14(d)(1) or 13(e)(1) of the Securities Exchange Act of 1934

(Amendment No. __)*

_____

(Name of Subject Company (issuer))

_____

(Names of Filing Persons (identifying status as offeror, issuer or other person))

_____

(Title of Class of Securities)

_____

(CUSIP Number of Class of Securities)

(Name, address, and telephone numbers of person authorized to receive notices and communications on behalf of filing persons)

Calculation of Filing Fee

Transaction valuation*	Amount of filing fee

* Set forth the amount on which the filing fee is calculated and state how it was determined.

[ ] Check the box if any part of the fee is offset as provided by Rule 0-11(a)(2) and identify the filing with which the offsetting fee was previously paid. Identify the previous filing by registration statement number, or the Form or Schedule and the date of its filing.

Amount Previously Paid:_____

Form or Registration No.:_____

Filing Party:_____

Date Filed:_____

[ ] Check the box if the filing relates solely to preliminary communications made before the commencement of a tender offer.

Check the appropriate boxes below to designate any transactions to which the statement relates:

[ ] third-party tender offer subject to Rule 14d-1.

[ ] issuer tender offer subject to Rule 13e-4.

[ ] going-private transaction subject to Rule 13e-3.

[ ] amendment to Schedule 13D under Rule 13d-2.

Check the following box if the filing is a final amendment reporting the results of the tender offer:[ ]

If applicable, check the appropriate box(es) below to designate the appropriate rule provision(s) relied upon:

[ ] Rule 13e-4(i) (Cross-Border Issuer Tender Offer)

[ ] Rule 14d-1(d) (Cross-Border Third-Party Tender Offer)

General Instructions:

A. File eight copies of the statement, including all exhibits, with the Commission if paper filing is permitted.

B. This filing must be accompanied by a fee payable to the Commission as required by §240.0-11.

C. If the statement is filed by a general or limited partnership, syndicate or other group, the information called for by Items 3 and 5—8 for a third-party tender offer and Items 5—8 for an issuer tender offer must be given with respect to: (i) each partner of the general partnership; (ii) each partner who is, or functions as, a general partner of the limited partnership; (iii) each member of the syndicate or group; and (iv) each person controlling the partner or member. If the statement is filed by a corporation or if a person referred to in (i), (ii), (iii) or (iv) of this Instruction is a corporation, the information called for by the items specified above must be given with respect to: (a) each executive officer and director of the corporation; (b) each person controlling the corporation; and (c) each executive officer and director of any corporation or other person ultimately in control of the corporation.

D. If the filing contains only preliminary communications made before the commencement of a tender offer, no signature or filing fee is required. The filer need not respond to the items in the schedule. Any pre-commencement communications that are filed under cover of this schedule need not be incorporated by reference into the schedule.

E. If an item is inapplicable or the answer is in the negative, so state. The statement published, sent or given to security holders may omit negative and not applicable responses. If the schedule includes any information that is not published, sent or given to security holders, provide that information or specifically incorporate it by reference under the appropriate item number and heading in the schedule. Do not recite the text of disclosure requirements in the schedule or any document published, sent or given to security holders. Indicate clearly the coverage of the requirements without referring to the text of the items.

F. Information contained in exhibits to the statement may be incorporated by reference in answer or partial answer to any item unless it would render the answer misleading, incomplete, unclear or confusing. A copy of any information that is incorporated by reference or a copy of the pertinent pages of a document containing the information must be submitted with this statement as an exhibit, unless it was previously filed with the Commission electronically on EDGAR. If an exhibit contains information responding to more than one item in the schedule, all information in that exhibit may be incorporated by reference once in response to the several items in the schedule for which it provides an answer. Information incorporated by reference is deemed filed with the Commission for all purposes of the Act.

G. A filing person may amend its previously filed Schedule 13D (§240.13d-101) on Schedule TO (§240.14d-100) if the appropriate box on the cover page is checked to indicate a combined filing and the information called for by the fourteen disclosure items on the cover page of Schedule 13D (§240.13d-101) is provided on the cover page of the combined filing with respect to each filing person.

H. The final amendment required by §240.14d-3(b)(2) and §240.13e-4(c)(4) will satisfy the reporting requirements of section 13(d) of the Act with respect to all securities acquired by the offeror in the tender offer.

I. Amendments disclosing a material change in the information set forth in this statement may omit any information previously disclosed in this statement.

J. If the tender offer disclosed on this statement involves a going-private transaction, a combined Schedule TO (§ 240.14d-100) and Schedule 13E-3 (§ 240.13e-100) may be filed with the Commission under cover of Schedule TO. The Rule 13e-3 box on the cover page of the Schedule TO must be checked to indicate a combined filing. All information called for by both schedules must be provided except that Items 1†3, 5, 8 and 9 of Schedule TO may be omitted to the extent those items call for information that duplicates the item requirements in Schedule 13E-3.

K. For purposes of this statement, the following definitions apply:

(1) The term *offeror* means any person who makes a tender offer or on whose behalf a tender offer is made;

(2) The term *issuer tender offer* has the same meaning as in Rule 13e-4(a)(2); and

(3) The term *third-party tender offer* means a tender offer that is not an issuer tender offer.

Special Instructions for Complying with Schedule TO:

Under Sections 13(e), 14(d) and 23 of the Act and the rules and regulations of the Act, the Commission is authorized to solicit the information required to be supplied by this schedule.

Disclosure of the information specified in this schedule is mandatory. The information will be used for the primary purpose of disclosing tender offer and going-private transactions. This statement will be made a matter of public record. Therefore, any information given will be available for inspection by any member of the public.

Because of the public nature of the information, the Commission can use it for a variety of purposes, including referral to other governmental authorities or securities self-regulatory organizations for investigatory purposes or in connection with litigation involving the Federal securities laws or other civil, criminal or regulatory statutes or provisions. I.R.S. identification numbers, if furnished, will assist the Commission in identifying security holders and, therefore, in promptly processing tender offer and going-private statements.

Failure to disclose the information required by this schedule, except for I.R.S. identification numbers, may result in civil or criminal action against the persons involved for violation of the Federal securities laws and rules.

Item 1. *Summary Term Sheet.*

Furnish the information required by Item 1001 of Regulation M-A (§ 229.1001 of this chapter) unless information is disclosed to security holders in a prospectus that meets the requirements of § 230.421(d) of this chapter.

Item 2. *Subject Company Information.*

Furnish the information required by Item 1002(a) through (c) of Regulation M-A (§ 229.1002 of this chapter).

Item 3. *Identity and Background of Filing Person.*

Furnish the information required by Item 1003(a) through (c) of Regulation M-A (§ 229.1003 of this chapter) for a third-party tender offer and the information required by Item 1003(a) of Regulation M-A (§ 229.1003 of this chapter) for an issuer tender offer.

Item 4. *Terms of the Transaction.*

Furnish the information required by Item 1004(a) of Regulation M-A (§ 229.1004 of this chapter) for a third-party tender offer and the information required by Item 1004(a) through (b) of Regulation M-A (§ 229.1004 of this chapter) for an issuer tender offer.

Item 5. *Past Contacts, Transactions, Negotiations and Agreements.*

Furnish the information required by Item 1005(a) and (b) of Regulation M-A (§ 229.1005 of this chapter) for a third-party tender offer and the information required by Item 1005(e) of Regulation M-A (§ 229.1005) for an issuer tender offer.

Item 6. *Purposes of the Transaction and Plans or Proposals.*

Furnish the information required by Item 1006(a) and (c)(1) through (7) of Regulation M-A (§ 229.1006 of this chapter) for a third-party tender offer and the information required by Item 1006(a) through (c) of Regulation M-A (§ 229.1006 of this chapter) for an issuer tender offer.

Item 7. *Source and Amount of Funds or Other Consideration.*

Furnish the information required by Item 1007(a), (b) and (d) of Regulation M-A (§ 229.1007 of this chapter).

Item 8. *Interest in Securities of the Subject Company.*

Furnish the information required by Item 1008 of Regulation M-A (§ 229.1008 of this chapter).

Item 9. *Persons/Assets, Retained, Employed, Compensated or Used.*

Furnish the information required by Item 1009(a) of Regulation M-A (§ 229.1009 of this chapter).

Item 10. *Financial Statements.*

If material, furnish the information required by Item 1010(a) and (b) of Regulation M-A (§ 229.1010 of this chapter) for the issuer in an issuer tender offer and for the offeror in a third-party tender offer.

Instructions to Item 10:

1. Financial statements must be provided when the offeror's financial condition is material to security holder's decision whether to sell, tender or hold the securities sought. The facts and circumstances of a tender offer, particularly the terms of the tender offer, may influence a determination as to whether financial statements are material, and thus required to be disclosed.

2. Financial statements are *not* considered material when: (a) the consideration offered consists solely of cash; (b) the offer is not subject to any financing condition; *and* either: (c) the offeror is a public reporting company under Section 13(a) or 15(d) of the Act that files reports electronically on EDGAR, or (d) the offer is for all outstanding securities of the subject class. Financial information may be required, however, in a two-tier transaction. *See* Instruction 5 below.

3. The filing person may incorporate by reference financial statements contained in any document filed with the Commission, solely for the purposes of this schedule, if: (a) the financial statements substantially meet the requirements of this item; (b) an express statement is made that the financial statements are incorporated by reference; (c) the information incorporated by reference is clearly identified by page, paragraph, caption or otherwise;and (d) if the information incorporated by reference is not filed with this schedule, an indication is made where the information may be inspected and copies obtained. Financial statements that are required to be presented in comparative form for two or more fiscal years or periods may not be incorporated by reference unless the material incorporated by reference includes the entire period for which the comparative data is required to be given. *See* General Instruction F to this schedule.

4. If the offeror in a third-party tender offer is a natural person, and such person's financial information is material, disclose the net worth of the offeror. If the offeror's net worth is derived from material amounts of assets that are not readily marketable or there are material guarantees and contingencies, disclose the nature and approximate amount of the individual's net worth that consists of illiquid assets and the magnitude of any guarantees or contingencies that may negatively affect the natural person's net worth.

5. Pro forma financial information is required in a negotiated third-party cash tender offer when securities are intended to be offered in a subsequent merger or other transaction in which remaining target securities are acquired and the acquisition of the subject company is significant to the offeror under § 210.11-01(b)(1) of this chapter. The offeror must disclose the financial information specified in Item 3(f) and Item 5 of Form S-4 (§ 239.25 of this chapter) in the schedule filed with the Commission, but may furnish only the summary financial information specified in Item 3(d), (e) and (f) of Form S-4 in the disclosure document sent to security holders. If pro forma financial information is required by this instruction, the historical financial statements specified in Item 1010 of Regulation M-A (§ 229.1010 of this chapter) are required for the bidder.

6. The disclosure materials disseminated to security holders may contain the summarized financial information specified by Item 1010(c) of Regulation M-A (§ 229.1010 of this chapter) instead of the financial information required by Item 1010(a) and (b). In that case, the financial information required by Item 1010(a) and (b) of Regulation M-A must be disclosed in the statement. If summarized financial information is disseminated to security holders, include appropriate instructions on how more complete financial information can be obtained. If the summarized financial information is prepared on the basis of a comprehensive body of accounting principles other than U.S. GAAP, the summarized financial information must be accompanied by a reconciliation as described in Instruction 8 of this Item.

7. If the offeror is not subject to the periodic reporting requirements of the Act, the financial statements required by this Item need not be audited if audited financial statements are not available or obtainable without unreasonable cost or expense. Make a statement to that effect and the reasons for their unavailability.

8. If the financial statements required by this Item are prepared on the basis of a comprehensive body of accounting principles other than U.S. GAAP, provide a reconciliation to U.S. GAAP in accordance with Item 17 of Form 20-F (§ 249.220f of this chapter), unless a reconciliation is unavailable or not obtainable without unreasonable cost or expense. At a minimum, however, when financial statements are prepared on a basis other than U.S. GAAP, a narrative description of all material variations in accounting principles, practices and methods used in preparing the non-U.S. GAAP financial statements from those accepted in the U.S. must be presented.

Item 11. *Additional Information.*

Furnish the information required by Item 1011(a) and (c) of Regulation M-A (§ 229.1011 of this chapter).

Item 12. *Exhibits.*

File as an exhibit to the Schedule all documents specified by Item 1016(a), (b), (d), (g) and (h) of Regulation M-A (§ 229.1016 of this chapter).

Item 13. *Information Required by Schedule 13E-3.*

If the Schedule TO is combined with Schedule 13E-3 (§ 240.13e-100), set forth the information required by Schedule 13E-3 that is not included or covered by the items in Schedule TO.

Signature

After due inquiry and to the best of my knowledge and belief, I certify that the information set forth in this statement is true, complete and correct.

_____

(Signature)

_____

(Name and title)

_____

(Date)

Instruction to Signature: The statement must be signed by the filing person or that person's authorized representative. If the statement is signed on behalf of a person by an authorized representative (other than an executive officer of a corporation or general partner of a partnership), evidence of the representative's authority to sign on behalf of the person must be filed with the statement. The name and any title of each person who signs the statement must be typed or printed beneath the signature. See §§ 240.12b-11 and 240.14d-1(h) with respect to signature requirements.

Schedule 14D-9
Solicitation/Recommendation Statement under Section 14(d)(4) of the Securities Exchange Act of 1934

SECURITIES AND EXCHANGE COMMISSION
Washington, D.C. 20549
SCHEDULE 14D-9

Solicitation/Recommendation Statement under Section 14(d)(4) of the Securities Exchange Act of 1934

(Amendment No.__)

_____

(Name of Subject Company)

_____

(Names of Persons Filing Statement)

_____

(Title of Class of Securities)

_____

(CUSIP Number of Class of Securities)

_____

(Name, address, and telephone numbers of person authorized to receive notices and communications on behalf of the persons filing statement)

[ ] Check the box if the filing relates solely to preliminary communications made before the commencement of a tender offer.

General Instructions

A. File eight copies of the statement, including all exhibits, with the Commission if paper filing is permitted.

B. If the filing contains only preliminary communications made before the commencement of a tender offer, no signature is required. The filer need not respond to the items in the schedule. Any pre-commencement communications that are filed under cover of this schedule need not be incorporated by reference into the schedule.

C. If an item is inapplicable or the answer is in the negative, so state. The statement published, sent or given to security holders may omit negative and not applicable responses. If the schedule includes any information that is not published, sent or given to security holders, provide that information or specifically incorporate it by reference under the appropriate item number and heading in the schedule. Do not recite the text of disclosure requirements in the schedule or any document published, sent or given to security holders. Indicate clearly the coverage of the requirements without referring to the text of the items.

D. Information contained in exhibits to the statement may be incorporated by reference in answer or partial answer to any item unless it would render the answer misleading, incomplete, unclear or confusing. A copy of any information that is incorporated by reference or a copy of the pertinent pages of a document containing the information must be submitted with this statement as an exhibit, unless it was previously filed with the Commission electronically on EDGAR. If an exhibit contains information responding to more than one item in the schedule, all information in that exhibit may be incorporated by reference once in response to the several items in the schedule for which it provides an answer. Information incorporated by reference is deemed filed with the Commission for all purposes of the Act.

E. Amendments disclosing a material change in the information set forth in this statement may omit any information previously disclosed in this statement.

Item 1. *Subject Company Information.*

Furnish the information required by Item 1002(a) and (b) of Regulation M-A (§ 229.1002 of this chapter).

Item 2. *Identity and Background of Filing Person.*

Furnish the information required by Item 1003(a) and (d) of Regulation M-A (§ 229.1003 of this chapter).

Item 3. *Past Contacts, Transactions, Negotiations and Agreements.*

Furnish the information required by Item 1005(d) of Regulation M-A (§ 229.1005 of this chapter).

Item 4. *The Solicitation or Recommendation.*

Furnish the information required by Item 1012(a) through (c) of Regulation M-A (§ 229.1012 of this chapter).

Item 5. *Person/Assets, Retained, Employed, Compensated or Used.*

Furnish the information required by Item 1009(a) of Regulation M-A (§ 229.1009 of this chapter).

Item 6. *Interest in Securities of the Subject Company.*

Furnish the information required by Item 1008(b) of Regulation M-A (§ 229.1008 of this chapter).

Item 7. *Purposes of the Transaction and Plans or Proposals.*

Furnish the information required by Item 1006(d) of Regulation M-A (§ 229.1006 of this chapter).

Item 8. *Additional Information.*

Furnish the information required by Item 1011(b) and (c) of Regulation M-A (§ 229.1011 of this chapter).

Item 9. *Exhibits.*

File as an exhibit to the Schedule all documents specified by Item 1016(a), (e) and (g) of Regulation M-A (§ 229.1016 of this chapter).

Signature. After due inquiry and to the best of my knowledge and belief, I certify that the information set forth in this statement is true, complete and correct.

———————————
(Signature)

———————————
(Name and title)

———————————
(Date)

Instruction to Signature: The statement must be signed by the filing person or that person's authorized representative. If the statement is signed on behalf of a person by an authorized representative (other than an executive officer of a corporation or general partner of a partnership), evidence of the representative's authority to sign on behalf of the person must be filed with the statement. The name and any title of each person who signs the statement must be typed or printed beneath the signature. See § 240.14d-1(h) with respect to signature requirements.

Schedule 15G
Information to be included in the document distributed pursuant to 17 CFR 240.15g-2

SECURITIES AND EXCHANGE COMMISSION
Washington, D.C. 20549
SCHEDULE 15G
Under the Securities Exchange Act of 1934

Instructions to Schedule 15G

A. Schedule 15G (Schedule) may be provided to customers in its entirety either on paper or electronically. It may also be provided to customers electronically through a link to the SEC's Web site.

1. If the Schedule is sent in paper form, the format and typeface of the Schedule must be reproduced exactly as presented. For example, words that are capitalized must remain capitalized, and words that are underlined or bold must remain underlined or bold. The typeface must be clear and easy to read. The Schedule may be reproduced either by photocopy or by printing.

2. If the Schedule is sent electronically, the e-mail containing the Schedule must have as a subject line "Important Information on Penny Stocks." The Schedule reproduced in the text of the
e-mail must be clear, easy-to-read type presented in a manner reasonably calculated to draw the customer's attention to the language in the document, especially words that are capitalized, underlined or in bold.

3. If the Schedule is sent electronically using a hyperlink to the SEC Web site, the e-mail containing the hyperlink must have as a subject line: "Important Information on Penny Stocks." Immediately before the hyperlink, the text of the e-mail must reproduce the following statement in clear, easy-to-read type presented in a manner reasonably calculated to draw the customer's attention to the words: "We are required by the U.S. Securities and Exchange Commission to give you the following disclosure statement: http://www.sec.gov/investor/schedule15g.htm. It explains some of the risks of investing in penny stocks. Please read it carefully before you agree to purchase or sell a penny stock."

B. Regardless of how the Schedule is provided to the customer, the communication must also provide the name, address, telephone number and e-mail address of the broker. E-mail messages may also include any privacy or confidentiality information that the broker routinely includes in e-mail messages sent to customers. No other information may be included in these communications, other than instructions on how to provide a signed and dated acknowledgement of receipt of the Schedule.

C. The document entitled "Important Information on Penny Stocks" must be distributed as Schedule 15G and must be no more than two pages in length if provided in paper form.

D. The disclosures made through the Schedule are in addition to any other disclosures that are required under the federal securities laws.

E. Recipients of the document must not be charged any fee for the document.

F. The content of the Schedule is as follows:

IMPORTANT INFORMATION ON PENNY STOCKS

The U.S. Securities and Exchange Commission (SEC) requires your broker to give this statement to you, and to obtain your signature to show that you have received it, before your first trade in a penny stock. This statement contains important information—and you should read it carefully before you sign it, and before you decide to purchase or sell a penny stock.

In addition to obtaining your signature, the SEC requires your broker to wait at least two business days after sending you this statement before executing your first trade to give you time to carefully consider your trade.

Penny stocks can be very risky.

Penny stocks are low-priced shares of small companies. Penny stocks may trade infrequently—which means that it may be difficult to sell penny stock shares once you have them. Because it may also be difficult to find quotations for penny stocks, they may be impossible to accurately price. *Investors in penny stock should be prepared for the possibility that they may lose their whole investment.*

While penny stocks generally trade over-the-counter, they may also trade on U.S. securities exchanges, facilities of U.S. exchanges, or foreign exchanges. You should learn about the market in which the penny stock trades to determine how much demand there is for this stock and how difficult it will be to sell. Be especially careful if your broker is offering to sell you newly issued penny stock that has no established trading market.

The securities you are considering have not been approved or disapproved by the SEC. Moreover, the SEC has not passed upon the fairness or the merits of this transaction nor upon the accuracy or adequacy of the information contained in any prospectus or any other information provided by an issuer or a broker or dealer.

Information you should get.

In addition to this statement, your broker is required to give you a statement of your financial situation and investment goals explaining why his or her firm has determined that penny stocks are a suitable investment for you. In addition, your broker is required to obtain your agreement to the proposed penny stock transaction.

Before you buy penny stock, federal law requires your salesperson to tell you the "*offer*" and the "*bid*" on the stock, and the "*compensation*" the salesperson and the firm receive for the trade. The firm also must send a confirmation of these prices to you after the trade. You will need this price information to determine what profit or loss, if any, you will have when you sell your stock.

The offer price is the wholesale price at which the dealer is willing to sell stock to other dealers. The bid price is the wholesale price at which the dealer is willing to buy the stock from other dealers. In its trade with you, the dealer may add a retail charge to these wholesale prices as compensation (called a "markup" or "markdown").

The difference between the bid and the offer price is the dealer's "*spread.*" A spread that is large compared with the purchase price can make a resale of a stock very costly. To be profitable when you sell, the bid price of your stock must rise above the amount of this spread *and* the compensation charged by both your selling and purchasing dealers. *Remember that if the dealer has no bid price, you may not be able to sell the stock after you buy it, and may lose your whole investment.*

After you buy penny stock, your brokerage firm must send you a monthly account statement that gives an estimate of the value of each penny stock in your account, if there is enough information to make an estimate. If the firm has not bought or sold any penny stocks for your account for six months, it can provide these statements every three months.

Additional information about low-priced securities—including penny stocks—is available on the SEC's Web site at *http://www.sec.gov/investor/pubs/microcapstock.htm*. In addition, your broker will send you a copy of this information upon request. The SEC encourages you to learn all you can before making this investment.

Brokers' duties and customer's rights and remedies.

Remember that your salesperson is not an impartial advisor—he or she is being paid to sell you stock. Do not rely only on the salesperson, but seek outside advice before you buy any stock. You can get the disciplinary history of a salesperson or firm from NASD at 1-800-289-9999 or contact NASD via the Internet at *www.nasd.com*. You can also get additional information from your state securities official. The North American Securities Administrators Association, Inc. can give you contact information for your state. You can reach NASAA at (202) 737-0900 or via the Internet at *www.nasaa.org.*

If you have problems with a salesperson, contact the firm's compliance officer. You can also contact the securities regulators listed above. Finally, if you are a victim of fraud, you may have rights and remedies under state and federal law. In addition to the regulators listed above, you also may contact the SEC with complaints at (800) SEC-0330 or via the Internet at help@-sec.gov.

FURTHER INFORMATION

THE SECURITIES BEING SOLD TO YOU HAVE NOT BEEN APPROVED OR DISAPPROVED BY THE SECURITIES AND EXCHANGE COMMISSION. MOREOVER, THE SECURITIES AND EXCHANGE COMMISSION HAS NOT PASSED UPON THE FAIRNESS OR THE MERITS OF THIS TRANSACTION NOR UPON THE ACCURACY OR ADEQUACY OF THE INFORMATION CONTAINED IN ANY PROSPECTUS OR ANY OTHER INFORMATION PROVIDED BY AN ISSUER OR A BROKER OR DEALER.

Generally, penny stock is a security that:
- is priced under five dollars;
- is *not* traded on a national stock exchange or on NASDAQ (the NASD's automated quotation system for actively traded stocks);
- may be listed in the "pink sheets" or the NASD OTC Bulletin Board;
- is issued by a company that has less than $5 million in net tangible assets and has been in business less than three years, by a company that has under $2 million in net tangible assets and has been in business for at least three years, or by a company that has revenues of $6 million for three years.

Use caution when investing in penny stocks:

1. *Do not make a hurried investment decision.* High-pressure sales techniques can be a warning sign of fraud. The salesperson is not an impartial advisor, but is paid for selling stock to you. The salesperson also does not have to watch your investment for you. Thus, you should think over the offer and seek outside advice. Check to see if the information given by the salesperson differs from other information you may have. Also, it is illegal for salespersons to promise that a stock will increase in value or is risk-free, or to guarantee against loss. If you think there is a problem, ask to speak with a compliance official at the firm, and, if necessary, any of the regulators referred to in this statement.

2. *Study the company issuing the stock.* Be wary of companies that have no operating history, few assets, or no defined business purpose. These may be sham or "shell" corporations. Read the prospectus for the company carefully before you invest. Some dealers fraudulently solicit investors' money to buy stock in sham companies, artificially inflate the stock prices, then cash in their profits before public investors can sell their stock.

3. *Understand the risky nature of these stocks.* You should be aware that you may lose part or all of your investment. Because of large dealer spreads, you will not be able to sell the stock immediately back to the dealer at the same price it sold the stock to you. In some cases, the stock may fall quickly in value. New companies, whose stock is sold in an "initial public offering," often are riskier investments. Try to find out if the shares the salesperson wants to sell you are part of such an offering. Your salesperson must give you a "prospectus" in an initial public offering, but the financial condition shown in the prospectus of new companies can change very quickly.

4. *Know the brokerage firm and the salespeople with whom you are dealing.* Because of the nature of the market for penny stock, you may have to rely solely on the original brokerage firm that sold you the stock for prices and to buy the stock back from you. Ask the National Association of Securities Dealers, Inc. (NASD) or your state securities regulator, which is a member of the North American Securities Administrators Association, Inc. (NASAA), about the licensing and

disciplinary record of the brokerage firm and the salesperson contacting you. The telephone numbers of the NASD and NASAA are listed on the first page of this document.

5. *Be cautious if your salesperson leaves the firm.* If the salesperson who sold you the stock leaves his or her firm, the firm may reassign your account to a new salesperson. If you have problems, ask to speak to the firm's branch office manager or a compliance officer. Although the departing salesperson may ask you to transfer your stock to his or her new firm, you do not have to do so. Get information on the new firm. Be wary of requests to sell your securities when the salesperson transfers to a new firm. Also, you have the right to get your stock certificate from your selling firm. You do not have to leave the certificate with that firm or any other firm.

YOUR RIGHTS

Disclosures to you. Under penalty of federal law, your brokerage firm must tell you the following information at two different times—*before* you agree to buy or sell a penny stock, and after the trade, by *written confirmation:*

- *The bid and offer price quotes for penny stock, and the number of shares to which the quoted prices apply.* The *bid* and *offer* quotes are the wholesale prices at which dealers trade among themselves. These prices give you an idea of the market value of the stock. The dealer must tell you these price quotes if they appear on an automated quotation system approved by the SEC. If not, the dealer must use its own quotes or trade prices. You should calculate the *spread*, the difference between the bid and offer quotes, to help decide if buying the stock is a good investment.

  A lack of quotes may mean that the market among dealers is not active. It thus may be difficult to resell the stock. You also should be aware that the actual price charged to you for the stock may differ from the price quoted to you for 100 shares. You should therefore determine, before you agree to a purchase, what the actual sales price (before the *markup*) will be for the exact number of shares you want to buy.

- *The brokerage firm's compensation for the trade.* A *markup* is the amount a dealer adds to the wholesale offer price of the stock and a *markdown* is the amount it subtracts from the wholesale bid price of the stock as *compensation.* A markup/markdown usually serves the same role as a broker's commission on a trade. Most of the firms in the penny stock market will be dealers, not brokers.

- *The compensation received by the brokerage firm's salesperson for the trade.* The brokerage firm must disclose to you, as a total sum, the cash compensation of your salesperson for the trade that is known at the time of the trade. The firm must describe in the written confirmation the nature of any other compensation of your salesperson that is unknown at the time of the trade.

In addition to the items listed above, your brokerage firm must send to you:

- *Monthly account statements.* In general, *your brokerage firm must send you a monthly statement* that gives an estimate of the value of each penny stock in your account, if there is enough information to make an estimate. If the firm has not bought or sold any penny stocks for your account for six months, it can provide these statements every three months.

- *A Written Statement of Your Financial Situation and Investment Goals.* In general, unless you have had an account with your brokerage firm for more than one year, or you have previously bought three different penny stocks from that firm, your brokerage firm must send you a written statement for you to sign that accurately describes your financial situation, your investment experience, and your investment goals, and that contains a statement of why your firm decided that penny stocks are a suitable investment for you. The firm also must get your written consent to buy the penny stock.

Legal remedies. If penny stocks are sold to you in violation of your rights listed above, or other federal or state securities laws, you may be able to cancel your purchase and get your money back. If the stocks are sold in a fraudulent manner, you may be able to sue the persons and firms that caused the fraud for damages. If you have signed an arbitration agreement, however, you may have to pursue your claim through arbitration. You may wish to contact an attorney. The SEC is not authorized to represent individuals in private litigation.

However, to protect yourself and other investors, you should report any violations of your brokerage firm's duties listed above and other securities laws to the SEC, the NASD, or your state securities administrator at the telephone numbers on the first page of this document. These bodies have the power to stop fraudulent and abusive activity of salespersons and firms engaged in the securities business. Or you can write to the SEC at 450 Fifth St., N.W., Washington, D.C. 20549; the NASD at 1735 K Street, N.W., Washington, D.C. 20006; or NASAA at 555 New Jersey Avenue, N.W., Suite 750, Washington, D.C. 20001. NASAA will give you the telephone number of your state's securities agency. If there is any disciplinary record of a person or a firm, the NASD, NASAA, or your state securities regulator will send you this information if you ask for it.

MARKET INFORMATION

The market for penny stocks. Penny stocks usually are not listed on an exchange or quoted on the NASDAQ system. Instead, they are traded between dealers on the telephone in the "over-the-counter" market. The NASD's OTC Bulletin Board also will contain information on some penny stocks. At times, however, price information for these stocks is not publicly available.

Market domination. In some cases, only one or two dealers, acting as "market makers," may be buying and selling a given stock. You should first ask if a firm is acting as a *broker* (your agent) or as a dealer. A *dealer* buys stock itself to fill your order or already owns the stock. A *market maker* is a dealer who holds itself out as ready to buy and sell stock on a regular basis. If the firm is a market maker, ask how many other market makers are dealing in the stock to see if the firm (or group of firms) dominates the market. When there are only one or two market makers, there is a risk that the dealer or group of dealers may control the market in that stock and set prices that are not based on competitive forces. In recent years, some market makers have created fraudulent markets in certain penny stocks, so that stock prices rose suddenly, but collapsed just as quickly, at a loss to investors.

Mark-ups and mark-downs. The actual price that the customer pays usually includes the mark-up or markdown. Markups and markdowns are direct profits for the firm and its salespeople, so you should be aware of such amounts to assess the overall value of the trade.

The "spread." The difference between the bid and offer price is the spread. Like a mark-up or mark-down, the spread is another source of profit for the brokerage firm and compensates the firm for the risk of owning the stock. A large spread can make a trade very expensive to an investor. For some penny stocks, the spread between the bid and offer may be a large part of the purchase price of the stock. Where the bid price is much lower than the offer price, the market value of the stock must rise substantially before the stock can be sold at a profit. Moreover, an investor may experience substantial losses if the stock must be sold immediately.

Example: If the bid is $0.04 per share and the offer is $0.10 per share, the spread (difference) is $0.06, which appears to be a small amount. But you would lose $0.06 on every share that you bought for $0.10 if you had to sell that stock immediately to the same firm. If you had invested $5,000 at the $0.10 offer price, the market maker's repurchase price, at $0.04 bid, would be only $2,000; thus you would lose $3,000, or more than half of your investment, if you decided to sell the stock. In addition, you would have to pay compensation (a "mark-up," "markdown," or commission) to buy and sell the stock.

In addition to the amount of the spread, the price of your stock must rise enough to make up for the compensation that the dealer charged you when it first sold you the stock. Then, when you want to resell the stock, a dealer again will charge compensation, in the form of a markdown. The dealer subtracts the markdown from the price of the stock when it buys the stock from you. Thus, to make a profit, the bid price of your stock must rise above the amount of the original spread, the markup, and the markdown.

Primary offerings. Most penny stocks are sold to the public on an ongoing basis. However, dealers sometimes sell these stocks in initial public offerings. You should pay special attention to stocks of companies that have never been offered to the public before, because the market for these stocks is untested. Because the offering is on a first-time basis, there is generally no market information about the stock to help determine its value. The federal securities laws generally require broker-dealers to give investors a "prospectus," which contains information

FORM 4

U.S. SECURITIES AND EXCHANGE COMMISSION
Washington, D.C. 20549
FORM 4

STATEMENT OF CHANGES IN BENEFICIAL OWNERSHIP OF SECURITIES

The Commission is authorized to solicit the information required by this form pursuant to Sections 16(a) and 23(a) of the Securities Exchange Act of 1934, Sections 17(a) and 20(a) of the Public Utility Holding Company Act of 1935, and Sections 30(h) and 38 of the Investment Company Act of 1940, and the rules and regulations thereunder.

Disclosure of information specified on this form is mandatory. The information will be used for the primary purpose of disclosing the transactions and holdings of directors, officers, and beneficial owners of registered companies. Information disclosed will be a matter of public record and available for inspection by members of the public. The Commission can use it in investigations or litigation involving the federal securities laws or other civil, criminal, or regulatory statutes or provisions, as well as for referral to other governmental authorities and self-regulatory organizations. Failure to disclose required information may result in civil or criminal action against persons involved for violations of the federal securities laws and rules.

GENERAL INSTRUCTIONS

1. When Form Must be Filed

(a) This Form must be filed before the end of the second business day following the day on which a transaction resulting in a change in beneficial ownership has been executed (see Rule 16a-1(a)(2) and Instruction 4 regarding the meaning of "beneficial owner," and Rule 16a-3(g) regarding determination of the date of execution for specified transactions). This Form and any amendment is deemed filed with the Commission or the Exchange on the date it is received by the Commission or the Exchange, respectively. See, however, Rule 16a-3(h) regarding delivery to a third party business that guarantees delivery of the filing no later than the specified due date.

(b) A reporting person no longer subject to section 16 of the Securities Exchange Act of 1934 ("Exchange Act") must check the exit box appearing on this Form. However, Form 4 and Form 5 obligations may continue to be applicable. *See* Rules 16a-3(f) and 16a-2(b). Form 5 transactions to date may be included on this Form and subsequent Form 5 transactions may be reported on a later Form 4 or Form 5, provided all transactions are reported by the required date.

(c) A separate Form shall be filed to reflect beneficial ownership of securities of each issuer, except that a single statement shall be filed with respect to the securities of a registered public utility holding company and all of its subsidiary companies.

(d) If a reporting person is not an officer, director, or 10% holder, the person should check "other" in Item 6 (Relationship of Reporting Person to Issuer) and describe the reason for reporting status in the space provided.

2. Where Form Must be Filed

(a) A reporting person must file this Form in electronic format via the Commission's Electronic Data Gathering Analysis and Retrieval System (EDGAR) in accordance with EDGAR rules set forth in Regulation S-T (17 CFR Part 232), except that a filing person that has obtained a hardship exception under Regulation S-T Rule 202 (17 CFR 232.202) may file the

Form in paper. For assistance with technical questions about EDGAR or to request an access code, call the EDGAR Filer Support Office at (202) 942-8900. For assistance with questions about the EDGAR rules, call the Office of EDGAR and Information Analysis at (202) 942-2940.

(b) At the time this Form or any amendment is filed with the Commission, file one copy with each Exchange on which any class of securities of the issuer is registered. If the issuer has designated a single Exchange to receive Section 16 filings, the copy shall be filed with that Exchange only.

(c) [Reserved.]

NOTE: If filing pursuant to a hardship exception under Regulation S-T Rule 202 (17 CFR 232.202), file three copies of this Form or any amendment, at least one of which is signed, with the Securities and Exchange Commission, 450 5th Street, NW, Washington, DC 20549. (Acknowledgement of receipt by the Commission may be obtained by enclosing a self-addressed stamped postcard identifying the Form or amendment filed.)

3. Class of Securities Reported

(a) (i) Persons reporting pursuant to Section 16(a) of the Exchange Act must report each transaction resulting in a change in beneficial ownership of any class of equity securities of the issuer and the beneficial ownership of that class of securities following the reported transaction(s), even though one or more of such classes may not be registered pursuant to Section 12 of the Exchange Act.

(ii) [Reserved.]

(iii) Persons reporting pursuant to Section 30(h) of the Investment Company Act of 1940 must report each transaction resulting in a change in beneficial ownership of any class of securities (equity or debt) of the registered closed-end investment company (other than "short-term paper" as defined in Section 2(a)(38) of the Investment Company Act) and the beneficial ownership of that class of securities following the reported transaction(s).

(b) The title of the security should clearly identify the class, even if the issuer has only one class of securities outstanding; for example, " Common Stock," "Class A Common Stock," "Class B Convertible Preferred Stock," etc.

(c) The amount of securities beneficially owned should state the face amount of debt securities (U.S. Dollars) or the number of equity securities, whichever is appropriate.

4. Transactions and Holdings Required to be Reported

(a) *General Requirements*

(i) Report, in accordance with Rule 16a-3(g): (1) all transactions not exempt from Section 16(b); (2) all transactions exempt from Section 16(b) pursuant to § 240.16b-3(d), § 240.16b-3(e), or § 240.16b-3(f); and (3) all exercises and conversions of derivative securities, regardless of whether exempt from Section 16(b) of the Act. Every transaction must be reported even though acquisitions and dispositions are equal. Report total beneficial ownership following the reported transaction(s) for each class of securities in which a transaction was reported.

Note: The amount of securities beneficially owned following the reported transaction(s) specified in Column 5 of Table I and Column 9 of Table II should reflect holdings reported or required to be reported by the date of the Form. Transactions and holdings eligible for deferred reporting on Form 5 need not be reflected in the month end total unless the transactions were reported earlier or are included on this Form.

(ii) Each transaction should be reported on a separate line. Transaction codes specified in Instruction 8 should be used to identify the nature of the transaction resulting in an acquisition or disposition of a security. A deemed execution date must be reported in Column 2A of Table I or Column 3A of Table II only if the execution date for the transaction is calculated pursuant to § 240.16a-3(g)(2) or § 240.16a-3(g)(3).

Note: Transactions reportable on Form 5 may, at the option of the reporting person, be reported on a Form 4 filed before the due date of the Form 5. (*See* Instruction 8 for the code for voluntarily reported transactions.)

(b) *Beneficial Ownership Reported (Pecuniary Interest)*

(i) Although for purposes of determining status as a ten percent holder, a person is deemed to beneficially own securities over which that person has voting or investment control (*see* Rule 16a-1(a)(1)), for reporting transactions and holdings, a person is deemed to be the beneficial owner of securities if that person has or shares the opportunity, directly or indirectly, to profit or share in any profit derived from a transaction in the securities ("pecuniary interest"). *See* Rule 16a-1(a)(2). *See also* Rule 16a-8 for the application of the beneficial ownership definition to trust holdings and transactions.

(ii) Both direct and indirect beneficial ownership of securities shall be reported. Securities beneficially owned directly are those held in the reporting person's name or in the name of a bank, broker or nominee for the account of the reporting person. In addition, securities held as joint tenants, tenants in common, tenants by the entirety, or as community property are to be reported as held directly. If a person has a pecuniary interest, by reason of any contract, understanding, or relationship (including a family relationship or arrangement), in securities held in the name of another person, that person is an indirect beneficial owner of the securities. *See* Rule 16a-1(a)(2)(ii) for certain indirect beneficial ownerships.

(iii) Report transactions in securities beneficially owned directly on separate lines from those beneficially owned indirectly. Report different forms of indirect ownership on separate lines. The nature of indirect ownership shall be stated as specifically as possible; for example, "By Self as Trustee for X," "By Spouse," "By X Trust," " By Y Corporation," etc.

(iv) In stating the amount of securities acquired, disposed of, or beneficially owned indirectly through a partnership, corporation, trust, or other entity, report the number of securities representing the reporting person's proportionate interest in transactions conducted by that entity or holdings of that entity. Alternatively, at the option of the reporting person, the entire amount of the entity's interest may be reported. *See* Rule 16a-1(a)(2)(ii) (B) and Rule 16a-1(a)(2)(iii).

(v) Where more than one beneficial owner of the same equity securities must report the same transaction on Form 4, such owners may file Form 4 individually or jointly. Joint and group filings may be made by any designated beneficial owner. Transactions with respect to securities owned separately by any joint or group filer are permitted to be included in the joint filing. Indicate only the name and address of the designated filer in Item 1 of Form 4 and attach a list of the names and addresses of each other reporting person. Joint and group filings must include all required information for each beneficial owner, and such filings must be signed by each beneficial owner, or on behalf of such owner by an authorized person.

If this Form is being filed in paper pursuant to a hardship exemption and the space provided for signatures is insufficient, attach a signature page. If this Form is being filed in paper, submit any attached listing of names or signatures on another Form 4, copy of Form 4 or separate page of 8 1/2 by 11 inch white paper, indicate the number of pages comprising the report (Form plus attachments) at the bottom of each report page (*e.g.*, 1 of 3, 2 of 3, 3 of 3), and include the name of the designated filer and information required by Items 2 and 3 of the Form on the attachment.

See Rule 16a-3(i) regarding signatures.

(c) *Non-Derivative and Derivative Securities*

(i) Report acquisitions or dispositions and holdings of non-derivative securities in Table I. Report acquisitions or dispositions and holdings of derivative securities (*e.g.*, puts, calls, options, warrants, convertible securities, or other rights or obligations to buy or sell securities) in Table II. Report the exercise or conversion of a derivative security in Table II (as a disposition of the derivative security) and report in Table I the holdings of the underlying security. Report acquisitions or dispositions and holdings of derivative securities that are both equity securities and convertible or exchangeable for other equity securities (*e.g.*, convertible preferred securities) only on Table II.

(ii) The title of a derivative security and the title of the equity security underlying the derivative security should be shown separately in the appropriate columns in Table II. The "puts" and "calls" reported in Table II include, in addition to separate puts and calls, any combination of the two, such as spreads and straddles. In reporting an option in Table II, state whether it represents a right to buy, a right to sell, an obligation to buy, or an obligation to sell the equity securities subject to the option.

(iii) Describe in the appropriate columns in Table II characteristics of derivative securities, including title, exercise or conversion price, date exercisable, expiration date, and the title and amount of securities underlying the derivative security. If the transaction reported is a purchase or sale of a derivative security, the purchase or sale price of that derivative security shall be reported in column 8. If the transaction is the exercise or conversion of a derivative security, leave column 8 blank and report the exercise or conversion price of the derivative security in column 2.

(iv) Securities constituting components of a unit shall be reported separately on the applicable table (e.g., if a unit has a non-derivative security component and a derivative security component, the non-derivative security component shall be reported in Table I and the derivative security component shall be reported in Table II). The relationship between individual securities comprising the unit shall be indicated in the space provided for explanation of responses. When securities are purchased or sold as a unit, state the purchase or sale price per unit and other required information regarding the unit securities.

5. Price of Securities

(a) Prices of securities shall be reported in U.S. dollars on a per share basis, not an aggregate basis, except that the aggregate price of debt shall be stated. Amounts reported shall exclude brokerage commissions and other costs of execution.

(b) If consideration other than cash was paid for the security, describe the consideration, including the value of the consideration, in the space provided for explanation of responses.

6. Additional Information

(a) If the space provided in the line items on the electronic Form is insufficient, use the space provided for footnotes. If the space provided for footnotes is insufficient, create a footnote that refers to an exhibit to the form that contains the additional information.

(b) If the space provided in the line items on the paper Form or space provided for additional comments is insufficient, attach another Form 4, copy of Form 4 or separate 8 1/2 by 11 inch white paper to Form 4, completed as appropriate to include the additional comments. Each attached page must include information required in Items 1, 2 and 3 of the Form. The number of pages comprising the report (Form plus attachments) shall be indicated at the bottom of each report page (e.g. 1 of 3, 2 of 3, 3 of 3).

(c) If one or more exhibits are included, whether due to a lack of space or because the exhibit is, by nature, a separate document (e.g., a power of attorney), provide a sequentially numbered list of the exhibits in the Form. Use the number "24" for any power of attorney and the number "99" for any other exhibit. If there is more than one of either such exhibit, then use numerical subparts. If the exhibit is being filed as a confirming electronic copy under Regulation S-T Rule 202(d) (17 CFR 232.202(d)), then place the designation "CE" (confirming exhibit) next to the name of the exhibit in the exhibit list. If the exhibit is being filed in paper pursuant to a hardship exception under Regulation S-T Rule 202 (17 CFR 232.202), then place the designation "P" (paper) next to the name of the exhibit in the exhibit list.

(d) If additional information is not reported as provided in paragraph (a), (b) or (c) of this instruction, whichever apply, it will be assumed that no additional information was provided.

7. Signature

(a) If the Form is filed for an individual, it shall be signed by that person or specifically on behalf of the individual by a person authorized to sign for the individual. If signed on behalf of the individual by another person, the authority of such person to sign the Form shall be confirmed to the Commission in writing in an attachment to the Form or as soon as practicable in an amendment by the individual for whom the Form is filed, unless such a confirmation still in effect is on file with the Commission. The confirming statement need only indicate that the reporting person authorizes and designates the named person or persons to file the Form on the reporting person's behalf, and state the duration of the authorization.

(b) If the Form is filed for a corporation, partnership, trust, or other entity, the capacity in which the individual signed shall be set forth (*e.g.*, John Smith, Secretary, on behalf of X Corporation).

8. Transaction Codes

Use the codes listed below to indicate in Table I, Column 3 and Table II, Column 4 the character of the transaction reported. Use the code that most appropriately describes the transaction. If the transaction is not specifically listed, use transaction Code "J" and describe the nature of the transaction in the space for explanation of responses. If a transaction is voluntarily reported earlier than required, place "V" in the appropriate column to so indicate; otherwise, the column should be left blank. If a transaction involves an equity swap or instrument with similar characteristics, use transaction Code "K" in addition to the code(s) that most appropriately describes the transaction, *e.g.*, "S/K" or "P/K."

General Transaction Codes

P-Open market or private purchase of non-derivative or derivative security
S-Open market or private sale of non-derivative or derivative security
V-Transaction voluntarily reported earlier than required

Rule 16b-3 Transaction Codes

A-Grant, award or other acquisition pursuant to Rule 16b3(d)
D-Disposition to the issuer of issuer equity securities pursuant to Rule 16b-3(e)
F-Payment of exercise price or tax liability by delivering or withholding securities incident to the receipt, exercise, or vesting of a security issued in accordance with Rule 16b-3
I-Discretionary transaction in accordance with Rule 16b3(f) resulting in acquisition or disposition of issuer securities
M-Exercise or conversion of derivative security exempted pursuant to Rule 16b-3

Derivative Securities Codes (Except for transactions exempted pursuant to Rule 16b-3)

C-Conversion of derivative security
E-Expiration of short derivative position
H-Expiration (or cancellation) of long derivative position with value received
O-Exercise of out-of-the-money derivative security
X-Exercise of in-the-money or at-the-money derivative security

Other Section 16(b) Exempt Transactions and Small Acquisition Codes (except for Rule 16b-3 codes above)

G-Bona fide gift
L-Small acquisition under Rule 16a-6
W-Acquisition or disposition by will or laws of descent and distribution
Z-Deposit into or withdrawal from voting trust

Other Transaction Codes

J-Other acquisition or disposition (describe transaction)
K-Transaction in equity swap or instrument with similar characteristics
U-Disposition pursuant to a tender of shares in a change of control transaction

9. Amendments

(a) If this Form is filed as an amendment in order to add one or more lines of transaction information to Table I or Table II of the Form being amended, provide each line being added, together with one or more footnotes, as necessary, to explain the addition of the line or lines. Do not repeat lines of transaction information that were disclosed in the original Form and are not being amended.

(b) If this Form is filed as an amendment in order to amend one or more lines of transaction information that already were disclosed in Table I or Table II of the Form being amended, provide the complete line or lines being amended, as amended, together with one or more footnotes, as necessary, to explain the amendment of the line or lines. Do not repeat lines of transaction information that were disclosed in the original Form and are not being amended.

(c) If this Form is filed as an amendment for any purpose other than or in addition to the purposes described in paragraphs (a) and (b) of this General Instruction 9, provide one or more footnotes, as necessary, to explain the amendment.

Form 4

FORM 4

☐ Check this box if no longer subject to Section 16. Form 4 or Form 5 obligations may continue. *See Instruction 1(b).*

(Print or Type Responses)

UNITED STATES SECURITIES AND EXCHANGE COMMISSION
Washington, D.C. 20549

STATEMENT OF CHANGES IN BENEFICIAL OWNERSHIP OF SECURITIES

Filed pursuant to Section 16(a) of the Securities Exchange Act of 1934, Section 17(a) of the Public Utility Holding Company Act of 1935 or Section 30(h) of the Investment Company Act of 1940

1. Name and Address of Reporting Person*

(Last)   (First)   (Middle)

(Street)

(City)   (State)   (Zip)

2. Issuer Name and Ticker or Trading Symbol

3. Date of Earliest Transaction Required to be Reported (Month/Day/Year)

4. If Amendment, Date Original Filed (Month/Day/Year)

5. Relationship of Reporting Person(s) to Issuer (Check all applicable)

____ Director   ____ 10% Owner
____ Officer (give title below)   ____ Other (specify below)

6. Individual or Joint/Group Filing (Check Applicable Line)
____ Form filed by One Reporting Person
____ Form filed by More than One Reporting Person

Table I — Non-Derivative Securities Acquired, Disposed of, or Beneficially Owned

1. Title of Security (Instr. 3)	2. Transaction Date (Month/Day/Year)	2A. Deemed Execution Date, if any (Month/Day/Year)	3. Transaction Code (Instr. 8)		4. Securities Acquired (A) or Disposed of (D) (Instr. 3, 4 and 5)			5. Amount of Securities Beneficially Owned Following Reported Transaction(s) (Instr. 3 and 4)	6. Ownership Form: Direct (D) or Indirect (I) (Instr. 4)	7. Nature of Indirect Beneficial Ownership (Instr. 4)
			Code	V	Amount	(A) or (D)	Price			

Reminder: Report on a separate line for each class of securities beneficially owned directly or indirectly.

* If the form is filed by more than one reporting person, *see* Instruction 4(b)(v).

(Over)

FORM 4 (continued)

Table II — Derivative Securities Acquired, Disposed of, or Beneficially Owned
(*e.g.,* puts, calls, warrants, options, convertible securities)

1. Title of Derivative Security (Instr. 3)	2. Conversion or Exercise Price of Derivative Security	3. Transaction Date (Month/Day/Year)	3A. Deemed Execution Date, if any (Month/Day/Year)	4. Transaction Code (Instr. 8)		5. Number of Derivative Securities Acquired (A) or Disposed of (D) (Instr. 3, 4, and 5)		6. Date Exercisable and Expiration Date (Month/Day/Year)		7. Title and Amount of Underlying Securities (Instr. 3 and 4)		8. Price of Derivative Security (Instr. 5)	9. Number of derivative Securities Beneficially Owned Following Reported Transaction(s) (Instr. 4)	10. Ownership Form of Derivative Security: Direct (D) or Indirect (I) (Instr. 4)	11. Nature of Indirect Beneficial Ownership (Instr. 4)
				Code	V	(A)	(D)	Date Exercisable	Expiration Date	Title	Amount or Number of Shares				

Explanation of Responses:

** Intentional misstatements or omissions of facts constitute Federal Criminal Violations.
See 18 U.S.C. 1001 and 15 U.S.C. 78ff(a).

Note: File three copies of this Form, one of which must be manually signed. If space is insufficient, *see* Instruction 6 for procedure.

Potential persons who are to respond to the collection of information contained in this form are not required to respond unless the form displays a currently valid OMB Number.

_____   _____
**Signature of Reporting Person   Date

REGULATION S-K—SELECTED PROVISIONS

17 C.F.R. §§ 229.10-229.802

N.B. The following is not a complete text of Regulation S-K. It omits a number of statutory provisions entirely, and also omits certain subsections of provisions that are partially included.

PART 229—STANDARD INSTRUCTIONS FOR FILING FORMS UNDER SECURITIES ACT OF 1933, SECURITIES EXCHANGE ACT OF 1934 AND ENERGY POLICY AND CONSERVATION ACT OF 1975— REGULATION S-K

Subpart 1—General

Item 10. General

(a) *Application of Regulation S-K.* This part (together with the General Rules and Regulations under the Securities Act of 1933, 15 U.S.C. 77a et seq., as amended ("Securities Act"), and the Securities Exchange Act of 1934, 15 U.S.C. 78a et seq., as amended ("Exchange Act") (Parts 230 and 240 of this chapter), the Interpretative Releases under these Acts (Parts 231 and 241 of this chapter) and the forms under these Acts (Parts 239 and 249 of this chapter)) states the requirements applicable to the content of the non-financial statement portions of:

(1) Registration statements under the Securities Act (Part 239 of this chapter) to the extent provided in the forms to be used for registration under such Act; and

(2) Registration statements under section 12 (subpart C of part 249 of this chapter), annual or other reports under sections 13 and 15(d) (subparts D and E of part 249 of this chapter), going-private transaction statements under section 13 (part 240 of this chapter), tender offer statements under sections 13 and 14 (part 240 of this chapter), annual reports to security holders and proxy and information statements under section 14 (part 240 of this chapter), and any other documents required to be filed under the Exchange Act, to the extent provided in the forms and rules under that Act.

(b) *Commission policy on projections.* The Commission encourages the use in documents specified in Rule 175 under the Securities Act (§ 230.175 of this chapter) and Rule 3b-6 under the Exchange Act (§ 240.3b-6 of this chapter) of management's projections of future economic performance that have a reasonable basis and are presented in an appropriate format. The guidelines set forth herein represent the Commission's views on important factors to be considered in formulating and disclosing such projections.

(1) *Basis for projections.* The Commission believes that management must have the option to present in Commission filings its good faith assessment of a registrant's future performance. Management, however, must have a reasonable basis for such an assessment. Although a history of operations or experience in projecting may be among the factors providing a basis for management's assessment, the Commission does not believe that a registrant always must have had such a history or experience in order to formulate projections with a reasonable basis. An outside review of management's projections may furnish additional support for having a reasonable basis for a projection. If management decides to include a report of such a review in a Commission filing, there also should be disclosure of the qualifications of the reviewer, the extent of the review, the relationship between the reviewer and the registrant, and other material factors concerning the process by which any outside review was sought or obtained. Moreover, in the case of a registration statement under the Securities Act, the reviewer would be deemed an expert and an appropriate consent must be filed with the registration statement.

(2) *Format for projections.* In determining the appropriate format for projections included in Commission filings, consideration must be given to, among other things, the financial items to be projected, the period to be covered, and the manner of presentation to be used. Although traditionally projections have been given for three financial items generally considered to be of primary importance to investors (revenues, net income (loss) and earnings (loss) per share), projection information need not necessarily be limited to these three items. However, management should take care to assure that the choice of items projected is not susceptible of misleading inferences through selective projection of only favorable items. Revenues, net income (loss) and earnings (loss) per share usually are presented together in order to avoid any misleading inferences that may arise when the individual items reflect contradictory trends. There may be instances, however, when it is appropriate to present earnings (loss) from continuing operations in addition to or in lieu of net income (loss). It generally would be misleading to present sales or revenue projections without one of the foregoing measures of income. The period that appropriately may be covered by a projection depends to a large extent on the particular circumstances of the company involved. For certain companies in certain industries, a projection covering a two or three year period may be entirely reasonable. Other companies may not have a reasonable basis for projections beyond the current year. Accordingly, management should select the period most appropriate in the circumstances. In addition, management, in making a projection, should disclose what, in its opinion, is the most probable specific amount or the most reasonable range for each financial item projected based on the selected assumptions. Ranges, however, should not be so wide as to make the disclosures meaningless. Moreover, several projections based on varying assumptions may be judged by management to be more meaningful than a single number or range and would be permitted.

(3) *Investor understanding.* (i) When management chooses to include its projections in a Commission filing, the disclosures accompanying the projections should facilitate investor understanding of the basis for and limitations of projections. In this regard investors should be cautioned against attributing undue certainty to management's assessment, and the Commission believes that investors would be aided by a statement indicating management's intention regarding the furnishing of updated projections. The Commission also believes that investor understanding would be enhanced by disclosure of the assumptions which in management's opinion are most significant to the projections or are the key factors upon which the financial results of the enterprise depend and encourages disclosure of assumptions in a manner that will provide a framework for analysis of the projection.

(ii) Management also should consider whether disclosure of the accuracy or inaccuracy of previous projections would provide investors with important insights into the limitations of projections. In this regard, consideration should be given to presenting the projections in a format that will facilitate subsequent analysis of the reasons for differences between actual and forecast results. An important benefit may arise from the systematic analysis of variances between projected and actual results on a continuing basis, since such disclosure may highlight for investors the most significant risk and profit-sensitive areas in a business operation.

(iii) With respect to previously issued projections, registrants are reminded of their responsibility to make full and prompt disclosure of material facts, both favorable and unfavorable, regarding their financial condition. This responsibility may extend to situations where management knows or has reason to know that its previously disclosed projections no longer have a reasonable basis.

(iv) Since a registrant's ability to make projections with relative confidence may vary with all the facts and circumstances, the responsibility for determining whether to discontinue or to resume making projections is best left to management. However, the Commission encourages registrants not to discontinue or to resume projections in Commission filings without a reasonable basis.

(c) *Commission policy on security ratings.* In view of the importance of security ratings ("ratings") to investors and the marketplace, the Commission permits registrants to disclose, on a voluntary basis, ratings assigned by rating organizations to classes of debt securities, convertible debt securities and preferred stock in registration statements and periodic reports. Set forth herein are the Commission's views on important matters to be considered in disclosing security ratings.

(1) *Securities Act filings.* (i) If a registrant includes in a registration statement filed under the Securities Act any rating(s) assigned to a class of securities, it should consider including: (A) any other rating intended for public dissemination assigned to such class by a nationally recognized statistical rating organization (NRSRO) ("additional NRSRO rating") that is available on the date of the initial filing of the document and that is materially different from any rating disclosed; and (B) the name of each rating organization whose rating is disclosed; each such rating organization's definition or description of the category in which it rated the class of securities; the relative rank of each rating within the assigning rating organization's overall classification system; and a statement informing investors that a security rating is not a recommendation to buy, sell or hold securities, that it may be subject to revision or withdrawal at any time by the assigning rating organization, and that each rating should be evaluated independently of any other rating. The registrant also should include the written consent of any rating organization that is not a NRSRO whose rating is included. With respect to the written consent of any NRSRO whose rating is included, see Rule 436(g) under the Securities Act (§ 230.436(g) of this chapter).

(ii) If a change in a rating already included is available subsequent to the filing of the registration statement, but prior to its effectiveness, the registrant should consider including such rating change in the final prospectus. If the rating change is material or if a materially different rating from any disclosed becomes available during this period, the registrant should consider amending the registration statement to include the rating change or additional rating and recirculating the preliminary prospectus.

(iii) If a materially different additional NRSRO rating or a material change in a rating already included becomes available during any period in which offers or sales are being made, the registrant should consider disclosing such additional rating or rating change by means of a post-effective amendment or sticker to the prospectus pursuant to Rule 424(b) under the Securities Act (§ 230.424(b) of this chapter), unless, in the case of a registration statement on Form S-3 (§ 239.13 of this chapter), it has been disclosed in a document incorporated by reference into the registration statement subsequent to its effectiveness and prior to the termination of the offering.

(2) *Exchange Act filings.* (i) If a registrant includes in a registration statement or periodic report filed under the Exchange Act any rating(s) assigned to a class of securities, it should consider including the information specified in paragraphs (c)(1)(i)(A) and (B) of this section.

(ii) If there is a material change in the rating(s) assigned by any NRSRO(s) to any outstanding class(es) of securities of a registrant subject to the reporting requirements of section 13(a) or 15(d) of the Exchange Act, the registrant should consider filing a report on Form 8-K (§ 249.308 of this chapter) or other appropriate report under the Exchange Act disclosing such rating change.

(d) [Reserved.]

(e) *Use of non-GAAP financial measures in Commission filings*. (1) Whenever one or more non-GAAP financial measures are included in a filing with the Commission:

(i) The registrant must include the following in the filing:

(A) A presentation, with equal or greater prominence, of the most directly comparable financial measure or measures calculated and presented in accordance with Generally Accepted Accounting Principles (GAAP);

(B) A reconciliation (by schedule or other clearly understandable method), which shall be quantitative for historical non-GAAP measures presented, and quantitative, to the extent available without unreasonable efforts, for forward-looking information, of the differences between the non-GAAP financial measure disclosed or released with the most directly comparable financial measure or measures calculated and presented in accordance with GAAP identified in paragraph (e)(1)(i)(A) of this section;

(C) A statement disclosing the reasons why the registrant's management believes that presentation of the non-GAAP financial measure provides useful information to investors regarding the registrant's financial condition and results of operations; and

(D) To the extent material, a statement disclosing the additional purposes, if any, for which the registrant's management uses the non-GAAP financial measure that are not disclosed pursuant to paragraph (e)(1)(i)(C) of this section; and

(ii) A registrant must not:

(A) Exclude charges or liabilities that required, or will require, cash settlement, or would have required cash settlement absent an ability to settle in another manner, from non-GAAP liquidity measures, other than the measures earnings before interest and taxes (EBIT) and earnings before interest, taxes, depreciation, and amortization (EBITDA);

(B) Adjust a non-GAAP performance measure to eliminate or smooth items identified as non-recurring, infrequent or unusual, when the nature of the charge or gain is such that it is reasonably likely to recur within two years or there was a similar charge or gain within the prior two years;

(C) Present non-GAAP financial measures on the face of the registrant's financial statements prepared in accordance with GAAP or in the accompanying notes;

(D) Present non-GAAP financial measures on the face of any pro forma financial information required to be disclosed by Article 11 of Regulation S-X (17 CFR 210.11-01 through 210.11-03); or

(E) Use titles or descriptions of non-GAAP financial measures that are the same as, or confusingly similar to, titles or descriptions used for GAAP financial measures; and

(iii) If the filing is not an annual report on Form 10-K or Form 20-F (17 CFR 249.220f), a registrant need not include the information required by paragraphs (e)(1)(i)(C) and (e)(1)(i)(D) of this section if that information was included in its most recent annual report on Form 10-K or Form 20-F or a more recent filing, provided that the required information is updated to the extent necessary to meet the requirements of paragraphs (e)(1)(i)(C) and (e)(1)(i)(D) of this section at the time of the registrant's current filing.

(2) For purposes of this paragraph (e), a non-GAAP financial measure is a numerical measure of a registrant's historical or future financial performance, financial position or cash flows that:

(i) Excludes amounts, or is subject to adjustments that have the effect of excluding amounts, that are included in the most directly comparable measure calculated and presented in accordance with GAAP in the statement of comprehensive income, balance sheet or statement of cash flows (or equivalent statements) of the issuer; or

(ii) Includes amounts, or is subject to adjustments that have the effect of including amounts, that are excluded from the most directly comparable measure so calculated and presented.

(3) For purposes of this paragraph (e), GAAP refers to generally accepted accounting principles in the United States, except that (i) in the case of foreign private issuers whose primary financial statements are prepared in accordance with non-U.S. generally accepted accounting principles, GAAP refers to the principles under which those primary financial statements are prepared; and (ii) in the case of foreign private issuers that include a non-GAAP financial measure derived from or based on a measure calculated in accordance with U.S. generally accepted accounting principles, GAAP refers to U.S. generally accepted accounting principles for purposes of the application of the requirements of this paragraph (e) to the disclosure of that measure.

(4) For purposes of this paragraph (e), non-GAAP financial measures exclude:

(i) operating and other statistical measures; and

(ii) ratios or statistical measures calculated using exclusively one or both of:

(A) Financial measures calculated in accordance with GAAP; and

(B) Operating measures or other measures that are not non-GAAP financial measures.

(5) For purposes of this paragraph (e), non-GAAP financial measures exclude financial measures required to be disclosed by GAAP, Commission rules, or a system of regulation of a government or governmental authority or self-regulatory organization that is applicable to the registrant. However, the financial measure should be presented outside of the financial statements unless the financial measure is required or expressly permitted by the standard-setter that is responsible for establishing the GAAP used in such financial statements.

(6) The requirements of paragraph (e) of this section shall not apply to a non-GAAP financial measure included in disclosure relating to a proposed business combination, the entity resulting therefrom or an entity that is a party thereto, if the disclosure is contained in a communication that is subject to § 230.425 of this chapter, § 240.14a-12 or § 240.14d-2(b)(2) of this chapter or § 229.1015 of this chapter.

(7) The requirements of paragraph (e) of this section shall not apply to investment companies registered under Section 8 of the Investment Company Act of 1940 (15 U.S.C. 80a-8).

Note to paragraph (e).

A non-GAAP financial measure that would otherwise be prohibited by paragraph (e)(1)(ii) of this section is permitted in a filing of a foreign private issuer if:

1. The non-GAAP financial measure relates to the GAAP used in the registrant's primary financial statements included in its filing with the Commission;

2. The non-GAAP financial measure is required or expressly permitted by the standard-setter that is responsible for establishing the GAAP used in such financial statements; and

3. The non-GAAP financial measure is included in the annual report prepared by the registrant for use in the jurisdiction in which it is domiciled, incorporated or organized or for distribution to its security holders.

(f) *Smaller Reporting Companies.* The requirements of this part apply to smaller reporting companies. A smaller reporting company may comply with either the requirements applicable to smaller reporting companies or the requirements applicable to other companies for each item, unless the requirements for smaller reporting companies specify that smaller reporting companies must comply with the smaller reporting company requirements. The following items of this part set forth requirements for smaller reporting companies that are different from requirements applicable to other companies:

Index of Scaled Disclosure Available to Smaller Reporting Companies

Item 101	Description of business
Item 201	Market price of and dividends on registrant's common equity and related stockholder matters
Item 301	Selected financial data
Item 302	Supplementary financial information
Item 303	Management's discussion and analysis of financial condition and results of operations
Item 305	Quantitative and qualitative disclosures about market risk
Item 402	Executive compensation
Item 404	Transactions with related persons, promoters and certain control persons
Item 407	Corporate governance
Item 503	Prospectus summary
Item 504	Use of proceeds
Item 601	Exhibits

(1) *Definition of Smaller Reporting Company.* As used in this part, the term *smaller reporting company* means an issuer that is not an investment company, an asset-backed issuer (as defined in §229.1101), or a majority-owned subsidiary of a parent that is not a smaller reporting company and that:

(i) Had a public float of less than $250 million; or

(ii) Had annual revenues of less than $100 million and either:

(A) No public float; or

(B) A public float of less than $700 million.

(2) *Determination:* Whether or not an issuer is a smaller reporting company is determined on an annual basis.

(i) For issuers that are required to file reports under section 13(a) or 15(d) of the Exchange Act:

(A) Public float is measured as of the last business day of the issuer's most recently completed second fiscal quarter and computed by multiplying the aggregate worldwide number of shares of its voting and non-voting common equity held by non-affiliates by the price at which the common equity was last sold, or the average of the bid and asked prices of common equity, in the principal market for the common equity;

(B) Annual revenues are as of the most recently completed fiscal year for which audited financial statements are available; and

(C) An issuer must reflect the determination of whether it came within the definition of smaller reporting company in its quarterly report on Form 10-Q for the first fiscal quarter of the next year, indicating on the cover page of that filing, and in subsequent filings for that fiscal year, whether it is a smaller reporting company, except that, if a determination based on public float indicates that the issuer is newly eligible to be a smaller reporting company, the issuer may choose to reflect this determination beginning with its first quarterly report on Form 10-Q following the determination, rather than waiting until the first fiscal quarter of the next year.

(ii) For determinations based on an initial registration statement under the Securities Act or Exchange Act for shares of its common equity:

(A) Public float is measured as of a date within 30 days of the date of the filing of the registration statement and computed by multiplying the aggregate worldwide number of shares of its voting and non-voting common equity held by non-affiliates before the registration plus, in the case of a Securities Act registration statement, the number of shares of its voting and non-voting common equity included in the registration statement by the estimated public offering price of the shares;

(B) Annual revenues are as of the most recently completed fiscal year for which audited financial statements are available; and

(C) The issuer must reflect the determination of whether it came within the definition of smaller reporting company in the registration statement and must appropriately indicate on the cover page of the filing, and subsequent filings for the fiscal year in which the filing is made, whether it is a smaller reporting company. The issuer must re-determine its status at the end of its second fiscal quarter and then reflect any change in status as provided in paragraph (f)(2)(i)(C) of this section. In the case of a determination based on an initial Securities Act registration statement, an issuer that was not determined to be a smaller reporting company has the option to re-determine its status at the conclusion of the offering covered by the registration statement based on the actual offering price and number of shares sold.

(iii) Once an issuer determines that it does not qualify for smaller reporting company status because it exceeded one or more of the current thresholds, it will remain unqualified unless when making its annual determination either:

(A) It determines that its public float was less than $200 million; or

(B) It determines that its public float and its annual revenues meet the requirements for subsequent qualification included in the following chart:

Prior Annual Revenues	Prior Public Float	
	None or less than $700 million	**$700 million or more**
Less than $100 million	**Neither threshold exceeded.**	**Public float—Less than $560 million; and Revenues—Less than $100 million.**
$100 million or more	**Public float—None or less than $700 million; and Revenues—Less than $80 million.**	**Public float—Less than $560 million; and Revenues—Less than $80 million.**

Instruction 1 to Paragraph (f): A registrant that qualifies as a smaller reporting company under the public float thresholds identified in paragraphs (f)(1)(i) and (f)(2)(iii)(A) of this section will qualify as a smaller reporting company regardless of its revenues.

Instruction 2 to Paragraph (f): A foreign private issuer is not eligible to use the requirements for smaller reporting companies unless it uses the forms and rules designated for domestic issuers and provides financial statements prepared in accordance with U.S. Generally Accepted Accounting Principles.

Subpart 100—Business

Item 101. Description of Business

(a) *General development of business.* Describe the general development of the business of the registrant, its subsidiaries and any predecessor(s) during the past five years, or such shorter period as the registrant may have been engaged in business. Information shall be disclosed for earlier periods if material to an understanding of the general development of the business.

(1) In describing developments, information shall be given as to matters such as the following: the year in which the registrant was organized and its form of organization; the nature and results of any bankruptcy, receivership or similar proceedings with respect to the registrant or any of its significant subsidiaries; the nature and results of any other material reclassification, merger or consolidation of the registrant or any of its significant subsidiaries; the acquisition or disposition of any material amount of assets otherwise than in the ordinary course of business; and any material changes in the mode of conducting the business.

(2) Registrants:

(i) Filing a registration statement on Form S-1 (§ 239.11 of this chapter) under the Securities Act or on Form 10 (§ 249.210 of this chapter) under the Exchange Act;

(ii) Not subject to the reporting requirements of section 13(a) or 15(d) of the Exchange Act immediately before the filing of such registration statement; and

(iii) That (including predecessors) have not received revenue from operations during each of the three fiscal years immediately before the filing of such registration statement, shall provide the following information:

(A) If the registration statement is filed prior to the end of the registrant's second fiscal quarter, a description of the registrant's plan of operation for the remainder of the fiscal year; or

(B) If the registration statement is filed subsequent to the end of the registrant's second fiscal quarter, a description of the registrant's plan of operation for the remainder of the fiscal year and for the first six months of the next fiscal year. If such information is not available, the reasons for its not being available shall be stated. Disclosure relating to any plan shall include such matters as:

(1) In the case of a registration statement on Form S-1, a statement in narrative form indicating the registrant's opinion as to the period of time that the proceeds from the offering will satisfy cash requirements and whether in the next six months it will be necessary to raise additional funds to meet the expenditures required for operating the business of the registrant; the specific reasons for such opinion shall be set forth and categories of expenditures and sources of cash resources shall be identified; however, amounts of expenditures and cash resources need not be provided; in addition, if the narrative statement is based on a cash budget, such budget shall be furnished to the Commission as supplemental information, but not as part of the registration statement;

(2) An explanation of material product research and development to be performed during the period covered in the plan;

(3) Any anticipated material acquisition of plant and equipment and the capacity thereof;

(4) Any anticipated material changes in number of employees in the various departments such as research and development, production, sales or administration; and

(5) Other material areas which may be peculiar to the registrant's business.

(b) [Reserved.]

(c) *Narrative description of business.* (1) Describe the business done and intended to be done by the registrant and its subsidiaries, focusing upon the registrant's dominant segment or each reportable segment about which financial information is presented in the financial statements. To the extent material to an understanding of the registrant's business taken as a whole, the description of each such segment shall include the information specified in paragraphs (c)(1)(i) through (x) of this Item. The matters specified in paragraphs (c)(1)(xi) through (xiii) of this Item shall be discussed with respect to the registrant's business in general; where material, the segments to which these matters are significant shall be identified.

(i) The principal products produced and services rendered by the registrant in the segment and the principal markets for, and methods of distribution of, the segment's principal products and services. In addition, state for each of the last three fiscal years the amount or percentage of total revenue contributed by any class of similar products or services which accounted for 10 percent or more of consolidated revenue in any of the last three fiscal years or 15 percent or more of consolidated revenue, if total revenue did not exceed $50,000,000 during any of such fiscal years.

(ii) A description of the status of a product or segment (*e.g.* whether in the planning stage, whether prototypes exist, the degree to which product design has progressed or whether further engineering is necessary), if there has been a public announcement of, or if the registrant otherwise has made public information about, a new product or segment that would require the investment of a material amount of the assets of the registrant or that otherwise is material. This paragraph is not intended to require disclosure of otherwise nonpublic corporate information the disclosure of which would affect adversely the registrant's competitive position.

(iii) The sources and availability of raw materials.

(iv) The importance to the segment and the duration and effect of all patents, trademarks, licenses, franchises and concessions held.

(v) The extent to which the business of the segment is or may be seasonal.

(vi) The practices of the registrant and the industry (respective industries) relating to working capital items (*e.g.*, where the registrant is required to carry significant amounts of inventory to meet rapid delivery requirements of customers or to assure itself of a continuous allotment of goods from suppliers; where the registrant provides rights to return merchandise; or where the registrant has provided extended payment terms to customers).

(vii) The dependence of the segment upon a single customer, or a few customers, the loss of any one or more of which would have a material adverse effect on the segment. The name of any customer and its relationship, if any, with the registrant or its subsidiaries shall be disclosed if sales to the customer by one or more segments are made in an aggregate amount equal to 10 percent or more of the registrant's consolidated revenues and the loss of such customer would have a material adverse effect on the registrant and its subsidiaries taken as a whole. The names of other customers may be included, unless in the particular case the effect of including the names would be misleading. For purposes of this paragraph, a group of customers under common control or customers that are affiliates of each other shall be regarded as a single customer.

(viii) The dollar amount of backlog orders believed to be firm, as of a recent date and as of a comparable date in the preceding fiscal year, together with an indication of the portion thereof not reasonably expected to be filled within the current fiscal year, and seasonal or other material aspects of the backlog. (There may be included as firm orders government orders that are firm but not yet funded and contracts awarded but not yet signed, provided an appropriate statement is added to explain the nature of such orders and the amount thereof. The portion of orders already included in sales or operating revenues on the basis of percentage of completion or program accounting shall be excluded.)

(ix) A description of any material portion of the business that may be subject to renegotiation of profits or termination of contracts or subcontracts at the election of the Government.

(x) Competitive conditions in the business involved including, where material, the identity of the particular markets in which the registrant competes, an estimate of the number of competitors and the registrant's competitive position, if known or reasonably available to the registrant. Separate consideration shall be given to the principal products or services or classes of products or services of the segment, if any. Generally, the names of competitors need not be disclosed. The registrant may include such names, unless in the particular case the effect of including the names would be misleading. Where, however, the registrant knows or has reason to know that one or a small number of competitors is dominant in the industry it shall be identified. The principal methods of competition (*e.g.*, price, service, warranty or product performance) shall be identified, and positive and negative factors pertaining to the competitive position of the registrant, to the extent that they exist, shall be explained if known or reasonably available to the registrant.

(xi) [Reserved.]

(xii) Appropriate disclosure also shall be made as to the material effects that compliance with Federal, State and local provisions which have been enacted or adopted regulating the discharge of materials into the environment, or otherwise relating to the protection of the environment, may have upon the capital expenditures, earnings and competitive position of the registrant and its subsidiaries. The registrant shall disclose any material estimated capital expenditures for environmental control facilities for the remainder of its current fiscal year and its succeeding fiscal year and for such further periods as the registrant may deem material.

(xiii) The number of persons employed by the registrant.

(d) [Reserved.]

(e) *Available Information*. Disclose the information in paragraphs (e)(1), (e)(2) and (e)(3) of this section in any registration statement you file under the Securities Act (15 U.S.C. 77a *et seq.*), and disclose the information in paragraph (e)(3) of this section in your annual report on Form 10-K (§ 249.310 of this chapter). Further disclose the information in paragraph (e)(4) of this section if you are an accelerated filer or a large accelerated filer (as defined in § 240.12b-2 of this chapter) filing an annual report on Form 10-K (§ 249.310 of this chapter):

(1) Whether you file reports with the Securities and Exchange Commission. If you are a reporting company, identify the reports and other information you file with the SEC.

(2) State that the SEC maintains an internet site that contains reports, proxy and information statements, and other information regarding issuers that file electronically with the SEC and state the address of that site (http://www.sec.gov).

(3) Disclose your internet address, if you have one.

(4)(i) Whether you make available free of charge on or through your Internet website, if you have one, your annual report on Form 10-K, quarterly reports on Form 10-Q (§ 249.308a of this chapter), current reports on Form 8-K (§ 249.308 of this chapter), and amendments to those reports filed or furnished pursuant to Section 13(a) or 15(d) of the Exchange Act (15 U.S.C. 78m(a) or 78o(d)) as soon as reasonably practicable after you electronically file such material with, or furnish it to, the SEC;

(ii) If you do not make your filings available in this manner, the reasons you do not do so (including, where applicable, that you do not have an Internet website); and

(iii) If you do not make your filings available in this manner, whether you voluntarily will provide electronic or paper copies of your filings free of charge upon request.

(f) *Reports to Security Holders*. Disclose the following information in any registration statement you file under the Securities Act:

(1) If the SEC's proxy rules or regulations, or stock exchange requirements, do not require you to send an annual report to security holders or to holders of American depository receipts, describe briefly the nature and frequency of reports that you will give to security holders. Specify whether the reports that you give will contain financial information that has been examined and reported on, with an opinion expressed "by" an independent public or certified public accountant.

(2) For a foreign private issuer, if the report will not contain financial information prepared in accordance with U.S. generally accepted accounting principles, you must state whether the report will include a reconciliation of this information with U.S. generally accepted accounting principles.

(g) *Enforceability of Civil Liabilities Against Foreign Persons*. Disclose the following if you are a foreign private issuer filing a registration statement under the Securities Act:

(1) Whether or not investors may bring actions under the civil liability provisions of the U.S. federal securities laws against the foreign private issuer, any of its officers and directors who are residents of a foreign country, any underwriters or experts named in the registration statement that are residents of a foreign country, and whether investors may enforce these civil liability provisions when the assets of the issuer or these other persons are located outside of the United States. The disclosure must address the following matters:

(i) The investor's ability to effect service of process within the United States on the foreign private issuer or any person;

(ii) The investor's ability to enforce judgments obtained in U.S. courts against foreign persons based upon the civil liability provisions of the U.S. federal securities laws;

(iii) The investor's ability to enforce, in an appropriate foreign court, judgments of U.S. courts based upon the civil liability provisions of the U.S. federal securities laws; and

(iv) The investor's ability to bring an original action in an appropriate foreign court to enforce liabilities against the foreign private issuer or any person based upon the U.S. federal securities laws.

(2) If you provide this disclosure based on an opinion of counsel, name counsel in the prospectus and file as an exhibit to the registration statement a signed consent of counsel to the use of its name and opinion.

(h) *Smaller Reporting Companies.* A smaller reporting company, as defined by § 229.10(f)(1), may satisfy its obligations under this Item by describing the development of its business during the last three years. If the smaller reporting company has not been in business for three years, give the same information for predecessor(s) of the smaller reporting company if there are any. This business development description should include:

(1) Form and year of organization;

(2) Any bankruptcy, receivership or similar proceeding; and

(3) Any material reclassification, merger, consolidation, or purchase or sale of a significant amount of assets not in the ordinary course of business.

(4) *Business of the Smaller Reporting Company.* Briefly describe the business and include, to the extent material to an understanding of the smaller reporting company:

(i) Principal products or services and their markets;

(ii) Distribution methods of the products or services;

(iii) Status of any publicly announced new product or service;

(iv) Competitive business conditions and the smaller reporting company's competitive position in the industry and methods of competition;

(v) Sources and availability of raw materials and the names of principal suppliers;

(vi) Dependence on one or a few major customers;

(vii) Patents, trademarks, licenses, franchises, concessions, royalty agreements or labor contracts, including duration;

(viii) Need for any government approval of principal products or services. If government approval is necessary and the smaller reporting company has not yet received that approval, discuss the status of the approval within the government approval process;

(ix) Effect of existing or probable governmental regulations on the business;

(x) [Reserved.]

(xi) Costs and effects of compliance with environmental laws (federal, state and local); and

(xii) Number of total employees and number of full-time employees.

(5) *Reports to Security Holders.* Disclose the following in any registration statement you file under the Securities Act of 1933:

(i) If you are not required to deliver an annual report to security holders, whether you will voluntarily send an annual report and whether the report will include audited financial statements;

(ii) Whether you file reports with the Securities and Exchange Commission. If you are a reporting company, identify the reports and other information you file with the Commission; and

(iii) State that the Commission maintains an internet site that contains reports, proxy and information statements, and other information regarding issuers that file electronically with the Commission and state the address of that site (http://www.sec.gov). Disclose your internet address, if available.

(6) *Foreign Issuers.* Provide the information required by Item 101(g) of Regulation S-K (§ 229.101(g)).

Instructions to Item 101. 1. In determining what information about the segments is material to an understanding of the registrant's business taken as a whole and therefore required to be disclosed pursuant to paragraph (c) of this Item, the registrant should take into account both quantitative and qualitative factors such as the significance of the matter to the registrant (*e.g.,* whether a matter with a relatively minor impact on the registrant's business is represented by management to be important to its future profitability), the pervasiveness of the matter (*e.g.,* whether it affects or may affect numerous items in the segment information), and the impact of the matter (*e.g.,* whether it distorts the trends reflected in the segment information). Situations may arise when information should be disclosed about a segment, although the information in quantitative terms may not appear significant to the registrant's business taken as a whole.

2. Base the determination of whether information about segments is required for a particular year upon an evaluation of interperiod comparability. For instance, interperiod comparability would require a registrant to report segment information in the current period even if not material under the criteria for reportability of FASB ASC Topic 280, Segment Reporting, if a segment has been significant in the immediately preceding period and the registrant expects it to be significant in the future.

3. The Commission, upon written request of the registrant and where consistent with the protection of investors, may permit the omission of any of the information required by this Item or the furnishing in substitution thereof of appropriate information of comparable character.

Item 102. Description of Property

State that the SEC maintains an internet site that contains reports, proxy and information statements, and other information regarding issuers that file electronically with the SEC and state the address of that site (http://www.sec.gov).

Instruction 1 to Item 102. This item requires information that will reasonably inform investors as to the suitability, adequacy, productive capacity, and extent of utilization of the principal physical properties of the registrant and its subsidiaries, to the extent the described properties are material. A registrant should engage in a comprehensive consideration of the materiality of its properties. If appropriate, descriptions may be provided on a collective basis; detailed descriptions of the physical characteristics of individual properties or legal descriptions by metes and bounds are not required and shall not be given.

Instruction 2 to Item 102. In determining materiality under this Item, the registrant should take into account both quantitative and qualitative factors. See Instruction 1 to Item 101 of Regulation S-K (§ 229.101).

Instruction 3 to Item 102. Registrants engaged in mining operations must refer to and, if required, provide the disclosure under §§ 229.1300 through 229.1305 (subpart 1300 of Regulation S-K), in addition to any disclosure required by this section.

Instruction 4 to Item 102. A registrant engaged in oil and gas producing activities shall provide the information required by Subpart 1200 of Regulation S-K.

Instruction 5 to Item 102. The definitions in § 210.4-10(a) of Regulation S-X [17 CFR 210] shall apply to this Item with respect to oil and gas operations.

Instruction 6 to Item 102. The attention of certain issuers engaged in oil and gas producing activities is directed to the information called for in Securities Act Industry Guide 4 (referred to in § 229.801(d)).

Instruction 7 to Item 102. The attention of issuers engaged in real estate activities is directed to the information called for in Guide 5 (§ 229.801(e) of this chapter).

Item 103. Legal Proceedings

Describe briefly any material pending legal proceedings, other than ordinary routine litigation incidental to the business, to which the registrant or any of its subsidiaries is a party or of which any of their property is the subject. Include the name of the court or agency in which the proceedings are pending, the date instituted, the principal parties thereto, a description of the factual basis alleged to underlie the proceeding and the relief sought. Include similar information as to any such proceedings known to be contemplated by governmental authorities.

Instructions to Item 103. 1. If the business ordinarily results in actions for negligence or other claims, no such action or claim need be described unless it departs from the normal kind of such actions.

2. No information need be given with respect to any proceeding that involves primarily a claim for damages if the amount involved, exclusive of interest and costs, does not exceed 10 percent of the current assets of the registrant and its subsidiaries on a consolidated basis. However, if any proceeding presents in large degree the same legal and factual issues as other proceedings pending or known to be contemplated, the amount involved in such other proceedings shall be included in computing such percentage.

3. Notwithstanding Instructions 1 and 2, any material bankruptcy, receivership, or similar proceeding with respect to the registrant or any of its significant subsidiaries shall be described.

4. Any material proceedings to which any director, officer or affiliate of the registrant, any owner of record or beneficially of more than five percent of any class of voting securities of the registrant, or any associate of any such director, officer, affiliate of the registrant, or security holder is a party adverse to the registrant or any of its subsidiaries or has a material interest adverse to the registrant or any of its subsidiaries also shall be described.

5. Notwithstanding the foregoing, an administrative or judicial proceeding (including, for purposes of A and B of this Instruction, proceedings which present in large degree the same issues) arising under any Federal, State or local provisions that have been enacted or adopted regulating the discharge of materials into the environment or primary [primarily] for the purpose of protecting the environment shall not be deemed "ordinary routine litigation incidental to the business" and shall be described if:

    A. Such proceeding is material to the business or financial condition of the registrant;

    B. Such proceeding involves primarily a claim for damages, or involves potential monetary sanctions, capital expenditures, deferred charges or charges to income and the amount involved, exclusive of interest and costs, exceeds 10 percent of the current assets of the registrant and its subsidiaries on a consolidated basis; or

C. A governmental authority is a party to such proceeding and such proceeding involves potential monetary sanctions, unless the registrant reasonably believes that such proceeding will result in no monetary sanctions, or in monetary sanctions, exclusive of interest and costs, of less than $100,000; provided, however, that such proceedings which are similar in nature may be grouped and described generically.

Item 104. Mine Safety Disclosure

(a) A registrant that is the operator, or that has a subsidiary that is an operator, of a coal or other mine shall provide the information specified below for the time period covered by the report:

(1) For each coal or other mine of which the registrant or a subsidiary of the registrant is an operator, identify the mine and disclose:

(i) The total number of violations of mandatory health or safety standards that could significantly and substantially contribute to the cause and effect of a coal or other mine safety or health hazard under section 104 of the Federal Mine Safety and Health Act of1977 (30 U.S.C. 814) for which the operator received a citation from the Mine Safety and Health Administration.

(ii) The total number of orders issued under section 104(b) of such Act (30 U.S.C.814(b)).

(iii) The total number of citations and orders for unwarrantable failure of the mine operator to comply with mandatory health or safety standards under section 104(d) of such Act (30 U.S.C. 814(d)).

(iv) The total number of flagrant violations under section 110(b)(2) of such Act (30U.S.C. 820(b)(2)).

(v) The total number of imminent danger orders issued under section 107(a) of such Act (30 U.S.C. 817(a)).

(vi) The total dollar value of proposed assessments from the Mine Safety and Health Administration under such Act (30 U.S.C. 801 et seq.).

Instruction to Item 104(a)(1)(vi): Registrants must provide the total dollar value of assessments proposed by MSHA relating to any type of violation during the period covered by the report, regardless of whether the registrant has challenged or appealed the assessment.

(vii) The total number of mining-related fatalities.

Instruction to Item 104(a)(1)(vii): Registrants must report all fatalities occurring at a coal or other mine during the period covered by the report unless the fatality has been determined by MSHA to be unrelated to mining activity.

(2) A list of coal or other mines, of which the registrant or a subsidiary of the registrant is an operator, that receive written notice from the Mine Safety and Health Administration of:

(i) A pattern of violations of mandatory health or safety standards that are of such nature as could have significantly and substantially contributed to the cause and effect of coal or other mine health or safety hazards under section 104(e) of such Act (30U.S.C. 814(e)); or

(ii) The potential to have such a pattern.

(3) Any pending legal action before the Federal Mine Safety and Health Review Commission involving such coal or other mine.

Instruction to Item 104(a)(3): The registrant must report the total number of legal actions that were pending before the Federal Mine Safety and Health Review Commission as of the last day of the time period covered by the report, as well as the aggregate number of legal actions instituted and the aggregate number of legal actions resolved during the reporting period. With respect to the total number of legal actions that were pending before the Federal Mine Safety and Health Review Commission as of the last day of the time period covered by the report, the registrant must also report the number of such legal actions that are:

1. Contests of citations and orders referenced in Subpart B of 29 CFR Part2700;

2. Contests of proposed penalties referenced in Subpart C of 29 CFR Part 2700;

3. Complaints for compensation referenced in Subpart D of 29 CFR Part 2700;

4. Complaints of discharge, discrimination or interference referenced in Subpart E of 29 CFR Part 2700;

5. Applications for temporary relief referenced in Subpart F of 29 CFR Part2700; and

6. Appeals of judges' decisions or orders to the Federal Mine Safety and Health Review Commission referenced in Subpart H of 29 CFR Part 2700.

(b) Definitions. For purposes of this Item:

(1) The term coal or other mine means a coal or other mine, as defined in section 3of the Federal Mine Safety and Health Act of 1977 (30 U.S.C. 802), that is subject to the provisions of such Act (30 U.S.C. 801 et seq.).

(2) The term operator has the meaning given the term in section 3 of the Federal Mine Safety and Health Act of 1977 (30 U.S.C. 802).

(3) The term subsidiary has the meaning given the term in Exchange Act Rule 12b-2(17 CFR 240.12b-2).

Instructions to Item 104:1.

The registrant must provide the information required by this Item as specified by § 229.601(b)(95) of this chapter. In addition, the registrant must provide a statement, in an appropriately captioned section of the periodic report, that the information concerning mine safety violations or other regulatory matters required by Section 1503(a) of the Dodd-Frank Wall Street Reform and Consumer Protection Act and this Item is included in exhibit 95 to the periodic report.

2. When the disclosure required by this item is included in an exhibit to an annual report on Form 10-K, the information is to be provided for the registrant's fiscal year.

Item 105. Risk Factors.

Where appropriate, provide under the caption "Risk Factors" a discussion of the most significant factors that make an investment in the registrant or offering speculative or risky. This discussion must be concise and organized logically. Do not present risks that could apply generically to any registrant or any offering. Explain how the risk affects the registrant or the securities being offered. Set forth each risk factor under a subcaption that adequately describes the risk. If the risk factor discussion is included in a registration statement, it must immediately follow the summary section. If you do not include a summary section, the risk factor section must immediately follow the cover page of the prospectus or the pricing information section that immediately follows the cover page. Pricing information means price and price-related information that you may omit from the prospectus in an effective registration statement based on Rule 430A (§ 230.430A(a) of this chapter). The registrant must furnish this information in plain English. See § 230.421(d) of Regulation C of this chapter.

Subpart 200—Securities of the Registrant

Item 201. Market Price of and Dividends on the Registrant's Common Equity and Related Stockholder Matters

(a) *Market information.*

(1)(i) Identify the principal United States market(s) and the corresponding trading symbol(s) for each class of the registrant's common equity. In the case of foreign registrants, also identify the principal foreign public trading market(s), if any, and the corresponding trading symbol(s) for each class of the registrant's common equity.

(ii) If the principal United States market for such common equity is not an exchange, indicate, as applicable, that any over-the-counter market quotations reflect inter-dealer prices, without retail mark-up, mark-down or commission and may not necessarily represent actual transactions.

(iii) Where there is no established public trading market for a class of common equity, furnish a statement to that effect and, if applicable, state the range of high and low bid information for each full quarterly period within the two most recent fiscal years and any subsequent interim period for which financial statements are included, or are required to be included by 17 CFR 210.3-01 through 210.3-20 (Article 3 of Regulation S–X), indicating the source of such quotations. Reference to quotations shall be qualified by appropriate explanation. For purposes of this Item the existence of limited or sporadic quotations should not of itself be deemed to constitute an "established public trading market."

(2) If the information called for by this paragraph (a) is being presented in a registration statement on Form S-1 (§ 239.11 of this chapter) under the Securities Act or on Form 10 (§ 249.210 of this chapter) under the Exchange Act relating to a class of common equity for which at the time of filing there is no established United States public trading market, indicate the amount(s) of common equity:

(i) [Reserved.]

(ii) That could be sold pursuant to § 230.144 of this chapter or that the registrant has agreed to register under the Securities Act for sale by security holders; or

(iii) That is being, or has been publicly proposed to be, publicly offered by the registrant (unless such common equity is being offered pursuant to an employee benefit plan or dividend reinvestment plan), the offering of which could have a material effect on the market price of the registrant's common equity.

(b) *Holders.* (1) Set forth the approximate number of holders of each class of common equity of the registrant as of the latest practicable date.

(2) If the information called for by this paragraph (b) is being presented in a registration statement filed pursuant to the Securities Act or a proxy statement or information statement filed pursuant to the Exchange Act that relates to an acquisition, business combination or other reorganization, indicate the effect of such transaction on the amount and percentage of present holdings of the registrant's common equity owned beneficially by (i) any person (including any group as that term is used in section 13(d)(3) of the Exchange Act) who is known to the registrant to be the beneficial owner of more than five percent of any class of the registrant's common equity and (ii) each director and nominee and (iii) all directors and officers as a group, and the registrant's present commitments to such persons with respect to the issuance of shares of any class of its common equity.

(c) *Dividends.* [Reserved.]

(2) Where registrants have a record of paying no cash dividends although earnings indicate an ability to do so, they are encouraged to consider the question of their intention to pay cash dividends in the foreseeable future and, if no such intention exists, to make a statement of that fact in the filing. Registrants which have a history of paying cash dividends also are encouraged to indicate whether they currently expect that comparable cash dividends will continue to be paid in the future and, if not, the nature of the change in the amount or rate of cash dividend payments.

(d) *Securities authorized for issuance under equity compensation plans.* (1) In the following tabular format, provide the information specified in paragraph (d)(2) of this Item as of the end of the most recently completed fiscal year with respect to compensation plans (including individual compensation arrangements) under which equity securities of the registrant are authorized for issuance, aggregated as follows:

(i) All compensation plans previously approved by security holders; and

(ii) All compensation plans not previously approved by security holders.

Equity Compensation Plan Information

Plan category	Number of securities to be issued upon exercise of outstanding options, warrants and rights (a)	Weighted-average exercise price of outstanding options, warrants and rights (b)	Number of securities remaining available for future issuance under equity compensation plans (excluding securities reflected in column (a)) (c)
Equity compensation plans approved by security holders			
Equity compensation plans not approved by security holders			
Total			

(2) The table shall include the following information as of the end of the most recently completed fiscal year for each category of equity compensation plan described in paragraph (d)(1) of this Item:

(i) The number of securities to be issued upon the exercise of outstanding options, warrants and rights (column (a));

(ii) The weighted-average exercise price of the outstanding options, warrants and rights disclosed pursuant to paragraph (d)(2)(i) of this Item (column (b)); and

(iii) Other than securities to be issued upon the exercise of the outstanding options, warrants and rights disclosed in paragraph (d)(2)(i) of this Item, the number of securities remaining available for future issuance under the plan (column (c)).

(3) For each compensation plan under which equity securities of the registrant are authorized for issuance that was adopted without the approval of security holders, describe briefly, in narrative form, the material features of the plan.

Instructions to Paragraph (d).

1. Disclosure shall be provided with respect to any compensation plan and individual compensation arrangement of the registrant (or parent, subsidiary or affiliate of the registrant) under which equity securities of the registrant are authorized for issuance to employees or non-employees (such as directors, consultants, advisors, vendors, customers, suppliers or lenders) in exchange for consideration in the form of goods or services as described in FASB ASC Topic 718, Compensation—Stock Compensation, and FASB ASC Subtopic 505-50, Equity—Equity-Based Payments to Non-Employees. No disclosure is required with respect to

(i) any plan, contract or arrangement for the issuance of warrants or rights to all security holders of the registrant as such on a pro rata basis (such as a stock rights offering) or

(ii) any employee benefit plan that is intended to meet the qualification requirements of Section 401(a) of the Internal Revenue Code (26 U.S.C. § 401(a)).

2. For purposes of this paragraph, an "individual compensation arrangement" includes, but is not limited to, the following: a written compensation contract within the meaning of "employee benefit plan" under § 230.405 of this chapter and a plan (whether or not set forth in any formal document) applicable to one person as provided under Item 402(a)(6)(ii) of Regulation S-K (§ 229.402(a)(6)(ii)).

3. If more than one class of equity security is issued under its equity compensation plans, a registrant should aggregate plan information for each class of security.

4. A registrant may aggregate information regarding individual compensation arrangements with the plan information required under paragraph (d)(1)(i) and (ii) of this item, as applicable.

5. A registrant may aggregate information regarding a compensation plan assumed in connection with a merger, consolidation or other acquisition transaction pursuant to which the registrant may make subsequent grants or awards of its equity securities with the plan information required under paragraph (d)(1)(i) and (ii) of this item, as applicable. A registrant shall disclose on an aggregated basis in a footnote to the table the information required under paragraph (d)(2)(i) and (ii) of this item with respect to any individual options, warrants or rights assumed in connection with a merger, consolidation or other acquisition transaction.

6. To the extent that the number of securities remaining available for future issuance disclosed in column (c) includes securities available for future issuance under any compensation plan or individual compensation arrangement other than upon the exercise of an option, warrant or right, disclose the number of securities and type of plan separately for each such plan in a footnote to the table.

7. If the description of an equity compensation plan set forth in a registrant's financial statements contains the disclosure required by paragraph (d)(3) of this item, a cross-reference to such description will satisfy the requirements of paragraph (d)(3) of this item.

8. If an equity compensation plan contains a formula for calculating the number of securities available for issuance under the plan, including, without limitation, a formula that automatically increases the number of securities available for issuance by a percentage of the number of outstanding securities of the registrant, a description of this formula shall be disclosed in a footnote to the table.

9. Except where it is part of a document that is incorporated by reference into a prospectus, the information required by this paragraph need not be provided in any registration statement filed under the Securities Act.

(e) *Performance Graph.* (1) Provide a line graph comparing the yearly percentage change in the registrant's cumulative total shareholder return on a class of common stock registered under section 12 of the Exchange Act (as measured by dividing the sum of the cumulative amount of dividends for the measurement period, assuming dividend reinvestment, and the difference between the registrant's share price at the end and the beginning of the measurement period; by the share price at the beginning of the measurement period) with:

(i) The cumulative total return of a broad equity market index assuming reinvestment of dividends, that includes companies whose equity securities are traded on the same exchange or are of comparable market capitalization; *provided, however,* that if the registrant is a company within the Standard & Poor's 500 Stock Index, the registrant must use that index; and

(ii) The cumulative total return, assuming reinvestment of dividends, of:

(A) A published industry or line-of-business index;

(B) Peer issuer(s) selected in good faith. If the registrant does not select its peer issuer(s) on an industry or line-of-business basis, the registrant shall disclose the basis for its selection; or

(C) Issuer(s) with similar market capitalization(s), but only if the registrant does not use a published industry or line-of-business index and does not believe it can reasonably identify a peer group. If the registrant uses this alternative, the graph shall be accompanied by a statement of the reasons for this selection.

(2) For purposes of paragraph (e)(1) of this Item, the term "measurement period" shall be the period beginning at the "measurement point" established by the market close on the last trading day before the beginning of the registrant's fifth preceding fiscal year, through and including the end of the registrant's last completed fiscal year. If the class of securities

has been registered under section 12 of the Exchange Act (15 U.S.C. 78*l*) for a shorter period of time, the period covered by the comparison may correspond to that time period.

(3) For purposes of paragraph (e)(1)(ii)(A) of this Item, the term "published industry or line-of-business index" means any index that is prepared by a party other than the registrant or an affiliate and is accessible to the registrant's security holders; *provided, however,* that registrants may use an index prepared by the registrant or affiliate if such index is widely recognized and used.

(4) If the registrant selects a different index from an index used for the immediately preceding fiscal year, explain the reason(s) for this change and also compare the registrant's total return with that of both the newly selected index and the index used in the immediately preceding fiscal year.

Instructions to Item 201(e):

1. In preparing the required graphic comparisons, the registrant should:

a. Use, to the extent feasible, comparable methods of presentation and assumptions for the total return calculations required by paragraph (e)(1) of this Item; *provided, however,* that if the registrant constructs its own peer group index under paragraph (e)(1)(ii)(B), the same methodology must be used in calculating both the registrant's total return and that on the peer group index; and

b. Assume the reinvestment of dividends into additional shares of the same class of equity securities at the frequency with which dividends are paid on such securities during the applicable fiscal year.

2. In constructing the graph:

a. The closing price at the measurement point must be converted into a fixed investment, stated in dollars, in the registrant's stock (or in the stocks represented by a given index) with cumulative returns for each subsequent fiscal year measured as a change from that investment; and

b. Each fiscal year should be plotted with points showing the cumulative total return as of that point. The value of the investment as of each point plotted on a given return line is the number of shares held at that point multiplied by the then prevailing share price.

3. The registrant is required to present information for the registrant's last five fiscal years, and may choose to graph a longer period; but the measurement point, however, shall remain the same.

4. Registrants may include comparisons using performance measures in addition to total return, such as return on average common shareholders' equity.

5. If the registrant uses a peer issuer(s) comparison or comparison with issuer(s) with similar market capitalizations, the identity of those issuers must be disclosed and the returns of each component issuer of the group must be weighted according to the respective issuer's stock market capitalization at the beginning of each period for which a return is indicated.

6. *Smaller Reporting Companies.* A registrant that qualifies as a smaller reporting company, as defined by § 229.10(f)(1), is not required to provide the information required by paragraph (e) of this Item.

7. The information required by paragraph (e) of this Item need not be provided in any filings other than an annual report to security holders required by Exchange Act Rule 14a-3 (17 CFR 240.14a-3) or Exchange Act Rule 14c-3 (17 CFR 240.14c-3) that precedes or accompanies a registrant's proxy or information statement relating to an annual meeting of security holders at which directors are to be elected (or special meeting or written consents in lieu of such meeting). Such information will not be deemed to be incorporated by reference into any filing under the Securities Act or the Exchange Act, except to the extent that the registrant specifically incorporates it by reference.

8. The information required by paragraph (e) of this Item shall not be deemed to be "soliciting material" or to be "filed" with the Commission or subject to Regulation 14A or 14C (17 CFR 240.14a-1–240.14a-104 or 240.14c-1–240.14c-101), other than as provided in this item, or to the liabilities of section 18 of the Exchange Act (15 U.S.C. 78r), except to the extent that the registrant specifically requests that such information be treated as soliciting material or specifically incorporates it by reference into a filing under the Securities Act or the Exchange Act.

Instructions to Item 201. [Reserved.]

Instruction 2 to Item 201. Bid information reported pursuant to this Item shall be adjusted to give retroactive effect to material changes resulting from stock dividends, stock splits and reverse stock splits

Instruction 3 to Item 201. The computation of the approximate number of holders of registrant's common equity may be based upon the number of record holders or also may include individual participants in security position listings. See Rule 17Ad-8 under the Exchange Act. The method of computation that is chosen shall be indicated.

Instruction 4 to Item 201. If the registrant is a foreign issuer, describe briefly:

A. Any governmental laws, decrees or regulations in the country in which the registrant is organized that restrict the export or import of capital, including, but not limited to, foreign exchange controls, or that affect the remittance of dividends or other payments to nonresident holders of the registrant's common equity; and

B. All taxes, including withholding provisions, to which United States common equity holders are subject under existing laws and regulations of the foreign country in which the registrant is organized. Include a brief description of pertinent provisions of any reciprocal tax treaty between such foreign country and the United States regarding withholding. If there is no such treaty, so state.

Instruction 5 to Item 201. If the registrant is a foreign private issuer whose common equity of the class being registered is wholly or partially in bearer form, the response to this Item shall so indicate together with as much information as the registrant is able to provide with respect to security holdings in the United States. If the securities being registered trade in the United States in the form of American Depositary Receipts or similar certificates, the response to this Item shall so indicate together with the name of the depositary issuing such receipts and the number of shares or other units of the underlying security representing the trading units in such receipts.

Item 202. Description of Registrant's Securities

(a) *Capital stock.* If capital stock is to be registered, state the title of the class and describe such of the matters listed in paragraphs (a)(1) through (5) as are relevant. A complete legal description of the securities need not be given.

(1) Outline briefly: (i) dividend rights; (ii) terms of conversion; (iii) sinking fund provisions; (iv) redemption provisions; (v) voting rights, including any provisions specifying the vote required by security holders to take action; (vi) any classification of the Board of Directors, and the impact of such classification where cumulative voting is permitted or required; (vii) liquidation rights; (viii) preemption rights; and (ix) liability to further calls or to assessment by the registrant and for liabilities of the registrant imposed on its stockholders under state statutes (*e.g.,* to laborers, servants or employees of the registrant), unless such disclosure would be immaterial because the financial resources of the registrant or other factors make it improbable that liability under such state statutes would be imposed; (x) any restriction on alienability of the securities to be registered; and (xi) any provision discriminating against any existing or prospective holder of such securities as a result of such security holder owning a substantial amount of securities.

(2) If the rights of holders of such stock may be modified otherwise than by a vote of a majority or more of the shares outstanding, voting as a class, so state and explain briefly.

(3) If preferred stock is to be registered, describe briefly any restriction on the repurchase or redemption of shares by the registrant while there is any arrearage in the payment of dividends or sinking fund installments. If there is no such restriction, so state.

(4) If the rights evidenced by, or amounts payable with respect to, the shares to be registered are, or may be, materially limited or qualified by the rights of any other authorized class of securities, include the information regarding such other securities as will enable investors to understand such limitations or qualifications. No information need be given, however, as to any class of securities all of which will be retired, provided appropriate steps to ensure such retirement will be completed prior to or upon delivery by the registrant of the shares.

(5) Describe briefly or cross-reference to a description in another part of the document, any provision of the registrant's charter or by-laws that would have an effect of delaying, deferring or preventing a change in control of the registrant and that would operate only with respect to an extraordinary corporate transaction involving the registrant [or any of its subsidiaries], such as a merger, reorganization, tender offer, sale or transfer of substantially all of its assets, or liquidation. Provisions and arrangements required by law or imposed by governmental or judicial authority need not be described or discussed pursuant to this paragraph (a)(5). Provisions or arrangements adopted by the registrant to effect, or further, compliance with laws or governmental or judicial mandate are not subject to the immediately preceding sentence where such compliance did not require the specific provisions or arrangements adopted.

(b) *Debt securities.* If debt securities are to be registered, state the title of such securities, the principal amount being offered, and, if a series, the total amount authorized and the total amount outstanding as of the most recent practicable date; and describe such of the matter listed in paragraphs (b)(1) through (10) as are relevant. A complete legal description of the securities need not be given. For purposes solely of this Item, debt securities that differ from one another only as to the interest rate or maturity shall be regarded as securities of the same class. Outline briefly:

(1) Provisions with respect to maturity, interest, conversion, redemption, amortization, sinking fund, or retirement;

(2) Provisions with respect to the kind and priority of any lien securing the securities, together with a brief identification of the principal properties subject to such lien;

(3) Provisions with respect to the subordination of the rights of holders of the securities to other security holders or creditors of the registrant; where debt securities are designated as subordinated in accordance with Instruction 1 to this Item, set forth the aggregate amount of outstanding indebtedness as of the most recent practicable date that by the terms of such debt securities would be senior to such subordinated debt and describe briefly any limitation on the issuance of such additional senior indebtedness or state that there is no such limitation;

(4) Provisions restricting the declaration of dividends or requiring the maintenance of any asset ratio or the creation or maintenance of reserves;

(5) Provisions restricting the incurrence of additional debt or the issuance of additional securities; in the case of secured debt, whether the securities being registered are to be issued on the basis of unbonded bondable property, the deposit of cash or otherwise; as of the most recent practicable date, the approximate amount of unbonded bondable property available as a basis for the issuance of bonds; provisions permitting the withdrawal of cash deposited as a basis for the issuance of bonds; and provisions permitting the release or substitution of assets securing the issue; *Provided, however,* That provisions permitting the release of assets upon the deposit of equivalent funds or the pledge of equivalent property, the release of property no longer required in the business, obsolete property, or property taken by eminent domain or the application of insurance moneys, and other similar provisions need not be described;

(6) The general type of event that constitutes a default and whether or not any periodic evidence is required to be furnished as to the absence of default or as to compliance with the terms of the indenture;

(7) Provisions relating to modification of the terms of the security or the rights of security holders;

(8) If the rights evidenced by the securities to be registered are, or may be, materially limited or qualified by the rights of any other authorized class of securities, the information regarding such other securities as will enable investors to understand the rights evidenced by the securities[;] to the extent not otherwise disclosed pursuant to this Item; no information need be given, however, as to any class of securities all of which will be retired, provided appropriate steps to ensure such retirement will be completed prior to or upon delivery by the registrant of the securities;

(9) If debt securities are to be offered at a price such that they will be deemed to be offered at an "original issue discount" as defined in paragraph (a) of Section 1273 of the Internal Revenue Code (26 U.S.C. 1273), or if a debt security is sold in a package with another security and the allocation of the offering price between the two securities may have the effect of offering the debt security at such an original issue discount, the tax effects thereof pursuant to sections 1271—1278; and

(10) The name of the trustee(s) and the nature of any material relationship with the registrant or with any of its affiliates; the percentage of securities of the class necessary to require the trustee to take action; and what indemnification the trustee may require before proceeding to enforce the lien.

(c) *Warrants and rights.* If the securities described are to be offered pursuant to warrants or rights state:

(1) The amount of securities called for by such warrants or rights;

(2) The period during which and the price at which the warrants or rights are exercisable;

(3) The amount of warrants or rights outstanding;

(4) Provisions for changes to or adjustments in the exercise price; and

(5) Any other material terms of such rights on [or] warrants.

(d) *Other securities.* If securities other than capital stock, debt, warrants or rights are to be registered, include a brief description (comparable to that required in paragraphs (a), (b) and (c) of Item 202) of the rights evidenced thereby.

(e) *Market information for securities other than common equity.* If securities other than common equity are to be registered and there is an established public trading market for such securities (as that term is used in Item 201 of Regulation S-K (§ 229.201 of this chapter)) provide market information with respect to such securities comparable to that required by paragraph (a) of Item 201 of Regulation S-K (§ 229.201).

(f) *American Depositary Receipts.* If Depositary Shares represented by American Depositary Receipts are being registered, furnish the following information:

(1) The name of the depositary and the address of its principal executive office.

(2) State the title of the American Depositary Receipts and identify the deposited security. Describe briefly the terms of deposit, including the provisions, if any, with respect to: (i) the amount of deposited securities represented by one unit of American Depositary Receipts; (ii) the procedure for voting, if any, the deposited securities; (iii) the collection and distribution of dividends; (iv) the transmission of notices, reports and proxy soliciting material; (v) the sale or exercise of rights; (vi) the deposit or sale of securities resulting from dividends, splits or plans of reorganization; (vii) amendment, extension or termination of the deposit; (viii) rights of holders of receipts to inspect the transfer books of the depositary and the list of holders of receipts; (ix) restrictions upon the right to deposit or withdraw the underlying securities; (x) limitation upon the liability of the depositary.

(3) Describe all fees and charges which may be imposed directly or indirectly against the holder of the American Depositary Receipts, indicating the type of service, the amount of fee or charges and to whom paid.

Instructions to Item 202. 1. Wherever the title of securities is required to be stated, there shall be given such information as will indicate the type and general character of the securities, including the following:

A. In the case of shares, the par or stated value, if any; the rate of dividends, if fixed, and whether cumulative or non-cumulative; a brief indication of the preference, if any; and if convertible or redeemable, a statement to that effect;

B. In the case of debt, the rate of interest; the date of maturity or, if the issue matures serially, a brief indication of the serial maturities, such as "maturing serially from 1955 to 1960"; if the payment of principal or interest is contingent, an appropriate indication of such contingency; a brief indication of the priority of the issue; and, if convertible or callable, a statement to that effect; or

C. In the case of any other kind of security, appropriate information of comparable character.

2. If the registrant is a foreign registrant, include (to the extent not disclosed in the document pursuant to Item 201 of Regulation S-K (§ 229.201) or otherwise) in the description of the securities:

A. A brief description of any limitations on the right of nonresident or foreign owners to hold or vote such securities imposed by foreign law or by the charter or other constituent document of the registrant, or if no such limitations are applicable, so state;

B. A brief description of any governmental laws, decrees or regulations in the country in which the registrant is organized affecting the remittance of dividends, interest and other payments to nonresident holders of the securities being registered;

C. A brief outline of all taxes, including withholding provisions, to which United States security holders are subject under existing laws and regulations of the foreign country in which the registrant is organized; and

D. A brief description of pertinent provisions of any reciprocal tax treaty between such foreign country and the United States regarding withholding or, if there is no such treaty, so state.

3. Section 305(a)(2) of the Trust Indenture Act of 1939, 15 U.S.C. 77aaa et seq., as amended ("Trust Indenture Act"), shall not be deemed to require the inclusion in a registration statement, prospectus, or annual report on Form 10-K of any information not required by this Item or Item 601(b)(4)(vi) of this chapter.

4. Where convertible securities or stock purchase warrants are being registered that are subject to redemption or call, the description of the conversion terms of the securities or material terms of the warrants shall disclose:

A. Whether the right to convert or purchase the securities will be forfeited unless it is exercised before the date specified in a notice of the redemption or call;

B. The expiration or termination date of the warrants;

C. The kinds, frequency and timing of notice of the redemption or call, including the cities or newspapers in which notice will be published (where the securities provide for a class of newspapers or group of cities in which the publication may be made at the discretion of the registrant, the registrant should describe such provision); and

D. In the case of bearer securities, that investors are responsible for making arrangements to prevent loss of the right to convert or purchase in the event of redemption of call, for example, by reading the newspapers in which the notice of redemption or call may be published.

5. The response to paragraph (f) shall include information with respect to fees and charges in connection with (A) the deposit or substitution of the underlying securities; (B) receipt and distribution of dividends; (C) the sale or exercise of rights; (D) the withdrawal of the underlying security; and (E) the transferring, splitting or grouping of receipts. Information

with respect to the right to collect the fees and charges against dividends received and deposited securities shall be included in response to this item.

6. For asset-backed securities, see also Item 1113 of Regulation AB (§ 229.1113).

> *Note to § 229.202*: If the securities being described have been accepted for listing on an exchange, the exchange may be identified. The document should not, however, convey the impression that the registrant may apply successfully for listing of the securities on an exchange or that, in the case of an underwritten offering, the underwriters may request the registrant to apply for such listing, unless there is reasonable assurance that the securities to be offered will be acceptable to a securities exchange for listing.

Subpart 300—Financial Information

Item 301. Selected Financial Data

Furnish in comparative columnar form the selected financial data for the registrant referred to below, for

(a) Each of the last five fiscal years of the registrant (or for the life of the registrant and its predecessors, if less), and

(b) Any additional fiscal years necessary to keep the information from being misleading.

(c) *Smaller Reporting Companies*. A registrant that qualifies as a smaller reporting company, as defined by § 229.10(f)(1), is not required to provide the information required by this Item.

(d) *Emerging Growth Company*. An emerging growth company, as defined in Rule 405 of the Securities Act of 1933 (§ 230.405 of this chapter) or Rule 12b-2 of the Securities Exchange Act of 1934 (§ 240.12b-2 of this chapter), that is providing the information called for by this Item in: (1) a Securities Act registration statement, need not present selected financial data for any period prior to the earliest audited financial statements presented in connection with the registrant's initial public offering of its common equity securities; or (2) a registration statement, periodic report, or other report filed under the Exchange Act, need not present selected financial data for any period prior to the earliest audited financial statements presented in connection with its first registration statement that became effective under the Exchange Act or the Securities Act.

Instructions to Item 301. 1. The purpose of the selected financial data shall be to supply in a convenient and readable format selected financial data which highlight certain significant trends in the registrant's financial condition and results of operations.

2. Subject to appropriate variation to conform to the nature of the registrant's business, the following items shall be included in the table of financial data: net sales or operating revenues; income (loss) from continuing operations; income (loss) from continuing operations per common share; total assets; long-term obligations and redeemable preferred stock (including long-term debt, capital leases, and redeemable preferred stock as defined in § 210.5-02.28(a) of Regulation S-X [17 CFR 210]; and cash dividends declared per common share. Registrants may include additional items which they believe would enhance an understanding of and would highlight other trends in their financial condition and results of operations.

Briefly describe, or cross-reference to a discussion thereof, factors such as accounting changes, business combinations or dispositions of business operations, that materially affect the comparability of the information reflected in selected financial data. Discussion of, or reference to, any material uncertainties should also be included where such matters might cause the data reflected herein not to be indicative of the registrant's future financial condition or results of operations.

3. All references to the registrant in the table of selected financial data and in this Item shall mean the registrant and its subsidiaries consolidated.

4. If interim period financial statements are included, or are required to be included by Article 3 of Regulation S-X, registrants should consider whether any or all of the selected financial data need to be updated for such interim periods to reflect a material change in the trends indicated; where such updating information is necessary, registrants shall provide

the information on a comparative basis unless not necessary to an understanding of such updating information.

5. A foreign private issuer shall disclose also the following information in all filings containing financial statements:

A. In the forepart of the document and as of the latest practicable date, the exchange rate into U.S. currency of the foreign currency in which the financial statements are denominated;

B. A history of exchange rates for the five most recent years and any subsequent interim period for which financial statements are presented setting forth the rates for period end, the average rates, and the range of high and low rates for each year, and

C. If equity securities are being registered, a five year summary of dividends per share stated in both the currency in which the financial statements are denominated and United States currency based on the exchange rates at each respective payment date.

6. A foreign private issuer shall present the selected financial data in the same currency as its financial statements. The issuer may present the selected financial data on the basis of the accounting principles used in its primary financial statements but in such case shall present this data also on the basis of any reconciliations of such data to United States generally accepted accounting principles and Regulation S-X made pursuant to Rule 4-01 of Regulation S-X (§ 210.4-01 of this chapter).

7. For purposes of this rule, the rate of exchange means the noon buying rate in New York City for cable transfers in foreign currencies as certified for customs purposes by the Federal Reserve Bank of New York. The average rate means the average of the exchange rates on the last day of each month during a year.

Item 302. Supplementary Financial Information

(a) *Selected quarterly financial data.* Registrants specified in paragraph (a)(5) of this Item shall provide the information specified below.

(1) Disclosure shall be made of net sales, gross profit (net sales less costs and expenses associated directly with or allocated to products sold or services rendered), income (loss) from continuing operations, per share data based upon income (loss) from continuing operations, net income (loss), per share data based upon net income (loss) and net income (loss) attributable to the registrant, for each full quarter within the two most recent fiscal years and any subsequent interim period for which financial statements are included or are required to be included by Article 3 of Regulation S-X (Part 210 of this chapter).

(2) When the data supplied pursuant to this paragraph (a) vary from the amounts previously reported on the Form 10-Q (§ 249.308a of this chapter) filed for any quarter, such as would be the case when a pooling of interests occurs or where an error is corrected, reconcile the amounts given with those previously reported and describe the reason for the difference.

(3) Describe the effect of any discontinued operations and unusual or infrequently occurring items recognized in each full quarter within the two most recent fiscal years and any subsequent interim period for which financial statements are included or are required to be included by 17 CFR 210.3-01 through 210.3-20 (Article 3 of Regulation S-X), as well as the aggregate effect and the nature of year-end or other adjustments which are material to the results of that quarter.

(4) If the financial statements to which this information relates have been reported on by an accountant, appropriate professional standards and procedures, as enumerated in the Statements of Auditing Standards issued by the Auditing Standards Board of the American Institute of Certified Public Accountants, shall be followed by the reporting accountant with regard to the data required by this paragraph (a).

(5) This paragraph (a) applies to any registrant, except a foreign private issuer, that has securities registered pursuant to sections 12(b) (15 U.S.C. § 78*l*(b)) (other than mutual life insurance companies) or 12(g) of the Exchange Act (15 U.S.C. § 78*l*(g)).

(b) *Information about oil and gas producing activities.* Registrants engaged in oil and gas producing activities shall present the information about oil and gas producing activities (as those activities are defined in Regulation S-X, § 210.4-10(a)) specified in FASB ASC Topic 932, Extractive Activities—Oil and Gas, if such oil and gas producing activities are regarded as significant under one or more of the tests set forth in FASB ASC Subtopic 932-235, Extractive Activities—Oil and Gas—Notes to Financial Statements, for "Significant Activities."

Instruction 1 to Paragraph (b). (a) FASB ASC Subtopic 932-235 disclosures that relate to annual periods shall be presented for each annual period for which a statement of comprehensive income (as defined in § 210.1-02 of Regulation S-X) is required, (b) FASB ASC Subtopic 932-235 disclosures required as of the end of an annual period shall be presented as of the date of each audited balance sheet required, and (c) FASB ASC Subtopic 932-235 disclosures required as of the beginning of an annual period shall be presented as of the beginning of each annual period for which a statement of comprehensive income (as defined in § 210.1-02 of Regulation S-X) is required.

Instruction 2 to Paragraph (b). This paragraph, together with § 210.4-10 of Regulation S-X, prescribes financial reporting standards for the preparation of accounts by persons engaged, in whole or in part, in the production of crude oil or natural gas in the United States, pursuant to Section 503 of the Energy Policy and Conservation Act of 1975 [42 U.S.C. 6383] ("EPCA") and Section 11(c) of the Energy Supply and Environmental Coordination Act of 1974 [15 U.S.C. 796] ("ESECA") as amended by Section 506 of EPCA. The application of this paragraph to those oil and gas producing operations of companies regulated for ratemaking purposes on an individual-company-cost-of-service basis may, however, give appropriate recognition to differences arising because of the effect of the ratemaking process.

Instruction 3 to Paragraph (b). Any person exempted by the Department of Energy from any recordkeeping or reporting requirements pursuant to Section 11(c) of ESECA, as amended, is similarly exempted from the related provisions of this paragraph in the preparation of accounts pursuant to EPCA. This exemption does not affect the applicability of this paragraph to filings pursuant to the federal securities laws.

(c) *Smaller Reporting Companies.* A registrant that qualifies as a smaller reporting company, as defined by § 229.10(f)(1), is not required to provide the information required by this Item.

Item 303. Management's Discussion and Analysis of Financial Condition and Results of Operations

(a) *Full fiscal years.* Discuss registrant's financial condition, changes in financial condition and results of operations. The discussion shall provide information as specified in paragraphs (a)(1) through (5) of this item and also shall provide such other information that the registrant believes to be necessary to an understanding of its financial condition, changes in financial condition and results of operations. Discussions of liquidity and capital resources may be combined whenever the two topics are interrelated. Where in the registrant's judgment a discussion of segment information and/or of other subdivisions (e.g., geographic areas) of the registrant's business would be appropriate to an understanding of such business, the discussion shall focus on each relevant, reportable segment and/or other subdivision of the business and on the registrant as a whole.

(1) *Liquidity.* Identify any known trends or any known demands, commitments, events or uncertainties that will result in or that are reasonably likely to result in the registrant's liquidity increasing or decreasing in any material way. If a material deficiency is identified, indicate the course of action that the registrant has taken or proposes to take to remedy the deficiency. Also identify and separately describe internal and external sources of liquidity, and briefly discuss any material unused sources of liquid assets.

(2) *Capital resources.* (i) Describe the registrant's material commitments for capital expenditures as of the end of the latest fiscal period, and indicate the general purpose of such commitments and the anticipated source of funds needed to fulfill such commitments.

(ii) Describe any known material trends, favorable or unfavorable, in the registrant's capital resources. Indicate any expected material changes in the mix and relative cost of such resources. The discussion shall consider changes between equity, debt and any off-balance sheet financing arrangements.

(3) *Results of operations.* (i) Describe any unusual or infrequent events or transactions or any significant economic changes that materially affected the amount of reported income from continuing operations and, in each case, indicate the extent to which income was so affected. In addition, describe any other significant components of revenues or expenses that, in the registrant's judgment, should be described in order to understand the registrant's results of operations.

(ii) Describe any known trends or uncertainties that have had or that the registrant reasonably expects will have a material favorable or unfavorable impact on net sales or revenues or income from continuing operations. If the registrant knows of events that will cause a material change in the relationship between costs and revenues (such as known future increases in costs of labor or materials or price increases or inventory adjustments), the change in the relationship shall be disclosed.

(iii) To the extent that the financial statements disclose material increases in net sales or revenues, provide a narrative discussion of the extent to which such increases are attributable to increases in prices or to increases in the volume or amount of goods or services being sold or to the introduction of new products or services.

(iv) For the three most recent fiscal years of the registrant, or for those fiscal years in which the registrant has been engaged in business, whichever period is shortest, discuss the impact of inflation and changing prices on the registrant's net sales and revenues and on income from continuing operations.

(4) *Off-balance sheet arrangements.* (i) In a separately-captioned section, discuss the registrant's off-balance sheet arrangements that have or are reasonably likely to have a current or future effect on the registrant's financial condition, changes in financial condition, revenues or expenses, results of operations, liquidity, capital expenditures or capital resources that is material to investors. The disclosure shall include the items specified in paragraphs (a) (4) (i) (A), (B), (C) and (D) of this Item to the extent necessary to an understanding of such arrangements and effect and shall also include such other information that the registrant believes is necessary for such an understanding.

(A) The nature and business purpose to the registrant of such off-balance sheet arrangements;

(B) The importance to the registrant of such off-balance sheet arrangements in respect of its liquidity, capital resources, market risk support, credit risk support or other benefits;

(C) The amounts of revenues, expenses and cash flows of the registrant arising from such arrangements; the nature and amounts of any interests retained, securities issued and other indebtedness incurred by the registrant in connection with such arrangements; and the nature and amounts of any other obligations or liabilities (including contingent obligations or liabilities) of the registrant arising from such arrangements that are or are reasonably likely to become material and the triggering events or circumstances that could cause them to arise; and

(D) Any known event, demand, commitment, trend or uncertainty that will result in or is reasonably likely to result in the termination, or material reduction in availability to the registrant, of its off-balance sheet arrangements that provide material benefits to it, and the course of action that the registrant has taken or proposes to take in response to any such circumstances.

(ii) As used in this paragraph (a) (4), the term *off-balance sheet arrangement* means any transaction, agreement or other contractual arrangement to which an entity unconsolidated with the registrant is a party, under which the registrant has:

(A) Any obligation under a guarantee contract that has any of the characteristics identified in FASB ASC paragraph 460-10-15-4 (Guarantees Topic), as may be modified or supplemented, and that is not excluded from the initial recognition and measurement provisions of FASB ASC paragraphs 460-10-15-7, 460-10-25-1, and 460-10-30-1;

(B) A retained or contingent interest in assets transferred to an unconsolidated entity or similar arrangement that serves as credit, liquidity or market risk support to such entity for such assets;

(C) Any obligation, including a contingent obligation, under a contract that would be accounted for as a derivative instrument, except that it is both indexed to the registrant's own stock and classified in stockholders' equity in the registrant's statement of financial position, and therefore excluded from the scope of FASB ASC Topic 815, Derivatives and edging, pursuant to FASB ASC subparagraph 815-10-15-74(a), as may be modified or supplemented; or

(D) Any obligation, including a contingent obligation, arising out of a variable interest (as defined in the FASB ASC Master Glossary) in an unconsolidated entity that is held by, and material to, the registrant, where such entity provides financing, liquidity, market risk or credit risk support to, or engages in leasing, hedging or research and development services with, the registrant.

(5) *Tabular disclosure of contractual obligations.* (i) In a tabular format, provide the information specified in this paragraph (a)(5) as of the latest fiscal year end balance sheet date with respect to the registrant's known contractual obligations specified in the table that follows this paragraph (a)(5)(i). The registrant shall provide amounts, aggregated by type of contractual obligation. The registrant may disaggregate the specified categories of contractual obligations using other categories suitable to its business, but the presentation must include all of the obligations of the registrant that fall within the specified categories. A presentation covering at least the periods specified shall be included. The tabular presentation may be accompanied by footnotes to describe provisions that create, increase or accelerate obligations, or other pertinent data to the extent necessary for an understanding of the timing and amount of the registrant's specified contractual obligations.

		Payments due by period			
Contractual Obligations	*Total*	*Less than 1 year*	*1–3 years*	*3–5 years*	*More than 5 years*
[Long–Term Debt Obligations]					
[Capital (Finance) Lease Obligations]					
[Operating Lease Obligations]					
[Purchase Obligations]					
[Other Long–Term Liabilities Reflected on the Registrant's Balance Sheet under GAAP]					
Total					

(ii) *Definitions*: The following definitions apply to this paragraph (a)(5):

(A) *Long-Term Debt Obligation* means a payment obligation under long-term borrowings referenced in FASB ASC paragraph 470-10-50-1 (Debt Topic), as may be modified or supplemented.

(B) *Capital Lease Obligation* means a payment obligation under a lease classified as a capital lease pursuant to FASB ASC Topic 840, Leases, as may be modified or supplemented.

(C) *Operating Lease Obligation* means a payment obligation under a lease classified as an operating lease and disclosed pursuant to FASB ASC Topic 840, as may be modified or supplemented.

(D) *Purchase Obligation* means an agreement to purchase goods or services that is enforceable and legally binding on the registrant that specifies all significant terms, including: fixed or minimum quantities to be purchased; fixed, minimum or variable price provisions; and the approximate timing of the transaction.

Instructions to Paragraph 303(a). 1. The registrant's discussion and analysis shall be of the financial statements and other statistical data that the registrant believes will enhance a reader's understanding of its financial condition, changes in financial condition, and results of operations. Generally, the discussion shall cover the periods covered by the financial statements included in the filing and the registrant.may use any presentation that in the registrant's judgment enhances a reader's understanding. A smaller reporting company's discussion shall cover the two-year period required in Article 8 of Regulation S-X and may use any presentation that in the registrant's judgment enhances a reader's understanding. For registrants providing financial statements covering three years in a filing, discussion about the earliest of the three years may be omitted if such discussion was already included in the registrant's prior filings on EDGAR that required disclosure in compliance with Item 303 of Regulation S-K, provided that registrants electing not to include a discussion of the earliest year must include a statement that identifies the location in the prior filing where the omitted discussion may be found. An emerging growth company, as defined in Rule 405 of the Securities Act (§ 230.405 of this chapter) or Rule 12b-2 of the Exchange Act (§ 240.12b-2 of this chapter), may provide the discussion required in paragraph (a) of this Item for its two most recent fiscal years if, pursuant to Section 7(a) of the Securities Act of 1933 (15 U.S.C 77g(a)), it provides audited financial statements for two years in a Securities Act registration statement for the initial public offering of the emerging growth company's common equity securities.

2. The purpose of the discussion and analysis shall be to provide to investors and other users information relevant to an assessment of the financial condition and results of operations of the registrant as determined by evaluating the amounts and certainty of cash flows from operations and from outside sources.

3. The discussion and analysis shall focus specifically on material events and uncertainties known to management that would cause reported financial information not to be necessarily indicative of future operating results or of future financial condition. This would include descriptions and amounts of (A) matters that would have an impact on future operations and have not had an impact in the past, and (B) matters that have had an impact on reported operations and are not expected to have an impact upon future operations.

4. Where the consolidated financial statements reveal material changes from year to year in one or more line items, the causes for the changes shall be described to the extent necessary to an understanding of the registrant's businesses as a whole; *Provided, however,* That if the causes for a change in one line item also relate to other line items, no repetition is required and a line-by-line analysis of the financial statements as a whole is not required or generally appropriate. Registrants need not recite the amounts of changes from year to year which are readily computable from the financial statements. The discussion shall not merely repeat numerical data contained in the consolidated financial statements.

5. The term "liquidity" as used in this Item refers to the ability of an enterprise to generate adequate amounts of cash to meet the enterprise's needs for cash. Except where it is otherwise clear from the discussion, the registrant shall indicate those balance sheet conditions or income or cash flow items which the registrant believes may be indicators of its liquidity condition. Liquidity generally shall be discussed on both a long-term and short-term basis. The issue of liquidity shall be discussed in the context of the registrant's own business or businesses. For example a discussion of working capital may be appropriate for certain manufacturing, industrial or related operations but might be inappropriate for a bank or public utility.

6. Where financial statements presented or incorporated by reference in the registration statement are required by § 210.4-08(e)(3) of Regulation S-X [17 CFR Part 210] to include disclosure of restrictions on the ability of both consolidated and unconsolidated subsidiaries to transfer funds to the registrant in the form of cash dividends, loans or advances, the discussion of liquidity shall include a discussion of the nature and extent of such restrictions and the impact such restrictions have had and are expected to have on the ability of the parent company to meet its cash obligations.

7. Any forward-looking information supplied is expressly covered by the safe harbor rule for projections. See Rule 175 under the Securities Act [17 CFR 230.175], Rule 3b-6 under the Exchange Act [17 CFR 240.3b-6] and Securities Act Release No. 6084 (June 25, 1979) (44 FR 33810).

8. Registrants are only required to discuss the effects of inflation and other changes in prices when considered material. This discussion may be made in whatever manner appears appropriate under the circumstances. All that is required is a brief textual presentation of management's views. No specific numerical financial data need be presented except as Rule 3-20(c) of Regulation S-X (§ 210.3-20(c) of this chapter) otherwise requires. However, registrants may elect to voluntarily disclose supplemental information on the effects of changing prices as provided for in FASB ASC Topic 255, Changing Prices, or through other supplemental disclosures. The Commission encourages experimentation with these disclosures in order to provide the most meaningful presentation of the impact of price changes on the registrant's financial statements.

9. Registrants that elect to disclose supplementary information on the effects of changing prices as specified by FASB ASC Topic 255 may combine such explanations with the discussion and analysis required pursuant to this Item or may supply such information separately with appropriate cross reference.

10. All references to the registrant in the discussion and in this Item shall mean the registrant and its subsidiaries consolidated.

11. Foreign private registrants also shall discuss briefly any pertinent governmental economic, fiscal, monetary, or potential policies or factors that have materially affected or could materially affect, directly or indirectly, their operations or investments by United States nationals.

12. If the registrant is a foreign private issuer, the discussion shall focus on the primary financial statements presented in the registration statement or report. There shall be a reference to the reconciliation to United States generally accepted accounting principles, and a discussion of any aspects of the difference between foreign and United States generally accepted accounting principles, not discussed in the reconciliation, that the registrant believes is necessary for an understanding of the financial statements as a whole.

13. The attention of bank holding companies is directed to the information called for in Guide 3 (§ 229.801(c) and § 229.802(c)).

14. The attention of property-casualty insurance companies is directed to the information called for in Guide 6 (§ 229.801(f)).

Instructions to Paragraph 303(a)(4):

1. No obligation to make disclosure under paragraph (a)(4) of this Item shall arise in respect of an off-balance sheet arrangement until a definitive agreement that is unconditionally binding or subject only to customary closing conditions exists or, if there is no such agreement, when settlement of the transaction occurs.

2. Registrants should aggregate off-balance sheet arrangements in groups or categories that provide material information in an efficient and understandable manner and should avoid repetition and disclosure of immaterial information. Effects that are common or similar with respect to a number of off-balance sheet arrangements must be analyzed in the aggregate to the extent the aggregation increases understanding. Distinctions in arrangements and their effects must be discussed to the extent the information is material, but the discussion should avoid repetition and disclosure of immaterial information.

3. For purposes of paragraph (a)(4) of this Item only, contingent liabilities arising out of litigation, arbitration or regulatory actions are not considered to be off-balance sheet arrangements.

4. Generally, the disclosure required by paragraph (a)(4) shall cover the most recent fiscal year. However, the discussion should address changes from the previous year where such discussion is necessary to an understanding of the disclosure.

5. In satisfying the requirements of paragraph (a)(4) of this Item, the discussion of off-balance sheet arrangements need not repeat information provided in the footnotes to the

financial statements, provided that such discussion clearly cross-references to specific information in the relevant footnotes and integrates the substance of the footnotes into such discussion in a manner designed to inform readers of the significance of the information that is not included within the body of such discussion.

(b) *Interim periods.* If interim period financial statements are included or are required to be included by Article 3 of Regulations S-X (17 CFR 210), a management's discussion and analysis of the financial condition and results of operations shall be provided so as to enable the reader to assess material changes in financial condition and results of operations between the periods specified in paragraphs (b) (1) and (2) of this Item. The discussion and analysis shall include a discussion of material changes in those items specifically listed in paragraph (a) of this Item, except that the impact of inflation and changing prices on operations for interim periods need not be addressed.

(1) *Material changes in financial condition.* Discuss any material changes in financial condition from the end of the preceding fiscal year to the date of the most recent interim balance sheet provided. If the interim financial statements include an interim balance sheet as of the corresponding interim date of the preceding fiscal year, any material changes in financial condition from that date to the date of the most recent interim balance sheet provided also shall be discussed. If discussions of changes from both the end and the corresponding interim date of the preceding fiscal year are required, the discussions may be combined at the discretion of the registrant.

(2) *Material changes in results of operations.* Discuss any material changes in the registrant's results of operations with respect to the most recent fiscal year-to-date period for which an income statement is provided and the corresponding year-to-date period of the preceding fiscal year. If the registrant is required to or has elected to provide an income statement for the most recent fiscal quarter, such discussion also shall cover material changes with respect to that fiscal quarter and the corresponding fiscal quarter in the preceding fiscal year. In addition, if the registrant has elected to provide an income statement for the twelve-month period ended as of the date of the most recent interim balance sheet provided, the discussion also shall cover material changes with respect to that twelve-month and the twelve-month period ended as of the corresponding interim balance sheet date of the preceding fiscal year. Notwithstanding the above, if for purposes of a registration statement a registrant subject to paragraph (b) of § 210.3-03 of Regulation S-X provides a statement of income for the twelve-month period ended as of the date of the most recent interim balance sheet provided in lieu of the interim income statements otherwise required, the discussion of material changes in that twelve-month period will be in respect to the preceding fiscal year rather than the corresponding preceding period.

Instructions to Paragraph (b) of Item 303.

Instruction 1 to Paragraph (b). If interim financial statements are presented together with financial statements for full fiscal years, the discussion of the interim financial information shall be prepared pursuant to this paragraph (b) and the discussion of the full fiscal year's information shall be prepared pursuant to paragraph (a) of this Item. Such discussions may be combined.

Instruction 2 to Paragraph (b). In preparing the discussion and analysis required by this paragraph (b), the registrant may presume that users of the interim financial information have read or have access to the discussion and analysis required by paragraph (a) for the preceding fiscal year.

Instruction 3 to Paragraph (b). The discussion and analysis required by this paragraph (b) is required to focus only on material changes. Where the interim financial statements reveal material changes from period to period in one or more significant line items, the causes for the changes shall be described if they have not already been disclosed: *Provided, however,* That if the causes for a change in one line item also relate to other line items, no repetition is required. Registrants need not recite the amounts of changes from period to period which are readily computable from the financial statements. The discussion shall not merely repeat numerical data contained in the financial statements. The information provided shall include that which is available to the registrant without undue effort or expense and which does not clearly appear in the registrant's condensed interim financial statements.

Instruction 4 to Paragraph (b). The registrant's discussion of material changes in results of operations shall identify any significant elements of the registrant's income or loss from continuing operations which do not arise from or are not necessarily representative of the registrant's ongoing business.

Instruction 5 to Paragraph (b). [Reserved.]

Instruction 6 to Paragraph (b). Any forward-looking information supplied is expressly covered by the safe harbor rule for projections. See Rule 175 under the Securities Act (17 CFR 230.175), Rule 3b-6 under the Exchange Act (17 CFR 249.3b-6) and Securities Act Release No. 6084 (June 25, 1979) (44 FR 38810).

Instruction 7 to Paragraph (b). The registrant is not required to include the table required by paragraph (a) (5) of this Item for interim periods. Instead, the registrant should disclose material changes outside the ordinary course of the registrant's business in the specified contractual obligations during the interim period.

Instruction 8 to Paragraph (b). The term statement of comprehensive income shall mean a statement of comprehensive income as defined in § 210.1-02 of Regulation S-X of this chapter.

(c) *Safe harbor.* (1) The safe harbor provided in Section 27A of the Securities Act of 1933 (15 U.S.C. 77z-2) and Section 21E of the Securities Exchange Act of 1934 (15 U.S.C. 78u-5) ("statutory safe harbors") shall apply to forward-looking information provided pursuant to paragraphs (a) (4) and (5) of this Item, provided that the disclosure is made by: an issuer; a person acting on behalf of the issuer; an outside reviewer retained by the issuer making a statement on behalf of the issuer; or an underwriter, with respect to information provided by the issuer or information derived from information provided by the issuer.

(2) For purposes of paragraph (c) of this Item only:

(i) All information required by paragraphs (a) (4) and (5) of this Item is deemed to be a *forward looking statement* as that term is defined in the statutory safe harbors, except for historical facts.

(ii) With respect to paragraph (a) (4) of this Item, the meaningful cautionary statements element of the statutory safe harbors will be satisfied if a registrant satisfies all requirements of that same paragraph (a) (4) of this Item.

(d) *Smaller Reporting Companies.* A smaller reporting company, as defined by § 229.10(f) (1), may provide the information required in paragraph (a) (3) (iv) of this Item for the last two most recent fiscal years of the registrant if it provides financial information on net sales and revenues and on income from continuing operations for only two years. A smaller reporting company is not required to provide the information required by paragraph (a) (5) of this Item.

Item 304. Changes in and Disagreements with Accountants on Accounting and Financial Disclosure

(a) (1) If during the registrant's two most recent fiscal years or any subsequent interim period, an independent accountant who was previously engaged as the principal accountant to audit the registrant's financial statements, or an independent accountant who was previously engaged to audit a significant subsidiary and on whom the principal accountant expressed reliance in its report, has resigned (or indicated it has declined to stand for re-election after the completion of the current audit) or was dismissed, then the registrant shall:

(i) State whether the former accountant resigned, declined to stand for re-election or was dismissed and the date thereof.

(ii) State whether the principal accountant's report on the financial statements for either of the past two years contained an adverse opinion or a disclaimer of opinion, or was qualified or modified as to uncertainty, audit scope, or accounting principles; and also describe the nature of each such adverse opinion, disclaimer of opinion, modification, or qualification.

(iii) State whether the decision to change accountants was recommended or approved by:

(A) any audit or similar committee of the board of directors, if the issuer has such a committee; or

(B) the board of directors, if the issuer has no such committee.

(iv) State whether during the registrant's two most recent fiscal years and any subsequent interim period preceding such resignation, declination or dismissal there were any disagreements with the former accountant on any matter of accounting principles or practices, financial statement disclosure, or auditing scope of procedure, which disagreement(s), if not resolved to the satisfaction of the former accountant, would have caused it to make reference to the subject matter of the disagreement(s) in connection with its report. Also, (A) describe each such disagreement; (B) state whether any audit or similar committee of the board of directors, or the board of directors, discussed the subject matter of each of such disagreements with the former accountant; and (C) state whether the registrant has authorized the former accountant to respond fully to the inquiries of the successor accountant concerning the subject matter of each of such disagreements and, if not, describe the nature of any limitation thereon and the reason therefore. The disagreements required to be reported in response to this Item include both those resolved to the former accountant's satisfaction and those not resolved to the former accountant's satisfaction. Disagreements contemplated by this Item are those that occur at the decision-making level, i.e., between personnel of the registrant responsible for presentation of its financial statements and personnel of the accounting firm responsible for rendering its report.

(v) Provide the information required by paragraphs (a)(1)(iv) of this Item for each of the kinds of events (even though the registrant and the former accountant did not express a difference of opinion regarding the event) listed in paragraphs (A) through (D) below, that occurred within the registrant's two most recent fiscal years and any subsequent interim period preceding the former accountant's resignation, declination to stand for re-election, or dismissal ("reportable events"). If the event led to a disagreement or difference of opinion, then the event should be reported as a disagreement under paragraph (a)(1)(iv) and need not be repeated under this paragraph.

(A) The accountant's having advised the registrant that the internal controls necessary for the registrant to develop reliable financial statements do not exist;

(B) the accountant's having advised the registrant that information has come to the accountant's attention that has led it to no longer be able to rely on management's representations, or that has made it unwilling to be associated with the financial statements prepared by management;

(C) (*1*) the accountant's having advised the registrant of the need to expand significantly the scope of its audit, or that information has come to the accountant's attention during the time period covered by Item 304(a)(1)(iv), that if further investigated may (*i*) materially impact the fairness or reliability of either: a previously issued audit report or the underlying financial statements; or the financial statements issued or to be issued covering the fiscal period(s) subsequent to the date of the most recent financial statements covered by an audit report (including information that may prevent it from rendering an unqualified audit report on those financial statements), or (*ii*) cause it to be unwilling to rely on management's representations or be associated with the registrant's financial statements, and (*2*) due to the accountant's resignation (due to audit scope limitations or otherwise) or dismissal, or for any other reason, the accountant did not so expand the scope of its audit or conduct such further investigation; or

(D) (*1*) the accountant's having advised the registrant that information has come to the accountant's attention that it has concluded materially impacts the fairness or reliability of either (*i*) a previously issued audit report or the underlying financial statements, or (*ii*) the financial statements issued or to be issued covering the fiscal period(s) subsequent to the date of the most recent financial statements covered by an audit report (including information that, unless resolved to the accountant's satisfaction, would prevent it from rendering an unqualified audit report on those financial statements), and (2) due to the accountant's resignation, dismissal or declination to stand for re-election, or for any other reason, the issue has not been resolved to the accountant's satisfaction prior to its resignation, dismissal or declination to stand for re-election.

(2) If during the registrant's two most recent fiscal years or any subsequent interim period, a new independent accountant has been engaged as either the principal accountant to audit the registrant's financial statements, or as an independent accountant to audit a significant subsidiary and on whom the principal accountant is expected to express reliance in its report, then the registrant shall identify the newly engaged accountant and indicate the date of such accountant's engagement. In addition, if during the registrant's two most recent fiscal years, and any subsequent interim period prior to engaging that accountant, the registrant (or someone on its behalf) consulted the newly engaged accountant regarding (i) either: the application of accounting principles to a specified transaction, either completed or proposed; or the type of audit opinion that might be rendered on the registrant's financial statements, and either a written report was provided to the registrant or oral advice was provided that the new accountant concluded was an important factor considered by the registrant in reaching a decision as to the accounting, auditing or financial reporting issue; or (ii) any matter that was either the subject of a disagreement (as defined in paragraph 304(a)(1)(iv) and the related instructions to this item) or a reportable event (as described in paragraph 304(a)(1)(v)), then the registrant shall:

(A) so state and identify the issues that were the subjects of those consultations;

(B) briefly describe the views of the newly engaged accountant as expressed orally or in writing to the registrant on each such issue and, if written views were received by the registrant, file them as an exhibit to the report or registration statement requiring compliance with this Item 304(a);

(C) state whether the former accountant was consulted by the registrant regarding any such issues, and if so, provide a summary of the former accountant's views; and

(D) request the newly engaged accountant to review the disclosure required by this Item 304(a) before it is filed with the Commission and provide the new accountant the opportunity to furnish the registrant with a letter addressed to the Commission containing any new information, clarification of the registrant's expression of its views, or the respects in which it does not agree with the statements made by the registrant in response to Item 304(a). The registrant shall file any such letter as an exhibit to the report or registration statement containing the disclosure required by this Item.

(3) The registrant shall provide the former accountant with a copy of the disclosures it is making in response to this Item 304(a) that the former accountant shall receive no later than the day that the disclosures are filed with the Commission. The registrant shall request the former accountant to furnish the registrant with a letter addressed to the Commission stating whether it agrees with the statements made by the registrant in response to this Item 304(a) and, if not, stating the respects in which it does not agree. The registrant shall file the former accountant's letter as an exhibit to the report or registration statement containing this disclosure. If the former accountant's letter is unavailable at the time of filing such report or registration statement, then the registrant shall request the former accountant to provide the letter as promptly as possible so that the registrant can file the letter with the Commission within ten business days after the filing of the report or registration statement. Notwithstanding the ten business day period, the registrant shall file the letter by amendment within two business days of receipt; if the letter is received on a Saturday, Sunday or holiday on which the Commission is not open for business, then the two business day period shall begin to run on and shall include the first business day thereafter. The former accountant may provide the registrant with an interim letter highlighting specific areas of concern and indicating that a more detailed letter will be forthcoming within the ten business day

period noted above. If not filed with the report or registration statement containing the registrant's disclosure under this Item 304(a), then the interim letter, if any, shall be filed by the registrant by amendment within two business days of receipt.

(b) If, (1) in connection with a change in accountants subject to paragraph (a) of this Item 304, there was any disagreement of the type described in paragraph (a)(1)(iv) or any reportable event as described in paragraph (a)(1)(v) of this Item; (2) during the fiscal year in which the change in accountants took place or during the subsequent fiscal year, there have been any transactions or events similar to those which involved such disagreement or reportable event and (3) such transactions or events were material and were accounted for or disclosed in a manner different from that which the former accountants apparently would have concluded was required, the registrant shall state the existence and nature of the disagreement or reportable event and also state the effect on the financial statements if the method had been followed which the former accountants apparently would have concluded was required. These disclosures need not be made if the method asserted by the former accountants ceases to be generally accepted because of authoritative standards or interpretations subsequently issued.

Instructions to Item 304: 1. The disclosure called for by paragraph (a) of this Item need not be provided if it has been previously reported (as that term is defined in Rule 12b-2 under the Exchange Act (§ 240.12b-2 of this chapter); the disclosure called for by paragraph (a) must be provided, however, notwithstanding prior disclosure, if required pursuant to Item 9 of Schedule 14A (§ 240.14a-101 of this chapter). The disclosure called for by paragraph (b) of this section must be furnished, where required, notwithstanding any prior disclosure about accountant changes or disagreements.

2. When disclosure is required by paragraph (a) of this section in an annual report to security holders pursuant to Rule 14a-3 (§ 240.14a-3 of this chapter) or Rule 14c-3 (§ 240.14c-3 of this chapter), or in a proxy or information statement filed pursuant to the requirements of Schedule 14A or 14C (§ 240.14a-101 or § 240.14c-101 of this chapter), in lieu of a letter pursuant to paragraph (a)(2)(D) or (a)(3), prior to filing such materials with or furnishing such materials to the Commission, the registrant shall furnish the disclosure required by paragraph (a) of this section to any former accountant engaged by the registrant during the period set forth in paragraph (a) of this section and to the newly engaged accountant. If any such accountant believes that the statements made in response to paragraph (a) of this section are incorrect or incomplete, it may present its views in a brief statement, ordinarily expected not to exceed 200 words, to be included in the annual report or proxy or information statement. This statement shall be submitted to the registrant within ten business days of the date the accountant receives the registrant's disclosure. Further, unless the written views of the newly engaged accountant required to be filed as an exhibit by paragraph (a)(2)(B) of this Item 304 have been previously filed with the Commission the registrant shall file a Form 8-K concurrently with the annual report or proxy or information statement for the purpose of filing the written views as exhibits thereto.

3. The information required by Item 304(a) need not be provided for a company being acquired by the registrant that is not subject to the filing requirements of either section 13(a) or 15(d) of the Exchange Act, or, because of section 12(i) of the Exchange Act, has not furnished an annual report to security holders pursuant to Rule 14a-3 Rule 14c-3 for its latest fiscal year.

4. The term "disagreements" as used in this Item shall be interpreted broadly, to include any difference of opinion concerning any matter of accounting principles or practices, financial statement disclosure, or auditing scope or procedure which (if not resolved to the satisfaction of the former accountant) would have caused it to make reference to the subject matter of the disagreement in connection with its report. It is not necessary for there to have been an argument to have had a disagreement, merely a difference of opinion. For purposes of this Item, however, the term disagreements does not include initial differences of opinion based on incomplete facts or preliminary information that were later resolved to the former accountant's satisfaction by, and providing the registrant and the accountant do not continue to have a difference of opinion upon, obtaining additional relevant facts or information.

5. In determining whether any disagreement or reportable event has occurred, an oral communication from the engagement partner or another person responsible for rendering the accounting firm's opinion (or their designee) will generally suffice as the accountant advising

the registrant of a reportable event or as a statement of a disagreement at the "decision-making level" within the accounting firm and require disclosure under this Item.

Item 305. Quantitative and Qualitative Disclosures About Market Risk

(a) Quantitative information about market risk.

(1) Registrants shall provide, in their reporting currency, quantitative information about market risk as of the end of the latest fiscal year, in accordance with one of the following three disclosure alternatives. In preparing this quantitative information, registrants shall categorize market risk sensitive instruments into instruments entered into for trading purposes and instruments entered into for purposes other than trading purposes. Within both the trading and other than trading portfolios, separate quantitative information shall be presented, to the extent material, for each market risk exposure category (i.e., interest rate risk, foreign currency exchange rate risk, commodity price risk, and other relevant market risks, such as equity price risk). A registrant may use one of the three alternatives set forth below for all of the required quantitative disclosures about market risk. A registrant also may choose, from among the three alternatives, one disclosure alternative for market risk sensitive instruments entered into for trading purposes and another disclosure alternative for market risk sensitive instruments entered into for other than trading purposes. Alternatively, a registrant may choose any disclosure alternative, from among the three alternatives, for each risk exposure category within the trading and other than trading portfolios. The three disclosure alternatives are:

(i) (A) (1) Tabular presentation of information related to market risk sensitive instruments; such information shall include fair values of the market risk sensitive instruments and contract terms sufficient to determine future cash flows from those instruments, categorized by expected maturity dates.

(2) Tabular information relating to contract terms shall allow readers of the table to determine expected cash flows from the market risk sensitive instruments for each of the next five years. Comparable tabular information for any remaining years shall be displayed as an aggregate amount.

(3) Within each risk exposure category, the market risk sensitive instruments shall be grouped based on common characteristics. Within the foreign currency exchange rate risk category, the market risk sensitive instruments shall be grouped by functional currency and within the commodity price risk category, the market risk sensitive instruments shall be grouped by type of commodity.

(4) See the Appendix to this Item for a suggested format for presentation of this information; and

(B) Registrants shall provide a description of the contents of the table and any related assumptions necessary to understand the disclosures required under paragraph (a) (1) (i) (A) of this Item 305; or

(ii) (A) Sensitivity analysis disclosures that express the potential loss in future earnings, fair values, or cash flows of market risk sensitive instruments resulting from one or more selected hypothetical changes in interest rates, foreign currency exchange rates, commodity prices, and other relevant market rates or prices over a selected period of time. The magnitude of selected hypothetical changes in rates or prices may differ among and within market risk exposure categories; and

(B) Registrants shall provide a description of the model, assumptions, and parameters, which are necessary to understand the disclosures required under paragraph (a) (1) (ii) (A) of this Item 305; or

(iii) (A) Value at risk disclosures that express the potential loss in future earnings, fair values, or cash flows of market risk sensitive instruments over a selected period of time, with a selected likelihood of occurrence, from changes in interest rates, foreign currency exchange rates, commodity prices, and other relevant market rates or prices;

(B) (1) For each category for which value at risk disclosures are required under paragraph (a) (1) (iii) (A) of this Item 305, provide either:

(i) The average, high and low amounts, or the distribution of the value at risk amounts for the reporting period; or

(ii) The average, high and low amounts, or the distribution of actual changes in fair values, earnings, or cash flows from the market risk sensitive instruments occurring during the reporting period; or

(iii) The percentage or number of times the actual changes in fair values, earnings, or cash flows from the market risk sensitive instruments exceeded the value at risk amounts during the reporting period;

(2) Information required under paragraph (a)(1)(iii)(B)(1) of this Item 305 is not required for the first fiscal year end in which a registrant must present Item 305 information; and

(C) Registrants shall provide a description of the model, assumptions, and parameters, which are necessary to understand the disclosures required under paragraphs (a)(1)(iii)(A) and (B) of this Item 305.

(2) Registrants shall discuss material limitations that cause the information required under paragraph (a)(1) of this Item 305 not to reflect fully the net market risk exposures of the entity. This discussion shall include summarized descriptions of instruments, positions, and transactions omitted from the quantitative market risk disclosure information or the features of instruments, positions, and transactions that are included, but not reflected fully in the quantitative market risk disclosure information.

(3) Registrants shall present summarized market risk information for the preceding fiscal year. In addition, registrants shall discuss the reasons for material quantitative changes in market risk exposures between the current and preceding fiscal years. Information required by this paragraph (a)(3), however, is not required if disclosure is not required under paragraph (a)(1) of this Item 305 for the current fiscal year. Information required by this paragraph (a)(3) is not required for the first fiscal year end in which a registrant must present Item 305 information.

(4) If registrants change disclosure alternatives or key model characteristics, assumptions, and parameters used in providing quantitative information about market risk (e.g., changing from tabular presentation to value at risk, changing the scope of instruments included in the model, or changing the definition of loss from fair values to earnings), and if the effects of any such change is material, the registrant shall:

(i) Explain the reasons for the change; and

(ii) Either provide summarized comparable information, under the new disclosure method, for the year preceding the current year or, in addition to providing disclosure for the current year under the new method, provide disclosures for the current year and preceding fiscal year under the method used in the preceding year.

Instructions to Paragraph 305(a).

1. Under paragraph 305(a)(1):

A. For each market risk exposure category within the trading and other than trading portfolios, registrants may report the average, high, and low sensitivity analysis or value at risk amounts for the reporting period, as an alternative to reporting year-end amounts.

B. In determining the average, high, and low amounts for the fiscal year under instruction 1.A. of the Instructions to Paragraph 305(a), registrants should use sensitivity analysis or value at risk amounts relating to at least four equal time periods throughout the reporting period (e.g., four quarter-end amounts, 12 month-end amounts, or 52 week-end amounts).

C. Functional currency means functional currency as defined by generally accepted accounting principles (see, e.g., FASB ASC Master Glossary).

D. Registrants using the sensitivity analysis and value at risk disclosure alternatives are encouraged, but not required, to provide quantitative amounts that reflect the aggregate market risk inherent in the trading and other than trading portfolios.

2. Under paragraph 305(a)(1)(i):

A. Examples of contract terms sufficient to determine future cash flows from market risk sensitive instruments include, but are not limited to:

i. Debt instruments—principal amounts and weighted average effective interest rates;

ii. Forwards and futures—contract amounts and weighted average settlement prices;

iii. Options—contract amounts and weighted average strike prices;

iv. Swaps—notional amounts, weighted average pay rates or prices, and weighted average receive rates or prices; and

v. Complex instruments—likely to be a combination of the contract terms presented in 2.A.i. through iv. of this Instruction;

B. When grouping based on common characteristics, instruments should be categorized, at a minimum, by the following characteristics, when material:

i. Fixed rate or variable rate assets or liabilities;

ii. Long or short forwards and futures;

iii. Written or purchased put or call options with similar strike prices;

iv. Receive fixed and pay variable swaps, receive variable and pay fixed swaps, and receive variable and pay variable swaps;

v. The currency in which the instruments' cash flows are denominated;

vi. Financial instruments for which foreign currency transaction gains and losses are reported in the same manner as translation adjustments under generally accepted accounting principles (see, e.g., FASB ASC paragraph 830-20-35-3 (Foreign Currency Matters Topic)); and

vii. Derivatives used to manage risks inherent in anticipated transactions;

C. Registrants may aggregate information regarding functional currencies that are economically related, managed together for internal risk management purposes, and have statistical correlations of greater than 75% over each of the past three years;

D. Market risk sensitive instruments that are exposed to rate or price changes in more than one market risk exposure category should be presented within the tabular information for each of the risk exposure categories to which those instruments are exposed;

E. If a currency swap eliminates all foreign currency exposures in the cash flows of a foreign currency denominated debt instrument, neither the currency swap nor the foreign currency denominated debt instrument are required to be disclosed in the foreign currency risk exposure category. However, both the currency swap and the foreign currency denominated debt instrument should be disclosed in the interest rate risk exposure category; and

F. The contents of the table and related assumptions that should be described include, but are not limited to:

i. The different amounts reported in the table for various categories of the market risk sensitive instruments (e.g., principal amounts for debt, notional amounts for swaps, and contract amounts for options and futures);

ii. The different types of reported market rates or prices (e.g., contractual rates or prices, spot rates or prices, forward rates or prices); and

iii. Key prepayment or reinvestment assumptions relating to the timing of reported amounts.

3. Under paragraph 305(a)(1)(ii):

A. Registrants should select hypothetical changes in market rates or prices that are expected to reflect reasonably possible near-term changes in those rates and prices. In this regard, absent economic justification for the selection of a different amount, registrants should use changes that are not less than 10 percent of end of period market rates or prices;

B. For purposes of instruction 3.A. of the Instructions to Paragraph 305(a), the term reasonably possible has the same meaning as defined by generally accepted accounting principles (see, e.g., FASB ASC Master Glossary);

C. For purposes of instruction 3.A. of the Instructions to Paragraph 305(a), the term near term means a period of time going forward up to one year from the date of the financial statements (see generally FASB ASC Master Glossary);

D. Market risk sensitive instruments that are exposed to rate or price changes in more than one market risk exposure category should be included in the sensitivity analysis disclosures for each market risk category to which those instruments are exposed;

E. Registrants with multiple foreign currency exchange rate exposures should prepare foreign currency sensitivity analysis disclosures that measure the aggregate sensitivity to changes in all foreign currency exchange rate exposures, including the effects of changes in both transactional currency/functional currency exchange rate exposures and functional currency/reporting currency exchange rate exposures. For example, assume a French division of a registrant presenting its financial statements in U.S. dollars ($US) invests in a deutschmark(DM)-denominated debt security. In these circumstances, the $US is the reporting currency and the DM is the transactional currency. In addition, assume this division determines that the French franc (FF) is its functional currency according to FASB ASC Topic 830, Foreign Currency Matters. In preparing the foreign currency sensitivity analysis disclosures, this registrant should report the aggregate potential loss from hypothetical changes in both the DM/FF exchange rate exposure and the FF/$US exchange rate exposure; and

F. Model, assumptions, and parameters that should be described include, but are not limited to, how loss is defined by the model (e.g., loss in earnings, fair values, or cash flows), a general description of the modeling technique (e.g., duration modeling, modeling that measures the change in net present values arising from selected hypothetical changes in market rates or prices, and a description as to how optionality is addressed by the model), the types of instruments covered by the model (e.g., derivative financial instruments, other financial instruments, derivative commodity instruments, and whether other instruments are included voluntarily, such as certain commodity instruments and positions, cash flows from anticipated transactions, and certain financial instruments excluded under instruction 3.C.ii. of the General Instructions to Paragraphs 305(a) and 305(b)), and other relevant information about the model's assumptions and parameters, (e.g., the magnitude and timing of selected hypothetical changes in market rates or prices used, the method by which discount rates are determined, and key prepayment or reinvestment assumptions).

4. Under paragraph 305(a)(1)(iii):

A. The confidence intervals selected should reflect reasonably possible near-term changes in market rates and prices. In this regard, absent economic justification for the selection of different confidence intervals, registrants should use intervals that are 95 percent or higher;

B. For purposes of instruction 4.A. of the Instructions to Paragraph 305(a), the term reasonably possible has the same meaning as defined by generally accepted accounting principles (see, e.g., FASB ASC Master Glossary);

C. For purposes of instruction 4.A. of the Instructions to Paragraphs 305(a), the term near term means a period of time going forward up to one year from the date of the financial statements (see generally FASB ASC Master Glossary);

D. Registrants with multiple foreign currency exchange rate exposures should prepare foreign currency value at risk analysis disclosures that measure the aggregate sensitivity to changes in all foreign currency exchange rate exposures, including the aggregate effects of changes in both transactional currency/functional currency exchange rate exposures and functional currency/reporting currency exchange rate exposures. For example, assume a French division of a registrant presenting its financial statements in U.S. dollars ($US) invests in a deutschmark(DM)-denominated debt security. In these circumstances, the $US is the reporting currency and the DM is the transactional currency. In addition, assume this division determines that the French franc (FF) is its functional currency according to FASB ASC Topic 830, Foreign Currency Matters. In preparing the foreign currency value at risk disclosures, this registrant should report the aggregate potential loss from hypothetical changes in both the DM/FF exchange rate exposure and the FF/$US exchange rate exposure; and

E. Model, assumptions, and parameters that should be described include, but are not limited to, how loss is defined by the model (e.g., loss in earnings, fair values, or cash flows), the type of model used (e.g., variance/covariance, historical simulation, or Monte Carlo simulation and a description as to how optionality is addressed by the model), the types of instruments covered by the model (e.g., derivative financial instruments, other financial instruments, derivative commodity instruments, and whether other instruments are included voluntarily, such as certain commodity instruments and positions, cash flows from anticipated transactions, and certain financial instruments excluded under instruction 3.C.ii. of the General Instructions to Paragraphs 305(a) and 305(b)), and other relevant information about the model's assumptions and parameters, (e.g., holding periods, confidence intervals, and, when appropriate, the methods used for aggregating value at risk amounts across market risk exposure categories, such as by assuming perfect positive correlation, independence, or actual observed correlation).

5. Under paragraph 305(a)(2), limitations that should be considered include, but are not limited to:

A. The exclusion of certain market risk sensitive instruments, positions, and transactions from the disclosures required under paragraph 305(a)(1) (e.g., derivative commodity instruments not permitted by contract or business custom to be settled in cash or with another financial instrument, commodity positions, cash flows from anticipated transactions, and certain financial instruments excluded under instruction 3.C.ii. of the General Instructions to Paragraphs 305(a) and 305(b)). Failure to include such instruments, positions, and transactions in preparing the disclosures under paragraph 305(a)(1) may be a limitation because the resulting disclosures may not fully reflect the net market risk of a registrant; and

B. The ability of disclosures required under paragraph 305(a)(1) to reflect fully the market risk that may be inherent in instruments with leverage, option, or prepayment features (e.g., options, including written options, structured notes, collateralized mortgage obligations, leveraged swaps, and options embedded in swaps).

(b) Qualitative information about market risk.

(1) To the extent material, describe:

(i) The registrant's primary market risk exposures;

(ii) How those exposures are managed. Such descriptions shall include, but not be limited to, a discussion of the objectives, general strategies, and instruments, if any, used to manage those exposures; and

(iii) Changes in either the registrant's primary market risk exposures or how those exposures are managed, when compared to what was in effect during the most recently completed fiscal year and what is known or expected to be in effect in future reporting periods.

(2) Qualitative information about market risk shall be presented separately for market risk sensitive instruments entered into for trading purposes and those entered into for purposes other than trading.

Instructions to Paragraph 305(b).

1. For purposes of disclosure under paragraph 305(b), primary market risk exposures means:

A. The following categories of market risk: interest rate risk, foreign currency exchange rate risk, commodity price risk, and other relevant market rate or price risks (e.g., equity price risk); and

B. Within each of these categories, the particular markets that present the primary risk of loss to the registrant. For example, if a registrant has a material exposure to foreign currency exchange rate risk and, within this category of market risk, is most vulnerable to changes in dollar/yen, dollar/pound, and dollar/peso exchange rates, the registrant should disclose those exposures. Similarly, if a registrant has a material exposure to interest rate risk and, within this category of market risk, is most vulnerable to changes in short-term U.S. prime interest rates, it should disclose the existence of that exposure.

2. For purposes of disclosure under paragraph 305(b), registrants should describe primary market risk exposures that exist as of the end of the latest fiscal year, and how those exposures are managed.

General Instructions to Paragraphs 305(a) and 305(b).

1. The disclosures called for by paragraphs 305(a) and 305(b) are intended to clarify the registrant's exposures to market risk associated with activities in derivative financial instruments, other financial instruments, and derivative commodity instruments.

2. In preparing the disclosures under paragraphs 305(a) and 305(b), registrants are required to include derivative financial instruments, other financial instruments, and derivative commodity instruments.

3. For purposes of paragraphs 305(a) and 305(b), derivative financial instruments, other financial instruments, and derivative commodity instruments (collectively referred to as "market risk sensitive instruments") are defined as follows:

A. Derivative financial instruments has the same meaning as defined by generally accepted accounting principles (see, e.g., FASB ASC Master Glossary), and includes futures, forwards, swaps, options, and other financial instruments with similar characteristics;

B. Other financial instruments means all financial instruments as defined by generally accepted accounting principles for which fair value disclosures are required (see, e.g., FASB ASC paragraph 825-10-50-8 (Financial Instruments Topic)), except for derivative financial instruments, as defined above;

C. i. Other financial instruments include, but are not limited to, trade accounts receivable, investments, loans, structured notes, mortgage-backed securities, trade accounts payable, indexed debt instruments, interest-only and principal-only obligations, deposits, and other debt obligations;

ii. Other financial instruments exclude employers' and plans' obligations for pension and other post-retirement benefits, substantively extinguished debt, insurance contracts, lease contracts, warranty obligations and rights, unconditional purchase obligations, investments accounted for under the equity method, noncontrolling interests in consolidated enterprises, and equity instruments issued by the registrant and classified in stockholders' equity in the statement of financial position (see, e.g., FASB ASC paragraph 825-10-50-8). For purposes of this item, trade accounts receivable and trade accounts payable need not be considered other financial instruments when their carrying amounts approximate fair value; and

D. Derivative commodity instruments include, to the extent such instruments are not derivative financial instruments, commodity futures, commodity forwards, commodity swaps, commodity options, and other commodity instruments with similar characteristics that are permitted by contract or business custom to be settled in cash or with another financial instrument. For purposes of this paragraph, settlement in cash includes settlement in cash of the net change in value of the derivative commodity instrument (e.g., net cash settlement based on changes in the price of the underlying commodity).

4. A. In addition to providing required disclosures for the market risk sensitive instruments defined in instruction 2. of the General Instructions to Paragraphs 305(a) and 305(b), registrants are encouraged to include other market risk sensitive instruments, positions, and transactions within the disclosures required under paragraphs 305(a) and 305(b). Such instruments, positions, and transactions might include commodity positions, derivative commodity instruments that are not permitted by contract or business custom to be settled in cash or with another financial instrument, cash flows from anticipated transactions, and certain financial instruments excluded under instruction 3.C.ii. of the General Instructions to Paragraphs 305(a) and 305(b).

B. Registrants that voluntarily include other market risk sensitive instruments, positions and transactions within their quantitative disclosures about market risk under the sensitivity analysis or value at risk disclosure alternatives are not required to provide separate market risk disclosures for any voluntarily selected instruments, positions, or transactions. Instead, registrants selecting the sensitivity analysis and value at risk disclosure alternatives are permitted to present comprehensive market risk disclosures, which reflect the combined market risk exposures inherent in both the required and any voluntarily selected instruments, position, or transactions. Registrants that choose the tabular presentation disclosure alternative should present voluntarily selected instruments, positions, or transactions in a manner consistent with the requirements in Item 305(a) for market risk sensitive instruments.

C. If a registrant elects to include voluntarily a particular type of instrument, position, or transaction in their quantitative disclosures about market risk, that registrant should include all, rather than some, of those instruments, positions, or transactions within those disclosures. For example, if a registrant holds in inventory a particular type of commodity position and elects to include that commodity position within their market risk disclosures, the registrant should include the entire commodity position, rather than only a portion thereof, in their quantitative disclosures about market risk.

5. A. Under paragraphs 305(a) and 305(b), a materiality assessment should be made for each market risk exposure category within the trading and other than trading portfolios.

B. For purposes of making the materiality assessment under instruction 5.A. of the General Instructions to Paragraphs 305(a) and 305(b), registrants should evaluate both:

i. The materiality of the fair values of derivative financial instruments, other financial instruments, and derivative commodity instruments outstanding as of the end of the latest fiscal year; and

ii. The materiality of potential, near-term losses in future earnings, fair values, and/or cash flows from reasonably possible near-term changes in market rates or prices.

iii. If either paragraphs B.i. or B.ii. in this instruction of the General Instructions to Paragraphs 305(a) and 305(b) are material, the registrant should disclose quantitative and qualitative information about market risk, if such market risk for the particular market risk exposure category is material.

C. For purposes of instruction 5.B.i. of the General Instructions to Paragraphs 305(a) and 305(b), registrants generally should not net fair values, except to the extent allowed under generally accepted accounting principles (see, e.g., FASB ASC Subtopic 210-20, Balance Sheet—Offsetting). For example, under this instruction, the fair value of assets generally should not be netted with the fair value of liabilities.

D. For purposes of instruction 5.B.ii. of the General Instructions to Paragraphs 305(a) and 305(b), registrants should consider, among other things, the magnitude of:

i. Past market movements;

ii. Reasonably possible, near-term market movements; and

iii. Potential losses that may arise from leverage, option, and multiplier features.

E. For purposes of instructions 5.B.ii and 5.D.ii of the General Instructions to Paragraphs 305(a) and 305(b), the term near term means a period of time going forward up to one year from the date of the financial statements (see FASB ASC Master Glossary).

F. For the purpose of instructions 5.B.ii. and 5.D.ii. of the General Instructions to Paragraphs 305(a) and 305(b), the term reasonably possible has the same meaning as defined by generally accepted accounting principles (see, e.g., FASB ASC Master Glossary).

6. For purposes of paragraphs 305(a) and 305(b), registrants should present the information outside of, and not incorporate the information into, the financial statements (including the footnotes to the financial statements). In addition, registrants are encouraged to provide the required information in one location. However, alternative presentation, such as inclusion of all or part of the information in Management's Discussion and Analysis, may be used at the discretion of the registrant. If information is disclosed in more than one location, registrants should provide cross-references to the locations of the related disclosures.

7. For purposes of the instructions to paragraphs 305(a) and 305(b), trading purposes means dealing and other trading activities measured at fair value with gains and losses recognized in earnings. In addition, anticipated transactions means transactions (other than transactions involving existing assets or liabilities or transactions necessitated by existing firm commitments) an enterprise expects, but is not obligated, to carry out in the normal course of business.

(c) Interim periods. If interim period financial statements are included or are required to be included by Article 3 of Regulation S-X (17 CFR 210), discussion and analysis shall be provided so as to enable the reader to assess the sources and effects of material changes in information that would be provided under Item 305 of Regulation S-K from the end of the preceding fiscal year to the date of the most recent interim balance sheet.

Instructions to Paragraph 305(c).

1. Information required under paragraph (c) of this Item 305 is not required until after the first fiscal year end in which this Item 305 is applicable.

(d) Safe Harbor.

(1) The safe harbor provided in Section 27A of the Securities Act of 1933 (15 U.S.C. 77z-2) and Section 21E of the Securities Exchange Act of 1934 (15 U.S.C. 78u-5) ("statutory safe harbors") shall apply, with respect to all types of issuers and transactions, to information provided pursuant to paragraphs (a), (b), and (c) of this Item 305, provided that the disclosure is made by: an issuer; a person acting on behalf of the issuer; an outside reviewer retained by the issuer making a statement on behalf of the issuer; or an underwriter, with respect to information provided by the issuer or information derived from information provided by the issuer.

(2) For purposes of paragraph (d) of this Item 305 only:

(i) All information required by paragraphs (a), (b)(1)(i), (b)(1)(iii), and (c) of this Item 305 is considered forward looking statements for purposes of the statutory safe harbors, except for historical facts such as the terms of particular contracts and the number of market risk sensitive instruments held during or at the end of the reporting period; and

(ii) With respect to paragraph (a) of this Item 305, the meaningful cautionary statements prong of the statutory safe harbors will be satisfied if a registrant satisfies all requirements of that same paragraph (a) of this Item 305.

(e) *Smaller Reporting Companies.* A smaller reporting company, as defined by § 229.10(f)(1), is not required to provide the information required by this Item.

General Instructions to Paragraphs 305(a), 305(b), 305(c), 305(d), and 305(e).

1. Bank registrants, thrift registrants, and non-bank and non-thrift registrants with market capitalizations on January 28, 1997 in excess of $2.5 billion should provide Item 305 disclosures in filings with the Commission that include annual financial statements for fiscal years ending after June 15, 1997. Non-bank and non-thrift registrants with market capitalizations on January 28, 1997 of $2.5 billion or less should provide Item 305 disclosures in filings with the Commission that include financial statements for fiscal years ending after June 15, 1998.

2.A. For purposes of instruction 1. of the General Instructions to Paragraphs 305(a), 305(b), 305(c), 305(d), and 305(e), bank registrants and thrift registrants include any registrant which has control over a depository institution.

B. For purposes of instruction 2.A. of the General Instructions to Paragraphs 305(a), 305(b), 305(c), 305(d), and 305(e), a registrant has control over a depository institution if:

i. The registrant directly or indirectly or acting through one or more other persons owns, controls, or has power to vote 25% or more of any class of voting securities of the depository institution;

ii. The registrant controls in any manner the election of a majority of the directors or trustees of the depository institution; or

iii. The Federal Reserve Board or Office of Thrift Supervision determines, after notice and opportunity for hearing, that the registrant directly or indirectly exercises a controlling influence over the management or policies of the depository institution.

C. For purposes of instruction 2.B. of the General Instructions to Paragraphs 305(a), 305(b), 305(c), 305(d), and 305(e), a depository institution means any of the following:

i. An insured depository institution as defined in section 3(c)(2) of the Federal Deposit Insurance Act (12 U.S.C.A. Sec. 1813(c));

ii. An institution organized under the laws of the United States, any State of the United States, the District of Columbia, any territory of the United States, Puerto Rico, Guam, American Somoa, or the Virgin Islands, which both accepts demand deposits or deposits that the depositor may withdraw by check or similar means for payment to third parties or others and is engaged in the business of making commercial loans.

D. For purposes of instruction 1. of the General Instructions to Paragraphs 305(a), 305(b), 305(c), 305(d) and 305(e), market capitalization is the aggregate market value of common equity as set forth in General Instruction I.B.1. of Form S-3; provided however, that common equity held by affiliates is included in the calculation of market capitalization; and provided further that instead of using the 60 day period prior to filing referenced in General Instruction I.B.1. of Form S-3, the measurement date is January 28, 1997.

Appendix to Item 305—Tabular Disclosures

The tables set forth below are illustrative of the format that might be used when a registrant elects to present the information required by paragraph (a)(1)(i)(A) of Item 305 regarding terms and information about derivative financial instruments, other financial instruments, and derivative commodity instruments. These examples are for illustrative purposes only. Registrants are not required to display the information in the specific format illustrated below. Alternative methods of display are permissible as long as the disclosure requirements of the section are satisfied. Furthermore, these examples were designed primarily to illustrate possible formats for presentation of the information required by the disclosure item and do not purport to illustrate the broad range of derivative financial instruments, other financial instruments, and derivative commodity instruments utilized by registrants.

Interest Rate Sensitivity

The table below provides information about the Company's derivative financial instruments and other financial instruments that are sensitive to changes in interest rates, including interest rate swaps and debt obligations. For debt obligations, the table presents principal cash flows and related weighted average interest rates by expected maturity dates. For interest rate swaps, the table presents notional amounts and weighted average interest rates by expected (contractual) maturity dates. Notional amounts are used to calculate the contractual payments to be exchanged under the contract. Weighted average variable rates are based on implied forward rates in the yield curve at the reporting date. The information is presented in U.S. dollar equivalents, which is the Company's reporting currency. The instrument's actual cash flows are denominated in both U.S. dollars ($US) and German deutschmarks (DM), as indicated in parentheses.

Liabilities

(7) (US$ Equivalent in millions)

| | December 31, 19X1 | | | | | | | |
| | *Expected maturity date* | | | | | | | |
	19X2	19X3	19X4	19X5	19X6	_Thereafter_	_Total_	_Fair value_
Long-term Debt:								
Fixed Rate ($US)	$XXX	$XXX	$XXX	$XXX	$XXX	$XXX	$XXXX	$X
Average interest rate	XX %	XX %	XX %	XX %	XX %	XX %	XX %	
Fixed Rate (DM)	XXX	XXX	XXX	XXX	XXX	XXX	XXX	X
Average interest rate	XX %	XX %	XX %	XX %	XX %	XX %	XX %	
Variable Rate ($US)	XXX	XXX	XXX	XXX	XXX	XXX	XXX	X
Average interest rate	XX %	XX %	XX %	XX %	XX %	XX %	XX %	

Interest Rate Derivatives

(7) (In millions)

	19X2	19X3	19X4	19X5	19X6	_Thereafter_	_Total_	_Fair value_
Interest Rate Swaps:								
Variable to Fixed ($US)	$XXX	$XXX	$XXX	$XXX	$XXX	$XXX	$XXXX	$X
Average pay rate	XX %	XX %	XX %	XX %	XX %	XX %	XX %	
Average receive rate	XX %	XX %	XX %	XX %	XX %	XX %	XX %	
Fixed to Variable ($US)	XXX	XXX	XXX	XXX	XXX	XXX	XXX	X
Average pay rate	XX %	XX %	XX %	XX %	XX %	XX %	XX %	
Average receive rate	XX %	XX %	XX %	XX %	XX %	XX %	XX %	

Exchange Rate Sensitivity

The table below provides information about the Company's derivative financial instruments, other financial instruments, and firmly committed sales transactions by functional currency and presents such information in U.S. dollar equivalents.[1] The table summarizes information on instruments and transactions that are sensitive to foreign currency exchange rates, including foreign currency forward exchange agreements, deutschmark (DM)-denominated debt obligations, and firmly committed DM sales transactions. For debt obligations, the table presents principal cash flows and related weighted average interest rates by expected maturity dates. For firmly committed DM-sales transactions, sales amounts are presented by the expected transaction date, which are not expected to exceed two years. For foreign currency forward exchange agreements, the table presents the notional amounts and weighted average exchange rates by expected (contractual) maturity dates. These notional amounts generally are used to calculate the contractual payments to be exchanged under the contract.

---

[1] The information is presented in U.S. dollars because that is the registrant's reporting currency.

December 31, 19X1

On-Balance Sheet Financial Instruments		*Expected maturity date*						*Total*	*Fair value*
	19X2	*19X3*	*19X4*	*19X5*	*19X6*	*Thereafter*		
(7) (US$ Equivalent in millions)									
$US Functional Currency[2]:									
Liabilities									
Long-Term Debt:									
Fixed Rate (DM)	$XXXX	$XXXX	$XXXX	$XXXX	$XXXX	$XXXX		$XXXX	$X
Average interest rate	XX	XX	XX	XX	XX	XX		XX	
(7) Expected maturity or transaction date Anticipated Transactions and Related Derivatives[3]									
(7) (US$ Equivalent in millions)									
$US Functional Currency:									
Firmly committed Sales Contracts (DM)	$XXXX	$XXXX	—	—	—	—		$XXXX	$X
Forward Exchange Agreements (Receive $US/Pay DM):									
Contract Amount	XXX	XXX	—	—	—	—		XXX	X
Average Contractual Exchange Rate	XX	XX	—	—	—	—		XX	—

[2] Similar tabular information would be provided for other functional currencies.

[3] Pursuant to General Instruction 4. to Items 305(a) and 305(b) of Regulation S-K, registrants may include cash flows from anticipated transactions and operating cash flows resulting from non-financial and non-commodity instruments.

Commodity Price Sensitivity

The table below provides information about the Company's corn inventory and futures contracts that are sensitive to changes in commodity prices, specifically corn prices. For inventory, the table presents the carrying amount and fair value at December 31, 19x1. For the futures contracts the table presents the notional amounts in bushels, the weighted average contract prices, and the total dollar contract amount by expected maturity dates, the latest of which occurs one year from the reporting date. Contract amounts are used to calculate the contractual payments and quantity of corn to be exchanged under the futures contracts.

December 31, 19X1

	Carrying amount	Fair value
(1) (In millions)		
On Balance Sheet Commodity Position and Related Derivatives		
Corn Inventory[4]	$XXX	$XXX

	Expected maturity 1992	*Fair value*
Related Derivatives		
Futures Contracts (Short):		
Contract Volumes (100,000 bushels)	XXX	—
Weighted Average Price (Per 100,000 bushels)	$X.XX	—
Contract Amount ($US in millions)	$XXX	$XXX

[4] Pursuant to General Instruction 4. to Items 305(a) and 305(b) of Regulation S-K, registrants may include information on commodity positions, such as corn inventory.

Item 306. [Reserved]

Item 307. Disclosure Controls and Procedures

Disclose the conclusions of the registrant's principal executive and principal financial officers, or persons performing similar functions, regarding the effectiveness of the registrant's disclosure controls and procedures (as defined in 240.13a-15(e) or 240.15d-15(e) of this chapter) as of the end of the period covered by the report, based on the evaluation of these controls and procedures required by paragraph (b) of § 240.13a-15 or § 240.15d-15 of this chapter.

Item 308. Internal Control Over Financial Reporting

(a) *Management's annual report on internal control over financial reporting.* Provide a report of management on the registrant's internal control over financial reporting (as defined in § 240.13a-15(f) or 240.15d-15(f) of this chapter) that contains:

(1) A statement of management's responsibility for establishing and maintaining adequate internal control over financial reporting for the registrant;

(2) A statement identifying the framework used by management to evaluate the effectiveness of the registrant's internal control over financial reporting as required by paragraph (c) of § 240.13a-15 or 240.15d-15 of this chapter;

(3) Management's assessment of the effectiveness of the registrant's internal control over financial reporting as of the end of the registrant's most recent fiscal year, including a statement as to whether or not internal control over financial reporting is effective. This discussion must include disclosure of any material weakness in the registrant's internal control over financial reporting identified by management. Management is not permitted to conclude that the registrant's internal control over financial reporting is effective if there are one or more material weaknesses in the registrant's internal control over financial reporting; and

(4) If the registrant is an accelerated filer or a large accelerated filer (as defined in §240.12b-2 of this chapter), or otherwise includes in its annual report a registered public accounting firm's attestation report on internal control over financial reporting, a statement that the registered public accounting firm that audited the financial statements included in the annual report containing the disclosure required by this Item has issued an attestation report on the registrant's internal control over financial reporting.

(b) *Attestation Report of the Registered Public Accounting Firm.* If the registrant, other than a registrant that is an emerging growth company, as defined in Rule 405 of the Securities Act of 1933 (§230.405 of this chapter) or Rule 12b-2 of the Securities Exchange Act of 1934 (§240.12b-2 of this chapter), is an accelerated filer or a large accelerated filer (as defined in §240.12b-2 of this chapter), provide the registered public accounting firm's attestation report on the registrant's internal control over financial reporting in the registrant's annual report containing the disclosure required by this Item.

(c) *Changes in internal control over financial reporting.* Disclose any change in the registrant's internal control over financial reporting identified in connection with the evaluation required by paragraph (d) of §240.13a-15 or 240.15d-15 of this chapter that occurred during the registrant's last fiscal quarter (the registrant's fourth fiscal quarter in the case of an annual report) that has materially affected, or is reasonably likely to materially affect, the registrant's internal control over financial reporting.

Instructions to Item 308

1. A registrant need not comply with paragraphs (a) and (b) of this Item until it either had been required to file an annual report pursuant to section 13(a) or 15(d) of the Exchange Act (15 U.S.C. 78m or 78o(d)) for the prior fiscal year or had filed an annual report with the Commission for the prior fiscal year. A registrant that does not comply shall include a statement in the first annual report that it files in substantially the following form: "This annual report does not include a report of management's assessment regarding internal control over financial reporting or an attestation report of the company's registered public accounting firm due to a transition period established by rules of the Securities and Exchange Commission for newly public companies."

2. The registrant must maintain evidential matter, including documentation, to provide reasonable support for management's assessment of the effectiveness of the registrant's internal control over financial reporting.

Subpart 400—Management and Certain Security Holders

Item 401. Directors, Executive Officers, Promoters and Control Persons

(a) *Identification of directors.* List the names and ages of all directors of the registrant and all persons nominated or chosen to become directors; indicate all positions and offices with the registrant held by each such person; state his term of office as director and any period(s) during which he has served as such; describe briefly any arrangement or understanding between him and any other person(s) (naming such person(s)) pursuant to which he was or is to be selected as a director or nominee.

Instructions to Paragraph (a) of Item 401. 1. Do not include arrangements or understandings with directors or officers of the registrant acting solely in their capacities as such.

2. No nominee or person chosen to become a director who has not consented to act as such shall be named in response to this Item. In this regard, with respect to proxy statements, see Rule 14a-4(d) under the Exchange Act (§240.14a-4(d) of this chapter).

3. If the information called for by this paragraph (a) is being presented in a proxy or information statement, no information need be given respecting any director whose term of office as a director will not continue after the meeting to which the statement relates.

4. With regard to proxy statements in connection with action to be taken concerning the election of directors, if fewer nominees are named than the number fixed by or

pursuant to the governing instruments, state the reasons for this procedure and that the proxies cannot be voted for a greater number of persons than the number of nominees named.

5. With regard to proxy statements in connection with action to be taken concerning the election of directors, if the solicitation is made by persons other than management, information shall be given as to nominees of the persons making the solicitation. In all other instances, information shall be given as to directors and persons nominated for election or chosen by management to become directors.

(b) *Identification of executive officers.* List the names and ages of all executive officers of the registrant and all persons chosen to become executive officers; indicate all positions and offices with the registrant held by each such person; state his term of office as officer and the period during which he has served as such and describe briefly any arrangement or understanding between him and any other person(s) (naming such person) pursuant to which he was or is to be selected as an officer.

Instructions to Paragraph (b) of Item 401. 1. Do not include arrangements or understandings with directors or officers of the registrant acting solely in their capacities as such.

2. No person chosen to become an executive officer who has not consented to act as such shall be named in response to this Item.

(c) *Identification of certain significant employees.* Where the registrant employs persons such as production managers, sales managers, or research scientists who are not executive officers but who make or are expected to make significant contributions to the business of the registrant, such persons shall be identified and their background disclosed to the same extent as in the case of executive officers. Such disclosure need not be made if the registrant was subject to section 13(a) or 15(d) of the Exchange Act or was exempt from section 13(a) by section 12(g)(2)(G) of such Act immediately prior to the filing of the registration statement, report, or statement to which this Item is applicable.

(d) *Family relationships.* State the nature of any family relationship between any director, executive officer, or person nominated or chosen by the registrant to become a director or executive officer.

Instruction to Paragraph 401(d). The term "family relationship" means any relationship by blood, marriage, or adoption, not more remote than first cousin.

(e) Business Experience. (1) Background. Briefly describe the business experience during the past five years of each director, executive officer, person nominated or chosen to become a director or executive officer, and each person named in answer to paragraph (c) of Item 401, including: each person's principal occupations and employment during the past five years; the name and principal business of any corporation or other organization in which such occupations and employment were carried on; and whether such corporation or organization is a parent, subsidiary or other affiliate of the registrant. In addition, for each director or person nominated or chosen to become a director, briefly discuss the specific experience, qualifications, attributes or skills that led to the conclusion that the person should serve as a director for the registrant at the time that the disclosure is made, in light of the registrant's business and structure. If material, this disclosure should cover more than the past five years, including information about the person's particular areas of expertise or other relevant qualifications. When an executive officer or person named in response to paragraph (c) of Item 401 has been employed by the registrant or a subsidiary of the registrant for less than five years, a brief explanation shall be included as to the nature of the responsibility undertaken by the individual in prior positions to provide adequate disclosure of his or her prior business experience. What is required is information relating to the level of his or her professional competence, which may include, depending upon the circumstances, such specific information as the size of the operation supervised.

(2) *Directorships.* Indicate any other directorships held, including any other directorships held during the past five years, by each director or person nominated or chosen to

become a director in any company with a class of securities registered pursuant to section 12 of the Exchange Act or subject to the requirements of section 15(d) of such Act or any company registered as an investment company under the Investment Company Act of 1940, 15 U.S.C. 80a-1, et seq., as amended, naming such company.

Instruction to Paragraph (e) of Item 401. For purposes of paragraph (e)(2), where the other directorships of each director or person nominated or chosen to become a director include directorships of two or more registered investment companies that are part of a "fund complex" as that term is defined in Item 22(a) of Schedule 14A under the Exchange Act (§ 240.14a-101 of this chapter), the registrant may, rather than listing each such investment company, identify the fund complex and provide the number of investment company directorships held by the director or nominee in such fund complex.

(f) *Involvement in certain legal proceedings.* Describe any of the following events that occurred during the past ten years and that are material to an evaluation of the ability or integrity of any director, person nominated to become a director or executive officer of the registrant:

(1) A petition under the Federal bankruptcy laws or any state insolvency law was filed by or against, or a receiver, fiscal agent or similar officer was appointed by a court for the business or property of such person, or any partnership in which he was a general partner at or within two years before the time of such filing, or any corporation or business association of which he was an executive officer at or within two years before the time of such filing;

(2) Such person was convicted in a criminal proceeding or is a named subject of a pending criminal proceeding (excluding traffic violations and other minor offenses);

(3) Such person was the subject of any order, judgment, or decree, not subsequently reversed, suspended or vacated, of any court of competent jurisdiction, permanently or temporarily enjoining him from, or otherwise limiting, the following activities:

(i) Acting as a futures commission merchant, introducing broker, commodity trading advisor, commodity pool operator, floor broker, leverage transaction merchant, any other person regulated by the Commodity Futures Trading Commission, or an associated person of any of the foregoing, or as an investment adviser, underwriter, broker or dealer in securities, or as an affiliated person, director or employee of any investment company, bank, savings and loan association or insurance company, or engaging in or continuing any conduct or practice in connection with such activity;

(ii) Engaging in any type of business practice; or

(iii) Engaging in any activity in connection with the purchase or sale of any security or commodity or in connection with any violation of Federal or State securities laws or Federal commodities laws;

(4) Such person was the subject of any order, judgment or decree, not subsequently reversed, suspended or vacated, of any Federal or State authority barring, suspending or otherwise limiting for more than 60 days the right of such person to engage in any activity described in paragraph (f)(3)(i) of this Item, or to be associated with persons engaged in any such activity;

(5) Such person was found by a court of competent jurisdiction in a civil action or by the Commission to have violated any Federal or State securities law, and the judgment in such civil action or finding by the Commission has not been subsequently reversed, suspended, or vacated;

(6) Such person was found by a court of competent jurisdiction in a civil action or by the Commodity Futures Trading Commmission to have violated any Federal commodities law, and the judgment in such civil action or finding by the Commodity Futures Trading Commission has not been subsequently reversed, suspended or vacated;

(7) Such person was the subject of, or a party to, any Federal or State judicial or administrative order, judgment, decree, or finding, not subsequently reversed, suspended or vacated, relating to an alleged violation of:

(i) Any Federal or State securities or commodities law or regulation; or

(ii) Any law or regulation respecting financial institutions or insurance companies including, but not limited to, a temporary or permanent injunction, order of disgorgement or restitution, civil money penalty or temporary or permanent cease-and desist order, or removal or prohibition order; or

(iii) Any law or regulation prohibiting mail or wire fraud or fraud in connection with any business entity; or

(8) Such person was the subject of, or a party to, any sanction or order, not subsequently reversed, suspended or vacated, of any self-regulatory organization (as defined in Section 3(a)(26) of the Exchange Act (15 U.S.C. 78c(a)(26))), any registered entity (as defined in Section 1(a)(29) of the Commodity Exchange Act (7 U.S.C. 1(a)(29))), or any equivalent exchange, association, entity or organization that has disciplinary authority over its members or persons associated with a member.

Instructions to Paragraph (f) of Item 401. 1. For purposes of computing the ten year period referred to in this paragraph, the date of a reportable event shall be deemed the date on which the final order, judgment or decree was entered, or the date on which any rights of appeal from preliminary orders, judgments, or decrees have lapsed. With respect to bankruptcy petitions, the computation date shall be the date of filing for uncontested petitions or the date upon which approval of a contested petition became final.

2. If any event specified in this paragraph (f) has occurred and information in regard thereto is omitted on the grounds that it is not material, the registrant may furnish to the Commission, at time of filing (or at the time preliminary materials are filed, or ten days before definitive materials are filed if preliminary filing is not required, pursuant to Rule 14a-6 or 14c-5 under the Exchange Act (§§240.14a-6 and 240.14c-5 of this chapter)), as supplemental information and not as part of the registration statement, report, or proxy or information statement, materials to which the omission relates, a description of the event and a statement of the reasons for the omission of information in regard thereto.

3. The registrant is permitted to explain any mitigating circumstances associated with events reported pursuant to this paragraph.

4. If the information called for by this paragraph (f) is being presented in a proxy or information statement, no information need be given respecting any director whose term of office as a director will not continue after the meeting to which the statement relates.

5. This paragraph (f)(7) shall not apply to any settlement of a civil proceeding among private litigants.

(g) *Promoters and Control Persons.* (1) Registrants, which have not been subject to the reporting requirements of section 13(a) or 15(d) of the Exchange Act (15 U.S.C. 78m(a) or 78o(d)) for the twelve months immediately prior to the filing of the registration statement, report, or statement to which this Item is applicable, and which had a promoter at any time during the past five fiscal years, shall describe with respect to any promoter, any of the events enumerated in paragraphs (f)(1) through (f)(6) of this Item that occurred during the past five years and that are material to a voting or investment decision.

(2) Registrants, which have not been subject to the reporting requirements of Section 13(a) or 15(d) of the Exchange Act for the twelve months immediately prior to the filing of the registration statement, report, or statement to which this Item is applicable, shall describe with respect to any control person, any of the events enumerated in paragraphs (f)(1) through (f)(6) of this section that occurred during the past five years and that are material to a voting or investment decision.

Instructions to Paragraph (g) of Item 401. 1. Instructions 1. through 3. to paragraph (f) shall apply to this paragraph (g).

2. Paragraph (g) shall not apply to any subsidiary of a registrant which has been reporting pursuant to Section 13(a) or 15(d) of the Exchange Act for the twelve months immediately prior to the filing of the registration statement, report or statement.

Instruction to Item 401. The information regarding executive officers called for by this Item need not be furnished in proxy or information statements prepared in accordance with Schedule 14A or Schedule 14C under the Exchange Act (§ 240.14a-101 and § 240.14c-101 of this chapter) if you are relying on General Instruction G of Form 10-K under the Exchange Act (§ 249.310 of this chapter), such information is furnished in a separate section captioned "Information about our Executive Officers," and is included in Part I of your annual report on Form 10-K.

Item 402. Executive Compensation.

(a) General.

(1) *Treatment of Foreign Private Issuers.* A foreign private issuer will be deemed to comply with this Item if it provides the information required by Items 6.B and 6.E.2 of Form 20-F (17 CFR 249.220f), with more detailed information provided if otherwise made publicly available or required to be disclosed by the issuer's home jurisdiction or a market in which its securities are listed or traded.

(2) *All Compensation Covered.* This Item requires clear, concise and understandable disclosure of all plan and non-plan compensation awarded to, earned by, or paid to the named executive officers designated under paragraph (a)(3) of this Item, and directors covered by paragraph (k) of this Item, by any person for all services rendered in all capacities to the registrant and its subsidiaries, unless otherwise specifically excluded from disclosure in this Item. All such compensation shall be reported pursuant to this Item, even if also called for by another requirement, including transactions between the registrant and a third party where a purpose of the transaction is to furnish compensation to any such named executive officer or director. No amount reported as compensation for one fiscal year need be reported in the same manner as compensation for a subsequent fiscal year; amounts reported as compensation for one fiscal year may be required to be reported in a different manner pursuant to this Item.

(3) *Persons Covered.* Disclosure shall be provided pursuant to this Item for each of the following (the "named executive officers"):

(i) All individuals serving as the registrant's principal executive officer or acting in a similar capacity during the last completed fiscal year ("PEO"), regardless of compensation level;

(ii) All individuals serving as the registrant's principal financial officer or acting in a similar capacity during the last completed fiscal year ("PFO"), regardless of compensation level;

(iii) The registrant's three most highly compensated executive officers other than the PEO and PFO who were serving as executive officers at the end of the last completed fiscal year; and

(iv) Up to two additional individuals for whom disclosure would have been provided pursuant to paragraph (a)(3)(iii) of this Item but for the fact that the individual was not serving as an executive officer of the registrant at the end of the last completed fiscal year.

Instructions to Item 402(a)(3).

1. *Determination of Most Highly Compensated Executive Officers.* The determination as to which executive officers are most highly compensated shall be made by reference to total compensation for the last completed fiscal year (as required to be disclosed pursuant to paragraph (c)(2)(x) of this Item) reduced by the amount required to be disclosed pursuant to paragraph (c)(2)(viii) of this Item, *provided*, *however*, that no disclosure need be provided

for any executive officer, other than the PEO and PFO, whose total compensation, as so reduced, does not exceed $100,000.

2. *Inclusion of Executive Officer of Subsidiary*. It may be appropriate for a registrant to include as named executive officers one or more executive officers or other employees of subsidiaries in the disclosure required by this Item. See Rule 3b-7 under the Exchange Act (17 CFR 240.3b-7).

3. *Exclusion of Executive Officer Due to Overseas Compensation*. It may be appropriate in limited circumstances for a registrant not to include in the disclosure required by this Item an individual, other than its PEO or PFO, who is one of the registrant's most highly compensated executive officers due to the payment of amounts of cash compensation relating to overseas assignments attributed predominantly to such assignments.

(4) *Information for Full Fiscal Year*. If the PEO or PFO served in that capacity during any part of a fiscal year with respect to which information is required, information should be provided as to all of his or her compensation for the full fiscal year. If a named executive officer (other than the PEO or PFO) served as an executive officer of the registrant (whether or not in the same position) during any part of the fiscal year with respect to which information is required, information shall be provided as to all compensation of that individual for the full fiscal year.

(5) *Omission of Table or Column*. A table or column may be omitted if there has been no compensation awarded to, earned by, or paid to any of the named executive officers or directors required to be reported in that table or column in any fiscal year covered by that table.

(6) *Definitions*. For purposes of this Item:

(i) The term *stock* means instruments such as common stock, restricted stock, restricted stock units, phantom stock, phantom stock units, common stock equivalent units or any similar instruments that do not have option-like features, and the term *option* means instruments such as stock options, stock appreciation rights and similar instruments with option-like features. The term *stock appreciation rights* ("*SARs*") refers to SARs payable in cash or stock, including SARs payable in cash or stock at the election of the registrant or a named executive officer. The term *equity* is used to refer generally to stock and/or options.

(ii) The term *plan* includes, but is not limited to, the following: Any plan, contract, authorization or arrangement, whether or not set forth in any formal document, pursuant to which cash, securities, similar instruments, or any other property may be received. A plan may be applicable to one person. Registrants may omit information regarding group life, health, hospitalization, or medical reimbursement plans that do not discriminate in scope, terms or operation, in favor of executive officers or directors of the registrant and that are available generally to all salaried employees.

(iii) The term *incentive plan* means any plan providing compensation intended to serve as incentive for performance to occur over a specified period, whether such performance is measured by reference to financial performance of the registrant or an affiliate, the registrant's stock price, or any other performance measure. An *equity incentive plan* is an incentive plan or portion of an incentive plan under which awards are granted that fall within the scope of FASB ASC Topic 718, Compensation—Stock Compensation. A *non-equity incentive plan* is an incentive plan or portion of an incentive plan that is not an equity incentive plan. The term *incentive plan award* means an award provided under an incentive plan.

(iv) The terms *date of grant* or *grant date* refer to the grant date determined for financial statement reporting purposes pursuant to FASB ASC Topic 718.

(v) *Closing market price* is defined as the price at which the registrant's security was last sold in the principal United States market for such security as of the date for which the closing market price is determined.

(b) *Compensation Discussion and Analysis*.

(1) Discuss the compensation awarded to, earned by, or paid to the named executive officers. The discussion shall explain all material elements of the registrant's compensation of the named executive officers. The discussion shall describe the following:

(i) The objectives of the registrant's compensation programs;

(ii) What the compensation program is designed to reward;

(iii) Each element of compensation;

(iv) Why the registrant chooses to pay each element;

(v) How the registrant determines the amount (and, where applicable, the formula) for each element to pay;

(vi) How each compensation element and the registrant's decisions regarding that element fit into the registrant's overall compensation objectives and affect decisions regarding other elements.

(vii) Whether and, if so, how the registrant has considered the results of the most recent shareholder advisory vote on executive compensation required by section 14A of the Exchange Act (15 U.S.C. 78n-1) or § 240.14a-20 of this chapter in determining compensation policies and decisions and, if so, how that consideration has affected the registrant's executive compensation decisions and policies.

(2) While the material information to be disclosed under Compensation Discussion and Analysis will vary depending upon the facts and circumstances, examples of such information may include, in a given case, among other things, the following:

(i) The policies for allocating between long-term and currently paid out compensation;

(ii) The policies for allocating between cash and non-cash compensation, and among different forms of non-cash compensation;

(iii) For long-term compensation, the basis for allocating compensation to each different form of award (such as relationship of the award to the achievement of the registrant's long-term goals, management's exposure to downside equity performance risk, correlation between cost to registrant and expected benefits to the registrant);

(iv) How the determination is made as to when awards are granted, including awards of equity-based compensation such as options;

(v) What specific items of corporate performance are taken into account in setting compensation policies and making compensation decisions;

(vi) How specific forms of compensation are structured and implemented to reflect these items of the registrant's performance, including whether discretion can be or has been exercised (either to award compensation absent attainment of the relevant performance goal(s) or to reduce or increase the size of any award or payout), identifying any particular exercise of discretion, and stating whether it applied to one or more specified named executive officers or to all compensation subject to the relevant performance goal(s);

(vii) How specific forms of compensation are structured and implemented to reflect the named executive officer's individual performance and/or individual contribution to these items of the registrant's performance, describing the elements of individual performance and/or contribution that are taken into account;

(viii) Registrant policies and decisions regarding the adjustment or recovery of awards or payments if the relevant registrant performance measures upon which they are based are restated or otherwise adjusted in a manner that would reduce the size of an award or payment;

(ix) The factors considered in decisions to increase or decrease compensation materially;

(x) How compensation or amounts realizable from prior compensation are considered in setting other elements of compensation (e.g., how gains from prior option or stock awards are considered in setting retirement benefits);

(xi) With respect to any contract, agreement, plan or arrangement, whether written or unwritten, that provides for payment(s) at, following, or in connection with any termination or change-in-control, the basis for selecting particular events as triggering payment (*e.g.*, the rationale for providing a single trigger for payment in the event of a change-in-control);

(xii) The impact of the accounting and tax treatments of the particular form of compensation;

(xiii) The registrant's equity or other security ownership requirements or guidelines (specifying applicable amounts and forms of ownership), and any registrant policies regarding hedging the economic risk of such ownership;

(xiv) Whether the registrant engaged in any benchmarking of total compensation, or any material element of compensation, identifying the benchmark and, if applicable, its components (including component companies); and

(xv) The role of executive officers in determining executive compensation.

Instructions to Item 402(b).

1. The purpose of the Compensation Discussion and Analysis is to provide to investors material information that is necessary to an understanding of the registrant's compensation policies and decisions regarding the named executive officers.

2. The Compensation Discussion and Analysis should be of the information contained in the tables and otherwise disclosed pursuant to this Item. The Compensation Discussion and Analysis should also cover actions regarding executive compensation that were taken after the registrant's last fiscal year's end. Actions that should be addressed might include, as examples only, the adoption or implementation of new or modified programs and policies or specific decisions that were made or steps that were taken that could affect a fair understanding of the named executive officer's compensation for the last fiscal year. Moreover, in some situations it may be necessary to discuss prior years in order to give context to the disclosure provided.

3. The Compensation Discussion and Analysis should focus on the material principles underlying the registrant's executive compensation policies and decisions and the most important factors relevant to analysis of those policies and decisions. The Compensation Discussion and Analysis shall reflect the individual circumstances of the registrant and shall avoid boilerplate language and repetition of the more detailed information set forth in the tables and narrative disclosures that follow.

4. Registrants are not required to disclose target levels with respect to specific quantitative or qualitative performance-related factors considered by the compensation committee or the board of directors, or any other factors or criteria involving confidential trade secrets or confidential commercial or financial information, the disclosure of which would result in competitive harm for the registrant. The standard to use when determining whether disclosure would cause competitive harm for the registrant is the same standard that would apply when a registrant requests confidential treatment of confidential trade secrets or confidential commercial or financial information pursuant to Securities Act Rule 406 (17 CFR 230.406) and Exchange Act Rule 24b-2 (17 CFR 240.24b-2), each of which incorporates the criteria for non-disclosure when relying upon Exemption 4 of the Freedom of Information Act (5 U.S.C. 552(b)(4)) and Rule 80(b)(4) (17 CFR 200.80(b)(4)) thereunder. A registrant is not required to seek confidential treatment under the procedures in Securities Act Rule 406 and Exchange Act Rule 24b-2 if it determines that the disclosure would cause competitive harm in reliance on this instruction; however, in that case, the registrant must discuss how difficult it will be for the executive or how likely it will be for the registrant to achieve the undisclosed target levels or other factors.

5. Disclosure of target levels that are non-GAAP financial measures will not be subject to Regulation G (17 CFR 244.100–102) and Item 10(e) (§ 229.10(e)); however, disclosure must be provided as to how the number is calculated from the registrant's audited financial statements.

6. In proxy or information statements with respect to the election of directors, if the information disclosed pursuant to Item 407(i) would satisfy paragraph (b)(2)(xiii) of this Item, a registrant may refer to the information disclosed pursuant to Item 407(i).

SUMMARY COMPENSATION TABLE

Name and Principal Position	Year	Salary ($)	Bonus ($)	Stock Awards ($)	Option Awards ($)	Non-Equity Incentive Plan Compensation ($)	Change in Pension Value and Nonqualified Deferred Compensation Earnings ($)	All Other Compensation ($)	Total ($)
(a)	(b)	(c)	(d)	(e)	(f)	(g)	(h)	(i)	(j)
PEO									
PFO									
A									
B									
C									

(c) *Summary Compensation Table.*

(1) *General.* Provide the information specified in paragraph (c)(2) of this Item, concerning the compensation of the named executive officers for each of the registrant's last three completed fiscal years, in a Summary Compensation Table in the tabular format specified below.

(2) The Table shall include:

(i) The name and principal position of the named executive officer (column (a));

(ii) The fiscal year covered (column (b));

(iii) The dollar value of base salary (cash and non-cash) earned by the named executive officer during the fiscal year covered (column (c));

(iv) The dollar value of bonus (cash and non-cash) earned by the named executive officer during the fiscal year covered (column (d));

Instructions to Item 402(c)(2)(iii) and (iv).

1. If the amount of salary or bonus earned in a given fiscal year is not calculable through the latest practicable date, a footnote shall be included disclosing that the amount of salary or bonus is not calculable through the latest practicable date and providing the date that the amount of salary or bonus is expected to be determined, and such amount must then be disclosed in a filing under Item 5.02(f) of Form 8-K (17 CFR 249.308).

2. Registrants shall include in the salary column (column (c)) or bonus column (column (d)) any amount of salary or bonus forgone at the election of a named executive officer under which stock, equity-based or other forms of non-cash compensation instead have been received by the named executive officer. However, the receipt of any such form of non-cash compensation instead of salary or bonus must be disclosed in a footnote added to the salary or bonus column and, where applicable, referring to the Grants of Plan-Based Awards Table (required by paragraph (d) of this Item) where the stock, option or non-equity incentive plan award elected by the named executive officer is reported.

(v) For awards of stock, the aggregate grant date fair value computed in accordance with FASB ASC Topic 718 (column (e));

(vi) For awards of options, with or without tandem SARs (including awards that subsequently have been transferred), the aggregate grant date fair value computed in accordance with FASB ASC Topic 718 (column (f));

Instruction 1 to Item 402(c)(2)(v) and (vi).

For awards reported in columns (e) and (f), include a footnote disclosing all assumptions made in the valuation by reference to a discussion of those assumptions in the registrant's financial statements, footnotes to the financial statements, or discussion in the Management's Discussion and Analysis. The sections so referenced are deemed part of the disclosure provided pursuant to this Item.

Instruction 2 to Item 402(c)(2)(v) and (vi).

If at any time during the last completed fiscal year, the registrant has adjusted or amended the exercise price of options or SARs previously awarded to a named executive officer, whether through amendment, cancellation or replacement grants, or any other means ("repriced"), or otherwise has materially modified such awards, the registrant shall include, as awards required to be reported in column (f), the incremental fair value, computed as of the repricing or modification date in accordance with FASB ASC Topic 718, with respect to that repriced or modified award.

Instruction 3 to Item 402(c)(2)(v) and (vi).

For any awards that are subject to performance conditions, report the value at the grant date based upon the probable outcome of such conditions. This amount should be consistent with the estimate of aggregate compensation cost to be recognized over the service period determined as of the grant date under FASB ASC Topic 718, excluding the effect of estimated forfeitures. In a footnote to the table, disclose the value of the award at the grant date assuming that the highest level of performance conditions will be achieved if an amount less than the maximum was included in the table.

(vii) The dollar value of all earnings for services performed during the fiscal year pursuant to awards under non-equity incentive plans as defined in paragraph (a)(6)(iii) of this Item, and all earnings on any outstanding awards (column (g));

Instructions to Item 402(c)(2)(vii).

1. If the relevant performance measure is satisfied during the fiscal year (including for a single year in a plan with a multi-year performance measure), the earnings are reportable for that fiscal year, even if not payable until a later date, and are not reportable again in the fiscal year when amounts are paid to the named executive officer.

2. All earnings on non-equity incentive plan compensation must be identified and quantified in a footnote to column (g), whether the earnings were paid during the fiscal year, payable during the period but deferred at the election of the named executive officer, or payable by their terms at a later date.

(viii) The sum of the amounts specified in paragraphs (c)(2)(viii)(A) and (B) of this Item (column (h)) as follows:

(A) The aggregate change in the actuarial present value of the named executive officer's accumulated benefit under all defined benefit and actuarial pension plans (including supplemental plans) from the pension plan measurement date used for financial statement reporting purposes with respect to the registrant's audited financial statements for the prior completed fiscal year to the pension plan measurement date used for financial statement reporting purposes with respect to the registrant's audited financial statements for the covered fiscal year; and

(B) Above-market or preferential earnings on compensation that is deferred on a basis that is not tax-qualified, including such earnings on nonqualified defined contribution plans;

Instructions to Item 402(c)(2)(viii).

1. The disclosure required pursuant to paragraph (c)(2)(viii)(A) of this Item applies to each plan that provides for the payment of retirement benefits, or benefits that will be paid primarily following retirement, including but not limited to taxqualified defined benefit plans and supplemental executive retirement plans, but excluding tax-qualified defined contribution plans and nonqualified defined contribution plans. For purposes of this disclosure, the registrant should use the same amounts required to be disclosed pursuant to paragraph (h)(2)(iv)

of this Item for the covered fiscal year and the amounts that were or would have been required to be reported for the executive officer pursuant to paragraph (h)(2)(iv) of this Item for the prior completed fiscal year.

2. Regarding paragraph (c)(2)(viii)(B) of this Item, interest on deferred compensation is above-market only if the rate of interest exceeds 120% of the applicable federal long-term rate, with compounding (as prescribed under section 1274(d) of the Internal Revenue Code, (26 U.S.C. 1274(d))) at the rate that corresponds most closely to the rate under the registrant's plan at the time the interest rate or formula is set. In the event of a discretionary reset of the interest rate, the requisite calculation must be made on the basis of the interest rate at the time of such reset, rather than when originally established. Only the above-market portion of the interest must be included. If the applicable interest rates vary depending upon conditions such as a minimum period of continued service, the reported amount should be calculated assuming satisfaction of all conditions to receiving interest at the highest rate. Dividends (and dividend equivalents) on deferred compensation denominated in the registrant's stock ("deferred stock") are preferential only if earned at a rate higher than dividends on the registrant's common stock. Only the preferential portion of the dividends or equivalents must be included. Footnote or narrative disclosure may be provided explaining the registrant's criteria for determining any portion considered to be above-market.

3. The registrant shall identify and quantify by footnote the separate amounts attributable to each of paragraphs (c)(2)(viii)(A) and (B) of this Item. Where such amount pursuant to paragraph (c)(2)(viii)(A) is negative, it should be disclosed by footnote but should not be reflected in the sum reported in column (h).

(ix) All other compensation for the covered fiscal year that the registrant could not properly report in any other column of the Summary Compensation Table (column (i)). Each compensation item that is not properly reportable in columns (c)—(h), regardless of the amount of the compensation item, must be included in column (i). Such compensation must include, but is not limited to:

(A) Perquisites and other personal benefits, or property, unless the aggregate amount of such compensation is less than $10,000;

(B) All "gross-ups" or other amounts reimbursed during the fiscal year for the payment of taxes;

(C) For any security of the registrant or its subsidiaries purchased from the registrant or its subsidiaries (through deferral of salary or bonus, or otherwise) at a discount from the market price of such security at the date of purchase, unless that discount is available generally, either to all security holders or to all salaried employees of the registrant, the compensation cost, if any, computed in accordance with FASB ASC Topic 718;

(D) The amount paid or accrued to any named executive officer pursuant to a plan or arrangement in connection with:

(1) Any termination, including without limitation through retirement, resignation, severance or constructive termination (including a change in responsibilities) of such executive officer's employment with the registrant and its subsidiaries; or

(2) A change in control of the registrant;

(E) Registrant contributions or other allocations to vested and unvested defined contribution plans;

(F) The dollar value of any insurance premiums paid by, or on behalf of, the registrant during the covered fiscal year with respect to life insurance for the benefit of a named executive officer; and

(G) The dollar value of any dividends or other earnings paid on stock or option awards, when those amounts were not factored into the grant date fair value required to be reported for the stock or option award in column (e) or (f); and

Instructions to Item 402(c)(2)(ix).

1. Non-equity incentive plan awards and earnings and earnings on stock and options, except as specified in paragraph (c)(2)(ix)(G) of this Item, are required to be reported elsewhere as provided in this Item and are not reportable as All Other Compensation in column (i).

2. Benefits paid pursuant to defined benefit and actuarial plans are not reportable as All Other Compensation in column (i) unless accelerated pursuant to a change in control; information concerning these plans is reportable pursuant to paragraphs (c)(2)(viii)(A) and (h) of this Item.

3. Any item reported for a named executive officer pursuant to paragraph (c)(2)(ix) of this Item that is not a perquisite or personal benefit and whose value exceeds $10,000 must be identified and quantified in a footnote to column (i). This requirement applies only to compensation for the last fiscal year. All items of compensation are required to be included in the Summary Compensation Table without regard to whether such items are required to be identified other than as specifically noted in this Item.

4. Perquisites and personal benefits may be excluded as long as the total value of all perquisites and personal benefits for a named executive officer is less than $10,000. If the total value of all perquisites and personal benefits is $10,000 or more for any named executive officer, then each perquisite or personal benefit, regardless of its amount, must be identified by type. If perquisites and personal benefits are required to be reported for a named executive officer pursuant to this rule, then each perquisite or personal benefit that exceeds the greater of $25,000 or 10% of the total amount of perquisites and personal benefits for that officer must be quantified and disclosed in a footnote. The requirements for identification and quantification apply only to compensation for the last fiscal year. Perquisites and other personal benefits shall be valued on the basis of the aggregate incremental cost to the registrant. With respect to the perquisite or other personal benefit for which footnote quantification is required, the registrant shall describe in the footnote its methodology for computing the aggregate incremental cost. Reimbursements of taxes owed with respect to perquisites or other personal benefits must be included in column (i) and are subject to separate quantification and identification as tax reimbursements (paragraph (c)(2)(ix)(B) of this Item) even if the associated perquisites or other personal benefits are not required to be included because the total amount of all perquisites or personal benefits for an individual named executive officer is less than $10,000 or are required to be identified but are not required to be separately quantified.

5. For purposes of paragraph (c)(2)(ix)(D) of this Item, an accrued amount is an amount for which payment has become due.

(x) The dollar value of total compensation for the covered fiscal year (column (j)). With respect to each named executive officer, disclose the sum of all amounts reported in columns (c) through (i).

Instructions to Item 402(c).

1. Information with respect to fiscal years prior to the last completed fiscal year will not be required if the registrant was not a reporting company pursuant to section 13(a) or 15(d) of the Exchange Act (15 U.S.C. 78m(a) or 78o(d)) at any time during that year, except that the registrant will be required to provide information for any such year if that information previously was required to be provided in response to a Commission filing requirement.

2. All compensation values reported in the Summary Compensation Table must be reported in dollars and rounded to the nearest dollar. Reported compensation values must be reported numerically, providing a single numerical value for each grid in the table. Where compensation was paid to or received by a named executive officer in a different currency, a footnote must be provided to identify that currency and describe the rate and methodology used to convert the payment amounts to dollars.

3. If a named executive officer is also a director who receives compensation for his or her services as a director, reflect that compensation in the Summary Compensation Table and provide a footnote identifying and itemizing such compensation and amounts. Use the categories in the Director Compensation Table required pursuant to paragraph (k) of this Item.

4. Any amounts deferred, whether pursuant to a plan established under section 401(k) of the Internal Revenue Code (26 U.S.C. 401(k)), or otherwise, shall be included in the appropriate column for the fiscal year in which earned.

GRANTS OF PLAN-BASED AWARDS*

Name	Grant Date	Estimated Future Payouts Under Non-Equity Incentive Plan Awards			Estimated Future Payouts Under Equity Incentive Plan Awards			All Other Stock Awards: Number of Shares of Stock or Units (#)	All Other Option Awards: Number of Securities Underlying Options (#)	Exercise or Base Price of Option Awards ($/Sh)	Grant Date Fair Value of Stock and Option Awards
		Threshold ($)	Target ($)	Maximum ($)	Threshold (#)	Target (#)	Maximum (#)				
(a)	(b)	(c)	(d)	(e)	(f)	(g)	(h)	(i)	(j)	(k)	(l)
PEO											
PFO											
A											
B											
C											

(d) *Grants of Plan-Based Awards Table.* (1) Provide the information specified in paragraph (d)(2) of this Item, concerning each grant of an award made to a named executive officer in the last completed fiscal year under any plan, including awards that subsequently have been transferred, in the following tabular format:

(2) The Table shall include:

(i) The name of the named executive officer (column (a));

(ii) The grant date for equity-based awards reported in the table (column (b)). If such grant date is different than the date on which the compensation committee (or a committee of the board of directors performing a similar function or the full board of directors) takes action or is deemed to take action to grant such awards, a separate, adjoining column shall be added between columns (b) and (c) showing such date;

(iii) The dollar value of the estimated future payout upon satisfaction of the conditions in question under non-equity incentive plan awards granted in the fiscal year, or the applicable range of estimated payouts denominated in dollars (threshold, target and maximum amount) (columns (c) through (e));

(iv) The number of shares of stock, or the number of shares underlying options to be paid out or vested upon satisfaction of the conditions in question under equity incentive plan awards granted in the fiscal year, or the applicable range of estimated payouts denominated in the number of shares of stock, or the number of shares underlying options under the award (threshold, target and maximum amount) (columns (f) through (h));

(v) The number of shares of stock granted in the fiscal year that are not required to be disclosed in columns (f) through (h) (column (i));

(vi) The number of securities underlying options granted in the fiscal year that are not required to be disclosed in columns (f) through (h) (column (j));

(vii) The per-share exercise or base price of the options granted in the fiscal year (column (k)). If such exercise or base price is less than the closing market price of the underlying security on the date of the grant, a separate, adjoining column showing the closing market price on the date of the grant shall be added after column (k); and

(viii) The grant date fair value of each equity award computed in accordance with FASB ASC Topic 718 (column (l)). If at any time during the last completed fiscal year, the registrant has adjusted or amended the exercise or base price of options, SARs or similar optionlike instruments previously awarded to a named executive officer, whether through amendment, cancellation or replacement grants, or any other means ("repriced"), or otherwise has materially modified such awards, the incremental fair value, computed as of the repricing or modification date in accordance with FASB ASC Topic 718, with respect to that repriced or modified award, shall be reported.

Instructions to Item 402(d).

1. Disclosure on a separate line shall be provided in the Table for each grant of an award made to a named executive officer during the fiscal year. If grants of awards were made to a named executive officer during the fiscal year under more than one plan, identify the particular plan under which each such grant was made.

2. For grants of incentive plan awards, provide the information called for by columns (c), (d) and (e), or (f), (g) and (h), as applicable. For columns (c) and (f), *threshold* refers to the minimum amount payable for a certain level of performance under the plan. For columns (d) and (g), *target* refers to the amount payable if the specified performance target(s) are reached. For columns (e) and (h), *maximum* refers to the maximum payout possible under the plan. If the award provides only for a single estimated payout, that amount must be reported as the *target* in columns (d) and (g). In columns (d) and (g), registrants must provide a representative amount based on the previous fiscal year's performance if the target amount is not determinable.

3. In determining if the exercise or base price of an option is less than the closing market price of the underlying security on the date of the grant, the registrant may use either the closing market price as specified in paragraph (a)(6)(v) of this Item, or if no market exists, any other formula prescribed for the security. Whenever the exercise or base price reported in column (k) is not the closing market price, describe the methodology for determining the exercise or base price either by a footnote or accompanying textual narrative.

4. A tandem grant of two instruments, only one of which is granted under an incentive plan, such as an option granted in tandem with a performance share, need be reported only in column (i) or (j), as applicable. For example, an option granted in tandem with a performance share would be reported only as an option grant in column (j), with the tandem feature noted either by a footnote or accompanying textual narrative.

5. Disclose the dollar amount of consideration, if any, paid by the executive officer for the award in a footnote to the appropriate column.

6. If non-equity incentive plan awards are denominated in units or other rights, a separate, adjoining column between columns (b) and (c) shall be added quantifying the units or other rights awarded.

7. Options, SARs and similar option-like instruments granted in connection with a repricing transaction or other material modification shall be reported in this Table. However, the disclosure required by this Table does not apply to any repricing that occurs through a pre-existing formula or mechanism in the plan or award that results in the periodic adjustment of the option or SAR exercise or base price, an antidilution provision in a plan or award, or a recapitalization or similar transaction equally affecting all holders of the class of securities underlying the options or SARs.

8. For any equity awards that are subject to performance conditions, report in column (l) the value at the grant date based upon the probable outcome of such conditions. This amount should be consistent with the estimate of aggregate compensation cost to be recognized over the service period determined as of the grant date under FASB ASC Topic 718, excluding the effect of estimated forfeitures.

(e) *Narrative Disclosure to Summary Compensation Table and Grants of Plan-Based Awards Table.*

(1) Provide a narrative description of any material factors necessary to an understanding of the information disclosed in the tables required by paragraphs (c) and (d) of this Item. Examples of such factors may include, in given cases, among other things:

(i) The material terms of each named executive officer's employment agreement or arrangement, whether written or unwritten;

(ii) If at any time during the last fiscal year, any outstanding option or other equity-based award was repriced or otherwise materially modified (such as by extension of exercise periods, the change of vesting or forfeiture conditions, the change or elimination of applicable performance criteria, or the change of the bases upon which returns are determined), a description of each such repricing or other material modification;

(iii) The material terms of any award reported in response to paragraph (d) of this Item, including a general description of the formula or criteria to be applied in determining the amounts payable, and the vesting schedule. For example, state where applicable that dividends will be paid on stock, and if so, the applicable dividend rate and whether that rate is preferential. Describe any performance-based conditions, and any other material conditions, that are applicable to the award. For purposes of the Table required by paragraph (d) of this Item and the narrative disclosure required by paragraph (e) of this Item, performance-based conditions include both performance conditions and market conditions, as those terms are defined in FASB ASC Topic 718; and

(iv) An explanation of the amount of salary and bonus in proportion to total compensation.

Instructions to Item 402(e)(1).

1. The disclosure required by paragraph (e)(1)(ii) of this Item would not apply to any repricing that occurs through a pre-existing formula or mechanism in the plan or award that results in the periodic adjustment of the option or SAR exercise or base price, an antidilution provision in a plan or award, or a recapitalization or similar transaction equally affecting all holders of the class of securities underlying the options or SARs.

2. Instructions 4 and 5 to Item 402(b) apply regarding disclosure pursuant to paragraph (e)(1) of target levels with respect to specific quantitative or qualitative performance-related factors considered by the compensation committee or the board of directors, or any other factors or criteria involving confidential trade secrets or confidential commercial or financial information, the disclosure of which would result in competitive harm for the registrant.

OUTSTANDING EQUITY AWARDS AT FISCAL YEAR-END

Name	Option Awards					Stock Awards			
	Number of Securities Underlying Unexercised Options (#) Exercisable	Number of Securities Underlying Unexercised Options (#) Unexercisable	Equity Incentive Plan Awards: Number of Securities Underlying Unexercised Unearned Options (#)	Option Exercise Price ($)	Option Expiration Date	Number of Shares or Units of Stock That Have Not Vested (#)	Market Value of Shares or Units of Stock That Have Not Vested ($)	Equity Incentive Plan Awards: Number of Unearned Shares, Units or Other Rights That Have Not Vested (#)	Equity Incentive Plan Awards: Market or Payout Value of Unearned Shares, Units or Other Rights That Have Not Vested ($)
(a)	(b)	(c)	(d)	(e)	(f)	(g)	(h)	(i)	(j)
PEO									
PFO									
A									
B									
C									

(2) Reserved.

(f) *Outstanding Equity Awards at Fiscal Year-End Table.* (1) Provide the information specified in paragraph (f)(2) of this Item, concerning unexercised options; stock that has not vested; and equity incentive plan awards for each named executive officer outstanding as of the end of the registrant's last completed fiscal year in the following tabular format:

(2) The Table shall include:

(i) The name of the named executive officer (column (a));

(ii) On an award-by-award basis, the number of securities underlying unexercised options, including awards that have been transferred other than for value, that are exercisable and that are not reported in column (d) (column (b));

(iii) On an award-by-award basis, the number of securities underlying unexercised options, including awards that have been transferred other than for value, that are unexercisable and that are not reported in column (d) (column (c));

(iv) On an award-by-award basis, the total number of shares underlying unexercised options awarded under any equity incentive plan that have not been earned (column (d)); exercise or base price (column (e));

(vi) For each instrument reported in columns (b), (c) and (d), as applicable, the expiration date (column (f));

(vii) The total number of shares of stock that have not vested and that are not reported in column (i) (column (g));

(viii) The aggregate market value of shares of stock that have not vested and that are not reported in column (j) (column (h));

(ix) The total number of shares of stock, units or other rights awarded under any equity incentive plan that have not vested and that have not been earned, and, if applicable the number of shares underlying any such unit or right (column (i)); and

(x) The aggregate market or payout value of shares of stock, units or other rights awarded under any equity incentive plan that have not vested and that have not been earned (column (j)).

Instructions to Item 402(f)(2).

1. Identify by footnote any award that has been transferred other than for value, disclosing the nature of the transfer.

2. The vesting dates of options, shares of stock and equity incentive plan awards held at fiscal-year end must be disclosed by footnote to the applicable column where the outstanding award is reported.

3. Compute the market value of stock reported in column (h) and equity incentive plan awards of stock reported in column (j) by multiplying the closing market price of the registrant's stock at the end of the last completed fiscal year by the number of shares or units of stock or the amount of equity incentive plan awards, respectively. The number of shares or units reported in columns (d) or (i), and the payout value reported in column (j), shall be based on achieving threshold performance goals, except that if the previous fiscal year's performance has exceeded the threshold, the disclosure shall be based on the next higher performance measure (target or maximum) that exceeds the previous fiscal year's performance. If the award provides only for a single estimated payout, that amount should be reported. If the target amount is not determinable, registrants must provide a representative amount based on the previous fiscal year's performance.

4. Multiple awards may be aggregated where the expiration date and the exercise and/or base price of the instruments is identical. A single award consisting of a combination of options, SARs and/or similar option-like instruments shall be reported as separate awards with respect to each tranche with a different exercise and/or base price or expiration date.

5. Options or stock awarded under an equity incentive plan are reported in columns (d) or (i) and (j), respectively, until the relevant performance condition has been satisfied. Once the relevant performance condition has been satisfied, even if the option or stock award is subject to forfeiture conditions, options are reported in column (b) or (c), as appropriate, until they are exercised or expire, or stock is reported in columns (g) and (h) until it vests.

(g) *Option Exercises and Stock Vested Table*. (1) Provide the information specified in paragraph (g)(2) of this Item, concerning each exercise of stock options, SARs and similar instruments, and each vesting of stock, including restricted stock, restricted stock units and similar instruments, during the last completed fiscal year for each of the named executive officers on an aggregated basis in the following tabular format:

OPTION EXERCISES AND STOCK VESTED

Name	Option Awards		Stock Awards	
	Number of Shares Acquired on Exercise (#)	Value Realized on Exercise ($)	Number of Shares Acquired on Vesting (#)	Value Realized on Vesting ($)
(a)	(b)	(c)	(d)	(e)
PEO				
PFO				
A				
B				
C				

(2) The Table shall include:

(i) The name of the executive officer (column (a));

(ii) The number of securities for which the options were exercised (column (b));

(iii) The aggregate dollar value realized upon exercise of options, or upon the transfer of an award for value (column (c));

(iv) The number of shares of stock that have vested (column (d)); and

(v) The aggregate dollar value realized upon vesting of stock, or upon the transfer of an award for value (column (e)).

Instruction to Item 402(g)(2).

Report in column (c) the aggregate dollar amount realized by the named executive officer upon exercise of the options or upon the transfer of such instruments for value. Compute the dollar amount realized upon exercise by determining the difference between the market price of the underlying securities at exercise and the exercise or base price of the options. Do not include the value of any related payment or other consideration provided (or to be provided) by the registrant to or on behalf of a named executive officer, whether in payment of the exercise price or related taxes. (Any such payment or other consideration provided by the registrant is required to be disclosed in accordance with paragraph (c)(2)(ix) of this Item.) Report in column (e) the aggregate dollar amount realized by the named executive officer upon the vesting of stock or the transfer of such instruments for value. Compute the aggregate dollar amount realized upon vesting by multiplying the number of shares of stock or units by the market value of the underlying shares on the vesting date. For any amount realized upon exercise or vesting for which receipt has been deferred, provide a footnote quantifying the amount and disclosing the terms of the deferral.

(h) *Pension Benefits*.

(1) Provide the information specified in paragraph (h)(2) of this Item with respect to each plan that provides for payments or other benefits at, following, or in connection with retirement, in the following tabular format:

PENSION BENEFITS

Name	Plan Name	Number of Years Credited Service (#)	Present Value of Accumulated Benefit ($)	Payments During Last Fiscal Year ($)
(a)	(b)	(c)	(d)	(e)
PEO				
PFO				
A				
B				
C				

(2) The Table shall include:

(i) The name of the executive officer (column (a));

(ii) The name of the plan (column (b));

(iii) The number of years of service credited to the named executive officer under the plan, computed as of the same pension plan measurement date used for financial statement reporting purposes with respect to the registrant's audited financial statements for the last completed fiscal year (column (c));

(iv) The actuarial present value of the named executive officer's accumulated benefit under the plan, computed as of the same pension plan measurement date used for financial statement reporting purposes with respect to the registrant's audited financial statements for the last completed fiscal year (column (d)); and

(v) The dollar amount of any payments and benefits paid to the named executive officer during the registrant's last completed fiscal year (column (e)).

Instructions to Item 402(h)(2).

1. The disclosure required pursuant to this Table applies to each plan that provides for specified retirement payments and benefits, or payments and benefits that will be provided primarily following retirement, including but not limited to tax-qualified defined benefit plans and supplemental executive retirement plans, but excluding tax-qualified defined contribution plans and nonqualified defined contribution plans. Provide a separate row for each such plan in which the named executive officer participates.

2. For purposes of the amount(s) reported in column (d), the registrant must use the same assumptions used for financial reporting purposes under generally accepted accounting principles, except that retirement age shall be assumed to be the normal retirement age as defined in the plan, or if not so defined, the earliest time at which a participant may retire under the plan without any benefit reduction due to age. The registrant must disclose in the accompanying textual narrative the valuation method and all material assumptions applied in quantifying the present value of the current accrued benefit. A benefit specified in the plan document or the executive's contract itself is not an assumption. Registrants may satisfy all or part of this disclosure by reference to a discussion of those assumptions in the registrant's financial statements, footnotes to the financial statements, or discussion in the Management's Discussion and Analysis. The sections so referenced are deemed part of the disclosure provided pursuant to this Item.

3. For purposes of allocating the current accrued benefit between tax qualified defined benefit plans and related supplemental plans, apply the limitations applicable to tax qualified defined benefit plans established by the Internal Revenue Code and the regulations thereunder that applied as of the pension plan measurement date.

4. If a named executive officer's number of years of credited service with respect to any plan is different from the named executive officer's number of actual years of service with the registrant, provide footnote disclosure quantifying the difference and any resulting benefit augmentation.

(3) Provide a succinct narrative description of any material factors necessary to an understanding of each plan covered by the tabular disclosure required by this paragraph. While material factors will vary depending upon the facts, examples of such factors may include, in given cases, among other things:

(i) The material terms and conditions of payments and benefits available under the plan, including the plan's normal retirement payment and benefit formula and eligibility standards, and the effect of the form of benefit elected on the amount of annual benefits. For this purpose, normal retirement means retirement at the normal retirement age as defined in the plan, or if not so defined, the earliest time at which a participant may retire under the plan without any benefit reduction due to age;

(ii) If any named executive officer is currently eligible for early retirement under any plan, identify that named executive officer and the plan, and describe the plan's early retirement payment and benefit formula and eligibility standards. For this purpose, early retirement means retirement at the early retirement age as defined in the plan, or otherwise available to the executive under the plan;

(iii) The specific elements of compensation (*e.g.*, salary, bonus, etc.) included in applying the payment and benefit formula, identifying each such element;

(iv) With respect to named executive officers' participation in multiple plans, the different purposes for each plan; and

(v) Registrant policies with regard to such matters as granting extra years of credited service.

NONQUALIFIED DEFERRED COMPENSATION

Name	Executive Contributions in Last FY ($)	Registrant Contributions in Last FY ($)	Aggregate Earnings in Last FY ($)	Aggregate Withdrawals/ Distributions ($)	Aggregate Balance at Last FYE ($)
(a)	(b)	(c)	(d)	(e)	(f)
PEO					
PFO					
A					
B					
C					

(i) *Nonqualified Defined Contribution and Other Nonqualified Deferred Compensation Plans.*

(1) Provide the information specified in paragraph (i)(2) of this Item with respect to each defined contribution or other plan that provides for the deferral of compensation on a basis that is not tax-qualified in the following tabular format:

(2) The Table shall include:

(i) The name of the executive officer (column (a));

(ii) The dollar amount of aggregate executive contributions during the registrant's last fiscal year (column (b));

(iii) The dollar amount of aggregate registrant contributions during the registrant's last fiscal year (column (c));

(iv) The dollar amount of aggregate interest or other earnings accrued during the registrant's last fiscal year (column (d));

(v) The aggregate dollar amount of all withdrawals by and distributions to the executive during the registrant's last fiscal year (column (e)); and

(vi) The dollar amount of total balance of the executive's account as of the end of the registrant's last fiscal year (column (f)).

Instruction to Item 402(i)(2).

Provide a footnote quantifying the extent to which amounts reported in the contributions and earnings columns are reported as compensation in the last completed fiscal year in the registrant's Summary Compensation Table and amounts reported in the aggregate balance at last fiscal year end (column (f)) previously were reported as compensation to the named executive officer in the registrant's Summary Compensation Table for previous years.

(3) Provide a succinct narrative description of any material factors necessary to an understanding of each plan covered by tabular disclosure required by this paragraph. While material factors will vary depending upon the facts, examples of such factors may include, in given cases, among other things:

(i) The type(s) of compensation permitted to be deferred, and any limitations (by percentage of compensation or otherwise) on the extent to which deferral is permitted;

(ii) The measures for calculating interest or other plan earnings (including whether such measure(s) are selected by the executive or the registrant and the frequency and manner in which selections may be changed), quantifying interest rates and other earnings measures applicable during the registrant's last fiscal year; and

(iii) Material terms with respect to payouts, withdrawals and other distributions.

(j) *Potential Payments Upon Termination or Change-in-Control.* Regarding each contract, agreement, plan or arrangement, whether written or unwritten, that provides for payment(s) to a named executive officer at, following, or in connection with any termination, including without limitation resignation, severance, retirement or a constructive termination of a named executive officer, or a change in control of the registrant or a change in the named executive officer's responsibilities, with respect to each named executive officer:

(1) Describe and explain the specific circumstances that would trigger payment(s) or the provision of other benefits, including perquisites and health care benefits;

(2) Describe and quantify the estimated payments and benefits that would be provided in each covered circumstance, whether they would or could be lump sum, or annual, disclosing the duration, and by whom they would be provided;

(3) Describe and explain how the appropriate payment and benefit levels are determined under the various circumstances that trigger payments or provision of benefits;

(4) Describe and explain any material conditions or obligations applicable to the receipt of payments or benefits, including but not limited to non-compete, non-solicitation, non-disparagement or confidentiality agreements, including the duration of such agreements and provisions regarding waiver of breach of such agreements; and

(5) Describe any other material factors regarding each such contract, agreement, plan or arrangement.

Instructions to Item 402(j).

1. The registrant must provide quantitative disclosure under these requirements, applying the assumptions that the triggering event took place on the last business day of the registrant's last completed fiscal year, and the price per share of the registrant's securities is the closing market price as of that date. In the event that uncertainties exist as to the provision of payments and benefits or the amounts involved, the registrant is required to make a reasonable estimate (or a reasonable estimated range of amounts) applicable to the payment or benefit and disclose material assumptions underlying such estimates or estimated ranges in its disclosure. In such event, the disclosure would require forward-looking information as appropriate.

2. Perquisites and other personal benefits or property may be excluded only if the aggregate amount of such compensation will be less than $10,000. Individual perquisites and personal benefits shall be identified and quantified as required by Instruction 4 to paragraph (c)(2)(ix) of this Item. For purposes of quantifying health care benefits, the registrant must use the assumptions used for financial reporting purposes under generally accepted accounting principles.

3. To the extent that the form and amount of any payment or benefit that would be provided in connection with any triggering event is fully disclosed pursuant to paragraph (h) or (i) of this Item, reference may be made to that disclosure. However, to the extent that the form or amount of any such payment or benefit would be enhanced or its vesting or other provisions accelerated in connection with any triggering event, such enhancement or acceleration must be disclosed pursuant to this paragraph.

4. Where a triggering event has actually occurred for a named executive officer and that individual was not serving as a named executive officer of the registrant at the end of the last completed fiscal year, the disclosure required by this paragraph for that named executive officer shall apply only to that triggering event.

5. The registrant need not provide information with respect to contracts, agreements, plans or arrangements to the extent they do not discriminate in scope, terms or operation, in favor of executive officers of the registrant and that are available generally to all salaried employees.

(k) *Compensation of Directors.*

(1) Provide the information specified in paragraph (k)(2) of this Item, concerning the compensation of the directors for the registrant's last completed fiscal year, in the following tabular format:

(2) The Table shall include:

(i) The name of each director unless such director is also a named executive officer under paragraph (a) of this Item and his or her compensation for service as a director is fully reflected in the Summary Compensation Table pursuant to paragraph (c) of this Item and otherwise as required pursuant to paragraphs (d) through (j) of this Item (column (a));

(ii) The aggregate dollar amount of all fees earned or paid in cash for services as a director, including annual retainer fees, committee and/or chairmanship fees, and meeting fees (column (b));

(iii) For awards of stock, the aggregate grant date fair value computed in accordance with FASB ASC Topic 718 (column (c));

DIRECTOR COMPENSATION

Name	Fees Earned or Paid in Cash ($)	Stock Awards ($)	Option Awards ($)	Non-Equity Incentive Plan Compensation ($)	Change in Pension Value and Nonqualified Deferred Compensation Earnings	All Other Compensation ($)	Total ($)
(a)	(b)	(c)	(d)	(e)	(f)	(g)	(h)
A							
B							
C							
D							
E							

(iv) For awards of options, with or without tandem SARs (including awards that subsequently have been transferred), the aggregate grant date fair value computed in accordance with FASB ASC Topic 718 (column (d));

Instruction to Item 402(k)(2)(iii) and (iv).

For each director, disclose by footnote to the appropriate column: the grant date fair value of each equity award computed in accordance with FASB ASC Topic 718; for each option, SAR or similar option like instrument for which the registrant has adjusted or amended the exercise or base price during the last completed fiscal year, whether through amendment, cancellation or replacement grants, or any other means ("repriced"), or otherwise has materially modified such awards, the incremental fair value, computed as of the repricing or modification date in accordance with FASB ASC Topic 718; and the aggregate number of stock awards and the aggregate number of option awards outstanding at fiscal year end. However, the disclosure required by this Instruction does not apply to any repricing that occurs through a pre-existing formula or mechanism in the plan or award that results in the periodic adjustment of the option or SAR exercise or base price, an antidilution provision in a plan or award, or a recapitalization or similar transaction equally affecting all holders of the class of securities underlying the options or SARs.

(v) The dollar value of all earnings for services performed during the fiscal year pursuant to non-equity incentive plans as defined in paragraph (a)(6)(iii) of this Item, and all earnings on any outstanding awards (column (e));

(vi) The sum of the amounts specified in paragraphs (k)(2)(vi)(A) and (B) of this Item (column (f)) as follows:

(A) The aggregate change in the actuarial present value of the director's accumulated benefit under all defined benefit and actuarial pension plans (including supplemental plans) from the pension plan measurement date used for financial statement reporting purposes with respect to the registrant's audited financial statements for the prior completed fiscal year to the pension plan measurement date used for financial statement reporting purposes with respect to the registrant's audited financial statements for the covered fiscal year; and

(B) Above-market or preferential earnings on compensation that is deferred on a basis that is not tax-qualified, including such earnings on nonqualified defined contribution plans;

(vii) All other compensation for the covered fiscal year that the registrant could not properly report in any other column of the Director Compensation Table (column (g)). Each compensation item that is not properly reportable in columns (b)—(f), regardless of the amount of the compensation item, must be included in column (g). Such compensation must include, but is not limited to:

(A) Perquisites and other personal benefits, or property, unless the aggregate amount of such compensation is less than $10,000;

(B) All "gross-ups" or other amounts reimbursed during the fiscal year for the payment of taxes;

(C) For any security of the registrant or its subsidiaries purchased from the registrant or its subsidiaries (through deferral of salary or bonus, or otherwise) at a discount from the market price of such security at the date of purchase, unless that discount is available generally, either to all security holders or to all salaried employees of the registrant, the compensation cost, if any, computed in accordance with FASB ASC Topic 718;

(D) The amount paid or accrued to any director pursuant to a plan or arrangement in connection with:

(*1*) The resignation, retirement or any other termination of such director; or

(*2*) A change in control of the registrant;

(E) Registrant contributions or other allocations to vested and unvested defined contribution plans;

(F) Consulting fees earned from, or paid or payable by the registrant and/or its subsidiaries (including joint ventures);

(G) The annual costs of payments and promises of payments pursuant to director legacy programs and similar charitable award programs;

(H) The dollar value of any insurance premiums paid by, or on behalf of, the registrant during the covered fiscal year with respect to life insurance for the benefit of a director; and

(I) The dollar value of any dividends or other earnings paid on stock or option awards, when those amounts were not factored into the grant date fair value required to be reported for the stock or option award in column (c) or (d); and

Instructions to Item 402(k)(2)(vii).

1. Programs in which registrants agree to make donations to one or more charitable institutions in a director's name, payable by the registrant currently or upon a designated event, such as the retirement or death of the director, are charitable awards programs or director legacy programs for purposes of the disclosure required by paragraph (k)(2)(vii)(G) of this Item. Provide footnote disclosure of the total dollar amount payable under the program and other material terms of each such program for which tabular disclosure is provided.

2. Any item reported for a director pursuant to paragraph (k)(2)(vii) of this Item that is not a perquisite or personal benefit and whose value exceeds $10,000 must be identified and quantified in a footnote to column (g). All items of compensation are required to be included in the Director Compensation Table without regard to whether such items are required to be identified other than as specifically noted in this Item.

3. Perquisites and personal benefits may be excluded as long as the total value of all perquisites and personal benefits for a director is less than $10,000. If the total value of all perquisites and personal benefits is $10,000 or more for any director, then each perquisite or personal benefit, regardless of its amount, must be identified by type. If perquisites and personal benefits are required to be reported for a director pursuant to this rule, then each perquisite or personal benefit that exceeds the greater of $25,000 or 10% of the total amount of perquisites and personal benefits for that director must be quantified and disclosed in a footnote. Perquisites and other personal benefits shall be valued on the basis of the aggregate incremental cost to the registrant. With respect to the perquisite or other personal benefit for which footnote quantification is required, the registrant shall describe in the footnote its methodology for computing the aggregate incremental cost. Reimbursements of taxes owed with respect to perquisites or other personal benefits must be included in column (g) and are subject to separate quantification and identification as tax reimbursements (paragraph (k)(2)(vii)(B) of this Item) even if the associated perquisites or other personal benefits are not required to be included because the total amount of all perquisites or personal benefits for an individual director is less than $10,000 or are required to be identified but are not required to be separately quantified.

(viii) The dollar value of total compensation for the covered fiscal year (column (h)). With respect to each director, disclose the sum of all amounts reported in columns (b) through (g).

Instruction to Item 402(k)(2).

Two or more directors may be grouped in a single row in the Table if all elements of their compensation are identical. The names of the directors for whom disclosure is presented on a group basis should be clear from the Table.

(3) *Narrative to Director Compensation Table.*

Provide a narrative description of any material factors necessary to an understanding of the director compensation disclosed in this Table. While material factors will vary depending upon the facts, examples of such factors may include, in given cases, among other things:

(i) A description of standard compensation arrangements (such as fees for retainer, committee service, service as chairman of the board or a committee, and meeting attendance); and

(ii) Whether any director has a different compensation arrangement, identifying that director and describing the terms of that arrangement.

Instruction to Item 402(k).

In addition to the Instruction to paragraphs (k)(2)(iii) and (iv) and the Instructions to paragraph (k)(2)(vii) of this Item, the following apply equally to paragraph (k) of this Item: Instructions 2 and 4 to paragraph (c) of this Item; Instructions to paragraphs (c)(2)(iii) and (iv) of this Item; Instructions to paragraphs (c)(2)(v) and (vi) of this Item; Instructions to paragraph (c)(2)(vii) of this Item; Instructions to paragraph (c)(2)(viii) of this Item; and Instructions 1 and 5 to paragraph (c)(2)(ix) of this Item. These Instructions apply to the columns in the Director Compensation Table that are analogous to the columns in the Summary Compensation Table to which they refer and to disclosures under paragraph (k) of this Item that correspond to analogous disclosures provided for in paragraph (c) of this Item to which they refer.

(*l*) *Smaller Reporting Companies and Emerging Growth Companies.* A registrant that qualifies as a "smaller reporting company," as defined by Item 10(f) (§ 229.10(f)(1)), or is an "emerging growth company," as defined in Rule 405 of the Securities Act (§ 230.405 of this chapter) or Rule 12b-2 of the Exchange Act (§ 240.12b-2 of this chapter), may provide the scaled disclosure in paragraphs (m) through (r) instead of paragraphs (a) through (k), (s), and (u) of this Item.

(m) *Smaller Reporting Companies—General.*

(1) *All Compensation Covered.* This Item requires clear, concise and understandable disclosure of all plan and non-plan compensation awarded to, earned by, or paid to the named executive officers designated under paragraph (m)(2) of this Item, and directors covered by paragraph (r) of this Item, by any person for all services rendered in all capacities to the smaller reporting company and its subsidiaries, unless otherwise specifically excluded from disclosure in this Item. All such compensation shall be reported pursuant to this Item, even if also called for by another requirement, including transactions between the smaller reporting company and a third party where a purpose of the transaction is to furnish compensation to any such named executive officer or director. No amount reported as compensation for one fiscal year need be reported in the same manner as compensation for a subsequent fiscal year; amounts reported as compensation for one fiscal year may be required to be reported in a different manner pursuant to this Item.

(2) *Persons Covered.* Disclosure shall be provided pursuant to this Item for each of the following (the "named executive officers"):

(i) All individuals serving as the smaller reporting company's principal executive officer or acting in a similar capacity during the last completed fiscal year ("PEO"), regardless of compensation level;

(ii) The smaller reporting company's two most highly compensated executive officers other than the PEO who were serving as executive officers at the end of the last completed fiscal year; and

(iii) Up to two additional individuals for whom disclosure would have been provided pursuant to paragraph (m)(2)(ii) of this Item but for the fact that the individual was not serving as an executive officer of the smaller reporting company at the end of the last completed fiscal year.

Instructions to Item 402(m)(2).

1. *Determination of Most Highly Compensated Executive Officers.* The determination as to which executive officers are most highly compensated shall be made by reference to total compensation for the last completed fiscal year (as required to be disclosed pursuant to paragraph (n)(2)(x) of this Item) reduced by the amount required to be disclosed pursuant to paragraph (n)(2)(viii) of this Item, *provided, however,* that no disclosure need be provided for any executive officer, other than the PEO, whose total compensation, as so reduced, does not exceed $100,000.

2. *Inclusion of Executive Officer of a Subsidiary.* It may be appropriate for a smaller reporting company to include as named executive officers one or more executive officers or other employees of subsidiaries in the disclosure required by this Item. See Rule 3b-7 under the Exchange Act (17 CFR 240.3b-7).

3. *Exclusion of Executive Officer Due to Overseas Compensation.* It may be appropriate in limited circumstances for a smaller reporting company not to include in the disclosure required by this Item an individual, other than its PEO, who is one of the smaller reporting company's most highly compensated executive officers due to the payment of amounts of cash compensation relating to overseas assignments attributed predominantly to such assignments.

(3) *Information for Full Fiscal Year.* If the PEO served in that capacity during any part of a fiscal year with respect to which information is required, information should be provided as to all of his or her compensation for the full fiscal year. If a named executive officer (other than the PEO) served as an executive officer of the smaller reporting company (whether or not in the same position) during any part of the fiscal year with respect to which information is required, information shall be provided as to all compensation of that individual for the full fiscal year.

(4) *Omission of Table or Column.* A table or column may be omitted if there has been no compensation awarded to, earned by, or paid to any of the named executive officers or directors required to be reported in that table or column in any fiscal year covered by that table.

(5) *Definitions.* For purposes of this Item:

(i) The term *stock* means instruments such as common stock, restricted stock, restricted stock units, phantom stock, phantom stock units, common stock equivalent units or any similar instruments that do not have option-like features, and the term *option* means instruments such as stock options, stock appreciation rights and similar instruments with option-like features. The term *stock appreciation rights* ("*SARs*") refers to SARs payable in cash or stock, including SARs payable in cash or stock at the election of the smaller reporting company or a named executive officer. The term *equity* is used to refer generally to stock and/or options.

(ii) The term *plan* includes, but is not limited to, the following: Any plan, contract, authorization or arrangement, whether or not set forth in any formal document, pursuant to which cash, securities, similar instruments, or any other property may be received. A plan may be applicable to one person. Smaller reporting companies may omit information regarding group life, health, hospitalization, or medical reimbursement plans that do not discriminate in scope, terms or operation, in favor of executive officers or directors of the smaller reporting company and that are available generally to all salaried employees.

(iii) The term *incentive plan* means any plan providing compensation intended to serve as incentive for performance to occur over a specified period, whether such performance is measured by reference to financial performance of the smaller reporting company or an affiliate, the smaller reporting company's stock price, or any other performance measure. An equity incentive plan is an incentive plan or portion of an incentive plan under which awards are granted that fall within the scope of FASB ASC Topic 718. A *non-equity incentive plan* is an incentive plan or portion of an incentive plan that is not an equity incentive plan. The term *incentive plan award* means an award provided under an incentive plan.

(iv) The terms *date of grant* or *grant date* refer to the grant date determined for financial statement reporting purposes pursuant to FASB ASC Topic 718.

(v) *Closing market price* is defined as the price at which the smaller reporting company's security was last sold in the principal United States market for such security as of the date for which the closing market price is determined.

(n) *Smaller Reporting Companies—Summary Compensation Table.* (1) *General.* Provide the information specified in paragraph (n)(2) of this Item, concerning the compensation of the named executive officers for each of the smaller reporting company's last two completed fiscal years, in a Summary Compensation Table in the tabular format specified below.

SUMMARY COMPENSATION TABLE

Name and principal position (a)	Year (b)	Salary ($) (c)	Bonus ($) (d)	Stock awards ($) (e)	Option awards ($) (f)	Nonequity incentive plan compensation ($) (g)	Nonqualified deferred compensation earnings ($) (h)	All other compensation ($) (i)	Total ($) (j)
PEO									
A									
B									

(2) The Table shall include:

(i) The name and principal position of the named executive officer (column (a));

(ii) The fiscal year covered (column (b));

(iii) The dollar value of base salary (cash and non-cash) earned by the named executive officer during the fiscal year covered (column (c));

(iv) The dollar value of bonus (cash and non-cash) earned by the named executive officer during the fiscal year covered (column (d));

Instructions to Item 402(n)(2)(iii) and (iv).

1. If the amount of salary or bonus earned in a given fiscal year is not calculable through the latest practicable date, a footnote shall be included disclosing that the amount of salary or bonus is not calculable through the latest practicable date and providing the date that the amount of salary or bonus is expected to be determined, and such amount must then be disclosed in a filing under Item 5.02(f) of Form 8-K (17 CFR 249.308).

2. Smaller reporting companies shall include in the salary column (column (c)) or bonus column (column (d)) any amount of salary or bonus forgone at the election of a named executive officer under which stock, equity-based or other forms of non-cash compensation instead have been received by the named executive officer. However, the receipt of any such form of non-cash compensation instead of salary or bonus must be disclosed in a footnote added to the salary or bonus column and, where applicable, referring to the narrative disclosure to the Summary Compensation Table (required by paragraph (o) of this Item) where the material terms of the stock, option or non-equity incentive plan award elected by the named executive officer are reported.

(v) For awards of stock, the dollar amount recognized for financial statement reporting purposes with respect to the fiscal year in accordance with FAS 123R (column (e));

(vi) For awards of options, with or without tandem SARs, the dollar amount recognized for financial statement reporting purposes with respect to the fiscal year in accordance with FAS 123R (column (f));

Instruction 1 to Item 402(n)(2)(v) and (n)(2)(vi). For awards reported in columns (e) and (f), include a footnote disclosing all assumptions made in the valuation by reference to a discussion of those assumptions in the smaller reporting company's financial statements, footnotes to the financial statements, or discussion in the Management's Discussion and Analysis. The sections so referenced are deemed part of the disclosure provided pursuant to this Item.

Instruction 2 to Item 402(n)(2)(v) and (n)(2)(vi). If at any time during the last completed fiscal year, the smaller reporting company has adjusted or amended the exercise price of options or SARs previously awarded to a named executive officer, whether through amendment, cancellation or replacement grants, or any other means ("repriced"), or otherwise has materially modified such awards, the smaller reporting company shall include, as awards required to be reported in column (f), the incremental fair value, computed as of the repricing or modification date in accordance with FASB ASC Topic 718, with respect to that repriced or modified award.

Instruction 3 to Item 402(n)(2)(v) and (vi). For any awards that are subject to performance conditions, report the value at the grant date based upon the probable outcome of such conditions. This amount should be consistent with the estimate of aggregate compensation cost to be recognized over the service period determined as of the grant date under FASB ASC Topic 718, excluding the effect of estimated forfeitures. In a footnote to the table, disclose the value of the award at the grant date assuming that the highest level of performance conditions will be achieved if an amount less than the maximum was included in the table.

(vii) The dollar value of all earnings for services performed during the fiscal year pursuant to awards under non-equity incentive plans as defined in paragraph (m)(5)(iii) of this Item, and all earnings on any outstanding awards (column (g));

Instructions to Item 402(n)(2)(vii).

1. If the relevant performance measure is satisfied during the fiscal year (including for a single year in a plan with a multi-year performance measure), the earnings are reportable for that fiscal year, even if not payable until a later date, and are not reportable again in the fiscal year when amounts are paid to the named executive officer.

2. All earnings on non-equity incentive plan compensation must be identified and quantified in a footnote to column (g), whether the earnings were paid during the fiscal year, payable during the period but deferred at the election of the named executive officer, or payable by their terms at a later date. (viii) Above-market or preferential earnings on compensation that is deferred on a basis that is not tax-qualified, including such earnings on nonqualified defined contribution plans (column (h));

Instruction to Item 402(n)(2)(viii). Interest on deferred compensation is above market only if the rate of interest exceeds 120% of the applicable federal long-term rate, with compounding (as prescribed under section 1274(d) of the Internal Revenue Code, (26 U.S.C. 1274(d))) at the rate that corresponds most closely to the rate under the smaller reporting company's plan at the time the interest rate or formula is set. In the event of a discretionary reset of the interest rate, the requisite calculation must be made on the basis of the interest rate at the time of such reset, rather than when originally established. Only the above-market portion of the interest must be included. If the applicable interest rates vary depending upon conditions such as a minimum period of continued service, the reported amount should be calculated assuming satisfaction of all conditions to receiving interest at the highest rate. Dividends (and dividend equivalents) on deferred compensation denominated in the smaller reporting company's stock ("deferred stock") are preferential only if earned at a rate higher than dividends on the smaller reporting company's common stock. Only the preferential portion of the dividends or equivalents must be included. Footnote or narrative disclosure may be provided explaining the smaller reporting company's criteria for determining any portion considered to be above-market.

(ix) All other compensation for the covered fiscal year that the smaller reporting company could not properly report in any other column of the Summary Compensation Table (column (i)). Each compensation item that is not properly reportable in columns (c) through (h), regardless of the amount of the compensation item, must be included in column (i). Such compensation must include, but is not limited to:

(A) Perquisites and other personal benefits, or property, unless the aggregate amount of such compensation is less than $10,000;

(B) All "gross-ups" or other amounts reimbursed during the fiscal year for the payment of taxes;

(C) For any security of the smaller reporting company or its subsidiaries purchased from the smaller reporting company or its subsidiaries (through deferral of salary or bonus, or otherwise) at a discount from the market price of such security at the date of purchase, unless that discount is available generally, either to all security holders or to all salaried employees of the smaller reporting company, the compensation cost, if any, computed in accordance with FASB ASC Topic 718;

(D) The amount paid or accrued to any named executive officer pursuant to a plan or arrangement in connection with:

(*1*) Any termination, including without limitation through retirement, resignation, severance or constructive termination (including a change in responsibilities) of such executive officer's employment with the smaller reporting company and its subsidiaries; or

(*2*) A change in control of the smaller reporting company;

(E) Smaller reporting company contributions or other allocations to vested and unvested defined contribution plans;

(F) The dollar value of any insurance premiums paid by, or on behalf of, the smaller reporting company during the covered fiscal year with respect to life insurance for the benefit of a named executive officer; and

(G) The dollar value of any dividends or other earnings paid on stock or option awards, when those amounts were not factored into the grant date fair value required to be reported for the stock or option award in column (e) or (f); and

Instructions to Item 402(n)(2)(ix).

1. Non-equity incentive plan awards and earnings and earnings on stock or options, except as specified in paragraph (n) (2) (ix) (G) of this Item, are required to be reported elsewhere as provided in this Item and are not reportable as All Other Compensation in column (i).

2. Benefits paid pursuant to defined benefit and actuarial plans are not reportable as All Other Compensation in column (i) unless accelerated pursuant to a change in control; information concerning these plans is reportable pursuant to paragraph (q) (1) of this Item.

3. Reimbursements of taxes owed with respect to perquisites or other personal benefits must be included in the columns as tax reimbursements (paragraph (n) (2) (ix) (B) of this Item) even if the associated perquisites or other personal benefits are not required to be included because the aggregate amount of such compensation is less than $10,000.

4. Perquisites and other personal benefits shall be valued on the basis of the aggregate incremental cost to the smaller reporting company.

5. For purposes of paragraph (n) (2) (ix) (D) of this Item, an accrued amount is an amount for which payment has become due.

(x) The dollar value of total compensation for the covered fiscal year (column (j)). With respect to each named executive officer, disclose the sum of all amounts reported in columns (c) through (i).

Instructions to Item 402(n).

1. Information with respect to the fiscal year prior to the last completed fiscal year will not be required if the smaller reporting company was not a reporting company pursuant to section 13(a) or 15(d) of the Exchange Act (15 U.S.C. 78m(a) or 78o(d)) at any time during that year, except that the smaller reporting company will be required to provide information for any such year if that information previously was required to be provided in response to a Commission filing requirement.

2. All compensation values reported in the Summary Compensation Table must be reported in dollars and rounded to the nearest dollar. Reported compensation values must be reported numerically, providing a single numerical value for each grid in the table. Where compensation was paid to or received by a named executive officer in a different currency, a footnote must be provided to identify that currency and describe the rate and methodology used to convert the payment amounts to dollars.

3. If a named executive officer is also a director who receives compensation for his or her services as a director, reflect that compensation in the Summary Compensation Table and provide a footnote identifying and itemizing such compensation and amounts. Use the categories in the Director Compensation Table required pursuant to paragraph (r) of this Item.

4. Any amounts deferred, whether pursuant to a plan established under section 401(k) of the Internal Revenue Code (26 U.S.C. 401(k)), or otherwise, shall be included in the appropriate column for the fiscal year in which earned.

(o) *Smaller Reporting Companies—Narrative Disclosure to Summary Compensation Table*. Provide a narrative description of any material factors necessary to an understanding of the information disclosed in the Table required by paragraph (n) of this Item. Examples of such factors may include, in given cases, among other things:

(1) The material terms of each named executive officer's employment agreement or arrangement, whether written or unwritten;

(2) If at any time during the last fiscal year, any outstanding option or other equity based award was repriced or otherwise materially modified (such as by extension of exercise periods, the change of vesting or forfeiture conditions, the change or elimination of applicable performance criteria, or the change of the bases upon which returns are determined), a description of each such repricing or other material modification;

(3) The waiver or modification of any specified performance target, goal or condition to payout with respect to any amount included in non-stock incentive plan compensation or payouts reported in column (g) to the Summary Compensation Table required by paragraph (n) of this Item, stating whether the waiver or modification applied to one or more specified named executive officers or to all compensation subject to the target, goal or condition;

(4) The material terms of each grant, including but not limited to the date of exercisability, any conditions to exercisability, any tandem feature, any reload feature, any tax-reimbursement feature, and any provision that could cause the exercise price to be lowered;

(5) The material terms of any non-equity incentive plan award made to a named executive officer during the last completed fiscal year, including a general description of the formula or criteria to be applied in determining the amounts payable and vesting schedule;

(6) The method of calculating earnings on nonqualified deferred compensation plans including nonqualified defined contribution plans; and

(7) An identification to the extent material of any item included under All Other Compensation (column (i)) in the Summary Compensation Table. Identification of an item shall not be considered material if it does not exceed the greater of $25,000 or 10% of all items included in the specified category in question set forth in paragraph (n)(2)(ix) of this Item. All items of compensation are required to be included in the Summary Compensation Table without regard to whether such items are required to be identified.

Instruction to Item 402(o). The disclosure required by paragraph (o)(2) of this Item would not apply to any repricing that occurs through a pre-existing formula or mechanism in the plan or award that results in the periodic adjustment of the option or SAR exercise or base price, an antidilution provision in a plan or award, or a recapitalization or similar transaction equally affecting all holders of the class of securities underlying the options or SARs.

(p) *Smaller Reporting Companies—Outstanding Equity Awards at Fiscal Year-End Table*. (1) Provide the information specified in paragraph (p)(2) of this Item, concerning unexercised options; stock that has not vested; and equity incentive plan awards for each named executive officer outstanding as of the end of the smaller reporting company's last completed fiscal year in the following tabular format:

Outstanding Equity Awards at Fiscal Year-End

Name (a)	Option awards					Stock awards			
	Number of securities underlying unexercised options (#) exercisable (b)	Number of securities underlying unexercised options (#) unexercisable (c)	Equity incentive plan awards: Number of securities underlying unexercised unearned options (#) (d)	Option exercise price ($) (e)	Option expiration date (f)	Number of shares or units of stock that have not vested (#) (g)	Market value of shares or units of stock that have not vested ($) (h)	Equity incentive plan awards: Number of unearned shares, units or other rights that have not vested (#) (i)	Equity incentive plan awards: Market or payout value of unearned shares, units or other rights that have not vested ($) (j)
PEO									
A									
B									

(2) The Table shall include:

(i) The name of the named executive officer (column (a));

(ii) On an award-by-award basis, the number of securities underlying unexercised options, including awards that have been transferred other than for value, that are exercisable and that are not reported in column (d) (column (b));

(iii) On an award-by-award basis, the number of securities underlying unexercised options, including awards that have been transferred other than for value, that are unexercisable and that are not reported in column (d) (column (c));

(iv) On an award-by-award basis, the total number of shares underlying unexercised options awarded under any equity incentive plan that have not been earned (column (d));

(v) For each instrument reported in columns (b), (c) and (d), as applicable, the exercise or base price (column (e));

(vi) For each instrument reported in columns (b), (c) and (d), as applicable, the expiration date (column (f));

(vii) The total number of shares of stock that have not vested and that are not reported in column (i) (column (g));

(viii) The aggregate market value of shares of stock that have not vested and that are not reported in column (j) (column (h));

(ix) The total number of shares of stock, units or other rights awarded under any equity incentive plan that have not vested and that have not been earned, and, if applicable the number of shares underlying any such unit or right (column (i)); and

(x) The aggregate market or payout value of shares of stock, units or other rights awarded under any equity incentive plan that have not vested and that have not been earned (column (j)).

Instructions to Item 402(p)(2).

1. Identify by footnote any award that has been transferred other than for value, disclosing the nature of the transfer.

2. The vesting dates of options, shares of stock and equity incentive plan awards held at fiscal-year end must be disclosed by footnote to the applicable column where the outstanding award is reported.

3. Compute the market value of stock reported in column (h) and equity incentive plan awards of stock reported in column (j) by multiplying the closing market price of the smaller reporting company's stock at the end of the last completed fiscal year by the number of shares or units of stock or the amount of equity incentive plan awards, respectively. The number of shares or units reported in column (d) or (i), and the payout value reported in column (j), shall be based on achieving threshold performance goals, except that if the previous fiscal year's performance has exceeded the threshold, the disclosure shall be based on the next higher performance measure (target or maximum) that exceeds the previous fiscal year's performance. If the award provides only for a single estimated payout, that amount should be reported. If the target amount is not determinable, smaller reporting companies must provide a representative amount based on the previous fiscal year's performance.

4. Multiple awards may be aggregated where the expiration date and the exercise and/or base price of the instruments is identical. A single award consisting of a combination of options, SARs and/or similar option-like instruments shall be reported as separate awards with respect to each tranche with a different exercise and/or base price or expiration date.

5. Options or stock awarded under an equity incentive plan are reported in columns (d) or (i) and (j), respectively, until the relevant performance condition has been satisfied. Once the relevant performance condition has been satisfied, even if the option or stock award is subject to forfeiture conditions, options are reported in column (b) or (c), as appropriate, until they are exercised or expire, or stock is reported in columns (g) and (h) until it vests.

(q) *Smaller Reporting Companies—Additional Narrative Disclosure.* Provide a narrative description of the following to the extent material:

(1) The material terms of each plan that provides for the payment of retirement benefits, or benefits that will be paid primarily following retirement, including but not limited to tax-qualified defined benefit plans, supplemental executive retirement plans, tax-qualified defined contribution plans and nonqualified defined contribution plans.

(2) The material terms of each contract, agreement, plan or arrangement, whether written or unwritten, that provides for payment(s) to a named executive officer at, following, or in connection with the resignation, retirement or other termination of a named executive officer, or a change in control of the smaller reporting company or a change in the named executive officer's responsibilities following a change in control, with respect to each named executive officer.

(r) *Smaller Reporting Companies—Compensation of Directors.* (1) Provide the information specified in paragraph (r)(2) of this Item, concerning the compensation of the directors for the smaller reporting company's last completed fiscal year, in the following tabular format:

Director Compensation

Name (a)	Fees earned or paid in cash ($) (b)	Stock awards ($) (c)	Option awards ($) (d)	Non-equity incentive plan compensation ($) (e)	Nonqualified deferred compensation earnings ($) (f)	All other compensation ($) (g)	Total ($) (h)
A							
B							
C							
D							
E							

(2) The Table shall include:

(i) The name of each director unless such director is also a named executive officer under paragraph (m) of this Item and his or her compensation for service as a director is fully reflected in the Summary Compensation Table pursuant to paragraph (n) of this Item and otherwise as required pursuant to paragraphs (o) through (q) of this Item (column (a));

(ii) The aggregate dollar amount of all fees earned or paid in cash for services as a director, including annual retainer fees, committee and/or chairmanship fees, and meeting fees (column (b));

(iii) For awards of stock, the aggregate grant date fair value computed in accordance with FASB ASC Topic 718 (column (c));

(iv) For awards of options, with or without tandem SARs (including awards that subsequently have been transferred), the aggregate grant date fair value computed in accordance with FASB ASC Topic 718 (column (d));

Instruction to Item 402(r)(2)(iii) and (iv). For each director, disclose by footnote to the appropriate column, the aggregate number of stock awards and the aggregate number of option awards outstanding at fiscal year end.

(v) The dollar value of all earnings for services performed during the fiscal year pursuant to non-equity incentive plans as defined in paragraph (m)(5)(iii) of this Item, and all earnings on any outstanding awards (column (e));

(vi) Above-market or preferential earnings on compensation that is deferred on a basis that is not tax-qualified, including such earnings on nonqualified defined contribution plans (column (f));

(vii) All other compensation for the covered fiscal year that the smaller reporting company could not properly report in any other column of the Director Compensation Table (column (g)). Each compensation item that is not properly reportable in columns (b) through (f), regardless of the amount of the compensation item, must be included in column (g) and must be identified and quantified in a footnote if it is deemed material in accordance with paragraph (o)(7) of this Item. Such compensation must include, but is not limited to:

(A) Perquisites and other personal benefits, or property, unless the aggregate amount of such compensation is less than $10,000;

(B) All "gross-ups" or other amounts reimbursed during the fiscal year for the payment of taxes;

(C) For any security of the smaller reporting company or its subsidiaries purchased from the smaller reporting company or its subsidiaries (through deferral of salary or bonus, or otherwise) at a discount from the market price of such security at the date of purchase, unless that discount is available generally, either to all security holders or to all salaried employees of the smaller reporting company, the compensation cost, if any, computed in accordance with FASB ASC Topic 718;

(D) The amount paid or accrued to any director pursuant to a plan or arrangement in connection with:

(*1*) The resignation, retirement or any other termination of such director; or

(*2*) A change in control of the smaller reporting company;

(E) Smaller reporting company contributions or other allocations to vested and unvested defined contribution plans;

(F) Consulting fees earned from, or paid or payable by the smaller reporting company and/or its subsidiaries (including joint ventures);

(G) The annual costs of payments and promises of payments pursuant to director legacy programs and similar charitable award programs;

(H) The dollar value of any insurance premiums paid by, or on behalf of, the smaller reporting company during the covered fiscal year with respect to life insurance for the benefit of a director; and

(I) The dollar value of any dividends or other earnings paid on stock or option awards, when those amounts were not factored into the grant date fair value required to be reported for the stock or option award in column (c) or (d); and

Instruction to Item 402(r)(2)(vii). Programs in which smaller reporting companies agree to make donations to one or more charitable institutions in a director's name, payable by the smaller reporting company currently or upon a designated event, such as the retirement or death of the director, are charitable awards programs or director legacy programs for purposes of the disclosure required by paragraph (r)(2)(vii)(G) of this Item. Provide footnote disclosure of the total dollar amount payable under the program and other material terms of each such program for which tabular disclosure is provided.

(viii) The dollar value of total compensation for the covered fiscal year (column (h)). With respect to each director, disclose the sum of all amounts reported in columns (b) through (g).

Instruction to Item 402(r)(2). Two or more directors may be grouped in a single row in the Table if all elements of their compensation are identical. The names of the directors for whom disclosure is presented on a group basis should be clear from the Table.

(3) *Narrative to Director Compensation Table.* Provide a narrative description of any material factors necessary to an understanding of the director compensation disclosed in this Table. While material factors will vary depending upon the facts, examples of such factors may include, in given cases, among other things:

(i) A description of standard compensation arrangements (such as fees for retainer, committee service, service as chairman of the board or a committee, and meeting attendance); and

(ii) Whether any director has a different compensation arrangement, identifying that director and describing the terms of that arrangement.

Instruction to Item 402(r). In addition to the Instruction to paragraph (r)(2)(vii) of this Item, the following apply equally to paragraph (r) of this Item: Instructions 2 and 4 to paragraph (n) of this Item; the Instructions to paragraphs (n)(2)(iii) and (iv) of this Item; the Instructions to paragraphs (n)(2)(v) and (vi) of this Item; the Instructions to paragraph (n)(2)(vii) of this Item; the Instruction to paragraph (n)(2)(viii) of this Item; the Instructions to paragraph (n)(2)(ix) of this Item; and paragraph (o)(7) of this Item. These Instructions apply to the columns in the Director Compensation Table that are analogous to the columns in the Summary Compensation Table to which they refer and to disclosures under paragraph (r) of this Item that correspond to analogous disclosures provided for in paragraph (n) of this Item to which they refer.

(s) *Narrative Disclosure of the Registrant's Compensation Policies and Practices as they Relate to the Registrant's Risk Management.* To the extent that risks arising from the registrant's compensation policies and practices for its employees are reasonably likely to have a material adverse effect on the registrant, discuss the registrant's policies and practices of compensating its employees, including non-executive officers, as they relate to risk management practices and risk-taking incentives. While the situations requiring disclosure will vary depending on the particular registrant and compensation policies and practices, situations that may trigger disclosure include, among others, compensation policies and practices: at a business unit of the company that carries a significant portion of the registrant's risk profile; at a business unit with compensation structured significantly differently than other units within the registrant; at a business unit that is significantly more profitable than others within the registrant; at a business unit where compensation expense is a significant percentage of the unit's revenues; and that vary significantly from the overall risk and reward structure of the registrant, such as when bonuses are awarded upon accomplishment of a task, while the income and risk to the registrant from the task extend over a significantly longer period of time. The purpose of this paragraph (s) is to provide investors material information concerning how the registrant compensates and incentivizes its employees that may create risks that are reasonably likely to have a material adverse effect on the registrant. While the information to be disclosed pursuant to this paragraph (s) will vary depending upon the nature of the registrant's business and the compensation approach, the following are examples of the issues that the registrant may need to address for the business units or employees discussed:

(1) The general design philosophy of the registrant's compensation policies and practices for employees whose behavior would be most affected by the incentives established by the policies and practices, as such policies and practices relate to or affect risk taking by employees on behalf of the registrant, and the manner of their implementation;

(2) The registrant's risk assessment or incentive considerations, if any, in structuring its compensation policies and practices or in awarding and paying compensation;

(3) How the registrant's compensation policies and practices relate to the realization of risks resulting from the actions of employees in both the short term and the long term, such as through policies requiring claw backs or imposing holding periods;

(4) The registrant's policies regarding adjustments to its compensation policies and practices to address changes in its risk profile;

(5) Material adjustments the registrant has made to its compensation policies and practices as a result of changes in its risk profile; and

(6) The extent to which the registrant monitors its compensation policies and practices to determine whether its risk management objectives are being met with respect to incentivizing its employees.

(t) *Golden Parachute Compensation.* (1) In connection with any proxy or consent solicitation material providing the disclosure required by section 14A(b)(1) of the Exchange Act (15 U.S.C. 78n-1(b)(1)) or any proxy or consent solicitation that includes disclosure under Item 14 of Schedule 14A (§ 240.14a-101) pursuant to Note A of Schedule 14A (excluding any proxy or consent solicitation of an "emerging growth company," as defined in Rule 405 of the Securities Act (§ 230.405 of this chapter) or Rule 12b-2 of the Exchange Act (§ 240.12b-2 of this chapter)), with respect to each named executive officer of the acquiring company and the target company, provide the information specified in paragraphs (t)(2) and (3) of this section regarding any agreement or understanding, whether written or unwritten, between such named executive officer and the acquiring company or target company, concerning any type of compensation, whether present, deferred or contingent, that is based on or otherwise relates to an acquisition, merger, consolidation, sale or other disposition of all or substantially all assets of the issuer, as follows:

Golden Parachute Compensation

Name	Cash ($)	Equity ($)	Pension/ NQDC ($)	Perquisites/ Benefits ($)	Tax Reimbursement ($)	Other ($)	Total ($)
(a)	(b)	(c)	(d)	(e)	(f)	(g)	(h)
PEO							
PFO							
A							
B							
C							

(2) The table shall include, for each named executive officer:

(i) The name of the named executive officer (column (a));

(ii) The aggregate dollar value of any cash severance payments, including but not limited to payments of base salary, bonus, and pro-rated non-equity incentive compensation plan payments (column (b));

(iii) The aggregate dollar value of:

    (A) Stock awards for which vesting would be accelerated;

    (B) In-the-money option awards for which vesting would be accelerated; and

    (C) Payments in cancellation of stock and option awards (column (c));

(iv) The aggregate dollar value of pension and nonqualified deferred compensation benefit enhancements (column (d));

(v) The aggregate dollar value of perquisites and other personal benefits or property, and health care and welfare benefits (column (e));

(vi) The aggregate dollar value of any tax reimbursements (column (f));

(vii) The aggregate dollar value of any other compensation that is based on or otherwise relates to the transaction not properly reported in columns (b) through (f) (column (g)); and

(viii) The aggregate dollar value of the sum of all amounts reported in columns (b) through (g) (column (h)).

Instructions to Item 402(t)(2).

1. If this disclosure is included in a proxy or consent solicitation seeking approval of an acquisition, merger, consolidation, or proposed sale or other disposition of all or substantially all the assets of the registrant, or in a proxy or consent solicitation that includes disclosure under Item 14 of Schedule 14A (§ 240.14a-101) pursuant to Note A of Schedule 14A, the disclosure provided by this table shall be quantified assuming that the triggering event took place on the latest practicable date, and that the price per share of the registrant's securities shall be determined as follows: If the shareholders are to receive a fixed dollar amount, the price per share shall be that fixed dollar amount, and if such value is not a fixed dollar amount, the price per share shall be the average closing market price of the registrant's securities over the first five business days following the first public announcement of the transaction. Compute the dollar value of in-the-money option awards for which vesting would be accelerated by determining the difference between this price and the exercise or base price of the options. Include only compensation that is based on or otherwise relates to the subject transaction. Apply Instruction 1 to Item 402(t) with respect to those executive officers for whom disclosure was required in the issuer's most recent filing with the Commission under the Securities Act (15 U.S.C. 77a et seq.) or Exchange Act (15 U.S.C. 78a et seq.) that required disclosure pursuant to Item 402(c).

2. If this disclosure is included in a proxy solicitation for the annual meeting at which directors are elected for purposes of subjecting the disclosed agreements or understandings to a shareholder vote under section 14A(a)(1) of the Exchange Act (15 U.S.C. 78n-1(a)(1)), the disclosure provided by this table shall be quantified assuming that the triggering event took place on the last business day of the registrant's last completed fiscal year, and the price per share of the registrant's securities is the closing market price as of that date. Compute the dollar value of in-the-money option awards for which vesting would be accelerated by determining the difference between this price and the exercise or base price of the options.

3. In the event that uncertainties exist as to the provision of payments and benefits or the amounts involved, the registrant is required to make a reasonable estimate applicable to the payment or benefit and disclose material assumptions underlying such estimates in its disclosure. In such event, the disclosure would require forward-looking information as appropriate.

4. For each of columns (b) through (g), include a footnote quantifying each separate form of compensation included in the aggregate total reported. Include the value of all perquisites and other personal benefits or property. Individual perquisites and personal benefits shall be identified and quantified as required by Instruction 4 to Item 402(c)(2)(ix) of this section. For purposes of quantifying health care benefits, the registrant must use the assumptions used for financial reporting purposes under generally accepted accounting principles.

5. For each of columns (b) through (h), include a footnote quantifying the amount payable attributable to a double-trigger arrangement (i.e., amounts triggered by a change-in-control for which payment is conditioned upon the executive officer's termination without cause or resignation for good reason within a limited time period following the change-in-control), specifying the time-frame in which such termination or resignation must occur in order for the amount to become payable, and the amount payable attributable to a single-trigger arrangement (i.e., amounts triggered by a change-in-control for which payment is not conditioned upon such a termination or resignation of the executive officer).

6. A registrant conducting a shareholder advisory vote pursuant to §240.14a-21(c) of this chapter to cover new arrangements and understandings, and/or revised terms of agreements and understandings that were previously subject to a shareholder advisory vote pursuant to §240.14a-21(a) of this chapter, shall provide two separate tables. One table shall disclose all golden parachute compensation, including both the arrangements and amounts previously disclosed and subject to a shareholder advisory vote under section 14A(a)(1) of the Exchange Act (15 U.S.C. 78n-1(a)(1)) and §240.14a-21(a) of this chapter and the new arrangements and understandings and/or revised terms of agreements and understandings that were previously subject to a shareholder advisory vote. The second table shall disclose only the new arrangements and/or revised terms subject to the separate shareholder vote under section 14A(b)(2) of the Exchange Act and §240.14a-21(c) of this chapter.

7. In cases where this Item 402(t)(2) requires disclosure of arrangements between an acquiring company and the named executive officers of the soliciting target company, the registrant shall clarify whether these agreements are included in the separate shareholder advisory vote pursuant to §240.14a-21(c) of this chapter by providing a separate table of all agreements and understandings subject to the shareholder advisory vote required by section 14A(b)(2) of the Exchange Act (15 U.S.C. 78n-1(b)(2)) and §240.14a-21(c) of this chapter, if different from the full scope of golden parachute compensation subject to Item 402(t) disclosure.

(3) Provide a succinct narrative description of any material factors necessary to an understanding of each such contract, agreement, plan or arrangement and the payments quantified in the tabular disclosure required by this paragraph. Such factors shall include, but not be limited to a description of:

(i) The specific circumstances that would trigger payment(s);

(ii) Whether the payments would or could be lump sum, or annual, disclosing the duration, and by whom they would be provided; and

(iii) Any material conditions or obligations applicable to the receipt of payment or benefits, including but not limited to non-compete, non-solicitation, non-disparagement or confidentiality agreements, including the duration of such agreements and provisions regarding waiver or breach of such agreements.

Instructions to Item 402(t).

1. A registrant that does not qualify as a "smaller reporting company," as defined by §229.10(f)(1) of this chapter, must provide the information required by this Item 402(t) with respect to the individuals covered by Items 402(a)(3)(i), (ii) and (iii) of this section. A registrant that qualifies as a "smaller reporting company," as defined by §229.10(f)(1) of this chapter, must provide the information required by this Item 402(t) with respect to the individuals covered by Items 402(m)(2)(i) and (ii) of this section.

2. The obligation to provide the information in this Item 402(t) shall not apply to agreements and understandings described in paragraph (t)(1) of this section with senior management of foreign private issuers, as defined in §240.3b-4 of this chapter.

Instruction to Item 402.

Specify the applicable fiscal year in the title to each table required under this Item which calls for disclosure as of or for a completed fiscal year.

(u) *Pay Ratio Disclosure—*

(1) *Disclose.*

(i) The median of the annual total compensation of all employees of the registrant, except the PEO of the registrant;

(ii) The annual total compensation of the PEO of the registrant; and

(iii) The ratio of the amount in paragraph (u)(1)(i) of this Item to the amount in paragraph (u)(1)(ii) of this Item. For purposes of the ratio required by this paragraph (u)(1)(iii), the amount in paragraph (u)(1)(i) of this Item shall equal one, or, alternatively, the ratio may be expressed narratively as the multiple that the amount in paragraph (u)(1)(ii) of this Item bears to the amount in paragraph (u)(1)(i) of this Item.

(2) For purposes of this paragraph (u):

(i) *Total compensation* for the median of annual total compensation of all employees of the registrant and the PEO of the registrant shall be determined in accordance with paragraph (c)(2)(x) of this Item. In determining the total compensation, all references to "named executive officer" in this Item and the instructions thereto may be deemed to refer instead, as applicable, to "employee" and, for non-salaried employees, references to "base salary" and "salary" in this Item and the instructions thereto may be deemed to refer instead, as applicable, to "wages plus overtime";

(ii) *Annual total compensation* means total compensation for the registrant's last completed fiscal year; and

(iii) *Registrant* means the registrant and its consolidated subsidiaries.

(3) For purposes of this paragraph (u), *employee* or *employee of the registrant* means an individual employed by the registrant or any of its consolidated subsidiaries, whether as a full-time, part-time, seasonal, or temporary worker, as of a date chosen by the registrant within the last three months of the registrant's last completed fiscal year. The definition of employee or employee of the registrant does not include those workers who are employed, and whose compensation is determined, by an unaffiliated third party but who provide services to the registrant or its consolidated subsidiaries as independent contractors or "leased" workers;

(4) For purposes of this paragraph (u), an employee located in a jurisdiction outside the United States (a "non-U.S. employee") may be exempt from the definition of employee or employee of the registrant under either of the following conditions:

(i) The employee is employed in a foreign jurisdiction in which the laws or regulations governing data privacy are such that, despite its reasonable efforts to obtain or process the information necessary for compliance with this paragraph (u), the registrant is unable to do so without violating such data privacy laws or regulations. The registrant's reasonable efforts shall include, at a minimum, using or seeking an exemption or other relief under any governing data privacy laws or regulations. If the registrant chooses to exclude any employees using this exemption, it shall list the excluded jurisdictions, identify the specific data privacy law or regulation, explain how complying with this paragraph (u) violates such data privacy law or regulation (including the efforts made by the registrant to use or seek an exemption or other relief under such law or regulation), and provide the approximate number of employees exempted from each jurisdiction based on this exemption. In addition, if a registrant excludes any non-U.S. employees in a particular jurisdiction under this exemption, it must exclude all non-U.S. employees in that jurisdiction. Further, the registrant shall obtain a legal opinion from counsel that opines on the inability of the registrant to obtain or process the information necessary for compliance with this paragraph (u) without violating the jurisdiction's laws or regulations governing data privacy, including the registrant's inability to obtain an exemption or other relief under any governing laws or regulations. The registrant shall file the legal opinion as an exhibit to the filing in which the pay ratio disclosure is included.

(ii) The registrant's non-U.S. employees account for 5% or less of the registrant's total employees. In that circumstance, if the registrant chooses to exclude any non-U.S. employees under this exemption, it must exclude all non-U.S. employees. Additionally, if a registrant's non-U.S. employees exceed 5% of the registrant's total U.S. and non-U.S. employees, it may exclude up to 5% of its total employees who are non-U.S. employees; *provided, however*, if a registrant excludes any non-U.S. employees in a particular jurisdiction, it must exclude all non-U.S. employees in that jurisdiction. If more than 5% of a registrant's employees are located in any one non-U.S. jurisdiction, the registrant may not exclude any employees in that jurisdiction under this exemption.

(A) In calculating the number of non-U.S. employees that may be excluded under this Item 402(u)(4)(ii) ("*de minimis*" exemption), a registrant shall count against the total any non-U.S. employee exempted under the data privacy law exemption under Item 402(u)(4)(i) ("data privacy" exemption). A registrant may exclude any non-U.S. employee from a jurisdiction that meets the data privacy exemption, even if the number of excluded employees exceeds 5% of the registrant's total employees. If, however, the number of employees excluded under the data privacy exemption equals or exceeds 5% of the registrant's total employees, the registrant may not use the *de minimis* exemption. Additionally, if the number of employees excluded under the data privacy exemption is less than 5% of the registrant's total employees, the registrant may use the *de minimis* exemption to exclude no more than the number of non-U.S. employees that, combined with the data privacy exemption, does not exceed 5% of the registrant's total employees.

(B) If a registrant excludes non-U.S. employees under the *de minimis* exemption, it must disclose the jurisdiction or jurisdictions from which those employees are being excluded, the approximate number of employees excluded from each jurisdiction under the *de minimis* exemption, the total number of its U.S. and non-U.S. employees irrespective of any exemption (data privacy or *de minimis*), and the total number of its U.S. and non-U.S. employees used for its *de minimis* calculation.

Instruction 1 to Item 402(u)—Disclosing the Date Chosen For Identifying the Median Employee. A registrant shall disclose the date within the last three months of its last completed fiscal year that it selected pursuant to paragraph (u)(3) of this Item to identify its median employee. If the registrant changes the date it uses to identify the median employee from the prior year, the registrant shall disclose this change and provide a brief explanation about the reason or reasons for the change.

Instruction 2 to Item 402(u)—Identifying the Median Employee.

A registrant is required to identify its median employee only once every three years and calculate total compensation for that employee each year; *provided that*, during a registrant's last completed fiscal year there has been no change in its employee population or employee compensation arrangements that it reasonably believes would result in a significant change to its pay ratio disclosure. If there have been no changes that the registrant reasonably believes would significantly affect its pay ratio disclosure, the registrant shall disclose that it is using the same median employee in its pay ratio calculation and describe briefly the basis for its reasonable belief. For example, the registrant could disclose that there has been no change in its employee population or employee compensation arrangements that it believes would significantly impact the pay ratio disclosure. If there has been a change in the registrant's employee population or employee compensation arrangements that the registrant reasonably believes would result in a significant change in its pay ratio disclosure, the registrant shall re-identify the median employee for that fiscal year. If it is no longer appropriate for the registrant to use the median employee identified in year one as the median employee in years two or three because of a change in the original median employee's circumstances that the registrant reasonably believes would result in a significant change in its pay ratio disclosure, the registrant may use another employee whose compensation is substantially similar to the original median employee based on the compensation measure used to select the original median employee.

Instruction 3 to Item 402(u)—Updating For the Last Completed Fiscal Year.

Pay ratio information (*i.e.*, the disclosure called for by paragraph (u)(1) of this Item) with respect to the registrant's last completed fiscal year is not required to be disclosed until the filing of its annual report on Form 10-K for that last completed fiscal year or, if later, the filing of a definitive proxy or information statement relating to its next annual meeting of shareholders (or written consents in lieu of such a meeting) following the end of such fiscal year; *provided that*, the required pay ratio information must, in any event, be filed as provided in General Instruction G(3) of Form 10-K (17 CFR 249.310) not later than 120 days after the end of such fiscal year.

Instruction 4 to Item 402(u)—Methodology and Use of Estimates.

1. Registrants may use reasonable estimates both in the methodology used to identify the median employee and in calculating the annual total compensation or any elements of total compensation for employees other than the PEO.

2. In determining the employees from which the median employee is identified, a registrant may use its employee population or statistical sampling and/or other reasonable methods.

3. A registrant may identify the median employee using annual total compensation or any other compensation measure that is consistently applied to all employees included in the calculation, such as information derived from the registrant's tax and/or payroll records. In using a compensation measure other than annual total compensation to identify the median employee, if that measure is

recorded on a basis other than the registrant's fiscal year (such as information derived from tax and/or payroll records), the registrant may use the same annual period that is used to derive those amounts. Where a compensation measure other than annual total compensation is used to identify the median employee, the registrant must disclose the compensation measure used.

4. In identifying the median employee, whether using annual total compensation or any other compensation measure that is consistently applied to all employees included in the calculation, the registrant may make cost-of-living adjustments to the compensation of employees in jurisdictions other than the jurisdiction in which the PEO resides so that the compensation is adjusted to the cost of living in the jurisdiction in which the PEO resides. If the registrant uses a cost-of-living adjustment to identify the median employee, and the median employee identified is an employee in a jurisdiction other than the jurisdiction in which the PEO resides, the registrant must use the same cost-of-living adjustment in calculating the median employee's annual total compensation and disclose the median employee's jurisdiction. The registrant also shall briefly describe the cost-of-living adjustments it used to identify the median employee and briefly describe the cost-of-living adjustments it used to calculate the median employee's annual total compensation, including the measure used as the basis for the cost-of-living adjustment. A registrant electing to present the pay ratio in this manner also shall disclose the median employee's annual total compensation and pay ratio without the cost-of-living adjustment. To calculate this pay ratio, the registrant will need to identify the median employee without using any cost-of-living adjustments.

5. The registrant shall briefly describe the methodology it used to identify the median employee. It shall also briefly describe any material assumptions, adjustments (including any cost-of-living adjustments), or estimates it used to identify the median employee or to determine total compensation or any elements of total compensation, which shall be consistently applied. The registrant shall clearly identify any estimates used. The required descriptions should be a brief overview; it is not necessary for the registrant to provide technical analyses or formulas. If a registrant changes its methodology or its material assumptions, adjustments, or estimates from those used in its pay ratio disclosure for the prior fiscal year, and if the effects of any such change are significant, the registrant shall briefly describe the change and the reasons for the change. Registrants must also disclose if they changed from using the cost-of-living adjustment to not using that adjustment and if they changed from not using the cost-of-living adjustment to using it.

6. Registrants may, at their discretion, include personal benefits that aggregate less than $10,000 and compensation under non-discriminatory benefit plans in calculating the annual total compensation of the median employee as long as these items are also included in calculating the PEO's annual total compensation. The registrant shall also explain any difference between the PEO's annual total compensation used in the pay ratio disclosure and the total compensation amounts reflected in the Summary Compensation Table, if material.

Instruction 5 to Item 402(u)—Permitted Annualizing Adjustments.

A registrant may annualize the total compensation for all permanent employees (full-time or part-time) that were employed by the registrant for less than the full fiscal year (such as newly hired employees or permanent employees on an unpaid leave of absence during the period). A registrant may not annualize the total compensation for employees in temporary or seasonal positions. A registrant may not make a full-time equivalent adjustment for any employee.

Instruction 6 to Item 402(u)—PEO Compensation Not Available.

A registrant that is relying on Instruction 1 to Item 402(c)(2)(iii) and (iv) in connection with the salary or bonus of the PEO for the last completed fiscal year, shall disclose that the pay ratio required by paragraph (u) of this Item is not calculable until the PEO salary or bonus, as applicable, is determined and shall disclose the date that the PEO's actual total compensation is expected to be determined. The disclosure required by paragraph (u) of this Item shall then be disclosed in the filing under Item 5.02(f) of Form 8-K (17 CFR 249.308) that discloses the PEO's salary or bonus in accordance with Instruction 1 to Item 402(c)(2)(iii) and (iv).

Instruction 7 to Item 402(u)—Transition Periods For Registrants.

1. Upon becoming subject to the requirements of Section 13(a) or 15(d) of the Exchange Act (15 U.S.C. 78m or 78o(d)), a registrant shall comply with paragraph (u) of this Item with respect to compensation for the first fiscal year following the year in which it became subject to such requirements, but not for any fiscal year commencing before January 1, 2017. The registrant may omit the disclosure required by paragraph (u) of this Item from any filing until the filing of its annual report on

Form 10-K (17 CFR 249.310) for such fiscal year or, if later, the filing of a proxy or information statement relating to its next annual meeting of shareholders (or written consents in lieu of such a meeting) following the end of such year; *provided that*, such disclosure shall, in any event, be filed as provided in General Instruction G(3) of Form 10-K not later than 120 days after the end of such fiscal year.

2. A registrant may omit any employees that became its employees as the result of the business combination or acquisition of a business for the fiscal year in which the transaction becomes effective, but the registrant must disclose the approximate number of employees it is omitting. Those employees shall be included in the total employee count for the triennial calculations of the median employee in the year following the transaction for purposes of evaluating whether a significant change had occurred. The registrant shall identify the acquired business excluded for the fiscal year in which the business combination or acquisition becomes effective.

3. A registrant shall comply with paragraph (u) of this Item with respect to compensation for the first fiscal year commencing on or after the date the registrant ceases to be a smaller reporting company, but not for any fiscal year commencing before January 1, 2017.

Instruction 8 to Item 402(u)—Emerging Growth Companies. A registrant is not required to comply with paragraph (u) of this Item if it is an emerging growth company as defined in Section 2(a)(19) of the Securities Act (15 U.S.C. 77(b)(a)(19)) or Section 3(a)(80) of the Exchange Act (15 U.S.C. 78c(a)(80)). A registrant shall comply with paragraph (u) of this Item with respect to compensation for the first fiscal year commencing on or after the date the registrant ceases to be an emerging growth company, but not for any fiscal year commencing before January 1, 2017.

Instruction 9 to Item 402(u)—Additional Information.

Registrants may present additional information, including additional ratios, to supplement the required ratio, but are not required to do so. Any additional information shall be clearly identified, not misleading, and not presented with greater prominence than the required ratio.

Instruction 10 to Item 402(u)—Multiple PEOs During the Year. A registrant with more than one non-concurrent PEO serving during its fiscal year may calculate the annual total compensation for its PEO in either of the following manners:

1. The registrant may calculate the compensation provided to each person who served as PEO during the year for the time he or she served as PEO and combine those figures; or

2. The registrant may look to the PEO serving in that position on the date it selects to identify the median employee and annualize that PEO's compensation.

Regardless of the alternative selected, the registrant shall disclose which option it chose and how it calculated its PEO's annual total compensation.

Instruction 11 to Item 402(u)—Employees' Personally Identifiable Information.

Registrants are not required to, and should not, disclose any personally identifiable information about that employee other than his or her compensation. Registrants may choose to generally identify an employee's position to put the employee's compensation in context, but registrants are not required to provide this information and should not do so if providing the information could identify any specific individual.

Item 403. Security Ownership of Certain Beneficial Owners and Management

(a) *Security ownership of certain beneficial owners.* Furnish the following information, as of the most recent practicable date, in substantially the tabular form indicated, with respect to any person (including any "group" as that term is used in section 13(d)(3) of the Exchange Act) who is known to the registrant to be the beneficial owner of more than five percent of any class of the registrant's voting securities. The address given in column (2) may be a business, mailing or residence address. Show in column (3) the total number of shares beneficially owned and in column (4) the percentage of class so owned. Of the number of shares shown in column (3), indicate by footnote or otherwise the amount known to be shares with respect to which such listed beneficial owner has the right to acquire beneficial ownership, as specified in Rule 13d-3(d)(1) under the Exchange Act (§ 240.13d-3(d)(1) of this chapter).

(1) Title of class	(2) Name and address of beneficial owner	(3) Amount and nature of beneficial ownership	(4) Percent of class

(b) *Security Ownership of Management.* Furnish the following information, as of the most recent practicable date, in substantially the tabular form indicated, as to each class of equity securities of the registrant or any of its parents or subsidiaries, including directors' qualifying shares, beneficially owned by all directors and nominees, naming them, each of the named executive officers as defined in Item 402(a)(3) (§ 229.402(a)(3)), and directors and executive officers of the registrant as a group, without naming them. Show in column (3) the total number of shares beneficially owned and in column (4) the percent of the class so owned. Of the number of shares shown in column (3), indicate, by footnote or otherwise, the amount of shares that are pledged as security and the amount of shares with respect to whichsuch persons have the right to acquire beneficial ownership as specified in § 240.13d-3(d)(1) of this chapter.

(1) Title of class	(2) Name of beneficial owner	(3) Amount and nature of beneficial ownership	(4) Percent of class

(c) *Changes in control.* Describe any arrangements, known to the registrant, including any pledge by any person of securities of the registrant or any of its parents, the operation of which may at a subsequent date result in a change in control of the registrant.

Instructions to Item 403. 1. The percentages are to be calculated on the basis of the amount of outstanding securities, excluding securities held by or for the account of the registrant or its subsidiaries, plus securities deemed outstanding pursuant to Rule 13d-3(d)(1) under the Exchange Act [17 CFR 240.13d-3(d)(1)]. For purposes of paragraph (b), if the percentage of shares beneficially owned by any director or nominee, or by all directors and officers of the registrant as a group, does not exceed one percent of the class so owned, the registrant may, in lieu of furnishing a precise percentage, indicate this fact by means of an asterisk and explanatory footnote or other similar means.

2. For the purposes of this Item, beneficial ownership shall be determined in accordance with Rule 13d-3 under the Exchange Act (§ 240.13d-3 of this chapter). Include such additional subcolumns or other appropriate explanation of column (3) necessary to reflect amounts as to which the beneficial owner has (A) sole voting power, (B) shared voting power, (C) sole investment power, or (D) shared investment power.

3. The registrant shall be deemed to know the contents of any statements filed with the Commission pursuant to section 13(d) or 13(g) of the Exchange Act. When applicable, a registrant may rely upon information set forth in such statements unless the registrant knows or has reason to believe that such information is not complete or accurate or that a statement or amendment should have been filed and was not.

4. For purposes of furnishing information pursuant to paragraph (a) of this Item, the registrant may indicate the source and date of such information.

5. Where more than one beneficial owner is known to be listed for the same securities, appropriate disclosure should be made to avoid confusion. For purposes of paragraph (b), in computing the aggregate number of shares owned by directors and officers of the registrant as a group, the same shares shall not be counted more than once.

6. Paragraph (c) of this Item does not require a description of ordinary default provisions contained in the charter, trust indentures or other governing instruments relating to securities of the registrant.

7. Where the holder(s) of voting securities reported pursuant to paragraph (a) hold more than five percent of any class of voting securities of the registrant pursuant to any voting trust or similar agreement, state the title of such securities, the amount held or to be held pursuant to the trust or agreement (if not clear from the table) and the duration of the agreement. Give the names and addresses of the voting trustees and outline briefly their voting rights and other powers under the trust or agreement.

Item 404. Transactions with Related Persons, Promoters and Certain Control Persons.

(a) *Transactions with Related Persons.* Describe any transaction, since the beginning of the registrant's last fiscal year, or any currently proposed transaction, in which the registrant was or is to be a participant and the amount involved exceeds $120,000, and in which any related person had or will have a direct or indirect material interest. Disclose the following information regarding the transaction:

(1) The name of the related person and the basis on which the person is a related person.

(2) The related person's interest in the transaction with the registrant, including the related person's position(s) or relationship(s) with, or ownership in, a firm, corporation, or other entity that is a party to, or has an interest in, the transaction.

(3) The approximate dollar value of the amount involved in the transaction.

(4) The approximate dollar value of the amount of the related person's interest in the transaction, which shall be computed without regard to the amount of profit or loss.

(5) In the case of indebtedness, disclosure of the amount involved in the transaction shall include the largest aggregate amount of principal outstanding during the period for which disclosure is provided, the amount thereof outstanding as of the latest practicable date, the amount of principal paid during the periods for which disclosure is provided, the amount of interest paid during the period for which disclosure is provided, and the rate or amount of interest payable on the indebtedness.

(6) Any other information regarding the transaction or the related person in the context of the transaction that is material to investors in light of the circumstances of the particular transaction.

Instructions to Item 404(a).

1. For the purposes of paragraph (a) of this Item, the term *related person* means:

a. Any person who was in any of the following categories at any time during the specified period for which disclosure under paragraph (a) of this Item is required:

i. Any director or executive officer of the registrant;

ii. Any nominee for director, when the information called for by paragraph (a) of this Item is being presented in a proxy or information statement relating to the election of that nominee for director; or

iii. Any immediate family member of a director or executive officer of the registrant, or of any nominee for director when the information called for by paragraph (a) of this Item is being presented in a proxy or information statement relating to the election of that nominee for director, which means any child, stepchild, parent, stepparent, spouse, sibling, mother-in-law, father-in-law, son-in-law, daughter- in-law, brother-in-law, or sister-in-law of such director, executive officer or nominee for director, and any person (other than a tenant or employee) sharing the household of such director, executive officer or nominee for director; and

b. Any person who was in any of the following categories when a transaction in which such person had a direct or indirect material interest occurred or existed:

i. A security holder covered by Item 403(a) (§ 229.403(a)); or

ii. Any immediate family member of any such security holder, which means any child, stepchild, parent, stepparent, spouse, sibling, mother-in-law, father-inlaw, son-in-law, daughter-in-law, brother-in-law, or sister-in-law of such security holder, and any person (other than a tenant or employee) sharing the household of such security holder.

2. For purposes of paragraph (a) of this Item, a *transaction* includes, but is not limited to, any financial transaction, arrangement or relationship (including any indebtedness or guarantee of indebtedness) or any series of similar transactions, arrangements or relationships.

3. The amount involved in the transaction shall be computed by determining the dollar value of the amount involved in the transaction in question, which shall include:

a. In the case of any lease or other transaction providing for periodic payments or installments, the aggregate amount of all periodic payments or installments due on or after the beginning of the registrant's last fiscal year, including any required or optional payments due during or at the conclusion of the lease or other transaction providing for periodic payments or installments; and

b. In the case of indebtedness, the largest aggregate amount of all indebtedness outstanding at any time since the beginning of the registrant's last fiscal year and all amounts of interest payable on it during the last fiscal year.

4. In the case of a transaction involving indebtedness:

a. The following items of indebtedness may be excluded from the calculation of the amount of indebtedness and need not be disclosed: amounts due from the related person for purchases of goods and services subject to usual trade terms, for ordinary business travel and expense payments and for other transactions in the ordinary course of business;

b. Disclosure need not be provided of any indebtedness transaction for the related persons specified in Instruction 1.b. to paragraph (a) of this Item; and

c. If the lender is a bank, savings and loan association, or broker-dealer extending credit under Federal Reserve Regulation T (12 CFR part 220) and the loans are not disclosed as nonaccrual, past due, restructured or potential problems (see Item III.C.1. and 2. of Industry Guide 3, Statistical Disclosure by Bank Holding Companies (17 CFR 229.802(c))), disclosure under paragraph (a) of this Item may consist of a statement, if such is the case, that the loans to such persons:

i. Were made in the ordinary course of business;

ii. Were made on substantially the same terms, including interest rates and collateral, as those prevailing at the time for comparable loans with persons not related to the lender; and

iii. Did not involve more than the normal risk of collectibility or present other unfavorable features.

5.a. Disclosure of an employment relationship or transaction involving an executive officer and any related compensation solely resulting from that employment relationship or transaction need not be provided pursuant to paragraph (a) of this Item if:

i. The compensation arising from the relationship or transaction is reported pursuant to Item 402 (§ 229.402); or

ii. The executive officer is not an immediate family member (as specified in Instruction 1 to paragraph (a) of this Item) and such compensation would have been reported under Item 402 (§ 229.402) as compensation earned for services to the registrant if the executive officer was a named executive officer as that term is defined in Item 402(a)(3) (§ 229.402(a)(3)), and such compensation had been approved, or recommended to the board of directors of the registrant for approval, by the compensation committee of the board of directors (or group of independent directors performing a similar function) of the registrant.

b. Disclosure of compensation to a director need not be provided pursuant to paragraph (a) of this Item if the compensation is reported pursuant to Item 402(k) (§ 229.402(k)).

6. A person who has a position or relationship with a firm, corporation, or other entity that engages in a transaction with the registrant shall not be deemed to have an indirect material interest within the meaning of paragraph (a) of this Item where:

a. The interest arises only:

i. From such person's position as a director of another corporation or organization that is a party to the transaction; or

ii. From the direct or indirect ownership by such person and all other persons specified in Instruction 1 to paragraph (a) of this Item, in the aggregate, of less than a ten percent equity interest in another person (other than a partnership) which is a party to the transaction; or iii. From both such position and ownership; or

b. The interest arises only from such person's position as a limited partner in a partnership in which the person and all other persons specified in Instruction 1 to paragraph (a) of this Item, have an interest of less than ten percent, and the person is not a general partner of and does not hold another position in the partnership.

7. Disclosure need not be provided pursuant to paragraph (a) of this Item if:

a. The transaction is one where the rates or charges involved in the transaction are determined by competitive bids, or the transaction involves the rendering of services as a common or contract carrier, or public utility, at rates or charges fixed in conformity with law or governmental authority;

b. The transaction involves services as a bank depositary of funds, transfer agent, registrar, trustee under a trust indenture, or similar services; or

c. The interest of the related person arises solely from the ownership of a class of equity securities of the registrant and all holders of that class of equity securities of the registrant received the same benefit on a pro rata basis.

(b) *Review, Approval or Ratification of Transactions with Related Persons*.

(1) Describe the registrant's policies and procedures for the review, approval, or ratification of any transaction required to be reported under paragraph (a) of this Item. While the material features of such policies and procedures will vary depending on the particular circumstances, examples of such features may include, in given cases, among other things:

(i) The types of transactions that are covered by such policies and procedures;

(ii) The standards to be applied pursuant to such policies and procedures;

(iii) The persons or groups of persons on the board of directors or otherwise who are responsible for applying such policies and procedures; and

(iv) A statement of whether such policies and procedures are in writing and, if not, how such policies and procedures are evidenced.

(2) Identify any transaction required to be reported under paragraph (a) of this Item since the beginning of the registrant's last fiscal year where such policies and procedures did not require review, approval or ratification or where such policies and procedures were not followed.

Instruction to Item 404(b).

Disclosure need not be provided pursuant to this paragraph regarding any transaction that occurred at a time before the related person became one of the enumerated persons in Instruction 1.a.i., ii., or iii. to Item 404(a) if such transaction did not continue after the related person became one of the enumerated persons in Instruction 1.a.i., ii., or iii. to Item 404(a).

(c) *Promoters and Certain Control Persons*.

(1) Registrants that are filing a registration statement on Form S-1 under the Securities Act (§ 239.11 of this chapter) or on Form 10 or Form 10-SB under the Exchange Act (§ 249.210 of this chapter) and that had a promoter at any time during the past five fiscal years shall:

(i) State the names of the promoter(s), the nature and amount of anything of value (including money, property, contracts, options or rights of any kind) received or to be received by each promoter, directly or indirectly, from the registrant and the nature and amount of any assets, services or other consideration therefore received or to be received by the registrant; and

(ii) As to any assets acquired or to be acquired by the registrant from a promoter, state the amount at which the assets were acquired or are to be acquired and the principle followed or to be followed in determining such amount, and identify the persons making the determination and their relationship, if any, with the registrant or any promoter. If the assets were acquired by the promoter within two years prior to their transfer to the registrant, also state the cost thereof to the promoter.

(2) Registrants shall provide the disclosure required by paragraphs (c)(1)(i) and (c)(1)(ii) of this Item as to any person who acquired control of a registrant that is a shell company, or any person that is part of a group, consisting of two or more persons that agree to act together for the purpose of acquiring, holding, voting or disposing of equity securities of a registrant, that acquired control of a registrant that is a shell company. For purposes of this Item, *shell company* has the same meaning as in Rule 405 under the Securities Act (17 CFR 230.405) and Rule 12b-2 under the Exchange Act (17 CFR 240.12b-2).

(d) *Smaller Reporting Companies.* A registrant that qualifies as a "smaller reporting company," as defined by § 229.10(f)(1), must provide the following information in order to comply with this Item:

(1) The information required by paragraph (a) of this Item for the period specified there for a transaction in which the amount involved exceeds the lesser of $120,000 or one percent of the average of the smaller reporting company's total assets at year end for the last two completed fiscal years;

(2) The information required by paragraph (c) of this Item; and

(3) A list of all parents of the smaller reporting company showing the basis of control and as to each parent, the percentage of voting securities owned or other basis of control by its immediate parent, if any.

Instructions to Item 404.

1. If the information called for by this Item is being presented in a registration statement filed pursuant to the Securities Act or the Exchange Act, information shall be given for the periods specified in the Item and, in addition, for the two fiscal years preceding the registrant's last fiscal year, unless the information is being incorporated by reference into a registration statement on Form S-4 (17 CFR 239.25), in which case, information shall be given for the periods specified in the Item.

2. A foreign private issuer will be deemed to comply with this Item if it provides the information required by Item 7.B. of Form 20-F (17 CFR 249.220f) with more detailed information provided if otherwise made publicly available or required to be disclosed by the issuer's home jurisdiction or a market in which its securities are listed or traded.

Item 405. Compliance With Section 16(a) of the Exchange Act

(a) *Reporting Obligation.* Every registrant having a class of equity securities registered pursuant to Section 12 of the Exchange Act (15 U.S.C. 78*l*) and every closed-end investment company registered under the Investment Company Act of 1940 (15 U.S.C. 80a-1 *et seq.*) must:

(1) Under the caption "Delinquent Section 16(a) Reports," identify each person who, at any time during the fiscal year, was a director, officer, beneficial owner of more than ten percent of any class of equity securities of the registrant registered pursuant to Section 12 of the Exchange Act, or any other person subject to Section 16 of the Exchange Act with respect to the registrant because of the requirements of Section 30 of the Investment Company Act ("reporting person") that failed to file on a timely basis reports required by Section 16(a) of the Exchange Act during the most recent fiscal year or prior fiscal years.

(2) For each such person, set forth the number of late reports, the number of transactions that were not reported on a timely basis, and any known failure to file a required form. A known failure to file would include, but not be limited to, a failure to file a Form 3, which is required of all reporting persons, and a failure to file a Form 5 in the absence of the written representation referred to in paragraph (b)(3) of this section, unless the registrant otherwise knows that no Form 5 is required.

Instruction 1 to Paragraph (a) of Item 405. If no disclosure is required, registrants are encouraged to exclude the caption "Delinquent Section 16(a) Reports."

Instruction 2 to Paragraph (a) of Item 405. The registrant is only required to disclose a failure to file timely once. For example, if in the most recently concluded fiscal year a reporting person filed a Form 4 disclosing a transaction that took place in the prior fiscal year, and should have been reported in that year, the registrant should disclose that late filing and transaction pursuant to this Item 405 with respect to the most recently concluded fiscal year, but not in material filed with respect to subsequent years.

(b) *Scope of the Inquiry.* In determining whether disclosure is required pursuant to paragraph (a) of this section, the registrant may rely only on the following:

(1) A review of Forms 3 and 4 (17 CFR 249.103 and 249.104) and amendments thereto filed electronically with the Commission during the registrant's most recent fiscal year;

(2) A review of Forms 5 (17 CFR 249.105) and amendments thereto filed electronically with the Commission with respect to the registrant's most recent fiscal year; and

(3) Any written representation from the reporting person that no Form 5 is required. The registrant must maintain the representation in its records for two years, making a copy available to the Commission or its staff upon request.

Item 406. Code of Ethics

(a) Disclose whether the registrant has adopted a code of ethics that applies to the registrant's principal executive officer, principal financial officer, principal accounting officer or controller, or persons performing similar functions. If the registrant has not adopted such a code of ethics, explain why it has not done so.

(b) For purposes of this Item 406, the term *code of ethics* means written standards that are reasonably designed to deter wrongdoing and to promote:

(1) Honest and ethical conduct, including the ethical handling of actual or apparent conflicts of interest between personal and professional relationships;

(2) Full, fair, accurate, timely, and understandable disclosure in reports and documents that a registrant files with, or submits to, the Commission and in other public communications made by the registrant;

(3) Compliance with applicable governmental laws, rules and regulations;

(4) The prompt internal reporting of violations of the code to an appropriate person or persons identified in the code; and

(5) Accountability for adherence to the code.

(c) The registrant must:

(1) File with the Commission a copy of its code of ethics that applies to the registrant's principal executive officer, principal financial officer, principal accounting officer or controller, or persons performing similar functions, as an exhibit to its annual report;

(2) Post the text of such code of ethics on its Internet website and disclose, in its annual report, its Internet address and the fact that it has posted such code of ethics on its Internet website; or

(3) Undertake in its annual report filed with the Commission to provide to any person without charge, upon request, a copy of such code of ethics and explain the manner in which such request may be made.

(d) If the registrant intends to satisfy the disclosure requirement under Item 5.05 of Form 8-K regarding an amendment to, or a waiver from, a provision of its code of ethics that applies to the registrant's principal executive officer, principal financial officer, principal accounting officer or controller, or persons performing similar functions and that relates to any element of the code of ethics definition enumerated in paragraph (b) of this Item by posting such information on its Internet website, disclose the registrant's Internet address and such intention.

Instructions to Item 406.

1. A registrant may have separate codes of ethics for different types of officers. Furthermore, a *code of ethics* within the meaning of paragraph (b) of this Item may be a portion of a broader document that addresses additional topics or that applies to more persons than those specified in paragraph (a). In satisfying the requirements of paragraph (c), a registrant need only file, post or provide the portions of a broader document that constitutes a *code of ethics* as defined in paragraph (b) and that apply to the persons specified in paragraph (a).

2. If a registrant elects to satisfy paragraph (c) of this Item by posting its code of ethics on its website pursuant to paragraph (c)(2), the code of ethics must remain accessible on its website for as long as the registrant remains subject to the requirements of this Item and chooses to comply with this Item by posting its code on its website pursuant to paragraph (c)(2).

3. A registrant that is an Asset-Backed Issuer (as defined in § 240.13a-14(g) and § 240.15d-14(g) of this chapter) is not required to disclose the information required by this Item.

Item 407. Corporate Governance.

(a) Director Independence. Identify each director and, when the disclosure called for by this paragraph is being presented in a proxy or information statement relating to the election of directors, each nominee for director, that is independent under the independence standards applicable to the registrant under paragraph (a)(1) of this Item. In addition, if such independence standards contain independence requirements for committees of the board of directors, identify each director that is a member of the compensation, nominating or audit committee that is not independent under such committee independence standards. If the registrant does not have a separately designated audit, nominating or compensation committee or committee performing similar functions, the registrant must provide the disclosure of directors that are not independent with respect to all members of the board of directors applying such committee independence standards.

(1) In determining whether or not the director or nominee for director is independent for the purposes of paragraph (a) of this Item, the registrant shall use the applicable definition of independence, as follows:

(i) If the registrant is a listed issuer whose securities are listed on a national securities exchange or in an inter-dealer quotation system which has requirements that a majority of the board of directors be independent, the registrant's definition of independence that it uses for determining if a majority of the board of directors is independent incompliance with the listing standards applicable to the registrant. When determining whether the members of a committee of the board of directors are independent, the registrant's definition of independence that it uses for determining if the members of that specific committee are independent in compliance with the independence standards applicable for the members of the specific committee in the listing standards of the national securities exchange or inter-dealer quotation system that the registrant uses for determining if a majority of the board of directors are independent. If the registrant does not have independence standards for a committee, the independence standards for that specific committee in the listing standards of the national securities exchange or inter-dealer quotation system that the registrant uses for determining if a majority of the board of directors are independent.

(ii) If the registrant is not a listed issuer, a definition of independence of a national securities exchange or of an inter-dealer quotation system which has requirements that a majority of the board of directors be independent, and state which definition is used. Whatever such definition the registrant chooses, it must use the same definition with respect to all directors and nominees for director. When determining whether the members of a specific committee of the board of directors are independent, if the national securities exchange or national securities association whose standards are used has independence standards for the members of a specific committee, use those committee specific standards.

(iii) If the information called for by paragraph (a) of this Item is being presented in a registration statement on Form S-1 (§ 239.11 of this chapter) under the Securities Act or on a Form 10 (§ 249.210 of this chapter) under the Exchange Act where the registrant has applied for listing with a national securities exchange or in an interdealer quotation system that has requirements that a majority of the board of directors be independent, the definition of independence that the registrant uses for determining if a majority of the board of directors is independent, and the definition of independence that the registrant uses for determining if members of the specific committee of the board of directors are independent, that is in compliance with the independence listing standards of the national securities exchange or inter-dealer quotation system on which it has applied for listing, or if the registrant has not adopted such definitions, the independence standards for determining if the majority of the board of directors is independent and if members of the committee of the board of directors are independent of that national securities exchange or inter-dealer quotation system.

(2) If the registrant uses its own definitions for determining whether its directors and nominees for director, and members of specific committees of the board of directors, are independent, disclose whether these definitions are available to security holders on the

registrant's Web site. If so, provide the registrant's Web site address. If not, include a copy of these policies in an appendix to the registrant's proxy statement or information statement that is provided to security holders at least once every three fiscal years or if the policies have been materially amended since the beginning of the registrant's last fiscal year. If a current copy of the policies is not available to security holders on the registrant's Web site, and is not included as an appendix to the registrant's proxy statement or information statement, identify the most recent fiscal year in which the policies were so included in satisfaction of this requirement.

(3) For each director and nominee for director that is identified as independent, describe, by specific category or type, any transactions, relationships or arrangements not disclosed pursuant to Item 404(a) (§ 229.404(a)), or for investment companies, Item 22(b) of Schedule 14A (§ 240.14a-101 of this chapter), that were considered by the board of directors under the applicable independence definitions in determining that the director is independent.

Instructions to Item 407(a).

1. If the registrant is a listed issuer whose securities are listed on a national securities exchange or in an inter-dealer quotation system which has requirements that a majority of the board of directors be independent, and also has exemptions to those requirements (for independence of a majority of the board of directors or committee member independence) upon which the registrant relied, disclose the exemption relied upon and explain the basis for the registrant's conclusion that such exemption is applicable. The same disclosure should be provided if the registrant is not a listed issuer and the national securities exchange or inter-dealer quotation system selected by the registrant has exemptions that are applicable to the registrant. Any national securities exchange or inter-dealer quotation system which has requirements that at least 50 percent of the members of a small business issuer's board of directors must be independent shall be considered a national securities exchange or inter-dealer quotation system which has requirements that a majority of the board of directors be independent for the purposes of the disclosure required by paragraph (a) of this Item.

2. Registrants shall provide the disclosure required by paragraph (a) of this Item for any person who served as a director during any part of the last completed fiscal year, except that no information called for by paragraph (a) of this Item need be given in a registration statement filed at a time when the registrant is not subject to the reporting requirements of section 13(a) or 15(d) of the Exchange Act (15 U.S.C. 78m(a) or 78o(d)) respecting any director who is no longer a director at the time of effectiveness of the registration statement.

3. The description of the specific categories or types of transactions, relationships or arrangements required by paragraph (a)(3) of this Item must be provided in such detail as is necessary to fully describe the nature of the transactions, relationships or arrangements.

(b) Board Meetings and Committees; Annual Meeting Attendance.

(1) State the total number of meetings of the board of directors (including regularly scheduled and special meetings) which were held during the last full fiscal year. Name each incumbent director who during the last full fiscal year attended fewer than 75 percent of the aggregate of:

(i) The total number of meetings of the board of directors (held during the period for which he has been a director); and

(ii) The total number of meetings held by all committees of the board on which he served (during the periods that he served).

(2) Describe the registrant's policy, if any, with regard to board members' attendance at annual meetings of security holders and state the number of board members who attended the prior year's annual meeting.

Instruction to Item 407(b)(2).

In lieu of providing the information required by paragraph (b)(2) of this Item in the proxy statement, the registrant may instead provide the registrant's Web site address where such information appears.

(3) State whether or not the registrant has standing audit, nominating and compensation committees of the board of directors, or committees performing similar functions. If the registrant has such committees, however designated, identify each committee member, state the number of committee meetings held by each such committee during the last fiscal year and describe briefly the functions performed by each such committee. Such disclosure need not be provided to the extent it is duplicative of disclosure provided in accordance with paragraph (c), (d) or (e) of this Item.

(c) *Nominating Committee.* (1) If the registrant does not have a standing nominating committee or committee performing similar functions, state the basis for the view of the board of directors that it is appropriate for the registrant not to have such a committee and identify each director who participates in the consideration of director nominees.

(2) Provide the following information regarding the registrant's director nomination process:

(i) State whether or not the nominating committee has a charter. If the nominating committee has a charter, provide the disclosure required by Instruction 2 to this Item regarding the nominating committee charter;

(ii) If the nominating committee has a policy with regard to the consideration of any director candidates recommended by security holders, provide a description of the material elements of that policy, which shall include, but need not be limited to, a statement as to whether the committee will consider director candidates recommended by security holders;

(iii) If the nominating committee does not have a policy with regard to the consideration of any director candidates recommended by security holders, state that fact and state the basis for the view of the board of directors that it is appropriate for the registrant not to have such a policy;

(iv) If the nominating committee will consider candidates recommended by security holders, describe the procedures to be followed by security holders in submitting such recommendations;

(v) Describe any specific minimum qualifications that the nominating committee believes must be met by a nominating committee-recommended nominee for a position on the registrant's board of directors, and describe any specific qualities or skills that the nominating committee believes are necessary for one or more of the registrant's directors to possess;

(vi) Describe the nominating committee's process for identifying and evaluating nominees for director, including nominees recommended by security holders, and any differences in the manner in which the nominating committee evaluates nominees for director based on whether the nominee is recommended by a security holder, and whether, and if so how, the nominating committee (or the board) considers diversity in identifying nominees for director. If the nominating committee (or the board) has a policy with regard to the consideration of diversity in identifying director nominees, describe how this policy is implemented, as well as how the nominating committee (or the board) assesses the effectiveness of its policy;

(vii) With regard to each nominee approved by the nominating committee for inclusion on the registrant's proxy card (other than nominees who are executive officers or who are directors standing for re-election), state which one or more of the following categories of persons or entities recommended that nominee: security holder, nonmanagement director, chief executive officer, other executive officer, third-party search firm, or other specified source. With regard to each such nominee approved by a nominating committee of an investment company, state which one or more of the following additional categories of persons or entities recommended that nominee: security holder, director, chief executive officer, other executive officer, or employee of the investment company's investment adviser, principal underwriter, or any affiliated person of the investment adviser or principal underwriter;

(viii) If the registrant pays a fee to any third party or parties to identify or evaluate or assist in identifying or evaluating potential nominees, disclose the function performed by each such third party; and

(ix) If the registrant's nominating committee received, by a date not later than the 120th calendar day before the date of the registrant's proxy statement released to security holders in connection with the previous year's annual meeting, a recommended nominee from a security holder that beneficially owned more than 5% of the registrant's voting common stock for at least one year as of the date the recommendation was made, or from a group of security holders that beneficially owned, in the aggregate, more than 5% of the registrant's voting common stock, with each of the securities used to calculate that ownership held for at least one year as of the date the recommendation was made, identify the candidate and the security holder or security holder group that recommended the candidate and disclose whether the nominating committee chose to nominate the candidate, *provided, however,* that no such identification or disclosure is required without the written consent of both the security holder or security holder group and the candidate to be so identified.

Instructions to Item 407(c)(2)(ix).

1. For purposes of paragraph (c)(2)(ix) of this Item, the percentage of securities held by a nominating security holder may be determined using information set forth in the registrant's most recent quarterly or annual report, and any current report subsequent thereto, filed with the Commission pursuant to the Exchange Act (or, in the case of a registrant that is an investment company registered under the Investment Company Act of 1940, the registrant's most recent report on Form N-CSR (§§ 249.331 and 274.128 of this chapter)), unless the party relying on such report knows or has reason to believe that the information contained therein is inaccurate.

2. For purposes of the registrant's obligation to provide the disclosure specified in paragraph (c)(2)(ix) of this Item, where the date of the annual meeting has been changed by more than 30 days from the date of the previous year's meeting, the obligation under that Item will arise where the registrant receives the security holder recommendation a reasonable time before the registrant begins to print and mail its proxy materials.

3. For purposes of paragraph (c)(2)(ix) of this Item, the percentage of securities held by a recommending security holder, as well as the holding period of those securities, may be determined by the registrant if the security holder is the registered holder of the securities. If the security holder is not the registered owner of the securities, he or she can submit one of the following to the registrant to evidence the required ownership percentage and holding period:

a. A written statement from the "record" holder of the securities (usually a broker or bank) verifying that, at the time the security holder made the recommendation, he or she had held the required securities for at least one year; or

b. If the security holder has filed a Schedule 13D (§ 240.13d-101 of this chapter), Schedule 13G (§ 240.13d-102 of this chapter), Form 3 (§ 249.103 of this chapter), Form 4 (§ 249.104 of this chapter), and/or Form 5 (§ 249.105 of this chapter), or amendments to those documents or updated forms, reflecting ownership of the securities as of or before the date of the recommendation, a copy of the schedule and/or form, and any subsequent amendments reporting a change in ownership level, as well as a written statement that the security holder continuously held the securities for the one-year period as of the date of the recommendation.

4. For purposes of the registrant's obligation to provide the disclosure specified in paragraph (c)(2)(ix) of this Item, the security holder or group must have provided to the registrant, at the time of the recommendation, the written consent of all parties to be identified and, where the security holder or group members are not registered holders, proof that the security holder or group satisfied the required ownership percentage and holding period as of the date of the recommendation.

Instruction to Item 407(c)(2).

For purposes of paragraph (c)(2) of this Item, the term nominating committee refers not only to nominating committees and committees performing similar functions, but also to groups of directors fulfilling the role of a nominating committee, including the entire board of directors.

(3) Describe any material changes to the procedures by which security holders may recommend nominees to the registrant's board of directors, where those changes were implemented after the registrant last provided disclosure in response to the requirements of paragraph (c)(2)(iv) of this Item, or paragraph (c)(3) of this Item.

Instructions to Item 407(c)(3).

1. The disclosure required in paragraph (c)(3) of this Item need only be provided in a registrant's quarterly or annual reports.

2. For purposes of paragraph (c)(3) of this Item, adoption of procedures by which security holders may recommend nominees to the registrant's board of directors, where the registrant's most recent disclosure in response to the requirements of paragraph (c)(2)(iv) of this Item, or paragraph (c)(3) of this Item, indicated that the registrant did not have in place such procedures, will constitute a material change.

(d) Audit Committee.

(1) State whether or not the audit committee has a charter. If the audit committee has a charter, provide the disclosure required by Instruction 2 to this Item regarding the audit committee charter.

(2) If a listed issuer's board of directors determines, in accordance with the listing standards applicable to the issuer, to appoint a director to the audit committee who is not independent (apart from the requirements in § 240.10A-3 of this chapter), including as a result of exceptional or limited or similar circumstances, disclose the nature of the relationship that makes that individual not independent and the reasons for the board of directors' determination.

(3)(i) The audit committee must state whether:

(A) The audit committee has reviewed and discussed the audited financial statements with management;

(B) The audit committee has discussed with the independent auditors the matters required to be discussed by the applicable requirements of the Public Company Accounting Oversight Board (PCAOB) and the Commission;

(C) The audit committee has received the written disclosures and the letter from the independent accountant required by applicable requirements of the Public Company Accounting Oversight Board regarding the independent accountant's communications with the audit committee concerning independence, and has discussed with the independent accountant the independent accountant's independence; and

(D) Based on the review and discussions referred to in paragraphs (d)(3)(i)(A) through (d)(3)(i)(C) of this Item, the audit committee recommended to the board of directors that the audited financial statements be included in the company's annual report on Form 10-K (17 CFR 249.310) (or, for closed-end investment companies registered under the Investment Company Act of 1940 (15 U.S.C. 80a-1 et seq.), the annual report to shareholders required by section 30(e) of the Investment Company Act of 1940 (15 U.S.C. 80a-29(e)) and Rule 30d-1 (17 CFR 270.30d-1) thereunder) for the last fiscal year for filing with the Commission.

(ii) The name of each member of the company's audit committee (or, in the absence of an audit committee, the board committee performing equivalent functions or the entire board of directors) must appear below the disclosure required by paragraph (d)(3)(i) of this Item.

(4)(i) If the registrant meets the following requirements, provide the disclosure in paragraph (d)(4)(ii) of this Item:

(A) The registrant is a listed issuer, as defined in § 240.10A-3 of this chapter;

(B) The registrant is filing either an annual report on Form 10-K (17 CFR 249.310 of this chapter), or a proxy statement or information statement pursuant to the Exchange Act (15 U.S.C. 78a et seq.) if action is to be taken with respect to the election of directors; and

(C) The registrant is neither:

(1) A subsidiary of another listed issuer that is relying on the exemption in § 240.10A-3(c)(2) of this chapter; nor

(2) Relying on any of the exemptions in § 240.10A-3(c)(4) through (c)(7) of this chapter.

(ii)(A) State whether or not the registrant has a separately-designated standing audit committee established in accordance with section 3(a)(58)(A) of the Exchange Act (15 U.S.C. 78c(a)(58)(A)), or a committee performing similar functions. If the registrant has such a committee, however designated, identify each committee member. If the entire board of directors is acting as the registrant's audit committee as specified in section 3(a)(58)(B) of the Exchange Act (15 U.S.C. 78c(a)(58)(B)), so state.

(B) If applicable, provide the disclosure required by § 240.10A-3(d) of this chapter regarding an exemption from the listing standards for audit committees.

(5) Audit Committee Financial Expert.

(i)(A) Disclose that the registrant's board of directors has determined that the registrant either:

(1) Has at least one audit committee financial expert serving on its audit committee; or

(2) Does not have an audit committee financial expert serving on its audit committee.

(B) If the registrant provides the disclosure required by paragraph (d)(5)(i)(A)(1) of this Item, it must disclose the name of the audit committee financial expert and whether that person is independent, as independence for audit committee members is defined in the listing standards applicable to the listed issuer.

(C) If the registrant provides the disclosure required by paragraph (d)(5)(i)(A)(2) of this Item, it must explain why it does not have an audit committee financial expert.

Instruction to Item 407(d)(5).

(i) If the registrant's board of directors has determined that the registrant has more than one audit committee financial expert serving on its audit committee, the registrant may, but is not required to, disclose the names of those additional persons. A registrant choosing to identify such persons must indicate whether they are independent pursuant to paragraph (d)(5)(i)(B) of this Item.

(ii) For purposes of this Item, an audit committee financial expert means a person who has the following attributes:

(A) An understanding of generally accepted accounting principles and financial statements;

(B) The ability to assess the general application of such principles in connection with the accounting for estimates, accruals and reserves;

(C) Experience preparing, auditing, analyzing or evaluating financial statements that present a breadth and level of complexity of accounting issues that are generally comparable to the breadth and complexity of issues that can reasonably be expected to be raised by the registrant's financial statements, or experience actively supervising one or more persons engaged in such activities;

(D) An understanding of internal control over financial reporting; and

(E) An understanding of audit committee functions.

(iii) A person shall have acquired such attributes through:

(A) Education and experience as a principal financial officer, principal accounting officer, controller, public accountant or auditor or experience in one or more positions that involve the performance of similar functions;

(B) Experience actively supervising a principal financial officer, principal accounting officer, controller, public accountant, auditor or person performing similar functions;

(C) Experience overseeing or assessing the performance of companies or public accountants with respect to the preparation, auditing or evaluation of financial statements; or

(D) Other relevant experience.

(iv) Safe Harbor.

(A) A person who is determined to be an audit committee financial expert will not be deemed an expert for any purpose, including without limitation for purposes of section 11 of the Securities Act (15 U.S.C. 77k), as a result of being designated or identified as an audit committee financial expert pursuant to this Item 407.

(B) The designation or identification of a person as an audit committee financial expert pursuant to this Item 407 does not impose on such person any duties, obligations or liability that are greater than the duties, obligations and liability imposed on such person as a member of the audit committee and board of directors in the absence of such designation or identification.

(C) The designation or identification of a person as an audit committee financial expert pursuant to this Item does not affect the duties, obligations or liability of any other member of the audit committee or board of directors.

Instructions to Item 407(d)(5).

1. The disclosure under paragraph (d)(5) of this Item is required only in a registrant's annual report. The registrant need not provide the disclosure required by paragraph (d)(5) of this Item in a proxy or information statement unless that registrant is electing to incorporate this information by reference from the proxy or information statement into its annual report pursuant to General Instruction G(3) to Form 10-K (17 CFR 249.310).

2. If a person qualifies as an audit committee financial expert by means of having held a position described in paragraph (d)(5)(iii)(D) of this Item, the registrant shall provide a brief listing of that person's relevant experience. Such disclosure may be made by reference to disclosures required under Item 401(e) (§ 229.401(e)).

3. In the case of a foreign private issuer with a two-tier board of directors, for purposes of paragraph (d)(5) of this Item, the term board of directors means the supervisory or non-management board. In the case of a foreign private issuer meeting the requirements of § 240.10A-3(c)(3) of this chapter, for purposes of paragraph (d)(5) of this Item, the term board of directors means the issuer's board of auditors (or similar body) or statutory auditors, as applicable. Also, in the case of a foreign private issuer, the term generally accepted accounting principles in paragraph (d)(5)(ii)(A) of this Item means the body of generally accepted accounting principles used by that issuer in its primary financial statements filed with the Commission.

4. A registrant that is an Asset-Backed Issuer (as defined in § 229.1101) is not required to disclose the information required by paragraph (d)(5) of this Item.

Instructions to Item 407(d).

1. The information required by paragraphs (d)(1)—(3) of this Item shall not be deemed to be "soliciting material," or to be "filed" with the Commission or subject to Regulation 14A or 14C (17 CFR 240.14a-1 through 240.14b-2 or 240.14c-1 through 240.14c-101), other than as provided in this Item, or to the liabilities of section 18 of the Exchange Act (15 U.S.C. 78r), except to the extent that the registrant specifically requests that the information be treated as soliciting material or specifically incorporates it by reference into a document filed under the Securities Act or the Exchange Act. Such information will not be deemed to be incorporated by reference into any filing under the Securities Act or the Exchange Act, except to the extent that the registrant specifically incorporates it by reference.

2. The disclosure required by paragraphs (d)(1)—(3) of this Item need only be provided one time during any fiscal year.

3. The disclosure required by paragraph (d)(3) of this Item need not be provided in any filings other than a registrant's proxy or information statement relating to an annual meeting of security holders at which directors are to be elected (or special meeting or written consents in lieu of such meeting).

(e) Compensation Committee.

(1) If the registrant does not have a standing compensation committee or committee performing similar functions, state the basis for the view of the board of directors that it is appropriate for the registrant not to have such a committee and identify each director who participates in the consideration of executive officer and director compensation.

(2) State whether or not the compensation committee has a charter. If the compensation committee has a charter, provide the disclosure required by Instruction 2 to this Item regarding the compensation committee charter.

(3) Provide a narrative description of the registrant's processes and procedures for the consideration and determination of executive and director compensation, including:

(i)(A) The scope of authority of the compensation committee (or persons performing the equivalent functions); and

(B) The extent to which the compensation committee (or persons performing the equivalent functions) may delegate any authority described in paragraph (e)(3)(i)(A) of this Item to other persons, specifying what authority may be so delegated and to whom;

(ii) Any role of executive officers in determining or recommending the amount or form of executive and director compensation; and

(iii) Any role of compensation consultants in determining or recommending the amount or form of executive and director compensation (other than any role limited to consulting on any broad-based plan that does not discriminate in scope, terms, or operation, in favor of executive officers or directors of the registrant, and that is available generally to all salaried employees; or providing information that either is not customized for a particular registrant or that is customized based on parameters that are not developed by the compensation consultant, and about which the compensation consultant does not provide advice) during the registrant's last completed fiscal year, identifying such consultants, stating whether such consultants were engaged directly by the compensation committee (or persons performing the equivalent functions) or any other person, describing the nature and scope of their assignment, and the material elements of the instructions or directions given to the consultants with respect to the performance of their duties under the engagement:

(A) If such compensation consultant was engaged by the compensation committee (or persons performing the equivalent functions) to provide advice or recommendations on the amount or form of executive and director compensation (other than any role limited to consulting on any broad-based plan that does not discriminate in scope, terms, or operation, in favor of executive officers or directors of the registrant, and that is available generally to all salaried employees; or providing information that either is not customized for a particular registrant or that is customized based on parameters that are not developed by the compensation consultant, and about which the compensation consultant does not provide advice) and the compensation consultant or its affiliates also provided additional services to the registrant or its affiliates in an amount in excess of $120,000 during the registrant's last completed fiscal year, then disclose the aggregate fees for determining or recommending the amount or form of executive and director compensation and the aggregate fees for such additional services. Disclose whether the decision to engage the compensation consultant or its affiliates for these other services was made, or recommended, by management, and whether the compensation committee or the board approved such other services of the compensation consultant or its affiliates.

executive officer during the past fiscal year shall be limited to the registrant's proxy or information statement.

(5) *Corporate governance—Material changes to procedures for nominating directors.* Disclose any material changes to the procedures by which security holders may recommend nominees to the registrant's board of directors, where those changes were implemented after the registrant last provided disclosure in response to the requirements of paragraph (c)(2)(iv) of this Item, or paragraph (c)(3) of this Item, or in response to the requirements of Exchange Act Rule 14a-8(i)(8) (§240.14a-8(i)(8) of this chapter).

Instruction to Item 407.

For purposes of this Item, the term *listed issuer* means an issuer whose securities are listed on a national securities exchange registered pursuant to Section 6 of the Exchange Act (15 U.S.C. 78f) or in an automated inter-dealer quotation system of a national securities association registered pursuant to Section 15A(a) of the Exchange Act (15 U.S.C. 78o-3(a)) that has requirements that a majority of the board of directors be independent.

[47 FR 11401, Mar. 16, 1982, as amended at 71 FR 6002, Feb. 1, 2006; 71 FR 39422, July 12, 2006; 71 FR 78350, Dec. 29, 2006; 72 FR 4167, Jan. 30, 2007; 74 FR 2145, Jan. 14, 2009; 74 FR 18616, Apr. 23, 2009; 74 FR 68352, Dec. 23, 2009; 75 FR 56787, Sept. 16, 2010; 78 FR 5064, Jan. 23, 2013; 84 FR 12707, Apr. 2, 2019]

Subpart 229.500—Registration Statement and Prospectus Provisions

§229.501 (Item 501) Forepart of Registration Statement and Outside Front Cover Page of Prospectus.

The registrant must furnish the following information in plain English. See §230.421(d) of Regulation C of this chapter.

(a) *Front cover page of the registration statement.* Where appropriate, include the delaying amendment legend from §230.473 of Regulation C of this chapter.

(b) *Outside front cover page of the prospectus.* Limit the outside cover page to the following information:

(1) The name of the registrant. If your name is the same as that of a company that is well known, include information to eliminate any possible confusion with the other company. If your name indicates a line of business in which you are not engaged or in which you are engaged only to a limited extent, include information to eliminate any misleading inference as to your business. In some circumstances, disclosure may not be sufficient, and you may have to change your name. You will not have to change your name if you are a subsidiary of another company and you include the name of the parent company in your prospectus.

(2) The title and amount of securities offered. Reserve a portion of this information for securities to be offered by selling security holders, if any.

(3) A description of the securities being registered, other than securities registered to be offered to employees, or securities with a basis for exemption from the registration requirements.

executive officer of another entity shall be accompanied by the disclosure called for by Item 404 with respect to that person.

Instruction to Item 407(e)(4).

For purposes of paragraph (e)(4) of this Item, the term entity shall not include an entity exempt from tax under section 501(c)(3) of the Internal Revenue Code (26 U.S.C. 501(c)(3)).

(5) Under the caption "Compensation Committee Report:"

(i) The compensation committee (or other board committee performing equivalent functions or, in the absence of any such committee, the entire board of directors) must state whether:

(A) The compensation committee has reviewed and discussed the Compensation Discussion and Analysis required by Item 402(b) (§ 229.402(b)) with management; and

(B) Based on the review and discussions referred to in paragraph (e)(5)(i)(A) of this Item, the compensation committee recommended to the board of directors that the Compensation Discussion and Analysis be included in the registrant's annual report on Form 10-K (§ 249.310 of this chapter), proxy statement on Schedule 14A (§ 240.14a- 101 of this chapter) or information statement on Schedule 14C (§ 240.14c-101 of this chapter).

(ii) The name of each member of the registrant's compensation committee (or other board committee performing equivalent functions or, in the absence of any such committee, the entire board of directors) must appear below the disclosure required by paragraph (e)(5)(i) of this Item.

Instructions to Item 407(e)(5).

1. The information required by paragraph (e)(5) of this Item shall not be deemed to be "soliciting material," or to be "filed" with the Commission or subject to Regulation 14A or 14C (17 CFR 240.14a-1 through 240.14b-2 or 240.14c-1 through 240.14c-101), other than as provided in this Item, or to the liabilities of section 18 of the Exchange Act (15 U.S.C. 78r), except to the extent that the registrant specifically requests that the information be treated as soliciting material or specifically incorporates it by reference into a document filed under the Securities Act or the Exchange Act.

2. The disclosure required by paragraph (e)(5) of this Item need not be provided in any filings other than an annual report on Form 10-K (§ 249.310 of this chapter), a proxy statement on Schedule 14A (§ 240.14a-101 of this chapter) or an information statement on Schedule 14C (§ 240.14c-101 of this chapter). Such information will not be deemed to be incorporated by reference into any filing under the Securities Act or the Exchange Act, except to the extent that the registrant specifically incorporates it by reference. If the registrant elects to incorporate this information by reference from the proxy or information statement into its annual report on Form 10-K pursuant to General Instruction G(3) to Form 10-K, the disclosure required by paragraph (e)(5) of this Item will be deemed furnished in the annual report on Form 10-K and will not be deemed incorporated by reference into any filing under the Securities Act or the Exchange Act as a result as a result of furnishing the disclosure in this manner.

3. The disclosure required by paragraph (e)(5) of this Item need only be provided one time during any fiscal year.

(f) Shareholder Communications

(1) State whether or not the registrant's board of directors provides a process for security holders to send communications to the board of directors and, if the registrant does not have such a process for security holders to send communications to the board of directors, state the basis for the view of the board of directors that it is appropriate for the registrant not to have such a process.

(2) If the registrant has a process for security holders to send communications to the board of directors:

(i) Describe the manner in which security holders can send communications to the board and, if applicable, to specified individual directors; and

(ii) If all security holder communications are not sent directly to board members, describe the registrant's process for determining which communications will be relayed to board members.

Instructions to Item 407(f).

1. In lieu of providing the information required by paragraph (f)(2) of this Item in the proxy statement, the registrant may instead provide the registrant's Web site address where such information appears.

2. For purposes of the disclosure required by paragraph (f)(2)(ii) of this Item, a registrant's process for collecting and organizing security holder communications, as well as similar or related activities, need not be disclosed provided that the registrant's process is approved by a majority of the independent directors or, in the case of a registrant that is an investment company, a majority of the directors who are not "interested persons" of the investment company as defined in section 2(a)(19) of the Investment Company Act of 1940 (15 U.S.C. 80a-2(a)(19)).

3. For purposes of this paragraph, communications from an officer or director of the registrant will not be viewed as "security holder communications." Communications from an employee or agent of the registrant will be viewed as "security holder communications" for purposes of this paragraph only if those communications are made solely in such employee's or agent's capacity as a security holder.

4. For purposes of this paragraph, security holder proposals submitted pursuant to § 240.14a-8 of this chapter, and communications made in connection with such proposals, will not be viewed as "security holder communications."

(g) *Smaller Reporting Companies and Emerging Growth Companies.*

(1) A registrant that qualifies as a "smaller reporting company," as defined by § 229.10(f)(1), is not required to provide:

(i) The disclosure required in paragraph (d)(5) of this Item in its first annual report filed pursuant to Section 13(a) or 15(d) of the Exchange Act (15 U.S.C. 78m(a) or 78o(d)) following the effective date of its first registration statement filed under the Securities Act (15 U.S.C. 77a *et seq.*) or Exchange Act (15 U.S.C. 78a *et seq.*); and

(ii) The disclosure required by paragraphs (e)(4) and (e)(5) of this Item.

(2) A registrant that qualifies as an "emerging growth company," as defined in Rule 405 of the Securities Act (§ 230.405 of this chapter) or Rule 12b-2 of the Exchange Act (§ 240.12b-2 of this chapter), is not required to provide the disclosure required by paragraph (e)(5) of this Item.

(h) Board Leadership Structure and Role in Risk Oversight. Briefly describe the leadership structure of the registrant's board, such as whether the same person serves as both principal executive officer and chairman of the board, or whether two individuals serve in those positions, and, in the case of a registrant that is an investment company, whether the chairman of the board is an "interested person" of the registrant as defined in section 2(a)(19) of the Investment Company Act (15 U.S.C. 80a-2(a)(19)). If one person serves as both principal executive officer and chairman of the board, or if the chairman of the board of a registrant that is an investment company is an "interested person" of the registrant, disclose whether the registrant has a lead independent director and what specific role the lead independent director plays in the leadership of the board. This disclosure should indicate why the registrant has determined that its leadership structure is appropriate given the specific characteristics or circumstances of the registrant. In addition, disclose the extent of the board's role in the risk oversight of the registrant, such as how the board administers its oversight function, and the effect that this has on the board's leadership structure.

Instructions to Item 407.

1. For purposes of this Item:

a. Listed issuer means a listed issuer as defined in § 240.10A-3 of this chapter;

b. National securities exchange means a national securities exchange registered pursuant to section 6(a) of the Exchange Act (15 U.S.C. 78f(a));

    c. Inter-dealer quotation system means an automated inter-dealer quotation system of a national securities association registered pursuant to section 15A(a) of the Exchange Act (15 U.S.C. 78o-3(a)); and

    d. National securities association means a national securities association registered pursuant to section 15A(a) of the Exchange Act (15 U.S.C. 78o-3(a)) that has been approved by the Commission (as that definition may be modified or supplemented).

    2. With respect to paragraphs (c)(2)(i), (d)(1) and (e)(2) of this Item, disclose whether a current copy of the applicable committee charter is available to security holders on the registrant's Web site, and if so, provide the registrant's Web site address. If a current copy of the charter is not available to security holders on the registrant's Web site, include a copy of the charter in an appendix to the registrant's proxy or information statement that is provided to security holders at least once every three fiscal years, or if the charter has been materially amended since the beginning of the registrant's last fiscal year. If a current copy of the charter is not available to security holders on the registrant's Web site, and is not included as an appendix to the registrant's proxy or information statement, identify in which of the prior fiscal years the charter was so included in satisfaction of this requirement.

Subpart 500—Registration Statement and Prospectus Provisions

Item 501. Forepart of Registration Statement and Outside Front Cover Page of Prospectus

    The registrant must furnish the following information in plain English. See § 230.421(d) of Regulation C of this chapter.

    (a) *Front Cover Page of the Registration Statement.* Where appropriate, include the delaying amendment legend from § 230.473 of Regulation C of this chapter.

    (b) *Outside Front Cover Page of the Prospectus.* Limit the outside cover page to one page. If the following information applies to your offering, disclose it on the outside cover page of the prospectus.

    (1) *Name.* The registrant's name. A foreign registrant must give the English translation of its name.

Instruction to Paragraph 501(b)(1): If your name is the same as that of a company that is well known, include information to eliminate any possible confusion with the other company. If your name indicates a line of business in which you are not engaged or in which you are engaged only to a limited extent, include information to eliminate any misleading inference as to your business.

    (2) *Title and amount of securities.* The title and amount of securities offered. Separately state the amount of securities offered by selling security holders, if any. If the underwriter has any arrangement with the issuer, such as an over-allotment option, under which the underwriter may purchase additional shares in connection with the offering, indicate that this arrangement exists and state the amount of additional shares that the underwriter may purchase under the arrangement. Give a brief description of the securities except where the information is clear from the title of the security. For example, you are not required to describe common stock that has full voting, dividend and liquidation rights usually associated with common stock.

    (3) *Offering price of the securities.* Where you offer securities for cash, the price to the public of the securities, the underwriter's discounts and commissions, the net proceeds you receive, and any selling shareholder's net proceeds. Show this information on both a per share or unit basis and for the total amount of the offering. If you make the offering on a minimum/maximum basis, show this information based on the total minimum and total maximum amount of the offering. You may present the information in a table, term sheet format, or other clear presentation. You may present the information in any format that fits the design of the cover page so long as the information can be easily read and is not misleading;

Instructions to paragraph 501(b)(3)

1. If a preliminary prospectus is circulated and you are not subject to the reporting requirements of Section 13(a) or 15 (d) of the Exchange Act, provide, as applicable:

(A) A bona fide estimate of the range of the maximum offering price and the maximum number of securities offered; or

(B) A bona fide estimate of the principal amount of the debt securities offered.

2. If it is impracticable to state the price to the public, explain the method by which the price is to be determined. Instead of explaining the method on the outside front cover page of the prospectus, you may state that the offering price will be determined by a particular method or formula that is described in the prospectus and include a cross-reference to the location of such disclosure in the prospectus, including the page number. Highlight the cross-reference by prominent type or in another manner. If the securities are to be offered at the market price, or if the offering price is to be determined by a formula related to the market price, indicate the market and market price of the securities as of the latest practicable date.

3. If you file a registration statement on Form S-8, you are not required to comply with this paragraph (b)(3).

(4) *Market For the Securities.* The national securities exchange(s) where the securities being offered are listed. If the securities being offered are not listed on a national securities exchange, the principal United States market(s) where the registrant, through the engagement of a registered broker-dealer, has actively sought and achieved quotation. In each case, also disclose the corresponding trading symbol(s) for the securities on such market(s).

(5) *Risk Factors.* A cross-reference to the risk factors section, including the page number where it appears in the prospectus. Highlight this cross-reference by prominent type or in another manner;

(6) *State Legend.* Any legend or statement required by the law of any state in which the securities are to be offered. You may combine this with any legend required by the SEC, if appropriate;

(7) *Commission Legend.* A legend that indicates that neither the Securities and Exchange Commission nor any state securities commission has approved or disapproved of the securities or passed upon the accuracy or adequacy of the disclosures in the prospectus and that any contrary representation is a criminal offense. You may use one of the following or other clear, plain language:

Example A: Neither the Securities and Exchange Commission nor any state securities commission has approved or disapproved of these securities or passed upon the adequacy or accuracy of this prospectus. Any representation to the contrary is a criminal offense.

Example B: Neither the Securities and Exchange Commission nor any state securities commission has approved or disapproved of these securities or determined if this prospectus is truthful or complete. Any representation to the contrary is a criminal offense.

(8) *Underwriting.* (i) Name(s) of the lead or managing underwriter(s) and an identification of the nature of the underwriting arrangements;

(ii) If the offering is not made on a firm commitment basis, a brief description of the underwriting arrangements. You may use any clear, concise, and accurate description of the underwriting arrangements. You may use the following descriptions of underwriting arrangements where appropriate:

Example A: Best efforts offering. The underwriters are not required to sell any specific number or dollar amount of securities but will use their best efforts to sell the securities offered.

Example B: Best efforts, minimum-maximum offering. The underwriters must sell the minimum number of securities offered (insert number) if any are sold. The underwriters are required to use only their best efforts to sell the maximum number of securities offered (insert number).

(iii) If you offer the securities on a best efforts or best efforts minimum/maximum basis, the date the offering will end, any minimum purchase requirements, and any arrangements to place the funds in an escrow, trust, or similar account. If you have not made any of these arrangements, state this fact and describe the effect on investors;

(9) *Date of Prospectus.* The date of the prospectus;

(10) *Prospectus "Subject to Completion" Legend.*

(i) If you use the prospectus before the effective date of the registration statement or if you use Rule 430A [§ 230.430A of this chapter] to omit pricing information and the prospectus is used before you determine the public offering price, include a prominent statement that:

(A) The information in the prospectus will be amended or completed;

(B) A registration statement relating to these securities has been filed with the Securities and Exchange Commission;

(C) The securities may not be sold until the registration statement becomes effective; and

(D) The prospectus is not an offer to sell the securities, and it is not soliciting an offer to buy the securities, in any state where offers or sales are not permitted.

(ii) The legend called for by paragraph (b)(10)(i) of this Item may be in the following or other clear, plain language:

> The information in this prospectus is not complete and may be changed. We may not sell these securities until the registration statement filed with the Securities and Exchange Commission is effective. This prospectus is not an offer to sell these securities and it is not soliciting an offer to buy these securities in any state where the offer or sale is not permitted.

(iii) Registrants may exclude the statement in paragraph (b)(10)(i)(D) of this Item if the offering is not prohibited by state law.

Item 502. Inside Front and Outside Back Cover Pages of Prospectus

The registrant must furnish this information in plain English. See § 230.421(d) of Regulation C of this chapter.

(a) *Table of Contents.* On either the inside front or outside back cover page of the prospectus, provide a reasonably detailed table of contents. It must show the page number of the various sections or subdivisions of the prospectus. Include a specific listing of the risk factors section required by Item 105 of this Regulation S-K (17 CFR 229.503). You must include the table of contents immediately following the cover page in any prospectus you deliver electronically.

(b) *Dealer Prospectus Delivery Obligation.* On the outside back cover page of the prospectus, advise dealers of their prospectus delivery obligation, including the expiration date specified by Section 4(3) of the Securities Act (15 U.S.C. 77d(3)) and § 230.174 of this chapter. If you do not know the expiration date on the effective date of the registration statement, include the expiration date in the copy of the prospectus you file under § 230.424(b) of this chapter. You do not have to include this information if dealers are not required to deliver a prospectus under § 230.174 of this chapter or Section 24(d) of the Investment Company Act (15 U.S.C. 80a-24). You may use the following or other clear, plain language:

Dealer Prospectus Delivery Obligation

Until (insert date), all dealers that effect transactions in these securities, whether or not participating in this offering, may be required to deliver a prospectus. This is in addition to the dealers' obligation to deliver a prospectus when acting as underwriters and with respect to their unsold allotments or subscriptions.

Item 503. Prospectus Summary

The registrant must furnish this information in plain English. See § 230.421(d) of Regulation C of this chapter.

(a) *Prospectus Summary.* Provide a summary of the information in the prospectus where the length or complexity of the prospectus makes a summary useful. The summary should be brief. The summary should not contain, and is not required to contain, all of the detailed information in the prospectus. If you provide summary business or financial information, even if you do not caption it as a summary, you still must provide that information in plain English.

Instruction to paragraph 503(a).

The summary should not merely repeat the text of the prospectus but should provide a brief overview of the key aspects of the offering. Carefully consider and identify those aspects of the offering that are the most significant and determine how best to highlight those points in clear, plain language.

(b) *Address and Telephone Number.* Include, either on the cover page or in the summary section of the prospectus, the complete mailing address and telephone number of your principal executive offices.

(c) [Reserved.]

Instruction to Item 503. For asset-backed securities, see also Item 1103 of Regulation AB (§ 229.1103).

Item 504. Use of Proceeds

State the principal purposes for which the net proceeds to the registrant from the securities to be offered are intended to be used and the approximate amount intended to be used for each such purpose. Where registrant has no current specific plan for the proceeds, or a significant portion thereof, the registrant shall so state and discuss the principal reasons for the offering.

Instructions to Item 504. 1. Where less than all the securities to be offered may be sold and more than one use is listed for the proceeds, indicate the order of priority of such purposes and discuss the registrant's plans if substantially less than the maximum proceeds are obtained. Such discussion need not be included if underwriting arrangements with respect to such securities are such that, if any securities are sold to the public, it reasonably can be expected that the actual proceeds will not be substantially less than the aggregate proceeds to the registrant shown pursuant to Item 501 of Regulation S-K (§ 229.501).

2. Details of proposed expenditures need not be given; for example, there need be furnished only a brief outline of any program of construction or addition of equipment. Consideration should be given as to the need to include a discussion of certain matters addressed in the discussion and analysis of registrant's financial condition and results of operations, such as liquidity and capital expenditures.

3. If any material amounts of other funds are necessary to accomplish the specified purposes for which the proceeds are to be obtained, state the amounts of such other funds needed for each such specified purpose and the sources thereof.

4. If any material part of the proceeds is to be used to discharge indebtedness, set forth the interest rate and maturity of such indebtedness. If the indebtedness to be discharged was incurred within one year, describe the use of the proceeds of such indebtedness other than short-term borrowings used for working capital.

5. If any material amount of the proceeds is to be used to acquire assets, otherwise than in the ordinary course of business, describe briefly and state the cost of the assets and, where such assets are to be acquired from affiliates of the registrant or their associates, give the names of the persons from whom they are to be acquired and set forth the principle followed in determining the cost to the registrant.

6. Where the registrant indicates that the proceeds may, or will, be used to finance acquisitions of other businesses, the identity of such businesses, if known, or, if not known, the nature of the businesses to be sought, the status of any negotiations with respect to the acquisition, and a brief description of such business shall be included. Where, however, pro forma financial statements reflecting such acquisition are not required by §§ 210.1-01 through 210.13-02 (Regulation S-X) of this chapter, including § 210.8-05 (Rule 8-05 of

Regulation S-X) of this chapter for smaller reporting companies, to be included in the registration statement, the possible terms of any transaction, the identification of the parties thereto or the nature of the business sought need not be disclosed, to the extent that the registrant reasonably determines that public disclosure of such information would jeopardize the acquisition. Where Regulation S-X, including § 210.8-04 (Rule 8-04 of Regulation S-X) of this chapter for smaller reporting companies, as applicable, would require financial statements of the business to be acquired to be included, the description of the business to be acquired shall be more detailed.

7. The registrant may reserve the right to change the use of proceeds, provided that such reservation is due to certain contingencies that are discussed specifically and the alternatives to such use in that event are indicated.

Item 505. Determination of Offering Price

(a) *Common equity.* Where common equity is being registered for which there is no established public trading market for purposes of paragraph (a) of Item 201 of Regulation S-K (§ 229.201(a)) or where there is a material disparity between the offering price of the common equity being registered and the market price of outstanding shares of the same class, describe the various factors considered in determining such offering price.

(b) *Warrants, rights and convertible securities.* Where warrants, rights or convertible securities exercisable for common equity for which there is no established public trading market for purposes of paragraph (a) of Item 201 of Regulation S-K (§ 229.201(a)) are being registered, describe the various factors considered in determining their exercise or conversion price.

Item 506. Dilution

Where common equity securities are being registered and there is substantial disparity between the public offering price and the effective cash cost to officers, directors, promoters and affiliated persons of common equity acquired by them in transactions during the past five years, or which they have the right to acquire, and the registrant is not subject to the reporting requirements of section 13(a) or 15(d) of the Exchange Act immediately prior to filing of the registration statement, there shall be included a comparison of the public contribution under the proposed public offering and the effective cash contribution of such persons. In such cases, and in other instances where common equity securities are being registered by a registrant that has had losses in each of its last three fiscal years and there is a material dilution of the purchasers' equity interest, the following shall be disclosed:

(a) The net tangible book value per share before and after the distribution;

(b) The amount of the increase in such net tangible book value per share attributable to the cash payments made by purchasers of the shares being offered; and

(c) The amount of the immediate dilution from the public offering price which will be absorbed by such purchasers.

Item 507. Selling Security Holders

If any of the securities to be registered are to be offered for the account of security holders, name each such security holder, indicate the nature of any position, office, or other material relationship which the selling security holder has had within the past three years with the registrant or any of its predecessors or affiliates, and state the amount of securities of the class owned by such security holder prior to the offering, the amount to be offered for the security holder's account, the amount and (if one percent or more) the percentage of the class to be owned by such security holder after completion of the offering.

Item 508. Plan of Distribution

(a) *Underwriters and underwriting obligation.* If the securities are to be offered through underwriters, name the principal underwriters, and state the respective amounts underwritten.

Identify each such underwriter having a material relationship with the registrant and state the nature of the relationship. State briefly the nature of the obligation of the underwriter(s) to take the securities.

Instruction to Paragraph 508(a). All that is required as to the nature of the underwriters' obligation is whether the underwriters are or will be committed to take and to pay for all of the securities if any are taken, or whether it is merely an agency or the type of "best efforts" arrangement under which the underwriters are required to take and to pay for only such securities as they may sell to the public. Conditions precedent to the underwriters' taking the securities, including "market-outs," need not be described except in the case of an agency or "best efforts" arrangement.

(b) *New underwriters.* Where securities being registered are those of a registrant that has not previously been required to file reports pursuant to section 13(a) or 15(d) of the Exchange Act, or where a prospectus is required to include reference on its cover page to material risks pursuant to Item 501 of Regulation S-K (§ 229.501), and any one or more of the managing underwriter(s) (or where there are no managing underwriters, a majority of the principal underwriters) has been organized, reactivated, or first registered as a broker-dealer within the past three years, these facts concerning such underwriter(s) shall be disclosed in the prospectus together with, where applicable, the disclosures that the principal business function of such underwriter(s) will be to sell the securities to be registered, or that the promoters of the registrant have a material relationship with such underwriter(s). Sufficient details shall be given to allow full appreciation of such underwriter(s) experience and its relationship with the registrant, promoters and their controlling persons.

(c) *Other distributions.* Outline briefly the plan of distribution of any securities to be registered that are to be offered otherwise than through underwriters.

(1) If any securities are to be offered pursuant to a dividend or interest reinvestment plan the terms of which provide for the purchase of some securities on the market, state whether the registrant or the participant pays fees, commissions, and expenses incurred in connection with the plan. If the participant will pay such fees, commissions and expenses, state the anticipated cost to participants by transaction or other convenient reference.

(2) If the securities are to be offered through the selling efforts of brokers or dealers, describe the plan of distribution and the terms of any agreement, arrangement, or understanding entered into with broker(s) or dealer(s) prior to the effective date of the registration statement, including volume limitations on sales, parties to the agreement and the conditions under which the agreement may be terminated. If known, identify the broker(s) or dealer(s) which will participate in the offering and state the amount to be offered through each.

(3) If any of the securities being registered are to be offered otherwise than for cash, state briefly the general purposes of the distribution, the basis upon which the securities are to be offered, the amount of compensation and other expenses of distribution, and by whom they are to be borne. If the distribution is to be made pursuant to a plan of acquisition, reorganization, readjustment or succession, describe briefly the general effect of the plan and state when it became or is to become operative. As to any material amount of assets to be acquired under the plan, furnish information corresponding to that required by Instruction 5 of Item 504 of Regulation S-K (§ 229.504).

(d) *Offerings on exchange.* If the securities are to be offered on an exchange, indicate the exchange. If the registered securities are to be offered in connection with the writing of exchange-traded call options, describe briefly such transactions.

(e) *Underwriter's compensation.* Provide a table that sets out the nature of the compensation and the amount of discounts and commissions to be paid to the underwriter for each security and in total. The table must show the separate amounts to be paid by the company and the selling shareholders. In addition, include in the table all other items considered by the Financial Industry Regulatory Authority ("FINRA") to be underwriting compensation for purposes of FINRA rules.

Instructions to paragraph 508(e)

1. The term "commissions" is defined in paragraph (17) of Schedule A of the Securities Act. Show separately in the table the cash commissions paid by the registrant and selling security holders. Also show in the table commissions paid by other persons. Disclose any finder's fee or similar payments in the table.

2. Disclose the offering expenses specified in Item 511 of Regulation S-K (17 CFR 229.511).

3. If the underwriter has any arrangement with the issuer, such as an over-allotment option, under which the underwriter may purchase additional shares in connection with the offering, indicate that this arrangement exists and state the amount of additional shares that the underwriter may purchase under the arrangement. Where the underwriter has such an arrangement, present maximum-minimum information in a separate column to the table, based on the purchase of all or none of the shares subject to the arrangement. Describe the key terms of the arrangement in the narrative.

(f) *Underwriter's representative on board of directors.* Describe any arrangement whereby the underwriter has the right to designate or nominate a member or members of the board of directors of the registrant. The registrant shall disclose the identity of any director so designated or nominated, and indicate whether or not a person so designated or nominated, or allowed to be designated or nominated by the underwriter is or may be a director, officer, partner, employee or affiliate of the underwriter.

(g) *Indemnification of underwriters.* If the underwriting agreement provides for indemnification by the registrant of the underwriters or their controlling persons against any liability arising under the Securities Act, furnish a brief description of such indemnification provisions.

(h) *Dealers' compensation.* State briefly the discounts and commissions to be allowed or paid to dealers, including all cash, securities, contracts or other considerations to be received by any dealer in connection with the sale of the securities. If any dealers are to act in the capacity of sub-underwriters and are to be allowed or paid any additional discounts or commissions for acting in such capacity, a general statement to that effect will suffice without giving the additional amounts to be sold.

(i) *Finders.* Identify any finder and, if applicable, describe the nature of any material relationship between such finder and the registrant, its officers, directors, principal stockholders, finders or promoters or the principal underwriter(s), or if there is a managing underwriter(s), the managing underwriter(s) (including, in each case, affiliates or associates thereof).

(j) *Discretionary accounts.* If the registrant was not, immediately prior to the filing of the registration statement, subject to the requirements of section 13(a) or 15(d) of the Exchange Act, identify any principal underwriter that intends to sell to any accounts over which it exercises discretionary authority and include an estimate of the amount of securities so intended to be sold. The response to this paragraph shall be contained in a pre-effective amendment which shall be circulated if the information is not available when the registration statement is filed.

(k) *Passive market making.* If the underwriters or any selling group members intend to engage in passive market making transactions as permitted by Rule 103 of Regulation M (§ 242.103 of this chapter), indicate such intention and briefly describe passive market making.

(l) *Stabilization and other transactions.* (1) Briefly describe any transaction that the underwriter intends to conduct during the offering that stabilizes, maintains, or otherwise affects the market price of the offered securities. Include information on stabilizing transactions, syndicate short covering transactions, penalty bids, or any other transaction that affects the offered security's price. Describe the nature of the transactions clearly and explain how the transactions affect the offered security's price. Identify the exchange or other market on which these transactions may occur. If true, disclose that the underwriter may discontinue these transactions at any time;

(2) If the stabilizing began before the effective date of the registration statement, disclose the amount of securities bought, the prices at which they were bought and the period

within which they were bought. If you use § 230.430A of this chapter, the prospectus you file under § 230.424(b) of this chapter or include in a post-effective amendment must contain information on the stabilizing transactions that took place before the determination of the public offering price; and

(3) If you are making a warrants or rights offering of securities to existing security holders and any securities not purchased by existing security holders are to be reoffered to the public, disclose in a supplement to the prospectus or in the prospectus used in connection with the reoffering:

(i) The amount of securities bought in stabilization activities during the offering period and the price or range of prices at which the securities were bought;

(ii) The amount of the offered securities subscribed for during the offering period;

(iii) The amount of the offered securities subscribed for by the underwriter during the offering period;

(iv) The amount of the offered securities sold during the offering period by the underwriter and the price or price ranges at which the securities were sold; and

(v) The amount of the offered securities that will be reoffered to the public and the public offering price.

Item 509. Interests of Named Experts and Counsel

If (a) any expert named in the registration statement as having prepared or certified any part thereof (or is named as having prepared or certified a report or valuation for use in connection with the registration statement), or (b) counsel for the registrant, underwriters or selling security holders named in the prospectus as having given an opinion upon the validity of the securities being registered or upon other legal matters in connection with the registration or offering of such securities, was employed for such purpose on a contingent basis, or at the time of such preparation, certification or opinion or at any time thereafter through the date of effectiveness of the registration statement or that part of the registration statement to which such preparation, certification or opinion relates, had, or is to receive in connection with the offering, a substantial interest, direct or indirect, in the registrant or any of its parents or subsidiaries or was connected with the registrant or any of its parents or subsidiaries as a promoter, managing underwriter (or any principal underwriter, if there are no managing underwriters), voting trustee, director, officer, or employee, furnish a brief statement of the nature of such contingent basis, interest, or connection.

Instructions to Item 509. 1. The interest of an expert (other than an accountant) or counsel will not be deemed substantial and need not be disclosed if the interest, including the fair market value of all securities of the registrant owned, received and to be received, or subject to options, warrants or rights received or to be received by the expert or counsel does not exceed $50,000. For the purpose of this Instruction, the term "expert" or counsel includes the firm, corporation, partnership or other entity, if any, by which such expert or counsel is employed or of which he is a member or of counsel to and all attorneys in the case of counsel, and all nonclerical personnel in the case of named experts, participating in such matter on behalf of such firm, corporation, partnership or entity.

2. Accountants, providing a report on the financial statements, presented or incorporated by reference in the registration statement, should note § 210.2-01 of Regulation S-X (17 CFR 210) for the Commission's requirements regarding "Qualification of Accountants" which discusses disqualifying interests.

Item 510. Disclosure of Commission Position on Indemnification for Securities Act Liabilities

In addition to the disclosure prescribed by Item 702 of Regulation S-K (§ 229.702), if the undertaking required by paragraph (h) of Item 512 of Regulation S-K (§ 229.512) is not required to be included in the registration statement because acceleration of the effective date of the registration statement is not being requested, and if waivers have not been obtained comparable to those specified in paragraph (h), a brief description of the indemnification provisions relating to directors, officers and controlling persons of the registrant against liability arising under the Securities Act (including any provision of the underwriting agreement which relates to indemnification of the underwriter or its controlling persons by the registrant against such liabilities where a director, officer or controlling person of the registrant is such an underwriter or controlling person thereof or a member of any firm which is such an underwriter) shall be included in the prospectus, together with a statement in substantially the following form:

Insofar as indemnification for liabilities arising under the Securities Act of 1933 may be permitted to directors, officers or persons controlling the registrant pursuant to the foregoing provisions, the registrant has been informed that in the opinion of the Securities and Exchange Commission such indemnification is against public policy as expressed in the Act and is therefore unenforceable.

Item 511. Other Expenses of Issuance and Distribution

Furnish a reasonably itemized statement of all expenses in connection with the issuance and distribution of the securities to be registered, other than underwriting discounts and commissions. If any of the securities to be registered are to be offered for the account of security holders, indicate the portion of such expenses to be borne by such security holder.

Instruction to Item 511. Insofar as practicable, registration fees, Federal taxes, States taxes and fees, trustees' and transfer agents' fees, costs of printing and engraving, and legal, accounting, and engineering fees shall be itemized separately. Include as a separate item any premium paid by the registrant or any selling security holder on any policy obtained in connection with the offering and sale of the securities being registered which insures or indemnifies directors or officers against any liabilities they may incur in connection with the registration, offering, or sale of such securities. The information may be given as subject to future contingencies. If the amounts of any items are not known, estimates, identified as such, shall be given.

Item 512. Undertakings

Include each of the following undertakings that is applicable to the offering being registered.

(a) *Rule 415 offering.*[1] Include the following if the securities are registered pursuant to Rule 415 under the Securities Act (§ 230.415 of this chapter):

The undersigned registrant hereby undertakes:

(1) To file, during any period in which offers or sales are being made, a post-effective amendment to this registration statement:

(i) To include any prospectus required by section 10(a)(3) of the Securities Act of 1933;

(ii) To reflect in the prospectus any facts or events arising after the effective date of the registration statement (or the most recent post-effective amendment thereof) which, individually or in the aggregate, represent a fundamental change in the information set forth in the registration statement. Notwithstanding the foregoing, any increase or decrease in volume of securities offered (if the total dollar value of securities offered would not exceed that which was registered) and any deviation from the low or high end of the estimated maximum offering range may be reflected in the form of prospectus filed with the Commission pursuant to Rule 424(b) (§ 230.424(b) of this chapter) if, in the aggregate, the changes in volume and price represent no more than a 20% change in the maximum

---

[1] Paragraph (a) reflects proposals made in Securities Act Release No. 6334 (Aug. 6, 1981).

aggregate offering price set forth in the "Calculation of Registration Fee" table in the effective registration statement;

(iii) To include any material information with respect to the plan of distribution not previously disclosed in the registration statement or any material change to such information in the registration statement;

Provided, however, That:

(A) Paragraphs (a) (1) (i) and (a) (1) (ii) of this section do not apply if the registration statement is on Form S-8 (§ 239.16b of this chapter), and the information required to be included in a post-effective amendment by those paragraphs is contained in reports filed with or furnished to the Commission by the registrant pursuant to section 13 or section 15 (d) of the Securities Exchange Act of 1934 (15 U.S.C. 78m or 78o (d)) that are incorporated by reference in the registration statement; and

(B) Paragraphs (a) (1) (i), (ii) and (iii) of this section do not apply if the registration statement is on Form S-3 (§ 239.13 of this chapter), Form SF-3 (§ 239.45 of this chapter), or Form F-3 (§ 239.33 of this chapter) and the information required to be included in a post-effective amendment by those paragraphs is contained in reports filed with or furnished to the Commission by the registrant pursuant to section 13 or section 15 (d) of the Securities Exchange Act of 1934 (15 U.S.C. 78m or 78o (d)) that are incorporated by reference in the registration statement as to a registration statement on Form S-3, Form SF-3 or Form F-3, or is contained in a form of prospectus filed pursuant to § 230.424 (b) of this chapter that is part of the registration statement.

(C) Provided further, however, that paragraphs (a) (1) (i) and (a) (1) (ii) do not apply if the registration statement is for an offering of asset-backed securities on Form S-1 (§ 239.11 of this chapter) or Form S-3 (§ 239.13 of this chapter) on Form SF-1 (§ 239.44 of this chapter) or Form SF-3 (§ 239.45 of this chapter), and the information required to be included in a post-effective amendment is provided pursuant to Item 1100 (c) of Regulation AB (§ 239.1100 (c)).

(2) That, for the purpose of determining any liability under the Securities Act of 1933, each such post-effective amendment shall be deemed to be a new registration statement relating to the securities offered therein, and the offering of such securities at that time shall be deemed to be the initial bona fide offering thereof.

(3) To remove from registration by means of a post-effective amendment any of the securities being registered which remain unsold at the termination of the offering.

(4) If the registrant is a foreign private issuer, to file a post-effective amendment to the registration statement to include any financial statements required by Item 8.A of Form 20-F (17 CFR 249.220f) at the start of any delayed offering or throughout a continuous offering. Financial statements and information otherwise required by Section 10 (a) (3) of the Act (15 U.S.C. 77j(a) (3)) need not be furnished, *provided* that the registrant includes in the prospectus, by means of a post-effective amendment, financial statements required pursuant to this paragraph (a) (4) and other information necessary to ensure that all other information in the prospectus is at least as current as the date of those financial statements. Notwithstanding the foregoing, with respect to registration statements on Form F-3 (§ 239.33 of this chapter), a post-effective amendment need not be filed to include financial statements and information required by Section 10 (a) (3) of the Act or Item 8.A of Form 20-F if such financial statements and information are contained in periodic reports filed with or furnished to the Commission by the registrant pursuant to section 13 or section 15 (d) of the Securities Exchange Act of 1934 that are incorporated by reference in the Form F-3.

(5) That, for the purpose of determining liability under the Securities Act of 1933 to any purchaser:

(i) If the registrant is relying on Rule 430B (§ 230.430B of this chapter):

(A) Each prospectus filed by the registrant pursuant to Rule 424(b) (3) (§ 230.424(b) (3) of this chapter) shall be deemed to be part of the registration statement as of the date the filed prospectus was deemed part of and included in the registration statement; and

(B) Each prospectus required to be filed pursuant to Rule 424(b)(2), (b)(5), or (b)(7) (§ 230.424(b)(2), (b)(5), or (b)(7) of this chapter) as part of a registration statement in reliance on Rule 430B relating to an offering made pursuant to Rule 415(a)(1)(i), (vii), or (x) (§ 230.415(a)(1)(i), (vii), or (x) of this chapter) for the purpose of providing the information required by section 10(a) of the Securities Act of 1933 shall be deemed to be part of and included in the registration statement as of the earlier of the date such form of prospectus is first used after effectiveness or the date of the first contract of sale of 314 securities in the offering described in the prospectus. As provided in Rule 430B, for liability purposes of the issuer and any person that is at that date an underwriter, such date shall be deemed to be a new effective date of the registration statement relating to the securities in the registration statement to which that prospectus relates, and the offering of such securities at that time shall be deemed to be the initial bona fide offering thereof. *Provided, however,* that no statement made in a registration statement or prospectus that is part of the registration statement or made in a document incorporated or deemed incorporated by reference into the registration statement or prospectus that is part of the registration statement will, as to a purchaser with a time of contract of sale prior to such effective date, supersede or modify any statement that was made in the registration statement or prospectus that was part of the registration statement or made in any such document immediately prior to such effective date; or

(ii) If the registrant is subject to Rule 430C (§ 230.430C of this chapter), each prospectus filed pursuant to Rule 424(b) as part of a registration statement relating to an offering, other than registration statements relying on Rule 430B or other than prospectuses filed in reliance on Rule 430A (§ 230.430A of this chapter), shall be deemed to be part of and included in the registration statement as of the date it is first used after effectiveness. *Provided, however,* that no statement made in a registration statement or prospectus that is part of the registration statement or made in a document incorporated or deemed incorporated by reference into the registration statement or prospectus that is part of the registration statement will, as to a purchaser with a time of contract of sale prior to such first use, supersede or modify any statement that was made in the registration statement or prospectus that was part of the registration statement or made in any such document immediately prior to such date of first use.

(iii) If the registrant is relying on § 230.430D of this chapter:

(A) Each prospectus filed by the registrant pursuant to §§ 230.424(b)(3) and (h) of this chapter shall be deemed to be part of the registration statement as of the date the filed prospectus was deemed part of and included in the registration statement; and

(B) Each prospectus required to be filed pursuant to § 230.424(b)(2), (b)(5), or (b)(7) of this chapter as part of a registration statement in reliance on § 230.430D of this chapter relating to an offering made pursuant to § 230.415(a)(1)(vii) or (a)(1)(xii) of this chapter for the purpose of providing the information required by section 10(a) of the Securities Act of 1933 (15 U.S.C. 77j(a)) shall be deemed to be part of and included in the registration statement as of the earlier of the date such form of prospectus is first used after effectiveness or the date of the first contract of sale of securities in the offering described in the prospectus. As provided in § 230.430D of this chapter, for liability purposes of the issuer and any person that is at that date an underwriter, such date shall be deemed to be a new effective date of the registration statement relating to the securities in the registration statement to which that prospectus relates, and the offering of such securities at that time shall be deemed to be the initial bona fide offering thereof. Provided, however, that no statement made in a registration statement or prospectus that is part of the registration statement or made in a document incorporated or deemed incorporated by reference into the registration statement or prospectus that is part of the registration statement will, as to a purchaser with a time of contract of sale prior to such effective date, supersede or modify any statement that was made in the registration statement or prospectus that was part of the registration statement or made in any such document immediately prior to such effective date; or

(6) That, for the purpose of determining liability of the registrant under the Securities Act of 1933 to any purchaser in the initial distribution of the securities:

The undersigned registrant undertakes that in a primary offering of securities of the undersigned registrant pursuant to this registration statement, regardless of the underwriting method used to sell the securities to the purchaser, if the securities are offered or sold to such purchaser by means of any of the following communications, the undersigned registrant will be a seller to the purchaser and will be considered to offer or sell such securities to such purchaser:

(i) Any preliminary prospectus or prospectus of the undersigned registrant relating to the offering required to be filed pursuant to Rule 424 (§ 230.424 of this chapter);

(ii) Any free writing prospectus relating to the offering prepared by or on behalf of the undersigned registrant or used or referred to by the undersigned registrant;

(iii) The portion of any other free writing prospectus relating to the offering containing material information about the undersigned registrant or its securities provided by or on behalf of the undersigned registrant; and

(iv) Any other communication that is an offer in the offering made by the undersigned registrant to the purchaser.

(7) If the registrant is relying on § 230.430D of this chapter, with respect to any offering of securities registered on Form SF-3 (§ 239.45 of this chapter), to file the information previously omitted from the prospectus filed as part of an effective registration statement in accordance with § 230.424(h) and § 230.430D of this chapter.

(b) *Filings incorporating subsequent Exchange Act documents by reference.* Include the following if the registration statement incorporates by reference any Exchange Act document filed subsequent to the effective date of the registration statement:

The undersigned registrant hereby undertakes that, for purposes of determining any liability under the Securities Act of 1933, each filing of the registrant's annual report pursuant to section 13(a) or section 15(d) of the Securities Exchange Act of 1934 (and, where applicable, each filing of an employee benefit plan's annual report pursuant to section 15(d) of the Securities Exchange Act of 1934) that is incorporated by reference in the registration statement shall be deemed to be a new registration statement relating to the securities offered therein, and the offering of such securities at that time shall be deemed to be the initial bona fide offering thereof.

(c) [Reserved.]

(d) [Reserved.]

(e) [Reserved.]

(f) [Reserved.]

(g) *Registration on Form S-4 or F-4 of securities offered for resale.* Include the following if the securities are being registered on Form S-4 or F-4 (§ 239.23, 25 or 34 of this chapter) in connection with a transaction specified in paragraph (a) of Rule 145 (§ 230.145 of this chapter).

(1) The undersigned registrant hereby undertakes as follows: that prior to any public reoffering of the securities registered hereunder through use of a prospectus which is a part of this registration statement, by any person or party who is deemed to be an underwriter within the meaning of Rule 145(c), the issuer undertakes that such reoffering prospectus will contain the information called for by the applicable registration form with respect to reofferings by persons who may be deemed underwriters, in addition to the information called for by the other Items of the applicable form.

(2) The registrant undertakes that every prospectus (i) that is filed pursuant to paragraph (1) immediately preceding, or (ii) that purports to meet the requirements of section

10(a)(3) of the Act and is used in connection with an offering of securities subject to Rule 415 (§ 230.415 of this chapter), will be filed as a part of an amendment to the registration statement and will not be used until such amendment is effective, and that, for purposes of determining any liability under the Securities Act of 1933, each such post-effective amendment shall be deemed to be a new registration statement relating to the securities offered therein, and the offering of such securities at that time shall be deemed to be the initial bona fide offering thereof.

(h) *Request for acceleration of effective date or filing of registration statement on Form S-8.* Include the following if acceleration is requested of the effective date of the registration statement pursuant to Rule 461 under the Securities Act (§ 230.461 of this chapter), or if the registration statement is filed on Form S-8, and: (1) any provision or arrangement exists whereby the registrant may indemnify a director, officer or controlling person of the registrant against liabilities arising under the Securities Act, or (2) the underwriting agreement contains a provision whereby the registrant indemnifies the underwriter or controlling persons of the underwriter against such liabilities and a director, officer or controlling person of the registrant is such an underwriter or controlling person thereof or a member of any firm which is such an underwriter, and (3) the benefits of such indemnification are not waived by such persons:

Insofar as indemnification for liabilities arising under the Securities Act of 1933 may be permitted to directors, officers and controlling persons of the registrant pursuant to the foregoing provisions, or otherwise, the registrant has been advised that in the opinion of the Securities and Exchange Commission such indemnification is against public policy as expressed in the Act and is, therefore, unenforceable. In the event that a claim for indemnification against such liabilities (other than the payment by the registrant of expenses incurred or paid by a director, officer or controlling person of the registrant in the successful defense of any action, suit or proceeding) is asserted by such director, officer or controlling person in connection with the securities being registered, the registrant will, unless in the opinion of its counsel the matter has been settled by controlling precedent, submit to a court of appropriate jurisdiction the question whether such indemnification by it is against public policy as expressed in the Act and will be governed by the final adjudication of such issue.

(i) Include the following in a registration statement permitted by Rule 430A under the Securities Act of 1933 [§ 230.430A of this chapter]:

The undersigned registrant hereby undertakes that:

(1) For purposes of determining any liability under the Securities Act of 1933, the information omitted from the form of prospectus filed as part of this registration statement in reliance upon Rule 430A and contained in a form of prospectus filed by the registrant pursuant to Rule 424(b)(1) or (4) or 497(h) under the Securities Act shall be deemed to be part of this registration statement as of the time it was declared effective.

(2) For the purpose of determining any liability under the Securities Act of 1933, each post-effective amendment that contains a form of prospectus shall be deemed to be a new registration statement relating to the securities offered therein, and the offering of such securities at that time shall be deemed to be the initial bona fide offering thereof.

(j) *Qualification of trust indentures under the Trust Indenture Act of 1939 for delayed offerings.* Include the following if the registrant intends to rely on Section 305(b)(2) of the Trust Indenture Act of 1939 for determining the eligibility of the trustee under indentures for securities to be issued, offered, or sold on a delayed basis by or on behalf of the registrant:

"The undersigned registrant hereby undertakes to file an application for the purpose of determining the eligibility of the trustee to act under subsection (a) of Section 310 of the Trust Indenture Act ("Act") in accordance with the rules and regulations prescribed by the Commission under Section 305(b)(2) of the Act."

(k) *Filings Regarding Asset-Backed Securities Incorporating by Reference Subsequent Exchange Act Documents by Third Parties.*Include the following if the registration statement incorporates by reference any Exchange Act document filed subsequent to the effective date of the registration statement pursuant to Item 1100(c) of Regulation AB (§ 229.1100(c)):

"The undersigned registrant hereby undertakes that, for purposes of determining any liability under the Securities Act of 1933, each filing of the annual report pursuant to section 13(a) or section 15(d) of the Securities Exchange Act of 1934 of a third party that is incorporated by reference in the registration statement in accordance with Item 1100(c)(1) of Regulation AB (17 CFR 229.1100(c)(1)) shall be deemed to be a new registration statement relating to the securities offered therein, and the offering of such securities at that time shall be deemed to be the initial bona fide offering thereof."

Subpart 600—Exhibits

Item 601. Exhibits

(a) *Exhibits and index required.*

(1) Subject to Rule 411(c) (§ 230.411(c) of this chapter) under the Securities Act and Rule 12b-32 (§ 240.12b-32 of this chapter) under the Exchange Act regarding incorporation of exhibits by reference, the exhibits required in the exhibit table shall be filed as indicated, as part of the registration statement or report.

(2) Each registration statement or report shall contain an exhibit index, which must appear before the required signatures in the registration statement or report. For convenient reference, each exhibit shall be listed in the exhibit index according to the number assigned to it in the exhibit table. If an exhibit is incorporated by reference, this must be noted in the exhibit index. Each exhibit identified in the exhibit index (other than an exhibit filed in eXtensible Business Reporting Language or an exhibit that is filed with Form ABS-EE) must include an active link to an exhibit that is filed with the registration statement or report or, if the exhibit is incorporated by reference, an active hyperlink to the exhibit separately filed on EDGAR. If a registration statement or report is amended, each amendment must include hyperlinks to the exhibits required with the amendment. For a description of each of the exhibits included in the exhibit table, see paragraph (b) of this section.

(3) This Item applies only to the forms specified in the exhibit table. With regard to forms not listed in that table, reference shall be made to the appropriate form for the specific exhibit filing requirements applicable thereto.

(4) If a material contract or plan of acquisition, reorganization, arrangement, liquidation or succession is executed or becomes effective during the reporting period reflected by a Form 10-Q or Form 10-K, it shall be filed as an exhibit to the Form 10-Q or Form 10-K filed for the corresponding period. Any amendment or modification to a previously filed exhibit to a Form 10, 10-K or 10-Q document shall be filed as an exhibit to a Form 10-Q or Form 10-K. Such amendment or modification need not be filed where such previously filed exhibit would not be currently required.

(5) Schedules (or similar attachments) to the exhibits required by this Item are not required to be filed provided that they do not contain information material to an investment or voting decision and that information is not otherwise disclosed in the exhibit or the disclosure document. Each exhibit filed must contain a list briefly identifying the contents of all omitted schedules. Registrants need not prepare a separate list of omitted information if such information is already included within the exhibit in a manner that conveys the subject matter of the omitted schedules and attachments. In addition, the registrant must provide a copy of any omitted schedule to the Commission or its staff upon request.

(6) The registrant may redact information from exhibits required to be filed by this Item if disclosure of such information would constitute a clearly unwarranted invasion of personal privacy (*e.g.*, disclosure of bank account numbers, social security numbers, home addresses, and similar information).

Instructions to Item 601. 1. If an exhibit to a registration statement (other than an opinion or consent), filed in preliminary form, has been changed only (A) to insert information as to interest, dividend or conversion rates, redemption or conversion prices, purchase or offering prices, underwriters' or dealers' commissions, names, addresses or participation of underwriters or similar matters, which information appears elsewhere in an amendment to the registration statement or a prospectus filed pursuant to Rule 424(b) under the Securities Act [§ 230.424(b) of this chapter], or (B) to correct typographical errors, insert signatures or make other similar immaterial changes, then, notwithstanding any contrary requirement of any rule or form, the registrant need not refile such exhibit as so amended. Any such incomplete exhibit may not, however, be incorporated by reference in any subsequent filing under any Act administered by the Commission.

2. In any case where two or more indentures, contracts, franchises, or other documents required to be filed as exhibits are substantially identical in all material respects except as to the parties thereto, the dates of execution, or other details, the registrant need file a copy of only one of such documents, with a schedule identifying the other documents omitted and setting forth the material details in which such documents differ from the document a copy of which is filed. The Commission may at any time in its discretion require filing of copies of any documents so omitted.

3. Only copies, rather than originals, need be filed of each exhibit required except as otherwise specifically noted.

4. *Electronic filings.* Whenever an exhibit is filed in paper pursuant to a hardship exemption (§§ 232.201 and 232.202 of this chapter), the letter "P" (paper) shall be placed next to the exhibit in the list of exhibits required by Item 601(a)(2) of this Rule. Whenever an electronic confirming copy of an exhibit is filed pursuant to a hardship exemption (§ 232.201 or § 232.202(d) of this chapter), the exhibit index should specify where the confirming electronic copy can be located; in addition, the designation "CE" (confirming electronic) should be placed next to the listed exhibit in the exhibit index.

Exhibit Table

Instructions to the Exhibit Table. 1. The exhibit table indicates those documents that must be filed as exhibits to the respective forms listed.

2. The "X" designation indicates the documents which are required to be filed with each form even if filed previously with another document. *Provided, however,* that such previously filed documents may be incorporated by reference to satisfy the filing requirements.

3. The number used in the far left column of the table refers to the appropriate subsection in paragraph (b) where a description of the exhibit can be found. Whenever necessary, alphabetical or numerical subparts may be used.

[Table Listing Exhibits has been omitted—EDS.]

(b) *Description of exhibits.* Set forth below is a description of each document listed in the exhibit tables. **[Many of the exhibit descriptions have been omitted—EDS.]**

(1) *Underwriting agreement—* . . .

(2) *Plan of acquisition, reorganization, arrangement, liquidation or succession—* . . .

(3) (i) *Articles of incorporation.* . . .

(ii) *Bylaws.* . . .

(4) *Instruments defining the rights of security holders, including indentures.* . . .

(5) *Opinion re legality*—(i) An opinion of counsel as to the legality of the securities being registered, indicating whether they will, when sold, be legally issued, fully paid and non-assessable, and, if debt securities, whether they will be binding obligations of the registrant.

(ii) If the securities being registered are issued under a plan and the plan is subject to the requirements of ERISA furnish either:

(A) An opinion of counsel which confirms compliance of the provisions of the written documents constituting the plan with the requirements of ERISA pertaining to such provisions; or

(B) A copy of the Internal Revenue Service determination letter that the plan is qualified under section 401 of the Internal Revenue Code; or

(iii) If the securities being registered are issued under a plan which is subject to the requirements of ERISA and the plan has been amended subsequent to the filing of (ii)(A) or (B) above, furnish either:

(A) An opinion of counsel which confirms compliance of the amended provisions of the plan with the requirements of ERISA pertaining to such provisions; or

(B) A copy of the Internal Revenue Service determination letter that the amended plan is qualified under section 401 of the Internal Revenue Code.

Note: Attention is directed to Item 8 of Form S-8 for exemptions to this exhibit requirement applicable to that Form.

(6) [Reserved.]

(7) *Correspondence from an independent accountant regarding non-reliance on a previously issued audit report or completed interim review.* Any written notice from the registrant's current or previously engaged independent accountant that the independent accountant is withdrawing a previously issued audit report or that a previously issued audit report or completed interim review, covering one or more years or interim periods for which the registrant is required to provide financial statements under Regulation S-X (part 210 of this chapter), should no longer be relied upon. In addition, any letter, pursuant to Item 4.02(c) of Form 8-K (§ 249.308 of this chapter), from the independent accountant to the Commission stating whether the independent accountant agrees with the statements made by the registrant describing the events giving rise to the notice.

(8) *Opinion re tax matters*—For filings on Form S-11 under the Securities Act (§ 239.18) or those to which Securities Act Industry Guide 5 applies, an opinion of counsel or of an independent public or certified public accountant or, in lieu thereof, a revenue ruling from the Internal Revenue Service, supporting the tax matters and consequences to the shareholders as described in the filing when such tax matters are material to the transaction for which the registration statement is being filed. This exhibit otherwise need only be filed with the other applicable registration forms where the tax consequences are material to an investor and a representation as to tax consequences is set forth in the filing. If a tax opinion is set forth in full in the filing, an indication that such is the case may be made in lieu of filing the otherwise required exhibit. Such tax opinions may be conditioned or may be qualified, so long as such conditions and qualifications are adequately described in the filing.

(9) *Voting trust agreement*— . . .

(10) *Material Contracts*

(i)(A) Every contract not made in the ordinary course of business that is material to the registrant and is to be performed in whole or in part at or after the filing of the registration statement or report. In addition, for newly reporting registrants, every contract not made in the ordinary course of business that is material to the registrant and that was entered into not more than two years before the date on which such registrant:

(*1*) First files a registration statement or report; or

(*2*) Completes a transaction that had the effect of causing it to cease being a public shell company.

(B) The only contracts that need to be filed are those to which the registrant or a subsidiary of the registrant is a party or has succeeded to a party by assumption or assignment or in which the registrant or such subsidiary has a beneficial interest.

(ii) If the contract is such as ordinarily accompanies the kind of business conducted by the registrant and its subsidiaries, it will be deemed to have been made in the ordinary course of business and need not be filed unless it falls within one or more of the following categories, in which case it shall be filed except where immaterial in amount or significance:

(A) Any contract to which directors, officers, promoters, voting trustees, security holders named in the registration statement or report, or underwriters are parties other than contracts involving only the purchase or sale of current assets having a determinable market price, at such market price;

(B) Any contract upon which the registrant's business is substantially dependent, as in the case of continuing contracts to sell the major part of registrant's products or services or to purchase the major part of registrant's requirements of goods, services or raw materials or any franchise or license or other agreement to use a patent, formula, trade secret, process or trade name upon which registrant's business depends to a material extent;

(C) Any contract calling for the acquisition or sale of any property, plant or equipment for a consideration exceeding 15 percent of such fixed assets of the registrant on a consolidated basis; or

(D) Any material lease under which a part of the property described in the registration statement or report is held by the registrant.

(iii) (A) Any management contract or any compensatory plan, contract or arrangement, including but not limited to plans relating to options, warrants or rights, pension, retirement or deferred compensation or bonus, incentive or profit sharing (or if not set forth in any formal document, a written description thereof) in which any director or any of the named executive officers of the registrant, as defined by Item 402(a)(3) (§ 229.402(a)(31), participates shall be deemed material and shall be filed; and any other management contract or any compensatory plan, contract, or arrangement in which any other executive officer of the registrant participates shall be filed unless immaterial in amount or significance.

(B) Any compensatory plan, contract or arrangement adopted without the approval of security holders pursuant to which equity may be awarded, including, but not limited to, options, warrants or rights (or if not set forth in any formal document, a written description thereof), in which any employee (whether or not an executive officer of the registrant) participates shall be filed unless immaterial in amount or significance. A compensation plan assumed by a registrant in connection with a merger, consolidation or other acquisition transaction pursuant to which the registrant may make further grants or awards of its equity securities shall be considered a compensation plan of the registrant for purposes of the preceding sentence.

(C) Notwithstanding paragraph (iii)(A) above, the following management contracts or compensatory plans, contracts or arrangements need not be filed:

(*1*) Ordinary purchase and sales agency agreements.

(*2*) Agreements with managers of stores in a chain organization or similar organization.

(*3*) Contracts providing for labor or salesmen's bonuses or payments to a class of security holders, as such.

(*4*) Any compensatory plan, contract or arrangement which pursuant to its terms is available to employees, officers or directors generally and which in operation provides for the same method of allocation of benefits between management and nonmanagement participants.

(*5*) Any compensatory plan, contract or arrangement if the registrant is a foreign private issuer that furnishes compensatory information under Item 402(a)(1) (§ 229.402(a)(1)) and the public filing of the plan, contract or arrangement, or portion thereof, is not required in the registrant's home country and is not otherwise publicly disclosed by the registrant.

(*6*) Any compensatory plan, contract, or arrangement if the registrant is a wholly owned subsidiary of a company that has a class of securities registered pursuant to section 12 or files reports pursuant to section 15(d) of the Exchange Act and is filing a report on Form 10-K or registering debt instruments or preferred stock which are not voting securities on Form S-2.

(iv) The registrant may redact provisions or terms of exhibits required to be filed by paragraph (b)(10) if those provisions or terms are both not material and would likely cause competitive harm to the registrant if publicly disclosed. If it does so, the registrant should mark the exhibit index to indicate that portions of the exhibit or exhibits have been omitted and include a prominent statement on the first page of the redacted exhibit that certain identified information has been excluded from the exhibit because it is both not material and would likely cause competitive harm to the registrant if publicly disclosed. The registrant also must indicate by brackets where the information is omitted from the filed version of the exhibit. If requested by the Commission or its staff, the registrant must promptly provide an unredacted copy of the exhibit on a supplemental basis. The Commission or its staff also may request the registrant to provide its materiality and competitive harm analyses on a supplemental basis. Upon evaluation of the registrant's supplemental materials, the Commission or its staff may request the registrant to amend its filing to include in the exhibit any previously redacted information that is not adequately supported by the registrant's materiality and competitive harm analyses. The registrant may request confidential treatment of the supplemental material submitted under this paragraph (b)(10)(iv) pursuant to Rule 83 (§ 200.83 of this chapter) while it is in the possession of the Commission or its staff. After completing its review of the supplemental information, the Commission or its staff will return or destroy it at the request of the registrant if the registrant complies with the procedures outlined in Rules 418 or 12b-4 (§ 230.418 or 240.12b-4 of this chapter).

Instruction 1 to Paragraph (b)(10) of Item 601: For purposes of paragraph (b)(10)(i) of this Item, a "newly reporting registrant" is:

1. Any registrant filing a registration statement that, at the time of such filing, is not subject to the reporting requirements of Section 13(a) or 15(d) of the Exchange Act, whether or not such registrant has ever previously been subject to the reporting requirements of Section 13(a) or 15(d),

2. Any registrant that has not filed an annual report since the revival of a previously suspended reporting obligation, and

3. Any registrant that:

    a. Was a shell company, other than a business combination related shell company, as defined in Rule 12b-2 under the Exchange Act (17 CFR 240.12b-2), immediately before completing a transaction that has the effect of causing it to cease being a shell company and

    b. Has not filed a registration statement or Form 8-K as required by Items 2.01 and 5.06 of that form, since the completion of such transaction.

4. For example, newly reporting registrants would include a registrant that is filing its first registration statement under the Securities Act or the Exchange Act, and a registrant that was a public shell company, other than a business combination related shell company, and completes a reverse merger transaction causing it to cease being a shell company.

Instruction 2 to Paragraph (b)(10): With the exception of management contracts, in order to comply with paragraph (b)(10)(iii) [*sic*] of this section, registrants need only file copies of the various compensatory plans and need not file each individual director's or executive officer's personal agreement under the plans unless there are particular provisions in such personal agreements whose disclosure in an exhibit is necessary to an investor's understanding of that individual's compensation under the plan.

Instruction 3 to Paragraph (b)(10): If a material contract is executed or becomes effective during the reporting period reflected by a Form 10-Q or Form 10-K, it must be filed as an exhibit to the Form 10-Q or Form 10-K filed for the corresponding period. See paragraph (a)(4) of this Item. With respect to quarterly reports on Form 10-Q, only those contracts executed or becoming effective during the most recent period reflected in the report must be filed.

    (11) [Reserved.]

    (12) [Reserved.]

    (13) *Annual or Quarterly Report to Security Holders.*

       (i) The registrant's annual report to security holders for its last fiscal year or its quarterly report to security holders, if all or a portion thereof is incorporated by reference in the filing. Such report, except for those portions thereof that are expressly incorporated by reference in the filing, is to be furnished for the information of the Commission and is not to be deemed "filed" as part of the filing. If the financial statements in the report have been incorporated by reference in the filing, the accountant's certificate must be manually signed in one copy. *See* Rule 439 (§ 230.439 of this chapter).

(ii) *Electronic Filings.* If all, or any portion, of the annual or quarterly report to security holders is incorporated by reference into any electronic filing, all, or such portion, of the annual or quarterly report to security holders so incorporated, must be filed in electronic format as an exhibit to the filing.

(14) *Code of ethics.* Any code of ethics, or amendment thereto, that is the subject of the disclosure required by § 229.406 (Item 406 of Regulation S-K) or Item 5.05 of Form 8-K (§ 249.308 of this chapter), to the extent that the registrant intends to satisfy the Item 406 or Item 5.05 requirements through filing of an exhibit.

(15) *Letter re unaudited interim financial information*—A letter, where applicable, from the independent accountant that acknowledges awareness of the use in a registration statement of a report on unaudited interim financial information that pursuant to Rule 436(c) under the Securities Act (§ 230.436(c) of this chapter) is not considered a part of a registration statement prepared or certified by an accountant or a report prepared or certified by an accountant within the meaning of sections 7 and 11 of that Act. Such letter may be filed with the registration statement, an amendment thereto, or a report on Form 10-Q which is incorporated by reference into the registration statement.

(16) *Letter re change in certifying accountant*—A letter from the registrant's former independent accountant regarding its concurrence or disagreement with the statements made by the registrant in the current report concerning the resignation or dismissal as the registrant's principal accountant.

(17) *Correspondence on departure of director.* Any written correspondence from a former director concerning the circumstances surrounding the former director's retirement, resignation, refusal to stand for re-election or removal, including any letter from the former director to the registrant stating whether the former director agrees with statements made by the registrant describing the former director's departure.

(18) *Letter re change in accounting principles*—Unless previously filed, a letter from the registrant's independent accountant indicating whether any change in accounting principles or practices followed by the registrant, or any change in the method of applying any such accounting principles or practices, which affected the financial statements being filed with the Commission in the report or which is reasonably certain to affect the financial statements of future fiscal years is to an alternative principle which in his judgment is preferable under the circumstances. No such letter need be filed when such change is made in response to a standard adopted by the Financial Accounting Standards Board that creates a new accounting principle, that expresses a preference for an accounting principle, or that rejects a specific accounting principle.

(19) [Reserved.]

(20) *Other documents or statements to security holders*—If the registrant makes available to its stockholders or otherwise publishes, within the period prescribed for filing the report, a document or statement containing information meeting some or all of the requirements of this form the information called for may be incorporated by reference to such published document or statement provided copies thereof are filed as an exhibit to the report on this form.

(21) *Subsidiaries of the registrant*—(i) List all subsidiaries of the registrant, the state or other jurisdiction of incorporation or organization of each, and the names under which such subsidiaries do business. This list may be incorporated by reference from a document which includes a complete and accurate list.

(ii) The names of particular subsidiaries may be omitted if the unnamed subsidiaries, considered in the aggregate as a single subsidiary, would not constitute a significant subsidiary as of the end of the year covered by this report. (See the definition of "significant subsidiary" in Rule 1-02(w) (17 CFR 210.1-02(w)) of Regulation S-X.) The names of consolidated wholly-owned multiple subsidiaries carrying on the same line of business, such as chain stores or small loan companies, may be omitted, provided the name of the immediate parent, the line of business, the number of omitted subsidiaries operating in the United States and the number operating in foreign countries are given. This instruction shall not apply, however, to banks, insurance companies, savings and loan associations or to any subsidiary subject to regulation by another Federal agency.

(22) *Subsidiary Guarantors and Issuers of Guaranteed Securities and Affiliates Whose Securities Collateralize Securities of the Registrant.* List each of the entities in paragraphs (b)(22)(i) and (ii) of this section under an appropriately captioned heading that identifies the associated securities. An entity need not be listed more than once so long as its role as issuer, co-issuer, or guarantor of a guaranteed security and/or as affiliate whose security is pledged as collateral for a registrant's security is clearly indicated with respect to each applicable security:

(i) For a registrant that is the parent company (as that term is defined in § 210.3-10(b)(1) of this chapter) and subject to § 210.13-01 of this chapter, each of the registrant's subsidiaries that is a guarantor, issuer, or co-issuer of the guaranteed security subject to Section 13(a) or 15(d) of the Securities Exchange Act of 1934, or the offer and sale of which is being registered under the Securities Act of 1933; and

(ii) For a registrant that is subject to § 210.13-02 of this chapter, each of the registrant's affiliates whose security is pledged as collateral for the registrant's security subject to Section 13(a) or Section 15(d) of the Securities Exchange Act of 1934, or the offer and sale of which is being registered under the Securities Act of 1933. For each affiliate, also identify the security or securities pledged as collateral.

(23) *Consents of experts and counsel*—(i) Securities Act filings—All written consents required to be filed shall be dated and manually signed. Where the consent of an expert or counsel is contained in his report or opinion or elsewhere in the registration statement or document filed therewith, a reference shall be made in the index to the report, the part of the registration statement or document or opinion, containing the consent.

(ii) Exchange Act reports—where the filing of a written consent is required with respect to material incorporated by reference in a previously filed registration statement under the Securities Act, such consent may be filed as an exhibit to the material incorporated by reference. Such consents shall be dated and manually signed.

(24) *Power of attorney*— . . .

(25) *Statement of eligibility of trustee*—(i) A statement of eligibility and qualification of each person designated to act as trustee under an indenture to be qualified under the Trust Indenture Act of 1939. Such statement of eligibility shall be bound separately from the other exhibits. . . .

(26) [Reserved.]

(27)through (30) [Reserved].

(31) *Rule 13a-14(a)/15d-14(a) Certifications.* The certifications required by Rule 13a-14(a) (17 CFR 240.13a-14(a)) or Rule 15d-14(a) (17 CFR 240.15d-14(a)) exactly as set forth below:

CERTIFICATIONS*

I [identify the certifying person], certify that:

1. I have reviewed this [specify report] of [identify registrant];

2. Based on my knowledge, this report does not contain any untrue statement of a material fact or omit to state a material fact necessary to make the statements made, in light of the circumstances under which such statements were made, not misleading with respect to the period covered by this report;

---

* Provide a separate certification for each principal executive officer and principal financial officer of the registrant. See Rules 13a-14(a) and 15d-14(a).

3. Based on my knowledge, the financial statements, and other financial information included in this report, fairly present in all material respects the financial condition, results of operations and cash flows of the registrant as of, and for, the periods presented in this report;

4. The registrant's other certifying officer(s) and I are responsible for establishing and maintaining disclosure controls and procedures (as defined in Exchange Act Rules 13a-15(e) and 15d-15(e)) and internal control over financial reporting (as defined in Exchange Act Rules 13a-15(f) and 15d-15(f)) for the registrant and have:

(a) Designed such disclosure controls and procedures, or caused such disclosure controls and procedures to be designed under our supervision, to ensure that material information relating to the registrant, including its consolidated subsidiaries, is made known to us by others within those entities, particularly during the period in which this report is being prepared;

(b) Designed such internal control over financial reporting, or caused such internal control over financial reporting to be designed under our supervision, to provide reasonable assurance regarding the reliability of financial reporting and the preparation of financial statements for external purposes in accordance with generally accepted accounting principles;

(c) Evaluated the effectiveness of the registrant's disclosure controls and procedures and presented in this report our conclusions about the effectiveness of the disclosure controls and procedures, as of the end of the period covered by this report based on such evaluation; and

(d) Disclosed in this report any change in the registrant's internal control over financial reporting that occurred during the registrant's most recent fiscal quarter (the registrant's fourth fiscal quarter in the case of an annual report) that has materially affected, or is reasonably likely to materially affect, the registrant's internal control over financial reporting; and

5. The registrant's other certifying officer(s) and I have disclosed, based on our most recent evaluation of internal control over financial reporting, to the registrant's auditors and the audit committee of the registrant's board of directors (or persons performing the equivalent functions):

(a) All significant deficiencies and material weaknesses in the design or operation of internal control over financial reporting which are reasonably likely to adversely affect the registrant's ability to record, process, summarize and report financial information; and

(b) Any fraud, whether or not material, that involves management or other employees who have a significant role in the registrant's internal control over financial reporting.

Date: ....

[Signature]..

[Title] ....

Rule 13a-14(d)/15d-14(d) Certifications. If an asset-backed issuer (as defined in § 229.1101), the certifications required by Rule 13a-14(d) (17 CFR 240.13a-14(d)) or Rule 15d-14(d) (17 CFR 240.15d-14(d)) exactly as set forth below: **[The description for this certification has been omitted—EDS.]**

(32) Section 1350 Certifications.

(i) The certifications required by Rule 13a-14(b) (17 CFR 240.13a-14 (b)) or Rule 15d-14(b) (17 CFR 240.15d-14(b)) and Section 1350 of Chapter 63 of Title 18 of the United States Code (18 U.S.C. 1350).

(ii) A certification furnished pursuant to this item will not be deemed "filed" for purposes of Section 18 of the Exchange Act (15 U.S.C. 78r), or otherwise subject to the liability of that section. Such certification will not be deemed to be incorporated by reference into any filing under the Securities Act or the Exchange Act, except to the extent that the registrant specifically incorporates it by reference.

(33) *Report on assessment of compliance with servicing criteria for asset-backed securities*. Each report on assessment of compliance with servicing criteria required by § 229.1122(a).

(34) *Attestation report on assessment of compliance with servicing criteria for asset-backed securities*. Each attestation report on assessment of compliance with servicing criteria for asset-backed securities required by § 229.1122(b).

(35) *Servicer compliance statement*. Each servicer compliance statement required by § 229.1123.

(36) *Certification For Shelf Offerings of Asset-Backed Securities*. Provide the certification required by General Instruction I.B.1.(a) of Form SF-3 (§ 239.45 of this chapter) exactly as set forth below:

Certification

I [identify the certifying individual] certify as of [the date of the final prospectus under § 230.424 of this chapter] that:

1. I have reviewed the prospectus relating to [title of all securities, the offer and sale of which are registered] (the "securities") and am familiar with, in all material respects, the following: The characteristics of the securitized assets underlying the offering (the "securitized assets"), the structure of the securitization, and all material underlying transaction agreements as described in the prospectus;

2. Based on my knowledge, the prospectus does not contain any untrue statement of a material fact or omit to state a material fact necessary to make the statements made, in light of the circumstances under which such statements were made, not misleading;

3. Based on my knowledge, the prospectus and other information included in the registration statement of which it is a part fairly present, in all material respects, the characteristics of the securitized assets, the structure of the securitization and the risks of ownership of the securities, including the risks relating to the securitized assets that would affect the cash flows available to service payments or distributions on the securities in accordance with their terms; and

4. Based on my knowledge, taking into account all material aspects of the characteristics of the securitized assets, the structure of the securitization, and the related risks as described in the prospectus, there is a reasonable basis to conclude that the securitization is structured to produce, but is not guaranteed by this certification to produce, expected cash flows at times and in amounts to service scheduled payments of interest and the ultimate repayment of principal on the securities (or other scheduled or required distributions on the securities, however denominated) in accordance with their terms as described in the prospectus.

5. The foregoing certifications are given subject to any and all defenses available to me under the federal securities laws, including any and all defenses available to an executive officer that signed the registration statement of which the prospectus referred to in this certification is part.

Date:_____

_____   [Signature]

_____   [Title]

The certification must be signed by the chief executive officer of the depositor, as required by General Instruction I.B.1.(a) of Form SF-3.

(37) through (94) [Reserved]

(95) Mine Safety Disclosure Exhibit. A registrant that is an operator, or that has a subsidiary that is an operator, of a coal or other mine must provide the information required by Item 104 of Regulation S-K (§ 229.104 of this chapter) in an exhibit to its Exchange Act annual or quarterly report. For purposes of this Item:

(1) The term coal or other mine means a coal or other mine, as defined in section 3 of the Federal Mine Safety and Health Act of 1977 (30 U.S.C. 802), that is subject to the provisions of such Act

(2) The term operator has the meaning given the term in section 3 of the Federal Mine Safety and Health Act of 1977 (30 U.S.C. 802).

(3) The term subsidiary has the meaning given the term in Exchange Act Rule 12b–2 (17 CFR 240.12b–2).

(96) *Technical Report Summary.*

(i) A registrant that, pursuant to §§ 229.1300 through 229.1305 (subpart 229.1300 of Regulation S-K), discloses information concerning its mineral resources or mineral reserves must file a technical report summary by one or more qualified persons that, for each material property, identifies and summarizes the scientific and technical information and conclusions reached concerning an initial assessment used to support disclosure of mineral resources, or concerning a preliminary or final feasibility study used to support disclosure of mineral reserves. At its election, a registrant may also file a technical report summary from a qualified person that identifies and summarizes the information reviewed and conclusions reached by the qualified person about the registrant's exploration results. Please refer to § 229.1302(b) (Item 1302(b) of Regulation S-K) for when a registrant must file the technical report summary as an exhibit to its Securities Act registration statement or Exchange Act registration statement or report.

(ii) The technical report summary must not include large amounts of technical or other project data, either in the report or as appendices to the report. The qualified person must draft the summary to conform, to the extent practicable, with the plain English principles set forth in § 230.421 or § 240.13a-20 of this chapter.

(iii) (A) A technical report summary that reports the results of a preliminary or final feasibility study must provide all of the information specified in paragraph (b)(96)(iii)(B) of this section. A technical report summary that reports the results of an initial assessment must, at a minimum, provide the information specified in paragraphs (b)(96)(iii)(B)(*1*) through (*11*) and (*20*) through (*25*) of this section, and may also include the information specified in paragraph (b)(96)(iii)(B)(*19*) of this section. A technical report summary that reports exploration results must, at a minimum, provide the information specified in paragraphs (b)(96)(iii)(B)(*1*) through (*9*) and (*20*) through (*25*) of this section.

(B) A qualified person must include the following information in the technical report summary, as required by paragraph (b)(96)(iii)(A) of this section, to the extent the information is material.

(*1*) *Executive Summary.* Briefly summarize the most significant information in the technical report summary, including property description (including mineral rights) and ownership, geology and mineralization, the status of exploration, development and operations, mineral resource and mineral reserve estimates, summary capital and operating cost estimates, permitting requirements, and the qualified person's conclusions and recommendations. The executive summary must be brief and should not contain all of the detailed information in the technical support summary.

(*2*) *Introduction.* Disclose:

(*i*) The registrant for whom the technical report summary was prepared;

(*ii*) The terms of reference and purpose for which the technical report summary was prepared, including whether the technical report summary's purpose was to report mineral resources, mineral reserves, or exploration results;

(*iii*) The sources of information and data contained in the technical report summary or used in its preparation, with citations if applicable;

(*iv*) The details of the personal inspection on the property by each qualified person or, if applicable, the reason why a personal inspection has not been completed; and

(*v*) That the technical report summary updates a previously filed technical report summary, identified by name and date, when applicable.

(*3*) *Property Description.*

(*i*) Describe the location of the property, accurate to within one mile, using an easily recognizable coordinate system. The qualified person must provide appropriate maps, with proper engineering detail (such as scale, orientation, and titles) to portray the location of the property. Such maps must be legible on the page when printed.

(*ii*) Disclose the area of the property.

(*iii*) Disclose the name or number of each title, claim, mineral right, lease, or option under which the registrant and its subsidiaries have or will have the right to hold or operate the property. If held by leases or options, the registrant must provide the expiration dates of such leases or options and associated payments.

(*iv*) Describe the mineral rights, and how such rights have been obtained at this location, indicating any conditions that the registrant must meet in order to obtain or retain the property.

(*v*) Describe any significant encumbrances to the property, including current and future permitting requirements and associated timelines, permit conditions, and violations and fines.

(*vi*) Disclose any other significant factors and risks that may affect access, title, or the right or ability to perform work on the property.

(*vii*) If the registrant holds a royalty or similar interest in the property, except as provided under §§ 229.1303(a)(3) and 229.1304(a)(2), the information in paragraph (b)(96)(iii)(B)(3) of this section must be provided for the property that is owned or operated by a party other than the registrant. In this event, for example, the report must address the documents under which the owner or operator holds or operates the property, the mineral rights held by the owner or operator, conditions required to be met by the owner or operator, significant encumbrances, and significant factors and risks relating to the property or work on the property.

(*4*) *Accessibility, Climate, Local Resources, Infrastructure and Physiography.* Describe:

(*i*) The topography, elevation, and vegetation;

(*ii*) The means of access to the property, including highways, towns, rivers, railroads, and airports;

(*iii*) The climate and the length of the operating season, as applicable; and

(*iv*) The availability of and required infrastructure, including sources of water, electricity, personnel, and supplies.

(*5*) *History.* Describe:

(*i*) Previous operations, including the names of previous operators, insofar as known; and

(*ii*) The type, amount, quantity, and general results of exploration and development work undertaken by any previous owners or operators.

(*6*) *Geological Setting, Mineralization, and Deposit.*

(*i*) Describe briefly the regional, local, and property geology and the significant mineralized zones encountered on the property, including a summary of the surrounding rock types, relevant geological controls, and the length, width, depth, and continuity of the mineralization, together with a description of the type, character, and distribution of the mineralization.

(*ii*) Each mineral deposit type that is the subject of investigation or exploration together with the geological model or concepts being applied in the investigation or forming the basis of the exploration program.

(*iii*) The qualified person must include at least one stratigraphic column and one cross-section of the local geology to meet the requirements of paragraph (b)(96)(iii)(B)(*6*) of this section.

(7) *Exploration.* Describe the nature and extent of all relevant exploration work, conducted by or on behalf of, the registrant.

(*i*) For all exploration work other than drilling, describe: The procedures and parameters relating to the surveys and investigations; the sampling methods and sample quality, including whether the samples are representative, and any factors that may have resulted in sample biases; the location, number, type, nature, and spacing or density of samples collected, and the size of the area covered; and the significant results of and the qualified person's interpretation of the exploration information.

(*ii*) For drilling, describe: The type and extent of drilling including the procedures followed; any drilling, sampling, or recovery factors that could materially affect the accuracy and reliability of the results; and the material results and interpretation of the drilling results. For a technical report summary to support disclosure of exploration results, the qualified person must provide information on all samples or drill holes to meet the requirements of this paragraph. If some information is excluded, the qualified person must identify the omitted information and explain why that information is not material.

(*iii*) For characterization of hydrogeology, describe: The nature and quality of the sampling methods used to acquire data on surface and groundwater parameters; the type and appropriateness of laboratory techniques used to test for groundwater flow parameters such as permeability, and include discussions of the quality control and quality assurance procedures; results of laboratory testing and the qualified person's interpretation, including any material assumptions, which must include descriptions of permeable zones or aquifers, flow rates, in-situ saturation, recharge rates and water balance; and the groundwater models used to characterize aquifers, including material assumptions used in the modeling.

(*iv*) For geotechnical data, testing and analysis, describe: The nature and quality of the sampling methods used to acquire geotechnical data; the type and appropriateness of laboratory techniques used to test for soil and rock strength parameters, including discussions of the quality control and quality assurance procedures; and results of laboratory testing and the qualified person's interpretation, including any material assumptions.

(*v*) Reports must include a plan view of the property showing locations of all drill holes and other samples.

(*vi*) The technical report summary must include a description of data concerning drilling, hydrogeology, or geotechnical data only to the extent such data is relevant and available.

Instruction 1 to Paragraph (b)(96)(iii)(B)(7): The technical report summary must comply with all disclosure standards for exploration results under §§ 229.1300 through 229.1305 (subpart 229.1300 of Regulation S-K).

Instruction 2 to Paragraph (b)(96)(iii)(B)(7): For a technical report summary to support disclosure of mineral resources or mineral reserves, the qualified person can meet the requirements of paragraph (b)(96)(iii)(B)(7)(*ii*) of this section by providing sampling (including drilling) plans, representative plans, and cross-sections of results.

Instruction 3 to Paragraph (b)(96)(iii)(B)(7): If disclosing an exploration target, provide such disclosure in a subsection of the *Exploration* section of the technical report summary that is clearly captioned as a discussion of an exploration target. That section must include all of the disclosure required under § 229.1302(c).

(*8*) *Sample Preparation, Analyses, and Security.* Describe:

(*i*) Sample preparation methods and quality control measures employed prior to sending samples to an analytical or testing laboratory, sample splitting and reduction methods, and the security measures taken to ensure the validity and integrity of samples;

(*ii*) Sample preparation, assaying and analytical procedures used, the name and location of the analytical or testing laboratories, the relationship of the laboratory to the registrant, and whether the laboratories are certified by any standards association and the particulars of such certification;

(*iii*) The nature, extent, and results of quality control procedures and quality assurance actions taken or recommended to provide adequate confidence in the data collection and estimation process;

(*iv*) The adequacy of sample preparation, security, and analytical procedures, in the opinion of the qualified person; and

(*v*) If the analytical procedures used are not part of conventional industry practice, a justification by the qualified person for why he or she believes the procedure is appropriate in this instance.

(*9*) *Data Verification.* Describe the steps taken by the qualified person to verify the data being reported on or which is the basis of this technical report summary, including:

(*i*) Data verification procedures applied by the qualified person;

(*ii*) Any limitations on or failure to conduct such verification, and the reasons for any such limitations or failure; and

(*iii*) The qualified person's opinion on the adequacy of the data for the purposes used in the technical report summary.

(*10*) *Mineral Processing and Metallurgical Testing.* Describe:

(*i*) The nature and extent of the mineral processing or metallurgical testing and analytical procedures;

(*ii*) The degree to which the test samples are representative of the various types and styles of mineralization and the mineral deposit as a whole;

(*iii*) The name and location of the analytical or testing laboratories, the relationship of the laboratory to the registrant, whether the laboratories are certified by any standards association and the particulars of such certification;

(*iv*) The relevant results including the basis for any assumptions or predictions about recovery estimates. Discuss any processing factors or deleterious elements that could have a significant effect on potential economic extraction; and

(*v*) The adequacy of the data for the purposes used in the technical report summary, in the opinion of the qualified person. If the analytical procedures used in the analysis are not part of conventional industry practice, the qualified person must state so and provide a justification for why he or she believes the procedure is appropriate in this instance.

(*11*) *Mineral Resource Estimates*. If this item is included, the technical report summary must:

(*i*) Describe the key assumptions, parameters, and methods used to estimate the mineral resources, in sufficient detail for a reasonably informed person to understand the basis for and how the qualified person estimated the mineral resources. The technical report summary must include mineral resource estimates at a specific point of reference selected by the qualified person. The selected point of reference must be disclosed in the technical report summary;

(*ii*) Provide the qualified person's estimates of mineral resources for all commodities, including estimates of quantities, grade or quality, cut-off grades, and metallurgical or processing recoveries. Unless otherwise stated, cut-off grades also refer to net smelter returns, pay limits, and other similar terms. The qualified person preparing the mineral resource estimates must round off, to appropriate significant figures chosen to reflect order of accuracy, any estimates of quantity and grade or quality. If the qualified person chooses to disclose mineral resources inclusive of mineral reserves, he or she must also clearly state the mineral resources exclusive of mineral reserves in the technical report summary;

(*iii*) Include the qualified person's estimates of cut-off grades based on assumed costs for surface or underground operations and commodity prices that provide a reasonable basis for establishing the prospects of economic extraction for mineral resources. The qualified person must disclose the price used for each commodity and explain, with particularity, his or her reasons for using the selected price, including the material assumptions underlying the selection. This explanation must include disclosure of the time frame used to estimate the commodity price and unit costs for cut-off grade estimation and the reasons justifying the selection of that time frame. The qualified person may use a price set by contractual arrangement, provided that such price is reasonable, and the qualified person discloses that he or she is using a contractual price when disclosing the price used;

(*iv*) Provide the qualified person's classification of mineral resources into inferred, indicated, and measured mineral resources in accordance with § 229.1302(d)(1)(iii)(A) (Item 1302(d)(1)(iii)(A) of Regulation S-K). The qualified person must disclose the criteria used to classify a resource as inferred, indicated, or measured and must justify the classification;

(*v*) Discuss the uncertainty in the estimates of inferred, indicated, and measured mineral resources, and explain the sources of uncertainty and how they were considered in the uncertainty estimates. The qualified person must consider all sources of uncertainty associated with each class of mineral resources. Sources of uncertainty that affect such reporting of uncertainty include sampling or drilling methods, data processing and handling, geologic modeling, and estimation. The qualified person must support the disclosure of uncertainty associated with each class of mineral resources with a list of all factors considered and explain how those factors contributed to the final conclusion about the level of uncertainty underlying the resource estimates. The qualified person is not required to use estimates of confidence limits derived from geostatistics or other numerical methods to support the disclosure of uncertainty surrounding mineral resource classification. If the qualified person chooses to use confidence limit estimates from geostatistics or other numerical methods, he or she should consider the limitations of these methods and adjust the estimates appropriately to reflect sources of uncertainty that are not accounted for by these methods;

(*vi*) When reporting the grade or quality for a multiple commodity mineral resource as metal or mineral equivalent, disclose the individual grade of each metal or mineral and the commodity prices, recoveries, and any other relevant conversion factors used to estimate the metal or mineral equivalent grade; and

(*vii*) Provide the qualified person's opinion on whether all issues relating to all relevant technical and economic factors likely to influence the prospect of economic extraction can be resolved with further work.

Instruction 1 to Paragraph (b)(96)(iii)(B)(11): The technical report summary must comply with all disclosure standards for mineral resources under §§ 229.1300 through 229.1305 (subpart 229.1300 of Regulation S-K).

Instruction 2 to Paragraph (b)(96)(iii)(B)(11): Sections 229.1303 and 229.1304 (Items 1303 and 1304 of Regulation S-K) notwithstanding, in this technical report summary mineral resource estimates may be inclusive of mineral reserves so long as this is clearly stated with equal prominence to the rest of the item.

(*12*) *Mineral Reserve Estimates*. If this item is included, the technical report summary must:

(*i*) Describe the key assumptions, parameters, and methods used to estimate the mineral reserves, in sufficient detail for a reasonably informed person to understand the basis for converting, and how the qualified person converted, indicated and measured mineral resources into the mineral reserves. The technical report summary must include mineral reserve estimates at a specific point of reference selected by the qualified person. The qualified person must disclose the selected point of reference in the technical report summary;

(*ii*) Provide the qualified person's estimates of mineral reserves for all commodities, including estimates of quantities, grade or quality, cut-off grades, and metallurgical or processing recoveries. The qualified person preparing the mineral resource estimates must round off, to appropriate significant figures chosen to reflect order of accuracy, any estimates of quantity and grade or quality;

(*iii*) Include the qualified person's estimates of cut-off grades based on detailed cut-off grade analysis that includes a long term price that provides a reasonable basis for establishing that the project is economically viable. The qualified person must disclose the price used for each commodity and explain, with particularity, his or her reasons for using the selected price, including the material assumptions underlying the selection. This explanation must include disclosure of the time frame used to estimate the price and costs and the reasons justifying the selection of that time frame. The qualified person may use a price set by contractual arrangement, provided that such price is reasonable, and the qualified person discloses that he or she is using a contractual price when disclosing the price used;

(*iv*) Provide the qualified person's classification of mineral reserves into probable and proven mineral reserves in accordance with § 229.1302(e)(2) (Item 1302(e)(2) of Regulation S-K);

(*v*) When reporting the grade or quality for a multiple commodity mineral reserve as metal or mineral equivalent, disclose the individual grade of each metal or mineral and the commodity prices, recoveries, and any other relevant conversion factors used to estimate the metal or mineral equivalent grade; and

(*vi*) Provide the qualified person's opinion on how the mineral reserve estimates could be materially affected by risk factors associated with or changes to any aspect of the modifying factors.

Instruction 1 to Paragraph (b)(96)(iii)(B)(12): The technical report summary must comply with all disclosure standards for mineral reserves under §§ 229.1300 through 1305 (subpart 229.1300 of Regulation S-K).

(*13*) *Mining Methods.* Describe the current or proposed mining methods and the reasons for selecting these methods as the most suitable for the mineral reserves under consideration. Include:

(*i*) Geotechnical and hydrological models, and other parameters relevant to mine designs and plans;

(*ii*) Production rates, expected mine life, mining unit dimensions, and mining dilution and recovery factors;

(*iii*) Requirements for stripping, underground development, and back-filling;

(*iv*) Required mining equipment fleet and machinery, and personnel; and

(*v*) At least one map of the final mine outline.

(*14*) *Processing and Recovery Methods.* Describe the current or proposed mineral processing methods and the reasons for selecting these methods as the most suitable for extracting the valuable products from the mineralization under consideration. Include:

(*i*) A description or flow sheet of any current or proposed process plant;

(*ii*) Plant throughput and design, equipment characteristics and specifications;

(*iii*) Current or projected requirements for energy, water, process materials, and personnel; and

(*iv*) If the processing method, plant design, or other parameter has never been used to commercially extract the valuable product from such mineralization, a justification by the qualified person for why he or she believes the approach will be successful in this instance.

Instruction 1 to Paragraph (b)(96)(iii)(B)(14): If the processing method, plant design, or other parameter has never been used to commercially extract the valuable product from such mineralization and is still under development, then no mineral resources or reserves can be disclosed on the basis of that method, design, or other parameter.

(*15*) *Infrastructure.* Describe the required infrastructure for the project, including roads, rail, port facilities, dams, dumps and leach pads, tailings disposal, power, water, and pipelines, as applicable. Include at least one map showing the layout of the infrastructure.

(*16*) *Market Studies.* Describe the market for the products of the mine, including justification for demand or sales over the life of the mine (or length of cash flow projections). Include:

(*i*) Information concerning markets for the property's production, including the nature and material terms of any agency relationships and the results of any relevant market studies, commodity price projections, product valuation, market entry strategies, and product specification requirements; and

(*ii*) Descriptions of all material contracts required for the issuer to develop the property, including mining, concentrating, smelting, refining, transportation, handling, hedging arrangements, and forward sales contracts. State which contracts have been executed and which are still under negotiation. For all contracts with affiliated parties, discuss whether the registrant obtained the same terms, rates or charges as could be obtained had the contract been negotiated at arm's length with an unaffiliated third party.

(*17*) *Environmental Studies, Permitting, and Plans, Negotiations, or Agreements with Local Individuals or Groups.* Describe the factors pertaining to environmental compliance, permitting, and local individuals or groups, which are related to the project. Include:

(*i*) The results of environmental studies (*e.g.*, environmental baseline studies or impact assessments);

(ii) Requirements and plans for waste and tailings disposal, site monitoring, and water management during operations and after mine closure;

(*iii*) Project permitting requirements, the status of any permit applications, and any known requirements to post performance or reclamation bonds;

(*iv*) Plans, negotiations, or agreements with local individuals or groups;

(*v*) Mine closure plans, including remediation and reclamation plans, and the associated costs;

(*vi*) The qualified person's opinion on the adequacy of current plans to address any issues related to environmental compliance, permitting, and local individuals or groups; and

(*vii*) Descriptions of any commitments to ensure local procurement and hiring.

(*18*) *Capital and Operating Costs.*

(*i*) Provide estimates of capital and operating costs, with the major components set out in tabular form. Explain and justify the basis for the cost estimates including any contingency budget estimates. State the accuracy level of the capital and operating cost estimates.

(*ii*) To assess the accuracy of the capital and operating cost estimates, the qualified person must take into account the risks associated with the specific engineering estimation methods used to arrive at the estimates. As part of this analysis, the qualified person must take into consideration the accuracy of the estimation methods in prior similar environments. The accuracy of capital and operating cost estimates must comply with § 229.1302 (Item 1302 of Regulation S-K).

(*19*) *Economic Analysis.*

(*i*) Describe the key assumptions, parameters, and methods used to demonstrate economic viability, and provide all material assumptions including discount rates, exchange rates, commodity prices, and taxes, royalties, and other government levies or interests applicable to the mineral project or to production, and to revenues or income from the mineral project.

(*ii*) Disclose the results of the economic analysis, including annual cash flow forecasts based on an annual production schedule for the life of project, and measures of economic viability such as net present value (NPV), internal rate of return (IRR), and payback period of capital.

(*iii*) Include sensitivity analysis results using variants in commodity price, grade, capital and operating costs, or other significant input parameters, as appropriate, and discuss the impact on the results of the economic analysis.

(*iv*) The qualified person may, but is not required to, include an economic analysis in an initial assessment. If the qualified person includes an economic analysis in an initial assessment, the qualified person must also include a statement, of equal prominence to the rest of this section, that, unlike mineral reserves, mineral resources do not have demonstrated economic viability. The qualified person may include inferred mineral resources in the economic analysis only if he or she satisfies the conditions set forth in § 229.1302(d)(4)(ii) (Item 1302(d)(4)(ii) of Regulation S-K).

(*20*) *Adjacent Properties*. Where applicable, a qualified person may include relevant information concerning an adjacent property if:

(*i*) Such information was publicly disclosed by the owner or operator of the adjacent property;

(*ii*) The source of the information is identified;

(*iii*) The qualified person states that he or she has been unable to verify the information and that the information is not necessarily indicative of the mineralization on the property that is the subject of the technical report summary; and

(*iv*) The technical report summary clearly distinguishes between the information from the adjacent property and the information from the property that is the subject of the technical report summary.

(*21*) *Other Relevant Data and Information*. Include any additional information or explanation necessary to provide a complete and balanced presentation of the value of the property to the registrant. Information included in this item must comply with §§ 299.1300 through 229.1305 (subpart 229.1300 of Regulation S-K).

(*22*) *Interpretation and Conclusions*. The qualified person must summarize the interpretations of and conclusions based on the data and analysis in the technical report summary. He or she must also discuss any significant risks and uncertainties that could reasonably be expected to affect the reliability or confidence in the exploration results, mineral resource or mineral reserve estimates, or projected economic outcomes.

(*23*) *Recommendations*. If applicable, the qualified person must describe the recommendations for additional work with associated costs. If the additional work program is divided into phases, the costs for each phase must be provided along with decision points at the end of each phase.

(*24*) *References*. Include a list of all references cited in the technical report summary in sufficient detail so that a reader can locate each reference.

(*25*) *Reliance on Information Provided By the Registrant*. If relying on information provided by the registrant for matters discussed in the technical report summary, as permitted under § 229.1302(f), provide the disclosure required pursuant to § 229.1302(f)(2).

(97) through (98) [Reserved].

(99) *Additional exhibits*—(i) Any additional exhibits which the registrant may wish to file shall be so marked as to indicate clearly the subject matters to which they refer.

(ii) If pursuant to Section 11(a) of the Securities Act (15 U.S.C. 77k(a)) an issuer makes generally available to its security holders an earnings statement covering a period of at least 12 months beginning after the effective date of the registration statement, and if such earnings statement is made available by "other methods" than those specified in paragraph (a) or (b) of § 230.158 of this chapter, it must be filed as an exhibit to the Form 10-Q or the Form 10-K, as appropriate, covering the period in which the earnings statement was released.

(100) [Reserved.]

(101) *Interactive Data File*. Where a registrant prepares its financial statements in accordance with either generally accepted accounting principles as used in the United States or International Financial Reporting Standards as issued by the International Accounting Standards Board, an Interactive Data File (§ 232.11 of this chapter) is:

(i) *Required to Be Submitted*. Required to be submitted to the Commission in the manner provided by § 232.405 of this chapter if the registrant is not registered under the Investment Company Act of 1940 (15 U.S.C. 80a-1 *et seq.*), except that an Interactive Data File:

(A) First is required for a periodic report on Form 10-Q (§ 249.308a of this chapter), Form 20-F (§ 249.220f of this chapter), or Form 40-F (§ 249.240f of this chapter), as applicable;

(B) Is required for a registration statement under the Securities Act only if the registration statement contains a price or price range; and

(C) Is required for a Form 8-K (§ 249.308 of this chapter):

(*1*) Only when the Form 8-K contains audited annual financial statements that are a revised version of financial statements that previously were filed with the Commission and that have been revised pursuant to applicable accounting standards to reflect the effects of certain subsequent events, including a discontinued operation, a change in reportable segments or a change in accounting principle. In such case, the Interactive Data File will be required only as to such revised financial statements regardless of whether the Form 8-K contains other financial statements;

(*2*) Except that a business development company as defined in Section 2(a)(48) of the Investment Company Act of 1940 (15 U.S.C. 80a-2(a)(48)) also is required to submit an Interactive Data File to the extent required by § 232.405(b)(3)(iii) of this chapter.

(ii) *Permitted to Be Submitted*. Permitted to be submitted to the Commission in the manner provided by Rule 405 of Regulation S-T (§ 232.405 of this chapter) if the:

(A) Registrant is not registered under the Investment Company Act of 1940 (15 U.S.C. 80a-1 *et seq.*); and

(B) Interactive Data File is not required to be submitted to the Commission under paragraph (b)(101)(i) of this section.

Instruction 1 to Paragraphs (b)(101)(i) and (ii): When an Interactive Data File is submitted as provided by § 232.405(a)(3)(i) of this chapter, the exhibit index must include the word "Inline" within the title description for any eXtensible Business Reporting Language (XBRL)-related exhibit.

(iii) Not permitted to be submitted to the Commission if the registrant is registered under the Investment Company Act of 1940 (15 U.S.C. 80a-1 *et seq.*).

(102) *Asset Data File*. An Asset Data File (as defined in § 232.11 of this chapter) filed pursuant to Item 1111(h)(3) of Regulation AB (§ 229.1111(h)(3)).

(103) *Asset Related Document*. Additional asset-level information or explanatory language pursuant to Item 1111(h)(4) and (5) of Regulation AB (§ 229.1111(h)(4) and (h)(5)).

(104) *Cover Page Interactive Data File*. A Cover Page Interactive Data File (as defined in § 232.11 of this chapter) as required by Rule 406 of Regulation S-T (17 CFR 232.406), and in the manner provided by the EDGAR Filer Manual.

(105) [Reserved].

(106) *Static Pool*. If not included in the prospectus filed in accordance with § 230.424(b)(2) or (5) and (h) of this chapter, static pool disclosure as required by § 229.1105.

Subpart 700—Miscellaneous

Item 701. Recent Sales of Unregistered Securities; Use of Proceeds from Registered Securities

Furnish the following information as to all securities of the registrant sold by the registrant within the past three years which were not registered under the Securities Act. Include sales of reacquired securities, as well as new issues, securities issued in exchange for property, services, or other securities, and new securities resulting from the modification of outstanding securities.

(a) *Securities sold*. Give the date of sale and the title and amount of securities sold.

(b) *Underwriters and other purchasers.* Give the names of the principal underwriters, if any. As to any such securities not publicly offered, name the persons or identify the class of persons to whom the securities were sold.

(c) *Consideration.* As to securities sold for cash, state the aggregate offering price and the aggregate underwriting discounts or commissions. As to any securities sold otherwise than for cash, state the nature of the transaction and the nature and aggregate amount of consideration received by the registrant.

(d) *Exemption from registration claimed.* Indicate the section of the Securities Act or the rule of the Commission under which exemption from registration was claimed and state briefly the facts relied upon to make the exemption available.

(e) *Terms of conversion or exercise.* If the information called for by this paragraph (e) is being presented on Form 8-K, Form 10-Q, Form 10-K or Form 10-D (§§ 249.308, 249.308a, 249.310 or § 249.312) under the Exchange Act, and where the securities sold by the registrant are convertible or exchangeable into equity securities, or are warrants or options representing equity securities, disclose the terms of conversion or exercise of the securities.

(f) *Use of Proceeds.* As required by § 230.463 of this chapter, following the effective date of the first registration statement filed under the Securities Act by an issuer, the issuer or successor issuer shall report the use of proceeds on its first periodic report filed pursuant to sections 13(a) and 15(d) of the Exchange Act (15 U.S.C. 78m(a) and 78o(d)) after effectiveness of its Securities Act registration statement, and thereafter on each of its subsequent periodic reports filed pursuant to sections 13(a) and 15(d) of the Exchange Act through the later of disclosure of the application of all the offering proceeds, or disclosure of the termination of the offering. If a report of the use of proceeds is required with respect to the first effective registration statement of the predecessor issuer, the successor issuer shall provide such a report. The information provided pursuant to paragraphs (f)(2) through (f)(4) of this Item need only be provided with respect to the first periodic report filed pursuant to sections 13(a) and 15(d) of the Exchange Act after effectiveness of the registration statement filed under the Securities Act. Subsequent periodic reports filed pursuant to sections 13(a) and 15(d) of the Exchange Act need only provide the information required in paragraphs (f)(2) through (f)(4) of this Item if any of such required information has changed since the last periodic report filed. In disclosing the use of proceeds in the first periodic report filed pursuant to the Exchange Act, the issuer or successor issuer should include the following information:

(1) The effective date of the Securities Act registration statement for which the use of proceeds information is being disclosed and the Commission file number assigned to the registration statement;

(2) If the offering has commenced, the offering date, and if the offering has not commenced, an explanation why it has not;

(3) If the offering terminated before any securities were sold, an explanation for such termination; and

(4) If the offering did not terminate before any securities were sold, disclose:

(i) Whether the offering has terminated and, if so, whether it terminated before the sale of all securities registered;

(ii) The name(s) of the managing underwriter(s), if any;

(iii) The title of each class of securities registered and, where a class of convertible securities is being registered, the title of any class of securities into which such securities may be converted;

(iv) For each class of securities (other than a class of securities into which a class of convertible securities registered may be converted without additional payment to the issuer) the following information, provided for both the account of the issuer and the account(s) of any selling security holder(s): the amount registered, the aggregate price of the offering amount registered, the amount sold and the aggregate offering price of the amount sold to date;

(v) From the effective date of the Securities Act registration statement to the ending date of the reporting period, the amount of expenses incurred for the issuer's account in connection with the issuance and distribution of the securities registered for underwriting discounts and commissions, finders'fees, expenses paid to or for underwriters, other expenses and total expenses. Indicate if a reasonable estimate for the amount of expenses incurred is provided instead of the actual amount of expense. Indicate whether such payments were:

(A) Direct or indirect payments to directors, officers, general partners of the issuer or their associates; to persons owning ten (10) percent or more of any class of equity securities of the issuer; and to affiliates of the issuer; or

(B) Direct or indirect payments to others;

(vi) The net offering proceeds to the issuer after deducting the total expenses described in paragraph (f)(4)(v) of this Item;

(vii) From the effective date of the Securities Act registration statement to the ending date of the reporting period, the amount of net offering proceeds to the issuer used for construction of plant, building and facilities; purchase and installation of machinery and equipment; purchases of real estate; acquisition of other business(es); repayment of indebtedness; working capital; temporary investments (which should be specified); and any other purposes for which at least five (5) percent of the issuer's total offering proceeds or $100,000 (whichever is less) has been used (which should be specified). Indicate if a reasonable estimate for the amount of net offering proceeds applied is provided instead of the actual amount of net offering proceeds used. Indicate whether such payments were:

(A) Direct or indirect payments to directors, officers, general partners of the issuer or their associates; to persons owning ten (10) percent or more of any class of equity securities of the issuer; and to affiliates of the issuer; or

(B) Direct or indirect payments to others; and

(viii) If the use of proceeds in paragraph (f)(4)(vii) of this Item represents a material change in the use of proceeds described in the prospectus, the issuer should describe briefly the material change.

Instructions. 1. Information required by this Item 701 need not be set forth as to notes, drafts, bills of exchange, or bankers' acceptances which mature not later than one year from the date of issuance.

2. If the sales were made in a series of transactions, the information may be given by such totals and periods as will reasonably convey the information required.

Item 702. Indemnification of Directors and Officers

State the general effect of any statute, charter provisions, by-laws, contract or other arrangements under which any controlling persons, director or officer of the registrant is insured or indemnified in any manner against liability which he may incur in his capacity as such.

Item 703. Purchases of Equity Securities by the Issuer and Affiliated Purchasers

(a) In the following tabular format, provide the information specified in paragraph (b) of this Item with respect to any purchase made by or on behalf of the issuer or any "affiliated purchaser," as defined in § 240.10b-18(a)(3) of this chapter, of shares or other units of any class of the issuer's equity securities that is registered by the issuer pursuant to section 12 of the Exchange Act (15 U.S.C. 78*l*).

ISSUER PURCHASES OF EQUITY SECURITIES

Period	(a) Total Number of Shares (or Units) Purchased	(b) Average Price Paid per Share (or Unit)	(c) Total Number of Shares (or Units) Purchased as Part of Publicly Announced Plans or Programs	(d) Maximum Number (or Approximate Dollar Value) of Shares (or Units) that May Yet Be Purchased Under the Plans or Programs
Month #1 (identify beginning and ending dates)				
Month #2 (identify beginning and ending dates)				
Month #3 (identify beginning and ending dates)				
Total				

(b) The table shall include the following information for each class or series of securities for each month included in the period covered by the report:

(1) The total number of shares (or units) purchased (column (a));

Instruction to paragraph (b)(1) of Item 703

Include in this column all issuer repurchases, including those made pursuant to publicly announced plans or programs and those not made pursuant to publicly announced plans or programs. Briefly disclose, by footnote to the table, the number of shares purchased other than through a publicly announced plan or program and the nature of the transaction (*e.g.*, whether the purchases were made in open-market transactions, tender offers, in satisfaction of the company's obligations upon exercise of outstanding put options issued by the company, or other transactions).

(2) The average price paid per share (or unit) (column (b));

(3) The total number of shares (or units) purchased as part of publicly announced repurchase plans or programs (column (c)); and

(4) The maximum number (or approximate dollar value) of shares (or units) that may yet be purchased under the plans or programs (column (d)).

Instructions to paragraphs (b)(3) and (b)(4) of Item 703

1. In the table, disclose this information in the aggregate for all plans or programs publicly announced.

2. By footnote to the table, indicate:

a. The date each plan or program was announced;

b. The dollar amount (or share or unit amount) approved;

c. The expiration date (if any) of each plan or program;

d. Each plan or program that has expired during the period covered by the table; and

e. Each plan or program the issuer has determined to terminate prior to expiration, or under which the issuer does not intend to make further purchases.

Instruction to Item 703

Disclose all purchases covered by this Item, including purchases that do not satisfy the conditions of the safe harbor of § 240.10b-18 of this chapter.

Subpart 800—List of Industry Guides

Item 801. Securities Act Industry Guides

(a) Guide 1. [Removed and reserved in Release No. 33-7300, May 31, 1996, effective July 15, 1996, 61 F.R. 30397.]

(b) [Reserved.]

(c) Guide 3. Statistical disclosure by bank holding companies.

(d) Guide 4. Prospectuses relating to interests in oil and gas programs.

(e) Guide 5. Preparation of registration statements relating to interests in real estate limited partnerships.

(f) Guide 6. Disclosures concerning unpaid claims and claim adjustment expenses of property-casualty underwriters.

Item 802. Exchange Act Industry Guides

(a) Guide 1. [Removed and reserved in Release No. 33-7300, May 31, 1996, effective July 15, 1996, 61 F.R. 30397.]

(b) [Reserved.]

(c) Guide 3. Statistical disclosure by bank holding companies.

(d) Guide 4. Disclosures concerning unpaid claims and claim adjustment expenses of property-casualty underwriters.

(e) [Reserved].

(f) [Reserved].

N.B. The following is not a complete text of Regulation S-X. It omits a number of statutory provisions entirely, and also omits certain subsections of provisions that are partially included.

Article 2—Qualifications and Reports of Accountants

Item 2-01. Qualifications of Accountants

Preliminary Note

Rule 2-01 is designed to ensure that auditors are qualified and independent of their audit clients both in fact and in appearance. Accordingly, the rule sets forth restrictions on financial, employment, and business relationships between an accountant and an audit client and restrictions on an accountant providing certain non-audit services to an audit client.

Rule 2-01(b) sets forth the general standard of auditor independence. Paragraphs (c)(1) to (c)(5) reflect the application of the general standard to particular circumstances. The rule does not purport to, and the Commission could not, consider all circumstances that raise independence concerns, and these are subject to the general standard in paragraph 2-01(b). In considering this standard, the Commission looks in the first instance to whether a relationship or the provision of a service: (a) creates a mutual or conflicting interest between the accountant and the audit client; (b) places the accountant in the position of auditing his or her own work; (c) results in the accountant acting as management or an employee of the audit client; or (d) places the accountant in a position of being an advocate for the audit client.

These factors are general guidance only and their application may depend on particular facts and circumstances. For that reason, Rule 2-01 provides that, in determining whether an accountant is independent, the Commission will consider all relevant facts and circumstances. For the same reason, registrants and accountants are encouraged to consult with the Commission's Office of the Chief Accountant before entering into relationships, including relationships involving the provision of services, that are not explicitly described in the Rule.

(a) The Commission will not recognize any person as a certified public accountant who is not duly registered and in good standing as such under the laws of the place of his residence or principal office. The Commission will not recognize any person as a public accountant who is not in good standing and entitled to practice as such under the laws of the place of his residence or principal office.

(b) The Commission will not recognize an accountant as independent, with respect to an audit client, if the accountant is not, or a reasonable investor with knowledge of all relevant facts and circumstances would conclude that the accountant is not, capable of exercising objective and impartial judgment on all issues encompassed within the accountant's engagement. In determining whether an accountant is independent, the Commission will consider all relevant circumstances, including all relationships between the accountant and the audit client, and not just those relating to reports filed with the Commission.

(c) This paragraph sets forth a non-exclusive specification of circumstances inconsistent with paragraph (b) of this section.

(1) *Financial relationships*. An accountant is not independent if, at any point during the audit and professional engagement period, the accountant has a direct financial interest or a material indirect financial interest in the accountant's audit client, such as:

(i) *Investments in audit clients*. An accountant is not independent when:

(A) The accounting firm, any covered person in the firm, or any of his or her immediate family members, has any direct investment in an audit client, such as stocks, bonds, notes, options, or other securities. The term *direct investment* includes an investment in an audit client through an intermediary if:

(*1*) The accounting firm, covered person, or immediate family member, alone or together with other persons, supervises or participates in the intermediary's investment decisions or has control over the intermediary; or

(*2*) The intermediary is not a diversified management investment company, as defined by Section 5(b)(1) of the Investment Company Act of 1940, 15 U.S.C. 80a-5(b)(1), and has an investment in the audit client that amounts to 20% or more of the value of the intermediary's total investments.

(B) Any partner, principal, shareholder, or professional employee of the accounting firm, any of his or her immediate family members, any close family member of a covered person in the firm, or any group of the above persons has filed a Schedule 13D or 13G (17 CFR 240.13d-101 or 240.13d-102) with the Commission indicating beneficial ownership of more than five percent of an audit client's equity securities or controls an audit client, or a close family member of a partner, principal, or shareholder of the accounting firm controls an audit client.

(C) The accounting firm, any covered person in the firm, or any of his or her immediate family members, serves as voting trustee of a trust, or executor of an estate, containing the securities of an audit client, unless the accounting firm, covered person in the firm, or immediate family member has no authority to make investment decisions for the trust or estate.

(D) The accounting firm, any covered person in the firm, any of his or her immediate family members, or any group of the above persons has any material indirect investment in an audit client. For purposes of this paragraph, the term *material indirect investment* does not include ownership by any covered person in the firm, any of his or her immediate family members, or any group of the above persons of 5% or less of the outstanding shares of a diversified management investment company, as defined by Section 5(b)(1) of the Investment Company Act of 1940, 15 U.S.C. 80a-5(b)(1), that invests in an audit client.

(E) The accounting firm, any covered person in the firm, or any of his or her immediate family members:

(*1*) Has any direct or material indirect investment in an entity where:

(*i*) An audit client has an investment in that entity that is material to the audit client and has the ability to exercise significant influence over that entity; or

(*ii*) The entity has an investment in an audit client that is material to that entity and has the ability to exercise significant influence over that audit client;

(*2*) Has any material investment in an entity over which an audit client has the ability to exercise significant influence; or

(*3*) Has the ability to exercise significant influence over an entity that has the ability to exercise significant influence over an audit client.

(ii) *Other financial interests in audit client*. An accountant is not independent when the accounting firm, any covered person in the firm, or any of his or her immediate family members has:

(A) *Loans/Debtor-Creditor Relationship*.

(*1*) Any loan (including any margin loan) to or from an audit client, or an audit client's officers, directors, or beneficial owners (known through reasonable inquiry) of the audit client's equity securities where such beneficial owner has significant influence over the audit client, except for the following loans obtained from a financial institution under its normal lending procedures, terms, and requirements:

(*i*) Automobile loans and leases collateralized by the automobile;

(*ii*) Loans fully collateralized by the cash surrender value of an insurance policy;

(*iii*) Loans fully collateralized by cash deposits at the same financial institution; and

(*iv*) A mortgage loan collateralized by the borrower's primary residence provided the loan was not obtained while the covered person in the firm was a covered person.

(*2*) For purposes of paragraph (c)(1)(ii)(A) of this section:

(*i*) The term *audit client* for a fund under audit excludes an y other fund that otherwise would be considered an *affiliate of the audit client*;

(*ii*) The term *fund* means: An investment company or an entity that would be an investment company but for the exclusions provided by Section 3(c) of the Investment Company Act of 1940 (15 U.S.C. 80a-3(c)); or a commodity pool as defined in Section 1a(10) of the U.S. Commodity Exchange Act, as amended [(7 U.S.C. 1-1a(10)], that is not an investment company or an entity that would be an investment company but for the exclusions provided by Section 3(c) of the Investment Company Act of 1940 (15 U.S.C. 80a-3(c)).

(B) *Savings and checking accounts*. Any savings, checking, or similar account at a bank, savings and loan, or similar institution that is an audit client, if the account has a balance that exceeds the amount insured by the Federal Deposit Insurance Corporation or any similar insurer, except that an accounting firm account may have an uninsured balance provided that the likelihood of the bank, savings and loan, or similar institution experiencing financial difficulties is remote.

(C) *Broker-dealer accounts*. Brokerage or similar accounts maintained with a broker-dealer that is an audit client, if:

(*1*) Any such account includes any asset other than cash or securities (within the meaning of "security" provided in the Securities Investor Protection Act of 1970 ("SIPA") (15 U.S.C. 78aaa *et seq.*));

(*2*) The value of assets in the accounts exceeds the amount that is subject to a Securities Investor Protection Corporation advance, for those accounts, under Section 9 of SIPA (15 U.S.C. 78fff-3); or

(*3*) With respect to non-U.S. accounts not subject to SIPA protection, the value of assets in the accounts exceeds the amount insured or protected by a program similar to SIPA.

(D) *Futures commission merchant accounts*. Any futures, commodity, or similar account maintained with a futures commission merchant that is an audit client.

(E) *Credit cards*. Any aggregate outstanding credit card balance owed to a lender that is an audit client that is not reduced to $10,000 or less on a current basis taking into consideration the payment due date and any available grace period.

(F) *Insurance products*. Any individual policy issued by an insurer that is an audit client unless:

(*1*) The policy was obtained at a time when the covered person in the firm was not a covered person in the firm; and

(*2*) The likelihood of the insurer becoming insolvent is remote.

(G) *Investment companies*.Any financial interest in an entity that is part of an investment company complex that includes an audit client.

(iii) *Exceptions*. Notwithstanding paragraphs (c)(1)(i) and (c)(1)(ii) of this section, an accountant will not be deemed not independent if:

(A) *Inheritance and gift.* Any person acquires an unsolicited financial interest, such as through an unsolicited gift or inheritance, that would cause an accountant to be not independent under paragraph (c)(1)(i) or (c)(1)(ii) of this section, and the financial interest is disposed of as soon as practicable, but no later than 30 days after the person has knowledge of and the right to dispose of the financial interest.

(B) *New audit engagement.* Any person has a financial interest that would cause an accountant to be not independent under paragraph (c)(1)(i) or (c)(1)(ii) of this section, and:

(*1*) The accountant did not audit the client's financial statements for the immediately preceding fiscal year; and

(*2*) The accountant is independent under paragraph (c)(1)(i) and (c)(1)(ii) of this section before the earlier of:

(*i*) Signing an initial engagement letter or other agreement to provide audit, review, or attest services to the audit client; or

(*ii*) Commencing any audit, review, or attest procedures (including planning the audit of the client's financial statements).

(C) *Employee compensation and benefit plans.* An immediate family member of a person who is a covered person in the firm only by virtue of paragraphs (f)(11)(iii) or (f)(11)(iv) of this section has a financial interest that would cause an accountant to be not independent under paragraph (c)(1)(i) or (c)(1)(ii) of this section, and the acquisition of the financial interest was an unavoidable consequence of participation in his or her employer's employee compensation or benefits program, provided that the financial interest, other than unexercised employee stock options, is disposed of as soon as practicable, but no later than 30 days after the person has the right to dispose of the financial interest.

(iv) *Audit clients' financial relationships.* An accountant is not independent when:

(A) *Investments by the audit client in the accounting firm.* An audit client has, or has agreed to acquire, any direct investment in the accounting firm, such as stocks, bonds, notes, options, or other securities, or the audit client's officers or directors are record or beneficial owners of more than 5% of the equity securities of the accounting firm.

(B) *Underwriting.* An accounting firm engages an audit client to act as an underwriter, broker-dealer, market-maker, promoter, or analyst with respect to securities issued by the accounting firm.

(2) *Employment relationships.* An accountant is not independent if, at any point during the audit and professional engagement period, the accountant has an employment relationship with an audit client, such as:

(i) *Employment at audit client of accountant.* A current partner, principal, shareholder, or professional employee of the accounting firm is employed by the audit client or serves as a member of the board of directors or similar management or governing body of the audit client.

(ii) *Employment at audit client of certain relatives of accountant.* A close family member of a covered person in the firm is in an accounting role or financial reporting oversight role at an audit client, or was in such a role during any period covered by an audit for which the covered person in the firm is a covered person.

(iii) *Employment at audit client of former employee of accounting firm.*

(A) A former partner, principal, shareholder, or professional employee of an accounting firm is in an accounting role or financial reporting oversight role at an audit client, unless the individual:

(*1*) Does not influence the accounting firm's operations or financial policies;

(*2*) Has no capital balances in the accounting firm; and

(*3*) Has no financial arrangement with the accounting firm other than one providing for regular payment of a fixed dollar amount (which is not dependent on the revenues, profits, or earnings of the accounting firm):

(*i*) Pursuant to a fully funded retirement plan, rabbi trust, or, in jurisdictions in which a rabbi trust does not exist, a similar vehicle; or

(*ii*) In the case of a former professional employee who was not a partner, principal, or shareholder of the accounting firm and who has been disassociated from the accounting firm for more than five years, that is immaterial to the former professional employee; and

(B) A former partner, principal, shareholder, or professional employee of an accounting firm is in a financial reporting oversight role at an issuer (as defined in section 10A(f) of the Securities Exchange Act of 1934 (15 U.S.C. 78j-1(f)), except an issuer that is an investment company registered under section 8 of the Investment Company Act of 1940 (15 U.S.C. 80a-8), unless the individual:

(1) Employed by the issuer was not a member of the audit engagement team of the issuer during the one year period preceding the date that audit procedures commenced for the fiscal period that included the date of initial employment of the audit engagement team member by the issuer;

(2) For purposes of paragraph (c)(2)(iii)(B)(1) of this section, the following individuals are not considered to be members of the audit engagement team:

(i) Persons, other than the lead partner and the concurring partner, who provided ten or fewer hours of audit, review, or attest services during the period covered by paragraph (c)(2)(iii)(B)(1) of this section;

(ii) Individuals employed by the issuer as a result of a business combination between an issuer that is an audit client and the employing entity, provided employment was not in contemplation of the business combination and the audit committee of the successor issuer is aware of the prior employment relationship;and

(iii) Individuals that are employed by the issuer due to an emergency or other unusual situation provided that the audit committee determines that the relationship is in the interest of investors;

(3) For purposes of paragraph (c)(2)(iii)(B)(1) of this section, audit procedures are deemed to have commenced for a fiscal period the day following the filing of the issuer's periodic annual report with the Commission covering the previous fiscal period; or

(C) A former partner, principal, shareholder, or professional employee of an accounting firm is in a financial reporting oversight role with respect to an investment company registered under section 8 of the Investment Company Act of 1940 (15 U.S.C. 80a-8), if

(*1*) The former partner, principal, shareholder, or professional employee of an accounting firm is employed in a financial reporting oversight role related to the operations and financial reporting of the registered investment company at an entity in the investment company complex, as defined in (f)(14) of this section, that includes the registered investment company;and

(*2*) The former partner, principal, shareholder, or professional employee of an accounting firm employed by the registered investment company or any entity in the investment company complex was a member of the audit engagement team of the registered investment company or any other registered investment company in the investment company complex during the one year period preceding the date that audit procedures commenced that included the date of initial employment of the audit engagement team member by the registered investment company or any entity in the investment company complex.

(*3*) For purposes of paragraph (c)(2)(iii)(C)(2) of this section, the following individuals are not considered to be members of the audit engagement team:

(*i*) Persons, other than the lead partner and concurring partner, who provided ten or fewer hours of audit, review or attest services during the period covered by paragraph (c)(2)(iii)(C)(2) of this section;

(*ii*) Individuals employed by the registered investment company or any entity in the investment company complex as a result of a business combination between a registered investment company or any entity in the investment company complex that is an audit client and the employing entity, provided employment was not in contemplation of the business combination and the audit committee of the registered investment company is aware of the prior employment relationship; and

(*iii*) Individuals that are employed by the registered investment company or any entity in the investment company complex due to an emergency or other unusual situation provided that the audit committee determines that the relationship is in the interest of investors.

(*4*) For purposes of paragraph (c) (2) (iii) (C) (*2*) of this section, audit procedures are deemed to have commenced the day following the filing of the registered investment company's periodic annual report with the Commission.

(iv) *Employment at accounting firm of former employee of audit client.* A former officer, director, or employee of an audit client becomes a partner, principal, shareholder, or professional employee of the accounting firm, unless the individual does not participate in, and is not in a position to influence, the audit of the financial statements of the audit client covering any period during which he or she was employed by or associated with that audit client.

(3) *Business relationships.* An accountant is not independent if, at any point during the audit and professional engagement period, the accounting firm or any covered person in the firm has any direct or material indirect business relationship with an audit client, or with persons associated with the audit client in a decision-making capacity, such as an audit client's officers, directors, or substantial stockholders. The relationships described in this paragraph do not include a relationship in which the accounting firm or covered person in the firm provides professional services to an audit client or is a consumer in the ordinary course of business.

(4) *Non-audit services.* An accountant is not independent if, at any point during the audit and professional engagement period, the accountant provides the following non-audit services to an audit client:

(i) *Bookkeeping or other services related to the accounting records or financial statements of the audit client.* Any service, unless it is reasonable to conclude that the results of these services will not be subject to audit procedures during an audit of the audit client's financial statements, including:

(A) Maintaining or preparing the audit client's accounting records;

(B) Preparing the audit client's financial statements that are filed with the Commission or that form the basis of financial statements filed with the Commission; or

(C) Preparing or originating source data underlying the audit client's financial statements.

(ii) *Financial information systems design and implementation.* Any service, unless it is reasonable to conclude that the results of these services will not be subject to audit procedures during an audit of the audit client's financial statements, including:

(A) Directly or indirectly operating, or supervising the operation of, the audit client's information system or managing the audit client's local area network; or

(B) Designing or implementing a hardware or software system that aggregates source data underlying the financial statements or generates information that is significant to the audit client's financial statements or other financial information systems taken as a whole.

(iii) *Appraisal or valuation services, fairness opinions, or contribution-in-kind reports.* Any appraisal service, valuation service, or any service involving a fairness opinion or contribution-in-kind report for an audit client, unless it is reasonable to conclude that the results of these services will not be subject to audit procedures during an audit of the audit client's financial statements.

(iv) *Actuarial services*. Any actuarially-oriented advisory service involving the determination of amounts recorded in the financial statements and related accounts for the audit client other than assisting a client in understanding the methods, models, assumptions, and inputs used in computing an amount, unless it is reasonable to conclude that the results of these services will not be subject to audit procedures during an audit of the audit client's financial statements.

(v) *Internal audit outsourcing services*. Any internal audit service that has been outsourced by the audit client that relates to the audit client's internal accounting controls, financial systems, or financial statements, for an audit client unless it is reasonable to conclude that the results of these services will not be subject to audit procedures during an audit of the audit client's financial statements.

(vi) *Management functions*. Acting, temporarily or permanently, as a director, officer, or employee of an audit client, or performing any decision-making, supervisory, or ongoing monitoring function for the audit client.

(vii) *Human resources*. (A) Searching for or seeking out prospective candidates for managerial, executive, or director positions;

(B) Engaging in psychological testing, or other formal testing or evaluation programs;

(C) Undertaking reference checks of prospective candidates for an executive or director position;

(D) Acting as a negotiator on the audit client's behalf, such as determining position, status or title, compensation, fringe benefits, or other conditions of employment; or

(E) Recommending, or advising the audit client to hire, a specific candidate for a specific job (except that an accounting firm may, upon request by the audit client, interview candidates and advise the audit client on the candidate's competence for financial accounting, administrative, or control positions).

(viii) *Broker-dealer, investment adviser, or investment banking services*. Acting as a broker-dealer (registered or unregistered), promoter, or underwriter, on behalf of an audit client, making investment decisions on behalf of the audit client or otherwise having discretionary authority over an audit client's investments, executing a transaction to buy or sell an audit client's investment, or having custody of assets of the audit client, such as taking temporary possession of securities purchased by the audit client.

(ix) *Legal services*. Providing any service to an audit client that, under circumstances in which the service is provided, could be provided only by someone licensed, admitted, or otherwise qualified to practice law in the jurisdiction in which the service is provided.

(x) *Expert services unrelated to the audit*. Providing an expert opinion or other expert service for an audit client, or an audit client's legal representative, for the purpose of advocating an audit client's interests in litigation or in a regulatory or administrative proceeding or investigation. In any litigation or regulatory or administrative proceeding or investigation, an accountant's independence shall not be deemed to be impaired if the accountant provides factual accounts, including in testimony, of work performed or explains the positions taken or conclusions reached during the performance of any service provided by the accountant for the audit client.

(5) *Contingent fees*. An accountant is not independent if, at any point during the audit and professional engagement period, the accountant provides any service or product to an audit client for a contingent fee or a commission, or receives a contingent fee or commission from an audit client.

(6) *Partner rotation*. (i) Except as provided in paragraph (c)(6)(ii) of this section, an accountant is not independent of an audit client when:

(A) Any audit partner as defined in paragraph (f) (7) (ii) of this section performs:

(*1*) The services of a lead partner, as defined in paragraph (f) (7) (ii) (A) of this section, or concurring partner, as defined in paragraph (f) (7) (ii) (B) of this section, for more than five consecutive years; or

(*2*) One or more of the services defined in paragraphs (f) (7) (ii) (C) and (D) of this section for more than seven consecutive years;

(B) Any audit partner:

(*1*) Within the five consecutive year period following the performance of services for the maximum period permitted under paragraph (c) (6) (i) (A) (*1*) of this section, performs for that audit client the services of a lead partner, as defined in paragraph (f) (7) (ii) (A) of this section, or concurring partner, as defined in paragraph (f) (7) (ii) (B) of this section, or a combination of those services, or

(*2*) Within the two consecutive year period following the performance of services for the maximum period permitted under paragraph (c) (6) (i) (A) (*2*) of this section, performs one or more of the services defined in paragraph (f) (7) (ii) of this section.

(ii) Any accounting firm with less than five audit clients that are issuers (as defined in section 10A(f) of the Securities Exchange Act of 1934 (15 U.S.C. 78j-1(f))) and less than ten partners shall be exempt from paragraph (c) (6) (i) of this section *provided* the Public Company Accounting Oversight Board conducts a review at least once every three years of each of the audit client engagements that would result in a lack of auditor independence under this paragraph.

(iii) For purposes of paragraph (c) (6) (i) of this section, an audit client that is an investment company registered under section 8 of the Investment Company Act of 1940 (15 U.S.C. 80a-8), does not include an affiliate of the audit client that is an entity in the same investment company complex, as defined in paragraph (f) (14) of this section, except for another registered investment company in the same investment company complex. For purposes of calculating consecutive years of service under paragraph (c) (6) (i) of this section with respect to investment companies in an investment company complex, audits of registered investment companies with different fiscal year-ends that are performed in a continuous 12-month period count as a single consecutive year.

(7) *Audit committee administration of the engagement.* An accountant is not independent of an issuer (as defined in section 10A(f) of the Securities Exchange Act of 1934 (15 U.S.C. 78j-1(f))), other than an issuer that is an Asset-Backed Issuer as defined in § 240.13a-14(g) and § 240.15d-14(g) of this chapter, or an investment company registered under section 8 of the Investment Company Act of 1940 (15 U.S.C. 80a-8), other than a unit investment trust as defined by section 4(2) of the Investment Company Act of 1940 (15 U.S.C. 80a-4(2)), unless:

(i) In accordance with Section 10A(i) of the Securities Exchange Act of 1934 (15 U.S.C. 78j-1(i)) either:

(A) Before the accountant is engaged by the issuer or its subsidiaries, or the registered investment company or its subsidiaries, to render audit or non-audit services, the engagement is approved by the issuer's or registered investment company's audit committee; or

(B) The engagement to render the service is entered into pursuant to pre-approval policies and procedures established by the audit committee of the issuer or registered investment company, *provided* the policies and procedures are detailed as to the particular service and the audit committee is informed of each service and such policies and procedures do not include delegation of the audit committees responsibilities under the Securities Exchange Act of 1934 to management; or

(C) With respect to the provision of services other than audit, review or attest services the pre-approval requirement is waived if:

(*1*) The aggregate amount of all such services provided constitutes no more than five percent of the total amount of revenues paid by the audit client to its accountant during the fiscal year in which the services are provided;

(*2*) Such services were not recognized by the issuer or registered investment company at the time of the engagement to be non-audit services; and

(*3*) Such services are promptly brought to the attention of the audit committee of the issuer or registered investment company and approved prior to the completion of the audit by the audit committee or by one or more members of the audit committee who are members of the board of directors to whom authority to grant such approvals has been delegated by the audit committee.

(ii) A registered investment company's audit committee also must pre-approve its accountant's engagements for non-audit services with the registered investment company's investment adviser (not including a sub-adviser whose role is primarily portfolio management and is sub-contracted or overseen by another investment adviser) and any entity controlling, controlled by, or under common control with the investment adviser that provides ongoing services to the registered investment company in accordance with paragraph (c)(7)(i) of this section, if the engagement relates directly to the operations and financial reporting of the registered investment company, except that with respect to the waiver of the pre-approval requirement under paragraph (c)(7)(i)(C) of this section, the aggregate amount of all services provided constitutes no more than five percent of the total amount of revenues paid to the registered investment company's accountant by the registered investment company, its investment adviser and any entity controlling, controlled by, or under common control with the investment adviser that provides ongoing services to the registered investment company during the fiscal year in which the services are provided that would have to be pre-approved by the registered investment company's audit committee pursuant to this section.

(8) *Compensation*. An accountant is not independent of an audit client if, at any point during the audit and professional engagement period, any audit partner earns or receives compensation based on the audit partner procuring engagements with that audit client to provide any products or services other than audit, review or attest services. Any accounting firm with fewer than ten partners and fewer than five audit clients that are issuers (as defined in section 10A(f) of the Securities Exchange Act of 1934 (15 U.S.C. 78j-1(f))) shall be exempt from the requirement stated in the previous sentence.

(d) *Quality controls*. An accounting firm's independence will not be impaired solely because a covered person in the firm is not independent of an audit client provided:

(1) The covered person did not know of the circumstances giving rise to the lack of independence;

(2) The covered person's lack of independence was corrected as promptly as possible under the relevant circumstances after the covered person or accounting firm became aware of it; and

(3) The accounting firm has a quality control system in place that provides reasonable assurance, taking into account the size and nature of the accounting firm's practice, that the accounting firm and its employees do not lack independence, and that covers at least all employees and associated entities of the accounting firm participating in the engagement, including employees and associated entities located outside of the United States.

(4) For an accounting firm that annually provides audit, review, or attest services to more than 500 companies with a class of securities registered with the Commission under Section 12 of the Securities Exchange Act of 1934 (15 U.S.C. 78*l*), a quality control system will not provide such reasonable assurance unless it has at least the following features:

(i) Written independence policies and procedures;

(ii) With respect to partners and managerial employees, an automated system to identify their investments in securities that might impair the accountant's independence;

(iii) With respect to all professionals, a system that provides timely information about entities from which the accountant is required to maintain independence;

(iv) An annual or on-going firm-wide training program about auditor independence;

(v) An annual internal inspection and testing program to monitor adherence to independence requirements;

(vi) Notification to all accounting firm members, officers, directors, and employees of the name and title of the member of senior management responsible for compliance with auditor independence requirements;

(vii) Written policies and procedures requiring all partners and covered persons to report promptly to the accounting firm when they are engaged in employment negotiations with an audit client, and requiring the firm to remove immediately any such professional from that audit client's engagement and to review promptly all work the professional performed related to that audit client's engagement; and

(viii) A disciplinary mechanism to ensure compliance with this section.

(e) (1) *Transition and grandfathering.* Provided the following relationships did not impair the accountant's independence under pre-existing requirements of the Commission, the Independence Standards, Board, or the accounting profession in the United States, the existence of the relationship on May 6, 2003, will not be deemed to impair an accountant's independence:

(i) Employment relationships that commenced at the issuer prior to May 6, 2003, as described in paragraph (c) (2) (iii) (B) of this section.

(ii) Compensation earned or received, as described in paragraph (c) (8) of this section during the fiscal year of the accounting firm that includes the effective date of this section.

(iii) Until May 6, 2004, the provision of services described in paragraph (c) (4) of this section provided those services are pursuant to contracts in existence on May 6, 2003.

(iv) The provision of services by the accountant under contracts in existence on May 6, 2003, that have not been pre-approved by the audit committee as described in paragraph (c) (7) of this section.

(v) Until the first day of the issuer's fiscal year beginning after May 6, 2003, by a "lead"' partner and other audit partner (other than the "concurring" partner) providing services in excess of those permitted under paragraph (c) (6) of this section. An accountant's independence will not be deemed to be impaired until the first day of the issuer's fiscal year beginning after May 6, 2004, by a "concurring" partner providing services in excess of those permitted under paragraph (c) (6) of this section. For the purposes of calculating periods of service under paragraph (c) (6) of this section:

(A) For the "lead" and "concurring" partner, the period of service includes time served as the "lead"' or "concurring" partner prior to May 6, 2003; and

(B) For audit partners other than the "lead" partner or "'concurring" partner, and for audit partners in foreign firms, the period of service does not include time served on the audit engagement team prior to the first day of issuer's fiscal year beginning on or after May 6, 2003.

(2) *Settling financial arrangements with former professionals.* To the extent not required by pre-existing requirements of the Commission, the Independence Standards Board, or the accounting profession in the United States, the requirement in paragraph (c) (2) (iii) of this section to settle financial arrangements with former professionals applies to situations that arise after the effective date of this section.

(f) *Definitions of terms.* For purposes of this section:

(1) *Accountant*, as used in paragraphs (b) through (e) of this section, means a registered public accounting firm, certified public accountant or public accountant performing services in connection with an engagement for which independence is required. References to the accountant include any accounting firm with which the certified public accountant or public accountant is affiliated.

(2) *Accounting firm* means an organization (whether it is a sole proprietorship, incorporated association, partnership, corporation, limited liability company, limited liability

partnership, or other legal entity) that is engaged in the practice of public accounting and furnishes reports or other documents filed with the Commission or otherwise prepared under the securities laws, and all of the organization's departments, divisions, parents, subsidiaries, and associated entities, including those located outside of the United States. Accounting firm also includes the organization's pension, retirement, investment, or similar plans.

(3) (i) *Accounting role* means a role in which a person is in a position to or does exercise more than minimal influence over the contents of the accounting records or anyone who prepares them.

(ii) *Financial reporting oversight role* means a role in which a person is in a position to or does exercise influence over the contents of the financial statements or anyone who prepares them, such as when the person is a member of the board of directors or similar management or governing body, chief executive officer, president, chief financial officer, chief operating officer, general counsel, chief accounting officer, controller, director of internal audit, director of financial reporting, treasurer, or any equivalent position.

(4) *Affiliate of the audit client* means:

(i) An entity that has control over the audit client, or over which the audit client has control, or which is under common control with the audit client, including the audit client's parents and subsidiaries;

(ii) An entity over which the audit client has significant influence, unless the entity is not material to the audit client;

(iii) An entity that has significant influence over the audit client, unless the audit client is not material to the entity; and

(iv) Each entity in the investment company complex when the audit client is an entity that is part of an investment company complex.

(5) *Audit and professional engagement period* includes both:

(i) The period covered by any financial statements being audited or reviewed (the "audit period"); and

(ii) The period of the engagement to audit or review the audit client's financial statements or to prepare a report filed with the Commission (the "professional engagement period"):

(A) The professional engagement period begins when the accountant either signs an initial engagement letter (or other agreement to review or audit a client's financial statements) or begins audit, review, or attest procedures, whichever is earlier; and

(B) The professional engagement period ends when the audit client or the accountant notifies the Commission that the client is no longer that accountant's audit client.

(iii) For audits of the financial statements of foreign private issuers, the "audit and professional engagement period" does not include periods ended prior to the first day of the last fiscal year before the foreign private issuer first filed, or was required to file, a registration statement or report with the Commission, provided there has been full compliance with home country independence standards in all prior periods covered by any registration statement or report filed with the Commission.

(6) *Audit client* means the entity whose financial statements or other information is being audited, reviewed, or attested and any affiliates of the audit client, other than, for purposes of paragraph (c) (1) (i) of this section, entities that are affiliates of the audit client only by virtue of paragraph (f) (4) (ii) or (f) (4) (iii) of this section.

(7) (i) *Audit engagement team* means all partners, principals, shareholders and professional employees participating in an audit, review, or attestation engagement of an audit client, including audit partners and all persons who consult with others on the audit

engagement team during the audit, review, or attestation engagement regarding technical or industry-specific issues, transactions, or events.

(ii) *Audit partner* means a partner or persons in an equivalent position, other than a partner who consults with others on the audit engagement team during the audit, review, or attestation engagement regarding technical or industry-specific issues, transactions, or events, who is a member of the audit engagement team who has responsibility for decision-making on significant auditing, accounting, and reporting matters that affect the financial statements, or who maintains regular contact with management and the audit committee and includes the following:

(A) The lead or coordinating audit partner having primary responsibility for the audit or review (the "lead partner");

(B) The partner conducting a quality review under applicable professional standards and any applicable rules of the Commission to evaluate the significant judgments and the related conclusions reached in forming the overall conclusion on the audit or review engagement ("Engagement Quality Reviewer" or "Engagement Quality Control Reviewer");

(C) Other audit engagement team partners who provide more than ten hours of audit, review, or attest services in connection with the annual or interim consolidated financial statements of the issuer or an investment company registered under section 8 of the Investment Company Act of 1940 (15 U.S.C. 80a-8); and

(D) Other audit engagement team partners who serve as the "lead partner" in connection with any audit or review related to the annual or interim financial statements of a subsidiary of the issuer whose assets or revenues constitute 20% or more of the assets or revenues of the issuer's respective consolidated assets or revenues.

(8) *Chain of command* means all persons who:

(i) Supervise or have direct management responsibility for the audit, including at all successively senior levels through the accounting firm's chief executive;

(ii) Evaluate the performance or recommend the compensation of the audit engagement partner; or

(iii) Provide quality control or other oversight of the audit.

(9) *Close family members* means a person's spouse, spousal equivalent, parent, dependent, nondependent child, and sibling.

(10) *Contingent fee* means, except as stated in the next sentence, any fee established for the sale of a product or the performance of any service pursuant to an arrangement in which no fee will be charged unless a specified finding or result is attained, or in which the amount of the fee is otherwise dependent upon the finding or result of such product or service. Solely for the purposes of this section, a fee is not a "contingent fee" if it is fixed by courts or other public authorities, or, in tax matters, if determined based on the results of judicial proceedings or the findings of governmental agencies. Fees may vary depending, for example, on the complexity of services rendered.

(11) *Covered persons in the firm* means the following partners, principals, shareholders, and employees of an accounting firm:

(i) The "audit engagement team";

(ii) The "chain of command";

(iii) Any other partner, principal, shareholder, or managerial employee of the accounting firm who has provided ten or more hours of non-audit services to the audit client for the period beginning on the date such services are provided and ending on the date the accounting firm signs the report on the financial statements for the fiscal year during which those services are provided, or who expects to provide ten or more hours of non-audit services to the audit client on a recurring basis; and

(iv) Any other partner, principal, or shareholder from an "office" of the accounting firm in which the lead audit engagement partner primarily practices in connection with the audit.

(12) *Group* means two or more persons who act together for the purposes of acquiring, holding, voting, or disposing of securities of a registrant.

(13) *Immediate family members* means a person's spouse, spousal equivalent, and dependents.

(14) *Investment company complex.*

(i) "Investment company complex" includes:

(A) An investment company and its investment adviser or sponsor;

(B) Any entity controlled by or controlling an investment adviser or sponsor in paragraph (f)(14)(i)(A) of this section, or any entity under common control with an investment adviser or sponsor in paragraph (f)(14)(i)(A) of this section if the entity:

(1) Is an investment adviser or sponsor; or

(2) Is engaged in the business of providing administrative, custodian, underwriting, or transfer agent services to any investment company, investment adviser, or sponsor; and

(C) Any investment company or entity that would be an investment company but for the exclusions provided by Section 3(c) of the Investment Company Act of 1940 (15 U.S.C. 80a-3(c)) that has an investment adviser or sponsor included in this definition by either paragraph (f)(14)(i)(A) or (f)(14)(i)(B) of this section.

(ii) An investment adviser, for purposes of this definition, does not include a subadviser whose role is primarily portfolio management and is subcontracted with or overseen by another investment adviser.

(iii) Sponsor, for purposes of this definition, is an entity that establishes a unit investment trust.

(15) *Office* means a distinct sub-group within an accounting firm, whether distinguished along geographic or practice lines.

(16) *Rabbi trust* means an irrevocable trust whose assets are not accessible to the accounting firm until all benefit obligations have been met, but are subject to the claims of creditors in bankruptcy or insolvency.

(17) *Audit committee* means a committee (or equivalent body) as defined in section 3(a)(58) of the Securities Exchange Act of 1934 (15 U.S.C. 78c(a)(58)).

Item 2-02. Accountants' reports and attestation reports on management's assessment of internal control over financial reporting

(a) *Technical requirements for accountants' reports.* The accountant's report (1) shall be dated; (2) shall be signed manually; (3) shall indicate the city and State where issued; and (4) shall identify without detailed enumeration the financial statements covered by the report.

(b) *Representations as to the audit included in accountants' reports.* The accountant's report (1) shall state the applicable professional standards under which the audit was conducted; and (2) shall designate any auditing procedures deemed necessary by the accountant under the circumstances of the particular case, which have been omitted, and the reasons for their omission. Nothing in this rule shall be construed to imply authority for the omission of any procedure which independent accountants would ordinarily employ in the course of an audit made for the purpose of expressing the opinions required by paragraph (c) of this section.

(c) *Opinions to be expressed in accountants' reports.* The accountant's report shall state clearly: (1) The opinion of the accountant in respect of the financial statements covered by the report and the accounting principles and practices reflected therein; and (2) the opinion of the accountant as to the consistency of the application of the accounting principles, or as to any changes in such principles which have a material effect on the financial statements.

(d) *Exceptions identified in accountants' reports.* Any matters to which the accountant takes exception shall be clearly identified, the exception thereto specifically and clearly stated, and, to the extent practicable, the effect of each such exception on the related financial statements given. (See § 101 of the Codification of Financial Reporting Policies.)

(e) Paragraph (e) of this section applies only to registrants that are providing financial statements in a filing for a period with respect to which Arthur Andersen LLP or a foreign affiliate of Arthur Andersen LLP ("Andersen") issued an accountants' report. Notwithstanding any other Commission rule or regulation, a registrant that cannot obtain an accountants' report that meets the technical requirements of paragraph (a) of this section after reasonable efforts may include in the document a copy of the latest signed and dated accountants' report issued by Andersen for such period in satisfaction of that requirement, if prominent disclosure that the report is a copy of the previously issued Andersen accountants' report and that the report has not been reissued by Andersen is set forth on such copy.

(f) *Attestation Report on Internal Control Over Financial Reporting.* (1) Every registered public accounting firm that issues or prepares an accountant's report for a registrant, other than a registrant that is neither an accelerated filer nor a large accelerated filer (as defined in § 240.12b-2 of this chapter), or is an emerging growth company, as defined in Rule 405 of the Securities Act (§ 230.405 of this chapter) or Rule 12b-2 of the Exchange Act (§ 240.12b-2 of this chapter), or an investment company registered under Section 8 of the Investment Company Act of 1940 (15 U.S.C. 80a-8), that is included in an annual report required by section 13(a) or 15(d) of the Securities Exchange Act of 1934 (15 U.S.C. 78a *et seq.*) containing an assessment by management of the effectiveness of the registrant's internal control over financial reporting must include an attestation report on internal control over financial reporting.

(2) If an attestation report on internal control over financial reporting is included in an annual report required by section 13(a) or 15(d) of the Securities Exchange Act of 1934 (15 U.S.C. 78a et seq.), it shall clearly state the opinion of the accountant, either unqualified or adverse, as to whether the registrant maintained, in all material respects, effective internal control over financial reporting, except in the rare circumstance of a scope limitation that cannot be overcome by the registrant or the registered public accounting firm which would result in the accounting firm disclaiming an opinion. The attestation report on internal control over financial reporting shall be dated, signed manually, identify the period covered by the report and indicate that the accountant has audited the effectiveness of internal control over financial reporting. The attestation report on internal control over financial reporting may be separate from the accountant's report.

(g) *Attestation Report on Assessment of Compliance with Servicing Criteria for Asset-Backed Securities.* The attestation report on assessment of compliance with servicing criteria for asset-backed securities, as required by § 240.13a-18(c) or 240.15d-18(c) of this chapter, shall be dated, signed manually, identify the period covered by the report and clearly state the opinion of the registered public accounting firm as to whether the asserting party's assessment of compliance with the servicing criteria is fairly stated in all material respects, or must include an opinion to the effect that an overall opinion cannot be expressed. If an overall opinion cannot be expressed, explain why.

Item 2-07. Communicaton with Audit Committees

(a) Each registered public accounting firm that performs for an audit client that is an issuer (as defined in section 10A(f) of the Securities Exchange Act of 1934 (15 U.S.C. 78j-1(f))), other than an issuer that is an Asset-Backed Issuer as defined in § 240.13a-14(g) and § 240.15d-14(g) of this chapter, or an investment company registered under section 8 of the Investment Company Act of 1940 (15 U.S.C. 80a-8), other than a unit investment trust as defined by section 4(2) of the Investment Company Act of 1940 (15 U.S.C. 80a-4(2)), any audit required under the securities laws shall report, prior to the filing of such audit report with the Commission (or in the case of a registered investment company, annually, and if the annual communication is not within 90 days prior to the filing, provide an update, in the 90 day period prior to the filing, of any changes to the previously reported information), to the audit committee of the issuer or registered investment company:

(1) All critical accounting policies and practices to be used;

(2) All alternative treatments within Generally Accepted Accounting Principles for policies and practices related to material items that have been discussed with management of the issuer or registered investment company, including:

(i) Ramifications of the use of such alternative disclosures and treatments; and

(ii) The treatment preferred by the registered public accounting firm;

(3) Other material written communications between the registered public accounting firm and the management of the issuer or registered investment company, such as any management letter or schedule of unadjusted differences;

(4) If the audit client is an investment company, all non-audit services provided to any entity in an investment company complex, as defined in 210.2-01(f)(14) of this section, that were not pre-approved by the registered investment company's audit committee pursuant to 210.2-01(c)(7) of this section.

(b) [Reserved]

REGULATION M

17 C.F.R. §§ 242.100-242.105

Rule	Subject
100	Definitions
101	Activities by distribution participants
102	Activities by issuers and selling security holders during a distribution
103	Nasdaq passive market making
104	Stabilizing and other activities in connection with an offering
105	Short Selling in connection with a public offering

PART 242—REGULATION M

Rule 100. Definitions

(a) Preliminary Note: Any transaction or series of transactions, whether or not effected pursuant to the provisions of Regulation M, remain subject to the antifraud and antimanipulation provisions of the securities laws, including, without limitation, Section 17(a) of the Securities Act of 1933 [15 U.S.C. 77q(a)] and Sections 9, 10(b), and 15(c) of the Securities Exchange Act of 1934 [15 U.S.C. 78i, 78j(b), and 78o(c)].

(b) For purposes of this section, the following definitions shall apply:

ADTV means the worldwide average daily trading volume during the two full calendar months immediately preceding, or any 60 consecutive calendar days ending within the 10 calendar days preceding, the filing of the registration statement; or, if there is no registration statement or if the distribution involves the sale of securities on a delayed basis pursuant to § 230.415 of this chapter, two full calendar months immediately preceding, or any consecutive 60 calendar days ending within the 10 calendar days preceding, the determination of the offering price.

Affiliated purchaser means:

(1) A person acting, directly or indirectly, in concert with a distribution participant, issuer, or selling security holder in connection with the acquisition or distribution of any covered security; or

(2) An affiliate, which may be a separately identifiable department or division of a distribution participant, issuer, or selling security holder, that, directly or indirectly, controls the purchases of any covered security by a distribution participant, issuer, or selling security holder, whose purchases are controlled by any such person, or whose purchases are under common control with any such person; or

(3) An affiliate, which may be a separately identifiable department or division of a distribution participant, issuer, or selling security holder, that regularly purchases securities for its own account or for the account of others, or that recommends or exercises investment discretion with respect to the purchase or sale of securities; *Provided, however*, That this paragraph (3) shall not apply to such affiliate if the following conditions are satisfied:

(i) The distribution participant, issuer, or selling security holder:

(A) Maintains and enforces written policies and procedures reasonably designed to prevent the flow of information to or from the affiliate that might result in a violation of §§ 242.101, 242.102, and 242.104; and

(B) Obtains an annual, independent assessment of the operation of such policies and procedures; and

(ii) The affiliate has no officers (or persons performing similar functions) or employees (other than clerical, ministerial, or support personnel) in common with the distribution participant, issuer, or selling security holder that direct, effect, or recommend transactions in securities; and

(iii) The affiliate does not, during the applicable restricted period, act as a market maker (other than as a specialist in compliance with the rules of a national securities exchange), or engage, as a broker or a dealer, in solicited transactions or proprietary trading, in covered securities.

Agent independent of the issuer means a trustee or other person who is independent of the issuer. The agent shall be deemed to be independent of the issuer only if:

(1) The agent is not an affiliate of the issuer; and

(2) Neither the issuer nor any affiliate of the issuer exercises any direct or indirect control or influence over the prices or amounts of the securities to be purchased, the timing of, or the manner in which, the securities are to be purchased, or the selection of a broker or dealer (other than the independent agent itself) through which purchases may be executed; *Provided, however*, That the issuer or its affiliate will not be deemed to have such control or influence solely because it revises not more than once in any three-month period the source of the shares to fund the plan, the basis for determining the amount of its contributions to a plan, or the basis for determining the frequency of its allocations to a plan, or any formula specified in a plan that determines the amount or timing of securities to be purchased by the agent.

Asset-backed security has the meaning contained in § 229.1101 of this chapter.

At-the-market offering means an offering of securities at other than a fixed price.

Business day refers to a 24 hour period determined with reference to the principal market for the securities to be distributed, and that includes a complete trading session for that market.

Completion of participation in a distribution. Securities acquired in the distribution for investment by any person participating in a distribution, or any affiliated purchaser of such person, shall be deemed to be distributed. A person shall be deemed to have completed its participation in a distribution as follows:

(1) An issuer or selling security holder, when the distribution is completed;

(2) An underwriter, when such person's participation has been distributed, including all other securities of the same class that are acquired in connection with the distribution, and any stabilization arrangements and trading restrictions in connection with the distribution have been terminated; *Provided, however*, That an underwriter's participation will not be deemed to have been completed if a syndicate overallotment option is exercised in an amount that exceeds the net syndicate short position at the time of such exercise; and

(3) Any other person participating in the distribution, when such person's participation has been distributed.

Covered security means any security that is the subject of a distribution, or any reference security.

Current exchange rate means the current rate of exchange between two currencies, which is obtained from at least one independent entity that provides or disseminates foreign exchange quotations in the ordinary course of its business.

Distribution means an offering of securities, whether or not subject to registration under the Securities Act, that is distinguished from ordinary trading transactions by the magnitude of the offering and the presence of special selling efforts and selling methods.

Distribution participant means an underwriter, prospective underwriter, broker, dealer, or other person who has agreed to participate or is participating in a distribution.

Electronic communications network has the meaning provided in § 242.600.

Employee has the meaning contained in Form S-8 (§ 239.16b of this chapter) relating to employee benefit plans.

Exchange Act means the Securities Exchange Act of 1934 (15 U.S.C. 78a et seq.).

Independent bid means a bid by a person who is not a distribution participant, issuer, selling security holder, or affiliated purchaser.

NASD means the National Association of Securities Dealers, Inc. or any of its subsidiaries.

Nasdaq means the electronic dealer quotation system owned and operated by The Nasdaq Stock Market, Inc.

Nasdaq security means a security that is authorized for quotation on Nasdaq, and such authorization is not suspended, terminated, or prohibited.

Net purchases means the amount by which a passive market maker's purchases exceed its sales.

Offering price means the price at which the security is to be or is being distributed.

Passive market maker means a market maker that effects bids or purchases in accordance with the provisions of § 242.103.

Penalty bid means an arrangement that permits the managing underwriter to reclaim a selling concession from a syndicate member in connection with an offering when the securities originally sold by the syndicate member are purchased in syndicate covering transactions.

Plan means any bonus, profit-sharing, pension, retirement, thrift, savings, incentive, stock purchase, stock option, stock ownership, stock appreciation, dividend reinvestment, or similar plan; or any dividend or interest reinvestment plan or employee benefit plan as defined in § 230.405 of this chapter.

Principal market means the single securities market with the largest aggregate reported trading volume for the class of securities during the 12 full calendar months immediately preceding the filing of the registration statement; or, if there is no registration statement or if the distribution involves the sale of securities on a delayed basis pursuant to § 230.415 of this chapter, during the 12 full calendar months immediately preceding the determination of the offering price. For the purpose of determining the aggregate trading volume in a security, the trading volume of depositary shares representing such security shall be included, and shall be multiplied by the multiple or fraction of the security represented by the depositary share. For purposes of this paragraph, depositary share means a security, evidenced by a depositary receipt, that represents another security, or a multiple or fraction thereof, deposited with a depositary.

Prospective underwriter means a person:

(1) Who has submitted a bid to the issuer or selling security holder, and who knows or is reasonably certain that such bid will be accepted, whether or not the terms and conditions of the underwriting have been agreed upon; or

(2) Who has reached, or is reasonably certain to reach, an understanding with the issuer or selling security holder, or managing underwriter that such person will become an underwriter, whether or not the terms and conditions of the underwriting have been agreed upon.

Public float value shall be determined in the manner set forth on the front page of Form 10-K (§ 249.310 of this chapter), even if the issuer of such securities is not required to file Form 10-K, relating to the aggregate market value of common equity securities held by non-affiliates of the issuer.

Reference period means the two full calendar months immediately preceding the filing of the registration statement or, if there is no registration statement or if the distribution involves the sale of securities on a delayed basis pursuant to § 230.415 of this chapter, the two full calendar months immediately preceding the determination of the offering price.

Reference security means a security into which a security that is the subject of a distribution ("subject security") may be converted, exchanged, or exercised or which, under the terms of the subject security, may in whole or in significant part determine the value of the subject security.

Restricted period means:

(1) For any security with an ADTV value of $100,000 or more of an issuer whose common equity securities have a public float value of $25 million or more, the period beginning on the later of one business day prior to the determination of the offering price or such time that a person becomes a distribution participant, and ending upon such person's completion of participation in the distribution; and

(2) For all other securities, the period beginning on the later of five business days prior to the determination of the offering price or such time that a person becomes a distribution participant, and ending upon such person's completion of participation in the distribution.

(3) In the case of a distribution involving a merger, acquisition, or exchange offer, the period beginning on the day proxy solicitation or offering materials are first disseminated to security holders, and ending upon the completion of the distribution.

Securities Act means the Securities Act of 1933 (15 U.S.C. 77a et seq.).

Selling security holder means any person on whose behalf a distribution is made, other than an issuer.

Stabilize or stabilizing means the placing of any bid, or the effecting of any purchase, for the purpose of pegging, fixing, or maintaining the price of a security.

Syndicate covering transaction means the placing of any bid or the effecting of any purchase on behalf of the sole distributor or the underwriting syndicate or group to reduce a short position created in connection with the offering.

30% ADTV limitation means 30 percent of the market maker's ADTV in a covered security during the reference period, as obtained from the NASD.

Underwriter means a person who has agreed with an issuer or selling security holder:

(1) To purchase securities for distribution; or

(2) To distribute securities for or on behalf of such issuer or selling security holder; or

(3) To manage or supervise a distribution of securities for or on behalf of such issuer or selling security holder.

Rule 101. Activities by Distribution Participants

(a) *Unlawful Activity.* In connection with a distribution of securities, it shall be unlawful for a distribution participant or an affiliated purchaser of such person, directly or indirectly, to bid for, purchase, or attempt to induce any person to bid for or purchase, a covered security during the applicable restricted period; *Provided, however,* That if a distribution participant or affiliated purchaser is the issuer or selling security holder of the securities subject to the distribution, such person shall be subject to the provisions of § 242.102, rather than this section.

(b) *Excepted Activity.* The following activities shall not be prohibited by paragraph (a) of this section:

(1) *Research.* The publication or dissemination of an information, opinion, or recommendation, if the conditions of § 230.138, § 230.139 or § 230.139b of this chapter are met; or

(2) *Transactions complying with certain other sections.* Transactions complying with § 242.103 or § 242.104; or

(3) *Odd-lot transactions.* Transactions in odd-lots; or transactions to offset odd-lots in connection with an odd-lot tender offer conducted pursuant to § 240.13e-4(h)(5) of this chapter; or

(4) *Exercises of securities.* The exercise of any option, warrant, right, or any conversion privilege set forth in the instrument governing a security; or

(5) *Unsolicited transactions.* Unsolicited brokerage transactions; or unsolicited purchases that are not effected from or through a broker or dealer, on a securities exchange, or through an inter-dealer quotation system or electronic communications network; or

(6) *Basket transactions.* (i) Bids or purchases, in the ordinary course of business, in connection with a basket of 20 or more securities in which a covered security does not comprise more than 5% of the value of the basket purchased; or

(ii) Adjustments to such a basket in the ordinary course of business as a result of a change in the composition of a standardized index; or

(7) *De minimis transactions.* Purchases during the restricted period, other than by a passive market maker, that total less than 2% of the ADTV of the security being purchased, or unaccepted bids; *Provided, however,* That the person making such bid or purchase has maintained and enforces written policies and procedures reasonably designed to achieve compliance with the other provisions of this section; or

(8) *Transactions in connection with a distribution.* Transactions among distribution participants in connection with a distribution, and purchases of securities from an issuer or selling security holder in connection with a distribution, that are not effected on a securities exchange, or through an interdealer quotation system or electronic communications network; or

(9) *Offers to sell or the solicitation of offers to buy.* Offers to sell or the solicitation of offers to buy the securities being distributed (including securities acquired in stabilizing), or securities offered as principal by the person making such offer or solicitation; or

(10) *Transactions in Rule 144A securities.* Transactions in securities eligible for resale under § 230.144A(d)(3) of this chapter, or any reference security, if the Rule 144A securities are sold in the United States solely to:

(i) Qualified institutional buyers, as defined in § 230.144A(a)(1) of this chapter, or purchasers that the seller and any person acting on behalf of the seller reasonably believes are qualified institutional buyers, in transactions exempt from registration under section 4(2) of the Securities Act (15 U.S.C. 77d(2)) or § 230.144A or § 230.500 *et seq.* of this chapter; or

(ii) Persons not deemed to be "U.S. persons" for purposes of § 230.902(o)(2) or § 230.902(o)(7) of this chapter, during distribution qualifying under paragraph (b)(10)(i) of this section.

(c) *Excepted Securities.* The provisions of this section shall not apply to any of the following securities:

(1) *Actively-traded securities.* Securities that have an ADTV value of at least $1 million and are issued by an issuer whose common equity securities have a public float value of at least $150 million; *Provided, however,* That such securities are not issued by the distribution participant or an affiliate of the distribution participant; or

(2) *Investment grade nonconvertible and asset-backed securities.* Nonconvertible debt securities, nonconvertible preferred securities, and asset-backed securities, that are rated by at least one nationally recognized statistical rating organization, as that term is used in § 240.15c3-1 of this chapter, in one of its generic rating categories that signifies investment grade; or

(3) *Exempted securities.* "Exempted securities" as defined in section 3(a)(12) of the Exchange Act (15 U.S.C. 78c(a)(12)); or

(4) *Face-amount certificates or securities issued by an open-end management investment company or unit investment trust.* Face-amount certificates issued by a face-amount certificate company, or redeemable securities issued by an open-end management investment company or a unit investment trust. Any terms used in this paragraph (c)(4) that are defined in the Investment Company Act of 1940 (15 U.S.C. 80a-1 et seq.) shall have the meanings specified in such Act.

(d) *Exemptive Authority.* Upon written application or upon its own motion, the Commission may grant an exemption from the provisions of this section, either unconditionally or on specified terms and conditions, to any transaction or class of transactions, or to any security or class of securities.

Rule 102. Activities by Issuers and Selling Security Holders During a Distribution

(a) *Unlawful Activity.* In connection with a distribution of securities effected by or on behalf of an issuer or selling security holder, it shall be unlawful for such person, or any affiliated purchaser of such person, directly or indirectly, to bid for, purchase, or attempt to induce any person to bid for or purchase, a covered security during the applicable restricted period; *Except That* if an affiliated purchaser is a distribution participant, such affiliated purchaser may comply with § 242.101, rather than this section.

(b) *Excepted Activity.* The following activities shall not be prohibited by paragraph (a) of this section:

(1) *Odd-lot transactions.* Transactions in odd-lots, or transactions to offset odd-lots in connection with an odd-lot tender offer conducted pursuant to § 240.13e-4 (h) (5) of this chapter; or

(2) *Transactions by closed-end investment companies.* (i) Transactions complying with § 270.23c-3 of this chapter; or

(ii) Periodic tender offers of securities, at net asset value, conducted pursuant to § 240.13e-4 of this chapter by a closed-end investment company that engages in a continuous offering of its securities pursuant to § 230.415 of this chapter; *provided, however,* That such securities are not traded on a securities exchange or through an inter-dealer quotation system or electronic communications network; or

(3) *Redemptions by commodity pools or limited partnerships.* Redemptions by commodity pools or limited partnerships, at a price based on net asset value, which are effected in accordance with the terms and conditions of the instruments governing the securities; *Provided, however,* That such securities are not traded on a securities exchange, or through an inter-dealer quotation system or electronic communications network; or

(4) *Exercises of securities.* The exercise of any option, warrant, right, or any conversion privilege set forth in the instrument governing a security; or

(5) *Offers to sell or the solicitation of offers to buy.* Offers to sell or the solicitation of offers to buy the securities being distributed; or

(6) *Unsolicited purchases.* Unsolicited purchases that are not effected from or through a broker or dealer, on a securities exchange, or through an inter-dealer quotation system or electronic communications network; or

(7) *Transactions in Rule 144A securities.* Transactions in securities eligible for resale under § 230.144A(d) (3) of this chapter, or any reference security, if the Rule 144A securities are sold in the United States solely to:

(i) Qualified institutional buyers, as defined in § 230.144A(a) (1) of this chapter, or purchasers that the seller and any person acting on behalf of the seller reasonably believes are qualified institutional buyers, in transactions exempt from registration under section 4(2) of the Securities Act (15 U.S.C. 77d(2)) or § 230.144A or § 230.500 *et seq.* of this chapter; or

(ii) Persons not deemed to be "U.S. persons" for purposes of § 230.902(o) (2) or § 230.902(o) (7) of this chapter, during a distribution qualifying under paragraph (b) (7) (i) of this section.

(c) *Plans.*

(1) Paragraph (a) of this section shall not apply to distributions of securities pursuant to a plan, which are made:

(i) Solely to employees or security holders of an issuer or its subsidiaries, or to a trustee or other person acquiring such securities for the accounts of such persons; or

(ii) To persons other than employees or security holders, if bids for or purchases of securities pursuant to the plan are effected solely by an agent independent of the issuer and the securities are from a source other than the issuer or an affiliated purchaser of the issuer.

(2) Bids for or purchases of any security made or effected by or for a plan shall be deemed to be a purchase by the issuer unless the bid is made, or the purchase is effected, by an agent independent of the issuer.

(d) *Excepted Securities.* The provisions of this section shall not apply to any of the following securities:

(1) *Actively-traded reference securities.* Reference securities with an ADTV value of at least $1 million that are issued by an issuer whose common equity securities have a public float value of at least $150 million; *Provided, however,* That such securities are not issued by the issuer, or any affiliate of the issuer, of the security in distribution.

(2) *Investment grade nonconvertible and asset-backed securities.* Nonconvertible debt securities, nonconvertible preferred securities, and asset-backed securities, that are rated by at least one nationally recognized statistical rating organization, as that term is used in § 240.15c3-1 of this chapter, in one of its generic rating categories that signifies investment grade; or

(3) *Exempted securities.* "Exempted securities" as defined in section 3(a)(12) of the Exchange Act (15 U.S.C. 78c(a)(12)); or

(4) *Face-amount certificates or securities issued by an open-end management investment company or unit investment trust.* Face-amount certificates issued by a face-amount certificate company, or redeemable securities issued by an open-end management investment company or a unit investment trust. Any terms used in this paragraph (d)(4) that are defined in the Investment Company Act of 1940 (15 U.S.C. 80a-1 et seq.) shall have the meanings specified in such Act.

(e) *Exemptive Authority.* Upon written application or upon its own motion, the Commission may grant an exemption from the provisions of this section, either unconditionally or on specified terms and conditions, to any transaction or class of transactions, or to any security or class of securities.

Rule 103. Nasdaq Passive Market Making

(a) *Scope of Section.* This section permits broker-dealers to engage in market making transactions in covered securities that are Nasdaq securities without violating the provisions of § 242.101; *Except That* this section shall not apply to any security for which a stabilizing bid subject to § 242.104 is in effect, or during any at-the-market offering or best efforts offering.

(b) *Conditions to be Met.*

(1) *General limitations.* A passive market maker must effect all transactions in the capacity of a registered market maker on Nasdaq. A passive market maker shall not bid for or purchase a covered security at a price that exceeds the highest independent bid for the covered security at the time of the transaction, except as permitted by paragraph (b)(3) of this section or required by a rule promulgated by the Commission or the NASD governing the handling of customer orders.

(2) *Purchase limitation.* On each day of the restricted period, a passive market maker's net purchases shall not exceed the greater of its 30% ADTV limitation or 200 shares (together, "purchase limitation"); *Provided, however,* That a passive market maker may purchase all of the securities that are part of a single order that, when executed, results in its purchase limitation being equalled or exceeded. If a passive market maker's net purchases equal or exceed its purchase limitation, it shall withdraw promptly its quotations from Nasdaq. If a passive market maker withdraws its quotations pursuant to this paragraph, it may not effect any bid or purchase in the covered security for the remainder of that day, irrespective of any later sales during that day, unless otherwise permitted by § 242.101.

(3) *Requirement to lower the bid.* If all independent bids for a covered security are reduced to a price below the passive market maker's bid, the passive market maker must lower its bid promptly to a level not higher than the then highest independent bid; *Provided, however,* That a passive market maker may continue to bid and effect purchases at its bid at a price exceeding the then highest independent bid until the passive market maker purchases

an aggregate amount of the covered security that equals or, through the purchase of all securities that are part of a single order, exceeds the lesser of two times the minimum quotation size for the security, as determined by NASD rules, or the passive market maker's remaining purchasing capacity under paragraph (b)(2) of this section.

(4) *Limitation on displayed size.* At all times, the passive market maker's displayed bid size may not exceed the lesser of the minimum quotation size for the covered security, or the passive market maker's remaining purchasing capacity under paragraph (b)(2) of this section; *Provided, however,* That a passive market maker whose purchasing capacity at any time is between one and 99 shares may display a bid size of 100 shares.

(5) *Identification of a passive market making bid.* The bid displayed by a passive market maker shall be designated as such.

(6) *Notification and reporting to the NASD.* A passive market maker shall notify the NASD in advance of its intention to engage in passive market making, and shall submit to the NASD information regarding passive market making purchases, in such form as the NASD shall prescribe.

(7) *Prospectus disclosure.* The prospectus for any registered offering in which any passive market maker intends to effect transactions in any covered security shall contain the information required in §§ 228.502, 228.508, 229.502, and 229.508 of this chapter.

(c) *Transactions at Prices Resulting From Unlawful Activity.* No transaction shall be made at a price that the passive market maker knows or has reason to know is the result of activity that is fraudulent, manipulative, or deceptive under the securities laws, or any rule or regulation thereunder.

Rule 104. Stabilizing and Other Activities in Connection With an Offering

(a) *Unlawful Activity.* It shall be unlawful for any person, directly or indirectly, to stabilize, to effect any syndicate covering transaction, or to impose a penalty bid, in connection with an offering of any security, in contravention of the provisions of this section. No stabilizing shall be effected at a price that the person stabilizing knows or has reason to know is in contravention of this section, or is the result of activity that is fraudulent, manipulative, or deceptive under the securities laws, or any rule or regulation thereunder.

(b) *Purpose.* Stabilizing is prohibited except for the purpose of preventing or retarding a decline in the market price of a security.

(c) *Priority.* To the extent permitted or required by the market where stabilizing occurs, any person stabilizing shall grant priority to any independent bid at the same price irrespective of the size of such independent bid at the time that it is entered.

(d) *Control of Stabilizing.* No sole distributor or syndicate or group stabilizing the price of a security or any member or members of such syndicate or group shall maintain more than one stabilizing bid in any one market at the same price at the same time.

(e) *At-the-Market Offerings.* Stabilizing is prohibited in an at-the-market offering.

(f) *Stabilizing Levels.*

(1) *Maximum stabilizing bid.* Notwithstanding the other provisions of this paragraph (f), no stabilizing shall be made at a price higher than the lower of the offering price or the stabilizing bid for the security in the principal market (or, if the principal market is closed, the stabilizing bid in the principal market at its previous close).

(2) *Initiating stabilizing.*

(i) *Initiating stabilizing when the principal market is open.* After the opening of quotations for the security in the principal market, stabilizing may be initiated in any market at a price no higher than the last independent transaction price for the security in the principal market if the security has traded in the principal market on the day stabilizing is initiated or on the most recent prior day of trading in the principal market and the current asked price in the principal market is equal to or greater than the last independent transaction price. If both conditions of the preceding sentence are not satisfied, stabilizing may be initiated in any market after the opening of quotations in the principal market at a price no higher than the highest current independent bid for the security in the principal market.

(ii) *Initiating stabilizing when the principal market is closed.*

(A) When the principal market for the security is closed, but immediately before the opening of quotations for the security in the market where stabilizing will be initiated, stabilizing may be initiated at a price no higher than the lower of:

(1) The price at which stabilizing could have been initiated in the principal market for the security at its previous close; or

(2) The most recent price at which an independent transaction in the security has been effected in any market since the close of the principal market, if the person stabilizing knows or has reason to know of such transaction.

(B) When the principal market for the security is closed, but after the opening of quotations in the market where stabilizing will be initiated, stabilizing may be initiated at a price no higher than the lower of:

(1) The price at which stabilization could have been initiated in the principal market for the security at its previous close; or

(2) The last independent transaction price for the security in that market if the security has traded in that market on the day stabilizing is initiated or on the last preceding business day and the current asked price in that market is equal to or greater than the last independent transaction price. If both conditions of the preceding sentence are not satisfied, under this paragraph (f)(2)(ii)(B)(2), stabilizing may be initiated at a price no higher than the highest current independent bid for the security in that market.

(iii) *Initiating stabilizing when there is no market for the security or before the offering price is determined.* If no bona fide market for the security being distributed exists at the time stabilizing is initiated, no stabilizing shall be initiated at a price in excess of the offering price. If stabilizing is initiated before the offering price is determined, then stabilizing may be continued after determination of the offering price at the price at which stabilizing then could be initiated.

(3) *Maintaining or carrying over a stabilizing bid.* stabilizing bid initiated pursuant to paragraph (f)(2) of this section, which has not been discontinued, may be maintained, or carried over into another market, irrespective of changes in the independent bids or transaction prices for the security.

(4) *Increasing or reducing a stabilizing bid.* A stabilizing bid may be increased to a price no higher than the highest current independent bid for the security in the principal market if the principal market is open, or, if the principal market is closed, to a price no higher than the highest independent bid in the principal market at the previous close thereof. A stabilizing bid may be reduced, or carried over into another market at a reduced price, irrespective of changes in the independent bids or transaction prices for the security. If stabilizing is discontinued, it shall not be resumed at a price higher than the price at which stabilizing then could be initiated.

(5) *Initiating, maintaining, or adjusting a stabilizing bid to reflect the current exchange rate.* If a stabilizing bid is expressed in a currency other than the currency of the principal market for the security, such bid may be initiated, maintained, or adjusted to reflect the current exchange rate, consistent with the provisions of this section. If, in initiating, maintaining, or adjusting a stabilizing bid pursuant to this paragraph (f)(5), the bid would be at or below the midpoint between two trading differentials, such stabilizing bid shall be adjusted downward to the lower differential.

(6) *Adjustments to stabilizing bid.* If a security goes ex-dividend, ex-rights, or ex-distribution, the stabilizing bid shall be reduced by an amount equal to the value of the dividend, right, or distribution. If, in reducing a stabilizing bid pursuant to this paragraph (f)(6), the bid would be at or below the midpoint between two trading differentials, such stabilizing bid shall be adjusted downward to the lower differential.

(7) *Stabilizing of components.* When two or more securities are being offered as a unit, the component securities shall not be stabilized at prices the sum of which exceeds the then permissible stabilizing price for the unit.

(8) *Special prices.* Any stabilizing price that otherwise meets the requirements of this section need not be adjusted to reflect special prices available to any group or class of persons (including employees or holders of warrants or rights).

(g) *Offerings With no U.S. Stabilizing Activities.*

(1) Stabilizing to facilitate an offering of a security in the United States shall not be deemed to be in violation of this section if all of the following conditions are satisfied:

(i) No stabilizing is made in the United States;

(ii) Stabilizing outside the United States is made in a jurisdiction with statutory or regulatory provisions governing stabilizing that are comparable to the provisions of this section; and

(iii) No stabilizing is made at a price above the offering price in the United States, except as permitted by paragraph (f)(5) of this section.

(2) For purposes of this paragraph (g), the Commission by rule, regulation, or order may determine whether a foreign statute or regulation is comparable to this section considering, among other things, whether such foreign statute or regulation: specifies appropriate purposes for which stabilizing is permitted; provides for disclosure and control of stabilizing activities; places limitations on stabilizing levels; requires appropriate recordkeeping; provides other protections comparable to the provisions of this section; and whether procedures exist to enable the Commission to obtain information concerning any foreign stabilizing transactions.

(h) *Disclosure and Notification.*

(1) Any person displaying or transmitting a bid that such person knows is for the purpose of stabilizing shall provide prior notice to the market on which such stabilizing will be effected, and shall disclose its purpose to the person with whom the bid is entered.

(2) Any person effecting a syndicate covering transaction or imposing a penalty bid shall provide prior notice to the self-regulatory organization with direct authority over the principal market in the United States for the security for which the syndicate covering transaction is effected or the penalty bid is imposed.

(3) Any person subject to this section who sells to, or purchases for the account of, any person any security where the price of such security may be or has been stabilized, shall send to the purchaser at or before the completion of the transaction, a prospectus, offering circular, confirmation, or other document containing a statement similar to that comprising the statement provided for in Item 502(d) of Regulation S-B (§ 228.502(d) of this chapter) or Item 502(d) of Regulation S-K (§ 229.502(d) of this chapter).

(i) *Recordkeeping Requirements.* A person subject to this section shall keep the information and make the notification required by § 240.17a-2 of this chapter.

(j) *Excepted Securities.* The provisions of this section shall not apply to:

(1) *Exempted Securities.* "Exempted securities," as defined in section 3(a)(12) of the Exchange Act (15 U.S.C. 78c(a)(12)); or

(2) *Transactions of Rule 144A securities.* Transactions in securities eligible for resale under § 230.144A(d)(3) of this chapter, if such securities are sold in the United States solely to:

(i) Qualified institutional buyers, as defined in § 230.144A(a)(1) of this chapter, or purchasers that the seller and any person acting on behalf of the seller reasonably believes are qualified institutional buyers, in a transaction exempt from registration under section 4(2) of the Securities Act (15 U.S.C. 77d(2)) or § 230.144A or § 230.500 *et seq.* of this chapter; or

(ii) Persons not deemed to be "U.S. persons" for purposes of § 230.902(o)(2) or § 230.902(o)(7) of this chapter, during a distribution qualifying under paragraph (j)(2)(i) of this section.

(k) *Exemptive Authority*. Upon written application or upon its own motion, the Commission may grant an exemption from the provisions of this section, either unconditionally or on specified terms and conditions, to any transaction or class of transactions, or to any security or class of securities.

Rule 105. Short Selling in Connection With a Public Offering

(a) *Unlawful Activity*. In connection with an offering of equity securities for cash pursuant to a registration statement or a notification on Form 1-A (§ 239.90 of this chapter) or Form 1-E (§ 239.200 of this chapter) filed under the Securities Act of 1933 ("offered securities"), it shall be unlawful for any person to sell short (as defined in § 242.200(a)) the security that is the subject of the offering and purchase the offered securities from an underwriter or broker or dealer participating in the offering if such short sale was effected during the period ("Rule 105 restricted period") that is the shorter of the period:

(1) Beginning five business days before the pricing of the offered securities and ending with such pricing; or

(2) Beginning with the initial filing of such registration statement or notification on Form 1-A or Form 1-E and ending with the pricing.

(b) *Excepted Activity*.

(1) *Bona Fide Purchase*. It shall not be prohibited for such person to purchase the offered securities as provided in paragraph (a) of this section if:

(i) Such person makes a bona fide purchase(s) of the security that is the subject of the offering that is:

(A) At least equivalent in quantity to the entire amount of the Rule 105 restricted period short sale(s);

(B) Effected during regular trading hours;

(C) Reported to an "effective transaction reporting plan" (as defined in § 242.600(b)(23)); and

(D) Effected after the last Rule 105 restricted period short sale, and no later than the business day prior to the day of pricing; and

(ii) Such person did not effect a short sale, that is reported to an effective transaction reporting plan, within the 30 minutes prior to the close of regular trading hours (as defined in § 242.600(b)(68)) on the business day prior to the day of pricing.

(2) *Separate Accounts*. Paragraph (a) of this section shall not prohibit the purchase of the offered security in an account of a person where such person sold short during the Rule 105 restricted period in a separate account, if decisions regarding securities transactions for each account are made separately and without coordination of trading or cooperation among or between the accounts.

(3) *Investment Companies*. Paragraph (a) of this section shall not prohibit an investment company (as defined by Section 3 of the Investment Company Act) that is registered under Section 8 of the Investment Company Act, or a series of such company (investment company) from purchasing an offered security where any of the following sold the offered security short during the Rule 105 restricted period:

(i) An affiliated investment company, or any series of such a company; or

(ii) A separate series of the investment company.

(c) *Excepted Offerings*. This section shall not apply to offerings filed under § 230.415 of this chapter or to offerings that are not conducted on a firm commitment basis.

(d) *Exemptive Authority*. Upon written application or upon its own motion, the Commission may grant an exemption from the provisions of this section, either unconditionally or on specified terms and conditions, to any transaction or class of transactions, or to any security or class of securities.

REGULATION SHO—REGULATION OF SHORT SALES

17 C.F.R. §§ 242.200 to 242.203

Rule 200. Definition of "Short Sale" and Marking Requirements

(a) The term short sale shall mean any sale of a security which the seller does not own or any sale which is consummated by the delivery of a security borrowed by, or for the account of, the seller.

(b) A person shall be deemed to own a security if:

(1) The person or his agent has title to it; or

(2) The person has purchased, or has entered into an unconditional contract, binding on both parties thereto, to purchase it, but has not yet received it; or

(3) The person owns a security convertible into or exchangeable for it and has tendered such security for conversion or exchange; or

(4) The person has an option to purchase or acquire it and has exercised such option; or

(5) The person has rights or warrants to subscribe to it and has exercised such rights or warrants; or

(6) The person holds a security futures contract to purchase it and has received notice that the position will be physically settled and is irrevocably bound to receive the underlying security.

(c) A person shall be deemed to own securities only to the extent that he has a net long position in such securities.

(d) A broker or dealer shall be deemed to own a security, even if it is not net long, if:

(1) The broker or dealer acquired that security while acting in the capacity of a block positioner; and

(2) If and to the extent that the broker or dealer's short position in the security is the subject of offsetting positions created in the course of bona fide arbitrage, risk arbitrage, or bona fide hedge activities.

(e) A broker-dealer shall be deemed to own a security even if it is not net long, if:

(1) The broker-dealer is unwinding index arbitrage position involving a long basket of stock and one or more short index futures traded on a board of trade or one or more standardized options contracts as defined in 17 CFR 240.9b-1(a)(4); and

(2) If and to the extent that the broker-dealer's short position in the security is the subject of offsetting positions created and maintained in the course of bonafide arbitrage, risk arbitrage, or bona fide hedge activities; and

(3) The sale does not occur during a period commencing at the time that the NYSE Composite Index has declined by two percent or more from its closing value on the previous day and terminating upon the end of the trading day. The two percent shall be calculated at the beginning of each calendar quarter and shall be two percent, rounded down to the

nearest 10 points, of the average closing value of the NYSE Composite Index for the last month of the previous quarter.

(f) In order to determine its net position, a broker or dealer shall aggregate all of its positions in a security unless it qualifies for independent trading unit aggregation, in which case each independent trading unit shall aggregate all of its positions in a security to determine its net position. Independent trading unit aggregation is available only if:

(1) The broker or dealer has a written plan of organization that identifies each aggregation unit, specifies its trading objective(s), and supports its independent identity;

(2) Each aggregation unit within the firm determines, at the time of each sale, its net position for every security that it trades;

(3) All traders in an aggregation unit pursue only the particular trading objective(s) or strategy(s) of that aggregation unit and do not coordinate that strategy with any other aggregation unit; and

(4) Individual traders are assigned to only one aggregation unit at any time.

(g) A broker or dealer must mark all sell orders of any equity security as "long," "short," or "short exempt."

(1) An order to sell shall be marked "long" only if the seller is deemed to own the security being sold pursuant to paragraphs (a) through (f) of this section and either:

(i) The security to be delivered is in the physical possession or control of the broker or dealer; or

(ii) It is reasonably expected that the security will be in the physical possession or control of the broker or dealer no later than the settlement of the transaction.

(2) A sale order shall be marked "short exempt" only if the provisions of § 242.201(c) or (d) are met.

(h) Upon written application or upon its own motion, the Commission may grant an exemption from the provisions of this section, either unconditionally or on specified terms and conditions, to any transaction or class of transactions, or to any security or class of securities, or to any person or class of persons.

Rule 201. Circuit Breaker

(a) Definitions. For the purposes of this section:

(1) The term *covered security* shall mean any NMS stock as defined in § 242.600(b)(48).

(2) The term *effective transaction reporting plan for a covered security* shall have the same meaning as in § 242.600(b)(23).

(3) The term *listing market* shall have the same meaning as the term "listing market" as defined in the effective transaction reporting plan for the covered security.

(4) The term *national best bid* shall have the same meaning as in § 42.600(b)(43).

(5) The term *odd lot* shall have the same meaning as in § 242.600(b)(51).

(6) The term *plan processor* shall have the same meaning as in § 242.600(b)(59).

(7) The term *regular trading hours* shall have the same meaning as in § 242.600(b)(68).

(8) The term *riskless principal* shall mean a transaction in which a broker or dealer, after having received an order to buy a security, purchases the security as principal at the same price to satisfy the order to buy, exclusive of any explicitly disclosed markup or markdown, commission equivalent, or other fee, or, after having received an order to sell, sells the security as principal at the same price to satisfy the order to sell, exclusive of any explicitly disclosed markup or markdown, commission equivalent, or other fee.

(9) The term *trading center* shall have the same meaning as in § 242.600(b)(82).

(b)(1) A trading center shall establish, maintain, and enforce written policies and procedures reasonably designed to:

(i) Prevent the execution or display of a short sale order of a covered security at a price that is less than or equal to the current national best bid if the price of that covered security decreases by 10% or more from the covered security's closing price as determined by the listing market for the covered security as of the end of regular trading hours on the prior day; and

(ii) Impose the requirements of paragraph (b)(1)(i) of this section for the remainder of the day and the following day when a national best bid for the covered security is calculated and disseminated on a current and continuing basis by a plan processor pursuant to an effective national market system plan.

(iii) Provided, however, that the policies and procedures must be reasonably designed to permit:

(A) The execution of a displayed short sale order of a covered security by a trading center if, at the time of initial display of the short sale order, the order was at a price above the current national best bid; and

(B) The execution or display of a short sale order of a covered security marked "short exempt" without regard to whether the order is at a price that is less than or equal to the current national best bid.

(2) A trading center shall regularly surveil to ascertain the effectiveness of the policies and procedures required by paragraph (b)(1) of this section and shall take prompt action to remedy deficiencies in such policies and procedures.

(3) The determination regarding whether the price of a covered security has decreased by 10% or more from the covered security's closing price as determined by the listing market for the covered security as of the end of regular trading hours on the prior day shall be made by the listing market for the covered security and, if such decrease has occurred, the listing market shall immediately notify the single plan processor responsible for consolidation of information for the covered security pursuant to § 242.603(b). The single plan processor must then disseminate this information.

(c) Following any determination and notification pursuant to paragraph (b)(3) of this section with respect to a covered security, a broker or dealer submitting a short sale order of the covered security in question to a trading center may mark the order "short exempt" if the broker or dealer identifies the order as being at a price above the current national best bid at the time of submission; provided, however:

(1) The broker or dealer that identifies a short sale order of a covered security as "short exempt" in accordance with this paragraph (c) must establish, maintain, and enforce written policies and procedures reasonably designed to prevent incorrect identification of orders for purposes of this paragraph; and

(2) The broker or dealer shall regularly surveil to ascertain the effectiveness of the policies and procedures required by paragraph (c)(1) of this section and shall take prompt action to remedy deficiencies in such policies and procedures.

(d) Following any determination and notification pursuant to paragraph (b)(3) of this section with respect to a covered security, a broker or dealer may mark a short sale order of a covered security "short exempt" if the broker or dealer has a reasonable basis to believe that:

(1) The short sale order of a covered security is by a person that is deemed to own the covered security pursuant to § 242.200, provided that the person intends to deliver the security as soon as all restrictions on delivery have been removed.

(2) The short sale order of a covered security is by a market maker to offset customer odd-lot orders or to liquidate an odd-lot position that changes such broker's or dealer's position by no more than a unit of trading.

(3) The short sale order of a covered security is for a good faith account of a person who then owns another security by virtue of which he is, or presently will be, entitled to acquire an equivalent number of securities of the same class as the securities sold; provided such sale, or the purchase which such sale offsets, is effected for the bona fide purpose of profiting from a current difference between the price of the security sold and the security owned and that such right of acquisition was originally attached to or represented by another security or was issued to all the holders of any such securities of the issuer.

(4) The short sale order of a covered security is for a good faith account and submitted to profit from a current price difference between a security on a foreign securities market and a security on a securities market subject to the jurisdiction of the United States, provided that the short seller has an offer to buy on a foreign market that allows the seller to immediately cover the short sale at the time it was made. For the purposes of this paragraph (d)(4), a depository receipt of a security shall be deemed to be the same security as the security represented by such receipt.

(5)(i) The short sale order of a covered security is by an underwriter or member of a syndicate or group participating in the distribution of a security in connection with an over-allotment of securities; or

(ii) The short sale order of a covered security is for purposes of a lay-off sale by an underwriter or member of a syndicate or group in connection with a distribution of securities through a rights or standby underwriting commitment.

(6) The short sale order of a covered security is by a broker or dealer effecting the execution of a customer purchase or the execution of a customer "long" sale on a riskless principal basis. In addition, for purposes of this paragraph (d)(6), a broker or dealer must have written policies and procedures in place to assure that, at a minimum:

(i) The customer order was received prior to the offsetting transaction;

(ii) The offsetting transaction is allocated to a riskless principal or customer account within 60 seconds of execution; and

(iii) The broker or dealer has supervisory systems in place to produce records that enable the broker or dealer to accurately and readily reconstruct, in a time-sequenced manner, all orders on which a broker or dealer relies pursuant to this exception.

(7) The short sale order is for the sale of a covered security at the volume weighted average price (VWAP) that meets the following criteria:

(i) The VWAP for the covered security is calculated by:

(A) Calculating the values for every regular way trade reported in the consolidated system for the security during the regular trading session, by multiplying each such price by the total number of shares traded at that price;

(B) Compiling an aggregate sum of all values; and

(C) Dividing the aggregate sum by the total number of reported shares for that day in the security.

(ii) The transactions are reported using a special VWAP trade modifier.

(iii) The VWAP matched security:

(A) Qualifies as an "actively-traded security" pursuant to § 242.101 and § 242.102; or

(B) The proposed short sale transaction is being conducted as part of a basket transaction of twenty or more securities in which the subject security does not comprise more than 5% of the value of the basket traded.

(iv) The transaction is not effected for the purpose of creating actual, or apparent, active trading in or otherwise affecting the price of any security.

(v) A broker or dealer shall be permitted to act as principal on the contraside to fill customer short sale orders only if the broker's or dealer's position in the covered security, as committed by the broker or dealer during the preopening period of a trading day and aggregated across all of its customers who propose to sell short the same security on a VWAP basis, does not exceed 10% of the covered security's relevant average daily trading volume.

(e) No self-regulatory organization shall have any rule that is not in conformity with, or conflicts with, this section.

(f) Upon written application or upon its own motion, the Commission may grant an exemption from the provisions of this section, either unconditionally or on specified terms and conditions, to any person or class of persons, to any transaction or class of transactions, or to any security or class of securities to the extent that such exemption is necessary or appropriate, in the public interest, and is consistent with the protection of investors.

Rule 203. Borrowing and Delivery Requirements

(a) Long Sales. (1) If a broker or dealer knows or has reasonable grounds to believe that the sale of an equity security was or will be effected pursuant to an order marked "long," such broker or dealer shall not lend or arrange for the loan of any security for delivery to the purchaser's broker after the sale, or fail to deliver a security on the date delivery is due.

(2) The provisions of paragraph (a)(1) of this section shall not apply:

(i) To the loan of any security by a broker or dealer through the medium of a loan to another broker or dealer;

(ii) If the broker or dealer knows, or has been reasonably informed by the seller, that the seller owns the security, and that the seller would deliver the security to the broker or dealer prior to the scheduled settlement of the transaction, but the seller failed to do so; or

(iii) If, prior to any loan or arrangement to loan any security for delivery, or failure to deliver, a national securities exchange, in the case of a sale effected thereon, or a national securities association, in the case of a sale not effected on an exchange, finds:

(A) That such sale resulted from a mistake made in good faith;

(B) That due diligence was used to ascertain that the circumstances specified in § 242.200(g) existed; and

(C) Either that the condition of the market at the time the mistake was discovered was such that undue hardship would result from covering the transaction by a "purchase for cash" or that the mistake was made by the seller's broker and the sale was at a permissible price under any applicable short sale price test.

(b) Short Sales. (1) A broker or dealer may not accept a short sale order in an equity security from another person, or effect a short sale in an equity security for its own account, unless the broker or dealer has:

(i) Borrowed the security, or entered into a bona-fide arrangement to borrow the security; or

(ii) Reasonable grounds to believe that the security can be borrowed so that it can be delivered on the date delivery is due; and

(iii) Documented compliance with this paragraph (b)(1).

(2) The provisions of paragraph (b)(1) of this section shall not apply to:

(i) A broker or dealer that has accepted a short sale order from another registered broker or dealer that is required to comply with paragraph (b)(1) of this section, unless the broker or dealer relying on this exception contractually undertook responsibility for compliance with paragraph (b)(1) of this section;

(ii) Any sale of a security that a person is deemed to own pursuant to § 242.200, provided that the broker or dealer has been reasonably informed that the person intends to deliver such security as soon as all restrictions on delivery have been removed. If the person has not delivered such security within 35 days after the trade date, the broker-dealer that effected the sale must borrow securities or close out the short position by purchasing securities of like kind and quantity;

(iii) Short sales effected by a market maker in connection with bona-fide market making activities in the security for which this exception is claimed; and

(iv) Transactions in security futures.

(3) If a participant of a registered clearing agency has a fail to deliver position at a registered clearing agency in a threshold security for thirteen consecutive settlement days, the participant shall immediately thereafter close out the fail to deliver position by purchasing securities of like kind and quantity:

(i) Provided, however, that a participant of a registered clearing agency that has a fail to deliver position at a registered clearing agency in a threshold security on the effective date of this amendment and which, prior to the effective date of this amendment, had been previously grandfathered from the close-out requirement in this paragraph (b)(3) (i.e., because the participant of a registered clearing agency had a fail to deliver position at a registered clearing agency on the settlement day preceding the day that the security became a threshold security), shall close out that fail to deliver position within thirty-five consecutive settlement days of the effective date of this amendment by purchasing securities of like kind and quantity;

(ii) Provided, however, that if a participant of a registered clearing agency has a fail to deliver position at a registered clearing agency in a threshold security that was sold pursuant to § 230.144 of this chapter for thirty-five consecutive settlement days, the participant shall immediately thereafter close out the fail to deliver position in the security by purchasing securities of like kind and quantity;

(iii) Provided, however, that a participant of a registered clearing agency that has a fail to deliver position at a registered clearing agency in a threshold security on the effective date of this amendment and which, prior to the effective date of this amendment, had been previously excepted from the close-out requirement in paragraph (b)(3) of this section (i.e., because the participant of a registered clearing agency had a fail to deliver position in the threshold security that is attributed to short sales effected by a registered options market maker to establish or maintain a hedge on options positions that were created before the security became a threshold security), shall immediately close out that fail to deliver position, including any adjustments to the fail to deliver position, within 35 consecutive settlement days of the effective date of this amendment by purchasing securities of like kind and quantity;

(iv) If a participant of a registered clearing agency has a fail to deliver position at a registered clearing agency in a threshold security for thirteen consecutive settlement days, the participant and any broker or dealer for which it clears transactions, including any market maker that would otherwise be entitled to rely on the exception provided in paragraph (b)(2)(iii) of this section, may not accept a short sale order in the threshold security from another person, or effect a short sale in the threshold security for its own account, without borrowing the security or entering into a bona-fide arrangement to borrow the security, until the participant closes out the fail to deliver position by purchasing securities of like kind and quantity;

(v) If a participant of a registered clearing agency entitled to rely on the 35 consecutive settlement day close-out requirement contained in paragraph (b)(3)(i), (b)(3)(ii), or (b)(3)(iii) of this section has a fail to deliver position at a registered clearing agency in the threshold security for 35 consecutive settlement days, the participant and any broker or dealer for which it clears transactions, including any market maker, that would otherwise be entitled to rely on the exception provided in paragraph (b)(2)(ii) of this section, may not accept a short sale order in the threshold security from another person, or effect a short sale in the threshold security for its own account, without borrowing the security or entering into a bona-fide arrangement to borrow the security, until the participant closes out the fail to deliver position by purchasing securities of like kind and quantity;

(vi) If a participant of a registered clearing agency reasonably allocates a portion of a fail to deliver position to another registered broker or dealer for which it clears trades or for which it is responsible for settlement, based on such broker or dealer's short position, then the provisions of this paragraph (b)(3) relating to such fail to deliver position shall apply to the portion of such registered broker or dealer that was allocated the fail to deliver position, and not to the participant; and

(vii) A participant of a registered clearing agency shall not be deemed to have fulfilled the requirements of this paragraph (b)(3) where the participant enters into an arrangement with another person to purchase securities as required by this paragraph (b)(3), and the participant knows or has reason to know that the other person will not deliver securities in settlement of the purchase.

(c) Definitions.

(1) For purposes of this section, the term market maker has the same meaning as in section 3(a)(38) of the Securities Exchange Act of 1934 ("Exchange Act") (15 U.S.C. 78c(a)(38)).

(2) For purposes of this section, the term participant has the same meaning as in section 3(a)(24) of the Exchange Act (15 U.S.C. 78c(a)(24)).

(3) For purposes of this section, the term registered clearing agency means a clearing agency, as defined in section 3(a)(23)(A) of the Exchange Act (15 U.S.C. 78c(a)(23)(A)), that is registered with the Commission pursuant to section 17A of the Exchange Act (15 U.S.C. 78q-1).

(4) For purposes of this section, the term security future has the same meaning as in section 3(a)(55) of the Exchange Act (15 U.S.C. 78c(a)(55)).

(5) For purposes of this section, the term settlement day means any business day on which deliveries of securities and payments of money may be made through the facilities of a registered clearing agency.

(6) For purposes of this section, the term threshold security means any equity security of an issuer that is registered pursuant to section 12 of the Exchange Act (15 U.S.C. 78l) or for which the issuer is required to file reports pursuant to section 15(d) of the Exchange Act (15 U.S.C. 78o(d)):

(i) For which there is an aggregate fail to deliver position for five consecutive settlement days at a registered clearing agency of 10,000 shares or more, and that is equal to at least 0.5% of the issue's total shares outstanding;

(ii) Is included on a list disseminated to its members by a self-regulatory organization; and

(iii) Provided, however, that a security shall cease to be a threshold security if the aggregate fail to deliver position at a registered clearing agency does not exceed the level specified in paragraph (c)(6)(i) of this section for five consecutive settlement days.

(d) Exemptive Authority. Upon written application or upon its own motion, the Commission may grant an exemption from the provisions of this section, either unconditionally or on specified terms and conditions, to any transaction or class of transactions, or to any security or class of securities, or to any person or class of persons.

REGULATION M-A—SELECTED PROVISIONS

17 C.F.R. §§ 229.1000 to 229.1016

N.B. The following is not a complete text of Regulation M-A. It omits a number of statutory provisions entirely, and also omits certain subsections of provisions that are partially included.

Subpart 1000—Mergers and Acquisitions (Regulation M-A)

Item 1000. Definitions

The following definitions apply to the terms used in Regulation M-A (§§ 229.1000 through 229.1016), unless specified otherwise:

(a) *Associate* has the same meaning as in § 240.12b-2 of this chapter;

(b) *Instruction C* means General Instruction C to Schedule 13E-3 (§ 240.13e-100 of this chapter) and General Instruction C to Schedule TO (§ 240.14d-100 of this chapter);

(c) *Issuer tender offer* has the same meaning as in § 240.13e-4 (a) (2) of this chapter;

(d) *Offeror* means any person who makes a tender offer or on whose behalf a tender offer is made;

(e) *Rule 13e-3 transaction* has the same meaning as in § 240.13e-3 (a) (3) of this chapter;

(f) *Subject company* means the company or entity whose securities are sought to be acquired in the transaction (*e.g.*, the target), or that is otherwise the subject of the transaction;

(g) *Subject securities* means the securities or class of securities that are sought to be acquired in the transaction or that are otherwise the subject of the transaction; and

(h) *Third-party tender offer* means a tender offer that is not an issuer tender offer.

Item 1001. Summary Term Sheet

Summary term sheet. Provide security holders with a summary term sheet that is written in plain English. The summary term sheet must briefly describe in bullet point format the most material terms of the proposed transaction. The summary term sheet must provide security holders with sufficient information to understand the essential features and significance of the proposed transaction. The bullet points must cross-reference a more detailed discussion contained in the disclosure document that is disseminated to security holders.

Instructions to Item 1001:

1. The summary term sheet must not recite all information contained in the disclosure document that will be provided to security holders. The summary term sheet is intended to serve as an overview of all material matters that are presented in the accompanying documents provided to security holders.

2. The summary term sheet must begin on the first or second page of the disclosure document provided to security holders.

3. Refer to Rule 421(b) and (d) of Regulation C of the Securities Act (§ 230.421 of this chapter) for a description of plain English disclosure.

Item 1002. Subject Company Information

(a) *Name and address.* State the name of the subject company (or the issuer in the case of an issuer tender offer), and the address and telephone number of its principal executive offices.

(b) *Securities.* State the exact title and number of shares outstanding of the subject class of equity securities as of the most recent practicable date. This may be based upon information in the most recently available filing with the Commission by the subject company unless the filing person has more current information.

(c) *Trading market and price.* Identify the principal market in which the subject securities are traded and state the high and low sales prices for the subject securities in the principal market (or, if there is no principal market, the range of high and low bid quotations and the source of the quotations) for each quarter during the past two years. If there is no established trading market for the securities (except for limited or sporadic quotations), so state.

(d) *Dividends.* State the frequency and amount of any dividends paid during the past two years with respect to the subject securities. Briefly describe any restriction on the subject company's current or future ability to pay dividends. If the filing person is not the subject company, furnish this information to the extent known after making reasonable inquiry.

(e) *Prior public offerings.* If the filing person has made an underwritten public offering of the subject securities for cash during the past three years that was registered under the Securities Act of 1933 or exempt from registration under Regulation A (§ 230.251 through § 230.263 of this chapter), state the date of the offering, the amount of securities offered, the offering price per share (adjusted for stock splits, stock dividends, etc. as appropriate) and the aggregate proceeds received by the filing person.

(f) *Prior stock purchases.* If the filing person purchased any subject securities during the past two years, state the amount of the securities purchased, the range of prices paid and the average purchase price for each quarter during that period. Affiliates need not give information for purchases made before becoming an affiliate.

Item 1003. Identity and Background of Filing Person

(a) *Name and address.* State the name, business address and business telephone number of each filing person. Also state the name and address of each person specified in Instruction C to the schedule (except for Schedule 14D-9 (§ 240.14d-101 of this chapter)). If the filing person is an affiliate of the subject company, state the nature of the affiliation. If the filing person is the subject company, so state.

(b) *Business and background of entities.* If any filing person (other than the subject company) or any person specified in Instruction C to the schedule is not a natural person, state the person's principal business, state or other place of organization, and the information required by paragraphs (c)(3) and (c)(4) of this section for each person.

(c) *Business and background of natural persons.* If any filing person or any person specified in Instruction C to the schedule is a natural person, provide the following information for each person:

(1) Current principal occupation or employment and the name, principal business and address of any corporation or other organization in which the employment or occupation is conducted;

(2) Material occupations, positions, offices or employment during the past five years, giving the starting and ending dates of each and the name, principal business and address of any corporation or other organization in which the occupation, position, office or employment was carried on;

(3) A statement whether or not the person was convicted in a criminal proceeding during the past five years (excluding traffic violations or similar misdemeanors). If the person was convicted, describe the criminal proceeding, including the dates, nature of conviction, name and location of court, and penalty imposed or other disposition of the case;

(4) A statement whether or not the person was a party to any judicial or administrative proceeding during the past five years (except for matters that were dismissed without sanction or settlement) that resulted in a judgment, decree or final order enjoining the person from future violations of, or prohibiting activities subject to, federal or state securities laws, or a finding of any violation of federal or state securities laws. Describe the proceeding, including a summary of the terms of the judgment, decree or final order; and

(5) Country of citizenship.

(d) *Tender offer.* Identify the tender offer and the class of securities to which the offer relates, the name of the offeror and its address (which may be based on the offeror's Schedule TO (§ 240.14d-100 of this chapter) filed with the Commission).

Instruction to Item 1003:

If the filing person is making information relating to the transaction available on the Internet, state the address where the information can be found.

Item 1004. Terms of the Transaction

(a) *Material terms.* State the material terms of the transaction.

(1) *Tender offers.* In the case of a tender offer, the information must include:

(i) The total number and class of securities sought in the offer;

(ii) The type and amount of consideration offered to security holders;

(iii) The scheduled expiration date;

(iv) Whether a subsequent offering period will be available, if the transaction is a third-party tender offer;

(v) Whether the offer may be extended, and if so, how it could be extended;

(vi) The dates before and after which security holders may withdraw securities tendered in the offer;

(vii) The procedures for tendering and withdrawing securities;

(viii) The manner in which securities will be accepted for payment;

(ix) If the offer is for less than all securities of a class, the periods for accepting securities on a pro rata basis and the offeror's present intentions in the event that the offer is oversubscribed;

(x) An explanation of any material differences in the rights of security holders as a result of the transaction, if material;

(xi) A brief statement as to the accounting treatment of the transaction, if material; and

(xii) The federal income tax consequences of the transaction, if material.

(2) *Mergers or Similar Transactions.* In the case of a merger or similar transaction, the information must include:

(i) A brief description of the transaction;

(ii) The consideration offered to security holders;

    (iii) The reasons for engaging in the transaction;

    (iv) The vote required for approval of the transaction;

    (v) An explanation of any material differences in the rights of security holders as a result of the transaction, if material;

    (vi) A brief statement as to the accounting treatment of the transaction, if material; and

    (vii) The federal income tax consequences of the transaction, if material.

Instruction to Item 1004(a):

If the consideration offered includes securities exempt from registration under the Securities Act of 1933, provide a description of the securities that complies with Item 202 of Regulation S-K (§ 229.202). This description is not required if the issuer of the securities meets the requirements of General Instructions I.A, I.B.1 or I.B.2, as applicable, or I.C. of Form S-3 (§ 239.13 of this chapter) and elects to furnish information by incorporation by reference; only capital stock is to be issued; and securities of the same class are registered under section 12 of the Exchange Act and either are listed for trading or admitted to unlisted trading privileges on a national securities exchange; or are securities for which bid and offer quotations are reported in an automated quotations system operated by a national securities association.

(b) *Purchases.* State whether any securities are to be purchased from any officer, director or affiliate of the subject company and provide the details of each transaction.

(c) *Different terms.* Describe any term or arrangement in the Rule 13e-3 transaction that treats any subject security holders differently from other subject security holders.

(d) *Appraisal rights.* State whether or not dissenting security holders are entitled to any appraisal rights. If so, summarize the appraisal rights. If there are no appraisal rights available under state law for security holders who object to the transaction, briefly outline any other rights that may be available to security holders under the law.

(e) *Provisions for unaffiliated security holders.* Describe any provision made by the filing person in connection with the transaction to grant unaffiliated security holders access to the corporate files of the filing person or to obtain counsel or appraisal services at the expense of the filing person. If none, so state.

(f) *Eligibility for listing or trading.* If the transaction involves the offer of securities of the filing person in exchange for equity securities held by unaffiliated security holders of the subject company, describe whether or not the filing person will take steps to assure that the securities offered are or will be eligible for trading on an automated quotations system operated by a national securities association.

Item 1005. Past Contacts, Transactions, Negotiations and Agreements

(a) *Transactions.* Briefly state the nature and approximate dollar amount of any transaction, other than those described in paragraphs (b) or (c) of this section, that occurred during the past two years, between the filing person (including any person specified in Instruction C of the schedule) and;

    (1) The subject company or any of its affiliates that are not natural persons if the aggregate value of the transactions is more than one percent of the subject company's consolidated revenues for:

    (i) The fiscal year when the transaction occurred; or

    (ii) The past portion of the current fiscal year, if the transaction occurred in the current year; and

Instruction to Item 1005(a)(1):

The information required by this Item may be based on information in the subject company's most recent filing with the Commission, unless the filing person has reason to believe the information is not accurate.

(2) Any executive officer, director or affiliate of the subject company that is a natural person if the aggregate value of the transaction or series of similar transactions with that person exceeds $60,000.

(b) *Significant corporate events.* Describe any negotiations, transactions or material contacts during the past two years between the filing person (including subsidiaries of the filing person and any person specified in Instruction C of the schedule) and the subject company or its affiliates concerning any:

(1) Merger;

(2) Consolidation;

(3) Acquisition;

(4) Tender offer for or other acquisition of any class of the subject company's securities;

(5) Election of the subject company's directors; or

(6) Sale or other transfer of a material amount of assets of the subject company.

(c) *Negotiations or contacts.* Describe any negotiations or material contacts concerning the matters referred to in paragraph (b) of this section during the past two years between:

(1) Any affiliates of the subject company; or

(2) The subject company or any of its affiliates and any person not affiliated with the subject company who would have a direct interest in such matters.

Instruction to paragraphs (b) and (c) of Item 1005:

Identify the person who initiated the contacts or negotiations.

(d) *Conflicts of interest.* If material, describe any agreement, arrangement or understanding and any actual or potential conflict of interest between the filing person or its affiliates and:

(1) The subject company, its executive officers, directors or affiliates;or

(2) The offeror, its executive officers, directors or affiliates.

Instruction to Item 1005(d):

If the filing person is the subject company, no disclosure called for by this paragraph is required in the document disseminated to security holders, so long as substantially the same information was filed with the Commission previously and disclosed in a proxy statement, report or other communication sent to security holders by the subject company in the past year. The document disseminated to security holders, however, must refer specifically to the discussion in the proxy statement, report or other communication that was sent to security holders previously. The information also must be filed as an exhibit to the schedule.

(e) *Agreements involving the subject company's securities.* Describe any agreement, arrangement, or understanding, whether or not legally enforceable, between the filing person (including any person specified in Instruction C of the schedule) and any other person with respect to any securities of the subject company. Name all persons that are a party to the agreements, arrangements, or understandings and describe all material provisions.

Instructions to Item 1005(e):

1. The information required by this Item includes: the transfer or voting of securities, joint ventures, loan or option arrangements, puts or calls, guarantees of loans, guarantees against loss, or the giving or withholding of proxies, consents or authorizations.

2. Include information for any securities that are pledged or otherwise subject to a contingency, the occurrence of which would give another person the power to direct the voting or disposition of the subject securities. No disclosure, however, is required about standard default and similar provisions contained in loan agreements.

Item 1006. Purpose of the Transaction and Plans or Proposals

(a) *Purposes.* State the purposes of the transaction.

(b) *Use of securities acquired.* Indicate whether the securities acquired in the transaction will be retained, retired, held in treasury, or otherwise disposed of.

(c) *Plans.* Describe any plans, proposals or negotiations that relate to or would result in:

(1) Any extraordinary transaction, such as a merger, reorganization or liquidation, involving the subject company or any of its subsidiaries;

(2) Any purchase, sale or transfer of a material amount of assets of the subject company or any of its subsidiaries;

(3) Any material change in the present dividend rate or policy, or indebtedness or capitalization of the subject company;

(4) Any change in the present board of directors or management of the subject company, including, but not limited to, any plans or proposals to change the number or the term of directors or to fill any existing vacancies on the board or to change any material term of the employment contract of any executive officer;

(5) Any other material change in the subject company's corporate structure or business, including, if the subject company is a registered closed-end investment company, any plans or proposals to make any changes in its investment policy for which a vote would be required by Section 13 of the Investment Company Act of 1940 (15 U.S.C. 80a-13);

(6) Any class of equity securities of the subject company to be delisted from a national securities exchange or cease to be authorized to be quoted in an automated quotations system operated by a national securities association;

(7) Any class of equity securities of the subject company becoming eligible for termination of registration under Section 12(g)(4) of the Act (15 U.S.C. 78*l*);

(8) The suspension of the subject company's obligation to file reports under Section 15(d) of the Act (15 U.S.C. 78o);

(9) The acquisition by any person of additional securities of the subject company, or the disposition of securities of the subject company; or

(10) Any changes in the subject company's charter, bylaws or other governing instruments or other actions that could impede the acquisition of control of the subject company.

(d) *Subject company negotiations.* If the filing person is the subject company:

(1) State whether or not that person is undertaking or engaged in any negotiations in response to the tender offer that relate to:

(i) A tender offer or other acquisition of the subject company's securities by the filing person, any of its subsidiaries, or any other person; or

(ii) Any of the matters referred to in paragraphs (c)(1) through (c)(3) of this section; and

(2) Describe any transaction, board resolution, agreement in principle, or signed contract that is entered into in response to the tender offer that relates to one or more of the matters referred to in paragraph (d)(1) of this section.

Instruction to Item 1006(d)(1):

If an agreement in principle has not been reached at the time of filing, no disclosure under paragraph (d)(1) of this section is required of the possible terms of or the parties to the transaction if in the opinion of the board of directors of the subject company disclosure would jeopardize continuation of the negotiations. In that case, disclosure indicating that negotiations are being undertaken or are underway and are in the preliminary stages is sufficient.

Item 1007. Source and Amount of Funds or Other Consideration

(a) *Source of funds.* State the specific sources and total amount of funds or other consideration to be used in the transaction. If the transaction involves a tender offer, disclose the amount of funds or other consideration required to purchase the maximum amount of securities sought in the offer.

(b) *Conditions.* State any material conditions to the financing discussed in response to paragraph (a) of this section. Disclose any alternative financing arrangements or alternative financing plans in the event the primary financing plans fall through. If none, so state.

(c) *Expenses.* Furnish a reasonably itemized statement of all expenses incurred or estimated to be incurred in connection with the transaction including, but not limited to, filing, legal, accounting and appraisal fees, solicitation expenses and printing costs and state whether or not the subject company has paid or will be responsible for paying any or all expenses.

(d) *Borrowed funds.* If all or any part of the funds or other consideration required is, or is expected, to be borrowed, directly or indirectly, for the purpose of the transaction:

(1) Provide a summary of each loan agreement or arrangement containing the identity of the parties, the term, the collateral, the stated and effective interest rates, and any other material terms or conditions of the loan; and

(2) Briefly describe any plans or arrangements to finance or repay the loan, or, if no plans or arrangements have been made, so state.

Instruction to Item 1007(d):

If the transaction is a third-party tender offer and the source of all or any part of the funds used in the transaction is to come from a loan made in the ordinary course of business by a bank as defined by Section 3(a)(6) of the Act (15 U.S.C. 78c), the name of the bank will not be made available to the public if the filing person so requests in writing and files the request, naming the bank, with the Secretary of the Commission.

Item 1008. Interest in Securities of the Subject Company (omitted)

Item 1009. Persons/Assets, Retained, Employed, Compensated or Used (omitted)

Item 1010. Financial Statements (omitted)

Item 1011. Additional information

(a) *Agreements, regulatory requirements and legal proceedings.* If material to a security holder's decision whether to sell, tender or hold the securities sought in the tender offer, furnish the following information:

(1) Any present or proposed material agreement, arrangement, understanding or relationship between the offeror or any of its executive officers, directors, controlling persons or subsidiaries and the subject company or any of its executive officers, directors, controlling persons or subsidiaries (other than any agreement, arrangement or understanding disclosed under any other sections of Regulation M-A (§§ 229.1000 through 229.1016));

Instruction to paragraph (a)(1):

In an issuer tender offer disclose any material agreement, arrangement, understanding or relationship between the offeror and any of its executive officers, directors, controlling persons or subsidiaries.

(2) To the extent known by the offeror after reasonable investigation, the applicable regulatory requirements which must be complied with or approvals which must be obtained in connection with the tender offer;

(3) The applicability of any anti-trust laws;

(4) The applicability of margin requirements under Section 7 of the Act (15 U.S.C. 78g) and the applicable regulations; and

(5) Any material pending legal proceedings relating to the tender offer, including the name and location of the court or agency in which the proceedings are pending, the date instituted, the principal parties, and a brief summary of the proceedings and the relief sought.

Instruction to Item 1011(a)(5):

A copy of any document relating to a major development (such as pleadings, an answer, complaint, temporary restraining order, injunction, opinion, judgment or order) in a material pending legal proceeding must be furnished promptly to the Commission staff on a supplemental basis.

(b) Furnish the information required by Item 402(t)(2) and (3) of this part (§ 229.402(t)(2) and (3)) and in the tabular format set forth in Item 402(t)(1) of this part (§ 229.402(t)(1)) with respect to each named executive officer

(1) Of the subject company in a Rule 13e-3 transaction; or

(2) Of the issuer whose securities are the subject of a third-party tender offer, regarding any agreement or understanding, whether written or unwritten, between such named executive officer and the subject company, issuer, bidder, or the acquiring company, as applicable, concerning any type of compensation, whether present, deferred or contingent, that is based upon or otherwise relates to the Rule 13e-3 transaction or third-party tender offer.

Instructions to Item 1011(b).

1. The obligation to provide the information in paragraph (b) of this section shall not apply where the issuer whose securities are the subject of the Rule 13e-3 transaction or tender offer is a foreign private issuer, as defined in § 240.3b-4 of this chapter, or an emerging growth company, as defined in Rule 405 of the Securities Act (§ 230.405 of this chapter) or Rule 12b-2 of the Exchange Act (§ 240.12b-2 of this chapter).

2. For purposes of Instruction 1 to Item 402(t)(2) of this part: If the disclosure is included in a Schedule 13E-3 (§ 240.13e-100 of this chapter) or Schedule 14D-9 (§ 240.14d-101 of this chapter), the disclosure provided by this table shall be quantified assuming that the triggering event took place on the latest practicable date and that the price per share of the securities of the subject company in a Rule 13e-3 transaction, or of the issuer whose securities are the subject of the third-party tender offer, shall be determined as follows: If the shareholders are to receive a fixed dollar amount, the price per share shall be that fixed dollar amount, and if such value is not a fixed dollar amount, the price per share shall be the average closing market price of such securities over the first five business days following the first public announcement of the transaction. Compute the dollar value of in-the-money option awards for which vesting would be accelerated by determining the difference between this price and the exercise or base price of the options. Include only compensation that is based on or otherwise relates to the subject transaction. Apply Instruction 1 to Item 402(t) with respect to those executive officers for whom disclosure was required in the most recent filing by the subject company in a Rule 13e-3 transaction or by the issuer whose securities are the subject of a third-party tender offer, with the Commission under the Securities Act (15 U.S.C. 77a et seq.) or Exchange Act (15 U.S.C. 78a et seq.) that required disclosure pursuant to Item 402(c).

(c) *Other material information.* Furnish such additional material information, if any, as may be necessary to make the required statements, in light of the circumstances under which they are made, not materially misleading.

Item 1012. The Solicitation or Recommendation (omitted)

Item 1013. Purposes, Alternatives, Reasons and Effects in a Going-Private Transaction.

(a) *Purposes.* State the purposes for the Rule 13e-3 transaction.

(b) *Alternatives.* If the subject company or affiliate considered alternative means to accomplish the stated purposes, briefly describe the alternatives and state the reasons for their rejection.

(c) *Reasons.* State the reasons for the structure of the Rule 13e-3 transaction and for undertaking the transaction at this time.

(d) *Effects.* Describe the effects of the Rule 13e-3 transaction on the subject company, its affiliates and unaffiliated security holders, including the federal tax consequences of the transaction.

Instructions to Item 1013:

1. Conclusory statements will not be considered sufficient disclosure in response to this Item 1013.

2. The description required by paragraph (d) of this Item 1013 must include a reasonably detailed discussion of both the benefits and detriments of the Rule 13e-3 transaction to the subject company, its affiliates and unaffiliated security holders. The benefits and detriments of the Rule 13e-3 transaction must be quantified to the extent practicable.

3. If this statement is filed by an affiliate of the subject company, the description required by paragraph (d) of this Item 1013 must include, but not be limited to, the effect of the Rule 13e-3 transaction on the affiliate's interest in the net book value and net earnings of the subject company in terms of both dollar amounts and percentages.

Item 1014. Fairness of the Going-Private Transaction.

(a) *Fairness.* State whether the subject company or affiliate filing the statement reasonably believes that the Rule 13e-3 transaction is fair or unfair to unaffiliated security holders. If any director dissented to or abstained from voting on the Rule 13e-3 transaction, identify the director, and indicate, if known, after making reasonable inquiry, the reasons for the dissent or abstention.

(b) *Factors Considered in Determining Fairness.* Discuss in reasonable detail the material factors upon which the belief stated in paragraph (a) of this Item 1014 is based and, to the extent practicable, the weight assigned to each factor. The discussion must include an analysis of the extent, if any, to which the filing person's beliefs are based on the factors described in Instruction 2 of this Item 1014, paragraphs (c), (d) and (e) of this Item 1014 and Item 1015 of Regulation M-A.

(c) *Approval of Security Holders.* State whether or not the transaction is structured so that approval of at least a majority of unaffiliated security holders is required.

(d) *Unaffiliated Representative.* State whether or not a majority of directors who are not employees of the subject company has retained an unaffiliated representative to act solely on behalf of unaffiliated security holders for purposes of negotiating the terms of the Rule 13e-3 transaction and/or preparing a report concerning the fairness of the transaction.

(e) *Approval of Directors.* State whether or not the Rule 13e-3 transaction was approved by a majority of the directors of the subject company who are not employees of the subject company.

(f) *Other Offers.* If any offer of the type described in paragraph (viii) of Instruction 2 to this Item 1014 has been received, describe the offer and state the reasons for its rejection.

Instructions to Item 1014:

1. A statement that the issuer or affiliate has no reasonable belief as to the fairness of the Rule 13e-3 transaction to unaffiliated security holders will not be considered sufficient disclosure in response to paragraph (a) of this Item 1014.

2. The factors that are important in determining the fairness of a transaction to unaffiliated security holders and the weight, if any, that should be given to them in a particular context will vary. Normally such factors will include, among others, those referred to in paragraphs (c), (d) and (e) of this Item 1014 and whether the consideration offered to unaffiliated security holders constitutes fair value in relation to:

(i) Current market prices;

(ii) Historical market prices;

(iii) Net book value;

(iv) Going concern value;

(v) Liquidation value;

(vi) Purchase prices paid in previous purchases disclosed in response to Item 1002(f) of Regulation M-A;

(vii) Any report, opinion, or appraisal described in Item 1015 of Regulation M-A; and

(viii) Firm offers of which the subject company or affiliate is aware made by any unaffiliated person, other than the filing persons, during the past two years for:

(A) The merger or consolidation of the subject company with or into another company, or vice versa;

(B) The sale or other transfer of all or any substantial part of the assets of the subject company; or

(C) A purchase of the subject company's securities that would enable the holder to exercise control of the subject company.

3. Conclusory statements, such as "The Rule 13e-3 transaction is fair to unaffiliated security holders in relation to net book value, going concern value and future prospects of the issuer" will not be considered sufficient disclosure in response to paragraph (b) of this Item 1014.

Item 1015. Reports, Opinions, Appraisals and Negotiations (omitted)

Item 1016. Exhibits (omitted)

REGULATION AC

17 C.F.R. §§ 242.500 to 242.505

Rule 500. Definitions

For purposes of Regulation AC (§§ 242.500 through 242.505 of this chapter) the term:

Covered person of a broker or dealer means an associated person of that broker or dealer but does not include:

(1) An associated person:

(i) If the associated person has no officers (or persons performing similar functions) or employees in common with the broker or dealer who can influence the activities of research analysts or the content of research reports; and

(ii) If the broker or dealer maintains and enforces written policies and procedures reasonably designed to prevent the broker or dealer, any controlling persons, officers (or persons performing similar functions), and employees of the broker or dealer from influencing the activities of research analysts and the content of research reports prepared by the associated person.

(2) An associated person who is an investment adviser:

(i) Not registered with the Commission as an investment adviser because of the prohibition of section 203A of the Investment Advisers Act of 1940 (15 U.S.C. 80b-3a); and

(ii) Not registered or required to be registered with the Commission as a broker or dealer.

Note to definition of covered person: An associated person of a broker or dealer who is not a covered person continues to be subject to the federal securities laws, including the anti-fraud provisions of the federal securities laws.

Foreign person means any person who is not a U.S. person.

Foreign security means a security issued by a foreign issuer for which a U.S. market is not the principal trading market.

Public appearance means any participation by a research analyst in a seminar, forum (including an interactive electronic forum), or radio or television or other interview, in which the research analyst makes a specific recommendation or provides information reasonably sufficient upon which to base an investment decision about a security or an issuer.

Registered broker or dealer means a broker or dealer registered or required to register pursuant to section 15 or section 15B of the Securities Exchange Act of 1934 (15 U.S.C. 78o or 78o-4) or a government securities broker or government securities dealer registered or required to register pursuant to section 15C(a)(1)(A) of the Securities Exchange Act of 1934 (15 U.S.C. 78o-5(a)(1)(A)).

Research analyst means any natural person who is primarily responsible for the preparation of the content of a research report.

Research report means a written communication (including an electronic communication) that includes an analysis of a security or an issuer and provides information reasonably sufficient upon which to base an investment decision.

Third party research analyst means:

(1) With respect to a broker or dealer, any research analyst not employed by that broker or dealer or any associated person of that broker or dealer; and

(2) With respect to a covered person of a broker or dealer, any research analyst not employed by that covered person, by the broker or dealer with whom that covered person is associated, or by any other associated person of the broker or dealer with whom that covered person is associated.

United States has the meaning contained in § 230.902(l) of this chapter.

U.S. person has the meaning contained in § 230.902(k) of this chapter.

Rule 501. Certifications in connection with research reports

(a) A broker or dealer or covered person that publishes, circulates, or provides a research report prepared by a research analyst to a U.S. person in the United States shall include in that research report a clear and prominent certification by the research analyst containing the following:

(1) A statement attesting that all of the views expressed in the research report accurately reflect the research analyst's personal views about any and all of the subject securities or issuers; and

(2) (i) A statement attesting that no part of the research analyst's compensation was, is, or will be, directly or indirectly, related to the specific recommendations or views expressed by the research analyst in the research report; or

(ii) A statement:

(A) Attesting that part or all of the research analyst's compensation was, is, or will be, directly or indirectly, related to the specific recommendations or views expressed by the research analyst in the research report;

(B) Identifying the source, amount, and purpose of such compensation; and

(C) Further disclosing that the compensation could influence the recommendations or views expressed in the research report.

(b) A broker or dealer or covered person that publishes, circulates, or provides a research report prepared by a third party research analyst to a U.S. person in the United States shall be exempt from the requirements of this section with respect to such research report if the following conditions are satisfied:

(1) The employer of the third party research analyst has no officers (or persons performing similar functions) or employees in common with the broker or dealer or covered person; and

(2) The broker or dealer (or, with respect to a covered person, the broker or dealer with whom the covered person is associated) maintains and enforces written policies and procedures reasonably designed to prevent the broker or dealer, any controlling persons, officers (or persons performing similar functions), and employees of the broker or dealer from influencing the activities of the third party research analyst and the content of research reports prepared by the third party research analyst.

Rule 502. Certifications in connection with public appearances

(a) If a broker or dealer publishes, circulates, or provides a research report prepared by a research analyst employed by the broker or dealer or covered person to a U.S. person in the

United States, the broker or dealer must make a record within thirty days after any calendar quarter in which the research analyst made a public appearance that contains the following:

(1) A statement by the research analyst attesting that the views expressed by the research analyst in all public appearances during the calendar quarter accurately reflected the research analyst's personal views at that time about any and all of the subject securities or issuers; and

(2) A statement by the research analyst attesting that no part of the research analyst's compensation was, is, or will be, directly or indirectly, related to the specific recommendations or views expressed by the research analyst in such public appearances.

(b) If the broker or dealer does not obtain a statement by the research analyst in accordance with paragraph (a) of this section:

(1) The broker or dealer shall promptly notify in writing its examining authority, designated pursuant to section 17(d) of the Securities Exchange Act of 1934 (15 U.S.C. 78q(d)) and 240.17d-2 of this chapter, that the research analyst did not provide the certifications specified in paragraph (a) of this section; and

(2) For 120 days following notification pursuant to paragraph (b)(1) of this section, the broker or dealer shall disclose in any research report prepared by the research analyst and published, circulated, or provided to a U.S. person in the United States that the research analyst did not provide the certifications specified in paragraph (a) of this section.

(c) In the case of a research analyst who is employed outside the United States by a foreign person located outside the United States, this section shall only apply to a public appearance while the research analyst is physically present in the United States.

(d) A broker or dealer shall preserve the records specified in paragraphs (a) and (b) of this section in accordance with § 240.17a-4 of this chapter and for a period of not less than 3 years, the first 2 years in an accessible place.

Rule 503. Certain foreign research reports

A foreign person, located outside the United States and not associated with a registered broker or dealer, who prepares a research report concerning a foreign security and provides it to a U.S. person in the United States in accordance with the provisions of § 240.15a-6(a)(2) of this chapter shall be exempt from the requirements of this regulation.

Rule 504. Notification to associated persons

A broker or dealer shall notify any person with whom that broker or dealer is associated who publishes, circulates, or provides research reports:

(a) Whether the broker or dealer maintains and enforces written policies and procedures reasonably designed to prevent the broker or dealer, any controlling persons, officers (or persons performing similar functions), or employees of the broker or dealer from influencing the activities of research analysts and the content of research reports prepared by the associated person; and

(b) Whether the associated person has any officers (or persons performing similar functions) or employees in common with the broker or dealer who can influence the activities of research analysts or the content of research reports and, if so, the identity of those persons.

Rule 505. Exclusion for news media

No provision of this Regulation AC shall apply to any person who:

(a) Is the publisher of any bona fide newspaper, news magazine or business or financial publication of general and regular circulation; and

(b) Is not registered or required to be registered with the Commission as a broker or dealer or investment adviser.

REGULATION FD

17 C.F.R. §§ 243.100-243.103

Rule	Subject
100	Regulation FD—General rule regarding selective disclosure
101	Definitions
102	No effect on antifraud liability
103	No effect on Exchange Act reporting status

Rule 100. Regulation FD—General Rule Regarding Selective Disclosure

(a) Whenever an issuer, or any person acting on its behalf, discloses any material non-public information regarding that issuer or its securities to any person described in paragraph (b)(1) of this section, the issuer shall make public disclosure of that information as provided in § 243.101(e):

(1) Simultaneously, in the case of an intentional disclosure; and

(2) Promptly, in the case of a non-intentional disclosure.

(b)(1) Except as provided in paragraph (b)(2) of this section, paragraph (a) of this section shall apply to a disclosure made to any person outside the issuer:

(i) Who is a broker or dealer, or a person associated with a broker or dealer, as those terms are defined in Section 3(a) of the Securities Exchange Act of 1934 (15 U.S.C. 78c(a));

(ii) Who is an investment adviser, as that term is defined in Section 202(a)(11) of the Investment Advisers Act of 1940 (15 U.S.C. 80b-2(a)(11)); an institutional investment manager, as that term is defined in Section 13(f)(6) of the Securities Exchange Act of 1934 (15 U.S.C. 78m(f)(6)), that filed a report on Form 13F (17 CFR 249.325) with the Commission for the most recent quarter ended prior to the date of the disclosure; or a person associated with either of the foregoing. For purposes of this paragraph, a "person associated with an investment adviser or institutional investment manager" has the meaning set forth in Section 202(a)(17) of the Investment Advisers Act of 1940 (15 U.S.C. 80b-2(a)(17)), assuming for these purposes that an institutional investment manager is an investment adviser;

(iii) Who is an investment company, as defined in Section 3 of the Investment Company Act of 1940 (15 U.S.C. 80a-3), or who would be an investment company but for Section 3(c)(1) (15 U.S.C. 80a-3(c)(1)) or Section 3(c)(7) (15 U.S.C.80a-3(c)(7)) thereof, or an affiliated person of either of the foregoing. For purposes of this paragraph, "affiliated person" means only those persons described in Section 2(a)(3)(C), (D), (E), and (F) of the Investment Company Act of 1940 (15 U.S.C. 80a-2(a)(3)(C), (D), (E), and (F)), assuming for these purposes that a person who would be an investment company but for Section 3(c)(1) (15 U.S.C. 80a-3(c)(1)) or Section 3(c)(7) (15 U.S.C. 80a-3(c)(7)) of the Investment Company Act of 1940 is an investment company; or

(iv) Who is a holder of the issuer's securities, under circumstances in which it is reasonably foreseeable that the person will purchase or sell the issuer's securities on the basis of the information.

(2) Paragraph (a) of this section shall not apply to a disclosure made:

(i) To a person who owes a duty of trust or confidence to the issuer (such as an attorney, investment banker, or accountant);

(ii) To a person who expressly agrees to maintain the disclosed information in confidence;

(iii) In connection with a securities offering registered under the Securities Act, other than an offering of the type described in any of Rule 415(a)(1)(i) through (vi) under the Securities Act (§ 230.415(a)(1)(i) through (vi) of this chapter) (except an offering of the type described in Rule 415(a)(1)(i) under the Securities Act (§ 230.415(a)(1)(i) of this chapter) also involving a registered offering, whether or not underwritten, for capital formation purposes for the account of the issuer (unless the issuer's offering is being registered for the purpose of evading the requirements of this section), if the disclosure is by any of the following means:

(A) A registration statement filed under the Securities Act, including a prospectus contained therein;

(B) A free writing prospectus used after filing of the registration statement for the offering or a communication falling within the exception to the definition of prospectus contained in clause (a) of section 2(a)(10) of the Securities Act;

(C) Any other Section 10(b) prospectus;

(D) A notice permitted by Rule 135 under the Securities Act (§ 230.135 of this chapter);

(E) A communication permitted by Rule 134 under the Securities Act (§ 230.134 of this chapter); or

(F) An oral communication made in connection with the registered securities offering after filing of the registration statement for the offering under the Securities Act.

Rule 101. Definitions

This section defines certain terms as used in Regulation FD (§ § 243.100-243.103).

(a) Intentional. A selective disclosure of material nonpublic information is "intentional" when the person making the disclosure either knows, or is reckless in not knowing, that the information he or she is communicating is both material and nonpublic.

(b) Issuer. An "issuer" subject to this regulation is one that has a class of securities registered under Section 12 of the Securities Exchange Act of 1934 (15 U.S.C. 78l), or is required to file reports under Section 15(d) of the Securities Exchange Act of 1934 (15 U.S.C. 78o(d)), including any closed-end investment company (as defined in Section 5(a)(2) of the Investment Company Act of 1940) (15 U.S.C. 80a-5(a)(2)), but not including any other investment company or any foreign government or foreign private issuer, as those terms are defined in Rule 405 under the Securities Act (§ 230.405 of this chapter).

(c) Person acting on behalf of an issuer. "Person acting on behalf of an issuer" means any senior official of the issuer (or, in the case of a closed-end investment company, a senior official of the issuer's investment adviser), or any other officer, employee, or agent of an issuer who regularly communicates with any person described in § 243.100(b)(1)(i), (ii), or (iii), or with holders of the issuer's securities. An officer, director, employee, or agent of an issuer who discloses material nonpublic information in breach of a duty of trust or confidence to the issuer shall not be considered to be acting on behalf of the issuer.

(d) Promptly. "Promptly" means as soon as reasonably practicable (but in no event after the later of 24 hours or the commencement of the next day's trading on the New York Stock Exchange) after a senior official of the issuer (or, in the case of a closed-end investment company, a senior official of the issuer's investment adviser) learns that there has been a non-intentional disclosure by the issuer or person acting on behalf of the issuer of information that the senior official knows, or is reckless in not knowing, is both material and nonpublic.

(e) Public disclosure. (1) Except as provided in paragraph (e)(2) of this section, an issuer shall make the "public disclosure" of information required by § 243.100(a) by furnishing to or filing with the Commission a Form 8-K (17 CFR 249.308) disclosing that information.

(2) An issuer shall be exempt from the requirement to furnish or file a Form 8-K if it instead disseminates the information through another method (or combination of methods) of disclosure that is reasonably designed to provide broad, non-exclusionary distribution of the information to the public.

(f) Senior official. "Senior official" means any director, executive officer (as defined in § 240.3b-7 of this chapter), investor relations or public relations officer, or other person with similar functions.

(g) Securities offering. For purposes of § 243.100(b)(2)(iv):

(1) Underwritten offerings. A securities offering that is underwritten commences when the issuer reaches an understanding with the broker-dealer that is to act as managing underwriter and continues until the later of the end of the period during which a dealer must deliver a prospectus or the sale of the securities (unless the offering is sooner terminated);

(2) Non-underwritten offerings. A securities offering that is not underwritten:

(i) If covered by Rule 415(a)(1)(x) (§ 230.415(a)(1)(x) of this chapter), commences when the issuer makes its first bona fide offer in a takedown of securities and continues until the later of the end of the period during which each dealer must deliver a prospectus or the sale of the securities in that takedown (unless the takedown is sooner terminated);

(ii) If a business combination as defined in Rule 165(f)(1) (§ 230.165(f)(1) of this chapter), commences when the first public announcement of the transaction is made and continues until the completion of the vote or the expiration of the tender offer, as applicable (unless the transaction is sooner terminated);

(iii) If an offering other than those specified in paragraphs (a) and (b) of this section, commences when the issuer files a registration statement and continues until the later of the end of the period during which each dealer must deliver a prospectus or the sale of the securities (unless the offering is sooner terminated).

Rule 102. No Effect on Antifraud Liability

No failure to make a public disclosure required solely by § 243.100 shall be deemed to be a violation of Rule 10b-5 (17 CFR 240.10b-5) under the Securities Exchange Act.

Rule 103. No Effect on Exchange Act Reporting Status

A failure to make a public disclosure required solely by § 243.100 shall not affect whether:

(a) For purposes of Forms S-2 (17 CFR 239.12), S-3 (17 CFR 239.13), S-8 (17 CFR 239.16b), and SF-3 (17 CFR 239.45) under the Securities Act, an issuer is deemed to have filed all the material required to be filed pursuant to Section 13 or 15(d) of the Securities Exchange Act of 1934 (15 U.S.C. 78m or 78o(d)) or, where applicable, has made those filings in a timely manner; or

(b) There is adequate current public information about the issuer for purposes of § 230.144(c) of this chapter (Rule 144(c)).

REGULATION G

17 C.F.R. § § 244.100-244.102

Rule	Subject
100	General rules regarding disclosure of non-GAAP financial measures
101	Definitions
102	No effect on antifraud liability

Rule 100. General Rules Regarding Disclosure of Non-GAAP Financial Measures

(a) Whenever a registrant, or person acting on its behalf, publicly discloses material information that includes a non-GAAP financial measure, the registrant must accompany that non-GAAP financial measure with:

(1) A presentation of the most directly comparable financial measure calculated and presented in accordance with Generally Accepted Accounting Principles (GAAP); and

(2) A reconciliation (by schedule or other clearly understandable method), which shall be quantitative for historical non-GAAP measures presented, and quantitative, to the extent available without unreasonable efforts, for forward-looking information, of the differences between the non-GAAP financial measure disclosed or released with the most comparable financial measure or measures calculated and presented in accordance with GAAP identified in paragraph (a)(1) of this section.

(b) A registrant, or a person acting on its behalf, shall not make public a non-GAAP financial measure that, taken together with the information accompanying that measure and any other accompanying discussion of that measure, contains an untrue statement of a material fact or omits to state a material fact necessary in order to make the presentation of the non-GAAP financial measure, in light of the circumstances under which it is presented, not misleading.

(c) This section shall not apply to a disclosure of a non-GAAP financial measure that is made by or on behalf of a registrant that is a foreign private issuer if the following conditions are satisfied:

(1) The securities of the registrant are listed or quoted on a securities exchange or inter-dealer quotation system outside the United States;

(2) The non-GAAP financial measure is not derived from or based on a measure calculated and presented in accordance with generally accepted accounting principles in the United States; and

(3) The disclosure is made by or on behalf of the registrant outside the United States, or is included in a written communication that is released by or on behalf of the registrant outside the United States.

(d) This section shall not apply to a non-GAAP financial measure included in disclosure relating to a proposed business combination, the entity resulting therefrom or an entity that is a party thereto, if the disclosure is contained in a communication that is subject to § 230.425 of this chapter, § 240.14a-12 or § 240.14d-2(b)(2) of this chapter or § 229.1015 of this chapter.

Notes to §244.100:

1. If a non-GAAP financial measure is made public orally, telephonically, by webcast, by broadcast, or by similar means, the requirements of paragraphs (a)(1)(i) and (a)(1)(ii) of this section will be satisfied if:

(i) The required information in those paragraphs is provided on the registrant's web site at the time the non-GAAP financial measure is made public; and

(ii) The location of the web site is made public in the same presentation in which the non-GAAP financial measure is made public.

2. The provisions of paragraph (c) of this section shall apply notwithstanding the existence of one or more of the following circumstances:

(i) A written communication is released in the United States as well as outside the United States, so long as the communication is released in the United States contemporaneously with or after the release outside the United States and is not otherwise targeted at persons located in the United States;

(ii) Foreign journalists, U.S. journalists or other third parties have access to the information;

(iii) The information appears on one or more web sites maintained by the registrant, so long as the web sites, taken together, are not available exclusively to, or targeted at, persons located in the United States; or

(iv) Following the disclosure or release of the information outside the United States, the information is included in a submission by the registrant to the Commission made under cover of a Form 6-K.

Rule 101. Definitions

This section defines certain terms as used in Regulation G (§§244.100 through 244.102).

(a)(1) *Non-GAAP financial measure.* A non-GAAP financial measure is a numerical measure of a registrant's historical or future financial performance, financial position or cash flows that:

(i) Excludes amounts, or is subject to adjustments that have the effect of excluding amounts, that are included in the most directly comparable measure calculated and presented in accordance with GAAP in the statement of income, balance sheet or statement of cash flows (or equivalent statements) of the issuer; or

(ii) Includes amounts, or is subject to adjustments that have the effect of including amounts, that are excluded from the most directly comparable measure so calculated and presented.

(2) A non-GAAP financial measure does not include operating and other financial measures and ratios or statistical measures calculated using exclusively one or both of:

(i) Financial measures calculated in accordance with GAAP; and

(ii) Operating measures or other measures that are not non-GAAP financial measures.

(3) A non-GAAP financial measure does not include financial measures required to be disclosed by GAAP, Commission rules, or a system of regulation of a government or governmental authority or self-regulatory organization that is applicable to the registrant.

(b) *GAAP.* GAAP refers to generally accepted accounting principles in the United States, except that (1) in the case of foreign private issuers whose primary financial statements are prepared in accordance with non-U.S. generally accepted accounting principles, GAAP refers to the principles under which those primary financial statements are prepared; and (2) in the case of foreign private issuers that include a non-GAAP financial measure derived from a measure calculated in accordance with U.S. generally accepted accounting principles, GAAP refers to U.S. generally accepted accounting principles for purposes of the application of the requirements of Regulation G to the disclosure of that measure.

(c) *Registrant.* A registrant subject to this regulation is one that has a class of securities registered under Section 12 of the Securities Exchange Act of 1934 (15 U.S.C. 78*l*), or is required to file reports under Section 15(d) of the Securities Exchange Act of 1934 (15 U.S.C. 78o(d)), excluding any investment company registered under Section 8 of the Investment Company Act of 1940 (15 U.S.C. 80a-8).

(d) *United States.* United States means the United States of America, its territories and possessions, any State of the United States, and the District of Columbia.

Rule 102. No Effect on Antifraud Liability

Neither the requirements of this Regulation G (17 CFR § 244.100 through 244.102) nor a person's compliance or non-compliance with the requirements of this Regulation shall in itself affect any person's liability under Section 10(b) (15 U.S.C. 78j(b)) of the Securities Exchange Act of 1934 or § 240.10b-5 of this chapter.

RULES OF PRACTICE AND INVESTIGATIONS—SELECTED PROVISIONS

17 C.F.R. § § 201.100-205.7

N.B. The following is not a complete text of the Rules of Practice and Investigations. It omits a number of statutory provisions entirely, and also omits certain subsections of provisions that are partially included.

SUBPART D—RULES OF PRACTICE
Part 201, Title 17, Code of Federal Regulations, September 7, 1995, 60 F.R. 46498
General Rules

Rule 100. Scope of the Rules of Practice

(a) Unless provided otherwise, these Rules of Practice govern proceedings before the Commission under the statutes that it administers.

(b) These rules do not apply to:

(1) Investigations, except where made specifically applicable by the Rules Relating to Investigations, part 203 of this chapter; or

(2) Actions taken by the duty officer pursuant to delegated authority under 17 CFR 200.43.

(3) Initiation of proceedings for SRO proposed rule changes under 17 CFR 201.700–701, except where made specifically applicable therein.

(c) The Commission, upon its determination that to do so would serve the interests of justice and not result in prejudice to the parties to the proceeding, may by order direct, in a particular proceeding, that an alternative procedure shall apply or that compliance with an otherwise applicable rule is unnecessary.

Rule 101. Definitions

(a) For purposes of these Rules of Practice, unless explicitly stated to the contrary:

(1) *Commission* means the United States Securities and Exchange Commission, or a panel of Commissioners constituting a quorum of the Commission, or a single Commissioner acting as duty officer pursuant to 17 CFR 200.42;

(2) *Counsel* means any attorney representing a party or any other person representing a party pursuant to § 201.102(b);

(3) *Disciplinary proceeding* means an action pursuant to § 201.102(e);

(4) *Enforcement proceeding* means an action, initiated by an order instituting proceedings, held for the purpose of determining whether or not a person is about to violate, has violated, has caused a violation of, or has aided or abetted a violation of any statute or rule administered by the Commission, or whether to impose a sanction as defined in Section 551(10) of the Administrative Procedure Act, 5 U.S.C. 551(10);

(5) *Hearing officer* means an administrative law judge, a panel of Commissioners constituting less than a quorum of the Commission, an individual Commissioner, or any other person duly authorized to preside at a hearing;

(6) *Interested division* means a division or an office assigned primary responsibility by the Commission to participate in a particular proceeding;

(7) *Order instituting proceedings* means an order issued by the Commission commencing a proceeding or an order issued by the Commission to hold a hearing;

(8) *Party* means the interested division, any person named as a respondent in an order instituting proceedings, any applicant named in the caption of any order, persons entitled to notice in a stop order proceeding as set forth in § 201.200(a)(2) or any person seeking Commission review of a decision;

(9) *Proceeding* means any agency process initiated:

(i) By an order instituting proceedings; or

(ii) By the filing, pursuant to § 201.410, of a petition for review of an initial decision by a hearing officer; or

(iii) By the filing, pursuant to § 201.420, of an application for review of a self-regulatory organization determination; or

(iv) By the filing, pursuant to § 201.430, of a notice of intention to file a petition for review of a determination made pursuant to delegated authority; or

(v) By the filing, pursuant to § 201.440, of an application for review of a determination by the Public Company Accounting Oversight Board; or

(vi) By the filing, pursuant to § 240.601 of this chapter, of an application for review of an action or failure to act in connection with the implementation or operation of any effective transaction reporting plan; or

(vii) By the filing, pursuant to § 240.608 of this chapter, of an application for review of an action taken or failure to act in connection with the implementation or operation of any effective national market system plan; or

(viii) By the filing, pursuant to Section 11A(b)(5) of the Securities Exchange Act of 1934, of an application for review of a determination of a registered securities information processor;

(10) *Secretary* means the Secretary of the Commission;

(11) *Temporary sanction* means a temporary cease-and-desist order or a temporary suspension of the registration of a broker, dealer, municipal securities dealer, government securities broker, government securities dealer, or transfer agent pending final determination whether the registration shall be revoked; and

(12) *Board* means the Public Company Accounting Oversight Board.

(b) [Reserved]

Rule 102. Appearance and Practice Before the Commission

A person shall not be represented before the Commission or a hearing officer except as stated in paragraphs (a) and (b) of this section or as otherwise permitted by the Commission or a hearing officer.

(a) *Representing oneself.* In any proceeding, an individual may appear on his or her own behalf.

(b) *Representing others.* In any proceeding, a person may be represented by an attorney at law admitted to practice before the Supreme Court of the United States or the highest court of any State (as defined in Section 3(a)(16) of the Exchange Act, 15 U.S.C. 78c(a)(16)); a member of a partnership may represent the partnership; a bona fide officer of a corporation, trust or association may represent the corporation, trust or association; and an officer or employee of a state commission or of a department or political subdivision of a state may represent the state commission or the department or political subdivision of the state.

(c) *Former Commission employees.* Former employees of the Commission must comply with the restrictions on practice contained in the Commission's Conduct Regulation, Subpart M, 17 CFR 200.735.

(d) *Designation of address for service; notice of appearance; power of attorney; withdrawal.*

(1) *Representing oneself.* When an individual first makes any filing or otherwise appears on his or her own behalf before the Commission or a hearing officer in a proceeding as defined in § 201.101(a), he or she shall file with the Commission, or otherwise state on the record, and keep current, an address at which any notice or other written communication required to be served upon him or her or furnished to him or her may be sent and a telephone number where he or she may be reached during business hours.

(2) *Representing others.* When a person first makes any filing or otherwise appears in a representative capacity before the Commission or a hearing officer in a proceeding as defined in § 201.101(a), that person shall file with the Commission, and keep current, a written notice stating the name of the proceeding; the representative's name, business address and telephone number; and the name and address of the person or persons represented.

(3) *Power of attorney.* Any individual appearing or practicing before the Commission in a representative capacity may be required to file a power of attorney with the Commission showing his or her authority to act in such capacity.

(4) *Withdrawal.* Any person seeking to withdraw his or her appearance in a representative capacity shall file a notice of withdrawal with the Commission or the hearing officer. The notice shall state the name, address, and telephone number of the withdrawing representative; the name, address, and telephone number of the person for whom the appearance was made; and the effective date of the withdrawal. If the person seeking to withdraw knows the name, address, and telephone number of the new representative, or knows that the person for whom the appearance was made intends to represent him- or herself, that information shall be included in the notice. The notice must be served on the parties in accordance with § 201.150. The notice shall be filed at least five days before the proposed effective date of the withdrawal.

(e) *Suspension and disbarment.*

(1) *Generally.* The Commission may censure a person or deny, temporarily or permanently, the privilege of appearing or practicing before it in any way to any person who is found by the Commission after notice and opportunity for hearing in the matter:

(i) Not to possess the requisite qualifications to represent others; or

(ii) To be lacking in character or integrity or to have engaged in unethical or improper professional conduct; or

(iii) To have willfully violated, or willfully aided and abetted the violation of any provision of the Federal securities laws or the rules and regulations thereunder.

(iv) With respect to persons licensed to practice as accountants, "improper professional conduct" under § 201.102(e)(1)(ii) means:

(A) Intentional or knowing conduct, including reckless conduct, that results in a violation of applicable professional standards; or

(B) Either of the following two types of negligent conduct:

(1) A single instance of highly unreasonable conduct that results in a violation of applicable professional standards in circumstances in which an accountant knows, or should know, that heightened scrutiny is warranted.

(2) Repeated instances of unreasonable conduct, each resulting in a violation of applicable professional standards, that indicate a lack of competence to practice before the Commission.

(2) *Certain professionals and convicted persons.* Any attorney who has been suspended or disbarred by a court of the United States or of any State; or any person whose license to practice as an accountant, engineer, or other professional or expert has been revoked or suspended in any State; or any person who has been convicted of a felony or a misdemeanor involving moral turpitude shall be forthwith suspended from appearing or practicing before the Commission. A disbarment, suspension, revocation or conviction within the meaning of this section shall be deemed to have occurred when the disbarring, suspending, revoking or convicting agency or tribunal enters its judgment or order, including a judgment or order on a plea of nolo contendere, regardless of whether an appeal of such judgment or order is pending or could be taken.

(3) *Temporary suspensions.* An order of temporary suspension shall become effective upon service on the respondent. No order of temporary suspension shall be entered by the Commission pursuant to paragraph (e)(3)(i) of this section more than 90 days after the date on which the final judgment or order entered in a judicial or administrative proceeding described in paragraph (e)(3)(i)(A) or (e)(3)(i)(B) of this section has become effective, whether upon completion of review or appeal procedures or because further review or appeal procedures are no longer available.

(i) The Commission, with due regard to the public interest and without preliminary hearing, may, by order, temporarily suspend from appearing or practicing before it any attorney, accountant, engineer, or other professional or expert who has been by name:

(A) Permanently enjoined by any court of competent jurisdiction, by reason of his or her misconduct in an action brought by the Commission, from violating or aiding and abetting the violation of any provision of the Federal securities laws or of the rules and regulations thereunder; or

(B) Found by any court of competent jurisdiction in an action brought by the Commission to which he or she is a party or found by the Commission in any administrative proceeding to which he or she is a party to have violated (unless the violation was found not to have been willful) or aided and abetted the violation of any provision of the Federal securities laws or of the rules and regulations thereunder.

(ii) Any person temporarily suspended from appearing and practicing before the Commission in accordance with paragraph (e)(3)(i) of this section may, within 30 days after service upon him or her of the order of temporary suspension, petition the Commission to lift the temporary suspension. If no petition has been received by the Commission within 30 days after service of the order, the suspension shall become permanent.

(iii) Within 30 days after the filing of a petition in accordance with paragraph (e)(3)(ii) of this section, the Commission shall either lift the temporary suspension, or set the matter down for hearing at a time and place designated by the Commission, or both, and, after opportunity for hearing, may censure the petitioner or disqualify petitioner from appearing or practicing before the Commission for a period of time or permanently. In every case in which the temporary suspension has not been lifted, every hearing held and other action taken pursuant to this paragraph (e)(3) shall be expedited in accordance with § 201.500. If the hearing is held before a hearing officer, the time limits set forth in § 201.540 will govern review of the hearing officer's initial decision.

(iv) In any hearing held on a petition filed in accordance with paragraph (e)(3)(ii) of this section, the staff of the Commission shall show either that the petitioner has been enjoined as described in paragraph (e)(3)(i)(A) of this section or that the petitioner has been found to have committed or aided and abetted violations as described in paragraph (e)(3)(i)(B) of this section and that showing, without more, may be the basis for censure or disqualification. Once that showing has been made, the burden shall be upon the petitioner to show cause why he or she should not be censured or temporarily or permanently disqualified from appearing and practicing before the Commission. In any such hearing, the petitioner may not contest any finding made against him or her or fact admitted by him or her in the judicial or administrative proceeding upon which the proceeding under this paragraph (e)(3) is predicated. A person who has consented to the entry of a permanent injunction as described in paragraph (e)(3)(i)(A) of this section without admitting the facts set forth in the complaint shall be presumed for all purposes under this paragraph (e)(3) to have been enjoined by reason of the misconduct alleged in the complaint.

(4) *Filing of prior orders*. Any person appearing or practicing before the Commission who has been the subject of an order, judgment, decree, or finding as set forth in paragraph (e)(3) of this section shall promptly file with the Secretary a copy thereof (together with any related opinion or statement of the agency or tribunal involved). Failure to file any such paper, order, judgment, decree or finding shall not impair the operation of any other provision of this section.

(5) *Reinstatement*.

(i) An application for reinstatement of a person permanently suspended or disqualified under paragraph (e)(1) or (e)(3) of this section may be made at any time, and the applicant may, in the Commission's discretion, be afforded a hearing; however, the suspension or disqualification shall continue unless and until the applicant has been reinstated by the Commission for good cause shown.

(ii) Any person suspended under paragraph (e)(2) of this section shall be reinstated by the Commission, upon appropriate application, if all the grounds for application of the provisions of that paragraph are subsequently removed by a reversal of the conviction or termination of the suspension, disbarment, or revocation. An application for reinstatement on any other grounds by any person suspended under paragraph (e)(2) of this section may be filed at any time and the applicant shall be accorded an opportunity for a hearing in the matter; however, such suspension shall continue unless and until the applicant has been reinstated by order of the Commission for good cause shown.

(6) *Other proceedings not precluded*. A proceeding brought under paragraph (e)(1), (e)(2) or (e)(3) of this section shall not preclude another proceeding brought under these same paragraphs.

(7) *Public hearings*. All hearings held under this paragraph (e) shall be public unless otherwise ordered by the Commission on its own motion or after considering the motion of a party.

(f) *Practice defined*. For the purposes of these Rules of Practice, practicing before the Commission shall include, but shall not be limited to:

(1) Transacting any business with the Commission; and

(2) The preparation of any statement, opinion or other paper by any attorney, accountant, engineer or other professional or expert, filed with the Commission in any registration statement, notification, application, report or other document with the consent of such attorney, accountant, engineer or other professional or expert.

PART 205—STANDARDS OF PROFESSIONAL CONDUCT FOR ATTORNEYS APPEARING AND PRACTICING BEFORE THE COMMISSION IN THE REPRESENTATION OF AN ISSUER

Rule 205.1. Purpose and Scope

This part sets forth minimum standards of professional conduct for attorneys appearing and practicing before the Commission in the representation of an issuer. These standards supplement applicable standards of any jurisdiction where an attorney is admitted or practices and are not intended to limit the ability of any jurisdiction to impose additional obligations on an attorney not inconsistent with the application of this part. Where the standards of a state or other United States jurisdiction where an attorney is admitted or practices conflict with this part, this part shall govern.

Rule 205.2. Definitions

For purposes of this part, the following definitions apply:

(a) *Appearing and practicing* before the Commission:

    (1) Means:

        (i) Transacting any business with the Commission, including communications in any form;

        (ii) Representing an issuer in a Commission administrative proceeding or in connection with any Commission investigation, inquiry, information request, or subpoena;

        (iii) Providing advice in respect of the United States securities laws or the Commission's rules or regulations thereunder regarding any document that the attorney has notice will be filed with or submitted to, or incorporated into any document that will be filed with or submitted to, the Commission, including the provision of such advice in the context of preparing, or participating in the preparation of, any such document; or

        (iv) Advising an issuer as to whether information or a statement, opinion, or other writing is required under the United States securities laws or the Commission's rules or regulations thereunder to be filed with or submitted to, or incorporated into any document that will be filed with or submitted to, the Commission; but

    (2) Does not include an attorney who:

        (i) Conducts the activities in paragraphs (a)(1)(i) through (a)(1)(iv) of this section other than in the context of providing legal services to an issuer with whom the attorney has an attorney-client relationship; or

        (ii) Is a non-appearing foreign attorney.

(b) *Appropriate response* means a response to an attorney regarding reported evidence of a material violation as a result of which the attorney reasonably believes:

    (1) That no material violation, as defined in paragraph (i) of this section, has occurred, is ongoing, or is about to occur;

    (2) That the issuer has, as necessary, adopted appropriate remedial measures, including appropriate steps or sanctions to stop any material violations that are ongoing, to prevent any material violation that has yet to occur, and to remedy or otherwise appropriately address any material violation that has already occurred and to minimize the likelihood of its recurrence; or

    (3) That the issuer, with the consent of the issuer's board of directors, a committee thereof to whom a report could be made pursuant to 205.3(b)(3), or a qualified legal compliance committee, has retained or directed an attorney to review the reported evidence of a material violation and either:

        (i) Has substantially implemented any remedial recommendations made by such attorney after a reasonable investigation and evaluation of the reported evidence; or

        (ii) Has been advised that such attorney may, consistent with his or her professional obligations, assert a colorable defense on behalf of the issuer (or the issuer's officer, director, employee, or agent, as the case may be) in any investigation or judicial or administrative proceeding relating to the reported evidence of a material violation.

(c) *Attorney* means any person who is admitted, licensed, or otherwise qualified to practice law in any jurisdiction, domestic or foreign, or who holds himself or herself out as admitted, licensed, or otherwise qualified to practice law.

(d) *Breach of fiduciary duty* refers to any breach of fiduciary or similar duty to the issuer recognized under an applicable federal or state statute or at common law, including but not limited to misfeasance, nonfeasance, abdication of duty, abuse of trust, and approval of unlawful transactions.

(e) *Evidence of a material violation* means credible evidence, based upon which it would be unreasonable, under the circumstances, for a prudent and competent attorney not to conclude that it is reasonably likely that a material violation has occurred, is ongoing, or is about to occur.

(f) *Foreign government issuer* means a foreign issuer as defined in 17 CFR 230.405 eligible to register securities on Schedule B of the Securities Act of 1933 (15 U.S.C. 77a *et seq.*, Schedule B).

(g) *In the representation of an issuer* means providing legal services as an attorney for an issuer, regardless of whether the attorney is employed or retained by the issuer.

(h) *Issuer* means an issuer (as defined in section 3 of the Securities Exchange Act of 1934 (15 U.S.C. 78c)), the securities of which are registered under section 12 of that Act (15 U.S.C. 78*l*), or that is required to file reports under section 15(d) of that Act (15 U.S.C.78o(d)), or that files or has filed a registration statement that has not yet become effective under the Securities Act of 1933 (15 U.S.C. 77a *et seq.*), and that it has not withdrawn, but does not include a foreign government issuer. For purposes of paragraphs (a) and (g) of this section, the term "issuer" includes any person controlled by an issuer, where an attorney provides legal services to such person on behalf of, or at the behest, or for the benefit of the issuer, regardless of whether the attorney is employed or retained by the issuer.

(i) *Material violation* means a material violation of an applicable United States federal or state securities law, a material breach of fiduciary duty arising under United States federal or state law, or a similar material violation of any United States federal or state law.

(j) *Non-appearing foreign attorney* means an attorney:

(1) Who is admitted to practice law in a jurisdiction outside the United States;

(2) Who does not hold himself or herself out as practicing, and does not give legal advice regarding, United States federal or state securities or other laws (except as provided in paragraph (j)(3)(ii) of this section); and

(3) Who:

(i) Conducts activities that would constitute appearing and practicing before the Commission only incidentally to, and in the ordinary course of, the practice of law in a jurisdiction outside the United States; or

(ii) Is appearing and practicing before the Commission only in consultation with counsel, other than a non-appearing foreign attorney, admitted or licensed to practice in a state or other United States jurisdiction.

(k) *Qualified legal compliance committee* means a committee of an issuer (which also may be an audit or other committee of the issuer) that:

(1) Consists of at least one member of the issuer's audit committee (or, if the issuer has no audit committee, one member from an equivalent committee of independent directors) and two or more members of the issuer's board of directors who are not employed, directly or indirectly, by the issuer and who are not, in the case of a registered investment company, "interested persons" as defined in section 2(a)(19) of the Investment Company Act of 1940 (15 U.S.C. 80a-2(a)(19));

(2) Has adopted written procedures for the confidential receipt, retention, and consideration of any report of evidence of a material violation under § 205.3;

(3) Has been duly established by the issuer's board of directors, with the authority and responsibility:

(i) To inform the issuer's chief legal officer and chief executive officer (or the equivalents thereof) of any report of evidence of a material violation (except in the circumstances described in § 205.3(b)(4));

     (ii) To determine whether an investigation is necessary regarding any report of evidence of a material violation by the issuer, its officers, directors, employees or agents and, if it determines an investigation is necessary or appropriate, to:

     (A) Notify the audit committee or the full board of directors;

     (B) Initiate an investigation, which may be conducted either by the chief legal officer (or the equivalent thereof) or by outside attorneys; and

     (C) Retain such additional expert personnel as the committee deems necessary; and

     (iii) At the conclusion of any such investigation, to:

     (A) Recommend, by majority vote, that the issuer implement an appropriate response to evidence of a material violation; and

     (B) Inform the chief legal officer and the chief executive officer (or the equivalents thereof) and the board of directors of the results of any such investigation under this section and the appropriate remedial measures to be adopted; and

     (4) Has the authority and responsibility, acting by majority vote, to take all other appropriate action, including the authority to notify the Commission in the event that the issuer fails in any material respect to implement an appropriate response that the qualified legal compliance committee has recommended the issuer to take.

     (l) *Reasonable* or *reasonably* denotes, with respect to the actions of an attorney, conduct that would not be unreasonable for a prudent and competent attorney.

     (m) *Reasonably believes* means that an attorney believes the matter in question and that the circumstances are such that the belief is not unreasonable.

     (n) *Report* means to make known to directly, either in person, by telephone, by e-mail, electronically, or in writing.

Rule 205.3. Issuer as Client

     (a) *Representing an issuer.* An attorney appearing and practicing before the Commission in the representation of an issuer owes his or her professional and ethical duties to the issuer as an organization. That the attorney may work with and advise the issuer's officers, directors, or employees in the course of representing the issuer does not make such individuals the attorney's clients.

     (b) *Duty to report evidence of a material violation.* (1) If an attorney, appearing and practicing before the Commission in the representation of an issuer, becomes aware of evidence of a material violation by the issuer or by any officer, director, employee, or agent of the issuer, the attorney shall report such evidence to the issuer's chief legal officer (or the equivalent thereof) or to both the issuer's chief legal officer and its chief executive officer (or the equivalents thereof) forthwith. By communicating such information to the issuer's officers or directors, an attorney does not reveal client confidences or secrets or privileged or otherwise protected information related to the attorney's representation of an issuer.

     (2) The chief legal officer (or the equivalent thereof) shall cause such inquiry into the evidence of a material violation as he or she reasonably believes is appropriate to determine whether the material violation described in the report has occurred, is ongoing, or is about to occur. If the chief legal officer (or the equivalent thereof) determines no material violation has occurred, is ongoing, or is about to occur, he or she shall notify the reporting attorney and advise the reporting attorney of the basis for such determination. Unless the chief legal officer (or the equivalent thereof) reasonably believes that no material violation has occurred, is ongoing, or is about to occur, he or she shall take all reasonable steps to cause the issuer to adopt an appropriate response, and shall advise the reporting attorney thereof. In lieu of causing an inquiry under this paragraph (b), a chief legal officer (or the equivalent thereof) may refer a report of evidence of a material violation to a qualified legal compliance committee under paragraph (c)(2) of this section if the issuer has duly established a qualified legal compliance committee prior to the report of evidence of a material violation.

(3) Unless an attorney who has made a report under paragraph (b)(1) of this section reasonably believes that the chief legal officer or the chief executive officer of the issuer (or the equivalent thereof) has provided an appropriate response within a reasonable time, the attorney shall report the evidence of a material violation to:

(i) The audit committee of the issuer's board of directors;

(ii) Another committee of the issuer's board of directors consisting solely of directors who are not employed, directly or indirectly, by the issuer and are not, in the case of a registered investment company, "interested persons" as defined in section 2(a)(19) of the Investment Company Act of 1940 (15 U.S.C. 80a-2(a)(19)) (if the issuer's board of directors has no audit committee); or

(iii) The issuer's board of directors (if the issuer's board of directors has no committee consisting solely of directors who are not employed, directly or indirectly, by the issuer and are not, in the case of a registered investment company, "interested persons" as defined in section 2(a)(19) of the Investment Company Act of 1940 (15 U.S.C. 80a-2(a)(19))).

(4) If an attorney reasonably believes that it would be futile to report evidence of a material violation to the issuer's chief legal officer and chief executive officer (or the equivalents thereof) under paragraph (b)(1) of this section, the attorney may report such evidence as provided under paragraph (b)(3) of this section.

(5) An attorney retained or directed by an issuer to investigate evidence of a material violation reported under paragraph (b)(1), (b)(3), or (b)(4) of this section shall be deemed to be appearing and practicing before the Commission. Directing or retaining an attorney to investigate reported evidence of a material violation does not relieve an officer or director of the issuer to whom such evidence has been reported under paragraph (b)(1), (b)(3), or (b)(4) of this section from a duty to respond to the reporting attorney.

(6) An attorney shall not have any obligation to report evidence of a material violation under this paragraph (b) if:

(i) The attorney was retained or directed by the issuer's chief legal officer (or the equivalent thereof) to investigate such evidence of a material violation and:

(A) The attorney reports the results of such investigation to the chief legal officer (or the equivalent thereof); and

(B) Except where the attorney and the chief legal officer (or the equivalent thereof) each reasonably believes that no material violation has occurred, is ongoing, or is about to occur, the chief legal officer (or the equivalent thereof) reports the results of the investigation to the issuer's board of directors, a committee thereof to whom a report could be made pursuant to paragraph (b)(3) of this section, or a qualified legal compliance committee; or

(ii) The attorney was retained or directed by the chief legal officer (or the equivalent thereof) to assert, consistent with his or her professional obligations, a colorable defense on behalf of the issuer (or the issuer's officer, director, employee, or agent, as the case may be) in any investigation or judicial or administrative proceeding relating to such evidence of a material violation, and the chief legal officer (or the equivalent thereof) provides reasonable and timely reports on the progress and outcome of such proceeding to the issuer's board of directors, a committee thereof to whom a report could be made pursuant to paragraph (b)(3) of this section, or a qualified legal compliance committee.

(7) An attorney shall not have any obligation to report evidence of a material violation under this paragraph (b) if such attorney was retained or directed by a qualified legal compliance committee:

(i) To investigate such evidence of a material violation; or

(ii) To assert, consistent with his or her professional obligations, a colorable defense on behalf of the issuer (or the issuer's officer, director, employee, or agent, as the case may be) in any investigation or judicial or administrative proceeding relating to such evidence of a material violation.

(8) An attorney who receives what he or she reasonably believes is an appropriate and timely response to a report he or she has made pursuant to paragraph (b)(1), (b)(3), or (b)(4) of this section need do nothing more under this section with respect to his or her report.

(9) An attorney who does not reasonably believe that the issuer has made an appropriate response within a reasonable time to the report or reports made pursuant to paragraph (b)(1), (b)(3), or (b)(4) of this section shall explain his or her reasons therefor to the chief legal officer (or the equivalent thereof), the chief executive officer (or the equivalent thereof), and directors to whom the attorney reported the evidence of a material violation pursuant to paragraph (b)(1), (b)(3), or (b)(4) of this section.

(10) An attorney formerly employed or retained by an issuer who has reported evidence of a material violation under this part and reasonably believes that he or she has been discharged for so doing may notify the issuer's board of directors or any committee thereof that he or she believes that he or she has been discharged for reporting evidence of a material violation under this section.

(c) *Alternative reporting procedures for attorneys retained or employed by an issuer that has established a qualified legal compliance committee.* (1) If an attorney, appearing and practicing before the Commission in the representation of an issuer, becomes aware of evidence of a material violation by the issuer or by any officer, director, employee, or agent of the issuer, the attorney may, as an alternative to the reporting requirements of paragraph (b) of this section, report such evidence to a qualified legal compliance committee, if the issuer has previously formed such a committee. An attorney who reports evidence of a material violation to such a qualified legal compliance committee has satisfied his or her obligation to report such evidence and is not required to assess the issuer's response to the reported evidence of a material violation.

(2) A chief legal officer (or the equivalent thereof) may refer a report of evidence of a material violation to a previously established qualified legal compliance committee in lieu of causing an inquiry to be conducted under paragraph (b)(2) of this section. The chief legal officer (or the equivalent thereof) shall inform the reporting attorney that the report has been referred to a qualified legal compliance committee. Thereafter, pursuant to the requirements under § 205.2(k), the qualified legal compliance committee shall be responsible for responding to the evidence of a material violation reported to it under this paragraph (c).

(d) *Issuer confidences.* (1) Any report under this section (or the contemporaneous record thereof) or any response thereto (or the contemporaneous record thereof) may be used by an attorney in connection with any investigation, proceeding, or litigation in which the attorney's compliance with this part is in issue.

(2) An attorney appearing and practicing before the Commission in the representation of an issuer may reveal to the Commission, without the issuer's consent, confidential information related to the representation to the extent the attorney reasonably believes necessary:

(i) To prevent the issuer from committing a material violation that is likely to cause substantial injury to the financial interest or property of the issuer or investors;

(ii) To prevent the issuer, in a Commission investigation or administrative proceeding from committing perjury, proscribed in 18 U.S.C. 1621; suborning perjury, proscribed in 18 U.S.C. 1622; or committing any act proscribed in 18 U.S.C. 1001 that is likely to perpetrate a fraud upon the Commission; or

(iii) To rectify the consequences of a material violation by the issuer that caused, or may cause, substantial injury to the financial interest or property of the issuer or investors in the furtherance of which the attorney's services were used.

Rule 205.4. Responsibilities of Supervisory Attorneys

(a) An attorney supervising or directing another attorney who is appearing and practicing before the Commission in the representation of an issuer is a supervisory attorney. An issuer's chief legal officer (or the equivalent thereof) is a supervisory attorney under this section.

(b) A supervisory attorney shall make reasonable efforts to ensure that a subordinate attorney, as defined in § 205.5(a), that he or she supervises or directs conforms to this part. To the extent a subordinate attorney appears and practices before the Commission in the representation of an issuer, that subordinate attorney's supervisory attorneys also appear and practice before the Commission.

(c) A supervisory attorney is responsible for complying with the reporting requirements in § 205.3 when a subordinate attorney has reported to the supervisory attorney evidence of a material violation.

(d) A supervisory attorney who has received a report of evidence of a material violation from a subordinate attorney under § 205.3 may report such evidence to the issuer's qualified legal compliance committee if the issuer has duly formed such a committee.

Rule 205.5. Responsibilities of a Subordinate Attorney

(a) An attorney who appears and practices before the Commission in the representation of an issuer on a matter under the supervision or direction of another attorney (other than under the direct supervision or direction of the issuer's chief legal officer (or the equivalent thereof)) is a subordinate attorney.

(b) A subordinate attorney shall comply with this part notwithstanding that the subordinate attorney acted at the direction of or under the supervision of another person.

(c) A subordinate attorney complies with § 205.3 if the subordinate attorney reports to his or her supervising attorney under § 205.3(b) evidence of a material violation of which the subordinate attorney has become aware in appearing and practicing before the Commission.

(d) A subordinate attorney may take the steps permitted or required by § 205.3(b) or (c) if the subordinate attorney reasonably believes that a supervisory attorney to whom he or she has reported evidence of a material violation under § 205.3(b) has failed to comply with § 205.3.

Rule 205.6. Sanctions and Discipline

(a) A violation of this part by any attorney appearing and practicing before the Commission in the representation of an issuer shall subject such attorney to the civil penalties and remedies for a violation of the federal securities laws available to the Commission in an action brought by the Commission thereunder.

(b) An attorney appearing and practicing before the Commission who violates any provision of this part is subject to the disciplinary authority of the Commission, regardless of whether the attorney may also be subject to discipline for the same conduct in a jurisdiction where the attorney is admitted or practices. An administrative disciplinary proceeding initiated by the Commission for violation of this part may result in an attorney being censured, or being temporarily or permanently denied the privilege of appearing or practicing before the Commission.

(c) An attorney who complies in good faith with the provisions of this part shall not be subject to discipline or otherwise liable under inconsistent standards imposed by any state or other United States jurisdiction where the attorney is admitted or practices.

(d) An attorney practicing outside the United States shall not be required to comply with the requirements of this part to the extent that such compliance is prohibited by applicable foreign law.

Rule 205.7. No Private Right of Action

(a) Nothing in this part is intended to, or does, create a private right of action against any attorney, law firm, or issuer based upon compliance or noncompliance with its provisions.

(b) Authority to enforce compliance with this part is vested exclusively in the Commission.

STAFF ACCOUNTING BULLETINS—SELECTED RELEASE

Release No.	Subject
99	Materiality

Release No. 99, August 12, 1999

Materiality

ACTION: Publication of Staff Accounting Bulletin

SUMMARY: This staff accounting bulletin expresses the views of the staff that exclusive reliance on certain quantitative benchmarks to assess materiality in preparing financial statements and performing audits of those financial statements is inappropriate; misstatements are not immaterial simply because they fall beneath a numerical threshold.

DATE: August 12, 1999

FOR FURTHER INFORMATION CONTACT: W. Scott Bayless, Associate Chief Accountant, or Robert E. Burns, Chief Counsel, Office of the Chief Accountant (202-942-4400), or David R. Fredrickson, Office of General Counsel (202-942-0900), Securities and Exchange Commission, 450 Fifth Street, N.W., Washington, D.C. 20549-1103; electronic addresses: BaylessWS@sec.gov; BurnsR@sec.gov; FredricksonD@sec.gov.

SUPPLEMENTARY INFORMATION: The statements in the staff accounting bulletins are not rules or interpretations of the Commission, nor are they published as bearing the Commission's official approval. They represent interpretations and practices followed by the Division of Corporation Finance and the Office of the Chief Accountant in administering the disclosure requirements of the Federal securities laws.

Part 211—(AMEND)

Accordingly, Part 211 of Title 17 of the Code of Federal Regulations is amended by adding Staff Accounting Bulletin No. 99 to the table found in Subpart B.

STAFF ACCOUNTING BULLETIN NO. 99

The staff hereby adds Section M to Topic 1 of the Staff Accounting Bulletin Series. Section M, entitled "Materiality," provides guidance in applying materiality thresholds to the preparation of financial statements filed with the Commission and the performance of audits of those financial statements.

1. Assessing materiality

Facts: During the course of preparing or auditing year-end financial statements, financial management or the registrant's independent auditor becomes aware of misstatements in a registrant's financial statements. When combined, the misstatements result in a 4% overstatement of net income and a $.02 (4%) overstatement of earnings per share. Because no item in the registrant's consolidated financial statements is misstated by more than 5%, management and the independent auditor conclude that the deviation from GAAP is immaterial and that the accounting is permissible.[1]

Question: Each Statement of Financial Accounting Standards adopted by the FASB states, "The provisions of this Statement need not be applied to immaterial items." In the staff's view, may a registrant or the auditor of its financial statements assume the immateriality of items that fall below a percentage threshold set by management or the auditor to determine whether amounts and items are material to the financial statements?

Interpretive Response: No. The staff is aware that certain registrants, over time, have developed quantitative thresholds as "rules of thumb" to assist in the preparation of their financial statements, and that auditors also have used these thresholds in their evaluation of whether items might be considered material to users of a registrant's financial statements. One rule of thumb in particular suggests that the misstatement or omission[2] of an item that falls under a 5% threshold is not material in the absence of particularly egregious circumstances, such as self-dealing or misappropriation by senior management. The staff reminds registrants and the auditors of their financial statements that exclusive reliance on this or any percentage or numerical threshold has no basis in the accounting literature or the law.

The use of a percentage as a numerical threshold, such as 5%, may provide the basis for a preliminary assumption that—without considering all relevant circumstances—a deviation of less than the specified percentage with respect to a particular item on the registrant's financial statements is unlikely to be material. The staff has no objection to such a "rule of thumb" as an initial step in assessing materiality. But quantifying, in percentage terms, the magnitude of a misstatement is only the beginning of an analysis of materiality; it cannot appropriately be used as a substitute for a full analysis of all relevant considerations. Materiality concerns the significance of an item to users of a registrant's financial statements. A matter is "material" if there is a substantial likelihood that a reasonable person would consider it important. In its Concepts Statement 2, the FASB stated the essence of the concept of materiality as follows:

The omission or misstatement of an item in a financial report is material if, in the light of surrounding circumstances, the magnitude of the item is such that it is probable that the judgment of a reasonable person relying upon the report would have been changed or influenced by the inclusion or correction of the item.[3]

This formulation in the accounting literature is in substance identical to the formulation used by the courts in interpreting the federal securities laws. The Supreme Court has held that a fact is material if there is -

a substantial likelihood that the . . . fact would have been viewed by the reasonable investor as having significantly altered the "total mix" of information made available.[4]

Under the governing principles, an assessment of materiality requires that one views the facts in the context of the "surrounding circumstances," as the accounting literature puts it, or the "total mix" of information, in the words of the Supreme Court. In the context of a misstatement of a

---

[1] AU 312 states that the auditor should consider audit risk and materiality both in (a) planning and setting the scope for the audit and (b) evaluating whether the financial statements taken as a whole are fairly presented in all material respects in conformity with GAAP. The purpose of this SAB is to provide guidance to financial management and independent auditors with respect to the evaluation of the materiality of misstatements that are identified in the audit process or preparation of the financial statements (i.e., (b) above). This SAB is not intended to provide definitive guidance for assessing "materiality" in other contexts, such as evaluations of auditor independence, as other factors may apply. There may be other rules that address financial presentation. See, e.g., Rule 2a-4, 17 CFR 270.2a-4, under the Investment Company Act of 1940.

[2] As used in this SAB, "misstatement" or "omission" refers to a financial statement assertion that would not be in conformity with GAAP.

[3] Concepts Statement 2, paragraph 132. See also Concepts Statement 2, Glossary of Terms—Materiality.

[4] TSC Industries v. Northway, Inc., 426 U.S. 438, 449 (1976). See also Basic, Inc. v. Levinson, 485 U.S. 224 (1988). As the Supreme Court has noted, determinations of materiality require "delicate assessments of the inferences a "reasonable shareholder" would draw from a given set of facts and the significance of those inferences to him . . . ." TSC Industries, 426 U.S. at 450.

financial statement item, while the "total mix" includes the size in numerical or percentage terms of the misstatement, it also includes the factual context in which the user of financial statements would view the financial statement item. The shorthand in the accounting and auditing literature for this analysis is that financial management and the auditor must consider both "quantitative" and "qualitative" factors in assessing an item's materiality.[5] Court decisions, Commission rules and enforcement actions, and accounting and auditing literature[6] have all considered "qualitative" factors in various contexts.

The FASB has long emphasized that materiality cannot be reduced to a numerical formula. In its Concepts Statement 2, the FASB noted that some had urged it to promulgate quantitative materiality guides for use in a variety of situations. The FASB rejected such an approach as representing only a "minority view, stating -

The predominant view is that materiality judgments can properly be made only by those who have all the facts. The Board's present position is that no general standards of materiality could be formulated to take into account all the considerations that enter into an experienced human judgment.[7]

The FASB noted that, in certain limited circumstances, the Commission and other authoritative bodies had issued quantitative materiality guidance, citing as examples guidelines ranging from one to ten percent with respect to a variety of disclosures.[8] And it took account of contradictory studies, one showing a lack of uniformity among auditors on materiality judgments, and another suggesting widespread use of a "rule of thumb" of five to ten percent of net income.[9] The FASB also considered whether an evaluation of materiality could be based solely on anticipating the market's reaction to accounting information.[10]

The FASB rejected a formulaic approach to discharging "the onerous duty of making materiality decisions"[11] in favor of an approach that takes into account all the relevant considerations. In so doing, it made clear that-

[M]agnitude by itself, without regard to the nature of the item and the circumstances in which the judgment has to be made, will not generally be a sufficient basis for a materiality judgment.[12]

Evaluation of materiality requires a registrant and its auditor to consider *all* the relevant circumstances, and the staff believes that there are numerous circumstances in which misstatements below 5% could well be material. Qualitative factors may cause misstatements of quantitatively small amounts to be material; as stated in the auditing literature:

As a result of the interaction of quantitative and qualitative considerations in materiality judgments, misstatements of relatively small amounts that come to the auditor's attention could have a material effect on the financial statements.[13]

Among the considerations that may well render material a quantitatively small misstatement of a financial statement item are -

---

[5] See, e.g., Concepts Statement 2, paragraphs 123-124; AU 312A.10 (materiality judgments are made in light of surrounding circumstances and necessarily involve both quantitative and qualitative considerations); AU 312A.34 ("Qualitative considerations also influence the auditor in reaching a conclusion as to whether misstatements are material."). As used in the accounting literature and in this SAB, "qualitative" materiality refers to the surrounding circumstances that inform an investor's evaluation of financial statement entries. Whether events may be material to investors for non-financial reasons is a matter not addressed by this SAB.

[6] See, e.g., Rule 1-02(o) of Regulation S-X, 17 CFR 210.1-02(o), Rule 405 of Regulation C, 17 CFR 230.405, and Rule 12b-2, 17 CFR 240.12b-2; AU 312A.10—.11, 317.13, 411.04 n. 1, and 508.36; In re Kidder Peabody Securities Litigation, 10 F. Supp. 2d 398 (S.D.N.Y.

1998); Parnes v. Gateway 2000, Inc., 122 F.3d 539 (8th Cir. 1997); In re Westinghouse Securities Litigation, 90 F.3d 696 (3d Cir. 1996); In the Matter of W.R. Grace & Co., Accounting and Auditing Enforcement Release ("AAER") 1140 (June 30, 1999); In the Matter of Eugene Gaughan, AAER 1141 (June 30, 1999); In the Matter of Thomas Scanlon, AAER 1142 (June 30, 1999); and In re Sensormatic Electronics Corporation, Sec. Act Rel. No. 7518 (March 25, 1998).

[7] Concepts Statement 2, paragraph 131.

[8] Concepts Statement 2, paragraphs 131 and 166.

[9] Concepts Statement 2, paragraph 167.

[10] Concepts Statement 2, paragraphs 168-169.

[11] Concepts Statement 2, paragraph 170.

[12] Concepts Statement 2, paragraph 125.

[13] AU 312.11.

- whether the misstatement arises from an item capable of precise measurement or whether it arises from an estimate and, if so, the degree of imprecision inherent in the estimate[14]
- whether the misstatement masks a change in earnings or other trends
- whether the misstatement hides a failure to meet analysts' consensus expectations for the enterprise
- whether the misstatement changes a loss into income or vice versa
- whether the misstatement concerns a segment or other portion of the registrant's business that has been identified as playing a significant role in the registrant's operations or profitability
- whether the misstatement affects the registrant's compliance with regulatory requirements
- whether the misstatement affects the registrant's compliance with loan covenants or other contractual requirements
- whether the misstatement has the effect of increasing management's compensation— for example, by satisfying requirements for the award of bonuses or other forms of incentive compensation
- whether the misstatement involves concealment of an unlawful transaction.

This is not an exhaustive list of the circumstances that may affect the materiality of a quantitatively small misstatement.[15] Among other factors, the demonstrated volatility of the price of a registrant's securities in response to certain types of disclosures may provide guidance as to whether investors regard quantitatively small misstatements as material. Consideration of potential market reaction to disclosure of a misstatement is by itself "too blunt an instrument to be depended on" in considering whether a fact is material.[16] When, however, management or the independent auditor expects (based, for example, on a pattern of market performance) that a known misstatement may result in a significant positive or negative market reaction, that expected reaction should be taken into account when considering whether a misstatement is material.[17]

For the reasons noted above, the staff believes that a registrant and the auditors of its financial statements should not assume that even small intentional misstatements in financial statements, for example those pursuant to actions to "manage" earnings, are immaterial.[18] While the intent of management does not render a misstatement material, it may provide significant evidence of materiality. The evidence may be particularly compelling where management has intentionally misstated items in the financial statements to "manage" reported earnings. In that instance, it presumably has done so believing that the resulting amounts and trends would be significant to users of the registrant's financial statements.[19] The staff believes that investors generally would

---

[14] As stated in Concepts Statement 2, paragraph 130:

Another factor in materiality judgments is the degree of precision that is attainable in estimating the judgment item. The amount of deviation that is considered immaterial may increase as the attainable degree of precision decreases. For example, accounts payable usually can be estimated more accurately than can contingent liabilities arising from litigation or threats of it, and a deviation considered to be material in the first case may be quite trivial in the second.

This SAB is not intended to change current law or guidance in the accounting literature regarding accounting estimates. *See, e.g.*, Accounting Principles Board Opinion 20, Accounting Changes 10, 11, 31-33 (July 1971).

[15] The staff understands that the Big Five Audit Materiality Task Force ("Task Force") was convened in March of 1998 and has made recommendations to the Auditing Standards Board including suggestions regarding communications with audit committees about unadjusted misstatements. *See* generally Big Five Audit Materiality Task Force. "Materiality in a Financial Statement Audit—Considering Qualitative Factors When Evaluating Audit Findings" (August 1998).

[16] See Concepts Statement 2, paragraph 169.

[17] If management does not expect a significant market reaction, a misstatement still may be material and should be evaluated under the criteria discussed in this SAB.

[18] Intentional management of earnings and intentional misstatements, as used in this SAB, do not include insignificant errors and omissions that may occur in systems and recurring processes in the normal course of business. See notes 37 and 49 infra.

[19] Assessments of materiality should occur not only at year-end, but also during the preparation of each quarterly or interim financial statement. See, e.g., In the Matter of Venator Group, Inc., AAER 1049 (June 29, 1998).

regard as significant a management practice to over- or under-state earnings up to an amount just short of a percentage threshold in order to "manage" earnings. Investors presumably also would regard as significant an accounting practice that, in essence, rendered all earnings figures subject to a management-directed margin of misstatement.

The materiality of a misstatement may turn on where it appears in the financial statements. For example, a misstatement may involve a segment of the registrant's operations. In that instance, in assessing materiality of a misstatement to the financial statements taken as a whole, registrants and their auditors should consider not only the size of the misstatement but also the significance of the segment information to the financial statements taken as a whole.[20] "A misstatement of the revenue and operating profit of a relatively small segment that is represented by management to be important to the future profitability of the entity"[21] is more likely to be material to investors than a misstatement in a segment that management has not identified as especially important. In assessing the materiality of misstatements in segment information—as with materiality generally—situations may arise in practice where the auditor will conclude that a matter relating to segment information is qualitatively material even though, in his or her judgment, it is quantitatively immaterial to the financial statements taken as a whole.[22]

Aggregating and Netting Misstatements

In determining whether multiple misstatements cause the financial statements to be materially misstated, registrants and the auditors of their financial statements should consider each misstatement separately and the aggregate effect of all misstatements.[23] A registrant and its auditor should evaluate misstatements in light of quantitative and qualitative factors and "consider whether, in relation to individual amounts, subtotals, or totals in the financial statements, they materially misstate the financial statements taken as a whole."[24] This requires consideration of—the significance of an item to a particular entity (for example, inventories to a manufacturing company), the pervasiveness of the misstatement (such as whether it affects the presentation of numerous financial statement items), and the effect of the misstatement on the financial statements taken as a whole . . . .[25]

Registrants and their auditors first should consider whether each misstatement is material, irrespective of its effect when combined with other misstatements. The literature notes that the analysis should consider whether the misstatement of "individual amounts" causes a material misstatement of the financial statements taken as a whole. As with materiality generally, this analysis requires consideration of both quantitative and qualitative factors.

If the misstatement of an individual amount causes the financial statements as a whole to be materially misstated, that effect cannot be eliminated by other misstatements whose effect may be to diminish the impact of the misstatement on other financial statement items. To take an obvious example, if a registrant's revenues are a material financial statement item and if they are materially overstated, the financial statements taken as a whole will be materially misleading even if the effect on earnings is completely offset by an equivalent overstatement of expenses.

Even though a misstatement of an individual amount may not cause the financial statements taken as a whole to be materially misstated, it may nonetheless, when aggregated with other

---

[20] See, e.g., In the Matter of W.R. Grace & Co., AAER 1140 (June 30, 1999).

[21] AU 9326.33.

[22] Id.

[23] The auditing literature notes that the "concept of materiality recognizes that some matters, either individually or in the aggregate, are important for fair presentation of financial statements in conformity with generally accepted accounting principles." AU 312.03. See also AU 312.04.

[24] AU 312.34. Quantitative materiality assessments often are made by comparing adjustments to revenues, gross profit, pretax and net income, total assets, stockholders' equity, or individual line items in the financial statements. The particular items in the financial statements to be considered as a basis for the materiality determination depend on the proposed adjustment to be made and other factors, such as those identified in this SAB. For example, an adjustment to inventory that is immaterial to pretax income or net income may be material to the financial statements because it may affect a working capital ratio or cause the registrant to be in default of loan covenants.

[25] AU 508.36.

misstatements, render the financial statements taken as a whole to be materially misleading. Registrants and the auditors of their financial statements accordingly should consider the effect of the misstatement on subtotals or totals. The auditor should aggregate all misstatements that affect each subtotal or total and consider whether the misstatements in the aggregate affect the subtotal or total in a way that causes the registrant's financial statements taken as a whole to be materially misleading.[26]

The staff believes that, in considering the aggregate effect of multiple misstatements on a subtotal or total, registrants and the auditors of their financial statements should exercise particular care when considering whether to offset (or the appropriateness of offsetting) a misstatement of an estimated amount with a misstatement of an item capable of precise measurement. As noted above, assessments of materiality should never be purely mechanical; given the imprecision inherent in estimates, there is by definition a corresponding imprecision in the aggregation of misstatements involving estimates with those that do not involve an estimate.

Registrants and auditors also should consider the effect of misstatements from prior periods on the current financial statements. For example, the auditing literature states,

Matters underlying adjustments proposed by the auditor but not recorded by the entity could potentially cause future financial statements to be materially misstated, even though the auditor has concluded that the adjustments are not material to the current financial statements.[27]

This may be particularly the case where immaterial misstatements recur in several years and the cumulative effect becomes material in the current year.

2. Immaterial misstatements that are intentional

Facts: A registrant's management intentionally has made adjustments to various financial statement items in a manner inconsistent with GAAP. In each accounting period in which such actions were taken, none of the individual adjustments is by itself material, nor is the aggregate effect on the financial statements taken as a whole material for the period. The registrant's earnings "management" has been effected at the direction or acquiescence of management in the belief that any deviations from GAAP have been immaterial and that accordingly the accounting is permissible.

Question: In the staff's view, may a registrant make intentional immaterial misstatements in its financial statements?

Interpretive Response: No. In certain circumstances, intentional immaterial misstatements are unlawful.

Considerations of the books and records provisions under the Exchange Act

Even if misstatements are immaterial,[28] registrants must comply with Sections 13(b)(2)—(7) of the Securities Exchange Act of 1934 (the "Exchange Act").[29] Under these provisions, each registrant with securities registered pursuant to Section 12 of the Exchange Act,[30] or required to file reports pursuant to Section 15(d),[31] must make and keep books, records, and accounts, which, in reasonable detail, accurately and fairly reflect the transactions and dispositions of assets of the registrant and must maintain internal accounting controls that are sufficient to provide reasonable assurances that, among other things, transactions are recorded as necessary to permit the preparation of financial statements in conformity with GAAP.[32] In this context, determinations of

---

[26] AU 312.34.

[27] AU 380.09.

[28] FASB Statements generally provide that "[t]he provisions of this Statement need not be applied to immaterial items." This SAB is consistent with that provision of the Statements. In theory, this language is subject to the interpretation that the registrant is free intentionally to set forth immaterial items in financial statements in a manner that plainly would be contrary to GAAP if the

misstatement were material. The staff believes that the FASB did not intend this result.

[29] 15 U.S.C. 78m(b)(2)—(7).

[30] 15 U.S.C. 78l.

[31] 15 U.S.C. 78o(d).

[32] Criminal liability may be imposed if a person knowingly circumvents or knowingly fails to implement a system of internal accounting controls or knowingly falsifies books, records or accounts. 15 U.S.C. 78m(4)

what constitutes "reasonable assurance" and "reasonable detail" are based not on a "materiality" analysis but on the level of detail and degree of assurance that would satisfy prudent officials in the conduct of their own affairs.[33] Accordingly, failure to record accurately immaterial items, in some instances, may result in violations of the securities laws.

The staff recognizes that there is limited authoritative guidance[34] regarding the "reasonableness" standard in Section 13(b)(2) of the Exchange Act. A principal statement of the Commission's policy in this area is set forth in an address given in 1981 by then Chairman Harold M. Williams.[35] In his address, Chairman Williams noted that, like materiality, "reasonableness" is not an "absolute standard of exactitude for corporate records."[36] Unlike materiality, however, "reasonableness" is not solely a measure of the significance of a financial statement item to investors. "Reasonableness," in this context, reflects a judgment as to whether an issuer's failure to correct a known misstatement implicates the purposes underlying the accounting provisions of Sections 13(b)(2)—(7) of the Exchange Act.[37]

In assessing whether a misstatement results in a violation of a registrant's obligation to keep books and records that are accurate "in reasonable detail," registrants and their auditors should consider, in addition to the factors discussed above concerning an evaluation of a misstatement's potential materiality, the factors set forth below.

- The significance of the misstatement. Though the staff does not believe that registrants need to make finely calibrated determinations of significance with respect to immaterial items, plainly it is "reasonable" to treat misstatements whose effects are clearly inconsequential differently than more significant ones.

- How the misstatement arose. It is unlikely that it is ever "reasonable" for registrants to record misstatements or not to correct known misstatements—even immaterial ones—as part of an ongoing effort directed by or known to senior management for the purposes of "managing" earnings. On the other hand, insignificant misstatements that arise from the operation of systems or recurring processes in the normal course of business generally will not cause a registrant's books to be inaccurate "in reasonable detail."[38]

(Footnote Continued)

and (5). See also Rule 13b2-1 under the Exchange Act, 17 CFR 240.13b2-1, which states, "No person shall, directly or indirectly, falsify or cause to be falsified, any book, record or account subject to Section 13(b)(2)(A) of the Securities Exchange Act."

[33] 15 U.S.C. 78m(b)(7). The books and records provisions of section 13(b) of the Exchange Act originally were passed as part of the Foreign Corrupt Practices Act ("FCPA"). In the conference committee report regarding the 1988 amendments to the FCPA, the committee stated:

The conference committee adopted the prudent man qualification in order to clarify that the current standard does not connote an unrealistic degree of exactitude or precision. The concept of reasonableness of necessity contemplates the weighing of a number of relevant factors, including the costs of compliance.

Cong. Rec. H2116 (daily ed. April 20, 1988).

[34] So far as the staff is aware, there is only one judicial decision that discusses Section 13(b)(2) of the Exchange Act in any detail, SEC v. World-Wide Coin Investments, Ltd., 567 F. Supp. 724 (N.D. Ga. 1983), and the courts generally have found that no private right of action exists under the accounting and books and records provisions of the Exchange Act. See e.g., Lamb v. Phillip Morris Inc., 915 F.2d 1024 (6th Cir. 1990) and JS Service Center Corporation v. General Electric Technical Services Company, 937 F. Supp. 216 (S.D.N.Y. 1996).

[35] The Commission adopted the address as a formal statement of policy in Securities Exchange Act Release No. 17500 (January 29, 1981), 46 FR 11544 (February 9, 1981), 21 SEC Docket 1466 (February 10, 1981).

[36] Id. at 46 FR 11546.

[37] Id.

[38] For example, the conference report regarding the 1988 amendments to the FCPA stated:

The Conferees intend to codify current Securities and Exchange Commission (SEC) enforcement policy that penalties not be imposed for insignificant or technical infractions or inadvertent conduct. The amendment adopted by the Conferees [Section 13(b)(4)] accomplishes this by providing that criminal penalties shall not be imposed for failing to comply with the FCPA's books and records or accounting provisions. This provision [Section 13(b)(5)] is meant to ensure that criminal penalties would be imposed where acts of commission or omission in keeping books or records or administering accounting controls have the purpose of falsifying books, records or accounts, or of circumventing the accounting controls set forth in the Act. This would include the deliberate falsification of books and records and other conduct calculated to evade the internal accounting controls requirement.

- The cost of correcting the misstatement. The books and records provisions of the Exchange Act do not require registrants to make major expenditures to correct small misstatements.[39] Conversely, where there is little cost or delay involved in correcting a misstatement, failing to do so is unlikely to be "reasonable."

- The clarity of authoritative accounting guidance with respect to the misstatement. Where reasonable minds may differ about the appropriate accounting treatment of a financial statement item, a failure to correct it may not render the registrant's financial statements inaccurate "in reasonable detail." Where, however, there is little ground for reasonable disagreement, the case for leaving a misstatement uncorrected is correspondingly weaker.

There may be other indicators of "reasonableness" that registrants and their auditors may ordinarily consider. Because the judgment is not mechanical, the staff will be inclined to continue to defer to judgments that "allow a business, acting in good faith, to comply with the Act's accounting provisions in an innovative and cost-effective way."[40]

The Auditor's Response to Intentional Misstatements

Section 10A(b) of the Exchange Act requires auditors to take certain actions upon discovery of an "illegal act."[41] The statute specifies that these obligations are triggered "whether or not [the illegal acts are] perceived to have a material effect on the financial statements of the issuer . . . ." Among other things, Section 10A(b)(1) requires the auditor to inform the appropriate level of management of an illegal act (unless clearly inconsequential) and assure that the registrant's audit committee is "adequately informed" with respect to the illegal act.

As noted, an intentional misstatement of immaterial items in a registrant's financial statements may violate Section 13(b)(2) of the Exchange Act and thus be an illegal act. When such a violation occurs, an auditor must take steps to see that the registrant's audit committee is "adequately informed" about the illegal act. Because Section 10A(b)(1) is triggered regardless of whether an illegal act has a material effect on the registrant's financial statements, where the illegal act consists of a misstatement in the registrant's financial statements, the auditor will be required to report that illegal act to the audit committee irrespective of any "netting" of the misstatements with other financial statement items.

The requirements of Section 10A echo the auditing literature. See, for example, SAS Nos. 54 and 99. Pursuant to paragraph 77 of SAS 99, if the auditor determines there is evidence that fraud may exist, the auditor must discuss the matter with the appropriate level of management that is at least one level above those involved, and with senior management and the audit committee. The auditor must report directly to the audit committee fraud involving senior management and fraud that causes a material misstatement of the financial statements. Paragraph 6 of SAS 99 states that "misstatements arising from fraudulent financial reporting are intentional misstatements or omissions of amounts or disclosures in financial statements designed to deceive financial statement users . . ."[42] SAS 99 further states that fraudulent financial reporting may involve falsification or alteration of accounting records; misrepresenting or omitting events, transactions or other information in the financial statements; and the intentional misapplication of accounting principles relating to amounts, classifications, the manner of presentation, or disclosures in the financial

---

(Footnote Continued)

Cong. Rec. H2115 (daily ed. April 20, 1988).

[39] As Chairman Williams noted with respect to the internal control provisions of the FCPA, "[t]housands of dollars ordinarily should not be spent conserving hundreds." 46 FR 11546.

[40] Id., at 11547.

[41] Section 10A(f) defines, for purposes of Section 10A, an "illegal act" as "an act or omission that violates any law, or any rule or regulation having the force of law." This is broader than the definition of an "illegal act" in AU 317.02, which states, "Illegal acts by clients do not

include personal misconduct by the entity's personnel unrelated to their business activities."

[42] An unintentional illegal act triggers the same procedures and considerations by the auditor as a fraudulent misstatement if the illegal act has a direct and material effect on the financial statements. See AU 110 n. 1, 317.05 and 317.07. Although distinguishing between intentional and unintentional misstatements is often difficult, the auditor must plan and perform the audit to obtain reasonable assurance that the financial statements are free of material misstatements in either case.

statements.[43] The clear implication of SAS 99 is that immaterial misstatements may be fraudulent financial reporting.[44]

Auditors that learn of intentional misstatements may also be required to (1) re-evaluate the degree of audit risk involved in the audit engagement, (2) determine whether to revise the nature, timing, and extent of audit procedures accordingly, and (3) consider whether to resign.[45]

Intentional misstatements also may signal the existence of reportable conditions or material weaknesses in the registrant's system of internal accounting control designed to detect and deter improper accounting and financial reporting.[46] As stated by the National Commission on Fraudulent Financial Reporting, also known as the Treadway Commission, in its 1987 report,

The tone set by top management—the corporate environment or culture within which financial reporting occurs—is the most important factor contributing to the integrity of the financial reporting process. Notwithstanding an impressive set of written rules and procedures, if the tone set by management is lax, fraudulent financial reporting is more likely to occur.[47]

An auditor is required to report to a registrant's audit committee any reportable conditions or material weaknesses in a registrant's system of internal accounting control that the auditor discovers in the course of the examination of the registrant's financial statements.[48]

GAAP precedence over industry practice

Some have argued to the staff that registrants should be permitted to follow an industry accounting practice even though that practice is inconsistent with authoritative accounting literature. This situation might occur if a practice is developed when there are few transactions and the accounting results are clearly inconsequential, and that practice never changes despite a subsequent growth in the number or materiality of such transactions. The staff disagrees with this argument. Authoritative literature takes precedence over industry practice that is contrary to GAAP.[49]

General comments

This SAB is not intended to change current law or guidance in the accounting or auditing literature.[50] This SAB and the authoritative accounting literature cannot specifically address all of

---

[43] Although the auditor is not required to plan or perform the audit to detect misstatements that are immaterial to the financial statements, SAS 99 requires the auditor to evaluate several fraud "risk factors" that may bring such misstatements to his or her attention. For example, an analysis of fraud risk factors under SAS 99 must include, among other things, consideration of management's interest in maintaining or increasing the registrant's stock price or earnings trend through the use of unusually aggressive accounting practices, whether management has a practice of committing to analysts or others that it will achieve unduly aggressive or clearly unrealistic forecasts, and the existence of assets, liabilities, revenues, or expenses based on significant estimates that involve unusually subjective judgments or uncertainties.

[44] In requiring the auditor to consider whether fraudulent misstatements are material, and in requiring differing responses depending on whether the misstatement is material, SAS 99 makes clear that fraud can involve immaterial misstatements. Indeed, a misstatement can be "inconsequential" and still involve fraud.

Under SAS 99, assessing whether misstatements due to fraud are material to the financial statements is a "cumulative process" that should occur both during and at the completion of the audit. SAS 99 further states

that this accumulation is primarily a "qualitative matter" based on the auditor's judgment. The staff believes that in making these assessments, management and auditors should refer to the discussion in Part 1 of this SAB.

[45] Auditors should document their determinations in accordance with SAS 96, SAS 99, and other appropriate sections of the audit literature.

[46] See, e.g., SAS 99.

[47] Report of the National Commission on Fraudulent Financial Reporting at 32 (October 1987). See also Report and Recommendations of the Blue Ribbon Committee on Improving the Effectiveness of Corporate Audit Committees (February 8, 1999).

[48] AU 325.02. See also AU 380.09, which, in discussing matters to be communicated by the auditor to the audit committee, states:

The auditor should inform the audit committee about adjustments arising from the audit that could, in his judgment, either individually or in the aggregate, have a significant effect on the entity's financial reporting process. For purposes of this section, an audit adjustment, whether or not recorded by the entity, is a proposed correction of the financial statements . . . .

[49] See AU 411.05.

[50] The FASB Discussion Memorandum, "Criteria for Determining Materiality," states that the financial

the novel and complex business transactions and events that may occur. Accordingly, registrants may account for, and make disclosures about, these transactions and events based on analogies to similar situations or other factors. The staff may not, however, always be persuaded that a registrant's determination is the most appropriate under the circumstances. When disagreements occur after a transaction or an event has been reported, the consequences may be severe for registrants, auditors, and, most importantly, the users of financial statements who have a right to expect consistent accounting and reporting for, and disclosure of, similar transactions and events. The staff, therefore, encourages registrants and auditors to discuss on a timely basis with the staff proposed accounting treatments for, or disclosures about, transactions or events that are not specifically covered by the existing accounting literature.

(Footnote Continued)

accounting and reporting process considers that "a great deal of the time might be spent during the accounting process considering insignificant matters .... If presentations of financial information are to be prepared economically on a timely basis and presented in a concise intelligible form, the concept of materiality is crucial." This SAB is not intended to require that misstatements arising from insignificant errors and omissions (individually and in the aggregate) arising from the normal recurring accounting close processes, such as a clerical error or an adjustment for a missed accounts payable invoice, always be corrected, even if the error is identified in the audit process and known to management. Management and the auditor would need to consider the various factors described elsewhere in this SAB in assessing whether such misstatements are material, need to be corrected to comply with the FCPA, or trigger procedures under Section 10A of the Exchange Act. Because this SAB does not change current law or guidance in the accounting or auditing literature, adherence to the principles described in this SAB should not raise the costs associated with recordkeeping or with audits of financial statements.

SARBANES-OXLEY ACT OF 2002

SARBANES-OXLEY ACT OF 2002
Selected Provisions

H.R.3763

One Hundred Seventh Congress

of the

United States of America

AT THE SECOND SESSION

Begun and held at the City of Washington on Wednesday,
the twenty-third day of January, two thousand and two
An Act

To protect investors by improving the accuracy and reliability of corporate disclosures made . pursuant to the securities laws, and for other purposes.

Be it enacted by the Senate and House of Representatives of the United States of America in Congress assembled,

SEC. 1.   SHORT TITLE; TABLE OF CONTENTS.

(a) SHORT TITLE—This Act may be cited as the "SarbanesOxley Act of 2002."

(b) TABLE OF CONTENTS—The table of contents for this Act is as follows:

SEC. 2. DEFINITIONS.

SEC. 3. COMMISSION RULES AND ENFORCEMENT.

(a) REGULATORY ACTION—The Commission shall promulgate such rules and regulations, as may be necessary or appropriate in the public interest or for the protection of investors, and in furtherance of this Act.

(b) ENFORCEMENT

(1) IN GENERAL—A violation by any person of this Act, any rule or regulation of the Commission issued under this Act, or any rule of the Board shall be treated for all purposes in the same manner as a violation of the Securities Exchange Act of 1934 (15 U.S.C. 78a et seq.) or the rules and regulations issued thereunder, consistent with the provisions of this Act, and any such person shall be subject to the same penalties, and to the same extent, as for a violation of that Act or such rules or regulations.

(2) INVESTIGATIONS, INJUNCTIONS, AND PROSECUTION OF OFFENSES—Section 21 of the Securities Exchange Act of 1934 (15 U.S.C. 78u) is amended—

(A) in subsection (a)(1), by inserting "the rules of the Public Company Accounting Oversight Board, of which such person is a registered public accounting firm or a person associated with such a firm," after "is a participant,";

(B) in subsection (d)(1), by inserting "the rules of the Public Company Accounting Oversight Board, of which such person is a registered public accounting firm or a person associated with such a firm," after "is a participant,";

(C) in subsection (e), by inserting "the rules of the Public Company Accounting Oversight Board, of which such person is a registered public accounting firm or a person associated with such a firm," after "is a participant,"; and

(D) in subsection (f), by inserting "or the Public Company Accounting Oversight Board" after "self-regulatory organization" each place that term appears.

(3) CEASE-AND-DESIST PROCEEDINGS—Section 21C(c)(2) of the Securities Exchange Act of 1934 (15 U.S.C. 78u-3(c)(2)) is amended by inserting "registered public accounting firm (as defined in section 2 of the Sarbanes-Oxley Act of 2002)," after "government securities dealer."

(4) ENFORCEMENT BY FEDERAL BANKING AGENCIES. Section 12(i) of the Securities Exchange Act of 1934 (15 U.S.C. 78l(i)) is amended by—

(A) striking "sections 12," each place it appears and inserting "sections 10A(m), 12"; and

(B) striking "and 16," each place it appears and inserting "and 16 of this Act, and sections 302, 303, 304, 306, 401(b), 404, 406, and 407 of the Sarbanes-Oxley Act of 2002."

(c) EFFECT ON COMMISSION AUTHORITY—Nothing in this Act or the rules of the Board shall be construed to impair or limit—

(1) the authority of the Commission to regulate the accounting profession, accounting firms, or persons associated with such firms for purposes of enforcement of the securities laws;

(2) the authority of the Commission to set standards for accounting or auditing practices or auditor independence, derived from other provisions of the securities laws or the rules or regulations thereunder, for purposes of the preparation and issuance of any audit report, or otherwise under applicable law; or

(3) the ability of the Commission to take, on the initiative of the Commission, legal, administrative, or disciplinary action against any registered public accounting firm or any associated person thereof.

TITLE I—PUBLIC COMPANY ACCOUNTING OVERSIGHT BOARD

SEC. 101. ESTABLISHMENT; ADMINISTRATIVE PROVISIONS.

(a) ESTABLISHMENT OF BOARD—There is established the Public Company Accounting Oversight Board, to oversee the audit of companies that are subject to the securities laws, and related matters, in order to protect the interests of investors and further the public interest in the preparation of informative, accurate, and independent audit reports. The Board shall be a body corporate, operate as a nonprofit corporation, and have succession until dissolved by an Act of Congress.

(b) STATUS—The Board shall not be an agency or establishment of the United States Government, and, except as otherwise provided in this Act, shall be subject to, and have all the powers conferred upon a nonprofit corporation by, the District of Columbia Nonprofit Corporation Act. No member or person employed by, or agent for, the Board shall be deemed to be an officer or employee of or agent for the Federal Government by reason of such service.

(c) DUTIES OF THE BOARD—The Board shall, subject to action by the Commission under section 107, and once a determination is made by the Commission under subsection (d) of this section—

(1) register public accounting firms that prepare audit reports for issuers, brokers, and dealers in accordance with section 102;

(2) establish or adopt, or both, by rule, auditing, quality control, ethics, independence, and other standards relating to the preparation of audit reports for issuers, brokers, and dealers in accordance with section 103;

(3) conduct inspections of registered public accounting firms, in accordance with section 104 and the rules of the Board;

(4) conduct investigations and disciplinary proceedings concerning, and impose appropriate sanctions where justified upon, registered public accounting firms and associated persons of such firms, in accordance with section 105;

(5) perform such other duties or functions as the Board (or the Commission, by rule or order) determines are necessary or appropriate to promote high professional standards among, and improve the quality of audit services offered by, registered public accounting firms and associated persons thereof, or otherwise to carry out this Act, in order to protect investors, or to further the public interest;

(6) enforce compliance with this Act, the rules of the Board, professional standards, and the securities laws relating to the preparation and issuance of audit reports and the obligations and liabilities of accountants with respect thereto, by registered public accounting firms and associated persons thereof; and

(7) set the budget and manage the operations of the Board and the staff of the Board.

(d) COMMISSION DETERMINATION—The members of the Board shall take such action (including hiring of staff, proposal of rules, and adoption of initial and transitional auditing and other professional standards) as may be necessary or appropriate to enable the Commission to determine, not later than 270 days after the date of enactment of this Act, that the Board is so organized and has the capacity to carry out the requirements of this title, and to enforce compliance with this title by registered public accounting firms and associated persons thereof. The Commission shall be responsible, prior to the appointment of the Board, for the planning for the establishment and administrative transition to the Board's operation.

(e) BOARD MEMBERSHIP

(1) COMPOSITION—The Board shall have 5 members, appointed from among prominent individuals of integrity and reputation who have a demonstrated commitment to the interests of investors and the public, and an understanding of the responsibilities for and nature of the financial disclosures required of issuers, brokers, and dealers under the securities laws and the obligations of accountants with respect to the preparation and issuance of audit reports with respect to such disclosures.

(2) LIMITATION—Two members, and only 2 members, of the Board shall be or have been certified public accountants pursuant to the laws of 1 or more States, provided that, if 1 of those 2 members is the chairperson, he or she may not have been a practicing certified public accountant for at least 5 years prior to his or her appointment to the Board.

(3) FULL-TIME INDEPENDENT SERVICE—Each member of the Board shall serve on a full-time basis, and may not, concurrent with service on the Board, be employed by any other person or engage in any other professional or business activity. No member of the Board may share in any of the profits of, or receive payments from, a public accounting firm (or any other person, as determined by rule of the Commission), other than fixed continuing payments, subject to such conditions as the Commission may impose, under standard arrangements for the retirement of members of public accounting firms.

(4) APPOINTMENT OF BOARD MEMBERS

(A) INITIAL BOARD—Not later than 90 days after the date of enactment of this Act, the Commission, after consultation with the Chairman of the Board of Governors of the Federal Reserve System and the Secretary of the Treasury, shall appoint the chairperson and other initial members of the Board, and shall designate a term of service for each.

(B) VACANCIES—A vacancy on the Board shall not affect the powers of the Board, but shall be filled in the same manner as provided for appointments under this section.

(5) TERM OF SERVICE

(A) IN GENERAL—The term of service of each Board member shall be 5 years, and until a successor is appointed, except that—

(i) the terms of office of the initial Board members (other than the chairperson) shall expire in annual increments, 1 on each of the first 4 anniversaries of the initial date of appointment; and

(ii) any Board member appointed to fill a vacancy occurring before the expiration of the term for which the predecessor was appointed shall be appointed only for the remainder of that term.

(B) TERM LIMITATION—No person may serve as a member of the Board, or as chairperson of the Board, for more than 2 terms, whether or not such terms of service are consecutive.

(6) REMOVAL FROM OFFICE—A member of the Board may be removed by the Commission from office, in accordance with section 107(d)(3), for good cause shown before the expiration of the term of that member.

(f) POWERS OF THE BOARD—In addition to any authority granted to the Board otherwise in this Act, the Board shall have the power, subject to section 107—

(1) to sue and be sued, complain and defend, in its corporate name and through its own counsel, with the approval of the Commission, in any Federal, State, or other court;

(2) to conduct its operations and maintain offices, and to exercise all other rights and powers authorized by this Act, in any State, without regard to any qualification, licensing, or other provision of law in effect in such State (or a political subdivision thereof);

(3) to lease, purchase, accept gifts or donations of or otherwise acquire, improve, use, sell, exchange, or convey, all of or an interest in any property, wherever situated;

(4) to appoint such employees, accountants, attorneys, and other agents as may be necessary or appropriate, and to determine their qualifications, define their duties, and fix their salaries or other compensation (at a level that is comparable to private sector self-regulatory, accounting, technical, supervisory, or other staff or management positions);

(5) to allocate, assess, and collect accounting support fees established pursuant to section 109, for the Board, and other fees and charges imposed under this title; and

(6) to enter into contracts, execute instruments, incur liabilities, and do any and all other acts and things necessary, appropriate, or incidental to the conduct of its operations and the exercise of its obligations, rights, and powers imposed or granted by this title.

(g) RULES OF THE BOARD—The rules of the Board shall, subject to the approval of the Commission—

(1) provide for the operation and administration of the Board, the exercise of its authority, and the performance of its responsibilities under this Act;

(2) permit, as the Board determines necessary or appropriate, delegation by the Board of any of its functions to an individual member or employee of the Board, or to a division of the Board, including functions with respect to hearing, determining, ordering, certifying, reporting, or otherwise acting as to any matter, except that—

(A) the Board shall retain a discretionary right to review any action pursuant to any such delegated function, upon its own motion;

(B) a person shall be entitled to a review by the Board with respect to any matter so delegated, and the decision of the Board upon such review shall be deemed to be the action of the Board for all purposes (including appeal or review thereof); and

(C) if the right to exercise a review described in subparagraph (A) is declined, or if no such review is sought within the time stated in the rules of the Board, then the action taken by the holder of such delegation shall for all purposes, including appeal or review thereof, be deemed to be the action of the Board;

(3) establish ethics rules and standards of conduct for Board members and staff, including a bar on practice before the Board (and the Commission, with respect to Board-related matters) of 1 year for former members of the Board, and appropriate periods (not to exceed 1 year) for former staff of the Board; and

(4) provide as otherwise required by this Act.

(h) ANNUAL REPORT TO THE COMMISSION—The Board shall submit an annual report (including its audited financial statements) to the Commission, and the Commission shall transmit a copy of that report to the Committee on Banking, Housing, and Urban Affairs of the Senate, and the Committee on Financial Services of the House of Representatives, not later than 30 days after the date of receipt of that report by the Commission.

SEC. 102. REGISTRATION WITH THE BOARD.

(a) MANDATORY REGISTRATION—It shall be unlawful for any person that is not a registered public accounting firm to prepare or issue, or to participate in the preparation or issuance of, any audit report with respect to any issuer, broker, or dealer.

(b) APPLICATIONS FOR REGISTRATION

(1) FORM OF APPLICATION—A public accounting firm shall use such form as the Board may prescribe, by rule, to apply for registration under this section.

(2) CONTENTS OF APPLICATIONS—Each public accounting firm shall submit, as part of its application for registration, in such detail as the Board shall specify—

(A) the names of all issuers, brokers, and dealers for which the firm prepared or issued audit reports during the immediately preceding calendar year, and for which the firm expects to prepare or issue audit reports during the current calendar year;

(B) the annual fees received by the firm from each such issuer, broker, or dealer for audit services, other accounting services, and non-audit services, respectively;

(C) such other current financial information for the most recently completed fiscal year of the firm as the Board may reasonably request;

(D) a statement of the quality control policies of the firm for its accounting and auditing practices;

(E) a list of all accountants associated with the firm who participate in or contribute to the preparation of audit reports, stating the license or certification number of each such person, as well as the State license numbers of the firm itself;

(F) information relating to criminal, civil, or administrative actions or disciplinary proceedings pending against the firm or any associated person of the firm in connection with any audit report;

(G) copies of any periodic or annual disclosure filed by an issuer, broker, or dealer with the Commission during the immediately preceding calendar year which discloses accounting disagreements between such issuer, broker, or dealer and the firm in connection with an audit report furnished or prepared by the firm for such issuer, broker, or dealer and

(H) such other information as the rules of the Board or the Commission shall specify as necessary or appropriate in the public interest or for the protection of investors.

(3) CONSENTS—Each application for registration under this subsection shall include—

(A) a consent executed by the public accounting firm to cooperation in and compliance with any request for testimony or the production of documents made by the Board in the furtherance of its authority and responsibilities under this title (and an agreement to secure and enforce similar consents from each of the associated persons of the public accounting firm as a condition of their continued employment by or other association with such firm); and

(B) a statement that such firm understands and agrees that cooperation and compliance, as described in the consent required by subparagraph (A), and the securing and enforcement of such consents from its associated persons, in accordance with the rules of the Board, shall be a condition to the continuing effectiveness of the registration of the firm with the Board.

(c) ACTION ON APPLICATIONS

(1) TIMING—The Board shall approve a completed application for registration not later than 45 days after the date of receipt of the application, in accordance with the rules of the Board, unless the Board, prior to such date, issues a written notice of disapproval to, or requests more information from, the prospective registrant.

(2) TREATMENT—A written notice of disapproval of a completed application under paragraph (1) for registration shall be treated as a disciplinary sanction for purposes of sections 105(d) and 107(c).

(d) PERIODIC REPORTS—Each registered public accounting firm shall submit an annual report to the Board, and may be required to report more frequently, as necessary to update the information contained in its application for registration under this section, and to provide to the Board such additional information as the Board or the Commission may specify, in accordance with subsection (b)(2).

(e) PUBLIC AVAILABILITY—Registration applications and annual reports required by this subsection, or such portions of such applications or reports as may be designated under rules of the Board, shall be made available for public inspection, subject to rules of the Board or the Commission, and to applicable laws relating to the confidentiality of proprietary, personal, or other information contained in such applications or reports, provided that, in all events, the Board shall protect from public disclosure information reasonably identified by the subject accounting firm as proprietary information.

(f) REGISTRATION AND ANNUAL FEES—The Board shall assess and collect a registration fee and an annual fee from each registered public accounting firm, in amounts that are sufficient to recover the costs of processing and reviewing applications and annual reports.

SEC. 103. AUDITING, QUALITY CONTROL, AND INDEPENDENCE STANDARDS AND RULES.

(a) AUDITING, QUALITY CONTROL, AND ETHICS STANDARDS

(1) IN GENERAL—The Board shall, by rule, establish, including, to the extent it determines appropriate, through adoption of standards proposed by 1 or more professional groups of accountants designated pursuant to paragraph (3)(A) or advisory groups convened pursuant to paragraph (4), and amend or otherwise modify or alter, such auditing and related attestation standards, such quality control standards, such ethics standards, and such independence standards to be used by registered public accounting firms in the preparation and issuance of audit reports, as required by this Act or the rules of the Commission, or as may be necessary or appropriate in the public interest or for the protection of investors.

(2) RULE REQUIREMENTS—In carrying out paragraph (1), the Board—

(A) shall include in the auditing standards that it adopts, requirements that each registered public accounting firm shall—

(i) prepare, and maintain for a period of not less than 7 years, audit work papers, and other information related to any audit report, in sufficient detail to support the conclusions reached in such report;

(ii) provide a concurring or second partner review and approval of such audit report (and other related information), and concurring approval in its issuance, by a qualified person (as prescribed by the Board) associated with the public accounting firm, other than the person in charge of the audit, or by an independent reviewer (as prescribed by the Board); and

(iii) in each audit report for an issuer, describe the scope of the auditor's testing of the internal control structure and procedures of the issuer, required by section 404(b), and present (in such report or in a separate report)—

(I) the findings of the auditor from such testing;

(II) an evaluation of whether such internal control structure and procedures—

(aa) include maintenance of records that in reasonable detail accurately and fairly reflect the transactions and dispositions of the assets of the issuer;

(bb) provide reasonable assurance that transactions are recorded as necessary to permit preparation of financial statements in accordance with generally accepted accounting principles, and that receipts and expenditures of the issuer are being made only in accordance with authorizations of management and directors of the issuer; and

(III) a description, at a minimum, of material weaknesses in such internal controls, and of any material noncompliance found on the basis of such testing.

(B) shall include, in the quality control standards that it adopts with respect to the issuance of audit reports, requirements for every registered public accounting firm relating to—

(i) monitoring of professional ethics and independence from issuers, brokers, and dealers on behalf of which the firm issues audit reports;

(ii) consultation within such firm on accounting and auditing questions;

(iii) supervision of audit work;

(iv) hiring, professional development, and advancement of personnel;

(v) the acceptance and continuation of engagements;

(vi) internal inspection; and

(vii) such other requirements as the Board may prescribe, subject to subsection (a)(1).

(3) AUTHORITY TO ADOPT OTHER STANDARDS

(A) IN GENERAL—In carrying out this subsection, the Board—

(i) may adopt as its rules, subject to the terms of section 107, any portion of any statement of auditing standards or other professional standards that the Board determines satisfy the requirements of paragraph (1), and that were proposed by 1 or more professional groups of accountants that shall be designated or recognized by the Board, by rule, for such purpose, pursuant to this paragraph or 1 or more advisory groups convened pursuant to paragraph (4); and

(ii) notwithstanding clause (i), shall retain full authority to modify, supplement, revise, or subsequently amend, modify, or repeal, in whole or in part, any portion of any statement described in clause (i).

(B) INITIAL AND TRANSITIONAL STANDARDS—The Board shall adopt standards described in subparagraph (A)(i) as initial or transitional standards, to the extent the Board determines necessary, prior to a determination of the Commission under section 101(d), and such standards shall be separately approved by the Commission at the time of that determination, without regard to the procedures required by section 107 that otherwise would apply to the approval of rules of the Board.

(C) TRANSITION PERIOD FOR EMERGING GROWTH COMPANIES. Any rules of the Board requiring mandatory audit firm rotation or a supplement to the auditor's report in which the auditor would be required to provide additional information about the audit and the financial statements of the issuer (auditor discussion and analysis) shall not apply to an audit of an emerging growth company, as defined in section 3 of the Securities Exchange Act of 1934. Any additional rules adopted by the Board after the date of enactment of this subparagraph shall not apply to an audit of any emerging growth company, unless the Commission determines that the application of such additional requirements is necessary or appropriate in the public interest, after considering the protection of investors and whether the action will promote efficiency, competition, and capital formation.

(4) ADVISORY GROUPS—The Board shall convene, or authorize its staff to convene, such expert advisory groups as may be appropriate, which may include practicing accountants and other experts, as well as representatives of other interested groups, subject to such rules as the Board may prescribe to prevent conflicts of interest, to make recommendations concerning the content (including proposed drafts) of auditing, quality control, ethics, independence, or other standards required to be established under this section.

(b) INDEPENDENCE STANDARDS AND RULES—The Board shall establish such rules as may be necessary or appropriate in the public interest or for the protection of investors, to implement, or as authorized under, title II of this Act.

(c) COOPERATION WITH DESIGNATED PROFESSIONAL GROUPS OF ACCOUNTANTS AND ADVISORY GROUPS

(1) IN GENERAL—The Board shall cooperate on an ongoing basis with professional groups of accountants designated under subsection (a)(3)(A) and advisory groups convened under subsection (a)(4) in the examination of the need for changes in any standards subject to its authority under subsection (a), recommend issues for inclusion on the agendas of such designated professional groups of accountants or advisory groups, and take such other steps as it deems appropriate to increase the effectiveness of the standard setting process.

(2) BOARD RESPONSES—The Board shall respond in a timely fashion to requests from designated professional groups of accountants and advisory groups referred to in paragraph (1) for any changes in standards over which the Board has authority.

(d) EVALUATION OF STANDARD SETTING PROCESS—The Board shall include in the annual report required by section 101(h) the results of its standard setting responsibilities during the period to which the report relates, including a discussion of the work of the Board with any designated professional groups of accountants and advisory groups described in paragraphs (3)(A) and (4) of subsection (a), and its pending issues agenda for future standard setting projects.

SEC. 104. INSPECTIONS OF REGISTERED PUBLIC ACCOUNTING FIRMS.

(a) IN GENERAL—

(1) Inspections Generally. The Board shall conduct a continuing program of inspections to assess the degree of compliance of each registered public accounting firm and associated persons of that firm with this Act, the rules of the Board, the rules of the Commission, or

professional standards, in connection with its performance of audits, issuance of audit reports, and related matters involving issuers.

(2) Inspections of Audit Reports For Brokers and Dealers.

(A) the Board may, by rule, conduct and require a program of inspection in accordance with paragraph (1), on a basis to be determined by the Board, of registered public accounting firms that provide one or more audit reports for a broker or dealer. The Board, in establishing such a program, may allow for differentiation among classes of brokers and dealers, as appropriate.

(B) if the Board determines to establish a program of inspection pursuant to subparagraph (A), the Board shall consider in establishing any inspection schedules whether differing schedules would be appropriate with respect to registered public accounting firms that issue audit reports only for one or more brokers or dealers that do not receive, handle, or hold customer securities or cash or are not a member of the Securities Investor Protection Corporation.

(C) any rules of the Board pursuant to this paragraph shall be subject to prior approval by the Commission pursuant to section 107(b) before the rules become effective, including an opportunity for public notice and comment.

(D) notwithstanding anything to the contrary in section 102 of this Act, a public accounting firm shall not be required to register with the Board if the public accounting firm is exempt from the inspection program which may be established by the Board under subparagraph (A).

(b) INSPECTION FREQUENCY

(1) IN GENERAL—Subject to paragraph (2), inspections required by this section shall be conducted—

(A) annually with respect to each registered public accounting firm that regularly provides audit reports for more than 100 issuers; and

(B) not less frequently than once every 3 years with respect to each registered public accounting firm that regularly provides audit reports for 100 or fewer issuers.

(2) ADJUSTMENTS TO SCHEDULES—The Board may, by rule, adjust the inspection schedules set under paragraph (1) if the Board finds that different inspection schedules are consistent with the purposes of this Act, the public interest, and the protection of investors. The Board may conduct special inspections at the request of the Commission or upon its own motion.

(c) PROCEDURES—The Board shall, in each inspection under this section, and in accordance with its rules for such inspections—

(1) identify any act or practice or omission to act by the registered public accounting firm, or by any associated person thereof, revealed by such inspection that may be in violation of this Act, the rules of the Board, the rules of the Commission, the firm's own quality control policies, or professional standards;

(2) report any such act, practice, or omission, if appropriate, to the Commission and each appropriate State regulatory authority; and

(3) begin a formal investigation or take disciplinary action, if appropriate, with respect to any such violation, in accordance with this Act and the rules of the Board.

(d) CONDUCT OF INSPECTIONS—In conducting an inspection of a registered public accounting firm under this section, the Board shall—

(1) inspect and review selected audit and review engagements of the firm (which may include audit engagements that are the subject of ongoing litigation or other controversy between the firm and 1 or more third parties), performed at various offices and by various associated persons of the firm, as selected by the Board;

(2) evaluate the sufficiency of the quality control system of the firm, and the manner of the documentation and communication of that system by the firm; and

(3) perform such other testing of the audit, supervisory, and quality control procedures of the firm as are necessary or appropriate in light of the purpose of the inspection and the responsibilities of the Board.

(e) RECORD RETENTION—The rules of the Board may require the retention by registered public accounting firms for inspection purposes of records whose retention is not otherwise required by section 103 or the rules issued thereunder.

(f) PROCEDURES FOR REVIEW—The rules of the Board shall provide a procedure for the review of and response to a draft inspection report by the registered public accounting firm under inspection. The Board shall take such action with respect to such response as it considers appropriate (including revising the draft report or continuing or supplementing its inspection activities before issuing a final report), but the text of any such response, appropriately redacted to protect information reasonably identified by the accounting firm as confidential, shall be attached to and made part of the inspection report.

(g) REPORT—A written report of the findings of the Board for each inspection under this section, subject to subsection (h), shall be—

(1) transmitted, in appropriate detail, to the Commission and each appropriate State regulatory authority, accompanied by any letter or comments by the Board or the inspector, and any letter of response from the registered public accounting firm; and

(2) made available in appropriate detail to the public (subject to section 105(b)(5)(A), and to the protection of such confidential and proprietary information as the Board may determine to be appropriate, or as may be required by law), except that no portions of the inspection report that deal with criticisms of or potential defects in the quality control systems of the firm under inspection shall be made public if those criticisms or defects are addressed by the firm, to the satisfaction of the Board, not later than 12 months after the date of the inspection report.

(h) INTERIM COMMISSION REVIEW

(1) REVIEWABLE MATTERS—A registered public accounting firm may seek review by the Commission, pursuant to such rules as the Commission shall promulgate, if the firm—

(A) has provided the Board with a response, pursuant to rules issued by the Board under subsection (f), to the substance of particular items in a draft inspection report, and disagrees with the assessments contained in any final report prepared by the Board following such response; or

(B) disagrees with the determination of the Board that criticisms or defects identified in an inspection report have not been addressed to the satisfaction of the Board within 12 months of the date of the inspection report, for purposes of subsection (g)(2).

(2) TREATMENT OF REVIEW—Any decision of the Commission with respect to a review under paragraph (1) shall not be reviewable under section 25 of the Securities Exchange Act of 1934 (15 U.S.C. 78y), or deemed to be "final agency action" for purposes of section 704 of title 5, United States Code.

(3) TIMING—Review under paragraph (1) may be sought during the 30-day period following the date of the event giving rise to the review under subparagraph (A) or (B) of paragraph (1).

SEC. 105. INVESTIGATIONS AND DISCIPLINARY PROCEEDINGS.

(a) IN GENERAL—The Board shall establish, by rule, subject to the requirements of this section, fair procedures for the investigation and disciplining of registered public accounting firms and associated persons of such firms.

(b) INVESTIGATIONS

(1) AUTHORITY—In accordance with the rules of the Board, the Board may conduct an investigation of any act or practice, or omission to act, by a registered public accounting firm, any associated person of such firm, or both, that may violate any provision of this Act, the rules of the Board, the provisions of the securities laws relating to the preparation and issuance of audit reports and the obligations and liabilities of accountants with respect thereto, including the rules of the Commission issued under this Act, or professional standards, regardless of how the act, practice, or omission is brought to the attention of the Board.

(2) TESTIMONY AND DOCUMENT PRODUCTION—In addition to such other actions as the Board determines to be necessary or appropriate, the rules of the Board may—

(A) require the testimony of the firm or of any person associated with a registered public accounting firm, with respect to any matter that the Board considers relevant or material to an investigation;

(B) require the production of audit work papers and any other document or information in the possession of a registered public accounting firm or any associated person thereof, wherever domiciled, that the Board considers relevant or material to the investigation, and may inspect the books and records of such firm or associated person to verify the accuracy of any documents or information supplied;

(C) request the testimony of, and production of any document in the possession of, any other person, including any client of a registered public accounting firm that the Board considers relevant or material to an investigation under this section, with appropriate notice, subject to the needs of the investigation, as permitted under the rules of the Board; and

(D) provide for procedures to seek issuance by the Commission, in a manner established by the Commission, of a subpoena to require the testimony of, and production of any document in the possession of, any person, including any client of a registered public accounting firm, that the Board considers relevant or material to an investigation under this section.

(3) NONCOOPERATION WITH INVESTIGATIONS

(A) IN GENERAL—If a registered public accounting firm or any associated person thereof refuses to testify, produce documents, or otherwise cooperate with the Board in connection with an investigation under this section, the Board may—

(i) suspend or bar such person from being associated with a registered public accounting firm, or require the registered public accounting firm to end such association;

(ii) suspend or revoke the registration of the public accounting firm; and

(iii) invoke such other lesser sanctions as the Board considers appropriate, and as specified by rule of the Board.

(B) PROCEDURE—Any action taken by the Board under this paragraph shall be subject to the terms of section 107(c).

(4) COORDINATION AND REFERRAL OF INVESTIGATIONS

(A) COORDINATION—The Board shall notify the Commission of any pending Board investigation involving a potential violation of the securities laws, and thereafter coordinate its work with the work of the Commission's Division of Enforcement, as necessary to protect an ongoing Commission investigation.

(B) REFERRAL—The Board may refer an investigation under this section—

(i) to the Commission;

(ii) to a self-regulatory organization, in the case of an investigation that concerns an audit report for a broker or dealer that is under the jurisdiction of such self-regulatory organization;

(iii) to any other Federal functional regulator (as defined in section 509 of the Gramm-Leach-Bliley Act (15 U.S.C. 6809)), in the case of an investigation that concerns an audit report for an institution that is subject to the jurisdiction of such regulator; and

(iv) at the direction of the Commission, to—

(I) the Attorney General of the United States;

(II) the attorney general of 1 or more States; and

(III) the appropriate State regulatory authority.

(5) USE OF DOCUMENTS

(A) CONFIDENTIALITY—Except as provided in subparagraph (B) and (C), all documents and information prepared or received by or specifically for the Board, and deliberations of the Board and its employees and agents, in connection with an inspection under section 104 or with an investigation under this section, shall be confidential and privileged as an evidentiary matter (and shall not be subject to civil discovery or other legal process) in any proceeding in any Federal or State court or administrative agency, and shall be exempt from disclosure, in the hands of an agency or establishment of the Federal Government, under the Freedom of Information Act (5 U.S.C. 552a), or otherwise, unless and until presented in connection with a public proceeding or released in accordance with subsection (c).

(B) AVAILABILITY TO GOVERNMENT AGENCIES—Without the loss of its status as confidential and privileged in the hands of the Board, all information referred to in subparagraph (A) may—

(i) be made available to the Commission; and

(ii) in the discretion of the Board, when determined by the Board to be necessary to accomplish the purposes of this Act or to protect investors, be made available to—

(I) the Attorney General of the United States;

(II) the appropriate Federal functional regulator (as defined in section 509 of the Gramm-LeachBliley Act (15 U.S.C. 6809)), other than the Commission, and the Director of the Federal Housing Finance Agency, with respect to an audit report for an institution subject to the jurisdiction of such regulator;

(III) State attorneys general in connection with any criminal investigation;

(IV) any appropriate State regulatory authority; and

(V) a self-regulatory organization, with respect to an audit report for a broker or dealer that is under the jurisdiction of such self-regulatory organization, each of which shall maintain such information as confidential and privileged.

(C) AVAILABILITY TO FOREIGN OVERSIGHT AUTHORITIES—Without the loss of its status as confidential and privileged in the hands of the Board, all information referred to in subparagraph (A) that relates to a public accounting firm that a foreign government has empowered a foreign auditor oversight authority to inspect or otherwise enforce laws with respect to, may, at the discretion of the Board, be made available to the foreign auditor oversight authority, if—

(i) the Board finds that it is necessary to accomplish the purposes of this Act or to protect investors;

(ii) the foreign auditor oversight authority provides—

(I) such assurances of confidentiality as the Board may request;

(II) a description of the applicable information systems and controls of the foreign auditor oversight authority; and

(III) a description of the laws and regulations of the foreign government of the foreign auditor oversight authority that are relevant to information access; and

(iii) the Board determines that it is appropriate to share such information.

(6) IMMUNITY—Any employee of the Board engaged in carrying out an investigation under this Act shall be immune from any civil liability arising out of such investigation in the same manner and to the same extent as an employee of the Federal Government in similar circumstances.

(c) DISCIPLINARY PROCEDURES

(1) NOTIFICATION; RECORDKEEPING—The rules of the Board shall provide that in any proceeding by the Board to determine whether a registered public accounting firm, or an associated person thereof, should be disciplined, the Board shall—

(A) bring specific charges with respect to the firm or associated person;

(B) notify such firm or associated person of, and provide to the firm or associated person an opportunity to defend against, such charges; and

(C) keep a record of the proceedings.

(2) PUBLIC HEARINGS—Hearings under this section shall not be public, unless otherwise ordered by the Board for good cause shown, with the consent of the parties to such hearing.

(3) SUPPORTING STATEMENT—A determination by the Board to impose a sanction under this subsection shall be supported by a statement setting forth—

(A) each act or practice in which the registered public accounting firm, or associated person, has engaged (or omitted to engage), or that forms a basis for all or a part of such sanction;

(B) the specific provision of this Act, the securities laws, the rules of the Board, or professional standards which the Board determines has been violated; and

(C) the sanction imposed, including a justification for that sanction.

(4) SANCTIONS—If the Board finds, based on all of the facts and circumstances, that a registered public accounting firm or associated person thereof has engaged in any act or practice, or omitted to act, in violation of this Act, the rules of the Board, the provisions of the securities laws relating to the preparation and issuance of audit reports and the obligations and liabilities of accountants with respect thereto, including the rules of the Commission issued under this Act, or professional standards, the Board may impose such disciplinary or remedial sanctions as it determines appropriate, subject to applicable limitations under paragraph (5), including—

(A) temporary suspension or permanent revocation of registration under this title;

(B) temporary or permanent suspension or bar of a person from further association with any registered public accounting firm;

(C) temporary or permanent limitation on the activities, functions, or operations of such firm or person (other than in connection with required additional professional education or training);

(D) a civil money penalty for each such violation, in an amount equal to—

(i) not more than $100,000 for a natural person or $2,000,000 for any other person; and

(ii) in any case to which paragraph (5) applies, not more than $750,000 for a natural person or $15,000,000 for any other person;

(E) censure;

(F) required additional professional education or training; or

(G) any other appropriate sanction provided for in the rules of the Board.

(5) INTENTIONAL OR OTHER KNOWING CONDUCT—The sanctions and penalties described in subparagraphs (A) through (C) and (D)(ii) of paragraph (4) shall only apply to—

(A) intentional or knowing conduct, including reckless conduct, that results in violation of the applicable statutory, regulatory, or professional standard; or

(B) repeated instances of negligent conduct, each resulting in a violation of the applicable statutory, regulatory, or professional standard.

(6) FAILURE TO SUPERVISE

(A) IN GENERAL—The Board may impose sanctions under this section on a registered accounting firm or upon any person who is, or at the time of the alleged failure reasonably to supervise was, a supervisory person of such firm, if the Board finds that—

(i) the firm has failed reasonably to supervise an associated person, either as required by the rules of the Board relating to auditing or quality control standards, or otherwise, with a view to preventing violations of this Act, the rules of the Board, the provisions of the securities laws relating to the preparation and issuance of audit reports and the obligations and liabilities of accountants with respect thereto, including the rules of the Commission under this Act, or professional standards; and

(ii) such associated person commits a violation of this Act, or any of such rules, laws, or standards.

(B) RULE OF CONSTRUCTION—No current or former supervisory person of a registered public accounting firm shall be deemed to have failed reasonably to supervise any other person for purposes of subparagraph (A), if—

(i) there have been established in and for that firm procedures, and a system for applying such procedures, that comply with applicable rules of the Board and that would reasonably be expected to prevent and detect any such violation by such associated person; and

(ii) such person has reasonably discharged the duties and obligations incumbent upon that person by reason of such procedures and system, and had no reasonable cause to believe that such procedures and system were not being complied with.

(7) EFFECT OF SUSPENSION

(A) ASSOCIATION WITH A PUBLIC ACCOUNTING FIRM It shall be unlawful for any person that is suspended or barred from being associated with a registered public accounting firm under this subsection willfully to become or remain associated with any registered public accounting firm, or for any registered public accounting firm that knew, or, in the exercise of reasonable care should have known, of the suspension or bar, to permit such an association, without the consent of the Board or the Commission.

(B) ASSOCIATION WITH AN ISSUER, BROKER, OR DEALER—It shall be unlawful for any person that is suspended or barred from being associated with an issuer, broker, or dealer under this subsection willfully to become or remain associated with any issuer, broker, or dealer in an accountancy or a financial management capacity, and for any issuer, broker, or dealer that knew, or in the exercise of reasonable care should have known, of such suspension or bar, to permit such an association, without the consent of the Board or the Commission.

(d) REPORTING OF SANCTIONS

(1) RECIPIENTS—If the Board imposes a disciplinary sanction, in accordance with this section, the Board shall report the sanction to—

(A) the Commission;

(B) any appropriate State regulator authority or any foreign accountancy licensing board with which such firm or person is licensed or certified; and

(C) the public (once any stay on the imposition of such sanction has been lifted).

(2) CONTENTS—The information reported under paragraph (1) shall include—

(A) the name of the sanctioned person;

(B) a description of the sanction and the basis for its imposition; and

(C) such other information as the Board deems appropriate.

(e) STAY OF SANCTIONS

(1) IN GENERAL—Application to the Commission for review, or the institution by the Commission of review, of any disciplinary action of the Board shall operate as a stay of any such disciplinary action, unless and until the Commission orders (summarily or after notice and opportunity for hearing on the question of a stay, which hearing may consist solely of the submission of affidavits or presentation of oral arguments) that no such stay shall continue to operate.

(2) EXPEDITED PROCEDURES—The Commission shall establish for appropriate cases an expedited procedure for consideration and determination of the question of the duration of a stay pending review of any disciplinary action of the Board under this subsection.

SEC. 106. FOREIGN PUBLIC ACCOUNTING FIRMS.

(a) APPLICABILITY TO CERTAIN FOREIGN FIRMS

(1) IN GENERAL—Any foreign public accounting firm that prepares or furnishes an audit report with respect to any issuer, broker, or dealer, shall be subject to this Act and the rules of the Board and the Commission issued under this Act, in the same manner and to the same extent as a public accounting firm that is organized and operates under the laws of the United States or any State, except that registration pursuant to section 102 shall not by itself provide a basis for subjecting such a foreign public accounting firm to the

jurisdiction of the Federal or State courts, other than with respect to controversies between such firms and the Board.

(2) BOARD AUTHORITY—The Board may, by rule, determine that a foreign public accounting firm (or a class of such firms) that does not issue audit reports nonetheless plays such a substantial role in the preparation and furnishing of such reports for particular issuers, brokers, or dealers that it is necessary or appropriate, in light of the purposes of this Act and in the public interest or for the protection of investors, that such firm (or class of firms) should be treated as a public accounting firm (or firms) for purposes of registration under, and oversight by the Board in accordance with, this title.

(b) PRODUCTION OF DOCUMENTS.

(1) PRODUCTION BY FOREIGN FIRMS— If a foreign public accounting firm performs material services upon which a registered public accounting firm relies in the conduct of an audit or interim review, issues an audit report, performs audit work, or conducts interim reviews, the foreign public accounting firm shall—

(A) produce the audit work papers of the foreign public accounting firm and all other documents of the firm related to any such audit work or interim review to the Commission or the Board, upon request of the Commission or the Board; and

(B) be subject to the jurisdiction of the courts of the United States for purposes of enforcement of any request for such documents.

(2) OTHER PRODUCTION— Any registered public accounting firm that relies, in whole or in part, on the work of a foreign public accounting firm in issuing an audit report, performing audit work, or conducting an interim review, shall—

(A) produce the audit work papers of the foreign public accounting firm and all other documents related to any such work in response to a request for production by the Commission or the Board; and

(B) secure the agreement of any foreign public accounting firm to such production, as a condition of the reliance by the registered public accounting firm on the work of that foreign public accounting firm.

(c) EXEMPTION AUTHORITY—The Commission, and the Board, subject to the approval of the Commission, may, by rule, regulation, or order, and as the Commission (or Board) determines necessary or appropriate in the public interest or for the protection of investors, either unconditionally or upon specified terms and conditions exempt any foreign public accounting firm, or any class of such firms, from any provision of this Act or the rules of the Board or the Commission issued under this Act.

(d) SERVICE OF REQUESTS OR PROCESS.

(1) IN GENERAL— Any foreign public accounting firm that performs work for a domestic registered public accounting firm shall furnish to the domestic registered public accounting firm a written irrevocable consent and power of attorney that designates the domestic registered public accounting firm as an agent upon whom may be served any request by the Commission or the Board under this section or upon whom may be served any process, pleadings, or other papers in any action brought to enforce this section.

(2) SPECIFIC AUDIT WORK— Any foreign public accounting firm that performs material services upon which a registered public accounting firm relies in the conduct of an audit or interim review, issues an audit report, performs audit work, or, performs interim reviews, shall designate to the Commission or the Board an agent in the United States upon whom may be served any request by the Commission or the Board under this section or upon whom may be served any process, pleading, or other papers in any action brought to enforce this section.

(e) SANCTIONS— A willful refusal to comply, in whole in or in part, with any request by the Commission or the Board under this section, shall be deemed a violation of this Act.

(f) OTHER MEANS OF SATISFYING PRODUCTION OBLIGATIONS— Notwithstanding any other provisions of this section, the staff of the Commission or the Board may allow a foreign public accounting firm that is subject to this section to meet production obligations under this section through alternate means, such as through foreign counterparts of the Commission or the Board.

(g) DEFINITION—In this section, the term "foreign public accounting firm" means a public accounting firm that is organized and operates under the laws of a foreign government or political subdivision thereof.

SEC. 107. COMMISSION OVERSIGHT OF THE BOARD.

(a) GENERAL OVERSIGHT RESPONSIBILITY—The Commission shall have oversight and enforcement authority over the Board, as provided in this Act. The provisions of section 17(a)(1) of the Securities Exchange Act of 1934 (15 U.S.C. 78q(a)(1)), and of section 17(b)(1) of the Securities Exchange Act of 1934 (15 U.S.C. 78q(b)(1)) shall apply to the Board as fully as if the Board were a "registered securities association" for purposes of those sections 17(a)(1) and 17(b)(1).

(b) RULES OF THE BOARD

(1) DEFINITION—In this section, the term "proposed rule" means any proposed rule of the Board, and any modification of any such rule.

(2) PRIOR APPROVAL REQUIRED—No rule of the Board shall become effective without prior approval of the Commission in accordance with this section, other than as provided in section 103(a)(3)(B) with respect to initial or transitional standards.

(3) APPROVAL CRITERIA—The Commission shall approve a proposed rule, if it finds that the rule is consistent with the requirements of this Act and the securities laws, or is necessary or appropriate in the public interest or for the protection of investors.

(4) PROPOSED RULE PROCEDURES—The provisions of paragraphs (1) through (3) of section 19(b) of the Securities Exchange Act of 1934 (15 U.S.C. 78s(b)) shall govern the proposed rules of the Board, as fully as if the Board were a "registered securities association" for purposes of that section 19(b), except that, for purposes of this paragraph—

(A) the phrase "consistent with the requirements of this title and the rules and regulations thereunder applicable to such organization" in section 19(b)(2) of that Act shall be deemed to read "consistent with the requirements of title I of the Sarbanes-Oxley Act of 2002, and the rules and regulations issued thereunder applicable to such organization, or as necessary or appropriate in the public interest or for the protection of investors"; and

(B) the phrase "otherwise in furtherance of the purposes of this title" in section 19(b)(3)(C) of that Act shall be deemed to read "otherwise in furtherance of the purposes of title I of the Sarbanes-Oxley Act of 2002."

(5) COMMISSION AUTHORITY TO AMEND RULES OF THE BOARD—The provisions of section 19(c) of the Securities Exchange Act of 1934 (15 U.S.C. 78s(c)) shall govern the abrogation, deletion, or addition to portions of the rules of the Board by the Commission as fully as if the Board were a "registered securities association" for purposes of that section 19(c), except that the phrase "to conform its rules to the requirements of this title and the rules and regulations thereunder applicable to such organization, or otherwise in furtherance of the purposes of this title" in section 19(c) of that Act shall, for purposes of this paragraph, be deemed to read "to assure the fair administration of the Public Company Accounting Oversight Board, conform the rules promulgated by that Board to the requirements of title I of the Sarbanes-Oxley Act of 2002, or otherwise further the purposes of that Act, the securities laws, and the rules and regulations thereunder applicable to that Board."

(c) COMMISSION REVIEW OF DISCIPLINARY ACTION TAKEN BY THE BOARD

(1) NOTICE OF SANCTION—The Board shall promptly file notice with the Commission of any final sanction on any registered public accounting firm or on any associated person thereof, in such form and containing such information as the Commission, by rule, may prescribe.

(2) REVIEW OF SANCTIONS—The provisions of sections 19(d)(2) and 19(e)(1) of the Securities Exchange Act of 1934 (15 U.S.C. 78s (d)(2) and (e)(1)) shall govern the review by the Commission of final disciplinary sanctions imposed by the Board (including sanctions imposed under section 105(b)(3) of this Act for noncooperation in an investigation of the Board), as fully as if the Board were a self-regulatory organization and the Commission were the appropriate regulatory agency for such organization for purposes of those sections 19(d)(2) and 19(e)(1), except that, for purposes of this paragraph—

(A) section 105(e) of this Act (rather than that section 19(d)(2)) shall govern the extent to which application for, or institution by the Commission on its own motion of, review of any disciplinary action of the Board operates as a stay of such action;

(B) references in that section 19(e)(1) to "members" of such an organization shall be deemed to be references to registered public accounting firms;

(C) the phrase "consistent with the purposes of this title" in that section 19(e)(1) shall be deemed to read "consistent with the purposes of this title and title I of the Sarbanes-Oxley Act of 2002";

(D) references to rules of the Municipal Securities Rulemaking Board in that section 19(e)(1) shall not apply; and (E) the reference to section 19(e)(2) of the Securities Exchange Act of 1934 shall refer instead to section 107(c)(3) of this Act.

(3) COMMISSION MODIFICATION AUTHORITY—The Commission may enhance, modify, cancel, reduce, or require the remission of a sanction imposed by the Board upon a registered public accounting firm or associated person thereof, if the Commission, having due regard for the public interest and the protection of investors, finds, after a proceeding in accordance with this subsection, that the sanction—

(A) is not necessary or appropriate in furtherance of this Act or the securities laws; or

(B) is excessive, oppressive, inadequate, or otherwise not appropriate to the finding or the basis on which the sanction was imposed.

(d) CENSURE OF THE BOARD; OTHER SANCTIONS

(1) RESCISSION OF BOARD AUTHORITY—The Commission, by rule, consistent with the public interest, the protection of investors, and the other purposes of this Act and the securities laws, may relieve the Board of any responsibility to enforce compliance with any provision of this Act, the securities laws, the rules of the Board, or professional standards.

(2) CENSURE OF THE BOARD; LIMITATIONS—The Commission may, by order, as it determines necessary or appropriate in the public interest, for the protection of investors, or otherwise in furtherance of the purposes of this Act or the securities laws, censure or impose limitations upon the activities, functions, and operations of the Board, if the Commission finds, on the record, after notice and opportunity for a hearing, that the Board—

(A) has violated or is unable to comply with any provision of this Act, the rules of the Board, or the securities laws; or

(B) without reasonable justification or excuse, has failed to enforce compliance with any such provision or rule, or any professional standard by a registered public accounting firm or an associated person thereof.

(3) CENSURE OF BOARD MEMBERS; REMOVAL FROM OFFICEThe Commission may, as necessary or appropriate in the public interest, for the protection of investors, or otherwise in furtherance of the purposes of this Act or the securities laws, remove from office or censure any person who is, or at the time of the alleged misconduct was, a member of the Board, if the Commission finds, on the record, after notice and opportunity for a hearing, that such member—

(A) has willfully violated any provision of this Act, the rules of the Board, or the securities laws;

(B) has willfully abused the authority of that member; or

(C) without reasonable justification or excuse, has failed to enforce compliance with any such provision or rule, or any professional standard by any registered public accounting firm or any associated person thereof.

SEC. 108. ACCOUNTING STANDARDS.

(a) AMENDMENT TO SECURITIES ACT OF 1933—Section 19 of the Securities Act of 1933 (15 U.S.C. 77s) is amended—

(1) by redesignating subsections (b) and (c) as subsections (c) and (d), respectively; and

(2) by inserting after subsection (a) the following:

"(b) RECOGNITION OF ACCOUNTING STANDARDS

"(1) IN GENERAL—In carrying out its authority under subsection (a) and under section 13(b) of the Securities Exchange Act of 1934, the Commission may recognize, as 'generally accepted' for purposes of the securities laws, any accounting principles established by a standard setting body—

"(A) that—

"(i) is organized as a private entity;

"(ii) has, for administrative and operational purposes, a board of trustees (or equivalent body) serving in the public interest, the majority of whom are not, concurrent with their service on such board, and have not been during the 2-year period preceding such service, associated persons of any registered public accounting firm;

"(iii) is funded as provided in section 109 of the Sarbanes-Oxley Act of 2002;

"(iv) has adopted procedures to ensure prompt consideration, by majority vote of its members, of changes to accounting principles necessary to reflect emerging accounting issues and changing business practices; and

"(v) considers, in adopting accounting principles, the need to keep standards current in order to reflect changes in the business environment, the extent to which international convergence on high quality accounting standards is necessary or appropriate in the public interest and for the protection of investors; and

"(B) that the Commission determines has the capacity to assist the Commission in fulfilling the requirements of subsection (a) and section 13(b) of the Securities Exchange Act of 1934, because, at a minimum, the standard setting body is capable of improving the accuracy and effectiveness of financial reporting and the protection of investors under the securities laws.

"(2) ANNUAL REPORT—A standard setting body described in paragraph (1) shall submit an annual report to the Commission and the public, containing audited financial statements of that standard setting body."

(b) COMMISSION AUTHORITY—The Commission shall promulgate such rules and regulations to carry out section 19(b) of the Securities Act of 1933, as added by this section, as it deems necessary or appropriate in the public interest or for the protection of investors.

(c) NO EFFECT ON COMMISSION POWERS—Nothing in this Act, including this section and the amendment made by this section, shall be construed to impair or limit the authority of the Commission to establish accounting principles or standards for purposes of enforcement of the securities laws.

(d) STUDY AND REPORT ON ADOPTING PRINCIPLES-BASED ACCOUNTING

(1) STUDY

(A) IN GENERAL—The Commission shall conduct a study on the adoption by the United States financial reporting system of a principlesbased accounting system.

SEC. 109. FUNDING.

(a) IN GENERAL—The Board, and the standard setting body designated pursuant to section 19(b) of the Securities Act of 1933, as amended by section 108, shall be funded as provided in this section.

(b) ANNUAL BUDGETS—The Board and the standard setting body referred to in subsection (a) shall each establish a budget for each fiscal year. The budget of the Board shall be subject to approval by the Commission.

(c) SOURCES AND USES OF FUNDS

(1) RECOVERABLE BUDGET EXPENSES—The budget of the Board, for each fiscal year of each of those 2 entities, shall be payable from annual accounting support fees, in accordance with subsections (d) and (e). Accounting support fees and other receipts of the Board and of such standard-setting body shall not be considered public monies of the United States.

(2) FUNDS GENERATED FROM THE COLLECTION OF MONETARY PENAL-TIES—Subject to the availability in advance in an appropriations Act, and notwithstanding subsection (j), all funds collected by the Board as a result of the assessment of monetary penalties shall be used to fund a merit scholarship program for undergraduate and graduate students enrolled in accredited accounting degree programs, which program is to be administered by the Board or by an entity or agent identified by the Board.

(d) ANNUAL ACCOUNTING SUPPORT FEE FOR THE BOARD

(1) ESTABLISHMENT OF FEE—The Board shall establish, with the approval of the Commission, a reasonable annual accounting support fee (or a formula for the computation thereof), as may be necessary or appropriate to establish and maintain the Board. Such fee may also cover costs incurred in the Board's first fiscal year (which may be a short fiscal year), or may be levied separately with respect to such short fiscal year.

(2) ASSESSMENTS—The rules of the Board under paragraph (1) shall provide for the equitable allocation, assessment, and collection by the Board (or an agent appointed by the Board) of the fee established under paragraph (1), among issuers, in accordance with subsection (g), and among brokers and dealers, in accordance with subsection (h), and allowing for differentiation among classes of issuers, brokers and dealers, as appropriate.

(3) BROKERS AND DEALERS— The Board shall begin the allocation, assessment, and collection of fees under paragraph (2) with respect to brokers and dealers with the payment of support fees to fund the first full fiscal year beginning after the date of enactment of the Investor Protection and Securities Reform Act of 2010.

(e) ANNUAL ACCOUNTING SUPPORT FEE FOR STANDARD SETTING BODY—The annual accounting support fee for the standard setting body referred to in subsection (a)—

(1) shall be allocated in accordance with subsection (g), and assessed and collected against each issuer, on behalf of the standard setting body, by 1 or more appropriate designated collection agents, as may be necessary or appropriate to pay for the budget and provide for the expenses of that standard setting body, and to provide for an independent, stable source of funding for such body, subject to review by the Commission; and

(2) may differentiate among different classes of issuers.

(f) LIMITATION ON FEE—The amount of fees collected under this section for a fiscal year on behalf of the Board or the standards setting body, as the case may be, shall not exceed the recoverable budget expenses of the Board or body, respectively (which may include operating, capital, and accrued items), referred to in subsection (c)(1).

(g) ALLOCATION OF ACCOUNTING SUPPORT FEES AMONG ISSUERS Any amount due from issuers (or a particular class of issuers) under this section to fund the budget of the Board or the standard setting body referred to in subsection (a) shall be allocated among and payable by each issuer (or each issuer in a particular class, as applicable) in an amount equal to the total of such amount, multiplied by a fraction—

(1) the numerator of which is the average monthly equity market capitalization of the issuer for the 12-month period immediately preceding the beginning of the fiscal year to which such budget relates; and

(2) the denominator of which is the average monthly equity market capitalization of all such issuers for such 12-month period.

(h) ALLOCATION OF ACCOUNTING SUPPORT FEES AMONG BROKERS AND DEALERS.

(1) OBLIGATION TO PAY— Each broker or dealer shall pay to the Board the annual accounting support fee allocated to such broker or dealer under this section.

(2) ALLOCATION— Any amount due from a broker or dealer (or from a particular class of brokers and dealers) under this section shall be allocated among brokers and dealers and payable by the broker or dealer (or the brokers and dealers in the particular class, as applicable).

(3) PROPORTIONALITY— The amount due from a broker or dealer shall be in proportion to the net capital of the broker or dealer (before or after any adjustments), compared to the total net capital of all brokers and dealers (before or after any adjustments), in accordance with rules issued by the Board.

(i) [Omitted; paragraph (h) [redesignated as (i)] amended existing law.]

(j) RULE OF CONSTRUCTION— Nothing in this section shall be construed to render either the Board, the standard setting body referred to in subsection (a), or both, subject to procedures in Congress to authorize or appropriate public funds, or to prevent such organization from utilizing additional sources of revenue for its activities, such as earnings from publication sales, provided that each additional source of revenue shall not jeopardize, in the judgment of the Commission, the actual and perceived independence of such organization.

(k) START-UP EXPENSES OF THE BOARD— From the unexpended balances of the appropriations to the Commission for fiscal year 2003, the Secretary of the Treasury is authorized to advance to the Board not to exceed the amount necessary to cover the expenses of the Board during its first fiscal year (which may be a short fiscal year).

TITLE II—AUDITOR INDEPENDENCE

SEC. 201. SERVICES OUTSIDE THE SCOPE OF PRACTICE OF AUDITORS.

(a) PROHIBITED ACTIVITIES—Section 10A of the Securities Exchange Act of 1934 (15 U.S.C. 78j-1) is amended by adding at the end the following: "(g) PROHIBITED ACTIVITIES— Except as provided in subsection (h), it shall be unlawful for a registered public accounting firm (and any associated person of that firm, to the extent determined appropriate by the Commission) that performs for any issuer any audit required by this title or the rules of the Commission under this title or, beginning 180 days after the date of commencement of the operations of the Public Company Accounting Oversight Board established under section 101 of the Sarbanes-Oxley Act of 2002 (in this section referred to as the 'Board'), the rules of the Board, to provide to that issuer, contemporaneously with the audit, any non-audit service, including—

"(1) bookkeeping or other services related to the accounting records or financial statements of the audit client;

"(2) financial information systems design and implementation;

"(3) appraisal or valuation services, fairness opinions, or contribution-in-kind reports;

"(4) actuarial services;

"(5) internal audit outsourcing services;

"(6) management functions or human resources;

"(7) broker or dealer, investment adviser, or investment banking services;

"(8) legal services and expert services unrelated to the audit; and

"(9) any other service that the Board determines, by regulation, is impermissible.

"(h) PREAPPROVAL REQUIRED FOR NON-AUDIT SERVICES—A registered public accounting firm may engage in any nonaudit service, including tax services, that is not described in any of paragraphs (1) through (9) of subsection (g) for an audit client, only if the activity is approved in advance by the audit committee of the issuer, in accordance with subsection (i)."

(b) EXEMPTION AUTHORITY—The Board may, on a case by case basis, exempt any person, issuer, public accounting firm, or transaction from the prohibition on the provision of services under section 10A(g) of the Securities Exchange Act of 1934 (as added by this section), to the extent that such exemption is necessary or appropriate in the public interest and is consistent with the protection of investors, and subject to review by the Commission in the same manner as for rules of the Board under section 107.

SEC. 202. PREAPPROVAL REQUIREMENTS.

Section 10A of the Securities Exchange Act of 1934 (15 U.S.C. 78j-1), as amended by this Act, is amended by adding at the end the following:

"(i) PREAPPROVAL REQUIREMENTS

"(1) IN GENERAL

"(A) AUDIT COMMITTEE ACTION—All auditing services (which may entail providing comfort letters in connection with securities underwritings or statutory audits required for insurance companies for purposes of State law) and non-audit services, other than as provided in subparagraph (B), provided to an issuer by the auditor of the issuer shall be preapproved by the audit committee of the issuer.

"(B) DE MINIMUS EXCEPTION—The preapproval requirement under subparagraph (A) is waived with respect to the provision of non-audit services for an issuer, if—

"(i) the aggregate amount of all such non-audit services provided to the issuer constitutes not more than 5 percent of the total amount of revenues paid by the issuer to its auditor during the fiscal year in which the nonaudit services are provided;

"(ii) such services were not recognized by the issuer at the time of the engagement to be non-audit services; and

"(iii) such services are promptly brought to the attention of the audit committee of the issuer and approved prior to the completion of the audit by the audit committee or by 1 or more members of the audit committee who are members of the board of directors to whom authority to grant such approvals has been delegated by the audit committee.

"(2) DISCLOSURE TO INVESTORS—Approval by an audit committee of an issuer under this subsection of a non-audit service to be performed by the auditor of the issuer shall be disclosed to investors in periodic reports required by section 13(a).

"(3) DELEGATION AUTHORITY—The audit committee of an issuer may delegate to 1 or more designated members of the audit committee who are independent directors of the board of directors, the authority to grant preapprovals required by this subsection. The decisions of any member to whom authority is delegated under this paragraph to preapprove an activity under this subsection shall be presented to the full audit committee at each of its scheduled meetings.

"(4) APPROVAL OF AUDIT SERVICES FOR OTHER PURPOSES In carrying out its duties under subsection (m)(2), if the audit committee of an issuer approves an audit service within the scope of the engagement of the auditor, such audit service shall be deemed to have been preapproved for purposes of this subsection."

SEC. 203. AUDIT PARTNER ROTATION.

Section 10A of the Securities Exchange Act of 1934 (15 U.S.C. 78j-1), as amended by this Act, is amended by adding at the end the following:

"(j) AUDIT PARTNER ROTATION—It shall be unlawful for a registered public accounting firm to provide audit services to an issuer if the lead (or coordinating) audit partner (having primary responsibility for the audit), or the audit partner responsible for reviewing the audit, has performed audit services for that issuer in each of the 5 previous fiscal years of that issuer."

SEC. 204. AUDITOR REPORTS TO AUDIT COMMITTEES.

Section 10A of the Securities Exchange Act of 1934 (15 U.S.C. 78j-1), as amended by this Act, is amended by adding at the end the following:

"(k) REPORTS TO AUDIT COMMITTEES—Each registered public accounting firm that performs for any issuer any audit required by this title shall timely report to the audit committee of the issuer—

"(1) all critical accounting policies and practices to be used;

"(2) all alternative treatments of financial information within generally accepted accounting principles that have been discussed with management officials of the issuer, ramifications of the use of such alternative disclosures and treatments, and the treatment preferred by the registered public accounting firm; and

"(3) other material written communications between the registered public accounting firm and the management of the issuer, such as any management letter or schedule of unadjusted differences."

SEC. 205. CONFORMING AMENDMENTS.

SEC. 206. CONFLICTS OF INTEREST.

Section 10A of the Securities Exchange Act of 1934 (15 U.S.C. 78j-1), as amended by this Act, is amended by adding at the end the following:

"(l) CONFLICTS OF INTEREST—It shall be unlawful for a registered public accounting firm to perform for an issuer any audit service required by this title, if a chief executive officer, controller, chief financial officer, chief accounting officer, or any person serving in an equivalent position for the issuer, was employed by that registered independent public accounting firm and participated in any capacity in the audit of that issuer during the 1-year period preceding the date of the initiation of the audit."

SEC. 207. STUDY OF MANDATORY ROTATION OF REGISTERED PUBLIC ACCOUNTING FIRMS.

SEC. 208. COMMISSION AUTHORITY.

(a) COMMISSION REGULATIONS—Not later than 180 days after the date of enactment of this Act, the Commission shall issue final regulations to carry out each of subsections (g) through (l) of section 10A of the Securities Exchange Act of 1934, as added by this title.

(b) AUDITOR INDEPENDENCE—It shall be unlawful for any registered public accounting firm (or an associated person thereof, as applicable) to prepare or issue any audit report with respect to any issuer, if the firm or associated person engages in any activity with respect to that issuer prohibited by any of subsections (g) through (l) of section 10A of the Securities Exchange Act of 1934, as added by this title, or any rule or regulation of the Commission or of the Board issued thereunder.

SEC. 209. CONSIDERATIONS BY APPROPRIATE STATE REGULATORY AUTHORITIES.

In supervising nonregistered public accounting firms and their associated persons, appropriate State regulatory authorities should make an independent determination of the proper standards applicable, particularly taking into consideration the size and nature of the business of the accounting firms they supervise and the size and nature of the business of the clients of those firms. The standards applied by the Board under this Act should not be presumed to be applicable for purposes of this section for small and medium sized nonregistered public accounting firms.

TITLE III—CORPORATE RESPONSIBILITY

SEC. 301. PUBLIC COMPANY AUDIT COMMITTEES.

Section 10A of the Securities Exchange Act of 1934 (15 U.S.C. 78f) is amended by adding at the end the following:

"(m) STANDARDS RELATING TO AUDIT COMMITTEES.

"(1) COMMISSION RULES

"(A) IN GENERAL—Effective not later than 270 days after the date of enactment of this subsection, the Commission shall, by rule, direct the national securities exchanges and national securities associations to prohibit the listing of any security of an issuer that is not in compliance with the requirements of any portion of paragraphs (2) through (6).

"(B) OPPORTUNITY TO CURE DEFECTS—The rules of the Commission under subparagraph (A) shall provide for appropriate procedures for an issuer to have an opportunity to cure any defects that would be the basis for a prohibition under subparagraph (A), before the imposition of such prohibition.

"(2) RESPONSIBILITIES RELATING TO REGISTERED PUBLIC ACCOUNTING FIRMS—The audit committee of each issuer, in its capacity as a committee of the board of directors, shall be directly responsible for the appointment, compensation, and oversight of the work of any registered public accounting firm employed by that issuer (including resolution of disagreements between management and the auditor regarding financial reporting) for the purpose of preparing or issuing an audit report or related work, and each such registered public accounting firm shall report directly to the audit committee.

"(3) INDEPENDENCE

"(A) IN GENERAL—Each member of the audit committee of the issuer shall be a member of the board of directors of the issuer, and shall otherwise be independent.

"(B) CRITERIA—In order to be considered to be independent for purposes of this paragraph, a member of an audit committee of an issuer may not, other than in his or her capacity as a member of the audit committee, the board of directors, or any other board committee—

"(i) accept any consulting, advisory, or other compensatory fee from the issuer; or

"(ii) be an affiliated person of the issuer or any subsidiary thereof.

"(C) EXEMPTION AUTHORITY—The Commission may exempt from the requirements of subparagraph (B) a particular relationship with respect to audit committee members, as the Commission determines appropriate in light of the circumstances.

"(4) COMPLAINTS—Each audit committee shall establish procedures for—

"(A) the receipt, retention, and treatment of complaints received by the issuer regarding accounting, internal accounting controls, or auditing matters; and

"(B) the confidential, anonymous submission by employees of the issuer of concerns regarding questionable accounting or auditing matters.

"(5) AUTHORITY TO ENGAGE ADVISERS—Each audit committee shall have the authority to engage independent counsel and other advisers, as it determines necessary to carry out its duties.

"(6) FUNDING—Each issuer shall provide for appropriate funding, as determined by the audit committee, in its capacity as a committee of the board of directors, for payment of compensation—

"(A) to the registered public accounting firm employed by the issuer for the purpose of rendering or issuing an audit report; and

"(B) to any advisers employed by the audit committee under paragraph (5)."

SEC. 302. CORPORATE RESPONSIBILITY FOR FINANCIAL REPORTS.

(a) REGULATIONS REQUIRED—The Commission shall, by rule, require, for each company filing periodic reports under section 13(a) or 15(d) of the Securities Exchange Act of 1934 (15 U.S.C. 78m, 78o(d)), that the principal executive officer or officers and the principal financial officer or officers, or persons performing similar functions, certify in each annual or quarterly report filed or submitted under either such section of such Act that—

(1) the signing officer has reviewed the report;

(2) based on the officer's knowledge, the report does not contain any untrue statement of a material fact or omit to state a material fact necessary in order to make the statements made, in light of the circumstances under which such statements were made, not misleading;

(3) based on such officer's knowledge, the financial statements, and other financial information included in the report, fairly present in all material respects the financial condition and results of operations of the issuer as of, and for, the periods presented in the report;

(4) the signing officers—

(A) are responsible for establishing and maintaining internal controls;

(B) have designed such internal controls to ensure that material information relating to the issuer and its consolidated subsidiaries is made known to such officers by others within those entities, particularly during the period in which the periodic reports are being prepared;

(C) have evaluated the effectiveness of the issuer's internal controls as of a date within 90 days prior to the report; and

(D) have presented in the report their conclusions about the effectiveness of their internal controls based on their evaluation as of that date;

(5) the signing officers have disclosed to the issuer's auditors and the audit committee of the board of directors (or persons fulfilling the equivalent function)—

(A) all significant deficiencies in the design or operation of internal controls which could adversely affect the issuer's ability to record, process, summarize, and report financial data and have identified for the issuer's auditors any material weaknesses in internal controls; and

(B) any fraud, whether or not material, that involves management or other employees who have a significant role in the issuer's internal controls; and

(6) the signing officers have indicated in the report whether or not there were significant changes in internal controls or in other factors that could significantly affect internal controls subsequent to the date of their evaluation, including any corrective actions with regard to significant deficiencies and material weaknesses.

(b) FOREIGN REINCORPORATIONS HAVE NO EFFECT—Nothing in this section 302 shall be interpreted or applied in any way to allow any issuer to lessen the legal force of the statement required under this section 302, by an issuer having reincorporated or having engaged in any other transaction that resulted in the transfer of the corporate domicile or offices of the issuer from inside the United States to outside of the United States.

(c) DEADLINE—The rules required by subsection (a) shall be effective not later than 30 days after the date of enactment of this Act.

SEC. 303. IMPROPER INFLUENCE ON CONDUCT OF AUDITS.

(a) RULES TO PROHIBIT—It shall be unlawful, in contravention of such rules or regulations as the Commission shall prescribe as necessary and appropriate in the public interest or for the protection of investors, for any officer or director of an issuer, or any other person acting under the direction thereof, to take any action to fraudulently influence, coerce, manipulate, or mislead any independent public or certified accountant engaged in the performance of an audit of the financial statements of that issuer for the purpose of rendering such financial statements materially misleading.

(b) ENFORCEMENT—In any civil proceeding, the Commission shall have exclusive authority to enforce this section and any rule or regulation issued under this section.

(c) NO PREEMPTION OF OTHER LAW—The provisions of subsection (a) shall be in addition to, and shall not supersede or preempt, any other provision of law or any rule or regulation issued thereunder.

(d) DEADLINE FOR RULEMAKING—The Commission shall—

(1) propose the rules or regulations required by this section, not later than 90 days after the date of enactment of this Act; and

(2) issue final rules or regulations required by this section, not later than 270 days after that date of enactment.

SEC. 304. FORFEITURE OF CERTAIN BONUSES AND PROFITS.

(a) ADDITIONAL COMPENSATION PRIOR TO NONCOMPLIANCE WITH COMMISSION FINANCIAL REPORTING REQUIREMENTS—If an issuer is required to prepare an accounting restatement due to the material noncompliance of the issuer, as a result of misconduct, with any financial reporting requirement under the securities laws, the chief executive officer and chief financial officer of the issuer shall reimburse the issuer for—

(1) any bonus or other incentive-based or equity-based compensation received by that person from the issuer during the 12-month period following the first public issuance or filing with the Commission (whichever first occurs) of the financial document embodying such financial reporting requirement; and

(2) any profits realized from the sale of securities of the issuer during that 12-month period.

(b) COMMISSION EXEMPTION AUTHORITY—The Commission may exempt any person from the application of subsection (a), as it deems necessary and appropriate.

SEC. 305. OFFICER AND DIRECTOR BARS AND PENALTIES.

(a) UNFITNESS STANDARD

(1) SECURITIES EXCHANGE ACT OF 1934—Section 21(d)(2) of the Securities Exchange Act of 1934 (15 U.S.C. 78u(d)(2)) is amended by striking "substantial unfitness" and inserting "unfitness."

(2) SECURITIES ACT OF 1933—Section 20(e) of the Securities Act of 1933 (15 U.S.C. 77t(e)) is amended by striking "substantial unfitness" and inserting "unfitness."

(b) EQUITABLE RELIEF—Section 21(d) of the Securities Exchange Act of 1934 (15 U.S.C. 78u(d)) is amended by adding at the end the following:

"(5) EQUITABLE RELIEF—In any action or proceeding brought or instituted by the Commission under any provision of the securities laws, the Commission may seek, and any Federal court may grant, any equitable relief that may be appropriate or necessary for the benefit of investors."

SEC. 306. INSIDER TRADES DURING PENSION FUND BLACKOUT PERIODS.

(a) PROHIBITION OF INSIDER TRADING DURING PENSION FUND BLACKOUT PERIODS

(1) IN GENERAL—Except to the extent otherwise provided by rule of the Commission pursuant to paragraph (3), it shall be unlawful for any director or executive officer of an

issuer of any equity security (other than an exempted security), directly or indirectly, to purchase, sell, or otherwise acquire or transfer any equity security of the issuer (other than an exempted security) during any blackout period with respect to such equity security if such director or officer acquires such equity security in connection with his or her service or employment as a director or executive officer.

(2) REMEDY

(A) IN GENERAL—Any profit realized by a director or executive officer referred to in paragraph (1) from any purchase, sale, or other acquisition or transfer in violation of this subsection shall inure to and be recoverable by the issuer, irrespective of any intention on the part of such director or executive officer in entering into the transaction.

(B) ACTIONS TO RECOVER PROFITS—An action to recover profits in accordance with this subsection may be instituted at law or in equity in any court of competent jurisdiction by the issuer, or by the owner of any security of the issuer in the name and in behalf of the issuer if the issuer fails or refuses to bring such action within 60 days after the date of request, or fails diligently to prosecute the action thereafter, except that no such suit shall be brought more than 2 years after the date on which such profit was realized.

(3) RULEMAKING AUTHORIZED—The Commission shall, in consultation with the Secretary of Labor, issue rules to clarify the application of this subsection and to prevent evasion thereof. Such rules shall provide for the application of the requirements of paragraph (1) with respect to entities treated as a single employer with respect to an issuer under section 414(b), (c), (m), or (o) of the Internal Revenue Code of 1986 to the extent necessary to clarify the application of such requirements and to prevent evasion thereof. Such rules may also provide for appropriate exceptions from the requirements of this subsection, including exceptions for purchases pursuant to an automatic dividend reinvestment program or purchases or sales made pursuant to an advance election.

(4) BLACKOUT PERIOD—For purposes of this subsection, the term "blackout period," with respect to the equity securities of any issuer—

(A) means any period of more than 3 consecutive business days during which the ability of not fewer than 50 percent of the participants or beneficiaries under all individual account plans maintained by the issuer to purchase, sell, or otherwise acquire or transfer an interest in any equity of such issuer held in such an individual account plan is temporarily suspended by the issuer or by a fiduciary of the plan; and

(B) does not include, under regulations which shall be prescribed by the Commission—

(i) a regularly scheduled period in which the participants and beneficiaries may not purchase, sell, or otherwise acquire or transfer an interest in any equity of such issuer, if such period is—

(i) incorporated into the individual account plan; and

(ii) timely disclosed to employees before becoming participants under the individual account plan or as a subsequent amendment to the plan; or

(ii) any suspension described in subparagraph (A) that is imposed solely in connection with persons becoming participants or beneficiaries, or ceasing to be participants or beneficiaries, in an individual account plan by reason of a corporate merger, acquisition, divestiture, or similar transaction involving the plan or plan sponsor.

(5) INDIVIDUAL ACCOUNT PLAN—For purposes of this subsection, the term "individual account plan" has the meaning provided in section 3(34) of the Employee Retirement Income Security Act of 1974 (29 U.S.C. 1002(34), except that such term shall not include a one-participant retirement plan (within the meaning of section 101(i)(8)(B) of such Act (29 U.S.C. 1021(i)(8)(B))).

(6) NOTICE TO DIRECTORS, EXECUTIVE OFFICERS, AND THE COMMISSION— In any case in which a director or executive officer is subject to the requirements of this subsection in connection with a blackout period (as defined in paragraph (4)) with respect to

any equity securities, the issuer of such equity securities shall timely notify such director or officer and the Securities and Exchange Commission of such blackout period.

(b) NOTICE REQUIREMENTS TO PARTICIPANTS AND BENEFICIARIES UNDER ERISA

(1) IN GENERAL—Section 101 of the Employee Retirement Income Security Act of 1974 (29 U.S.C. 1021) is amended by redesignating the second subsection (h) as subsection (j), and by inserting after the first subsection (h) the following new subsection:

"(i) NOTICE OF BLACKOUT PERIODS TO PARTICIPANT OR BENEFICIARY UNDER INDIVIDUAL ACCOUNT PLAN

"(1) DUTIES OF PLAN ADMINISTRATOR—In advance of the commencement of any blackout period with respect to an individual account plan, the plan administrator shall notify the plan participants and beneficiaries who are affected by such action in accordance with this subsection.

"(2) NOTICE REQUIREMENTS

"(A) IN GENERAL—The notices described in paragraph (1) shall be written in a manner calculated to be understood by the average plan participant and shall include—

"(i) the reasons for the blackout period,

"(ii) an identification of the investments and other rights affected,

"(iii) the expected beginning date and length of the blackout period,

"(iv) in the case of investments affected, a statement that the participant or beneficiary should evaluate the appropriateness of their current investment decisions in light of their inability to direct or diversify assets credited to their accounts during the blackout period, and

"(v) such other matters as the Secretary may require by regulation.

"(B) NOTICE TO PARTICIPANTS AND BENEFICIARIES Except as otherwise provided in this subsection, notices described in paragraph (1) shall be furnished to all participants and beneficiaries under the plan to whom the blackout period applies at least 30 days in advance of the blackout period.

"(C) EXCEPTION TO 30-DAY NOTICE REQUIREMENT In any case in which—

'(i) a deferral of the blackout period would violate the requirements of subparagraph (A) or (B) of section 404(a)(1), and a fiduciary of the plan reasonably so determines in writing, or

"(ii) the inability to provide the 30 day advance notice is due to events that were unforeseeable or circumstances beyond the reasonable control of the plan administrator, and a fiduciary of the plan reasonably so determines in writing,

subparagraph (B) shall not apply, and the notice shall be furnished to all participants and beneficiaries under the plan to whom the blackout period applies as soon as reasonably possible under the circumstances unless such a notice in advance of the termination of the blackout period is impracticable.

"(D) WRITTEN NOTICE—The notice required to be provided under this subsection shall be in writing, except that such notice may be in electronic or other form to the extent that such form is reasonably accessible to the recipient.

"(E) NOTICE TO ISSUERS OF EMPLOYER SECURITIES SUBJECT TO BLACKOUT PERIOD—In the case of any blackout period in connection with an individual account plan, the plan administrator shall provide timely notice of such blackout period to the issuer of any employer securities subject to such blackout period.

"(3) EXCEPTION FOR BLACKOUT PERIODS WITH LIMITED APPLICABILITY–In any case in which the blackout period applies only to 1 or more participants or beneficiaries in connection with a merger, acquisition, divestiture, or similar transaction involving the plan or plan sponsor and occurs solely in connection with becoming or ceasing to be a participant or beneficiary under the plan by reason of such merger, acquisition, divestiture, or transaction, the requirement of this subsection that the notice be provided to all participants and beneficiaries shall be treated as met if the notice required under paragraph (1) is provided to such participants or beneficiaries to whom the blackout period applies as soon as reasonably practicable.

"(4) CHANGES IN LENGTH OF BLACKOUT PERIOD—If, following the furnishing of the notice pursuant to this subsection, there is a change in the beginning date or length of the blackout period (specified in such notice pursuant to paragraph (2)(A)(iii)), the administrator shall provide affected participants and beneficiaries notice of the change as soon as reasonably practicable. In relation to the extended blackout period, such notice shall meet the requirements of paragraph (2)(D) and shall specify any material change in the matters referred to in clauses (i) through (v) of paragraph (2)(A).

"(5) REGULATORY EXCEPTIONS—The Secretary may provide by regulation for additional exceptions to the requirements of this subsection which the Secretary determines are in the interests of participants and beneficiaries.

"(6) GUIDANCE AND MODEL NOTICES—The Secretary shall issue guidance and model notices which meet the requirements of this subsection.

"(7) BLACKOUT PERIOD—For purposes of this subsection—

"(A) IN GENERAL—The term 'blackout period' means, in connection with an individual account plan, any period for which any ability of participants or beneficiaries under the plan, which is otherwise available under the terms of such plan, to direct or diversify assets credited to their accounts, to obtain loans from the plan, or to obtain distributions from the plan is temporarily suspended, limited, or restricted, if such suspension, limitation, or restriction is for any period of more than 3 consecutive business days.

"(B) EXCLUSIONS—The term 'blackout period' does not include a suspension, limitation, or restriction—

"(i) which occurs by reason of the application of the securities laws (as defined in section 3(a)(47) of the Securities Exchange Act of 1934),

"(ii) which is a change to the plan which provides for a regularly scheduled suspension, limitation, or restriction which is disclosed to participants or beneficiaries through any summary of material modifications, any materials describing specific investment alternatives under the plan, or any changes thereto, or

"(iii) which applies only to 1 or more individuals, each of whom is the participant, an alternate payee (as defined in section 206(d)(3)(K)), or any other beneficiary pursuant to a qualified domestic relations order (as defined in section 206(d)(3)(B)(i)).

"(8) INDIVIDUAL ACCOUNT PLAN

"(A) IN GENERAL—For purposes of this subsection, the term 'individual account plan' shall have the meaning provided such term in section 3(34), except that such term shall not include a one-participant retirement plan.

"(B) ONE-PARTICIPANT RETIREMENT PLAN—For purposes of subparagraph (A), the term 'oneparticipant retirement plan' means a retirement plan that—

"(i) on the first day of the plan year—

"(I) covered only the employer (and the employer's spouse) and the employer owned the entire business (whether or not incorporated), or

"(II) covered only one or more partners (and their spouses) in a business partnership (including partners in an S or C corporation (as defined in section 1361(a) of the Internal Revenue Code of 1986)),

"(ii) meets the minimum coverage requirements of section 410(b) of the Internal Revenue Code of 1986 (as in effect on the date of the enactment of this paragraph) without being combined with any other plan of the business that covers the employees of the business,

"(iii) does not provide benefits to anyone except the employer (and the employer's spouse) or the partners (and their spouses), "(iv) does not cover a business that is a member of an affiliated service group, a controlled group of corporations, or a group of businesses under common control, and

"(v) does not cover a business that leases employees."

(2) ISSUANCE OF INITIAL GUIDANCE AND MODEL NOTICE—The Secretary of Labor shall issue initial guidance and a model notice pursuant to section 101(i)(6) of the Employee Retirement Income Security Act of 1974 (as added by this subsection) not later than January 1, 2003. Not later than 75 days after the date of the enactment of this Act, the Secretary shall promulgate interim final rules necessary to carry out the amendments made by this subsection.

(3) CIVIL PENALTIES FOR FAILURE TO PROVIDE NOTICE—Section 502 of such Act (29 U.S.C. 1132) is amended—

(A) in subsection (a)(6), by striking "(5), or (6)" and inserting "(5), (6), or (7)";

(B) by redesignating paragraph (7) of subsection (c) as paragraph (8); and

(C) by inserting after paragraph (6) of subsection (c) the following new paragraph:

"(7) The Secretary may assess a civil penalty against a plan administrator of up to $100 a day from the date of the plan administrator's failure or refusal to provide notice to participants and beneficiaries in accordance with section 101(i). For purposes of this paragraph, each violation with respect to any single participant or beneficiary shall be treated as a separate violation."

(8) PLAN AMENDMENTS—If any amendment made by this subsection requires an amendment to any plan, such plan amendment shall not be required to be made before the first plan year beginning on or after the effective date of this section, if—

(A) during the period after such amendment made by this subsection takes effect and before such first plan year, the plan is operated in good faith compliance with the requirements of such amendment made by this subsection, and

(B) such plan amendment applies retroactively to the period after such amendment made by this subsection takes effect and before such first plan year.

(c) EFFECTIVE DATE—The provisions of this section (including the amendments made thereby) shall take effect 180 days after the date of the enactment of this Act. Good faith compliance with the requirements of such provisions in advance of the issuance of applicable regulations thereunder shall be treated as compliance with such provisions.

SEC. 307. RULES OF PROFESSIONAL RESPONSIBILITY FOR ATTORNEYS.

Not later than 180 days after the date of enactment of this Act, the Commission shall issue rules, in the public interest and for the protection of investors, setting forth minimum standards of professional conduct for attorneys appearing and practicing before the Commission in any way in the representation of issuers, including a rule—

(1) requiring an attorney to report evidence of a material violation of securities law or breach of fiduciary duty or similar violation by the company or any agent thereof, to the chief legal counsel or the chief executive officer of the company (or the equivalent thereof); and

(2) if the counsel or officer does not appropriately respond to the evidence (adopting, as necessary, appropriate remedial measures or sanctions with respect to the violation), requiring the attorney to report the evidence to the audit committee of the board of directors of the issuer or to another committee of the board of directors comprised solely of directors not employed directly or indirectly by the issuer, or to the board of directors.

SEC. 308. FAIR FUNDS FOR INVESTORS.

(a) CIVIL PENALTIES TO BE USED FOR THE RELIEF OF VICTIMS— If, in any judicial or administrative action brought by the Commission under the securities laws, the

Commission obtains a civil penalty against any person for a violation of such laws, or such person agrees, in settlement of any such action, to such civil penalty, the amount of such civil penalty shall, on the motion or at the direction of the Commission, be added to and become part of a disgorgement fund or other fund established for the benefit of the victims of such violation.

(b) ACCEPTANCE OF ADDITIONAL DONATIONS—The Commission is authorized to accept, hold, administer, and utilize gifts, bequests and devises of property, both real and personal, to the United States for a disgorgement fund or other fund described in subsection (a). Such gifts, bequests, and devises of money and proceeds from sales of other property received as gifts, bequests, or devises shall be deposited in such fund and shall be available for allocation in accordance with subsection (a).

(c) STUDY REQUIRED

(1) SUBJECT OF STUDY—The Commission shall review and analyze—

(A) enforcement actions by the Commission over the five years preceding the date of the enactment of this Act that have included proceedings to obtain civil penalties or disgorgements to identify areas where such proceedings may be utilized to efficiently, effectively, and fairly provide restitution for injured investors; and

(B) other methods to more efficiently, effectively, and fairly provide restitution to injured investors, including methods to improve the collection rates for civil penalties and disgorgements.

(d) [Omitted.]

(e) DEFINITION—As used in this section, the term "disgorgement fund" means a fund established in any administrative or judicial proceeding described in subsection (a).

TITLE IV—ENHANCED FINANCIAL DISCLOSURES

SEC. 401. DISCLOSURES IN PERIODIC REPORTS.

(a) DISCLOSURES REQUIRED—Section 13 of the Securities Exchange Act of 1934 (15 U.S.C. 78m) is amended by adding at the end the following:

"(i) ACCURACY OF FINANCIAL REPORTS—Each financial report that contains financial statements, and that is required to be prepared in accordance with (or reconciled to) generally accepted accounting principles under this title and filed with the Commission shall reflect all material correcting adjustments that have been identified by a registered public accounting firm in accordance with generally accepted accounting principles and the rules and regulations of the Commission.

"(j) OFF-BALANCE SHEET TRANSACTIONS—Not later than 180 days after the date of enactment of the Sarbanes-Oxley Act of 2002, the Commission shall issue final rules providing that each annual and quarterly financial report required to be filed with the Commission shall disclose all material off-balance sheet transactions, arrangements, obligations (including contingent obligations), and other relationships of the issuer with unconsolidated entities or other persons, that may have a material current or future effect on financial condition, changes in financial condition, results of operations, liquidity, capital expenditures, capital resources, or significant components of revenues or expenses."

(b) COMMISSION RULES ON PRO FORMA FIGURES—Not later than 180 days after the date of enactment of the Sarbanes-Oxley Act fo 2002, the Commission shall issue final rules providing that pro forma financial information included in any periodic or other report filed with the Commission pursuant to the securities laws, or in any public disclosure or press or other release, shall be presented in a manner that—

(1) does not contain an untrue statement of a material fact or omit to state a material fact necessary in order to make the pro forma financial information, in light of the circumstances under which it is presented, not misleading; and

(2) reconciles it with the financial condition and results of operations of the issuer under generally accepted accounting principles.

(c) STUDY AND REPORT ON SPECIAL PURPOSE ENTITIES

(1) STUDY REQUIRED—The Commission shall, not later than 1 year after the effective date of adoption of off-balance sheet disclosure rules required by section 13(j) of the Securities Exchange Act of 1934, as added by this section, complete a study of filings by issuers and their disclosures to determine—

(A) the extent of off-balance sheet transactions, including assets, liabilities, leases, losses, and the use of special purpose entities; and

(B) whether generally accepted accounting rules result in financial statements of issuers reflecting the economics of such offbalance sheet transactions to investors in a transparent fashion.

(2) REPORT AND RECOMMENDATIONS—Not later than 6 months after the date of completion of the study required by paragraph (1), the Commission shall submit a report to the President, the Committee on Banking, Housing, and Urban Affairs of the Senate, and the Committee on Financial Services of the House of Representatives, setting forth—

(A) the amount or an estimate of the amount of off-balance sheet transactions, including assets, liabilities, leases, and losses of, and the use of special purpose entities by, issuers filing periodic reports pursuant to section 13 or 15 of the Securities Exchange Act of 1934;

(B) the extent to which special purpose entities are used to facilitate off-balance sheet transactions;

(C) whether generally accepted accounting principles or the rules of the Commission result in financial statements of issuers reflecting the economics of such transactions to investors in a transparent fashion;

(D) whether generally accepted accounting principles specifically result in the consolidation of special purpose entities sponsored by an issuer in cases in which the issuer has the majority of the risks and rewards of the special purpose entity; and

(E) any recommendations of the Commission for improving the transparency and quality of reporting off-balance sheet transactions in the financial statements and disclosures required to be filed by an issuer with the Commission.

SEC. 402. ENHANCED CONFLICT OF INTEREST PROVISIONS.

(a) PROHIBITION ON PERSONAL LOANS TO EXECUTIVES

Section 13 of the Securities Exchange Act of 1934 (15 U.S.C. 78m), as amended by this Act, is amended by adding at the end the following:

"(k) PROHIBITION ON PERSONAL LOANS TO EXECUTIVES

"(1) IN GENERAL—It shall be unlawful for any issuer (as defined in section 2 of the Sarbanes Oxley Act of 2002), directly or indirectly, including through any subsidiary, to extend or maintain credit, to arrange for the extension of credit, or to renew an extension of credit, in the form of a personal loan to or for any director or executive officer (or equivalent thereof) of that issuer. An extension of credit maintained by the issuer on the date of enactment of this subsection shall not be subject to the provisions of this subsection, provided that there is no material modification to any term of any such extension of credit or any renewal of any such extension of credit on or after that date of enactment.

"(2) LIMITATION—Paragraph (1) does not preclude any home improvement and manufactured home loans (as that term is defined in section 5 of the Home Owners' Loan Act (12 U.S.C. 1464)), consumer credit (as defined in section 103 of the Truth in Lending Act (15 U.S.C. 1602)), or any extension of credit under an open end credit plan (as defined in section 103 of the Truth in Lending Act (15 U.S.C. 1602)), or a charge card (as defined in section 127(c)(4)(e) of the Truth in Lending Act (15 U.S.C. 1637(c)(4)(e))), or any extension of credit by a broker or dealer registered under section 15 of this title to an employee of that broker or dealer to buy, trade, or carry securities, that is permitted under rules or regulations of the Board of Governors of the Federal Reserve System pursuant to section 7 of this title (other than an extension of credit that would be used to purchase the stock of that issuer), that is—

"(A) made or provided in the ordinary course of the consumer credit business of such issuer;

"(B) of a type that is generally made available by such issuer to the public; and

"(C) made by such issuer on market terms, or terms that are no more favorable than those offered by the issuer to the general public for such extensions of credit.

"(3) RULE OF CONSTRUCTION FOR CERTAIN LOANS—Paragraph (1) does not apply to any loan made or maintained by an insured depository institution (as defined in section 3 of the Federal Deposit Insurance Act (12 U.S.C. 1813)), if the loan is subject to the insider lending restrictions of section 22(h) of the Federal Reserve Act (12 U.S.C. 375b)."

SEC. 403. DISCLOSURES OF TRANSACTIONS INVOLVING MANAGEMENT AND PRINCIPAL STOCKHOLDERS.

(a) AMENDMENT—Section 16 of the Securities Exchange Act of 1934 (15 U.S.C. 78p) is amended by striking the heading of such section and subsection (a) and inserting the following:

"SEC. 16. DIRECTORS, OFFICERS, AND PRINCIPAL STOCKHOLDERS.

"(a) DISCLOSURES REQUIRED

"(1) DIRECTORS, OFFICERS, AND PRINCIPAL STOCKHOLDERS REQUIRED TO FILE—Every person who is directly or indirectly the beneficial owner of more than 10 percent of any class of any equity security (other than an exempted security) which is registered pursuant to section 12, or who is a director or an officer of the issuer of such security, shall file the statements required by this subsection with the Commission (and, if such security is registered on a national securities exchange, also with the exchange).

"(2) TIME OF FILING—The statements required by this subsection shall be filed—

"(A) at the time of the registration of such security on a national securities exchange or by the effective date of a registration statement filed pursuant to section 12(g);

"(B) within 10 days after he or she becomes such beneficial owner, director, or officer;

"(C) if there has been a change in such ownership, or if such person shall have purchased or sold a security-based swap agreement (as defined in section 206(b) of the Gramm-Leach-Bliley Act (15 U.S.C. 78c note)) involving such equity security, before the end of the second business day following the day on which the subject transaction has been executed, or at such other time as the Commission shall establish, by rule, in any case in which the Commission determines that such 2-day period is not feasible.

"(3) CONTENTS OF STATEMENTS—A statement filed—

"(A) under subparagraph (A) or (B) of paragraph (2) shall contain a statement of the amount of all equity securities of such issuer of which the filing person is the beneficial owner; and

"(B) under subparagraph (C) of such paragraph shall indicate ownership by the filing person at the date of filing, any such changes in such ownership, and such purchases and sales of the security-based swap agreements as have occurred since the most recent such filing under such subparagraph.

"(4) ELECTRONIC FILING AND AVAILABILITY—Beginning not later than 1 year after the date of enactment of the Sarbanes-Oxley Act of 2002—

"(A) a statement filed under subparagraph (C) of paragraph (2) shall be filed electronically;

"(B) the Commission shall provide each such statement on a publicly accessible Internet site not later than the end of the business day following that filing; and

"(C) the issuer (if the issuer maintains a corporate website) shall provide that statement on that corporate website, not later than the end of the business day following that filing."

(b) EFFECTIVE DATE—The amendment made by this section shall be effective 30 days after the date of the enactment of this Act.

SEC. 404. MANAGEMENT ASSESSMENT OF INTERNAL CONTROLS.

(a) RULES REQUIRED—The Commission shall prescribe rules requiring each annual report required by section 13(a) or 15(d) of the Securities Exchange Act of 1934 (15 U.S.C. 78m or 78o(d)) to contain an internal control report, which shall—

(1) state the responsibility of management for establishing and maintaining an adequate internal control structure and procedures for financial reporting; and

(2) contain an assessment, as of the end of the most recent fiscal year of the issuer, of the effectiveness of the internal control structure and procedures of the issuer for financial reporting.

(b) INTERNAL CONTROL EVALUATION AND REPORTING—With respect to the internal control assessment required by subsection (a), each registered public accounting firm that prepares or issues the audit report for the issuer, other than an issuer that is an emerging growth company (as defined in section 3 of the Securities Exchange Act of 1934), shall attest to, and report on, the assessment made by the management of the issuer. An attestation made under this subsection shall be made in accordance with standards for attestation engagements issued or adopted by the Board. Any such attestation shall not be the subject of a separate engagement.

(c) EXEMPTION FOR SMALLER ISSUERS— Subsection (b) shall not apply with respect to any audit report prepared for an issuer that is neither a "large accelerated filer" nor an "accelerated filer" as those terms are defined in Rule 12b-2 of the Commission (17 C.F.R. 240.12b-2).

SEC. 405. EXEMPTION.

Nothing in section 401, 402, or 404, the amendments made by those sections, or the rules of the Commission under those sections shall apply to any investment company registered under section 8 of the Investment Company Act of 1940 (15 U.S.C. 80a-8).

SEC. 406. CODE OF ETHICS FOR SENIOR FINANCIAL OFFICERS.

(a) CODE OF ETHICS DISCLOSURE—The Commission shall issue rules to require each issuer, together with periodic reports required pursuant to section 13(a) or 15(d) of the Securities Exchange Act of 1934, to disclose whether or not, and if not, the reason therefor, such issuer has adopted a code of ethics for senior financial officers, applicable to its principal financial officer and comptroller or principal accounting officer, or persons performing similar functions.

(b) CHANGES IN CODES OF ETHICS—The Commission shall revise its regulations concerning matters requiring prompt disclosure on Form 8-K (or any successor thereto) to require the immediate disclosure, by means of the filing of such form, dissemination by the Internet or by other electronic means, by any issuer of any change in or waiver of the code of ethics for senior financial officers.

(c) DEFINITION—In this section, the term "code of ethics" means such standards as are reasonably necessary to promote—

(1) honest and ethical conduct, including the ethical handling of actual or apparent conflicts of interest between personal and professional relationships;

(2) full, fair, accurate, timely, and understandable disclosure in the periodic reports required to be filed by the issuer; and

(3) compliance with applicable governmental rules and regulations.

(d) DEADLINE FOR RULEMAKING—The Commission shall—

(1) propose rules to implement this section, not later than 90 days after the date of enactment of this Act; and

(2) issue final rules to implement this section, not later than 180 days after that date of enactment.

SEC. 407. DISCLOSURE OF AUDIT COMMITTEE FINANCIAL EXPERT.

(a) RULES DEFINING "FINANCIAL EXPERT"—The Commission shall issue rules, as necessary or appropriate in the public interest and consistent with the protection of investors, to require each issuer, together with periodic reports required pursuant to sections 13(a) and 15(d) of the Securities Exchange Act of 1934, to disclose whether or not, and if not, the reasons therefor, the audit committee of that issuer is comprised of at least 1 member who is a financial expert, as such term is defined by the Commission.

(b) CONSIDERATIONS—In defining the term "financial expert" for purposes of subsection (a), the Commission shall consider whether a person has, through education and experience as a public accountant or auditor or a principal financial officer, comptroller, or principal accounting officer of an issuer, or from a position involving the performance of similar functions—

(1) an understanding of generally accepted accounting principles and financial statements;

(2) experience in—

(A) the preparation or auditing of financial statements of generally comparable issuers; and

(B) the application of such principles in connection with the accounting for estimates, accruals, and reserves;

(3) experience with internal accounting controls; and

(4) an understanding of audit committee functions.

(c) DEADLINE FOR RULEMAKING—The Commission shall—

(1) propose rules to implement this section, not later than 90 days after the date of enactment of this Act; and

(2) issue final rules to implement this section, not later than 180 days after that date of enactment.

SEC. 408. ENHANCED REVIEW OF PERIODIC DISCLOSURES BY ISSUERS.

(a) REGULAR AND SYSTEMATIC REVIEW—The Commission shall review disclosures made by issuers reporting under section 13(a) of the Securities Exchange Act of 1934 (including reports filed on Form 10-K), and which have a class of securities listed on a national securities exchange or traded on an automated quotation facility of a national securities association, on a regular and systematic basis for the protection of investors. Such review shall include a review of an issuer's financial statement.

(b) REVIEW CRITERIA—For purposes of scheduling the reviews required by subsection (a), the Commission shall consider, among other factors—

(1) issuers that have issued material restatements of financial results;

(2) issuers that experience significant volatility in their stock price as compared to other issuers;

(3) issuers with the largest market capitalization;

(4) emerging companies with disparities in price to earning ratios;

(5) issuers whose operations significantly affect any material sector of the economy; and

(6) any other factors that the Commission may consider relevant.

(c) MINIMUM REVIEW PERIOD—In no event shall an issuer required to file reports under section 13(a) or 15(d) of the Securities Exchange Act of 1934 be reviewed under this section less frequently than once every 3 years.

SEC. 409. REAL TIME ISSUER DISCLOSURES.

Section 13 of the Securities Exchange Act of 1934 (15 U.S.C. 78m), as amended by this Act, is amended by adding at the end the following:

"(l) REAL TIME ISSUER DISCLOSURES—Each issuer reporting under section 13(a) or 15(d) shall disclose to the public on a rapid and current basis such additional information concerning material changes in the financial condition or operations of the issuer, in plain English, which may include trend and qualitative information and graphic presentations, as the Commission determines, by rule, is necessary or useful for the protection of investors and in the public interest."

TITLE V—ANALYST CONFLICTS OF INTEREST

SEC. 501. TREATMENT OF SECURITIES ANALYSTS BY REGISTERED SECURITIES ASSOCIATIONS AND NATIONAL SECURITIES EXCHANGES.

(a) RULES REGARDING SECURITIES ANALYSTS—The Securities Exchange Act of 1934 (15 U.S.C. 78a et seq.) is amended by inserting after section 15C the following new section:

"SEC. 15D. SECURITIES ANALYSTS AND RESEARCH REPORTS.

"(a) ANALYST PROTECTIONS—The Commission, or upon the authorization and direction of the Commission, a registered securities association or national securities exchange, shall have adopted, not later than 1 year after the date of enactment of this section, rules reasonably designed to address conflicts of interest that can arise when securities analysts recommend equity securities in research reports and public appearances, in order to improve the objectivity of research and provide investors with more useful and reliable information, including rules designed—

"(1) to foster greater public confidence in securities research, and to protect the objectivity and independence of securities analysts, by—

"(A) restricting the prepublication clearance or approval of research reports by persons employed by the broker or dealer who are engaged in investment banking activities, or persons not directly responsible for investment research, other than legal or compliance staff;

"(B) limiting the supervision and compensatory evaluation of securities analysts to officials employed by the broker or dealer who are not engaged in investment banking activities; and

"(C) requiring that a broker or dealer and persons employed by a broker or dealer who are involved with investment banking activities may not, directly or indirectly, retaliate against or threaten to retaliate against any securities analyst employed by that broker or dealer or its affiliates as a result of an adverse, negative, or otherwise unfavorable research report that may adversely affect the present or prospective investment banking relationship of the broker or dealer with the issuer that is the subject of the research report, except that such rules may not limit the authority of a broker or dealer to discipline a securities analyst for causes other than such research report in accordance with the policies and procedures of the firm;

"(2) to define periods during which brokers or dealers who have participated, or are to participate, in a public offering of securities as underwriters or dealers should not publish or otherwise distribute research reports relating to such securities or to the issuer of such securities;

"(3) to establish structural and institutional safeguards within registered brokers or dealers to assure that securities analysts are separated by appropriate informational partitions within the firm from the review, pressure, or oversight of those whose involvement in investment banking activities might potentially bias their judgment or supervision; and

"(4) to address such other issues as the Commission, or such association or exchange, determines appropriate.

"(b) DISCLOSURE—The Commission, or upon the authorization and direction of the Commission, a registered securities association or national securities exchange, shall have adopted, not later than 1 year after the date of enactment of this section, rules reasonably designed to require each securities analyst to disclose in public appearances, and each registered broker or dealer to disclose in each research report, as applicable, conflicts of interest that are known or should have been known by the securities analyst or the broker or dealer, to exist at the time of the appearance or the date of distribution of the report, including—

"(1) the extent to which the securities analyst has debt or equity investments in the issuer that is the subject of the appearance or research report;

"(2) whether any compensation has been received by the registered broker or dealer, or any affiliate thereof, including the securities analyst, from the issuer that is the subject of the appearance or research report, subject to such exemptions as the Commission may determine appropriate and necessary to prevent disclosure by virtue of this paragraph of material non-public information regarding specific potential future investment banking transactions of such issuer, as is appropriate in the public interest and consistent with the protection of investors;

"(3) whether an issuer, the securities of which are recommended in the appearance or research report, currently is, or during the 1-year period preceding the date of the appearance or date of distribution of the report has been, a client of the registered broker or dealer, and if so, stating the types of services provided to the issuer;

"(4) whether the securities analyst received compensation with respect to a research report, based upon (among any other factors) the investment banking revenues (either generally or specifically earned from the issuer being analyzed) of the registered broker or dealer; and

"(5) such other disclosures of conflicts of interest that are material to investors, research analysts, or the broker or dealer as the Commission, or such association or exchange, determines appropriate.

"(c) DEFINITIONS—In this section—

"(1) the term 'securities analyst' means any associated person of a registered broker or dealer that is principally responsible for, and any associated person who reports directly or indirectly to a securities analyst in connection with, the preparation of the substance of a research report, whether or not any such person has the job title of 'securities analyst'; and

"(2) the term 'research report' means a written or electronic communication that includes an analysis of equity securities of individual companies or industries, and that provides information reasonably sufficient upon which to base an investment decision."

(b) ENFORCEMENT—Section 21B(a) of the Securities Exchange Act of 1934 (15 U.S.C. 78u-2(a)) is amended by inserting "15D," before "15B."

(c) COMMISSION AUTHORITY—The Commission may promulgate and amend its regulations, or direct a registered securities association or national securities exchange to promulgate and amend its rules, to carry out section 15D of the Securities Exchange Act of 1934, as added by this section, as is necessary for the protection of investors and in the public interest.

TITLE VI—COMMISSION RESOURCES AND AUTHORITY

SEC. 601. AUTHORIZATION OF APPROPRIATIONS.

Section 35 of the Securities Exchange Act of 1934 (15 U.S.C. 78kk) is amended to read as follows:

"SEC. 35. AUTHORIZATION OF APPROPRIATIONS.

"In addition to any other funds authorized to be appropriated to the Commission, there are authorized to be appropriated to carry out the functions, powers, and duties of the Commission, $776,000,000 for fiscal year 2003, of which—

"(1) $102,700,000 shall be available to fund additional compensation, including salaries and benefits, as authorized in the Investor and Capital Markets Fee Relief Act (Public Law 107123; 115 Stat. 2390 et seq.);

"(2) $108,400,000 shall be available for information technology, security enhancements, and recovery and mitigation activities in light of the terrorist attacks of September 11, 2001; and

"(3) $98,000,000 shall be available to add not fewer than an additional 200 qualified professionals to provide enhanced oversight of auditors and audit services required by the Federal securities laws, and to improve Commission investigative and disciplinary efforts with respect to such auditors and services, as well as for additional professional support staff necessary to strengthen the programs of the Commission involving Full Disclosure and Prevention and Suppression of Fraud, risk management, industry technology review, compliance, inspections, examinations, market regulation, and investment management."

SEC. 602. APPEARANCE AND PRACTICE BEFORE THE COMMISSION.

The Securities Exchange Act of 1934 (15 U.S.C. 78a et seq.) is amended by inserting after section 4B the following:

"SEC. 4C. APPEARANCE AND PRACTICE BEFORE THE COMMISSION.

"(a) AUTHORITY TO CENSURE—The Commission may censure any person, or deny, temporarily or permanently, to any person the privilege of appearing or practicing before the Commission in any way, if that person is found by the Commission, after notice and opportunity for hearing in the matter—

"(1) not to possess the requisite qualifications to represent others;

"(2) to be lacking in character or integrity, or to have engaged in unethical or improper professional conduct; or

"(3) to have willfully violated, or willfully aided and abetted the violation of, any provision of the securities laws or the rules and regulations issued thereunder.

"(b) DEFINITION—With respect to any registered public accounting firm or associated person, for purposes of this section, the term 'improper professional conduct' means—

"(1) intentional or knowing conduct, including reckless conduct, that results in a violation of applicable professional standards; and

"(2) negligent conduct in the form of—

"(A) a single instance of highly unreasonable conduct that results in a violation of applicable professional standards in circumstances in which the registered public accounting firm or associated person knows, or should know, that heightened scrutiny is warranted; or

"(B) repeated instances of unreasonable conduct, each resulting in a violation of applicable professional standards, that indicate a lack of competence to practice before the Commission."

SEC. 603. FEDERAL COURT AUTHORITY TO IMPOSE PENNY STOCK BARS.

(a) Securities Exchange Act of 1934—Section 21(d) of the Securities Exchange Act of 1934 (15 U.S.C. 78u(d)), as amended by this Act, is amended by adding at the end the following:

"(6) AUTHORITY OF A COURT TO PROHIBIT PERSONS FROM PARTICIPATING IN AN OFFERING OF PENNY STOCK

"(A) IN GENERAL—In any proceeding under paragraph (1) against any person participating in, or, at the time of the alleged misconduct who was participating in, an offering of penny stock, the court may prohibit that person from participating in an offering of penny stock, conditionally or unconditionally, and permanently or for such period of time as the court shall determine.

"(B) DEFINITION—For purposes of this paragraph, the term 'person participating in an offering of penny stock' includes any person engaging in activities with a broker, dealer, or issuer for purposes of issuing, trading, or inducing or attempting to induce the purchase or sale of, any penny stock. The Commission may, by rule or regulation, define such term to include other activities, and may, by rule, regulation, or order, exempt any person or class of persons, in whole or in part, conditionally or unconditionally, from inclusion in such term."

(b) Securities Act of 1933—Section 20 of the Securities Act of 1933 (15 U.S.C. 77t) is amended by adding at the end the following:

"(g) AUTHORITY OF A COURT TO PROHIBIT PERSONS FROM PARTICIPATING IN AN OFFERING OF PENNY STOCK

"(1) IN GENERAL—In any proceeding under subsection (a) against any person participating in, or, at the time of the alleged misconduct, who was participating in, an offering of penny stock, the court may prohibit that person from participating in an offering of penny stock, conditionally or unconditionally, and permanently or for such period of time as the court shall determine.

"(2) DEFINITION—For purposes of this subsection, the term 'person participating in an offering of penny stock' includes any person engaging in activities with a broker, dealer, or issuer for purposes of issuing, trading, or inducing or attempting to induce the purchase or sale of, any penny stock. The Commission may, by rule or regulation, define such term to include other activities, and may, by rule, regulation, or order, exempt any person or class of persons, in whole or in part, conditionally or unconditionally, from inclusion in such term."

SEC. 604. QUALIFICATIONS OF ASSOCIATED PERSONS OF BROKERS AND DEALERS.

TITLE VII—STUDIES AND REPORTS

SEC. 701. GAO STUDY AND REPORT REGARDING CONSOLIDATION OF PUBLIC ACCOUNTING FIRMS.

SEC. 702. COMMISSION STUDY AND REPORT REGARDING CREDIT RATING AGENCIES.

SEC. 703. STUDY AND REPORT ON VIOLATORS AND VIOLATIONS.

SEC. 704. STUDY OF ENFORCEMENT ACTIONS.

SEC. 705. STUDY OF INVESTMENT BANKS.

TITLE VIII—CORPORATE AND CRIMINAL FRAUD ACCOUNTABILITY

SEC. 801. SHORT TITLE.

This title may be cited as the "Corporate and Criminal Fraud Accountability Act of 2002."

SEC. 802. CRIMINAL PENALTIES FOR ALTERING DOCUMENTS.

(a) IN GENERAL—Chapter 73 of title 18, United States Code, is amended by adding at the end the following:

"Sec. 1519. Destruction, alteration, or falsification of records in Federal investigations and bankruptcy

"Whoever knowingly alters, destroys, mutilates, conceals, covers up, falsifies, or makes a false entry in any record, document, or tangible object with the intent to impede, obstruct, or influence the investigation or proper administration of any matter within the jurisdiction of any department or agency of the United States or any case filed under title 11, or in relation to or contemplation of any such matter or case, shall be fined under this title, imprisoned not more than 20 years, or both.

"Sec. 1520. Destruction of corporate audit records

"(a)(1) Any accountant who conducts an audit of an issuer of securities to which section 10A(a) of the Securities Exchange Act of 1934 (15 U.S.C. 78j-1(a)) applies, shall maintain all audit or review workpapers for a period of 5 years from the end of the fiscal period in which the audit or review was concluded.

"(2) The Securities and Exchange Commission shall promulgate, within 180 days, after adequate notice and an opportunity for comment, such rules and regulations, as are reasonably necessary, relating to the retention of relevant records such as workpapers, documents that form the basis of an audit or review, memoranda, correspondence, communications, other documents, and records (including electronic records) which are created, sent, or received in connection with an audit or review and contain conclusions, opinions, analyses, or financial data relating to such an audit or review, which is conducted by any accountant who conducts an audit of an issuer of securities to which section 10A(a) of the Securities Exchange Act of 1934 (15 U.S.C. 78j-1(a)) applies. The Commission may, from time to time, amend or supplement the rules and regulations that it is required to promulgate under this section, after adequate notice and an opportunity for comment, in order to ensure that such rules and regulations adequately comport with the purposes of this section.

"(b) Whoever knowingly and willfully violates subsection (a)(1), or any rule or regulation promulgated by the Securities and Exchange Commission under subsection (a)(2), shall be fined under this title, imprisoned not more than 10 years, or both.

"(c) Nothing in this section shall be deemed to diminish or relieve any person of any other duty or obligation imposed by Federal or State law or regulation to maintain, or refrain from destroying, any document."

(b) CLERICAL AMENDMENT—The table of sections at the beginning of chapter 73 of title 18, United States Code, is amended by adding at the end the following new items:

"1519. Destruction, alteration, or falsification of records in Federal investigations and bankruptcy.

"1520. Destruction of corporate audit records."

SEC. 803. DEBTS NONDISCHARGEABLE IF INCURRED IN VIOLATION OF SECURITIES FRAUD LAWS.

SEC. 804. STATUTE OF LIMITATIONS FOR SECURITIES FRAUD.

(a) IN GENERAL—Section 1658 of title 28, United States Code, is amended—

(1) by inserting "(a)" before "Except"; and

(2) by adding at the end the following:

"(b) Notwithstanding subsection (a), a private right of action that involves a claim of fraud, deceit, manipulation, or contrivance in contravention of a regulatory requirement concerning the securities laws, as defined in section 3(a)(47) of the Securities Exchange Act of 1934 (15 U.S.C. 78c(a)(47)), may be brought not later than the earlier of—

"(1) 2 years after the discovery of the facts constituting the violation; or

"(2) 5 years after such violation."

(b) EFFECTIVE DATE—The limitations period provided by section 1658(b) of title 28, United States Code, as added by this section, shall apply to all proceedings addressed by this section that are commenced on or after the date of enactment of this Act.

(c) NO CREATION OF ACTIONS—Nothing in this section shall create a new, private right of action.

SEC. 805. REVIEW OF FEDERAL SENTENCING GUIDELINES FOR OBSTRUCTION OF JUSTICE AND EXTENSIVE CRIMINAL FRAUD.

SEC. 806. PROTECTION FOR EMPLOYEES OF PUBLICLY TRADED COMPANIES WHO PROVIDE EVIDENCE OF FRAUD.

(a) IN GENERAL—Chapter 73 of title 18, United States Code, is amended by inserting after section 1514 the following:

"Sec. 1514A. Civil action to protect against retaliation in fraud cases

"(a) WHISTLEBLOWER PROTECTION FOR EMPLOYEES OF PUBLICLY TRADED COMPANIES—No company with a class of securities registered under section 12 of the Securities Exchange Act of 1934 (15 U.S.C. 78l), or that is required to file reports under section 15(d) of the Securities Exchange Act of 1934 (15 U.S.C. 78o(d)), or any officer, employee, contractor, subcontractor, or agent of such company, may discharge, demote, suspend, threaten, harass, or in any other manner discriminate against an employee in the terms and conditions of employment because of any lawful act done by the employee—

"(1) to provide information, cause information to be provided, or otherwise assist in an investigation regarding any conduct which the employee reasonably believes constitutes a violation of section 1341, 1343, 1344, or 1348, any rule or regulation of the Securities and Exchange Commission, or any provision of Federal law relating to fraud against shareholders, when the information or assistance is provided to or the investigation is conducted by—

"(A) a Federal regulatory or law enforcement agency;

"(B) any Member of Congress or any committee of Congress; or

"(C) a person with supervisory authority over the employee (or such other person working for the employer who has the authority to investigate, discover, or terminate misconduct); or

"(2) to file, cause to be filed, testify, participate in, or otherwise assist in a proceeding filed or about to be filed (with any knowledge of the employer) relating to an alleged violation of section 1341, 1343, 1344, or 1348, any rule or regulation of the Securities and Exchange Commission, or any provision of Federal law relating to fraud against shareholders.

"(b) ENFORCEMENT ACTION

"(1) IN GENERAL—A person who alleges discharge or other discrimination by any person in violation of subsection (a) may seek relief under subsection (c), by—

"(A) filing a complaint with the Secretary of Labor; or

"(B) if the Secretary has not issued a final decision within 180 days of the filing of the complaint and there is no showing that such delay is due to the bad faith of the claimant, bringing an action at law or equity for de novo review in the appropriate district court of the United States, which shall have jurisdiction over such an action without regard to the amount in controversy.

"(2) PROCEDURE

"(A) IN GENERAL—An action under paragraph (1)(A) shall be governed under the rules and procedures set forth in section 42121(b) of title 49, United States Code.

"(B) EXCEPTION—Notification made under section 42121(b)(1) of title 49, United States Code, shall be made to the person named in the complaint and to the employer.

"(C) BURDENS OF PROOF—An action brought under paragraph (1)(B) shall be governed by the legal burdens of proof set forth in section 42121(b) of title 49, United States Code.

"(D) STATUTE OF LIMITATIONS—An action under paragraph (1) shall be commenced not later than 90 days after the date on which the violation occurs.

"(c) REMEDIES

"(1) IN GENERAL—An employee prevailing in any action under subsection (b)(1) shall be entitled to all relief necessary to make the employee whole.

"(2) COMPENSATORY DAMAGES—Relief for any action under paragraph (1) shall include—

"(A) reinstatement with the same seniority status that the employee would have had, but for the discrimination;

"(B) the amount of back pay, with interest; and

"(C) compensation for any special damages sustained as a result of the discrimination, including litigation costs, expert witness fees, and reasonable attorney fees.

"(d) RIGHTS RETAINED BY EMPLOYEE—Nothing in this section shall be deemed to diminish the rights, privileges, or remedies of any employee under any Federal or State law, or under any collective bargaining agreement."

(b) CLERICAL AMENDMENT—The table of sections at the beginning of chapter 73 of title 18, United States Code, is amended by inserting after the item relating to section 1514 the following new item:

"1514A. Civil action to protect against retaliation in fraud cases."

SEC. 807. CRIMINAL PENALTIES FOR DEFRAUDING SHAREHOLDERS OF PUBLICLY TRADED COMPANIES.

(a) IN GENERAL—Chapter 63 of title 18, United States Code, is amended by adding at the end the following:

"Sec. 1348. Securities fraud

"Whoever knowingly executes, or attempts to execute, a scheme or artifice—

"(1) to defraud any person in connection with any security of an issuer with a class of securities registered under section 12 of the Securities Exchange Act of 1934 (15 U.S.C. 78l) or that is required to file reports under section 15(d) of the Securities Exchange Act of 1934 (15 U.S.C. 78o(d)); or

"(2) to obtain, by means of false or fraudulent pretenses, representations, or promises, any money or property in connection with the purchase or sale of any security of an issuer with a class of securities registered under section 12 of the Securities Exchange Act of 1934 (15 U.S.C. 78l) or that is required to file reports under section 15(d) of the Securities Exchange Act of 1934 (15 U.S.C. 78o(d));

shall be fined under this title, or imprisoned not more than 25 years, or both."

(b) CLERICAL AMENDMENT—The table of sections at the beginning of chapter 63 of title 18, United States Code, is amended by adding at the end the following new item:

"1348. Securities fraud."

TITLE IX—WHITE-COLLAR CRIME PENALTY ENHANCEMENTS

SEC. 901. SHORT TITLE.

This title may be cited as the "White-Collar Crime Penalty Enhancement Act of 2002."

SEC. 902. ATTEMPTS AND CONSPIRACIES TO COMMIT CRIMINAL FRAUD OFFENSES.

(a) IN GENERAL—Chapter 63 of title 18, United States Code, is amended by inserting after section 1348 as added by this Act the following:

"**Sec. 1349. Attempt and conspiracy**

"Any person who attempts or conspires to commit any offense under this chapter shall be subject to the same penalties as those prescribed for the offense, the commission of which was the object of the attempt or conspiracy.

(b) CLERICAL AMENDMENT—The table of sections at the beginning of chapter 63 of title 18, United States Code, is amended by adding at the end the following new item:

"1349. Attempt and conspiracy."

SEC. 903. CRIMINAL PENALTIES FOR MAIL AND WIRE FRAUD.

(a) MAIL FRAUD—Section 1341 of title 18, United States Code, is amended by striking "five" and inserting "20".

(b) WIRE FRAUD—Section 1343 of title 18, United States Code, is amended by striking "five" and inserting "20".

SEC. 904. CRIMINAL PENALTIES FOR VIOLATIONS OF THE EMPLOYEE RETIREMENT INCOME SECURITY ACT OF 1974.

Section 501 of the Employee Retirement Income Security Act of 1974 (29 U.S.C. 1131) is amended—

(1) by striking "$5,000" and inserting "$100,000";

(2) by striking "one year" and inserting "10 years"; and

(3) by striking "$100,000" and inserting "$500,000."

SEC. 905. AMENDMENT TO SENTENCING GUIDELINES RELATING TO CERTAIN WHITE-COLLAR OFFENSES.

SEC. 906. CORPORATE RESPONSIBILITY FOR FINANCIAL REPORTS.

(a) IN GENERAL—Chapter 63 of title 18, United States Code, is amended by inserting after section 1349, as created by this Act, the following:

"**Sec. 1350. Failure of corporate officers to certify financial reports**

(a) CERTIFICATION OF PERIODIC FINANCIAL REPORTS—Each periodic report containing financial statements filed by an issuer with the Securities Exchange Commission pursuant to section 13(a) or 15(d) of the Securities Exchange Act of 1934 (15 U.S.C. 78m(a) or 78o(d)) shall be accompanied by a written statement by the chief executive officer and chief financial officer (or equivalent thereof) of the issuer.

"(b) CONTENT—The statement required under subsection (a) shall certify that the periodic report containing the financial statements fully complies with the requirements of section 13(a) or 15(d) of the Securities Exchange Act pf 1934 (15 U.S.C. 78m or 78o(d)) and that information contained in the periodic report fairly presents, in all material respects, the financial condition and results of operations of the issuer.

"(c) CRIMINAL PENALTIES—Whoever—

"(1) certifies any statement as set forth in subsections (a) and (b) of this section knowing that the periodic report accompanying the statement does not comport with all the requirements set forth in this section shall be fined not more than $1,000,000 or imprisoned not more than 10 years, or both; or

"(2) willfully certifies any statement as set forth in subsections (a) and (b) of this section knowing that the periodic report accompanying the statement does not comport with all the requirements set forth in this section shall be fined not more than $5,000,000, or imprisoned not more than 20 years, or both."

(b) CLERICAL AMENDMENT—The table of sections at the beginning of chapter 63 of title 18, United States Code, is amended by adding at the end the following:

"1350. Failure of corporate officers to certify financial reports."

TITLE X—CORPORATE TAX RETURNS

SEC. 1001. SENSE OF THE SENATE REGARDING THE SIGNING OF CORPORATE TAX RETURNS BY CHIEF EXECUTIVE OFFICERS.

It is the sense of the Senate that the Federal income tax return of a corporation should be signed by the chief executive officer of such corporation.

TITLE XI—CORPORATE FRAUD ACCOUNTABILITY

SEC. 1101. SHORT TITLE.

This title may be cited as the "Corporate Fraud Accountability Act of 2002."

SEC. 1102. TAMPERING WITH A RECORD OR OTHERWISE IMPEDING AN OFFICIAL PROCEEDING.

Section 1512 of title 18, United States Code, is amended—

(1) by redesignating subsections (c) through (i) as subsections (d) through (j), respectively; and

(2) by inserting after subsection (b) the following new subsection:

"(c) Whoever corruptly—

"(1) alters, destroys, mutilates, or conceals a record, document, or other object, or attempts to do so, with the intent to impair the object's integrity or availability for use in an official proceeding; or

"(2) otherwise obstructs, influences, or impedes any official proceeding, or attempts to do so, shall be fined under this title or imprisoned not more than 20 years, or both."

SEC. 1103. TEMPORARY FREEZE AUTHORITY FOR THE SECURITIES AND EXCHANGE COMMISSION.

(a) IN GENERAL—Section 21C(c) of the Securities Exchange Act of 1934 (15 U.S.C. 78u-3(c)) is amended by adding at the end the following:

"(3) TEMPORARY FREEZE

"(A) IN GENERAL

"(i) ISSUANCE OF TEMPORARY ORDERWhenever, during the course of a lawful investigation involving possible violations of the Federal securities laws by an issuer of publicly traded securities or any of its directors, officers, partners, controlling persons, agents, or employees, it shall appear to the Commission that it is likely that the issuer will make extraordinary payments (whether compensation or otherwise) to any of the foregoing persons, the Commission may petition a Federal district court for a temporary order requiring the issuer to escrow, subject to court supervision, those payments in an interest-bearing account for 45 days.

"(ii) STANDARD—A temporary order shall be entered under clause (i), only after notice and opportunity for a hearing, unless the court determines that notice and hearing prior to entry of the order would be impracticable or contrary to the public interest.

"(iii) EFFECTIVE PERIOD—A temporary order issued under clause (i) shall—

"(I) become effective immediately;

"(II) be served upon the parties subject to it; and

"(III) unless set aside, limited or suspended by a court of competent jurisdiction, shall remain effective and enforceable for 45 days.

"(iv) EXTENSIONS AUTHORIZED—The effective period of an order under this subparagraph may be extended by the court upon good cause shown for not longer than 45 additional days, provided that the combined period of the order shall not exceed 90 days.

"(B) PROCESS ON DETERMINATION OF VIOLATIONS

"(i) VIOLATIONS CHARGED—If the issuer or other person described in subparagraph (A) is charged with any violation of the Federal securities laws before the expiration of the effective period of a temporary order under subparagraph (A) (including any applicable extension period), the order shall remain in effect, subject to court approval, until the conclusion of any legal proceedings related thereto, and the affected issuer or other person, shall have the right to petition the court for review of the order.

"(ii) VIOLATIONS NOT CHARGED—If the issuer or other person described in subparagraph (A) is not charged with any violation of the Federal securities laws before the expiration of the effective period of a temporary order under subparagraph (A) (including any applicable extension period), the escrow shall terminate at the expiration of the 45-day effective period (or the expiration of any extension period, as applicable), and the disputed payments (with accrued interest) shall be returned to the issuer or other affected person."

(b) TECHNICAL AMENDMENT—Section 21C(c)(2) of the Securities Exchange Act of 1934 (15 U.S.C. 78u-3(c)(2)) is amended by striking "This" and inserting "paragraph (1)."

SEC. 1104. AMENDMENT TO THE FEDERAL SENTENCING GUIDELINES.

(a) REQUEST FOR IMMEDIATE CONSIDERATION BY THE UNITED STATES SENTENCING COMMISSION—Pursuant to its authority under section 994(p) of title 28, United States Code, and in accordance with this section, the United States Sentencing Commission is requested to—

(1) promptly review the sentencing guidelines applicable to securities and accounting fraud and related offenses;

(2) expeditiously consider the promulgation of new sentencing guidelines or amendments to existing sentencing guidelines to provide an enhancement for officers or directors of publicly traded corporations who commit fraud and related offenses; and

(3) submit to Congress an explanation of actions taken by the Sentencing Commission pursuant to paragraph (2) and any additional policy recommendations the Sentencing Commission may have for combating offenses described in paragraph (1).

(b) CONSIDERATIONS IN REVIEW—In carrying out this section, the Sentencing Commission is requested to—

(1) ensure that the sentencing guidelines and policy statements reflect the serious nature of securities, pension, and accounting fraud and the need for aggressive and appropriate law enforcement action to prevent such offenses;

(2) assure reasonable consistency with other relevant directives and with other guidelines;

(3) account for any aggravating or mitigating circumstances that might justify exceptions, including circumstances for which the sentencing guidelines currently provide sentencing enhancements;

(4) ensure that guideline offense levels and enhancements for an obstruction of justice offense are adequate in cases where documents or other physical evidence are actually destroyed or fabricated;

(5) ensure that the guideline offense levels and enhancements under United States Sentencing Guideline 2B1.1 (as in effect on the date of enactment of this Act) are sufficient for a fraud offense when the number of victims adversely involved is significantly greater than 50;

(6) make any necessary conforming changes to the sentencing guidelines; and

(7) assure that the guidelines adequately meet the purposes of sentencing as set forth in section 3553(a)(2) of title 18, United States Code.

(c) EMERGENCY AUTHORITY AND DEADLINE FOR COMMISSION ACTION—The United States Sentencing Commission is requested to promulgate the guidelines or amendments provided for under this section as soon as practicable, and in any event not later than the 180 days after the date of enactment of this Act, in accordance with the procedures sent forth in section 21(a) of the Sentencing Reform Act of 1987, as though the authority under that Act had not expired.

SEC. 1105. AUTHORITY OF THE COMMISSION TO PROHIBIT PERSONS FROM SERVING AS OFFICERS OR DIRECTORS.

(a) SECURITIES EXCHANGE ACT OF 1934—Section 21C of the Securities Exchange Act of 1934 (15 U.S.C. 78u-3) is amended by adding at the end the following:

"(f) AUTHORITY OF THE COMMISSION TO PROHIBIT PERSONS FROM SERVING AS OFFICERS OR DIRECTORS—In any cease-and-desist proceeding under subsection (a), the Commission may issue an order to prohibit, conditionally or unconditionally, and permanently or for such period of time as it shall determine, any person who has violated section 10(b) or the rules or regulations thereunder, from acting as an officer or director of any issuer that has a class of securities registered pursuant to section 12, or that is required to file reports pursuant to section 15(d), if the conduct of that person demonstrates unfitness to serve as an officer or director of any such issuer."

(b) SECURITIES ACT OF 1933—Section 8A of the Securities Act of 1933 (15 U.S.C. 77h-1) is amended by adding at the end of the following:

"(f) AUTHORITY OF THE COMMISSION TO PROHIBIT PERSONS FROM SERVING AS OFFICERS OR DIRECTORS—In any cease-and-desist proceeding under subsection (a), the Commission may issue an order to prohibit, conditionally or unconditionally, and permanently or for such period of time as it shall determine, any person who has violated section 17(a)(1) or the rules or regulations thereunder, from acting as an officer or director of any issuer that has a class of securities registered pursuant to section 12 of the Securities Exchange Act of 1934, or that is required to file reports pursuant to section 15(d) of that Act, if the conduct of that person demonstrates unfitness to serve as an officer or director of any such issuer."

SEC. 1106. INCREASED CRIMINAL PENALTIES UNDER SECURITIES EXCHANGE ACT OF 1934.

Section 32(a) of the Securities Exchange Act of 1934 (15 U.S.C. 78ff(a)) is amended—

(1) by striking "$1,000,000, or imprisoned not more than 10 years" and inserting "$5,000,000, or imprisoned not more than 20 years"; and

(2) by striking "$2,500,000" and inserting "$25,000,000."

SEC. 1107. RETALIATION AGAINST INFORMANTS.

(a) IN GENERAL—Section 1513 of title 18, United States Code, is amended by adding at the end the following:

"(e) Whoever knowingly, with the intent to retaliate, takes any action harmful to any person, including interference with the lawful employment or livelihood of any person, for providing to a law enforcement officer any truthful information relating to the commission or possible commission of any Federal offense, shall be fined under this title or imprisoned not more than 10 years, or both."

Speaker of the House of Representatives.

Vice President of the United States and

President of the Senate.

END

INVESTMENT ADVISERS ACT OF 1940—SELECTED PROVISIONS

15 U.S.C. §§ 80b-1 et seq.

N.B. The following is not a complete text of the Investment Advisers Act of 1940. It omits a number of statutory provisions entirely, and also omits certain subsections of provisions that are partially included.

Sec. 201. FINDINGS

Upon the basis of facts disclosed by the record and report of the Securities and Exchange Commission made pursuant to section 30 of the Public Utility Holding Company Act of 1935, and facts otherwise disclosed and ascertained, it is hereby found that investment advisers are of national concern, in that among other things—

(1) their advice, counsel, publications, writings, analyses, and reports are furnished and distributed, and their contracts, subscription agreements, and other arrangements with clients are negotiated and performed, by the use of the mails and means and instrumentalities of interstate commerce;

(2) their advice, counsel, publications, writings, analyses, and reports customarily relate to the purchase and sale of securities traded on national securities exchanges and in interstate over-the-counter markets, securities issued by companies engaged in business in interstate commerce, and securities issued by national banks and member banks of the Federal Reserve System; and

(3) the foregoing transactions occur in such volume as substantially to affect interstate commerce, national securities exchanges, and other securities markets, the national banking system and the national economy.

Sec. 202. DEFINITIONS

(a) When used in this title, unless the context otherwise requires, the following definitions shall apply: . . .

1071

(11) [Investment Adviser]

"Investment adviser" means any person who, for compensation, engages in the business of advising others, either directly or through publications or writings, as to the value of securities or as to the advisability of investing in, purchasing, or selling securities, or who, for compensation and as part of a regular business, issues or promulgates analyses or reports concerning securities; but does not include: (A) a bank, or any bank holding company as defined in the Bank Holding Company Act of 1956, which is not an investment company, except that the term "investment adviser" includes any bank or bank holding company to the extent that such bank or bank holding company serves or acts as an investment adviser to a registered investment company, but if, in the case of a bank, such services or actions are performed through a separately identifiable department or division, the department or division, and not the bank itself, shall be deemed to be the investment adviser; (B) any lawyer, accountant, engineer, or teacher whose performance of such services is solely incidental to the practice of his profession; (C) any broker or dealer whose performance of such services is solely incidental to the conduct of his business as a broker or dealer and who receives no special compensation therefor; (D) the publisher of any bona fide newspaper, news magazine or business or financial publication of general and regular circulation; (E) any person whose advice, analyses, or reports relate to no securities other than securities which are direct obligations of or obligations guaranteed as to principal or interest by the United States, or securities issued or guaranteed by corporations in which the United States has a direct or indirect interest which shall have been designated by the Secretary of the Treasury, pursuant to Section 3(a)(12) of the Securities Exchange Act of 1934, as exempted securities for the purposes of that Act; (F) any nationally recognized statistical rating organization, as that term is defined in section 3(a)(62) of the Securities Exchange Act of 1934, unless such organization engages in issuing recommendations as to purchasing, selling, or holding securities or in managing assets, consisting in whole or in part of securities, on behalf of others; (G) any family office, as defined by rule, regulation, or order of the Commission, in accordance with the purposes of this title; or (H) such other persons not within the intent of this paragraph, as the Commission may designate by rules and regulations or order.

Sec. 203. REGISTRATION OF INVESTMENT ADVISERS

(a) Except as provided in subsection (b) and section 203A, it shall be unlawful for any investment adviser, unless registered under this section, to make use of the mails or any means or instrumentality of interstate commerce in connection with his or its business as an investment adviser.

(b) The provisions of subsection (a) shall not apply to—

(1) Any investment adviser, other than an investment adviser who acts as an investment adviser to any private fund, all of whose clients are residents of the State within which such investment adviser maintains his or its principal office and place of business, and who does not furnish advice or issue analyses or reports with respect to securities listed or admitted to unlisted trading privileges on any national securities exchange;

(2) Any investment adviser whose only clients are insurance companies;

(3) Any investment adviser that is a foreign private adviser;

(4) Any investment adviser that is a charitable organization as defined in section 3(c)(10(B) of the Investment Company Act of 1940, or is a trustee, director, officer, employee, or volunteer of such a charitable organization acting within the scope of such person's employment or duties with such organization, whose advice, analyses, or reports are provided only to one or more of the following:

(A) any such charitable organization;

(B) a fund that is excluded from the definition of an investment company under section 3(c)(10(B) of the Investment Company Act of 1940; or

(C) a trust or other donative instrument described in section 3(c)(10(B) of the Investment Company Act of 1940, or the trustees, administrators, settlors (or potential settlors), or beneficiaries of any such trust or other instrument;

(5) any plan described in section 414(e) of the Internal Revenue Code of 1986, any person or entity eligible to establish and maintain such a plan under the Internal Revenue Code of 1986, or any trustee, director, officer, or employee of or volunteer for any such plan or person, if such person or entity, acting in such capacity, provides investment advice exclusively to, or with respect to, any plan, person, or entity or any company, account, or fund that is excluded from the definition of an investment company under section 3(c)(14) of the Investment Company Act of 1940;

(6)(A) any investment adviser that is registered with the Commodity Futures Trading Commission as a commodity trading advisor whose business does not consist primarily of acting as an investment adviser, as defined in section 202(a)(11) of this title, and that does not act as an investment adviser to—

(i) an investment company registered under title I of this Act; or

(ii) a company which has elected to be a business development company pursuant to section 54 of title I of this Act and has not withdrawn its election or

(B) Any investment adviser that is registered with the Commodity Futures Trading Commission as a commodity trading advisor and advises a private fund, provided that, if after the date of enactment of the Investor Protection and Securities Reform Act of 2010, the business of the advisor should become predominately the provision of securities-related advice, then such adviser shall register with the Commission;

(7) Any investment adviser, other than any entity that has elected to be regulated or is regulated as a business development company pursuant to section 54 of the Investment Company Act of 1940 (15 U.S.C. 80a-54), who solely advises—

(A) Small business investment companies that are licensees under the Small Business Investment Act of 1958;

(B) Entities that have received from the Small Business Administration notice to proceed to qualify for a license as a small business investment company under the Small Business Investment Act of 1958, which notice or license has not been revoked; or

(C) Applicants that are affiliated with 1 or more licensed small business investment companies described in subparagraph (A) and that have applied for another license under the Small Business Investment Act of 1958, which application remains pending; or

(8) Any investment adviser, other than an entity that has elected to be regulated or is regulated as a business development company pursuant to section 54 of the Investment Company Act of 1940 (15 U.S.C. 80a-53), who solely advises—

(A) Rural business investment companies (as defined in section 384A of the Consolidated Farm and Rural Development Act (7 U.S.C. 2009cc)); or

(B) Companies that have submitted to the Secretary of Agriculture an application in accordance with section 384D(b) of the Consolidated Farm and Rural Development Act (7 U.S.C. 2009cc-3(b)) that—

(i) Have received from the Secretary of Agriculture a letter of conditions, which has not been revoked; or

(ii) Are affiliated with 1 or more rural business investment companies described in subparagraph (A).

(c)(1) An investment adviser, or any person who presently contemplates becoming an investment adviser, may be registered by filing with the Commission an application for registration in such form and containing such of the following information and documents as the Commission, by rule, may prescribe as necessary or appropriate in the public interest or for the protection of investors:

(A) the name and form of organization under which the investment adviser engages or intends to engage in business; the name of the State or other sovereign power under which such investment adviser is organized; the location of his or its principal office, principal business office, and branch offices, if any; the names and addresses of his or its partners, officers, directors, and persons performing similar functions or, if such an investment adviser be an individual, of such individual; and the number of his or its employees;

(B) the education, the business affiliations for the past ten years, and the present business affiliations of such investment adviser and of his or its partners, officers, directors, and persons performing similar functions and of any controlling person thereof;

(C) the nature of the business of such investment adviser, including the manner of giving advice and rendering analyses or reports;

(D) a balance sheet certified by an independent public accountant and other financial statements (which shall, as the Commission specifies, be certified);

(E) the nature and scope of the authority of such investment adviser with respect to clients' funds and accounts;

(F) the basis or bases upon which such investment adviser is compensated;

(G) whether such investment adviser, or any person associated with such investment adviser, is subject to any disqualification which would be a basis for denial, suspension, or revocation of registration of such investment adviser under the provisions of subsection (e) of this section; and

(H) a statement as to whether the principal business of such investment adviser consists or is to consist of acting as investment adviser and a statement as to whether a substantial part of the business of such investment adviser, consists or is to consist of rendering investment supervisory services.

(2) Within forty-five days of the date of the filing of such application (or within such longer period as to which the applicant consents) the Commission shall—

(A) by order grant such registration; or

(B) institute proceedings to determine whether registration should be denied. Such proceedings shall include notice of the grounds for denial under consideration and opportunity for hearing and shall be concluded within one hundred twenty days of the date of the filing of the application for registration. At the conclusion of such proceedings the Commission, by order, shall grant or deny such registration. The Commission may extend the time for conclusion of such proceedings for up to ninety days if it finds good cause for such extension and publishes its reasons for so finding or for such longer period as to which the applicant consents.

The Commission shall grant such registration if the Commission finds that the requirements of this section are satisfied and that the applicant is not prohibited from registering as an investment adviser under section 203A. The Commission shall deny such registration if it does not make such a finding or if it finds that if the applicant were so registered, its registration would be subject to suspension or revocation under subsection (e) of this section.

(d) Any provision of this title (other than subsection (a) of this section) which prohibits any act, practice, or course of business if the mails or any means or instrumentality of interstate commerce are used in connection therewith, shall also prohibit any such act, practice, or course of business by any investment adviser registered pursuant to this section or any person acting on behalf of such an investment adviser, irrespective of any use of the mails or any means or instrumentality of interstate commerce in connection therewith.

(e) The Commission, by order, shall censure, place limitations on the activities, functions, or operations of, suspend for a period not exceeding twelve months, or revoke the registration of any investment adviser if it finds, on the record after notice and opportunity for hearing, that such censure, placing of limitations, suspension, or revocation is in the public interest and that such investment adviser, or any person associated with such investment adviser, whether prior to or subsequent to becoming so associated—

(1) has willfully made or caused to be made in any application for registration or report required to be filed with the Commission under this title, or in any proceeding before the Commission with respect to registration, any statement which was at the time and in the light of the circumstances under which it was made false or misleading with respect to any

material fact, or has omitted to state in any such application or report any material fact which is required to be stated therein.

(2) has been convicted within ten years preceding the filing of any application for registration or at any time thereafter of any felony or misdemeanor or of a substantially equivalent crime by a foreign court of competent jurisdiction which the Commission finds—

(A) involves the purchase or sale of any security, the taking of a false oath, the making of a false report, bribery, perjury, burglary, any substantially equivalent activity however denominated by laws of the relevant foreign government, or conspiracy to commit any such offense;

(B) Arises out of the conduct of the business of a broker, dealer, municipal securities dealer, investment adviser, bank, insurance company, government securities broker, government securities dealer, fiduciary, transfer agent, credit rating agency, foreign person performing a function substantially equivalent to any of the above, or entity or person required to be registered under the Commodity Exchange Act or any substantially equivalent statute or regulation;

(C) involves the larceny, theft, robbery, extortion, forgery, counterfeiting, fraudulent concealment, embezzlement, fraudulent conversion, or misappropriation of funds or securities; or substantially equivalent activity however denominated by the laws of the relevant foreign government
or

(D) involves the violation of sections 152, 1341, 1342, or 1343 or chapter 25 or 47 of title 18, United States Code, or a violation of substantially equivalent foreign statute.

(3) has been convicted during the 10-year period preceding the date of filing of any application for registration, or at any time thereafter, of—

(A) any crime that is punishable by imprisonment for 1 or more years, and that is not described in paragraph (2); or

(B) a substantially equivalent crime by a foreign court of competent jurisdiction.

(4) is permanently or temporarily enjoined by order, judgment, or decree of any court of competent jurisdiction, including any foreign court of competent jurisdiction, from acting as an investment adviser, underwriter, broker, dealer, municipal securities dealer, government securities broker, government securities dealer, transfer agent foreign person performing a function substantially equivalent to any of the above, or entity or person required to be registered under the Commodity Exchange Act or any substantially equivalent statute or regulation, or as an affiliated person or employee of any investment company, bank, insurance company foreign entity substantially equivalent to any of the above, or entity or person required to be registered under the Commodity Exchange Act or any substantially equivalent statute or regulation, or from engaging in or continuing any conduct or practice in connection with any such activity, or in connection with the purchase or sale of any security.

(5) has willfully violated any provision of the Securities Act of 1933, the Securities Exchange Act of 1934, the Investment Company Act of 1940, this title, the Commodity Exchange Act, or the rules, or regulations under any such statutes or any rule of the Municipal Securities Rulemaking Board, or is unable to comply with any such provision.

(6) has willfully aided, abetted, counseled, commanded, induced, or procured the violation by any other person of any provision of the Securities Act of 1933, the Securities Exchange Act of 1934, the Investment Company Act of 1940, this title, the Commodity Exchange Act, the rules or regulations under any of such statutes, or the rules of the Municipal Securities Rulemaking Board, or has failed reasonably to supervise, with a view to preventing violations of the provisions of such statutes, rules, and regulations, another person who commits such a violation, if such other person is subject to his supervision. For the purposes of this paragraph no person shall be deemed to have failed reasonably to supervise any person, if—

(A) there have been established procedures, and a system for applying such procedures, which would reasonably be expected to prevent and detect, insofar as practicable, any such violation by such other person, and

(B) such person has reasonably discharged the duties and obligations incumbent upon him by reason of such procedures and system without reasonable cause to believe that such procedures and system were not being complied with.

(7) is subject to any order of the Commission barring or suspending the right of the person to be associated with an investment adviser;

(8) has been found by a foreign financial regulatory authority to have—

(A) made or caused to be made in any application for registration or report required to be filed with a foreign securities authority, or in any proceeding before a foreign securities authority with respect to registration, any statement that was at the time and in light of the circumstances under which it was made false or misleading with respect to any material fact, or has omitted to state in any application or report to a foreign securities authority any material fact that is required to be stated therein;

(B) violated any foreign statute or regulation regarding transactions in securities or contracts of sale of a commodity for future delivery traded on or subject to the rules of a contract market or any board of trade; or

(C) aided, abetted, counseled, commanded, induced, or procured the violation by any other person of any foreign statute or regulation regarding transactions in securities or contracts of sale of a commodity for future delivery traded on or subject to the rules of a contract market or any board of trade, or has been found, by the foreign financial regulatory authority, to have failed reasonably to supervise, with a view to preventing violations of statutory provisions, and rules and regulations promulgated thereunder, another person who commits such a violation, if such other person is subject to his supervision; or

(9) is subject to any final order of a State securities commission (or any agency or officer performing like functions), State authority that supervises or examines banks, savings associations, or credit unions, State insurance commission (or any agency or office performing like functions), an appropriate Federal banking agency (as defined in section 3 of the Federal Deposit Insurance Act (12 U.S.C. 1813(q))), or the National Credit Union Administration, that—

(A) bars such person from association with an entity regulated by such commission, authority, agency, or officer, or from engaging in the business of securities, insurance, banking, savings association activities, or credit union activities; or

(B) constitutes a final order based on violations of any laws or regulations that prohibit fraudulent, manipulative, or deceptive conduct.

(f) The Commission, by order, shall censure or place limitations on the activities of any person associated, seeking to become associated, or, at the time of the alleged misconduct, associated or seeking to become associated with, or, at the time of the alleged misconduct, associated or seeking to become associated an investment adviser, or suspend for a period not exceeding 12 months or bar any such person from being associated with an investment adviser, broker, dealer, municipal securities dealer, municipal advisor, transfer agent, or nationally recognized statistical rating organization if the Commission finds, on the record after notice and opportunity for hearing, that such censure, placing of limitations, suspension, or bar is in the public interest and that such person has committed or omitted any act or omission enumerated in paragraph (1), (5), (6), (8), or (9) of subsection (e) or has been convicted of any offense specified in paragraph (2) or (3) of subsection (e) within ten years of the commencement of the proceedings under this subsection, or is enjoined from any action, conduct, or practice specified in paragraph (4) of subsection (e). It shall be unlawful for any person as to whom such an order suspending or barring him from being associated with an investment adviser is in effect willfully to become, or to be, associated with an investment adviser without the consent of the Commission, and it shall be unlawful for any investment adviser to permit such a person to become, or remain, a person associated with him without the consent of the Commission, if such investment adviser knew, or in the exercise of reasonable care, should have known, of such order.

(g) Any successor to the business of an investment adviser registered under this section shall be deemed likewise registered hereunder, if within thirty days from its succession to such business it shall file an application for registration under this section, unless and until the Commission, pursuant to subsection (c) or subsection (e) of this section, shall deny registration to or revoke or suspend the registration of such successor.

(h) Any person registered under this section may, upon such terms and conditions as the Commission finds necessary in the public interest or for the protection of investors, withdraw from registration by filing a written notice of withdrawal with the Commission. If the Commission finds that any person registered under this section, or who has pending an application for registration filed under this section, is no longer in existence, is not engaged in business as an investment adviser, or is prohibited from registering as an investment adviser under section 203A, the Commission shall by order cancel the registration of such person.

[Money Penalties in Administrative Proceedings]

(i) MONEY PENALTIES IN ADMINISTRATIVE PROCEEDINGS.—

(1) IN GENERAL.—In any proceeding instituted pursuant to subsection (e) or (f) against any person, the Commission may impose a civil penalty if it finds, on the record after notice and opportunity for hearing that such penalty is in the public interest, that such person—

(i) has willfully violated any provision of the Securities Act of 1933, the Securities Exchange Act of 1934, the Investment Company Act of 1940, or this title, or the rules or regulations thereunder;

(ii) has willfully aided, abetted, counseled, commanded, induced, or procured such a violation by any other person;

(iii) has willfully made or caused to be made in any application for registration or report required to be filed with the Commission under this title, or in any proceeding before the Commission with respect to registration, any statement which was, at the time and in the light of the circumstances under which it was made, false or misleading with respect to any material fact, or has omitted to state in any such application or report any material fact which was required to be stated therein; or

(iv) has failed reasonably to supervise, within the meaning of subsection (e)(6) of this title, with a view to preventing violations of the provisions of this title and the rules and regulations thereunder, another person who commits such a violation, if such other person is subject to his supervision;

(B) CEASE-AND-DESIST PROCEEDINGS.—In any proceeding instituted pursuant to subsection (k) against any person, the Commission may impose a civil penalty if the Commission finds, on the record, after notice and opportunity for hearing, that such person—

(i) Is violating or has violated any provision of this title, or any rule or regulation issued under this title; or

(ii) Is or was a cause of the violation of any provision of this title, or any rule or regulation issued under this title.

[Maximum Amount of Penalty]

(2) MAXIMUM AMOUNT OF PENALTY.—

(A) FIRST TIER.—The maximum amount of penalty for each act or omission described in paragraph (1) shall be $5,000 for a natural person or $50,000 for any other person.

(B) SECOND TIER.—Notwithstanding subparagraph (A), the maximum amount of penalty for each such act or omission shall be $50,000 for a natural person or $250,000 for any other person if the act or omission described in paragraph (1) involved fraud, deceit, manipulation, or deliberate or reckless disregard of a regulatory requirement.

(C) THIRD TIER.—Notwithstanding subparagraphs (A) and (B), the maximum amount of penalty fr each such act or omission shall be $100,000 for a natural person or $500,000 for any other person if—

(i) the act or omission described in paragraph (1) involved fraud, deceit, manipulation, or deliberate or reckless disregard of a regulatory requirement; and

(ii) such act or omission directly or indirectly resulted in substantial losses or created a significant risk of substantial losses to other persons or resulted in substantial pecuniary gain to the person who committed the act or omission.

[Public Interest]

(3) DETERMINATION OF PUBLIC INTEREST.—In considering under this section whether a penalty is in the public interest, the Commission may consider—

(A) whether the act or omission for which such penalty is assessed involved fraud, deceit, manipulation, or deliberate or reckless disregard of a regulatory requirement;

(B) the harm to other persons resulting either directly or indirectly from such act or omission;

(C) the extent to which any person was unjustly enriched, taking into account any restitution made to persons injured by such behavior;

(D) whether such person previously has been found by the Commission, another appropriate regulatory agency, or a self-regulatory organization to have violated the Federal securities laws, State securities laws, or the rules of a self-regulatory organization, has been enjoined by a court of competent jurisdiction from violations of such laws or rules, or has been convicted by a court of competent jurisdiction of violations of such laws or of any felony or misdemeanor described in section 203(e)(2) of this title;

(E) the need to deter such person and other persons from committing such acts or omissions; and

(F) such other matters as justice may require.

[Ability to Pay]

(4) EVIDENCE CONCERNING ABILITY TO PAY.—In any proceeding in which the Commission may impose a penalty under this section, a respondent may present evidence of the respondent's ability to pay such penalty. The Commission may, in its discretion, consider such evidence in determining whether such penalty is in the public interest. Such evidence may relate to the extent of such person's ability to continue in business and the collectability of a penalty, taking into account any other claims of the United States or third parties upon such person's assests and the amount of such person's assets.

[Accounting and Disgorgement.]

(j) AUTHORITY TO ENTER AN ORDER REQUIRING AN ACCOUNTING AND DISGORGEMENT.—In any proceeding in which the Commission may impose a penalty under this section, the Commission may enter an order requiring accounting and disgorgement, including reasonable interest. The Commission is authorized to adopt rules, regulations, and orders concerning payments to investors, rates of interest, periods of accrual, and such other matters as it deems appropriate to implement this subsection.

[Cease-and-Desist Proceedings]

(k) CEASE.-AND-DESIST PROCEEDINGS.—

(1) AUTHORITY OF THE COMMISSION.—If the Commission finds, after notice and opportunity for hearing, that any person is violating, has violated, or is about to violate any provision of this title, or any rule or regulation thereunder, the Commission may publish its findings and enter an order requiring such person, and any other person that is, was, or would be a cause of the violation, due to an act or omission the person knew or should have known would contribute to such violation, to cease and desist from committing or causing such violation and any future violation of the same provision, rule, or regulation. Such order may, in addition to requiring a person to cease and desist from committing or causing a violation, require such person to comply, or to take steps to effect compliance, with such provision, rule, or regulation, upon such terms and conditions and within such time as the Commission may specify in such order. Any such order may, as the Commission deems appropriate, require future compliance or steps to effect future compliance, either perma-

nently or for such period of time as the Commission may specify, with such provision rule, or regulation with respect to any security, any issuer, or any other person.

[Hearing]

(2) HEARING.—The notice instituting proceedings pursuant to paragraph (1) shall fix a hearing date not earlier than 30 days nor later than 60 days after service of the notice unless an earlier or a later date is set by the Commission with the consent of any respondent so served.

[Temporary Order]

(3) TEMPORARY ORDER.—

(A) IN GENERAL.—Whenever the Commission determines that the alleged violation or threatened violation specified in the notice instituting proceedings pursuant to paragraph (1), or the continuation thereof, is likely to result in significant dissipation or conversion of assets, significant harm to investors, or substantial harm to the public interest, including, but not limited to, losses to the Securities Investor Protection Corporation, prior to the completion of the proceedings, the Commission may enter a temporary order requiring the respondent to cease and desist from the violation or threatened violation and to take such action to prevent the violation or threatened violation and to prevent dissipation or conversion of assets, significant harm to investors, or substantial harm to the public interest as the Commission deems appropriate pending completion of such proceedings. Such an order shall be entered only after notice and opportunity for a hearing, unless the Commission, notwithstanding section 211(c) of this title, determines that notice and hearing prior to entry would be impracticable to contrary to the public interest. A temporary order shall become effective upon service upon the respondent and, unless set aside, limited, or suspended by the Commission or a court of competent jurisdiction, shall remain effective and enforceable pending the completion of the proceedings.

(B) APPLICABILITY.—This paragraph shall apply only to a respondent that acts, or, at the time of the alleged misconduct acted, as a broker, dealer, investment adviser, investment company, municipal securities dealer, government securities broker, government securities dealer, or transfer agent, or is, or was at the time of the alleged misconduct, an associated person of, or a person seeking to become associated with, any of the foregoing.

(4) REVIEW OF TEMPORARY ORDERS.—

(A) COMMISSION REVIEW.—At any time after the respondent has been served with a temporary cease-and-desist order pursuant to paragraph (3), the respondent may apply to the Commission to have the order set aside, limited or suspended. If the respondent has been served with a temporary cease-and-desist order entered without a prior Commission hearing, the respondent may, within 10 days after the date on which the order was served, request a hearing on such application and the Commission shall hold a hearing and render a decision on such application at the earliest possible time.

(B) JUDICIAL REVIEW.—Within—

(i) 10 days after the date the respondent was served with a temporary cease-and-desist order entered with a prior Commission hearing, or

(ii) 10 days after the Commission renders a decision on an application and hearing under subparagraph (A), with respect to any temporary cease-and-desist order entered without a prior Commission hearing,

the respondent may apply to the United States district court for the district in which the respondent resides or has its principal office or principal place of business, or for the District of Columbia, for an order setting aside, limiting, or suspending the effectiveness or enforcement of the order, and the court shall have jurisdiction to enter such an order. A respondent served with a temporary cease-and-desist order entered without a prior Commission hearing may not apply to the court except after hearing and decision by the Commission on the respondent's application under subparagraph (A) of this paragraph.

(C) NO AUTOMATIC STAY OF TEMPORARY ORDER.—The commencement of proceedings under subparagraph (B) of this paragraph shall not, unless specifically ordered by the court, operate as a stay of the Commission's order.

(D) EXCLUSIVE REVIEW.—Section 213 of this title shall not apply to a temporary order entered pursuant to this section.

(5) AUTHORITY TO ENTER AN ORDER REQUIRING AN ACCOUNTING AND DISGORGEMENT.—In any cease-and-desist proceeding under paragraph (1), the Commission may enter an order requiring accounting and disgorgement, including reasonable interest. The Commission is authorized to adopt rules, regulations, and orders concerning payments to investors, rates of interest, periods of accrual, and such other matters as it deems appropriate to implement this subsection.

(*l*) Exemption of Venture Capital Fund Advisers.—

(1) In General.—No investment adviser that acts as an investment adviser solely to 1 or more venture capital funds shall be subject to the registration requirements of this title with respect to the provision of investment advice relating to a venture capital fund. Not later than 1 year after the date of enactment of this subsection, the Commission shall issue final rules to define the term "venture capital fund" for purposes of this subsection. The Commission shall require such advisers to maintain such records and provide to the Commission such annual or other reports as the Commission determines necessary or appropriate in the public interest or for the protection of investors.

(2) Advisers of SBICS.—For purposes of this subsection, a venture capital fund includes an entity described in subparagraph (A), (B), or (C) of subsection (b)(7) (other than an entity that has elected to be regulated or is regulated as a business development company pursuant to section 54 of the Investment Company Act of 1940).

(3) Advisers of RBICS.—For purposes of this subsection, a venture capital fund includes an entity described in subparagraph (A) or (B) of subsection (b)(8) (other than an entity that has elected to be regulated as a business development company pursuant to section 54 of the Investment Company Act of 1940 (15 U.S.C. 80a-53)).

(m) Exemption of and Reporting By Certain Private Fund Advisers.—

(1) In General.—The Commission shall provide an exemption from the registration requirements under this section to any investment adviser of private funds, if each of such investment adviser acts solely as an adviser to private funds and has assets under management in the United States of less than $150,000,000.

(2) Reporting.—The Commission shall require investment advisers exempted by reason of this subsection to maintain such records and provide to the Commission such annual or other reports as the Commission determines necessary or appropriate in the public interest or for the protection of investors.

(3) Advisers of SBICS.—For purposes of this subsection, the assets under management of a private fund that is an entity described in subparagraph (A), (B), or (C) of subsection (b)(7) (other than an entity that has elected to be regulated or is regulated as a business development company pursuant to section 54 of the Investment Company Act of 1940) shall be excluded from the limit set forth in paragraph (1).

(4) Advisers of RBICS.—For purposes of this subsection, the assets under management of a private fund that is an entity described in subparagraph (A) or (B) of subsection (b)(8) (other than an entity that has elected to be regulated or is regulated as a business development company pursuant to section 54 of the Investment Company Act of 1940 (15 U.S.C. 80a-53)) shall be excluded from the limit set forth in paragraph (1).

(n) REGISTRATION AND EXAMINATION OF MID-SIZED PRIVATE FUND ADVISERS.—In prescribing regulations to carry out the requirements of this section with respect to investment advisers acting as investment advisers to mid-sized private funds, the Commission shall take into account the size, governance, and investment strategy of such funds to determine whether they pose systemic risk, and shall provide for registration and examination procedures with respect to the investment advisers of such funds which reflect the level of systemic risk posed by such funds.

Sec. 203A. STATE AND FEDERAL RESPONSIBILITIES

(a) Advisers Subject to State Authorities.—

(1) In general.—No investment adviser that is regulated or required to be regulated as an investment adviser in the State in which it maintains its principal office and place of business shall register under section 203, unless the investment adviser—

(A) has assets under management of not less than $25,000,000, or such higher amount as the Commission may, by rule, deem appropriate in accordance with the purposes of this title; or

(B) is an adviser to an investment company registered under title I of this Act.

(2) Treatment of Mid-sized Investment Advisers.—

(A) In General.—No investment adviser described in subparagraph (B) shall register under section 203, unless the investment adviser is an adviser to an investment company registered under the Investment Company Act of 1940, or a company which has elected to be a business development company pursuant to section 54 of the Investment Company Act of 1940, and has not withdrawn the election, except that, if by effect of this paragraph an investment adviser would be required to register with 15 or more States, then the adviser may register under section 203.

(B) Covered Persons.—An investment adviser described in this subparagraph is an investment adviser that—

(i) Is required to be registered as an investment adviser with the securities commissioner (or any agency or office performing like functions) of the State in which it maintains its principal office and place of business and, if registered, would be subject to examination as an investment adviser by any such commissioner, agency, or office; and

(ii) Has assets under management between—

(I) The amount specified under subparagraph (A) of paragraph (1), as such amount may have been adjusted by the Commission pursuant to that subparagraph; and

(II) $100,000,000, or such higher amount as the Commission may, by rule, deem appropriate in accordance with the purposes of this title.

(3) Definition.—For purposes of this subsection, the term "assets under management" means the securities portfolios with respect to which an investment adviser provides continuous and regular supervisory or management services.

(b) Advisers Subject to Commission Authority.—

(1) In general.—No law of any State or political subdivision thereof requiring the registration, licensing, or qualification as an investment adviser or supervised person of an investment adviser shall apply to any person—

(A) that is registered under section 203 as an investment adviser, or that is a supervised person of such person, except that a State may license, register, or otherwise qualify any investment adviser representative who has a place of business located within that State;

(B) that is not registered under section 203 because that person is excepted from the definition of an investment adviser under section 202(a)(11); or

(C) That is not registered under section 203 because that person is exempt from registration as provided in subsection (b)(7) of such section, or is a supervised person of such person; or

(D) That is not registered under section 203 because that person is exempt from registration as provided in subsection (b)(8) of such section, or is a supervised person of such person.

(2) Limitation.—Nothing in this subsection shall prohibit the securities commission (or any agency or office performing like functions) of any State from investigating and bringing

enforcement actions with respect to fraud or deceit against an investment adviser or person associated with an investment adviser.

(c) Exemptions.—Notwithstanding subsection (a), the Commission, by rule or regulation upon its own motion, or by order upon application, may permit the registration with the Commission of any person or class of persons to which the application of subsection (a) would be unfair, a burden on interstate commerce, or otherwise inconsistent with the purposes of this section.

(d) State Assistance.—Upon request of the securities commissioner (or any agency or officer performing like functions) of any State, the Commission may provide such training, technical assistance, or other reasonable assistance in connection with the regulation of investment advisers by the State.

Sec. 204A. PREVENTION OF MISUSE OF NONPUBLIC INFORMATION

Every investment adviser subject to section 204 of this title shall establish, maintain, and enforce written policies and procedures reasonably designed, taking into consideration the nature of such investment adviser's business, to prevent the misuse in violation of this Act or the Securities Exchange Act of 1934, or the rules or regulations thereunder, of material, nonpublic information by such investment adviser or any person associated with such investment adviser. The Commission, as it deems necessary or appropriate in the public interest or for the protection of investors, shall adopt rules or regulations to require specific policies or procedures reasonably designed to prevent misuse in violation of this Act or the Securities Exchange Act of 1934 (or the rules or regulations thereunder) of material, nonpublic information.

Sec. 205. INVESTMENT ADVISORY CONTRACTS

(a) No investment adviser registered or required to be registered with the Commission shall enter into, extend, or renew any investment advisory contract, or in any way perform any investment advisory contract entered into, extended, or renewed on or after the effective date of this title, if such contract—

(1) provides for compensation to the investment adviser on the basis of a share of capital gains upon or capital appreciation of the funds or any portion of the funds of the client;

(2) fails to provide, in substance, that no assignment of such contract shall be made by the investment adviser without the consent of the other party to the contract; or

(3) fails to provide, in substance, that the investment adviser, if a partnership, will notify the other party to the contract of any change in the membership of such partnership within a reasonable time after such change.

(b) Paragraph (1) of this section shall not

(1) be construed to prohibit an investment advisory contract which provides for compensation based upon the total value of a fund averaged over a definite period, or as of definite dates, or taken as of a definite date;

(2) apply to an investment advisory contract with—

(A) an investment company registered under title I of this Act, or

(B) any other person (except a trust, governmental plan, collective trust fund, or separate account referred to in section 3(c)(11) of title I of this Act), provided that the contract relates to the investment of assets in excess of $1 million,

if the contract provides for compensation based on the asset value of the company or fund under management averaged over a specified period and increasing and decreasing proportionately with the investment performance of the company or fund over a specified period in relation to the investment record of an appropriate index of securities prices or such other measure of investment performance as the Commission by rule, regulation, or order may specify;

(3) apply with respect to any investment advisory contract between an investment adviser and a business development company, as defined in this title, if (A) the compensation provided for in such contract does not exceed 20 per centum of the realized capital gains upon the funds of the business development company over a specified period or as of definite dates, computed net of all realized capital losses and unrealized capital depreciation, and the condition of section 61(a)(4)(B)(iii) of title I of this Act is satisfied, and (B) the business development company does not have outstanding any option, warrant, or right issued pursuant to section 61(a)(4)(B) of title I of this Act and does not have a profit-sharing plan described in section 57(n) of title I of this Act;

(4) apply to an investment advisory contract with a company excepted from the definition of an investment company under section 3(c)(7) of title I of this Act; or

(5) apply to an investment advisory contract with a person who is not a resident of the United States.

(c) For purposes of paragraph (2) of subsection (b), the point from which increases and decreases in compensation are measured shall be the fee which is paid or earned when the investment performance of such company or fund is equivalent to that of the index or other measure of performance, and an index of securities prices shall be deemed appropriate unless the Commission by order shall determine otherwise.

(d) As used in paragraphs (2) and (3) of this subsection (a), "investment advisory contract" means any contract or agreement whereby a person agrees to act as investment adviser or to manage any investment or trading account of another person other than an investment company registered under title I of this Act.

(e) The Commission, by rule or regulation, upon its own motion, or by order upon application, may conditionally or unconditionally exempt any person or transaction, or any class or classes of persons or transactions, from subsection (a)(1), if and to the extent that the exemption relates to an investment advisory contract with any person that the Commission determines does not need the protections of subsection (a)(1), on the basis of such factors as financial sophistication, net worth, knowledge of and experience in financial matters, amount of assets under management, relationship with a registered investment adviser, and such other factors as the Commission determines are consistent with this section. With respect to any factor used in any rule or regulation by the Commission in making a determination under this subsection, if the Commission uses a dollar amount test in connection with such factor, such as a net asset threshold, the Commission shall, by order, not later than 1 year after the date of enactment of the Private Fund Investment Advisers Registration Act of 2010, and every 5 years thereafter, adjust for the effects of inflation on such test. Any such adjustment that is not a multiple of $100,000 shall be rounded to the nearest multiple of $100,000.

(f) AUTHORITY TO RESTRICT MANDATORY PREDISPUTE ARBITRATION.—The Commission, by rule, may prohibit, or impose conditions or limitations on the use of, agreements that require customers or clients of any investment adviser to arbitrate any future dispute between them arising under the Federal securities laws, the rules and regulations thereunder, or the rules of a self-regulatory organization if it finds that such prohibition, imposition of conditions, or limitations are in the public interest and for the protection of investors.

Sec. 206. PROHIBITED TRANSACTIONS BY INVESTMENT ADVISERS

It shall be unlawful for any investment adviser, by use of the mails or any means or instrumentality of interstate commerce, directly or indirectly—

(1) to employ any device, scheme, or artifice to defraud any client or prospective client;

(2) to engage in any transaction, practice, or course of business which operates as a fraud or deceit upon any client or prospective client;

(3) acting as principal for his own account, knowingly to sell any security to or purchase any security from a client, or acting as broker for a person other than such client, knowingly to effect any sale or purchase of any security for the account of such client, without disclosing to such client in writing before the completion of such transaction the capacity in

which he is acting and obtaining the consent of the client to such transaction. The prohibitions of this paragraph (3) shall not apply to any transaction with a customer of a broker or dealer if such broker or dealer is not acting as an investment adviser in relation to such transaction; or

(4) to engage in any act, practice, or course of business which is fraudulent, deceptive, or manipulative. The Commission shall, for the purposes of this paragraph (4) by rules and regulations define, and prescribe means reasonably designed to prevent, such acts, practices, and courses of business as are fraudulent, deceptive, or manipulative.

Sec. 206A. EXEMPTIONS

The Commission, by rules and regulations, upon its own motion, or by order upon application, may conditionally or unconditionally exempt any person or transaction or any class or classes or persons, or transactions, from any provision or provisions of this title or of any rule or regulation thereunder, if and to the extent that such exemption is necessary or appropriate in the public interest and consistent with the protection of investors and the purposes fairly intended by the policy and provisions of this title.

ADVISERS ACT RULES—SELECTED PROVISIONS

17 C.F.R. §§ 275.204-3—275.206(4)-7

N.B. The following is not a complete text of the Advisers Act Rules. It omits a number of statutory provisions entirely, and also omits certain subsections of provisions that are partially included.

Rule 203(b)(3)-1. Definition of "Client" of an Investment Adviser [*Removed.*]

Rule 203(l)-1. Venture Capital Fund Defined.

(a) *Venture Capital Fund Defined.* For purposes of section 203(*l*) of the Act (15 U.S.C. 80b-3(*l*)), a venture capital fund is any entity described in subparagraph (A), (B), or (C) of section 203(b)(7) of the Act (15 U.S.C. 80b-3(b)(7)) (other than an entity that has elected to be regulated or is regulated as a business development company pursuant to section 54 of the Investment Company Act of 1940 (15 U.S.C. 80a-53)) or any private fund that:

(1) Represents to investors and potential investors that it pursues a venture capital strategy;

(2) Immediately after the acquisition of any asset, other than qualifying investments or short-term holdings, holds no more than 20 percent of the amount of the fund's aggregate capital contributions and uncalled committed capital in assets (other than short-term holdings) that are not qualifying investments, valued at cost or fair value, consistently applied by the fund;

(3) Does not borrow, issue debt obligations, provide guarantees or otherwise incur leverage, in excess of 15 percent of the private fund's aggregate capital contributions and uncalled committed capital, and any such borrowing, indebtedness, guarantee or leverage is for a non-renewable term of no longer than 120 calendar days, except that any guarantee by the private fund of a qualifying portfolio company's obligations up to the amount of the value of the private fund's investment in the qualifying portfolio company is not subject to the 120 calendar day limit;

(4) Only issues securities the terms of which do not provide a holder with any right, except in extraordinary circumstances, to withdraw, redeem or require the repurchase of such securities but may entitle holders to receive distributions made to all holders pro rata; and

(5) Is not registered under section 8 of the Investment Company Act of 1940 (15 U.S.C. 80a-8), and has not elected to be treated as a business development company pursuant to section 54 of that Act (15 U.S.C. 80a-53).

(b) Certain Pre-Existing Venture Capital Funds. For purposes of section 203(l) of the Act (15 U.S.C. 80b-3(l)) and in addition to any venture capital fund as set forth in paragraph (a) of this section, a venture capital fund also includes any private fund that:

(1) Has represented to investors and potential investors at the time of the offering of the private fund's securities that it pursues a venture capital strategy;

(2) Prior to December 31, 2010, has sold securities to one or more investors that are not related persons, as defined in § 275.206(4)-2(d)(7), of any investment adviser of the private fund; and

(3) Does not sell any securities to (including accepting any committed capital from) any person after July 21, 2011.

(c) Definitions. For purposes of this section:

(1) Committed capital means any commitment pursuant to which a person is obligated to:

(i) Acquire an interest in the private fund; or

(ii) Make capital contributions to the private fund.

(2) Equity security has the same meaning as in section 3(a)(11) of the Securities Exchange Act of 1934 (15 U.S.C. 78c(a)(11)) and § 240.3a11-1 of this chapter.

(3) Qualifying investment means:

(i) An equity security issued by a qualifying portfolio company that has been acquired directly by the private fund from the qualifying portfolio company;

(ii) Any equity security issued by a qualifying portfolio company in exchange for an equity security issued by the qualifying portfolio company described in paragraph (c)(3)(i) of this section; or

(iii) Any equity security issued by a company of which a qualifying portfolio company is a majority-owned subsidiary, as defined in section 2(a)(24) of the Investment Company Act of 1940 (15 U.S.C. 80a-2(a)(24)), or a predecessor, and is acquired by the private fund in exchange for an equity security described in paragraph (c)(3)(i) or (c)(3)(ii) of this section.

(4) Qualifying portfolio company means any company that:

(i) At the time of any investment by the private fund, is not reporting or foreign traded and does not control, is not controlled by or under common control with another company, directly or indirectly, that is reporting or foreign traded;

(ii) Does not borrow or issue debt obligations in connection with the private fund's investment in such company and distribute to the private fund the proceeds of such borrowing or issuance in exchange for the private fund's investment; and

(iii) Is not an investment company, a private fund, an issuer that would be an investment company but for the exemption provided by § 270.3a-7 of this chapter, or a commodity pool.

(5) Reporting or foreign traded means, with respect to a company, being subject to the reporting requirements under section 13 or 15(d) of the Securities Exchange Act of 1934 (15 U.S.C. 78m or 78o(d)), or having a security listed or traded on any exchange or organized market operating in a foreign jurisdiction.

(6) Short-term holdings means cash and cash equivalents, as defined in § 270.2a51-1(b)(7)(i) of this chapter, U.S. Treasuries with a remaining maturity of 60 days or less, and shares of an open-end management investment company registered under section 8 of the Investment Company Act of 1940 (15 U.S.C. 80a-8) that is regulated as a money market fund under § 270.2a-7 of this chapter.

Note: For purposes of this section, an investment adviser may treat as a private fund any issuer formed under the laws of a jurisdiction other than the United States that has not offered or sold its securities in the United States or to U.S. persons in a manner inconsistent with being a private fund, provided that the adviser treats the issuer as a private fund under the Act (15 U.S.C. 80b) and the rules there under for all purposes.

Rule 203(m)-1. Private Fund Adviser Exemption.

(a) United States Investment Advisers. For purposes of section 203(m) of the Act(15 U.S.C. 80b-3(m)), an investment adviser with its principal office and place of business in the United States is exempt from the requirement to register under section203 of the Act if the investment adviser:

(1) Acts solely as an investment adviser to one or more qualifying private funds; and

(2) Manages private fund assets of less than $150 million.

(b) Non-United States Investment Advisers. For purposes of section 203(m) of the Act (15 U.S.C. 80b-3(m)), an investment adviser with its principal office and place of business outside of the United States is exempt from the requirement to register under section 203 of the Act if:

(1) The investment adviser has no client that is a United States person except for one or more qualifying private funds; and

(2) All assets managed by the investment adviser at a place of business in the United States are solely attributable to private fund assets, the total value of which is less than$150 million.

(c) Frequency of Calculations. For purposes of this section, calculate private fund assets annually, in accordance with General Instruction 15 to Form ADV (§ 279.1 of this chapter).

(d) Definitions. For purposes of this section:

(1) *Assets under management* means the regulatory assets under management as determined under Item 5.F of Form ADV (§ 279.1 of this chapter), except the following shall be excluded from the definition of assets under management for purposes of this section:

(i) The regulatory assets under management attributable to a private fund that is an entity described in subparagraph (A), (B), or (C) of section 203(b)(7) of the Act (15 U.S.C. 80b-3(b)(7)) (other than an entity that has elected to be regulated or is regulated as a business development company pursuant to section 54 of the Investment Company Act of 1940 (15 U.S.C. 80a-53)); and

(ii) The regulatory assets under management attributable to a private fund that is an entity described in subparagraph (A) or (B) of section 203(b)(8) of the Act (15 U.S.C. 80b-3(b)(8)) (other than an entity that has elected to be regulated or is regulated as a business development company pursuant to section 54 of the Investment Company Act of 1940 (15 U.S.C. 80a-53).

(2) Place of business has the same meaning as in § 275.222-1(a).

(3) Principal office and place of business of an investment adviser means the executive office of the investment adviser from which the officers, partners, or managers of the investment adviser direct, control, and coordinate the activities of the investment adviser.

(4) Private fund assets means the investment adviser's assets under management attributable to a qualifying private fund.

(5) Qualifying private fund means any private fund that is not registered under section 8 of the Investment Company Act of 1940 (15 U.S.C. 80a-8) and has not elected to be treated as a business development company pursuant to section 54 of that Act (15U.S.C. 80a-53). For purposes of this section, an investment adviser may treat as a private fund an issuer that qualifies for an exclusion from the definition of an "investment company," as defined in section 3 of the Investment Company Act of 1940(15 U.S.C. 80a-3), in addition to those provided by section 3(c)(1) or 3(c)(7) of that Act(15 U.S.C. 80a-3(c)(1) or 15 U.S.C. 80a-3(c)(7)), provided that the investment adviser treats the issuer as a private fund under the Act (15 U.S.C. 80b) and the rules there under for all purposes.

(6) Related person has the same meaning as in § 275.206(4)-2(d)(7).

(7) United States has the same meaning as in § 230.902(l) of this chapter.(8) United States person means any person that is a U.S. person as defined in§ 230.902(k) of this chapter, except that any discretionary account or similar account that is held for the benefit of a United States person by a dealer or other professional fiduciary is a United States person if the dealer or professional fiduciary is a related person of the investment adviser relying on this section and is not organized, in corporated, or (if an individual) resident in the United States.

Rule 204-3. Delivery of Brochures and Brochure Supplements.

(a) *General Requirements.* If you are registered under the Act as an investment adviser, you must deliver a brochure and one or more brochure supplements to each client or prospective client that contains all information required by Part 2 of Form ADV [17 CFR 279.1].

(b) *Delivery Requirements.* Subject to paragraph (g), you (or a supervised person acting on your behalf) must:

(1) Deliver to a client or prospective client your current brochure before or at the time you enter into an investment advisory contract with that client.

(2) Deliver to each client, annually within 120 days after the end of your fiscal year and without charge, if there are material changes in your brochure since your last annual updating amendment:

(i) A current brochure, or

(ii) The summary of material changes to the brochure as required by Item 2 of Form ADV, Part 2A that offers to provide your current brochure without charge, accompanied by the Web site address (if available) and an e-mail address (if available) and telephone number by which a client may obtain the current brochure from you, and the Web site address for obtaining information about you through the Investment Adviser Public Disclosure (IAPD) system.

(3) Deliver to each client or prospective client a current brochure supplement for a supervised person before or at the time that supervised person begins to provide advisory services to the client; provided, however, that if investment advice for a client is provided by a team comprised of more than five supervised persons, a current brochure supplement need only be delivered to that client for the five supervised persons with the most significant responsibility for the day-to-day advice provided to that client. For purposes of this section, a supervised person will provide advisory services to a client if that supervised person will:

(i) Formulate investment advice for the client and have direct client contact; or

(ii) Make discretionary investment decisions for the client, even if the supervised person will have no direct client contact.

(4) Deliver the following to each client promptly after you create an amended brochure or brochure supplement, as applicable, if the amendment adds disclosure of an event, or materially revises information already disclosed about an event, in response to Item 9 of Part 2A of Form ADV or Item 3 of Part 2B of Form ADV (Disciplinary Information), respectively, (i) the amended brochure or brochure supplement, as applicable, along with a statement describing the material facts relating to the change in disciplinary information, or (ii) a statement describing the material facts relating to the change in disciplinary information.

(c) *Exceptions to Delivery Requirement.*

(1) You are not required to deliver a brochure to a client:

(i) That is an investment company registered under the Investment Company Act of 1940 [15 U.S.C. 80a-1 to 80a-64] or a business development company as defined in that Act, provided that the advisory contract with that client meets the requirements of section 15(c) of that Act [15 U.S.C. 80a-15(c)]; or

(ii) Who receives only impersonal investment advice for which you charge less than $500 per year.

(2) You are not required to deliver a brochure supplement to a client:

(i) To whom you are not required to deliver a brochure under subparagraph (c)(1) of this section;

(ii) Who receives only impersonal investment advice; or

(iii) Who is an officer, employee, or other person related to the adviser that would be a "qualified client" of your firm under § 275.205-3(d)(1)(iii).

(d) *Wrap Fee Program Brochures.*

(1) If you are a sponsor of a wrap fee program, then the brochure that paragraph (b) of this section requires you to deliver to a client or prospective client of the wrap fee program

must be a wrap fee program brochure containing all the information required by Part 2A, Appendix 1 of Form ADV. Any additional information in a wrap fee program brochure must be limited to information applicable to wrap fee programs that you sponsor.

(2) You do not have to deliver a wrap fee program brochure if another sponsor of the wrap fee program delivers, to the client or prospective client of the wrap fee program, a wrap fee program brochure containing all the information required by Part 2A, Appendix 1 of Form ADV.

Note to Paragraph (d): A wrap fee program brochure does not take the place of any brochure supplements that you are required to deliver under paragraph (b) of this section.

(e) *Multiple Brochures.* If you provide substantially different advisory services to different clients, you may provide them with different brochures, so long as each client receives all information about the services and fees that are applicable to that client. The brochure you deliver to a client may omit any information required by Part 2A of Form ADV if the information does not apply to the advisory services or fees that you will provide or charge, or that you propose to provide or charge, to that client.

(f) *Other Disclosure Obligations.* Delivering a brochure or brochure supplement in compliance with this section does not relieve you of any other disclosure obligations you have to your advisory clients or prospective clients under any federal or state laws or regulations.

(g) *Definitions.* For purposes of this section:

(1) Impersonal investment advice means investment advisory services that do not purport to meet the objectives or needs of specific individuals or accounts.

(2) Current brochure and current brochure supplement mean the most recent revision of the brochure or brochure supplement, including all amendments to date.

(3) Sponsor of a wrap fee program means an investment adviser that is compensated under a wrap fee program for sponsoring, organizing, or administering the program, or for selecting, or providing advice to clients regarding the selection of, other investment advisers in the program.

(4) Supervised person means any of your officers, partners or directors (or other persons occupying a similar status or performing similar functions) or employees, or any other person who provides investment advice on your behalf.

(5) Wrap fee program means an advisory program under which a specified fee or fees not based directly upon transactions in a client's account is charged for investment advisory services (which may include portfolio management or advice concerning the selection of other investment advisers) and the execution of client transactions.

Rule 205-3. Exemption from the Compensation Prohibition of Section 205(a)(1) for Investment Advisers

(a) *General.* The provisions of section 205(a)(1) of the Act (15 U.S.C. 80b-5(a)(1)) will not be deemed to prohibit an investment adviser from entering into, performing, renewing or extending an investment advisory contract that provides for compensation to the investment adviser on the basis of a share of the capital gains upon, or the capital appreciation of, the funds, or any portion of the funds, of a client, *Provided,* That the client entering into the contract subject to this section is a qualified client, as defined in paragraph (d)(1) of this section.

(b) *Identification of the client.* In the case of a private investment company, as defined in paragraph (d)(3) of this section, an investment company registered under the Investment Company Act of 1940, or a business development company, as defined in section 202(a)(22) of the Act (15 U.S.C. 80b-2(a)(22)), each equity owner of any such company (except for the investment adviser entering into the contract and any other equity owners not charged a fee on the basis of a share of capital gains or capital appreciation) will be considered a client for purposes of paragraph (a) of this section.

(c) Transition Rules.—

(1) Registered Investment Advisers. If a registered investment adviser entered into a contract and satisfied the conditions of this section that were in effect when the contract was entered into, the adviser will be considered to satisfy the conditions of this section; Provided, however, that if a natural person or company who was not a party to the contract becomes a party (including an equity owner of a private investment company advised by the adviser), the conditions of this section in effect at that time will apply with regard to that person or company.

(2) Registered Investment Advisers that were Previously Not Registered. If an investment adviser was not required to register with the Commission pursuant to section 203 of the Act (15 U.S.C. 80b-3) and was not registered, section 205(a)(1) of the Act will not apply to an advisory contract entered into when the adviser was not required to register and was not registered, or to an account of an equity owner of a private investment company advised by the adviser if the account was established when the adviser was not required to register and was not registered; Provided, however, that section 205(a)(1) of the Act will apply with regard to a natural person or company who was not a party to the contract and becomes a party (including an equity owner of a private investment company advised by the adviser) when the adviser is required to register.

(3) Certain Transfers of Interests. Solely for purposes of paragraphs (c)(1) and (c)(2) of this section, a transfer of an equity ownership interest in a private investment company by gift or bequest, or pursuant to an agreement related to a legal separation or divorce, will not cause the transferee to "become a party" to the contract and will not cause section 205(a)(1) of the Act to apply to such transferee.

(d) *Definitions.* For the purposes of this section:

(1) The term "qualified client" means:

(i) A natural person who, or a company that, immediately after entering into the contract has at least $1,000,000 under the management of the investment adviser;

(ii) A natural person who, or a company that, the investment adviser entering into the contract (and any person acting on his behalf) reasonably believes, immediately prior to entering into the contract, either:

(A) Has a net worth (together, in the case of a natural person, with assets held jointly with a spouse) of more than $2,000,000. For purposes of calculating a natural person's net worth:

(1) The person's primary residence must not be included as an asset;

(2) Indebtedness secured by the person's primary residence, up to the estimated fair market value of the primary residence at the time the investment advisory contract is entered into may not be included as a liability (except that if the amount of such indebtedness outstanding at the time of calculation exceeds the amount outstanding 60 days before such time, other than as a result of the acquisition of the primary residence, the amount of such excess must be included as a liability); and

(3) Indebtedness that is secured by the person's primary residence in excess of the estimated fair market value of the residence must be included as a liability; or

(B) Is a qualified purchaser as defined in section 2(a)(51)(A) of the Investment Company Act of 1940 (15 U.S.C. 80a-2(a)(51)(A)) at the time the contract is entered into; or

(iii) A natural person who immediately prior to entering into the contract is:

(A) An executive officer, director, trustee, general partner, or person serving in a similar capacity, of the investment adviser; or

(B) An employee of the investment adviser (other than an employee performing solely clerical, secretarial or administrative functions with regard to the investment adviser) who, in connection with his or her regular functions or duties, participates in the investment activities of such investment adviser, provided that such employee has been performing such functions and duties for or on behalf of the investment adviser, or substantially similar functions or duties for or on behalf of another company for at least 12 months.

(2) The term "company" has the same meaning as in section 202(a)(5) of the Act (15 U.S.C. 80b-2(a)(5)), but does not include a company that is required to be registered under the Investment Company Act of 1940 but is not registered.

(3) The term "private investment company" means a company that would be defined as an investment company under section 3(a) of the Investment Company Act of 1940 (15 U.S.C. 80a-3(a)) but for the exception provided from that definition by section 3(c)(1) of such Act (15 U.S.C. 80a-3(c)(1)).

(4) The term "executive officer" means the president, any vice president in charge of a principal business unit, division or function (such as sales, administration or finance), any other officer who performs a policy-making function, or any other person who performs similar policy-making functions, for the investment adviser.

(e) Inflation Adjustments. Pursuant to section 205(e) of the Act, the dollar amounts specified in paragraphs (d)(1)(i) and (d)(1)(ii)(A) of this section shall be adjusted by order of the Commission, on or about May 1, 2016 and issued approximately every five years thereafter. The adjusted dollar amounts established in such orders shall be computed by:

(1) Dividing the year-end value of the Personal Consumption Expenditures Chain-Type Price Index (or any successor index thereto), as published by the United States Department of Commerce, for the calendar year preceding the calendar year in which the order is being issued, by the year-end value of such index (or successor) for the calendar year 1997;

(2) For the dollar amount in paragraph (d)(1)(i) of this section, multiplying $750,000 times the quotient obtained in paragraph (e)(1) of this section and rounding the product to the nearest multiple of $100,000; and

(3) For the dollar amount in paragraph (d)(1)(ii)(A) of this section, multiplying $1,500,000 times the quotient obtained in paragraph (e)(1) of this section and rounding the product to the nearest multiple of $100,000.

Rule 206(4)-1. Advertisements by Investment Advisers

(a) It shall constitute a fraudulent, deceptive, or manipulative act, practice, or course of business within the meaning of section 206(4) of the Act [15 U.S.C. 80b-6(4)] for any investment adviser registered or required to be registered under section 203 of the Act [15 U.S.C. 80b-3], directly or indirectly, to publish, circulate, or distribute any advertisement:

(1) Which refers, directly or indirectly, to any testimonial of any kind concerning the investment adviser or concerning any advice, analysis, report or other service rendered by such investment adviser; or

(2) Which refers, directly or indirectly, to past specific recommendations of such investment adviser which were or would have been profitable to any person; *provided, however,* that this shall not prohibit an advertisement which sets out or offers to furnish a list of all recommendations made by such investment adviser within the immediately preceding period of not less than one year if such advertisement, and such list if it is furnished separately: (A) state the name of each such security recommended, the date and nature of each such recommendation (e.g., whether to buy, sell or hold), the market price at that time, the price at which the recommendation was to be acted upon, and the market price of each such security as of the most recent practicable date, and (B) contain the following cautionary legend on the first page thereof in print or type as large as the largest print or type used in the body or text thereof: "it should not be assumed that recommendations made in the future will be profitable or will equal the performance of the securities in this list"; or

(3) Which represents, directly or indirectly, that any graph, chart, formula or other device being offered can in and of itself be used to determine which securities to buy or sell, or when to buy or sell them; or which represents, directly or indirectly, that any graph, chart, formula or other device being offered will assist any person in making his own decisions as to which securities to buy or sell, or when to buy or sell them, without prominently disclos-

ing in such advertisement the limitations thereof and the difficulties with respect to its use; or

(4) which contains any statement to the effect that any report, analysis, or other service will be furnished free or without charge, unless such report, analysis or other service actually is or will be furnished entirely free and without any condition or obligation, directly or indirectly; or

(5) which contains any untrue statement of a material fact, or which is otherwise false or misleading.

(b) For the purposes of this rule the term "advertisement" shall include any notice, circular, letter or other written communication addressed to more than one person, or any notice or other announcement in any publication or by radio or television, which offers (1) any analysis, report, or publication concerning securities, or which is to be used in making any determination as to when to buy or sell any security, or which security to buy or sell, or (2) any graph, chart, formula or other device to be used in making any determination as to when to buy or sell any security, or which security to buy or sell, or (3) any other investment advisory service with regard to securities.

Rule 206(4)-4. Financial and Disciplinary Information that Investment Advisers Must Disclose to Clients

[Removed and Reserved. SEC Release No. IA-3060; July 28, 2010. Effective: October 12, 2010.]

Rule 206(4)-5. Political Contributions By Certain Investment Advisers

(a) *Prohibitions.* As a means reasonably designed to prevent fraudulent, deceptive or manipulative acts, practices, or courses of business within the meaning of section 206(4) of the Act (15 U.S.C. 80b-6(4)), it shall be unlawful:

(1) For any investment adviser registered (or required to be registered) with the Commission, or unregistered in reliance on the exemption available under section 203(b)(3) of the Advisers Act (15 U.S.C. 80b-3(b)(3)), or that is an exempt reporting adviser, as defined in section 275.204-4(a), to provide investment advisory services for compensation to a government entity within two years after a contribution to an official of the government entity is made by the investment adviser or any covered associate of the investment adviser (including a person who becomes a covered associate within two years after the contribution is made); and

(2) For any investment adviser registered (or required to be registered) with the Commission, or unregistered in reliance on the exemption available under section 203(b)(3) of the Advisers Act (15 U.S.C. 80b-3(b)(3)), or that is an exempt reporting adviser, or any of the investment adviser's covered associates:

(i) To provide or agree to provide, directly or indirectly, payment to any person to solicit a government entity for investment advisory services on behalf of such investment adviser unless such person is:

(A) A regulated person; or

(B) An executive officer, general partner, managing member (or, in each case, a person with a similar status or function), or employee of the investment adviser; and

(ii) To coordinate, or to solicit any person or political action committee to make, any:

(A) Contribution to an official of a government entity to which the investment adviser is providing or seeking to provide investment advisory services; or

(B) Payment to a political party of a State or locality where the investment adviser is providing or seeking to provide investment advisory services to a government entity.

(b) *Exceptions.*

(1) *De Minimis Exception.* Paragraph (a)(1) of this section does not apply to contributions made by a covered associate, if a natural person, to officials for whom the covered associate was entitled to vote at the time of the contributions and which in the aggregate do not exceed $350 to any one official, per election, or to officials for whom the covered associate was not entitled to vote at the time of the contributions and which in the aggregate do not exceed $150 to any one official, per election.

(2) *Exception For Certain New Covered Associates.* The prohibitions of paragraph (a)(1) of this section shall not apply to an investment adviser as a result of a contribution made by a natural person more than six months prior to becoming a covered associate of the investment adviser unless such person, after becoming a covered associate, solicits clients on behalf of the investment adviser.

(3) *Exception For Certain Returned Contributions.*

(i) An investment adviser that is prohibited from providing investment advisory services for compensation pursuant to paragraph (a)(1) of this section as a result of a contribution made by a covered associate of the investment adviser is excepted from such prohibition, subject to paragraphs (b)(3)(ii) and (b)(3)(iii) of this section, upon satisfaction of the following requirements:

(A) The investment adviser must have discovered the contribution which resulted in the prohibition within four months of the date of such contribution;

(B) Such contribution must not have exceeded $350; and

(C) The contributor must obtain a return of the contribution within 60 calendar days of the date of discovery of such contribution by the investment adviser.

(ii) In any calendar year, an investment adviser that has reported on its annual updating amendment to Form ADV (17 CFR 279.1) that it has more than 50 employees is entitled to no more than three exceptions pursuant to paragraph (b)(3)(i) of this section, and an investment adviser that has reported on its annual updating amendment to Form ADV that it has 50 or fewer employees is entitled to no more than two exceptions pursuant to paragraph (b)(3)(i) of this section.

(iii) An investment adviser may not rely on the exception provided in paragraph (b)(3)(i) of this section more than once with respect to contributions by the same covered associate of the investment adviser regardless of the time period. (c) Prohibitions as Applied to Covered Investment Pools. For purposes of this section, an investment adviser to a covered investment pool in which a government entity invests or is solicited to invest shall be treated as though that investment adviser were providing or seeking to provide investment advisory services directly to the government entity.

(d) *Further Prohibition.* As a means reasonably designed to prevent fraudulent, deceptive or manipulative acts, practices, or courses of business within the meaning of section 206(4) of Advisers Act (15 U.S.C. 80b-6(4)), it shall be unlawful for any investment adviser registered (or required to be registered) with the Commission, or unregistered in reliance on the exemption available under section 203(b)(3) of the Advisers Act (15 U.S.C. 80b-3(b)(3)), or that is an exempt reporting adviser, or any of the investment adviser's covered associates to do anything indirectly which, if done directly, would result in a violation of this section.

(e) *Exemptions.* The Commission, upon application, may conditionally or unconditionally exempt an investment adviser from the prohibition under paragraph (a)(1) of this section. In determining whether to grant an exemption, the Commission will consider, among other factors:

(1) Whether the exemption is necessary or appropriate in the public interest and consistent with the protection of investors and the purposes fairly intended by the policy and provisions of the Advisers Act (15 U.S.C. 80b);

(2) Whether the investment adviser:

(i) Before the contribution resulting in the prohibition was made, adopted and implemented policies and procedures reasonably designed to prevent violations of this section; and

(ii) Prior to or at the time the contribution which resulted in such prohibition was made, had no actual knowledge of the contribution; and

(iii) After learning of the contribution:

(A) Has taken all available steps to cause the contributor involved in making the contribution which resulted in such prohibition to obtain a return of the contribution; and

(B) Has taken such other remedial or preventive measures as may be appropriate under the circumstances;

(3) Whether, at the time of the contribution, the contributor was a covered associate or otherwise an employee of the investment adviser, or was seeking such employment;

(4) The timing and amount of the contribution which resulted in the prohibition;

(5) The nature of the election (e.g., Federal, State or local); and

(6) The contributor's apparent intent or motive in making the contribution which resulted in the prohibition, as evidenced by the facts and circumstances surrounding such contribution.

(f) *Definitions.* For purposes of this section:

(1) *Contribution* means any gift, subscription, loan, advance, or deposit of money or anything of value made for:

(i) The purpose of influencing any election for Federal, State or local office;

(ii) Payment of debt incurred in connection with any such election; or

(iii) Transition or inaugural expenses of the successful candidate for State or local office.

(2) *Covered associate of an investment adviser* means:

(i) Any general partner, managing member or executive officer, or other individual with a similar status or function;

(ii) Any employee who solicits a government entity for the investment adviser and any person who supervises, directly or indirectly, such employee; and

(iii) Any political action committee controlled by the investment adviser or by any person described in paragraphs (f)(2)(i) and (f)(2)(ii) of this section.

(3) *Covered investment pool* means:

(i) An investment company registered under the Investment Company Act of 1940 (15 U.S.C. 80a) that is an investment option of a plan or program of a government entity; or

(ii) Any company that would be an investment company under section 3(a) of the Investment Company Act of 1940 (15 U.S.C. 80a-3(a)), but for the exclusion provided from that definition by either section 3(c)(1), section 3(c)(7) or section 3(c)(11) of that Act (15 U.S.C. 80a-3(c)(1), (c)(7) or (c)(11)).

(4) Executive officer of an investment adviser means:

(i) The president;

(ii) Any vice president in charge of a principal business unit, division or function (such as sales, administration or finance);

(iii) Any other officer of the investment adviser who performs a policy-making function; or

(iv) Any other person who performs similar policy-making functions for the investment adviser.

(5) *Government entity* means any State or political subdivision of a State, including:

(i) Any agency, authority, or instrumentality of the State or political subdivision;

(ii) A pool of assets sponsored or established by the State or political subdivision or any agency, authority or instrumentality thereof, including, but not limited to a "defined benefit plan" as defined in section 414(j) of the Internal Revenue Code (26 U.S.C. 414(j)), or a State general fund;

(iii) A plan or program of a government entity; and

(iv) Officers, agents, or employees of the State or political subdivision or any agency, authority or instrumentality thereof, acting in their official capacity.

(6) *Official* means any person (including any election committee for the person) who was, at the time of the contribution, an incumbent, candidate or successful candidate for elective office of a government entity, if the office:

(i) Is directly or indirectly responsible for, or can influence the outcome of, the hiring of an investment adviser by a government entity; or

(ii) Has authority to appoint any person who is directly or indirectly responsible for, or can influence the outcome of, the hiring of an investment adviser by a government entity.

(7) *Payment* means any gift, subscription, loan, advance, or deposit of money or anything of value.

(8) *Plan or program of a government entity* means any participant-directed investment program or plan sponsored or established by a State or political subdivision or any agency, authority or instrumentality thereof, including, but not limited to, a "qualified tuition plan" authorized by section 529 of the Internal Revenue Code (26 U.S.C. 529), a retirement plan authorized by section 403(b) or 457 of the Internal Revenue Code (26 U.S.C. 403(b) or 457), or any similar program or plan.

(9) *Regulated person* means:

(i) An investment adviser registered with the Commission that has not, and whose covered associates have not, within two years of soliciting a government entity:

(A) Made a contribution to an official of that government entity, other than as described in paragraph (b)(1) of this section; and

(B) Coordinated or solicited any person or political action committee to make any contribution or payment described in paragraphs (a)(2)(ii)(A) and (B) of this section; or

(ii) A "broker," as defined in section 3(a)(4) of the Securities Exchange Act of 1934 (15 U.S.C. 78c(a)(4)) or a "dealer," as defined in section 3(a)(5) of that Act (15 U.S.C. 78c(a)(5)), that is registered with the Commission, and is a member of a national securities association registered under section 15A of that Act (15 U.S.C. 78o-3), provided that:

(A) The rules of the association prohibit members from engaging in distribution or solicitation activities if certain political contributions have been made; and

(B) The Commission, by order, finds that such rules impose substantially equivalent or more stringent restrictions on broker-dealers than this section imposes on investment advisers and that such rules are consistent with the objectives of this section.

(10) *Solicit* means:

(i) With respect to investment advisory services, to communicate, directly or indirectly, for the purpose of obtaining or retaining a client for, or referring a client to, an investment adviser; and

(ii) With respect to a contribution or payment, to communicate, directly or indirectly, for the purpose of obtaining or arranging a contribution or payment.

Rule 206(4)-6. Proxy Voting

If you are an investment adviser registered or required to be registered under section 203 of the Act (15 U.S.C. 80b-3), it is a fraudulent, deceptive, or manipulative act, practice or course of business within the meaning of section 206(4) of the Act (15 U.S.C. 80b-6(4)), for you to exercise voting authority with respect to client securities, unless you:

(a) Adopt and implement written policies and procedures that are reasonably designed to ensure that you vote client securities in the best interest of clients, which procedures must include how you address material conflicts that may arise between your interests and those of your clients;

(b) Disclose to clients how they may obtain information from you about how you voted with respect to their securities; and

(c) Describe to clients your proxy voting policies and procedures and, upon request, furnish a copy of the policies and procedures to the requesting client.

Rule 206(4)-7. Compliance procedures and practices

If you are an investment adviser registered or required to be registered under section 203 of the Investment Advisers Act of 1940 (15 U.S.C. 80b-3), it shall be unlawful within the meaning of section 206 of the Act (15 U.S.C. 80b-6) for you to provide investment advice to clients unless you:

(a) *Policies and procedures.* Adopt and implement written policies and procedures reasonably designed to prevent violation, by you and your supervised persons, of the Act and the rules that the Commission has adopted under the Act;

(b) *Annual review.* Review, no less frequently than annually, the adequacy of the policies and procedures established pursuant to this section and the effectiveness of their implementation; and

(c) *Chief compliance officer.* Designate an individual (who is a supervised person) responsible for administering the policies and procedures that you adopt under paragraph (a) of this section.

Rule 206(4)-8. Pooled Investment Vehicles

(a) *Prohibition.* It shall constitute a fraudulent, deceptive, or manipulative act, practice, or course of business within the meaning of section 206(4) of the Act (15 U.S.C. 80b6(4)) for any investment adviser to a pooled investment vehicle to:

(1) Make any untrue statement of a material fact or to omit to state a material fact necessary to make the statements made, in the light of the circumstances under which they were made, not misleading, to any investor or prospective investor in the pooled investment vehicle; or

(2) Otherwise engage in any act, practice, or course of business that is fraudulent, deceptive, or manipulative with respect to any investor or prospective investor in the pooled investment vehicle.

(b) *Definition.* For purposes of this section "pooled investment vehicle" means any investment company as defined in section 3(a) of the Investment Company Act of 1940 (15 U.S.C. 80a-3(a)) or any company that would be an investment company under section 3(a) of that Act but for the exclusion provided from that definition by either section 3(c)(1) or section 3(c)(7) of that Act (15 U.S.C. 80a-3(c)(1) or (7)).

INVESTMENT COMPANY ACT OF 1940—SELECTED PROVISIONS

15 U.S.C. §§ 80a-1 et seq.

N.B. The following is not a complete text of the Investment Company Act of 1940. It omits a number of statutory provisions entirely, and also omits certain subsections of provisions that are partially included.

Act	15 U.S.C. Section	Subject
1	80a-1	Findings and declaration of policy
2(a)	80a-2	General definitions
		(3) Affiliated person
		(9) Control
		(19) Interested person
		(35) Sales load
		(36) Security
		(53) Credit Rating Agency
3	80a-3	Definition of investment company
8	80a-8	Registration of investment companies
9	80a-9	Ineligibility of certain affiliated persons and underwriters
10	80a-10	Affiliations or interest of Directors, Officers, and Employees
12	80a-12	Functions and activities of investment companies
13	80a-13	Changes in investment policy
15	80a-15	Investment advisory and underwriting contracts
17	80a-17	Transactions of certain affiliated persons and underwriters
18	80a-18	Capital structure
22	80a-22	Distribution, redemption, and repurchase of redeemable securities
36	80a-35	Breach of fiduciary duty
42	80a-41	Enforcement of title

Sec. 1. FINDINGS AND DECLARATION OF POLICY

(a) Upon the basis of facts disclosed by the record and reports of the Securities and Exchange Commission made pursuant to section 30 of the Public Utility Holding Company Act of 1935, and facts otherwise disclosed and ascertained, it is hereby found that investment companies are affected with a national public interest in that, among other things—

(1) the securities issued by such companies, which constitute a substantial part of all securities publicly offered, are distributed, purchased, paid for, exchanged, transferred, redeemed, and repurchased by use of the mails and means and instrumentalities of interstate commerce, and in the case of the numerous companies which issue redeemable securities this process of distribution and redemption is continuous;

(2) the principal activities of such companies—investing, reinvesting, and trading in securities—are conducted by use of the mails and means and instrumentalities of interstate commerce, including the facilities of national securities exchanges, and constitute a substantial part of all transactions effected in the securities markets of the Nation;

(3) such companies customarily invest and trade in securities issued by, and may dominate and control or otherwise affect the policies and management of, companies engaged in business in interstate commerce;

(4) such companies are media for the investment in the national economy of a substantial part of the national savings and may have a vital effect upon the flow of such savings into the capital markets; and

(5) the activities of such companies, extending over many States, their use of the instrumentalities of interstate commerce and the wide geographic distribution of their security holders, make difficult, if not impossible, effective State regulation of such companies in the interest of investors.

(b) Upon the basis of facts disclosed by the record and reports of the Securities and Exchange Commission made pursuant to section 30 of the Public Utility Holding Company Act of 1935, and facts otherwise disclosed and ascertained, it is hereby declared that the national public interest and the interest of investors are adversely affected—

(1) when investors purchase, pay for, exchange, receive dividends upon, vote, refrain from voting, sell, or surrender securities issued by investment companies without adequate, accurate, and explicit information, fairly presented, concerning the character of such securities and the circumstances, policies, and financial responsibility of such companies and their management;

(2) when investment companies are organized, operated, managed, or their portfolio securities are selected, in the interest of directors, officers, investment advisers, depositors, or other affiliated persons thereof, in the interest of underwriters, brokers, or dealers, in the interest of special classes of their security holders, or in the interest of other investment companies or persons engaged in other lines of business, rather than in the interest of all classes of such companies' security holders;

(3) when investment companies issue securities containing inequitable or discriminatory provisions, or fail to protect the preferences and privileges of the holders of their outstanding securities;

(4) when the control of investment companies is unduly concentrated through pyramiding or inequitable methods of control, or is inequitably distributed, or when investment companies are managed by irresponsible persons;

(5) when investment companies, in keeping their accounts, in maintaining reserves, and in computing their earnings and the asset value of their outstanding securities, employ unsound or misleading methods, or are not subjected to adequate independent scrutiny;

(6) when investment companies are reorganized, become inactive, or change the character of their business, or when the control or management thereof is transferred, without the consent of their security holders;

(7) when investment companies by excessive borrowing and the issuance of excessive amounts of senior securities increase unduly the speculative character of their junior securities; or

(8) when investment companies operate without adequate assets or reserves.

It is hereby declared that the policy and purposes of this title, in accordance with which the provisions of this title shall be interpreted, are to mitigate and, so far as is feasible, to eliminate the conditions enumerated in this section which adversely affect the national public interest and the interest of investors.

Sec. 2. GENERAL DEFINITIONS

(a) When used in this title, unless the context otherwise requires—

(3) [Affiliated Person]

"Affiliated person" of another person means (A) any person directly or indirectly owning, controlling, or holding with power to vote, 5 per centum or more of the outstanding voting securities of such other person; (B) any person 5 per centum or more of whose outstanding voting securities are directly or indirectly owned, controlled, or held with power to vote, by such other person; (C) any person directly or indirectly controlling, controlled by, or under common control with, such other person; (D) any officer, director, partner, copartner, or employee of such other person; (E) if such other person is an investment company, any investment adviser thereof or any member of an advisory board thereof; and (F) if such other person is an unincorporated investment company not having a board of directors, the depositor thereof.

(9) Control

"Control" means the power to exercise a controlling influence over the management or policies of a company, unless such power is solely the result of an official position with such company.

Any person who owns beneficially, either directly or through one or more controlled companies, more than 25 per centum of the voting securities of a company shall be presumed to control such company. Any person who does not so own more than 25 per centum of the voting securities of any company shall be presumed not to control such company. A natural person shall be presumed not to be a controlled person within the meaning of this title. Any such presumption may be rebutted by evidence, but except as hereinafter provided, shall continue until a determination to the contrary made by the Commission by order either on its own motion or on application by an interested person. If an application filed hereunder is not granted or denied by the Commission within sixty days after filing thereof, the determination sought by the application shall be deemed to have been temporarily granted pending final determination of the Commission thereon. The Commission, upon its own motion or upon application, may by order revoke or modify any order issued under this paragraph whenever it shall find that the determination embraced in such original order is no longer consistent with the facts.

(19) [Interested Person]

"Interested person" of another person means—

(A) when used with respect to an investment company—

(i) any affiliated person of such company,

(ii) any member of the immediate family of any natural person who is an affiliated person of such company,

(iii) any interested person of any investment adviser of or principal underwriter for such company,

(iv) any person or partner or employee of any person who at any time since the beginning of the last two completed fiscal years of such company has acted as legal counsel for such company,

(v) any person or any affiliated person of a person (other than a registered investment company) that, at any time during the 6-month period preceding the date of the determination of whether that person or affiliated person is an interested person, has executed any portfolio transactions for, engaged in any principal transactions with, or distributed shares for—

(I) the investment company;

(II) any other investment company having the same investment adviser as such investment company or holding itself out to investors as a related company for purposes of investment or investor services; or

(III) any account over which the investment company's investment adviser has brokerage placement discretion,

(vi) any person or any affiliated person of a person (other than a registered investment company) that, at any time during the 6-month period preceding the date of the determination of whether that person or affiliated person is an interested person, has loaned money or other property to—

(I) the investment company;

(II) any other investment company having the same investment adviser as such investment company or holding itself out to investors as a related company for purposes of investment or investor services; or

(III) any account for which the investment company's investment adviser has borrowing authority, and

(vii) any natural person whom the Commission by order shall have determined to be an interested person by reason of having had, at any time since the beginning of the last two completed fiscal years of such company, a material business or professional relationship with such company or with the principal executive officer of such company or with any other investment company having the same investment adviser or principal underwriter or with the principal executive officer of such other investment company:

Provided, That no person shall be deemed to be an interested person of an investment company solely by reason of (aa) his being a member of its board of directors or advisory board or an owner of its securities, or (bb) his membership in the immediate family of any person specified in clause (aa) of this proviso; and

(B) when used with respect to an investment adviser of or principal underwriter for any investment company—

(i) any affiliated person of such investment adviser or principal underwriter,

(ii) any member of the immediate family of any natural person who is an affiliated person of such investment adviser or principal underwriter,

(iii) any person who knowingly has any direct or indirect beneficial interest in, or who is designated as trustee, executor, or guardian of any legal interest in, any security issued either by such investment adviser or principal underwriter or by a controlling person of such investment adviser or principal underwriter,

(iv) any person or partner or employee of any person who at any time since the beginning of the last two completed fiscal years of such investment company has acted as legal counsel for such investment adviser or principal underwriter,

(v) any person or any affiliated person of a person (other than a registered investment company) that, at any time during the 6-month period preceding the date of the determination of whether that person or affiliated person is an interested person, has executed any portfolio transactions for, engaged in any principal transactions with, or distributed shares for—

(I) any investment company for which the investment adviser or principal underwriter serves as such;

(II) any investment company holding itself out to investors, for purposes of investment or investor services, as a company related to any investment company for which the investment adviser or principal underwriter serves as such; or

(III) any account over which the investment adviser has brokerage placement discretion,

(vi) any person or any affiliated person of a person (other than a registered investment company) that, at any time during the 6-month period preceding the date of the determination of whether that person or affiliated person is an interested person, has loaned money or other property to—

(I) any investment company for which the investment adviser or principal underwriter serves as such;

(II) any investment company holding itself out to investors, for purposes of investment or investor services, as a company related to any investment company for which the investment adviser or principal underwriter serves as such; or

(III) any account for which the investment adviser has borrowing authority, and

(vii) any natural person whom the Commission by order shall have determined to be an interested person by reason of having had at any time since the beginning of the last two completed fiscal years of such investment company a material business or professional relationship with such investment adviser or principal underwriter or with the principal executive officer or any controlling person of such investment adviser or principal underwriter.

For the purposes of this paragraph (19), "member of the immediate family" means any parent, spouse of a parent, child, spouse of a child, spouse, brother or sister, and includes step and adoptive relationships. The Commission may modify or revoke any order issued under clause (vi) of subparagraph (A) or (B) of this paragraph whenever it finds that such order is no longer consistent with the facts. No order issued pursuant to clause (vii) of subparagraph (A) or (B) of this paragraph shall become effective until at least sixty days after the entry thereof, and no such order shall affect the status of any person for the purposes of this title or for any other purpose for any period prior to the effective date of such order.

(35) [Sales Load]

"Sales load" means the difference between the price of a security to the public and that portion of the proceeds from its sale which is received and invested or held for investment by the issuer (or in the case of a unit investment trust, by the depositor or trustee), less any portion of such difference deducted for trustee's or custodian's fees, insurance premiums, issue taxes, or administrative expenses or fees which are not properly chargeable to sales or promotional activities. In the case of a periodic payment plan certificate, "sales load" includes the sales load on any investment company securities in which the payments made on such certificate are invested, as well as the sales load on the certificate itself.

(36) [Security]

"Security" means any note, stock, treasury stock, security future, bond, debenture, evidence of indebtedness, certificate of interest or participation in any profit-sharing agreement, collateral-trust certificate, preorganization certificate or subscription, transferable share, investment contract, voting-trust certificate, certificate of deposit for a security, fractional undivided interest in oil, gas, or other mineral rights, any put, call, straddle, option, or privilege on any security (including a certificate of deposit) or on any group or index of securities (including any interest therein or based on the value thereof), or any put, call, straddle, option, or privilege entered into on a national securities exchange relating to foreign currency, or, in general, any interest or instrument commonly known as a "security," or any certificate of interest or participation in, temporary or interim certificate for, receipt for, guarantee of, or warrant or right to subscribe to or purchase, any of the foregoing.

(53) [Credit Rating Agency]

The term "credit rating agency" has the same meaning as in section 3 of the Securities Exchange Act of 1934.

(54) [Commodity Pool, Commodity Pool Operator, Commodity Trading Advisor, Major Swap Participant, Swap, Swap Dealer, Swap Execution Facility]

The terms "commodity pool", "commodity pool operator", "commodity trading advisor", "major swap participant", "swap", "swap dealer", and "swap execution facility" have the same meanings as in section 1a of the Commodity Exchange Act (7 U.S.C. 1a).

Sec. 3. DEFINITION OF INVESTMENT COMPANY

(a) (1) When used in this title, "investment company" means any issuer which—

    (A) is or holds itself out as being engaged primarily, or proposes to engage primarily, in the business of investing, reinvesting, or trading in securities;

    (B) is engaged or proposes to engage in the business of issuing face-amount certificates of the installment type, or has been engaged in such business and has any such certificate outstanding; or

    (C) is engaged or proposes to engage in the business of investing, reinvesting, owning, holding, or trading in securities, and owns or proposes to acquire investment securities having a value exceeding 40 per centum of the value of such issuer's total assets (exclusive of Government securities and cash items) on an unconsolidated basis.

(2) As used in this section, "investment securities" includes all securities except (A) Government securities, (B) securities issued by employees' securities companies, and (C) securities issued by majority-owned subsidiaries of the owner which (i) are not investment companies, and (ii) are not relying on the exception from the definition of investment company in paragraph (1) or (7) of subsection (c).

(b) Notwithstanding paragraph (1)(C) of subsection (a), none of the following persons is an investment company within the meaning of this title:

(1) Any issuer primarily engaged, directly or through a wholly-owned subsidiary or subsidiaries, in a business or businesses other than that of investing, reinvesting, owning, holding, or trading in securities.

(2) Any issuer which the Commission, upon application by such issuer, finds and by order declares to be primarily engaged in a business or businesses other than that of investing, reinvesting, owning, holding, or trading in securities either directly or (A) through majority-owned subsidiaries or (B) through controlled companies conducting similar types of businesses. The filing of an application under this paragraph in good faith by an issuer other than a registered investment company shall exempt the applicant for a period of sixty days from all provisions of this title applicable to investment companies as such. For cause shown, the Commission by order may extend such period of exemption for an additional period or periods. Whenever the Commission, upon its own motion or upon application, finds that the circumstances which gave rise to the issuance of an order granting an application under this paragraph no longer exist, the Commission shall by order revoke such order.

(3) Any issuer all the outstanding securities of which (other than short-term paper and directors' qualifying shares) are directly or indirectly owned by a company excepted from the definition of investment company by paragraph (1) or (2) of this subsection.

(c) Notwithstanding subsection (a), none of the following persons is an investment company within the meaning of this title:

(1) Any issuer whose outstanding securities (other than short-term paper) are beneficially owned by not more than one hundred persons (or, in the case of a qualifying venture capital fund, 250 persons) and which is not making and does not presently propose to make a public offering of its securities. Such issuer shall be deemed to be an investment company for purposes of the limitations set forth in subparagraphs (A)(i) and (B)(i) of section 12(d)(1) governing the purchase or other acquisition by such issuer of any security issued by any registered investment company and the sale of any security issued by any registered open-end investment company to any such issuer. For the purposes of this paragraph:

(A) Beneficial ownership by a company shall be deemed to be beneficial ownership by one person, except that, if such company owns 10 per centum or more of the outstanding voting securities of the issuer, and is or, but for the exception provided for in this paragraph or paragraph (7), would be an investment company, the beneficial ownership shall be deemed to be that of the holders of such company's outstanding securities (other than short-term paper).

(B) Beneficial ownership by any person who acquires securities or interests in securities of an issuer described in the first sentence of this paragraph shall be deemed to be beneficial ownership by the person from whom such transfer was made, pursuant to such rules and regulations as the Commission shall prescribe as necessary or appropriate in the public interest and consistent with the protection of investors and the purposes fairly intended by the policy and provisions of this title, where the transfer was caused by legal separation, divorce, death, or other involuntary event.

(C)(i) The term "qualifying venture capital fund" means a venture capital fund that has not more than $10,000,000 in aggregate capital contributions and uncalled committed capital, with such dollar amount to be indexed for inflation once every 5 years by the Commission, beginning from a measurement made by the Commission on a date selected by the Commission, rounded to the nearest $1,000,000.

(ii) The term "venture capital fund" has the meaning given the term in section 275.203(*l*)-1 of title 17, Code of Federal Regulations, or any successor regulation.

(2) (A) Any person primarily engaged in the business of underwriting and distributing securities issued by other persons, selling securities to customers, acting as broker, and acting as market intermediary, or any one or more of such activities, whose gross income normally is derived principally from such business and related activities.

(B) For purposes of this paragraph—

(i) the term "market intermediary" means any person that regularly holds itself out as being willing contemporaneously to engage in, and that is regularly engaged in, the business of entering into transactions on both sides of the market for a financial contract or one or more such financial contracts; and

(ii) the term "financial contract" means any arrangement that—

(I) takes the form of an individually negotiated contract, agreement, or option to buy, sell, lend, swap, or repurchase, or other similar individually negotiated transaction commonly entered into by participants in the financial markets;

(II) is in respect of securities, commodities, currencies, interest or other rates, other measures of value, or any other financial or economic interest similar in purpose or function to any of the foregoing; and

(III) is entered into in response to a request from a counter party for a quotation, or is otherwise entered into and structured to accommodate the objectives of the counter party to such arrangement.

(3) Any bank or insurance company; any savings and loan association, building and loan association, cooperative bank, homestead association, or similar institution, or any receiver, conservator, liquidator, liquidating agent, or similar official or person thereof or therefor; or any common trust fund or similar fund maintained by a bank exclusively for the collective investment and reinvestment of moneys contributed thereto by the bank in its capacity as a trustee, executor, administrator, or guardian, if—

(A) such fund is employed by the bank solely as an aid to the administration of trusts, estates, or other accounts created and maintained for a fiduciary purpose;

(B) except in connection with the ordinary advertising of the bank's fiduciary services, interests in such fund are not—

(i) advertised; or

(ii) offered for sale to the general public; and

(C) fees and expenses charged by such fund are not in contravention of fiduciary principles established under applicable Federal or State law.

(4) Any person substantially all of whose business is confined to making small loans, industrial banking, or similar businesses.

(5) Any person who is not engaged in the business of issuing redeemable securities, face-amount certificates of the installment type or periodic payment plan certificates, and who is primarily engaged in one or more of the following businesses: (A) Purchasing or otherwise acquiring notes, drafts, acceptances, open accounts receivable, and other obligations representing part or all of the sales price of merchandise, insurance, and services; (B) making loans to manufacturers, wholesalers, and retailers of, and to prospective purchasers of, specified merchandise, insurance, and services; and (C) purchasing or otherwise acquiring mortgages and other liens on and interests in real estate.

(6) Any company primarily engaged, directly or through majority-owned subsidiaries, in one or more of the businesses described in paragraphs (3), (4), and (5), or in one or more of such businesses (from which not less than 25 per centum of such company's gross income during its last fiscal year was derived) together with an additional business or businesses other than investing, reinvesting, owning, holding, or trading in securities.

(7) (A) Any issuer, the outstanding securities of which are owned exclusively by persons who, at the time of acquisition of such securities, are qualified purchasers, and which is not making and does not at that time propose to make a public offering of such securities. Securities that are owned by persons who received the securities from a qualified purchaser as a gift or bequest, or in a case in which the transfer was caused by legal separation, divorce,

death, or other involuntary event, shall be deemed to be owned by a qualified purchaser, subject to such rules, regulations, and orders as the Commission may prescribe as necessary or appropriate in the public interest or for the protection of investors.

(B) Notwithstanding subparagraph (A), an issuer is within the exception provided by this paragraph if—

(i) in addition to qualified purchasers, outstanding securities of that issuer are beneficially owned by not more than 100 persons who are not qualified purchasers, if—

(I) such persons acquired any portion of the securities of such issuer on or before September 1, 1996; and

(II) at the time at which such persons initially acquired the securities of such issuer, the issuer was excepted by paragraph (1); and

(ii) prior to availing itself of the exception provided by this paragraph—

(I) such issuer has disclosed to each beneficial owner, as determined under paragraph (1), that future investors will be limited to qualified purchasers, and that ownership in such issuer is no longer limited to not more than 100 persons; and

(II) concurrently with or after such disclosure, such issuer has provided each beneficial owner, as determined under paragraph (1), with a reasonable opportunity to redeem any part or all of their interests in the issuer, notwithstanding any agreement to the contrary between the issuer and such persons, for that person's proportionate share of the issuer's net assets.

(C) Each person that elects to redeem under subparagraph (B)(ii)(II) shall receive an amount in cash equal to that person's proportionate share of the issuer's net assets, unless the issuer elects to provide such person with the option of receiving, and such person agrees to receive, all or a portion of such person's share in assets of the issuer. If the issuer elects to provide such persons with such an opportunity, disclosure concerning such opportunity shall be made in the disclosure required by subparagraph (B)(ii)(I).

(D) An issuer that is excepted under this paragraph shall nonetheless be deemed to be an investment company for purposes of the limitations set forth in subparagraphs (A)(i) and (B)(i) of section 12(d)(1) relating to the purchase or other acquisition by such issuer of any security issued by any registered investment company and the sale of any security issued by any registered open-end investment company to any such issuer.

(E) For purposes of determining compliance with this paragraph and paragraph (1), an issuer that is otherwise excepted under this paragraph and an issuer that is otherwise excepted under paragraph (1) shall not be treated by the Commission as being a single issuer for purposes of determining whether the outstanding securities of the issuer excepted under paragraph (1) are beneficially owned by not more than 100 persons or whether the outstanding securities of the issuer excepted under this paragraph are owned by persons that are not qualified purchasers. Nothing in this subparagraph shall be construed to establish that a person is a bona fide qualified purchaser for purposes of this paragraph or a bona fide beneficial owner for purposes of paragraph (1).

(8) [Repealed.]

(9) Any person substantially all of whose business consists of owning or holding oil, gas, or other mineral royalties or leases, or fractional interests therein, or certificates of interest or participation in or investment contracts relative to such royalties, leases, or fractional interests.

(10)(A) Any company organized and operated exclusively for religious, educational, benevolent, fraternal, charitable, or reformatory purposes—

(i) no part of the net earnings of which inures to the benefit of any private shareholder or individual; or

(ii) which is or maintains a fund described in subparagraph (B).

(B) For the purposes of subparagraph (A)(ii), a fund is described in this subparagraph if such fund is a pooled income fund, collective trust fund, collective investment fund, or similar fund maintained by a charitable organization exclusively for the collective investment and reinvestment of one or more of the following:

(i) assets of the general endowment fund or other funds of one or more charitable organizations;

(ii) assets of a pooled income fund;

(iii) assets contributed to a charitable organization in exchange for the issuance of charitable gift annuities;

(iv) assets of a charitable remainder trust or of any other trust, the remainder interests of which are irrevocably dedicated to any charitable organization;

(v) assets of a charitable lead trust;

(vi) assets of a trust, the remainder interests of which are revocably dedicated to or for the benefit of 1 or more charitable organizations, if the ability to revoke the dedication is limited to circumstances involving—

(I) an adverse change in the financial circumstances of a settlor or an income beneficiary of the trust;

(II) a change in the identity of the charitable organization or organizations having the remainder interest, provided that the new beneficiary is also a charitable organization; or

(III) both the changes described in subclauses (I) and (II);

(vii) assets of a trust not described in clauses (i) through (v), the remainder interests of which are revocably dedicated to a charitable organization, subject to subparagraph (C); or

(viii) such assets as the Commission may prescribe by rule, regulation, or order in accordance with section 6(c).

(C) A fund that contains assets described in clause (vii) of subparagraph (B) shall be excluded from the definition of an investment company for a period of 3 years after the date of enactment of this subparagraph, but only if—

(i) such assets were contributed before the date which is 60 days after the date of enactment of this subparagraph; and

(ii) such assets are commingled in the fund with assets described in one or more of clauses (i) through (vi) and (viii) of subparagraph (B).

(D) For purposes of this paragraph—

(i) a trust or fund is "maintained" by a charitable organization if the organization serves as a trustee or administrator of the trust or fund or has the power to remove the trustees or administrators of the trust or fund and to designate new trustees or administrators;

(ii) the term "pooled income fund" has the same meaning as in section 642(c)(5) of the Internal Revenue Code of 1986;

(iii) the term "charitable organization" means an organization described in paragraphs (1) through (5) of section 170(c) or section 501(c)(3) of the Internal Revenue Code of 1986;

(iv) the term "charitable lead trust" means a trust described in section 170(f)(2)(B), 2055(e)(2)(B), or 2522(c)(2)(B) of the Internal Revenue Code of 1986;

(v) the term "charitable remainder trust" means a charitable remainder annuity trust or a charitable remainder unitrust, as those terms are defined in section 664(d) of the Internal Revenue Code of 1986; and

(vi) the term "charitable gift annuity" means an annuity issued by a charitable organization that is described in section 501(m)(5) of the Internal Revenue Code of 1986.

(11) Any employee's stock bonus, pension, or profit-sharing trust which meets the requirements for qualification under section 401 of the Internal Revenue Code of 1986 or; any governmental plan described in section 3(a)(2)(C) of the Securities Act of 1933;

or any collective trust fund maintained by a bank consisting solely of assets of such trusts or governmental plans, or both; or any separate account the assets of which are derived solely from (A) contributions under pension or profit-sharing plans which meet the requirements of section 401 of the Internal Revenue Code of 1986 or the requirements for deduction of the employer's contribution under section 404(a)(2) of such Code, (B) contributions under governmental plans in connection with which interests, participations, or securities are exempted from the registration provisions of section 5 of the Securities Act of 1933 by section 3(a)(2)(C) of such Act, and (C) advances made by an insurance company in connection with the operation of such separate account.

(12) Any voting trust the assets of which consist exclusively of securities of a single issuer which is not an investment company.

(13) Any security holders' protective committee or similar issuer having outstanding and issuing no securities other than certificates of deposit and short-term paper.

[Church Plans]

(14) Any church plan described in section 414(e) of the Internal Revenue Code of 1986, if, under any such plan, no part of the assets may be used for, or diverted to, purposes other than the exclusive benefit of plan participants or beneficiaries, or any company or account that is—

(A) established by a person that is eligible to establish and maintain such a plan under section 414(e) of the Internal Revenue Code of 1986; and

(B) substantially all of the activities of which consist of—

(i) managing or holding assets contributed to such church plans or other assets which are permitted to be commingled with the assets of church plans under the Internal Revenue Code of 1986; or

(ii) administering or providing benefits pursuant to church plans.

Sec. 8. REGISTRATION OF INVESTMENT COMPANIES

(a) Any investment company organized or otherwise created under the laws of the United States or of a State may register for the purposes of this title by filing with the Commission a notification of registration, in such form as the Commission shall by rules and regulations prescribe as necessary or appropriate in the public interest or for the protection of investors. An investment company shall be deemed to be registered upon receipt by the Commission of such notification of registration.

(b) Every registered investment company shall file with the Commission, within such reasonable time after registration as the Commission shall fix by rules and regulations, an original and such copies of a registration statement, in such form and containing such of the following information and documents as the Commission shall by rules and regulations prescribe as necessary or appropriate in the public interest or for the protection of investors:

(1) a recital of the policy of the registrant in respect of each of the following types of activities, such recital consisting in each case of a statement whether the registrant reserves freedom of action to engage in activities of such type, and if such freedom of action is reserved, a statement briefly indicating, insofar as is practicable, the extent to which the registrant intends to engage therein: (A) the classification and subclassifications, as defined in sections 4 and 5, within which the registrant proposes to operate; (B) borrowing money; (C) the issuance of senior securities; (D) engaging in the business of underwriting securities issued by other persons; (E) concentrating investments in a particular industry or group of industries; (F) the purchase and sale of real estate and commodities, or either of them; (G) making loans to other persons; and (H) portfolio turnover (including a statement showing the aggregate dollar of purchases and sales of portfolio securities, other than Government securities, in each of the last three full fiscal years preceding the filing of such registration statement);

(2) a recital of all investment policies of the registrant, not enumerated in paragraph (1), which are changeable only if authorized by shareholder vote;

(3) a recital of all policies of the registrant, not enumerated in paragraphs (1) and (2), in respect of matters which the registrant deems matters of fundamental policy;

(4) the name and address of each affiliated person of the registrant; the name and principal address of every company, other than the registrant, of which each such person is an officer, director, or partner; a brief statement of the business experience for the preceding five years of each officer and director of the registrant; and

(5) the information and documents which would be required to be filed in order to register under the Securities Act of 1933 and the Securities Exchange Act of 1934 all securities (other than short-term paper) which the registrant has outstanding or proposes to issue.

(c) The Commission shall make provision, by permissive rules and regulations or order, for the filing of the following, or so much of the following as the Commission may designate, in lieu of the information and documents required pursuant to subsection (b):

(1) copies of the most recent registration statement filed by the registrant under the Securities Act of 1933 and currently effective under such Act, or if the registrant has not filed such a statement, copies of a registration statement filed by the registrant under the Securities Exchange Act of 1934 and currently effective under such Act;

(2) copies of any reports filed by the registrant pursuant to section 13 or 15(d) of the Securities Exchange Act of 1934; and

(3) a report containing reasonably current information regarding the matters included in copies filed pursuant to paragraphs (1) and (2), and such further information regarding matters not included in such copies as the Commission is authorized to require under subsection (b).

(d) If the registrant is a unit investment trust substantially all of the assets of which are securities issued by another registered investment company, the Commission is authorized to prescribe for the registrant, by rules and regulations or order, a registration statement which eliminates inappropriate duplication of information contained in the registration statement filed under this section by such other investment company.

(e) If it appears to the Commission that a registered investment company has failed to file the registration statement required by this section or a report required pursuant to section 30(a) or (b), or has filed such a registration statement or report but omitted therefrom material facts required to be stated therein, or has filed such a registration statement or report in violation of section 34(b), the Commission shall notify such company by registered mail or by certified mail of the failure to file such registration statement or report, or of the respects in which such registration statement or report appears to be materially incomplete or misleading, as the case may be, and shall fix a date (in no event earlier than thirty days after the mailing of such notice) prior to which such company may file such registration statement or report or correct the same. If such registration statement or report is not filed or corrected within the time so fixed by the Commission or any extension thereof, the Commission, after appropriate notice and opportunity for hearing, and upon such conditions and with such exemptions as it deems appropriate for the protection of investors, may by order suspend the registration of such company until such statement or report is filed or corrected, or may by order revoke such registration, if the evidence establishes—

(1) that such company has failed to file a registration statement required by this section or a report required pursuant to section 30(a) or (b), or has filed such a registration statement or report but omitted therefrom material facts required to be stated therein, or has filed such a registration statement or report in violation of section 34(b); and

(2) that such suspension or revocation is in the public interest.

(f) Whenever the Commission, on its own motion or upon application, finds that a registered investment company has ceased to be an investment company, it shall so declare by order and upon the taking effect of such order the registration of such company shall cease to be in effect. If necessary for the protection of investors, an order under this subsection may be made upon appropriate conditions. The Commission's denial of any application under this subsection shall be by order.

Sec. 9. INELIGIBILITY OF CERTAIN AFFILIATED PERSONS AND UNDERWRITERS

(a) It shall be unlawful for any of the following persons to serve or act in the capacity of employee, officer, director, member of an advisory board, investment adviser, or depositor of any registered investment company, or principal underwriter for any registered open-end company, registered unit investment trust, or registered face amount certificate company.

(1) any person who within 10 years has been convicted of any felony or misdemeanor involving the purchase or sale of any security or arising out of such person's conduct as an underwriter, broker, dealer, investment adviser, municipal securities dealer, government securities broker, government securities dealer, bank, transfer agent, or entity or person required to be registered under the Commodity Exchange Act, or as an affiliated person, salesman, or employee of any investment company, bank, insurance company, or entity or person required to be registered under the Commodity Exchange Act;

(2) any person who, by reason of any misconduct, is permanently or temporarily enjoined by order, judgment, or decree of any court of competent jurisdiction from acting as an underwriter, broker, dealer, investment adviser, municipal securities dealer, government securities broker, government securities dealer, bank, transfer agent, or entity or person required to be registered under the Commodity Exchange Act, or as an affiliated person, salesman, or employee of any investment company, bank, insurance company, or entity or person required to be registered under the Commodity Exchange Act, or from engaging in or continuing any conduct or practice in connection with any such activity or in connection with the purchase or sale of any security; or

(3) a company any affiliated person of which is ineligible, by reason of paragraph (1) or (2), to serve or act in the foregoing capacities.

For the purposes of paragraphs (1), (2), and (3) of this subsection, the term "investment adviser" shall include an investment adviser as defined in title II of this Act.

(b) The Commission may, after notice and opportunity for hearing, by order prohibit, conditionally or unconditionally, either permanently or for such period of time as it in its discretion shall deem appropriate in the public interest, any person from serving or acting as an employee, officer, director, member of an advisory board, investment adviser or depositor of, or principal underwriter for, a registered investment company or affiliated person of such investment adviser, depositor, or principal underwriter, if such person—

(1) has willfully made or caused to be made in any registration statement, application or report filed with the Commission under this title any statement which was at the time and in the light of the circumstances under which it was made false or misleading with respect to any material fact, or has omitted to state in any such registration statement, application, or report any material fact which was required to be stated therein;

(2) has willfully violated any provision of the Securities Act of 1933, or of the Securities Exchange Act of 1934, or of title II of this Act, or of this title, or of the Commodity Exchange Act, or of any rule or regulation under any of such statutes;

(3) has willfully aided, abetted, counseled, commanded, induced, or procured the violation by any other person of the Securities Act of 1933, or of the Securities Exchange Act of 1934, or of title II of this Act, or of this title, or of the Commodity Exchange Act, or of any rule of regulation under any of such statutes;

(4) has been found by a foreign financial regulatory authority to have—

(A) made or caused to be made in any application for registration or report required to be filed with a foreign securities authority, or in any proceeding before a foreign securities authority with respect to registration, any statement that was at the time and in light of the circumstances under which it was made false or misleading with respect to any material fact, or has omitted to state in any application or report to a foreign securities authority any material fact that is required to be stated therein;

(B) violated any foreign statute or regulation regarding transactions in securities or contracts of sale of a commodity for future delivery traded on or subject to the rules of a contract market or any board of trade; or

(C) aided, abetted, counseled, commanded, induced, or procured the violation by any other person of any foreign statute or regulation regarding transactions in securities or contracts of sale of a commodity for future delivery traded on or subject to the rules of a contract market or any board of trade;

(5) within 10 years has been convicted by a foreign court of competent jurisdiction of a crime, however denominated by the laws of the relevant foreign government, that is substantially equivalent to an offense set forth in paragraph (1) of subsection (a); or

(6) by reason of any misconduct, is temporarily or permanently enjoined by any foreign court of competent jurisdiction from acting in any of the capacities, set forth in paragraph (2) of subsection (a), or a substantially equivalent foreign capacity, or from engaging in or continuing any conduct or practice in connection with any such activity or in connection with the purchase or sale of any security.

(c) Any person who is ineligible, by reason of subsection (a), to serve or act in the capacities enumerated in that subsection, may file with the Commission an application for an exemption from the provisions of that subsection. The Commission shall by order grant such application, either unconditionally or on an appropriate temporary or other conditional basis, if it is established that the prohibitions of subsection (a), as applied to such person, are unduly or disproportionately severe or that the conduct of such person has been such as not to make it against the public interest or protection of investors to grant such application.

(d) MONEY PENALTIES IN ADMINISTRATIVE PROCEEDINGS.—

(1) AUTHORITY OF COMMISSION.—

(A) IN GENERAL.—In any proceeding instituted pursuant to subsection (b) against any person, the Commission may impose a civil penalty if it finds, on the record after notice and opportunity for hearing, that such penalty is in the public interest, and that such person—

(i) has willfully violated any provision of the Securities Act of 1933, the Securities Exchange Act of 1934, the Investment Advisers Act of 1940, or this title, or the rules or regulations thereunder;

(ii) has willfully aided, abetted, counseled, commanded, induced, or procured such a violation by any other person; or

(iii) has willfully made or caused to be made in any registration statement, application, or report required to be filed with the Commission under this title, any statement which was, at the time and in the light of the circumstances under which it was made false or misleading with respect to any material fact, or has omitted to state in any such registration statement, application, or report any material fact which was required to be stated therein;

(B) CEASE-AND-DESIST PROCEEDINGS.—In any proceeding instituted pursuant to subsection (f) against any person, the Commission may impose a civil penalty if the Commission finds, on the record, after notice and opportunity for hearing, that such person—

(i) Is violating or has violated any provision of this title, or any rule or regulation issued under this title; or

(ii) Is or was a cause of the violation of any provision of this title, or any rule or regulation issued under this title.

(2) MAXIMUM AMOUNT OF PENALTY.—

(A) FIRST TIER.—The maximum amount of penalty for each act or omission described in paragraph (1) shall be $5,000 for a natural person or $50,000 for any other person.

(B) SECOND TIER.—Notwithstanding subparagraph (A), the maximum amount of penalty for each such act or omission shall be $50,000 for a natural person or $250,000 for any other person if the act or omission described in paragraph (1) involved fraud, deceit, manipulation, or deliberate or reckless disregard of a regulatory requirement.

(C) THIRD TIER.—Notwithstanding subparagraphs (A) and (B), the maximum amount of penalty for each such act or omission shall be $100,000 for a natural person or $500,000 for any other person if—

(i) the act or omission described in paragraph (1) involved fraud, deceit, manipulation, or deliberate or reckless disregard of a regulatory requirement; and

(ii) such act or omission directly or indirectly resulted in substantial losses or created a significant risk of substantial losses to other persons or resulted in substantial pecuniary gain to the person who committed the act or omission.

(3) DETERMINATION OF PUBLIC INTEREST.—In considering under this section whether a penalty is in the public interest, the Commission may consider—

(A) whether the act or omission for which such penalty is assessed involved fraud, deceit, manipulation, or deliberate or reckless disregard of a regulatory requirement;

(B) the harm to other persons resulting either directly or indirectly from such act or omission;

(C) the extent to which any person was unjustly enriched, taking into account any restitution made to persons injured by such behavior;

(D) whether such person previously has been found by the Commission, another appropriate regulatory agency, or a self-regulatory organization to have violated the Federal securities laws, State securities laws, or the rules of a self-regulatory organization, has been enjoined by a court of competent jurisdiction from violations of such laws or rules, or has been convicted by a court of competent jurisdiction of violations of such laws or of any felony or misdemeanor described in section 203(e)(2) of the Investment Advisers Act of 1940;

(E) the need to deter such person and other persons from committing such acts or omissions; and

(F) such other matters as justice may require.

(4) EVIDENCE CONCERNING ABILITY TO PAY.—In any proceeding in which the Commission may impose a penalty under this section, a respondent may present evidence of the respondent's ability to pay such penalty. The Commission may, in its discretion, consider such evidence in determining whether such penalty is in the public interest. Such evidence may relate to the extent of such person's ability to continue in business and the collectability of a penalty, taking into account any other claims of the United States or third parties upon such person's assets and the amount of such person's assets.

(e) AUTHORITY TO ENTER AN ORDER REQUIRING AN ACCOUNTING AND DISGORGEMENT.—In any proceeding in which the Commission may impose a penalty under this section, the Commission may enter an order requiring accounting and disgorgement, including reasonable interest. The Commission is authorized to adopt rules, regulations, and orders concerning payments to investors, rates of interest, periods of accrual, and such other matters as it deems appropriate to implement this subsection.

(f) CEASE-AND-DESIST PROCEEDINGS.—

(1) AUTHORITY OF THE COMMISSION.—If the Commission finds, after notice and opportunity for hearing, that any person is violating, has violated, or is about to violate any provision of this title, or any rule or regulation thereunder, the Commission may publish its findings and enter an order requiring such person, and any other person that is, was, or would be a cause of the violation, due to an act or omission the person knew or should have known would contribute to such violation, to cease and desist from committing or causing such violation and any future violation of the same provision, rule, or regulation. Such order may, in addition to requiring a person to cease and desist from committing or causing a violation, require such person to comply, or to take steps to effect compliance, with such provision, rule, or regulation, upon such terms and conditions and within such time as the Commission may specify in such order. Any such order may, as the Commission deems appropriate, require future compliance or steps to effect future compliance, either permanently or for such period of time as the Commission may specify, with such provision, rule, or regulation with respect to any security, any issuer, or any other person.

(2) HEARING.—The notice instituting proceedings pursuant to paragraph (1) shall fix a hearing date not earlier than 30 days nor later than 60 days after service of the notice unless an earlier or a later date is set by the Commission with the consent of any respondent so served.

(3) TEMPORARY ORDER.—

(A) IN GENERAL.—Whenever the Commission determines that the alleged violation or threatened violation specified in the notice instituting proceedings pursuant to paragraph (1), or the continuation thereof, is likely to result in significant dissipation or conversion of assets, significant harm to investors, or substantial harm to the public interest, including, but not limited to, losses to the Securities Investor Protection Corporation, prior to the completion of the proceeding, the Commission may enter a temporary order requiring the respondent to cease and desist from the violation or threatened violation and to take such action to prevent the violation or threatened violation and to prevent dissipation or conversion of assets, significant harm to investors, or substantial harm to the public interest as the Commission deems appropriate pending completion of such proceedings. Such an order shall be entered only after notice and opportunity for a hearing, unless the Commission, notwithstanding section 40(a) of this title, determines that notice and hearing prior to entry would be impracticable or contrary to the public interest. A temporary order shall become effective upon service upon the respondent and, unless set aside, limited, or suspended by the Commission or a court of competent jurisdiction, shall remain effective and enforceable pending the completion of the proceedings.

(B) APPLICABILITY.—This paragraph shall apply only to a respondent that acts, or, at the time of the alleged misconduct acted, as a broker, dealer, investment adviser, investment company, municipal securities dealer, government securities broker, government securities dealer, or transfer agent, or is, or was at the time of the alleged misconduct, an associated person of, or a person seeking to become associated with, any of the foregoing.

(4) REVIEW OF TEMPORARY ORDERS.—

(A) COMMISSION REVIEW.—At any time after the respondent has been served with a temporary cease-and-desist order pursuant to paragraph (3), the respondent may apply to the Commission to have the order set aside, limited, or suspended. If the respondent has been served with a temporary cease-and-desist order entered without a prior Commission hearing, the respondent may, within 10 days after the date on which the order was served, request a hearing on such application and the Commission shall hold a hearing and render a decision on such application at the earliest possible time.

(B) JUDICIAL REVIEW.—Within—

(i) 10 days after the date the respondent was served with a temporary cease-and-desist order entered with a prior Commission hearing, or

(ii) 10 days after the Commission renders a decision on an application and hearing under subparagraph (A), with respect to any temporary cease-and-desist order entered without a prior Commission hearing.

the respondent may apply to the United States district court for the district in which the respondent resides or has its principal place of business, or for the District of Columbia, for an order setting aside, limiting, or suspending the effectiveness or enforcement of the order, and the court shall have jurisdiction to enter such an order. A respondent served with a temporary cease-and-desist order entered without a prior Commission hearing may not apply to the court except after hearing and decision by the Commission on the respondent's application under subparagraph (A) of this paragraph.

(C) NO AUTOMATIC STAY OF TEMPORARY ORDER.—The commencement of proceedings under subparagraph (B) of this paragraph shall not, unless specifically ordered by the court, operate as a stay of the Commission's order.

(D) EXCLUSIVE REVIEW.—Section 43 of this title shall not apply to a temporary order entered pursuant to this section.

(5) AUTHORITY TO ENTER AN ORDER REQUIRING AN ACCOUNTING AND DISGORGEMENT.—In any cease-and-desist proceeding under subsection (f)(1), the Commission may enter an order requiring accounting and disgorgement, including reasonable interest. The Commission is authorized to adopt rules, regulations, and orders concerning payments to investors,

rates of interest, periods of accrual, and such other matters as it deems appropriate to implement this subsection.

(g) For the purposes of this section, the term "investment adviser" includes a corporate or other trustee performing the functions of an investment adviser.

Sec. 10. AFFILIATIONS OR INTEREST OF DIRECTORS, OFFICERS, AND EMPLOYEES

(a) No registered investment company shall have a board of directors more than 60 per centum of the members of which are persons who are interested persons of such registered company.

(b) No registered investment company shall—

(1) employ as regular broker any director, officer, or employee of such registered company, or any person of which any such director, officer, or employee is an affiliated person, unless a majority of the board of directors of such registered company shall be persons who are not such brokers or affiliated persons of any of such brokers;

(2) use as a principal underwriter of securities issued by it any director, officer, or employee of such registered company or any person of which any such director, officer, or employee is an interested person, unless a majority of the board of directors of such registered company shall be persons who are not such principal underwriters or interested persons of any of such principal underwriters; or

(3) have as director, officer, or employee any investment banker, or any affiliated person of an investment banker, unless a majority of the board of directors of such registered company shall be persons who are not investment bankers or affiliated persons of any investment banker. For the purposes of this paragraph, a person shall not be deemed an affiliated person of an investment banker solely by reason of the fact that he is an affiliated person of a company of the character described in section 12(d)(3)(A) and (B).

(c) No registered investment company shall have a majority of its board of directors consisting of persons who are officers, directors, or employees of any one bank (together with its affiliates and subsidiaries) or any one bank holding company (together with its affiliates and subsidiaries) (as such terms are defined in section 2 of the Bank Holding Company Act of 1956), except that, if on March 15, 1940, any registered investment company had a majority of its directors consisting of persons who are directors, officers, or employees of any one bank, such company may continue to have the same percentage of its board of directors consisting of persons who are directors, officers, or employees of such bank.

(d) Notwithstanding subsections (a) and (b)(2) of this section, a registered investment company may have a board of directors all the members of which, except one, are interested persons of the investment adviser of such company, or are officers or employees of such company, if—

(1) such investment company is an open-end company;

(2) such investment adviser is registered under title II of this Act and is engaged principally in the business of rendering investment supervisory services as defined in title II;

(3) no sales load is charged on securities issued by such investment company;

(4) any premium over net asset value charged by such company upon the issuance of any such security, plus any discount from net asset value charged on redemption thereof, shall not in the aggregate exceed 2 per centum;

(5) no sales or promotion expenses are incurred by such registered company;but expenses incurred in complying with laws regulating the issue or sale of securities shall not be deemed sales or promotion expenses;

(6) such investment adviser is the only investment adviser to such investment company, and such investment adviser does not receive a management fee exceeding 1 per

centum per annum of the value of such company's net assets averaged over the year or taken as of a definite date or dates within the year;

(7) all executive salaries and executive expenses and office rent of such investment company are paid by such investment adviser; and

(8) such investment company has only one class of securities outstanding, each unit of which has equal voting rights with every other unit.

(e) If by reason of the death, disqualification, or bona fide resignation of any director or directors, the requirements of the foregoing provisions of this section or of section 15(f)(1) in respect of directors shall not be met by a registered investment company, the operation of such provision shall be suspended as to such registered company—

(1) for a period of thirty days if the vacancy or vacancies may be filled by action of the board of directors;

(2) for a period of sixty days if a vote of stockholders is required to fill the vacancy or vacancies; or

(3) for such longer period as the Commission may prescribe, by rules and regulations upon its own motion or by order upon application, as not inconsistent with the protection of investors.

(f) No registered investment company shall knowingly purchase or otherwise acquire, during the existence of any underwriting or selling syndicate, any security (except a security of which such company is the issuer) a principal underwriter of which is an officer, director, member of an advisory board, investment adviser, or employee of such registered company, or is a person (other than a company of the character described in section 12(d)(3)(A) and (B)) of which any such officer, director, member of an advisory board, investment adviser, or employee is an affiliated person, unless in acquiring such security such registered company is itself acting as a principal underwriter for the issuer. The Commission, by rules and regulations upon its own motion or by order upon application, may conditionally or unconditionally exempt any transaction or classes of transactions from any of the provisions of this subsection, if and to the extent that such exemption is consistent with the protection of investors.

(g) In the case of a registered investment company which has an advisory board, such board, as a distinct entity, shall be subject to the same restrictions as to its membership as are imposed upon a board of directors by this section.

(h) In the case of a registered management company which is an unincorporated company not having a board of directors, the provisions of this section shall apply as follows:

(1) the provisions of subsection (a), as modified by subsection (e), shall apply to the board of directors of the depositor of such company;

(2) the provisions of subsections (b) and (c), as modified by subsection (e), shall apply to the board of directors of the depositor and of every investment adviser of such company; and

(3) the provisions of subsection (f) shall apply to purchases and other acquisitions for the account of such company of securities a principal underwriter of which is the depositor or an investment adviser of such company, or an affiliated person of such depositor or investment adviser.

Sec. 12. FUNCTIONS AND ACTIVITIES OF INVESTMENT COMPANIES

(a) It shall be unlawful for any registered investment company, in contravention of such rules and regulations or orders as the Commission may prescribe as necessary or appropriate in the public interest or for the protection of investors—

(1) to purchase any security on margin, except such short-term credits as are necessary for the clearance of transactions;

(2) to participate on a joint or a joint and several basis in any trading account in securities, except in connection with an underwriting in which such registered company is a participant; or

(3) to effect a short sale of any security, except in connection with an underwriting in which such registered company is a participant.

(b) It shall be unlawful for any registered open-end company (other than a company complying with the provisions of section 10(d)) to act as a distributor of securities of which it is the issuer, except through an underwriter, in contravention of such rules and regulations as the Commission may prescribe as necessary or appropriate in the public interest or for the protection of investors.

(c) It shall be unlawful for any registered diversified company to make any commitment as underwriter, if immediately thereafter the amount of its outstanding underwriting commitments, plus the value of its investments in securities of issuers (other than investment companies) of which it owns more than 10 per centum of the outstanding voting securities, exceeds 25 per centum of the value of its total assets.

[Ownership of Stock of Other Investment Companies]

(d)(1)(A) It shall be unlawful for any registered investment company (the "acquiring company") and any company or companies controlled by such acquiring company to purchase or otherwise acquire any security issued by any other investment company (the "acquired company"), and for any investment company (the "acquiring company") and any company or companies controlled by such acquiring company to purchase or otherwise acquire any security issued by any registered investment company (the "acquired company"), if the acquiring company and any company or companies controlled by it immediately after such purchase or acquisition own in the aggregate—

(i) more than 3 per centum of the total outstanding voting stock of the acquired company;

(ii) securities issued by the acquired company having an aggregate value in excess of 5 per centum of the value of the total assets of the acquiring company; or

(iii) securities issued by the acquired company and all other investment companies (other than Treasury stock of the acquiring company) having an aggregate value in excess of 10 per centum of the value of the total assets of the acquiring company.

(B) It shall be unlawful for any registered open-end investment company (the "acquired company"), any principal underwriter therefor, or any broker or dealer registered under the Securities Exchange Act of 1934, knowingly to sell or otherwise dispose of any security issued by the acquired company to any other investment company (the "acquiring company") or any company or companies controlled by the acquiring company, if immediately after such sale or disposition—

(i) more than 3 per centum of the total outstanding voting stock of the acquired company is owned by the acquiring company and any company or companies controlled by it; or

(ii) more than 10 per centum of the total outstanding voting stock of the acquired company is owned by the acquiring company and other investment companies and companies controlled by them.

(C) It shall be unlawful for any investment company (the "acquiring company") and any company or companies controlled by the acquiring company to purchase or otherwise acquire any security issued by a registered closed-end investment company, if immediately after such purchase or acquisition the acquiring company, other investment companies having the same investment adviser, and companies controlled by such investment companies, own more than 10 per centum of the total outstanding voting stock of such close-end company.

(D) The provisions of this paragraph shall not apply to a security received as a dividend or as a result of an offer of exchange approved pursuant to section 11 or of a plan of reorganization of any company (other than a plan devised for the purpose of evading the foregoing provisions).

(E) The provisions of this paragraph shall not apply to a security (or securities) purchased or acquired by an investment company if—

(i) the depositor of, or principal underwriter for, such investment company is a broker or dealer registered under the Securities Exchange Act of 1934, or a person controlled by such a broker or dealer;

(ii) such security is the only investment security held by such investment company (or such securities are the only investment securities held by such investment company, if such investment company is a registered unit investment trust that issues two or more classes or series of securities, each of which provides for the accumulation of shares of a different investment company);and

(iii) the purchase or acquisition is made pursuant to an arrangement with the issuer of, or principal underwriter for, the issuer of the security whereby such investment company is obligated—

(aa) either to seek instructions from its security holders with regard to the voting of all proxies with respect to such security and to vote such proxies only in accordance with such instructions, or to vote the shares held by it in the same proportion as the vote of all other holders of such security, and

(bb) in the event that such investment company is not a registered investment company, to refrain from substituting such security unless the Commission shall have approved such substitution in the manner provided in section 26 of this Act.

(F) The provisions of this paragraph shall not apply to securities purchased or otherwise acquired by a registered investment company if—

(i) immediately after such purchase or acquisition not more than 3 per centum of the total outstanding stock of such issuer is owned by such registered investment company and all affiliated persons of such registered investment company; and

(ii) such registered investment company has not offered or sold after January 1, 1971, and is not proposing to offer or sell any security issued by it through a principal underwriter or otherwise at a public offering price which includes a sales load of more than 1½ per centum.

No issuer of any security purchased or acquired by a registered investment company pursuant to this subparagraph shall be obligated to redeem such security in an amount exceeding 1 per centum of such issuer's total outstanding securities during any period of less than thirty days. Such investment company shall exercise voting rights by proxy or otherwise with respect to any security purchased or acquired pursuant to this subparagraph in the manner prescibed by subparagraph (E) of this subsection.

(G) (i) This paragraph does not apply to securities of a registered open-end investment company or a registered unit investment trust (hereafter in this subparagraph referred to as the "acquired company") purchased or otherwise acquired by a registered open-end investment company or a registered unit investment trust (hereafter in this subparagraph referred to as the "acquiring company") if—

(I) the acquired company and the acquiring company are part of the same group of investment companies;

(II) the securities of the acquired company, securities of other registered open-end investment companies and registered unit investment trusts that are part of the same group of investment companies, Government securities, and short-term paper are the only investments held by the acquiring company;

(III) with respect to—

(aa) securities of the acquired company, the acquiring company does not pay and is not assessed any charges or fees for distribution-related activities, unless the acquiring company does not charge a sales load or other fees or charges for distribution-related activities; or (bb) securities of the acquiring company, any sales loads and other distribution-related fees charged, when aggregated with any sales load and distribution-related fees paid by the acquiring company with respect to securities of the acquired company, are not excessive under rules adopted pursuant to section 22(b) or section 22(c) by a securities association registered under section 15A of the Securities Exchange Act of 1934, or the Commission;

(IV) the acquired company has a policy that prohibits it from acquiring any securities of registered open-end investment companies or registered unit investment trusts in reliance on this subparagraph or subparagraph (F); and

(V) such acquisition is not in contravention of such rules and regulations as the Commission may from time to time prescribe with respect to acquisitions in accordance with this subparagraph, as necessary and appropriate for the protection of investors.

(ii) For purposes of this subparagraph, the term "group of investment companies" means any 2 or more registered investment companies that hold themselves out to investors as related companies for purposes of investment and investor services.

(H) For the purposes of this paragraph, the value of an investment company's total assets shall be computed as of the time of a purchase or acquisition or as closely thereto as is reasonably possible.

(I) In any action brought to enforce the provisions of this paragraph, the Commission may join as a party the issuer of any security purchased or otherwise acquired in violation of this paragraph (1), and the court may issue any order with respect to such issuer as may be necessary or appropriate for the enforcement of the provisions of this paragraph.

(J) The Commission, by rule or regulation, upon its own motion or by order upon application, may conditionally or unconditionally exempt any person, security, or transaction, or any class or classes of persons, securities, or transactions from any provision of this paragraph, if and to the extent that such exemption is consistent with the public interest and the protection of investors.

[Ownership of Outstanding Voting Stock of Insurance Companies]

(2) It shall be unlawful for any registered investment company and any company or companies controlled by such registered investment company to purchase or otherwise acquire any security (except a security received as a dividend or as a result of a plan of reorganization of any company, other than a plan devised for the purpose of evading the provisions of this paragraph) issued by any insurance company of which such registered investment company and any company or companies controlled by such registered company do not, at the time of such purchase or acquisition, own in the aggregate at least 25 per centum of the total outstanding voting stock, if such registered company and any company or companies controlled by it own in the aggregate, or as a result of such purchase or acquisition will own in the aggregate, more than 10 per centum of the total outstanding voting stock of such insurance company.

[Brokers, Dealers, Underwriters or Investment Advisers]

(3) It shall be unlawful for any registered investment company and any company or companies controlled by such registered investment company to purchase or otherwise acquire any security issued by or any other interest in the business of any person who is a broker, a dealer, is engaged in the business of underwriting, or is either an investment adviser of an investment company or an investment adviser registered under title II of this Act, unless (A) such person is a corporation all the outstanding securities of which (other than short-term paper, securities representing bank loans, and directors' qualifying shares) are, or after such acquisition will be, owned by one or more registered investment companies; and (B) such person is primarily engaged in the business of underwriting and distributing securities issued by other persons, selling securities to customers, or any one or more of such or related activities, and the gross income of such person normally is derived principally from such business or related activities.

(e) Notwithstanding any provisions of this title, any registered investment company may hereafter purchase or otherwise acquire any security issued by any one corporation engaged or proposing to engage in the business of underwriting, furnishing capital to industry, financing promotional enterprises, purchasing securities of issuers for which no ready market is in existence, and reorganizing companies or similar activities; provided—

(1) That the securities issued by such corporation (other than short-term paper and securities representing bank loans) shall consist solely of one class of common stock and shall have been originally issued or sold for investment to registered investment companies only;

(2) That the aggregate cost of the securities of such corporation purchased by such registered investment company does not exceed 5 per centum of the value of the total assets of such registered company at the time of any purchase or acquisition of such securities; and

(3) That the aggregate paid-in capital and surplus of such corporation does not exceed $100,000,000.

For the purpose of paragraph (1) of section 5(b) any investment in any such corporation shall be deemed to be an investment in an investment company.

(f) Notwithstanding any provisions of this Act, any registered face-amount certificate company may organize not more than two face-amount certificate companies and acquire and own all or any part of the capital stock thereof only if such stock is acquired and held for investment: *Provided,* That the aggregate cost to such registered company of all such stock so acquired shall not exceed six times the amount of the minimum capital stock requirement provided in subdivision (1) of subsection (a) of section 28 for a face-amount company organized on or after March 15, 1940: *And provided further,* That the aggregate cost to such registered company of all such capital stock issued by face-amount certificate companies organized or otherwise created under laws other than the laws of the United States or any State thereof shall not exceed twice the amount of the minimum capital stock requirement provided in subdivision (1) of subsection (a) of section 28 for a company organized on or after March 15, 1940. Nothing contained in this subsection shall be deemed to prevent the sale of any such stock to any other person if the original purchase was made by such registered face-amount certificate company in good faith for investment and not for resale.

(g) Notwithstanding the provisions of this section any registered investment company and any company or companies controlled by such registered company may purchase or otherwise acquire from another investment company or any company or companies controlled by such registered company more than 10 per centum of the total outstanding voting stock of any insurance company owned by any such company or companies, or may acquire the securities of any insurance company if the Commission by order determines that such acquisition is in the public interest because the financial condition of such insurance company will be improved as a result of such acquisition or any plan contemplated as a result thereof. This section shall not be deemed to prohibit the promotion of a new insurance company or the acquisition of the securities of any newly created insurance company by a registered investment company, alone or with other persons. Nothing contained in this section shall in any way affect or derogate from the powers of any insurance commissioner or similar official or agency of the United States or any State, or to affect the right under State law of any insurance company to acquire securities of any other insurance company or insurance companies.

Sec. 13. CHANGES IN INVESTMENT POLICY

(a) No registered investment company shall, unless authorized by the vote of a majority of its outstanding voting securities—

(1) change its subclassification as defined in section 5(a)(1) and (2) of this title or its subclassification from a diversified to a nondiversified company;

(2) borrow money, issue senior securities, underwrite securities issued by other persons, purchase or sell real estate or commodities or make loans to other persons, except in

each case in accordance with the recitals of policy contained in its registration statement in respect thereto;

(3) deviate from its policy in respect of concentration of investments in any particular industry or group of industries as recited in its registration statement, deviate from any investment policy which is changeable only if authorized by shareholder vote, or deviate from any policy recited in its registration statement pursuant to section 8(b)(3);

(4) change the nature of its business so as to cease to be an investment company.

(b) In the case of a common-law trust of the character described in section 16(c), either written approval by holders of a majority of the outstanding shares of beneficial interest or the vote of a majority of such outstanding shares cast in person or by proxy at a meeting called for the purpose shall for the purposes of subsection (a) be deemed the equivalent of the vote of a majority of the outstanding voting securities, and the provisions of paragraph (42) of section 2(a) as to a majority shall be applicable to the votes cast at such a meeting.

Sec. 15. INVESTMENT ADVISORY AND UNDERWRITING CONTRACTS

(a) It shall be unlawful for any person to serve or act as investment advisor of a registered investment company, except pursuant to a written contract, which contract, whether with such registered company or with an investment adviser of such registered company, has been approved by the vote of a majority of the outstanding voting securities of such registered company, and—

(1) precisely describes all compensation to be paid thereunder;

(2) shall continue in effect for a period more than two years from the date of its execution, only so long as such continuance is specifically approved at least annually by the board of directors or by vote of a majority of the outstanding voting securities of such company;

(3) provides, in substance, that it may be terminated at any time, without the payment of any penalty, by the board of directors of such registered company or by vote of a majority of the outstanding voting securities of such company on not more than sixty days' written notice to the investment adviser; and

(4) provides, in substance, for its automatic termination in the event of its assignment.

(b) It shall be unlawful for any principal underwriter for a registered open-end company to offer for sale, sell, or deliver after sale any security of which such company is the issuer, except pursuant to a written contract with such company, which contract—

(1) shall continue in effect for a period, more than two years from the date of its execution, only so long as such continuance is specifically approved at least annually by the board of directors or by vote of a majority of the outstanding voting securities of such company; and

(2) provides, in substance, for its automatic termination in the event of its assignment.

(c) In addition to the requirements of subsection (a) and (b) of this section, it shall be unlawful for any registered investment company having a board of directors to enter into, renew, or perform any contract or agreement, written or oral, whereby a person undertakes regularly to serve or act as investment adviser of or principal underwriter for such company unless the terms of such contract or agreement and any renewal thereof have been approved by the vote of a majority of directors, who are not parties to such contract or agreement or interested persons of any such party, cast in person at a meeting called for the purpose of voting on such approval. It shall be the duty of the directors of a registered investment company to request and evaluate, and the duty of an investment adviser to such company to furnish, such information as may reasonably be necessary to evaluate the terms of any contract whereby a person undertakes regularly to serve or act as investment adviser of such company. It shall be unlawful for the directors of a registered investment company, in connection with their evaluation of the terms of any contract whereby a person undertakes regularly to serve or act as investment adviser of such company, to take into account the purchase price or other consideration any person may have paid in connection with a transaction of the type referred to in paragraph (1), (3), or (4) of subsection (f).

(d) In the case of a common-law trust of the character described in section 16(c), either written approval by holders of a majority of the outstanding shares of beneficial interest or the vote of a majority of such outstanding shares cast in person or by proxy at a meeting called for the purpose shall for the purposes of this section be deemed the equivalent of the vote of a majority of the outstanding voting securities, and the provisions of paragraph (42) of section 2(a) as to a majority shall be applicable to the vote cast at such a meeting.

(e) Nothing contained in this section shall be deemed to require or contemplate any action by an advisory board of any registered company or by any of the members of such a board.

(f) (1) An investment adviser, or a corporate trustee performing the functions of an investment adviser, of a registered investment company or an affiliated person of such investment adviser or corporate trustee may receive any amount or benefit in connection with a sale of securities of, or a sale of any other interest in, such investment adviser or corporate trustee which results in an assignment of an investment advisory contract with such company or the change in control of or identity of such corporate trustee, if—

(A) for a period of three years after the time of such action, at least 75 per centum of the members of the board of directors of such registered company or such corporate trustee (or successor thereto, by reorganization or otherwise) are not (i) interested persons of the investment adviser of such company or such corporate trustee, or (ii) interested persons of the predecessor investment adviser or such corporate trustee; and

(B) there is not imposed an unfair burden on such company as a result of such transactions or any express or implied terms, conditions, or understandings applicable thereto.

(2) (A) For the purpose of paragraph (1) (A) of this subsection, interested persons of a corporate trustee shall be determined in accordance with section 2(a) (19) (B): Provided, That no person shall be deemed to be an interested person of a corporate trustee solely by reason of (i) his being a member of its board of directors or advisory board or (ii) his membership in the immediate family of any person specified in clause (i) of this subparagraph.

(B) For the purpose of paragraph (1) (B) of this subsection, an unfair burden on a registered investment company includes any arrangement, during the two-year period after the date on which any such transaction occurs, whereby the investment adviser or corporate trustee or predecessor or successor investment advisers or corporate trustee or any interested person of any such adviser or any such corporate trustee receives or is entitled to receive any compensation directly or indirectly (i) from any person in connection with the purchase or sale of securities or other property to, from, or on behalf of such company, other than bona fide ordinary compensation as principal underwriter for such company, or (ii) from such company or its security holders for other than bona fide investment advisory or other services.

(3) If—

(A) an assignment of an investment advisory contract with a registered investment company results in a successor investment adviser to such company, or if there is a change in control of or identity of a corporate trustee of a registered investment company, and such adviser or trustee is then an investment adviser or corporate trustee with respect to other assets substantially greater in amount than the amount of assets of such company, or

(B) as a result of a merger of, or a sale of substantially all the assets by, a registered investment company with or to another registered investment company with assets substantially greater in amount, a transaction occurs which would be subject to paragraph (1) (A) of this subsection,

such discrepancy in size of assets shall be considered by the Commission in determining whether or to what extent an application under section 6(c) for exemption from the provisions of paragraph (1) (A) should be granted.

(4) Paragraph (1) (A) of this section shall not apply to a transaction in which a controlling block of outstanding voting securities of an investment adviser to a registered investment company or of a corporate trustee performing the functions of an investment adviser to a registered investment company is—

(A) distributed to the public and in which there is, in fact, no change in the identity of the persons who control such investment adviser or corporate trustee, or

(B) transferred to the investment adviser or the corporate trustee, or an affiliated person or persons of such investment adviser or corporate trustee, or is transferred from the investment adviser or corporate trustee to an affiliated person or persons of the investment adviser or corporate trustee: Provided, That (i) each transferee (other than such adviser or trustee) is a natural person and (ii) the transferees (other than such adviser or trustee) owned in the aggregate more than 25 per centum of such voting securities for a period of at least six months prior to such transfer.

Sec. 17. TRANSACTIONS OF CERTAIN AFFILIATED PERSONS AND UNDERWRITERS

(a) It shall be unlawful for any affiliated person or promoter of or principal underwriter for a registered investment company (other than a company of the character described in section 12(d)(3)(A) and (B), or any affiliated person of such a person, promoter, or principal underwriter, acting as principal—

(1) knowingly to sell any security or other property to such registered company or to any company controlled by such registered company, unless such sale involves solely (A) securities of which the buyer is the issuer, (B) securities of which the seller is the issuer and which are part of a general offering to the holders of a class of its securities, or (C) securities deposited with the trustee of a unit investment trust or periodic payment plan by the depositor thereof;

(2) knowingly to purchase from such registered company, or from any company controlled by such registered company, any security or other property (except securities of which the seller is the issuer);

(3) to borrow money or other property from such registered company or from any company controlled by such registered company (unless the borrower is controlled by the lender) except as permitted in section 21(b); or

(4) to loan money or other property to such registered company, or to any company controlled by such registered company, in contravention of such rules, regulations, or orders as the Commission may, after consultation with and taking into consideration the views of the Federal banking agencies (as defined in section 3 of the Federal Deposit Insurance Act), prescribe or issue consistent with the protection of investors.

(b) Notwithstanding subsection (a), any person may file with the Commission an application for an order exempting a proposed transaction of the applicant from one or more provisions of that subsection. The Commission shall grant such application and issue such order of exemption if evidence establishes that—

(1) the terms of the proposed transaction, including the consideration to be paid or received, are reasonable and fair and do not involve overreaching on the part of any person concerned;

(2) the proposed transaction is consistent with the policy of each registered investment company concerned, as recited in its registration statement and reports filed under this title; and

(3) the proposed transaction is consistent with the general purposes of this title.

(c) Notwithstanding subsection (a), a person may, in the ordinary course of business, sell to or purchase from any company merchandise or may enter into a lessor-lessee relationship with any person and furnish the services incident thereto.

(d) It shall be unlawful for any affiliated person of or principal underwriter for a registered investment company (other than a company of the character described in section 12(d)(3)(A) and

(B)), or any affiliated person of such a person or principal underwriter, acting as principal to effect any transaction in which such registered company, or a company controlled by such registered company, is a joint or a joint and several participant with such person, principal underwriter, or affiliated person, in contravention of such rules and regulations as the Commission may prescribe for the purpose of limiting or preventing participation by such registered or controlled company on a basis different from or less advantageous than that of such other participant. Nothing contained in this subsection shall be deemed to preclude any affiliated person from acting as manager of any underwriting syndicate or other group in which such registered or controlled company is a participant and receiving compensation therefor.

(e) It shall be unlawful for any affiliated person of a registered investment company, or any affiliated person of such person—

(1) acting as agent, to accept from any source any compensation (other than a regular salary or wages from such registered company) for the purchase or sale of any property to or for such registered company or any controlled company thereof, except in the course of such person's business as an underwriter or broker; or

(2) acting as broker, in connection with the sale of securities to or by such registered company or any controlled company thereof, to receive from any source a commission, fee, or other remuneration for effecting such transaction which exceeds (A) the usual and customary broker's commission if the sale is effected on a securities exchange, or (B) 2 per centum of the sales price if the sale is effected in connection with a secondary distribution of such securities, or (C) 1 per centum of the purchase or sale price of such securities if the sale is otherwise effected unless the Commission shall, by rules and regulations or order in the public interest and consistent with the protection of investors, permit a larger commission.

(f) CUSTODY OF SECURITIES.—

(1) Every registered management company shall place and maintain its securities and similar investments in the custody of (A) a bank or banks having the qualification prescribed in paragraph (1) of section 26(a) of this title for the trustees of unit investment trusts; or (B) a company which is a member of a national securities exchange as defined in the Securities Exchange Act of 1934, subject to such rules and regulations as the Commission may from time to time prescribe for the protection of investors; or (C) such registered company, but only in accordance with such rules and regulations or orders as the Commission may from time to time prescribe for the protection of investors.

(2) Subject to such rules, regulations, and orders as the Commission may adopt as necessary or appropriate for the protection of investors, a registered management company or any such custodian, with the consent of the registered management company for which it acts as custodian, may deposit all or any part of the securities owned by such registered management company in a system for the central handling of securities established by a national securities exchange or national securities association registered with the Commission under the Securities Exchange Act of 1934, or such other person as may be permitted by the Commission, pursuant to which system all securities of any particular class or series of any issuer deposited within the system are treated as fungible and may be transferred or pledged by bookkeeping entry without physical delivery of such securities.

(3) Rules, regulations, and orders of the Commission under this subsection, among other things, may make appropriate provision with respect to such matters as the earmarking, segregation, and hypothecation of such securities and investments, and may provide for or require periodic or other inspections by any or all of the following: Independent public accountants, employees and agents of the Commission, and such other persons as the Commission may designate.

(4) No member of a national securities exchange which trades in securities for its own account may act as custodian except in accordance with rules and regulations prescribed by the Commission for the protection of investors.

(5) If a registered company maintains its securities and similar investments in the custody of a qualified bank or banks, the cash proceeds from the sale of such securities

and similar investments and other cash assets of the company shall likewise be kept in the custody of such a bank or banks, or in accordance with such rules and regulations or orders as the Commission may from time to time prescribe for the protection of investors, except that such a registered company may maintain a checking account in a bank or banks having the qualifications prescribed in paragraph (1) of section 26(a) of this title for the trustees of unit investment trusts with the balance of such account or the aggregate balances of such accounts at no time in excess of the amount of the fidelity bond, maintained pursuant to section 17(g) of this title, covering the officers or employees authorized to draw on such account or accounts.

(6) The Commission may, after consultation with and taking into consideration the views of the Federal banking agencies (as defined in section 3 of the Federal Deposit Insurance Act), adopt rules and regulations, and issue orders, consistent with the protection of investors, prescribing the conditions under which a bank, or an affiliated person of a bank, either of which is an affiliated person, promoter, organizer, or sponsor of, or principal underwriter for, a registered management company, may serve as custodian of that registered management company.

(g) The Commission is authorized to require by rules and regulations or orders for the protection of investors that any officer or employee of a registered management investment company who may singly, or jointly with others, have access to securities or funds of any registered company, either directly or through authority to draw upon such funds or to direct generally the disposition of such securities (unless the officer or employee has such access solely through his position as an officer or employee of a bank) be bonded by a reputable fidelity insurance company against larceny and embezzlement in such reasonable minimum amounts as the Commission may prescribe.

(h) After one year from the effective date of this title, neither the charter, certificate of incorporation, articles of association, indenture of trust, nor the by-laws of any registered investment company, nor any other instrument pursuant to which such a company is organized or administered, shall contain any provision which protects or purports to protect any director or officer of such company against any liability to the company or to its security holders to which he would otherwise be subject by reason of willful misfeasance, bad faith, gross negligence or reckless disregard of the duties involved in the conduct of his office.

(i) After one year from the effective date of this title no contract or agreement under which any person undertakes to act as investment adviser of, or principal underwriter for, a registered investment company shall contain any provision which protects or purports to protect such person against any liability to such company or its security holders to which he would otherwise be subject by reason of willful misfeasance, bad faith, or gross negligence, in the performance of his duties, or by reason of his reckless disregard of his obligations and duties under such contract or agreement.

(j) It shall be unlawful for any affiliated person of or principal underwriter for a registered investment company or any affiliated person of an investment adviser of or principal underwriter for a registered investment company, to engage in any act, practice, or course of business in connection with the purchase or sale, directly or indirectly, by such person of any security held or to be acquired by such registered investment company in contravention of such rules and regulations as the Commission may adopt to define, and prescribe means reasonably necessary to prevent, such acts, practices, or courses of business as are fraudulent, deceptive or manipulative. Such rules and regulations may include requirements for the adoption of codes of ethics by registered investment companies and investment advisers of, and principal underwriters for, such investment companies establishing such standards as are reasonably necessary to prevent such acts, practices, or courses of business.

Sec. 18. CAPITAL STRUCTURE

(a) It shall be unlawful for any registered closed-end company to issue any class of senior security, or to sell any such security of which it is the issuer, unless—

    (1) if such class of senior security represents an indebtedness—

(A) immediately after such issuance or sale, it will have an asset coverage of at least 300 per centum;

(B) provision is made to prohibit the declaration of any dividend (except a dividend payable in stock of the issuer), or the declaration of any other distribution, upon any class of the capital stock of such investment company, or the purchase of any such capital stock, unless, in every such case, such class of senior securities has at the time of the declaration of any such dividend or distribution or at the time of any such purchase an asset coverage of at least 300 per centum after deducting the amount of such dividend, distribution, or purchase price, as the case may be, except that dividends may be declared upon any preferred stock if such senior security representing indebtedness has an asset coverage of at least 200 per centum at the time of declaration thereof after deducting the amount of such dividend; and

(C) provision is made either—

(i) that, if on the last business day of each of twelve consecutive calendar months such class of senior securities shall have an asset coverage of less than 100 per centum, the holders of such securities voting as a class shall be entitled to elect at least a majority of the members of the board of directors of such registered company, such voting right to continue until such class of senior security shall have an asset coverage of 110 per centum or more on the last business day of each of three consecutive calendar months, or

(ii) that, if on the last business day of each of twenty-four consecutive calendar months such class of senior securities shall have an asset coverage of less than 100 per centum, an event of default shall be deemed to have occurred;

(2) if such class of senior security is a stock—

(A) immediately after such issuance or sale it will have an asset coverage of at least 200 per centum;

(B) provision is made to prohibit the declaration of any dividend (except a dividend payable in common stock of the issuer), or the declaration of any other distribution, upon the common stock of such investment company, or the purchase of any such common stock, unless in every such case such class of senior security has at the time of the declaration of any such dividend or distribution or at the time of any such purchase an asset coverage of at least 200 per centum after deducting the amount of such dividend, distribution or purchase price, as the case may be;

(C) provision is made to entitle the holders of such senior securities, voting as a class, to elect at least two directors at all times, and, subject to the prior rights, if any, of the holders of any other class of senior securities outstanding, to elect a majority of the directors if at any time dividends on such class of securities shall be unpaid in an amount equal to two full years' dividends on such securities, and to continue to be so represented until all dividends in arrears shall have been paid or otherwise provided for;

(D) provision is made requiring approval by the vote of a majority of such securities, voting as a class, of any plan of reorganization adversely affecting such securities or of any action requiring a vote of security holders as in section 13(a) provided; and

(E) such class of stock shall have complete priority over any other class as to distribution of assets and payment of dividends, which dividends shall be cumulative.

(b) The asset coverage in respect of a senior security provided for in subsection (a) may be determined on the basis of values calculated as of a time within forty-eight hours (not including Sundays or holidays) next preceding the time of such determination. The time of issue or sale shall, in the case of an offering of such securities to existing stockholders of the issuer, be deemed to be the first date on which such offering is made, and in all other cases shall be deemed to be the time, as of which a firm commitment to issue or sell and to take or purchase such securities shall be made.

(c) Notwithstanding the provisions of subsection (a) it shall be unlawful for any registered closed-end investment company to issue or sell any senior security representing indebtedness if immediately thereafter such company will have outstanding more than one class of senior security representing indebtedness, or to issue or sell any senior security which is a stock if immediately thereafter such company will have outstanding more than one class of senior security which is a stock, except that (1) any such class of indebtedness or stock may be issued in one or more series: *Provided,* That no such series shall have a preference or priority over any other series upon the distribution of the assets of such registered closed-end company or in respect of the payment of interest or dividends, and (2) promissory notes or other evidences of indebtedness issued in consideration of any loan, extension, or renewal thereof, made by a bank or other person and privately arranged, and not intended to be publicly distributed, shall not be deemed to be a separate class of senior securities representing indebtedness within the meaning of this subsection (c).

(d) It shall be unlawful for any registered management company to issue any warrant or right to subscribe to or purchase a security of which such company is the issuer, except in the form of warrants or rights to subscribe expiring not later than one hundred and twenty days after their issuance and issued exclusively and ratably to a class or classes of such company's security holders; except that any warrant may be issued in exchange for outstanding warrants in connection with a plan of reorganization.

(e) The provisions of this section 18 shall not apply to any senior securities issued or sold by any registered closed-end company—

(1) for the purpose of refunding through payment, purchase, redemption, retirement, or exchange, any senior security of such registered investment company except that no senior security representing indebtedness shall be so issued or sold for the purpose of refunding any senior security which is a stock; or

(2) pursuant to any plan of reorganization (other than for refunding as referred to in paragraph (1) of this subsection), provided—

(A) that such senior securities are issued or sold for the purpose of substituting or exchanging such senior securities for outstanding senior securities, and if such senior securities represent indebtedness they are issued or sold for the purpose of substituting or exchanging such senior securities for outstanding senior securities representing indebtedness, of any registered investment company which is a party to such plan of reorganization; or

(B) that the total amount of such senior securities so issued or sold pursuant to such plan does not exceed the total amount of senior securities of all the companies which are parties to such plan, and the total amount of senior securities representing indebtedness so issued or sold pursuant to such plan does not exceed the total amount of senior securities representing indebtedness of all such companies, or, alternatively, the total amount of such senior securities so issued or sold pursuant to such plan does not have the effect of increasing the ratio of senior securities representing indebtedness to the securities representing stock or the ratio of senior securities representing stock to securities junior thereto when compared with such ratios as they existed before such reorganization.

(f)(1) It shall be unlawful for any registered open-end company to issue any class of senior security or to sell any senior security of which it is the issuer, except that any such registered company shall be permitted to borrow from any bank: *Provided,* that immediately after any such borrowing there is an asset coverage of at least 300 per centum for all borrowings of such registered company: *And provided further,* that in the event that such asset coverage shall at any time fall below 300 per centum such registered company shall, within three days thereafter (not including Sundays and holidays) or such longer period as the Commission may prescribe by rules and regulations, reduce the amount of its borrowings to an extent that the asset coverage of such borrowings shall be at least 300 per centum.

(2) "Senior security" shall not, in the case of a registered open-end company, include a class or classes or a number of series of preferred or special stock each of which is preferred over all other classes or series in respect of assets specifically allocated to that class or series: *Provided,* That (A) such company has outstanding no class or series of stock which is

not so preferred over all other classes or series, or (B) the only other outstanding class of the issuer's stock consists of a common stock upon which no dividend (other than a liquidating dividend) is permitted to be paid and which in the aggregate represents not more than one-half of 1 per centum of the issuer's outstanding voting securities. For the purpose of insuring fair and equitable treatment of the holders of the outstanding voting securities of each class or series of stock of such company, the Commission may by rule, regulation, or order direct that any matter required to be submitted to the holders of the outstanding voting securities of such company shall not be deemed to have been effectively acted upon unless approved by the holders of such percentage (not exceeding a majority) of the outstanding voting securities of each class or series of stock affected by such matter as shall be prescribed in such rule, regulation, or order.

(g) Unless otherwise provided: "Senior security" means any bond, debenture, note, or similar obligation or instrument constituting a security and evidencing indebtedness, and any stock of a class having priority over any other class as to distribution of assets or payment of dividends;and "senior security representing indebtedness" means any senior security other than stock.

The term "senior security" when used in subparagraphs (B) and (C) of paragraph (1) of subsection (a), shall not include any promissory note or other evidence of indebtedness issued in consideration of any loan, extension, or renewal thereof, made by a bank or other person and privately arranged, and not intended to be publicly distributed; nor shall such term, when used in this section 18, include any such promissory note or other evidence of indebtedness in any case where such a loan is for temporary purposes only and in an amount not exceeding 5 per centum of the value of the total assets of the issuer at the time when the loan is made. A loan shall be presumed to be for temporary purposes if it is repaid within sixty days and is not extended or renewed; otherwise it shall be presumed not to be for temporary purposes. Any such presumption may be rebutted by evidence.

(h) "Asset coverage" of a class of senior security representing an indebtedness of an issuer means the ratio which the value of the total assets of such issuer, less all liabilities and indebtedness not represented by senior securities, bears to the aggregate amount of senior securities representing indebtedness of such issuer. "Asset coverage" of a class of senior security of an issuer which is a stock means the ratio which the value of the total assets of such issuer, less all liabilities and indebtedness not represented by senior securities, bears to the aggregate amount of senior securities representing indebtedness of such issuer plus the aggregate of the involuntary liquidation preference of such class of senior security which is a stock. The involuntary liquidation preference of a class of senior security which is a stock shall be deemed to mean the amount to which such class of senior security would be entitled on involuntary liquidation of the issuer in preference to a security junior to it.

(i) Except as provided in subsection (a) of this section, or as otherwise required by law, every share of stock hereafter issued by a registered management company (except a common-law trust of the character described in section 16(c)) shall be a voting stock and have equal voting rights with every other outstanding voting stock: *Provided,* That this subsection shall not apply to shares issued pursuant to the terms of any warrant or subscription right outstanding on March 15, 1940, or any firm contract entered into before March 15, 1940, to purchase such securities from such company nor to shares issued in accordance with any rules, regulations, or orders which the Commission may make permitting such issue.

(j) Notwithstanding any provision of this title, it shall be unlawful, after the date of enactment of this title, for any registered face-amount certificate company—

(1) to issue, except in accordance with such rules, regulations, or orders as the Commission may prescribe in the public interest or as necessary or appropriate for the protection of investors, any security other than (A) a face-amount certificate; (B) a common stock having a par value and being without preference as to dividends or distributions and having at least equal voting rights with any outstanding security of such company; or (C) short-term payment or promissory notes or other indebtedness issued in consideration of any loan, extension, or renewal thereof, made by a bank or other person and privately arranged and not intended to be publicly offered;

(2) if such company has outstanding any security, other than such face-amount certificates, common stock, promissory notes, or other evidence of indebtedness, to make any distribution or declare or pay any dividend on any capital security in contravention of such rules and regulations or orders as the Commission may prescribe in the public interest or as necessary or appropriate for the protection of investors or to insure the financial integrity of such company, to prevent the impairment of the company's ability to meet its obligations upon its face-amount certificates; or

(3) to issue any of its securities except for cash or securities including securities of which such company is the issuer.

(k) The provisions of subparagraphs (A) and (B) of paragraph (1) of subsection (a) of this section shall not apply to investment companies operating under the Small Business Investment Act of 1958, and the provisions of paragraph (2) of said subsection shall not apply to such companies so long as such class of senior security shall be held or guaranteed by the Small Business Administration.

Sec. 22. DISTRIBUTION, REDEMPTION, AND REPURCHASE OF REDEEMABLE SECURITIES

(a) A securities association registered under section 15A of the Securities Exchange Act of 1934 may prescribe, by rules adopted and in effect in accordance with said section and subject to all provisions of said section applicable to the rules of such an association—

(1) a method or methods for computing the minimum price at which a member thereof may purchase from any investment company any redeemable security issued by such company and the maximum price at which a member may sell to such company any redeemable security issued by it or which he may receive for such security upon redemption, so that the price in each case will bear such relation to the current net asset value of such security computed as of such time as the rules may prescribe; and

(2) a minimum period of time which must elapse after the sale or issue of such security before any resale to such company by a member or its redemption upon surrender by a member;

[(a) continued] in each case for the purpose of eliminating or reducing so far as reasonably practicable any dilution of the value of other outstanding securities of such company or any other result of such purchase, redemption, or sale which is unfair to holders of such other outstanding securities;and said rules may prohibit the members of the association from purchasing, selling, or surrendering for redemption any such redeemable securities in contravention of said rules.

(b) (1) Such a securities association may also, by rules adopted and in effect in accordance with said section 15A, and notwithstanding the provisions of subsection (b) (6) thereof but subject to all other provisions of said section applicable to the rules of such an association, prohibit its members from purchasing, in connection with a primary distribution of redeemable securities of which any registered investment company is the issuer, any such security from the issuer or from any principal underwriter except at a price equal to the price at which such security is then offered to the public less a commission, discount, or spread which is computed in conformity with a method or methods, and within such limitations as to the relation thereof to said public offering price, as such rules may prescribe in order that the price at which such security is offered or sold to the public shall not include an excessive sales load but shall allow for reasonable compensation for sales personnel, broker-dealers, and underwriters, and for reasonable sales loads to investors. The Commission shall on application or otherwise, if it appears that smaller companies are subject to relatively higher operating costs, make due allowance therefor by granting any such company or class of companies appropriate qualified exemptions from the provisions of this section.

(2) At any time after the expiration of eighteen months from the date of enactment of the Investment Company Amendments Act of 1970, the Commission may alter or supplement the rules of any securities association as may be necessary to effectuate the purposes of this subsection in the manner provided by section 19(c) of the Securities Exchange Act of 1934.

(3) If any provision of this subsection is in conflict with any provision of any law of the United States in effect on the date this subsection takes effect, the provisions of this subsection shall prevail.

(c) The Commission may make rules and regulations applicable to registered investment companies and to principal underwriters of, and dealers in, the redeemable securities of any registered investment company, whether or not members of any securities association, to the same extent, covering the same subject matter, and for the accomplishment of the same ends as are prescribed in subsection (a) of this section in respect of the rules which may be made by a registered securities association governing its members. Any rules and regulations so made by the Commission, to the extent that they may be inconsistent with the rules of any such association, shall so long as they remain in force supersede the rules of the association and be binding upon its members as well as all other underwriters and dealers to whom they may be applicable.

(d) No registered investment company shall sell any redeemable security issued by it to any person except either to or through a principal underwriter for distribution or at a current public offering price described in the prospectus, and, if such class of security is being currently offered to the public by or through an underwriter, no principal underwriter of such security and no dealer shall sell any such security to any person except a dealer, a principal underwriter, or the issuer, except at a current public offering price described in the prospectus. Nothing in this subsection shall prevent a sale made (i) pursuant to an offer of exchange permitted by section 11 including any offer made pursuant to section 11(b); (ii) pursuant to an offer made solely to all registered holders of the securities, or of a particular class or series of securities issued by the company proportionate to their holdings or proportionate to any cash distribution made to them by the company (subject to appropriate qualifications designed solely to avoid issuance of fractional securities);or (iii) in accordance with rules and regulations of the Commission made pursuant to subsection (b) of section 12.

(e) No registered investment company shall suspend the right of redemption, or postpone the date of payment or satisfaction upon redemption of any redeemable security in accordance with its terms for more than seven days after the tender of such security to the company or its agent designated for that purpose for redemption, except—

(1) for any period (A) during which the New York Stock Exchange is closed other than customary week-end and holiday closings or (B) during which trading on the New York Stock Exchange is restricted;

(2) for any period during which an emergency exists as a result of which (A) disposal by the company of securities owned by it is not reasonably practicable or (B) it is not reasonably practicable for such company fairly to determine the value of its net assets; or

(3) for such other periods as the Commission may by order permit for the protection of security holders of the company.

The Commission shall by rules and regulations determine the conditions under which (i) trading shall be deemed to be restricted and (ii) an emergency shall be deemed to exist within the meaning of this subsection.

(f) No registered open-end company shall restrict the transferability or negotiability of any security of which it is the issuer except in conformity with the statements with respect thereto contained in its registration statement nor in contravention of such rules and regulations as the Commission may prescribe in the interest of the holders of all of the outstanding securities of such investment company.

(g) No registered open-end company shall issue any of its securities (1) for services; or (2) for property other than cash or securities (including securities of which such registered company is the issuer), except as a dividend or distribution to its security holders or in connection with a reorganization.

Sec. 36. BREACH OF FIDUCIARY DUTY

(a) The Commission is authorized to bring an action in the proper district court of the United States, or in the Unites States court of any territory or other place subject to the jurisdiction of the

United States, alleging that a person who is, or at the time of the alleged misconduct was, serving or acting in one or more of the following capacities has engaged within five years of the commencement of the action or is about to engage in any act or practice constituting a breach of fiduciary duty involving personal misconduct in respect of any registered investment company for which such person so serves or acts, or at the time of the alleged misconduct, so served or acted—

(1) as officer, director, member of any advisory board, investment adviser, or depositor; or

(2) as principal underwriter, if such registered company is an open-end company, unit investment trust, or face-amount certificate company.

If such allegations are established, the court may enjoin such person from acting in any or all such capacities either permanently or temporarily and award such injunctive or other relief against such person as may be reasonable and appropriate in the circumstances, having due regard to the protection of investors and to the effectuation of the policies declared in section 1(b) of this title.

(b) For the purposes of this subsection, the investment adviser of a registered investment company shall be deemed to have a fiduciary duty with respect to the receipt of compensation for services, or of payments of a material nature, paid by such registered investment company, or by the security holders therof, to such investment adviser or any affiliated person of such investment adviser. An action may be brought under this subsection by the Commission, or by a security holder of such registered investment company on behalf of such company, against such investment adviser, or any affiliated person of such investment adviser, or any other person enumerated in subsection (a) of this section who has a fiduciary duty concerning such compensation or payments, for breach of fiduciary duty in respect of such compensation or payments paid by such registered investment company or by the security holders thereof to such investment adviser or person. With respect to any such action the following provisions shall apply:

(1) It shall not be necessary to allege or prove that any defendant engaged in personal misconduct, and the plaintiff shall have the burden of proving a breach of fiduciary duty.

(2) In any such action approval by the board of directors of such investment company of such compensation or payments, or of contracts or other arrangements providing for such compensation or payments, and ratification or approval of such compensation or payments, or of contracts or other arrangements providing for such compensation or payments, by the shareholders of such investment company, shall be given such consideration by the court as is deemed appropriate under all the circumstances.

(3) No such action shall be brought or maintained against any person other than the recipient of such compensation or payments, and no damages or other relief shall be granted against any person other than the recipient of such compensation or payments. No award of damages shall be recoverable for any period prior to one year before the action was instituted. Any award of damages against such recipient shall be limited to the actual damages resulting from the breach of fiduciary duty and shall in no event exceed the amount of compensation or payments received from such investment company, or the security holders therof, by such recipient.

(4) This subsection shall not apply to compensation or payments made in connection with transactions subject to section 17 of this title, or rules, regulations, or orders thereunder, or to sales loads for the acquisition of any security issued by a registered investment company.

(5) Any action pursuant to this subsection may be brought only in an appropriate district court of the United States.

(6) No finding by a court with respect to a breach of fiduciary duty under this subsection shall be made a basis (A) for a finding of a violation of this title for the purposes of sections 9 and 49 of this title, section 15 of the Securities Exchange Act of 1934, or section 203 of title II of this Act, or (B) for an injunction to prohibit any person from serving in any of the capacities enumerated in subsection (a) of this section.

(c) For the purposes of subsections (a) and (b) the term "investment adviser" includes a corporate or other trustee performing the functions of an investment adviser.

Sec. 42. ENFORCEMENT OF TITLE

(a) The Commission may make such investigations as it deems necessary to determine whether any person has violated or is about to violate any provision of this title or of any rule, regulation, or order hereunder, or to determine whether any action in any court or any proceeding before the Commission shall be instituted under this title against a particular person or persons, or with respect to a particular transaction or transactions. The Commission shall permit any person to file with it a statement in writing, under oath or otherwise as the Commission shall determine, as to all the facts and circumstances concerning the matter to be investigated.

(b) For the purpose of any investigation or any other proceeding under this title, any member of the Commission, or any officer thereof designated by it, is empowered to administer oaths and affirmations, subpena witnesses, compel their attendance, take evidence, and require the production of any books, papers, correspondence, memoranda, contracts, agreements, or other records which are relevant or material to the inquiry. Such attendance of witnesses and the production of any such records may be required from any place in any State or in any Territory or other place subject to the jurisdiction of the United States at any designated place of hearing.

(c) In case of contumacy by, or refusal to obey a subpena issued to, any person, the Commission may invoke the aid of any court of the United States within the jurisdiction of which such investigation or proceeding is carried on, or where such person resides or carries on business, in requiring the attendance and testimony of witnesses and the production of books, papers, correspondence, memoranda, contracts, agreements, and other records. And such court may issue an order requiring such person to appear before the Commission or member or officer designated by the Commission, there to produce records, if so ordered, or to give testimony touching the matter under investigation or in question; any failure to obey such order of the court may be punished by such court as a contempt thereof. All process in any such case may be served in the judicial district whereof such person is an inhabitant or wherever he may be found. Any person who without just cause shall fail or refuse to attend and testify or to answer any lawful inquiry or to produce books, papers, correspondence, memoranda, contracts, agreements, or other records, if in his or its power so to do, in obedience to the subpena of the Commission, shall be guilty of a misdemeanor, and upon conviction shall be subject to a fine of not more than $1,000 or to imprisonment for a term of not more than one year, or both.

[Violations Enjoined]

(d) Whenever it shall appear to the Commission that any person has engaged or is about to engage in any act or practice constituting a violation of any provision of this title, or of any rule, regulation, or order hereunder, it may in its discretion bring an action in the proper district court of the United States, or the proper United States court of any Territory or other place subject to the jurisdiction of the United States, to enjoin such acts or practices and to enforce compliance with this title or any rule, regulation, or order hereunder. Upon a showing that such person has engaged or is about to engage in any such act or practice, a permanent or temporary injunction or decree or restraining order shall be granted without bond. In any proceeding under this subsection to enforce compliance with section 7, the court as a court of equity may, to the extent it deems necessary or appropriate, take exclusive jurisdiction and possession of the investment company or companies involved and the books, records, and assets thereof, wherever located; and the court shall have jurisdiction to appoint a trustee, who with the approval of the court shall have power to dispose of any or all of such assets, subject to such terms and conditions as the court may prescribe. The Commission may transmit such evidence as may be available concerning any violation of the provisions of this title, or of any rule, regulation, or order thereunder, the Attorney General, who, in his discretion, may institute the appropriate criminal proceedings under this title.

(e) MONEY PENALTIES IN CIVIL ACTIONS.—

(1) AUTHORITY OF COMMISSION.—Whenever it shall appear to the Commission that any person has violated any provision of this title, the rules or regulations thereunder, or a cease-and-desist order entered by the Commission pursuant to section 9(f) of this title, the Commission may bring an action in a United States district court to seek, and the court shall have jurisdiction to impose, upon a proper showing, a civil penalty to be paid by the person who committed such violation.

(2) AMOUNT OF PENALTY.—

(A) FIRST TIER.—The amount of the penalty shall be determined by the court in light of the facts and circumstances. For each violation, the amount of the penalty shall not exceed the greater of (i) $5,000 for a natural person or $50,000 for any other person, or (ii) the gross amount of pecuniary gain to such defendant as a result of the violation.

(B) SECOND TIER.—Notwithstanding subparagraph (A), the amount of penalty for each such violation shall not exceed the greater of (i) $50,000 for a natural person or $250,000 for any other person, or (ii) the gross amount of pecuniary gain to such defendant as a result of the violation, if the violation described in paragraph (1) involved fraud, deceit, manipulation, or deliberate or reckless disregard of a regulatory requirement.

(C) THIRD TIER.—Notwithstanding subparagraphs (A) and (B), the amount of penalty for each such violation shall not exceed the greater of (i) $100,000 for a natural person or $500,000 for any other person, or (ii) the gross amount of pecuniary gain to such defendant as a result of the violation, if—

(I) the violation described in paragraph (1) involved fraud, deceit, manipulation, or deliberate or reckless disregard of a regulatory requirement; and

(II) such violation directly or indirectly resulted in substantial losses or created a significant risk of substantial losses to other persons.

(3) PROCEDURES FOR COLLECTION.—

(A) PAYMENT OF PENALTY TO TREASURY.—A penalty imposed under this section shall be payable into the Treasury of the United States, except as otherwise provided in section 308 of the Sarbanes-Oxley Act of 2002 and Section 21F of the Securities Exchange Act of 1934.

(B) COLLECTION OF PENALTIES.—If a person upon whom such a penalty is imposed shall fail to pay such penalty within the time prescribed in the court's order, the Commission may refer the matter to the Attorney General who shall recover such penalty by action in the appropriate United States district court.

(C) REMEDY NOT EXCLUSIVE.—The actions authorized by this subsection may be brought in addition to any other action that the Commission or the Attorney General is entitled to bring.

(D) JURISDICTION AND VENUE.—For purposes of section 44 of this title, actions under this paragraph shall be actions to enforce a liability or a duty created by this title.

(4) SPECIAL PROVISIONS RELATING TO A VIOLATION OF A CEASE-AND-DESIST ORDER.—In an action to enforce a cease-and-desist order entered by the Commission pursuant to section 9(f), each separate violation of such order shall be a separate offense, except that in the case of a violation through a continuing failure to comply with the order, each day of the failure to comply shall be deemed a separate offense.

INVESTMENT COMPANY ACT RULES—SELECTED PROVISIONS

17 C.F.R. §§ 270.2a-4—270.38a-1

N.B. The following is not a complete text of the Investment Company Act Rules. It omits a number of statutory provisions entirely, and also omits certain subsections of provisions that are partially included.

Rule 0-1. Definition of terms used in this part

(a) As used in the rules and regulations prescribed by the Commission pursuant to the Investment Company Act of 1940, unless the context otherwise requires: . . .

(6) (i) A person is an independent legal counsel with respect to the directors who are not interested persons of an investment company ("disinterested directors") if:

(A) A majority of the disinterested directors reasonably determine in the exercise of their judgment (and record the basis for that determination in the minutes of their meeting) that any representation by the person of the company's investment adviser, principal underwriter, administrator ("management organizations"), or any of their control persons, since the beginning of the fund's last two completed fiscal years, is or was sufficiently limited that it is unlikely to adversely affect the professional judgment of the person in providing legal representation to the disinterested directors; and

(B) The disinterested directors have obtained an undertaking from such person to provide them with information necessary to make their determination and to update promptly that information when the person begins to represent, or materially increases his representation of, a management organization or control person.

(ii) The disinterested directors are entitled to rely on the information obtained from the person, unless they know or have reason to believe that the information is materially false or incomplete. The disinterested directors must re-evaluate their determination no less frequently than annually (and record the basis accordingly), except as provided in paragraph (iii) of this section.

(iii) After the disinterested directors obtain information that the person has begun to represent, or has materially increased his representation of, a management organization (or any of its control persons), the person may continue to be an independent legal counsel, for purposes of paragraph (a)(6)(i) of this section, for no longer than three months unless during that period the disinterested directors make a new determination under that paragraph.

(iv) For purposes of paragraphs (a)(6)(i)-(iii) of this section:

(A) The term person has the same meaning as in section 2(a)(28) of the Act (15 U.S.C. 80a-2(a)(28)) and, in addition, includes a partner, co-member, or employee of any person; and

(B) The term control person means any person (other than an investment company) directly or indirectly controlling, controlled by, or under common control with any of the investment company's management organizations.

(7) Fund governance standards. The board of directors of an investment company ("fund") satisfies the fund governance standards if:

(i) At least seventy-five percent of the directors of the fund are not interested persons of the fund ("disinterested directors") or, if the fund has three directors, all but one are disinterested directors;

(ii) The disinterested directors of the fund select and nominate any other disinterested director of the fund;

(iii) Any person who acts as legal counsel for the disinterested directors of the fund is an independent legal counsel as defined in paragraph (a)(6) of this section;

(iv) A disinterested director serves as chairman of the board of directors of the fund, presides over meetings of the board of directors and has substantially the same responsibilities as would a chairman of a board of directors;

(v) The board of directors evaluates at least once annually the performance of the board of directors and the committees of the board of directors, which evaluation must include a consideration of the effectiveness of the committee structure of the fund board and the number of funds on whose boards each director serves;

(vi) The disinterested directors meet at least once quarterly in a session at which no directors who are interested persons of the fund are present; and

(vii) The disinterested directors have been authorized to hire employees and to retain advisers and experts necessary to carry out their duties.

Rule 2a-4. Definition of "Current Net Asset Value" for use in Computing Periodically the Current Price of Redeemable Security

(a) The current net asset value of any redeemable security issued by a registered investment company used in computing periodically the current price for the purpose of distribution, redemption, and repurchase means an amount which reflects calculations, whether or not recorded in the books of account, made substantially in accordance with the following, with estimates used where necessary or appropriate:

(1) Portfolio securities with respect to which market quotations are readily available shall be valued at current market value, and other securities and assets shall be valued at fair value as determined in good faith by the board of directors of the registered company.

(2) Changes in holdings of portfolio securities shall be reflected no later than in the first calculation on the first business day following the trade date.

(3) Changes in the number of outstanding shares of the registered company resulting from distributions, redemptions, and repurchases shall be reflected no later than in the first calculation on the first business day following such change.

(4) Expenses, including any investment advisory fees, shall be included to date of calculation. Appropriate provision shall be made for Federal income taxes if required.

Investment companies which retain realized capital gains designated as a distribution to shareholders shall comply with paragraph (h) of § 210.6-03 of Regulation S-X.

(5) Dividends receivable shall be included to date of calculation either at ex-dividend dates or record dates, as appropriate.

(6) Interest income and other income shall be included to date of calculation.

(b) The items which would otherwise be required to be reflected by subparagraphs (4) and (6) above need not be so reflected if cumulatively, when netted, they do not amount to as much as 1 cent per outstanding share.

(c) Notwithstanding the requirements of paragraph (a) above, any interim determination of current net asset value between calculations made as of the close of the New York Stock Exchange on the preceding business day and the current business day may be estimated so as to reflect any change in current net asset value since the closing calculation on the preceding business day.

Rule 2a-7. Money Market Funds

(a) *Definitions*—

(1) *Acquisition* (or *acquire*) means any purchase or subsequent rollover (but does not include the failure to exercise a demand feature).

(2) *Amortized cost method* of valuation means the method of calculating an investment company's net asset value whereby portfolio securities are valued at the fund's acquisition cost as adjusted for amortization of premium or accretion of discount rather than at their value based on current market factors.

(3) *Asset-backed security* means a fixed income security (other than a government security) issued by a special purpose entity (as defined in this paragraph (a)(3)), substantially all of the assets of which consist of qualifying assets (as defined in this paragraph (a)(3)). Special purpose entity means a trust, corporation, partnership or other entity organized for the sole purpose of issuing securities that entitle their holders to receive payments that depend primarily on the cash flow from qualifying assets, but does not include a registered investment company. Qualifying assets means financial assets, either fixed or revolving, that by their terms convert into cash within a finite time period, plus any rights or other assets designed to assure the servicing or timely distribution of proceeds to security holders.

(4) *Business day* means any day, other than Saturday, Sunday, or any customary business holiday.

(5) *Collateralized fully* has the same meaning as defined in § 270.5b-3(c)(1) except that § 270.5b-3(c)(1)(iv)(C) shall not apply.

(6) *Conditional demand feature* means a demand feature that is not an unconditional demand feature. A conditional demand feature is not a guarantee.

(7) *Conduit security* means a security issued by a municipal issuer (as defined in this paragraph (a)(7)) involving an arrangement or agreement entered into, directly or indirectly, with a person other than a municipal issuer, which arrangement or agreement provides for or secures repayment of the security. Municipal issuer means a state or territory of the United States (including the District of Columbia), or any political subdivision or public instrumentality of a state or territory of the United States. A conduit security does not include a security that is:

(i) Fully and unconditionally guaranteed by a municipal issuer;

(ii) Payable from the general revenues of the municipal issuer or other municipal issuers (other than those revenues derived from an agreement or arrangement with a person who is not a municipal issuer that provides for or secures repayment of the security issued by the municipal issuer);

(iii) Related to a project owned and operated by a municipal issuer; or

(iv) Related to a facility leased to and under the control of an industrial or commercial enterprise that is part of a public project which, as a whole, is owned and under the control of a municipal issuer.

(8) *Daily liquid assets* means:

(i) Cash;

(ii) Direct obligations of the U.S. Government;

(iii) Securities that will mature, as determined without reference to the exceptions in paragraph (i) of this section regarding interest rate readjustments, or are subject to a demand feature that is exercisable and payable, within one business day; or

(iv) Amounts receivable and due unconditionally within one business day on pending sales of portfolio securities.

(9) *Demand feature* means a feature permitting the holder of a security to sell the security at an exercise price equal to the approximate amortized cost of the security plus accrued interest, if any, at the later of the time of exercise or the settlement of the transaction, paid within 397 calendar days of exercise.

(10) *Demand feature issued by a non-controlled person* means a demand feature issued by:

(i) A person that, directly or indirectly, does not control, and is not controlled by or under common control with the issuer of the security subject to the demand feature (control means "control" as defined in section 2(a)(9) of the Act) (15 U.S.C. 80a-2(a)(9)); or

(ii) A sponsor of a special purpose entity with respect to an asset-backed security.

(11) *Eligible security means a security*:

(i) With a remaining maturity of 397 calendar days or less that the fund's board of directors determines presents minimal credit risks to the fund, which determination must include an analysis of the capacity of the security's issuer or guarantor (including for this paragraph (a)(11)(i) the provider of a conditional demand feature, when applicable) to meet its financial obligations, and such analysis must include, to the extent appropriate, consideration of the following factors with respect to the security's issuer or guarantor:

(A) Financial condition;

(B) Sources of liquidity;

(C) Ability to react to future market-wide and issuer- or guarantor-specific events, including ability to repay debt in a highly adverse situation; and

(D) Strength of the issuer or guarantor's industry within the economy and relative to economic trends, and issuer or guarantor's competitive position within its industry.

(ii) That is issued by a registered investment company that is a money market fund; or

(iii) That is a government security.

Note to Paragraph (a)(11): For a discussion of additional factors that may be relevant in evaluating certain specific asset types see Investment Company Act Release No. IC-31828 (9/16/15).

(12) *Event of insolvency* has the same meaning as defined in § 270.5b-3(c)(2).

(13) *Floating rate security* means a security the terms of which provide for the adjustment of its interest rate whenever a specified interest rate changes and that, at any time until the final maturity of the instrument or the period remaining until the principal amount can be recovered through demand, can reasonably be expected to have a market value that approximates its amortized cost.

(14) *Government money market fund* means a money market fund that invests 99.5 percent or more of its total assets in cash, government securities, and/or repurchase agreements that are collateralized fully.

(15) *Government security* has the same meaning as defined in section 2(a)(16) of the Act (15 U.S.C. 80a-2(a)(16)).

(16) *Guarantee*:

(i) Means an unconditional obligation of a person other than the issuer of the security to undertake to pay, upon presentment by the holder of the guarantee (if required), the principal amount of the underlying security plus accrued interest when due or upon default, or, in the case of an unconditional demand feature, an obligation that entitles the holder to receive upon the later of exercise or the settlement of the transaction the approximate amortized cost of the underlying security or securities, plus accrued interest, if any. A guarantee includes a letter of credit, financial guaranty (bond) insurance, and an unconditional demand feature (other than an unconditional demand feature provided by the issuer of the security).

(ii) The sponsor of a special purpose entity with respect to an asset-backed security shall be deemed to have provided a guarantee with respect to the entire principal amount of the asset-backed security for purposes of this section, except paragraphs (a)(12)(iii) (definition of eligible security), (d)(2)(iii) (credit substitution), (d)(3)(iv)(A) (fractional guarantees) and (e) (guarantees not relied on) of this section, unless the money market fund's board of directors has determined that the fund is not relying on the sponsor's financial strength or its ability or willingness to provide liquidity, credit or other support to determine the quality (pursuant to paragraph (d)(2) of this section) or liquidity (pursuant to paragraph (d)(4) of this section) of the asset-backed security, and maintains a record of this determination (pursuant to paragraphs (g)(7) and (h)(6) of this section).

(17) *Guarantee issued by a non-controlled person* means a guarantee issued by:

(i) A person that, directly or indirectly, does not control, and is not controlled by or under common control with the issuer of the security subject to the guarantee (control means "control" as defined in section 2(a)(9) of the Act) (15 U.S.C. 80a-2(a)(9))); or

(ii) A sponsor of a special purpose entity with respect to an asset-backed security.

(18) *Illiquid security* means a security that cannot be sold or disposed of in the ordinary course of business within seven calendar days at approximately the value ascribed to it by the fund.

(19) *Penny-rounding method* of pricing means the method of computing an investment company's price per share for purposes of distribution, redemption and repurchase whereby the current net asset value per share is rounded to the nearest one percent.

(20) *Refunded security* has the same meaning as defined in § 270.5b-3(c)(4) [sic; should be § 270.5b-3(c)(5)].

(21) *Retail money market fund* means a money market fund that has policies and procedures reasonably designed to limit all beneficial owners of the fund to natural persons.

(22) *Single state fund* means a tax exempt fund that holds itself out as seeking to maximize the amount of its distributed income that is exempt from the income taxes or other taxes on investments of a particular state and, where applicable, subdivisions thereof.

(23) *Tax exempt fund* means any money market fund that holds itself out as distributing income exempt from regular federal income tax.

(24) *Total assets* means, with respect to a money market fund using the Amortized Cost Method, the total amortized cost of its assets and, with respect to any other money market fund, means the total value of the money market fund's assets, as defined in section 2(a)(41) of the Act (15 U.S.C. 80a-2(a)(41)) and the rules thereunder.

(25) *Unconditional demand feature* means a demand feature that by its terms would be readily exercisable in the event of a default in payment of principal or interest on the underlying security or securities.

(26) *United States dollar-denominated* means, with reference to a security, that all principal and interest payments on such security are payable to security holders in United States dollars under all circumstances and that the interest rate of, the principal amount to be repaid, and the timing of payments related to such security do not vary or float with the value

of a foreign currency, the rate of interest payable on foreign currency borrowings, or with any other interest rate or index expressed in a currency other than United States dollars.

(27) *Variable rate security* means a security the terms of which provide for the adjustment of its interest rate on set dates (such as the last day of a month or calendar quarter) and that, upon each adjustment until the final maturity of the instrument or the period remaining until the principal amount can be recovered through demand, can reasonably be expected to have a market value that approximates its amortized cost.

(28) *Weekly liquid assets* means:

(i) Cash;

(ii) Direct obligations of the U.S. Government;

(iii) Government securities that are issued by a person controlled or supervised by and acting as an instrumentality of the government of the United States pursuant to authority granted by the Congress of the United States that:

(A) Are issued at a discount to the principal amount to be repaid at maturity without provision for the payment of interest; and

(B) Have a remaining maturity date of 60 days or less.

(iv) Securities that will mature, as determined without reference to the exceptions in paragraph (i) of this section regarding interest rate readjustments, or are subject to a demand feature that is exercisable and payable, within five business days; or

(v) Amounts receivable and due unconditionally within five business days on pending sales of portfolio securities.

(b) *Holding Out and Use of Names and Titles*—

(1) *Holding Out*. It shall be an untrue statement of material fact within the meaning of section 34(b) of the Act (15 U.S.C. 80a-33(b)) for a registered investment company, in any registration statement, application, report, account, record, or other document filed or transmitted pursuant to the Act, including any advertisement, pamphlet, circular, form letter, or other sales literature addressed to or intended for distribution to prospective investors that is required to be filed with the Commission by section 24(b) of the Act (15 U.S.C. 80a-24(b)), to hold itself out to investors as a money market fund or the equivalent of a money market fund, unless such registered investment company complies with this section.

(2) *Names*. It shall constitute the use of a materially deceptive or misleading name or title within the meaning of section 35(d) of the Act (15 U.S.C. 80a-34(d)) for a registered investment company to adopt the term "money market" as part of its name or title or the name or title of any redeemable securities of which it is the issuer, or to adopt a name that suggests that it is a money market fund or the equivalent of a money market fund, unless such registered investment company complies with this section.

(3) *Titles*. For purposes of paragraph (b)(2) of this section, a name that suggests that a registered investment company is a money market fund or the equivalent thereof includes one that uses such terms as "cash," "liquid," "money," "ready assets" or similar terms.

(c) *Pricing and Redeeming Shares*—

(1) *Share Price Calculation*.

(i) The current price per share, for purposes of distribution, redemption and repurchase, of any redeemable security issued by a government money market fund or retail money market fund, notwithstanding the requirements of section 2(a)(41) of the Act (15 U.S.C. 80a-2(a)(41)) and of §§ 270.2a-4 and 270.22c-1 thereunder, may be computed by use of the amortized cost method and/or the penny-rounding method. To use these methods, the board of directors of the government or retail money market fund must determine, in good faith, that it is in the best interests of the fund and its shareholders to maintain a stable net asset value per share or stable price per share, by virtue of either the amortized cost method and/or the penny-rounding method. The government or retail money market fund may continue to use such methods only so long as the board of directors believes that they fairly reflect the market-based net asset value per share and the fund complies with the other requirements of this section.

(ii) Any money market fund that is not a government money market fund or a retail money market fund must compute its price per share for purposes of distribution, redemption and repurchase by rounding the fund's current net asset value per share to a minimum of the fourth decimal place in the case of a fund with a $1.0000 share price or an equivalent or more precise level of accuracy for money market funds with a different share price (e.g. $10.000 per share, or $100.00 per share).

(2) *Liquidity Fees and Temporary Suspensions of Redemptions.* Except as provided in paragraphs (c)(2)(iii) and (v) of this section, and notwithstanding sections 22(e) and 27(i) of the Act (15 U.S.C. 80a-22(e) and 80a-27(i)) and § 270.22c-1:

(i) *Discretionary Liquidity Fees and Temporary Suspensions of Redemptions.* If, at any time, the money market fund has invested less than thirty percent of its total assets in weekly liquid assets, the fund may institute a liquidity fee (not to exceed two percent of the value of the shares redeemed) or suspend the right of redemption temporarily, subject to paragraphs (c)(2)(i)(A) and (B) of this section, if the fund's board of directors, including a majority of the directors who are not interested persons of the fund, determines that the fee or suspension of redemptions is in the best interests of the fund.

(A) *Duration and Application of Discretionary Liquidity Fee.* Once imposed, a discretionary liquidity fee must be applied to all shares redeemed and must remain in effect until the money market fund's board of directors, including a majority of the directors who are not interested persons of the fund, determines that imposing such liquidity fee is no longer in the best interests of the fund. Provided however, that if, at the end of a business day, the money market fund has invested thirty percent or more of its total assets in weekly liquid assets, the fund must cease charging the liquidity fee, effective as of the beginning of the next business day.

(B) *Duration of Temporary Suspension of Redemptions.* The temporary suspension of redemptions must apply to all shares and must remain in effect until the fund's board of directors, including a majority of the directors who are not interested persons of the fund, determines that the temporary suspension of redemptions is no longer in the best interests of the fund. Provided, however, that the fund must restore the right of redemption on the earlier of:

(1) The beginning of the next business day following a business day that ended with the money market fund having invested thirty percent or more of its total assets in weekly liquid assets; or

(2) The beginning of the next business day following ten business days after suspending redemptions. The money market fund may not suspend the right of redemption pursuant to this section for more than ten business days in any rolling ninety calendar day period.

(ii) *Default Liquidity Fees.* If, at the end of a business day, the money market fund has invested less than ten percent of its total assets in weekly liquid assets, the fund must institute a liquidity fee, effective as of the beginning of the next business day, as described in paragraphs (c)(2)(ii)(A) and (B) of this section, unless the fund's board of directors, including a majority of the directors who are not interested persons of the fund, determines that imposing the fee is not in the best interests of the fund.

(A) *Amount of Default Liquidity Fee.* The default liquidity fee shall be one percent of the value of shares redeemed unless the money market fund's board of directors, including a majority of the directors who are not interested persons of the fund, determines, at the time of initial imposition or later, that a higher or lower fee level is in the best interests of the fund. A liquidity fee may not exceed two percent of the value of the shares redeemed.

(B) *Duration and Application of Default Liquidity Fee.* Once imposed, the default liquidity fee must be applied to all shares redeemed and shall remain in effect until the money market fund's board of directors, including a majority of the directors who are not interested persons of the fund, determines that imposing such liquidity fee is not in the best interests of the fund. Provided however, that if, at the end of a business day, the money market fund has invested thirty percent or more of its total assets in weekly liquid assets, the fund must cease charging the liquidity fee, effective as of the beginning of the next business day.

(iii) *Government Money Market Funds.* The requirements of paragraphs (c)(2)(i) and (ii) of this section shall not apply to a government money market fund. A government money market fund may, however, choose to rely on the ability to impose liquidity fees and suspend redemptions consistent with the requirements of paragraph (c)(2)(i) and/or (ii) of this section and any other requirements that apply to liquidity fees and temporary suspensions of redemptions (e.g., Item 4(b)(1)(ii) of Form N-1A (§ 274.11A of this chapter)).

(iv) *Variable Contracts.* Notwithstanding section 27(i) of the Act (15 U.S.C. 80a-27(i)), a variable insurance contract issued by a registered separate account funding variable insurance contracts or the sponsoring insurance company of such separate account may apply a liquidity fee or temporary suspension of redemptions pursuant to paragraph (c)(2) of this section to contract owners who allocate all or a portion of their contract value to a subaccount of the separate account that is either a money market fund or that invests all of its assets in shares of a money market fund.

(v) *Master Feeder Funds.* Any money market fund (a "feeder fund") that owns, pursuant to section 12(d)(1)(E) of the Act (15 U.S.C. 80a-12(d)(1)(E)), shares of another money market fund (a "master fund") may not impose liquidity fees or temporary suspensions of redemptions under paragraphs (c)(2)(i) and (ii) of this section, provided however, that if a master fund, in which the feeder fund invests, imposes a liquidity fee or temporary suspension of redemptions pursuant to paragraphs (c)(2)(i) and (ii) of this section, then the feeder fund shall pass through to its investors the fee or redemption suspension on the same terms and conditions as imposed by the master fund.

(d) *Risk-Limiting Conditions*—

(1) *Portfolio Maturity.* The money market fund must maintain a dollar-weighted average portfolio maturity appropriate to its investment objective; provided, however, that the money market fund must not:

(i) Acquire any instrument with a remaining maturity of greater than 397 calendar days;

(ii) Maintain a dollar-weighted average portfolio maturity ("WAM") that exceeds 60 calendar days; or

(iii) Maintain a dollar-weighted average portfolio maturity that exceeds 120 calendar days, determined without reference to the exceptions in paragraph (i) of this section regarding interest rate readjustments ("WAL").

(2) *Portfolio Quality*—

(i) *General.* The money market fund must limit its portfolio investments to those United States dollar-denominated securities that at the time of acquisition are eligible securities.

(ii) *Securities Subject to Guarantees.* A security that is subject to a guarantee may be determined to be an eligible security based solely on whether the guarantee is an eligible security, provided however, that the issuer of the guarantee, or another institution, has undertaken to promptly notify the holder of the security in the event the guarantee is substituted with another guarantee (if such substitution is permissible under the terms of the guarantee).

(iii) *Securities Subject to Conditional Demand Features.* A security that is subject to a conditional demand feature ("underlying security") may be determined to be an eligible security only if:

(A) The conditional demand feature is an eligible security;

(B) The underlying security or any guarantee of such security is an eligible security, except that the underlying security or guarantee may have a remaining maturity of more than 397 calendar days.

(C) At the time of the acquisition of the underlying security, the money market fund's board of directors has determined that there is minimal risk that the circumstances that would result in the conditional demand feature not being exercisable will occur; and

(1) The conditions limiting exercise either can be monitored readily by the fund or relate to the taxability, under federal, state or local law, of the interest payments on the security; or

(2) The terms of the conditional demand feature require that the fund will receive notice of the occurrence of the condition and the opportunity to exercise the demand feature in accordance with its terms; and

(D) The issuer of the conditional demand feature, or another institution, has undertaken to promptly notify the holder of the security in the event the conditional demand feature is substituted with another conditional demand feature (if such substitution is permissible under the terms of the conditional demand feature).

(3) *Portfolio Diversification—*

(i) *Issuer Diversification.* The money market fund must be diversified with respect to issuers of securities acquired by the fund as provided in paragraphs (d)(3)(i) and (ii) of this section, other than with respect to government securities.

(A) *Taxable and National Funds.* Immediately after the acquisition of any security, a money market fund other than a single state fund must not have invested more than:

(1) Five percent of its total assets in securities issued by the issuer of the security, provided, however, that with respect to paragraph (d)(3)(i)(A) of this section, such a fund may invest up to twenty-five percent of its total assets in the securities of a single issuer for a period of up to three business days after the acquisition thereof; provided, further, that the fund may not invest in the securities of more than one issuer in accordance with the foregoing proviso in this paragraph (d)(3)(i)(A)(1) at any time; and

(2) Ten percent of its total assets in securities issued by or subject to demand features or guarantees from the institution that issued the demand feature or guarantee, provided, however, that a tax exempt fund need only comply with this paragraph (d)(3)(i)(A)(2) with respect to eighty-five percent of its total assets, subject to paragraph (d)(3)(iii) of this section.

(B) *Single State Funds.* Immediately after the acquisition of any security, a single state fund must not have invested:

(1) With respect to seventy-five percent of its total assets, more than five percent of its total assets in securities issued by the issuer of the security; and

(2) With respect to seventy-five percent of its total assets, more than ten percent of its total assets in securities issued by or subject to demand features or guarantees from the institution that issued the demand feature or guarantee, subject to paragraph (d)(3)(iii) of this section.

(ii) *Issuer Diversification Calculations.* For purposes of making calculations under paragraph (d)(3)(i) of this section:

(A) *Repurchase Agreements.* The acquisition of a repurchase agreement may be deemed to be an acquisition of the underlying securities, provided the obligation of the seller to repurchase the securities from the money market fund is collateralized fully and the fund's board of directors has evaluated the seller's creditworthiness.

(B) *Refunded Securities.* The acquisition of a refunded security shall be deemed to be an acquisition of the escrowed government securities.

(C) *Conduit Securities.* A conduit security shall be deemed to be issued by the person (other than the municipal issuer) ultimately responsible for payments of interest and principal on the security.

(D) *Asset-Backed Securities—*

(1) *General.* An asset-backed security acquired by a fund ("primary ABs") shall be deemed to be issued by the special purpose entity that issued the asset-backed security, provided, however:

    (i) *Holdings of Primary ABS.* Any person whose obligations constitute ten percent or more of the principal amount of the qualifying assets of the primary ABS ("ten percent obligor") shall be deemed to be an issuer of the portion of the primary ABS such obligations represent; and

    (ii) *Holdings of Secondary ABS.* If a ten percent obligor of a primary ABS is itself a special purpose entity issuing asset-backed securities ("secondary ABs"), any ten percent obligor of such secondary ABS also shall be deemed to be an issuer of the portion of the primary ABS that such ten percent obligor represents.

(2) *Restricted Special Purpose Entities.* A ten percent obligor with respect to a primary or secondary ABS shall not be deemed to have issued any portion of the assets of a primary ABS as provided in paragraph (d)(3)(ii)(D)(1) of this section if that ten percent obligor is itself a special purpose entity issuing asset-backed securities ("restricted special purpose entity"), and the securities that it issues (other than securities issued to a company that controls, or is controlled by or under common control with, the restricted special purpose entity and which is not itself a special purpose entity issuing asset-backed securities) are held by only one other special purpose entity.

(3) *Demand Features and Guarantees.* In the case of a ten percent obligor deemed to be an issuer, the fund must satisfy the diversification requirements of paragraph (d)(3)(iii) of this section with respect to any demand feature or guarantee to which the ten percent obligor's obligations are subject.

(E) *Shares of Other Money Market Funds.* A money market fund that acquires shares issued by another money market fund in an amount that would otherwise be prohibited by paragraph (d)(3)(i) of this section shall nonetheless be deemed in compliance with this section if the board of directors of the acquiring money market fund reasonably believes that the fund in which it has invested is in compliance with this section.

(F) *Treatment of Certain Affiliated Entities*—

(1) *General.* The money market fund, when calculating the amount of its total assets invested in securities issued by any particular issuer for purposes of paragraph (d)(3)(i) of this section, must treat as a single issuer two or more issuers of securities owned by the money market fund if one issuer controls the other, is controlled by the other issuer, or is under common control with the other issuer, provided that "control" for this purpose means ownership of more than 50 percent of the issuer's voting securities.

(2) *Equity Owners of Asset-Backed Commercial Paper Special Purpose Entities.* The money market fund is not required to aggregate an asset-backed commercial paper special purpose entity and its equity owners under paragraph (d)(3)(ii)(F)(1) of this section provided that a primary line of business of its equity owners is owning equity interests in special purpose entities and providing services to special purpose entities, the independent equity owners' activities with respect to the SPEs are limited to providing management or administrative services, and no qualifying assets of the special purpose entity were originated by the equity owners.

(3) *Ten Percent Obligors.* For purposes of determining ten percent obligors pursuant to paragraph (d)(3)(ii)(D)(1)(i) of this section, the money market fund must treat as a single person two or more persons whose obligations in the aggregate constitute ten percent or more of the principal amount of the qualifying assets of the primary ABS if one person controls the other, is controlled by the other person, or is under common control with the person, provided that "control" for this purpose means ownership of more than 50 percent of the person's voting securities.

(iii) *Diversification Rules For Demand Features and Guarantees.* The money market fund must be diversified with respect to demand features and guarantees acquired by the fund as provided in paragraphs (d)(3)(i), (iii), and (iv) of this section, other than with respect to a demand feature issued by the same institution that issued the underlying security, or with respect to a guarantee or demand feature that is itself a government security.

(A) *General.* Immediately after the acquisition of any demand feature or guarantee, any security subject to a demand feature or guarantee, or a security directly issued by the issuer of a demand feature or guarantee, a money market fund must not have invested more than ten percent of its total assets in securities issued by or subject to demand features or guarantees from the institution that issued the demand feature or guarantee, subject to paragraphs (d)(3)(i) and (d)(3)(iii)(B) of this section.

(B) *Tax Exempt Funds.* Immediately after the acquisition of any demand feature or guarantee, any security subject to a demand feature or guarantee, or a security directly issued by the issuer of a demand feature or guarantee (any such acquisition, a "demand feature or guarantee acquisition"), a tax exempt fund, with respect to eighty-five percent of its total assets, must not have invested more than ten percent of its total assets in securities issued by or subject to demand features or guarantees from the institution that issued the demand feature or guarantee; provided that any demand feature or guarantee acquisition in excess of ten percent of the fund's total assets in accordance with this paragraph must be a demand feature or guarantee issued by a non-controlled person.

(iv) *Demand Feature and Guarantee Diversification Calculations—*

(A) *Fractional Demand Features or Guarantees.* In the case of a security subject to a demand feature or guarantee from an institution by which the institution guarantees a specified portion of the value of the security, the institution shall be deemed to guarantee the specified portion thereof.

(B) *Layered Demand Features or Guarantees.* In the case of a security subject to demand features or guarantees from multiple institutions that have not limited the extent of their obligations as described in paragraph (d)(3)(iv)(A) of this section, each institution shall be deemed to have provided the demand feature or guarantee with respect to the entire principal amount of the security.

(v) *Diversification Safe Harbor.* A money market fund that satisfies the applicable diversification requirements of paragraphs (d)(3) and (e) of this section shall be deemed to have satisfied the diversification requirements of section 5(b)(1) of the Act (15 U.S.C. 80a-5(b)(1)) and the rules adopted thereunder.

(4) *Portfolio Liquidity.* The money market fund must hold securities that are sufficiently liquid to meet reasonably foreseeable shareholder redemptions in light of the fund's obligations under section 22(e) of the Act (15 U.S.C. 80a-22(e)) and any commitments the fund has made to shareholders; provided, however, that:

(i) *Illiquid Securities.* The money market fund may not acquire any illiquid security if, immediately after the acquisition, the money market fund would have invested more than five percent of its total assets in illiquid securities.

(ii) *Minimum Daily Liquidity Requirement.* The money market fund may not acquire any security other than a daily liquid asset if, immediately after the acquisition, the fund would have invested less than ten percent of its total assets in daily liquid assets. This provision does not apply to tax exempt funds.

(iii) *Minimum Weekly Liquidity Requirement.* The money market fund may not acquire any security other than a weekly liquid asset if, immediately after the acquisition, the fund would have invested less than thirty percent of its total assets in weekly liquid assets.

(e) *Demand Features and Guarantees Not Relied Upon.* If the fund's board of directors has determined that the fund is not relying on a demand feature or guarantee to determine the quality (pursuant to paragraph (d)(2) of this section), or maturity (pursuant to paragraph (i) of this section), or liquidity of a portfolio security (pursuant to paragraph (d)(4) of this section), and maintains a record of this determination (pursuant to paragraphs (g)(3) and (h)(7) of this section), then the fund may disregard such demand feature or guarantee for all purposes of this section.

(f) *Defaults and Other Events—*

(1) *Adverse Events.* Upon the occurrence of any of the events specified in paragraphs (f)(1)(i) through (iii) of this section with respect to a portfolio security, the money market fund shall dispose of such security as soon as practicable consistent with achieving an orderly disposition of the security, by sale, exercise of any demand feature or otherwise, absent a finding by the board of directors that disposal of the portfolio security would not be in the best interests of the money market fund (which determination may take into account, among other factors, market conditions that could affect the orderly disposition of the portfolio security):

(i) The default with respect to a portfolio security (other than an immaterial default unrelated to the financial condition of the issuer);

(ii) A portfolio security ceases to be an eligible security (e.g., no longer presents minimal credit risks); or

(iii) An event of insolvency occurs with respect to the issuer of a portfolio security or the provider of any demand feature or guarantee.

(2) *Notice to the Commission.* The money market fund must notify the Commission of the occurrence of certain material events, as specified in Form N-CR (§ 274.222 of this chapter).

(3) *Defaults For Purposes of Paragraphs (f)(1) and (2) of this Section.* For purposes of paragraphs (f)(1) and (2) of this section, an instrument subject to a demand feature or guarantee shall not be deemed to be in default (and an event of insolvency with respect to the security shall not be deemed to have occurred) if:

(i) In the case of an instrument subject to a demand feature, the demand feature has been exercised and the fund has recovered either the principal amount or the amortized cost of the instrument, plus accrued interest;

(ii) The provider of the guarantee is continuing, without protest, to make payments as due on the instrument; or

(iii) The provider of a guarantee with respect to an asset-backed security pursuant to paragraph (a)(16)(ii) of this section is continuing, without protest, to provide credit, liquidity or other support as necessary to permit the asset-backed security to make payments as due.

(g) *Required Procedures.* The money market fund's board of directors must adopt written procedures including the following:

(1) *Funds Using Amortized Cost.* In the case of a government or retail money market fund that uses the amortized cost method of valuation, in supervising the money market fund's operations and delegating special responsibilities involving portfolio management to the money market fund's investment adviser, the money market fund's board of directors, as a particular responsibility within the overall duty of care owed to its shareholders, shall establish written procedures reasonably designed, taking into account current market conditions and the money market fund's investment objectives, to stabilize the money market fund's net asset value per share, as computed for the purpose of distribution, redemption and repurchase, at a single value.

(i) *Specific Procedures.* Included within the procedures adopted by the board of directors shall be the following:

(A) *Shadow Pricing.* Written procedures shall provide:

(1) That the extent of deviation, if any, of the current net asset value per share calculated using available market quotations (or an appropriate substitute that reflects current market conditions) from the money market fund's amortized cost price per share, shall be calculated at least daily, and at such other intervals that the board of directors determines appropriate and reasonable in light of current market conditions;

(2) For the periodic review by the board of directors of the amount of the deviation as well as the methods used to calculate the deviation; and

(3) For the maintenance of records of the determination of deviation and the board's review thereof.

(B) *Prompt Consideration of Deviation*. In the event such deviation from the money market fund's amortized cost price per share exceeds 1/2 of 1 percent, the board of directors shall promptly consider what action, if any, should be initiated by the board of directors.

(C) *Material Dilution or Unfair Results*. Where the board of directors believes the extent of any deviation from the money market fund's amortized cost price per share may result in material dilution or other unfair results to investors or existing share-holders, it shall cause the fund to take such action as it deems appropriate to eliminate or reduce to the extent reasonably practicable such dilution or unfair results.

(ii) [Reserved]

(2) *Funds Using Penny Rounding*. In the case of a government or retail money market fund that uses the penny rounding method of pricing, in supervising the money market fund's operations and delegating special responsibilities involving portfolio management to the money market fund's investment adviser, the money market fund's board of directors, as a particular responsibility within the overall duty of care owed to its shareholders, must establish written procedures reasonably designed, taking into account current market con-ditions and the money market fund's investment objectives, to assure to the extent reason-ably practicable that the money market fund's price per share as computed for the purpose of distribution, redemption and repurchase, rounded to the nearest one percent, will not deviate from the single price established by the board of directors.

(3) *Ongoing Review of Credit Risks*. The written procedures must require the adviser to provide ongoing review of whether each security (other than a government security) con-tinues to present minimal credit risks. The review must:

(i) Include an assessment of each security's credit quality, including the capacity of the issuer or guarantor (including conditional demand feature provider, when applicable) to meet its financial obligations; and

(ii) Be based on, among other things, financial data of the issuer of the portfolio security or provider of the guarantee or demand feature, as the case may be, and in the case of a security subject to a conditional demand feature, the issuer of the security whose financial condition must be monitored under paragraph (d)(2)(iii) of this section, whether such data is publicly available or provided under the terms of the security's governing documents.

(4) *Securities Subject to Demand Features or Guarantees*. In the case of a security subject to one or more demand features or guarantees that the fund's board of directors has deter-mined that the fund is not relying on to determine the quality (pursuant to paragraph (d)(2) of this section), maturity (pursuant to paragraph (i) of this section) or liquidity (pursuant to paragraph (d)(4) of this section) of the security subject to the demand feature or guarantee, written procedures must require periodic evaluation of such determination.

(5) *Adjustable Rate Securities Without Demand Features*. In the case of a variable rate or floating rate security that is not subject to a demand feature and for which maturity is determined pursuant to paragraph (i)(1), (i)(2) or (i)(4) of this section, written procedures shall require periodic review of whether the interest rate formula, upon readjustment of its interest rate, can reasonably be expected to cause the security to have a market value that approximates its amortized cost value.

(6) *Ten Percent Obligors of Asset-Backed Securities*. In the case of an asset-backed security, written procedures must require the fund to periodically determine the number of ten percent obligors (as that term is used in paragraph (d)(3)(ii)(D) of this section) deemed to be the issuers of all or a portion of the asset-backed security for purposes of paragraph (d)(3)(ii)(D) of this section; provided, however, written procedures need not require per-iodic determinations with respect to any asset-backed security that a fund's board of direc-tors has determined, at the time of acquisition, will not have, or is unlikely to have, ten percent obligors that are deemed to be issuers of all or a portion of that asset-backed

security for purposes of paragraph (d)(3)(ii)(D) of this section, and maintains a record of this determination.

(7) *Asset-Backed Securities Not Subject to Guarantees.* In the case of an asset-backed security for which the fund's board of directors has determined that the fund is not relying on the sponsor's financial strength or its ability or willingness to provide liquidity, credit or other support in connection with the asset-backed security to determine the quality (pursuant to paragraph (d)(2) of this section) or liquidity (pursuant to paragraph (d)(4) of this section) of the asset-backed security, written procedures must require periodic evaluation of such determination.

(8) *Stress Testing.* Written procedures must provide for:

(i) *General.* The periodic stress testing, at such intervals as the board of directors determines appropriate and reasonable in light of current market conditions, of the money market fund's ability to have invested at least ten percent of its total assets in weekly liquid assets, and the fund's ability to minimize principal volatility (and, in the case of a money market fund using the amortized cost method of valuation or penny rounding method of pricing as provided in paragraph (c)(1) of this section, the fund's ability to maintain the stable price per share established by the board of directors for the purpose of distribution, redemption and repurchase), based upon specified hypothetical events that include, but are not limited to:

(A) Increases in the general level of short-term interest rates, in combination with various levels of an increase in shareholder redemptions;

(B) An event indicating or evidencing credit deterioration, such as a downgrade or default of particular portfolio security positions, each representing various portions of the fund's portfolio (with varying assumptions about the resulting loss in the value of the security), in combination with various levels of an increase in shareholder redemptions;

(C) A widening of spreads compared to the indexes to which portfolio securities are tied in various sectors in the fund's portfolio (in which a sector is a logically related subset of portfolio securities, such as securities of issuers in similar or related industries or geographic region or securities of a similar security type), in combination with various levels of an increase in shareholder redemptions; and

(D) Any additional combinations of events that the adviser deems relevant.

(ii) A report on the results of such testing to be provided to the board of directors at its next regularly scheduled meeting (or sooner, if appropriate in light of the results), which report must include:

(A) The date(s) on which the testing was performed and an assessment of the money market fund's ability to have invested at least ten percent of its total assets in weekly liquid assets and to minimize principal volatility (and, in the case of a money market fund using the amortized cost method of valuation or penny rounding method of pricing as provided in paragraph (c)(1) of this section to maintain the stable price per share established by the board of directors); and

(B) An assessment by the fund's adviser of the fund's ability to withstand the events (and concurrent occurrences of those events) that are reasonably likely to occur within the following year, including such information as may reasonably be necessary for the board of directors to evaluate the stress testing conducted by the adviser and the results of the testing. The fund adviser must include a summary of the significant assumptions made when performing the stress tests.

(h) *Recordkeeping and Reporting—*

(1) *Written Procedures.* For a period of not less than six years following the replacement of existing procedures with new procedures (the first two years in an easily accessible place), a written copy of the procedures (and any modifications thereto) described in this section must be maintained and preserved.

(2) *Board Considerations and Actions.* For a period of not less than six years (the first two years in an easily accessible place) a written record must be maintained and preserved of the

board of directors' considerations and actions taken in connection with the discharge of its responsibilities, as set forth in this section, to be included in the minutes of the board of directors' meetings.

(3) *Credit Risk Analysis.* For a period of not less than three years from the date that the credit risks of a portfolio security were most recently reviewed, a written record must be maintained and preserved in an easily accessible place of the determination that a portfolio security is an eligible security, including the determination that it presents minimal credit risks at the time the fund acquires the security, or at such later times (or upon such events) that the board of directors determines that the investment adviser must reassess whether the security presents minimal credit risks.

(4) *Determinations With Respect to Adjustable Rate Securities.* For a period of not less than three years from the date when the assessment was most recently made, a written record must be preserved and maintained, in an easily accessible place, of the determination required by paragraph (g)(5) of this section (that a variable rate or floating rate security that is not subject to a demand feature and for which maturity is determined pursuant to paragraph (i)(1), (i)(2) or (i)(4) of this section can reasonably be expected, upon readjustment of its interest rate at all times during the life of the instrument, to have a market value that approximates its amortized cost).

(5) *Determinations With Respect to Asset-Backed Securities.* For a period of not less than three years from the date when the determination was most recently made, a written record must be preserved and maintained, in an easily accessible place, of the determinations required by paragraph (g)(6) of this section (the number of ten percent obligors (as that term is used in paragraph (d)(3)(ii)(D) of this section) deemed to be the issuers of all or a portion of the asset-backed security for purposes of paragraph (d)(3)(ii)(D) of this section). The written record must include:

(i) The identities of the ten percent obligors (as that term is used in paragraph (d)(3)(ii)(D) of this section), the percentage of the qualifying assets constituted by the securities of each ten percent obligor and the percentage of the fund's total assets that are invested in securities of each ten percent obligor; and

(ii) Any determination that an asset-backed security will not have, or is unlikely to have, ten percent obligors deemed to be issuers of all or a portion of that asset-backed security for purposes of paragraph (d)(3)(ii)(D) of this section.

(6) *Evaluations With Respect to Asset-Backed Securities Not Subject to Guarantees.* For a period of not less than three years from the date when the evaluation was most recently made, a written record must be preserved and maintained, in an easily accessible place, of the evaluation required by paragraph (g)(7) of this section (regarding asset-backed securities not subject to guarantees).

(7) *Evaluations With Respect to Securities Subject to Demand Features or Guarantee*s. For a period of not less than three years from the date when the evaluation was most recently made, a written record must be preserved and maintained, in an easily accessible place, of the evaluation required by paragraph (g)(4) of this section (regarding securities subject to one or more demand features or guarantees).

(8) *Reports With Respect to Stress Testing.* For a period of not less than six years (the first two years in an easily accessible place), a written copy of the report required under paragraph (g)(8)(ii) of this section must be maintained and preserved.

(9) *Inspection of Records.* The documents preserved pursuant to paragraph (h) of this section are subject to inspection by the Commission in accordance with section 31(b) of the Act (15 U.S.C. 80a-30(b)) as if such documents were records required to be maintained pursuant to rules adopted under section 31(a) of the Act (15 U.S.C. 80a-30(a)).

(10) *Web Site Disclosure of Portfolio Holdings and Other Fund Information.* The money market fund must post prominently on its Web site the following information:

(i) For a period of not less than six months, beginning no later than the fifth business day of the month, a schedule of its investments, as of the last business day or subsequent calendar day of the preceding month, that includes the following information:

(A) With respect to the money market fund and each class of redeemable shares thereof:

(1) The WAM; and

(2) The WAL.

(B) With respect to each security held by the money market fund:

(1) Name of the issuer;

(2) Category of investment (indicate the category that identifies the instrument from among the following: U.S. Treasury Debt; U.S. Government Agency Debt; Non-U.S. Sovereign, Sub-Sovereign and Supra-National debt; Certificate of Deposit; Non-Negotiable Time Deposit; Variable Rate Demand Note; Other Municipal Security; Asset Backed Commercial Paper; Other Asset Backed Securities; U.S. Treasury Repurchase Agreement, if collateralized only by U.S. Treasuries (including Strips) and cash; U.S. Government Agency Repurchase Agreement, collateralized only by U.S. Government Agency securities, U.S. Treasuries, and cash; Other Repurchase Agreement, if any collateral falls outside Treasury, Government Agency and cash; Insurance Company Funding Agreement; Investment Company; Financial Company Commercial Paper; and Non-Financial Company Commercial Paper. If Other Instrument, include a brief description);

(3) CUSIP number (if any);

(4) Principal amount;

(5) The maturity date determined by taking into account the maturity shortening provisions in paragraph (i) of this section (i.e., the maturity date used to calculate WAM under paragraph (d)(1)(ii) of this section);

(6) The maturity date determined without reference to the exceptions in paragraph (i) of this section regarding interest rate readjustments (i.e., the maturity used to calculate WAL under paragraph (d)(1)(iii) of this section);

(7) Coupon or yield; and

(8) Value.

(ii) A schedule, chart, graph, or other depiction, which must be updated each business day as of the end of the preceding business day, showing, as of the end of each business day during the preceding six months:

(A) The percentage of the money market fund's total assets invested in daily liquid assets;

(B) The percentage of the money market fund's total assets invested in weekly liquid assets; and

(C) The money market fund's net inflows or outflows.

(iii) A schedule, chart, graph, or other depiction showing the money market fund's net asset value per share (which the fund must calculate based on current market factors before applying the amortized cost or penny-rounding method, if used), rounded to the fourth decimal place in the case of funds with a $1.000 share price or an equivalent level of accuracy for funds with a different share price (e.g., $10.00 per share), as of the end of each business day during the preceding six months, which must be updated each business day as of the end of the preceding business day.

(iv) A link to a Web site of the Securities and Exchange Commission where a user may obtain the most recent 12 months of publicly available information filed by the money market fund pursuant to § 270.30b1-7.

(v) For a period of not less than one year, beginning no later than the same business day on which the money market fund files an initial report on Form N-CR (§ 274.222 of this chapter) in response to the occurrence of any event specified in Parts C, E, F, or G of Form N-CR, the same information that the money market fund is required to report to the Commission on Part C (Items C.1, C.2, C.3, C.4, C.5, C.6, and C.7), Part E (Items E.1, E.2, E.3, and E.4), Part F (Items F.1 and F.2), or Part G of Form N-CR concerning such event, along with the following statement: "The Fund was required to disclose additional information about this event [or "these events," as appropriate] on Form N-CR and to file this form with the Securities and Exchange Commission. Any Form N-CR filing submitted by the Fund is available on the EDGAR Database on the Securities and Exchange Commission's Internet site at http://www.sec.gov."

(11) *Processing of Transactions*. A government money market fund and a retail money market fund (or its transfer agent) must have the capacity to redeem and sell securities issued by the fund at a price based on the current net asset value per share pursuant to § 270.22c-1. Such capacity must include the ability to redeem and sell securities at prices that do not correspond to a stable price per share.

(i) *Maturity of Portfolio Securities*. For purposes of this section, the maturity of a portfolio security shall be deemed to be the period remaining (calculated from the trade date or such other date on which the fund's interest in the security is subject to market action) until the date on which, in accordance with the terms of the security, the principal amount must unconditionally be paid, or in the case of a security called for redemption, the date on which the redemption payment must be made, except as provided in paragraphs (i)(1) through (i)(8) of this section:

(1) *Adjustable Rate Government Securities*. A government security that is a variable rate security where the variable rate of interest is readjusted no less frequently than every 397 calendar days shall be deemed to have a maturity equal to the period remaining until the next readjustment of the interest rate. A government security that is a floating rate security shall be deemed to have a remaining maturity of one day.

(2) *Short-Term Variable Rate Securities*. A variable rate security, the principal amount of which, in accordance with the terms of the security, must unconditionally be paid in 397 calendar days or less shall be deemed to have a maturity equal to the earlier of the period remaining until the next readjustment of the interest rate or the period remaining until the principal amount can be recovered through demand.

(3) *Long-Term Variable Rate Securities*. A variable rate security, the principal amount of which is scheduled to be paid in more than 397 calendar days, that is subject to a demand feature, shall be deemed to have a maturity equal to the longer of the period remaining until the next readjustment of the interest rate or the period remaining until the principal amount can be recovered through demand.

(4) *Short-Term Floating Rate Securities*. A floating rate security, the principal amount of which, in accordance with the terms of the security, must unconditionally be paid in 397 calendar days or less shall be deemed to have a maturity of one day, except for purposes of determining WAL under paragraph (d)(1)(iii) of this section, in which case it shall be deemed to have a maturity equal to the period remaining until the principal amount can be recovered through demand.

(5) *Long-Term Floating Rate Securities*. A floating rate security, the principal amount of which is scheduled to be paid in more than 397 calendar days, that is subject to a demand feature, shall be deemed to have a maturity equal to the period remaining until the principal amount can be recovered through demand.

(6) *Repurchase Agreements*. A repurchase agreement shall be deemed to have a maturity equal to the period remaining until the date on which the repurchase of the underlying securities is scheduled to occur, or, where the agreement is subject to demand, the notice period applicable to a demand for the repurchase of the securities.

(7) *Portfolio Lending Agreements*. A portfolio lending agreement shall be treated as having a maturity equal to the period remaining until the date on which the loaned securities are scheduled to be returned, or where the agreement is subject to demand, the notice period applicable to a demand for the return of the loaned securities.

(8) *Money Market Fund Securities*. An investment in a money market fund shall be treated as having a maturity equal to the period of time within which the acquired money market fund is required to make payment upon redemption, unless the acquired money market fund has agreed in writing to provide redemption proceeds to the investing money market fund

within a shorter time period, in which case the maturity of such investment shall be deemed to be the shorter period.

(j) *Delegation*. The money market fund's board of directors may delegate to the fund's investment adviser or officers the responsibility to make any determination required to be made by the board of directors under this section other than the determinations required by paragraphs (c)(1) (board findings), (c)(2)(i) and (ii) (determinations related to liquidity fees and temporary suspensions of redemptions), (f)(1) (adverse events), (g)(1) and (2) (amortized cost and penny rounding procedures), and (g)(8) (stress testing procedures) of this section.

(1) *Written Guidelines*. The board of directors must establish and periodically review written guidelines (including guidelines for determining whether securities present minimal credit risks as required in paragraphs (d)(2) and (g)(3) of this section) and procedures under which the delegate makes such determinations.

(2) *Oversight*. The board of directors must take any measures reasonably necessary (through periodic reviews of fund investments and the delegate's procedures in connection with investment decisions and prompt review of the adviser's actions in the event of the default of a security or event of insolvency with respect to the issuer of the security or any guarantee or demand feature to which it is subject that requires notification of the Commission under paragraph (f)(2) of this section by reference to Form N-CR (§ 274.222 of this chapter)) to assure that the guidelines and procedures are being followed.

Rule 3a-1. Certain Prima Facie Investment Companies

Notwithstanding section 3(a)(1)(C) of the Act (15 U.S.C. 80a-3(a)(1)(c)), an issuer will be deemed not to be an investment company under the Act; *Provided*, That:

(a) No more than 45 percent of the value (as defined in section 2(a)(41) of the Act) of such issuer's total assets (exclusive of Government securities and cash items) consists of, and no more than 45 percent of such issuer's net income after taxes (for the last four fiscal quarters combined) is derived from, securities other than:

(1) Government securities;

(2) Securities issued by employees' securities companies;

(3) Securities issued by majority-owned subsidiaries of the issuer (other than subsidiaries relying on the exclusion from the definition of investment companies in section 3(b)(3) or section 3(c)(1) of the Act) which are not investment companies; and

(4) Securities issued by companies:

(i) Which are controlled primarily by such issuer;

(ii) Through which such issuer engages in a business other than that of investing, reinvesting, owning, holding or trading in securities; and

(iii) Which are not investment companies;

(b) The issuer is not an investment company as defined in section 3(a)(1)(A) or 3(a)(1)(B) of the Act (15 U.S.C. 80a-3(a)(1)(A) or 80a-3(a)(1)(B)) and is not a special situation investment company; and

(c) The percentages described in paragraph (a) of this section are determined on an unconsolidated basis, except that the issuer shall consolidate its financial statements with the financial statements of any wholly-owned subsidiaries.

Rule 12b-1. Distribution of Shares by Registered Open-End Management Investment Company

(a)(1) Except as provided in this section, it shall be unlawful for any registered open-end management investment company (other than a company complying with the provisions of section 10(d) of the Act [15 U.S.C. 80a-10(d)]) to act as a distributor of securities of which it is the issuer, except through an underwriter.

(2) For purposes of this section, such a company will be deemed to be acting as a distributor of securities of which it is the issuer, other than through an underwriter, if it engages directly or indirectly in financing any activity which is primarily intended to result in the sale of shares issued by such company, including, but not necessarily limited to, advertising, compensation of underwriters, dealers, and sales personnel, the printing and mailing of prospectuses to other than current shareholders, and the printing and mailing of sales literature.

(b) A registered, open-end management investment company ("company") may act as a distributor of securities of which it is the issuer, *Provided* That any payments made by such company in connection with such distribution are made pursuant to a written plan describing all material aspects of the proposed financing of distribution and that all agreements with any person relating to implementation of the plan are in writing, *and further provided* That:

(1) Such plan has been approved by a vote of at least a majority of the outstanding voting securities of such company, if adopted after any public offering of the company's voting securities or the sale of such securities to persons who are not affiliated persons of the company, affiliated persons of such persons, promoters of the company, or affiliated persons of such promoters;

(2) Such plan, together with any related agreements, has been approved by a vote of the board of directors of such company, and of the directors who are not interested persons of the company and have no direct or indirect financial interest in the operation of the plan or in any agreements related to the plan, cast in person at a meeting called for the purpose of voting on such plan or agreements; and

(3) Such plan or agreement provides, in substance:

(i) That it shall continue in effect for a period of more than one year from the date of its execution or adoption only so long as such continuance is specifically approved at least annually in the manner described in paragraph (b)(2);

(ii) That any person authorized to direct the disposition of monies paid or payable by such company pursuant to the plan or any related agreement shall provide to the company's board of directors, and the directors shall review, at least quarterly, a written report of the amounts so expended and the purposes for which such expenditures were made; and

(iii) In the case of a plan, that it may be terminated at any time by vote of a majority of the members of the board of directors of the company who are not interested persons of the company and have no direct or indirect financial interest in the operation of the plan or in any agreements related to the plan or by vote of a majority of the outstanding voting securities of such company; and

(iv) In the case of an agreement related to a plan,

(A) That it may be terminated at any time, without the payment of any penalty, by vote of a majority of the members of the board of directors of such company who are not interested persons of the company and have no direct or indirect financial interest in the operation of the plan or in any agreements related to the plan or by vote of a majority of the outstanding voting securities of such company on not more than sixty days' written notice to any other party to the agreement, and

(B) For its automatic termination in the event of its assignment; and

(4) Such plan provides that it may not be amended to increase materially the amount to be spent for distribution without shareholder approval and that all material amendments of the plan must be approved in the manner described in paragraph (b)(2);

(5) Such plan is implemented and continued in a manner consistent with the provisions of paragraphs (c), (d), and (e) of this section;

(c) A registered open-end management investment company may rely on the provisions of paragraph (b) of this section only if its board of directors satisfies the fund governance standards as defined in § 270.0-1(a)(7);

(d) In considering whether a registered open-end management investment company should implement or continue a plan in reliance on paragraph (b) of this section, the directors of such company shall have a duty to request and evaluate, and any person who is a party to any agreement with such company relating to such plan shall have a duty to furnish, such information as may reasonably be necessary to an informed determination of whether such plan should be implemented or continued; in fulfilling their duties under this paragraph the directors should consider and give appropriate weight to all pertinent factors, and minutes describing the factors considered and the basis for the decision to use company assets for distribution must be made and preserved in accordance with paragraph (f) of this section;

NOTE: For a discussion of factors which may be relevant to a decision to use company assets for distribution, see Investment Company Act Releases Nos. 10862, September 7, 1979, and 11414, October 28, 1980.

(e) A registered open-end management investment company may implement or continue a plan pursuant to paragraph (b) of this section only if the directors who vote to approve such implementation or continuation conclude, in the exercise of reasonable business judgment and in light of their fiduciary duties under state law and under sections 36(a) and (b) [15 U.S.C. 80a-35(a) and (b)] of the Act, that there is a reasonable likelihood that the plan will benefit the company and its shareholders;

(f) A registered open-end management investment company must preserve copies of any plan, agreement or report made pursuant to this section for a period of not less than six years from the date of such plan, agreement or report, the first two years in an easily accessible place;

(g) If a plan covers more than one series or class of shares, the provisions of the plan must be severable for each series or class, and whenever this section provides for any action to be taken with respect to a plan, that action must be taken separately for each series or class affected by the matter. Nothing in this paragraph (g) shall affect the rights of any purchase class under § 270.18f-3(f)(2)(iii); and

(h) Notwithstanding any other provision of this section, a company may not:

(1) Compensate a broker or dealer for any promotion or sale of shares issued by that company by directing to the broker or dealer:

(i) The company's portfolio securities transactions; or

(ii) Any remuneration, including but not limited to any commission, mark-up, mark-down, or other fee (or portion thereof) received or to be received from the company's portfolio transactions effected through any other broker (including a government securities broker) or dealer (including a municipal securities dealer or a government securities dealer); and

(2) Direct its portfolio securities transactions to a broker or dealer that promotes or sells shares issued by the company, unless the company (or its investment adviser):

(i) Is in compliance with the provisions of paragraph (h)(1) of this section with respect to that broker or dealer; and

(ii) Has implemented, and the company's board of directors (including a majority of directors who are not interested persons of the company) has approved, policies and procedures reasonably designed to prevent:

(A) The persons responsible for selecting brokers and dealers to effect the company's portfolio securities transactions from taking into account the brokers' and dealers' promotion or sale of shares issued by the company or any other registered investment company; and

(B) The company, and any investment adviser and principal underwriter of the company, from entering into any agreement (whether oral or written) or other understanding under which the company directs, or is expected to direct, portfolio securities transactions, or any remuneration described in paragraph (h)(1)(ii) of this section, to a broker (including a government securities broker) or dealer (including a municipal securities dealer or a government securities dealer) in consideration for the promotion or sale of shares issued by the company or any other registered investment company.

Rule 17a-6. Exemption for Transactions with Portfolio Affiliates.

(a) A transaction to which a Fund, or a company controlled by a Fund, and a Portfolio Affiliate of the Fund are parties is exempt from the provisions of section 17(a) of the Act (15 U.S.C. 80a-17(a)), provided that none of the following persons is a party to the transaction, or has a direct or indirect Financial Interest in a party to the transaction other than the Fund:

(1) An officer, director, employee, investment adviser, member of an advisory board, depositor, promoter of or principal underwriter for the Fund;

(2) A person directly or indirectly controlling the Fund;

(3) A person directly or indirectly owning, controlling or holding with power to vote five percent or more of the outstanding voting securities of the Fund;

(4) A person directly or indirectly under common control with the Fund, other than:

(i) A Portfolio Affiliate of the Fund; or

(ii) A Fund whose sole interest in the transaction or a party to the transaction is an interest in the Portfolio Affiliate; or

(5) An affiliated person of any of the persons mentioned in paragraphs (a)(1)-(4) of this section, other than the Fund or a Portfolio Affiliate of the Fund.

(b) *Definitions.*

(1) *Financial Interest.*

(i) The term *Financial Interest* as used in this section does not include:

(A) Any interest through ownership of securities issued by the Fund;

(B) Any interest of a wholly-owned subsidiary of a Fund;

(C) Usual and ordinary fees for services as a director;

(D) An interest of a non-executive employee;

(E) An interest of an insurance company arising from a loan or policy made or issued by it in the ordinary course of business to a natural person;

(F) An interest of a bank arising from a loan or account made or maintained by it in the ordinary course of business to or with a natural person, unless it arises from a loan to a person who is an officer, director or executive of a company which is a party to the transaction, or from a loan to a person who directly or indirectly owns, controls, or holds with power to vote, five percent or more of the outstanding voting securities of a company which is a party to the transaction;

(G) An interest acquired in a transaction described in paragraph (d)(3) of § 270.17d-1; or

(H) Any other interest that the board of directors of the Fund, including a majority of the directors who are not interested persons of the Fund, finds to be not material, provided that the directors record the basis for that finding in the minutes of their meeting.

(ii) A person has a Financial Interest in any party in which it has a Financial Interest, in which it had a Financial Interest within six months prior to the transaction, or in which it will acquire a Financial Interest pursuant to an arrangement in existence at the time of the transaction.

(2) *Fund* means a registered investment company or separate series of a registered investment company.

(3) *Portfolio Affiliate of a Fund* means a person that is an affiliated person (or an affiliated person of an affiliated person) of a Fund solely because the Fund, a Fund under common control with the Fund, or both:

(i) Controls such person (or an affiliated person of such person); or

(ii) Owns, controls, or holds with power to vote five percent or more of the outstanding voting securities of such person (or an affiliated person of such person).

Rule 17a-7. Exemption of Certain Purchase or Sale Transactions Between an Investment Company and Certain Affiliated Persons Thereof

A purchase or sale transaction between registered investment companies or separate series of registered investment companies, which are affiliated persons, or affiliated persons of affiliated persons, of each other, between separate series of a registered investment company, or between a registered investment company or a separate series of a registered investment company and a person which is an affiliated person of such registered investment company (or affiliated person of such person) solely by reason of having a common investment adviser or investment advisers which are affiliated persons of each other, common directors, and/or common officers, is exempt from section 17(a) of the Act; *Provided*, That:

(a) The transaction is a purchase or sale, for no consideration other than cash payment against prompt delivery of a security for which market quotations are readily available;

(b) The transaction is effected at the independent current market price of the security. For purposes of this paragraph the "current market price" shall be:

(1) If the security is an "NMS stock" as that term is defined in 17 CFR 242.600, the last sale price with respect to such security reported in the consolidated transaction reporting system ("consolidated system") or the average of the highest current independent bid and lowest current independent offer for such security (reported pursuant to 17 CFR 242.602) if there are no reported transactions in the consolidated system that day; or

(2) If the security is not a reported security, and the principal market for such security is an exchange, then the last sale on such exchange or the average of the highest current independent bid and lowest current independent offer on such exchange if there are no reported transactions on such exchange that day; or

(3) If the security is not a reported security and is quoted in the NASDAQ System, then the average of the highest current independent bid and lowest current independent offer reported on Level 1 of NASDAQ; or

(4) For all other securities, the average of the highest current independent bid and lowest current independent offer determined on the basis of reasonable inquiry;

(c) The transaction is consistent with the policy of each registered investment company and separate series of a registered investment company participating in the transaction, as recited in its registration statement and reports filed under the Act;

(d) No brokerage commission, fee (except for customary transfer fees), or other remuneration is paid in connection with the transaction;

(e) The board of directors of the investment company, including a majority of the directors who are not interested persons of such investment company, (1) adopts procedures pursuant to which such purchase or sale transactions may be effected for the company, which are reasonably designed to provide that all the conditions of this section in paragraphs (a) through (d) have been complied with, (2) makes and approves such changes as the board deems necessary, and (3) determines no less frequently than quarterly that all such purchases or sales made during the preceding quarter were effected in compliance with such procedures;

(f) The board of directors of the investment company satisfies the fund governance standards defined in § 270.0-1(a)(7).

(g) The investment company (1) maintains and preserves permanently in an easily accessible place a written copy of the procedures (and any modifications thereto) described in paragraph (e) of this section, and (2) maintains and preserves for a period not less than six years from the end of the fiscal year in which any transactions occurred, the first two years in an easily accessible place, a written record of each such transaction setting forth a description of the security purchased or sold, the identity of the person on the other side of the transaction, the terms of the purchase or sale transaction, and the information or materials upon which the determinations described in paragraph (e)(3) of this section were made.

Rule 17d-1. Applications Regarding Joint Enterprises or Arrangements and Certain Profit-Sharing Plans

(a) No affiliated person of or principal underwriter for any registered investment company (other than a company of the character described in Section 12(d)(3)(A) and (B) of the Act) and no affiliated person of such a person or principal underwriter, acting as principal, shall participate in, or effect any transaction in connection with, any joint enterprise or other joint arrangement or profit-sharing plan in which any such registered company, or a company controlled by such registered company, is a participant, and which is entered into, adopted or modified subsequent to the effective date of this rule, unless an application regarding such joint enterprise, arrangement or profit-sharing plan has been filed with the Commission and has been granted by an order entered prior to the submission of such plan or modification to security holders for approval, or prior to such adoption or modification if not so submitted, except that the provisions of this rule shall not preclude any affiliated person from acting as manager of any underwriting syndicate or other group in which such registered or controlled company is a participant and receiving compensation therefor.

(b) In passing upon such applications, the Commission will consider whether the participation of such registered or controlled company in such joint enterprise, joint arrangement or profit-sharing plan on the basis proposed is consistent with the provisions, policies and purposes of the Act and the extent to which such participation is on a basis different from or less advantageous than that of other participants.

(c) "Joint enterprise or other joint arrangement or profit-sharing plan" as used in this rule shall mean any written or oral plan, contract, authorization or arrangement, or any practice or understanding concerning an enterprise or undertaking whereby a registered investment company or a controlled company thereof and any affiliated person of or a principal underwriter for such registered investment company, or any affiliated person of such a person or principal underwriter, have a joint or a joint and several participation, or share in the profits of such enterprise or undertaking, including, but not limited to, any stock option or stock purchase plan, but shall not include an investment advisory contract subject to Section 15 of the Act.

(d) Notwithstanding the requirements of paragraph (a) of this section, no application need be filed pursuant to this section with respect to any of the following:

(1) Any profit-sharing, stock option or stock purchase plan provided by any controlled company which is not an investment company for its officers, directors or employees, or the purchase of stock or the granting, modification or exercise of options pursuant to such a plan, provided:

(*a*) no individual participates therein who is either; (i) an affiliated person of any investment company which is an affiliated person of such controlled company; or (ii) an affiliated person of the investment adviser or principal underwriter of such investment company; and

(*b*) no participant has been an affiliated person of such investment company, its investment adviser or principal underwriter during the life of the plan and for six months prior to, as the case may be: (i) institution of the profit-sharing plan; (ii) the purchase of stock pursuant to a stock purchase plan; or (iii) the granting of any options pursuant to a stock option plan.

(2) Any plan provided by any registered investment company or any controlled company for its officers or employees if such plan has been qualified under Section 401 of the Internal Revenue Code of 1954 and all contributions paid under said plan by the employer qualify as deductible under Section 404 of said Code.

(3) Any loan or advance of credit to, or acquisition of securities or other property of, a small business concern, or any agreement to do any of the foregoing, ("Investments") made by a bank and a small business investment company (SBIC) licensed under the Small Business Investment Act of 1958, whether such transactions are contemporaneous or separated in time, where the bank is an affiliated person of either (i) the SBIC or (ii) an affiliated person of the SBIC; but reports containing pertinent details as to investments and

transactions relating thereto shall be made at such time, on such forms and by such persons as the Commission may from time to time prescribe.

(4) The issuance by a registered investment company which is licensed by the Small Business Administration ("SBA") pursuant to the Small Business Investment Company Act of 1958 of stock options which qualify under Section 422 of the Internal Revenue Code, as amended, and which conform to § 107.805(b) of Chapter I of Title 13 of the Code of Federal Regulations.

(5) Any joint enterprise or other joint arrangement or profit-sharing plan ("joint enterprise") in which a registered investment company or a company controlled by such a company, is a participant, and in which a Portfolio Affiliate (as defined in 270.17a-6(b)(3)) of such registered investment company is also a participant, provided that:

(i) None of the persons identified in § 270.17a-6(a) is a participant in the joint enterprise, or has a direct or indirect Financial Interest in a participant in the joint enterprise (other than the registered investment company);

(ii) *Financial Interest.*

(A) The term *Financial Interest* as used in this section does not include:

(*1*) Any interest through ownership of securities issued by the registered investment company;

(*2*) Any interest of a wholly-owned subsidiary of the registered investment company;

(*3*) Usual and ordinary fees for services as a director;

(*4*) An interest of a non-executive employee;

(*5*) An interest of an insurance company arising from a loan or policy made or issued by it in the ordinary course of business to a natural person;

(*6*) An interest of a bank arising from a loan to a person who is an officer, director, or executive of a company which is a participant in the joint transaction or from a loan to a person who directly or indirectly owns, controls, or holds with power to vote, five percent or more of the outstanding voting securities of a company which is a participant in the joint transaction;

(*7*) An interest acquired in a transaction described in paragraph (d)(3) of this section; or

(*8*) Any other interest that the board of directors of the investment company, including a majority of the directors who are not interested persons of the investment company, finds to be not material, provided that the directors record the basis for that finding in the minutes of their meeting.

(B) A person has a Financial Interest in any party in which it has a Financial Interest, in which it had a Financial Interest within six months prior to the investment company's participation in the enterprise, or in which it will acquire a Financial Interest pursuant to an arrangement in existence at the time of the investment company's participation in the enterprise.

(6) The receipt of securities and/or cash by an investment company or a controlled company thereof and an affiliated person of such investment company or an affiliated person of such person pursuant to a plan of reorganization: *Provided*, That no person identified in § 270.17a-6(a)(1) or any company in which such a person has a direct or indirect Financial Interest (as defined in paragraph (d)(5)(ii) of this section):

(i) has a direct or indirect financial interest in the corporation under reorganization, except owning securities of the class or classes owned by such investment company or controlled company;

(ii) receives pursuant to such plan any securities or other property, except securities of the same class and subject to the same terms as the securities received by such investment company or controlled company, and/or cash in the same proportion as is received by the investment company or controlled company based on securities of the company under reorganization owned by such persons; and

(iii) is, or has a direct or indirect financial interest in any person (other than such investment company or controlled company) who is, (A) purchasing assets from the company under reorganization or (B) exchanging shares with such person in a transaction not in compliance with the standards described in this paragraph (d)(6).

(7) Any arrangement regarding liability insurance policies (other than a bond required pursuant to rule 17g-1 (§ 270.17g-1) under the Act); *Provided,* That:

(i) the investment company's participation in the joint liability insurance policy is in the best interests of the investment company;

(ii) the proposed premium for the joint liability insurance policy to be allocated to the investment company, based upon its proportionate share of the sum of the premiums that would have been paid if such insurance coverage were purchased separately by the insured parties, is fair and reasonable to the investment company;

(iii) The joint liability insurance policy does not exclude coverage for bona fide claims made against any director who is not an interested person of the investment company, or against the investment company if it is a co-defendant in the claim with the disinterested director, by another person insured under the joint liability insurance policy;

(iv) the board of directors of the investment company, including a majority of the directors who are not interested persons with respect thereto, determine no less frequently than annually that the standards described in paragraphs (i) and (ii) have been satisfied; and

(v) The board of directors of the investment company satisfies the fund governance standards defined in § 270.0-1(a)(7).

(8) An investment adviser's bearing expenses in connection with a merger, consolidation or purchase or sale of substantially all of the assets of a company which involves a registered investment company of which it is an affiliated person.

Rule 17j-1. Personal Investment Activity of Investment Company Personnel

(a) *Definitions.* For purposes of this section:

(1) *Access Person* means:

(i) Any Advisory Person of a Fund or of a Fund's investment adviser. If an investment adviser's primary business is advising Funds or other advisory clients, all of the investment adviser's directors, officers, and general partners are presumed to be Access Persons of any Fund advised by the investment adviser. All of a Fund's directors, officers, and general partners are presumed to be Access Persons of the Fund.

(ii) Any director, officer or general partner of a principal underwriter who, in the ordinary course of business, makes, participates in or obtains information regarding, the purchase or sale of Covered Securities by the Fund for which the principal underwriter acts, or whose functions or duties in the ordinary course of business relate to the making of any recommendation to the Fund regarding the purchase or sale of Covered Securities.

(2) *Advisory Person* of a Fund or of a Fund's investment adviser means:

(i) Any director, officer, general partner or employee of the Fund or investment adviser (or of any company in a control relationship to the Fund or investment adviser) who, in connection with his or her regular functions or duties, makes, participates in, or obtains information regarding, the purchase or sale of Covered Securities by a Fund, or whose functions relate to the making of any recommendations with respect to such purchases or sales; and

(ii) Any natural person in a control relationship to the Fund or investment adviser who obtains information concerning recommendations made to the Fund with regard to the purchase or sale of Covered Securities by the Fund.

(3) *Control* has the same meaning as in section 2(a)(9) of the Act [15 U.S.C. 80a-2(a)(9)].

(4) *Covered Security* means a security as defined in section 2(a)(36) of the Act [15 U.S.C. 80a-2(a)(36)], except that it does not include:

(i) Direct obligations of the Government of the United States;

(ii) Bankers' acceptances, bank certificates of deposit, commercial paper and high quality short-term debt instruments, including repurchase agreements; and

(iii) Shares issued by open-end Funds.

(5) *Fund* means an investment company registered under the Investment Company Act.

(6) An *Initial Public Offering* means an offering of securities registered under the Securities Act of 1933 [15 U.S.C. 77a], the issuer of which, immediately before the registration, was not subject to the reporting requirements of sections 13 or 15(d) of the Securities Exchange Act of 1934 [15 U.S.C. 78m or 78o(d)].

(7) *Investment Personnel* of a Fund or of a Fund's investment adviser means:

(i) Any employee of the Fund or investment adviser (or of any company in a control relationship to the Fund or investment adviser) who, in connection with his or her regular functions or duties, makes or participates in making recommendations regarding the purchase or sale of securities by the Fund.

(ii) Any natural person who controls the Fund or investment adviser and who obtains information concerning recommendations made to the Fund regarding the purchase or sale of securities by the Fund.

(8) A *Limited Offering* means an offering that is exempt from registration under the Securities Act of 1933 pursuant to section 4(a)(2) or Section 4(5) or section 4(a)5 [77d(a)(2) or 77d(a)(5)] or pursuant to rule 504 or rule 506 [17 CFR 230.504 or 230.506] under the Securities Act of 1933.

(9) *Purchase or sale of a Covered Security* includes, among other things, the writing of an option to purchase or sell a Covered Security.

(10) *Security Held or to be Acquired* by a Fund means:

(i) Any Covered Security which, within the most recent 15 days:

(A) Is or has been held by the Fund; or

(B) Is being or has been considered by the Fund or its investment adviser for purchase by the Fund; and

(ii) Any option to purchase or sell, and any security convertible into or exchangeable for, a Covered Security described in paragraph (a)(10)(i) of this section.

(11) *Automatic Investment Plan* means a program in which regular periodic purchases (or withdrawals) are made automatically in (or from) investment accounts in accordance with a predetermined schedule and allocation. An Automatic Investment Plan includes a dividend reinvestment plan.

(b) *Unlawful Actions.* It is unlawful for any affiliated person of or principal underwriter for a Fund, or any affiliated person of an investment adviser of or principal underwriter for a Fund, in connection with the purchase or sale, directly or indirectly, by the person of a Security Held or to be Acquired by the Fund:

(1) To employ any device, scheme or artifice to defraud the Fund;

(2) To make any untrue statement of a material fact to the Fund or omit to state a material fact necessary in order to make the statements made to the Fund, in light of the circumstances under which they are made, not misleading;

(3) To engage in any act, practice or course of business that operates or would operate as a fraud or deceit on the Fund; or

(4) To engage in any manipulative practice with respect to the Fund.

(c) *Code of Ethics.*

(1) *Adoption and Approval of Code of Ethics.*

(i) Every Fund (other than a money market fund or a Fund that does not invest in Covered Securities) and each investment adviser of and principal underwriter for the Fund, must adopt a written code of ethics containing provisions reasonably necessary to prevent its Access Persons from engaging in any conduct prohibited by paragraph (b) of this section.

(ii) The board of directors of a Fund, including a majority of directors who are not interested persons, must approve the code of ethics of the Fund, the code of ethics of each investment adviser and principal underwriter of the Fund, and any material changes to these codes. The board must base its approval of a code and any material changes to the code on a determination that the code contains provisions reasonably necessary to prevent Access Persons from engaging in any conduct prohibited by paragraph (b) of this section. Before approving a code of a Fund, investment adviser or principal underwriter or any amendment to the code, the board of directors must receive a certification from the Fund, investment adviser or principal underwriter that it has adopted procedures reasonably necessary to prevent Access Persons from violating the Fund's, investment adviser's, or principal underwriter's code of ethics. The Fund's board must approve the code of an investment adviser or principal underwriter before initially retaining the services of the investment adviser or principal underwriter. The Fund's board must approve a material change to a code no later than six months after adoption of the material change.

(iii) If a Fund is a unit investment trust, the Fund's principal underwriter or depositor must approve the Fund's code of ethics, as required by paragraph (c)(1)(ii) of this section. If the Fund has more than one principal underwriter or depositor, the principal underwriters and depositors may designate, in writing, which principal underwriter or depositor must conduct the approval required by paragraph (c)(1)(ii) of this section, if they obtain written consent from the designated principal underwriter or depositor.

(2) *Administration of Code of Ethics.*

(i) The Fund, investment adviser and principal underwriter must use reasonable diligence and institute procedures reasonably necessary to prevent violations of its code of ethics.

(ii) No less frequently than annually, every Fund (other than a unit investment trust) and its investment advisers and principal underwriters must furnish to the Fund's board of directors, and the board of directors must consider, a written report that:

(A) Describes any issues arising under the code of ethics or procedures since the last report to the board of directors, including, but not limited to, information about material violations of the code or procedures and sanctions imposed in response to the material violations; and

(B) Certifies that the Fund, investment adviser or principal underwriter, as applicable, has adopted procedures reasonably necessary to prevent Access Persons from violating the code.

(3) *Exception for Principal Underwriters.* The requirements of paragraphs (c)(1) and (c)(2) of this section do not apply to any principal underwriter unless:

(i) The principal underwriter is an affiliated person of the Fund or of the Fund's investment adviser; or

(ii) An officer, director or general partner of the principal underwriter serves as an officer, director or general partner of the Fund or of the Fund's investment adviser.

(d) *Reporting Requirements of Access Persons.*

(1) *Reports Required.* Unless excepted by paragraph (d)(2) of this section, every Access Person of a Fund (other than a money market fund or a Fund that does not invest in Covered Securities) and every Access Person of an investment adviser of or principal underwriter for the Fund, must report to that Fund, investment adviser or principal underwriter:

(i) *Initial Holdings Reports*. No later than 10 days after the person becomes an Access Person (which information must be current as of a date no more than 45 days prior to the date the person becomes an Access Person):

(A) The title, number of shares and principal amount of each Covered Security in which the Access Person had any direct or indirect beneficial ownership when the person became an Access Person;

(B) The name of any broker, dealer or bank with whom the Access Person maintained an account in which any securities were held for the direct or indirect benefit of the Access Person as of the date the person became an Access Person; and

(C) The date that the report is submitted by the Access Person.

(ii) *Quarterly Transaction Reports*. No later than 30 days after the end of a calendar quarter, the following information:

(A) With respect to any transaction during the quarter in a Covered Security in which the Access Person had any direct or indirect beneficial ownership:

(1) The date of the transaction, the title, the interest rate and maturity date (if applicable), the number of shares and the principal amount of each Covered Security involved;

(2) The nature of the transaction (*i.e.*, purchase, sale or any other type of acquisition or disposition);

(3) The price of the Covered Security at which the transaction was effected;

(4) The name of the broker, dealer or bank with or through which the transaction was effected; and

(5) The date that the report is submitted by the Access Person.

(B) With respect to any account established by the Access Person in which any securities were held during the quarter for the direct or indirect benefit of the Access Person:

(1) The name of the broker, dealer or bank with whom the Access Person established the account;

(2) The date the account was established; and

(3) The date that the report is submitted by the Access Person.

(iii) *Annual Holdings Reports*. Annually, the following information (which information must be current as of a date no more than 45 days before the report is submitted):

(A) The title, number of shares and principal amount of each Covered Security in which the Access Person had any direct or indirect beneficial ownership;

(B) The name of any broker, dealer or bank with whom the Access Person maintains an account in which any securities are held for the direct or indirect benefit of the Access Person; and

(C) The date that the report is submitted by the Access Person.

(2) *Exceptions from Reporting Requirements*.

(i) A person need not make a report under paragraph (d)(1) of this section with respect to transactions effected for, and Covered Securities held in, any account over which the person has no direct or indirect influence or control.

(ii) A director of a Fund who is not an "interested person" of the Fund within the meaning of section 2(a)(19) of the Act [15 U.S.C. 80a-2(a)(19)], and who would be required to make a report solely by reason of being a Fund director, need not make:

(A) An initial holdings report under paragraph (d)(1)(i) of this section and an annual holdings report under paragraph (d)(1)(iii) of this section; and

(B) A quarterly transaction report under paragraph (d)(1)(ii) of this section, unless the director knew or, in the ordinary course of fulfilling his or her official duties as a Fund director, should have known that during the 15-day period immediately before or after the director's transaction in a Covered Security, the Fund purchased or sold the Covered Security, or the Fund or its investment adviser considered purchasing or selling the Covered Security.

(iii) An Access Person to a Fund's principal underwriter need not make a report to the principal underwriter under paragraph (d)(1) of this section if:

(A) The principal underwriter is not an affiliated person of the Fund (unless the Fund is a unit investment trust) or any investment adviser of the Fund; and

(B) The principal underwriter has no officer, director or general partner who serves as an officer, director or general partner of the Fund or of any investment adviser of the Fund.

(iv) An Access Person to an investment adviser need not make a separate report to the investment adviser under paragraph (d)(1) of this section to the extent the information in the report would duplicate information required to be recorded under § 275.204-2(a)(13) of this chapter.

(v) An Access Person need not make a quarterly transaction report under paragraph (d)(1)(ii) of this section if the report would duplicate information contained in broker trade confirmations or account statements received by the Fund, investment adviser or principal underwriter with respect to the Access Person in the time period required by paragraph (d)(1)(ii), if all of the information required by that paragraph is contained in the broker trade confirmations or account statements, or in the records of the Fund, investment adviser or principal underwriter.

(vi) An Access Person need not make a quarterly transaction report under paragraph (d)(1)(ii) of this section with respect to transactions effected pursuant to an Automatic Investment Plan.

(3) *Review of Reports*. Each Fund, investment adviser and principal underwriter to which reports are required to be made by paragraph (d)(1) of this section must institute procedures by which appropriate management or compliance personnel review these reports.

(4) *Notification of Reporting Obligation*. Each Fund, investment adviser and principal underwriter to which reports are required to be made by paragraph (d)(1) of this section must identify all Access Persons who are required to make these reports and must inform those Access Persons of their reporting obligation.

(5) *Beneficial Ownership*. For purposes of this section, beneficial ownership is interpreted in the same manner as it would be under § 240.16a-1(a)(2) of this chapter in determining whether a person is the beneficial owner of a security for purposes of section 16 of the Securities Exchange Act of 1934 [15 U.S.C. 78p] and the rules and regulations thereunder. Any report required by paragraph (d) of this section may contain a statement that the report will not be construed as an admission that the person making the report has any direct or indirect beneficial ownership in the Covered Security to which the report relates.

(e) *Pre-approval of Investments in IPOs and Limited Offerings*. Investment Personnel of a Fund or its investment adviser must obtain approval from the Fund or the Fund's investment adviser before directly or indirectly acquiring beneficial ownership in any securities in an Initial Public Offering or in a Limited Offering.

(f) *Recordkeeping Requirements*.

(1) Each Fund, investment adviser and principal underwriter that is required to adopt a code of ethics or to which reports are required to be made by Access Persons must, at its principal place of business, maintain records in the manner and to the extent set out in this paragraph (f), and must make these records available to the Commission or any representative of the Commission at any time and from time to time for reasonable periodic, special or other examination:

(A) A copy of each code of ethics for the organization that is in effect, or at any time within the past five years was in effect, must be maintained in an easily accessible place;

(B) A record of any violation of the code of ethics, and of any action taken as a result of the violation, must be maintained in an easily accessible place for at least five years after the end of the fiscal year in which the violation occurs;

(C) A copy of each report made by an Access Person as required by this section, including any information provided in lieu of the reports under paragraph (d)(2)(v) of this section, must be maintained for at least five years after the end of the fiscal year in which the report is made or the information is provided, the first two years in an easily accessible place;

(D) A record of all persons, currently or within the past five years, who are or were required to make reports under paragraph (d) of this section, or who are or were responsible for reviewing these reports, must be maintained in an easily accessible place; and

(E) A copy of each report required by paragraph (c)(2)(ii) of this section must be maintained for at least five years after the end of the fiscal year in which it is made, the first two years in an easily accessible place.

(2) A Fund or investment adviser must maintain a record of any decision, and the reasons supporting the decision, to approve the acquisition by investment personnel of securities under paragraph (e), for at least five years after the end of the fiscal year in which the approval is granted.

Rule 22c-1. Pricing of Redeemable Securities for Distribution, Redemption and Repurchase

(a) No registered investment company issuing any redeemable security, no person designated in such issuer's prospectus as authorized to consummate transactions in any such security, and no principal underwriter of, or dealer in, any such security shall sell, redeem, or repurchase any such security except at a price based on the current net asset value of such security which is next computed after receipt of a tender of such security for redemption or of an order to purchase or sell such security; *Provided*, That:

(1) This paragraph shall not prevent a sponsor of a unit investment trust (hereinafter referred to as the "Trust") engaged exclusively in the business of investing in eligible trust securities (as defined in Rule 14a-3(b) [17 CFR 270.14a-3(b)]) from selling or repurchasing Trust units in a secondary market at a price based on the offering side evaluation of the eligible trust securities in the Trust's portfolio, determined at any time on the last business day of each week, effective for all sales made during the following week, if on the days that such sales or repurchases are made the sponsor receives a letter from a qualified evaluator stating, in its opinion, that:

(i) in the case of repurchases, the current bid price is not higher than the offering side evaluation, computed on the last business day of the previous week; and

(ii) in the case of resales, the offering side evaluation, computed as of the last business day of the previous week, is not more than one-half of one percent ($5.00 on a unit representing $1,000 principal amount of eligible trust securities) greater than the current offering price.

(2) This paragraph shall not prevent any registered investment company from adjusting the price of its redeemable securities sold pursuant to a merger, consolidation or purchase of substantially all of the assets of a company which meets the conditions specified in § 270.17a-8.

(3) Notwithstanding this paragraph (a), a registered open-end management investment company (but not a registered open-end management investment company that is regulated as a money market fund under § 270.2a-7 or an exchange-traded fund as defined in paragraph (a)(3)(v)(A) of this section) (a "fund") may use swing pricing to adjust its current net asset value per share to mitigate dilution of the value of its outstanding redeemable securities as a result of shareholder purchase or redemption activity, provided that it has estab-

lished and implemented swing pricing policies and procedures in compliance with the paragraphs (a)(3)(i) through (v) of this section.

(b) For the purposes of this section, (1) the current net asset value of any such security shall be computed no less frequently than once daily, Monday through Friday, at the specific time or times during the day that the board of directors of the investment company sets, in accordance with paragraph (e) of this section, except on:

(i) days on which changes in the value of the investment company's portfolio securities will not materially affect the current net asset value of the investment company's redeemable securities;

(ii) days during which no security is tendered for redemption and no order to purchase or sell such security is received by the investment company; or

(iii) customary national business holidays described or listed in the prospectus and local and regional business holidays listed in the prospectus; and

(2) a "qualified evaluator" shall mean any evaluator which represents it is in a position to determine, on the basis of an informal evaluation of the eligible trust securities held in the Trust's portfolio, whether—

(i) the current bid price is higher than the offering side evaluation, computed on the last business day of the previous week, and

(ii) the offering side evaluation, computed as of the last business day of the previous week, is more than one-half of one percent ($5.00 on a unit representing $1,000 principal amount of eligible trust securities) greater than the current offering price.

(c) Notwithstanding the provisions above, any registered separate account offering variable annuity contracts, any person designated in such account's prospectus as authorized to consummate transactions in such contracts, and any principal underwriter of or dealer in such contracts shall be permitted to apply the initial purchase payment for any such contract at a price based on the current net asset value of such contract which is next computed:

(1) Not later than two business days after receipt of the order to purchase by the insurance company sponsoring the separate account ("insurer"), if the contract application and other information necessary for processing the order to purchase (collectively, "application") are complete upon receipt; or

(2) Not later than two business days after an application which is incomplete upon receipt by the insurer is made complete, *Provided,* That, if an incomplete application is not made complete within five business days after receipt,

(i) The prospective purchaser shall be informed of the reasons for the delay, and

(ii) The initial purchase payment shall be returned immediately and in full, unless the prospective purchaser specifically consents to the insurer retaining the purchase payment until the application is made complete.

(3) As used in this section:

(i) "Prospective Purchaser" shall mean either an individual contract-owner or an individual participant in a group contract.

(ii) "Initial Purchase Payment" shall refer to the first purchase payment submitted to the insurer by, or on behalf of, a prospective purchaser.

(d) The board of directors shall initially set the time or times during the day that the current net asset value shall be computed, and shall make and approve such changes as the board deems necessary.

Rule 22c-2. Redemption fees for redeemable securities

(a) Redemption Fee. It is unlawful for any fund issuing redeemable securities, its principal underwriter, or any dealer in such securities, to redeem a redeemable security issued by the fund within seven calendar days after the security was purchased, unless it complies with the following requirements:

(1) Board Determination. The fund's board of directors, including a majority of directors who are not interested persons of the fund, must either:

(i) Approve a redemption fee, in an amount (but no more than two percent of the value of shares redeemed) and on shares redeemed within a time period (but no less than seven calendar days), that in its judgment is necessary or appropriate to recoup for the fund the costs it may incur as a result of those redemptions or to otherwise eliminate or reduce so far as practicable any dilution of the value of the outstanding securities issued by the fund, the proceeds of which fee will be retained by the fund; or

(ii) Determine that imposition of a redemption fee is either not necessary or not appropriate.

(2) Shareholder Information. With respect to each financial intermediary that submits orders, itself or through its agent, to purchase or redeem shares directly to the fund, its principal underwriter or transfer agent, or to a registered clearing agency, the fund (or on the fund's behalf, the principal underwriter or transfer agent) must either:

(i) Enter into a shareholder information agreement with the financial intermediary (or its agent); or

(ii) Prohibit the financial intermediary from purchasing in nominee name on behalf of other persons, securities issued by the fund. For purposes of this paragraph, "purchasing" does not include the automatic reinvestment of dividends.

(3) Recordkeeping. The fund must maintain a copy of the written agreement under paragraph (a)(2)(i) of this section that is in effect, or at any time within the past six years was in effect, in an easily accessible place.

(b) Excepted Funds. The requirements of paragraph (a) of this section do not apply to the following funds, unless they elect to impose a redemption fee pursuant to paragraph (a)(1) of this section:

(1) Money market funds;

(2) Any fund that issues securities that are listed on a national securities exchange; and

(3) Any fund that affirmatively permits short-term trading of its securities, if its prospectus clearly and prominently discloses that the fund permits short-term trading of its securities and that such trading may result in additional costs for the fund.

(c) Definitions. For the purposes of this section:

(1) Financial intermediary means:

(i) Any broker, dealer, bank, or other person that holds securities issued by the fund, in nominee name;

(ii) A unit investment trust or fund that invests in the fund in reliance on section 12(d)(1)(E) of the Act (15 U.S.C. 80a-12(d)(1)(E)); and

(iii) In the case of a participant-directed employee benefit plan that owns the securities issued by the fund, a retirement plan's administrator under section 3(16)(A) of the Employee Retirement Income Security Act of 1974 (29 U.S.C. 1002(16)(A)) or any person that maintains the plan's participant records.

(iv) Financial intermediary does not include any person that the fund treats as an individual investor with respect to the fund's policies established for the purpose of eliminating or reducing any dilution of the value of the outstanding securities issued by the fund.

(2) Fund means an open-end management investment company that is registered or required to register under section 8 of the Act (15 U.S.C. 80a-8), and includes a separate series of such an investment company.

(3) Money market fund means an open-end management investment company that is registered under the Act and is regulated as a money market fund under § 270.2a-7.

(4) Shareholder includes a beneficial owner of securities held in nominee name, a participant in a participant-directed employee benefit plan, and a holder of interests in a fund or unit investment trust that has invested in the fund in reliance on section 12(d)(1)(E)

(1) *Policies and procedures.* Adopt and implement written policies and procedures reasonably designed to prevent violation of the Federal Securities Laws by the fund, including policies and procedures that provide for the oversight of compliance by each investment adviser, principal underwriter, administrator, and transfer agent of the fund;

(2) *Board approval.* Obtain the approval of the fund's board of directors, including a majority of directors who are not interested persons of the fund, of the fund's policies and procedures and those of each investment adviser, principal underwriter, administrator, and transfer agent of the fund, which approval must be based on a finding by the board that the policies and procedures are reasonably designed to prevent violation of the Federal Securities Laws by the fund, and by each investment adviser, principal underwriter, administrator, and transfer agent of the fund;

(3) *Annual review.* Review, no less frequently than annually, the adequacy of the policies and procedures of the fund and of each investment adviser, principal underwriter, administrator, and transfer agent and the effectiveness of their implementation;

(4) *Chief compliance officer.* Designate one individual responsible for administering the fund's policies and procedures adopted under paragraph (a)(1):

(i) Whose designation and compensation must be approved by the fund's board of directors, including a majority of the directors who are not interested persons of the fund;

(ii) Who may be removed from his or her responsibilities by action of (and only with the approval of) the fund's board of directors, including a majority of the directors who are not interested persons of the fund;

(iii) Who must, no less frequently than annually, provide a written report to the board that, at a minimum, addresses:

(A) The operation of the policies and procedures of the fund and each investment adviser, principal underwriter, administrator, and transfer agent of the fund, any material changes made to those policies and procedures since the date of the last report, and any material changes to the policies and procedures recommended as a result of the annual review conducted pursuant to paragraph (a)(3) of this section; and

(B) Each Material Compliance Matter that occurred since the date of the last report; and

(iv) Who must, no less frequently than annually, meet separately with the fund's independent directors.

(b) *Unit investment trusts.* If the fund is a unit investment trust, the fund's principal underwriter or depositor must approve the fund's policies and procedures and chief compliance officer, must receive all annual reports, and must approve the removal of the chief compliance officer from his or her responsibilities.

(c) *Undue influence prohibited.* No officer, director, or employee of the fund, its investment adviser, or principal underwriter, or any person acting under such person's direction may directly or indirectly take any action to coerce, manipulate, mislead, or fraudulently influence the fund's chief compliance officer in the performance of his or her duties under this section.

(d) *Recordkeeping.* The fund must maintain:

(1) A copy of the policies and procedures adopted by the fund under paragraph (a)(1) that are in effect, or at any time within the past five years were in effect, in an easily accessible place; and

(2) Copies of materials provided to the board of directors in connection with their approval under paragraph (a)(2) of this section, and written reports provided to the board of directors pursuant to paragraph (a)(4)(iii) of this section (or, if the fund is a unit investment trust, to the fund's principal underwriter or depositor, pursuant to paragraph (b) of this section) for at least five years after the end of the fiscal year in which the documents were provided, the first two years in an easily accessible place; and

(3) Any records documenting the fund's annual review pursuant to paragraph (a)(3) of this section for at least five years after the end of the fiscal year in which the annual review was conducted, the first two years in an easily accessible place.

(e) *Definitions*. For purposes of this section:

(1) *Federal Securities Laws* means the Securities Act of 1933 (15 U.S.C. 77a-aa), the Securities Exchange Act of 1934 (15 U.S.C. 78a-mm), the Sarbanes-Oxley Act of 2002 (Pub. L. 107-204, 116 Stat. 745 (2002)), the Investment Company Act of 1940 (15 U.S.C. 80a), the Investment Advisers Act of 1940 (15 U.S.C. 80b), Title V of the Gramm-Leach-Bliley Act (Pub. L. No. 106-102, 113 Stat. 1338 (1999), any rules adopted by the Commission under any of these statutes, the Bank Secrecy Act (31 U.S.C. 5311-5314; 5316-5332) as it applies to funds, and any rules adopted thereunder by the Commission or the Department of the Treasury.

(2) A *Material Compliance Matter* means any compliance matter about which the fund's board of directors would reasonably need to know to oversee fund compliance, and that involves, without limitation:

(i) A violation of the Federal Securities Laws by the fund, its investment adviser, principal underwriter, administrator or transfer agent (or officers, directors, employees or agents thereof),

(ii) A violation of the policies and procedures of the fund, its investment adviser, principal underwriter, administrator or transfer agent, or

(iii) A weakness in the design or implementation of the policies and procedures of the fund, its investment adviser, principal underwriter, administrator or transfer agent.